1 MONTH OF
FREE
READING

at

www.ForgottenBooks.com

By purchasing this book you are eligible for one month membership to ForgottenBooks.com, giving you unlimited access to our entire collection of over 1,000,000 titles via our web site and mobile apps.

To claim your free month visit:

www.forgottenbooks.com/free783245

ISBN 978-0-483-99355-6
PIBN 10783245

THE

LITERARY PANORAMA,

AND

National Register :

A

REVIEW	REGISTER	MAGAZINE
OF	OF	OF
BOOKS,	EVENTS,	VARIETIES :

COMPRISING

INTERESTING INTELLIGENCE

FROM

THE VARIOUS DISTRICTS OF THE UNITED KINGDOM;

THE

British Connexions

IN

AMERICA,	THE EAST INDIES,	WESTERN
AFRICA,	THE WEST INDIES,	ASIA, &c.

AND FROM

~ALL PARTS OF THE WORLD.

AMERICA, U. S.	DENMARK,	HUNGARY,	PORTUGAL,
AMERICA, SPANISH,	EGYPT,	ITALY,	PRUSSIA,
ARABIA,	FRANCE,	NEW HOLLAND,	RUSSIA,
AUSTRIA,	GERMANY,	NORWAY,	SPAIN,
BRAZIL,	GREECE,	PERSIA,	SWEDEN,
CHINA,	HOLLAND,	POLAND,	TURKEY, &c.

NEW SERIES.—VOLUME THE NINTH.

Turning with easy eye thou may'st behold——
From India and the golden Chersonese
And utmost Indian Isle Taprobane,
From Gallia, Gades, and the British west,
Germans and Scythians, and Sarmatians north,
Beyond Danubius to the Tauric pool :
ALL NATIONS—— MILTON.—*Paradise Regained.*

LONDON:

Published by SIMPKIN and MARSHALL, Stationers' Court, and
C. TAYLOR, No. 108, Hatton Garden, Holborn:

Printed by Plummer and Brewis,

Love Lane, Eastcheap.

1819.

ADDRESS.

THE difficulty of a first address, whether personal or literary, is acknowledged by all; but the difficulty of a last address is infinitely greater; and at this moment we find it even oppressive. It is not enough to acknowledge with the utmost deference, the singular favours with which our Work has been honoured from the most illustrious quarters; we should be extremely ungrateful not to recollect, also, that general patronage which has distinguished it, from its commencement. But, mutability is the character of all terrestrial things. In the course of fifteen or twenty years, persons as well as properties change; nor is the LITERARY PANORAMA an exception. Of the Gentlemen originally engaged in conducting it, some have been called to distant situations, which they now fill with honour and advantage, as principals; some have obeyed the call general to mortals, leaving their coadjutors to lament their loss; and the survivors, though still at their posts, plead in declining health an undeniable apology for diminished exertions.

But, our duties are not diminished; and finding ourselves, under existing circumstances, unable to accomplish all the purposes we have ever had, and still have in view, we have coalesced with another Work of the same principles and sentiments as our own; and we trust that the connection will justify the adage, VIS UNITA FORTIOR.

When the LITERARY PANORAMA was instituted, the condition of Britain was that of extreme pressure from external violence: from a foe at once malignant beyond common malice, and tyrannical beyond common oppression: we have seen that foe subdued; and we have had the honour to foretell the progress of his downfal, almost step by step, and month by month; we have seen his ruin ensured by his excess, and his friends—friends at least to his fortune, repulsed from his side by his own haughtiness, till " his star" set in blood. We have seen the ferocious become a supplicant and a prisoner, although his inveterate decrees were among the first public events, which it was our duty to record. We found our Country involved in war : with infinite satisfaction we leave it in peace. We then did our duty, by supporting with our humble powers the means of national protection; and we have subsequently discharged the same duty by giving a faithful and free opinion on the conduct incumbent on our countrymen, in order to secure the most valuable advantages offered them by the present tranquillity.

Our Readers will have perceived that of late our attention has been much increased in reference to British Commerce, and to the acquisition of intelligence from various quarters of the globe: these communications will be continued, and with invigorated effect ; including also the continuation of that Continental Intelligence for which our Work has stood pre-eminent. They will now be transferred to .

THE NEW MONTHLY MAGAZINE,

AND

LITERARY PANORAMA,

PUBLISHED BY MR. COLBURN, PUBLIC LIBRARY, CONDUIT STREET; BELL AND BRADFUTE, EDINBURGH; AND J. CUMMING, DUBLIN.

To this connexion we entreat permission to refer our valued Correspondents, as well literary as commercial; and, again expressing our gratitude to them, and to the Public at large, for numerous and highly valued favours, we most respectfully take our leave.

July 1, 1819.

TO THE READERS AND FRIENDS OF

THE LITERARY PANORAMA.

THE Proprietors of the NEW MONTHLY MAGAZINE beg leave to acquaint the Readers and Friends of the LITERARY PANORAMA, that in consequence of the union which has taken place between that work and the New Monthly Magazine, those important Political and Commercial Papers which have hitherto distinguished the Literary Panorama, will in future appear *exclusively* in the New Monthly Magazine, the next Number of which will be published on the 1st of August, under the title of

The New Monthly Magazine,

AND LITERARY PANORAMA,

Embellished with a fine Portrait, accompanied by a Memoir, of the Right Hon. G. CANNING, M. P.; and enriched by a variety of Original Communications; Biographical Memoirs; Poetical Compositions; Criticisms on New Publications; Literary and Scientific Intelligence; Inventions; Discoveries; New Acts, Parliamentary Reports; Reviews of Fine Arts, Music, and the Drama; Literary, Medical, Chemical, Agricultural, and Commercial Reports; Historical Digest of Political Events; Incidents; Promotions, Births, Marriages, Deaths, &c.

For the information of those who may be unacquainted with the progress of this Work, it may be proper to state, that it has uniformly sustained a high literary character, men of the first eminence having from its commencement been strenuous in enriching its pages with their communications; and that independent of its being a faithful chronicle of the great political events of the times, and an

accurate record of domestic and family history, it forms
a complete register of every novelty in the arts, sciences,
and letters, equally acceptable to the scholar and the
philosopher, to the man of leisure and the man of business.
Established on the principles of sound patriotism, it peculiarly recommends itself to all real lovers of their country,
as a popular vehicle for the dissemination of political
truth, and as the best antidote to a Magazine distinguished
for sentiments tending to encourage disaffection and
infidently, and consequently subversive of all our existing political, religious, and social institutions.

THE HALF YEARLY VOLUME

For 1819, just completed, is illustrated with Portraits of

WILLIAM WORDSWORTH, Esq.
REV. R. C. MATURIN,
S. T. COLERIDGE, Esq.
LADY CAROLINE LAMB,
SIR JOHN FLEMING LEICESTER,
MADAME DE GENLIS.

AND CONTAINS THE FOLLOWING INTERESTING PAPERS:

ORIGINAL COMMUNICATIONS.

Lord Byron's Juvenile Poems, with numerous specimens, English
Bards and Scotch Reviewers; Culloden Anecdotes, John Roy
Stewart, James M'Gregor, Mr. Grant. &c. &c.; Knights
Templars, enemies to Christianity, Cambrian Antiquities; Sir
Samuel Romilly on Public Schools; New Pilgrim's Progress; the
Pythagorean Reformers; Remarkable Confession of a condemned
Malefactor; Seetzen's Travels in Arabia Felix; On the Language
of an Historian; Causes of the Variation in the Climate; Hamlet
and the Grave-digger; Anecdotes of Eminent Persons, Walter
Scott, Richard Gough, David Garrick, P. Curran, Lord Avon-
more, &c. &c.; Dog of Galloway; Medicinal Properties of Gold;
Fossil Tree; Captain Duff on the Dry-rot; Monsieur Dupin on
the Breakwater at Plymouth; Mount Edgecombe; the Jetee of
Cherburg; Original Critique of Dr. Johnson on Grainger's Poem
of the Sugar Cane; Mr. Jenkin on Planetary Motion; New
Theory of Gravitation; Hungarian Gypsies; Sabina, or Scenes at
the Toilette of a Roman Lady of Fashion; Sketches of Trinidad
and the Mouth of the Oronoco; Professor Pictet on the use of

Machinery in Manufactures; Increase of the Poor Rates; Con-. duct of Historians; Memoirs of Peter Gale Faux, Stenographer and Patriot; A Cockney Pastoral; M. G. Lewis's Letter to his Father in defence of the Monk; Observations on the Annals of the Fine Arts; Red Snow; Dwarf of Naples; Remarks on the Copyright Act; The Vampire, a Tale; A Pedestrian Tour round Florence; Luther's Goblet; Plan for supply of London with Provisions; Madame de Stael on the Life and Writings of Camoens; Fashionable Phraseology; Currents and Whirlpools; on the Establishment of a Public Market for Literature; The Newtonian System defended; Origin of Whig and Tory; Fascinating Power of Serpents; Pearl Fishery of Panama; Marriage of Figaro; Character of Cleopatra by Madame de Stael; Tour of the Austrian Archdukes in England; On the Theatrical Representations of the Ancients; Ghent in 1817; On the Practicability of a NE. and NW. Passage into the Pacific Ocean; Remarks on a late Exhibition of Chalk Drawings; Mr. Treadgold on the Decay of Timber; National Medals; Whale Fishery: The Italians, Mr. Bucke and Mr. Kean; Who was Junius?; Modern Standard of Genius; Lord Byron's Travels in Greece; Remarkable Prophecy of the Appearance of Luther; Memoir of Sir Peter Leicester, the celebrated Antiquary: also of Mr. Lee, the Arabic Professor; Considerations on the Poor Laws; Curious particulars of Sir R. Maxwell, of Orchardston; On the Poetry of Walter Scott; Life of Tom Brown the elder; Monsieur Biot's Voyage to the Shetland Islands; on the Practicability of Cash Payments by the Bank; Portrait of Aspasia, by Madame de Stael; Sir H. Davy on the Herculaneum MSS.; The Eloquence of Silence; Evils of Exquisite Sensibility; Spring, a Poem, from the German of Von Kleist; On the American Trade with China; On Ringing out the old Year; Notices of Danish Literature; English Manners in the 17th Century; Professor Bode's Remarks on Meteorology; Memoir of the Life and Writings of Von Kleist; Saving Banks first established at Hamburgh; On Blight, and the Transmigration of Insects; Condition of the Highland Peasantry; The Bishop of Norwich and the Moravian Episcopacy; Who was Junius? second letter; Anecdotes of John Cleland; Remarkable Events in English History; Allegorical Declaration of Love; A Peep into a Barber's Shop of Antiquity; &c. &c. &c.

REVIEW OF NEW BOOKS,

With interesting Extracts.

Hon. Horace Walpole's Letters to the Rev. W. Cole, &c. Gourgaud's Campaign of 1815; Antar, an Arabian Tale; Stebbing's Minstrel of the Glen; Present State of Musical Instruction; Barrow's Arctic Voyages; Time's Telescope for 1819; Clapham on the Pentateuch; Monk's Vindication of the University of Cambridge; Ferrari on Singing; Golowin's Japan; Human Life, a Poem, by Mr. Rogers; Art of French Conversation; Ximenes, and other Poems; Memoirs of Las Casas; Valpy's Delphin Classics; Campbell's Specimens of the British Poets; Durovernum, by Arthur Brooke; Clarke's Scandinavia; Fitzclarence's Route across India; Captain Burney's History of North-Eastern Discoveries; Watkins's Memoirs of her Majesty Queen of Great Britain; Junius Unmasked; Junius with his Vizor up; Elements of Natural Philosophy, by J. Mitchell; Food for Youth; A defence of the Church against Professor Monk, &c. by Sir J. E. Smith, M. D.; Speech of Lieut.-General Thornton on the Catholic Question; The Wrongs of Man, a Satire; Nautical Essays, or a Scriptural View of the Ocean; Shepherd's Observance of the Lord's Day; Redford and Riche's History of Uxbridge; The Patriot Father, by Kotzebue; Treasures of Thought, from Madame de Stael; The Priory of Birkenhead; Jamieson's Conversations on History; Blaine's Elements of Medical Logic; Principles of Punctuation, by Cecil Hardy; An Eulogium on Sir Samuel Romilly, by M. Benjamin de Constant; Letters addressed to a late Duchess; The Banquet, a Poem; &c. &c.

FINE ARTS.

Propriety of encouraging Artists of our own Country; Luke Clennell; On the Annals of the Arts; British Gallery; Patronage of British Genius; Anti-British Prejudices; Remarks on an Exhibition of Chalk Drawings; Spring Garden Exhibition of Paintings; Sir J. F. Leicester's Picture Gallery; Backler's Window for St. James's Church: Exhibition of the Royal Academy, Somerset-House; Mr Fawkes's Exhibition of Drawing's; &c. &c.

USEFUL ARTS.

Adiaphonon, a new Musical Instrument; New discovery in Optics; Velocipede; American Water-Burner; Cast Iron rendered Malleable; Iron Boat; Paper from Alga Marina; Pyroligneous Acid; Power of the Screw; Portable Gas-Bags; Moirée Metallique; Distillation of Coal; Felt rendered Impenetrable; Tar Lamp; Improved Bank Notes; A new Life Boat; Sorbic Acid; Linen Thread from the Flos of Nettles; &c. &c. &c.

RURAL ECONOMY.

Leverage to propel Ploughs, by Mr. Thomas; Ackerman's Moveable Axles; Sugar in Potatoes; Mathew's Safe Coach; Prevention of Dry Rot; Means of detecting Adulteration of Flour; Mr. Doncaster on Spade Agriculture; &c. &c.

OBITUARY, WITH ANECDOTES, &c.

Sir Philip Francis, K.B.; Mr. John Courtois; Earl Paulet; F. W. Blagdon, Esq.; Earl of Errol; Dr. Wolcot; Augustus von Kotzebue; George Henry Harlow; Francisco Manuel; Richard Baker, the Conjurer; James Sandy; John Sackehouse, the Esquimaux who accompanied Captain Ross to the North;—&c.

ADDRESS.

THE commencement of a new Volume imposes on the Proprietors and Editors of the LITERARY PANORAMA, the grateful task of expressing their acknowledgements for the support and encouragement, which it has received for upwards of ten years. During that eventful period, they reflect with pleasure that their journal has been the vehicle of more information connected with the domestic concerns and the national commerce of Britain, than any of its competitors for public favour. At the same time they can confidently appeal to their past labours in proof of their successful pains, in delineating the condition and resources of the great powers of the eastern and western hemispheres, and in furnishing *early* and *important* information relative to the transactions which have taken place in the theatre of Europe. But while these momentous topics have justly claimed their primary attention, it has been the aim of the editors to render the Literary Panorama, a valuable repository of information on every subject, whether connected with literature, the Fine or Useful Arts, Philanthropic Plans and Institutions, &c. &c. that can interest either the legislator or the private individual. To the success with which this department of the Literary Panorama has been conducted the Editors have on various occasions received the most satisfactory testimonials.

In looking forward to the future, they have no new promises to make, no new plans to develope. By their old Friends and Patrons, they trust the LITERARY PANORAMA will be found to evince the same priority and interest of information which characterize its former volumes. But, as this Address may fall into the hands of some, who may not be fully acquainted with its plan, the Editors and Proprietors beg respectfully to recapitulate its principal features.

The LITERARY PANORAMA, then, comprizes

I. A Monthly compendium of National Papers and Parliamentary Reports, illustrative of the History, Statistics, and Commerce of the British Empire.

II. An universal Epitome of interesting and useful Intelligence from all Quarters of the Globe.

III. A Review of Books,—not the productions of Britain only, but those of all civilized countries. For the improvement of this department, new and extensive arrangements have been made, by which we' shall be enabled, in future, to give more ample notices of Foreign Literature, and, especially that of the Westo show to these people their own strength, and the incapacity of Spain to give them protection or enforce obedience. The groundwork was, however, laid in the jealous and oppressive system adopted at a more early period by the kings of Spain, whose policy it seemed to be to keep within as narrow limits as circumstances would permit the intelligence, wealth, and population of that part of America subject to their dominion, as the surest means of preserving an empire which they considered the great source of their wealth and power.

The revolution, having been auspiciously commenced in the city of Buenos Ayres, was warmly and zealously supported by the mass of the people descended from the Spaniards; but the native Spaniards, as well those domesticated in the country as those in the service of the king, were almost all opposed to it, particularly at the time and under the circumstances it took place. Dissensions were the immediate result, and their long standing jealousy and distrust of each other have by subsequent events been heightened into deadly hostility, which time alone can wear away. These dissensions have been considered as one of the causes that produced those which subsequently took place among the patriots themselves, and which have been most serious obstacles in the progress of revolution. Other obstacles, however, have been presented by the royal government in Peru, which has hitherto not only been able to sustain itself there, but has found means, by enlisting the native Peruvians, in its service, to send at different times considerable armies into the upper provinces on the river La Plata, where the war has been carried on from the commencement of the revolution to the present day with various success; the great extent and peculiar character of the country, and the want of resources, having prevented either party from making a decisive blow of the contest. When we came away, the advantage in that quarter was on the side of the Spaniards, as they were in possession of the provinces of Upper Peru, which had to a certain degree at least, joined in the revolution, and some of which are represented in the Congress. Every where else they have been obliged to yield up the government and abandon the country, or submit to the ruling power. The peculiar situation of Monte Video, on the east side of the river La Plata, open to the sea, and strongly fortified, enabled the Spanish naval and military forces, at an early period in the revolution, to make a stand there: they were ultimately obliged to surrender it; not, however, until long-protracted, and perhaps ill directed, efforts on the part of the assailants, had given rise to many jarring incidents between those who came from the opposite shores of the rivers; probably the effect, in part at least, of ancient jealousies, kept alive by the individual interest of different leaders; these have been followed by the individual interest of different generals; and have been followed by events calculated to produce a still greater alienation; and although several

attempts have been made to bring about a union, they have hitherto been unsuccessful. The provinces of the "Banda Oriental" and the "Entre Rios," on the eastern side of the river, under the direction of General Artigas, are now at war with those on the western side, under the Government of the Congress at Buenos-Ayres.

This war has originated from a combination of causes in which both parties have, perhaps, something to complain of, and something to blame themselves for.

General Artigas and his followers profess a belief that it is the intention of the Government of Buenos-Ayres to put them down, and oblige them to submit to such arrangements as will deprive them of the privileges of self-government, to which they claim to have a right. They say, however, that they are willing to unite with the people on the western side of the river; but not in such a way as will subject them to what they call the tyranny of the city of Buenos-Ayres. On the other hand, it is stated that this is merely a pretext; that the real object of General Artigas and some of the principal officers is to prevent a union on any terms, and to preserve the power they have acquired, by giving an erroneous excitement to the people who follow them. That it is wished and intended to place these provinces on a footing with the others. That the respectable portion of their inhabitants are aware of this fact, and anxious for a union; but are prevented from openly expressing their sentiments from a fear of General Artigas, whose power is uncontrolled by law or justice; and hence the propriety and necessity of aiding them to resist it. Armies have accordingly been marched within the present year into these provinces; but they were not joined by a number of the inhabitants, and were defeated with great loss.

This war is evidently a source of great injury and regret; and, at the same time, of extraordinary irritation to both parties; for, independently of other causes of recrimination, each accuses the other of having brought about that state of things which threatens to place a most important and valuable portion of their country in the hands of a foreign power, who has invaded it with a regular and well-appointed army, and is gradually taking possession of commanding points, from which it may be difficult for their united force hereafter to dislodge them. That they will unite is, I think, to be calculated on, unless some event disastrous to the cause of the revolution itself takes place; for their mutual interest requires a union. But more of moderation and discretion may be necessary to bring it about than is at this time to be expected from the irritated feelings of some of the principal personages on both sides.

The city of Santa-Fé, and a small district of country around it, also refuses to acknowledge the authority of the Government of Buenos-Ayres.

In Paraguay the events of the revolution

have differed from those in any other province, as the inhabitants of that country have uniformly resisted the efforts of the other provinces to unite them. After having aided the Spanish authorities placed over them, to repel a military force which had been sent to overthrow them, they themselves expelled from their country these authorities, and established a Government of their own, totally unconnected with that of the other provinces, with whom they manifest an unwillingness to keep up even a commercial intercourse. This has given rise to a suspicion in the minds of some that there is a secret predilection among them for the ancient order of things. But from what is said of their cold and calculating character—from the safe position of their country, and its capacity to supply its own wants, it is probable that their object is to husband their resources, and profit by the exertions of others, without giving their own in aid of them; and possibly, in case of ultimate failure, to place their conduct in a less objectionable point of view before the Government of Spain. Whatever may have been their motives, they have hitherto contrived to escape in a great measure the evils of war.

Their resources, in men and money, are said to be considerable, and no country is more independent of foreign supplies.

Their conduct furnishes a striking contrast to that of the people of Buenos-Ayres, who entered into the revolution with unbounded zeal and energy, and ever have been ready to meet the difficulties of so great an undertaking. This circumstance connected with their local situation, greater resources, and more general information, and perhaps the fact of their having been the first to get power into their hands, have had the effect to give them a controlling influence over the revolutionary government, which has not failed to excite, in some degree, the jealousy of the other provinces, and amongst themselves a feeling of superiority little calculated to allay their jealousy. Great evils were at one time apprehended from this state of things; but the Congress which met at Tucuman, in March, 1816, composed of deputies from the several provinces then united, assumed the sovereign power of the country, boldly declared its absolute independence, and adopted a provisional form of government, which is understood to have the effect of allaying dissensions, and of introducing a more regular administration of public affairs.

It will be seen from the documents in your possession, that this provisional constitution recognizes many of the principles of free government: but with such drawbacks are little calculated to enforce them in practice. Great allowances are doubtless to be made for the circumstances of the times, and the danger and difficulty of tearing up ancient institutions, or of adapting new principles to them. But, after due allowance for all these considerations, it did not appear to me that so much had been done for the cause of civil liberty as might have been expected, or that those in power

were its strongest advocates. It is generally admitted, however, that some changes for the better have been made. Much care seems to be taken to educate the rising generation, and as those who are now coming on the theatre of action have grown up since the commencement of the revolution, and have had the advantages of the light thrown in by it, it is fair to suppose that they will be better prepared to support and administer a free government than those whose habits were formed under the colonial government of Spain.

The commerce and manufactures of the country have grown beyond its agriculture.—Various causes, however, have contributed to lessen some branches of manufacture since the revolution, but commerce is understood to have been increased by it. A much greater variety and quantity of foreign goods are imported, and a greater demand is opened for the productions of the country. The city of Buenos-Ayres is the seat of this commerce. From it, foreign and some domestic goods, are spread through the interior, as far as Chili and Upper Peru, and, in return, the various productions are drawn to it. This trade is carried on principally by land, as is that between the different provinces, though some small portion of it finds its way up and down the large rivers from the La Plata, which is itself not so much a river as a great bay. The abundance of cattle, horses, and mules, and of some other animals peculiar to the country, which are used in the mountainous regions of Peru, furnish facilities for transportation not to be found in any other country so little improved; hence the price of transportation is very low, and the internal trade greater than it otherwise would be, though it had been materially lessened in some important branches by the war with Peru, and the system adopted in Paraguay.

The export and import trade is principally in the hands of the British, though the United States and other nations participate in it to a certain degree. It is depended on as the great source of revenue to the State; hence they have been tempted to make the duties very high, and to lay them upon both imports and exports, with the exception of lumber and military stores. This circumstance, connected with the fact that payment is demanded at the custom-house before the goods are delivered, has led to a regular system of smuggling, which is said to be carried to great excess, and doubtless occasions the official returns to fall short of the actual amount of the trade. This may be the reason why they were not given to us. The articles imported are almost every variety of European and East India goods, principally from England; rum, sugar, coffee, tobacco, cotton, and timber from Brazil; lumber of almost every description, cod-fish, furniture, gin, and some smaller articles, from the United States, together with the military stores; which however, find their way into this country directly from Europe, and are thus furnished at a cheaper rate than we can sell them. The principal articles of export are taken from the various animals of the country, tame and wild, from the ox to the chinchilla; copper from Chili, and some of the precious metals, drawn principally from Peru; but as gold is worth 17 dollars the ox, and passed by tale at that rate, very little of it is exported; hence the currency of the country is gold; for they have no paper money. The "Libranzas," or bills of credit, issued by the Government, are, however, an article of traffic among the merchants, as they are received in payment of one half of the duties. No distinction is made in favour of the trade of any nation, save only that the British merchants have some peculiar facilities granted them in relation to their letters, which are an object of taxation, at least so far as applies to those sent out of the country.

In the official statements given to us, to which I beg leave generally to refer for information as to the foreign relations, the productions, military and naval force, revenue, and population, the latter is stated at 1,300,000 exclusive of Indians. This is understood as comprehending the population of all the provinces; but, as some of them are not under the Government at Buenos Ayres, I have thought it proper to annex the several estimates I have collected of the population of each province, as they may serve to give some general information on that point. The most immediate difficulty felt by the Government, whilst we were in the country, seemed to arise from the want of money; for, although the debt was small, their credit was low. It had not been found practicable to adopt a system of finance adequate to the exigencies of the times, though it would seem, from the statements given to us, that the revenue of the last year exceeded the expences. The important events of the present year in Chili, of which you are informed, will doubtless have the effect to raise the credit of the country, and to lessen the pressure upon it, at least for a time, and will probably leave the Government more at leisure to attend to its internal affairs.

When we came away, it was understood that a committee of the Congress was engaged in drafting a new constitution, the power of forming and adopting it being exclusively vested in the Congress. Whether it will assume a federal or a national character, is somewhat doubtful, as there are evidently two parties in the country, whose views in this respect are very different, and it is believed that they are both represented in the Congress. The one party is in favour of a consolidated or national government; the other wishes for a federal government, somewhat upon the principles of that of the United States. The probability seems to be, that, although there might be a a majority of the people in the province generally in favour of the federal system, it would not be adopted upon the ground that it was not so well calculated as a national government to provide for the common defence, the great object now in view. The same general reason may be urged, perhaps, for giving to the latter, should it be adopted, less of a republican character than probably would have been given to it in more quiet and peaceful times. There is danger too, as the power of forming and adopting the constitution is placed in the hands of a few, that the rights and privileges of the people may not be so well understood or attended to as they would have been had the people themselves had a more immediate agency in the affair. It is not to be doubted, however, that it will at least have a republican form, and be bottomed upon the principles of independence, which is contended for by all descriptions of politicians in the country who have taken part in the revolution, and will, it is believed, be supported by them, in any event, to the last extremity.

Their means of defence, of which they are fully aware, are, in proportion to their numbers, greater perhaps than those of almost any other people, and the duration and the events of the war have strengthened the general determination never to submit to Spain. This determination rests upon the recollection of former sufferings and deprivations; upon a consciousness of their ability to defend and to govern themselves; and upon a conviction that, in case of submission on any terms, they would, sooner or later, be made to feel the vengeance of the mother country. These considerations doubtless have the most weight upon those who have taken a leading part. They, of course, use all their influence to enforce them, and thus to keep up the spirit of the revolution. In this they have probably had the less difficulty, as although the sufferings of the people have been great, particularly in military service, and in raising contributions necessary for that service, yet the incubus of Spanish power being thrown off, and with it that train of followers who filled up almost every avenue to wealth and consequence, the higher classes have been awakened to a sense of advantages they did not before enjoy. They have seen their commerce freed from legal restraints, their articles of export become more valuable, their supplies furnished at a lower rate, and all the offices of Government, or other employments, laid open to them as fair objects of competition. The lower classes have found their labour more in demand, and better paid for; and their importance in society greater than it formerly was.

They are yet, however, from their indolence, general want of education, and the great mixture of "casts" among them, in a degraded state, but little felt in the affairs of the Government. The stimulus now given will operate to produce a change in them for the better, and, it is to be presumed, will gradually have its effect, as their docility, intelligence, and activity, when called into service, give evidence that they are not deficient in natural or physical powers.

Labour, as it becomes more general, will become less irksome to individuals, and the gradual acquisition of property which must necessarily result from it in such a country, under a good Government, will doubtless produce the happy effects there which it has uniformly produced elsewhere, and more especially in countries where the population is small when compared to the extent of territory.

I am very sensible that I may have been led into errors of fact, or inference. In that case I can plead honesty of intention, and the difficulty of collecting at a single point, and within a limited time, correct information; or of analyzing that which was collected, respecting a people in a state of revolution, who are spread over an immense country, and whose habits, institutions, and language, are so different from our own.

I have only to add, that we were politely received by the Supreme Director, who made every profession for our Government, and every offer of accommodation to us, as its agents, which we had a right to expect, and that the people manifested on all occasions the most friendly dispositions.

Estimate of the population of the province of Buenos Ayres, Cordova, Tucuman, Mendoza, or Cuyo, and Salta, under the names of the different towns or districts which send Representatives to the Congress.

By an imperfect census, taken, it is believed, in 1815, Buenos Ayres contained 93,100, excluding troops and transient persons, and Indians.

	By more recent estimates, excluding Indians.	Excluding Indians.	Including Indians.
Buenos Ayres	105,000	120,000	150,000
Cordova	75,000	75,000	100,000
Tucuman	45,000	45,000	20,000*
Santiago del Estero	45,000	60,000	
Valle de Callamarca	36,000	40,000	
Rioja	20,000	20,000	
San Juan	34,000	34,000	
Mendoza	38,000	38,000	
San Luis	16,000	16,000	
Injuy	25,000	25,000	
Salta	50,000	50,000	
	489,000	523,000	

PROVINCES OF UPPER PERU.

Cochabamba	100,000	120,000	200,000
Potosi	112,000	112,000	250,000
Plata, or Chorcas	112,000	112,000	175,000
La Paz			800,000
Puno { under the name of Santa Cruz de la	120,000		30,000†
Sierra			150,000†
Quiro			50,000†
Paraguay			300,000
Banda Oriental and Entre Rios }	50,000		

* Probably the town only.

† Under the various names of Santa Cruz de la Sierra Majos, and Chequitos.

Note.—It is not understood that any part of the province of Corrientes, or that of the city or district of Santa Fee, is included in this estimate; and some districts of some of the other provinces may be omitted.

Together with the Reports from our Commissioners, were transmitted to Congress the several documents therein referred to.

As we attach considerable importance to these Reports, we shall in our following Numbers continue them with such remarks as their contents and tenor may suggest.

Political and Literary Anecdotes of his own Times. By Dr. William King, Principal of St. Mary's Hall, Oxon. 8vo. 8s. 6d. Murray, London, 1818.

This work, though small in bulk, is rich in amusing anecdote, and when once taken up is not hastily to be thrown aside. Its author, Dr. King, was born at Stepney, near London, in 1685, and died in 1763. He was an accomplished scholar, and was highly esteemed for his wit, humour, and independent spirit.

The present volume we learn from the editor's prefatory advertisement, was discovered in the possession of two ladies relations of the author. Of its authenticity there can be no doubt; as from a comparison of the hand-writing of the original manuscript with that which is well ascertained to be Dr. King's, in the account books of St. Mary's Hall, Oxford, (of which he was for many years the principal) there is every reason to suppose it to have been written by Dr. K. himself, and to have been intended for publication.

These "Anecdotes," though desultory are exceedingly curious. They contain a very striking character of the pretender, together with many interesting particulars relative to the jacobite party, to which Dr. King was strongly attached, and with the leaders of which he was intimately acquainted. Many pleasant stories of the great men and literary characters, contemporaries of Dr. King, are here recorded, with some elegant criticisms on the latin poets. We select a few instances for the amusement of our readers.

Who amongst all the modern writers is to be more esteemed and admired than Monsieur Fenelon, Archbishop of Cambray, and author of Telemachus, whose piety, politeness and humanity were equal to his great learning? Ramsay, the author of *Cyrus*, who was educated in Monsieur Fenelon's Family, acquainted me with an anecdote which hath ever made me reverence the memory of this excellent man. Some *German* officers who were prisoners at *Cambray* were invited to dine with the Archbishop, whose table was always open to the officers of the *French* garrison, of which a certain number dined with him every day. The *Germans* during the dinner were continually calling for bumpers of wine. The *French* seemed to sneer at this behaviour of the *German* officers, and looked on them with a kind of contempt: which Monsieur Fenelon observing called for an half-pint glass of Burgundy, (which perhaps was more than be had ever taken at one meal before,) and drank it off to the health of the prisoners. This was a handsome compliment to the *Germans*, and a proper reprimand to his own countrymen. But, as soon as the *German* officers were gone, he thus admonished the *French* gentlemen. "You should endeavour to divest yourselves of all national prejudices, and never condemn the customs and manners of a foreign people, because they are altogether different from your own. I am a true *French*-man, and love my country; but I love mankind better than my country."

It is well known that during Sir Robert Walpole's administration corruption was carried to a most disgraceful extent in Parliament. Dr. King, (who it will be recollected was a zealous jacobite) boldly ascribes all our national misfortunes since the accession of the House of Brunswick to that administration.

It is certain that all our national misfortunes since the accession of the House of Hanover must be chiefly ascribed to Walpole's administration. He unhinged all the principles and morals of our people, and changed the government into a system of corruption. He openly ridiculed virtue and merit, and promoted no man to any employment of profit or honour, who had scruples of conscience, or refused implicitly to obey his commands. He was a ready speaker, understood the business of parliament, and knew how to manage an House of Commons, which however was not a very difficult task, if it be considered that a majority of the members were of his own nomination. He seemed to have great resolution; and yet he was once so much intimidated by the clamours of the people without doors, that he thought it expedient

to give up one of his most favorite schemes. He had besides some difficulties to encounter through his whole administration, which were not known to the public. A friend of mine who dined with him one day *tete-a-tete* took occasion to compliment him on the great honour and power which he enjoyed as prime minister. "Doctor," says he, "I have great power it is true, but I have two cursed drawbacks, *Hanover*, and the * * * avarice." This minister who thought he had established himself beyond a possibility of being shaken, fell at last by his too great security: if he may be said to fall who went out of employment with an Earldom and a pension of 4000l, or 5000l. a year.

Other anecdotes of profligate corruption are recorded, for which we refer to the volume itself, but there is so much good sense in the following observations on a custom, now growing into some degree of disuse, that we cannot withhold them from our readers, who (we think) cannot fail to be amused with the stories with which they are enlivened.

The custom of giving money to servants is now become such a grievance, that it seems to demand the interposition of the legislature totally to abolish it. How much are foreigners astonished when they observe that a man cannot dine at any house in *England*, not even with his father or his brother, or with any other of his nearest relations, or most intimate friends and companions, unless he pay for his dinner? But how can they behold without indignation or contempt a man of quality standing by his guests, while they are distributing money to a double row of his servants? If, when I am invited to dine with any of my acquaintance, I were to send the master of the house a sirloin of beef for a present, it would be considered as a gross affront; and yet as soon as I shall have dined or before I leave the house, I must be obliged to pay for the sirloin, which was brought to his table or placed on the sideboard. For I contend, that all the money which is bestowed on the servants, is given to the master. For if the servants' wages were increased in some proportion to their vails (which is the practice of a few great families, the D. of Norfolk's, Mr. Spencer's, Sir Francis Dashwood's, &c.) this scandalous custom might be totally extinguished. I remember a Lord Poor, a roman catholic Peer in *Ireland*, who lived upon a small pension which Q. Anne had granted him: he was a man of honour, and well esteemed, and had formerly been an officer of some distinction in the service of *France*. The Duke of

Ormonde had often invited him to dinner, and he as often excused himself. At last the Duke kindly expostulated with him, and would know the reason why he so constantly refused to be one of his guests. My Lord Poor then honestly confessed that he could not afford it: but, says he, if your Grace will put a guinea into my hands as often as you are pleased to invite me to dine, I will not decline the honour of waiting on you. This was done, and my Lord was afterwards a frequent guest in St. James's Square. For my part, whenever I am invited to the table of any of my noble friends, I have the vanity to imagine that my company is desired for the sake of my conversation, and there is certainly no reason why I should give the servants money because I give the master pleasure. Besides I have observed the servants of every great house consider these vails to be as much their due as the fees which are claimed in the Custom-house, or in any other public office. And therefore they make no distinction between a gentleman of 200l. a year and one of 2000l. although they look on the former as inferior in every respect to themselves. *Maxima quæque domus servis est plena superbis* is an axiom which will hold true to the end of the world. Upon the whole if this custom which is certainly a disgrace to our country, is to continue in force, I think it may at least be practised in a better manner. Suppose there were written in large gold letters over the door of every man of rank : The fees for dining here are three half crowns (or ten shillings) to be paid to the porter on entering the house: Peers or Peeresses to pay what more they think proper. By this regulation two inconveniences would be avoided : first the difficulty of distinguishing amongst a great number the quality of the servants. I who am near sighted have sometimes given the footman what I designed for the butler, and the butler has had only the footman's fee: for which the butler treated me with no small contempt, until an opportunity offered of correcting my error. But secondly this method would prevent the shame which every master of a family cannot help feeling whilst he sees his guests giving about their shillings and half crowns to his servants. He may then conduct them boldly to his door, and take his leave with a good grace. My Lord Taaffe of *Ireland* a general officer in the *Austrian* service, came into *England* a few years ago on account of his private affairs. When his friends who had dined with him were going away, he always attended them to the door, and if they offered any money to the servant who opened it (for he never suffered but one servant to appear,) he

always prevented them, saying in his manner of speaking *English*, "If you do give, give it to me, for it was I that did buy the dinner."

The following anecdote relative to Oliver Cromwell, has we believe never before been published. To us at least it is perfectly new, and it exhibits a pleasing trait in the character of that extraordinary man.

In the civil war my grandfather Sir William Smyth was governor of * Hillesdon House, near Buckingham, where the King had a small garrison. This place was besieged and taken by Cromwell. But the officers capitulated to march out with their arms, baggage, &c. As soon as they were without the gate, one of Cromwell's soldiers snatched off Sir William Smyth's hat. He immediately complained to Cromwell of the fellow's insolence and breach of the capitulation. "Sir," says Cromwell, "if you can point out the man, or I can discover him, I promise you he shall not go unpunished. In the mean time (taking off a new beaver which he had on his head) be pleased to accept of this hat instead of your own."

We must conclude our extracts with the following anecdotes relative to the Pretender, with whom our author had a conversation in September 1750.

September 1750, I received a note from my Lady Primrose, who desired to see me immediately. As soon as I waited on her she led me into her dressing-room and presented me to———†. If I was surprised to find him there, I was still more astonished when he acquainted me with the motives which had induced him to hazard a journey to England at this juncture. The impatience of his friends who were in exile had formed a scheme which was impracticable ; but although it had been as feasible as they had represented it to him, yet no preparation had been made, nor was any thing ready to carry it into execution. He was soon convinced that he had been deceived, and therefore, after a stay in London of five days only, he returned to the place from whence he came. As I had some long conversations with him here, and for some years after held a constant correspondence with him, not indeed by letters but by messengers‡, who were occasionally

---

* The siege of Hillesdon House is nowhere mentioned by my Lord Clarendon. The noble historian and Sir W. Smyth were not good friends.

† The Pretender.

‡ These were not common couriers, but gentlemen of fortune, honour, and veracity, and on whose relations I could entirely depend.

dispatched to him; and as during this intercourse I informed myself of all particulars relating to him and of his whole conduct, both in public and private life, I am perhaps as well qualified as any man in England to draw a just character of him; and I impose this task on myself not only for the information of posterity, but for the sake of many worthy gentlemen whom I shall leave behind me, who are at present attached to his name, and who have formed their ideas of him from public report, but more particularly from those great actions which he performed in Scotland. As to his person he is tall and well made, but stoops a little, owing perhaps to the great fatigue which he underwent in his northern expedition. He has an handsome face and good eyes; (I think * his busts which about this time were commonly in London, are more like him than any of his pictures which I have yet seen;) but in polite company he would not pass for a genteel man. He hath a quick apprehension, and speaks *French*, *Italian*, and *English*, the last with a little of a foreign accent. As to the rest very little care seems to have been taken of his education. He had not made the belles lettres or any of the finer arts his study which surprised me much considering his preceptors and the noble opportunities he must have always had in that nursery † of all the elegant and liberal arts and science. But I was still more astonished when I found him unacquainted with the history and constitution of *England*, in which he ought to have been very early instructed. I never heard him express any noble or benevolent sentiments, the certain indications of a great soul and a good heart; or discover any sorrow or compassion for the misfortunes of so many worthy men who had suffered in his cause‡. But the most odious part of his

character is his love of money, a vice which I do not remember to have been imputed by our historians to any of his ancestors, and is the certain index of a base and little mind. I know it may be urged in his vindication that a prince in exile ought to be an economist. And so he ought; but nevertheless his purse should be always open, as long as there is any thing in it, to relieve the necessities of his friends and adherents. King Charles the second during his banishment would have shared the last pistole in his pocket with his little family. But I have known this gentleman with two thousand Louis d'ors in his strong box pretend he was in great distress, and borrow money from a lady in Paris, who was not in affluent circumstances. His most faithful servants, who had closely attended him in all his difficulties were ill rewarded. Two Frenchmen who had left every thing to follow his fortune, who had been sent as couriers through half Europe, and executed their commissions with great punctuality and exactness, were suddenly discharged without any faults imputed to them, or any recompense for their past service. To this spirit of avarice may be added his insolent manner of treating his immediate dependants, very unbecoming a great prince, and a sure prognostic of what might be expected from him if ever he acquired sovereign power. Sir J. Harrington * and † Col. Goring who suffered themselves to be imprisoned with him, rather than desert him, when the rest of his family and attendants fled, were afterwards obliged to quit his service on account of his illiberal behaviour. But there is one part of his character, which I must particularly insist on, since it occasioned the defection of the most powerful of his friends and adherents in England, and by some concurring accidents totally blasted all his hopes and pretensions. When he was in Scotland, he had a mistress whose

---

* He came one evening to my lodgings and drank tea with me : my servant after he was gone said to me, " that he thought my new visitor very like Prince Charles." " Why," said I. " have you ever seen Prince Charles ? " " No sir," replied the fellow, " but this gentleman, whoever he may be, exactly resembles the busts which are sold in Red lion-street, and are said to be the busts of Prince Charles." The truth is, these busts were taken in plaster of Paris from his face.

† Rome. His governor was a protestant, and I am apt to believe purposely neglected his education, of which it is surmised he made a merit to the English ministry ; for he was always supposed to be their pensioner. The Chevalier Ramsay the author of Cyrus was Prince Charles' preceptor for about a year, but a court faction removed him.

‡ As to his religion he is certainly free from all bigotry and superstition, and would readily conform to the religion of the country. With the catholics he is catholic ; with the protestants

he is a protestant ; and to convince the latter of his sincerity, he often carried an English Common Prayer-book in his pocket ; and sent to Gordon (whom I have mentioned before) a nonjuring clergyman, to christen the first child he had by Mrs. W.

* Sir J. Harrington remained in banishment till the accession of the present King George III. No man is better acquainted with the private history and character of Prince Charles, and if ever he reads what I have here written, I am confident that he will readily vouch the truth of my narrative.

† Goring upon quitting his service was recommended by my Lord Marshall to the King of Prussia, who immediately gave him a command in his army equal to his pretensions. Goring died soon after, and his loss was greatly lamented by his Prussian Majesty, who honoured him with a character in a letter to my Lord Marshal.

name is Walkenshaw, and whose sister was at that time and is still housekeeper at Leicester House. Some years after he was released from his prison and conducted out of France, he sent for this girl who soon acquired such a dominion over him that she was acquainted with all his schemes, and trusted with his most secret correspondence. As soon as this was known in England, all those persons of distinction who were attached to him were greatly alarmed; they imagined that this wench had been placed in his family by the English ministers, and considering her sister's situation they seemed to have some ground for their suspicion; wherefore they dispatched a gentleman to *Paris*, where the Prince then was, who had instructions to insist that Mrs. Walkenshaw should be removed to a convent for a certain term; but her gallant absolutely refused to comply with this demand, and although Mr. M'Namara the gentleman who was sent to him, who has a natural eloquence and an excellent understanding, urged the most cogent reasons, and used all the arts of persuasion to induce him to part with his mistress, and even proceeded so far as to assure him according to his instructions, that an immediate interruption of all correspondence with his most powerful friends in England, and in short that the ruin of his interest which was now daily increasing, would be the infallible consequence of his refusal, yet he continued inflexible, and all M'Namara's intreaties and remonstrances were ineffectual. M'Namara staid in Paris some days beyond the time prescribed him, endeavouring to reason the Prince into a better temper, but finding him obstinately persevere in his first answer he took his leave with concern and indignation, saying as he passed out, "what has your family done, Sir, thus to draw down the vengeance of heaven on every branch of it through so many ages?" It is worthy of remark that in all the conferences which M'Namara had with the Prince on this occasion, the latter declared that it was not a violent passion or indeed any particular regard [*] which attached him to Mrs.

Walkenshaw, and that he could see her removed from him without any concern, but he would not receive directions in respect to his private conduct from any man alive. When M'Namara returned to London and reported the Prince's answer to the gentlemen [*] who had employed him, they were astonished and confounded. However they soon resolved on the measures which they were to pursue for the future, and determined no longer to serve a man who could not be pursuaded to serve himself, and chose rather to endanger the lives of his best and most faithful friends than part with an harlot, whom as he had often declared he neither loved nor esteemed. If ever that old adage *Quos Jupiter vult perdere*, &c. could be properly applied to any person, whom could it so well fit as the gentleman of whom I have been speaking? for it is difficult by any other means to account for such a sudden infatuation. [†] He was indeed soon afterwards made sensible of his misconduct, when it was too late to repair it; for from this era may truly be dated the ruin of his cause, which for the future can only subsist in the N—n—ing congregations, which are generally formed of the meanest people, from whom no danger to the present government need ever be apprehended.

---

[*] These were all men of fortune and distinction and many of them persons of the first quality, who attached themselves to — as to a person who they imagined might be made the instrument of saving their country. They were sensible that by Walpole's administration the English government was become a system of corruption, and that Walpole's successors who pursued his plan without any of his abilities, had reduced us to such a deplorable situation, that our commercial interest was sinking, our colonies in danger of being lost, and Great Britain, which, if her powers were properly ‡ exerted, was able to give laws to other nations, was become the contempt of all Europe.

[*] As they were afterwards in Mr. Pitt's administration.

[†] He was soon made acquainted with the defection which immediately followed upon the report of his answer. He endeavoured to excuse himself by blaming the gentleman who had been sent to him; he pretended the message had not been properly delivered, that he had been treated rudely and insolently, &c. But this was not the case. Mr. M'Namara addressed him in the most respectful manner, and though he spoke firmly, as he knew the consequence of the Prince's refusal, yet he could not have treated him with more deference if he had been on the throne. The Prince's accusation of M'Namara was very unjust, as well as ungrateful, for M'Namara had been often with him, and had served him with great zeal and fidelity on many important occasions, both at home and abroad.

---

[*] I believe he spoke truth when he declared he had no esteem for his northern mistress, although she had been his companion for so many years. She had no elegance of manners and as they had both contracted an odious habit of drinking, so they exposed themselves very frequently, not only to their own family but to all their neighbours. They often quarrelled and sometimes fought: they were some of these drunken scenes which probably occasioned the report of his madness.

Curiosities of Literature. Vol. 3, 8vo. 12s. Murray, London, 1817.

THE two first volumes of this amusing and instructive publication, have for many years been before the public, and the repeated impressions they have undergone, sufficiently attest the estimation in which they are deservedly held. The third volume, which is entirely new, is not inferior to the two preceding, in the variety and interesting nature of the articles which it contains; and it exhibits the same taste in selection and extensive reading, which uniformly characterizes all Mr. D'Israeli's productions.

The present volume comprises upwards of thirty articles, historical, critical, biographical, literary, and miscellaneous, and treating on the following subjects, viz. The Pantomimical Characters—Extempore Comedies—Massinger, Milton, and the Italian Theatre—Songs of Trades, or Songs for the People—Introducers of Exotic Flowers, Fruits, &c.—Usurers of the Seventeenth Century—Chidiock Tichbourne (a Roman Catholic's History)—Elizabeth and her Parliament—Anecdotes of Prince Henry the son of James I. when a child—The Diary of a Master of the Ceremonies—Diaries, Moral, Historical, and Critical—Licenceers of the Press—Of Anagrams and Echo Verses—Orthography of Proper Names—Names of our Streets—Secret History of Edward Vere, Earl of Oxford—Ancient Cookery and Cooks—Ancient and Modern Saturnalia—Reliquiæ Gethinianæ—Robinson Crusoe—Catholic and Protestant Dramas—The History of the Theatre during its Suppression—Drinking Customs in England—On Literary Anecdotes—Condemned Poets—Acajou and Zirphile, of its Preface—Tom o' Bedlams—Introduction of Tea, Coffee, and Chocolate—Charles the First's Love of the Fine Arts—Secret History of Charles I. and his Queen Henrietta—The Minister the Cardinal Duke of Richelieu—The Minister, Duke of Buckingham, Lord Admiral, Lord General, &c. &c. &c.—Felton the Political Assassin—Johnson's Hints for the Life of Pope.

Where every article presents abundant materials for selection, it is difficult to extract a part, without impairing the interest of the whole; we shall, therefore, confine our specimens to a few passages from Mr. D'Israeli's 'Anecdotes of Prince Henry, the Son of James I. when a Child,' (drawn up from a manuscript memoir of him, written by one of his attendants,) and from his 'Secret History of Charles the First, and his Queen Henrietta,' which may be consulted with advantage by the future historian of that eventful period.

"Prince Henry in his childhood rarely wept, and endured pain without a groan. When a boy wrestled with him in earnest, and threw him, he was not 'seen to whine or weep at the hurt.' His sense of justice was early; for when his playmate, the little Earl of Mar, ill-treated one of his pages, Henry reproved his puerile friend: 'I love you because you are my Lord's son and my cousin; but, if you be not better conditioned, I will love such an one better,' naming the child that had complained of him."

"His martial character was perpetually discovering itself. When asked what instrument he liked best? he answered, 'a trumpet.' We are told that none of his age could dance with more grace, but that he never delighted in dancing; while he performed his heroical exercises with pride and delight, more particularly when before the King, the Constable of Castile, and other ambassadors. He was instructed by his master to handle and toss the pike, to march and hold himself in an affected style of stateliness, according to the martinets of those days; but he soon rejected such petty and artificial fashions; yet, to shew that his dislike arose from no want of skill in a trifling accomplishment, he would sometimes resume it only to laugh at it, and instantly return to his own natural demeanour. On one of these occasions one of these martinets observing that they could never be good soldiers unless they always kept true order and measure in marching, 'What then must they do,' cried Henry, 'when they wade through a swift-running water?' In all things freedom of action from his own native impulse, he preferred to the settled rules of his teachers; and when his physician told him that he rode too fast, he replied, 'Must I ride by rules of physic?' When he was eating a cold capon in cold weather, the physician told him that that was not meat for the weather. 'You may see, doctor,' said Henry, 'that my cook is no astronomer.' And when the same physician observing him eat cold and hot meat together, protested against it, 'I cannot mind that now,' said the royal boy facetiously, 'though they should have run at tilt together in my belly.' "

"Born in Scotland, and heir to the crown of England, at a time when the mutual jealousies of the two nations were running so high, the boy often had occasion to express the unity of affection, which was really in his heart. Being questioned by a nobleman, whether, after his father, he had rather be King of England or Scotland? he asked, "which of them was best?' being answered, that it was England, 'Then,' said the Scottish-born Prince, 'would I have both!' And once in reading this verse in Virgil,

Tros Tyriusve mihi nullo discrimine agetur.

the boy said he would make use of that verse for himself, with a slight alteration, thus—

'Anglus Scotusne mihi nullo discrimine agetur.'

" He was careful to keep alive the same feeling for another part of the British dominions, and the young Prince appears to have been regarded with great affection by the Welsh; for when once the Prince asked a gentleman at what mark he should shoot? the courtier pointed with levity at a Welshman who was present. 'Will you see then,' said the princely boy, 'how I will shoot at Welshmen?' Turning his back from him, the Prince shot his arrow in the air.— When a Welshman, who had taken a large carouse, in the fulness of his heart and his head, in the presence of the King, said that the Prince should have 40,000 Welshmen to wait upon him, against any King in Christendom; the King, not a little jealous, hastily inquired, 'To do what?' the little Prince turned away the momentary alarm by his facetiousness,— 'To cut off the heads of 40,000 leeks.'

"His bold and martial character was discovered in minute circumstances like these. Eating in the King's presence a dish of milk, the King asked him why he ate so much child's meat? 'Sir, it is also man's meat,' Henry replied;—and immediately after having fed heartily on a partridge, the King observed, that that meat would make him a coward, according to the prevalent notions of the age respecting diet; to which the young Prince replied, 'Though it be but a cowardly fowl, it shall not make me a coward.'—Once taking up strawberries with two spoons, when one might have sufficed, our infant Mars gaily exclaimed, 'The one I use as a rapier, and the other as a dagger.' "

It is well known that great pains were taken, in order to give the future sove-

reign of Britain (as he was expected to be) a suitable education, and his preceptor, Adam Newton, appears to have filled his office with no servility to the capricious fancies of his royal pupil.

"Desirous, however, of cherishing the generous spirit and playful humour of Henry, his Tutor encouraged a freedom of jesting with him, which appears to have been carried at times to a degree of momentary irritability on the side of the Tutor, by the keen humour of the boy. While the royal pupil held his master in equal reverence and affection, the gaiety of his temper sometimes twitched the equability or the gravity of the Preceptor. When Newton, wishing to set an example to the Prince in heroic exercises, one day practised the pike, and tossing it with such little skill as to have failed in the attempt, the young Prince telling him of his failure, Newton obviously lost his temper, observing, that 'to find fault was an evil humour.' 'Master, I take the humour of you.' 'It becomes not a Prince,' observed Newton. 'Then,' retorted the young Prince, 'doth it worse become a Prince's Master!'—Some of these harmless bickerings are amusing. When his Tutor, playing at shuffle-board with the Prince, blamed him for changing so often, and taking up a piece, threw it on the board, and missed his aim, the Prince smiling, exclaimed, 'Well thrown, Master;' on which the Tutor, a little vexed, said, 'he would not strive with a Prince at shuffle-board.' Henry observed, 'Yet you gownsmen should be best at such exercises, which are not meet for men who are more stirring.' The Tutor, a little irritated, said, 'I am meet for whipping of boys.' 'You vaunt then,' retorted the Prince, 'that which a ploughman or cart-driver can do better than you.' 'I can do more,' said the Tutor, 'for I can govern foolish children.' On which the Prince, who, in his respect for his Tutor, did not care to carry the jest farther, rose from table, and in a low voice to those near him said, 'He had need be a wise man that could do that.'—Newton was sometimes severe in his chastisements; for when the Prince was playing at Goff, and having warned his Tutor, who was standing by in conversation, that he was going to strike the ball, and having lifted up the Goff-club, some one observing, 'Beware, Sir, that you hit not Mr. Newton;' the Prince drew back the club, but smilingly observed, 'Had I done so, I had but paid my debts.'—At another time, when the princely boy was amusing himself with the sports of a child, his Tutor wishing to draw him to more manly exercises, amongst other things, said to him, in good humour, 'God send you a wise wife!' 'That she may govern you and me!' said the Prince. The Tutor observed, that 'he had one of his own;' the Prince replied, 'But mine, if I have one, would govern your wife, and by that means would govern both you and me.'—Henry, at this early age, excelled in a quickness of reply, combined with reflection, which marks the precocity of his intellect. His Tutor having laid a wager with the Prince that he could not refrain from standing with his back to the fire, and seeing him forget himself once or twice, standing in that posture, the Tutor said, 'Sir, the wager is won, you have failed twice;' Master,' replied Henry, 'Saint Peter's cock crew thrice.'—A Musician having played a voluntary in his presence, was requested to play the same again. 'I could not for the kingdom of Spain,' said the musician, 'for this were harder than for a preacher to repeat word by word a sermon that he had not learnt by rote.' A clergyman standing by, observed that he thought a Preacher might do that: 'Perhaps,' rejoined the young Prince, 'for a bishoprick!'

"The natural facetiousness of his temper appears frequently in the good humour with which the little Prince was accustomed to treat his domestics. The Prince had two of opposite characters, who were frequently set by the ears for the sake of the sport; the one, Murray, nick-named 'the taylor,' loved his liquor; and the other was a stout 'trencherman.' The King desired the Prince to put an end to these brawls, and to make the men agree; and that the agreement should be written and transcribed by both. 'Then,' said the Prince, 'must the drunken taylor subscribe it with chalk, for he cannot write his name, and then I will make them agree upon this condition—that the trencherman shall go into the cellar and drink with Will Murray, and Will Murray shall make a great wallet for the trencherman to carry his victuals in.'—One of his servants having cut the Prince's finger, and sucking out the blood with his mouth, that it might heal the more easily, the young Prince, who expressed no displeasure at the accident, said to him pleasantly, 'If, which God forbid! my father, myself, and the rest of his kindred should fail, you might claim the crown, for you have now in you the blood royal.'—Our little Prince once resolved on a hearty game of play, and for this purpose only admitted his young gentlemen, and ex-

cluded the men: it happened that an old servant, not aware of the injunction, entered the apartment, on which the Prince told him he might play too; and when the Prince was asked why he admitted this old man rather than the other men, he rejoined, 'Because he had a right to be of their number, for *Senex bis puer.*'

"Nor was our little Prince susceptible of gross flattery, for when once he wore white shoes, and one said that he longed to kiss his foot, the Prince said to the fawning courtier, 'Sir, I am not the Pope;' the other replied that he would not kiss the Pope's foot, except it were to bite off his great toe. The Prince gravely rejoined: 'At Rome you would be glad to kiss his foot, and forget the rest.'

"It was then the mode, when the King or the Prince travelled, to sleep with their suite at the houses of the nobility; and the loyalty and zeal of the host were usually displayed in the reception given to the royal guest. It happened that in one of these excursions the Prince's servants complained that they had been obliged to go to bed supperless, through the pinching parsimony of the house, which the little Prince at the time of hearing seemed to take no great notice of. The next morning the lady of the house, coming to pay her respects to him, she found him turning a volume that had many pictures in it; one of which was a painting of a company sitting at a banquet: this he shewed her. 'I invite you, Madam, to a feast.' 'To what feast?' she asked. 'To this feast,' said the boy. 'What, would your highness give me but a painted feast?' Fixing his eye on her, he said, 'No better, Madam, is found in this house.' There was a delicacy and greatness of spirit in this ingenious reprimand, far excelling the wit of a child.

"According to this anecdote-writer, it appears that James I. probably did not delight in the martial dispositions of his son, and whose habits and opinions were, in all respects, forming themselves opposite to his own tranquil and literary character. The writer says that, 'his Majesty, with the tokens of love to him, would sometimes interlace sharp speeches, and other demonstrations of fatherly severity.' Henry, who however lived, though he died early, to become a patron of ingenious men, and a lover of genius, was himself at least as much enamoured of the pike, as of the pen. The King, to rouse him to study, told him, that if he did not apply more diligently to his book, his brother, Duke Charles, who seemed already attached to study, would prove more able for governmentand for the cabinet, and that himself would be only fit for field-exercises and military affairs. To his father, the little Prince made no reply: but, when his tutor one day reminded him of what his father had said, to stimulate our young Prince to literary diligence, Henry asked, whether he thought his brother would prove so good a scholar? His tutor replied, that he was so likely to prove. 'Then,' rejoined our little Prince, 'will I make Charles Archbishop of Canterbury.'

"Our Henry was devoutly pious and rigid, in never permitting before him any licentious language or manners. It is well known that James I. had a habit of swearing,—innocent expletives in conversation, which, in truth, only expressed the warmth of his feelings; but, in that age, when Puritanism had already possessed half the nation, an oath was considered as nothing short of blasphemy. Henry once made a keen allusion to this verbal frailty of his father's; for when he was told that some hawks were to be sent to him, but it was thought the King would intercept some of them, the little Prince replied, 'He may do as he pleases, for he shall not be put to the oath for the matter.' The King once asking him, what were the best verses he had learned in the first book of Virgil, the little Prince answered, These:

Réx erat Æeas nobis quo justior alter
Nec pietate fuit, nec bello major et armis.

"Such are a few of the puerile anecdotes of a Prince who died in early youth, gleaned from a contemporary manuscript, by an eye and ear witness. They are trifles, but trifles consecrated by his name. They are genuine, and the philosopher knows how to value the indications of a great and heroic character. There are among them some, which may occasion an inattentive reader to forget, that they are all the speeches and the actions of a child!'

The secret history of Charles I. and his Queen Henrietta is drawn from manuscript letters of the times, and from the printed "Ambassades du Marechal Bassompierre." They shew how bigotted she was to the Romish faith, and how faithfully she educated her two sons in its tenets; but they also shew that Charles I. was by no means the weak, uxorious monarch he is represented by many writers.

"When Henrietta was on her way to England, a Legate from Rome arrested her at Amiens, requiring the Princess to undergo a penance, which was to last sixteen days, for marrying Charles without the

papal dispensation. The Queen stopped her journey, and wrote to inform the King of the occasion. Charles, who was then waiting for her at Canterbury, replied, that if Henrietta did not instantly proceed, he would return alone to London. Henrietta doubtless sighed for the Pope and the penance, but she set off the day she received the King's letter. The King, either by his wisdom or his impatience, detected the aim of the Roman Pontiff, who, had he been permitted to arrest the progress of a Queen of England for sixteen days in the face of all Europe, would thus have obtained a tacit supremacy over a British Monarch."

"By the marriage-contract, Henrietta was to be allowed a household establishment, composed of her own people; and this had been contrived to be not less than a small French colony, exceeding three hundred persons. It composed, in fact, a French faction, and looks like a covert project of Richelieu's to further his intrigues here, by opening a perpetual correspondence with the discontented Catholics of England. In the instructions of Bassompierre, one of the alleged objects of the marriage is the general good of the Catholic religion, by affording some relief to those English who professed it. If, however, that great Statesman ever entertained this political design, the simplicity and pride of the Roman Priests here completely overturned it; for in their blind zeal they dared to extend their domestic tyranny over Majesty itself.

"The French party had not long resided here, ere the mutual jealousies between the two nations broke out. All the English who were not Catholics, were soon dismissed from their attendance on the Queen, by herself; while Charles was compelled by the popular cry, to forbid any English Catholics to serve the Queen, or to be present at the celebration of her mass. The King was even obliged to employ poursuivants or king's messengers, to stand at the door of her chapel to seize on any of the English who entered there, while on these occasions the French would draw their swords to defend these concealed Catholics. 'The Queen and her's' became an odious distinction in the nation. Such were the indecent scenes exhibited in public; they were not less reserved in private. The following anecdote of saying a grace before the King, at his own table, in a most indecorous race run between the Catholic priest and the King's chaplain, is given in a manuscript letter of the times.

"'The King and Queen dining together

in the presence, Mr. Hacket (chaplain to the Lord Keeper Williams) being then to say grace, the Confessor would have prevented him, but that Hacket shoved him away; whereupon the Confessor went to the Queen's side, and was about to say grace again, but that the King pulling the dishes unto him, and the carvers falling to their business hindered. When dinner was done, the Confessor thought, standing by the Queen, to have been before Mr. Hacket, but Mr. Hacket again got the start. The Confessor, nevertheless, begins his grace as loud as Mr. Hacket, with such a confusion, that the King in great passion instantly rose from the table, and, taking the Queen by the hand, retired into the bed-chamber.' It is with difficulty we conceive how such a scene of priestly indiscretion should have been suffered at the table of an English Sovereign."

"One of the articles in the contract of marriage was, that the Queen should have a chapel at St. James's, to be built and consecrated by her French Bishop; the Priests became very importunate, declaring that without a chapel mass could not be performed with the state it ought before a Queen. The King's answer is not that of a man inclined to Popery. 'If the queen's closet, where they now say mass, is not large enough, let them have it in the great chamber; and, if the great chamber is not wide enough, they might use the garden; and, if the garden would not serve their turn, then was the park the fittest place.'

"The French Priests and the whole party feeling themselves slighted, and sometimes worse treated, were breeding perpetual quarrels among themselves, grew weary of England, and wished themselves away; but many having purchased their places with all their fortune, would have been ruined by the breaking up of the establishment. Bassompierre alludes to the broils and clamours of these French strangers, which exposed them to the laughter of the English Court; and one cannot but smile in observing, in one of the dispatches of this great mediator between two Kings and a Queen, addressed to the Minister, that one of the greatest obstacles which he had found in this difficult negotiation, arose from the bed-chamber women! The French King being desirous of having two additional women to attend the English Queen, his sister, the Ambassador declares, that 'it would be more expedient rather to diminish than to increase the number; for they all live so ill together, with such rancorous jealousies

and enmities, that I have more trouble to make them agree than I shall find to accommodate the differences between the two Kings. Their continual bickerings, and often their vituperative language, occasion the English to entertain the most contemptible and ridiculous opinions of our nation. I shall not, therefore, insist on this point, unless it shall please his Majesty to renew it.'

"The French Bishop was under the age of thirty, and his authority was imagined to have been irreverently treated by two beautiful viragos in that civil war of words which was raging; one of whom, Madame St. George, was in high favour, and most intolerably hated by the English. Yet such was English gallantry, that the King presented this lady on her dismission with several thousand pounds and jewels. There was something inconceivably ludicrous in the notions of the English, of a Bishop hardly of age, and the gravity of whose character was probably tarnished by French gesture and vivacity. This French establishment was daily growing in expence and number; a manuscript letter of the times states that it cost the King 240*l.* a day, and had increased from three-score persons to four hundred and forty, besides children!

It was one evening that the King suddenly appeared, and, summoning the French household, commanded them to take their instant departure—the carriages were prepared for their removal. In doing this, Charles had to resist the warmest intreaties, and even the vehement anger of the Queen, who is said in her rage to have broken several panes of the window of the apartment to which the King dragged her, and confined her from them.

"The scene which took place among the French people, at the sudden announcement of the King's determination, was remarkably indecorous. They instantly flew to take possession of all the Queen's wardrobe and jewels; they did not leave her, it appears, a change of linen, since it was with difficulty she procured one as a favour, according to some manuscript letters of the times. One of their extraordinary expedients was that of inventing bills; for which they pretended they had engaged themselves on account of the Queen, to the amount of 10,000*l.* which the Queen at first owned to, but afterwards acknowledged the debts were fictitious ones. Among these items was one of 400*l.* for necessaries for her Majesty; an Apothecary's bill for drugs of 800*l.*; and another of 150*l.* for 'the Bishop's unholy water,' as the writer expresses it. The young French

Bishop attempted by all sorts of delays to avoid this ignominious expulsion; till the King was forced to send his yeomen of the guards to turn them out from Somerset-house, where the juvenile French Bishop, at once protesting against it, and mounting the steps of the coach, took his departure, 'head and shoulders.' It appears, that to pay the debts and the pensions, besides sending the French troops free home, cost 50,000*l*.

"In a long procession of nearly forty coaches, after four days tedious travelling they reached Dover; but the spectacle of these impatient foreigners so reluctantly quitting England, gesticulating their sorrows or their quarrels, exposed them to the derision, and stirred up the prejudices of the common people. As Madame St. George, whose vivacity is always described extravagantly French, was stepping into the boat, one of the mob could not resist the satisfaction of flinging a stone at her French cap; an English courtier who was conducting her, instantly quitted his charge, ran the fellow through the body, and quietly returned to the boat. The man died on the spot; but no further notice appears to have been taken of the inconsiderate gallantry of this English courtier."

This transaction took place in 1626, and, four years afterwards, the French court attempted to introduce a bishop and physician about the Queen's person, but Charles I. absolutely prohibited it. From the preceding narrative of secret history,

"Charles I. does not appear so weak a slave to his Queen, as our writers echo from each other; and those who make Henrietta so important a personage in the cabinet, appear to have been imperfectly acquainted with her real talents. Charles, indeed, was deeply enamoured of the Queen, for he was inclined to strong personal attachments; and 'the temperance of his youth, by which he had lived so free from personal vice,' as May the parliamentary historian expresses it, even the gay levity of Buckingham seems never, in approaching the King, to have violated. Charles admired in Henrietta all those personal graces which he himself wanted; her vivacity in conversation enlivened his own seriousness, and her gay volubility the defective utterance of his own; while the versatility of her manners relieved his own formal habits. Doubtless the Queen exercised the same power over this Monarch which vivacious females are privileged by nature to possess over their husbands; she was often listened to, and her

suggestions were sometimes approved; but the fixed and systematic principles of the character and the government of this Monarch must not be imputed to the intrigues of a mere lively and volatile woman; we must trace them to a higher source; to his own inherited conceptions of the Regal rights, if we would seek for truth, and read the history of human nature in the history of Charles I.

Should Mr. D'Israeli's 'Miscellanies' survive many of the sources whence its contents are derived, they will be much more valuable to posterity than to the present times. His work is happily calculated for those who possess but few books, and but little leisure for reading.

A Narrative of a Journey of five thousand miles through the eastern and western States of America, contained in eight Reports, addressed to the thirty-nine English families, by whom the Author was deputed in June 1817, to ascertain whether any, and what part of the United States would be suitable for their residence; with Remarks on Mr. Birkbeck's Notes and Letters. By Henry Bradshaw Fearon, 8vo. 10s. 6d. Longman and Co. London, 1818.

In our last volume* we offered to our readers a general, though necessarily brief sketch of the multifarious contents of this interesting work, and had an opportunity of corroborating part of his statements. There were, however, two or three topics connected with the government and politics of the United States, to which, from want of [time and space, we were prevented from directing our attention. We shall, therefore, resume our notice of Mr. Fearon's volume, in order to supply that deficiency, and shall avail ourselves of the opportunity thus presented to us, of giving some important facts relative to the actual state of improvements in that country, which we have lately received, and on the authenticity of which our readers may confidently rely.

During Mr. Fearon's residence at Philadelphia, an election took place for the office of Governor of Pennsylvania,

---

who is possessed of very considerable patronage, having not fewer than forty or fifty offices, more or less lucrative, at his disposal. In a country like the United States, which boasts of such perfect freedom in its constitution, we simple Englishmen would expect to find the utmost fairness and impartiality in election. Mr. Fearon, however, undeceives us in this respect; and we learn that they are managed with as much dexterity on the other side of the Atlantic, as the most virulent reformists affirm to take place in Great Britain. But we shall let our author speak for himself.

The political parties, existing at Philadelphia are as follows:

"1st. The violent democrats, denominated 'Patent Democrats.'

"2d. The moderate democrats, called by the names of 'Independent Republicans,' 'Democrats of the Revolutions', and 'Old Schoolmen.'

"3d. Federalists, denominated also 'Tories,' 'Hartford Conventionalists,' and 'Blue Light Men.'

"4th. No party men called "Quids."

"The present candidates for the office of governor are each of them of the democratic party. General Hiester is of the moderate faction, and is also supported against his opponent by the federalists and quids. Mr. Finlay has the powerful aid of the unyielding democrats; and, though he is in a minority in the proportion of one to three within the city of Philadelphia, little doubt is entertained of his election's having been carried by a large majority through the State at large. All that are citizens, whether native or naturalized, of the age of twenty-one years and upwards, and who have paid their taxes, have the right of voting. It is not necessary that a man should be a householder in order to pay taxes, there being a direct or poll tax of 9s. per annum, which alone, when paid by men possessed of the previous qualification of citizenship, establishes the right to vote. The general election is preceded by an election in the different wards of officers called inspectors, whose business it is to receive the ballot ticket of voters: parties try their strength in this first step. I witnessed the mode of voting: the persons choosing inspectors attend at a stated place in their own ward, and deliver in their ballot through a window. The number assembled at any one time did not exceed twenty. There was no noise, no confusion, in fact, not even con-

versation. I was astonished to witness the anxiety felt by leading men, that their party should be elected inspectors. The eventful choice at the general election seemed, in fact in their estimation, actually to rest upon the having 'Inspectors' of their own party. I remarked to them that it could be of no consequence of what party these gentlemen were, as they were protected from partial or corrupt conduct by the mode of voting being by ballot. One of them informed me afterwards, that the fact of the inspectors being on one side or the other, had been calculated to make a difference of upwards of 200 votes in a particular section! arising from the reception of improper, and the rejection of good votes. The means by which an inspector can affect this, though the mode is by ballot, is said to be remarkably exact. That there may be some truth in this statement, would seem probable from a scene which I witnessed in the evening. I called upon the gentleman before alluded to. His room was completely crammed with the managers of the forthcoming election; and here, instead of finding that the general anxiety was at all connected with the advancement of correct political principles, I heard the following conversation:

"I'll bet you fifty (dollars) on Heister in Chesnut ward."

"What majority will you give him?"

"One fourth."

"Give old Sour Kraut (Heister) a hundred and thirty, and I'll take you."

"Done."

"What will you give Finlay in Lower Delaware ward?"

"One hundred."

"And what to Heister?"

"Three hundred."

"Give Bill three and a half, and I'll take you for five hundred."

"No: I'll give him three and half for a pair of boots."

"'Guess I'll take you for a pair and a hat.—What for Dock ward?"

"I won't bet on Dock: they're all a set of d——d Tories."

"Will you give Joe four hundred in South Mulberry?"

"I won't take Joe, I guess, in that ward?"

"What will you give Billy in South Mulberry?"

"A couple of hundred."

"Done for five hundred."

All. "What majority upon the whole election, Friend ——, will you advise us to give?"

Fr. "You must be cautious in your majorities. We do not know how Beaver and Dauphin (the counties of Dauphin and Beaver) may turn out.—Mind! save yourselves. If you find Billy (Finlay) going down, take up Sour Kraut (Heister.)

Elections are *managed*, it appears, and even governed by a species of meeting, termed a "*Caucus,*" of the precise nature of which Mr. Fearon could not obtain a correct account, but which he thus describes:

Candidates do not personally appear. Those who wish to be chosen obtain, as a preliminary step, what is termed "The Appointment." This is said to secure them the support of the whole of that party from which "the appointment" emanates. An announcement, called "The Ticket," issues from this Caucus a few days before the election; in this case there were three of these "tickets," severally headed, *Federal, Republican,* and *Democratic.* The federalists sent to an acquaintance of mine their "ticket," enclosed in the following circular letter; though I would remark, that *canvassing,* in the English meaning of that word, is not allowed:

"Fellow Citizen,
"The exercise of the elective franchise is
"at all times a privilege of the highest
"value:—on the present occasion every
"federalist has an opportunity to aid in
"dispelling prejudices—in lessening the
"malignity of party spirit—*in restoring
"the right of free election, and of resisting
"those dangerous abuses in government, in-
"troduced by office holders, which, if not
"promptly and steadily checked, threaten to
"become inveterate and irremediable.* Let
"every man be vigilant, active, and firm
"on this day, and success will crown our
"efforts.
"The inspectors have resolved to open
"the poll precisely at nine o'clock.
".*October* 14, 1817."

The democratic party adopt the same mode. I enclose you two of their circulars. These documents, as well as others which will follow, are, perhaps, better calculated than any other plan which I could adopt, to put you in possession of the state of parties, their mode of conduct and feeling towards each other, and also the general political condition of the whole people.

(CIRCULAR.)
"Sir,
"We enclose the *Democratic* Ticket,
"which is recommended by the delegates
"and conferrees fairly chosen, after *public
"notice.* We request you to vote it, and
"give it all the support to which you

"may deem it entitled. We consider
"this election as involving the most im-
"portant consequences. Federalism, con-
"scious of its own feebleness and inability
"to wrestle with the strength of demo-
"cracy, has made a *union* with a few
"disappointed men; hoping through them
"to turn over, not only the city and dis-
"trict, but the State and Union to Federal
"misrule.
"Be careful to bring with you your *re-
"ceipt* for COUNTY TAX. If a naturalized
"citizen, be sure to bring your CERTIFI-
"CATE of naturalization, as it will, in all
"probability, be required. These cau-
"tions are deemed more than ever ne-
"cessary, from the shameful conduct and
"persecuting spirit manifested by the Fe-
"deral Judges, at the late ward election.
"Be on the ground early. It is of im-
"portance, that every citizen votes, be-
"cause it may be that a vote would
"carry a candidate.
"Philadelphia, October 6, 1815."

DEMOCRATIC ADDRESS.

"Citizens, Democrats, Americans! *This
"is the day of the General Election!* If you
"value your own happiness, your political
"characters, your liberties, or your Re-
"publican institutions, every man to the
"poll, and vote the Democratic Ticket; it
"is headed with the name of the patriot
"WILLIAM FINDLAY. Citizens! the times
"are momentous! the seducers from the
"Democratic ranks have joined with our
"old inveterate political enemies to put
"down Democracy. It is an unholy
"league between apostates and political
"traitors on the one part, and on the
"other the anglo-federalists, the monar-
"chists, the aristocrats, the Hartford
"conventionalists, the blue-light men, the
"embargo-breakers, the Henryites, the
"men who in time of Peace cried out
"for war! war! but who in time of war
"called themselves the peace party. —
"Huzza for WILLIAM FINDLAY, and no
"bribery.—A long pull, a strong pull,
"and a pull altogether."

FEDERAL ADDRESS.

"WILLIAM FINDLAY,
"1. A selfish politician, who never served
"his country, and always on the look out
"for office. 2. An apostate federalist and
"time server. 3. A constant office hun-
"ter. 4. A treasury broker and public
"defaulter, who exchanged and used pub-
"lic money for his own benefit. 5. One
"who holds morality in contempt, and
"practices the maxim, that the end jus-
"tifies the means. 6. One who has

" resorted to the basest falsehoods to sup-
" port himself. 7. One who intrigued
" and bargained for the office, and openly
" electioneered for himself. 8. A state in-
" quisitor, who would gag, if not immo-
" late every man, not of his own sect.
" 9. A man who has blended the public
" money with his own, and is yet to ac-
" count for misdemeanor in office. 10.
" A barbarian, who holds that ' the study
" of the law disqualifies a man from being
" a judge.' "

" Take notice who are the friends of
" WILLIAM FINDLAY,— 1. Traitors and
" apostates. 2. Inveterate aristocrats. 3.
" Office-hunters. 4. Cormorants for the
" loaves and fishes, and friends only to
" themselves. 5. Fugitives from British
" gaols and justice.
" Take care!!!—WILLIAM FINDLAY's
" election will be sure, 1. If the Repub-
" licans stay at home. 2. If they are neg-
" ligent or timid on the election ground.
" 3. If election, like treasury frauds, are
" not detected and prevented.
" Take advice,—1. Look well to your
" tickets. 2. Look well to your boxes.
" 3 Look well to your tallies. 4. Look
" well to your returns; and 5. Look well
" to those who vote, that they are qua-
" lified."

On the day of election our author
was early on the spot where it was
to be made.

The place appointed to receive votes
for the city (exclusive of Southwark and
the northern liberties), was in the State-
house—the same building in which that
immortal document was passed—THE DE-
CLARATION OF INDEPENDENCE! There
were two inspectors for each ward of the
city placed at separate windows. The
electors delivered in their votes from the
street. The ground was what is here
called manned; that is, persons in the interest of the parties have written on their
hat or breast, " Federal Ticket," or " Democratic Ticket,"soliciting citizens as they
approach the poll " to vote their ticket;"
for which purpose they are prepared to
furnish them with the printed balloting
list of their party. The neighbouring
public-houses were, of course, occupied by
the electioneerers. I resolved to devote to
this as much of my time as possible, in
obtaining an insight into the character
and mind of this people, and to observe
them acting in their political capacity.
They were all betting upon the election;
but few, if any appeared to care one straw
about principle. Old General Barker,

(whom I had heard the previous evening
make a most able speech in favour of Mr.
Findlay, at a public meeting of the democrats) was travelling about to the several depots of leading characters. I
could hardly credit my sight that he was
the same person whom I had heard the
previous evening, His chief employment
during the day seemed drinking rum and
gin with any and every body. I made
some remarks to him concerning his speech:
he pleasantly answered, " My good fellow,
I did as well as I could, I guess: they
made me open the ball." This old general was the companion in arms of Washington: he has been both sheriff and
mayor: he has the character of possessing
a good heart, and very improvident generosity.

The election terminated throughout
the State in *one day*; and though the
excitement of party and pecuniary feeling, by the universality of gambling on
this occasion was very great, yet we
have much pleasure in stating that
there was no confusion or disturbance.
In a subsequent part of his volume,
Mr. Fearon recurs again to the subject
of elections, and takes notice of a very
striking remark in all the electioneering
addresses which he has seen, that the defeated party invariably complains of the
corrupt influence of *Caucus*, which he
informs us from an American writer, is

" a cant term for those private meetings
" which are held by the political parties,
" previous to elections, for the purpose of
" agreeing upon candidates for office, or
" concerting any measure which they de-
" sign carrying at the subsequent public
" meeting." The other day I called upon
" a resident of this city, a person of some
political importance. Aware that the
subject is already and very variously discussed throughout the States, I casually enquired, " Who do you think, Sir, will be
your next president ?" He gave no reply,
except by a significant nod. I followed up
my enquiry by " Do you think, Sir, Mr.
Adams will be selected ?" To which he
answered, with decided confidence, " No;
" I guess not, Sir; we have the man, we
" have the man, we know our man.—Craw-
" ford (the present secretary of the treasu-
" ry) had it in caucus last time, within a
" few." I enquired what he meant by
having it in caucus; for that Mr. Munroe
was elected by an overwhelming majority.
His answer was, " Ah! I guess you don't
" understand our modes; when you have
" been here a few years, you will compre-

" heed these things. Only mind, I tell you " Adams never can be president; for he " will not be able to do any thing with " caucus." From minute enquiry, I understood that this thing called caucus, was practically invented by Mr. John Adams, during his presidentship; and that it is now universally practised in the election to every office in America. Since the first choice of Mr. Jefferson, the presidential elections are managed by private meetings (or caucus) of the democratic members of congress, previous to elections: they settle among themselves who shall be president. This is what is called getting " the appointment in caucus," and an instance never occurs of the votes being in opposition to caucus. When they have determined upon who they wish to be president, they send circulars to their different States, pointing out, by a kind of *congé d'élire*, who they have resolved should be elected; and as the right of voting for presidents is confined to a very limited number, there is no instance of the caucus being disobeyed. Mr. Munroe being a democrat was, as a matter of course, voted for by the democratic States; and those of New England being federal, would not, I believe, give a vote upon the occasion. It appears that the members of the Washington caucus were almost equally divided between Mr. Crawford and Mr. Munroe; but that some accommodation being agreed upon, the latter got " the appointment." Had his rival obtained this, he and not Mr. Munroe would have been voted for by the democratic States, as a matter of course. These are alarming facts; for thus we see that the very men (the members of congress) who are directly excluded by the constitution from voting, become, by means of a secret something unknown to that constitution, and at variance with both its letter and spirit, the real electors to the presidentship. How necessary are the most unceasing vigilance, and the greatest degree of public principle and public virtue, to preserve even the best institutions from gross perversion! No oligarchy can be more dangerous than this, which deludes the people with a belief that they are all-powerful, and the electors of their chief magistrate, while virtually they are the mere tools of a faction, and have not a voice in the matter.

So much for the boasted independence of the United States.

Although slavery is confined chiefly to the southern States, yet there is a most degrading traffic carried on in the persons of Europeans, who, emigrating from Europe without money, pay for their passage by binding themselves to the captain, who receives the produce of their labour for a certain number of years. These are termed *Redemptioners*, and are disposed of by public advertisements, as regularly as the black slaves in any of the West Indian islands. Mr. Fearon has given some interesting information relative to this degrading traffic, for which our readers must consult his work. In one instance a gentleman of Philadelphia, who wanted an old couple to take care of his house, had a man, his wife, and daughter offered him for sale. He purchased them, and they proved to be his father, his mother, and sister!

. . . .

We now invite our readers to the particulars adverted to, at the commencement of this article, and which we trust will be found not unworthy of their attention, especially as they embrace various topics of information, which it did not fall within Mr. Fearon's plan to collect.

Agriculture is an important pursuit in the United States; and the example of the parent country, in instituting agricultural societies, and exhibitions has been recently followed in America, and with very beneficial results, particularly since the late war with this country. Among these, the Philadelphia agricultural society, which has published four volumes of its papers, has decidedly taken the lead. The state of New York boasts of not fewer than thirteen agricultural societies, most of which have annual cattle shows: but the Massachussetts agricultural society is stated to us, to hold the pre-eminence in activity, in the more northern part of the American Union. In Virginia several similar societies have been established, and not before they were wanted: for the agriculture of that State is in a deplorably bad state. In Kentucky also, which is but a newly formed State, societies have been established, and at Lexington there is one, which we understand is conducted with great spirit. Of the activity and attention here given to the improvement of their breeds of cattle, our readers will form an idea from the high prices paid for prime stock. One instance has been communicated to us, of an individual who imported from this country two bulls of the Hereford and Teeswater breeds, each of which was sold for the sum of *two thousand dollars.* In the vicinity of Philadelphia the Alderney breed is in pefection.

For the conveyance of the produce of the various States, excellent turnpike-roads are forming in every direction; our readers need not be told, that, though the invention of the steam engine is not of American origin, yet its application to the propulsion of vessels was first made by an American, (Mr. Fulton); and that most, if not all their great rivers are navigated with facility and dispatch by means of steam-boats. In order to complete the line of internal navigation, various schemes have been proposed for connecting the lakes and rivers of the United States by means of canals. The spirit of internal improvement in this respect is universal. The State of New York, in particular, is engaged in one grand operation; the construction of a canal to form a junction of Lake Erie with the waters of Hudson River. Eighty miles of it (we believe the whole length is between two and three hundred miles) were to be completed by the end of last year; and five thousand men, with fifteen hundred horses are at work upon this noble undertaking. And the canal between the rivers Chesapeak and Delaware is expected to be finished in the course of the present year.

Education, though in many places still defective, is fast spreading throughout the Union. Its *theory* is British, though without the solidity of enquiry and variety of assistance, which are offered in this country by professors, and authors who have treated on the various branches of science. Colleges and schools however, are multiplying in every direction. The system of tuition invented by Pestalozzi, at Berne, in Switzerland, was transplanted to Philadelphia, some years since, by Joseph Neef, formerly a co-adjutor of Pestalozzi's. At first, it promised the happiest success; but, from some cause or other, it fell to the ground, and the establishment was destroyed. The Lancasterian, or British and Foreign School

Society's method of teaching, however, is advancing steadily. A model school has been established at New York, where the plan of tuition has for some time been attempted under the direction of a master sent from England by that society. And the arrival of Mr. Joseph Lancaster in America, is there considered as forming a new era in its history. In the winter of 1817, the State of Pensylvania set a noble example to the rest of the Union, by passing a law to establish schools upon his system throughout that State; and at this time, Mr. L. is actually engaged by the directors of the public schools for the city and county of Philadelphia, personally to superintend a large model-school now building, in which an example will be given to the Union of his plan of procedure. Ample funds are provided by the State, in order to defray the expenses.

Correspondent with the progress of education is the taste for reading, especially in the great towns of the northern and middle States. In America all are politicians, and almost every man is either a federalist or a democrat. The eagerness of the people for news far surpasses even that of our own country; and we believe we are not incorrect in stating that nearly four hundred papers minister to this voracious appetite for novelty, which is gratified by the great cheapness of these vehicles of intelligence. Independently of reprints of several English Journals of the highest character, nearly thirty periodical publications announce, for the most part every month, the progress of science and general literature.

The reading of the Americans is, with few exceptions, English; the high price of paper, labour, and taxes in this country has been very favourable to the reprinting of English works in America. Every English production of celebrity whatever its size may be, is there immediately re-printed, and sold for one-fourth of its original price British Novels and Poetry are the favorite objects of perusal; and while we now write, a Philadelphia bookseller's prospectus lies before us, announcing are-print of Lady Morgan's " France" in one volume 8vo, for two dollars and a half, with a notice that " the above edition contains the French words and phrases as in the London, with an English translation of each in the page where it occurs." The same bookseller has announced, " the first American edition of Dr. Johnson's Dictionary, in two volumes, 4to, or four volumes 8vo. with the addition of the Standard of Pronunciation in Walker's Critical Pronouncing Dictionary." We cannot but wish that this, or some other work had been undertaken earlier, as it would, perhaps, have prevented the intrusion of those Americanisms, which at first render it difficult to an Englishman to converse with a native-born American. Each of the large Cyclopædias of this country is reprinting, either at New York or Philadelphia, at the expense of one or two opulent booksellers of those cities. And the establishment for several years past of book fairs, similar to those of Frankford and Leipsic, (which are alternately held at New York and Philadelphia) has greatly tended to facilitate the circulation of books. We are not acquainted with the actual number of volumes annually published in those cities ; but we know that, four years ago, the books, printed annually at Philadelphia alone, amounted to 500,000.

The original productions of the Americans, however, are comparatively few, Medicine, Law, the Geology and Topography of the United States, and especially Divinity, form the principal subjects of transatlantic literature. Much controversial discussion, indeed, has been carried on in the United States during the last 2 or 3 years. In the state of Massachussetts, Unitarianism is the prevalent doctrine, which has been attacked with great warmth. In Philadelphia Dr. White, Bishop of the Protestant Episcopal church in the commonwealth of Pennsylvania, has published " Comparative Views of the Controversy between the Calvanists and Arminians," which are written with great vigour and ability. The reverend author opposes the former denomination of Christians, but with singular candour and mildness ; but his work is not entirely free from Americanisms. The Rev. J. R. Wilson has

published an "Historical Sketch of Opinions on the Atonement from the Incarnation of Christ to the present time," in one volume, 8vo. which contains a detailed exposition of the doctrine of the Covenanters, among whom he is a minister. The Rev. Dr. Wharton, of Burlington, (New Jersey) has published a " View of the Controversy between the Protestant and Roman Catholic Churches," 8vo. This gentleman, we believe was formerly a Catholic priest, and chaplain to a Roman Catholic congregation at Worcester in Worcester in this country. He is said to be both an able controversialist, and an elegant writer. The system of divinity composed by the late Dr. Dwight, it will be sufficient here barely to mention, as it is on the eve of republication in this city. In short, so numerous are the theological productions of the United States, that they give full employment to a " Quarerly Theological Review," edited at Philadelphia, by the Rev. Ezra Stiles Ely. In connexion with theological literature, we may add that Professor Griesbach's critical edition of the New Testament (Leipsic, 1805) has been reprinted at Cambridge, in New England, in two handsome volumes 8vo. at the press of Messrs. Wells and Hilliard. The typography of the large paper copies is truly beautiful, and is not unworthy of any European printer.

In the benevolent work of circulating the scriptures " through every nation, kindred, and language," the American Bible Society has shewn itself to be an able and active associate of the parent British and Foreign Bible Society. " The formation of this society (to use the language of its committee) " was hailed as a great and glorious era in the history of the country: and its means of accomplishing the important end of its formation, have been increased with more than ordinary rapidity." In justification of this statement, it may be observed, that at the close of its first year, (May 1817) it numbered more than eighty auxillia. New societies are consequently forming, and the number now in existence, we believe, considerably exceeds two hundred. It may be proper to add, that the treasurer of the American National Society publishes the amounts of his receipts every month, and that they are three, four, and sometimes five thousand dollars per month.

· Various neat editions of the Roman Classics, which of course follow the most correct text of European editors, sufficiently attest the growing attention of the Americans to classical literature; and their late reprint of Ernesti's edition of Cicero's Works, in 20 volumes, 12mo. is highly creditable for its accuracy and neatness. But amid the multifarious productions of the American press, it is not a little singular that no authentic statistical work relative to the Union has hitherto issued from it. Mr. Bristed, an Englishman by birth, (who since his residence at New York, has become a barrister there) has published a book, which *he calls* " the Resources of the United States," and which has been reprinted in this city. Some good ideas as it unquestionably does contain; but it is replete with mistakes, and in every page there is abundant evidence of the greatest negligence in the collection of facts. We had intended to have given our readers an analysis of the London edition; but it is so little worth it, that this brief notice will be abundantly sufficient. We will only add, that Mr. Bristed's blunders have been severely exposed in several American Journals, and particularly in the Analectic Magazine published at Philadelphia, and the North American Review edited at Boston, to which the most distinguished literary characters of the Union contribute their assistance.

In the *belles lettres,* the Americans have given but few specimens of native talent; nor is this at all to be wondered at. The United States are even yet but an infant independent power; and with the exception of the oldest settled parts which we believe are usually termed *Old America,* the inhabitants of the more recently settled districts are too fully occupied in the necessary arts of life, to be able to spare time for lighter pursuits; politics, however, always excepted. Hence it is only within the last year that an original trea-

tise on the Belles Lettres has made its appearance, from the pen of Mr. Adams, in 2 volumes, 8vo. And their standard works in poetry are very few. " The Columbiad" of Mr. Barlow, reprinted in this country a few years since, though not destitute of some fine passages, is, upon the whole, a heavy production. The late Dr. Dwight's poems entitled " Greenfield Hill," and " The Conquest of Canaan," are very superior productions. Both of them, we believe, have been reprinted in this country; and of the latter, our readers may see a fine passage in the seventh volume of Mr. Campbell's recent work intitled " Specimens of the British Poets." The only *recent* productions of the American Muse, which we have seen, are Mr. Pierpoint's " Airs of Palestine," which contain some exquisite passages, and the " Backwoodsman," of Mr. Paulsen who holds a high rank among the native bards of America. Of these, as well as of some other works noticed in the course of this article, we shall endeavour to procure copies, and hope at no great distance of time to present analyses of them to our readers.

We cannot close this article without noticing the efforts making in America for civilizing the original inhabitants, or native Indians, as they are usually termed, and also for the benefit of the African negroes. The benevolent work of civilizing the former originated with the Philanthropic Society of Friends, but of late years it has been taken up by the American Government, and is now proceeding steadily and successfully under agents appointed by it.

With respect to the African Negroes, the import traffic in whom the American Government followed the example of Great Britain in prohibiting, several societies have been formed in their behalf in various States of the Union. The object of these benevolent institutions is, to educate African youth in a knowledge of the scriptures in their original languages and in general science; and, thus instructed, to send them forth, as missionaries, to carry the word of life to not fewer than fifty millions of Africans, of whom twenty millions are computed to be of the proper Negro race. The institutions, which we are now noticing, are yet but in their infancy; but from the wisdom with which they appear to be conducted, and from the sober piety of the distinguished individuals who have projected them, we are warranted to augur, in progress of time, the happiest results to that long enslaved and much injured part of mankind.

History of the City of Dublin, from the earliest accounts to the present time: containing its Annals, Antiquities, Ecclesiastical History and Charters, &c. &c. &c. By the late J. Warburton, Deputy Keeper of the Records in Birmingham Tower: the late Rev. J. Whitelaw, M. R. I. A. and the Rev. Robert Walsh, M. R. I. A. with numerous plates, plans, and maps, 4to. two vols. 5l. 5s. Large Paper, 8l. 8s. Cadell and Davies, London. 1818.

This work supplies an important chasm in the topography of the British Empire. From a variety of causes, Ireland, until within these few years, was almost a *terra incognita* to the generality of readers; and though the recent works of Mr. Wakefield, Mr. Curwen, (of whose valuable labours we gave an account in our last volume), and a few other Writers, have contributed to make known its political state and resources, yet the paucity of the *native* historians and topographers has been such, that we are now, for the first time since the commencement of our labours, called to give an analysis of a history of the City of Dublin, executed with the skill and ability which its importance requires.

The work now under our consideration was originally undertaken by Mr. Warburton, Deputy Keeper of the Records of Birmingham Tower, in the Castle of Dublin, and the Rev. James Whitelaw, Vicar of St. Catherine's in that City. For its antient history Mr. Warburton furnished such documents, as, from his employment, he had access to; and it was proposed to Mr. Whitelaw, to methodize and arrange them, and to add an account of modern Dublin. The death of Mr. Warburton consigned to Mr. Whitelaw an unfinished account, which he was

proceeding to complete, when his lamented death also consigned it to Mr. Walsh, when scarcely half the work was finished. By the latter Gentleman therefore it has been completed, who has honourably stated the proportions executed by his predecessors.

Besides a sketch of the exemplary life and public labours of the Rev. James Whitelaw, who fell a victim to the unwearied discharge of his ministerial duties, the first volume (to which we shall at present invite our readers' attention), contains a brief introductory account of the reduction of Ireland in the reign of King Henry II., together with a Chronological List of the Lords-Lieutenants and other Chief Governors, from that period to the present time. To this succeeds the *antient* history of the City of Dublin and its Castle, franchises, &c. &c. interspersed with extracts from numerous documents and charters: next follows a history of the Archiepiscopal See and its Bishops, and of the religious houses which existed previously to the Reformation. The *modern* history of Dublin is then presented to us, comprising a copious and interesting account of the city, its bay, and harbour; its situation, extent, and population; its public edifices, both civil and ecclesiastical; its seminaries; and various benevolent institutions.

In a volume presenting so great a variety of important and interesting topics it is difficult to select. We apprehend, however, that we shall gratify our readers most by giving them some idea of the *modern* state of the Metropolis of the Sister Island.

DUBLIN, the capital of Ireland, in population and extent the second city of the British empire, and probably the seventh in Europe*, is situate on the river Anna Liffey, and at a small distance from its mouth, to which it will probably, at no very distant period, extend: it stands nearly in the south-eastern extremity of an immense plain, stretching considerably above one hundred English miles across, the island from sea to sea, in some parts diversified with gentle eminences, but no where interrupted by mountains: bounded on the east by the Irish sea, where it rises into the elevated peninsula of Howth,

* The European cities that exceed Dublin in extent and population, are London, Paris, Constantinople, Vienna, Moscow, and Naples.

this plain terminates westward at the bay of Galway, and the lofty mountains that tower over the great lakes of Mask and Corrib ; and its greatest breadth, may be considered as extending nearly fifty miles from that mass of mountains occupying the confines of the counties of Dublin and Wicklow, about four miles south of this city, to the mountains of Carlingford and the Fewes on the confines of Lowth and Armagh, which with Sliew and Donard, the loftiest summit of the mountains of Mourne in Downe, though distant about sixty English miles. are frequently visible from the vicinity of Dublin; a circumstance, however, which is almost an unerring indication of approaching rain. Over that mass of mountains south of Dublin. and which is not distinguished by any general appellation, in clear weather, others still more elevated are visible, of which the most remarkable is the conical mountain, called from its form the Great Sugar-loaf.

From the south side of this mass issues the river Liffey, which, encreased by the King's river, of nearly equal magnitude, and running with a rapid stream through a region of mountains and bogs, enters this plain, through which it flows with a course so circuitous that though it runs nearly 71 English miles, including its numerous windings, yet the distance from its source to its mouth in the bay of Dublin does not exceed ten miles: in the upper part of its course it forms a beautiful cascade, where the torrent is precipitated into a gloomy abyss called Pul-a-fooka, or the Devil's hole. In Kildare its innumerable sinuosities are richly wooded ; and entering the county of Dublin, it approaches the capital through a deep glen, whose lofty, and in some parts precipitous banks, present the most interesting scenery to the eye of the traveller: the tide, which carries vessels of burden up to the city, just reaches its western edge, where a fall prevents further ascent, which circumstance, with its frequent shallows and rapids, renders it, though in many parts deep and gentle, totally useless in extending inland navigation from the capital : it is subject to floods, which sometimes rise to a dangerous height, overflow its banks to a considerable distance, frequently carry away the bridges that cross it, and meeting the ascending tide, sometimes lay the city quays under water: in summer, however, it is reduced to an inconsiderable stream, which on the recess of the tide presents to the spectator a channel nearly empty, and at once disgusting to the sight and smell: at its mouth it receives the Dodder from

Kippure, one of the eminences of the southern mass, which, though nothing more than a mountain torrent, is, of great importance to the capital. The other streams which pay their tribute to the Liffey are inconsiderable; that which watering the vicinity of Finglas, visits Glasnevin and Ballybough, seems at present to have no distinctive appellation, though formerly called the Tulkan or Tolekan; and the stream passing by Kilmainham, was formerly called the Cammock, a name at present equally forgotten.

The Castle of Dublin, the viceregal residence, and nearly the central point of Dublin, is in 53° 20′ 38½′ north latitude, and in 6° 17′ 29″ west longitude, from the meridian of Greenwich.

Dublin covers an area of about 1264 English acres, on which stood in the year 1798, 14,854 inhabited, with 1202 waste houses, containing a population of 170,805 souls, or 11.5 nearly to an inhabited house.

The Liffey divides the city into two unequal parts; the southern division, containing nearly 785 acres and 112,497 souls, and the northern only 478 acres and 58,308 souls.

Of the above area, nearly 146 acres were waste ground, and 36 covered by the Liffey, so that the total area of Dublin, occupied by buildings, was 1,117 acres, and the average population of each acre 153 souls.

To the above total, viz.   170,805

We must add for Spring-garden, a suburb beyond the circular road   1,286
For the Garrison, about   ..   7,000
Royal Hospital   400
Foundling Hospital   558
St. Patrick's Hospital   ..   155
House of Industry   1,657
Trinity College   529

Total population of Dublin in } 182,370
1798.   ...

The density of population, however, varies exceedingly, not only in Dublin, but in all cities that can boast of any considerable degree of antiquity. Our ancestors, in times of turbulence and confusion, more anxious for security than studious of convenience and elegance, crowded their habitations together, so as not to occupy a space too large for the purposes of defence. As domestic tranquillity became better secured, they gradually extended their quarters; persons of wealth and condition abandoned their former residence to the poorer class of citizens, built more airy houses in more spacious streets, and gradually refined ·into that state of elegance that now prevails. Hence it happens, that in the ancient parts of most cities, the population is dense in proportion both to the number of houses and the space that they occupy; while in the more modern parts, the train of servants, ever attendant on opulence and luxury, gives a population, great indeed in proportion to the number of houses, but inconsiderable, if we regard the area they occupy in extensive back grounds and spacious streets. The population of Dublin was accordingly found to be most crowded within the walls of the ancient city, comprehending the parishes of St. Werburgb, St. John, St. Michael, St. Nicholas within, the eastern part of St. Audeon, and the deanery of Christ-church. This space, containing an area of nearly forty-five acres English, had in 1682, according to Sir William Petty, 1145 houses, and in 1788, 1179 houses, and 15,683 inhabitants, which give an average of 349 souls nearly to an acre, and 13.3 to a house. The density of population however varies within this space, for in the parish of St. Michael it amounts to 439 souls to an acre, and almost 16 to a house. Notwithstanding the unprecedented rise in the price of foreign timber, and the apprehensions generally entertained of the effects which the union might have on the prosperity of this city, a considerable number of houses have been built since 1798, and its present population is not short of 190,000 souls, though we cannot pretend to speak with any degree of precision on this subject, no survey having latterly been made

We have not room to describe the squares, the Castle, and other public edifices that adorn this splendid city; but we cannot pass in silence its numerous and well-conducted charitable foundations, of which few capitals in Europe have, in proportion to their population, a greater number than Dublin has at present.

Nearly *seventy schools*, and other asylums, are copiously described in the course of this work, besides more than twenty medical hopitals, infirmaries, &c. Of eleven of the most considerable of these ample accounts are given in the first volume, viz. 1. The Blue Coat Hospital, founded by King Charles II. for the education of the children, sons or grandsons of reduced free citizens, nearly two hundred of whom are constantly on this foundation;—2. The Foundling Hospital, established in the early part of the last century, and in which there constantly appear to be upwards of 6000 foundlings; the excellent arrangements· of this institution are detailed at considerable length, and it is satisfactorily vindicated from the exceptions of Mr. Malthus.—3. The Hibernian Society's School for Educating the children of soldiers, five hundred of whom, upon the average, are constantly provided for. The economy and discipline of this school are intended to be assimilated as nearly as possible to the Asylum for the children of our gallant soldiers at Chelsea.—4. The Hibernian Marine Society's School, for the children of decayed seamen.—5. The House of Industry.—6. The Bedford Asylum for industrious children.—7. Penitentiary for the Reform of young criminals of the male sex.—8. Penitentiary for adult female convicts.—9. The Incorporated Society for promoting English Protestant Schools.—10. The Schools founded and endowed in the reign of Charles II. by the benevolent and munificent Erasmus Smith, Esq.—And, lastly, the Royal Hospital at Kilmainham, which, in its design and object, is the same as the noble monument of national gratitude at Chelsea.

The systems of education, domestic management, revenue, and expenditure of these various excellent charities, are detailed with considerable minuteness; and as public attention has of late years been much directed to the Penitentiary established at Millbank, near Westminster, we shall conclude an account of the first volume of this work, with the following extracts relative to the Penitentiaries at Dublin. The

Penitentiary, for the reform of young criminals of the Male Sex, was opened during the administration of his excellency Earl Hardwicke, in the year 1801, for the reception and reform of such young criminals under the age of 15 as were actually convicted, and under sentence of transportation. But though such was the original object of the institution, the majority of· boys received into it have been of different descriptions; namely, such as were detected in acts of theft, and committed in consequence thereof by magistrates without trial; others strongly suspected of being engaged in vicious and criminal courses; apprentices eloping from their masters, and otherwise miscon-ducting themselves. Some boys, appa-rently in danger of being involved in cri-minal practices, have been received at the instance of their parents. From the annual returns made by the governors, there is ground for concluding that the course of discipline, instruction, and in-dustry, pursued in this establishment, has been productive of salutary effects in many instances; but as the mistaken lenity of magistrates had frequently in former years induced them to discharge the per-sons so committed, before a sufficient time had elapsed to work a complete reform, there is reason to fear that the institution had, in consequence of this in-terference, not been productive of all the benefits to society which might otherwise have resulted from it. This inconvenience is however no longer complained of, and the magistrates at present do not discharge any boy, without the consent and appro-bation of the governors.

About sixteen boys generally are per-manently on the day-school list; and whenever a boy is unemployed at his trade, he is sent to school to receive instruction. There is also a Sunday school holden, at which all the boys attend. A clergyman, called " Clerical Visitor," has the superintendence of this penitentiary, with an annual salary of 120l.

The state of manufactures and industry, and the general state of the institution, will appear from the annexed report.

Since its formation in 1801, to 31st Dec. 1811, were admitted.

Young Convicts sentenced to transportation	69
Young criminals committed by magistrates	518
	587
Of those have been appren-ticed to trades	50
Pardoned by the Lord Lieute-nant	22
Enlisted in the army and navy by his Excellency's per-mission	99
Discharged by order of magis-trates	264
Transferred to the House of Industry for good conduct	63
Died	5
Escaped	16
Remained in the penitentiary	68
	587

State of Employment in the Penitentiary.

Weavers	18
Winders	30
Shoemakers	12
Boys taught to read and write only	8
	68

Gross Produce of the Labour of Boys.
Year ending 31st December 1811,
£111 19 0.

The Penitentiary for Adult Female Convicts, was placed under the direction of the Governors of the Dublin House of In-dustry, on the 1st December, 1809. Its object is the reception and employment of female convicts sentenced to transporta-tion: they are provided with bedsteads, beds, sheets, and blankets, and receive two meals daily of nutritive food. Those who are capable of industry, are usefully employed in making barrack bedding, and receive one-half of the profits of their labour. Since 1st December, 1809, 103 convicts have been admitted, of whom 26 have been reformed, and pardoned by his Grace the Lord-Lieutenant, 12 removed to the infirmary in the House of Industry, 5 remanded to Newgate as incorrigible, 2 died, 3 discharged in consequence of the time of their confinement having expired, 55 remain in the house.—Total 103.

The present State is as follows :

Number of female convicts, 5th Jan. 1812	55
Children of ditto, under two years of age	2
	57
Employed at weaving	22
Needle work	27
In the infirmary	4
As nurses	2
Children of Convicts	2
	56

Gross Amount of Labour of Female Convicts.
For twelve months, ending 31st Dec. 1811,
£424 5s. d.

These penitentiaries at present occupy buildings belonging to the police of the City of Dublin, and are situated in Smith-field, at some distance from the House of Industry; the temporary use of which has been given to the governors for this purpose: this department however is to be greatly enlarged, and additional ground has been purchased, on which the necessary buildings are to be erected without delay, on a plan prepared by Mr. Francis Johnson, and approved of by government. The surround-ing wall of this extensive edifice, which will be 40 feet high and 30 from the interior buildings, will enclose an area of nearly 5¼ English acres, presenting a front of 707 feet to Grange Gorman-lane, with a depth of 342 feet, and so constructed, that guards stationed at a very few points on its summit, will command the entire circumference. Ex-clusive of apartments for the proper officers, board-room, chapels for divine service, in-firmaries, kitchens, &c. this edifice, which consists of three stories, will contain spa-cious workshops cells for solitary confinement, with airing-grounds for 125 males and as many females, who are to be all convicts under sentence of transportation; the sexes will be perfectly separated, the convicts divided into four classes, each of which will have its distinct and separate airing ground, and the apartments of the keepers are so situated as to command an uninterrupted view of the work-shops under their respective inspection. The situation is elevated and airy, open on the north to the country, and on the south overlooking the city; and through the ground runs the stream called the Bradogue, with a lively course in a channel 6 feet wide by 7 feet high, and covered with a substantial arch, a circumstance of much importance, as its water may be occasionally diverted by means of sluices to cleanse the sewers necessary in so extensive a building.

(To be Continued.)

Charenton ; or the Follies of the Age : a Philosophical Romance. By M. de Lourdoueix. Translated from the French, 8vo. 7s. 6d. Baldwin, Cradock, and Joy, London, 1818.

The French press is continually teeming with a variety of literary works, by men of talents, and upon all subjects, which, for the moment, amuse and are admired. Few of them are sufficiently interesting to foreigners to be translated ; yet some pass unnoticed, which, both for their information and style deserve attention, and would gratify the general reader. Of this description is the volume now under consideration, which we think likely to interest the attention of the British Public: for, not only at this period, but at all times, in an historical as well as relative point of view, the affairs of France must be of importance to all civilized nations, and especially to Great Britain. This work, which comes from the pen of a writer greatly esteemed in his own country, is conceived with much ingenuity ; and the narrative, though short, is very agreeable. A young man, here called Monsieur Joseph, the son of a wholesale dealer at Paris, after spending several years in Germany, returns to the paternal roof, so entirely absorbed in mental speculations,. and exhibits so many marks of hypochondria; that his father, by the advice of a physician,

causes him to be conveyed to *Charenton,* the principal public establishment near Paris, for insane persons. Here the author lays the scene of his adventures ; and some of the supposed inhabitants of this place are his dramatis personæ. In the imaginary dialogues with them, the author gives a view of the political state of France, of its parties, of the natural tendency of the age to the general interests of mankind, and of the ultimate object of civilization in its silent progress towards universal good. The dialogues are sustained with much vigour of fancy, but are too long to admit of any one being extracted *entire ;* and a few detached passages would not, we think, do justice to the ingenious author. In the course of his residence at Charenton, Monsieur Joseph begins to imagine himself infected with the malady of the place; and accordingly sits down to write his "Halluciuations." As the chapter, thus intitled, appears to contain the author's deliberate opinions relative to the existing state of politics and parties of France, and as we think it gives, in a small compass, a more accurate and temperate view of them, than we have hitherto seen, we shall extract his observations on *Parties* in general, and on the conduct and politics of two of the most active of them; viz. The *Ultras* and *Liberals.*

Of Parties.

It is no problematical remark, that a fact, however unjust, however absurd it may be, cannot triumph for ever so short time on the earth without establishing a consequent interest.

Thus, in 1790, insurrection destroyed feodality, the interest of feodality nevertheless survives, and the interest of insurrection takes root. Bonaparte destroys insurrection, but the interest of insurrection survives, and the interest of usurpation takes root. In 1814 the legitimate government triumphs, but the interest of usurpation survives.

All these interests exist concurrently, and form parties. These parties are designated by a sort of nick names, which the public has stamped upon them without their leave. Such as are in the interest of feodality are called *Ultras,* those in the interest of insurrection are called *Jacobins,* those in the interest of usurpation are called *Bonapartists.*

Of the Ultras.

It is said that there cannot be *Ultra-royalists*, as one cannot love the king too much. This would be true if by *Ultras* was understood those who carried their love for the king to excess; but this name is given to those who have passed royalty, who are *beyond* it. Now as it is indisputable that when we are passed a place, we are no longer in that place, so when one has passed or gone beyond royalty, one is no longer royalist.—For example:

The day after the dissolution of the Chamber of 1815, I met a titled person whom I had known during the three months, when the same wishes the same dangers, the same efforts, united all the friends of legitimate loyalty. This person drew a most frightful picture of public affairs to me; according to him La Vendée was rising, the south was in arms, the Jacobins were talking of deposing the king, and the ministers, in concert with them, had gained the federates of the Faubourgs. In short, the throne was to be overturned in less than eight days. If that be the case, said I to him, it only remains for us to buy swords and large white cockades, and go and be killed on the staircase of the palace. " I'll not wear the white cockade again," replied he, " *till it shall please God to take our good king to himself.*" Was this man a royalist ?

More than once has the interest of feodality been armed in France against royalty: they who are *Ultras* now would have been *Leaguers* in the time of Henry III; those who were then *Leaguers* would be *Ultras*. Has not the Viscount de B. declared in a late publication that he would have joined the League, if he had been alive under Henry IV ?

If you ask an *Ultra* what he wants, he will tell you what he does not want.—Why ?—Because the man who is governed by an interest is impelled by a secret force which with him takes the place of judgment and reason, and only shows him obstacles without indicating to him the ulterior object.—Thus, he does not want Mr. Such-a-one to be in place, because Mr. Such-a-one is an advocate for the equality of rights, and it will be impossible *to advance* as long as Mr. Such-a-one is in power. —He does not want Mr. Such-a-one to remain in France, because Mr. Such-a-one, who is an enemy to royalty, is still a greater enemy to feodality.

But to come at the knowledge of the object of this party, remove for a moment the obstacles they point to you, and observe them *advance*, you will soon see whither they tend.

In 1815, the electors, through hatred of the men in the interest of usurpation, threw themselves into the arms of the federal party : and the Chamber of Deputies was composed of *Ultras*. From that moment the roofs of the hall daily resounded with declarations in favour of the ancient social system : a thousand arguments were advanced against the sale of corporate property, against the sale of the state forests, against the fiscal system, *against all the results of centralization,* in favour of the distinct incorporation and independence of the clergy, in favour of the old landed system, *in favour of every thing tending to the renewal of local interests.* All the proposed laws that had no tendency to establish such interests did not pass, why ?—because the Chamber of 1815 wished to UNDO THE REVOLUTION, and because the object of the Revolution, taking the word in its largest acceptation, is the centralization and unity of interests: from that moment all things, and all men, that stand in the way of the re-establishment of the ancient social system were fiercely attacked.— There were great shouts for purifying the administration, the army, the courts of justice ; from that moment the government *ceased to advance, or rather began to retrograde,* because it was hurried into a contrary direction to the operation of civilization, and because, instead of making a progress towards the results of the good principle, it was returning towards the results of the good principle, it was returning towards the interests of fact, towards institutions sprung from feodal usurpation and the federal league, all children of bad principle. The dissolution of the Chamber of 1815 was therefore indispensably necessary, and then the government began again *to advance.*

Of the politics of the Ultras.—The *Ultras* have advantages in their position which determine their politics. They were overturned by insurrection at the same time as royalty ; they were exposed to every kind of persecution, to the most infamous spoliations: they had for enemies the enemies of social order, men who profaned churches, erected altars to crime, and devoted virtue to the scaffold. Their blood gloriously mingled with the blood of martyrs and of kings. United by a common persecution with royalty and religion, the world has been accustomed to confound them with all that is august and sacred. The prejudice in regard to them being such as to make one forget that they had a distinct individual interest in opposing insurrection, it must appear strange to men who exist in a middle region of ideas, that the nobles having done every thing *for the king*, the king should not do every thing for them; that having lost their rights by the same blow which destroyed the rights of royalty, they should not resume them when royalty resumes it own.

All this may furnish the party with many arguments which will not be without weight in the opinion of the multitude; but though the vulgar can perceive only this lower king of justice, there is a higher species of Justice which alone ought to influence kings.

From the situation of the *Ultras*, it becomes their policy to put on the cloke of royalism to combat with men and things opposed to their party: it is for the king's interest therefore that they doom the French of the new system to exile; it is through royalism that they ask power, employments, and honours for themselves only; in short, it is for love of the king that they attack the king's government, labour to turn public opinion against it, do their utmost to make all the works of wisdom appear unjust and prejudicial to the state; and as it is difficult to reconcile such efforts with the respect they profess for the sovereign, they affect to make no mention of the king's name in their public accusations, but to designate only his ministers; a political foolery, which they the more readily adopt, as in fact it is not the person of the monarch which is in their way, but his government, that is to say, his ministers; and when they find in their conduct nothing to ground their animosity upon, they impute secret views to them, a resource ever ready for accusers who have no other.

One of the most usual practices of this party consists in confounding, in the mere acceptation of the word *Revolution*, the crimes, follies, and misfortunes that sprung from the insurrection of 93 with institutions which time has unfolded, which the nineteenth century has adopted, and which the charter has consecrated: thus, with them, the Septembriser and the Constitutional Royalist; he who killed the king and he who would lay down his life in defending him, are equally *Revolutionists*; the man who overthrew, and the man who is endeavouring to re-establish monarchy, are both *Jacobins*; and as *Revolutionists* and *Jacobins* are beings not very estimable, we must abjure the improvements of the age we live in, or be silent, if we wish not to be blackened in the drawing-rooms where the *Ultras* prevail.

The ministry fear the *Ultras*, and with some reason, for the *Ultras* are honourable persons, and their personal character gives

a weight to their political character; but all the harm they can do to the government is reduced to harassing them: having against them the age, which they cannot prevent from advancing, they are forced to follow its progress to harass it; so that they are themselves going further from the point to which they want to bring back society; and so we have seen their first writers entering into all the constitutional principles, and arming themselves with the charter to attack a government suitable to the times; the last resource of a party not strong enough to attack its enemy in front, and which, in abandoning its entrenchments, has made its existence dependent on the existence of the laws of exceptions which serve as a pretext for its attacks.

The secret wish of the *Ultras* is to make themselves masters of the administrations, in order to influence the elections, and have the whole legislative power; differing in this from the Jacobins, who desire to have power over the elections for the purpose of turning out the Ministers, and composing the administration according to their own views.

The saying, trivial as it is, *Go out of that place that I may go into it*, is the motto of all parties.

In the preceding observations it is proper we should apprize our readers, that the author speaks *only* of those Ultras who form an *opposition party* acting against the government of the King of France; and whose numbers are diminishing daily.

The *Liberals* are a junction of the Jacobins and Bonapartists; and their political principles and conduct are thus developed by our author.

In France, says he, we too easily suffer parties to usurp words to which notions of public good are affixed: we know how dearly we have paid for the words *national*, *patriot*, &c. &c. on the banners of the monsters who destroyed the *nation* and ruin the *country*; and we are not yet aware what the word *liberal*, on the banners of men in the interest of fact, will cost us. If is to this deplorable easiness we must impute the real corruption into which our political language has fallen. Is there a word that has among us determinate sense, and which, in certain mouths, signifies precisely the contrary of the signification given in our old dictionaries? The word *philosophy* formerly signified *the love of wisdom*; it has served among us moderns as a prototype of every kind of extravagance, and may now almost be construed *the love of*

G

folly. The word *liberty* signified, under Robespierre, and also under the consulate, *oppression, slavery.* The expression, *liberal ideas,* means at present, *outrage, military system,* &c. &c.—So that one might say of a certain personage, that he is as *philosophical as an ax, and as liberal as a bayonet.*

This diverging of signification was the more easy as the opposite parties laboured respectively to effect it: the *Jacobins* and *Bonapertists* to cover their turpitude with respectable garments; the *Ultras,* that those respectable garments might be soiled in touching the filth of Jacobinism. The former thought of making friends in this age, by concealing themselves under the cloke of liberal ideas: the latter of disgusting the age with liberal ideas, by muffling in their cloke men devoted to its hatred and contempt.

And such is the confusion into which we have been plunged by these parties, that if we praise *philosophy* we may be accused of extolling *folly;* that if we decry *philosophy,* we may be accused of decrying wisdom; that if we extol the *revolution,* we may be told that we are boasting of scaffolds and anarchy; if we speak degradingly of it, we shall be told that we are enemies to the progress of knowledge, and to the natural rights consecrated by the charter; and, in fine, if we praise *liberal ideas,* we shall be accused of being *Jacobins;* and of being *Ultras,* if we speak against them.

Compelled as the Jacobins and Bonapartists were to unite their strength against legitimacy, they could not but choose a common banner. It was requisite that the word for this banner should be sufficiently vague, to comprehend all the notions opposed to the old order of things: the word *liberal* was inscribed upon them, and the party took the field.

The head quarters of this party are established in some gilt offices of the Chaussée-d'Antin; there it is that the measures to be taken for the common interest are discussed; there it is that the news, the anecdotes, the bons-mots to be circulated in public, for the purpose of flattering the popular passions, and maintaining the hatred and hopes of subaltern members, are fabricated; there it is that men and things of the royal party are blackened, disfigured, and dressed grotesquely to be afterwards *thrown to the beasts;* there it is that the apotheoses of brethren who fall into the hands of the Prevotal courts and courts-martial are decreed; in a word, it is there that all that is to be done and said through the day is determined upon, just as the commanders

of regiments regulate every morning the duty of the officers of their garrison.

The leaders of this kind of tribunate possess great influence, because, by means of the profession which they exercise, they hold the fortunes of all. They have their orators, on whom they bestow property to render them eligible to the chamber of deputies. They have their songsters, who undertake to make respectable magistrates unpopular, and to make the little girls and shopmen of the *Rue Vivienne* laugh at kings and priests. They have their journals, which, not being able to attack things, make themselves amends by tearing the protectors of them to pieces; in fine, they would, upon need, find sufficient force for a *coup-de-main* among the men of the military system, whose hopes they buoy with the most officious zeal.

Just as the *Ultras* could not war against the age, but by attaching themselves to its progress, and entering into the constitutional principles, so the *Liberals,* in order to attack the government, have been compelled to enter little by little into the principles of royalty; it is thus that the journals of the faction daily make concessions, a single one of which is enough to overturn all their secret maxims; it is thus that the leaders of the party, to make their cloke thicker, call themselves *the first grenadiers of the hereditary magistrate.* But look under this cloke, and you will see, collected in file, all the men of insurrection, from the Jacobin of 93, to the federate of the hundred days; you will see men of the ax and of the sabre, eagles and red caps.

And how should you be encouraged by the language of these men, when your enemies are not alarmed by it; when they, whose whole life the sight of the king accuses, are not terrified at hearing the name of the king proclaimed by their leaders and their tribunes?..........

If ever they are able, by means of the elections, to have a majority in the chamber, they will strive to obtain the administration.

If they succeed in obtaining the administration, they will seize all the employments.

Once masters of all the posts, they will tell you their secret.

But is this secret of theirs still a secret to us? Did not one of their orators let it slip last year, in the chamber of the deputies? Did he not say, IT IS USURPATION ALONE THAT CAN TRANQUILLIZE THE INTERESTS OF USURPATION?

It is not difficult to draw the inference of this proposition, and both parties have accordingly done it, the one very loudly, the other very low.

Therefore, cried the *Ultras*, sacrifice the interests of usurpation, since you cannot secure them but by placing an usurper on the throne.

Therefore, muttered, *in petto*, the *Liberals*, Let us place an usurper on the throne, since it is the only way to tranquillize the interests of usurpation.

It would, in fact, be difficult for the government to get out of this dilemma, were the major proposition so just as the deduction : the question is not about tranquillizing the interests of usurpation, but leaving them undisturbed; which is a very different thing. The matter is to act as you would with fire, to leave it its prey, but not to throw to it what it has not taken. It is proper to devote to oblivion the faults of the revolution; but this oblivion can only by extended over men, and over events accomplished, not to the principles which produced those events, and which would produce others of the same kind. We are not to sacrifice moral order altogether to the perishable interests of a party. The concession we make to the past cannot compromise the future; in short, if we would adopt the avowed object of the revolution, we would not make interests triumph, which, as I have demonstrated, are completely opposed to that object.

But we are already reaping the fruit of the firm conduct which the government has maintained in regard to parties. The necessity which has compelled the factions to abandon their entrenchments, and to arm themselves, these with constitutional, and those with monarchical principles, is a great step towards the triumph of order. Though there is every reason to suspect the candour of their language, this important truth does not the less follow, that the more they advance with the age, the more impossible will they find it to return to the points which they have abandoned. The time is not so distant as is thought, when we shall be able to say, that there are no more parties in France, though there are party men; there will be no longer, properly speaking, *Jacobinism, Bonapartism*, or *Feudalism*, but merely *Jacobins, Bonapartists*, and *Ultras*. That is, let the government persevere, and the question will be soon confined to individuals; and to predict the end of our embarrassments, we shall have only to consult Buffon's tables of mortality. The anti-social interests depending only upon lives, the fund will be very soon annihilated.

Copious as these extracts are, we could with pleasure have enlarged them, if the limits of our journal would allow of their extension. The adventures of Monsieur Joseph are terminated, naturally enough, by one of the insane patients setting fire to Charenton; in consequence of which he effects his escape to his paternal home, where he promises to abandon his vagaries, and and is, of course, affectionately received.

It is impossible not to be amused as well as informed by this ingenious production. Though decided in its opinions, it is moderate, impartial, and, what is no mean recommendation, it is evidently *well translated*. The volume is illustrated with several engravings, in which those who are conversant with the great political actors in the *national Theatre of France*, will probably recognize the countenances of some well-known characters.

Lectures on the Principles and Institutions of the Roman Catholic Religion; with an appendix, containing historical and critical Illustrations. By Joseph Fletcher, M. A. 2d edit. revised, corrected, and enlarged, 8vo. 9s. Baldwin and Co. London, 1818.

A treatise on the subjects discussed in this valuable work, would be interesting at all times; but it is peculiarly intitled to attention at the present time, when the claims of our Roman Catholic fellow subjects are about to be submitted to the consideration of Parliament. As the first edition of this work was disposed of, before we could present our readers with an account of it, we seize the earliest opportunity of announcing to them the second impression.

Mr. Fletcher informs us that the substance of his ' *Lectures*' was delivered, some years since. in a series of discourses to his congregation, in consequence of the zealous efforts of the Roman Catholic Priest, then resident in Blackburn, (Lancashire) in the public vindication of his own principles ; and that Mr. F. has been induced to publish these Lectures from the attacks which have been repeatedly made on the Protestant faith, as well as from apprehensions of therevival of the Papal religion, and also that the rising generation may be well informed on the reasons of our secession from the Church of Rome. The topics which Mr. F. has treated are, 1. The authority of the church. 2. Oral Tradition. 3. Papal Supremacy. 4. Transubstantiation and the sacrifice of the Mass. 5. The Sacrament of the Church of Rome. 6. The Invocation of Saints, and the use of Images. 7. Purgatory and the Doctrine of Merit. 8. The Roman Catholic Hierarchy. 9. The Genus and Tendency of the Papal Religion.—A copious appendix is subjoined illustrating at length various subjects which are incidentally noticed in the Lecturers and a useful analysis of them is prefixed, which will enable the reader with facility to refer to any particular points.

From a careful examination of Mr. Fletcher's volume, we have no hesitation in saying, that it is a faithful exposition and defence of the principles on which the Protestant secession is founded. He has drawn his statements of Roman Catholic tenets from the creeds, confessions, and canons of that church, and from the writings of its ablest advocates, and he has refuted them with uncommon vigour and eloquence.

A Treatise on Soils and Manures, as founded on actual experience, and combined with the leading principles of agriculture, in which the theory and doctrines of Sir Humphrey Davy, and other eminent Agricultural Chemists are rendered familiar to the experienced farmer by a practised Agriculturist : 8vo. 5s. Cadell and Davis. London, 1818.

It is only of late years that the connexion between agriculture and chemistry has been considered with that attention which the subject so justly demands. The benefits, indeed, that may be derived from the union of chemical skill with the extensive observation of agricultural facts, are perhaps incalculable. At present, the state of knowledge, among the generality of farmers, is not such as to enable them to reap much advantage from chemical experiments, and the chemist has, himself, but few opportunities of applying his knowledge to practical purposes in

this way. Lord Dundonald, we believe, was one of the first who thus applied chemistry to the improvement of agriculture; and Sir Humphrey Davy has conferred an additional obligation on the farming interest, by the publication of his Elements of Agricultural Chemistry.

In the Treatise now under consideration, the leading doctrines of Sir H. Davy are brought under review, in order that such as are obviously well founded, or tenable against superficial objections, may be recommended to general practice; and that such as are open to objection, may be subjected to the test of experience in so plain a shape, as shall bring them within the grasp of the practical agriculturist, who may have formed no previous acquaintance with chemical science.

After a few preliminary observations on the use and bases of soils, and a definition of terms for them, the Author treats on the various means by which soils may be improved ; such as the admixture of earths, draining, paring, and burning, turning in green crops as manure, fallowing, irrigation. The application of earths as manures, the introduction of mineral and saline substances as manures, and the application, in the way of manure, of substances that are *not*, as well as of those which *are* excrementitious.

The work is written with considerable perspicuity, and in a manner which we think cannot fail to engage the attention of that important class of persons for whose use it is more immediately designed.

The Elements of Experimental Chemistry. By William Henry, M.D. F.R.S. The Eighth Edition. 8vo. with Plates, 2 vols. £1 8s. Baldwin and Co. London. 1818.

Although this is only a new edition of a well known work, published long before the commencement of our journal, we deem it proper to introduce it to the notice of our readers, on account of the very considerable and important additions which it has received, and also of our high opinion of its value, as the best elementary work on *experimental chemistry* perhaps, that is extant in our language. From a comparison of the present work with former editions, we can with confidence state, that the author has spared no pains to render his work worthy of the public favour, by incorporating into it every new fact, and by continuing the history of chemical discovery to the latest possible period, which the publication would admit. The instructions for conducting the various chemical experiments, are drawn up with singular precision; and various useful hints are given for performing them with *safety to the operator.* The plates, nine in number, are beautifully executed by Lowry; and the value of the work is greatly enhanced by the collection of chemical tables that are appended to it, and which are more numerous as well as more copious, than are to be found in any other treatise on this very important science.

Times' Telescope for 1819; *or, a complete Guide to the Almanach, containing an Explanation of Saints' Days; comparative Chronology; Astronomical Occurrences; Naturalists' Diary; a Description of Fruit Trees, and a compendium of Chemistry.* 12mo. Sherwood and Co·

This elegant work is replete with amusement and instruction, and fully supports the character we have given of the five former volumes; they who take a peep through Time's Telescope for 1819, will not repent the money they have paid for this gratification. It is an acceptable Christmas present for youth of both sexes.

BANKRUPTS, *Jan.* 22.

Atherton, T. Liverpool, tanner, at the George Inn, Liverpool. *Sols.* Adlington and Gregory, Bedford row, London, and Mr. Radcliffe, Lipool.

Bell, J. Church street, Spitalfields, bombazeen manufacturer. *Sol.* Mr. James, Bucklersbury.

Booth, J. Oxford street, grocer. *Sol.* Mr Hindman, Basinghall street.

Brown, J. Leeds, straw hat manufacturer. *Sol.* Mr. Ashley. Lord Mayor's Court office, Royal Exchange.

Carver, J. and Peet, W. Basinghall street, merchants. *Sols.* Jacomb and Bently, Basinghall st.

Cowley, T. Bolton-le-Moors, Lancashire, warehouseman. *Sols.* Milne and Parry, Temple, London·

Davis, N. Gloucester Terrace, New road, Whitechapel, merchant. *Sol.* Mr. Blandford, Bruton street, New Bond st.

Durham, J. Lower Shadwell-street, carcass-butcher. *Sols* Bull, and Co. Holles-street, Cavendish-street.

Fitzgerald, T. St. Catherine street, ship owner. *Sol.* Mr Pulley, Crown court, Broad st.

Gardner, N. and H. Gloucester, bankers and corn dealers. *Sol.* Mr. Becke, Devonshire street, Queen square, London; and Mr. Gardner, Gloucester.

Hardie, A. Union court, Broad street, merchant. *Sols* Nind and Cotterill, Throgmorton street.

Hudson, Upper Thames street, earthenwareman. *Sols.* Jacomb and Bently, Basinghall st.

Hughes, S. Liverpool, liquor merehant. . *Sol.* Mr. Hughes, Liverpool. *Sols.* Ducie and John, Palsgrave place, Temple bar, London.

Keats, T. M. Poultry, hat manufacturer. *Sol.* Mr. Blandford, Bruton street, Bond st.

Kernot, J. Castle street, Leicester fields, druggist. *Sol.* Mr Hindham, Basinghall st·

Lutey, T. Wapping, master mariner. *Sols.* Gregson and Fonnereau, Angel court, Throgmorton street.

Merchant, J. Shepton Mallet, Somersetshire, innkeeper, at the George Inn, Shepton Mallet. *Sols.* Mr. Burfood, Temple, London; and Mr. Biggins, Shepton Mallet.

Oxenham, J· T. Oxford street, mangle maker. *Sols.* Kearsey and Spurr, Bishopsgate street, Within.

Richards, D. Man's row, Bow common, manufacturing chemist. *Sol.* Mr. Venner, Upper Thornhaugh street, Bedford square.

Richards, H. Beaconsfield, Buckinghamshire, carpenter. *Sol.* Mr. Tucker, Bartlett's buildings, Holborn.

Russell, J. Lambeth, timber merchant. *Sols.* Loxley and Sons, Cheapside.

Still, J. South Island place, Brixton, Surrey, merchant. *Sol.* Mr. Leachman, Basinghall;st.

Swan, R. Gainsborough, Lincoln, merchant. *Sols.* Eicke and Evan, Aldermanbury.

Vertue, S. Mark lane, corn merchant, *Sols.* Sudlow, Francis, and Urquhart, Monument yard.

Wattson, J Gravesend, Kent, coach-master, *Sol.* Mr. Yatman, Arundel street, Strand,

Williams, H. Duke street, Bloomsbury, wine merchant. *Sol.* Mr. Younger, Wellclose sq.

BANKRUPTS, *Jan.* 26.

Andrews, R. Bristol, Baker. *Sols.* Poole and Grinfield, Grays Inn.

Brocklebank, S. Liverpool, merchant. *Sols.* Taylor and Roscoe, Temple.

Budden, J. Bristol, Liquor merchant. *Sols.* Edmunds, Lincoln's Inn·

Cole, E. Shrewsbury, Hop merchant. *Sol.* R. Griffiths, Southampton buildings·

Force, J. Walcot, dealer. *Sol.* Highmoor. Scott's yard.

Harman, J. Norwich, manufacturer. *Sol.* Nelson, Barnard's Inn.

Hulme, W. Leeh, grocer. *Sols.* Dewbury and Hardewood, Conduit st.

Jones, E Great Sutton street, coal merchant. *Sol* Cartle, Cursitor street.

Nicholls, B. A. Lloyd's Coffee House, Insurance broker. *Sols.* Reardon and Davis, Corbet court.

Noble, M. Lancaster. *Sols.* Alexander and Holme, New Inn.

Russell A. Tewkesbury, Linen draper. *Sol.* Cardale and Young, Gray's Inn.

Literary Register.

Authors, Editors, and Publishers are particularly requested to forward to the Literary Panorama Office, *Post Paid, on or before the 19th day of each Month, the Titles, Prices, and other particulars of the Works in hand, or published, for this department of the work.*

ANTIQUITIES.

Mr. Britton announces a " History and Description of Lichfield Cathedral, to be illustrated with 16 engravings, from Drawings, by F. Mackenzie ; among which is one representing the justly famed monument, by Chantrey, of the Children of Mrs. Robinson. This History is to be finished in the present year, and form a portion of the Author's Series of " The Cathedral Antiquities of England."

Miscellaneous Antiquities, No. 8, (in Continuation of the Bibliotheca Topographica Britannica) handsomely printed in 4to. Price £3 2s. a New Edition, corrected, enlarged, and embellished with numerous Plates, of a Comment on the Fifth Journey of Antoninus through Britain ; in which the Situation of Durobrivæ, the Seventh Station there mentioned, is discussed ; and Castor, in Northamptonshire, is shewn, from various Remains of Roman Antiquity, to have an undoubted claim to that situation. Also a Dissertation on an Image of Jupiter found there. Printed from the Original Manuscript. By the Rev. Kennet Gibson, late Curate of Castor.

To which is subjoined, The Parochial History of Castor, and its Dependencies, to the present time ; with an Account of Marham, and several other places in the neighbourhood of Castor. By Richard Gough, Esq.

٭٭٭ Of this Work (which is wanting in most of the Sets of the Bibliotheca Topographica Britannica) only one hundred copies are re-printed on Demy Quarto ; and Twenty-five on Imperial Quarto, Price £4 4s.

EDUCATION.

The Child's Introduction to Thorough Bass, in Conversations of a Fortnight, between a Mother and a Daughter of Ten Years Old.

II.

Elements of Astronomy, familiarly explaining the general Phænomena of the Heavenly Bodies, and the Theory of the Tides : to which is subjoined a complete Set of Questions for Examination. For the Use of Private Students, as well as of Seminaries. Intended as a Companion to the " School Geography" of the same Author. By Joseph Guy, formerly Professor of Geography at the Royal Military College, Great Marlow. In royal 18mo. illustrated by 18 beautiful plates, price 5s. bound in red.

III.

A Short History of France, for Young Persons. By a Daughter of the late Mrs. Trimmer. In 12mo. embellished with Six Plates from Original Designs.

Arithmetic for Children, by the Author of Letters for Young Persons in Humble Life, will soon appear.

The Youth's Spelling, Pronouncing, and explanatory Theological Dictionary of the New Testament, in which all the words of the four leading parts of speech, in the New Testament, are arranged under their respective heads, & the explanations given in as simple, clear, and concise a manner as possible.

To which is added, an Essay, by way of introduction, on the several parts of speech ; and also a correct Alphabetical Index. 12mo. 7s. fine paper, 9s.

HISTORY.

Shakh Mansur will soon publish, in 8vo. a History of Seyd Said, Sultan of Muscat, with an account of the countries and people on the shores of the Persian gulf, particularly of the Wahabees.

Horæ Britannicæ ; or, Studies in Ancient British History. By John Hughes, 2 vols. 8vo. 18s.

MEDICINE.

The Dublin Hospital Reports and Communications in Medicine and Surgery, volume the second, will soon appear.

Dr. John Bacon, of Gloucester, has in the press, an Inquiry respecting some of the Diseases of the Serous Membranes of the Abdomen and Thorax.

Mr. Thomas Alcock is preparing for publication, some Observations on Inflammation of the Mucous Membrane of the Respiratory Organs.

Translations of the Association of Fellows and Licentiates of the King's and Queen's College of Physicians in Ireland. vol. 2. 8vo. 16s.

MISCELLANIES.

Transactions of the Royal Society of Dublin, 4to. vol. 12, part 2.

Mr. Hazlitt has in the press, Lectures on the Comic Genius and Writers of Great Britain, now delivering at the Surry Institution.

A New Edition of Lord Bacon's Works, in 12 vols. small 8vo enriched with portraits, and the Latin part of them translated into English, by Dr. Peter Shaw, M.D. Will be ready early in March.

NATURAL HISTORY AND PHILOSOPHY.

Mr. James Mitchell has in the press, Elements of Natural Philosophy, Illustrated by experiments that may be performed without regular apparatus.

Mr. Geo. Samonelle has in the press, The Entomologist's Pocket Compendium: containing, an Introduction to the Knowledge of British Insects ; the Apparatus used, and the best means of obtaining and preserving them ; the Genera of Linnè ; together with the modern Method of arranging the Classes Crustacea, Myriapoda, Spiders, Mites, and Insects, according to their Affinities and Structure, after the System of Dr. Leach. Also, an Explanation of the Terms used in Entomology : a Kalendar of the Time, and Situations where usually found, of nearly 3000 Species ; and Instructions for collecting and fitting up Objects for the Microscope. Illustrated with Twelve Plates.

The Miscellaneous Works, in prose and verse, of George Hardinge, Esq. M. A. F. R. S. F. S. A. senior Justice of the Counties of Bredon, Glamorgan, and Ranor, in 3 vols. 8vo. with a portrait of the Author, price 2l. 2s. boards.

By Abraham Rees, D.D. F.R.S. &c. vol. 3, part 1, with part E of additional plates, of the new Cyclopædia ; or Universal Dictionary of Arts, Sciences, and Literature.

By James Millar, M.D. the Encyclopædia Edinensis, vol. 2, part 5. 4to. price 8s.

The Fables of Æsop and others, with 188 designs of Fables, and 187 curious tailpieces, engraved on wood by Thomas Bewick. Imperial paper, 1l. 11s. 6d ; royal paper, 1l. 1s ; demy paper 16s. boards.

Remarks on the Liberty of the Press in Great Britain ; together with Observations on the late Trials of Watson, Hone, &c.

Translated from the German of the celebrated F. Gentz, Aulic Counsellor to the Emperor of Germany, and author of the Balance of Power in Europe, &c. 8vo. 4s.

Letters on the Importance, Duty, and Advantages of Early Rising ; addressed to heads of Families, the man of business, the lover of nature, the student, and the Christian ; 8vo. 6s.

A Defence of Dr. Jonathan Swift, Dean of St. Patrick's, Dublin ; in answer to certain observations on his life and writings, in the 32d number of the Edinburgh Review ; 8vo. price 3s.

The Soul of Mr. Pitt ; developing that by giving the Funded Proprietors the Permissive Faculty of claiming Debentures, transferable to the Bearer, eighteen millions of Taxes may be taken off, and the 3 per Cent. Consols be constantly above 100l. 8vo. 1s. 6d.

POLITICAL ECONOMY.

Mr. H. A. Mitchell, of Newcastle, will soon publish, in octavo, a Treatise concerning Credit and Political Expediency ; tending to shew that there is no real national debt.

FINE ARTS.

Authentic Busts of Shakspeare, Camden, and B. Jonson. The Busts that have been commonly sold, professing to represent the features of these estimable writers, are notoriously devoid of authenticity, truth, and likeness. Although they may serve to amuse children, as any other plaster, or wax dolls, would ; they are unworthy of a place in the library of a man of taste and literature. To supplant such things, J. Britton engaged Mr. William Scoular to make reduced Models from the Monumental Busts at Westminster and Stratford Church, and these he has executed with fidelity and taste. They are 18 inches in height, by 12 inches in width ; each is fixed to a pedestal of three books, and each is preserved by a thin wash of paint, in stone colour, by which means they can be always kept clean. The price is Two Guineas each ; or Five Guineas for the Three.

Annals of Parisian Typography : containing an Account of the earliest Typographical Establishments ; and Notices and Illustrations of the most remarkable Productions of the Parisian Gothic Press. Compiled principally to shew its general Character, and its particular, Influence upon the early English Press. By the Rev. William Parr Creswell, large paper, 1l. 1s. 8vo. 14s.

BIOGRAPHY.

The Annual Biography and Obituary for 1819, with Silhouette portraits, 8vo. 15s.

The Life and Adventures of Antar, a celebrated Bedowen Chief, Warrior, and Poet, who flourished a few Years prior to the Mahommedan Era. Now first translated from the original Arabic, by Terrick Hamilton, Esq. Oriental Secretary to the British Embassy to Constantinople. Crown 8vo. 9s. 6d.

Memoirs of the First Thirty-two Years of the Life of James Hardy Vaux, now transported for the second Time, and for Life, to New South Wales. Written by Himself, 2 vols. 12mo. 12s.

NOVELS.

Frances ; or, the Two Mothers; a Tale. By M. S. in 3 vols. 12mo, 15s. boards.

The Charms of Dandyism ; or, Living in Style. By Olivia Morland, chief of the female dandies. Edited by Capt. Ashe, author of " The Spirit of the Book," &c. In 3 vols. 12mo.

Coraly ; a novel. In 3 vols. 12mo. 10s. 6d. boards.

Miss Hutton, author of the Miser Married, will soon publish Oakwood Hall, in 3 vols.

☞The Countess of Carrick, a tale, by Carolan, is in the press, and will be published in a few days.

POETRY.

Durovernum ; or, Sketches Historical and Descriptive of Canterbury; with other Poems. By Arthur Brooke, Esq. foolscap 8vo. 7s.

Human Life ; a Poem ; by Samuel Rogers, Esq. author of the Pleasures of Memory. Neatly printed in small 4to

Tales of the Hall ; by George Crabbe, LL.B. 8vo.

A Churchman's second Epistle, with notes and illustrations ; by the author of Religio Clerici. 8vo Also a third edition of the first part, with the addition of notes and illustrations.

Mr. J. H. Church will soon publish, in duodecimo, Angelo, or the Moss-grown Cell, a poem, in 4 cantos.

James Montgomery, Esq. is preparing for the press, Greenland and other poems.

THEOLOGY.

A Dissertation on the Scheme of Human Redemption, as developed in the Law and in the Gospel By the Rev. John Leveson Hamilton, A. B. 8vo. 12s.

Sermons on the Parables and Miracles of Jesus Christ. By Edward William Grinfield, M.A. 8vo. 10s.

Plain and Practical Sermons. By the Rev. John Boudier, M.A. 9s. boards.

A new edition of the late Rev. John Cennick's Discourses, adapted to village and domestic Worship, is in the press, revised and corrected, with recommendatory preface, and life, by Matthew Wilks.

Dr. William Barrow will soon publish a volume of Familiar Dissertations on Theological and Moral Subjects.

The Rev. H. Marriott has in the press a second volume of Sermons, expressly adapted to be read in families

Speedily will be published, in an octavo volume, the Principles of pretended Reformers in Church and State. This work will comprise a view, 1st. of the principles and practices of pretended Reformers in Church and State, which caused the rebellion against King Charles the First: 2d. Of the Principles and Practices of pretended Reformers during the rebellion and subsequent usurpation : and, 3d. of the Principles and Practices of pretended Reformers at the present time. By Arthur H. Kenney, D.D. Dean of Achonry, and late Fellow of Trinity College, Dublin.

Shortly will be published, by subscription, Immanuel's Crown ; or, the Divinity of Christ established ; by the Rev. Richard Newman, Faversham, Kent.

TOPOGRAPHY.

The History and Antiquities of the Town of Newark, the Sidnacester of the Romans ; interspersed with Biographical Sketches, and Pedigrees of some of the principal Families, and profusely embellished with engravings. By W. Dickinson, Esq. 4to. 2l. 2s.

A brief Account of the Guildhall of the City of London. By J. B. Nichols, F.S.A. embellished with an internal view, by J. C. Buckler ; and an original view of the old front, by Schnebbelie ; and dedicated to the Right Hon. the Lord Mayor and Corporation. 8vo. 5s.

VOYAGES AND TRAVELS.

A Classical Tour through Italy and Sicily, tending to illustrate some districts which have not been described by Mr. Eustace, in his Classical Tour. By Sir Richard Colt Hoare, Bart. 4to. 2l. 2s.

An Account of the Mission from Cape Coast Castle to the Kingdom of Ashantee, in Africa: comprising its History, Laws, Superstitions, Customs, Architecture, Trade, &c. To which is added, a Translation, from the Arabic, of an Account of Mr. Park's Death, &c. By Thomas Edward Bowdich, Esq. Conductor and Chief of the Embassy. With a map, and several plates of architecture, Costumes, Processions, &c. in 4to.

The Narrative of an Attempt to discover a Passage over the North Pole to Behring's Straits. By Capt David Buchan, Commander of his Majesty's Ships Dorothea and Trent. In 4to. with plates

The fourth volume of M. Humboldt's Personal Narrative of Travels to the Equinoctial Regions is in considerable forwardness.

Foreign Literary Gazette.

AUSTRIA.

Musical Institutions.

At Vienna, the amateurs of music are endeavouring to establish a Musical Conservatory on a new plan, suggested by M. de Mosel. As the first part of this plan, and till the whole can be carried into execution, they have instituted a school for singing: the conduct of which is entrusted to the celebrated Salieri.

The Manager in Distress.

The Manager of the Imperial Theatre at Vienna, has circulated an appeal to dramatic authors, to excite them to furnish him with new pieces, principally such as admit of *grand spectacle*; such as melodramas, or operas of enchantment; not, however, to the exclusion of comedies, tragedies, heroical operas and regular dramas. The authors will affix their own prices to their works, which they will settle with the manager, who engages to allow them further a certain portion of the receipts brought by their performances, and the number of their representations. The decision on their pieces to be fixed by well-known persons of taste and talents, and not to be delayed beyond two months.

In the Royal Gymnasia of Offen and Pesth, which two cities are only separated by the Danube, the number of students was, in 1817, at Offen, 375; and at Pesth, 701, together 1076. If to these be added the number of those who frequented the University of Pesth, which in 1817 was 771, the total will amount to 1847; which exceeds by more than half the number in the University of Berlin.

The new Gymnasium of Carlowitz, in Syrmia, reckoned 164 students in the whole of its six classes. In the two upper classes the ancient Greek language has been taught since 1817.

The Emperor visited this Gymnasium in the course of his last journey into Dalmatia, in 1817, and was pleased to declare his satisfaction with the state in which he found it, to the Director, Dr. Rumy. This gentleman has been elected corresponding member of the Societies of Rural Economy at Munich, that of Clagenfurth, in Carinthia, and that of the Georgicon of Kesthely. The Chancellor of Transylvania, Count Sam. de Telecky, also the Counsellor de Czerey, and the Archbishop of Carlowitz, have furnished considerable sums to promote the publication of Dr. Rumy's *Monumenta Hungarica.*

The Royal Society of Sciences at Goettingen, has recently elected as an honorary member, Stephanus de Stratimirovicz, the Greek Archbishop (not united to the Catholic Church), and Metropolitan at Carlowitz.

Medical Qualification.

In the kingdom now called the Lombardo Venetian, an ordonnance lately published, enjoins that in future no person shall be admitted Physician, Surgeon, Apothecary, or to the practice of Midwifery, who has not studied in one of the Universities or Institutions of the Empire, and who has not passed the usual examinations, and obtained a diploma.

Useful Work extensively circulated.

A singular honour, as it appears to us, has been conferred on a work of Professor Rudtorfer, entitled *Armamentarium Chirurgicum.* Descriptions and Figures of all the instruments of surgery, ancient and modern, four numbers in folio, with thirty plates, Vienna. By a decree of January 27, 1818, the Emperor has ordered that one copy of this work shall be sent at the expence of the Government, to all the public Libraries of Vienna, Milan, and Venice,—also, to all the Universities and Lyceums of the Monarchy, wherever there is a school of surgery;—and further, to every regiment and corps of the army.

PUBLIC INSTRUCTION.

The state of Public Instruction in the Empire of Austria, has lately been reported on to the following effect:—

In Hungary and Transilvania, there existed till recently, sixty-three Gymnasia, for the instruction of Catholic youth, of which forty were superintended by the Piarists, or Congregation of Pious Scholastic establishments. At the close of 1817, this Order reckoned 355 members, dispersed in 27 houses, two of which were in Transilvania. The other Gymnasia of these countries, are under the Orders of Saint Benedict, of the Premonstratenses, of Saint Francis, of Saint Augustin, and of the Citeaux.

Instructive Journal proposed.

The Polytechnical Institution of Vienna, proposes to publish a Journal under the title of ' The Journal of the Polytechnical Institution of Vienna,' comprising Natural Philosophy, Chemistry, the Mechanic Arts, the Fine Arts, Manufactures, and Commerce, and such other studies as belong to, or coincide with, those branches of knowledge and practice.

The Society of Rural Economy at Vien-

E

na, continues to publish its Memoirs at its own expence, quarto size.

DENMARK.

Ancient Writing illustrated: arrow-headed Characters.

Dr. Munter, at Copenhagen, has recently published *Versuch*, &c. an Essay on the cunei-formed Inscriptions at Persepolis. The labours and ingenuity of this gentleman are spoken of by Mr. Rich, the British resident at Bagdad, in a very respectful manner. This work makes one volume in 8vo. It should appear, from various specimens, that the same kind of characters was used at Nineveh, as well as at Babylon.

Royal Munificence in favour of Science.

The King of Denmark has granted a pension of eight hundred crowns, during two years, to four men of letters, to enable them to travel into foreign parts, for the benefit of making observations. The gentlemen at present thus honoured and benefited, are Messrs. Rask, philologist; Ingemann, poet; Clauzen, divine; and Henry Gorde, of Kiel, naturalist. Dr. Zeise, a naturalist, and the botanist, Schow, have also obtained additional means to continue their travels and studies abroad.

His Majesty has also given to the Society of Rural Economy of Denmark, the sum of 40,000 crowns, destined for the encouragement of Agriculture, principally in the province of Zealand.

The King has also ordered to be sent to the British Museum, a complete copy of the *Flora Danica.*

Fine Arts: Exhibition.

The last Exhibition of Pictures by the Academy of Fine Arts at Copenhagen, comprised 83 numbers. Among which were remarked several subjects taken from the History of Denmark, and Northern Mythology. Several pictures of animals and landscapes were highly admired.

Other Times other Patrons.

The Danish Sculptor, Thorwaldsen, at Rome, has proposed to the government of his country, the purchase of a series of bas reliefs, representing the *Triumph of Alexander.* These bas reliefs were ordered eight or ten years ago for the Imperial Palace at Rome; but, by the course of events, they have remained on the hands of the artists. The sum asked for them is 15,000 scudi. Endeavours are making to raise this sum by voluntary subscription.

M. Thorwaldsen has very lately finished four bas-reliefs, intended to ornament the royal residence of Christiansburgh, at Copenhagen.

FRANCE.

Military Madness not National Glory.

We lately gave a hint in our article on Military Eloquence, on the happy suitability of many addresses by the French generals to their armies, stimulating them to those energies which suited the purposes of their officers; not satisfied with this, the French press has lately put forth a collection of proclamations, reports, letters, and bulletins of the French armies, beginning from 1792, under the title of *Monument à la Gloire Nationale.* This assumption has been criticized by the French journalists, who appear to be at a loss to conceive by what means the fabrications, falsities, bombast, and incoherencies of the armies, under the Legislative Assembly, and especially under the Convention, maddened as they were by insane commissaries, can be thought to contribute to the National Glory.

Gallic Prejudices: England abused.

Some time ago, a work was published in France, by an officer who had been prisoner in England, in which he described the natives of our country as lost to all sense of honour, integrity, decorum, and patriotism; and the females especially, as given to vices of all kinds, and without exception to intoxication and indecency. The better part of the French public scouted the author and his work, (they are both dead since; for which reason we do not name them,) but that contempt has not hindered a certain Olivier de la Blatrie, chief of a battalion, Knight of St. Louis, and of the Legion of Honour, &c. from repeating similar nonsense. His countrymen describe his work as a compendium of the manners of the lowest classes of the London mob, which the writer mistakes for——the people of England.

Idle Tales counteracted.

Among the well-intentioned works which have lately issued from the French press, we must place *Les petits Peureux corrigés,* The little Alarmists corrected, intended to guard children from the effects of idle stories about ghosts, apparitions, spectres, and other fantastical appearances, with plates. We have described this as a well-intentioned work; but, if it were possible to maintain a strict silence on such subjects, and to prevent them from being mentioned in the hearing of children, we should infinitely prefer it. As we are not yet so happy as to have banished such worse than idle tales, we are at least obliged to gentlemen who endeavour to correct their injurious consequences.

BELGIUM,
Deaf and Dumb, v. The Blind.

A question was incidentally proposed by the Chevalier and professor Guyot, (who is Director of the Institution for the Deaf and Dumb, at Groningen,) to his friend Dr. Hartmann to this effect: " Which would be the least unfortunate, the blind or the deaf and dumb, supposing them to be cut off from all society, and left to themselves in a desert island,—or supposing them amidst their compatriots, vegetating in indigence—or enjoying a certain proportion of the goods of fortune?—And which of the two is the most susceptible of being rendered useful to Society?"

The question appeared to be so difficult, yet so interesting, that Dr. Hartmann consulted a judicious friend on it: that friend decided contrary to Dr. Hartmann's opinion. The Dr. has now given his view of the question to the public, in a pamphlet entitled—"The condition of those born blind, compared with that of those born deaf and dumb."—Brussels. The Dr. exerts himself in favour of those born blind; yet with great attention to the deaf and dumb. It is likely that different judgments may be formed on this enquiry, according to the individual subjects with which the person prying his judgment may have been familiar. This, however, is a generally received opinion, that the blind, whether from their birth, or rendered so by accident, are usually more lively, than those who are deaf and dumb, whether from their birth, or from accidents to which they have subsequently been subjected.

GERMANY.
Accidental Discovery: ancient History.

It is well known that some of the most curious documents illustrative of past times, have been discovered occupying the place of covers to later works; and it is probable that former good fortune in this way has excited, and will continue to excite the curious. Mr. Dibdin has recorded several instances in his Bibliographical Researches; and we presume that his hints have been taken, and may turn to good account: One instance to this purpose we find in the following article:

On the covers of some old books, in which the accounts of the Convent of St. Michael, at Lexenbargh, were formerly kept, has lately been discovered Fragments of the Annals of the Eleventh century, which the Antiquaries of Germany have deemed curious. They are very legibly written, and the writing is evidently of the early part of the twelfth century. The order of events is much the same with that in the *Chronographus Saxo*, published by Leibnitz; but the style is more concise. The period extends from 1066 to 1130.

ITALY.
Fasti Consolari complete.

It is well known that the *Fasti Consolari Capitolini* are of great use to the learned, in settling various points of Antiquity: we therefore have a satisfaction in reporting, that the first volume of a complete collection of them has appeared at Milan. These fragments were discovered at different times in the course of the Sixteenth century; and the Editor, Sig. Bartolomeo Borghesi, proposes to arrange and illustrate the whole. The work will form three volumes, in quarto.

English History favoured.

Hume's History of England, which had been formerly translated into Italian, has been again translated into that language; and the first volume of the work has appeared, in octavo, under the direction of Ginseppe Picotti, at Venice.

The Chronicle of Eusebius translated from the Armenian into Latin, as we have heretofore announced, is actually proceeding at the press. It will form one volume, in quarto.

Marginal Notes : valuable.

There are few means of instruction more valuable than the remarks made by men of learning for their own use, on the margins of works which they have carefully perused. It is well known that the hints of professor Porson of this nature have been collected with great assiduity: Those also of the famous Bentley, afford a fund of instruction, and are now an addition of no small interest to the pages of the Classical Journal.

The Abbate Luigi de Angelis, professor and librarian at Sienna, has collected the numerous additions and corrections made at different times in the margin of the various editions of the *Vocabulario della Crusca*, by several learned men of the greatest merit. These are sufficiently numerous to form three volumes, in 8vo. The work is in the press.

The Bible, with Notes and Comments.

We are glad to see that the Bible makes its way in the Church of Rome; no doubt in emulation of the exertions made by Protestants. The Archbishop of Florence has lately given his approbation to an Edition translated from the Vulgate into Italian, and accompanied by notes. This copy contains both the Old and the New Testament. It is in progress of printing at Turin, and will form twenty-three volumes, in 8vo.

Mosaic Pictures, on a large scale.

Sig. Raffaelli has succeeded in forming at Milan, a considerable establishment for performing works in Mosaic, especially on a large scale : at present this establishment is occupied in executing a copy of Leonardo da Vinci's famous picture of the Last Supper. This Mosaic will cost 24,000 ducats: it is, unquestionably, one of the largest of its kind ; since it measures 30 feet in length, by 15 feet in height. It is for the Empéror of Austria.

Mosaic is a kind of work in which by means of small pieces of glass, figures and representations of all kinds are produced. It is the most tedious of operations; but has the advantage of being indestructible by the air, or by ordinary accidents. It was much practised by the Ancients, and some of their Mosaics, more than two thousand years old, are yet remaining in good condition.

Clementine Museum: new edition.

Joseph Molini and Co. at Florence, announce a new edition of the *Museo Pio-Clementino* of Ennio Quirino Visconti, this edition will be directed by the Father Abbate Giovanni Battista Zenoni, the worthy successor of the Abbate Lanzi, The first ten plates will be accompanied with the explanatory text of the author, who was prevented by death from continuing his labours. As several of the plates inserted in the first edition were ill-drawn, new drawings have been made, by able artists at Rome, of these subjects, under direction of the editors. The work will be published in volumes, each containing forty plates. The number of plates will regulate the price ; yet not exceeding in the whole that of the Florentine Gallery, which was published in numbers each containing six plates.

Roman Numerals: their Origin.

Professor Mattheis at Rome, has lately published an interesting memoir, which he had read at the Roman Academy of Archaiology, on the origin of the Roman numeral figures. It is in Quarto ; and is illustrated by a plate executed by the process of lithography.

PRUSSIA.
New Subjects for Novels.

The Revolution in Spanish America has already furnished the prolific pen of the novelist, Julian Voss, at Berlin, with a subject, which he calls *Der Mooonch, &c.* The dying Monk of Peru. He has extended his story to Two Volumes, 8vo.

The way of the World in the Country.

The Tricks of the Town have given occasion to many novels and romances, not wholly works of imagination : a German writer has attempted to turn the tables on the country, in a novel in Two Volumes, which he entitles *Klein-Staedterien, &c.* The tricks of villages and hamlets ; containing Anecdotes and Historiettes.

RUSSIA.
Lyceum at Odessa.

In 1816, the Emperor of Russia founded a Lyceum at Odessa. The instruction there bestowed is divided into *preparatory*, which lasts from six to ten years,—*literary*, from ten to sixteen years;—and *scientific*, from sixteen to eighteen years.

To this Lyceum are united a Pedagogic Institution, for the instruction of School Masters, with two Supplementary Schools one of Jurisprudence and Political Economy, the other of Commercial Science.— There are also two Primary Schools. If we are not mistaken, this Lyceum bears the name of the Duke of Richelieu, formerly, Governor of Odessa.

Volcanic Island.

According to letters from Petersburgh, advices had been received there, of a new *Volcanic Island* having been raised among the Aleutian islands, not far from Unalaschka. This phenomenon appeared in the midst of a storm, attended with flames and smoke. After the sea was calmed, a boat was sent from Unalaschka, with twenty Russian hunters in her, who landed on this island, June 1, 1814. They found it full of crevices, and precipices. The surface was cooled to the depth of a few yards; but below that depth it was still hot. No water was found on any part of it. The vapours rising from it were not injurious: and the sea lions had begun to take up their residence in it. Another visit was paid to it in 1815. Its height was then diminished. It is about two miles in length, they have given it the name of *Boguslaw.*

SAXONY.

The Saxons have many able men among them, in the art of Machinery: the following, if correct, deserves notice by our civil engineers.

Beschreinburg, &c. Description on a Mill, worked by water ; but, which does not require running water, invented by J. F. Lange, 4to. with a plate. Leipsic. 1818.

SWITZERLAND.
The Helvetic Society of Natural Science

of which we have heretofore informed our readers, held its assembly last summer, at Lausanne, July 27, 28, 29. M. de Chavannes, President.

These days were spent in hearing lectures on scientific subjects, in botanizing around the environs, and in various philosophical experiments. The place of meeting for next July is appointed to be at St. Gall; and for the following year at Geneva.

ADVANTAGES OF PERIODICAL LITERATURE.

However the sneers of ill-founded criticism may have slighted or thrown into the shade, Periodical Literature, its advantages have been sensibly felt by every man of thought or of discretion. Men who are informed can now more readily convey instruction and improvement to the world than heretofore; and add thereby so much to the general stock of human happiness. The learning of early times was too long locked up from general use, and was almost as if placed in some *Sanctum sanctorum*, accessible only to the privileged High Priests. The common wants were unattended to by the affluent, morally as well as physically speaking; and the general mind remained in all its native wildness; on fancy pruned, no imagination regulated, no faculty of the mind called into proper action or display. Before the divine invention of Printing the dissemination of knowledge was attended with a world of difficulty, and yet it must still be owned, that the learning of the early and middle ages possessed but little charms to arrest the fancy, or to satisfy the judgment. Polemics chiefly occupied the learned, or metaphysics of little use, and still less understood. Theology ranged at its side the ablest men, of the times, and speculations about grace or the procession of the Holy Spirit occupied the labors of the monastery and the college. The discovery of the Justinian code gave however a new turn to enquiry, and the thoughts of the learned were directed to legislation. Nothing was written but in Latin:—medicine and physics—theology and ethics, were all discussed and taught in that language. It will be seen that all could not have had it in their power to become sufficient masters of it to receive or to convey instruction, and hence did the people so long remain ignorant of the first principles of philosophy or religion. The learning of the people did not pass beyond the anvil or the plough, or the servile obedience to their rulers, which was invariably pressed on their attention. But such disgraceful

darkness could not always hold its wide and terrible dominion. Too long had ignorance held sway— that Cadmus of society, that begets disorders, and leaves to the aspiring the uncontrolled ascendant; whilst to the humble it produced that barbarous degradation in which he was so long enchained.

But the invention of Printing soon changed the face of things. Treasures withheld for ages were scattered to the world,—if not with profusion, at all events, with an unsparing hand; and rapid improvement amply recompensed the inspired artist for his discovery, and the learned for their labors. In passing, however, it must be observed, that to the Monks we are entirely indebted for the preservation of the classic authors. Many have asserted, that what we now read as the works of venerated names, were the fabrications of the cloister; but if the fact be so, they do a singular credit to their authors. We merely notice this, to rescue from general calumny a body of people, who have deserved well of classical literature, and its patrons,—however their bigotry in religious matters, may subject them to the charge of selfish illiberality.

With Printing commenced an almost insatiable disposition to enquiry. Principles long established, became doubted and discussed; scholastic disputation was indulged in, almost to excess; but the sphere of general knowledge was enlarged, and the powers of the human mind became more acute and better known. If theology had hitherto absorbed the greater attention of the informed; metaphysics now almost cast the disputants into the shade—the celebrated *Thomists* and *Scotists*, as they were termed. With Printing also came the glorious *reformation*. But as soon as the zeal of parties was worn out—after celibacy was decreed immoral—and self-interpretation of the scriptures allowed to all,—the illiterate—the insane—the fanatic and wise man, the combatants left the field of controversy to the Descartes or Mallebranches. The ardour of enquiry opened to itself new channels—and men soon pushed their researches even to the discussion of an Almighty Providence. His laws were debated — his nature and attributes examined —and his motives for man's creation not very ceremoniously scrutinized. Finite capacities attempted to scan infinity itself; until in the inquiry—the mind startled at its daring, and lost itself in the labyrinth, into which its pride had unfortunately tempted it. Fatigued, however, with contentions on mind, its elements, its powers, and its uses,—Nature in her works, in her bowels, and general phenomena, arrested attention: and in this new and entertaining field, men speedily launched their barks—and gained considerably by their adventuring.

But it is not here intended to trace the progress of mind, or descant upon the vastness of those discoveries, which have tended so much to improve and civilize mankind. The task is too difficult to be attempted within the space which can be allotted to such essays; even were the materials for such an effort within the writers immediate reach. But it must still be observed, that Magazines, the great vehicles of periodical literature, have been of the most considerable utility and importance. A Magazine will be read, when the more bulky volume is neglected ; suited as its articles generally are, to " grave and gay, to lively and severe." The adventurer in the field of science, or general literature, first launches his little bark on the smooth sea of some amusing, and un-hypercritical Magazine; before he ventures into acknowledged publication—that sea, which may possibly be far " beyond his depth." If his daring be greater, and the shaft of criticism be levelled at his labors; though his sensibility be wounded, or his pride insulted—he still attempts, because he is as yet not publicly known; and his vanity prompts him to hazard, without much danger, a new, and, perhaps, a more fortunate production. A Magazine is the first asylum that opens its friendly door to genius, however garbed it be ; and relieves it frequently from that embarrassment, into which the *res angusta domi* may have unfortunately plunged it. A Magazine is a general granary, into which a public stock is thrown, whence every one may freely draw, and at a price much below that of the ordinary market.

(To be continued.)

THE PLEASURES AND PAINS OF. EDITORS OF PERIODICALS
(A SKETCH.)

" Delightful task."—*Thomson.*
" Hail plural Unit "—*Colman.*

Even in the immense metropolis there are not more than a score or two, and in the chief places of the kingdom not a greater number than from one to five of the entire population, who know any thing of the pleasures we are about to describe. To the great majority of readers, therefore, this exposition must possess the grand charm of novelty.

' Nothing could inspire us with *greater*

delight than to be able to state that that ' eminent artist E. F. has arrived in safety ' from Italy, where the contemplation of ' the great masters has added new powers ' even to his magic pencil.'

' The public will learn with the same ' *heartfelt satisfaction* which WE feel in an- ' nouncing it, that the accomplished Miss ' G. H. has recovered from her indisposi- ' tion, and will immediately resume her ' duties in the fashionable world.'

' WE are at once *astonished and enrap-* ' *tured* by J. K.'s last lecture on the diseases ' of the bladder. WE understand he begins ' his new course on the 1st of April next.'

And so on through the whole alphabet, and the whole circle of literature, arts and sciences.

In the first place, the joys of Editors are very widely spread and general ; in fact, they are made the happiest of living creatures—by being requested to publish such intimations as the following, sent to them expressly, as it should seem for their gratification.

' WE *rejoice* to hear that the MS. poem ' of A. B. is in such a state of forwardness ' that it may positively be expected to issue ' from the press this winter.'

' It gives, or affords, us the *highest plea-* ' *sure* to be able to state that Mr. C. D. in- ' tends to add another book to his exquisite ' treatise on morbid affections.'

WE are, it is true, sometimes *said to be sorry*, but in that case there is invariably a hope attached to *us*, a land of promise at the end of the desert;—thus

' WE are sorry to find that the Rev. L. M. is prevented by the gout from finish- ' ing his grand work on the prophecies; but ' have reason to hope that the delay will be ' short, and the publication rendered more ' perfect every day it remains in the hands ' of its classic author.'

' ' WE lament to learn that N. O's fa- ' mous picture of the *Bombardment** of ' Jerusalem will not grace the ensuing Ex- ' hibition; but the lovers of the arts will be ' consoled with us on being informed that ' it may be seen at his residence No. 717, ' next door to the Ophthalmia Hospital in ' the Regent's Park, and that many sublime ' touches have recently been added to this ' masterly composition.'

Being compelled ex officio to sympathize in print with all the hypothetical happiness (heaven knows how few in reality!) of Authors, Artists, Players, Lecturers, Publishers, Picture-dealers, Cognoscenti, Exhibitors, Teachers, Fiddlers, and Hunters after popularity of every kind; feeling all

* Why not bombard Jerusalem.

their little troubles, and more than partaking in all their great hopes; watching their motions, as it were, and recording their progress with a *maternal* anxiety; comforting the public when they are not immediately prominent, with the assurance that they will shortly be so, and being enraptured with their stupendous merits when they do come forward with any labour—these are the mere first links of *our* intimate connexion with every thing in the above lines.

Our opinions are of mighty importance. After seeing the midnight lamp expire in reading P.'s MSS. preparing for the press, we are rapped out of bed at seven o'clock by Q. determined not to present his Medals to the world without consulting us on the merits (so that *we* too must " stand the hazard") of the dye. ·R. invites *us* to inspect his show-room six miles off, in a miry suburb, before he erects his national monument to the memory of Tom Thumb the Great, *our* knowledge of the original and historical information rendering our judgment on the subject so truly desirable. Our meals are interrupted, our retirement broken in upon, our most precious time consumed, our very sick-rooms invaded, by the discoverers of curious papers found where they never were lost, the liberal possessors and ready retailers of scientific information which happens to be no news, the writers of poetry according to their own nomenclature, and the projectors of the most immortal schemes that ever an ungrateful world slighted as absurd and ridiculous.

Then the multitude of especial favours that *we* receive—each in his sphere! Being chosen as the most appropriate channel for a highly (self) interesting communication: —the publishers of long Essays written in haste and in want of our kind correction: —the most excellent Paper for an exposition of the greatest consequence to our readers in the improvement of S. T's patent:—the respectable medium for answering U's attack on V's important letter :— the valuable journal for widely disseminating a specimen of W's intended publication on a question of universal attraction!

It must be confessed that our enjoyments are occasionally chequered with some slight regrets. *We* find elegiac poets very hard hearted, and if we affront them, or even pastoral writers, by not immediately inserting their productions, we are sure of a severe scolding, a heavy postage, and anger everlasting. Antiquarians are also obdurate dogs to deal with : if disappointed on the ensuing day of publication, there is no escaping their research and remonstrance. In vain do we bury ourselves in the darkest corner of our study, and en-

trench ourselves behind the lies of our servants " *not at home*," we are invariably dug out, and suffer exposure. Authors, whom our consciences will not allow us to praise, charge us with prejudice, partiality, corruption, illiberality, malevolence, and all the deadly sins of human nature. Artists are perhaps still more intolerant and greedy of praise. Their appetites for flattery are only equalled by their immeasurable irritability; and woe be to that Critic who does not discover in every daub the colouring of Titian, combined with the grandeur of Michael Angelo; in every plaster-model the fancied fire of Phidias, and the imagined beauty of Praxiteles Indeed, we have ascertained that most public characters have such capacious stomachs, for applause, that there is no risk of surfeiting them with panegyric ; but, on the contrary much danger of being thought churls and niggardly starvlings for not giving enough. Reviews must be puffs—criticisms must observe no blemishes—biographies must make men angels!

Then we are occasionally sore beset with temptations. A pretty poetress has just finished her first attempt, " *Stanzas to a favourite Goldfinch*;" and with down-cast blue eyes, a heaving bosom, and a faltering voice, entreats to see it in print. We are martyred between the *writer* and the *writing.* Such a supplicant, what man can deny—such a composition, what Editor can insert! A philanthropist has a plan for the relief of the poor—have we not charity to give it place? A reformer produces a scheme for remedying all abuses—have we not patriotism to find room for it! An enthusiast would preach mankind into one blessed group of loving brethren—the Sermons are long and perhaps tedious, but surely our humanity cannot reject them!

And it is often in vain to endeavour to elude these applications with, " Your poetry is charming, but it wants a little polishing to fit it for the public eye"—' Will you be so good as make the necessary alterations.' " It would delight us, but take the merit from you, which must not be."—' Oh, I am not self-sufficient, and shall be happy to have my errors rectified.' "We will point out two or three slight defects in your exquisite ideas - - - so and so - - - et cetera." The verses are taken to be altered and we are never forgiven.

And then the Stage and its people! Heaven defend *us* from it and them! The theatre is a bottomless gulf for panegyric; the more that is poured in the more void it appears, and there is no return. *One* Shakspeare, who knew them well, has told us we had better have a bad epitaph after our death, than their ill report while we live; and yet there it no avoiding the latter by the sacrifice of truths on the altar of flattery, though we butcher hecatombs. What is the death of a monarch to an actor's taking leave, overcome by his feelings, supported by his friends, and all the audience, who have them, snivelling into their white handkerchiefs! What is the march of a general at the head of a victorious army, to the peregrinations of a third-rate mime through the provinces! As for the great heroes—if Critics do not laud them with more than eastern adulation, woe betide them, their motives are base, and they are the private foes of persons they never saw but on the public stage. Dreading some tragic end to our labours, we dare say no more of these tyrants, who carry the mockery of their profession into their course with real life.

"That is really a fine group, Mr. Sculptor—the attitudes are easy, the pyramidal form studied without affectation, the animals spirited, and the human figures full of nature." 'But is there no point at which your admirable judgment could oblige me by suggesting an improvement?' "The whole, we have said, is excellent, yet as no work is absolute faultless, it does seem possible to amend the anatomy of that horse's limbs, and thus improve its position—the armour of one of the knights too is rather heterogeneous, being semi-barbaric, semi-Greek, like the St. George on a *Pistrucci* crown"—'Oh, I beg your pardon, Gentlemen, I am sorry to differ from such superior minds, but I have *particularly* regarded the form and attitude of *that* horse, which is indeed the best part of the design, and the armour, I assure you, is classically accurate.' We are doomed ignorant pretenders as soon as our backs are turned, and the monument graces St. Paul's, with a crooked-legged Bucephalus and a painted Pict in an Athenian helmet:—very much on a par with the rest of the national monuments (of want of taste) in that Cathedral.

The Painter is equally solicitous for advice, alias praise, and equally wedded to his own system. "That *sky* is *green*"—Ah! that was necessary for the contrast with these *black* rocks. "The natural colour is *blue*." 'Surely you would not have a picture look *black* and *blue!*' "But these trees are heavy and brown." 'I must have a neutral tint in that bright sunset.'—A picture is entirely yellow, purple, and gold—it is a fine effort of colour. Another has men, women, and babes at the breast, all muscular as Samsons or Herculeses—it is a noble display of anatomical knowledge. A third has men of stone, and dead children of iron-grey—it is the grand gusto, half-tint, and not amenable to the laws of nature! We could swell the catalogue, but might be thought personal.

"This is a new mechanical invention—a fire and water escape, so that you are in no danger in your garret, should your house catch fire, nor in your cellar if it should be flooded. "Observe how the machinery moves." 'Yes, in the air, but either fire or water would destroy the very principle of its motion'—"I am sorry that you do not seem to understand the mechanical forces."—'We are sorry that you do not seem to understand the force of our argument'—"It is very easy to object to useful speculations, but not so easy to escape from the terrors of flood or horrors of conflagration!" 'Sir, we would rather trust to the resource of Gulliver among the Lilliputians, in both cases, than to your silly machine—Good by t'ye.'

We might dramatize a hundred other scenes in which the situation of the Editors of periodical works invariably resembles that of handsome women—most perseveringly courted, and little attended to when they come to advise. But we have said enough on the subject; and instead of resorting, as the Fair would do, to a certain lecture, we shall drop the curtain, behind which our readers have had a peep such as they may not have had before.

The Gatherer.

No. XXV.

"I am but a gatherer, and dealer in other men's stuff."

Eclipses for the Year 1819.

TO THE EDITORS.

SIRS.—The insertion of the following observations will oblige one of your constant readers:—

I am surprised why the Almanack writers give an account of only four eclipses for the year 1819, when it is known there will be six; and for the sake of your curious readers I will here prove it.

It is well known to those who understand astronomy, that when at the true conjunction of the sun and moon, the moon's true latitude is less than the sum of the semi-diameter of the earth's disk and penumbra, then the sun must and will be eclipsed. The first eclipse which they have omitted will be of the sun; it will happen on Lady Day, the 25th of March; the true conjunction of the sun and moon will be between eleven and twelve at night:

	l	g
Semidiameter of earth's disk	53	95
Semidiameter of penumbra	32	4
Sum	90	99
Moon's true latitude south desc.	85	43
Difference	4	46 less

shews the sun will then be eclipsed. The other eclipse which they have omitted will be also of the sun; it will be on the 19th day of October; the true conjunction of the sun and moon will be between three and four in the morning:

	l	n
Semidiameter of earth's disk	55	96
Semidiameter of penumbra	31	33
Sum	87	59
Moon's true lat. south asc.	75	1
Difference less 19	58 sun eclip.	

JOHN NORMAN.

It is to be noticed that although there will be at least four eclipses this year neither of them is visible to us; they will no doubt excite much astonishment and fear in the coast of New Zealand, New Holland, Guinea, California, and Japan, and especially in Madagascar, on the 3d October, where the moon will rise eclipsed, and in the Sandwich Islands it will set eclipsed; it will have the same appearance in Persia, the Caspian Sea, and west of Poland. Whatever appearances the moon ever assumes they are always interesting to the followers of Mahomet.

HORACE.

The singular esteem which some learned critics have always expressed for the works of Horace, became at last so fashionable, that scarce a man who affected the character of a polite scholar ever travelled ten miles from home without an Horace in his pocket. The late E. of S. was such an admirer of Horace, that his whole conversation consisted of quotations out of that poet, in which he often discovered his want of skill in the latin tongue, and always his want of taste. But the man whom I looked on (if I may be allowed the expression,) as Horace-mad, was one Dr. Douglas a physician of some note in London; I made an acquaintance with this gentleman on purpose that I might have a sight of his curious library, (if it might be called a library) which was a large room full of all the editions of Horace which had ever been published, as well as the several translations of that author into the modern languages. If there were any other books in the room, as there were a small number, they were only there for the sake of Horace, and were on no other account valuable to

the possessor, but because they contained some parts of Horace which had been published with select pieces or excerpta out of other latin authors for the use of schools, or because the translations of some of the odes and satires were printed in miscellanies, and were not to be found any where else. However I must acknowledge that the Doctor understood his author, whom he had studied with great care and application. Amongst other of his criticisms, he favoured me with the perusal of a dissertation on the first ode, and a defence of Dr. Hare's famous emendation of "*Te doctarum*," &c. instead of "*Me*."

VIRGIL.

Although Virgil was a court poet, and a favorite of Augustus, and was not only rewarded but enriched by that Emperor's bounty, yet his principles were republican. He retained a secret veneration for the patriot senators, and abhorred that venality and corruption by which the first Cæsar overturned the liberties of his country, and fixed his usurpation. There are two passages, one in the 6th and the other in the 8th book of the Æneid, which sufficiently prove my assertion. And I have sometimes wondered why Tucca and Varius did not expunge them, out of a compliment to the prince, but it is probable that their principles of government (for they were both men of a distinguished character) were the same as the poet's, whose work they were commissioned to revise.

Vendidit hic auro patriam, dominumque potentem
Imposuit.

Portrait of an ancient Dandy.

It was never forgotten by others, not apparently by himself, that the Lord Chancellor Hatton was brought to Queen Elizabeth's notice by his dancing, and even after he had attained this dignity of Lord Chancellor he laid aside his gown to dance at the wedding of his nephew. The circumstance is pleasantly alluded to by Gray, in the description of Stoke-pogie's house, with which his "Long Story" opens:

Full oft within these spacious walls,
When he had fifty winters o'er him,
My grave Lord Keeper led the brawls,
The seal and maces danced before him.

His bushy beard and shoe-strings green,
His high-crown'd hat and satin doublet,
Moved the stout heart of England's Queen,
Tho' Pope and Spaniard could not trouble it.

Instance of Vanity.

Vanitus, a man possessed of more money than sense, called a coach from a stand in London, and throwing himself all along upon the seat, told the coachman to drive

The Gatherer.

home. "Home sir, exclaimed the astonished driver, where is that your honour pleases to call *home* ?" "Bless me coachee, (replied the thing, with apparent surprise) I thought I was directing John my own coachman : it is so seldom I ride in a hack." A desire to display a consequence before a low bred man, who can neither know nor care any thing about you, indicates a mind of very narrow dimensions, but a vanity of insufferable extent.

Remarkable Absence.

A very absent divine finding his sight begin to fail, purchased a pair of spectacles, and on the first day of using them preached for a brother clergyman, but was observed to have them at the top of his forehead during the whole sermon. "So you have at last taken to spectacles, Doctor," said a friend after the service. "Yes, returned the unconscious absentee, I found I could not do without them, and I wonder now I never used them till to day."

Reverse of Fortune.

In the papers lately was given the trial of J. Robinson, a cotton spinner, at the Salford quarter sessions, for a conspiracy in conjunction with other cotton spinners, to raise their wages during the late turnout. This man with his elder brother and two other persons, built that large pile of buildings which stands on the banks of the Irwell at Manchester, still known by the name of Robinson's Factory. In this they carried on an extensive and lucrative business for many years; they also purchased large estates in Yorkshire, and the elder brother commenced building a wall of three miles in extent, round his park and mansion. They failed, however, from over speculation, and the brother who was the principal in the firm is now an inmate of the poor house; the other is reduced to the humble situation of a journeyman spinner.

Manure.

In a letter of Mr. Dinsdale to the editor of the *Annals of Philosophy*, we find a complaint of the ill management of manure by the majority of farmers, which is at once very just and of very old standing. They collect their manure of all descriptions in a corner of the yard, where they suffer it to remain uncovered, and the liquid and most valuable part to be drained away, and to emit exhalations, which however they might benefit the soil, are extremely insalubrious to themselves and their cattle. They even suffer dung to be carted on the land in a raw and unfermented state, there to lie in small heaps, until entirely exhausted of its goodness by the sun and wind. Instead of this unprofitable practice, they are advised, as they have so long and often been before, to pay more attention to the fermentative process on their dunghills, to stir them more frequently, and to keep them covered that they may not suffer exhaustion by the air. Sods or sward are recommended as the best covering. Dung treated in the superior manner, Mr. D. warrants will prove more powerfully contributory to vegetation, than all the boasted powers of *muriate of soda* (common salt.) The Chinese farmers (undoubted economists in some respects, and arrant bunglers in others) keep their dung in vats or deep trenches well lined, in a constantly liquid state, to obtain which, if they have not sufficient urine, they substitute water. They steep the whole of their seed corn in liquid manure, in order to promote its fecundity, sometimes adding to the steep *nitrate* of potass.

Marriage of Lord ——.

The marriage of this eminent Lawyer is not generally known, although it took place so far back as October last, at Gretna-Green. It is certain that little notice of this remarkable event has yet appeared in the public prints. In October his Lordship arrived at Gretna, accompanied by Miss ——, the present Lady ——, by whom he had had several children out of the pale of wedlock. He was dressed in fashionable female attire, with a large Leghorn bonnet and long veil. On the arrival of the officiating Priest of the Temple of Hymen, his Lordship threw off his dress and appeared in *propria persona*, and the usual ceremony being gone through, the parties were declared man and wife! His Lordship again put on his female vestments, and was on the point of taking his departure, when his son, the Hon. ——, made his appearance in a chaise and four; but the knot was tied, and shortly after the new married couple drove off. The bride is about 35 years old; the Noble bridegroom nearly 70. The object of this very extraordinary step is said to be for the purpose of legalising the children of this connection, who, according to Scottish law, cease to be illegitimate on the marriage of their parent at any time.

Shakspeare.

The following very singular reasons have been assigned by Mr. C. Butler, as grounds for a belief that Shakspeare was a Roman Catholic :—

"May the writer premise a suspicion, which, from internal evidence, he has long entertained, that Shakspeare was a Roman Catholic. Not one of his works contains the slightest reflections on Popery; or any of its practices; or any eulogy of the Re-

'ormation. His panegyric on Queen Elizabeth is cautiously expressed; whilst Queen Catharine is placed in a state of veneration; and nothing can exceed the skill with which Griffiths draws the panegyric of Wolsey. The Ecclesiastic is never presented by Shakspeare in a degrading point of view. The jolly monk, the irregular nun, never appears in his drama. It is not natural to suppose, that the topics on which at that time, those who criminated Popery loved so much to dwell, must have often solicited his notice, and invited him to employ his muse upon them, as subjects likely to engage the favourable attention, both of the Sovereign and the subject? Does not his abstinence from these justify a suspicion, *that a Popish feeling* withheld him from them? Milton made the gunpowder conspiracy the theme of a regular poem. *Shakspeare is altogether silent on it.*"—Butler's Memoirs of the English Catholics, vol. ii. p. 322.

We will only oppose a single observation to Mr. Butler's "suspicion." Shakspeare was buried *at his own desire in a Protestant Church*, with this rather ominous inscription, which we recommend to Mr. Butler's perusal:—

Good Friend, for Jesus' sake forbear
To dig the dust inclosed here.
Blest be the Man that spares these stones,
And curst be he that moves my bones.

Welsh Indians.

In the Cosmography, written by Peter Heylyn, and printed early in the 17th century, is the following paragraph relative to the first discovery of America:—"Finally, in the History of Wales, writ by David Powell, it is reported that Madoc, the son of Owen Gwineth, Prince of Wales, of purpose to decline engaging in a civil war raised in that estate, in the year 1170, put himself to sea, and after a long course of navigation came into this country, where, after he had left his men, and fortified some places of advantage in it, he returned home for more supplies, which he carried with him in ten barks; but neither he nor they were looked after by the rest of the nation. To which some add, that there is still some smattering of the Welsh or British tongue to be found amongst them; as that a bird with a white head is called Pengwin and the like; in which regard some sorry statesmen went about to entitle Queen Elizabeth unto the soverignty of these countries. Others, more wise, dissuaded from that vain ambition, considering that Welshmen, as well others, might be cast upon those parts by force of tempest, and easily implant some few words of their own among the people there inhabiting. And though I must

needs say for the honour of Wales, that they have more grounds for what they say, when those which look for this new world in the Atlantis of Plato, the Atlantick Islands of Aristotle and Plutarch, or the discoveries of Hanno the Carthagenian: yet I am not so far convinced of the truth thereof, the use of the mariner's compass being not so ancient (without which such a voyage could not be performed), but that I may conclude with more satisfaction, that this country was unknown to former ages."

Saffron supposed to prevent Sea Sickness.

M. Cadet, who spent part of the summer of 1817 in London, mentions that when he crossed the channel from Calais to Dover, he observed an English gentleman with a bag of Saffron suspended over his stomach. On enquiring the reason, he was told by the gentleman that it was a practice which he always followed when crossing the channel, because it preserved him from sea sickness. The remedy was found out, he said, in the following way. A small merchant, who had occasion to make frequent voyages, was always tormented with sea sickness when on ship-board. One day he embarked, after purchasing a pound of saffron, which he put under his shirt in order to avoid paying duty for it. He escaped without experiencing any sea sickness, though the sea was rough. Ascribing this lucky escape to the saffron, he communicated his discovery to several of his friends, who made repeated trials of the remedy, and always with success.

HINTS, PLANS, and PROCEEDINGS
OF
Benevolence.
——— *Homo sum:*
Humanum nihil a me alienum puto.

GENERAL PENSION SOCIETY.

Some few days since the General Quarterly Meeting of the Pension Society for the relief of the decayed Artizans, Mechanics, and their Widows, was held at the Albion Tavern, Aldersgate-street. The room appropriated to this proceeding was nearly filled by respectable persons, many of whom were ladies.

The Lord Mayor took the Chair, and after the minutes of a former meeting had been read, they proceeded to the order of the day.

The Lord Mayor then addressed the company, and read a letter from His Royal Highness the Duke of Kent, expressive of his satisfaction at the progress of the institution. The letter was followed by very loud applause.

It was a pleasing reflection, observed the Lord Mayor, that the greatest characters in this country were daily found among them, promoting every effort to benefit the objects of charity. Adverting to the proceedings of the Institution, he said that they had charitably placed on the Pension List a most respectable decayed mechanic, 79 years of age, another of 66, a woman of 80, and a woman of 60. They had bestowed bread on six persons, all of the most respectable characters. He expressed a hope that he should have the pleasure of seeing this charity extended, and many more persons provided for. He called upon them to exert their zeal, and to spare no pains to accomplish the object they all had in view—Loud applause

The Secretary then reported the state of Subscriptions since the establishment of the institution in February last, and after the election of Directors and other routine business, the meeting adjourned.

The object of the above Institution is to relieve distressed artizans and mechanics, upwards of 60 years of age, by a pension of 13L per annum, and poor widows of such persons with 7l. 16s. payable by the Directors of their Monthly Meetings. The pensioners are elected by ballot.

Encouragement of Industry, and Reduction of Poors' Rates.

It is hoped that the attention of the Legislature will be attracted to the impolitic duty of 5s. a thousand imposed upon draining-bricks: as this duty is paid in an early stage of the process of making, it is levied equally upon those which are spoilt as upon those which prove fit for use. This tax is, therefore, a greater obstruction to the progress of agricultural improvement than might be supposed by those who judge only from the rate of its assessment: moreover, losses must be more frequent if the bricks are manufactured without the usual buildings, and under the superintendence of an individual only wanting a supply for his own purposes, than if the business were conducted upon an extensive scale, professedly with a view to sale. But where draining-tiles are not within a reasonable distance, it is contemplated that each proprietor may burn upon his own premises as many draining-bricks as are required for his estate. By adopting this method, the expence of carriage (a most material consideration) will be avoided; and, while poors' rates will be reduced, and employment be diffused amongst the lower orders in making bricks and in land-draining, the value of property will be greatly augmented by the improvement. It would also appear to have been an oversight, to levy a duty upon draining-bricks, since draining-tiles are exempt from duty on account of their utility for agricultural drainage; the same reasons which are urged in favour of exempting draining-tiles from duty are equally applicable to draining-bricks; and as the latter requires less skill, and no building, the work may be resorted to as an employment for the poor in any part of the country where clay is to be found, and therefore is the more entitled to the exemption.

Bible Societies.

The cause of the British and Foreign Bible Society has very particularly flourished in the western counties in England, during the past year. Numerous Bible Associations have been formed, and attended with the most happy circumstances of success amongst the different classes of the poor. The Earl of Liverpool, when travelling in the West, in the course of the past Summer, observed that, he was persuaded, from accurate observation upon facts, more advantage was to be expected in regard to the amelioration of the character, circumstances, and morals of the poor of this country, from the influence of the Bible Associations, than from any other project which had been suggested. As such, that he in common with several other principal Members of the Cabinet, hoped to see the universal establishment of these Societies, being fully convinced of their manifest tendency to improve both the temporal and moral condition of the national population.

The Labouring Poor.

Mr. Arthur Young, in a letter dated Bradford Hall, Sept. 2, 1816, says; "In the counties of Rutland and Lincoln, the practice is to attach land to cottages, sufficient to support that number of cows which the cottager is able to purchase; they are tenants to the chief landlords, and not sub-tenants to the farmers; yet these latter are very generally friends to the system: well they may be so, for the poor rates are next to nothing when compared with such as are found in parishes wherein this advantageous system is not established. In the late minute inquiries made by the Board of Agriculture into the state of the labouring poor throughout the kingdom, many persons were written to, who reside in the districts where this system is common; and it was found by their replies, that the practice stands the test of present distress, as well as it supported the opposite difficulties of extreme scarcity.—It is much to be regretted, that so admirable an example is not copied in every part of the kingdom. In those counties where no such practice is met with, it is very rare indeed to meet a labourer who has saved any money, their reliance is entirely on the parish, and their present earnings dissipated in the alehouse. Not so in Lincolnshire; the men who wish to marry save their money to buy cows? and girls who wish to have husbands take the same means to secure them. Sobriety, industry, and economy are thus secured, and children are trained from their infancy to the cultivation of a garden and attending cattle, instead of starving with unemployed spinning wheels. No subject can better deserve the attention of men of considerable landed property. If some change of management, decisive in its nature, do not take take place, poors' rates will continue to increase, till they will absorb the whole landed revenue of the kingdom."

For the Encouragement of Industry, and reduction of Poors' rates.

The public we doubt not will have much gratification in learning that the Committee for the Encouragement of industry, and reduction of Poors' rates are daily receiving communications of the greatest importance, from every part of the country. Two much praise cannot be bestowed on the indefatigable exertions of *Mr. Benjamin Wills*, the Secretary of the Committee. The Meetings of the Committee, it may be useful to state, are held at the Kings Head, Poultry.

New Lanark, Jan. 15 1819.

Yesterday being the anniversary of the re-establishment in this village of the practical system of kindness, to supersede the necessity for punishment, introduced by Mr. Owen, the inhabitants to commemorate a day which secured to them so many well-devised means of improvement and enjoyment, spent the evening as usual in rejoicings of various kinds. They commenced, on a signal being given, by an almost instantaneous illumination of the whole village, which, placed in the romantic valley, produced an extraordinary effect, and from the distant hills appeared like enchantment. It continued about two hours, during which the village band played national airs in the area belonging to the infant school, which is in the middle of the establishment. When these ceased, seven of the public rooms were thrown open, for the amusement of the population, and it was soon found that five would scarcely accommodate those who wished to join the merry dance, and two of them were filled with young persons of both sexes, from 10 to 14 years of age. Refreshments were served to the whole of them, and the dancing rooms contained between ten and eleven hundred. The old and young were meat and clean, and without disorder or confusion of any kind, they appeared to enjoy themselves to their hearts' content. But the unaffected good humour and happiness which prevailed throughout the evening cannot be imagined by those who have not seen young persons in this situation in life, trained on a principle of kindness without any fear of punishment. No one could witness it without wishing that others could be permitted to enjoy similar advantages.

Account of the Harmonites.

The Dutch Society, formed by Frederick Rap, a Minister of the Gospel, settled some years ago in the Western part of Pennsylvania, made extensive improvements on lands they purchased at a reduced price, built a town with a number of good brick houses, which they called Harmony. They also planted a vineyard, made wines, &c. established almost all kinds of mechanism, and cultivated the land very extensively as their Society increased. Many of their Dutch friends joined them in a few years and placed all their property into the hands of Frederick Rap, their spiritual teacher, leader, and protector. They willingly submitted to his government and laws, which they delighted in. All their property, like that of Shakers, was one common stock, to feed the hungry and clothe the naked of such as joined them in a destitute situation. Their discipline was strict, prohibiting them from keeping bad company, drinking ardent spirits, or marrying; all which they considered sinful.

Their society becoming large, and the climate not suiting for their vineyards, they made extensive purchases of land on the Wabash, in the state of Indiana, where they are making rapid improvements. They have lately sold property to the amount of one hundred thousand dollars, exclusive of which, it is said, they have upwards of two millions of dollars in gold and silver. They have purchased upwards of one hundred thousand acres of land on the Wabash, at two dollars per acre, which from their industry and neatness of improvements will no doubt in a few years be worth from twenty to fifty dollars per acre. Their town is called New Harmony. —The climate is well suited to vineyards, and they will doubtless soon be able to supply that country with the best of wines, malt liquor, &c. All kinds of mechanical business will be carried on as before. This will greatly improve that part of the State, and of course render the adjoining lands more valuable. Persons therefore who wish to remove to that state, will do well to make their purchases soon, as the numerous emigrants to that country will soon take up all the unoccupied land, or at least greatly raise its value. From exploring the western country, and hearing the different opinions of the people, I am induced to believe that Iudiana is the most desirable state west of the Alleghany. Its climate is healthy, its soil productive, and its laws salutary.

On Punishment of Death.

The following observations are so interesting and relate so immediately to a subject of the first moral and political importance— *the punishment of death*—that we insert them with pleasure.

We are not advocates for exciting an improper commiseration for the criminal, for bestowing upon delinquency that share of public attention—we had almost said *favour*, which is withheld from virtuous poverty and unavoidable misfortune. It is one of the worst effects of the existing system that it tends to merge our horror and indignation for the crime in pity for the culprit, and to hinder our acquiescence in the administration of justice. The disproportion of the sentence to the guilt of the offender, in cases where the punishment of death is awarded to crimes without violence, is so revolting to humanity, that it renders the best part of society conspirators in their hearts against the laws of their country. 'They who would rejoice at the correction of a thief are yet shocked at the thought of destroying him. His crime sinks to nothing compared with his misery, and severity defeats itself by exciting pity.'

Respect for the laws is, next to religious principle, by far the most important and salutary restraint upon human passions that can be brought to act upon a civilized community; it is in fact the chief bond which holds society together. The fear of punishment is but remotely concerned in producing this subordination to law: in the absence of other restraints of a moral nature, this fear is found wholly inefficacious to deter from the dreadful venture of setting the consequences of crime at defiance. That which is of all dreadful things the most dreadful—*death*, is daily encountered with a hardihood which leaves no room for surprise, that even when arrayed in all the terrific ceremonial of punishment, the fear of death should scarcely be effectual to re-

press the mis-directed spirit of enterprise, much less to control the inveterate habits of the hardened and the desperate. 'There is no passion in the mind of man so weak,' remarks Lord Bacon, 'but it mates and masters the fear of death.' Certainly hanging is not punishment enough, is not terrible enough, to ensure obedience to the laws. Torture is not enough, it has been tried and proved to be not enough to overcome the bold contempt which, in the absence of moral fear, is felt by the offender towards his judges, whose utmost vengeance can, be knows, but wrest from him his life. Respect for the laws is a very different principle, and one more deeply seated in our nature than this animal fear : it springs from a sense of justice, and from the conscious need of that protection which the laws alone can afford. Conscience and self-interest are alike implicated in our solicitude for the maintenance of their authority ; and punishment, when conformable to our ideas of what the laws justly require as the sanction of that authority, is viewed with unmixed approbation, not only as the proper mark of infamy set upon the offence, but as the pledge of our own safety.

This respect for the laws is found to be in many instances not totally destroyed, even where the fear of punishment has not sufficed to deter from the commission of crime. Often the culprit will acknowledge the equity of his sentence, and his acquiescence in the law by which he suffers is, in such cases, followed by a salutary contrition for the wrong he has done to society. This idea of punishment, as a thing deserved and right, being once destroyed, no degree of severity will impart to the sanction of the law the force of a moral restraint. Punishment becomes efficient as a preventative of crime, chiefly as it contributes to render crime itself infamous, by striking in with the secret decision of conscience, and proclaiming before the world what the offender himself dreads to hear as the anticipated sentence of the tribunal of God. But when the penalty is as excessive as its execution is uncertain, it is not very likely that either the moral fear, or the servile dread of punishment, will be very efficacious in preventing crime. Could any expedient be devised, more directly adapted to divest of all its impressive majesty, the awful ceremonial of doom than the practice of our criminal courts, where the audience are accustomed to hear the sentence of death passed upon their fellow creatures, upon whom it is never intended to be executed, upon whom the spectators know that it is never intended to be executed, while the culprit himself is confident that it is merely a piece of legal form.

A very striking instance of the gross impropriety of this practical fiction was on one occasion referred to in the House of Commons, by an honourable member who had himself been an eye witness of the scene. Upon the home circuit some years ago, a young woman was tried for having stolen to the amount of forty shillings in a dwelling house. It was her first offence, and was attended by many circumstances of extenuation. The prosecutor appeared as he stated, from a sense of duty, the witnesses very reluctantly gave their evidence, and the jury still more reluctantly their verdict of guilty. It was impossible not to observe the interest excited in the court. The Judge passed sentence of death. She instantly fell lifeless at the bar. Lord Kenyon whose sensibility was not impaired by the sad duties of his office, cried out in great agitation from the bench, "*I don't mean to hang you; will nobody tell her I don't mean to hang her?*" 'I then felt,' continued the honourable relater of the fact, ' as I now feel that this was passing sentence, not upon the prisoner but upon the law. I ask whether an English Judge ought to be placed in a situation where it is imperative upon him to pass sentence of death, when he has not the remotest intention to order the sentence to be carried into execution.'

Original Poetry.

LINES TO THE YEAR 1818.

Peace to thee still!—tho' through thy devious way,
Few gleams of light have cheered my lurid day;
Few hours were happy, and few hopes fulfill'd,
Fate made me sport, and hurl'd me where she will'd.
Thy vernal season gave no spring to me,
Thy yellow ripeness no emblossom'd tree,
On whose rich branch, faint hopes might yet recline—
Thy harvest plenty, saw no plenty mine,
Thy brumal blasts—of all thy pow'rs alone
Pictur'd my fate:—but these,—with thee are
—gone!

What toil, what pain, what visions or designs
Alternate press'd me, through thy changing signs,
What days of sorrow, and what nights of care,
What storms endur'd, what yielding to despair,
What torturing day thoughts, and what broken sleep,
What frenzy—houseless,—yet not known to weep—

When drizzling rain—and vice tormented stroll,
Cros'd on my path—and fired my tumult soul.
What vain attempts to reason want to sense,
What doubts and cavils at Omnipotence—
What harrowing feelings, vultures each to each,
Without one balm, one anodyne to reach
The gangreen wounds felt at the bosoms core,
When pride kept watch at misery's squalid door,
And all the world beside—the leaden throng
Cull'd pleasures flower amid the flow of song—
Felt all the bliss that love returned imparts,
And all the sunshine of enraptured hearts,
The friendly welcome—and the outstretch'd hand,
The joy—bright eye that all can understand—
The thousand somethings that give life its charm
To which we cling—to which our feeling's warm;
But reft of these, complaint were now in vain—
To bear in secret is voluptuous pain!
And little boots it—now with thee inurn'd
To tell what hopes, or fears my bosom burn'd,
Lost in the grave, to which all haste apace,
The instinct animal—as the reasoning race.

But if chagrin'd with thee and with thy way,
There may be some who felt thy kindlier sway—
Some who embarking in the tempest sea
Of, chart-less, yet desired philosophy—
Have reached the haven which they eager sought,
And homeward turning—joyous tidings brought:
Some too who reckless of thy flying pace
In sloth consumed their few important days,
Thou may'st have summoned e'er 'twas yet too late,
Inspir'd to rise, and shun their perilous fate—
Woke into transport, grateful to above,
And vow'd henceforth to walk in peace and love!

There may be some to whom thy reign was mild,
Whose star rose brightly—and at setting smil'd,
Who sprung from want—above their fellows tow'r'd,
Met thousands' envy—but in fortune flower'd,
Looked on earth's crowd—as crowds should ever be,
Alike offensive to the wise and free,
Fickle and foaming, turbulent and still,
Like veering winds—that sleep or rage at will,
The slaves of passion—impulse, or of state,
Dangerous alike in triumph or defeat!

There may be some a trusty friend who've found,
Friend! once to me how grateful was the sound
Like music breathing o'er the listening stream?
Sweet as young love in sympathy's first dream?
Warm as devotion fired, by beauty's touch,
Kind as compassion, and more constant much!
But now whose memory like the twilight ray,
Melts into night—and vanishes away—.
Leaves not a trace, or if a trace it leave
That wounds life's peace—or blesses, to deceive!

Friend! oh what insult in the hackney'd name,
Our natures glory—and our natures shame,
A fluttering insect—with a painted breast,
A travelling swallow, seeking wintry nest,

A bane—a bliss—an honor, a disgrace,
A saintly Proteus only to be base—
An idol worshipped only to destroy
Life's discord—harmony, life's grief and joy!
Strange compound—friend!—I loath the once
   loved name,
Its sound, its mention, nay its thought brings
   shame,
Tho' once twas mine—to prize man's friendship
   high,
And in my heart to fold it: 'twas the eye
Thro' which life's visions all in bliss were seen,
Toils resting place—and sorrows breast of green,
The ambrosial dew to nourish all that live,
The source of hope—and all that Heaven
   could give!
A sound—a joy, that in one syllable
Gave more than language e'er combin'd to tell!
But fond idolater at th' alluring shrine,
Too easy trusting—it was early mine,
To meet just vengeance from that steel of
   thine,
Not hardened in the furnace—for such part,
But by cold frowns—and slights that reach the
   heart,
By many a shrug, and eye-lash curl'd—and look,
I'd rather feed the unsparing worm than—
   brook,
By—but 'tis pass'd: the name shan't cheat again,
It once lent joy—now welcome be its pain!

Peace to thee still! whate'er thy wrongs to me,
There have been thousands blessed by thine
   and thee,
Some exile homeward may his course have bent,
Joy in his eye, and in his heart content,
His feathery step—as light as dews that rest
On flowers that blush and bloom for beauty's
   breast—
That by surprise his early friends and sire,
Mourning his fate around their chirping fire,
May hail in speechless agony of joy,
Their unexpected, but their long—loved boy!

Perhaps some Xaltes timorous, fair and young,
The village pride, and boast of every tongue,
With lips and looks, as ripe for wedded bliss,
As fondling ivy, when the elm 'twill kiss—
With jetty locks that veil her snow-white breast,
And eyes that tell, what words had ne'er ex-
   press'd—

Perhaps to her—that long in secret sigh'd,
O'er vows by Laura pledged her as his bride,
E'er yet he ploughed the oceans billowy tide,
But now forlorn, or wan from brooding thought,
Some distant gleams of joy thou may'st have
   brought,
Some guardian stem, to prop the drooping
   flow'r,
E'er pluck'd by fate, in some disast'rous hour,
Some kindly ray—to light life's weary scene—
And give in Lara all he once had been,
A faithful swain! by destiny remov'd,
Too long from home, from friends, and her
   he lov'd,
But in her arms once more, to live and die—
His bliss her smile;—her all, his smiles reply!
And bounteous still to many a labouring elf,
Without one thought beyond the bounds of
   self—

Thou may'st have yielded all he wish'd of good,
By night repose—by day, small toil and food,
A pipe and glass at festival or wake;
For wife some treat—and for his boys a cake!

And unconfined to bounties, such as these,
Thou may'st have soothed the pay of grief to
   ease,
Have lightened sorrow to the widowed heart,
Fed orphan babes—and played a father's part!
Led blushing maidens to the nuptial shrine,
Warmed their young pulse, and taught them
   how divine,
To pluck the arrow from afflictions breast,
And lend to wedded joy its chiefest zest;
Their offspring in the path of Heaven to place,
Doves to their mates—and glory to their race!

And unforgetful too of nobler ends,
Thou may'st have men link'd with their kind as
   friends,
Have patriots fired to seek their country's good
By virtuous laws—and virtuous means pursu'd.
Have check'd for e'er, the march of giant war,
Sought nations peace—and giv'n its guardian
   star,
Bade arts advance, the sciences revive,
And drooping genius—o'er its ashes live!
Wreath'd merits urn, with flow'rs that mark
   thy care,
Greenly to bloom—and live immortal there!

What rapid strides to wisdom and to truth,
Thou may'st have made, amid our frolic youth,
What light held out, to teach the waxen mind
The march of thought—and in its progress find,
That vice however prosperous brings decay,
And glory fades like mists before the day—
That human knowledge, ample as earth's scope,
Is only useful, when it clings to hope,
And 'firms our bliss in him—whose endless
   reign,
Shall be the measure of the bliss we'll gain,
If in our earth's sojourn—his path were trod,
And prov'd as th' image of the Christian's God!
What various blessings to the world's vast
   throng,
Thou may'st have brought, how many a theme
   for song,
What mirth and joy entwining pleasures glass,
What juicy goblets it was thine to pass—
What sportive dance to Moroca's merry sons,
What laughing jest, and jollity that crowns,
The humble recreations of the poor;—
What minstrels welcomed at the muses' door,
What strains 'twas thine to give them, and
   what spell,
O'er all;—is more than verse like mine can tell!

Peace to thee still! and may the nascent year,
Not wheel less kindly through its changing
   sphere,
May every tear 'twas thine to start—and sigh
By that which follows be repaid with joy—
And joy continu to delight and bless;
All who can feel the warmth of happiness!
May the full horn be spread throughout the
   land,
And meek ey'd peace, with all her virtuous
   band;

Watch o'er our isle—and crime and faction brave,
Freedom her all   nd her friend—the wave!
May (too vain wish) mankind contention flee,
And live for th' interest of humanity!

CONRAD.

TO THE MEMORY OF MY FRIEND.

A —— C ——— e,

Oh! weep not his fate, tho' untimely his fall;
His deeds still shall live, and his mem'ry recall
Some scenes of the past; while th sword on his head
Its dews in compassion, a requiem shall shed!

Nor rude be the tongue, that descants o'er his doom;
The gentlest and bravest must bend to the tomb—

His years tho' not brilliant—not idly had flown,
His spring-time was gloom, and his summer is—gone!

His life's closing hour was yet soft as the breath
Of summer eve fading in night o'er the heath—
To sleep from its labor—like nature to rest,
And wake with the " morrow"—both blessing and bless'd.

Tho' unalive he flies, yet one friend to his worth,
Now wreathe this rude garland, to deck his cold curfh;
Whilst fate o'er his path-way, once strewing but ease,
Now gives him the hope, which he wrung from despair.

London, Nov. 1818.   F. M.

LINES

ADDRESSED TO A LADY ON HER BIRTH-DAY,
ACCOMPANIED BY AN ORNAMENTAL COMB
FOR HER HEAD!

What gift that's worthy can I make,
For sweet Miss Mary Ann to take—
I'd gladly g ve some Jewel rare,
To ornament her not brown Hair
But Jewels she's already got—
Two Brilliants in her *Head* I wot,
Which indicate that there you'l find,
What " far surpasses show"—the Mind!
Yet some small Tribute I would pay
On this return of natal Day,
Some thing of *use* as well as *show*
A Comb appears, quite " comme il faut"
Tho' Teeth it hâh, it will not Iife
Yet keeps the Hair both smooth and tight;
And tho' it neither speaks nor sees
You surely may discern with ease,
In spite of idle, vain pretence,
It very near approaches *Sense*!

BRAINS.

A FRAGMENT.

We toil and fret our life-time through,
For praise or fame that quickly flies,
Nor think that all, like morning's dew,
Shines for an hour—then fades and dies!

Oh, did we in our youthhood's prime,
But learn the wise and only lore—
To bend our thoughts to after-time,
Content were our's, for evermore!

But, lur'd by gay and phantom shades,
We urge our way as feelings lead;
Nor dream the brightest glory fades;
That worms will on our greatness feed.

But yet, perhaps, 'tis fated so!
And while on earth we're doom'd to toil,
The belief is sweet—that deeds below
May flourish in a kindlier soil.!

And after all, when life is o'er,
And cold, among our sires we sleep,
Some vision may those scenes restore,
Which love and virtue blooming keep.

X. Y. Z.

TO KALIA.

Tho' Kalia, love, thou art afar,
Whilst Want's drear eye looks on my lot,
And with the leaden world I war,
Thy form and worth are unforgot.

'Mid all my woes, one sigh to thee
Is worth a world of joy beside:
I'm still the child of minstrelsy,
And want or care in vain may chide.

Life has its cares,—it still has bliss,
But only that which Kalia gives;
As oft as mem'ry grants the kiss,
On which alone her Lara lives.

'Tis not, my girl, because to day
We meet not, that we love the less;
The hour will come, when we may say,
How absence adds to happiness!

Our fates may bid us still to part,
And wealth impose its severing chain,
But love still rules the faithful heart,
And whispers Hope—" we'll meet again."

Perhaps, by others' eye impress'd,
Thy heart may wander far from me,
But, Kalia, lips by Lara press'd,
Will tell if thou act faithlessly.

Yet, lovely girl, I cannot dream
That pride or wealth could alter thee;
Whose pow'r but like the moonlight beam,
Dies as it falls, tho' shiningly.

And still, tho' fate may bid us part,
And wealth impose its severing chain,
Yet Love, that rules the faithful heart,
Still whispers Hope—" we'll meet again."

LARA.

To C—— E—— G————

Accept, dear maid, this gift of mine—
" Affection," pow'r supreme, divine!
From whose sweet source on earth doth flow,
All that is best of Heaven below.
To thy young mind, oh may it prove
The guide to future virtuous love !
And in thy love, thy choice be bless'd
With one, whose love thou lov'st the best:
And when a wedded wife become,
May bliss reign o'er thy peaceful home.

W. H—g—th.

F

INTERESTING INTELLIGENCE FROM THE BRITISH SETTLEMENTS IN INDIA.

CALCUTTA.

HINDOO FESTIVAL; DEATH.

The Festival of *Rut'h Jattra* was held on Monday the 13th July, on which occasion four men were unfortunately crushed to death under the wheels of the Rot'h. Whether this was a voluntary sacrifice, or the effect of accident, has not been ascertained. The body of a fifth was also entangled among the wheels, and was with difficulty extricated from that perilous situation.

AJMERE: TOWN AND FORT, DESCRIBED.

" The Town, Fort, and district of Ajmere were surrendered to Brigadier Knox on the 9th of June. This is a very important acquisition, in every point of view. It removes the Mahrattas, and their influence completely from Rajpootana, and will give that devoted Country an opportunity of recovering its prosperity under the protection and benign influence of the British Government. From its commanding position it is a military post of much consequence, guarding the route across the desert by Bickanere and Maultaun. It also opens a direct and safe intercourse from the provinces of Agra and Delhi with Guzerat.—Poker, the celebrated place of Hindoo worship, where one of the principal Horse fairs in Hindeostan was formerly held, is close to Ajmere, and no doubt will soon be re-established,—at this the very best description of saddle, carriage and Cavalry Horses were formerly procured, viz. the Jungle Tazee, the Cutch and Cutteawar horses; also horses from Damaun, a district west of the Indus, from Kabul, Kandahar, Persia and Tartary. The people who bring down these horses will naturally carry back the value, in the produce of the provinces of Hindoostan,— hence we may fairly hope to see in the course of a few years, Ajmere become a great and flourishing commercial city. An event however has lately taken place, which may retard the accomplishment of this gratifying prospect:—the City of Maultaun and the country around it, has for some years been governed by an Afghan chieftain, who paid only a nominal obedience to the King of Kabul: it was the interest of this Chief to keep upon good terms with the British Government; and had his power continued, there is no doubt but he would have encouraged and protected as far as he was able, the intercourse across the desert with Kabul, Persia and Tartary.

Runjeet Singh, the Seikh Chief of Lahore, has long been desirous of obtaining possession of Maultaun; and though several time foiled, he has lately succeeded. The Nabob who defended it was killed, and the town and district is now completely in the possession of the Seikhs; and as they have shut up the intercourse through the Punjaub with the Northern nations of Asia, they will no doubt follow the same policy with the route across the desert; hence all intercourse with these Nations will be completely cut off, except by the sea port of Curratchy and Belochistan. *Mettoreh, July 4. 1818.*

MADRAS.

HORSE STEALING.

The following charge will shew that the native Hindoos are not deficient in the tricks of finished knavery, and natural Genious: or, that they have made the most laudable! proficiency 'in the dextrous professions, under European tutors and example.

Abdul Kawder, was charged with the offence of horse stealing—a very novel offence in this country—but which is made a capital felony by Stat. 1st Ed. 6. c. 12, 2d and 3d Ed. 6. c. 33 and 31 Eliz. c. 12— on account of the great difficulty of guarding this species of property and the great facility with which it is carried beyond the reach of the owner. It appears in the present case, that the prisoner on the 15th April last, came to the prosecutor, who is a horse dealer at Madras, and told him there was a person at Triplicane, one of the Nabob's people, who wanted to purchase a horse; in consequence of which, the prosecutor delivered a horse with a saddle on it to his own horse keeper, with special directions to him not to deliver the horse to the supposed purchaser, without receiving the price which he set on it, which was thirty Star Pagodas; and to accompany the prisoner to Triplicane, and bring back either the horse or the price. However, it appeared, that the prisoner as soon as he got near the Government Gardens, contrived to mount the horse, and rode away with him, telling the horse keeper, in whose charge he was, that he would go to the supposed purchaser and bring him the price; and desired him to wait there till he returned; but instead of that it appeared, that the prisoner immediately went and sold the saddle to a Fackier, at Triplicane, for four rupees, and took off the horse to the Zillah of Chittore, where he sold him to one Syed Meeram, in whose possession he was found, for three pagodas and a half, and never returned to the horse keeper, who waited for him a day and night at the Government Gardens: and the prisoner having absconded from his usual dwelling was at length, after several days' search taken in the Zillah of Chittore.

UNCOMMON WEATHER: THE EPIDEMIC.

The same extraordinary weather continues to prevail on this Coast, which has been experienced for the last six weeks. The Country has been literally inundated with rain, and the Rivers, both to the Northward and Southward, are as much out as during the Monsoon. Meanwhile we are happy to learn that Madras continues as healthy as during the same season of any former period, and we are glad to add the name of Bombay. It is with pleasure also we mention that by letters which have been received from the Northward during the week, it appears, that the accounts of the *Cholera Morbus* are of rather a more favorable nature. At *Jonins*, the malady had much abated that sanguine hopes were entertained that it would soon disappear altogether. The Epidemic is said to have reached Poonah, but few deaths had been occasioned by it. So much has been written on the subject of the cure of this disorder, in the last *ten* or *twelve* months, that we apprehend it must ere this be pretty well understood, and require no further elucidation; for if the many hundred elaborate letters prescribing a proper treatment for it have not yet effected that object, we must conclude this Epidemic to be invincible, and above the common controul of the science of Medicine. *Madras, August* 11.

BOMBAY.

WIDOW NOT BURNED.

We are rejoiced to learn, that, through the influence of the Resident at Baroda Futteh Sing's favourite wife was prevailed upon not to sacrifice herself on the funeral pile of her husband; an example, which we trust, will have its influence in checking, and ultimately abolishing that horrid practice, wherever the influence of the British Government may predominate.

PROGRESS OF THE EPIDEMIC.

We should be happy to report the cessation, or at least, the abatement of the disorder that has lately visited several districts of the Indian territory: but the fact is otherwise. We have perused several opinions as to the cause and origin of this disease; but none that are beyond controversy. The mode of treatment, also, is varied, according to the opposite theories of the practisioners; but, none has hitherto been so fortunate as to discover a specific.

Bombay Gazette—July 22, 1818.

The Cholera Morbus, we are concerned to hear has broken out with great violence at Jaulnah and Aurungabad, and the number of fatal cases we regret to say have been numerous. At Vizagapatam, Nelapilly and the greater part of the eastern coast of the Peninsula it has committed dreadful ravages, and as it appears to be characterized by properties peculiarly epidemic, we are happy to have it in our power to lay before our readers, many judicious remarks, that have been kindly furnished us, relative to a disease that has been so fatal to the native population in different parts of India, and it is confidently hoped that should we not possess the means of arresting its progress, yet the precautions taken by the faculty may be such as to ensure at least the most prompt Medical assistance; and for the purpose, we have been requested to suggest, the propriety of erecting Palls, or Sheds, in different parts of the Bazars, and Villages, where native assistants, may be always at hand to administer relief. We agree most heartily with our Brother Editor, that more attention to cleanliness among the natives even of the Presidency, is most desirable, and to effect so praiseworthy an object, (now become so imperious) with the least possible delay, we doubt not that the Magistrates' attentions, and exertions, will be applied to the promotion of that object.

Letters from Jaulnah state, that no less than thirty nine of the Royal Scots, have fallen victims to the Cholera, besides a number of natives.

We are extremely sorry to state that our letters from Nagpore of the beginning of June represent the sickness, that is now prevailing in that part of India, to be of a very serious and alarming nature. This disorder, which of course has received the name of Cholera Morbus, first appeared in the camp of Colonel Adams on the 30th ultimo, the day on which his corps reached Nagpore. On that day fifteen Sepoys and a great number of camp followers died of it. The inhabitants of Nagpore had been suffering from it grievously, for a fortnight before Colonel Adams reached the Capital, and the mortality among them is stated by our intelligent correspondent as at the rate of 25 per diem.

' The pestilence has nearly depopulated the beautiful valley of the Nerbuddah, and

It has spread all over Berar; our hospitals are completely crowded, and a most heart-rending sight it is, that presents itself in them; the groans of the dying—the lamentations of the friends of those already gone, and the doolies crowding to the place with fresh victims, has an awful effect, which can better be conceived than described. Dr. Corbyn's practice was adopted at first, but without success, and hence doubts are entertained of its infallibility; and I think on fair grounds: As to Dr. Tytler's 'New Rice Theory,' if it has not yet been overthrown, we have here proof positive of its erroneousness. Neither the sepoys nor camp-followers use rice of any kind, nor will they were do it where Otta is procurable; as it always is here; and the Madras Sepoys who prefer rice as much as oor's dislike it, have not, I believe suffered near so much. It appears to me to differ considerably from what it was described to be, in the various discussions upon it. The vomiting is easily subdued, and is never as had been described. Besides, the patient throws up almost pure water in general, free from the least tincture of bile. Those afflicted with it, are in the extremest torture you can conceive, and cry out that their whole inside is burning, particularly the liver; and it is always preceded by pains in the head, stomach and limbs. I hope our medical gentlemen will make their opinions and practice public, because it appears, there are several peculiarities in the disease now raging. That it is not infectious is proved beyond a doubt, for the officers daily visit the hospitals several times, touching and conversing with the sick, and feel no bad effects from this exercise of their humanity.

PERSIA BY WAY OF INDIA.

EUROPEAN ARTIST, FAVOURED BY THE SHAH.

Sir Robert Ker Porter, the once celebrated Panoramic artist, who since married a Russian Lady of rank, purposes, in the course of his travels in Persia, to visit Bushire; for the purpose of explaining some remains of an ancient architecture in its vicinity. He has been favoured with an audience, by his Persian Majesty and has been permitted to take a full length, likeness, of that august individual, he will shortly return to St. Petersburgh via Tabriz.

HONOURS REJECTED.

Eskander Khan, a Persian nobleman, of the Court of the Prince of Fars, attended by an Arab Shaikh, of some influence, bearing an honorary dress and sword, from his Royal highness to the Shaikh of Bahrein; lately returned disgusted with their reception, and wholly unsuccessful in the objects of their mission. The Shaikh accepted the dress and its accompaniment, but declined acknowledging the supremacy of Persia, by either paying the most trifling tribute, or allowing the coin of the island to bear the title or legend of his Persian Majesty; no gift was made in return for the royal donation, nor were the bearers of it, as is usual, fed during the period of their residence, at the public expense.

⁎ The reader will observe the mark of independence as referring to the coin; but the acceptance of the dress implied no subjection.

CHINA.

A PRIME MINISTER OF STATE DEGRADED.

(From Milne's Indo Chinese Gleaner.)

SUICIDES.

Peking Gazette, March 28, 1817.—It appears that a person holding a situation of the first rank, viz. Treasurer of the Fuh-Kien province, from an apprehension of being brought to trial for receiving improper fees, hanged himself. There was found in his bosom a statement of his case, written with his own hand.

The crime of self murder is perhaps as common in China as in any part of the world; it often arises from a principle of revenge, a motive which in many countries would not prompt to the foul deed, because the bad passion could not be gratified by the act. In China, those who by harsh usage, insulting and indecent language to females, fill the mind of a person with alarm, &c. and thus cause suicide, are amenable to the law, and are disgraced and punished according to the degree of guilt.

PUNISHMENT FOR REBELLION.

April 1.—In Shan-Tung, a man concerned in the rebellion of 1813, was put to a slow and ignominious death, by having his body slowly cut to pieces.

PECULATION IN PERFECTION.

The Censor of Keang-Nan reports to his Majesty, that the sums of money granted from the Imperial Treasury, for the relief of districts, in times of drought and famine, are so swallowed up by peculation, that little or nothing ever reaches the distressed people for whom the grants are intended.

REBELLION IN EMBRIO.

June 1, 1817.—An insurrection has taken place in the province of Yun-Nan. The insurgents are called by the Government

Lee-Fei, Monkey Banditti. The Foo-yuen of Canton, recently appointed, is prevented from undertaking the duties of his situation, being called away to quell the insurrection.

BLOODY ANIMOSITY.

June 19.—At the southern part of Fuh Keen, two families, or as that word (in Chinese) denotes in its most extensive sense, two clans, in the spring of the year, fell out in consequence of some verbal altercation. One family name was *Tsae,* and the other *Wang.* Each collected as many of his clan as he could, and rushing to arms of various kinds, fought with each other till eight men were killed, and 40 houses belonging to Tsae were burnt to ashes. The police seized a number of the parties; but so bitter was their animosity, that *Wang* again attacked the other party and killed several, which obliged the government to call in the aid of the military.

EARTHQUAKE DESTRUCTIVE.

August 12.—By a Peking Gazette of May the 2d, it appears by letters from Chang-Ming, the Viceroy of Szechuen province, on the western frontier of China, where a persecution of the Christians occurred about two years ago, that on the borders of that province, at a place called Chang-Ruh, an earthquake happened in April last. Upwards of 1,100 houses fell, and crushed to death beneath their ruins 2,800 and more persons, Chinese and foreigners, old and young, men and women, with a number of the Lama Priests. His Imperial Majesty expresses strong feelings of commiseration for the sufferers; and in addition to the 5,000 taels of silver which the Viceroy has already distributed to the houseless survivors, he directs 3,000 or 4,000 more to be added; and closes by particular care to be used in the distribution, that the people may actually receive it, instead of its being embezzled in its progress, as is too often the case; that Chin Poo Gae Lee Yuen, his universal affection for the black heads (i. e. the people) may be seconded by those entrusted with his Majesty's bounty.

PRIME MINISTERS DEGRADED.

for giving honest Advice.

Peking, July 20, 1817. — SIR—I have picked up an Imperial document which I beg to offer to you; and I am encouraged to do so, from a conviction, that whatever tends to illustrate the character of the human mind; the features of our common humanity, in regions but little known to our countrymen, will be acceptable to you.

The paper which I send you herewith refers to the Chinese friend of Lord Macartney, Sung Ta-jin, late Prime Minister of State in China. I once exchanged a few words with the old gentleman, and therefore may feel perhaps a little adventitious interest in his fate, but it is not so much to tell you of his fate, as to let you see the mode of thinking exhibited by himself, and by his master also, who is in several respects the greatest Sovereign upon earth, though I fear, neither the wisest nor the happiest of mortals.

On the day on which I have dated my letter, the following manifesto was received from his Imperial Majesty, Kea-King, i. e. " The Excellent and the Blessed;—the worthy to be congratulated." Alas! in many respects his situation seems far from being enviable.

The Shang Yu, or Edict from on high, runs thus :—

" In the 43rd year of Keen-lung, that eminent, illustrious and pure Sovereign, with profound respect visited the Shing-King, i. e, the affluent capital of his ancestors, in Man-chow Tartary. He there repeatedly declared his will to future generations, commanding his posterity to cherish the most affectionate regard for the region of Leaou, their ancient territory. Our Imperial family (said he) has through successive generations gladly repaired to the capital of their ancestors, as I have seen with my own eyes. Should hereafter many unfaithful Minister, deviate so far from what is correct, as to insinuate that these visits are unsuitable, let him, agreeably to the law enacted, in cases of rebelling against the commands of the Sovereign, be exterminated. Extend not to him pardon.

" I (Kea-King), with respect, receiving the sacred instructions, thus communicated, have determined to go next autumn, 1818, to the three mountains (in Manchow Tartary), and perform the grand sepulchral obsequies, to give scope to the thoughts of filial piety which possess my mind. I have accordingly frequently spoken of it to my Ministers, but have not explicitly sent down my Imperial will.

" This summer drought has existed, and there is still a want of rain, and yesterday, the Minister of State, Sung-Yuen, sent up a statement, in which he affirmed, that the cause of the present drought was my wish to visit the capital of my ancestors; that the Imperial Saints caused the drought as a sign from heaven intended to stop me from my purpose,—and so on. This really is an extreme degree of the strange wild nonsense which a man utters in his dreams.

Among the six questions for self-examination, which the ancient King, Ching-T'Hang* put to himself, in a case of drought, was his having visited the tombs of his ancestors, one? To utter language like the above, a year before the thing spoken of is to take place, and thereby agitate the minds of all, is indeed a great breach of the duties of a Prime Minister Supposing that next year there should be a scarcity in Peking and Man-chow Tartary, I would not wait till I was requested to desist. What difficulty would I have to send down my pleasure to defer the period of my departure?

"Last year, because Meën-ko tried to stop me from going to the autumnal hunt, I gave orders that if any one framed superficial tales to hinder me from my purpose, he should be punished according to military law; and now this summer Sung-Yuen, in consequence of a little drought, presumes to hinder me from going next year to the tombs to perform the great sepulchral obsequies; a thing which is of much greater importance than the autumnal hunt.

"If this statement of Sung's had been subsequent to my declaring publicly my intention, I certainly would have dealt with him according to the weighty canons of the state; I would have reverently received the law enacted by his late Majesty, and considering the present case as rebellion against the Imperial commands, would have instantly executed the sentence of the law (and punished him with death.) But as the present is a time of distressing drought, as we are desirous now to mitigate the punishment of criminals, and finally, as he has committed this deed antecedently to my public avowal of my intention, I delivered him over to the great officers of the Privy Council, that they may meet with the Board of Appointments, and being assembled in council, might determine what is to be done.

* Ching T'Hang lived 1743 years, B. C. In his time were seven years of famine, which synchronise with the seven years of famine in Egypt Ching-T'Hang examined himself by six interrogatories. Has there been irregularity in my government? Have the people been suffered to neglect their duties? Have luxurious palaces been built? Have crowds of women been collected in them for vicious purposes? Have extravagant presents been given? Have slanderers or flatterers been encouraged?

Among these, as his Majesty very truly observes, there is nothing said of visiting the tombs of ancestors.—The passage thus incidentally quoted, is remarkable from another cause. Ching-T'Hang was advised to accompany his prayers by a human sacrifice; and he determined on being himself the victim; but he had scarcely enunciated the words of self-examination and confession before abundant showers of rain fell.

"They have this day reported their opinion to be, that he should be deprived of his rank and office. This is what his crime really deserves; it is indeed lenient, and but a slight manifestation of my displeasure.

"I never make a man an offender for a word; but the present is such a glaring disobedience to the commands of Holy Majesty, that it is impossible not to punish it.

"It is hereby ordered, that Sung-Yuen be deprived of his situations, as Minister of State; as one of the great officers who stand in the Imperial presence; as one of the great officers who wait upon and guard the Imperial person; as Too-Tung, and every species of public service; that he be reduced to wear a button of the sixth rank; and be sent to the eight standards (of wandering shepherds) at Cha-ha-urh, there to fill for the present the situation of Adjutant General. Let his name be retained on the books, and if for eight years he commit no error, let him again be eligible for his former situation. I have punished him with humanity, to which I was compelled by the pain of mind which it gave to myself. This heart could not relinquish the hope of saving him from plebeian defilement. Probably all the officers under heaven will credit this.

"Let this document be recorded and preserved by the office of Shang-Shoo.— And let the Imperial sons and grand children receive it with implicit veneration. Let them not slight it. Make it generally known to all persons, within (China Proper) and beyond it."

During April his Majesty was to repair in person to the Tung-ling, or Eastern Tombs of his ancestors, there to perform the usual rites of sacrifice.

IMPERIAL APPREHENSIONS.

His Majesty's mind seems much occupied about the approach of the 24th year of his reign, when he will have reached the age of three score; the period will arrive in 1819. The Chinese cycle of 60 years, being much present to the minds of all persons, the completion of a cycle acquires a degree of importance like that of a new year, which is so general amongst mankind, or like the jubilee of the Jews. The phraseology his Majesty uses is, "I shall have performed a circuit of the cycle." A grand procession is to take place, the Kings and nobles of Tartary, the Governors of Provinces and the Ministers of State, are to prepare congratulations in prose and in verse. Besides these and a few other persons none are allowed to present odes or other compositions, for he says, many are anxious to do so in the hope of obtaining rewards. Those who do write must be brief and to the purpose; for on reaching his 50th year, which was observed as completing "Five decades," he remembers that an officer of Keang Soo Province, sent a composition which was nothing else but a string of quotations from the Yihking, but not one word applicable to the occasion. Of such productions he wishes to have no more. It seems like imagining His Majesty's death; but certainly, it is possible he may never see the completion of the cycle. From the uncertainty of human life, it is rather a delicate thing to begin to prepare so long before hand. However, he says, he still finds his health unimpaired. He has given orders to fit up suitably the idol temples at Zehol, where on such occasions he goes in person to burn incense.

NEW SOUTH WALES.

VACCINATION EFFECTED.

We have received intelligence from New South Wales to the 7th of March; but the Journals, as usual, do not contain much information, likely to excite general interest. We are happy to find, however, that packets of Vaccine matter had been received from the Mauritius, which had enabled the government to diffuse the benefit of the Jennerian discovery, throughout New South Wales.

BANK NOTES;

PLAN FOR PREVENTING FORGERY.

The subject of endeavours to prevent Forgery of Bank Notes, occupies at this moment the most ingenious Artist's, and the most considerate minds. Notwithstanding what is reported on a plan that bids fair to answer this desirable purpose, we think it our duty to insert the following observations, by Mr. Barber Beaumont. They shew at least a cultivated taste and a benevolent heart. We have inspected a variety of patterns and schemes offered with the same intent. But, we trust, that the most effectual, and therefore the most satisfactory, is that now in preparation.

"The proprietors of the Plymouth Dock Bank, about eighteen years since were forged upon; they, in consequence, had a handsome vignette designed, and engraved by an eminent historical engraver. He has engraved several successive plates for them, and they have never been imitated. But the partners, some years since, wishing to have a distinct appearance between their notes and bills, had a new plate engraved for the latter, with only an ornamental cypher instead of the vignette. This was no sooner issued that it was imitated, whereupon they immediately discontinued the use of the cypher plate, and adopted the vignette, and since then they have had no forgeries on them. The artist tells me that he and other historical engravers have engraved vignettes for several Country Bankers, and that he never heard of a forgery having been attempted of any of the plates.

It is well known that the engraving may be done upon softened steel as well as on copper; it is also ascertained that when engraved, the steel plates may be hardened to a high degree without injury, and that so prepared they will yield an immense number of impressions without any sensible wearing. I have heard some practical men say they will bear a million impressions, others reckon upon a hundred thousand. A plate executed as I suppose, would cost 80l. so that taking the minimum of impressions, viz. 100,000, the expence of using fine historical engravings on steel would be 30l. for 100,000 impressions.

The present copper-plates, I suppose, cost the Bank about 3l. each, and yield about 5000 impressions; the expense then of using bad writing engravings on copper is 60l. for 100,000 impressions, just double the expence of plates on the preventive system. This view only draws into comparison the relative expences of the opposite description of engravings; but a far more important saving would be produced by superseding the necessity of the expence of criminal prosecutions, and of the attendant corps of spies and informers.

A further effect of this system in preventing forgeries would be found in all the notes of one kind for a *long period of years* being taken from *one plate*, whence a person having a genuine note might compare it with the *minutiæ* of another suspected to be forged, and as it would be impossible even for the artist who had engraved an original plate, to follow, in a copy, the length, sweep, depth, and a number of the strokes in his original, a detection would be easily made, even by those who know nothing of the arts.

My preventive of forgeries then consists in *combining* the use of the *finest historical engravings*, which so few men can execute, with the use of *plates of extraordinary durability*.

National Register:

FOREIGN.

Foreign Jews.

"The state of the Jews on the Continent," says Mr. Cox, (the fellow traveller of Mr. Way) in a letter to a friend in this country, "affords an encouraging prospect and one which ought to stimulate us in our efforts to promote their conversion: after making full allowance for several instances of ignorance, bigotry, scepticism, and worldly mindedness, it may still be added, that a spirit of enquiry on divine subjects pervades, not merely several individuals and families, but even *whole synagogues.* I refer to what are called the Reformed Jews."—"It is encouraging to behold so large a body of the most enlightened and respectable Jews acknowledging the necessity of a radical change among them, rejecting the Talmud as a scene of blasphemy and absurdity; and confessing that, in their own houses, they occasionally read and approve parts of the New Testament. Not a few who profess their belief in Christ as a true prophet, though they inconsistently decline hailing him as the promised Messiah. At Hamburgh, the most respectable Jews are arranging plans for a new Synagogue, and have engaged an enlightened teacher, who instructs the children in the Old Testament, in a most impressive and spiritual manner. Most of our Hebrew Tracts and Testaments have been thankfully received. Many Jews themselves applied for them. A Jewish burgher, at Posen, said to us, 'the Lord be with you!' and added, 'the majority of the Jews are evidently wrong: the reformed party attempt a reformation by means which cannot accomplish it; and the Christian religion is, I verily believe, the only thing that can produce among us that moral change which we all stand so much in need of.' The observation of another Jew is equally striking; 'Why,' said he, 'do you not impress upon Christians, that, pure and divine as their religion is, it cannot lead them to felicity, unless it influence their hearts and lives. I am persuaded, that a great part of the Jews would have embraced the Christian religion, if Christians had manifested toward them that brotherly love and exemplary conduct which the the pure and exalted principles of Christ inculcate."

ALGIERS,

Nov. 26.—The plague has entirely ceased its ravages in our unfortunate country; but it carries off at Constantine from 40 to 60 persons daily, and it prevails at Bega, which gives reason to entertain fear that it may yet again burst out at Algiers. It appears certain that the number of persons who have fallen victims to it here is not less than 24,000, and in the country parts 29,000.

AMERICA.

Washington, Nov. 28.—The slave trade continues to flourish on the ocean, in spite of stipulation to relinquish, and alliances to put it down. Accounts received from Havannah, of the most recent dates, announce the following arrivals: Oct. 29, ship Jupiter, from Africa, 337 slaves; brig San Josef, 403 slaves; brig Brilliant, 345 slaves; Vengador, 490 slaves; schooner Astrea, 143 slaves. Nov. 1. Circassiana, 126 slaves—upwards of 1500 in one day. Most of these poor wretches, we fear, will find their way to the Louisiana market. We wish that the Spanish character of the ships be not a mere cover for American capital employed in this execrable traffic.

SOUTH AMERICA.

It is said that the Court of Rio Janeiro has refused to give up Monte Video, until restitution is made of Olivenza and other Cantons which formerly belonged to Portugal.

ASIA.

There is only one tree at Hilla, the ruins of Babylon, which is called by the natives *Athelè.* They maintain that it flourished in the ancient city, and that God purposely preserved it for Ali to tie up his horse after the battle of Hilla. It is an evergreen resembling the *lignum vitæ*, and so uncommon in the country that there is said to be only one other of the same kind at Bussora. *Rich's Memoir.*

Some time ago a large lion came every evening from the banks of the Euphrates, and took his stand on a bridge over a canal near Bagdat, to the terror of travellers. He was at last shot by a Zobeide Arab. —*Ibid.*

BAVARIA.

Extraordinary Occurrence.—Extract of a letter from Bavaria:—We have witnessed here a superb funeral of the Baron Hornstein, a Courtier; but the result is what induces me to mention it in my letter. Two days after, the workmen entered the Mausoleum, when they witnessed an object which petrified them! At the door of the sepulchre lay a body covered with blood—it was the mortal remains of this favourite of Courts and Princes. The Baron was buried alive! On recovering from his trance he had forced the lid of the coffin, and endeavoured to escape from the charnel-house—it was impossible! and therefore, in a fit of desperation, as it is supposed, he dashed his brains out against the wall. The Royal Family, and indeed the whole city, are plunged in grief at the horrid catastrophe.

CHINA.

Number and Treatment of Criminals.

In the close of 1816, there were in various prisons of the Chinese Empire, 10,270 criminals convicted of capital offences, and awaiting the Imperial order, to carry into effect the sentence of death. They consisted of persons who had been respited at various times, either from their crimes being less atrocious than those consigned immediately to the sword of the executioner; or on whose guilt there still hung some shadow of doubt. The sufferings of criminals detained in prison for years are very great. The Chinese in their boat state are not very cleanly in their dwelling houses. In prisons, criminals are at night chained to inclined boards on which they sleep, and without the power of removing from thence to any appropriate place to perform the offices of nature; hence their prisons become at once disgusting and unhealthy in the highest degree. Money can procure some alleviation, and the prisoners of long standing, attack in the most ferocious manner, unhappy persons who newly enter. They seize them by the arms and legs, and bite them, to extort money from them.

Observance of the Emperor's Birth-day.

PEKING,

May 2, 1817.—The Emperor's commands to the following effect, have been most respectfully received.

" In the 24th year of my reign, the anniversary of my 60th year occurs. It has been the usage of the Mung-Koo kings and nobles to make willow images of Buddah and present them. But the place in which these are dedicated, is already full of them, and if they be added to every ten years, they will be so crowded as to shew a want of respect. Let all the Mung-koo kings and nobles be informed, that when the time shall arrive, there is no occasion to adhere pertinaciously to former usage, and to present images of Buddah, but let them appropriate the money which they would spend on these to the repair and beautifying of the temples at Je-ho, where I constantly demand to bless the place and to burn incense. Thus they will display their feeling of Chinese veneration. Respect this."

Chinese Gleaner, III. p. 55.

COPENHAGEN.

Dec. 27.—In the night of the 21st, a singular meteor was seen in Fulmen, in the south-west. It was a ball of fire about the size of the moon, with a ring round it, from which there issued for several hours, small sparks like stars, which had an effect not unlike what is called Roman fire.

FROM ST. DOMINGO,

Extract from the *Charleston Courier* of the 9th ult.—" By the schooner *Martha*, Kielen, arrived yesterday, ten days from Cape Henry, we learn that two severe and destructive earthquakes were experienced in that island on the 20th ultimo, which destroyed several houses, and swallowed up five individuals."

EUROPE.

Amount of the Army and Navy.

In a statistical survey of Europe, lately published at Vienna, it is estimated that the armed force of Europe, on the peace establishment, consists of 1,798,000 men, and on a war establishment of 3,608,000. The marine is calculated at 462 vessels of the line, 370 frigates, and 1,922 vessels of lesser rank.

GHENT,

Jan. 7.—English agents are said to be travelling along the coast of the Baltic and northern provinces of Germany, to purchase 90,000 loads of timber for the service of the British navy. Eighty cubic feet are reckoned to a load, which, at the lowest price, would make a sum of 3,600,000 rix dollars.

HUDSON'S BAY.

Red Snow.—This curious substance, which has so much attracted the public attention, is stated to have been found lying upon the surface of snow lodged in ravines for upwards of 100 miles along the coast of Baffin's Bay. Considerable quantities were collected, and brought to this country in bottles, containing likewise the water of the snow upon which it had originally lain, as well as other substances apparently foreign, and having no connexion with the colouring matter. The following observations are founded upon experiments made upon minute quantities only, and are to be understood to apply to the colouring substance separated nearly from all foreign ingredients.

On opening the phial containing the substance diffused through the snow water, a very offensive odour, similar to that of putrid sea-weed, or excrement, was perceptible. After standing some time, the colouring matter slowly subsided, leaving the water colourless.—When examined with a magnifier, it appeared to consist of minute particles, more or less globular, and of a brownish red colour. Separated and dried upon a filter, the red colour gradually disappeared, and was succeeded by a yellowish green hue. The smell also was different, and somewhat resembled train oil. It was insoluble in alcohol, caustic potash, and indeed in all other menstrua tried, even when assisted by heat. Nitric acid, assisted by heat, rendered it green; if concentrated, and in excess, this acid decomposed it entirely; and when the excess of acid was expelled by heat, a greenish yellow residuum, without the least trace of the pink hue afforded by lithic acid under similar circumstances, was obtained. Chlorine bleached it immediately.

When exposed to heat alone, it yielded a dense white smoke, which was very inflammable. The charcoal left, after incineration, afforded a very minute quantity of ashes, containing traces of lime, iron, and silex, the last two of which were probably extraneous.

From these observations it is evident that this substance does not owe its colour and other properties to lithic acid, or oxide of iron. It seems, on the contrary, to be an organized substance; and the most general as well as probable opinion respecting its nature appears to be, that it is a production of some cryptogamous plant. The naturalist, therefore, will probably be better enabled to explain its origin and nature than the chemist.

From the circumstance of the red colour disappearing by exposure to the air, it seems to have undergone some change by keeping.

IAUN.

Dec. 27.—It is yet impossible to state with accuracy the purposes of those armed bands which, from the mountains of the Sierra Morena, have descended upon La Mancha, where they have committed various ravages. Of this we are certain, that they are very numerous, and that a great proportion of them consists of men who have served in the army or among the Guerillas. They have even proceeded so far as to levy heavy contributions at Santa Cruz, and even at Madridejos, in the centre of the Province. Several travellers whom they took were liberated after two or three days' detention. In consequence of these hostile demonstrations, Government has marched several bodies of troops to Ciudad Rea., Almapo, and other situations on the plain at the foot of the mountains.

MALTA.

Dec. 15.—On the 10th inst., arrived here, from Tunis, a zebeck, under Neapolitan colours, which place, the master reports he left on the 5th instant; at which date, the plague raged there with great violence, and that from 200 to 300 persons died daily. This vessel was ordered off, and sailed the same day (10th inst.) from hence from Syracuse.

PRUSSIA.

Immense Number of Suicides.

A very general notion is entertained that more suicides are committed in England than in any other countries; and day after day the newspapers are filled with communications in which this always assumed as an undoubted fact. The late publication of Mr. Kamptz, of Berlin, founded on official Returns, in the towns of Prussia, proves that the suicides are more numerous than they are in England.— For instance:—

	Population.	Suicides in 1817.
Berlin	166,584	77
Potsdam (not including the Military)	15,426	57
Frankfort on the Oder	12,500	41
Breslau	63,029	58
Leignitz	10,000	35
Reichenbach	3,500	56
Magdeburg	27,869	50
Merseburg	6,000	39
Dusseldorf	15,000	24

SICILY.

A letter from Naples, dated December 8, says that Mount Vesuvius exhibits one of those terrible spectacles which too often alarm that unfortunate city. The crater opened with a dreadful noise, after having darted forth whirlwinds of fire, and of inflammable matter, it vomited lava over the adjoining country, as far as the foot of the village of Torre Del Grecco.

THE ISLAND OF SUMATRA.

By the arrival of the *Kingston*, from Java, intelligence of much importance as affecting British interests in the Indian Seas has been received. The Governor of Fort Marlborough has displayed his characteristic energy and activity since his arrival in Sumatra, and has anxiously endeavoured to extend the British influence over the whole of that valuable and extensive island. Sumatra has hitherto been very little known. The European establishments are entirely on the coast—Europeans had never penetrated into the interior. All attempts to do so, indeed, were reckoned desperate; no European would embark in them. The population of the interior were considered as savages, and the mountains impassable, and yet the natives would still bring down their gold and cassia, and camphor, &c.

for which Sumatra had from the earliest ages been famous. The Governor felt there was but one alternative, and that was to open the road by going himself. His enterprise was crowned with success. He penetrated into the interior in three different directions; to the southward inland of Mauna, to the important provinces occupied by a people called the Passummahs; to the northward to Menangcabon, the far-famed capital of the Malay Empire; and inland to Bencoolen, across the island to Palembang.

The result has been the discovery of a mine of wealth—a country highly cultivated, and abounding in precious metals. The Passummahs are an athletic fine race of men, as superior to the people on the coast as it is possible to conceive; they are agricultural and numerous. At Menangcabon he was gratified with a population and country fully equal to any part of Java. Within the space of 20 miles the population does not fall short of a million. In short, it is the Governor's opinion, that, with a little encouragement, far greater resources are to be found in Sumatra than the British could have derived from Java; but much remains to be done. A Central Government must be established, the whole island must be brought under control, and the avenues of commerce, now closed up, reopened. Our readers are aware, that Menangcabon was the place whence all the gold that gave Melano the name of the Golden Chersonasis was carried.

The discoveries have not, however, been made without great personal risk and fatigue. The country could only be explored on foot—mountains 6,000 feet high were to be crossed, and rocks, precipices, and forests, to be traversed. For many nights the party had no shelter, but the leaves they could collect after their day's journey, and their journies were seldom less than from 20 to 30 miles a day over the very worst roads that ever were passed. In this expedition the Governor was accompanied by Lady Raffles. She was occasionally carried on a man's back, but generally walked, as the roads were too bad to admit of her being carried in a chair. Doctor Arnold, Physician and Naturalist, fell a sacrifice to the fatigue, and died of a violent fever. Dr. Horsfield, who accompanied the Governor to Menangcabon, was, on the 12th of August, the date of our last intelligence from Fort Marlborough, dangerously ill, with a dysentery, but we hope his life will be spared to carry home the important collections he has made, both in Java and Sumatra.

As this was the first appearance of the European authority in the interior, Lady Raffles was the most peaceable standard the party could hoist. It was impossible for the natives to consider their object warlike, when the Governor proceeded unarmed, and confided his wife to their hospitality.

They found the country beautiful and magnificent. Sir Thomas Stamford Raffles has thrown the trade open, and reformed all the establishments. Treaties have been entered into with the Princes of Menangcabon.

TURKEY.

We learn from Bucharest, that on the 31st of last month, about ten in the evening, a most brilliant meteor, probably of an electric nature, made its appearance. The light was perceived even in rooms where candles were burning. Several persons who observed it affirmed, that it had the appearance of a globe of fire resembling a falling star; that afterwards it became longer, and ended in a faint light, which disappeared in two minutes, leaving a trace of a reddish purple like a long tail. A courier, who arrived on the 1st of November from Jassy, saw it exactly in the same form, and with the same splendour, when he was on the road of Moldavia, 180 wersts (120 miles) from Bucharest. This probably is the same phenomenon which was seen at half-past eight in the evening of the same day, in the neighbourhood of the bath of Hercules, near Mehadia, in the Bannat, in the south east part of the horizon. It had the form above described, and a great number of sparks fell from it, but without any sensible detonation, and shed over the whole country a brilliant light, which lasted five minutes. After this there was observed, for a longer time, an illuminated longish body, with a black spot, which separating in the middle, formed two irregular still luminous masses, which gradually diminished and at length vanished. The firmament was serene and star-light; the air was calm. The thermometer, which was in the morning at seven o'clock, $1\frac{1}{2}$, and at noon nine, stood, at the moment of the phenomenon, at 11 of Reaumur: the barometer at 28.

FROM THE TURKISH FRONTIERS.

Dec. 16.—The last victory over the Wechabites puts an end to the war at once. Ibrahim Pacha, who commanded the Turkish army, sends the captain chief Abdallah to Constantinople, but he first had his head shaved, and all his teeth pulled out.

National Register:
BRITISH.

Christenings and Burials.

A general Bill of all the Christenings and Burials in the parishes within the Bills of Mortality for the year 1818.

Christened, males 12,530, females 11,703, in all 24,233; buried, males 9,883, females 9,822, in all 19,705. Whereof have died,

Under two yrs. of age	5,381	Sixty and seventy	1,585
Between two and five	1,813	Seventy and eighty	1,271
Five and ten	803	Eighty and ninety	722
Ten and twenty	763	Ninety and a hundred	175
Twenty and thirty	1,453	A hundred	1
Thirty and forty	1,844	A hundred and one	1
Forty and fifty	2,040	A hundred and two	1
Fifty and sixty	1,966	A hundred and eight	1

Decreased in the burials this year, 863.

Macbeth's Castle.

This venerable and stupendous remain of Scottish antiquity, in which the interesting discovery (the supposed Jacob's Stone) lately recited by us, has been made, is seated among the Sidlaw Hills, in the parish of Collace, a few miles to the North of the City of Perth. On the proud eminence, Dunsinnan Hill, on which Macbeth bid defiance to fate; he is said to have built a fortress on its summit, the literal interpretation of which is "Fort Emmett." To this he betook himself, secure, as he thought, from all danger. The situation of Dunsinnan is strong by nature, and he is said to have made it impregnable by art. The hill is insulated, deep on all sides, and difficult of access. The area on which Macbeth's Castle stood on this eminence is 168 yards in length, by 160 in breadth near the Eastern, and 56 near the Western extreme. Its foundations, so far as can be discerned, exhibit two concentric circles, somewhat elliptical. There seems to have a fosse facing the North-east, joined to the rampart; and an esplanade facing the South-east, encompassed with an outer wall, joined the rampart likewise.

Extraordinary Bridge.

The new iron bridge intended to be thrown over the Menai-strait, in Wales, will be 1,000 feet in length, and will be suspended between two rocks, at the height of 140 feet above the surface of the water.

ANTIQUITIES.

The three ancient Tumuli, called the Chronicle Hills, upon Got Moor, near Whittlesford, Cambridgeshire, were lately levelled, to make room for some modern improvements. The central Tumulus was eight feet high, and above 80 feet in diameter; the other were much lower, and all were connected by a wall constructed of flints and pebbles. Its length was four rods, its thickness 30 inches, and it had three abutments upon its eastern side. Beyond this wall, at the distance of 12 rods to the east, was found an ancient well made with clunch, nine feet in diameter, full of flints and tiles of a curious shape, so formed as to lap over each other. Some of these tiles had a hole in the centre, and from their general appearance, it was believed that they had been used in an aqueduct. In this well were found two Buck's or Elk's horns, of very large size. Upon opening the tumuli, the workmen removed, from the larger one, four human skeletons, which were found lying upon their backs, about two feet from the bottom. Some broken pieces of terra cotta, with red and with black glazing, were also found. In opening the northern tumulus, and in removing the wall upon its eastern side, such an innumerable quantity of the bones of a small quadruped was found that they were actually stratified to the depth of four inches, so that the workmen took out whole shovels filled with these bones; and the same were also found near other sepulchres about an hundred yards to the north of the Chronicle Hills. The most singular circumstance is, that there is no living animal now in the country, to which these bones, thus deposited by millions, may be anatomically referred. The bones of the jaw correspond with those of the Castor, or Beaver, as found in a fossil state in the bogs near Chatteris; but the first are incomparably smaller. Like those of the Beaver, they are furnished with two upper and two lower incisors, and with four grinders on each side. Nothing like these minute bones has, however, been yet known to exist in a fossil state. One of the Professors of this University, after a careful examination of the spot, believing them to have belonged to the Lemming, which sometimes descends in moving myriads from the mountains of Lapland, transmitted several of them to London, to Sir Joseph Banks, and to Sir Everard Home, who have confirmed his conjecture. According to these gentlemen there exists a creature of this species, called a Shrew Mouse, which is exceedingly destructive to young plantations. About two years ago the Commissioners of Forests wrote to Sir Joseph Banks, to know what could be done to get rid of them.

About 100 yards to the north of the Chronicle Hills, there were found two other sepulchres, in which human skeletons were found in soroi, constructed of flints and pebbles, put together with fine gravel.

In the first soros (which was five feet square, and eight feet deep, brought to a point with pebbles), were found two skeletons. The uppermost appeared to he of a larger size. Under the skull was found the blade of a poinard or knife. The head of this skeleton rested upon the body of the other. The soros was full of dirt; and patches of a white unctuous substance, like spermaceti, adhered to the flints. It had an oak bottom, black as oak, but stained with the green oxide of copper, owing to the decomposition of an ancient bronze vessel. Large iron nails, reduced almost to all oxide, were also found here. In the other soros (which was four feet square, within its circular wall, and eight feet deep), a human skeleton was found; and another below it in a sitting posture, with an erect spear, the point of which was of iron. Nails were found here, but no wood; as in the other soros. Here the small quadruped bones were found in great abundance.

The mode of burial exhibited by those ancient sepulchres, added to the fact of the bronze reliques found within one of them, and also that no Roman coins have ever been discovered among the other ruins plead strongly for the superior antiquity of the people here interred; and lead to a conclusion, that the Chronicle Hills were rather Celtic than Roman Tombs.

Gas Lights.

Mr. Patterson, of Montrose, has been making experiments on Gas Light, the result of which is likely to become very beneficial. His mode of obtaining the Gas from the coal is said to differ very little from that commonly practised; but his method of preserving and storing up the gas in air-tight bags, and dealing it out in portions as it is needed, is what appears most worthy of notice. He has stated to the Provost the practicability of lighting the public lamps of the town, on his plan, at less than half the common expence; and proposes with a small apparatus, not exceeding the trifling expense of £5, to satisfy the magistrate on that subject. He proposes to have a gasometer under every lamp, in the form of a column, of a capacity sufficient to contain as much gas as will burn eight hours, and on a plan quite different from the common gasometer. These are to be charged with gas every day from the bags; by means of a kind of bellows, and in less time than one could trim the oil and wick lamps. Thus the great expence and inconvenience of pipes conveying the gas through the town would be saved; and the disagreeable smell, which unavoidably rises from these pipes, be also prevented. By the same method the gas might be retailed to families, and kept in portable gas ometers move able about the house at pleasure.

The King.

The Bulletin issued at the usual period of the month, by the Physicians in attendance on his Majesty states his general health to be good, although without any abatement whatsoever of his mental disorder.

Public report says, the comforts of his Majesty are not as particularly taken care of as the nation we are satisfied would wish them to be: air and exercise are essential to those comforts, and however his Majesty may have been hitherto neglected, it is to be hoped that the notoriety of the fact will lead to more attention for the future!—

The Prince Regent has latterly spent a considerable portion of his time at the Pavilion at Brighton, and for the other branches of the Royal Family, they seem quietly pursuing those modes of life which keep them out of the reach of observation.

Old Bailey Sessions.

Before the Middlesex Jury withdrew, at the last Old Bailey Sessions, they presented to the Court the following paper:

"We, the Middlesex Jury, being on the eve of terminating our most painful duties, most respectfully wish to represent to your Lordships, that the verdicts which we have given on the evidence which has been submitted to us, will, when reported to his Majesty's Privy Council, be considered as only the decision of fallible men. That we are convinced that all sanguinary punishments have not only a tendency to destroy those principles of humanity which it is our duty to cultivate, but that, by their frequent occurrence, they render the heart callous: one instance of which has been brought before us, of a youth having picked a gentleman's pocket, while the dreadful sentence of the law was recently carrying into effect on four unfortunate persons.

"We disdain all visionary ideas and principles, 'We live to improve, or we live in vain.' With these feelings and sentiments, we most earnestly request, that when these cases are reported, you will urge this divine injunction—'I will have mercy, and not sacrifice.'"

(Signed)   PHILIP JACOB, Foreman, and the other eleven Jurymen.

AN ABSTRACT,

Of the Laws relative to Morality with the legal Penalities

AS TO PROPHANATION OF THE LORD'S DAY.

Offences.—Persons who meet *out* of their own parish for any sport or pastime, or who shall use any unlawful exercise or pastime in their own parish.

Penalties.— 3s. 4d. to the poor, or to be set in the stocks for 3 hours.—1 Charles 1. c. 1.

Offences.—If any carrier, waggoner, carman, drover with cattle, butcher, higgler, or either servants shall travel on the Lord's day. Fish carriages allowed.—2 George 3, c. 16.

Penalties.—20s. for every offence, to the use of the poor.—3 Charles 1, c. 1. and 29 Charles 2, c. 7.

Offences.—If any butcher, or any for him, shall kill any beast, or sell any vietuals.*

Penalties.—6s. 8d. for every offence.—3 Charles 1, c. 1.

Two witnesses required; and information within 6 months.

Offences.—If any shoemaker shall shew with intent to sell any boots, shoes, &c.

Penalties.—The value of every such pair, and 3s. 4d. for every pair.—1 James, c. 22, s. 28, 46, 50.

• N. B. This does not extend to victuallers, or eating houses ; or to bakers selling bread, or baking meat within certain hours. The following notice has lately been given from *Butchers' Hall.*—" Numerous applications having been made to the Court of Assistants of this Company requesting their exertions to *prevent the practice of Butchers exposing their Meat for sale on Sunday;* the Court think it right to give notice, that the Master, Wardens, and assistants of the Butchers' Company have, by their Charter of Incorporation, the control over persons exercising the trade in the City of London, and within two miles thereof, and that by their 43d.bye law, penalties are imposed for keeping open shop, offering for sale, or selling meat on Sundays. This Court, although strongly impressed with the necessity of checking so gross a violation of the Sabbath, will, with reluctance, adopt coercive measures to improve it ; they rather wish the trade to unite, and at once discontinue the practice. The Public are also most materially interested in the subject ; for it is a fact, that the profligate part of the labouring classes will continue in an alehouse on the Saturday night, spending their money, and destroying their health and morals, so long as meat can be obtained on the Sunday, by which their families, as well as themselves, are the sufferers.

Offences.—If any person shall follow or exercise his ordinay calling on a Sunday.

Penalties.—5s. or to stand in the stocks two hours.—29 Charles 2, c. 7.

Offences.—If any person shall cry or put to sale and wares, fruit, goods, &c. except milk and mackrel only, before and after divine service.

Penalties.—The goods, &c. to the use of the poor.—29 Charles 2, c. 7. 11. and 11 William, c. 24.

Offences.—No person shall open any house, or other place which shall be used for public entertainmet or amusement, or for publicly debating on any subject to which persons shall be admitted by payment of money, or by tickets sold for money.

Penalties.—£200. The conductor £100 The door-keeper, servant, or other person, who may deliver the tickets, or receive the money, £50. each.—21 George 3, c. 49.

Offences—Any person advertising any such public entertainment, amusement, or meeting, or any person publishing the same.

Penalties.—£50. for every offence.—21 George 3, c. 49.

DRUNKENNESS.

Offences.—If any person be convicted of being drunk.

Penalties.—5s. for the first offence, or to sit in the stocks six hours.—4 James, c. 5.

Offences. —No person to continue drinking or tippling in a public house on the Sabbath-day.

Penalties.—3s. 4d.—James, c. 5. 32 Geo. 3. c. 45.

Offences.—No Inn-keeper, or alehouse-keeper, shall suffer any one to continue drinking or tippling in his house, except such person be a traveller, or invited by a traveller, or a labourer who stays one hour to dinner, or who lodges in the house.

Penalties.—10s. and disabled three years from keeping a public house.—1 James, c. 9. 21. James, c. 7.

Offences.—If any alehouse-keeper be convicted of drunkenness.

Penalties.—Disabled from keeping a public house three years, besides the above penalties.

PROPHANE SWEARING.

Offences.—If any person be convicted of prophanely cursing or swearing.

Penalties.—For a labourer, soldier, or seaman, 1s. every other person under a gentleman, 2s. every gentleman or person of superior rank, 5s. second offence double third, triple. In default of payment to be sent to the house of correction.

The act to be read in all the parish churches and public chapels, the Sunday after every quarter day.

Penalties.—To neglect this, £5.—19 Geo. 2, c. 21.

OBSCENE BOOKS AND PRINTS.

Offences.—Persons selling obscene books and prints.

Penalties.—May be indicted, imprisoned, and put in the pillory.

FALSE WEIGHTS AND MEASURES.

Offences.—Persons using false weights or measures.

Penalties.—40s. for every offence.—35 Geo. 3, c. 102. and 37 Geo. 3, c. 143. Of may be punished by indictment, fine, and imprisonment.

CRUELTY TO ANIMALS.

Offences.—Any cattle-driver who shall misbehave himself in the driving, care, or management of cattle, or be the means of any mischief by them.

Penalties.—Fine 20s. or not less than 5s. or in default, be committed to the house or correction not exceeding one month.

CULTIVATION of WASTE LANDS by CRIMINALS.

To the Editor of the Literary Panorama.

SIR,—Having seen several Letters inserted in the *Times* paper, on the subject of the high prices of the necessaries of life, I did not notice in any of them a circumstance which, it is presumed, must operate not a little in keeping up the rents paid by the tenants to their landlords. At no time, perhaps, have the proprietors of estates throughout the United Kingdom borrowed so much money on their securities, and that on so disadvantageous terms as at the present. If this is admitted, what hopes can be entertained of a reduction of rents?

When the demands of the nation became excessive, recourse to supply these demands was had to the Income Tax. This tax occasioned many, from pride and other motives, to give in a statement of income beyond the fact; and as the nation became loaded with debt, so also did many of the men of property in a certain ratio.

It may not here be irrelevant to draw your attention to the extraordinary influence which the Bank of England appears to have over the nation; as long as this is the case, how can we look for cash payments. The perishable substance of its circulating medium must be extremely productive. Fire, shipwrecks, and many other circumstances, tend to increase its wealth. These hints are evident to the meanest capacity.

I shall now endeavour to point out the means of rectifying these evils by referring to the fundamental cause of power in a nation. The larger a well-cultivated superfice of country is, the more inhabitants it can support, and consequently the greater will be its means of resistance in case of danger. The non-cultivated lands of our *home* possessions are very considerable, and they could be enlarged by artificial exertions, as the indefatigable Dutch people had clearly manifested to the world many years ago. An alteration in our penal laws would enable us the better to cultivate the former lands, and to recover from the sea the latter.

Large buildings as penitentiaries might be erected, and as the nation, we must be aware, cannot now feel it convenient to carry on such expensive works, may it not be hoped that the great emporium of wealth, the Bank of England, would make the advances required. Government would have the means of granting ample security from the sale of such lands made arable: for instance, suppose a commencement was made on Bagshot Heath. A canal might be run with facility communicating to the metropolis, and the soil of the latter, which can now be obtained merely for taking away, could be transported to the former. There are other projects which I keep in reserve that would tend to accomplish this important measure.

I come now to the delicate measure of avoiding hard labour to all criminals by way of punishment.

Criminals for capital offences, not murder, to be sentenced to be branded on the right cheek *indelibly*, and to hard labour for life.

Criminals for transportable offences to be sentenced to hard labour for a certain number of years.

Criminals for minor offences to be sentenced to hard labour for a given time.

Let human nature be appealed to, and I am inclined to assert that the above punishments for capital offences would be more salutary in producing the desired effect of restoring good order, than the too common display of executions.

When the entire face of this country is fully made to produce as much provisions as the common order of things can expect, it may be very fairly considered that such means would be found adequate to support a population equal to its defence.

AGRICOLA.

POLITICAL PERISCOPE.

Panorama Office, January 29, 1819.

With whatever interest or expectation we may look to the persons or characters which figure in the deliberative assemblies of other countries, or those eminent stations which in all nations confer dignity and power, it is certain that our anxiety principally rests on the legislature of our own country; and is never more effectually stimulated than on the meeting of a new Parliament.

The duties of a Member of the British Senate are always arduous; nor is it easy to discharge them with satisfaction at once to the content and feelings of an individual's own mind, to the satisfaction of his constituents, and to that of the nation at large. We cannot believe of the public, speaking generally, that any arguments are necessary to excite their candour in behalf of their representatives; though we know that there are persons in the world, who make no allowances for insuperable obstacles, but think that to propose what they deem an excellent plan is the same thing as to ensure its execution. But plans which appear singularly happy to those with whom they have originated, may not be received with the same warmth of affection by those to whom they are newly communicated; and this it certain, that the more thoroughly a proposal be scrutinized in the first instance, if it will stand the scrutiny, the more likely is it to prove satisfactory when called into extensive operation. We chiefly address this consideration to that numerous class of very benevolent persons, who are always intent on improvements in Politics; and who not infrequently express their disappointments in the language of complaint.— *Why cannot they do so and so?* Without further preface we proceed to record the opening of the present Session of Parliament, which took place at the time appointed, Jan. 14. In the House of Lords, the Chancellor being ill, Mr. Baron Richards sat as Speaker, by patent from H. R. H. the Prince Regent. In the House of Commons, the same gentleman as was placed in the Chair after the retirement of the present Lord Colchester, (Mr. Manners Sutton) was again elected to that truly dignified and arduous situation, with a unanimity the most grateful and honorable to his talents and character.

The house met at 12 o'clock, when the Lord-Chancellor took the oaths and his seat.

His Royal Highness the Prince Regent did not come down to the house, but five commissioners were appointed to read the Royal speech, viz. the Lord-Chancellor, the Archbishop of Canterbury, Marquis Camden, the Earl of Harroby and Westmorland. At a quarter before 3 o'clock Sir Thomas Tyrwhitt, the Usher of the Black Rod, was sent to the House of Commons, in the usual form, to the House of Peers. The following Speech was then read by the Lord-Chancellor from the wool-sack:—

My Lords, and Gentlemen,

We are commanded by His Royal Highness the Prince Regent to express to you the deep regret which He feels in the continuance of His Majesty's lamented indisposition.

In announcing to you the severe calamity with which it has pleased Divine Providence to visit the Prince Regent, the Royal Family, and the nation, by the death of Her Majesty the Queen of the United Kingdom, His Royal Highness has commanded us to direct your attention to the consideration of such measures as this melancholy event has rendered necessary and expedient with respect to the care of His Majesty's sacred person.

We are directed to inform you, that the negociations which have taken place at Aix-la-Chapelle, have led to the evacuation of the French territory by the Allied armies.

The Prince Regent has given orders, that the convention concluded on this purpose, as well as the other documents connected with this arrangement, shall be laid before you; And he is persuaded, that you will view with peculiar satisfaction the intimate union which so happily subsists amongst the powers who were parties to these transactions, and the unvaried disposition which has been manifested in all their proceedings for the preservation of the peace and tranquillity of Europe.

The Prince Regent has commanded us further to acquaint you, that a Treaty has been concluded between His Royal Highness and the government of the United States of America, for the Renewal, for a further term of years, of the commercial convention now subsisting between the two na- tions, and for the amicable adjustment of several Points of mutual importance to the interests of both countries; and, as soon as the ratifications shall have been exchanged, His Royal Highness will give directions that a copy of this Treaty shall be laid before you.

Gentlemen of the House of Commons,

The Prince Regent has directed that the estimates for the current year shall be laid before you.

His Royal Highness feels assured, that you will learn with satisfaction the extent of reduction which the present situation of Europe, and the circumstances of the British empire, have enabled His Royal Highness to effect in the naval and military establishments of the country.

His Royal Highness has also the gratification of announcing to you, a considerable and progressive improvement of the revenue in its most important branches.

My Lords, and Gentlemen,

The Prince Regent has directed to be laid before you such papers as are necessary to shew the origin and result of the war in the East Indies.

His Royal Highness commands us to inform you, that the operations undertaken by the Governor General in Council against the Pindarries were dictated by the strictest principles of self defence; and that in the extended hostilities which followed upon those operations, the Mahrattah Princes were in every instance the aggressors. Under the provident and skilful superintendance of the Marquis of Hastings the campaign was marked in every point by brilliant achievements and successes; and His Majesty's forces, and those of the East India Company, (native as well as Europeans), rivalled each other in sustaining the reputation of the British arms.

The Prince Regent has the greatest pleasure in being able to inform you, that the trade, commerce, and manufactures of the country are in a most flourishing condition.

The favourable change which has so rapidly taken place in the internal circumstances of the United Kingdom affords the strongest proof of the solidity of its resources.

To cultivate and improve the advantages of our present situation will be the object of your deliberations; and His Royal Highness has commanded us to assure you of His disposition to concur and co-operate in whatever may be best calculated to secure to His Majesty's subjects the full benefits of that state of peace which, by the blessing of Providence, has been so happily re-established throughout Europe.

On this communication we do not allow ourselves to offer any comment, further than to say, that custom has warranted the Royal Speaker in putting the most favourable construction on the state of public affairs; and it must be recollected that the document will be read and canvassed, not only in every cabinet of Europe, but throughout the world. Even those gentlemen who indulge themselves in discovering sins of omission and commission in similar discourses, would be the first to complain, and vehemently too, should they contain those melancholy and despondent representations which these political critics think proper to adduce as correctives of the evils to be dreaded from official and national flattery.

The addresses were as usual echoes of the speech; and the praises bestowed on the memory of Her late Majesty were nothing more than must have been anticipated by all who had any means of knowing her general conduct, her benevolence, and her strict sense of personal honour and public decorum.

The most prominent measure as yet brought forward, is the proposal for placing H. R. H. the Duke of York in the same confidential care of His Majesty's person, as was entrusted to the late Queen. As there can scarcely be two sentiments on the subject, this is all we shall report at present on it.

The internal state of the country will, no doubt, be accurately sifted:—already the state of the criminal laws, of the national currency, of the Bank, especially in respect to the endeavours of that Body to render the crime of forgery more difficult, if not impracticable, and on this subject we have the pleasure of reporting from private information, that a plan is in progress, which (it is hoped) may prove effectual. We understand that the Directors have so far approved of it as to advance fifteen hundred or two thousand pounds, as an assistance in perfecting the machinery employed in preparing the article.

If our information be correct it cannot be imitated but by an expensive machinery, and the public may presume that no man who is able to advance two or three thousand pounds on the object, would be willing to direct his property, or his skill, to such a nefarious purpose. We know that the principal in this undertaking has relinquished an extensive business, in order to devote his whole time and attention to the perfection of his plan. This will be understood (we hope) by the Country Bankers; together with the hint, that it merely concerns them; as those who find forgery in one . direction beyond their powers, will not fail to forge in another direction—the trade in such fabrications having been reduced to a system, on the principle of division of labour.

Here we ought to congratulate on Country that the National Revenues have not only suffered no falling off, but have increased, in a regular and progressive ratio. We had much rather that they should rise steadily and keep rising, than rise suddenly, to sink again. The whole *bonus* for the years 1818 is considerable.

Official Statement.—Abstract of the New Produce of the Revenue of Great Britain for the Quarters ending 5th of Jan. 1818 and 1819, respectively, exclusive of arrear of War Duties :—

	1818.	1819.
Customs	£3,017,621	2,465,664
Excise	5,499,672	6,238,940
Stamps	1,566,532	1,530,532
Post Office	349,000	319,000
Assessed Taxes	2,260,017	2,303,778
Land Taxes	233,604	502,266
Miscellaneous	255,318	133,381
	£18.271,764	13,398,761

Government will by no means sanction the Petition that prays for an alteration in the Corn Laws: we believe this will not prove totally unexpected by the favourers of that application. Those most intimately concerned, may recollect the information they haved received to that effect, from our humble opinion.

Since our last, the French Ministry has been entirely changed; but no change that we perceive has taken place in the Councils of that kingdom, by which its neighbours may be affected. The Public Funds had declined, to the great detriment of many individuals; nor less, if we rightly conjecture, of the Public Credit, notwithstanding the endeavours of the then Minister to support them. That personage thought that a portion of the National income might properly be employed for this purpose. It may be generally safe; but some of it will be recovered with great difficulty.

Another part of our work has hinted at the effects of the depreciation of the French funds on indiscreet individuals among ourselves: sorry we are to say, that the same venturesome spirit is again at work: too much English money has gone over to France; and too much is still going over. However, the French funds rise gradually, and from their steady rise, the sanguine augur the best results. We might, possibly, agree with them; did we not know

that art and finesse is the darling sin of Frenchmen—and French Statesmen.

Spain has been thrown into mourning by an event too nearly resembling that by which the British Nation was deeply afflicted, in the loss of the princess Charlotte. The young Queen, from whom an heir was anxiously expected, died with her offspring, not advanced to maturity, at what may be called a moment's notice. It is true, that apoplexy may strike any one, at any time; but so many premature *accouchemens* as we have heard of, must have some cause, not founded in nature; —but, we fear—in fashion.

A decease more analogous to the usual course of nature, is that of the former Queen of Spain * of whom we have had occasion to speak somewhat harshly in a time past. Much of the late (we might say, of the present) embarassments of Spain have been attributed to her impeddence; if justice allows us to employ in speaking of the dead, a term for which we mght have substituted one more severe, in speaking of the living.

As to the Political affairs of Spain, we leave the task of explaining them to those who understand them. They are too perplexed and too perplexing, to come within the limits of our humble apprehension. Her contention with her Colonies engage all observers; but those who are not willing to be deceived, can discern but one probable issue to these miseries. It is well known, so far as concerns ourselves, that we mingle much pity with our censures.

From the Continent we hear little, and

---

* Maria Theresa, of Parma, Queen of Charles IV. of Spain and mother of Ferdinand VII. who died at Rome on the 4th of this month, was born at Parma, on the 9th of December, 1751, and was married on the 4th of September, 1765. She was the daughter of Don Philip, Duke of Parma and Placenati. She bore to her husband, Charles IV. six children, three of whom were Princes, namely, the present King of Spain, born in 1784; the Infant Don Carlos, born in 1788; and the Infant Don Francisco de Paulo, born in 1794; and three Princesses, namely, the present Queen of Portugal, born in 1774; the Queen of Etruria, now Duchess of Lucca, born in 1782; and the Hereditary Princess of Naples, born in 1789 Louisa Maria Theresa participated in all the vicissitudes which followed the event known under the name of the revolution of Aranjuez. She came to Bayonne during the scene of the forced abdication of the Bourbons of Spain, accompanied her husband afterwards from Spain to Compeigne, from Compiegne to Marseilles, and from Marseilles to Rome, where she died.

therefore conclude all is well. The Royal family of Wirtemburgh has suffered the sudden loss of the Queen, who formerly visited this country as Duchess of Oldenburgh, in company with her brother, the Emperor of Russia. We leave the improvement of these speaking events to the moralist.

The natural course of observation does not lead us immediately to America, but we believe that our Political intercourse with that country comes next in order at the present moment. The congress of the United States of North America is engaged in discussing the conduct of a General, who without the sanction of his Government executed two British subjects, not responsible to him, and apparently not guilty of the treason with which he accused them: we have not enlarged on this subject, because it appears to be probable that the Government will disavow the proceeding: perhaps—still more.

The affairs of South America continue embroiled. though we have lately heard less of fighting and murder in cold blood than heretofore.

South Africa is, we apprehend, getting forward in population, and civilization, in commerce and comfort; we expect from thence very interesting news,—almost daily

India we believe is pretty well settled, except Ceylon; which still gives occasion to very troublesome operations. But if our suspicions be not wholly groundless, China is likely to witness the disturbance of her tranquillity. Already are several provinces either in open insurgence, or in that discontented state which usually precedes political turbulence. In short, we have suspected for some time past, that the Chinese would be glad to see the Tartar Dynasty, now on the throne, displaced:—but what measures may have been taken for this purpose by the "black-heads," we know not.

Here we close our article:—a few years, perhaps, it may be the duty of the Panorama to advert to events in the powerful state of New Holland, or Van Diemen's Land; or to report the sailing of numerous fleets from the Society islands, (as we have from the Sandwich islands) or perhaps the arrival of Japanese, or Javanese, or Sumatran vessels, in considerable numbers, in the river Thames: But this were to extend our speculations too far at present; Observers we may be but we are not prophets; we watch the course of events as they rise, but what is below the horizon, as it must be matter of conjecture, we remit to its proper place, when it becomes matter of record.

Commercial Chronicle.

STATE OF TRADE,
Lloyd's Coffee House, Jan. 20, 1819.

The commercial world in the course of the present month has been thrown into more than a single state of alarm, by the interruption of the usual course of payments of some of our greatest mercantile houses. We have repeatedly hinted at the hazards incurred by adventurous speculations in financial operations going on abroad. At Paris, the principal seat of those operations, many houses of supposed property, and some of established credit, have found themselves incapable of fulfilling their engagements. Even the cautious Hollanders have had their share of the burden; but the German houses it is thought, have generally escaped pretty well.

If report may be credited,—but we do not always credit report, in full—a single house in the city of London, for many days together, lost, by speculation in the French funds, the *moderate* sum of thirty thousand pounds *per diem !* That this loss was incurred, we doubt not; but, that if fell on a single house, ultimately, we much doubt. It is more probable, that it fell on a list of supporters, who stood pledged to each other.

To give some idea of the extent to which mercantile accompts are carried in the metropolis, it is sufficient to say, that the outstanding acceptances of a firm—not that already alluded to—were no less than six hundred thousand pounds ! of which about half were about to become clamourous: admitting that a proportionate sum was not accepted for,—at what amount may we estimate the whole? at nine hundred thousand pounds—or at a million ?

The first symptom of this suspension was a hint from the Bank, by *not doing* an assortment of bills sent in for discount. As nobody doubts, either the intelligence on the prudence of the Bank, those in the secret soon understood the signal. On examination, however, it is ascertained that the assets of the firm are ample, and more than sufficient to meet demands: and the Bank has been induced to afford assistance, on the security of additional names. The real amount of this assistance, *pro tempore*, is, with great propriety, known to few; but the public journals have stated it at one hundred and fifty, or two hundred thousand pounds.

We some time ago had occasion to record some *sweeping* deficiencies among the dealers in hops; if we took any delight in such events, the Corn Market would this month have afforded us gratification; several houses have been severe sufferers: and this, too, if we mistake not, was first discovered by the same *not doings* as we have already hinted at.

Perhaps, the sufferings of the principals in thése extensive speculations, are not the proper subjects of extreme regret; but, they cannot suffer alone: those who are connected with them, and dependent on them—they are the real sufferers.

It is impossible, that when an eminent house *stops*, the evil should be wholly remedied, by its resumption of payments, though only a few days have intervened; the shock has been felt by its connexions; and by *their* connexions; and a dozen houses totter; of which half are sure to fall. Credit is a delicate thing; and we remember reading, in a French author, an account of a public body that was certainly ruined, after a considerable lapse of time (if we rightly remember, some years), because it had once suspended its payments for a single day.

It has been justly observed, that at this moment, so intimately are the affairs of all Europe blended, that a misfortune cannot happen in one metropolis, or seat of trade, but it immediately is felt in others. ˙ We presume, that the history of the month as we have referred to it, justifies this opinion; and there is roaan to think, that it has been especially experience among those universal. ˙

Dealers, agents, factors, and brokers, the Jewish people. They have connexions every where: and several among their most eminent men, bankers, and others, in foreign parts, have fallen victims, either to their own indiscretion, or to the uncontrollable course of events.

The foregoing report on the state of the speculators on the Corn Market, will have partly prepared the reader to expect rather a heavy account of the state of the market itself. Prime English corn is by no means superabundant. Foreign corn is offered at the lower rate of the market, yet the inclination of the buyers does not lie that way. Taking the whole together, it is probable, that the averages will be found to have been for a sufficient length of time below the import price, to allow the closing of the ports, in the course of the month of February. This, has been foreseen, and is foreseen; in consequence, the stocks on hand are allowed to accumulate; and are, certainly, very considerable. The demand for BARLEY has abated: that article, therefore, declines. OATS are in good supply. The most remarkable incident, lately,—at least, the newest incident—is an abundant supply of BEANS from an unusual quarter, the Mediterranean. This was so unlooked for, that at first, the vessels were thought to be contraband, by the Port officers. That, however, was cleared up; and they were admitted. The arrivals are now extensive; and the price of the article has fallen at least five shillings per quarter.

Accounts from Jamaica have brought intelligence of a violent and disastrous hurricane in that island. Now Jamaica is so seldom annoyed by these disagreeable visitants, that it is usually supposed to be out of the lines of hurricanes.—In this instance, it has not proved so. We are aware of the danger of trusting to first reports of damages done; and when they state a loss of half, or of one third of the crop, we are willing to hope that the deficiency will prove to be greatly overrated. Be that as it may prove: the Governor, has, no doubt, opened the ports to free importation of every kind of provisions: and, among others, the article of RICE has felt the advantage. Not less than 5,000 bags of East India Rice were bought up immediately; at an advance of 1*s.* or 2*s.* per cwt. That quantity, however, was deemed a sufficient supply; and what has been since offered for sale, at the same price, has been wholly withdrawn for want of buyers; but,

Commercial Chronicle.

the old price would; probably, have been given.

IRISH PROVISIONS.—There is a little doing in Beef and Pork, and no variation in the currency. A general opinion was entertained that the extensive public sales of Butter, lately advertised, would depress the prices; the result has, however, been rather favourable, and, as the greater proportion of the supplies have been shipped eagerly some time ago, on account of the high prices of London, it is expected the Imports will now be rather limited; the holders are anticipating an advance; there is, however, little or no business doing by private contract.—The following are the particulars of the latest public sales.

70 Frks. Carlow butter, 1st. 111s. a 113s.
00 Waterford ditto, 1st, 99s. a 101 .; 2nd, 93s.
800 Dublin ditto, 1st, 103s. a 104s.
300 Cork ditto, 3rds, 93s. a 94s.
316 Limerick ditto, 1st, 97s.; 2nd, 92s. a 93s.
250 French ditto. *Withdrawn.*
25 Bales singed Waterford Bacon, 64s.

709 Frks. Waterford butter, 1st quality, 93s. a 103s.; 2nd, 99s. a 93s.
450 Carlow ditto, 1st, 100s. a 110s. 6d. and 115s. 6d. a 118s. 6d.
300 Dublin ditto, 1st, 101s. a 105s.
164 Newry ditto, 1st, 98s. a 101s.
45 casks Friesland ditto, 88s. a 100s.
125 bales Waterford bacon, 58s. a 60s.
35 Middles ditto, 57s. a 58s.

From this statement our readers will infer, that no very universal, or very extensive, exportations to the afflicted island have as yet taken place.

The holders of SUGAR feel that kind of suspense which might be expected: they, too, doubt the full extent of the first accounts: yet that some, and even a considerable deficiency may be expected they cannot presume to deny. Under these circumstances, they are not anxious to effect sales; nor will they listen to any turn in favour of the buyer. The demand has for some time past been limited; but now seems to be rather improving: such, at least, is the general feeling of those concerned. The stock of Sugars at Liverpool is understood to be short, and some say, very short; insomuch that it is expected the demand on London would be greatly increased, from quarters

which used to look to the out ports for supply. The GOOD sugars, certainly will meet an advance in price.

On the other hand—the demand from the Continent is not only suspended, but the prices at their markets are much below those in London. Orders sent, are consequently, not many; and these are conditioned on such low terms as cannot be complied with. Foreign Sugars are therefore, at the moment, little other than a blank at the market.

Refined Goods are in improved demand. Lumps have experienced an advance of 1s. to 2s. and several considerable parcels of loaves have been taken out of the market. On the whole appearances are deemed favourable for the trade.

COFFEE has lately excited little interest. The former currency has given way; and attempts have been resorted to both by private contract, and by public sale, to dispose of quantities. They have, however, met with but indifferent success, unless attended with a deduction of 3s. or even 4s. from what had been formerly obtained. As this disposition is general, the prices of the article may be considered as declining.

RUM has experienced, or rather is experiencing an improved market. The quantity taken by government, which is understood to be 50,000 gallons more than was advertised for, has greatly contributed to this; because the contractors being bound to deliver, are under the necessity of resorting to the holders. This has given a briskness to demand and delivery, which is equally lively and extensive. There are also, considerable orders for shipping; to which must be added the effect of the reports from Jamaica: so that, on the whole this article may be stated, in considerable request.

BRANDY and HOLLANDS continue much as they were: the best qualities are the most sure of obtaining attention.

Oils continue to decline in prices; Greenland oil is gone down 1l. to 2l. per ton. Oil from the Southern Whale fishery has declined considerably. The late arrivals of Cape Oil have not yet found their market; but are expected soon to be put to public sale, except the heavy state of the market should otherwise determine.

Naval stores have declined : very considerable arrivals of Rough Turpentine are announced: the last considerable parcel sold, realised 15s. 6d. Spirits are, also lower: but in Pitch and Rosin, no variation worth mentioning.

In HEMP and FLAX there is a slight decline; but there seems to be more business doing; and the purchases looking forward to the spring supply, are reported to be extensive. Though the immediate price, therefore, may be perhaps, 20s. lower, yet the anticipated price is likely to suffer no depression.

TALLOW is a very heavy Article and not likely to improve : the prices are much depressed.

We shall now proceed to set before our readers abstracts and information received from foreign parts. We hope to be able greatly to enlarge this branch of our COMMERCIAL CHRONICLE; and from genuine sources of Mercantile Connection. Measures are taken to this effect; and we shall take a pleasure in communicating the results, which we doubt not be found equally interesting and Instructive.

ST. PETERSBURG, 10—22 Dec. 1818. —Business was perhaps never so void of all activity, owing to most extraordinary weather, which for the last week has been so mild as to exclude all winter communication with the interior, so necessary for the distribution of goods. Tallow has advanced to 180 rs. money down for yellow candle, soap tallow 170 rs. money, some few contracts for hemp have been made at 85 money down. Exchange on London, 12 ⅛.

NAPLES, 29 Dec. 1818.— Coffee is now not so brisk as it was : wheat is dull, as well as all kinds of grain. This Government have given notice that they will discount merchants' bills at five per cent. per annum.

HAMBRO', 5 Jan.—Generally speaking we continue exceedingly dull in business, and, with the exception of coffee and sugar, there is very little doing in Colonial articles; it is however, hoped that on account of the approach of spring, as well as on account of a sudden decline of

discount, which from 9¼ to 10 per Cent. within a few days past has fallen to 5 to 5¼ per Cent. Corn has experienced a great fall lately, and a further decline is anticipated, as soon as our river becomes free from ice.

AGRICULTURAL REPORT.

ESSEX.—The Wheat plants were never more promising at this season of the year, and in this part of the country, the slug and wire-worm so little complained of. The Peas, so early planted as noticed in our last report, now more resemble the month of April than that of January. Many pieces of that kind of Pulse should the land be sufficiently dry, will be fit for the hoe in a little time. Beans of all kinds are by some already planted. In a few instances Oats are actually in a state of vegetation. Indeed all agricultural performances in the fields are very forward, and the lands were never known to be in better condition for Spring seed. Plants of Tares are full and every way good. Just here, little can be said about Lambs at present.

Bankrupts and Certificates in the order of their dates, with their Attornies.

BANKRUPTS, Jan. 2.

Bedells W. Kinghton, Radnor, woolstapler Sols. Jenkins and Co. New inn.
Cater S. and Co. Watling st. warehousemen. Sols. Chapman and Co. Little st. Thomas Apostle, Queen st.
Chambers R. Market Rasen, Lincolnshire, currier. Sol. Eyre, Gray's inn lane.
Jenkins T. Whitchurch, Glamorganshire, timber merchant. Sols. Jenkins and Co. New inn.
Longman F. G. Norwich, maltster. Sol. Abbott' Roll's yard, Chancery lane.
Oulet J. Charlotte st. Fitzroy sq. jeweller. Sol. Poole, Adam's ct. Old Broad st.
Perry J. Stockport, Chester, muslin manufacturer. Sols. Wright and Co. Temple.
Sumner T Preston, Lancaster, corn merchant' Sol. Blakelock, Serjeant's inn.
Thomas W. Cheapside, tailor. Sols. Amory and Co. Lothbury.
Tully F. Bristol, baker. Sols. Poole and Co Gray's inn.
Wheeler D. Hyde st. Bloomsbury, colouring maker. Sol. Grimaldi, Copthall ct.

CERTIFICATES, Jan. 25.

J. Bragg, Birmingham, tye maker. J. Spreat, Exeter, coal merchant. W. Stephenson, Preston, linen draper. J. Bentley, cornbill, watch maker. C. Sivsac, Wilmot st. Brunswick sq. merchant. J. A. Butler, Blackheath, master mariner. J. Bowman, Crooked lane, wine merchant. J. Langford, Ludgate st chemist. W. Holttum, Long lane, Bermondsey, carpenter.

BANKRUPTCY ENLARGED, Jan. 6.

J. Marshall, North Hall, Leeds, clothier.
T. Stead, Blackfriars' road, woollen draper.

BANKRUPTS.

Blomerly W. Bolton, Lancaster, cotton manufacturer. *Sol.* Meddowcroft, Gray's inn.

Bryant W. Greenwich, coach master. *Sols.* Clarke and Co. Chancery lane.

Flinders J. Nottingham, hosier. *Sol.* Farren, Threadneedle street.

Gilson R. Bawtry, York, victualler. *Sol.* Knowles, New inn.

Johnson R. Plymouth, grocer. *Sol.* Bowden, Aldermanbury.

Peyton W. Lincoln's inn fields, wine merchant. *Sol* Hartley, Bridge street, Blackfriars.

Smith W. Moffatt st. City road. *Sol.* Dobson, Chancery lane.

Unwin R. Chapel en le Frith, Derby, timber merchant. *Sols.* Blagrave and Co. Symond's inn.

CERTIFICATES, *Jan.* 26.

C. Fowler, Sculcoates, York, merchant. J. Ladbroke, Draycote, Warwick, farmer. J. W. Middlewood, Whitechapel, perfumer. S Brown, Chesterfield, grocer. J. Wilson, Rathbone place, bookseller. W. Torkington, Pendleton, Lancaster, joiner. S. Williams and Co. Lilypot lane, straw hat manufacturer. J. Barker, Sheffield, cordwainer. A. Hardman, Bolton, Lancaster, muslin manufacturer.

BANKRUPTS, *Jan.* 9.

Chapman R. Hammersmith, surgeon. *Sols* Gatty and Co. Angel ct. Throgmorton st.

Hogg J. E. Bread st. warehouseman. *Sols* Knight and Co. Basinghall st.

Perkins J. Tiverton, Devon, timber merchant. *Sol.* Birkett, cloak lane.

Richmond T. Bell yard, Carey st. plumber. *Sol.* Fisher, Inner Temple lane.

Robinson J. Holywell, Flintshire, butcher. *Sols.* Lowe and Co. Southampton buildings, Chancery lane.

Rogers J. Old Broad st. merchant. *Sol.* Cottle, Aldermanbury.

Stiff W. Rotherwick, Southampton, shopkeeper. *Sol.* Bridger, Angel ct. Throgmorton st.

Thompson W. H. Liverpool, merchant. *Sols.* Lowe and Co. Southampton buildings, chancery lane.

CERTIFICATES, *Jan.* 30.

J. Upton, Park street, Southwark, baker. R. Dean, Poultry, hosier. J. Nowill, Jewry street, stationer. G. Lancaster, Barbadoes, merchant. C. L. Sparkes, Southbersted, Sussex, shopkeeper. W. Dean, Broad street, Ratcliffe, common brewer.

BANKRUPTCY SUPERSEDED, *Jan.* 12.

M. Ohren, Broad st. Ratcliffe.

BANKRUPTS.

Atkinson J. Darlston, Cumberland, cotton manufacturer. *Sol.* Birkett, Cloak lane.

Blackborn J. Witham, Essex, corn factor. *Sol.* Carter, Staple inn.

Everett W. Cambridge, corn merchant. *Sol.* Croft, Chancery lane.

Friday R. Isleworth, barge master. *Sols.* Ney and Co. Mincing lane.

Ingram L. Cheapside, hatter. *Sol.* Birkett, Cloak lane.

Jacob J. Gravel lane, Houndsditch, tobacconist, *Sol.* Norton, Commercial Chambers, Minories.

Kendrick J. Chaddesby Corbett, Worcester, miller. *Sols.* Lodington and Co. Temple.

Paterson M. Halifax, dyer. *Sols.* Morton and Co. Gray's inn square.

Phillips T. Bread st. hill, merchant. *Sol.* Clarke, Bishopsgate st. without.

Venus J. Shadwell, victualler. *Sols.* Robinson and Co. Austin Friars.

CERTIFICATES, *Feb.* 2.

W. Talbot, George yard, Lombard street, merchant. E. Wilcocks, Aldersgate street, ironmonger. W. Bell, Brampton, Cumberland, brandy merchant. F. Marsden, Wakefield, York, cabinet maker. W. and J. Fowler, Tamworth, Stafford, paper makers. J. S. Colbroke, Plympton, Devon, Maltster. E. Watson, Hitchin, Lincoln, corn dealer. W. Smith, Leicester, woolstapler.

BANKRUPTS, *Jan.* 16.

Cassels R. St. Swithin's lane, merchant. *Sol.* Poole, Adam's ct. Old Broad st.

Churchill J. Stanhope st. Clare market, brewer. *Sol.* Brown, Mincing lane.

Daniels W. Bishop Stortford, Hertfordshire, malt factor. *Sol.* Makinson, Temple.

Davey J. Foulsham, Norfolk, ironmonger. *Sols.* Tilson and Co. Coleman st.

Flint W. Old Bailey, printer. *Sols.* Amory and Co. Louthbury.

Gardiner D. Chiswell st. Finsbury sq. hatter. *Sol.* Clabon, Mark lane.

Hayward H. Great Portland st. paper hanger. *Sol* Archer, Southampton buildings, Chancery lane.

Jennyns J. C. Catherine st. Strand, dealer. *Sol.* Comerford, Copthall ct.

Lush E. Sherborne, Dorsetshire, linen draper. *Sols* King and Co. Gray's inn sq.

Lumley W. Jermyn st. St. James's wine merchant. *Sol.* Osbaldiston, London st. Fenchurch st.

Morgan W. Bristol, victualler. *Sol.* King, Sergeant's inn.

Parsons S. Hanover st. Long acre, coach plater. *Sols.* Robins and Co. Sergeant's inn.

Pidding J. J. High Holborn, stock broker. *Sol.* Guy, Howard st. Strand.

Power J. and Co. Finsbury sq. merchants. *Sol.* Warne, Change alley.

Wilson J. H. Upper Belgrave place, Pimlico, picture dealer. *Sol.* Newcomb, Vine st. Piccadilly.

Young T. Paddington green, St. Marylebone, grocer. *Sol.* Shuter, Mill bank street, Westminster.

CERTIFICATES. *Feb.* 6.

H. Horner, Leeds, merchant. J. Mackay, Warwick street, Golden square, saddle maker. W. Kewley, Manchester, appraiser. T. Fitch, Highgate, butcher. W. Randall, High Holborn, grocer. F Strube, Castle street, Westminster, dealer. H. Wilkinson, Great Eccleston, Lancashire, tanner. J. Burch, Jewry street, stationer. C. A. Pullan, Leeds, merchant. N. Birkinshaw, Derby, timber merchant. F. Lear, Strand, Brush maker J. White, Portland street, Portland place, merchant.

BANKRUPTS, *Jan.* 19.

Bradshaw R. Manchester, check manufacturer. *Sol.* Shaw, Ely plac, Holborn.

Brunner J. Birmingham, patten manufacturer. *Sol.* Bousfield, Bouverie street.

Collins F. New Fishbourne, Sussex, mealman *Sol.* Hume, Holborn court, Gray's inn

David J. Threadneedle street, merchant. *Sols.* Knight and Co. Threadneedle street.

Lucy H. Tupsleys, Hereford, builder. *Sol.* Pewtriss, Gray's inn.

Ritchie T. Air street, Piccadilly, merchant. *Sols.* Young and Co. St. Mildred's court, Poultry.

PRICES CURRENT, Feb. 20, 1819.

	£. s. d.	£. s. d.
American pot-ash, per cwt	0　0　0	to 2　10　0
Ditto　pearl	3　0　0	0　0　0
Barilla	1　13　0	0　0　0
Brandy, Cogniac, bond. gal.	0　5　6	0　5　9
Camphire, refined....lb.	0　4　10	0　5　0
Ditto unrefined··cwt.	10　10　0	13　0　0
Cochineal, fine black, lb.	1　7　0	11　1　0
Ditto, East India	0　5　6	0　6　6
Coffee, fine bond....cwt.	7　2	8　0　0
Ditto ordinary	6　0	6　16　0
Cotton Wool, Surinam, lb.	0　1　9	0　1　11
Ditto　Jamaica..	0　1　3	0　1　6
Ditto　Smyrna ..	0　1　0	0　1　3
Ditto　East-India	0　0　8	0　1　1
Currants, Zant....cwt..	5　0　0	4　11　0
Elephants' Teeth	31　0　0	38　0　0
——————Scrivelloes	20　0　0	20　0　0
Flax, Riga........ton	86　0　0	90　0　0
Ditto Petersburgh ..	72　0　0	73　6　0
Galls, Turkey....cwt··	11　11　0	12　0　0
Geneva, Holl. bond. gal.	0　3　8	0　3　9
Ditto, English	9　6　6	1　0　0
Gum Arabic, Turkey, cwt.	9　10　0	10　0　0
Hemp, Riga......ton	52　0　0	0　0　0
Ditto Petersburgh	0　0　0	4　10　0
Indigo Caraccas .. lb.	0　10　0	0　10　6
Ditto East India	0　7　8	0　9　3
Iron British bars ·· ton.	12　10　0	13　0　0
Ditto Swedish c.c.n.d.	21　0　0	22　10　0
Ditto Swed· 2nd sort	16　0　0	17　0　0
Lead in pigs...... fod	0　0　0	26　0　0
Ditto red··.··· ton	0　0　0	27　0　0
Ditto white......ton	0　0　0	40　0　0
Logwood··········· ton	8　10　0	9　0　0
Madder, Dutch crop, cwt.	6　0　0	7　0　0
Mahogany............ft.	0　1　6	0　2　0
Oil, Lucca··24 gal. jar	17　0　0	19　0　0
Ditto Florence, ½ chest	2　10　0	3　2　0
Ditto whale··········32	0　0　0	0　0　0
Ditto spermaceti··ton	66　0　0	88　0　0
Pitch, Stockholm ·· cwt.	0　11　0	0　0　0
Raisins, bloom ...., cwt.	0　0　0	4　15　0
Rice, Carolina bond····	2　5　0	2　7　0
Rum, Jamaica bond gal.	0　3　4	0　3　6
Ditto Leeward Island··0	3　0	0　3　2
Saltpetre, East India, cwt.	1　16　0	1　18　0
Silk, thrown, Italian, lb.	2　19　0	3　10　0
Silk,···raw,...Ditto..	1　16　0	2　8　0
Tallow, Russia, white ..	0　0　0	3　9　0
Ditto——, yellow··	3　12　0	3　13　0
Tar, Stockholm....bar.	1　0　0	1　3　0
Tin in blocks......cwt.	4　12　6	0　0　0
Tobacco, Maryland, lb.	0　0　11	0　1　2
Ditto Virginia	0　0　0	0　0　10
Wax, Guinea······cwt.	9　0　0	9　10　0
Whale-fins (Greenl) ton	100　0　0	0　0　0
Wine :		
Red Port, bond pipe ··	39　0　0	50　0　0
Ditto Lisbon	38　0　0	44　0　0
Ditto Madeira	60　0　0	70　0　0
Ditto Mountain········	26　0　0	33　0　0
Ditto Calcavella ······	0　0　0	0　0　0
Ditto Sherry ······butt	30　0　0	66　0　0
Ditto Claret ············26	0　0　0	65　0　0

Fire-Office Shares, &c. Feb. 21.

Canals.

	£. s.	£. s.
Chesterfield ....Div. 5l.....	102　—　—	— —
Coventry .... (Div. 44l.) ..	970　—　—	— —
Croydon	5　10　—	— —
Crinan	2　2　—	— —
Ellesmere and Chester (D.21.)	66　—　—	— —
Grand Junction ...(Div. 6l.)..	250　—　—	— —
Grand Surry	52　—　—	— —
Ditto (optional) Loan Div. 5l.	100　—　—	— —
Huddersfield	13　10　—	— —
Kennett and Avon	22　15　—	— —
Leeds and Liverpool (Div 10l.)	325　—　—	— —
Lancaster......Div. 1l.	26　—　—	— —
Oxford ....Div.31l.	690　—　—	— —
Peakforest	63　—　—	61　—
Stratford & Avon..........	10　—　—	— —
Thames and Medway	33　—　—	— —

Docks.

Commercial ....Div. 3l. 10s.	63　—　—	— —
East India........Div. 71l...	180　—　—	— —
London ......Div. 3l....	81　—　—	— —
West India ....Div.10l.....	196　—　—	— —

Insurance Companies.

Albion...... 500sh...£50 pd.	48　—　—	— —
County	—　—　—	— —
Eagle··········50 5pd.·····	2　10　—	— —
Globe·········Div. 6l.	130　—　—	— —
Hope·········50 5pd ·····	4　6　—	— —
Imperial ····500 50pd.	95　—　—	— —
London Fire ··············	27　—　—	— —
London Ship ··············	21　5　—	— —
Royal Exchange··Div. 10 ..	259　—　—	— —
Rock·······50.·2pd·····	4　4　—	— —
Union Fire Life··100l. 20 pd.	33　—　—	— —

Water Works.

Grand Junction..............42	—　—　—	— —
London Bridge....Div. 3l. 10s.52	10　60　—	— —
Manchester and Salford 36	10　—　—	— —
Portsmouth and Farlington 50l.	10　10　—	— —
Ditto (New) 50l.··Div. 6····33	—　6　2	— —
South London ···············	19　—　—	— —
West Middlesex··100··········	45　—　—	— —

Bridges.

Southwark ··············60	—　—　—	— —
Waterloo..................10	—　—　—	— —
Ditto Old Annuities 60 all pd·35	10　—　—	— —
Ditto New do. 40 all pd. ··25	—　—　—	— —
Vauxhall Bonds, 97 pd......	98　—　—	— —

Literary Institutions.

London, 75gs..................50	—　—　—	— —
Russel, 25gs..................13	—　—　—	— —
Surry, 30gs. ·················10	—　—　—	— —

Mines.

British Copper Comp. 100 sh.··—	—　—　—	— —
Beeralstone Lead and Silver....16	—　—　—	— —
Butspill ......10 pd.·············	—　—　—	— —
Great Hewas......15 pd.....25	—　—　—	— —

Roads.

Highgate Archway············	4　5　—	— —

Miscellaneous.

Auction Mart................21	—　—　—	— —
Five per cent. City Bonds.....107	—　—　—	— —
Chelsea 10 sh. Div. Div. 12 ··	—　—　—	— —
Lon. Commer. gate Rom 100p 34—	—　—　—	— —
Lon.) Flour Comp. 14 pd.....	1　19　—	1　5
East London · 100l. sh	—　—　—	— —
Gas Light and Coke Company 75	—　—　—	— —

METEOROLOGICAL TABLE.

	8 o'clock Morning	Noon.	11 o'clock Night.	Height of Barom. Inches.	Dryness by Leslie's Barom.	
Dec. 21	48	48	37	30,22	8	Fair
22	28	28	30	,52	0	Foggy
23	32	37	28	,35	0	Foggy
24	27	30	27	,22	7	Fair
25	27	37	38	,06	0	Cloudy
26	35	35	35	22,90	6	Cloudy
27	35	40	40	30,14	7	Fair
28	40	43	35	,52	8	Fair
29	35	39	30	,58	7	Fair
30	28	36	34	,45	4	Cloudy
31	28	35	32	,42	6	Fair
Jan. 1	32	30	32	,49	0	Foggy
2	32	39	38	,45	0	Foggy
3	40	43	32	,33	9	Fair
4	28	40	35	,26	9	Fair
5	32	42	40	,24	0	Foggy
6	40	42	40	,08	9	Fair
7	41	47	45	29,77	10	Cloudy
8	37	44	40	,88	8	Fair
9	44	45	45	,62	0	Rain
10	43	50	54	,76	15	Fair
11	45	47	38	,84	16	Fair
12	40	50	45	30,17	13	Fair
13	45	47	42	29,99	13	Fair
14	46	52	50	,95	0	Rain
15	47	50	40	,84	14	Fair
16	39	42	41	30,27	15	Fair
17	47	50	42	29,38	23	Stormy
18	41	42	39	,55	21	Fair
19	36	46	40	,80	20	Fair
20	37	44	41	,50	18	Fair

London Premiums of Insurance.

Aberdeen, Dundee, Perth, &c. 15s. 9d. to 20s.
Africa, 2gs.
Amelia Island, 0gs. to 0gs.
American States, 2½gs. to 5gs.
Belfast, Cork, Dublin, 20s. to 25s.
Brazils, 2gs.
Hamburgh, &c. 2gs. to 3gs.
Cadiz, Lisbon, Oporto, 30s.
Canada
Cape of Good Hope, 2gs. to 2½gs.
Constantinople, Smyrna, &c. 2gs. to 50s.
East-India (Co. ships) 3gs.
———— out and home, 6gs.
France, 30gs.
Gibraltar, 25 to 30s.
Gottenburgh, 3gs. to 4gs.
Greenland, out and home,
Holland 25s. to 50s.
Honduras, &c. 2gs.
Jamaica, 35s. to 40s.
Leeward Islands, 25s. to 30s.
Madeira, 20s. to 30s.
Malta, Italian States, &c. 35s. to 40s.
Malaga, 30s. to 40s.
Newfoundland,
Portsmouth, Falmouth, Plymouth, 20s.
River Plate, 2gs.
Southern Fishery, out and home, 10gs.
Stockholm, Petersburgh, Riga, &c. 6gs. to 8gs.

LONDON MARKETS.

PRICE OF BREAD.

				s.	d.
The Peck Loaf to weigh 17lb. 6oz.				4s	0d
The Half ditto	ditto	8	11	2	0
The Quar. ditto	ditto	4	5	1	0
The half ditto	ditto	2	2¼	0	6

POTATOES.

Kidney...... 8 0 0 | Ox Nobles .. 7 0 0
Champions .. 7 0 0 | Apple 7 0 0
ONIONS, per Bushel, 2s 0d to 3s 6d

MEAT.

Smithfield, per stone of 8b. to sink the Offal

		Beef	mut.	veal.	pork	lamb
1819.		s. d.	s. d.	s. d.	s. d.	s. d.
Jan.	27 ..	5 0	6 4	6 8	7 0	0 0
	..	5 4	6 8	7 0	7 0	0 0
	..	5 2	5 2	7 6	7 0	0 0
	..	5 2	6 4	7 0	6 8	0 0

SUGAR.

Lumps ordinary or large 32 to 40 lbs... 103
Fine or Canary, 24 to 30 lbs. 106
Loaves, fine........................ 120
Powder, ordinary, 9 to 11lbs.......... 108

COTTON TWIST.

Jan. 19.   Mule 1st quality, No. 40   3s. 2
    ————No. 120   7s. 9
    ————2d quality, No. 40   2s. 9d.
Discount—15 a 22½ per cent.

COALS, *delivered at* 13s. *per chald. advance.*

	Sunderland.			Newcastle.	
Dec. 27. ..	35s 0d to 44 0		36s 0d to 45 0	
Jan. 6. ..	35s 3	42 6	36s 6d	44 3
13. ..	32s 6	42 6	32s 6d	44 3
20. ..	30s 6	40 6	31s 9d	41 0

LEATHER.

Butts, 50 to 56lb. 24 | Calf Skins 30 to
Dressing Hides .. 21 | 45lb. per doz. 42
Crop hides for cut, 21 | Ditto 50 to 70.. —
Flat Ordinary .. 16 | Seals, Large.... 100

SOAP; yellow, 100s.; mottled 112s.; curd 116s.
CANDLES; per doz. 14s. 0d. ; moulds 15s. 0d.

Course of Exchange.

Bilboa	39	Palermo, per oz 130d.	
Amsterdam, C.F. 11-7		Leghorn	51¾
Ditto at sight	11-4	Genoa	47¼
Rotterdam	11-8	Venice,	24-80
Hamb. us. 2½	33-9	Naples	42¼
Altona us. 2½	33-10	Lisbon	58
Paris, 3d. d.	23-50	Oporto	58
Ditto, 2 us.	23 80	Rio Janeiro	65
Madrid	40½	Dublin	10
Cadiz	40⅜	Cork	10
Agio Bank of Holland, 2 per cent.			

HAY and STRAW.—AT SMITHFIELD.

	Hay.	Straw.	Clover.
	£. s. d.	£. s. d.	£. s. d.
Dec. 20 ..	8 0 0	2 14 0	9 9 0
27 ..	8 0 0	2 0 0	9 0 0
Jan. 4..	8 0 0	2 16 0	9 0 0
11 ..	8 0 0	2 0 0	9 0 0

Price of STOCKS, from 21st December, to 21th January, 1819.

1819. Dec.	Bank Stock.	3 p. Cent. Reduced.	3 p. Cent Consols.	4 p. Cent. Consols.	Navy 5 p. Cent	Irish 5 p. Cent	Long Annuities.	Imperial 3 p. Cent,	Ditto Annuities.	India Stock.	India Bonds.	South Sea Stock.	Excheq. Bills.	Consols for Acc.
22	—	78⅛ ¼	Shut.	94¾	Shut	106¼	20	—	—	—	78	—	15p	78⅞
23	—	77⅞	—	95	—	—	20 1-16	76	—	—	78	—	15p	79
24	267½	77⅞	—	94⅞	—	—	20	—	—	—	77	—	16p	79
25	Chri	tmas day	—	—	—	—	—	—	—	—		—		
26	St S	tephen	—	—		—	—	—	—	—		—		
28	—	77⅞	—	94⅞	—	—	20	—	—	—	78	—	16p	78⅞
29	268	77¾ ⅞	—	94⅞	—	—	20	—	—	—	78	—	16p	78⅞
30	267	77¾ ⅞	—	94¾	108½	—	20	—	—	—	79	—	18p	79⅛
31	268	77¾ 8	—	95	108½	—	20 1-16	—	—	—	80	—	18p	79⅜
Jan.														
1	—	78⅛ ¼	—	95¼	—	—	—	—	—	—		—	17p	79⅛
2	—	78⅛	—	95¼	108½	—	20 1-16	—	—	—	90	—	18p	79⅜
4	268	77⅞ 8⅛	—	95¼	108½	—	20 1-16	—	—	—	90	—	19p	79¼
5	267¼	78⅛ ¼	—	95⅛	—	—	20 1-16	—	—	—	95	—	20p	79¼
6	Epip	hany	—	—	—	—	—	—	—	—		—		
7	268¼	78¼ 7¾	77⅞ ⅛	95⅞	105⅞	—	20⅛	—	—	—	93	85	20p	79½
8	268	78⅛ 8¼	77¾ ⅞	95¾	105⅞	—	20⅛	—	—	—	93	—	20p	79¼
9	—	78⅛	77¾ ⅞	95¾	106	106¾	20⅛	—	—	—	92	—	21p	79
11	—	78¼ ⅛	77⅞	95¾	106	—	20 3-16	—	—	—	90	—	20p	79⅛
12	268	78½ ⅜	77¾	96¼	106½	—	20⅛	—	—	—	88	—	20p	79⅜
13	—	78⅜	77⅞ 8⅛	96⅜	106½	—	20 5-16	76⅛	—	—	88	—	21p	79⅝
14	—	78½	78 7⅞	96¾	106½	—	20 5-16	—	—	—	87	—	21p	77⅝
15	269	78½ ¾	77¾ 8⅛	96½	106½	—	20 5-16	76¾	—	—	87	86⅞	21d	79⅝
16	—	78⅝ ¾	78⅛ 7⅞	97	1'6½	—	20 5-16	—	—	—	88	86¾	20p	79⅝
18	—	78⅝	78⅛	97	106½	—	20 5-16	—	—	--	88	86¾	20p	79⅝
19	269	78¾ 79	78¼ ⅛	97	106¼	—	20⅞	—	—	233¼	88	—	20p	79
20	—	78⅞	78¼ 8	97⅛	106⅝	—	20⅞	77⅛	—	232½	88	86¼	20p	78⅝
21	—	78¾ 9	78⅛	97¼	106½	—	20⅞	—	—	233¾	88	—	20p	79

IRISH FUNDS.

Nov.	Irish Bank Stock.	Government Debenture 3½ per ct.	Government Stock, 3½ per ct.	Government Debenture 4 per ct.	Government Stock. 5 per ct.	Treasury Bills.	Grand Canal Stock.	Grand Canal Loan, 4 per ct.	Grand Canal Loan, 6 per ct	City Dublin Bonds.	Royal Canal Loan 6per cent.	Omnium.
24	—	88¼	86	—	107¼	—	—	—	—	—	—	
27	—	88¼	86	—	107¼	—	—	—	—	—	—	
28	—	88¼	86	—	106¾	—	—	—	—	—	—	
30	—	88¼	86¾					51½	77½			
4	—	89½	86¾	—	106⅞	—	—	—	—	—	—	
D. 5	251	89⅞	86⅞	—	107⅛	—	—	—	—	—	—	

AMERICAN FUNDS.

	IN LONDON. Dec. 24.	Jan. 1. 5.	8.	AT NEW YORK. Nov. 23.		Dec. 11
7 per Cent.	—	—	—	—	105	105
Bank Shares	24 10	24 10	24	—	110	115
Louisiana	—	—	—	par	par	par
Old 6 per Cent.	—	—	—	par	par	par
New 6 per Cent.	102	102	102	102	103½	100

Prices of the FRENCH FUNDS From Oct. 20, to Nov. 18.

1818	5 per Cent. consols fr.	c.	Bank Actions. fr.	c.
Dec 18	64		1500	—
21	65		1520	—
24	63		1490	—
26	63		1485	—
29	66	—	1445	—
Jan. 2	66	80	1490	—
5	67	75	1500	—
8	67	50	1505	—
11	67	10	1485	—
13	67	70	1470	—
18	68	30	1520	—
20	67	85	1495	—

By J. M. Richardson, 23, Cornhill.

THE

LITERARY PANORAMA,

AND

National Register:

For MARCH, 1819.

NATIONAL AND PARLIAMENTARY NOTICES,

(British and Foreign,)

PROSPECTIVE AND RETROSPECTIVE.

PRESENT STATE OF CHILI.

ABSTRACT

OF

Mr. BLAND'S REPORT

ON THE PRESENT STATE OF THE

PROVINCE OF CHILI,

IN SOUTH AMERICA;

Laid before the Congress of North America, by order of the President, November, 1818.

WHEN we gave in our last Number the Report of Mr. Graham, addressed to the President of the United States of North America, and by him laid before the Congress, we observed, that it was one of three, which had been procured by the American Government, for the purpose of obtaining correct and official information. It was a wise step in the President to send out this Mission; and the Agents selected, appear to have executed the charge entrusted to them, with great fidelity and diligence.

Arrived at Buenos-Ayres, it was evident that a more extensive excursion than was possible by the River Plate, or limited to the provinces adjoining, was not only desirable, but was in fact necessary. For, although

VOL. IX. No. 54.

that city, as a metropolis, with its new Government, might be for the moment in a prosperous condition, yet the resources requisite to support that prosperity, must, no doubt, be drawn from extensive intercourse with the interior; and from distant provinces. Among these, Chili presented itself, with prominent importance. The disposition of Chili, then, was to be ascertained; and for this purpose one of the American Commissioners, was deputed to the revolutionary rulers, who then held the reins of Governmental power.

The entire Report of this gentleman, Mr Bland, has not been published; and indeed it is so long, that our pages must needs be content with an abstract. That service has been performed for us by an American pen; and we present it in the form in which it has reached our hands. We give it somewhat out of its proper order, because there is absolutely nothing known concerning Chili, that is worthy of confidence; and because we hazarded a slight speculation on the duration of the power and influence of Buenos-Ayres over Chili, with which this report is in unison. We shall now endeavour to authenticate our observations, by adducing a few facts, the consequences of which are obvious.

G

Where Nature has interposed geographical boundaries to countries, and has marked those countries by distinct and permanent characters, though human power may incidentally violate the limits, and extend itself beyond them, in spite of Nature, yet the violation will not be of long continuance. Where vast oceans, trackless deserts, or impassible mountains, interpose a barrier, they will continue to perform their office, though, occasionally, they may be overcome. The adventurous and the energetic may encounter their difficulties successfully; but, the bulk of mankind are neither adventurous nor energetic; and if such be the disposition of a certain generation, their successors are sure to manifest other qualities, and to become quiescent and stationary.

Mr. Bland travelled from Buenos-Ayres to Mendoza, a distance of about 900 miles, by the usual road. This station is on the eastern side of the Andes; but, the Andes, themselves, are shut up by severe frost, during four months of the year; and are at all times difficult to pass. The mules which are used in this passage, when experienced in it, are tolerably safe; and the same may be said of the guides; but, if either the one or the other be *new*, or unaccustomed to the precipices, and chasms, which are of tremendous height and depth, the danger is absolutely terrific. From Buenos-Ayres to Mendoza, is a continued plain, of easy ascent; from Mendoza to St. Jago de Chili, is little other than a continued chain of mountains and valleys, of all dimensions, and forms.

It is not without reason, then, that Mr. Bland agrees with us, in supposing, that the connexion between the two countries, or rather the power and influence of Buenos-Ayres over Chili, will not be lasting. And if this actuating political principle be not lasting, the commercial connexion will certainly follow its fate. A passage shut up for four months in the year, a passage at all times extremely difficult, and so

constructed by nature, as to be defended by a handful of troops, which may bid defiance to whole armies, commits to its possessors a controuling power that no supposeable authority will be able to overcome. Mr. Bland thinks this connexion is at present to the disadvantage of the Chilians; on this we give no opinion.

The estimate of the commerce of the country, as to imports, furnished by this gentleman, agrees with what we have stated: he reports the whole at about four millions of dollars, of which two millions were from England. And, indeed, it must be evident, that while the seas are open, our countrymen can offer infinitely the best, the most valuable, and the most profitable assortments of goods. The passage round Cape Horn is now so greatly familiarized to our intrepid mariners, that we no longer shudder at the tempests and dangers which formerly distinguished our perusal of Lord Anson's Voyage. We have now, also, possession of the Cape of Good Hope, which in time, may afford facilities, by way of *depôt*, at least, not to be thought contemptible, by those who know how to turn them to advantage.

While the exports are wheat, flour, cordage, tallow and beef, the trade of this country with North America, is not likely to increase very greatly. These are commodities which America herself furnishes; and the principle of barter, or interchange, does not seem to be very applicable to such commerce. The gold of this country is washed out of the earth, in the valley of Quillota, which for several feet in depth, is intermixed with this metal; which is found in great purity. How far the supply might be increased, is at present uncertain: but considering the premium borne by gold in Europe, it may become of consequence to the prov' The silver mines are considered as bei very rich: and the Chilians take ca to report their belief that the mines Potosi, in Peru, are exhausted.

The most extraordinary particular the whole, is, that this same valley

Quillota is abundantly productive of corn, hemp, and cordage, of the finest qualities; which are generally transported on mules to Valparaiso, from whence it is distant about thirty miles. Fruit trees, of every description, flourish also in this valley; and they derive much of their fertility and excellence from the practice of irrigation; trenches being cut to every tree (or, the trees being planted in trenches) which are kept constantly moist, throughout the dry season. This advantage gives them an incontestible superiority. The valley of Quillota is situated between St. Jago and the town of Valparaiso, which is the general port to the whole province. It is rendered the more striking in point of appearance, by the contrast of the sterile mountains around it.

But, the province of Chili has a natural connexion with another province, that in spite of apparent obstacles will long continue to operate. Peru is destitute of those articles, corn, hemp, and cordage, in which Chili abounds: insomuch, that during certain periods of enmity, between the two provinces, corn was sold in Peru at twelve or fourteen dollars the (English) bushel. While, on the other hand, Chili is equally destitute of sugar, coffee, and the thousand *et ceteras*, which contribute to the enjoyments of social life: Six or seven shillings was at that time no unusual price for a pound of sugar, or of coffee. While the same authority was paramount over both provinces, this intercourse was mutually beneficial; and, should they once more combine their respective interests, this commerce will resume its former activity, and become the source of equal gratification to both.

Very different are the sentiments which breathe in Mr. Bland's Report, on the disposition of Chili. He describes an intervening desert of upwards of 300 miles extent, as affording a protection to the Chilians from any invasion by land from Peru;—and doubtless, this same desert affords a protection to the Peruvians from any invasion by land from Chili.—" A superior

naval force, says Mr. B., is indispensable to enable the Chilians to invade Peru; for the desert of Attacama prevents them from marching thither by land." Such are the attendants on revolutionary movements! Nothing but marchings, and invasions. It is not enough that Buenos-Ayres should change its masters, but Chili, also, shall be assisted with two thousand negroes and other forces, to establish new authorities : nor is it enough that Chili shall establish new authorities, Peru, also, must be invaded. At the present moment, Peru, it is presumed, affords the greatest proportion of resources in shipping and sailors :—the disposition of the people is another question.

But, before Peru be invaded, it should seem to be the policy of Chili to see that all is well at home. Mr. B. informs us, that taking the population of Chili at 1,200,000, one third of this population is adverse to " the Patriots," and still retains sentiments of loyalty. It would not, therefore, be very safe for any considerable force to be detached against Peru, or any where else out of the country, lest this party should take the advantage, and obtain the superiority.——

For, it will hardly be thought that the new authorities of Chili, should under-estimate the strength of their adherents ; and we should not be at all surprized to learn, that the true proportion of opinions was much nearer to numerical equality.

A much more pressing danger, to Chili, is that arising from the parties which have alternately risen to power and sunk to bondage, in the short space of a few revolving years. These rival parties, the Carreras, on the one side, and the Lorrains, (called also, we believe, the Roses) on the other, not only suffered their animosities to rise to counteraction and broils, but went so far as to cut each other to pieces in set battles: insomuch that they lost sight of their common enemy, the Spanish Royalists, and suffered their adversaries to invade their country, before the unnatural delirium had sub-sided. There are those who go so far as to affirm, that at the Battle of Ran-cagua, alluded to by Mr. Bland, the young Carreras, at the head of his regiment, had not sufficient compunc-tion at the destruction of his rivals by the Spanish bayonet, (though it cost the loss of the battle) to step forward to their relief from the ruin that sur-rounded them. If this single fact be truly stated, it speaks more than volumes for the unhappy fate of Chili, which ever be the party that holds the reins of Government. It agrees with Mr. Bland's observation, that the Lor-rains, when in power, had sacrificed two of the most distinguished of the Carreras, under judicial forms, to gra-tify the vengeance of the reigning faction.

The amount of the population is certainly stated at the highest in the official communication of the govern-ment of Chili to Mr. Bland. The amount of the army, if well disposed, well appointed, and well disciplined fighting men, are referred to, is taken much beyond the highest, even at the medium intended to be adopted. The Spanish force by which the Chilians were overcome, answered but little to our ideas of regular troops; and we have no reason to conclude that their opponents had any advantage over them, in these respects. Nor does it appear that the resources of the Chi-lians have since been so ample, as to place the question of their power to make better provision for their army, beyond all doubt, or suspicion.

On the contrary, the poverty of the Government is acknowledged : it has prompted the rulers to lay hands on the property of the Church : that this property was enormous, we have reason to believe; nor are reasons wanting to persuade us, that it was but too often diverted from purposes professedly pious, to the promotion of dissoluteness and gross immoralities. A late English traveller, who visited both Lima and St. Jago, affirms that the most respectable authority (to which he might have added, public report) de-scribes the monks and nuns of the several religious houses, as living the most profligate and licentious lives possible. Our readers have seen (COMP. LIT. PAN. 'N. S. Vol. V. p. 556.) an instance of similar imputations on the Clergy of Brazil, in the travels of M. Koster ; whose work affords others to the same purpose. Nor is the language of Dr. Robertson too harsh, when speaking of the priests in these countries, he says, " the giddy, the profligate, the avaricious, to whom the rigid discipline of a convent is intolerable, consider a mission to America, as a relief from mortification and bondage. There they soon obtain some parochial charge ; and by their situation, far removed from the inspec-tion of their monastic superiors, and exempt by their character, from the jurisdiction of the diocesan, they are hardly subject to control. According to the testimony of the most zealous Catholics, many of the regular clergy in the Spanish settlements, are not only destitute of the virtues becoming their profession, but regardless of that external decorum and respect, for the opinion of mankind, which preserve a semblance of worth, where the reality is wanting. Secure of impunity, some regulars, in contempt of their vow of poverty, engage openly in commerce, and are so rapaciously eager in amassing wealth, that they become the most grievous oppressors of the Indians, whom it was their duty to have pro-tected. Others with no less flagrant violation of their vow of chastity, indulge with little disguise in the most dissolute licentiousness."

Things are not mended, since the days alluded to by Dr. Robertson ; and revolutionary times are, of all others, the least adapted to efficient improvement of morals, professional or popular. We cannot wonder, that, ac-cording to Mr. Bland, neither monks nor nuns, have been treated with much ceremony ; but, we do not observe that any better materials for building up truly religious houses, are put in their place.

If the happiness of a people be not promoted by change in their government, of what advantage is such a change ? and how can public happiness be promoted, when morals are dissolute and religion is debased ? We hinted, in our last, at 'the consideration due to these subjects; and whatever turn affairs may take, we should be glad to think that these humble observations had fallen into hands capable of realizing their spirit, and disposed to organize their intention.

We conclude these slight suggestions by hinting, that it cannot be supposed that Mr. O'Higgins would fail to put the best possible face on things under his government, when conversing with the agent of a foreign power, which it was evidently his interest, and beyond question his wish and endeavour to conciliate. He would, naturally, do his utmost to maintain a respectable attitude.

Mr. Bland appears to have reported with sufficient fairness and impartiality. We have added a few additional particulars, derived from such sources of information as have reached our hands. Not to be mistaken, in some things, in reference to countries so distant, and so different from our own, is scarcely to be expected. And to form an opinion on such slender materials, is often more likely to mislead those who confide in it, than the frank acknowledgement of having hitherto formed no opinion at all. We do not perceive, in spite of the boastings of their agents, that the revolutionists are wonderfully strong; but, we perceive, clearly, and we presume, that others must perceive it, too, that the mother country is wonderfully weak; that her interests, if they are not to be entirely abandoned, require a support which can only be rendered at a prodigious, in fact, at an unprecedented expence.

That literature should obtain countenance amid the din of arms and national conflict, was hardly to be expected ; yet (the power of literature in influencing and guiding opinion has been found, of late years, so great, that no practised politician will despise it. The press was introduced for the first time into Chili, at the commencement of the revolution; the birth of one, was the birth of the other. But, the press is not free: each party, when in power, published according to its heart's desire, and nothing but sentiments, or communications which suited its party purposes; other printing presses were not saleable articles; and the American speculators in the commodity missed their object. Books are of little value where readers are few : nevertheless, this introduction of the means of access to the human mind, will have its consequences; and hereafter Chili may become respectable as a seat of general literature.

Our readers will remark for themselves a variety of minor particulars, on which we cannot now dilate. They have their importance; and eventually may become of great political moment. We are at a loss to discover what interest the chief and long established families in this Spanish settlement, take in the actual state of things : nor can we draw auguries as to their permanence, while it is acknowledged that rival factions have so bitterly contended for the sovereignty. The faction now depressed, may possibly recover strength; and that now in authority, unless supported by the general voice, may find its sway flit away from before its eyes, like a phantom. We are, however, bound to make our acknowledgments to Mr. Bland, for his instructive Report, and to the gentleman who has favoured the public with the following able abridgment of it.

ABSTRACT

OF

Mr. Bland's Report concerning Chili.

Mr. Bland was, in pursuance of instructions from the President, left by his colleagues, Mr. Rodney, and Mr. Graham, at Buenos-Ayres; whence, on the 15th of April, 1818, he departed for Chili, and on the 20th of the same month arrived at Mendoza, on the eastern side of the Andes, having travelled, by the way of the post-road, a distance of about 900 miles. He left Mendoza on the 29th of April, and, crossing the Andes, reached Santiago de Chili on the 5th of May; the whole route being, perhaps, about 1,200 miles. At this latter place Mr. Bland presented himself to Don Antonio Jose Irisarri, Secretary of State, through whom he obtained an interview with Don Bernardo O'Higgins, the Supreme Director of Chili. He was received with much cordiality by the Director, with whom he had, at different times, very interesting conversations, touching the present and future probable condition of Chili, and the friendly sentiments which the United States entertained towards that country.

In the several interviews which Mr. Bland had with the Supreme Director, he represented to him the good disposition which the Government of the United States cherished towards the independent authorities of Chili, and the cause in which they are engaged; the sympathy which the free citizens of North America felt for the sufferings of those who were contending for liberty and emancipation from the yoke of Old Spain in the southern part of the American continent; and portrayed to him the benefits to be derived from the establishment of the representative system, by the immediate formation of a Congress.

To these observations O'Higgins answered, that he was not insensible to the friendship of the United States; that it was his intention to institute a free government as soon as Chili was entirely freed of her enemies, and sufficiently tranquillized for the purpose; but that the present moment was inauspicious for the commencement of so great a work; that in times of public peril the presence of a Congress had been found extremely pernicious; that Mexico had been lost by a Congress; that the Congress of Venezuela once lost that country; and that Buenos-Ayres had been endangered by a Congress: lately, indeed, he admitted, the latter had learnt to act in more concert, and with greater propriety

The Supreme Director having intimated that it was expected the United States would recognize the independence of Chili, and that the Chilians would grant special favours in commerce to the nation (and it would be gratifying if the United States should be the nation) first making such recognition, Mr. Bland replied, that the single object of his mission was to make inquiry as to the true posture of affairs in Chili; that the United States would be thankful for any favours of the kind, but that they did not ask for them; that all they desired was to be put on a footing with other nations, and were willing to rely, as to any advantages in commerce and navigation, on the skill and industry of their merchants and seamen; that he had repaired to Santiago in order to procure, upon the spot, accurate knowledge

of the country, of its institutions, and of its capacities in peace and war; that the Government of the United States only wished to see its way clearly, and would make no improper use of this information; and that any particulars communicated to him from authority might be considered as confidential, or otherwise, just as the Supreme Director might deem proper.

The Supreme Director, O'Higgins, admitted the propriety of authentic information, in order that the Government of the United States might act intelligently with regard to South American affairs, and told Mr. Bland that he would cause an official statement to be made out respecting the condition and resources of Chili, and placed in his hands for that purpose; which promise the Supreme Director complied with.

During the intercourse between Mr. Bland and O'Higgins, the former explained to the latter the motives which actuated the President in the seizure of Amelia Island, and in driving the banditti from Galveston; and told him, that the freebooters who had been forced from those places were not the only armed vessels whose officers and crews had interrupted the lawful commerce of the United States, for that some of the privateers cruising under regular Patriot commissions had committed depredations upon their trade; that the United States would, at all hazards, defend the fair traffic of her citizens; and that they would do so even against the Chilians, however painful it might be to crush in the germ a growing intimacy between the two people, and which promised to be in the sequel fruitful of benefits to them both.

O'Higgins did not even know where Amelia Island and Galveston were situated, until Mr. Bland explained the positions to him. He decidedly approved of the conduct of the President in driving off the pirates from thence, inasmuch as it tended to preserve the character of the Patriot cause from imputations of an injurious nature: he had heard of outrages committed by private armed vessels sailing under some of the independent flags of South America; but that, whatever might have been the behaviour of the vessels acting under commissions from other states, no charge of the kind could justly be brought against the Chilians; that in fact, with the exception of some fishing-boats, it was not until very lately that the Government of Chili had any vessels of war under its control; and that he had taken great care, by giving proper instructions, and by placing suitable superintending officers on board, to prevent any departure from the rules of naval warfare prescribed by the law of nations.

In one of the conversations which took place, Mr. Bland told the Supreme Director, that when he was at Rio Janeiro (where, it will be recollected, the commissioners touched, on their way to Buenos-Ayres,) he had learnt through Mr. Sumter, the Minister of the United States, from the Spanish Minister resident there, that Great Britain had been induced to take an active part in favour of Old Spain, and had influenced the Allied Sovereigns of Europe to interpose for the adjustment of differences between her and her colonies; and that the plan of adjustment was to be something like that which had been formerly rejected by the Cortes, and might be found in a work that had been published in England, entitled, " An Outline of the Revolution in Spanish America."

At first O'Higgins did not believe in the truth of the information which Mr. Bland had received; he said that the British would hardly do so, as they wanted the commerce of Spanish America: but shortly after, meeting with him again, the Supreme Director said he was then convinced of it; for he had seen Capt. Shirriff, of the British frigate *Andromache*, in Santiago, who had told him that he had in his possession papers on the subject, with which he was going to Lima, in Peru. O'Higgins further remarked, that all attempts to reconcile the South Americans, short of the acknowledgment of their independence, would be fruitless; and that a return to allegiance under the government of Old Spain was wholly out of the question.

On the 9th July Mr. Bland, having received the statistical information which the Supreme Director had promised him, took leave of him and of the Secretary of State Irisarri. O'Higgins expressed his intention of writing a letter to the President; but whether he did so or not, Mr. Bland had not distinctly related.

On the 10th of July Mr. Bland left Santiago de Chili; on the 11th he arrived at Valparaiso; and on the 15th of July he sailed thence in the brig *America*, Captain Daniel Rea, and arrived, by the way of Cape Horn, at Philadelphia, on the 29th of October, 1818.

The narrative of Mr. Bland's communications with the Supreme Director forms but a small portion of his Report concerning Chili. He furnishes in addition a very copious description of that region of our hemisphere, in which he now and then lets his fancy get the better of his judgment. But, from the mass of pages which he has written, circumstances of a highly interesting complexion may be selected.

From Mr. Bland's account, it would seem that Chili is a country (excluding the Magellanic tract, or New Chili) of about 1,000 miles in extent on the sea coast; that it has many excellent ports convenient for foreign trade; that it is a country fruitful in grain, wine, and oil, and productive in gold, silver, copper, and tin; that it is destined to be the granary of that part of the world; that its population is about 1,200,000 souls; that

800,000 of these are under the domination of the Patriots, the remainder being under the jurisdiction of the Royalists; that there are about 50,000 Indian slaves in all Chili; and but very few slaves of the African race. All the mechanical arts and agriculture are in a rude state, and the roads and pathways in a neglected condition. The principal articles of export are the metals already mentioned, together with wheat, flour, hemp, cordage, hides, tallow, jerked beef, vecunia, guanaco, chinchilla skins, figs, raisins, &c. Of 4,000,000 of dollars' worth of imports, in the course of last year, two millions in value were from England, one from the United States, and one from Buenos-Ayres. The articles furnished from the United States are chiefly tobacco, windsor chairs, saddlery and furniture. Of European commodities, Mr. Bland thinks the manufactures of France and Germany are preferred. The stocks of cattle are numerous and fine; the horses are active, spirited, serviceable, and cheap; but the mules are the common beasts of burden. The soil and climate of Chili are different in different places: from the Straits of Chacao to the river Biobio it is woody, fertile, and salubrious, and is inhabited by the Araucanians, or natives; from the Biobio to the river Maule, the country is the same, but the population is Spanish: from the Maule to the Aconcagua, still fertile, but no forests: from the valley of Aconcagua the mine country presents itself, which is less fruitful on the surface: after the mine country, the dreary desert of Atacama, upwards of 300 miles extent, affords a protection to the Chilians from any invasion by land from Peru. From the Straits of Chacao to the river Maule, it rains at any season; at Santiago di Chili there is no rain for seven months in the year; and beyond Copiapo rains are hardly known. Mr. Bland divides the country into two regions—the one variable and humid, and the other invariable and dry. Fuel, in some parts, is scarce; but it is said there is plenty of pit-coal on the banks of the Biobio, near Conception. The Archipelago of Ancud, or Chiloe, contains 47 islands; it is a considerable fishery, and will be a nursery for seamen. There are only three carriage roads in all Chili. The fertile part of the soil is situated in valleys, surrounded for the most part by hills and mountains; and the inhabitants of these valleys communicate with each other principally by mule paths. Mr. Bland describes the people generally as being " mild, amiable, brave, and uninformed." Santiago is the capital, and contains about 40,000 souls. The Royalists have possession of Penco, and a considerable district around Conception, which is their strong hold; they retain, also, Valdivia and Chiloe. The patriot army, at a medium, (for Mr. Irisarri and Mr. Bland differ on this point) is about 6,000 strong, 2,000 of which are negroes from Buenos-Ayres; there are no Chilian officers in it, however, above the rank of Captain, with the exception of O'Higgins, who is a Brigadier under San Martin, and Colonel Raymon Freyere. The navy consists of but three or four indifferent vessels, but would be increased by the addition of two new ships of war, to be called *San Martin* and *Chacabuco*, built at New York, and for which purpose Messrs. Aguirre and Gomez were, a considerable time since, sent to the United States from Buenos-Ayres with money. A superior naval force is indispensable to enable the Chilians to invade Peru, for the desert of Atacama prevents them from marching thither by land. The Chilians have no seamen of their own.

The revenue of the Government in Chili is derived from duties on imports and exports; from an excise which is laid upon almost every thing that is sold; from a direct tax, the mines, papal bulls, printed indulgences for the living and. the dead, a crusade tax, tithes, forfeited estates of the Jesuits, voluntary contributions, and from confiscated estates of the enemies of the Patriot cause. The officers of the customs and the judges of the commercial courts receive no regular salaries, and a duty is imposed on merchandise to compensate them; in addition, traders quicken their exertions by presents or bribes. There are 10,000 monks and nuns in the country. The church holds one-third of the landed property of the state. The church lands are farmed out to tenants, who let them again to under tenants, and these last work them with slaves: thus three sets of idlers are supported upon the product of the industry of the labouring class. In addition to their landed estates, the religious institutions have what are called their *censos*, or money lent out at an interest of five *per* cent per annum, to the amount of ten millions of dollars. Besides their share of the tithes, which the state still permits them to draw, the clergy have the anuats, or first fruits, which yield to each curate between two and three hundred dollars per annum.

The government of Chili, it seems, is needy, and has made some progress towards laying hands on the enormous property of the priests. Indeed neither monks nor nuns, according to Mr. Bland, are treated with much ceremony; some of the former have been turned out of their dwelling-places, which have been occupied for military purposes, and some of them have been tried for treasonable practices.

The most immediately interesting part of the Report is that which gives the history of the Chilian Revolution, and the change of parties among the Patriots. There have, it appears, been two powerful factions in that country of the revolutionists themselves. At the head of one were the Carreras; the Larrains formed the other, with O'Higgins at their head. At the beginning of the contest for independence, the Carrera faction prevailed. It would seem, however, this

party did not manage affairs in a judicious manner; for at the battle of Rancagua, against the Royalists, fought on the 2d of October, 1814, the Patriots were entirely defeated, and fled over the Andes. They were rallied at Mendoza by San Martin, who identified himself with the Larrain faction; and, having obtained a reinforcement of 2,000 negroes from Buenos-Ayres, crossed the mountains, and, on the 12th February, 1816, fought the battle of Chacabuco, defeated the Royalists, and took their commander, Marco, prisoner. This may be called the second epoch of the revolution in Chili. The Carrera party was, of course, put down, and the Larrains, with O'Higgins as chief, confirmed themselves in power by the victory of Mapo, obtained on the 5th April, 1818. It is greatly to the dishonour of the Larrains that they seized this moment of success to put to death two of the most distinguished of the Carreras. They were sacrificed under judicial forms, and on the pretext of treason. Their execution was a foul and bloody murder, to gratify the vengeance of the reigning faction.

The closest intimacy subsists between the Governments of Chili and Buenos-Ayres. O'Higgins told Mr. Bland, that there was nothing which Buenos-Ayres could ask of Chili that would not be granted; and that Buenos-Ayres would act in like manner towards Chili. All the inhabitants of Buenos-Ayres are naturalized citizens of Chili. The Supreme Director, by way of characterizing the intimacy, said they were as two bodies actuated by one soul. Mr. Bland thinks, however, that this connexion is to the disadvantage of the Chilians, and conceives that it will not be lasting.

Under the faction of the Carreras, at the commencement of the revolution, the press, for the first time, was introduced into Chili. Before that period all books and papers, prior to their entrance into the country, were inspected and approved by the Holy Inquisition in Spain or at Lima. The name of the first paper was the *Aurora*. It was printed weekly, at a printing-office sent from New York, and managed by three citizens of the United States. It was edited by Camila Henriquez, now of Buenos-Ayres. The opposite party also published a paper, which they called the *Aurora*. It was edited by Irisarri; but at this time there are four weekly papers issued at Santiago: and none are published any where else in Chili; their names are the *Ministerial Gazette*, which is the acknowledged paper of the Government, *El Argos*, *El Duende*, and *El Sol*. They are all printed at the same press, and edited by clerks and officers of the Government. Two other printing-presses had been carried there for sale, but they were not saleable articles. Newspapers and pamphlets are conveyed free of postage, and books are imported free of duty.

The reader may recollect that, after the battle of Maypu, the Viceroy of Peru was desirous of effecting an exchange of prisoners, and sent on board the United States' sloop of war *Ontario*, Captain Biddle, from Lima, an officer to Valparaiso and Santiago for the purpose. It turned out, however, on investigation, that the Royalists had a few or no Chilian prisoners; that those which they formerly had, having been confined in one of the islands of the Archipelago of Chiloe, were released by the Patriots after the battle of Chacabuco. The Patriots, on the contrary, had about 8,000 Royalist prisoners, and were willing they should be exchanged for any prisoners which the Royalists held belonging to Buenos-Ayres; but, owing to some contempt manifested in relation to the Patriot authorities, no cartel was agreed upon.

Incidentally speaking of Peru, Mr. Bland says, that one-third of the population of that country are whites of unmixed blood, and two-thirds are mulattoes and negroes; the latter, in general, as well informed as the whites.

Observations on Criminal Jurisprudence, and the Reformation of Criminals; with an Appendix, containing the latest Reports of the State Prisons or Penitentiaries of Philadelphia, New York, and Massachussetts; and other Documents. By William Roscoe, Esq. 8vo. 9s. Cadell and Davies, London, 1819.

THAT the Criminal Law of England is in a state that imperiously calls for revision, is a fact, which needs only to be mentioned, to be universally admitted. " Sanguinary statutes, operative only in deforming our jurisprudence, and investing judges with discretion never originally intended, but rendered necessary by a nugatory severity, cannot be suffered to remain standing amid the general stir of education and improvement. So many of our statutes have been made in particular and temporary exigencies, in moments of excited public feeling, and transient fits of legislation,—with so little regard to system or proportion, and little connexion between law and natural sentiment, that every motive of policy, justice, and decency," requires some change to be made in our criminal law, so far as it relates to capital punishments and to the mode in which it is administered. Some of the more grossly severe acts have been expunged from the statute book, through

the generous and persevering efforts of the late much-lamented Sir Samuel Romilly. Much, however, remains to be done; and Mr. Roscoe has, most seasonably, offered the valuable work to the consideration of the public, of which we hasten to offer our readers a brief analysis.

The first topic discussed by Mr. R. is, *the motives and ends of Punishment*. In this section he strongly and ably combats the notion that anger is not only allowable in criminal jurisprudence, but that attempts to extirpate it must be vain, and, if successful, would be injurious. He further contends, and with much force of argument, that it is only the calm exercise of reason, by removing the inducement, or correcting the disposition to crimes, or by taking a sincere interest in the welfare of the offender, and convincing him that the evils he experiences are the unavoidable consequences of his own misconduct, and are inflicted upon him for his own good,—that we can expect to produce any beneficial effect. Upon the practicability of this is founded the great plan of modern improvement, called *the penitentiary system*, the advantages of which are every day becoming more apparent; and which, when perfected by experience, cannot fail to produce the happiest and most important results on the moral character and condition of mankind.

In the sections " *on punishments by way of example*," and " *on the prevention of crimes*," our author shews the inadequacy of extreme severity, and urges various moral considerations; which, if duly considered, will not merely prevent the commission of crimes, but will greatly improve the condition of the country. The inefficacy of the existing laws, which inflict the *punishment of death* for various crimes as well as of those which impose *punishments of inferior degree*, are next considered, and illustrated by many authentic facts, drawn from the evidence laid before various committees of the House of Commons within the last two or three years.

The section, which discusses "*proposed improvements in Criminal Law*," is little more than a statement of the difficulties experienced by Beccaria and other eminent writers who have treated on crimes and punishments; but the two following sections, on the *origin* and *present state of the Penitentiaries in America*, on the *Penitentiary system on the Continent of Europe*, and also in *this Country*, present a rich collection of most important facts. The

Price of STOCKS, from 21st December, to 21th January, 1819.

1819. Dec.	Bank Stock.	3 p. Cent. Reduced.	3 p. Cent. Consols.	4 p. Cent. Consols.	Navy 5 p. Cent.	Irish 5 p. Cent	Long Annuities.	Imperial 3 p. Cent,	Ditto Annuities.	India Stock.	India Bonds.	South Sea Stock.	Excheq. Bills.	Consols for Acc.
22	—	78¼ ⅛	Shut.	94¾	Shut	106¼	20	—	—	—	78	—	15p	78⅞
23	—	77⅞ ⅝	—	95	—	—	20 1-16	76	—	—	78	—	15p	79
24	267½	77⅝ ⅜	—	94⅞	—	—	20	—	—	—	77	—	16p	79
25	Christmas day		—	—	—	—	—	—	—	—		—		
26	St. Stephen		—	—		—	—	—	—	—		—		
28	—	77¾	—	94⅞	—	—	20	—	—	—	78	—	16p	78⅞
29	268	77½ ¼	—	94⅞	—	—	20	—	—	—	78	—	16p	78⅞
30	267	77½ ¼	—	94¾	108½	—	20	—	—	—	79	—	18p	79⅛
31	268	77¾ 8	—	95	108½	—	20 1-16	—	—	—	80	—	18p	79⅜
Jan.														
1	—	78¾ ½	—	95⅛	—	—	—	—	—	—		—	17p	79½
2	—	78⅞	—	95¼	108½	—	20 1-16	—	—	—	90	—	18p	79⅜
4	268	77⅞ 8⅛	—	95⅛	108½	—	20 1-16	—	—	—	90	—	19p	79¼
5	267¼	78⅛ ¼	—	95⅜	—	—	20 1-16	—	—	—	95	—	20p	79¼
6	Epiphany		—	—	—	—	—	—	—	—		—		
7	268¼	78¼ 7¾	77¾ ½	95⅝	105⅞	—	20⅛	—	—	—	93	85	20p	79¼
8	268	78⅞ 8¼	77½ ⅝	95⅛	105⅞	—	20⅛	—	—	—	93	—	20p	79¼
9	—	78⅛	77¼ ⅛	95¾	106	106¾	20⅛	—	—	—	92	—	21p	79
11	—	78⅛ ⅛	77⅞ ⅝	95⅞	106	—	20 3-16	—	—	—	90	—	20p	79⅛
12	268	78⅛	77½ ¾	96⅛	106½	—	20¼	—	—	—	88	—	20p	79⅜
13	—	78⅜	77⅞ 8⅛	96⅜	106½	—	20 5-16	76⅛	—	—	88	—	21p	79⅜
14	—	78⅜	78 7⅞	96⅜	106½	—	20 5-16	—	—	—	87	—	21p	77⅞
15	269	78⅜	77¾ 8⅛	96½	106½	—	20 5-16	76¾	—	—	87	86⅞	21d	79⅜
16	—	78⅝ ¾	78⅛ 7⅞	97	106½	—	20 5-16	—	—	—	88	86¼	20p	79⅜
18	—	78⅝	78⅛	97	106½	—	20 5-16	—	—	—	88	86¼	20p	79⅝
19	269	78⅝ 79	78⅛ ⅜	97	106½	—	20⅜	—	—	233¼	88	—	20p	79
20	—	78⅝	78⅛ 8	97½	106¾	—	20⅜	77⅛	—	232½	88	86¼	20p	78⅝
21	—	78¾ 9	78⅛ ⅜	97½	106⅞	—	20⅞	—	—	233¾	88	—	20p	79

IRISH FUNDS.

Nov.	Irish Bank Stock.	Government Debenture 3½ per ct.	Government Stock, 3½ per ct.	Government Debenture 4 per ct.	Government Stock. 5 per ct.	Treasury Bills.	Grand Canal Stock.	Grand Canal Loan, 4 per ct.	Grand Canal Loan, 6 per ct	City Dublin Bonds.	Royal Canal Loan 6per cent.	Omnium.
24	—	88¼	86	—	107¼	—	—	—	—	—	—	
27	—	88⅞	86	—	107¼	—	—	—	—	—	—	
28	—	88⅞	86	—	106¾	—	—	—	—	—	—	
30	—	88⅞	86¾					51½	77½			
4	—	89¼	86⅞	—	106⅞	—	—	—	—	—	—	
D. 5	251	89⅞	86⅞	—	107⅛	—	—	—	—	—	—	

Prices of the FRENCH FUNDS From Oct. 20, to Nov. 18.

1813 Dec	5 per Cent. consols fr.	c.	Bank Actions. fr.	c.
18	64		1500	—
21	65		1520	—
24	63		1490	—
26	63		1485	—
29	66	—	1445	—
Jan.				
2	66	80	1490	—
5	67	75	1500	—
8	67	50	1505	—
11	67	10	1485	—
13	67	70	1470	—
18	68	30	1520	—
20	67	85	1495	—

AMERICAN FUNDS.

	IN LONDON. Dec. 24.	Jan. 1. 5.	8.	AT NEW YORK. Nov. 23.		Dec .11
7 per Cent...........	—	—	—	—	105	105
Bank Shares	24 10	24 10	24	—	110	115
Louisiana	—	—	—	par	par	par
Old 6 per Cent.	—	—	—	par	par	par
New 6 per Cent.......	102	102	102	102	103½	100

By J. M. Richardson, 23, Cornhill.

THE

LITERARY PANORAMA,

AND

𝔑ational 𝔑egister:

For *MARCH*, 1819.

NATIONAL AND PARLIAMENTARY NOTICES,

(𝔅ritish and 𝔉oreign,)

PROSPECTIVE AND RETROSPECTIVE.

PRESENT STATE OF CHILI.

ABSTRACT

OF

Mr. BLAND'S REPORT

ON THE PRESENT STATE OF THE

PROVINCE OF CHILI,

IN SOUTH AMERICA;

Laid before the Congress of North America, by order of the President, November, 1818.

WHEN we gave in our last Number the Report of Mr. Graham, addressed to the President of the United States of North America, and by him laid before the Congress, we observed, that it was one of three, which had been procured by the American Government, for the purpose of obtaining correct and official information. It was a wise step in the President to send out this Mission; and the Agents selected, appear to have executed the charge entrusted to them, with great fidelity and diligence.

Arrived at Buenos-Ayres, it was evident that a more extensive excursion than was possible by the River Plate, or limited to the provinces adjoining, was not only desirable, but was in fact necessary. For, although

that city, as a metropolis, with its new Government, might be for the moment in a prosperous condition, yet the resources requisite to support that prosperity, must, no doubt, be drawn from extensive intercourse with the interior; and from distant provinces. Among these, Chili presented itself, with prominent importance. The disposition of Chili, then, was to be ascertained; and for this purpose one of the American Commissioners, was deputed to the revolutionary rulers, who then held the reins of Governmental power.

The entire Report of this gentleman, Mr Bland, has not been published; and indeed it is so long, that our pages must needs be content with an abstract. That service has been performed for us by an American pen; and we present it in the form in which it has reached our hands. We give it somewhat out of its proper order, because there is absolutely nothing known concerning Chili, that is worthy of confidence; and because we hazarded a slight speculation on the duration of the power and influence of Buenos-Ayres over Chili, with which this report is in unison. We shall now endeavour to authenticate our observations, by adducing a few facts, the consequences of which are obvious.

Where Nature has interposed geographical boundaries to countries, and has marked those countries by distinct and permanent characters, though human power may incidentally violate the limits, and extend itself beyond them, in spite of Nature, yet the violation will not be of long continuance. Where vast oceans, trackless deserts, or impassible mountains, interpose a barrier, they will continue to perform their office, though, occasionally, they may be overcome. The adventurous and the energetic may encounter their difficulties successfully; but, the bulk of mankind are neither adventurous nor energetic; and if such be the disposition of a certain generation, their successors are sure to manifest other qualities, and to become quiescent and stationary.

Mr. Bland travelled from Buenos-Ayres to Mendoza, a distance of about 900 miles, by the usual road. This station is on the eastern side of the Andes; but, the Andes, themselves, are shut up by severe frost, during four months of the year; and are at all times difficult to pass. The mules which are used in this passage, when experienced in it, are tolerably safe; and the same may be said of the guides; but, if either the one or the other be *new*, or unaccustomed to the precipices, and chasms, which are of tremendous height and depth, the danger is absolutely terrific. From Buenos-Ayres to Mendoza, is a continued plain, of easy ascent; from Mendoza to St. Jago de Chili, is little other than a continued chain of mountains and valleys, of all dimensions, and forms.

It is not without reason, then, that Mr. Bland agrees with us, in supposing, that the connexion between the two countries, or rather the power and influence of Buenos-Ayres over Chili, will not be lasting. And if this actuating political principle be not lasting, the commercial connexion will certainly follow its fate. A passage shut up for four months in the year, a passage at all times extremely difficult, and so

constructed by nature, as to be defended by a handful of troops, which may bid defiance to whole armies, commits to its possessors a controuling power, that no supposeable authority will be able to overcome. Mr. Bland thinks this connexion is at present to the disadvantage of the Chilians; on this we give no opinion.

The estimate of the commerce of the country, as to imports, furnished by this gentleman, agrees with what we have stated: he reports the whole at about four millions of dollars, of which two millions were from England. And, indeed, it must be evident, that while the seas are open, our countrymen can offer infinitely the best, the most valuable, and the most profitable assortments of goods. The passage round Cape Horn is now so greatly familiarized to our intrepid mariners, that we no longer shudder at the tempests and dangers which formerly distinguished our perusal of Lord Anson's Voyage. We have now, also, possession of the Cape of Good Hope, which in time, may afford facilities, by way of *depôt*, at least, not to be thought contemptible, by those who know how to turn them to advantage.

While the exports are wheat, flour, cordage, tallow and beef, the trade of this country with North America, is not likely to increase very greatly. These are commodities which America herself furnishes; and the principle of barter, or interchange, does not seem to be very applicable to such commerce. The gold of this country is washed out of the earth, in the valley of Quillota, which for several feet in depth, is intermixed with this metal; which is found in great purity. How far the supply might be increased, is at present uncertain: but considering the premium borne by gold in Europe, it may become of consequence to the province. The silver mines are considered as being very rich: and the Chilians take care to report their belief that the mines of Potosi, in Peru, are exhausted.

The most extraordinary particular of the whole, is, that this same valley of

Quillota is abundantly productive of corn, hemp, and cordage, of the finest qualities; which are generally transported on mules to Valparaiso, from whence it is distant about thirty miles. Fruit trees, of every description, flourish also in this valley; and they derive much of their fertility and excellence from the practice of irrigation; trenches being cut to every tree (or, the trees being planted in trenches) which are kept constantly moist, throughout the dry season. This advantage gives them an incontestible superiority. The valley of Quillota is situated between St. Jago and the town of Valparaiso, which is the general port to the whole province. It is rendered the more striking in point of appearance, by the contrast of the sterile mountains around it.

But, the province of Chili has a natural connexion with another province, that in spite of apparent obstacles will long continue to operate. Peru is destitute of those articles, corn, hemp, and cordage, in which Chili abounds: insomuch, that during certain periods of enmity, between the two provinces, corn was sold in Peru at twelve or fourteen dollars the (English) bushel. While, on the other hand, Chili is equally destitute of sugar, coffee, and the thousand *et ceteras*, which contribute to the enjoyments of social life: Six or seven shillings was at that time no unusual price for a pound of sugar, or of coffee. While the same authority was paramount over both provinces, this intercourse was mutually beneficial; and, should they once more combine their respective interests, this commerce will resume its former activity, and become the source of equal gratification to both.

Very different are the sentiments which breathe in Mr. Bland's Report, on the disposition of Chili. He describes an intervening desert of upwards of 300 miles extent, as affording a protection to the Chilians from any invasion by land from Peru;—and doubtless, this same desert affords a protection to the Peruvians from any invasion by land from 'Chili.——" A superior

naval force, says Mr. B., is indispensable to enable the Chilians to invade Peru; for the desert of Attacama prevents them from marching thither by land." Such are the attendants on revolutionary movements! Nothing but marchings, and invasions. It is not enough that Buenos-Ayres should change its masters, but Chili, also, shall be assisted with two thousand negroes and other forces, to establish new authorities: nor is it enough that Chili shall establish new authorities, Peru, also, must be invaded. At the present moment, Peru, it is presumed, affords the greatest proportion of resources in shipping and sailors:—the disposition of the people is another question.

But, before Peru be invaded, it should seem to be the policy of Chili to see that all is well at home. Mr. B. informs us, that taking the population of Chili at 1,200,000, one third of this population is adverse to " the Patriots," and still retains sentiments of loyalty. It would not, therefore, be very safe for any considerable force to be detached against Peru, or any where else out of the country, lest this party should take the advantage, and obtain the superiority.——

For, it will hardly be thought that the new authorities of Chili, should under-estimate the strength of their adherents; and we should not be at all surprized to learn, that the true proportion of opinions was much nearer to numerical equality.

A much more pressing danger, to Chili, is that arising from the parties which have alternately risen to power and sunk to bondage, in the short space of a few revolving years. These rival parties, the Carreras, on the one side, and the Lorrains, (called also, we believe, the Roses) on the other, not only suffered their animosities to rise to counteraction and broils, but went so far as to cut each other to pieces in set battles: insomuch that they lost sight of their common enemy, the Spanish Royalists, and suffered their adversaries to invade their country,

before the unnatural delirium had subsided. There are those who go so far
as to affirm, that at the Battle of Ran-
cagua, alluded to by Mr. Bland, the
young Carreras, at the head of his
regiment, had not sufficient compunc-
tion at the destruction of his rivals by
the Spanish bayonet, (though it cost
the loss of the battle) to step forward
to their relief from the ruin that surrounded them. If this single fact be
truly stated, it speaks more than
volumes for the unhappy fate of Chili,
which ever be the party that holds the
reins of Government. It agrees with
Mr. Bland's observation, that the Lor-
rains, when in power, had sacrificed
two of the most distinguished of the
Carreras, under judicial forms, to gratify the vengeance of the reigning
faction.

The amount of the population is
certainly stated at the highest in the
official communication of the government of Chili to Mr. Bland. The
amount of the army, if well disposed,
well appointed, and well disciplined
fighting men, are referred to, is taken
much beyond the highest, even at the
medium intended to be adopted. The
Spanish force by which the Chilians
were overcome, answered but little to
our ideas of regular troops; and we
have no reason to conclude that their
opponents had any advantage over
them, in these respects. Nor does it
appear that the resources of the Chilians have since been so ample, as to
place the question of their power to
make better provision for their army,
beyond all doubt, or suspicion.

On the contrary, the poverty of the
Government is acknowledged : it has
prompted the rulers to lay hands on
the property of the Church : that this
property was enormous, we have reason
to believe; nor are reasons wanting to
persuade us, that it was but too often
diverted from purposes professedly
pious, to the promotion of dissoluteness
and gross immoralities. A late
English traveller, who visited both
Lima and St. Jago, affirms that the
most respectable authority (to which he
might have added, public report) describes the monks and nuns of the
several religious houses, as living the
most profligate and licentious lives
possible. Our readers have seen
(COMP. LIT. PAN. 'N. S. Vol. V. p.
556.) an instance of similar imputations
on the Clergy of Brazil, in the travels
of M. Koster; whose work affords
others to the same purpose. Nor is
the language of Dr. Robertson too
harsh, when speaking of the priests in
these countries, he says, " the giddy,
the profligate, the avaricious, to whom
the rigid discipline of a convent is
intolerable, consider a mission to
America, as a relief from mortification
and bondage. There they soon obtain
some parochial charge; and by their
situation, far removed from the inspection of their monastic superiors, and
exempt by their character, from the
jurisdiction of the diocesan, they are
hardly subject to control. According
to the testimony of the most zealous
Catholics, many of the regular clergy
in the Spanish settlements, are not
only destitute of the virtues becoming
their profession, but regardless of that
external decorum and respect, for the
opinion of mankind, which preserve a
semblance of worth, where the reality
is wanting. Secure of impunity, some
regulars, in contempt of their vow of
poverty, engage openly in commerce,
and are so rapaciously eager in amassing
wealth, that they become the most
grievous oppressors of the Indians,
whom it was their duty to have protected. Others with no less flagrant
violation of their vow of chastity,
indulge with little disguise in the most
dissolute licentiousness."

Things are not mended, since the
days alluded to by Dr. Robertson;
and revolutionary times are, of all
others, the least adapted to efficient
improvement of morals, professional or
popular. We cannot wonder, that, according to Mr. Bland, neither monks
nor nuns, have been treated with much
ceremony ; but, we do not observe that
any better materials for building up
truly religious houses, are put in their
place.

If the happiness of a people be not promoted by change in their government, of what advantage is such a change? and how can public happiness be promoted, when morals are dissolute and religion is debased? We hinted, in our last, at the consideration due to these subjects; and whatever turn affairs may take, we should be glad to think that these humble observations had fallen into hands capable of realizing their spirit, and disposed to organize their intention.

We conclude these slight suggestions by hinting, that it cannot be supposed that Mr. O'Higgins would fail to put the best possible face on things under his government, when conversing with the agent of a foreign power, which it was evidently his interest, and beyond question his wish and endeavour to to conciliate. He would, naturally, do his utmost to maintain a respectable attitude.

Mr. Bland appears to have reported with sufficient fairness and impartiality. We have added a few additional particulars, derived from such sources of information as have reached our hands. Not to be mistaken, in some things, in reference to countries so distant, and so different from our own, is scarcely to be expected. And to form an opinion on such slender materials, is often more likely to mislead those who confide in it, than the frank acknowledgement of having hitherto formed no opinion at all. We do not perceive, in spite of the boastings of their agents, that the revolutionists are wonderfully strong; but, we perceive, clearly, and we presume, that others must perceive it, too, that the mother country is wonderfully weak; that her interests, if they are not to be entirely abandoned, require a support which can only be rendered at a prodigious, in fact, at an unprecedented expence.

That literature should obtain countenance amid the din of arms and national conflict, was hardly to be expected; yet [the power of literature in influencing and guiding opinion has been found, of late years, so great, that no practised politician will despise it. The press was introduced for the first time into Chili, at the commencement of the revolution; the birth of one, was the birth of the other. But, the press is not free: each party, when in power, published according to its heart's desire, and nothing but sentiments, or communications which suited its party purposes; other printing presses were not saleable articles; and the American speculators in the commodity missed their object. Books are of little value where readers are few: nevertheless, this introduction of the means of access to the human mind, will have its consequences; and hereafter Chili may become respectable as a seat of general literature.

Our readers will remark for themselves a variety of minor particulars, on which we cannot now dilate. They have their importance; and eventually may become of great political moment. We are at a loss to discover what interest the chief and long established families in this Spanish settlement, take in the actual state of things: nor can we draw auguries as to their permanence, while it is acknowledged that rival factions have so bitterly contended for the sovereignty. The faction now depressed, may possibly recover strength; and that now in authority, unless supported by the general voice, may find its sway flit away from before its eyes, like a phantom. We are, however, bound to make our acknowledgments to Mr. Bland, for his instructive Report, and to the gentleman who has favoured the public with the following able abridgment of it.

ABSTRACT

OF

Mr. Bland's Report concerning Chili.

Mr. Bland was, in pursuance of instructions from the President, left by his colleagues, Mr. Rodney, and Mr. Graham, at Buenos-Ayres; whence, on the 15th of April, 1818, he departed for Chili, and on the 20th of the same month arrived at Mendoza, on the eastern side of the Andes, having travelled, by the way of the post-road, a distance of about 900 miles. He left Mendoza on the 29th of April, and, crossing the Andes, reached Santiago de Chili on the 5th of May; the whole route being, perhaps, about 1,200 miles. At this latter place Mr. Bland presented himself to Don Antonio Jose Irisarri, Secretary of State, through whom he obtained an interview with Don Bernardo O'Higgins, the Supreme Director of. Chili. He was received with much cordiality by the Director, with whom he had, at different times, very interesting conversations, touching the present and future probable condition of Chili, and the friendly sentiments which the United States entertained towards that country.

In the several interviews which Mr. Bland had with the Supreme Director, he represented to him the good disposition which the Government of the United States cherished towards the independent authorities of Chili, and the cause in which they are engaged; the sympathy which the free citizens of North America felt for the sufferings of those who were contending for liberty and emancipation from the yoke of Old Spain in the southern part of the American continent; and portrayed to him the benefits to be derived from the establishment of the representative system, by the immediate formation of a Congress.

To these observations O'Higgins answered, that he was not insensible to the friendship of the United States; that it was his intention to institute a free government as soon as Chili was entirely freed of her enemies, and sufficiently tranquillized for the purpose; but that the present moment was inauspicious for the commencement of so great a work; that in times of public peril the presence of a Congress had been found ex tremely pernicious; that Mexico had been lost by a Congress; that the Congress of Venezuela once lost that country; and that Buenos-Ayres had been endangered by a Congress: lately, indeed, he admitted, the latter had learnt to act in more concert, and with greater propriety

The Supreme Director having intimated that it was expected the United States would recognize the independence of Chili, and that the Chilians would grant special favours in commerce to the nation (and it would be gratifying if the United States should be the nation) first making such recognition, Mr. Bland replied, that the single object of his mission was to make inquiry as to the true posture of affairs in Chili; that the United States would be thankful for any favours of the kind, but that they did not ask for them; that all they desired was to be put on a footing with other nations, and were willing to rely, as to any advantages in commerce and navigation, on the skill and industry of their merchants and seamen; that he had repaired to Santiago in order to procure, upon the spot, accurate knowledge of the country, of its institutions, and of its capacities in peace and war; that the Government of the United States only wished to see its way clearly, and would make no improper use of this information; and that any particulars communicated to him from authority might be considered as confidential, or otherwise, just as the Supreme Director might deem proper.

The Supreme Director, O'Higgins, admitted the propriety of authentic information, in order that the Government of the United States might act intelligently with regard to South American affairs, and told Mr. Bland that he would cause an official statement to be made out respecting the condition and resources of Chili, and placed in his hands for that purpose; which promise the Supreme Director complied with.

During the intercourse between Mr. Bland and O'Higgins, the former explained to the latter the motives which actuated the President in the seizure of Amelia Island, and in driving the banditti from Galveston; and told him, that the freebooters who had been forced from those places were not the only armed vessels whose officers and crews had interrupted the lawful commerce of the United States, for that some of the privateers cruising under regular Patriot commissions had committed depredations upon their trade; that the United States would, at all hazards, defend the fair traffic of her citizens; and that they would do so even against the Chilians, however painful it might be to crush in the germ a growing intimacy between the two people, and which promised to be in the sequel fruitful of benefits to them both.

O'Higgins did not even know where Amelia Island and Galveston were situated, until Mr. Bland explained the positions to him. He decidedly approved of the conduct of the President in driving off the pirates from thence, inasmuch as it tended to preserve the character of the Patriot cause from imputations of an injurious nature: he had heard of outrages .committed by private armed vessels sailing under some of the independent flags 'of South America; but that, whatever might have been the behaviour of the vessels acting under commissions from other states, no charge of the kind could justly be brought against the Chilians; that in fact, with the exception of some fishing-boats, it was not until very lately that the Government of Chili had any vessels of war under its control; and that he had taken great care, by giving proper instructions, and by placing suitable superintending officers on board, to prevent any departure from the rules of naval warfare prescribed by the law of nations.

In one of the conversations which took place, Mr. Bland told the Supreme Director, that when he was at Rio Janeiro (where, it will be recollected, the commissioners touched, on their way to Buenos-Ayres,) he had learnt through Mr. Sumter, the Minister of the United States, from the Spanish Minister resident there, that Great Britain had been induced to take an active part in favour of Old Spain, and had influenced the Allied Sovereigns of Europe to interpose for the adjustment of differences between her and her colonies; and that the plan of adjustment was to be something like that which had been formerly rejected by the Cortes, and might be found in a work that had been published in England, entitled, " An Outline of the Revolution in Spanish America."

At first O'Higgins did not believe in the truth of the information which Mr. Bland had received; he said that the British would hardly do so, as they wanted the commerce of Spanish America: but shortly after, meeting with him again, the Supreme Director said he was then convinced of it; for he had seen Capt. Shirriff, of the British frigate *Andromache*, in Santiago, who had told him that he had in his possession papers on the subject, with which he was going to Lima, in Peru. O'Higgins further remarked, that all attempts to reconcile the South Americans, short of the acknowledgment of their independence, would be fruitless; and that a return to allegiance under the government of Old Spain was wholly out of the question.

On the 9th July Mr. Bland, having received the statistical information which the Supreme Director had promised him, took leave of him and of the Secretary of State Irisarri. O'Higgins expressed his intention of writing a letter to the President; but whether he did so or not, Mr. Bland had not distinctly related.

On the 10th of July Mr. Bland left Santiago de Chili; on the 11th he arrived at Valparaiso; and on the 15th of July he sailed thence in the brig *America*, Captain Daniel Rea, and arrived, by the way of Cape Horn, at Philadelphia, on the 29th of October, 1818.

The narrative of Mr. Bland's communications with the Supreme Director forms but a small portion of his Report concerning Chili. He furnishes in addition a very copious description of that region of our hemisphere, in which he now and then lets his fancy get the better of his judgment. But, from the mass of pages which he has written, circumstances of a highly interesting complexion may be selected.

From Mr. Bland's account, it would seem that Chili is a country (excluding the Magellanic tract, or New Chili) of about 1,000 miles in extent on the sea coast; that it has many excellent ports convenient for foreign trade; that it is a country fruitful in grain, wine, and oil, and productive in gold, silver, copper, and tin; that it is destined to be the granary of that part of the world; that its population is about 1,200,000 souls; that

800,000 of these are under the domination of the Patriots, the remainder being under the jurisdiction of the Royalists; that there are about 50,000 Indian slaves in all Chili, and but very few slaves of the African race. All the mechanical arts and agriculture are in a rude state, and the roads and pathways in a neglected condition. The principal articles of export are the metals already mentioned, together with wheat, flour, hemp, cordage, hides, tallow, jerked beef, vecuna, guanaca, chinchilla skins, figs, raisins, &c. Of 4,000,000 of dollars' worth of imports, in the course of last year, two millions in value were from England, one from the United States, and one from Buenos-Ayres. The articles furnished from the United States are chiefly tobacco, windsor chairs, saddlery and furniture. Of European commodities, Mr. Bland thinks the manufactures of France and Germany are preferred. The stocks of cattle are numerous and fine; the horses are active, spirited, serviceable, and cheap; but the mules are the common beasts of burden. The soil and climate of Chili are different in different places: from the Straits of Chacao to the river Biobio it is woody, fertile, and salubrious, and is inhabited by the Araucanians, or natives; from the Biobio to the river Maule, the country is the same, but the population is Spanish; from the Maule to the Aconcagua, still fertile, but no forests: from the valley of Aconcagua the mine country presents itself, which is less fruitful on the surface: after the mine country, the dreary desert of Atacama, upwards of 300 miles extent, affords a protection to the Chilians from any invasion by land from Peru. From the Straits of Chacao to the river Maule, it rains at any season; at Santiago di Chili there is no rain for seven months in the year; and beyond Copiapo rains are hardly known. Mr. Bland divides the country into two regions—the one variable and humid, and the other invariable and dry. Fuel, in some parts, is scarce; but it is said there is plenty of pit-coal on the banks of the Biobio, near Conception. The Archipelago of Ancud, or Chiloe, contains 47 islands; it is a considerable fishery, and will be a nursery for seamen. There are only three carriage roads in all Chili. The fertile part of the soil is situated in valleys, surrounded for the most part by hills and mountains; and the inhabitants of these valleys communicate with each other principally by mule paths. Mr. Bland describes the people generally as being " mild, amiable, brave, and uninformed." Santiago is the capital, and contains about 40,000 souls. The Royalists have possession of Penco, and a considerable district around Conception, which is their strong hold; they retain, also, Valdivia and Chiloe. The patriot army, at a medium, (for Mr. Irisarri and Mr. Bland differ on this point) is about 6,000 strong, 2,000 of which are negroes from Buenos-Ayres; there are no Chilian officers in it, however, above the rank of Captain, with the exception of O'Higgins, who is a Brigadier under San Martin, and Colonel Raymon Freyere. The navy consists of but three or four indifferent vessels, but would be increased by the addition of two new ships of war, to be called *San Martin* and *Chacabuco*, built at New York, and for which purpose Messrs. Aguirre and Gomez were, a considerable time since, sent to the United States from Buenos-Ayres with money. A superior naval force is indispensable to enable the Chilians to invade Peru, for the desert of Atacama prevents them from marching thither by land. The Chilians have no seamen of their own.

The revenue of the Government in Chili is derived from duties on imports and exports; from an excise which is laid upon almost every thing that is sold; from a direct tax, the mines, papal bulls, printed indulgences for the living and, the dead, a crusade tax, tithes, forfeited estates of the Jesuits, voluntary contributions, and from confiscated estates of the enemies of the Patriot cause. The officers of the customs and the judges of the commercial courts receive no regular salaries, and a duty is imposed on merchandise to compensate them; in addition, traders quicken their exertions by presents or bribes. There are 10,000 monks and nuns in the country. The church holds one-third of the landed property of the state. The church lands are farmed out to tenants, who let them again to under tenants, and these last work them with slaves: thus three sets of idlers are supported upon the product of the industry of the labouring class. In addition to their landed estates, the religious institutions have what are called their *censos*, or money lent out at an interest of five per cent per annum, to the amount of ten millions of dollars. Besides their share of the tithes, which the state still permits them to draw, the clergy have the annats, or first fruits, which yield to each curate between two and three hundred dollars per annum.

The government of Chili, it seems, is needy, and has made some progress towards laying hands on the enormous property of the priests. Indeed neither monks nor nuns, according to Mr. Bland, are treated with much ceremony; some of the former have been turned out of their dwelling-places, which have been occupied for military purposes, and some of them have been tried for treasonable practices.

The most immediately interesting part of the Report is that which gives the history of the Chilian Revolution, and the change of parties among the Patriots. There have, it appears, been two powerful factions in that country of the revolutionists themselves. At the head of one were the Carreras; the Larrains formed the other, with O'Higgins at their head. At the beginning of the contest for independence, the Carrera faction prevailed. It would seem, however, this

party did not manage affairs in a judicious manner; for at the battle of Rancagua, against the Royalists, fought on the 2d of October, 1814, the Patriots were entirely defeated, and fled over the Andes. They were rallied at Mendoza by San Martin, who identified himself with the Larrain faction; and, having obtained a reinforcement of 2,000 negroes from Buenos-Ayres, crossed the mountains, and, on the 12th February, 1816, fought the battle of Chacabuco, defeated the Royalists, and took their commander, Marco, prisoner. This may be called the second epoch of the revolution in Chili. The Carrera party was, of course, put down, and the Larrains, with O'Higgins as chief, confirmed themselves in power by the victory of Mapu, obtained on the 5th April, 1818. It is greatly to the dishonour of the Larrains that they seized this moment of success to put to death two of the most distinguished of the Carreras. They were sacrificed under judicial forms, and on the pretext of treason. Their execution was a foul and bloody murder, to gratify the vengeance of the reigning faction.

The closest intimacy subsists between the Governments of Chili and Buenos-Ayres. O'Higgins told Mr. Bland, that there was nothing which Buenos-Ayres could ask of Chili that would not be granted; and that Buenos-Ayres would act in like manner towards Chili. All the inhabitants of Buenos-Ayres are naturalized citizens of Chili. The Supreme Director, by way of characterizing the intimacy, said they were as two bodies actuated by one soul. Mr. Bland thinks, however, that this connexion is to the disadvantage of the Chilians, and conceives that it will not be lasting.

Under the faction of the Carreras, at the commencement of the revolution, the press, for the first time, was introduced into Chili. Before that period all books and papers, prior to their entrance into the country, were inspected and approved by the Holy Inquisition in Spain or at Lima. The name of the first paper was the *Aurora*. It was printed weekly, at a printing-office sent from New York, and managed by three citizens of the United States. It was edited by Camilia Henriquez, now of Buenos-Ayres. The opposite party also published a paper, which they called the *Aurora*. It was edited by Irisarri; but at this time there are four weekly papers issued at Santiago: and none are published any where else in Chili; their names are the *Ministerial Gazette*, which is the acknowledged paper of the Government, *El Argos*, *El Duende*, and *El Sol*. They are all printed at the same press, and edited by clerks and officers of the Government. Two other printing-presses had been carried there for sale, but they were not saleable articles. Newspapers and pamphlets are conveyed free of postage, and books are imported free of duty.

The reader may recollect that, after the battle of Maypu, the Viceroy of Peru was desirous of effecting an exchange of prisoners, and sent on board the United States' sloop of war *Ontario*, Captain Biddle, from Lima, an officer to Valparaiso and Santiago for the purpose. It turned out, however, on investigation, that the Royalists had a few or no Chilian prisoners; that those which they formerly had, having been confined in one of the islands of the Archipelago of Chiloe, were released by the Patriots after the battle of Chacabuco. The Patriots, on the contrary, had about 8,000 Royalist prisoners, and were willing they should be exchanged for any prisoners which the Royalists held belonging to Buenos-Ayres; but, owing to some contempt manifested in relation to the Patriot authorities, no cartel was agreed upon.

Incidentally speaking of Peru, Mr. Bland says, that one-third of the population of that country are whites of unmixed blood, and two-thirds are mulattoes and negroes; the latter, in general, as well informed as the whites.

Observations on Criminal Jurisprudence, and the Reformation of Criminals; with an Appendix, containing the latest Reports of the State Prisons or Penitentiaries of Philadelphia, New York, and Massachussetts; and other Documents. By William Roscoe, Esq. 8vo. 9s. Cadell and Davies, London, 1819.

THAT the Criminal Law of England is in a state that imperiously calls for revision, is a fact, which needs only to be mentioned, to be universally admitted. "Sanguinary statutes, operative only in deforming our jurisprudence, and investing judges with discretion never originally intended, but rendered necessary by a nugatory severity, cannot be suffered to remain standing amid the general stir of education and improvement. So many of our statutes have been made in particular and temporary exigencies, in moments of excited public feeling, and transient fits of legislation,—with so little regard to system or proportion, and little connexion between law and natural sentiment, that every motive of policy, justice, and decency," requires some change to be made in our criminal law, so far as it relates to capital punishments and to the mode in which it is administered. Some of the more grossly severe acts have been expunged from the statute book, through

the generous and persevering efforts of the late much-lamented Sir Samuel Romilly. Much, however, remains to be done; and Mr. Roscoe has, most seasonably, offered the valuable work to the consideration of the public, of which we hasten to offer our readers a brief analysis.

The first topic discussed by Mr. R. is, *the motives and ends of Punishment.* In this section he strongly and ably combats the notion that anger is not only allowable in criminal jurisprudence, but that attempts to extirpate it must be vain, and, if successful, would be injurious. He further contends, and with much force of argument, that it is only the calm exercise of reason, by removing the inducement, or correcting the disposition to crimes, or by taking a sincere interest in the welfare of the offender, and convincing him that the evils he experiences are the unavoidable consequences of his own misconduct, and are inflicted upon him for his own good,—that we can expect to produce any beneficial effect. Upon the practicability of this is founded the great plan of modern improvement, called *the penitentiary system,* the advantages of which are every day becoming more apparent; and which, when perfected by experience, cannot fail to produce the happiest and most important results on the moral character and condition of mankind.

In the sections " *on punishments by way of example,*" and " *on the prevention of crimes,*" our author shews the inadequacy of extreme severity, and urges various moral considerations; which, if duly considered, will not merely prevent the commission of crimes, but will greatly improve the condition of the country. The inefficacy of the existing laws, which inflict the *punishment of death* for various crimes as well as of those which impose *punishments of inferior degree,* are next considered, and illustrated by many authentic facts, drawn from the evidence laid before various committees of the House of Commons within the last two or three years.

The section, which discusses "*proposed improvements in Criminal Law,*" is little more than a statement of the difficulties experienced by Beccaria and other eminent writers who have treated on crimes and punishments; but the two following sections, on the *origin* and *present state of the Penitentiaries in America,* on the *Penitentiary system on the Continent of Europe, and also in this Country,* present a rich collection of most important facts. The

State of Pennsylvania had the distinguished honour of originating Penitentiaries in America: the success attending the Penitentiary at Philadelphia induced some benevolent individuals at New York to procure the enactment of a law in 1796 in that State for erecting a similar edifice.

"By this law, which has since received several amendments, all those crimes (excepting *treason* and *murder*, which continue capital) that were before punished with death, were punishable by imprisonment for life ; all offences above the degree of petty larceny, are punishable for the first offence by imprisonment, for a term not exceeding fourteen years, and for a second offence for life. Petty larcenies for a term not exceeding one year ; and persons guilty of a second offence, were to have their punishment augmented for a time not exceeding three years. All persons convicted might also be subjected to hard labour, or solitude, or both, at the discretion of the court. Forfeiture of goods and lands, except for treason, deodands, and corporal punishments, were wholly abolished.

"For the management of the prison, seven inspectors were appointed by the governor and council during pleasure No salaries were paid to them ; actuated by principles of benevolence, and a love of justice and humanity, they offered the voluntary contribution of their services. They sought no other recompense than those feelings which accompany the exertions of good men for the benefit of society. It was their duty to inquire into and inspect the general state of the prison ; to see that the keepers were attentive and faithful in the discharge of their several duties ; that cleanliness, decency, and order, were every where maintained ; that the prisoners were treated with justice and humanity ; to listen to their complaints and communications ; to admonish the bad, applaud the good, and encourage all to amendment and reformation ; and to give them such advice as might awake virtuous sensibility, and promote their moral and religious improvement."

"Under such directions, the Penitentiary at New York was as successful in its operation as that at Philadelphia ; and similar establishments, under the name of State prisons, have since been founded in *Massachusetts, Vermont, Connecticut, New Jersey, Maryland, Virginia,* and other places."

"For some time after their commencement, these establishments appear to have answered every purpose which their promoters had in view. Most of them were conducted by persons who undertook their management without the inducement of salaries, or any other interested motive, and under their direction they continued for a course of years to be productive of the most beneficial effects. There is, however, reason to apprehend, that as these institutions were, from various causes, deprived of this assistance, a relaxation of discipline took place ; and that as the terms of commitment began to expire, or the prisoners were discharged on pardon as reformed, the number of those recommitted *for new offences* began to increase. This circumstance, combining with the rapid increase of population in every part of the United States, occasioned such an influx of prisoners, that the buildings became inadequate to their reception, or at least to afford that accommodation which is indispensable to their utility.

" The mere want of sufficient accommodations for the prisoners is not *the only cause* of the present unfavourable state of the Penitentiaries in America. Perhaps a still more substantial one may be found in the injudicious practice of receiving a *second,* a *third,* and even a *fourth* time, into these institutions, such criminals as have already undergone a series of discipline, and have been discharged before the expiration of their sentence as persons effectually reformed.

"It is indeed impossible to conceive any proceeding more derogatory to the character, and destructive of the benefits of these institutions, than this repeated and inefficient attempt. By the reception of a criminal for a *second* offence, who has already been discharged *as reclaimed,* the establishment confesses its own inutility, and is no longer a school of reform, but a *receptacle and shelter for acknowledged guilt.* The prisoners confined under the expectation of being reclaimed, finding themselves intermixed with abandoned profligates, who have gone through the same process without effect, will despair of their own recovery, or be induced to relax in their efforts ; and finding that such criminals can again be received, will have no higher wish than to imitate their example. Nor can it be contended, that there is any motive to operate upon the mind of the discharged criminal, with sufficient force to deter him from the perpetration of future offences, while he contemplates, as the worst consequence, his recommitment to a place with which he is already well acquainted, and which, by long habit, he has learnt to render tolerable, if not agreeable.

"In fact, the readmission into a Penitentiary of any person who has been discharged as *reformed*, affixes a stigma on the character of the establishment itself; because such person may be presumed to have availed himself of the credit given him by the institution, to impose upon others, and in all probability to commit crimes, which otherwise it would not have been in his power to do; thereby not only throwing discredit on such institution, but making it, in a manner accessary to his offence.

We have not room for many particulars relative to the Penitentiary system, practised generally on the continent; but the following information relative to the prisons of Paris, which were visited in 1814 and 1815 by the Hon. G. Bennet, M. P. is too valuable not to be transplanted to our pages. This gentleman stated to the Committee of the House of Commons, that

"Though little advance has been made in France towards a penitentiary system, yet that the greatest pains seem every where to be taken to keep the prisoners in a state of active and useful labour; and that, under proper restrictions and regulations, there seems to be no trade that cannot with safety be received within the walls of a prison."— "That in the prison of *St. Pelagie*, where persons are confined for small offences, not *condamnés aux fers*, the imprisonment is for various terms, none above ten years" "There were three hundred and fifty criminals, varying from all ages, from ten years old to sixty. A general system of work is introduced; there was hardly any one idle; work is found by manufacturers in Paris, and a person is in each workshop, to watch over and instruct the workmen. The trades at work were —*stocking-makers, tailors, shoe-makers, button-makers, cardings, cotton-spinning and carding, carpenters, goldsmiths, and jewellers.* Of the earnings, one-third goes for their food; one-third forms a purse given to them at their discharge; and one-third every fourth day or week for pocket money. They work from eight in the morning, in winter, to eight at night, with two hours of interval for dinner and exercise, from eleven to one; and from five in the morning in summer to seven in the evening." "No irons used except for refractory prisoners. Ordinary punishment, solitary confinement in a cell for two or three days. No one allowed to be struck. The friends of the prisoners can visit them twice a week by an order from the police." The regulations seem upon the whole to be good; food sufficient; and a visiting magistrate daily goes round to hear all complaints.

In the *St. Lazare* there were eight hundred and eighty women under sentence. "The common crime was domestic theft, and the majority of the prisoners servants in Paris." "The system of correctional police seems to be good. In twenty years about twelve hundred have been discharged, out of whom about two hundred have again been confined; and many persons who have been there are now living rich and respectable at Paris. The prison is inspected daily. Mass is performed once a week, on Sundays. No prayers on week days. No religious or moral instruction whatever. A general system of labour prevails throughout the prison. From one hundred to one hundred and thirty in each work-room, under one inspector. *Needle-work, spinning, winding, shawl-making,* and *embroidery.* Their earnings are divided into three parts. One for the government, one for the purse to be given them on their discharge, which sometimes amounts to three or four hundred francs, and one payable to them every fifteen days. The directors of the house make their arrangements with the contractors for the work. It is done at a cheaper rate than by free-labour. The prisoners were well dressed in prison dresses; neat and comfortable. The fault of the establishment appeared to be in the numbers; a want of classification; and consequently the penitentiary system was not as effective as it ought to be.

"In the *Bicêtre*, six hundred and eighty-two persons of all descriptions were confined, four hundred of whom were at work in different trades. Some earned as high as thirty or forty sous a day. The earnings were divided in thirds as before mentioned. No irons used, but the prison was in general dirty and offensive.— The chief defects in these establishments, in many respects so creditable to the country, seem to be the want of separate sleeping rooms, and an inattention to cleanliness— circumstances of the most indispensable importance to the health and improvement of the prisoners, and to the success of any Penitentiary."

Of the Penitentiary at Milbank we deem it unnecessary to extract any particulars, as our former volumes have presented our readers with the more remarkable circumstances, at the times they occurred; but the account of the gaol at Liverpool is in many respects so interesting that we cannot withhold it from our readers. This gaol, Mr. Roscoe informs us, has been erected about thirty years.

"Mr. Howard saw it in its progress in the year 1787, and expressed his opinion, that " *with a view to security, health, reformation, and convenience, it would be one of the first borough gaols in the kingdom.*"

"It is enclosed with a stone wall, twenty-one feet high, and consists of six wings, all converging in a semicircle, towards the chapel and the governor's house.

"Of these wings, three only are at present occupied for the purposes of the borough. In these are confined prisoners for debt, sued by process in the Borough Court, persons fined under the Dock Police Acts, and such delinquents as the Borough magistrates think proper to commit.

"The other three wings are now let by the Corporation to the County, as a House of Correction; and, at present, contain 343 prisoners, of whom 84 are females; all of whom are now employed in various kinds of work, under a regulated system of labour, as directed by the magistrates, and carried into execution by Mr. Thomas Amos, the present governor. This plan commenced in June, 1817, since which it has been carried on with an increasing prospect of utility. The employments for the males are *weaving, winding cotton, coopers' work, tailors, shoe-makers, clog-makers,* &c. For some of these, new work-shops were requisite, which have been erected by the prisoners, as *bricklayers, joiners,* &c. The women are employed in *knitting, sewing, picking cotton,* &c. in making slops, or cloathing for seamen, and for exportation to the colonies. Their own cloathing (except woollens) is also manufactured in the house. Children are first instructed in spinning and winding, and are afterwards put to the looms or other kinds of labour.

"The criminal is allowed *one-fourth* of his earnings for his own use; half of this is paid him *weekly,* the other half is reserved till his discharge. Till this plan of a small *weekly* payment was adopted, an inducement was evidently wanting; but this produced a striking effect.

"A Chaplain is appointed, who performs the church service every Sunday, and reads prayers once in the week days.

"The occupation of this building by the county is, however, only of a temporary nature; a House of Correction or Penitentiary, upon a still larger scale, having been commenced, and being now in great forwardness, in the township of Kirkdale, within two miles of Liverpool. This building will, when finished, consist of two half segments of an ellipsis, placed at a considerable distance from each other, but united at the ends by ranges of building, one side of which will form the Sessions House for this part of the county; the other, the Governor's House and other accommodations. The Chapel will be placed in the centre. This building is so constructed, as to afford every convenience for the proper classification of offenders. There will be a separate cell for every criminal by night, and a work-shop where he will be employed, either alone or with others, according to the nature of his business, by day. The work-shops will be erected on the outside of the two elliptical segments, leaving a sufficient passage between. The building is placed near a healthy village, in an elevated situation, and will afford every accommodation for carrying the penitentiary system into full effect; and from the encouragement already given, and the constant attention paid by the county magistrates, seconded by the judicious, firm, and conciliating measures adopted by the governor, there is every reason to hope that when the opportunities of improvement and reformation shall be increased by the additional conveniences of the new building, this establishment will vie with any in the kingdom.

"In the mean time, an earnest and highly commendable attempt is now making, to combine with the habits of order and industry amongst the convicts at Liverpool, a regular plan of intellectual and moral instruction. For this purpose a number of ladies, of the Society of Friends, have associated together, and have undertaken to instruct these unfortunate women in useful occupations, and to superintend and direct their labours; thereby rendering what was considered as their punishment, the means of their reformation and future welfare. This idea was suggested by the success of the beneficent efforts of Mrs. Fry, in reclaiming the prisoners in Newgate. On her recent visit to Liverpool, she found many persons who, from similar motives, had followed her generous and enlightened example, and had constituted a committee, and applied to the magistrates for their encouragement and support. By her assistance and advice, the assent of the magistrates was obtained ; and a matron was appointed to carry into effect the directions of the committee The convicts entered into the plan not only with willingness, but with cheerfulness. They chose monitors from amongst themselves to regulate their proceedings. The inactivity and disorder incident to gaols,have been effectually banished ; and the whole now presents a scene of peaceful industry, where their labours are relieved by reading select portions of scripture, or by intervals of necessary refreshment and repose."

The last section, *on the discipline of a Penitentiary*, contains many important suggestions which do not admit of abridgement. The appendix comprises numerous reports concerning the state of Penitentiaries and Penitentiary discipline in various parts of the world, which are either quoted or referred to in the preceeding part of the work: From these we could with pleasure have made ample extracts, if our time and space would have permitted ; the accounts of the moral and religious reformation on board several of the Hulks, will prove highly gratifying to every virtuous and benevolent mind.

Mr. Roscoe's name will doubtless ensure to his work an extensive circulation. The enlarged, humane, and philosophic views, which he has taken of the various subjects treated by him, do equal honour to his head and his heart ; and we trust that his suggestions will meet with that attention they so eminently deserve, in the approaching parliamentary discussions relative to the present sanguinary complexion of our criminal laws

---

A Treatise on the Importance of extending the British Fisheries ; containing a description of the Iceland Fisheries, and of the Newfoundland Fishery and Colony ; together with remarks and propositions for the better supply of the Metropolis and the Interior, with cured and fresh Fish. By S. Phelps, 8vo. 6s. Simpkin and Marshall ; London, 1818.

The importance of the Fisheries, not only as a profitable source of commerce, but especially as a nursery for seamen, is now so fully admitted that we should consider it a waste of our readers time and patience were we to enter into a particular consideration of them. The situation of the British coasts, indeed, is the most advantageous for catching fish in the World. The Scottish Islands, particularly those to the north and west, lie most commodiously for carrying on the fishing trade to perfection ; and the various creeks, coasts, bays, rivers, and lakes of Scotland, are replenished with the greatest abundance of the finest fish. The unfortunate monarch. Charles I, was so sensible of the advantages to be derived from fisheries, that he began the experiment, together with a company of merchants ; but the civil war soon frustrated that project. Charles II. made a similar attempt ; but his pressing wants caused him to withdraw his money from the concern, which soon after fell to the ground. Since the Union with Scotland, every successful attempts have been made to retrieve the fisheries ; and those carried on by British Capital and industry in other parts of the world. have been protected by various acts of the legislature. Deeply convinced of the great value of the fisheries both in a commercial and also in a political point of view,. Mr. Phelps has offered in the volume, now under consideration, numerous important facts, all of which concur to shew the necessity of extending the British Fisheries.

The first place to which our attention is directed, is the island of Iceland ; the bays and rivers of which are full of fish, and in such abundance that the natives do not fish on the outward banks, where the greatest quantities of the finest fish are to be caught ; but confine themselves to the bays or fiords, where they catch an inferior kind of fish in small boats. The Icelandic Rivers, it appears, contain abundance of very fine salmon, and it is stated that *one single* river in Iceland will produce as much salmon as all the rivers of England and Scotland.

As the trade with Iceland is now open, and the British Government has granted a bounty of £3 per ton on the Iceland fishery, our author recommends the establishment of an *Iceland Fishing Company*, under the following peculiar advantages.

"1st, The supply of fish is inexhaustible, 2d. The fishing grounds round Iceland are at no greater distance from the shores of Scotland and Ireland than the south banks of Newfoundland are from St. John's where the fish is cured."

sence of carbonic acid, or to the admixture of muriat and sulphat of magnesia; and it rarely contains much of either.

"As a pretty strong proof of the efficacy of rock salt for curing fish and meat, I have known hundreds of tons crushed and sold as bay salt for that purpose, without any complaint; and had it been known to be rock salt, it would certainly not have been used. This salt had been made foul by dirt, to give it the colour and appearance of bay salt.

"The Dutch purchase large quantities of Cheshire salt, which they mix with the bay salt, and some prefer it thus mixed to the bay salt alone, which they say is so strong that it burns the dry salt fish; but the best practice is to use fine salt in the first operation of curing, and large-grained salt in the finishing and packing.

Mr. Phelps states that a *small* admixture of the nitrate of potash, or saltpetre, with common salt, will have the most efficacious effect in curing, corning, and preserving all kinds of fish.

"It will," says he, give the fish a colour, clearness, and flavour, not to be obtained by any other method, and it will preserve it much longer and better than the fish cured in the common way, which, after a while, turns yellow, black, and rancid; on the contrary, the longer fish cured in this way is reasonably kept, the better will be its flavour; the same as the ling, cured at the Scilly islands, which, at two and three years old, has the best flavour; but the common salt fish at two years old is good for very little.

"Care should be taken to mix the saltpetre regularly with the other salt, which would be best done in solution, and one pound of nitrat of potash to one hundred weight of salt would be quite sufficient. It would add greatly to the quality of the large fishery salt, made by slow evaporation, in Cheshire, if it were judiciously introduced in the process of making that salt."

As the fisheries cannot be carried on to a great extent, and with full success, without the fostering aid and protection of government, and without regulations similar to those adopted by the admiralty of Holland; Mr. Phelps is of opinion, that it would be highly beneficial to the success of our fisheries, if government would appoint commissioners and a board for that purpose. The ultimate returns of benefit to government and to the country would amply repay, and justly warrant, the expense of such an establishment.

We have not room to follow this truly patriotic writer through all his suggestions relative to the fisheries. The whole volume abounds with facts, somewhat desultory indeed in their arrangment, but so important in their results, that we cannot too earnestly recommend it to the attention of our legislators, as well as to all who take an interest in the real welfare of their country.

Narrative of a Residence in Algiers By Signor Pananti, with Notes and Illustrations, by Edward Blaquiere, Esq. R. N. 4to. £2 2s. Colburn, London, 1818.

EVERY thing relative to the piratical maritime States of Barbary has of late become peculiarly interesting. In the manners, government, and religion of the singular people who inhabit them, there has always been much to excite curiosity; and that curiosity has been increased since the severe and deserved castigation inflicted upon Algiers, by the gallant Lord Exmouth, in 1816. Few, however, of the various individuals, who have returned home from a miserable captivity among the savage inhabitants of the Barbary States, have presented to the public any well-written narrative of their sufferings.

Signor Pananti, however, forms an exception to the generality of liberated captives, and in the volume now under consideration he has produced a deeply interesting and well written work; and has had the rare felicity of falling into the hands of an able and intelligent translator. After residing some time in England, where he had taken refuge during the revolutionary storm, which a very few years since overwhelmed his country, he was, in an evil hour, prevailed upon by some pretended friends to quit his hospitable asylum; and on his return to Italy, in a Sicilian vessel, he was captured by a fleet of Algerine corsairs. This heart-rending catastrophe, and the treatment he received from his ferocious captors, are thus powerfully described:

" No sooner (says he) was the infidel flag descried, than all was terror and dismay on board the Sicilian. I know not what chilling hand oppresses the Christian heart, on the appearance of Barbary corsairs: like the head of Medusa, it seemed to petrify every person on board. It was now that, as in all great disasters, instead of mutual support and encouragement, a sentiment of hatred is instantly generated; the fire of discord bursts forth amongst the companions of misfortune, and intestine war is kindled on public desolation. One of our men, who had been in slavery at Sallee, and who preserved the sad remembrance, inspired with a feeling of desperation, rushed up to the Captain, and would have certainly plunged a stiletto in his heart, had not myself and the passengers promptly interfered. Another, still more infuriated, seized a fire-brand, and was, by absolute force alone, prevented from applying it to the powder-magazine; some were for destroying themselves on board, others proposed jumping into the sea, and thus defeating the triumph of their enemies. This state of suffering and despair having subsided, it was shortly succeeded by a deep and mournful silence; after which the sailors were observed to descend, one by one, into the hold, there to await the event. As to us passengers, we remained on deck, deeply meditating on, and watching our approaching ruin.

" The shouts of the barbarians are heard close to us. They appear on deck in swarms, with haggard looks and naked scimetars, prepared for boarding; this is preceded by a gun, the sound of which was like the harbinger of death to the trembling captives, all of whom expected to be instantly sunk; it was the signal for a good prize. A second gun announced the capture, and immediately after they sprung aboard in great numbers. Their first movements were confined to a menacing display of their bright sabres and attaghans, with an order for us to make no resistance, and surrender; which it was hardly necessary to repeat: we had only to obey; and this ceremony being ended, our new visitors assumed a less austere tone, crying out in their *lingua Franca,* ' *No pauro !* *No pauro?*' (don't be afraid !) After this, rum was called for, then the keys of our trunks; when, dividing our party into two divisions, one was ordered into the pirate's boat, and conveyed into the admiral's frigate, while the others remained behind, under the care of several Moors, who had taken charge of the vessel. I was amongst the number of those transferred, and, in putting off from the brig, joined my companions in a speechless adieu of those we left behind.

" On gaining the frigate, we had no sooner got upon deck, than the barbarians uttered a cry of victory, usual when any captures are made. A savage joy seemed to play on their cadaverous aspects. A passage being opened for us between the armed Turks and Moorish sailors, we were conducted into the presence of the grand *Rais,* supreme commander of the Algerine squadron. He was seated between the captains of the five other frigates, who had assembled in close council to deliberate on the measures necessary to be taken with us, and to combine future operations. We were interrogated in brief and haughty terms, but neither insult nor rudeness was offered to any one of the party. The grand *Rais* very *civilly* asked us for our money, watches, rings, and every other article of value we had about our persons; in order, as he obligingly observed, to save them from the rapacity of the people of the Black Sea, who formed a considerable part of his crew; and who he candidly said were all *ladri.* He then deposited our respective property in a small box, faithfully assuring us that all should be returned on our leaving the vessel. During the distribution in the box, he repeated, alternately looking at the captives, ' *questo per ti*;' (this is for you,) ' *questi altro per ti* ;' but perhaps in his heart, ' and all this is for me !' we were then ordered to retire; and, placed upon a mat in the Rais's outer cabin, began to reflect on our new situation. When supper was served, it consisted of a black-looking paste, in an immense pan, which being placed on the deck, was immediately surrounded by a host of hungry Moors and negroes, indiscriminately mixed together, and making common cause for the laudable purpose of emptying the platter; which, if ever so well inclined to partake of, was a forlorn hope to us afflicted and over-ceremonious visitors; who, at this patriarchal repast, might with propriety be com-of fish, and in giving instruction how and and where to lay their nets.

"3dly. The Dutch kept the same fishermen employed the whole year round, in different fisheries and on different stations; for herrings are not found at the same time off the north of Iceland, the coasts of Scotland, and at Yarmouth, but succeed each other. The same with other fish according to their seasons.

"It appears, also, that another great cause of the superior success and extent of their fisheries was, that they fished in large companies or fleets, and made a kind of joint stock concern of their captures. For instance, off Iceland, there would be seldom less than 1000 to 1200 vessels fishing at the same stations; each shared alike, and on their return home they had merchants ready to contract for forty or fifty cargoes together to ship for foreign markets; whereas it is difficult to find a market for a single cargo, or a purchaser who would enter upon such an enterprize.

"Supposing a single vessel to be sent out to Iceland, and to return with a full cargo of fish;—what is the owner to do with the fish when he has got it? He has no connexion in the trade; and instead of receiving the value of his cargo, and returning again to the same employment, he must go to a foreign market, where he is also a stranger, and a new trader, and where he must sell his fish at any price that is offered, consequently he is no better off abroad than at home. This shows the importance of fishing companies and fishing stations, which still admit of ramifications, that would give occupation and support to numberless individuals of different descriptions. What makes the value of our oyster fisheries, but being carried on by extensive companies?

"The establishment of an Iceland fishing company is the more to be recommended, as its object is not to obtain a monopoly, but to extend the British fisheries generally, and thereby give regular employment to multitudes of the lower classes of the community (particularly seamen out of employ) and also to furnish a more abundant supply of a very desirable article of food; which can only be effected by the joint exertions and support of persons of high consideration and distinction. The efforts

of single individuals would be inadequate and unavailing; and unless prompt and powerful means are adopted, this trade, so natural and advantageous to the British interest, will again fall exclusively into the hands of the Dutch, or be alienated to the Norwegians.

"Some people may remark that our fisheries are already too extensive, and allege as a proof the present distressed state of our colony and fishery at Newfoundland; but this is by no means a proof. The local disadvantages, distance, and expence of our Newfoundland fishery operate against that fishery; but the demand for fish will always exceed the supply to be obtained, if it can be brought to market at a cheap rate, and of a good quality."

Mr. Phelps has given an interesting account of the introduction of the British trade with Iceland, for which we must refer our readers to his volume. There is, however, so much weight in his observations on the impolicy of the existing duties on salt, as tending to impede the progress of the fisheries, that we are tempted to extract some of his remarks.

"The greatest obstacle, which can possibly be named to impede or annoy the fishing trade, is certainly the duty on salt: for though it may be obtained duty free for that purpose, yet the waiting for permits and the attendance of excise officers; the danger of transport, the fear of mistakes, and of incurring heavy penalties, are such tremendous considerations, that few are bold enough to run such risks; and numberless cargoes of fish are not taken and cured in consequence.

"By having proper fishing stations this evil might in some measure be avoided; but it is a pity there should be any impediment to an object of such national and individual importance.

"Sir Thomas Bernard seems to have entered into a full examination of this subject, and, in recommending a commutation for the salt duties, he says, "The commutation should be so calculated as not to subject the individual to more than what he is now charged under the existing salt duties: for example, if a householder's in salt be at present thirty

be an advantage to him to pay only twenty shillings a-year in lieu of it;" and he endeavours to establish the fact, "that every family upon an average pays at least thirty shillings annually for salt." If this statement of Sir T. Bernard be correct, twenty-nine shillings out of the thirty ought to go to government for duties; and if this be the case, the revenue must, some way or other, be defrauded in this article to an immense extent, for if twenty shillings *salt tax* were laid on every taxable householder, in lieu of the duties on salt, government would be gainers and the householders also; and here would immediately be *a commutation for the salt duties;* and some additional amount could also be laid on the great consumers of salt, in cases where it would not oppress them.

"The cottager and the fishermen would then be free indeed, and none would be sufferers but a few poor excise officers, who may be pensioned, and permitted to retire upon half-pay, or become fish curers, or other useful members of the community.

"The bay salt is made in low situations, near the banks of the sea, from whence the salt water is let into long reservoirs or canals, the same as at the salt works at Lymington and other places, and the process is carried on nearly the same, with this only difference, that the salt water to make bay salt is entirely evaporated by the sun, and at Lymington, when the salt water is evaporated to a certain degree of concentration, it is conducted to the salt pans, where the process is finished by boiling.

"In this process of boiling, the bittern salts, or sulphats and muriats of magnesia and lime, which are contained in sea water, fall first to the bottom of the pans, or remain in the mother waters, and the salt which is taken up by the ladles is nearly pure and white sea or culinary salt; but, by the hasty boiling down of the brine, it has not time to form regular and large crystals.

"The newprocess in Cheshire for making large salt for the fisheries is, to evaporate the brine by a very slow heat, in very large pans, by which more regular and larger crystals are obtained.

"The finishing process of making baysalt, when the brine or salt water is evaporated

in the pits, by the heat of the sun, to a sufficient consistence, though not dry, is, to shovel into large heaps, in a pyramidical or conical form, on the dry land, on the banks of the canals or pits; and there, by repose, it regularly grains or crystallizes, and the deliquescent salts and moisture drain from it; and, although muriat of soda does not appear to contain carbonic acid, yet the presence of that acid seems necessary to its crystallization, as is the case with all neutral salts; and this is the only distinction there can possibly be between the quality of bay salt and the common salt made in England.

"I conceive, therefore, that the *rock salt* of Cheshire is as good, in every respect, for the purpose of curing fish of all kinds, as the bay, or foreign salt; but if, by experience, it should be found otherwise, it can only arise from the crystals being broken by crushing the rock salt; by which some part falls to powder, and some is large and unequal; and the fine part, when employed in curing, will sooner dissolve, and is termed weaker than the large salt.

"Salt, made by a strong heat, or by being fused, is more deliquescent, and does not decrepitate in the fire like large-grained or bay salt; which shows the disengagement of an elastic fluid, or carbonic acid.

"If large-grained salt, made after the new process, were exposed to the air, as soon as taken from the pans, in pyramids or cones, the same as the bay salt, I should conceive it would be even superior to bay salt, which naturally contains a great deal of foul and extraneous matter; but the regulations of the excise laws prohibit this method.

"The Cheshire salt is some of the purest native or crude salt in the world. The brine and rock salt of Cheshire do not contain the sulphat or muriat of magnesia in a degree like sea water; nor sulphat of lime, like most salt gems or rock salt. In fine, if it be admitted that the purer salt is, the better it is for curing or preserving fish or meat, no salt in the world can be better than the Cheshire is, when properly made. If, on the contrary, bay salt, or sea salt, should still be found preferable to Cheshire salt, it must be owing either to the per-sence of carbonic acid, or to the admixture of muriat and sulphat of magnesia; and it rarely contains much of either.

"As a pretty strong proof of the efficacy of rock salt for curing fish and meat, I have known hundreds of tons crushed and sold as bay salt for that purpose, without any complaint; and had it been known to be rock salt, it would certainly not have been used. This salt had been made foul by dirt, to give it the colour and appearance of bay salt.

"The Dutch purchase large quantities of Cheshire salt, which they mix with the bay salt, and some prefer it thus mixed to the bay salt alone, which they say is so strong that it burns the dry salt fish; but the best practice is to use fine salt in the first operation of curing, and large-grained salt in the finishing and packing.

Mr. Phelps states that a *small* admixture of the nitrate of potash, or saltpetre, with common salt, will have the most efficacious effect in curing, corning, and preserving all kinds of fish.

"It will," says he, give the fish a colour, clearness, and flavour, not to be obtained by any other method, and it will preserve it much longer and better than the fish cured in the common way, which, after a while, turns yellow, black, and rancid; on the contrary, the longer fish cured in this way is reasonably kept, the better will be its flavour; the same as the ling, cured at the Scilly islands, which, at two and three years old, has the best flavour; but the common salt fish at two years old is good for very little.

"Care should be taken to mix the salt-petre regularly with the other salt, which would be best done in solution, and one pound of nitrat of potash to one hundred weight of salt would be quite sufficient. It would add greatly to the quality of the large fishery salt, made by slow evaporation, in Cheshire, if it were judiciously introduced in the process of making that salt."

As the fisheries cannot be carried on to a great extent, and with full success, without the fostering aid and protection of government, and without regulations similar to those adopted by the admiralty of Holland; Mr. Phelps is of opinion, that it would be highly beneficial to the success of our fisheries, if government would appoint commissioners and a board for that purpose. The ultimate returns of benefit to government and to the country would amply repay, and justly warrant, the expense of such an establishment.

We have not room to follow this truly patriotic writer through all his suggestions relative to the fisheries. The whole volume abounds with facts, somewhat desultory indeed in their arrangement, but so important in their results, that we cannot too earnestly recommend it to the attention of our legislators, as well as to all who take an interest in the real welfare of their country.

Narrative of a Residence in Algiers By Signor Pananti, with Notes and Illustrations, by Edward Blaqniere, Esq. R. N. 4to. £2 2s. Colburn, London, 1818.

EVERY thing relative to the piratical maritime States of Barbary has of late become peculiarly interesting. In the manners, government, and religion of the singular people who inhabit them, there has always been much to excite curiosity; and that curiosity has been increased since the severe and deserved castigation inflicted upon Algiers, by the gallant Lord Exmouth, in 1816. Few, however, of the various individuals, who have returned home from a miserable captivity among the savage inhabitants of the Barbary States, have presented to the public any well-written narrative of their sufferings.

Signor Pananti, however, forms an exception to the generality of liberated captives, and in the volume now under consideration he has produced a deeply interesting and well written work; and has had the rare felicity of falling into the hands of an able and intelligent translator. After residing some time in England, where he had taken refuge during the revolutionary storm, which a very few years since overwhelmed his country, he was, in an evil hour, prevailed upon by some pretended friends to quit his hospitable asylum; and on his return to Italy, in a Sicilian vessel; he was captured by a fleet of Algerine corsairs. This heart-rending catastrophe, and the treatment he received from his ferocious captors, are thus powerfully, described:

"No sooner (says he) was the infidel flag descried, than all was terror and dismay on board the Sicilian. I know not what chilling hand oppresses the Christian heart, on the appearance of Barbary corsairs: like the head of Medusa, it seemed to petrify every person on board. It was now that, as in all great disasters, instead of mutual support and encouragement, a sentiment of hatred is instantly generated; the fire of discord bursts forth amongst the companions of misfortune, and intestine war is kindled on public desolation. One of our men, who had been in slavery at Sallee, and who preserved the sad remembrance, inspired with a feeling of desperation, rushed up to the Captain, and would have certainly plunged a stiletto in his heart, had not myself and the passengers promptly interfered. Another, still more infuriated, seized a fire-brand, and was, by absolute force alone, prevented from applying it to the powder-magazine; some were for destroying themselves on board, others proposed jumping into the sea, and thus defeating the triumph of their enemies. This state of suffering and despair having subsided, it was shortly succeeded by a deep and mournful silence; after which the sailors were observed to descend, one by one, into the hold, there to await the event. As to us passengers, we remained on deck, deeply meditating on, and watching our approaching ruin.

"The shouts of the barbarians are heard close to us. They appear on deck in swarms, with haggard looks and naked scimetars, prepared for boarding; this is preceded by a gun, the sound of which was like the harbinger of death to the trembling captives, all of whom expected to be instantly sunk; it was the signal for a good prize. A second gun announced the capture, and immediately after they sprung aboard in great numbers. Their first movements were confined to a menacing display of their bright sabres and attaghans, with an order for us to make no resistance, and surrender; which it was hardly necessary to repeat: we had only to obey; and this ceremony being ended, our new visitors assumed a less austere tone, crying

out in their *Dingua Franca*, ' *No pauro ! No pauro!*' (don't be afraid !). After this, rum was called for, then the keys of our trunks; when, dividing our party into two divisions, one was ordered into the pirate's boat, and conveyed into the admiral's frigate, while the others remained behind, under the care of several Moors, who had taken charge of the vessel. I was amongst the number of those transferred, and, in putting off from the brig, joined my companions in a speechless adieu of those we left behind.

"On gaining the frigate, we had no sooner got upon deck, than the barbarians uttered a cry of victory, usual when any captures are made. A savage joy seemed to play on their cadaverous aspects. A passage being opened for us between the armed Turks and Moorish sailors, we were conducted into the presence of the grand *Rais*, supreme commander of the Algerine squadron. He was seated between the captains of the five other frigates, who had assembled in close council to deliberate on the measures necessary to be taken with us, and to combine future operations. We were interrogated in brief and haughty terms, but neither insult nor rudeness was offered to any one of the party. The grand *Rais* very *civilly* asked us for our money, watches, rings, and every other article of value we had about our persons; in order, as he obligingly observed, to save them from the rapacity of the people of the Black Sea, who formed a considerable part of his crew; and who he candidly said were all *ladri*. He then deposited our respective property in a small box, faithfully assuring us that all should be returned on our leaving the vessel. During the distribution in the box, he repeated, alternately looking at the captives, ' *questo per ti*,' (this is for you,) ' *questi altro per ti*;' but perhaps in his heart, ' and all this is for me!' we were then ordered to retire; and, placed upon a mat in the *Rais's* outer cabin, began to reflect on our new situation. When supper was served, it consisted of a black-looking paste, in an immense pan, which being placed on the deck, was immediately surrounded by a host of hungry Moors and negroes, indiscriminately mixed together, and making common cause for the laudable purpose of emptying the platter; which, if ever so well inclined to partake of, was a forlorn hope to us afflicted and over-ceremonious visitors; who, at this patriarchal repast, might with propriety be compared to the timid spaniel, who vainly attempts to come in for a part of the bone thrown to the famished mastiff. Soon after sun-set, we were ordered to descend by a species of trap leading into the hold, which had infinitely more the appearance of a sepulchre than a place destined for living beings. There it was necessary to extend our wearied limbs, over blocks, cables, and other ship's tackling, which made ours a bed of thorns indeed! In this suffocating state, the bitterest reflections presented themselves to our sleepless imaginations. After being, as it were, on the eve of touching the paternal shore, what was now to become of us? Born and educated in a civilized country, long accustomed to share the protection of British liberty and law,. we were now captives of the vilest slaves, and perhaps doomed to drag out the remainder of our wretched days in dreary captivity amongst inexorable Moors! The poor sailors, too, all fathers of families, who looked to them alone for support and consolation, seemed totally incapable of bearing up against the misery of their situation.

" The crew of the pirate was composed of almost every race sent forth by the African continent, with the addition of several of the Levantine banditti, who are yearly imported from Smyrna, and other parts of Turkey, for the service of the regencies; and there was as great a diversity of colour, as nations, from the flat-nosed natives of Tombuctoo, to the white and ferocious descendants of the Almehades. By way of rendering the scene still more obnoxious, this motley crew were all either affected with some corroding humour, or swarming with vermin. Constantly expecting that a plague, the natural companion of so much filth, would break out, and doomed to see these stupid fatalists with lighted lamps, and pipes, in every part of the vessel: our anxiety between such a consoling choice of evils is not to be easily described, and made me often wish for the tub of Diogenes. As to the gloomy hole, in which we went through the painful ceremony of attempting to sleep, it could only be described in the language of the immortal author of the Inferno. Packed together like herrings, our bed was worse than that of Procrustes. Stretched along the deck in the manner of the Turks, compelled to eat our wretched meal with the lowest of the crew, we were invariably obliged to wait, till our black and tawny companions had filled their mouths from the dish with their filthy fingers. Cusrousu was the unvarying diet, and our beverage consisted of putrid water, which was handed round in an earthen pitcher, to us all in common."

At length the captors and captives arrived at Algiers. On approaching the anchorage, a shout of savage joy ran through the piratical frigate, and marked the satisfaction of the barbarians. As soon as they landed, the Rais, their conqueror, marche themd in ostentatious triumph through the city, to the council of regency; which had met in order to determine on the respective fates of the unhappy captives. The following passage in which Signor Pananti had delineated the anxieties of this trying moment, is one of the most deeply interesting in the whole volume.

" A large awning being extended in front of the house, the scene shortly opened; exhibiting the Members of the Regency, in barbarous pomp and horrid majesty, seated before us; accompanied by the *Ulemas*, or expounders of the law, and principal Agas of the Divan. We were then, without further ceremony or preamble, asked for our papers, which were duly examined; nor was that canting gravity wanting on this occasion, which is usually assumed to justify acts of rapine and plunder. The documents were then presented to the English Consul, whose presence is always required at these examinations, to verify any claim he may have to make. This gentleman soon saw the insufficiency of our documents, but, stimulated by the goodness of his heart and sentiments of pity for persons in our unhappy condition, he made every possible exertion to extricate us from the appalling destiny with which we were now threatened. The circumstance of some of the party being natives of a country united to the dominions of France did not restrain the Consul's generous efforts: we were unfortunate, and that was sufficient to insure the protection of an Englishman. But Rais Hamida boldly sustained the remorseless law of piracy; drawing the finest distinction imaginable between domiciliation and nationality, he proved himself a most able jurisconsult, according, at least, to the African code of public laws.

' A good prize! prisoners! slaves!' was now murmured through the council.

and soon communicated to the crowd assembled without, which, by its cries and vociferations, seemed to demand such a decision. The British Consul then formally demanded the English lady and her two children ; upon this being accorded, the Chevalier Rossi, her husband, advanced a few steps, and with dignified courage supported his claim to liberation, on the principle of having married an English woman, and of also being the father of two British subjects. This application being successful, he soon rejoined his anxious wife and children. Another attempt was now made in favour of us all by the Consul, but without effect :—this was followed by a cry in the hall of *'schiavi ! schiavi !'* (slaves, slaves ;) which horrible word was echoed by the multitude. The Members of the Council then rose ; and on the assembly being dissolved, the Consul and his attendants, together with Chevalier Rossi and family, departed ; leaving us devoted victims in a state of almost immoveable insensibility, as one who scarcely hears the thunder, when he is enveloped by the lurid glare of lightning which precedes it.

"Before we had recovered from our stupor, we were led off under the Grand *Serivano* and *Guardian Basha*, who led us through a considerable part of the city, followed by a great number of spectators. It being Friday, the Moorish sabbath, hundreds of infidels, in coming from the mosques, were soon attracted in every direction, to enjoy this new spectacle of degraded Christianity.

"Arrived at the palace of the Pasha, inhabited by the Dey, the first object that struck our eyes were six bleeding heads, ranged along before the entrance ! ! ! And as if this dreadful sight were not sufficient of itself to harrow up the soul, it was still farther aggravated by the necessity of stepping over them, in order to pass into the court. They were the heads of some turbulent Agas, who had dared to murmur against the Dey. A dead silence reigned throughout the building, in which Suspicion seemed to have fixed her abode, while fear was depicted in every countenance. Being ordered to arrange ourselves before the Dey's window, to feast the despot's eyes, he soon approached, looked at us with a mingled smile of exultation and contempt, then making a sign with his hand, we were ordered to depart; and after a third circuit of the town, arrived before a large dark-looking building. It was the great *Bagno*, or

house of reception for Christian slaves. Hence one of its pompous titles, *Bajos os Esclavos*. Every fibre trembled, and our limbs shook under us, as we traversed the horrid receptacle. The first words of the keeper, after we had entered, were, ' Whoever is brought into this place becomes a slave !' In passing the dank and filthy court-yard we were surrounded by a multitude of slaves, bearing about them all the signs of abandoned sufferers. They were ragged, lank, and haggard, with the head drooping, eyes sunk and distorted, cheeks imprinted by the furrows of protracted wretchedness, which seemed to have withered the soul, and by destroying the finer feelings of their nature, left no trace of pity for the sufferings of others : so that we passed without the slightest manifestation of that sympathy so naturally expected in such a situation. Exhausted by long confinement, and wrapped up in a sense of their own melancholy fate, our appearance was viewed with a stupid indifference, unaccompanied by any fellow feeling. During the few intervals unoccupied in the public works, they remain shut up, wandering about like pallid spectres in this house of darkness and of sorrow."

[To be concluded in our next Number.]

A Collection of Statutes, connected with the General Administration of the Law ; arranged according to the Order of Subjects, with Notes, by D. E. Evans, Esq. Barrister at Law, and Vice-Chancellor of the County Palatine of Lancaster, 8vo. 8 vols. £8.   Butterworth and Son; London, 1818.

THE Statutes at large form an indispensable part of the library of every individual, who is desirous of forming a comprehensive view of the *existing* Laws of his country; but unfortunately their bulk (for the latest and best edition consist of seventeen ponderous quarto tomes,) and their price (nearly £60,) operate as prohibitions to the acquisition of them. The multiplicity and variety of our laws was well exposed by the late Earl of Stanhope, when he submitted to the House of Lords a proposition for causing them to be reduced into one common system. What has been done towards accomplishing so desirable an object, we have at present no means of ascertaining. But, what Lord Stanhope hoped and wished to see effected, has in some degree been achieved by the learned and indefatigable editor of the work, which we are now to introduce to our readers.

In this collection Mr. Evans has endeavoured to bring together, in a moderate compass, the several statutes which are connected with the ordinary course of professional and magisterial practice, accompanied by a very few others which appeared to possess an interest as matter of historical curiosity.

In order to accomplish this purpose, he has excluded all statutes relating to the functions of the different officers of government—to matters of revenue, (with the exception of the land revenue of the crown)—to naval and military subjects, and other objects of partial and limited interest.

The following general synopsis of its contents will convince our readers how much important matter is here successfully brought together.

VOL. I.

Part I.—Persons and Corporations.

Class.
1 Aliens, Denizens, and Naturalization.
2 Statutes relating to the Clergy.

Class.
3 Marriage.
4 Parent and Child.
5 Corporations.

Part II.—Real Estates.

1 Miscellaneous Statutes concerning Real Estates.
2 Tithes.
3 Approvement and inclosure of commons.
4 Joint Tenants, Coparceners, and Tenants in Common.
5 Mortmain and Charitable Uses.

6 Conveyances by Infants, Lunatics, &c.
7 Fraudulent Conveyances.
8 Leases.
9 Uses.
10 Fines and Recoveries.
11 Wills.
12 Land Revenues of the Crown.

Addenda to Part I. and II.

VOL. II.

Part III.—Personal Property and Contracts.

1 Patents, Literary Property, &c.
2 Navigation, Ship Owners, and Mariners.
3 Insurance.
4 Bills of Exchange, and Promissory Notes.
5 Usury.

6 Annuities.
7 Gaming.
8 Stockjobbing.
9 Sale of Offices.
10 Buying of Titles.
11 Transfer of Stock.
12 Restitution of Stolen Property.
13 Executors and Administrators.

Part IV.—Courts and Civil Proceedings.

1 General Courts of Common Law—Judges.
2 Attornies.

3 Original Writ, Process, Arrest, Imprisonment, Bail, Appearance.

VOL. III.

4 Outlawry.
5 Privilege of Parliament.
6 Pleadings, &c.
7 Set off.
8 Limitations
9 Juries and Trials.
10 Evidence.
11 Costs.
12 Judgment, Execution, Statutes, Recognizances.
13 Error and false Judgment
14 Miscellaneous Sta-

tutes respecting Civil Actions and Proceedings.
15 Wales, Counties Palatine, Liberties.
16 Inferior Courts.
17 Statutes relating to Personal Liberty.
18 Real Actions.
19 Distress, Replevin, and Matter, relating to Landlord and Tenant.

VOL. IV.

20 Actions against Justices of Peace and other Officers.
21 Hue and Cry, and actions against the Hundred.
22 Penal Actions and Informations.

23 King's Debts.
24 Ecclesiastical and Maritime Courts.
25 Courts of Equity.
Addenda to the preceding Classes of Part IV.
26 Bankrupts.

VOL. V.

Part V.—Criminal Law.

1 Statutes relating to Religion and Ecclesiastical Supremacy.
2 Treason and other Offences affecting the State.
3 Offences relating to Coin.
4 Homicide.

5 Rape, Forcible Marriage, Polygamy, &c.
6 Riots, and Offences attended with malice or violence. Obstruction of public Officers.

VOL. VI.

VOL. VII.

Part VI.—Justices of Peace.

VOL. VIII.

In general, Mr. Evans has inserted the Articles without abridgment, as they appear in the ordinary editions of the Statutes: and where some parts only of a statute are applicable to the general design of the work, the others which relate to limited or temporary objects, are omitted, or are merely noticed by inserting the marginal abstracts.

In some cases the titles only are inserted as sufficiently declaring the object of the act, as in cases of acts by which others are continued or made perpetual, or where the mention of such acts may be considered as merely pointing out, in a general manner, the course and progress of the law upon subjects in respect of which it would be foreign from the principal design of the work to include the entire contents. To several statutes, Mr. Evans has added notes of the cases which have been decided upon their construction. In some instances, these notes are applied immediately to the particular expressions upon the construction of which questions have taken place. —In others they assume the character of a dissertation or a digest of the law, as applicable to the general subject.—In the composition of these notes as much attention seems to have been paid to conciseness as was consistent with perspicuity:—And in the examination of some questions, the editor has interposed his own views, and canvassed with freedom, (but without transgressing the limits of respect,) the conclusions of judical authority. In others, he has ventured to suggest an alteration of the subsisting law, or to offer such opinions as have occurred to him, with regard to legislative enquiry.

This is a brief outline of Mr. Evans's arduous and laborious work. Of the utility of his design, there can be but one opinion; and the manner in which it is executed is such will not detract from Mr. Evans's well-earned reputation, as an acute and able lawyer.

Some errors occur in the cross-references; but these will doubtless be removed in a future edition. The work is very handsomely printed; and, considering the vast mass of matter comprised within the moderate compass of eight large octavo volumes,—it is a cheap one,—a circumstance that is of no mean consequence to the purchaser of books, and especially of law books.

The Banquet, in Three Cantos, with Notes, 8vo. 5s. 6d. London, 1819, Baldwin, Cradock and Joy.

" LA critique est est aisée—la pratique difficile," said a French wit of the last century;—had he lived in the present, he would have been induced to reverse the position—such exuberance of invention, such fertility of imagination as it has become our good fortune to witness, our forefathers could have had no conception of; and, confined within the narrow limits of vulgar common sense and judgment, their sober faculties would no doubt have been completely bewildered in the airy flights of modern imagination.

To transcribe into the most unintelligible phraseology, the wild ravings of a disordered brain is an occupation, now neither uncommon nor extraordinary; and to receive with profound veneration what they are unable to comprehend, was ever the characteristic feature of the multitude; a general smile of contempt would be passed on him who should dare avow his inaptitude to understand a *modern fashionable* author's meaning. When literature has arrived at this pitch, the task of the critic ought in fact to be at an end, but as his opinion is still called for, hard indeed is the burthen imposed on him! whether the new works are to be judged by the old established rules, or whether new rules are to be framed and adapted to the fresh-raised fabrics of romantic inspiration,—is yet a question undecided in the empire of British taste.

In this state of things, therefore, it is with sincere pleasure that we hail the publication of a work in which something like classical information may be traced to the author—who evidently gives a preference to the wits of our Augustan period above the more fashionable writers of the day. Although this dereliction of modern theories may not recommend him to the generality of readers, yet to such as are not alarmed by so formidable a censure as we have ventured to pass upon him, we can with confidence announce a real gratification from the perusal of this work. Lest too much gravity should be anticipated from the pen of one so strangely biassed, we quote a passage or two among many others, that may counteract so erroneous an opinion.

Now to his task;—the carpet clear—behold!
The drawing-room its yawning valves unfold.
Encircling chairs encumber all the floor
And raps,with long pulsations,drum the door.
O'er the spruce lawn, the sprucer files approach,
In slender vis-a-vis, and ampler coach:—
As through the hall the company advance,
Silent they cast a wistful, side-long glance;
" Mirth in each eye, and hunger in each breast,
" The plates they view—and fancy all the rest."

Canto II. 255.

Although the subject is by no means susceptible of being treated in a very serious light, we find if any thing too much disposition to pun and ridicule in the author; who, carried away by a ready and lively wit, is apt perhaps to indulge in too many puns and quaint allusions, which tho' very well at proper distances, lose much of their effect by so numerous a distribution, as in this passage:

What would you covet more?
Your *Cape* behind, your *Côte Rotie* before:
In your strong *Tent* you may defy the age,
Or find some solace in your *Hermitage.*
Or if these fail you, there is your *Chateau,*
By knowing connoisseurs, sirnamed *Margot.*—

Canto III. 401.

Not so however in the following, where the hypoclondriac is admirably painted.

Avoid to ask the valetudinarian,
Who with capricious phlegm atrabilarian.
(*atrabiliarian*)
Cross, whimsical, irresolate, and shy,
Sees all your dainties with distemper'd eye;
Who, willing slave of Epidaurus' God,
Looks, ere he eat, for his physician's nod;
Before he takes a mouthful on his plate
Must try it by *apothecary's weight;*
Your ramekins too rich;— your mutton mean;—
Your fricassee too fat;—your leveret lean;—
Your craw-fish cold;—your harrico too hot;—
Your hash a thousand morbid ills has got.—
Such fill their mouths with arguments, excuses,
Of every meat will tell you the abuses,

With sophisms cramm'd, and aphorisms
　plenty,
And for one dram will give you scruples twenty;
By little eating, hope to grow the stronger,
And starve themselves to death to live the
　longer.

Nor in the following delineation of a
cook.

How singularly fortunate, who can
This *Rara Avis* meet, this proper man;
Who, conscious of his own unrivall'd powers,
Far over all his fellow-*creatures* towers;
Who, bred originally to the—*bar*,
Thinks he may treat his master on the par;
Like his profession, luminous and bright,
And, *in his own opinion*, always right.
His pride to kindle, not to quench a flame,
And wake the passions, not by reason tame:
With ample range of powers, and powers of
　range,
And well prepared this side or that to change:
Still in the vehemence of action cool
Who tries with patience, and condemns by
　rule,
As grave, as dignified, as those, and big,
Who wear a larger, not a whiter wig:
He sends alike, with firm unfaltering breath,
The tenderest fowl, or toughest ox to death.—
No Persian Sultan, whose despotic power
Takes any subject's head at any hour,
Can with a more imperious air confine,
Or to the bow-string his satrap consign,
Then he a goose to execution sends,
And not one muscle of his brow unbends!'
His visage grave, his aspect rough and stern,
Yet will his reddening cheek unconscious
　burn.　　　　　　　Canto II. 199.

To those wits, whose own genius is
not always at hand, upon a *pinch*, to
help them out with the joke that labours for utterance, this work must be
valuable, as they will find several not
inelegant witticisms, *ready-made* and
adapted to various occasions.

We by no means mention this as a
principal recommendation of the poem,
as we acknowledge that it has much
higher claims, and contains in many
passages that simplicity and force,
which is only to be found in our best
writers.

We shall only mention the opening
of the 3rd Canto.

Ah! where is now the care-constructed pile,
On which the blooming valleys used to smile?
Whose firm foundation, bedded in the rock,
Seem'd to defy the elemental shock;
Whose lofty head, on taper columns rear'd,
Towering o'er thick surrounding mists ap-
　pear'd:

To shield whose sacred walls, vast hills arose,
Capacious walls—as high almost as those:
Far from whose towers, incensed with fre-
　quent smoke,
The raging tempest howl'd, and harmless
　broke:
Whose glittering spires the lake would oft
　behold,
Deck'd, by the orient sun, in flaming gold.
　　　　　　　　　Canto III. 1.

＊　　＊　　＊　　＊　　＊　　＊
＊　＊　＊　The broken key-stone thrown
Far underneath the arch in which it shone,
While its dependant brothers, o'er their
　mate,
Bend trembling forward to partake its fate:
　　　　　　　　　Canto III. 25.

＊　　＊　　＊　　＊　　＊　　＊
The fretted bossage, from the ceiling ript,
Crumbles to powder in the yawning crypt.
With tinkling bell, the browsing wethers
　climb
Where, once, the hollow belfry toll'd its
　chime:
The ravens, with funereal cawings, hang
Where matin peals their cheerful carols rang;
Where sculptured tracery carved the storied
　dome,
The chough and jackdaw build their fetid
　home:
The ivy clings around the oaken stalls,
And matted misseltoe festoons the halls:
Who that surveys but must their lot deplore,
And breathe a wish, that wishes could restore;
Vain thought!—far otherwise!—for shortly
　must
The sad spectator here subscribe his dust:
The mite of earth thou must contribute too,
That other worms may moralize—on you.
The tardy hand of Time these ruins saves,
To heap their fragments on more recent
　graves:
　　　　　　　　　Canto III. 33.

The notes contain many entertaining
anecdotes, and much pains have been
taken to compress into a small compass, and without ostentation, many of
the most remarkable passages relating
to the subject, from Plato, Plutarch,
Aulus Gellius, Athenæus, and other
antient authors, together with several
amusing anecdotes from modern writers.
We select one, from the latter, illustrative of the following precept.

Custom, good sense, must teach you to select
Your phrase, your dish; and what you should
　reject.

Mr. Delille, in 1786, dining with his friend
Marmontel, related the following anecdote,
respecting the observance of fashionable cus-

town at table. The conversation turned on that multitude of indispensable trifles which are necessary to enable a man to mix in good society without being laughed at. "They are really innumerable," added Delille; "and what is most vexatious is, that all the wit and good sense in the world would never be sufficient, by themselves, to perfect you in these desirable accomplishments. A short time since," pursued he, "the Abbé Cosson, Professor of *Belles Lettres* at the College Mazarin, was describing to me a dinner to which he had been invited a few days before, where there were many persons of the first rank, blue ribbons, Marshals of France, &c. at the house of the Abbé Radouvilliers at Versailles. 'I will lay you any wager,' said I, 'that during this self-same dinner you were not guilty of less than an hundred improprieties.' —'What do you mean?' said the Abbé, quite startled; 'I am sure I did every thing like every body else.'—'What presumption!—now I dare say you did no one thing like any body there. But let us see—first of all, what did you do with your napkin when you sat down to table?'—'With my napkin? why, like others I unfolded it, spread it before me, and fastened it by one corner to a button hole of my coat.'—'Well, my good friend, you were the only person there that did so. Your napkin should not have been displayed in this way, it should have been thrown carelessly across your knee.— Pray in what manner did you take your soup?'—'Like every body else, I believe, with my spoon in one hand, and my fork in the other.'— 'Pleasant, indeed! your fork!—who would think of eating soup with a fork.— Well, go on;— after your soup, what did you eat?'—'A fresh egg.'—'And what became of the shell?'— 'Why, the servant took it away to be sure.' —'What, without breaking it?'—'Yes, without breaking it.'—'Shocking! remember never to eat an egg again without crushing the shell.'—'After that I asked for some bouilli.— Bouilli! you must never ask for bouilli, you must ask for beef.'—'Now, what next?'—'I requested the master of the house to send me some fowl.'—'Worse and worse. You should have asked for chicken, pullet, poult,—any thing but fowl. This expression is entirely confined to the *basse cour.* But what did you call for when you wanted to drink?'—'Why, like every one else, I asked for red wine or white wine, as I happened to want.'—'This was wrong again, you may call for Champagne or Hock, or Burgundy; never for wine. Then tell me in what way you ate your bread?'—'Certainly, as every one else does; I cut it as neatly as I could with my knife.'—'Bless me! do you not know that people always break their bread, never cut it? Go on; how did you manage your coffee?'—'For once I am sure I was right; it was scalding hot, and I poured it into the saucer to cool it.'—'Nobody else would have thought of doing such a

thing; we always drink coffee out of the cup, and never out of the saucer. From these specimens I think the probability is, my dear Cosson, that you neither uttered a word nor performed a single action any otherwise than diametrically contrary to the most obvious and established principles.'

"The Abbé was thunderstruck," continued Mr. Delille, " and for six weeks afterwards did little else but inquire of every body he happened to meet, how far I was right in the information I had given him."

Mr. Delille himself was indebted to a female friend for his initiation into these mysteries. He had long felt embarrassed in the great world where his talents were esteemed, and where those who are most admired for their genius are often most ridiculed for their awkwardness.

Although the Abbé Cosson was deficient in attention to the manners of the great, he was not wanting in *presence d'esprit.* Having breakfasted one day with an intimate acquaintance, where he met with some pastry which appeared to him excellent, the taste recurred to him the following morning. He went back to his friend at an early hour, and said to him very seriously—" My dear sir, some company that I did not expect have called to breakfast with me; do me the favour to lend me your *pye!*"

On the whole, we conceive our readers will not be displeased with us for recommending the book to their notice; which, as it does not depend on any of the ephemeral topics of the day, is likely to become a lasting favourite.

Reflections on the Liberty of the Press in Great Britain. Translated from the German of the celebrated E. Von Gentz, Aulic Counsellor to the Emperor of Austria, &c. &c. 8vo. 4s. Bohte and Co. London, 1819.

We have not forgotten that, when almost every other voice upon the Continent was hushed in admiration or in fear of Napoleon Buonaparte, then every where victorious—and when eyes which should have looked defiance, were turned towards his dispensing greatness in adulation or expectancy— that it was to M. Gentz more than to any other individual, that Europe owed the resuscitation and cherishing of that spirit of resistance which has led to his signal overthrow, and to the re-establishment of peace and liberty; —or that this distinguished statesman has been invariably the liberal and unanswerable advocate of England, whenever she has been, in ignorance or in envy, charged with aiming only at commercial monopoly, or with attempting to establish her own prosperity upon the ruin of other states. But, with a full sense of his claims upon our respect and gratitude, we must express our regret that he has written the pamphlet before us, and our entire dissent from his opinions upon the subject of the Liberty of the Press. It seems that great importance is, by the nations of the Continent, very naturally attached to the freedom of the Press, which has induced M. Gentz to attempt to prove, that it is a good which is mixed with so much evil, that even in England it would be better that a censorship should be established. His statements are, however, clear and candid; his mind appears to be entirely free from any bias towards arbitrary power; and, in deference to his high and well-earned reputation, we do not therefore hesitate to extract passages wholly at variance with our own opinions. The author's object and sentiments will distinctly appear in the following passage :—

" In all European States, England alone excepted, the press has, until very recently, been constantly regulated by measures of Police.* The privileges possessed by the English writers were not, in former times, regarded as subjects of censure or reproach for other governments. It was readily perceived that they were intimately interwoven with all the remaining peculiarities of the British Constitution, and that, were they detached from it, or removed to another soil, where they would be in contradiction with the form of government, the legislation, the administration of justice, and the national manners, they could not be expected to thrive. But as the human mind, along with the actual possession of a higher cultivation, and the chimerical notion of more extended faculties, has become accustomed to see, in ancient regulations, nothing but ancient fetters, the wish to emancipate the press from the dominion of the police, has been actively and

strongly expressed throughout all Europe."

The difficulty of " fixing the liberty of the press by positive ordinances," leads our author to propose as a question—

" Does the system, which prevents the abuse of the press by police legislation, or that which punishes its abuse, when committed, by penal laws, deserve to be preferred ?"

Among the evils of the latter, the following is, perhaps, the most strikingly expressed, but is very far from being conclusive :—

" If, in any remarkable case, general attention be excited,—by public accusations, provisional arrests, and all the solemn apparatus of a judicial trial, having perhaps at last a tragical issue, when all is agitation, and the far-famed guarantee of literary freedom is on every side calumniated as a feeble bulwark, a treacherous snare, and an instrument of the basest tyranny. The momentary terror, however, soon passes away. Every author, even the individual most conscious of having overstepped all bounds, and who may have dared all the vengeance of the laws, hopes, as far as regards himself, to be able to weather the storm; and, as the thunderbolt falls on but few heads, and seldom on the most criminal, the hope is not wholly unfounded. Even in the most extreme case, the progress of the trial presents many chances of deliverance. The defendant may rely on the ability of his counsel, on his own talents and eloquence, or on the preponderance of the popular feeling in his favour. Many see, in a trial of this kind, only the means of acquiring celebrity, and regard even the threatened punishment (especially before its effects are felt) as a new claim to the approbation and sympathy of all who entertain similar sentiments, or as an honourable martyrdom." '

The difficulty of defining libel is next strongly urged ; and it is argued, that in trials for that offence, the Judge must necessarily extend his judicial functions, and become, in point of fact, a Censor, and therefore that this duty might be better confided to some authority in the state.

" The duty of pronouncing judgment on a publication, with respect to its effects on the public interest, the mischief it may,

---

* This assertion is slightly qualified in a note.

under certain circumstances, create, and the danger to which it may expose the general tranquillity ; or of deciding on any of the relations which may subsist between the author and the public authority, is either not at all, or very remotely connected with the other functions of a Judge. This duty is entirely of a political nature ; it implies a knowledge of state affairs, of political relations, both foreign and domestic, of public life in general, and of the whole constitution of society, which can only be possessed by one who has a decided inclination, or has paid particular attention to studies of this kind. To desire an ordinary Tribunal of Justice to pronounce judgment on the political tendency of a publication, is not more hazardous than to call for its decision on the value of a picture or a musical composition."

M. Gentz is here singularly unfortunate in his illustrations ; for the value of pictures and of musical compositions is determined frequently in our Courts by the verdicts of juries, which give entire satisfaction.—Of Mr. Fox's Bill, declaring the jury, in cases of libel, competent to give a general verdict of guilty, or not guilty, upon the whole matter in issue, M. Gentz speaks as of an evil smaller than some others which presented themselves :

" The decision of Parliament, in the year 1792, is still viewed as the common triumph of the rights of Juries and the Liberty of the Press, and is consequently regarded, by the friends of both, as a most fortunate event. Whether it is proved to be such, by its results, is a question to which, on account of the diversity of views and feelings, very different and opposite answers may be expected. We shall not conceal our own opinion on the subject, however little it may correspond with the favourite notions of the day. We must, however, in the first place, remark that this Parliamentary decision might appear justifiable, even to those who entertain a more unfavourable opinion of its practical effects than we do: for there is still another question behind ; namely, whether the opposite decision would not have been attended with worse consequences. What might not have happened had the Parliament allowed the old wavering and equivocal practice to continue, or had, by a solemn decision, sanctioned the maxim that Juries, in actions for libel, were only competent to pronounce on the fact of the publication?—The Judicial Power,

which, in these stormy times, has too often bad to share the fate of the other authorities, would have become, in the highest degree, odious and suspected. The inevitable consequences of every public prosecution against offences of the press—the analyzing of the offensive article, the defence of the accused, usually more bold and always more mischievous than the libel itself, the scandal of the public discussion, the sophistry of the Counsel, the contest of the Crown Advocates with the Defendant, and often of the Judge with the Jury, in short, all the various circumstances which, in these dangerous proceedings, are of far greater importance, and are attended with far more serious consequences than any verdict of acquittal or condemnation can be —would have remained unchanged. The Jury would still, as they had formerly done, have sometimes acquitted the defendant, contrary to all legal evidence, on the ground of the proof of the acts of printing and publication being insufficient ; or in the case of that being impossible, would, by a dry return of NOT-GUILTY, have reduced the Judge to the perplexing alternative of either setting the defendant at liberty, with the fullest conviction of his guilt, or declaring the verdict invalid. The licentiousness of the press would not have been restrained, whilst the remedies against it would have been still further degraded in public opinion. Thus according to our view of the subject, the Parliament of 1792, by throwing the whole responsibility on the Jury, made choice of the lesser evil."

As our extracts are intended merely as specimens of the work, and as we can by no means attempt to follow the author through all his reasonings, we conclude with one passage, in which a certain class of our political writers is, at least, properly appreciated.

" The Constitution of Great Britain has maintained itself not by, but in spite of, the degenerate liberty of the press— But why should a question of this kind be driven to its utmost extremity? Why calculate how large a dose of corrupting and destroying matter a state may receive without accomplishing its destruction? If the licentiousness of the Press do not actually threaten the existence of England, is it not evil to poison all the sources both public and private of her moral life ? The disorganizing principles which the periodical pamphleteers, particularly those of the common order, instil into the lower classes of the people, are truly alarming in their nature; but still more alarming, when it is considered that the men who promulgate them exercise an unbounded controul over the opinion of millions of readers, who cannot procure the antidote of better. writings. Those perfidious demagogues incessantly address the people, in declamations on violated rights, deluded hopes, and real or imaginary sufferings. Every burthen which may fall heavy on individuals, every accidental difficulty, every inconvenience, produced by the change of times and circumstances, is represented as the immediate effect of the incapability, selfishness, and culpable blundering of the administration. The most criminal and absurd designs are imputed to the Ministers; and lest the oppressed should delay to seek redress, at their own hands, the future is painted to them in blacker colours than the present; thus, a thick cloud of dejection, bitterness and discontent, is spread over the nation; men's minds are filled with hostile aversions and gloomy anxieties; and the poor man is, at last, deprived of comfort, cheerfulness, and all enjoyment of life. Every feeling of satisfaction and security, and of confidence in the government, the tranquil and willing obedience of the people, their steady resignation under unavoidable sacrifices, and all the fruits and ornaments of a good constitution, are falsified, perverted, and discouraged by the 'harpy hands of these iniquitous scribblers. That neither the intellectual nor moral cultivation of the people can prosper in such a state of political corruption is self-evident. —Is this then a trifling evil?"

On these observations of M. Gentz, we have only room to remark, that he is alarmed on our account without reason; for the English character, formed, as it has been, under our free Constitution, and enlightened by our free press, is to these vipers but a file which they seek in vain to gnaw. The admission of M. Gentz, that our's is the only nation which is sound enough to bear this liberty, is, indeed, sufficiently flattering; but so far from regarding it as a source of *danger*, we feel that it is to us SECURITY AND STRENGTH. The monarch is never in ignorance of the real 'sentiments of the people; the Ministers collect the public voice, and dare not disregard its warnings; but, on the other hand, they feel assured that the

clamour of the disaffected, or disappointed few, will never be mistaken for the voice of the many, and that they never appeal in vain to the loyalty and good sense of the nation; while detection, exposure, and shame, are heaped upon the heads of those wretches who gain a miserable livelihood by their seditious attempts to disturb an order of things, which it is the interest of every true lover of rational liberty to support. With us, observes the eloquent Curran, "Sedition speaks ' aloud, and walks abroad—the demagogue goes forth, but the public eye is upon him; he frets his busy hour upon the stage; but soon . weariness, or punishment, or disappointment, bear him down, or drive him off, and he appears no more. · But how does the work of sedition go forward in countries, where public communication is not open to the people? Night after night the muffled rebel steals forth in the dark, and casts another and another brand upon the pile, to which, when the hour of fatal maturity shall arrive, he will apply the flame."

An Inquiry, whether Crime and Misery are produced or prevented by our present System of Prison Discipline. By Thomas Fowell Buxton, Esq. M. P. 8vo. 5s. 12mo. 2s. 6d. Arch, London, 1818.

Notes on a Visit made to some of the Prisons in Scotland and the North of England, with some general Observations on Prison Discipline. By Joseph John Gurney, 12mo. 3s. 6d. London, 1819.

The design of Mr. Buxton's very interesting publication, is sufficiently indicated by its title. To the "inquiry" which he instituted, he has given but too plain an answer, by his descriptions of several ill-regulated prisons: at the same time, however, he has presented to us some · instances of a more favourable kind. As the most material of Mr. B's accounts of prisons have been laid before the public, in numerous extracts, which have been inserted in the daily journals, we shall not detain our readers with any passages from his widely circulated book; but shall simply remark, that, upon the whole view of his case, he has most fully established the following important proposition, viz. *that, by those jails on the one hand, which are conducted on bad principles, crime and misery are produced and multiplied: and, on the other hand, that prisons, in which the prisoners are classified, inspected, instructed, and employed, have a powerful tendency to that, by which crime and misery will certainly be lessened, viz. the reformation of criminals.*

To strengthen and confirm this proposition by a variety of additional facts, is the chief object of Mr. Bevan's " Notes", which were taken in company with his sister, the well known and benevolent Mrs. Elizabeth Fry, during a journey through the north of England, and in part of Scotland, performed in the months of August and September of the last year. These notes, (our author informs us,) so far as respects all the more important prisons visited by him, have been read to the respective jailors, and have been carefully corrected since the date of his visit, by gentlemen on the spot. They may therefore be considered *accurate,* and will be found to dwell less on the minute details of each prison, than on particulars which are most connected with considerations of an important and interesting nature.

Upwards of thirty prisons were visited by these benevolent travellers; and the accounts of some of them are as gratifying, as those of others are painful, to the feelings of the benevolent mind. We shall select two or three examples, of each class, and shall then call our reader's attention to Mr. Bevan's very important observations on prison discipline.

Doncaster Jail.—" This jail consists of a small court-yard, two rooms on the ground floor, and two others above them; the rooms severally furnished with a small bed, and measuring thirteen feet square. Of the lower rooms, one is for male criminals of all descriptions, the other for male vagrants; of the upper rooms, one for females, whether debtors, vagrants, or criminals; the other for male debtors.

" Fifteen persons have at times been locked up together for the night in the apartment allotted to male criminals, that apartment measuring, as before stated, thirteen feet square. The state of these poor wretches, when thus situated, must have been in a very high degree miserable and unhealthy. In the male vagrants' room there is no light when the door is shut, except through a hole in the door, and of course no ventilation. The criminals in this jail are ironed; they are allowed eightpence per day and firing, but neither clothing nor soap. They are totally unemployed, and receive no instruction whatever. Forty persons have been confined in this jail at once; but at this time there were only five prisoners here. The doors of the four rooms being necessarily kept open during the day, *the prisoners of all descriptions, debtors and criminals, male and female, associate freely together.* Who can wonder that crimes increase? Who does not perceive the tendency of such an association to convert into felons the vagrant, the misdemeant, the debtor? One of the vagrants at this time in the prison was a Scotch woman, who having lost her husband, and having herself just recovered from a serious illness, was travelling homewards in company with her little child. she complained bitterly of her situation. " What could I do?" she said—" I dared not steal; I liked not to beg: destitute and afflicted, what could I do, but apply to the magistrates for a pass? The consequence is, that I am shut up for a week in prison, and exposed, perhaps, to the worst and most vicious of men." The case speaks for itself."

In justice, however, to the intelligent magistrates of Doncaster, it ought to be known that they are anxious to correct these lamentable abuses. Mr. Bevan was informed that they have in contemplation to erect a new prison. We cordially join in his benevolent wish,— "May they be encouraged to do this justice to themselves and the public!"

Berwick Borough Jail.—" Nothing can be much more defective than this small prison, It consists of two large boarded rooms in the upper story of the Court-house: one for debtors, the other for criminals—a simple wooden door between them.

"Connected with these day-rooms, is a small range of sleeping-cells. The whole prison is so exceedingly insecure, that the criminals cannot be permitted to make use of their day-room except in the presence of the jailer. Thus they are almost constantly confined in their comfortless sleeping-cells. Nor is this provision deemed sufficient; when their cases are bad, *they are chained to the wall.* The injustice and barbarity of such a mode of confinement are too conspicuous to require a comment. Neither criminals nor debtors have any airing-ground. The prison allowance is six-pence per day. No cloathing is allowed, nor is there any provision for medical attendance or religious instruction. The last of these defects is probably remedied ere now, by the voluntary kindness of a clergyman, the vicar of the town, who informed us of his resolution to visit the prisoners weekly, without any remuneration:—such an example is well worthy of being followed."

In Dunbar Jail, which is as deplorably filthy and wretched as any which Mr. B. visited, happily no one was confined. Very different, however, was the case with the County Jail at Haddington, which he found crowded with prisoners, in consequence of a riot that had taken place in the neighbourhood. And seldom indeed have we seen any poor creatures so wretchedly circumstanced.

"That part of the prison which is allotted to criminals and vagrants consists of four cells on the ground floor, measuring respectively thirteen feet by eight, and one on the second story,

measuring eleven feet by seven. It is difficult to conceive any thing more entirely miserable than these cells. Very dark—excessively dirty—clay floors—no fire places—straw in one corner for a bed, with perhaps a single rug—a tub in each of them, the receptacle of all filth. In one of the cells we observed three men who had been engaged in the riot; in another, a woman (the wife of one of them) and two boys; in a third, two more men and a woman (the wife of one of them). We understood that one of these women was a prisoner, the other a visitor; but have since been informed by the jailer that they were both visitors.

" None of the prisoners were ironed, except one man, who had attempted to break prison. This unfortunate person was fastened to a long iron bar. His legs, being passed through rings attached to the bar, were kept about two feet asunder, which distance might be increased to *three feet and a half* at the pleasure of the jailer. This cruel and shameful mode of confinement, which prevented the man from undressing, or from resting with any comfort to himself during the night, and which, by the constant separation of the legs, amounted to torture, had been continued for several days. We earnestly entreated for his deliverance, but apparently without effect.

" Another scene of still greater barbarity was in reserve for us. In the fourth cell—a cell as miserable as the rest—was a young man in a state of lunacy. No one knew who he was or whence he came; but having had the misfortune to frequent the premises of some gentleman in the neighbourhood, and to injure his garden seats, and being considered mischievous, he was consigned to this abominable dungeon, where he had been, at the date of our visit, in unvaried solitary confinement, for eighteen months. W. Horne, Esq. the sheriff of the county, has kindly engaged to ameliorate, as far as lies in his power, the situation of this most afflicted individual. It is most obvious that his present place of confinement is in every respect improper.

" No cloathing is allowed in this prison; no medical man attends it; no chaplain visits it. Its miserable inmates never leave their cells, for there is no change of rooms and no airing-ground; nor can they be under any one's constant and immediate care, for the jailer lives away from the prison. They can however keep up an almost unchecked communication with the people of the town, as the small grated windows of their cells all of them look upon the streets. We observed a lad on the outside of the prison, seated on a ledge of the wall, in close conversation with the three men who had been committed for rioting. The prisoners were at this time allowed nothing but water and four pennyworth of bread daily. I have since learned from the jailer that this was a short allowance by way of punishment for refractory conduct, and they usually have eightpence a day. Those who were in the jail when we visited it appeared in a remarkably careless and insensible state of mind. This we could not but attribute partly to the hardships and neglect which they here experience.

"I have yet to describe the most objectionable point of this terrible prison, namely, its accommodations for those debtors who are not burgesses. There were at this time three men of this description in the prison; shortly before there had been five; and at one time seven. These unhappy persons, innocent as they are of any punishable offence,—be they many, or be they few, be they healthy or be they sick,—are confined day and night, without any change or intermission whatsoever, in *a closet containing one small bed, and not quite nine feet square.*

" As we passed through Haddingtonshire, we were struck with the richness and fertility of the country, and with the uncommon abundance of the crops which it produces. It is considered one of the wealthiest counties in Scotland. Surely, then, we may indulge the pleasing expectation, that the inhabitants of this county, and especially its very liberal magistrates, will no longer suffer it to continue without such a prison as will tend to the reformation of offenders; such a one, at any rate, as will not, like their present jail, violate the common principles of justice and humanity.

Aberdeen County Jail.—" The defects of this jail have often been observed; and Neild went so far as to offer the magistrates pecuniary assistance, to encourage the building of a new prison. Baillie Garden, to whom we were introduced, and who received us with much civility, informed us that a sum of money had already been raised for this purpose, and that the new building would probably be commenced at an early period. In the mean time the present jail is a scene of unusual misery.

" It is a very ancient square tower, forming a mass of rude masonry, the walls of great thickness, and the interior so contrived as to exclude all convenience and comfort from its inmates. You ascend up a narrow winding stone staircase, with which most of the cells, where the prisoners are in custody, are immediately connected. In these cells they pass their whole time, there being no airing-ground in the prison, and no separate accommodations for sleeping.

" We were first introduced to a small room, about fifteen feet long by eight in breadth, set apart for female criminals. There were four women in it, a man, (the husband of one of them) and a child. The room was most offensively close and very dirty: there were two beds in it; in one lay the man, in the other an elderly woman, both ill; the child also looked very sickly. We thought we perceived symptoms in these invalids of jail fever; and indeed it was scarcely possible that so many persons should continue night and day together in so very close an apartment, without the production of fever and infection. The impropriety of the man's being thus confined in company with the women needs no remark.

" There are three more cells for criminals. In the first were two men who had been sentenced to transportation;

in the second, three others. Both these cells are small, cold, close, and very dirty; fitted up with the usual accommodation of tubs, but without fireplaces. I am informed, however, that a stove is placed in each of them during the winter months. Some of the men appeared sickly, and most of them hardened and indifferent to their situation: one of them (a desperate offender) was fastened by the legs to an iron bar, like the poor wretch whom we saw at Haddington. The third cell is, we hope, but seldom used; it is a black hole perfectly dark, and without any ventilation but through a small opening in the wall. In this jail the tried prisoners are not separated from the untried. Their food appeared to us very insufficient, for they are allowed only one pound and a half of bread with a pennyworth of milk per day; also a little cloathing on particular occasions. Their bedding is a straw mattress, and two blankets on each bed. A chaplain attends the prison three times in the week.

"The accommodations for debtors are miserably insufficient. They consist of two very small rooms on the same floor—a landing-place connecting them —and a little sleeping-room immediately above them. The debtors who are confined in this contracted place are of course constantly varying in number; but as far as I can recollect, there were twelve of them here when we visited them. They appeared crowded together; and crowded together they continue, day and night, without change.

"To crown all its other defects, this prison is so insecure, that four of the criminals, already described, have since made their escape from it.

"Can any one doubt its being necessary that a new jail should be built at Aberdeen?

"We proceeded from the jail to

The Bridewell.

"The Bridewell for the town and county of Aberdeen is a house of labour, to which are sent criminals of various descriptions, who have been sentenced to a term of imprisonment.

"It is quite new and of considerable extent, built, like other houses at Aberdeen, of excellent granite, and well situated on the out-skirts of the town. The several stories of this building consist respectively of a long gallery, with small but commodious and airy cells on each side. Every gallery is divided in the middle by the central stone staircase, the men prisoners being confined on one side of the house, the women on the other. The cells on one side of the galleries are for sleeping, those on the other for working. Every prisoner occupies a sleeping and a working-cell, the Bridewell being intended only for solitary confinement. The working-cells are comfortably warmed by steam. There is a Bible placed in every sleeping-cell—a provision which ought to be adopted in every prison. The bedding is excellent—a straw mattrass, two sheets, two blankets, a rug and a pillow, for each person. Of these articles, the sheets and the pillow might perhaps be spared with advantage. We observed in this Bridewell a good chapel, in which divine worship takes place once every week. In the highest story there is also a commodious infirmary, used chiefly as a nursery for the children of the female prisoners. The prisoners are properly clothed and well fed. They have porridge for breakfast, bread and milk for supper, and soup containing oatmeal and garden-stuff for dinner, except on one day in the week, when they are allowed broth with beef in it. In case of unruly conduct in the prison, they are punished by being placed for a certain number of hours in a perfectly dark cell. The men are employed in weaving; the women in weaving, spinning, and picking oakum. They work under the superintendance of one inspector, whose business is to watch over all, and to instruct in the art of weaving, those who are ignorant of it. The earings of the prisoners are first applied to their own maintenance in the prison, and are the means of reducing the annual expence of the establishment to a comparatively trifling sum. If any prisoner earns more than his maintenance,

I

he has credit for the surplus in account; half of it is given to him when he leaves the prison, and half on the receipt of a certificate of good conduct six months afterwards.

" The prisoners are allowed to take exercise in a walled garden at certain times of the day.

" This Bridewell was built for the accommodation of sixty Prisoners: there were forty in it at this time. The governor, James Watson, a very intelligent man, has known many instances of reformation produced amongst his prisoners. He has known them to acquire in the Bridewell not only the art of weaving, but the habits of industry; and this has led to a respectable settlement in life after they have left the prison. Scarcely any thing indeed seems wanted to render this institution a school of reform, but more religious instruction—more of that kind care, which a few benevolent and religious persons, if permitted to visit them daily might easily extend over these prisoners individually.

" The jail being quite full, several persons who had not been tried were confined, at this time, in one of the galleries of the Bridewell. It grieved us to observe how very different was their situation from that of the other prisoners; for their allowance was only fourpence per day, and they were totally without employment.

" It appears not a little surprising that the magistrates of this town and county, whose attention has been so laudably and so successfully directed to the erection and management of their Bridewell, should so long have continued satisfied with their Jail. It is a great error to suppose that those who are sentenced to a limited period of confinement are the only class of prisoners with whom it is worth while to try the experiment of employment. The system is of equal importance to those, who have yet to take their trial, and to those, who after trial are kept in prison until the opportunity arrives for their being sent to the hulks or transported. Prisoners under these or any other circumstances will for the most part be willing to labour, if permitted to receive a fair proportion of their own earnings. It is earnestly to be desired that the new jail about to be erected at Aberdeen may be so built as to afford every facility for this essential object.

" Another circumstance with which the visitor of prisons at Aberdeen is much impressed, is the large number of criminals as compared with that in the prisons of the neighbouring counties.

" In all the jails of Forfarshire we found not one offender against the laws, except a solitary deserter; whereas in the prisons of Aberdeen there were upwards of sixty criminals. It appeared on enquiry, that a large proportion of these offenders (I allude principally to those in the Bridewell) belonged to the city of Aberdeen; and I believe the fact may be accounted for, chiefly by some large cotton factories, in which upwards of five thousand persons of both sexes work together in large companies. The manufacturing poor at Dundee work separately, each in his own cottage; and at Dundee there are no criminals. It is indeed true that the prisoners in the Aberdeen Bridewell are committed mostly for petty offences; but how easy is the progress from such offences to crimes of a serious nature !"

[To be concluded in our next Number.]

A Brief Memoir of her late Majesty, Queen Charlotte; with Authentic Anecdotes, and a Poetical Appendix, by Thomas Williams, 18mo. with a Portrait, 2s. 6d. Simpkin and Marshall, London, 1819.

A concise, but well written sketch of the Life of her late Majesty, whose exemplary character, as a wife and a mother, is delineated with much truth and correctness. Many pleasing anecdotes of her private life and benevolence are interspersed. An elegant and faithful portrait ornaments this neatly printed little work; which, we think, must prove an acceptable addition to the juvenile library.

***

Elements of Astronomy, familiarly explaining the General Phænomena of the Heavenly Bodies, and the Theory of the Tides: illustrated with 18 copper plates, &c. &c. By Joseph Guy, 18mo. 5s. bound. Baldwin, Cradock, and Joy, London, 1819.

It is only of late years, since the course of education has been enlarged, that the very interesting Science of Astronomy has been generally taught in the superior classes of schools. Many valuable treatises on this subject we unquestionably possess; but their bulk and price necessarily place them beyond the reach of juvenile students. While Mr. Guy acknowledges his obligations to the labours of his predecessors, he modestly offers his little volume as a " handmaid to them :" It is, however, much more than this, and in fact presents to the reader a compendious but full abstract of the present state of the Science of Astronomy. Mr. G. has successfully avoided two evils, of very common occurrence,—that of *extreme brevity* on the one hand, and *too great prolixity* on the other. His work is illustrated by eighteen plates, exhibiting the various phenomena of the heavenly bodies with singular beauty and accuracy.

***

Sermons, preached in the Parish Church of High Wycombe, Bucks, 8vo. 2d. Edition, 10s. 6d. Longman and Co. London, 1818.

These discourses are of no common value; seldom, indeed, does it fall to our lot, to peruse Sermons, better adapted for domestic or private reading. They are of moderate length, earnest, practical, and affectionate; and, though not originally designed for publication, they are such compositions as will not disgrace the literary character of their author, who has been honoured with a most numerous list of respectable subscribers. Since this article was written, a *third* edition of Mr. Bradley's Volume has issued from the Press.

***

Profitable Amusement for Children; or Familiar Tales, containing useful Instruction with pleasing Entertainment, by the Author of " Learning better than House and Land," 18mo. 2s. W. Darton, London, 1818.

Though not announced in the title page, this amusing little volume is the production of the veteran tutor of youth, Dr. Carey, who has conferred an additional obligation on the rising generation in the present little volume; which contains a number of very pleasing and instructive tales, particularly adapted for children in the middle and lower classes of life.

***

The First Step to the French Tongue, designed as an easy Introduction to, and consisting entirely of, the Verbs; with practical Exercises, by A. Picquot. 12mo. 1s. Law and Whittaker, London.

A perfect knowledge of the nature and conjugation of the French Verbs is indispensable to the student of that elegant, and universally spoken language; but the *irregularities* are so numerous, as to render the acquisition of this knowledge exceedingly difficult; so that he, who attempts to simplify this particular branch of the language, confers no small obligation, both on the tutor and the pupil. This, Mr. Picquot has successfully accomplished in the present little volume, which will be found to contain all that is necessary for the knowledge of the French Verbs. Their formation is explained with much perspicuity; and the rules laid down, are illustrated by a series of easy and appropriate exercises; which (we think) will enable the diligent student soon to perfect himself in the knowledge of the verbs, and to express himself with that ease, correctness, and precision, for which the French language is eminently distinguished.

Literary Register.

Authors, Editors, and Publishers, are particularly requested to forward to the Literary Panorama Office, post paid, on, or before the 19th day of each month, the titles, prices, and other particulars of works in hand or published, for this department of the Work.

. . . .

BOOKS ANNOUNCED FOR PUBLICATION.

BIOGRAPHY.

The second or concluding part of Dr. Watkins' Memoir of her late Majesty, may be expected early in the present month.

Memoirs of John Duke of Marlborough; with his Original Correspondence, collected from the Family records at Blenheim, and other authentic sources. By William Coxe, M. A. F. R. S. F. S. A. Archdeacon of Wilts, and Rector of Bemerton. Vol. III. in 4to. with Plates.

The Rev. John Evans, of Islington, is printing a Memoir of the late Rev. Dr. Wm. Richards, with some account of the Rev. Roger Williams, founder of the state of Rhode Island.

Mr. Ryan has in the press, a Biographical Dictionary of the worthies of Ireland; from the earliest period to the present time. To be completed in three volumes, the first of which will be published early in March.

EDUCATION.

A translation of Abbe Guilles' Treatise on the Amusement and Instruction of the Blind, with engravings, is in the press.

Mr. Picquot, author of the Universal Geography, is printing, a Chronological Abridgment of the History of Modern Europe, compiled from the best historians.

Maternal Conversations, by Madame Dufresnoy, on beauty, passion, courage, justice, clemency, moderation, &c. will soon appear.

First Lessons in Latin, designed as an introduction to Eutropius and Phædrus, by the Rev. John Evans, will be published very soon.

Mr. Boileau will shortly publish the art of French Conversation, exemplified on a new plan with an introduction, &c.

An interesting little book for children is in the press, entitled, the Well Educated Doll; calculated to amuse and instruct; embellished with ten engravings.

HISTORY.

The Rev. John Lingard, author of the Antiquities of the Anglo-Saxon Church, will soon publish, in two quarto volumes, a History of England from the Invasion by the Romans to the Accession of Henry VIII.

Charles Mills, esq. author of a History of Mohammedanism, is preparing a History of the Crusades, undertaken for the recovery of the Holy Land.

Mr. S. Fleming proposes to publish, in a quarto volume, the Life of Demosthenes; with an account of the age of Philip of Macedon, and Alexander the Great.

HORTICULTURE.

The Gardener's Remembrancer, exhibiting the Nature of Vegetable Life and Vegetation; together with the Practical Methods of Gardening in all its branches. By James Mac Phail, Twenty Years Gardener and Steward to the late Earl of Liverpool.

MATHEMATICS AND NATURAL PHILOSOPHY.

Mr. Peter Nicholson will soon publish a Course of the Mathematical Sciences, adapted to succeed the study of arithmetic in public schools.

Preparing for publication by subscription, (10s. 6d.) the Elements of Radiant and Fixed Matter, in 8vo.

MEDICINE.

Sir Arthur Clark has nearly ready for publication, an Essay on Warm, Cold, and Vapour Bathing; with observations on Sea Bathing, &c.

Speedily will be published, a series of Engravings, representing the Bones of the Human Skeleton, with the Skeletons of some of the Lower Animals, by Edward Mitchell, Engraver, Edinburgh. The explanatory references by John Barclay, M.D. Lecturer on Anatomy, Fellow of the Royal College of Physicians, and of the Royal Society of Edinburgh, &c. &c. Part I. Imperial 4to.

Observations on the Nature and Treatment of the Epidemic Fever, at present prevailing in the Metropolis, as well as in most Parts of the United Kingdom. To which are added, Remarks on some of the opinions of Dr. Bateman, in his late treatise on that subject. By Henry Clutterbuck, M.D. Licentiate of the Royal College of Physicians, and one of the Physicians to the General Dispensary. In 8vo.

MISCELLANIES.

Mr. Martin, of Liverpool, has, in the press, a View of the Intellectual Powers of Man, with observations on their cultivation.

Charles Phillips, esq. will soon publish, Specimens of Irish Eloquence, with biographical notices, and a preface.

A series of Letters by the Hon. Lady Spenser to her Niece, the late Duchess of Devonshire, shortly after her marriage, is preparing for publication.

Speeches by the Right Hon. John Philpot Curran, late Master of the Rolls in Ireland. An edition greatly enlarged by the addition of his speech on the Trial of the Shearesses, and other speeches never before collected. With a Memoir and Portrait. In one large volume 8vo.

Sixty 'Curious and Authentic Narratives and Anecdotes, respecting extraordinary characters; illustrative of the tendency of Credulity and Fanaticism,&c. &c. By John Cecil, foolscap 8vo.

The Hermit in London, or Sketches of English Manners, in three volumes, will soon appear.

The Humourist; a collection of Entertaining Tales, Bons Mots, Epigrams, &c; with coloured plates by Cruikshank, is nearly ready.

Four numbers of a new cheap periodical work have appeared, entitled the British Magazine, chiefly devoted to the interests of the Society for the Improvement of Prison Discipline, and for the Reformation of Juvenile Offenders, the Society for the Promotion of Permanent and Universal Peace, and the Society for diffusing information on the subject of capital punishment.

The Rev. John Evans has in the press, Essays, Biographical, Literary, Moral, and Critical, which will soon appear.

NOVELS.

A new Satirical Novel is forthcoming, entitled London, or a Month at Steven's. By a resident.

Oakwood Hall: a Novel, 3 Vols. 12mo By Miss Hutton, Author of the Miser Married.

Correction, a Novel. Second Edition. 3 Vols. 12mo.

A Traveller's Tale of the Last Century. In 3 Vols 12mo. By Miss Spence, Author of Letters from the Highlands, &c.

In the press and will speedily be published handsomely printed in 3 Vols. 12mo. "The Intriguing Beauty, and the Beauty without Intrigue."

Mondouro, a Novel.

Hesitation; or to Marry or not to Marry. In 3 Vols. By the Author of the Bachelor and Married Man, &c.

POETRY.

Mr. Hogg, the Ettrick Shepherd, has in the press, the Jacobite Poetical Relicks of Scotland, during the struggles in 1715 and 1745.

Mr. P. B. Shelley has in the press, Rosalind and Helen, a tale; with other poems.

Mr. C. Dibdin will soon publish, Young Arthur, or the Child of Mystery, a metrical romance.

The Poetical Remains of the late Dr. John Leyden, with Memoirs of his Life. By the Rev. James Morton, In 8vo.

The Lament of Napoleon; Misplaced Love; and Minor Poems by S. R. Jackson, will be published in the course of the month.

J. Brown, esq. has in the press a poem, entitled, the Stage; addressed to Mr. Farren; containing strictures on various actors.

POLITICS.

Political Essays. By William Hazlitt, in 8vo.

THEOLOGY.

No. II. of Mr. Bellamy's New Translation of the Bible, from the Original Hebrew, including the Books of Exodus, Leviticus, and part of Numbers, will be published in the course of this month.

The Baptists self-convicted, by the Rev. William Anderson, of Dunstable; in his Remarks on the Editor of Calmet's Dictionary of the Holy Bible. By the editor of Calmer.

The Rev. Charles Simeon, M. A. Fellow of King's College, Cambridge, has issued proposals for publishing by subscription, (in 10 or 11 Volumes, demy 8vo. price 10s. 6d. each) Horæ Homileticæ, or discourses (in the form of Skeletons) upon the whole Scriptures, containing altogether, at least 1200; similar to, but distinct from, those in the five Volumes already published. No part of the Work will be put to press till June next in order that some estimate may be formed of the number required The first four volumes will be ready for delivery at Michaelmas next; the second four at Lady-Day 1820; and the remainder at the Michaelmas following. Those who subscribe for six Copies will be entitled to a seventh, gratis. The entire profits will be given to aid the Jewish Cause, and one or two other religious institutions.

In the press, a new edition of "The Enthusiasm of Methodists and Papists considered." By Bishop Lavington, with notes and an introduction, by the Rev. R. Polwhele. 8vo.

Familiar Dissertations on Theological and Moral Subjects. By the Rev. W. Barrow, L. L. D. F. R. S. and Prebendary of the Collegiate Church of Southwell. In 8vo.

The Rev. B. Kennicott will soon publish an Analysis of the Fifth Book of Hooker's Ecclesiastical Polity.

Prof. Paxton, of Edinburgh, will soon publish, Illustrations of Scripture, in two octavo volumes.

TOPOGRAPHY.

A general History of the County of

York. By Thomas Dunham Whitaker, L. L. D. F. S. A. Vicar of Whalley, and Rector of Heysham, in Lancashire. Part I.

Mr. W. B. Taylor is preparing an Historical account of the University of Dublin, illustrated by engravings, in the same style as those of Oxford and Cambridge.

VOYAGES AND TRAVELS.

Captain James Burney, of the royal navy, is printing an Historical Review of the Maritime Discoveries of the Russians, and of the attempts that have been made to discover a north-east passage to China.

A voyage up the Persian Gulph, and a Journey overland from India to England, in 1817; containing an Account of Arabia Felix, Arabia Deserta, Persia, Mesopotamia, Babylon, Bagdad, Kuordistan. Armenia, Asia Minor, &c. &c. By William Heude, Esq. of the Madras Military Establishment. In 4to. illustrated by Plates.

The Personal Narrative of M. De Humboldt's Travels to the Equinoctial Regions of the New Continent, during the Years 1799-1804. Translated by Helen Maria Williams, under the immediate inspection of the Author. Volume IV. In 8vo.

The Recollections of Japan, by Captain Golownin, are expected to appear in the course of a few days. They will be accompanied by a Chronological Account of the Rise, Decline, and Renewal, of British Commercial Intercourse with that Country.

~~~~~~~~~

BOOKS PUBLISHED.

CLASSICAL LITERATURE.

ΗΡΩΔΙΑΝΟΥ ΕΠΙΜΕΡΙΣΜΟΙ Herodiani Partitiones E. Codd. Parisinis edidit Jo. Fr. Boissonade. 8vo. 12s.

The DELPHIN CLASSICS, with the VARIORUM NOTES; intitled the REGENT'S EDITION. No. 1, P. VIRGILII MARONIS Opera Omnia, ex. ed. Chr. G. HEYNE, cum Variis lectionibus, interpretatione, notis Variorum, et Indice locupletissimo, accurate recensita. Curantect Impnmente, A. J. VALPY.

The price is now raised to new Subscribers, 19s. each part. On the 1st of April it will be raised to 20s. and on the 1st of June, to 21s. large paper double Eight months, will be allowed from the 6th of February, to persons now abroad, and fifteen months for India. Subscribers always remain at the price they originally enter. Any *original* Subscribers may change their small for large paper, on or before the 1st of April, at the first price. Twelve numbers will be published in the year, each number containing 672 pages.

The ŒDIPUS ROMANUS, or an Attempt to prove, from the principles of reasoning adopted by the Right Hon Sir William Drummond, in his *Œdipus Judaicus*, that the Twelve Cæsars are the Twelve Signs of the Zodiac. Addressed to the higher and literary Classes of Society. By the Rev. George Townsend, A. M. of Trinity College, Cambridge.

The second and concluding volume of Mr. Baynes's Translation of Ovid's Epistles, 8vo. 12s.

Gradus ad Parnassum ; a new edition, with the verses and phrases omitted ; the translation of the words given, also their formation. Many new words are added ; with various other Improvements, 12mo. 7s. 6d.

DRAMA.

The House of Atreus, and the House of Laius ; Tragedies founded on the Greek Drama ; with a Preface, on the peculiarities of its structure and moral principles ; and other Poems. By John Smith, formerly of King's College, Cambridge. 8vo. 10s. 6d.

EDUCATION.

Elements of Astronomy, familiarly explaining the general Phænomena of the Heavenly Bodies, and the Theory of the Tides : to which is subjoined, a complete Set of Questions for Examination. For the use of Private Students as well as of Public Seminaries. By Joseph Guy, formerly Professor of Geography at the Royal Military College, Great Marlow. Illustrated by 18 plates, royal 18mo. 6s.

Questions on the Chronology of English History, adapted to Dr. Valpy's Poetical Chronology, by the Rev. J. Evans, 12mo.

The School-Fellows ; by the author of " the Twin Sisters ;" second edition, 4s.

Family Suppers, or Evening Tales for Young People ; by Madame Delafay ; second edition, with sixteen engravings, 2 vols. 7s.

A Father's First Lessons ; by Jauffret, author of " the Travels of Rolando," &c. second edition, with five engravings, 3s. 6d.

The National Spelling-Book, or Guide to English Spelling and Pronunciation, divided and accented agreeably to the approved methods of Walker, Jones, and Sheridan ; by B. Tabart. 1s. 6d.

Infantine Stories ; consisting of words of one, two, and three syllables ; by Mrs. Fenwick ; embellished with engravings ; fifteenth edition, 2s. 6d.

The Bee and the Butterfly ; by Miss Sandham, author of " the School-Fellows," " Twin Sisters," &c. new edition, 2s. 6d.

The Juvenile Geography and Poetical Gazetteer, with views of the principal towns ; by J. Bissett. 2s. 6d.

Le Curé de Wakefield ; translated into French, by J. A. Voullaire, new edition 3s. 6d.

HISTORY.

The Parliamentary History of England, from the earliest Period to the Year 1803. Volume XXXIV, comprising the period from 1798 to 1800. royal 8vo. 1s. 1s. 6d.

Essays on the Institutions, Government, and Manners of the States of Ancient Greece. By Henry David Hill, D. D. Professor of Greek in the University of St. Andrews, 12mo. 7s.

MEDICINE AND SURGERY.

The Dublin Hospital Reports, and Communications in Medicine and Surgery. Vol. 2, 8vo. 13s.

A System of Pathological and operative Surgery, founded on Anatomy ; illustrated by Drawings of Diseased Structure, and Plans of Operation. By Robert Allen, Fellow of the Royal Colleges of Surgeons of London and Edinburgh, &c. &c. Volume 1, (to be completed in 3 volumes) 8vo. 12s. 6d.

MISCELLANEOUS.

Observations on Ackermann's Patent Moveable Axles to four-wheeled Carriages : containing an engraved elevation of the Carriage. with Plans and Sections, conveying accurate Ideas of this superior Improvement. 8vo. 3s.

A Series of Familiar Letters on Angling, Shooting, and Coursing. By Robert Lascelles, Esq. with plates, royal 8vo. 10s. 6d.

Specimens in Eccentric Circular Turning, with Practical Instructions for producing corresponding Pieces in that Art. By J. J. H. Ibbetson, with numerous Engravings, 8vo. 1l. 1s.

NATURAL PHILOSOPHY.

Elements of Natural Philosophy, Illustrated throughout with Copper and Wood Engravings, by James Mitchell, M.A. 12mo.

NOVELS.

Campbell ; or, the Scottish Probationer, in 3 vols. 12mo. 1l.

Emily ; or, the Wife's First Error ; and Beauty and Ugliness ; or, the Father's

Prayers and the Mother's Prophecy; two Tales. By Elizabeth Bennett, in 4 vols. 12mo. £1.

Zeal and Experience; a Tale, 8vo 10s. 6d.

POETRY.

Specimens of the British Poets, with Biographical and Critical Notices, and an Essay on English Poetry. By Thomas Campbell, Esq. author of the Pleasures of Hope. 7 vols. cr°wn 8vo. 3l. 13s. 6d.

Human Life; a Poem. By Samuel Rogers, Esq. author of the Pleasures of Memory. Small 4to. 12s. 6d.

The Messiah; part 2, by Mr. Cottle, foolscap 8vo. 6s.

A Churchman's Second Epistle. By the author of Religio Clerici. With notes and illustrations, 8vo. 5s. 6d.

Emigration; a Poem, in imitation of the third Satire of Juvenal. In 8vo price 1s. 6d.

A seventh Volume of the Collected Works of the Right Hon. Lord Byron, containing the third and fourth Cantos of Childe Harold. Foolscap 8vo. 7s.

The Banquet; a Poem in three Cantos, with notes; embellished with a frontispiece, and engraved titlepage, 8vo. 5s 6d.

POLITICS AND POLITICAL ECONOMY.

A Letter to the Right Hon. Robert Peel, M.P. for the University of Oxford, on the pernicious Effects of a variable standard of Value, especially as it regards the lower orders and the Poor Laws. By one of his Constituents.

Notes on a Visit made to some of the Prisons in Scotland and the North of England, in company with Elizabeth Fry; with some general observations on the subject of Prison Disipline. By Joseph John Gurney, 12mo. 3s. 6d.

Thoughts on the Funding and Paper System, and particularly the Bank Restriction, as connected with the National Distresses, with Remarks on the Observations of Mr. Preston and Sir John Sinclair. By N. J. Denison, Esq 8vo. price 3s. 6d.

The Principles and Practices of pretended Reformers in Church and State. By Arthur Kenney, D.D. Dean of Achonry, and late Fellow of Trinity College, Dublin; 8vo. 10s. 6d.

THEOLOGY.

Part VI. of the Fourth Edition of Calmet's Dictionary of the Bible, with the fragments and plates. 6s.

Remarks on Scepticism, especially as it is connected with the Subject of Organisation and Life. Being an Answer to some recent Works, both of French and English Physiologists. By Thomas Rennell, M.A. Christian Advocate in the University of Cambridge, and Vicar of Kensington, Middlesex. 8vo.

Novi Testamenti Græci Jesu Christi Tameion; alias Concordantiæ, ita concinnatum, ut et loca reperiendi, et vocum veras significatioues, et significationum diversitates per collationem investigandi, ducis instar esse possit. Opera Erasimi Schmidii, Græc. Lat. et Mathem. Prof. Accedit nova præfati o Ernesti Salamonis Cypriani. Handsomly printed at the Glasgow University Press, in 2 vols. 8vo. 1l. 10s.

The Life of Jesus Christ, including his Apocryphal History, from the Spurious Gospels, unpublished Manuscripts, &c. Embellished with a Head of Jesus, 8vo. 7s.

TRANSACTIONS OF SOCIETIES.

Transactions of the Literary Society of Bombay; containing Papers and Essays by Sir James Mackintosh, Sir John Malcolm, Sir George Staunton, H. Salt, Esq. Baron Wrede, &c. &c. &c. with plates, 4to. 2l. 12s. 6d.

Medico-Chirugical Translations, published by the Medical and Chirurgical Society. Volume IX. Part II, 8vo. 7s.

The Transactions of the Horticultural Society of London, part II, of volume III. With plates, 4to. 1l. 6s. 6d.

TOPOGRAPHY.

Enchiridion Romæ; or, Manual of detached Remarks ou the Buildings, Pictures. Statues, Inscriptions, &c. of Ancient and Modern Rome. By S. Weston, F. R. S. S. A. foolscap 8vo. 5s. 6d.

VOYAGES AND TRAVELS.

Letters from the North of Italy, addressed to Henry Hallam, Esq. relating principally to the Administration, Climate, Manners, Language, and Literature of that Country. By William Stewart Rose. In 2 vols. 8vo. 18s.

The Tour of Africa; containing a concise Account of all the Countries in that Quarter of the Globe, hitherto visited by Europeans; with the Manners and Customs of the Inhabitants; selected from the best Authors, and arranged by Catherine Hutton, with a map, 8vo. 12s.

Occurrences during Six Months Residence in the Province of Calabria Ulteriore, in the Kingdom of Naples, in the years 1809, 1810; containing a Description of the Country, Remarks on the Manners and Customs of the Inhabitants, and Observations on the Conduct of the French toward them, with instances of their oppression, &c. By Lieut. P. J. Elmhirst R. N. 8vo. 6s.

foreign Literary Gazette.

AUSTRIA.
Institution of Schools for general Instruction.

The method of mutual instruction, (Bell and Lancaster's system,) has recently been introduced into Austria, by the exertions, and under the patronage of Field Marshall Bianchi, Duke of Casa Lanza, who has established a school at his own expence, the superintendence of which, he has confided to M. Hauzza. The first essays were made on forty grenadiers of the Field Marshall's division; and were attended with complete success. This new school has subsequently been taken under the special protection of Prince Aloisius of Lichtenstein.

Paper bleached by new process.

M. J. G. Uffenheimer, at Vienna, has invented a new method of whitening paper; for which he has obtained an exclusive privilege during six years. We hope, that this process, whatever it be, will be free from all injurious effects on the substance of the paper; and from all principles of discolouration in after years; both which defects, we are sorry to say, have attended attempts made by new processes, among ourselves.

Bas-relief on Mummy Case.

We believe, that the external cases, which enclosed the mummies found in Egypt, were always painted; but the figures on them were not raised: however, if we may believe an article from Trieste, the brothers Rosetti, a name well known to all who have visited Cairo, presented to the Emperor of Austria, at the time of his stay at Trieste, the covering of a mummy sarcophagus, which is ornamented with figures in bas-relief: they allude, of course, to the Egyptian mythology. This covering, which belonged to the corpse of a young man, has been added to the cabinet of antiquities at Vienna.

New Bathing Machine.

Dr. Weidlich, of Vienna, has lately received from the Government, an exclusive privilege, to continue during six years, for the construction of a new bathing machine, of his invention: the nature of it we are not yet acquainted with.

FRANCE.
Genius and Study, Cautions to.

De l'Hygiène des gens de lettres, &c. On the Health of Men of Letters, or an Essay Medico-Philosophical on the most proper means to develope natural talents, and a disposition for the sciences, without injury to health, and without contracting disorders. By Stephen Brunaud, M.D. of Strasburgh.

Perhaps somewhat of sympathy with the subject of this work, induces us to report it with distinction. We know so well the bad habits contracted by inconsiderate students, the carelessness and indifference with which they allow the approaches of disorders, which at length become fixed in the constitution, that we cannot but receive with a certain degree of partiality, every attempt to warn the incautious ere it be too late, and to check, if possible, the further progress of such distressing drawbacks from human life and comfort. The most ingenious are the most exposed to them: they attack, and they undermine talent, intelligence, and industry.

It is acknowledged that the class of persons intended to be benefitted by the writer, is among the most important to society; and the subject has engaged the attention of able physicians. Tissot's Work is well known; but, that rather treats on the remedies for disorders, than on the means of prevention; whereas Dr. Brunard endeavours to regulate enquiry from an earlier stage. He adverts to the personal disposition, to the gradual opening and expansion of the understanding, to the dangers attending a forced or precocious developement of the mental powers, and to the proper education of those powers, as they successively are able to receive it. It must be acknowledged, that in some of our schools, and in not a few of our families, this is too little considered: the young mind is frequently forced forward, at the expence of the youthful person; and the progress of nature is worse than merely interrupted; it is disordered, disturbed, and injured.

Dr. B. considers the inconveniences attending the giving a wrong direction to native talent; and hints at means by which the real disposition of genius may be discerned: he thinks the free course of genius should not be interrupted, or misdirected. He considers how far study may be pursued; and when the labours of the mind must be suspended. He directs his views to the influence of music—to the relaxation found in those societies in which men of letters usually delight, and that of which female society is the source. He gives directions concerning air, exercise, clothing, food, sleep, and various natural occasions. Not omitting the passions of the mind, with proper precautions against their prevalence and excess. The influence of climate, of seasons, of the progress of life, are felt by men of letters with no small force; and often these causes act in a manner little suspected, and therefore undetected, and not provided against. The attention due to each of these causes of complaints, is strongly enforced by the writer.

But, perhaps, not the least curious article in this performance, is the list of learned men, who in different climes and ages, have attained to the extremity of human life: among the ancients, Herodian, the rhetorician Gorgias, Hippocrates, [109] exceed a hundred years among the moderns Fontenelle. Others have advanced far towards the same limits; and the list might be increased.

We could be glad should this meet the eye of some of our hard students, that it might produce on them its *full* effect. We have known many more who have shortened their lives by their intemperance in quest of knowledge, than we have known who prolonged their lives by the placidity of their employment. The dictate of genius is "forward," think nothing done, while any thing remains undone: but genius should lend a *willing* and obedient ear to the cautionary lessons of prudence; or the evening of life will severely suffer for imprudences committed during the anticipations of the morning.

Agriculture: advantages of Irrigation in dry summers.

The last summer was so uncommonly dry throughout Europe, that the attention of the observant was principally directed to the contemplation of its effects, and the phenomena resulting from them; some of these we have already mentioned. But,

it was natural, that those gentlemen who had usually directed their attention to agriculture, should, on this occasion, avail themselves of the advantages attending the practice of irrigation, to impress the public mind most strongly in favour of proceedings which they most warmly patronized. Agriculturists observe, very justly, that no greater service can be rendered to the art they study, than the discovery of means to water lands which are too dry, and to drain lands which are too wet. The first of these practices, as we have had occasion to record, in the early numbers of our journal, is no where so perfectly executed as among the districts at the foot of the Pyrennean mountains, and along the vallies of Piedmont. It was therefore natural to enquire how these districts had fared in a season so dry as the last. A Report on this subject has appeared from the Paris press, in the form of a letter from M. le Compte François de Neufchâteau to the Society of Agriculture, Arts and Commerce of the department of the eastern Pyrennees, instituted at Perpignan, on irrigation, and other objects of rural economy. The canals for watering the lower grounds, which form the principal subject of this pamphlet, appear to have been productive of great advantage, and the writer regrets the non-execution of a navigation canal, which was projected in 1710 to promote the intercourse between Languedoc and Rousillon, which would have afforded still greater resources for irrigation.

The author adds reflections on various other subjects; on the impulse given by liberty to the exertions of a people; on the observations made by Mr. Birkbeck on the agriculture of France; and on the particularities in French husbandry, which render it not favourite among the English; and this, certainly, is not the least curious article treated on by this eminent *literato*, and *ci-devant* minister.

GERMANY.

Secrets in Dyeing and Colouring.

We know not well what confidence to place in the pretensions of the following work; *Laboratorium*, &c. The Chemical Laboratory, or Collection of secret and important procedures relating to dyeing, to printing on stuffs and cloths, to whitster-ing, finishing, &c. by P. Bernard, Nuremberg, 1818. If this volume, contains accounts of any management more beneficial than is usual in our manufactories, it may deserve especial attention.

ITALY.

Shakespeare's Works: translation of.

At Turin is announced, a complete edition of the Works, or Theatre of Shakespeare. Each volume will contain two or three plays; which will be accompanied by prefaces from the pen of Aug. G. Schlegel, translated into Italian, with critical and historical notes, by M. Leoni.

It is but just, that while the Italian poets form a part of the studies of the polite, in all countries, and in our own particularly, our bards also should become familiar in Italy. We anticipate much information and pleasure from the Mr. Schlegel's accompaniments.

Monument of the Poet Dante.

A subscription has been proposed at Florence, for the purpose of erecting a monument to Dante. The execution of the sculpture is confided to Ricei. So few poets preserve their reputation for several centuries, that such a tribute to eminence is perhaps, among the most honourable, that can be devised: our Shakespeare was thus honoured, and a few others have been equally happy; but, generally speaking, this late distinction is sparingly granted.

Monument to the Poet Camoens.

This may be a proper place to observe that a monument to the memory of the Portuguese poet, Camoens, has been proposed, and the proposal has been supported with alacrity by some of our own countrymen: this has called forth the zeal of certain of the Portuguese nation, resident among us, who in public advertisements have claimed the honour, as properly belonging to their country, exclusively, and have called on their compatriots to come forward freely, and execute by their own powers and zeal, what foreigners deem it an honour to assist in.

New Journal, the Diario.

At Bologna, a new periodical work is announced, under the title of *Diario;* it will be published three times in a week; and will contain the usual assemblage of news, literary notices, discoveries, new and old, notices from writers, artists, &c.

Manufactures favoured.

The manufacturers of Tuscany have engaged the attention of the Academy of Fine Arts at Florence; who committed the subject to the third class of the members of their institution: that class has lately made a report, which is certainly interesting to their constituents and their country.

New Mechanical Inventions.

Lately has been published at Rome, the first number, containing seven plates, of a work purporting to be Mechanic and Hydraulic constructions, invented by Paulo-Maria Asters. Among others, this number contains the description of a machine, which the author calls a flying ladder; intended to raise men, or weights, to the summit of a tower, or other high building.

Ancient Vases: collections of.

The King of Naples has lately purchased the collection of vases formed by the canon Vivenzio, at Nola, for the sum of 30,000 ducats. This forms a very considerable and conspicuous addition to the Royal Museum.

A similar accession to the Imperial Cabinet at Vienna has lately taken place, by the transfer of Count de Lamberg's valuable collection; which has been obtained by the Emperor, at a very moderate price. It is to be hoped that these valuable articles will remain in their present situation, secure from fraud, fire, and foes.

Medical investigation of the Plague.

Although we hope and trust, it will please Providence to protect our country from the horrors of the plague, yet it may be proper to notice what information other countries afford on the subject. We therefore record a work published at Naples, which, on account of its importance, has been translated into several languages, under the title of *Storia della Peste:* &c. The History of the Plague at Noja, by Dr. Vitangelo Morea, 8vo. pp. 488. This history is very minute, and is accompanied with philosophical and chemical observations on the state of the atmosphere, during the progress of the disease. Noja is a little town in Puglia, distant 153 Italian miles from Naples.

POLAND.

University inaugurated.

The University of Warsaw, which has been open since the month of October, 1817, was solemnly inaugurated May 14, 1818. The discourses pronounced on this interesting occasion, which were in the Polish language, have been printed at Warsaw, in four sheets, 4to.

Conservators of Cracow University.

The University of Cracow, which, our readers may recollect, was placed under the protection of the three powers, who guaranteed the independence of the city of Cracow, in the treaties signed at Vienna, has lately chosen three conservators, to which, every year a report will be addressed on the progress made in the studies of the place, and on the course pursued. The present conservators, are, for Austria, Prince Metternich; for Russia, the Count de Novosilzow; and for Prussia, Prince Antony Radzivil, Governor General of the principality of Posen.

RUSSIA.

Translations of History of Russia.

The History of Russia, published by M. de Karamsin, which has been twice reprinted in its original language, the Russian, has lately been translated into French by two authors, at the same time. The first of these translations is by M. de St. Thomas: the second has been executed under the inspection of the author, by Professor Jeauffret. These two translations have been published at Petersburgh; a German translation is also in progress. Has any attention been paid to this work among the English literati capable of translating it?

Journal : Benevolence to Military.

Since 1814 there has been printed at Petersburgh, a journal in the German language, superintended by the Chevalier Pessarovius. This journal, on account of its merit, is translated into the Russian language; and its profits are devoted wholly (after deducting necessary expences) to the benefit of wounded and invalid soldiers. The sale is so considerable, that the editor has already had the satisfaction of distributing among these suffering heroes, the sum of 500,000 rubles, in Bank paper.

Dorpat, University.

The University of Dorpat, reckons, at this time, twenty five professors in ordinary, and ten extraordinary. The number of students is about three hundred. The building for containing the library, which is newly erected, is divided into several galleries and halls, which are already furnished with nearly 30,000 volumes.

SICILY.

Earthquake, description of.

In this island has lately been published, Memoria sul tremoto, &c. A Memoir historical and philosophical on the earthquake that took place at Catania, February 20, 1818. This history is by Dr. Agatino Longo. From the royal press at Catania, 8vo.

SPAIN.

Original Inhabitants : Basque.

We are exceedingly glad to record an article from a country that too seldom appears in this department of our work : that the learned Spaniards are absolutely idle, we do not believe; but, that their labours are very much lost to the public and the world, is but too evident.

In 1806, Don Juan Baptista de Erro, published an alphabet of what he conceived to be the primitive language. Very lately has appeared at Madrid, from the same learned hand, El Mundo primitivo, &c. The primitive World, or a Philosophical examination of the antiquity and the civilization of the Basque nation. In the first of these works the author exerted himself to prove that the Basque people were the first who inhabited Spain. In the present work, he endeavours to trace the first ages of the world, with the ideas of those ages on the formation of the universe, by taking the Basque appellatives as examples; and referring them to things, to numbers, and to the diverse productions of the three kingdoms of Nature.

SWITZERLAND.

Rural Economy : Implements.

M. Fellenberg at Hofwyl, continues to publish his Communications on the important subject of rural economy. The institution of this spirited patriot was reported in the PANORAMA from its first conception and opening: the attention of the British public has also been lately called to it from the public notice taken of it by one of our most conspicuous senators, who had made his observations on the spot. His report was highly favourable. We can only acquaint our readers, that M. Fellenberg's work contains descriptions of newly invented instruments for sowing, of new experiments made on milk, on irrigation, on change of earth, &c. &c.

Che Gatherer.

No. XXVI.

"I am but a gatherer, and dealer in other men's stuff."

The Palm-Tree Nation.

A recent traveller in South America, speaking of the little islands of the Orinoco, observes, they are evidently formed by the alluvial depositions of the river; they are under the water during the rainy season, but still are covered with palms, &c. Cocoa trees, which furnish the islanders at once with their food and their beverage—a bark, which they weave, and wood for their little articles of furniture and their canoes. The existence of the tribe of Gouaraouns seems connected with that of the family of the Palms, in the same manner that certain species of birds and insects are allied to particular trees and flowers. Four or five feet above high water-mark they plait together the young shoots to make their platform, which they cover with large mats. The roofs of these aerial huts are covered with leaves of the same tree, to which they fasten their canoes. These Indians are in number about ten thousand. They are tall, strong, and well made; less indolent than the other savages of South America; passionately fond of dancing; gay, social, and hospitable. They are not taciturn like their neighbours—their language, soft and harmonious, is rich, if we compare it with the other tribes. They are dexterous fishers—have dogs of a kind similar to those of our shepherds, which they keep for the purpose of catching fish in the shallows; they caress these animals, and treat them with much kindness. Their little trade con-

sists in fish, nets, hammocks, and baskets. They are at peace with all the world, even with the Spanish Government, who have long ago renounced the project of reducing them to subjection.

Anecdote of Goldsmith.

Goldsmith was always plain in his appearance; but when a boy, and immediately after suffering heavily from the small pox, he was particularly ugly. When he was about seven years old, a Fiddler, who reckoned himself a wit, happened to be playing to some company in Mrs. Goldsmith's house. During a pause between two sets of Country dances, little Oliver surprised the party, by jumping up suddenly, and dancing round the room. Struck with the grotesque appearance of the ill-favoured child, the fiddler exclaimed "Æsop," and the company burst into laughter; when Oliver turned to them, with a smile, and repeated the following couplet:

Heralds proclaim aloud, all saying,
See Æsop dancing, and his Monkey playing.

A Modern Æneas.

A Mr. Æneas M'D—— having once, it is said, dined with Dr. Troy, the titular archbishop of Dublin, he availed himself of the opportunity of imbibing more wine than he could with safety carry. As he was returning home, some watchmen thought proper to be dissatisfied with his conduct, and brought him to a watch-house; happily, he met the learned Lord N. who, after making a few inquiries, rebuked these heedless guardians of the night, observing that they were little aware of the dignity of the personage with whom they had presumed to interfere; that the charges they had preferred against him must be unfounded, for that he was no other, than the *pious Æneas*, returning from the sack of *Troy.*"

Dandyana: Definitions.

A Scottish Dandy.—Extract from Jamieson's *Dictionary of the Scottish Language:*—" DANDIE, DANDY—A principal person or THING; what is NICE, fine, or possessing supereminence, in whatever way. SC.

They'd gie the hag to dolefu' care,
And laugh at ilka DANDY.

R. GARNOWAY's Poems.

This word claims a very ancient etymon. 1st. dandi and Sue. Goth. daenne, signify liberal, munificent.   Sue. Goth. Dandis-folk.   Dandemaen is a title of honour or respect." We hope this etymology will not be lost upon our *dandy* readers.

In Hindoostanee, Dandy signifies a *boatman.* Of these people some are Abou-gines, and others are Lubbas *(Lubbers?)* of the Mohammedan Sect.   Their avoca-tion is laborious, but they are contented. Their dress consists of a piece of a cotton wrapped round the middle.

Modern Dandy.—By some writers, the thing is considered not to be an animal at all, but neither more nor less than a *suit of clothes,* endowed by some un-known species of magic or mechanism, with habits and faculties analogous in ap-pearance to some of those which belong to animal life. These, it is said, are chiefly confined to a locomotive power, a kind of mock instinct, by which it distinguishes and congregates with its kind, and a faculty of uttering articulate, though *un-meaning* sounds.

Spanish Dandies.—At the Tertulias or evening parties, the men stand in groups, or walk about the apartment, excepting some decided *curutacoé* or ladies' men, (Dandies?) and such as are only in the earlier stages of attendance upon the glance of a peculiar Donna. These lean upon the chairs of the ladies, are sometimes seated by them, and are armed with the *fan* of their favourites, in the twirling and flirting of which they generally display a feminine dexterity. Let not the possession of this accomplishment excite contempt: for it is highly necessary for a young man in Spa-nish society, to understand the hidden meaning of the different movements of this organ of female wit; by the use of which the Spanish lady expresses the passions which agitate her mind, whether jealousy, resentment, or pleasure; and by which she encourages or repels the too timid or too enterprising lover; and from the know-ledge of their meaning, the power of ex-pressing it, is but a step.

Roman Dandyism.—Tiberius, Emperor of Rome, speaking in the Senate, nearly 1800 years ago, concerning the growth of luxury, said—" How shall we reform the taste for Dress, which, according to the reigning fassion is so exquisitely nice, that the sexes are scarcely distinguish-able?"---*Tacitus.*

Religion of the Gipsies.

THEY profess to be of the National Religion; but their notion of religion is confined to repeating the Lord's prayer, and even this attainment is the honourable distinction of a few. They seldom attend any place of public worship, nor do they seek to impress religious sentiments on the minds of their children. They are very willing that their infants should be christened, if it can be done without trouble or expense; and, in cases where money is plentiful, the marriage ceremony is performed with due solemnity: but for the most part, marriage is merely a mu-tual pledging of faith, and names are given to their children without calling in the aid of a spiritual instrument. Indiffer-ence to all systems of faith and to all ritual observances is, indeed, one of the most striking features of the gipsey cha-racter throughout the world. They have every where attained to Voltaire's standard of perfection---they belong to no religion, but are ready to profess any. In Italy, they call themselves good Catholics; in the Protestant States of Germany they are Lutherans: in Russia, Moldavia, and Wallachia, they are Votaries of the Greek Church; in the dominions of the Grand Seignior, they believe in Mohammed and the Koran. But the Turks seem to enter-tain some doubts concerning the sound-ness of their faith; for, in the neighbour-hood of Constantinople they make them pay the poll tax, which is imposed upon believers.

Qualities of a General.

General Donadieu, whose name so fre-quently appears in the French papers, met with a remarkable rebuff from Mar-shal Gouvion St. Cyr, the late Minister at War, shortly before the recent change of Ministers. Being desirous to prefer a complaint against one of the many officers with whom he had had personal differ-ences, the General went to the War-office, but was stopped by the sentinel, who told him that his orders were peremptory, and that no person whatever was to be admit-ted at that hour to the Marshal. The

General, however, pushed by, and entered the Minister's apartment, where he found him deeply engaged in business; he was, however, proceeding to relate his complaint, when he was stopped by the Minister, with the enquiry of how he obtained admittance, and whether the sentinel had not informed him that he could not pass? "Oh, yes!" replied General Donadieu, "but I did not regard that." "General," rejoined the Minister, "I have long seen that you did not know how to command, and it is now equally clear that you do not know how to obey.—A soldier should have known that a private on duty was to be supported in his discharge of it as much as if he were a General; I beg, General, that you will retire."

Invention of Coaches.

The first coach ever seen in England formed part of the equipage of Henry Fitzalban, the last Earl of Arundel of that name, who died in 1579. It was invented by the French; as was the Post chaise also, which was first introduced in England by the son of the well known writer on husbandry, Mr. Jethro Tull. Hackney coaches were first established in London by Capt. Bailey, in 1634, and in the same year Hackney chairs or Sedans were introduced by Sir Sanders Duncombe, Knt. who was a great traveller; and had most probably seen them at Sedan, in France, where Dr. Johnson supposes that they were first made.

Brewer, in his "Beauties of Middlesex," observes in a note, that "It is familiarly said, that Hackney, on account of its numerous respectable inhabitants, was the first place near London provided with coaches of hire for the accommodation of families, and that thence arises the term *Hackney Coaches.* This appears quite futile; the word *Hackney,* as applied to a hireling, is traced to a remote British origin, and was certainly used in its present sense long before that village became conspicuous for wealth or population." In 1637, the number of Hackney coaches in London; was confined to 50; in 1652 to 200; in 1654 to 300; in 1661 to 400; in 1694 to 700; in 1710 to 800; in 1771 to 1,000; and in 1802 1,100. In imitation of our Hackney Coaches, Niocholas Sauvage introduced the *fiacres* at Paris, in the year 1650.

The *hammer cloth* is an ornamental covering of the coach-box; Mr. S. Pegge says, "The Coachman formerly used to carry a *hammer,* pincers, a few nails, &c. in a leathern pouch belonging to his box, and this cloth was devised for the hiding of them from public view."

Beautiful Simile.

So the struck Eagle, stretcht upon the plain, [again, No more through rolling clouds to soar View'd his own feather on the fatal dart, And wing'd the shaft that quiver'd in his heart. [feel Keen were his pangs, but keener far, to He nurs'd the pinion that impell'd the steel, Whilst the same plumage which nad warm'd his nest, [breast. Drank the last life-drop of his bleeding BYRON.

Mr. Rogers and Junius.

When the late Sir Philip Francis was, not long before his death, at Hollandhouse, the Lady of the mansion induced Mr. Rogers, the poet, to ask the Knight if he were really the author of "Junius's Letters." The Bard, knowing the Knight's austere character, addressed him with modest hesitation, asking if he might be permitted to propose a question. The Knight, evidently anticipating what was to come, exclaimed in a severe tone, "At your peril, Sir." Mr. Rogers immediately retired, and returning to tell Lady Holland the success of his mission, observed, that "if Sir Philip were really Junius, he was certainly Junius *Brutus.*"

Luther a Hunting.

This exercise was probably taken by the great reformer more for health than for pleasure, as indeed may be collected from his own curious account of it. "I was," says he, "lately two days a hunting, in which amusement I found both pleasure and pain. We killed a brace of hares, and took some unhappy partridges; a very pretty employment, truly, for an idle man! However, I could not forbear theologizing amidst dogs and nets; for, thought I to myself, do not we, in hunting innocent animals to death with dogs, very much resemble the devil, who, by crafty wiles and the instruments of wicked priests, is perpetually seeking whom he may devour? Again: We happened to take a leveret alive, which I put into my pocket, with an intent to preserve it; yet we were not gone far, before the dogs seized upon it, as it was in my pocket, and worried it. Just so the pope and the devil rage furiously to destroy the souls that I have saved, in spite of all my endeavours to prevent them. In short, I am tired of hunting these little innocent beasts; and had rather be employed, as I have been for some time, in spearing bears, wolves, tigers, and foxes; that is, in opposing and confounding wicked and impious divines, who resemble those savage animals in their qualities."

Habit—Custom.

Mr. Southey, in his *Omniana,* has the following anecdote on the force of habit. An Emir had bought a left eye of a glass eye-maker, supposing that he would be able to see with it. The man begged him to give it a little time; he could not expect that it would see all at once, as well as the right eye, which had been so many years in the habit of it! Custom, says somebody, is a great thing—I say it is every thing.

Knighthood.

Knighthood was originally conferred in England by the priest at the altar, after confession, and the consecration of the sword, during the Saxon Heptarchy. The first Knight made by the Sovereign with the sword of state, was Athelstan, on whom Alfred conferred this new dignity. The custom of Ecclesiastics conferring Knighthood, was abolished at a Synod, held at Westminster, in 1,100; and in the reign of Henry III. 1154, all persons having a yearly income of ten pounds were obliged to be knighted, or pay a fine to be excused.

The late Marie Antoinette.

A correspondent in the *Quotidienne,* adverting to the death of the late Antoinette, Queen of France, gives the following piquant anecdote, as one which has hitherto escaped all the historians of this disastrous period:—When the Royal Family, arrested in their attempted flight from France, were on their return from Varennes to Paris, the Dauphin having re-

marked on the buttons of M. Barnave, one of the Deputies appointed by the National Assembly to attend the Royal prisoners, the device *To live free, or die,* turned to his mother and said, "Mamma, what does that mean, to live free?" "My son, replied the Queen, it is to go where you please."—"Ah, mamma, rejoined the infant quickly, then we are not free." Her Majesty bade him be silent, but Barnave was much moved, and from this and other circumstances during the journey, returned full of grief and repentance to Paris, where he soon afterwards paid with his head for his desertion from the colours of the revolution.

Great and Little Napoleons.

The manuscript Memoirs of Gen. Rapp contain the following anecdote :—When Buonaparte was at Schoenbrunn, he used sometimes to amuse himself with a game at *vingt-et-un.* One evening, in which he had been very lucky, he shook the pieces of gold he had won in his hand, and said—"The Germans love these little Napóleons, don't they?" "Yes, replied Rapp, they do Sire; but then they are not at all fond of the *Great* one."

Spiders—Zinc.

Nothing can be more curious than the discoveries made by the Microscope, relative to the spider's thread and method of weaving. Leuwenhoeck states that he found 4 millions of these not thicker than the hairs of his beard, and each of these are now said to be compounded of 4 finer threads, which come from the insect's body in the manner that wire is drawn through a plate pierced with holes.—Another recent discovery, if possible more surprising is, that spiders feed on sulphate of zinc.

HINTS, PLANS, and PROCEEDINGS
OF
Benevolence.

Homo sum:
Humanum nihil a me alienum puto.

BOMBAY NATIVE SCHOOLS.

To the friends of mankind, and to those who are warmed with zeal for the promotion of its highest and most important interests, it will doubtless be in the greatest degree gratifying to know, that the president and members of the Bombay School committee, after having provided for the education of European and Christian children of both sexes, powerfully supported by the munificent and charitable aid of government and the public, under this presidency, have at length turned their serious consideration to the means best calculated for extending the blessings of intellectual cultivation to the native children of India.

The result of this consideration has been the invention and proposal of a plan for the attainment of an object of such pure philanthropy, so palpably beneficial, so flattering to the native character, and so tender of peculiar prejudices, which should never be openly and rudely assailed, that it has already met with the complete approbation of the assemblies or punchaets of two classes of the native inhabitants of this island, not the least powerful from numbers and wealth. The committee also having completely agreed on the most eligible plan, its execution was so far advanced that one English school was ex pected to be opened in the course of a week.

A Mahommedan youth, the son of a sepoy in the office of the chief secretary to government, who has received instruction for about a year at the central school in the town of Bombay, gave, in the course of a rigid examination, such proofs of capacity to convey to his countrymen the rudiments of tuition in English on the plan of Bell, that the first class of upwards of twenty Parsee children were to be placed under his care. A prospectus of the proposed plan has been translated into the Persian, Hindoostanee and Guzerattee languages; which were printed for the purpose of distribution, in order to diffuse among the native inhabitants a more general knowledge of the means about to be offered them, of educating their children in any of their respective dialects, more extensively, economically, and effectually, than they have hitherto been enabled to do.

A teacher of the Guzerattee has declared himself ready to attend the central school, in order to prepare himself for instruction on Bell's plan: the committee has deter-

mined to address the Calcutta school society, for books, tables, &c. to be translated here into the dialects peculiar to this part of India; which, as well as English books, the committee have determined to furnish gratuitously to the native schools, and also generally to extend toward them such other aid as may be in their power.

Even in the article of native books, however, the committee and promoters of the plan are not altogether unaided by native enterprize; fifty copies of an elementary Guzerattee work, comprizing the alphabet, the concise vocabulary, the rudiments of arithmetic, accounts, the forms of letter writing, bonds, obligations, leases, and interest tables, which are now printing by a Parsee inhabitant of Bombay, have been subscribed for, as well as the same number of copies of a translation into the same language of a Persian work, containing an easy epitome of the lives and remarkable sayings of the Grecian philosophers.

CALCUTTA SCHOOL BOOK SOCIETY.

Even the natives subscribe to this institution, although the sentiments, which the Society's books contain, aim at the ruin of the Hindoo system of religion. There is nothing which will more certainly effect the destruction of superstition, than these schools. Each succeeding generation will feel their influence more and more, until the contracted, and absurd ideas of the heathen, will be renounced. Already in the schools, have the highest and lowest castes mingled together. The Soodras have been placed above the Brahmin youth, without exciting the anger or chagrin of the latter. If these events continue to take place, for any length of time, the sacred thread of the Brahmins will be esteemed as nothing, and thrown by with disgust. The Church School Society have 3000 children under their direction; and the Baptists have more than 6000. These children will acquire more lofty ideas than their ancestors possessed; nor can we suppose that the time is far distant, when they will have a mean opinion of their sacred books, which assert that the world is made of seven continents, and seven oceans, and that Hindoostan is the centre. When they find the true geography of the globe, what will they think of their shasters?

PROGRESS OF MISSIONS.

In the last number of the "Missionary Register," we have an interesting and comprehensive Survey of the Protestant Missionary Stations throughout the world, in their geographical order: the extent and importance of which are described in the following introductory observations.

Supposing a person to visit in succession these various stations, his course might first be directed to Western Africa, comprehending that portion of the Continent which lies between Morocco and the Line. Crossing the Line, he would enter on that part of Africa which, lying south of the Line, may be classed in Missionary Records as *South Africa;* and which should be considered as including the islands that lie off its south-eastern coast. Passing up the coast of *Eastern Africa,* the Christian beholds, with hope of better days, as he works his way up the Red Sea, on the one hand Abyssinia and Nubia and Upper Egypt, and *Arabia* on the other. On entering the *Mediterranean,* after surveying Syria and the Holy Land, he passes by Lower Egypt, throughout the Barbary States; and then taking his station for a time in Malta, as the centre of this great scene of holy labour, he visits in succession, the Ionian Islands, Greece, the Archipelago, and the Lesser Asia. Passing into the *Black Sea,* and contemplating, as promising spheres of Christian Exertion, its Turkish and Russian Shores, he may make his way, by the Russian Provinces lying between the Black and the Caspian Seas—while he anticipates the final happiness of *Persia,* partly through these Provinces, and partly by means of the maritime and continental access to that kingdom from Western India—into the almost boundless plains of *Northern Asia,* comprehending the Provinces of that quarter belonging to Russia, with the widely-extended regions inhabited by Tartar and other Tribes, whether independent or connected with any of the neighbouring Powers. By the great country of *Thibet,* he may proceed to *China;* connected with which vast sphere of labour is *India beyond the Ganges;* whence, returning to the great scene of British Influence and Power, *India within the Ganges,* he may afterward traverse the whole series of *Asiatic Islands,* from the Laccadive and Maldive to Japan. From these, his course would lie through the Insular Continents, as they may be denominated, of *Australasia,* and the numerous groupes of *Polynesia.* Passing on, and contemplating the great Continent of *South America,* with earnest prayers for the rising of the Sun of Righteousness on that dreary region, he may reach Guiana, the solitary portion of that Quarter of the World where Protestant Christians are labouring for the good of the Heathen; and then, winding his course among the Islands and Shores of the *West Indies,* and passing through the Tribes of the *North-American Indians,* he may finish his vast survey, by contemplating, with admiration, the Triumphs of the Cross on the inhospitable shores of *Labrador* and of *Greenland.*

ASSOCIATION FOR THE RELIEF OF
THE POOR.
Report, Jan. 13, 1819.

The distribution of Coals at 9d. per bushel, and Potatoes at 14lbs. for 3d, commenced on the 12th of January, and continued to the 8th of April 1818, inclusive, in which period three hundred and thirty chaldrons of Coals, and about seventy-four tons of Potatoes, were delivered at the City Public Kitchen, to applicants bringing recommendatory Tickets from the Subscribers, being a larger distribution for the time, than had been witnessed in any former Winter. It is estimated that not less than two thousand five hundred families, consisting of about twelve thousand five hundred individuals, participated of this very salutary relief, which was received with sincere gratitude and humble acknowledgement; and the Committee are convinced it materially alleviated the sufferings and distress of great numbers of the industrious but necessitous poor, who were deserving of this bountiful assistance.

From the precaution which the Committee recommended to the Subscribers, of not giving more than one or two Tickets per week, according to the number in family, with an inquiry into the necessities of the applicants, it is believed impositions and abuses of the charity, are not numerous, considering the great extent of its operations. The loss sustained to the Fund of the Association on the distribution of Coals and Potatoes for the last Winter, and the consequent advantage to the Poor, including all contingent expences, amounted to 672l. 5s. 9d.

The Committee desire duly to acknowledge the continued liberality of the Subscribers, which has enabled them to render such extensive assistance to the necessitous and distressed, residing in various parts of the Metropolis; and they trust, a conviction of the substantial aid afforded to the poor, from the peculiar mode of relief adopted by the Society, has much tended to excite the generous contributions of the affluent and humane.

That such liberality is dictated by a wise policy, as well as by Christian compassion, cannot be doubted; for one class of the community cannot greatly suffer, without entailing a proportion of its misery on the other classes: hence arise an increase of the Poor's Rates, and what is still worse, a frightful increase of crimes—whatever therefore tends to rescue the indigent from absolute want, to make them more comfortable and contented, is advantageously felt by every rank above them in various ways, whilst it affords grateful satisfaction to the contributors.

An Appeal in behalf of the Family of the late Mr. Blagdon.

If the mourning relatives of the hero, who perishes in the field of glory, be entitled to the protection of a grateful country, the bereaved family of a man who devoted, and even sacrificed, his life to the cause of loyalty, and of all that is dear to Britons, may be allowed to raise its prayer, in the hope that it will neither be unheard nor unanswered. About the year 1808, Mr. Blagdon, the lamented individual in behalf of whose widow and children this *appeal* is most respectfully made, embarked the whole of his little property in the *Phœnix* weekly newspaper. The declared object of that publication was, to arrest the appalling progress of sedition, which then threatened, by its demoralizing effects upon society, to overturn the State, with all its ancient and glorious institutions. From the peculiar circumstances of the times, the work failed; and the projector was involved in ruin. The liberal aid, however, of some private friends, who loved the man, and admired his principles, enabled him, partially, to overcome his

difficulties, and to re-enter the lists of political warfare. Again, Mr. Blagdon was unsuccessful; and, a second time, he was stripped of his all—even his Looks, and his household furniture.

In attempting to establish his two papers (the *Phœnix*, and the *Political Register*) Mr. Blagdon expended the sum of nearly 3,500l. His ever-active, ever-buoyant spirit rose superior to misfortune; but, notwithstanding his incessant and indefatigable exertions for the support of his family, and for the liquidation of pecuniary claims against him, the doors of a prison were closed upon his worn and harassed frame. From this severe and complicated ruin, he never completely emerged. His personal liberty was indeed obtained; but his high sense of honour and integrity never again permitted him to feel himself free; and the remainder of his life presented only the melancholy display of a liberal mind, struggling, anxiously but unavailingly, against the inroads of poverty, and the attacks of disease.

By mental suffering, by repeated attacks of a liver complaint, and by the loss of rest, incurred through a sedulous attention on her husband, during his protracted illness, Mrs. Blagdon's health is greatly impaired. She and her four children (two girls and two boys, within the ages of 9 and 14) are totally unprovided for. Without money, without property of any description, without friends or relatives so situated as to be able to assist them, their sole reliance is on the benevolence of those who can feel for the widow and the fatherless.—The immediate object of this *appeal* is, to endeavour to raise such a fund as may enable Mrs. Blagdon to complete the education of her children, that they may be enabled to fill, with credit to themselves, and advantage to the community, whatever stations it may be their lot to hold.

References are respectfully offered to the following individuals, by whom the contributions of benevolence will be most gratefully received:—N. Byrne, Esq. Morning Post Office; J. Taylor, Esq. Sun Office, 112, Strand; at the Courier Office, 348, Strand; S. Cock, Esq. 2, Frederick Place, Old Jewry; Mr. M'Millan, 6 Bow Street, Covent Garden; Mr. Purser, 1, Finch Lane, Cornhill; Mr. Colburn, Library, Conduit Street, Hanover Square; the Banking-houses of Messrs. Birch and Chambers, 160, New Bond Street; Messrs. Hoare, Barnett, and Co., 62, Lombard Street; Messrs. Crickitt, Bacon, and Co., Ipswich, Suffolk; and Mr. Harral, Park Cottage, Ipswich, Suffolk.

List of the principal works written or edited by Mr. Blagdon.—The Phœnix Weekly Newspaper, 2 vols. 4to;—The Weekly Political Register, 2 vols. 8vo.;—History of Ancient and Modern India, 1 vol. folio;—The Modern Geographer; or, a Complete System of Geography, 5 vols. 8vo.;—The Life and Exploits of Admiral Lord Nelson, &c. 1 vol. 4to.;—The Life of George Morland, 1 vol. folio;—Translations of the Voyages and Travels of Denon, in Egypt; Golberry, in Africa; and Pallas, in Russia, 8 vols.;—Translations, &c. of Modern Contemporary Voyages and Travels, 11 vols. 8vo.—The Life and Transactions of our Saviour, 1 vol. royal 8vo.;—A Complete History of Christian Martyrdom, &c. with copious original Historical Notes, [a condensed, but elaborate edition of Fox's Martyrs, bearing the name of Milner] 1 vol. royal 8vo.;—Flowers of Literature, 7 vols.;—Mœriana, 2 vols.; various political pamphlets, &c. &c. &c.

HIBERNIAN SOCIETY

For Establishing Schools, and Circulating the Holy Scriptures in Ireland.

APPENDIX TO REPORT, 1818.

ALTHOUGH the Annual Report of the Hibernian Society, read at the General Meeting in May last, was connected with an Appendix of considerable length and importance; yet the Committee of this Institution feel it to be their duty to add to those communications a selection of the interesting intelligence which has since been received, in order that Individuals and Auxiliary Institutions who patronize this Society may know, that it pleases God to continue his blessing on the "work and labour of love," which they have undertaken in Ireland.

When the nature of the operations of the Hibernian Society is considered, in connexion with the places in which they are carried on, it might justly be expected that the results would be very interesting

and important. To afford the elements of useful education, and the benefits of scriptural instruction to children, who are immersed in ignorance and depravity; to introduce the inspired volume to the rising generation of a country, in which they have been prevented from seeing its glorious light, and hearing its joyful sound; and, by the instruction thus given to the children, to extend these high advantages to their parents and friends, who have hitherto been sunk in darkness and superstion;—these are means and exertions, which, if pursued with activity, must, with the divine blessing, produce a gradually increasing developement of intellectual benefits and moral and religious usefulness, in the highest degree gratifying and beneficial.

The truth of these observations has been proved ever since the Hibernian Society commenced its benevolent undertakings in Ireland; and its successive Reports have evidenced that its objects are worthy of especial consideration, and that its operations have been remarkably important and successful.

The number of the Society's Schools in Ireland, as stated in the last Report, was 392, and the number of Children taught therein, 32,516. The Treasurer was then above seven hundred pounds in advance. Since that time the Schools and the Scholars have increased; additional expenses are incurred thereby, and the claims of the Society on public generosity and christian benevolence, are rendered more urgent and impressive. Annual Subscriptions, Donations, Collections, and especially assistance from Auxiliary Institutions, are therefore earnestly solicited; and the Committee indulge the hope and expectation, that the interesting and important intelligence, which is conveyed in the following extracts, taken chiefly from the correspondence, during the last three months, of one who is daily in communication with the individuals employed in the service of the Society, will make this occasional communication very acceptable, and this appeal to public philanthropy very successful.

BENEFIT OF ALLOWING LAND TO THE POOR.

The good affects of allowing the poor labourer a small spot of ground, to be cultivated in his leisure hours, as a means of reducing the poor's-rate, are exemplified in the following extract from a letter inserted in The New Times:—

The hard-working, the meritorious and virtuous Isaac and Betty Stuckey, with a family of eight children, had an abhorrence of burthening a parish with a farthing expense, and a dread of losing their independence, although they had not a bit of meat for six months together, and were often strangers to a loaf of bread. Isaac, the husband, an excellent workman, earned eight shillings a week, but he was allowed to hire, even at double the value, half an acre of ground, where, with his spade, he laboured morning and night, before and after his daily work at the farm. To this generous half acre, poor Betty, the wife, when she could steal a few hours, would run with the spade to lessen her husband's toil. Isaac never murmured—Betty never complained. Visiting this family on a Sunday, since their case was published, and nearly 100l. contributed for them, I found the man with his Bible before him, his wife and children around him! Give, said the grateful people, ten thousand thanks to our unknown benevolent friends. On receiving between thirty and forty pounds, they had purchased hemp, had profited by working it 20l. With 40l. more in the hands of the treasurer, pigs, poultry, vegetables, and a rack, stored with bacon, this family are ready to hire a farm of about fifty acres. This good man, and thousands besides, assure me, that one acre of ground, at a fair rent, would afford more real relief, and tend more to the happiness of the labouring poor than all the poor-rates that are paid."

INTERESTING INTELLIGENCE FROM THE BRITISH SETTLEMENTS IN INDIA.

CALCUTTA.

PRINCELY LIBERALITY.

The following generous trait in the character of the Marquess of Hastings, deserves to be universally known. As Commander-in-Chief, he became entitled to a very large share of the rich booty acquired in the late campaign. No one could, in his military character possess a fairer title to this

property; for the Marquess both planned and directed the whole war in its general outline and almost in its minutest details: he took the field in person; he met the most alarming contingencies with coolness and promptitude; he kept the whole machine in regulated and equable movement, accelerating or restraining as occasion required, the daily movements of the separate detachments. If, under such circumstances, Lord Hastings had declined to suffer the allotment of his legal share to be made, he would perhaps have compromised the rights of his successors in command. Accordingly the Noble Marquess directed the usual division of the booty to be made; but reflecting that he had in his own person united the supreme civil and military authority—that as Governor-General, he had resolved upon the war, which, as Commander-in-Chief, he had directed—a feeling of personal delicacy precluded him from benefiting by this great accession of fortune. He was unwilling that even those who in the present or in future times might be most ignorant of his real character, should ever have the slightest ground to suspect that his public measures could have been in any degree affected by his private interest; and he therefore most magnanimously threw the whole of his share into the portion of the subalterns and privates.

FISH v. WASHERMAN.

The following singular circumstance occurred a few months since at Garden-Reach, near Calcutta. A washerman engaged in his occupation on the edge of a tank, was immersing a piece of cloth which he held in his hand in the water, when a large fish sprang forward, seized the cloth and the man's arm in his mouth, and was triumphantly swimming off with his prey. Fortunately, however, a person close by at the time caught hold of the washerman's quivering leg, and dragged both man and fish on shore! The animal was immediately taken to the Police Thana to be exhibited! It weighed a maund and a half, and was about six feet in length, of the species commonly called Sowlee. The washerman's arm was considerably lacerated.

STATE OF MORALS.

The following is an extract from the presentment of the grand Jury to Sir Edw. Hyde East, and the other judges of the

Supreme Court, dated June 29, 1818, adverting to a complaint on the part of the magistrates, that the powers with which they are at present invested are insufficient for the suppression of crime. "The complaint in question, if the grand jury understand it rightly, has reference to a want of the requisite authority for the prevention, rather than for the detection or punishment of offences. Of the fact they have no doubt, that the facilities of secreting and vending stolen property in Calcutta are greatly increased, by the free influx of strangers of all characters and from all parts of India, who establish themselves here as shopkeepers and tradesmen, and are in no way under the observance or control of the police; and they are equally well satisfied, that the daily increasing number of gaming houses and other places of resort for the idle and profligate, which the magistrates have no power to regulate or suppress, has eminently tended to demoralize the middle and lower classes of the population, and to increase the frequency of crime. The state of society in this great city seems indisputably to require, that the magistrate should be armed at least with the fullest powers committed to the ministers of police in any other city of the British dominions. And the Grand Jury are not without hope, that a system of regulation adapted to local circumstances may yet be devised, which shall essentially counteract the mischiefs complained of, and serve as a permanent check on the dissolute and depraved habits of a numerous class of the community, without materially trenching on the liberties, or disturbing the peace or comfort of the honest and industrious inhabitants."

BOMBAY.

DISTRESSES AT SEA.

The following detail of the calamities experienced by the officers and crew of the brig Fly from Batavia, is given in the Bombay Hurkaru. The crew of the brig Fly, which arrived here a few days ago from Batavia, had a most providential escape from suffering the severest of calamities. A few days after she had sailed, in March last, her captain died at sea, and the command devolving on officers not so well experienced in the navigation of those seas, they deviated from their course, and drifted about with various winds and cur-

rents for a considerable time; insomuch that their small supply of provisions was soon expended. When their distress became so urgent, they were compelled to have recourse for their food to three monkies, which were on board, and which constituted the whole subsistence of seven men for three days. This wretched provision being also consumed, they remained without any food whatever, until nature being nearly exhausted, one of the crew proposed to cast lots, that one might be sacrificed to furnish sustenance for the remainder. This being resolved upon, the lot fell upon the individual who proposed this remedy. Though ready to submit to his fate, and fainting from weakness, the desire of preserving life roused him to exert his feeble powers in one last effort. Hope gave him encouragement and he mounted up aloft, praying that he might descry some vessel or some land to save him from death, and his partners from such a shocking alternative to save themselves. His anxious eyes however long exerted their utmost powers in vain; despair seized him, all prospect of relief had fled, and he was about to descend to meet his destiny, when kind Providence answered his prayers and restored him to life. He discerned a sail at a distance; he hailed his brethren; they summoned all their remaining strength, made signal of distress, and bore up towards the vessel in sight, which proved to be the Endeavour, Capt. Rojerson, from Bombay, and by whom they were supplied with every thing their deplorable situation required, compatible with their own condition; the Endeavour's stock of provisions being also very low, and having suffered so much from stress of weather, that she was compelled to return to this river, which she entered in company with the Fly.

WOMAN BURIED ALIVE.

Bombay Gazette, Aug. 11.—We learn from a letter in one of the papers of the week, that a woman was lately buried alive with her deceased husband, near Isherah, within a few miles of Calcutta. The ceremonies accompanying this shocking spectacle, as they are detailed by an eye-witness, bespeak an inhumanity and cruelty truly deplorable. We had imagined that this mode of immolation was not required and scarcely countenanced by the Hindu law; but happening so close under the eye of public authority, we must conclude that it is according to law and usage. The bodies were placed upright in a hole dug for the purpose, and the earth was thrown in by handfuls around them and trodden down by the woman's oldest son, a youth of about 19. When it reached above the head of the miserable victim, a shout of joy and exultation was raised by the unfeeling multitude.

CHINA.

JEWS; INTERESTING FACT.

It has long been the opinion of some learned men, that part of the TEN TRIBES had found their way to China, and settled in the province of Ho-NAN. The following extract from the notes of the Rev. R. Morrison's journey to Peking, is submitted to the consideration of the reader. "[While in the interior,] October 10th, had a conversation with a Mahomedan gentleman, who informed me, that at KAE-FUNG FOO, in the province of Ho-NAN, there are a few families denominated the TEAOU-KIN-KEAOU, or the sect that plucks out the sinew from all the meat which they eat. They have a LE-PAE-OZE, or House of Worship, and observe the eighth day as a Sabbath." The fact of the existence of a few insulated families in the very heart of the Chinese empire, observing religious ceremonies that bear some resemblance to those observed by the Jews, and that seem so widely different from any of the Chinese ceremonies of Worship, is a very interesting one, and highly deserving of farther investigation. *Chinese Gleaner.*

Poetry.

SATIRES IN INDIA.
From the Asiatic Magazine.

[The following nervous and elegant Satires abound in strains of genuine Poetry, and display an intimate knowledge of the human heart; though written expressly for the meridian of CALCUTTA, they will, we doubt not, be acceptable to a large portion of our readers, for AUGUSTA is not without many an original whose portraits is here, " and one to the life."]

'Nothing so true as what you once let fall,
Most Women have no characters at all.'
                                    Pope.

WHAT! 'Women have no characters!—away!—
Plead not the sanction of a Poet's lay.

Can rash assertion dare the test of time,
Because it boasts the harmony of rhyme?
Shall raptured list'ners still as truth receive,
What the fond heart delights to disbelieve?
Not all the pleasing witchery of song,
Can e'er enslave, or lead the soul along.
TRUTH claims her heav'nly sway—her powers
     appear,
Bursttbe Bard's spells, and disenchant the ear?

Is there not feeling in the Woman's heart?—
Claims not affection there its purer part?
Is there not Mildness, Life's sad path to
     smooth,
And Love's endearments, still each care to
     sooth?
'Tis—WOMAN!—this thy character, indeed!
These are thy charms, that willing captives
     lead.
And tho' awhile the mem'ry of deceit
May bid some once fond heart in rancour beat,
May waken cold misanthrophy and spleen,
'Till man ungrateful fly from Beauty's scene,—
Ah! yet again one dear alluring smile,
One beaming glance of love shall still beguile;
While the dark joyless frown shall cease to
     lower,
And throbbing feelings own again thy power.

In every fancied bliss, that Youth can rear,
In ev'ry hope of Joy for future year,
'Mid hours of expectation, when the breast
Pants for some moment dearer than the rest,
Then, then, it is, that WOMAN seems alone,
The fair possessor of our Fancy's throne;
Then, then, it is, we breathe the anxious sigh,
We think of some fond glance from dewy eye;
We dream of soft caresses fondly given,
Of Beauty—Tenderness—best boons of
     Heaven!
And still, the dear,—the cherish'd dream to
     crown,
We hope—ah! pant, to call these charms
     our own!

In genial clime like this, where every ray,
That bursts, unceasing from the orb of day,
Gives the fond heart to all the fire of love,
And all the passions fierceness bids it prove.
Hear yonder Lover to the winds complain,
Though warm his vows, those vows are all in
     vain,

Proud Beauty scorns his true, though humble prayers,
And only smiles, when Wealth or Grandeur glares.

But oft complaint is rash, and wide from truth :
Observe yon am'rous boy—yon beardless youth ;
He singles out an object of desire,
Burns with a thoughtless flame, or,—feigns the fire ;
Then stung, at last, with well deserv'd neglect,
He rails to find, that Prudence can reject.

Yet other ills—alas !—our Youth assert,
(And grant—Oh Heaven! their tales the truth pervert)—
That there are Fair, who pant to try their power,
And playful search for sweets, from flower to flower ;
Who strive to wake th' impassion'd Lover's sigh,
And catch the thrilling langour of his eye ;
Who listen smiling to his tale of pain,
While melting looks half tell that Tale again.
—Or when his hand, in trembling touch of Love,
With timid pressure would their kindness move,
Then that dear kindness—fearful to deny,
Bids a soft hand, in gentler squeeze reply.
Thus—have we heard—the glowing force is play'd,
'Till some fond fool, enamour'd of a maid,
Half urg'd to Frenzy, ventures to propose ;
And paints a dismal picture of his woes ;
Repulse appals him!——the lov'd fair explains ;
The fool's refus'd—and laugh'd at for his pains !

Selina boasts each charm, that Poets seek,
The softest dye of Love illumes her cheek ;
The milder graces on her steps await,
Lark in her form, and ambush in her gait ;
There is that angel something in her eye,
That men adore, nor can its witch'ry fly——
That soft retiring look—that timid glance,
Which more than ev'ry lure bids Love advance—

The sweet, half-childish semblance of alarm,
Which sighs to cling to fond Protection's arm
That ev'ry seeming wakefulness of heart,
When tears of tenderness, too prompt to starts,
Flow at a word from glist'ning orbs of light,
'Till Beauty, gemm'd with feeling, beams more bright !
Oh! who would think, beneath a guise so soft,
Beats a proud heart, that pants to soar aloft,
That ever sighs for conquest, and for power,
And like some haughty hermit in his bower,
'Mid well-feign'd lowliness, allures a name,
And seeming still to shun it—grasps at fame ?

But let us turn from this the Lover's gaze,
Nor judge our Fair ones, by a Lover's praise,
Seek we the walks of calm domestic life,
And view awhile the Mother and the Wife,
And here are they, whom Eulogy may claim,
Worthy, as e'er her trumpet gave to fame,
Perchance there be, that Satire best may suit,
And Satire sings, when Eulogy is mute,
But—blest the thought ! how long may Satire roam !
And find no resting-place in Indian home.

Ere blooming MIRA left her humble home,
Or ever-dream'd from native bower to roam,
Then ev'ry Sunday deck'd in best array,
Prayer-book in hand, to Church she tripp'd away ;
Smil'd, as she caught each young admirer's stare,
And read their eyes, more deeply than the prayer.
Full many a dashing Clerk had sigh'd his pain,
Full many a spruce apprentice own'd her reign.
At home—her samplers rang'd in order fair,
And counterpanes of patch-work, prov'd her care ;
Her younger brother's shirts, so neatly made
So neatly mark'd, her industry betray'd ;
While smiling guests declar'd her tarts and pies,
Confess'd her skill, and claim'd the housewife's prize.
She was fair MIRA—when an Uncle came,
Rich as a Nabob—fraught with wealth and fame,

Fresh from the East ; and then her heart was
    fir'd,
The dream of Indian pomp her soul inspir'd:
Nor long her wishes vain—her Uncle's care,
Bade his lov'd niece some master's lessons
    share ;
'Till soon, how chang'd in ev'ry art to please!
She painted skies all blue, and greener trees ;
Could rattle, ' Ah vous dirai je' with an air,
And dress'd in newest, gayest ' *style of Hair* !'

Thus all accomplish'd, next o'er seas con-
    vey'd,
'Mid gay Calcutta's scenes, appear'd the maid;
Where, first attacks of fierce Musqitos o'er,
The damsel learnt to prize her Beauty's power;
And ere one year could steal upon her charms,
A wealthy suitor gain'd her to his arms!

Now see glad MIRA—blest in wish of
    pride,
The fair one's envy—and a JUDGE's bride !
She, who once pass'd each Hackney-coaches'
    stand,
And sigh'd in vain,—hath chariots at com-
    mand ;
She, to whom frock of chintz gave happiness,
Now shines in lace, and scorns a humbler dress:
With crowds of vain admirers at her sway,
'Mid listless elegance consumes the day ;
To think of once-dear friends, can never deign,
And lives the gayest of Calcutta's train.

But mark fair STELLA--ornament of worth !
Of milder manners— tho' of prouder birth ;
In her the Lady—Sister—Friend combine,
In her the Wife's more moral virtues shine.
How bright the welcome of her sparkling eye,
How kind her greeting in Society !
And (blest the truth !) that where one MIRA's
    seen,
A host of STELLAS deck our Indian scene.
            [*To be Continued.*]

TO THE WOOD ANEMONE,
BY THE AUTHOR OF " NIGHT,"
(A Descriptive Poem.)

Why dost thou close thine eye ?
Demurest Mourner! why ?

Say, did the fragrant night-breeze rudely kiss
Thy drooping forehead fair,
And press thy dewy hair
With amorous touch, embracing all amiss ?
And, therefore, flow'ret meek,
Glow on thy snowy cheek
Hues, less to shame than angry scorn allied,
Yet, lovely as the bloom
Of Even, on the tomb
Of one who injur'd liv'd, and slander'd died ?
Or, didst thou fondly meet
His soft-lip hybla-sweet?
And therefore doth the cold and loveless cloud
Thy wanton kissing chide ?
And therefore would'st thou hide
Thy burning blush, thy cheek so sweetly
    bow'd ?
Or, while the daisey slept,
Say, hast thou waked and wept,
Because thy Lord, the Lord of love and light,
Had left thy pensive smile ?
What western charms beguile
The fire-hair'd youth, forth from whose
    eyelids bright,
Are cast o'er nights deep sky
Her gems that flame on high ?
That Husband, whose warm glance thy soul
    reveres,
No flow'ret of the west
Detains on harlot breast ;
The envious cloud withholds him from thy
    tears.

EXTEMPORE LINES ON Mr. KEAN.
(By the Same.)

When long the Drama, in a sordid age,
Had droop'd, an exile ; to the desert stage,
Impassion'd Nature, weeping as she smil'd,
Led, by the trembling hand, her darling
    child :—
Even from the worms, upstarted buried Spleen,
While Shakespeare's dust, in transport, mur-
    mur'd ' Kean !'

INSCRIPTION FOR MY DAUGHTER'S
HOUR-GLASS.

Mark the golden grains that pass
Brightly thro' this channel'd glass,

Men uring by their ceaseless fall
Heaven's most precious gift to all!
Busy, till its sand be done,
See the shining current run ;
But, th' allotted numbers shed,
Another hour of life hath fled!
Its task perform'd, its travail past,
Like mortal man it rests at last!—
Yet let some hand invert its frame
And all its powers return the same,
Whilst any golden grains remain
'Twill work its little hour again.—
But who shall turn the glass for Man,
When all his golden grains have ran ?
Who shall collect his scatter'd sand,
Dispersed by Time's unsparing hand ?—
Never can one grain be found,
Howe'er we anxious search around!

Then, Daughters, since this truth is plain,
That Time once gone ne'er comes again,
Improv'd bid every moment pass—
See how the sand rolls down your glass.
                                    J. M. C.

National Register:

FOREIGN.

AFRICA: NORTH.

Plague at Tunis and Algiers.

Official accounts received from Gibraltar, dated the 18th Jan. state, that the deaths at Tunis, occasioned by the plague, amounted daily to above 600. At Algiers there were fresh attacks of the pestilence in December. The deaths by the plague at Tunis, according to official returns, from the 1st of November to the 1st of December, were 12,117!

AFRICA: WESTERN.

Pirates:—Slave Trade.

Sierra-Leone, Dec. 15.—We are happy to say, that Sir G. Collier has arrived on the coast, in his Majesty's ship Tartar; and we sincerely hope he will prove successful, not only in clearing these seas from the numerous pirates which have infested the whole line of coast from hence to Bonna, during the last two years, but that we shall hear no more of the slave trade, which, during the same period, has been carried on with such success and facility, by the Spaniards, French, and Portuguese, for want of a man of war.

Since February, 1818, no vessel of war has appeared at the British settlements on the Gold Coast: the last arrival of any force was his Majesty's ship Semiramis, Com. Sir J. Yeo; since whose return the slave ships have anchored and carried on their abominable trade within sight of the British forts, to the number of 6, 7, or 8 vessels at a time, with impunity.

Gold Trade.

We have to lament that our gold trade has declined very much of late on the coast, in consequence of a protracted warfare between the Ashantees and the natives of Buntucco. It is from these two principal states that we derive most of our gold, the Fantee nation acting more as intermediate agents than principals in such barters.

Consul at Ashantee.

Government having considered the trade of Ashantee of sufficient importance to induce them to send out a Consul to that country; it is hoped that he will have some influence in bringing them to terms of accommodation, and directing their minds to the less sanguinary employment of commerce.—For an interesting account of the Ashantees, consult LIT. PAN. vol. vii. p. 472.

Timbuctoo visited.

A young French traveller, nephew of Count Mollieu, Ex-Minister, has succeeded in reaching Timbuctoo by way of Senegal. His family has just received a letter from him, in which he announces his safe arrival in that celebrated town, hitherto almost unknown to Europeans, and which the unfortunate Mungo Park twice vainly attempted to reach.

AMERICA: UNITED STATES.

Emigrants from Europe.

A bill has been brought into the House of Representatives to prevent the sufferings of emigrants from Europe, in their passage from the United States. Of 5000 who sailed from Antwerp and Holland, in the year 1817, one thousand died on the passage. In one instance, a Captain sailed from a Dutch port with 1287 passengers in a single ship; he shortly after put into the Texel: in the interval 400 perished, and 300 more died before the vessel reached Philadelphia. The bill restricts the number of passengers to two for every five tons burthen.

American character of Emigrants.

New York is the great place of rendezvous for emigrants from all quarters; and Mr. Alderman Mesier, in a speech lately delivered to the Grand Jury of New York, after adverting to various offences which prevail, and their causes, adds, "The vicious habits of our city have, in some measure, their origin in the mixed character of our population. To this source may be referred many novel offences, as also the artifice with which they are perpetrated. Exotic vices, from the various nurseries of Europe, have been transplanted here, and professors of iniquity have found in this land of their adoption, talents equal to the practice of every improvement in villany which the old school has invented." So much for the virtuous and moral population, whom taxation and tyranny, as we are told, have driven across the Atlantic!

Wonderful Animal.

The naturalists of North America have been fortunate enough (they tell us) to discover that the mammoth still exists—the living mammoth—amongst the western wildernesses of that great continent. The bones of this enormous animal, though often found in the fossil state, have never, from time immemorial, that we can learn, been seen in actual motion. Those who descried the monster must have been hideously frightened; although it appears that they had their senses enough about them, to ascertain that he was not at all carnivorously given—a fact, indeed, which, if these travellers of the Mississippi had not been convinced of by their own escape from his jaws, they might have been assured of on the word of Cuvier, and others: they say it was graminivorous, or, rather, lignivorous, eating the *trunks* of trees! But all this time, was the animal really and undoubtedly a mammoth? We are told it had no horns, but was shaped somewhat "like a huge wild boar," about 15 feet high, or so. Now we have our private suspicions, that the beast in question wore

upon its shoulders the head of a cock, and carried at its other extremity a tail resembling that of a bull, so as to have been in all respects a rival not unworthy of that "most delicate monster," the Sea Serpent; one disturbing the coasts of the new world, the other devouring its forests; while the authority in favour of each is precisely equal as to weight and importance.

EGYPT.
Ancient City Discovered.

A French traveller now in Egypt has discovered, at a distance of about nine hours' journey from the Red Sea, an ancient city built in the mountains, between the 24th and 25th degrees of latitude. There are still 800 houses in existence. Among the ruins are found temples dedicated to various divinities. There are eleven statues, and various ruins of others. He has also discovered the ancient stations that were appointed on the route through the Desert, going from the Red Sea to the Valley of the Nile. These stations are at regular distances of nine hours between each. This route is undoubtedly one of those traversed by the commerce of India —a commerce which was so flourishing at the time of the *Lagides,* and under the first Emperors. The situation is now ascertained of the emerald mine, of which no certain knowledge was had for several ages.

M. Belzoni—Report contradicted.

A letter from Naples, from a source worthy of credit, contradicts the intelligence circulated by the English Journals, and repeated by those of the Continent, of the death of M. Belzoni. Lord Belmore, who has for some time past resided at Naples, and where he has lately arrived after a long and important journey in Egypt, Palestine, Syria, and Troy, has received letters from M. Belzoni, dated from Thebes, in Upper Egypt, the 27th October. He is pursuing his researches in Egypt with the greatest activity, and has already made various important discoveries. Lord Belmore himself advanced one hundred and fifty leagues above the cataracts, into Nubia; he passed six weeks at Thebes, where he daily employed about a hundred Arabs in searching. The discoveries he has made are very precious.

His journey will prove of great utility to geographers, as he has been careful to ascertain the distances of the different places he visited. He intends to publish an account of his travels on his arrival in England.

FRANCE.

Not to be believed!

Paris, Feb. 7.—The wife of an Englishman of distinction recently died in Paris. The husband was inconsolable for his loss, and would not quit the mortal remains of his once dear partner. He directed the preparations for the funeral, and accompanied the sepulchral procession to the burial-ground of Pere-la Chaise. On arriving there, he requested that a spot of ground might be assigned him for the grave. He was told the price of it would be 100 francs per yard, and a donation of 50 francs to the poor. "You will require two yards," said they, "consequently you must pay 250 francs." At these words, the Englishman took out of his pocket two pieces of 20 francs each, and pointing to the coffin containing the body of his late wife, in a weeping voice answered—*"Let her be interred upright!"*

French Telegraph.

Intelligence can be received from Calais at Paris, between which are 27 telegraphs, in 3 minutes.

Lisle	- - 22	-	-	2
Strasburg	- - 45	-	-	6¼
Lyons	- - 50	-	-⎱	8
Brest	- - 80	-	-⎰	

Antiquities at Arles.

Some inhabitants of the town of Arles having dug a spot of ground which the diminution of the waters of the Rhone had left uncovered, and which had been inundated from time immemorial, have found, amongst other relics of antiquity, a vase three feet high, and not less remarkable for the elegance of its shape than the perfection of its ornaments; a noble fragment of architecture, several coins, and a medal struck to celebrate the marriage of Constantine, with a great number of funeral urns, lacrymatories, and earthen lamps. The Prefect of the Department has immediately ordered regular excavations to be made in that piece of ground, in the neighbourhood of which, it may be recollected

that the fine statue, known under the appellation of the Venus of Arles, was found many years ago, and which probably still contains many precious chefs d'œuvre of antiquity.

Statue of Mad. L. Buonaparte.

At a private sale, lately at Paris, the statue in marble, by Canova, of Mad. Letitia Buonaparte, was purchased for the Duke of Devonshire, at the price of 36,000 francs. A Russian Prince had given a commission to bid for it, but limited the amount of his bidding to 24,000 francs.

GERMANY.

Leipsic Fair.

Leipsic, Jan. 23.—The new year's fair has turned out very ill; and though some business was done towards the conclusion, it was not sufficient to have much influence. Money is scarce, and many limit their expences more than is advantageous; others must limit them, in order to struggle through life with misery and want. The badness of the fair was chiefly caused by the new Prussian tariff of customs, and the consequent regulations which were put in force exactly during the fair, and may be said to beleaguer Leipsic on three sides. Every thing may, indeed, be imported into Prussia, but the duties on importation and consumption are so high, that every body hesitates to import any thing. The market-people, who bring provisions to the city, take no goods back with them. Many persons think, that by degrees things will be so managed, that many of the disadvantages will be avoided; but others are of opinion that the system of high duties will be modified or even abolished, because it will not produce to Prussia the revenue it expects, and is, besides, as inconsistent with a confederation of states as with the Act of the Confederation. The Russian and Polish merchants thought of conveying their goods through Bohemia, but first applied at Berlin, and another regulation was immediately made with respect to Russia and Poland.

The approaching Seasons.

A German astronomer has predicted the weather of the present year. The spring, he says, will commence early; the months of March and April will be very fine; all the harvests will be abundant, the cherries and prunes alone will fail; the wine will be of excellent quality, and above all, very saccharine; but there will be less of it than in 1818; there will be some dry fogs in the month of August, and the month of September will have some very cold days in it. Those who live near volcanoes, must be on their guard, for there will be many eruptions, preceded by earthquakes. Two comets will approach our planet, but will not cause any evil.

HANOVER.
Commerce Encouraged.

The Hanoverian Government is zealously encouraging the introduction into that kingdom of the trade which the system adopted by the Customs' department of Holland, and the new tariff enforced by the Prussian Government, have excluded from Belgium and the Rhenish provinces. They are also actively employed in improving the means of commercial intercourse, by making new roads, and repairing others. The customs' duties of that State are favourable to trade. The inhabitants look forward with anxiety to the expected establishment of the Provincial States.

INDIES: WEST.
Slave-Cruelties.

From Dominica some painful documents have been communicated, relative to the treatment of the unfortunate slaves. The facts appear to have been printed by order of the House of Commons, on the authority of the Governor of Dominica; and the publication of them forms the subject of "much surprise" on the part of the Colonial House of Assembly, as also of a civil, though rather a cool, correspondence between the speaker of that Body and Governor Maxwell. When we read of a boy of 15 years of age being tortured by a chain of iron round the neck, fastened by a padlock, and weighing 22lb.; of two infant girls only 12 years old, much marked by the cart-whip, fastened together with *iron chains round the neck;* of an old man, 60 years of age, severely beaten and placed in the stocks under a heavy chain; finally of a male child about 12 years old, loaded with an iron collar, chains, and log of wood, weighing 26lb.!—when we read of such abominations as these practised by men who call themselves Christians, we

must wish that either the accounts may be grossly exaggerated, or that the inflictors of such cruelties might, for a little time be forced to change conditions with their slaves, if it were only to teach them the use of power by making them feel its abuses.

Princess of Wales.

A letter from Milan, dated in January, says—The Princess of Wales is making preparations for a trip to the Holy Land. The Baron and young Austin (who is always addressed by the title of Prince) accompany her Royal Highness, together with a vast suite. The Princess told the Marchioness of Douglas that it was her intention to be absent six months; and that she meant to visit all the places of note in Egypt.—During the Princess's absence her new palace will proceed. Two gentlemen lately arrived from England, and had a long conference with her Royal Highness.

RUSSIA.
Peasantry Affranchised.

The 24th of December last, being the anniversary of the birth of the Emperor Alexander, was celebrated in Courland, in a very remarkable manner, that is to say, by reading, after divine service, the ordinance relative to the affranchisement of the peasantry; which took place in all the churches throughout that province.

Gulf of Finland navigable.

Petersburgh, Jan. 14.—The Gulf of Finland is as open to navigation as in the middle of summer, a circumstance never before known at this period: there is not a single flake of ice in the roads of Narva.

Hangman wanted.

The two executioners of the law in St. Petersburgh having died, the municipal authority vainly offered their places to others—no Russian could be found to accept them.

SPAIN.
Death of Charles V.

He survived the Queen only 16 days, and it is probable that her death, after a union of 54 years, might hasten the catastrophe of his own.

CHARLES V. recently deceased, was in the 71st year of his age. He was born at

Naples, the 11th Nov. 1748. He was the son of Charles III. and of Maria Amelia, of Saxony. He became Prince of Asturias in 1759, when his father succeeded to the throne of Spain, on the death of his (the father's) brother, Ferdinand VI. He married, at the age of 17, Maria Louisa of Parma, whose sway over him never ceased during their long union. He ascended the throne of Spain, the 14th December, 1788, and reigned till the 19th March, 1808, the day of his first abdication in favour of his son, an abdication which had nothing in it of a voluntary character. When the melancholy journey to Bayonne took place, King Ferdinand withdrew his claims to the crown, which Charles IV., constrained by superior force, surrendered immediately into the hands of Buonaparte. He had, during six years, a pension of 2,000,000 francs, but which was not regularly paid. He resided a short time.at Fontainbleau and Compeigne; he then established himself, with the Queen and Prince of Peace, at Marseilles, from whence he went to Rome in 1811. After the fall of Buonaparte, Charles IV. again solemnly renounced the Crown, in a treaty concluded with his son, the present King of Spain, who settled on him a pension of 3,000,000 francs, and agreed to pay his debts.

SWEDEN.
Mildness of the Season.

The accounts both from Sweden and Norway exhibit the unexampled fact, that up to the last month, there has been neither frost nor snow in these remote and hitherto inhospitable regions; but that the primroses blossom and the gooseberry-trees are green under the 59th degree of latitude. It is curious enough, that the mildness of the weather should be lamented as a hindrance to the ordinary communications and necessary business of the winter season; yet, in Sweden it seems that iron-ore cannot be conveyed to the forges; and in Russia, the usual merchandise hardly finds its way from the interior of the Empire to the capital, owing to the want of snow.

Herd of Rein-Deer.

Christiania, Jan. 1.—Within these few days we have had the pleasure of seeing here a drove of about 200 reindeer, among which were some white ones, or, as they are called, Siberian, with their keepers, and the dogs employed to guard them. They passed through on their way to the Rocky Mountains of the district of Stavanger, where an inhabitant of that place, who followed them, will attempt to naturalize these animals, which, for a long time, have not been seen there tame, and as domestic animals. This person has purchased these reindeer mostly in Russian Lapland, beyond Tornea, and some in Swedish Lapland. With much trouble they have been conducted this long journey, having been on the way ever since the month of March. In Aamodt, in the Osterthal, want of snow obliged him to leave behind the least necessary part of the baggage, as tents, fur-clothes, snow-shoes, and kitchen utensils. About 20 reindeer were killed on the journey for food; the owner and the driver having subsisted the whole time on the flesh and milk of these animals. In these unknown regions and large forests, as well as in the frequent fogs, he was obliged to direct his course by the compass, as if at sea. This person does not mean to content himself with this one expedition; when he has safely arrived at his own home, he will return to Lapland to fetch another drove. The plan to people these desert rocks with reindeer is equally remarkable and useful. An idea like this, and the resolution to execute it, occur but rarely. Up to Christmas there had been no sign of winter in the country about Drammen; no cold, snow, or ice, but mild spring weather, such as is usual in the month of May.

Smuggling Prevented.

Stockholm, Jan. 22.—To impede smuggling from the neighbouring ports, it has been ordered, that no sugar, coffee, tobacco, or wine, or arrack, shall be imported into the kingdom, in open vessels of any size, or in decked vessels under 25 lasts' burden, on pain of forfeiture of vessel and cargo, and a fine of 500 Banco dollars; and no magazine goods, except salt, corn, and hemp, shall be either exported or imported in such vessels. All those, however, who can prove that their goods were laden within the Sound before the 1st of April next, or without the Sound, before the 1st of May next, are excepted.

TURKEY.

Barbarous Cruelties.

We learn by the Dutch and Flanders mail, that a series of inhuman, though not unlooked for, spectacles were exhibited at Constantinople, on the 16th of December, and the following days. The Chief of the Wechabites and his Minister, who had been expected for some time, were then brought in chains to the Turkish capital, and led through the streets in barbarous triumph. They were next sent to prison and put to the torture; they were afterwards beheaded *in the Sultan's presence,* their bodies exposed during three days, and finally delivered up to be torn to pieces by the populace. Such horrors are scarcely to be conceived but in a country which is inaccessible to the progress of civilization. The religion of Mahomet was ingeniously constructed for prolonging the fierce character of the century which gave it birth, amongst the people to whom it was promulgated. The author of the Koran devised it as an instrument of inflaming or subjugating, at his own pleasure, the passions of a worse than semi-barbarous race; and under the cloke of religious doctrine he introduced an inexorable and perpetual bar to the improvement of knowledge, laws, or manners. When we hear, therefore, of torture being applied in Turkey, whether for judicial or vindictive purposes, we can only blame that dreadful system of faith and Government which has shut up the conscience and the intellect of society, and made immoveable ignorance the test of true devotion.

A Thousand Heads exposed.

Constantinople, Dec. 15.—The Pacha of Diarbech has sent to Constantinople a circumstantial report of his expedition against the rebels of Mardin. This report has been accompanied by a thousand heads, severed from the vanquished. These sanguinary trophies have been exposed, as usual, at the gate of the Seraglio. The Tartar who brought them has obtained a pelisse of honour; presents have also been sent to the Pacha.

National Register:

BRITISH.

THE KING.

WINDSOR CASTLE, FEB. 6.—His Majesty has enjoyed an uninterrupted state of good bodily health, and has been very tranquil during the last month, but his Majesty's disorder remains unchanged.

Bank Documents.

Several important papers connected with the Bank of England have been laid before Parliament, of which the following are abstracts:—

An account of the total amount of Bank notes and Bank post bills in circulation, from the 30th of December, 1817, to the 26th of January, 1819:

Bank notes of 5l. and upwards	18,668,660
Bank post bills	1,701,610
Bank notes under 5l. . . .	7,613,610

Total, 19th January, 1819 £27,983,889

Balances.

From the second paper it appears, that on the 15th of December, 1818, there were in the hands of the Bank balances of Customs to the amount of 86,593l.; of Excise to the amount of 28,216l. The total amount in their hands from the above sources of revenue, from the 1st of January to the 15th of December, inclusive, was 10,890,928l., and the average in their hands, on the 1st and 15th days of each month in the year, is 453,788l.

The total from the Postmaster-general's account was 652,929l. Average 27,205l.

Total from the different departments of Government, including the balances of the Accountant-general of the Court of Chancery, 34,984,304l. Average 1,457,679l.

Total of all public balances not specified in the preceding 457,622l. No average is given.

Of balances from unclaimed Dividends, including Lottery Prizes, there remained in the hands of the Bank on the 15th December, 1818, 141,507l.: total of the above for the year, 18,406,861l. 766,952l.

The amount of Sovereigns issued to the latest period to which the account could be made up, is 3,799,869; Half Sovereigns, 1,410,390*l.*

Forgeries.

The number of forged notes which were detected by the Bank of England, from the 10th of April, 1818, to the 28th of January, 1819, 23,104. Of these 21,562 were of 1*l.*; of 2*l.* there were 670; of 10*l.* there were 77; of 15*l. none;* of 20*l.* there were 19; and of notes above 20*l.* there was but one forged note.

The aggregate amount of Guineas, Half-guineas, and Seven-shilling pieces issued from the Bank of England, from the ·5th Jan. 1816 to the latest period to which the same can be made up, was 701,419*l.*19*s.*

The total number of Guineas, Half-guineas, and Seven-shilling pieces, cannot be ascertained.

The following is an account of the number of persons prosecuted by the Bank of England, for forging notes of the Bank of England, or for knowingly uttering or possessing forged notes, from the 10th of April, 1818, to the 28th of January, 1819:—

Number of persons capitally convicted for knowingly uttering forged Bank notes of 5*l.* and upwards . . . 2

For knowingly uttering forged Bank notes of 1*l.* and 2*l.* 25

For knowingly possessing forged Bank notes of 5*l.* and upwards . . . 3

For knowingly possessing forged Bank notes of 1*l.* and 2*l.* 84

Number of persons prosecuted capitally for knowingly uttering forged Bank notes of 5*l.* and upwards, but who were acquitted . . . . . Nil.

For knowingly uttering forged Bank notes of 1*l.* and 2*l.* but acquitted . 8

For knowingly possessing forged Bank notes of 1*l.* and 2*l.* but acquitted 1

Total number prosecuted 123

The number of persons prosecuted by the officers of his Majesty's Mint, for counterfeiting the legal coin of the realm, or for uttering counterfeit coin, between the 10th of April, 1818, and the 28th of January, 1819, has been 273.

The average amount of Bank notes in circulation in the half-year from January to June, inclusive, 1797, was 10,821,574*l.*

Ditto from July to December in the same year, 11,218,084*l.*

Ditto from January to June, 1817, 27,339,768*l.*

Ditto from July to Dec. 29,210,035*l.*

Ditto from January to June, 1818, 27,954,558*l.*

Ditto from July to Dec. 26,487,859*l.*'

Weights and Measures.

The commercial world will learn with satisfaction, that a plan has been commenced, under the auspices of the British Government, for determining the relative contents of the weights and measures of all trading countries. This important object is to be accomplished by procuring from abroad correct copies of foreign standards, and comparing them with those of England at his Majesty's Mint. Such a comparison, which could be effected only at a moment of universal peace, has never been attempted on a plan sufficiently general or systematic; and hence the errors and contradictions which abound in tables of foreign weights and measures, even in works of the highest authority. In order, therefore, to remedy an inconvenience so perplexing in commerce, Viscount Castlereagh has, by the recommendation of the Board of Trade, issued a circular, dated March 16, 1818, directing all the British Consuls abroad to send home copies of the principal standards used within their respective consulates, verified by the proper authorities, and accompanied by explanatory papers and other documents relative to the subject. Most of his Lordship's orders have been already executed in a very full and satisfactory manner. The despatches and packages transmitted on the occasion are deposited at the Royal Mint, where the standards are to be forthwith compared.

Ascertaining the Longitude.

An inquiry has lately been made by order of the Lords of the Admiralty, on an improved mode of working the calculations necessary to ascertain the Longitude of ships at sea. The plan is from observations of the positions of various stars, which promises to reduce the errors into so narrow a compass, that the actual certainty may be almost said to be discovered. Capt. Robert Tucker, R. N. is the inventor of this new method, which requires only six lines of figures.

Cultivation of Flax.

A premium of 50*l.* has been offered by the Prince Regent, as Duke of Cornwall and Lord of the Forest of Dartmoor, to the person who, this year, shall cultivate the greatest number of acres in flax.

Ropes to be made of Grass.

An experiment has been tried in Portsmouth Dock-yard, to ascertain if a grass, the common produce of New Zealand, and which may be cut down three times a year, is applicable to making large and small ropes. A favourable report, we understand, is made of it. The article is strong and pliable, and very silky in its nature. It can be brought into this country at less than 8*l.* per ton; one-seventh of the cost of hemp.

Gas Manufacture.

It is one of the important results of chemical science, that the various products from the distillation of coal amount to nearly six times the price of the original article. A chaldron of Newcastle coals which costs about 3*l.* will produce—

1¼ Chaldrons of Coke, at 21s.	£1	11	6
12 Gallons of Tar, at 10d. .	0	10	0
18 Gallons of Ammonial Liquor at 6d.	0	9	0
20,000 cubic ft. of Gas, at 15s. per 1000 cubic ft. . . .	15	0	0
	£17	10	6

Copper produced in England.

England produces more copper than any other country, and in Cornwall a much greater quantity is raised than in any other district of Britain. The total quantity annually obtained in the British islands is about 20,000 quintals; in Russia 67,000; in Austria 50,000; in Sweden 22,000; in Westphalia 17,000; in Denmark 8000; in Bavaria, 3,000; in France 2,500; in Saxony 1,300; and smaller quantities in some other countries; making a total of about 380,000 quintals. It is a fact worthy of remark, that Cornwall, which now furnishes not much less than half this amount, produced no copper only a century ago.

Case of Venetian Windows.

In an appeal lately made against the supplementary charges on windows, in Bath, the Commissioners of that city unanimously decided against the extra charges, declaring all Venetian windows made previously to the year 1785 chargeable only as one window, and Venetian windows made subsequently to that period chargeable as two windows only. The appellants, to the number of upwards of 700, are, by this decision, relieved; subject, however, to a case for the opinion of the Judges.

Annual Commitments.

The annual commitments for trial in England and Wales have advanced from the year 1805 to the year 1817, both inclusive, in the frightful progression of 4605 to 13,932.

Cattle consumed in London.

The consumption of sheep and lambs in London in 12 months, has been lately estimated at the number of 10,062,700. The number of horned cattle slaughtered, 164,000; and by the inspectors' return, it appears, the number of horses' hides produced at Leadenhall market, amounted to 12,900.

Climbing Boys.

The Report of Colonel Stephenson, Surveyor-general of the Board of Works (addressed to Henry Hobhouse, Esq. one of the Under-Secretaries of State for the Home Department), as to the practicability of superseding the practice of climbing boys by the use of machinery, is on the whole favourable to the use of machines, though the result of the experiments is, that the three Royal Architects concur in opinion, that climbing-boys cannot be at present totally dispensed with. Colonel Stephenson directed an intelligent clerk, Mr. Davis, to superintend experiments, in order to ascertain the truth. Mr. Davis reports, that the flues of the metropolis may be divided into four classes.' For the first class, the machines now in use are quite efficient; for part of the second class, they are also competent; and for the remainder of this class the ball and brush is perfectly efficient. In the third class, where the ascent is at all preserved, the ball and brush act effectually, as they do even in the fourth class, where there are no parts entirely level. The proportions of the different classes he found to be as under:—Out of 1,000 fixes, 910 are of the first class, 50 of the second, 30 of the third, and 10 of the fourth.

Galvanic Phenomena.

On the 4th of November last, various galvanic experiments were made on the body of the murderer Clydesdale, by Dr. Ure, of Glasgow, with a voltaic battery of 270 pair of 4-inch plates. The results were truly apalling. On moving the rod from the hip to the heel, the knee being previously bent, the leg was thrown out with such violence as nearly to overturn one of the assistants, who in vain attempted to prevent its extension! In the second experiment, the rod was applied to the phrenic nerve in the neck, when laborious breathing instantly commenced; the heaved and fell; the belly was protruded and collapsed, with the relaxing and retiring diaphragm; and it is thought, that but from the complete evacuation of the blood, pulsation might have occurred! In the third experiment, the supra-orbital nerve was touched, when every muscle in the murderer's face "was thrown into fearful action." The scene was hideous—several of the spectators left the room, and one gentleman actually fainted from terror or sickness. In the fourth experiment, the transmitting of the electral power from the spinal marrow to the ulmar nerve at the elbow, the fingers were instantly put in motion, and the agitation of the arm was so great, that the corpse seemed to point to the different spectators, some of whom thought it had come to life! Dr. Ure appears to be of opinion, that had not incisions been made in the blood-vessels of the neck, and the spinal marrow been lacerated, the criminal might have been restored to life!

Women Parsons.

A new sect of Methodists, distinguished by the appellation of Briantists, have lately taken rise, and are making considerable progress among the inhabitants of Cornwall. Their high-priest, it appears, was once a rigid disciple of Wesley: but on account of some disagreement taking place, he dissented from them, and instituted a sect of his own. In order, therefore, that his own followers may differ as much as possible from the tenets of the Wesleyans, he has adopted a new mode of instruction, which is no other than allowing *women to preach!*

Servants Frightened.

The servant-maids in Caernarvon have, for the last month, been greatly alarmed at finding, on opening the street-doors in the morning, a paper parcel on the steps, containing various sums of money in silver, of the old coinage. It will scarcely be believed, but some have been so timid, as to call in the aid of the passenger, to take it off. Nearly twenty pounds have been distributed in this way.

Horses, Carnivorous.

An instance has lately been mentioned of a young horse which preferred roasted or boiled meat to grass or corn. His dam was killed by an unfortunate accident, when the foal was five weeks old: he was fed by the dairy-maid, with cow's milk, and soon familiarly followed her to the kitchen. He was afterwards offered slices of beef, mutton, veal, or lamb, which he accepted like a dog: he did not like pork, but all kinds of fowl or game were highly agreeable to him. In different parts of India, the horses in an encampment are served with boiled sheep's heads, as a mess more nutritive than grain, when they have an extraordinary fatigue to undergo. May not this account admit of practical application? When grain and fodder are scarce, the worst cattle might be killed, and boiled into strong soup, cutting the flesh small, among straw, hay, or other vegetable provender. During scarcity, the cattle of Iceland go to the shores, and feed on fish.

Sagacity of a Hedgehog.

The Ayr Journal mentions a circumstance of a hedgehog being seen to cross the high road, near Garbestown, carrying on its back six pheasant's eggs, which upon examination were found to be pilfered from a pheasant's nest. The ingenuity of the creature was very conspicuous, as several of the remaining eggs were holed, which must have been done by it, when in the act of rolling itself over the nest, in order to make as many adhere to its prickles as possible. After watching the motions of the urchin for a short time longer, it was seen to deliberately crawl into a furze-bush, where its nest was, and where the shells of several eggs were strewed around, which had at some former period been conveyed hither in the same manner.

Population of the World.

The Table of Population and Territory of the present civilized world, as lately exhibited, gives to China 200 millions and 1,200,000 square miles of territory; to Great Britain, 20 millions of population, and 100,000 square miles; and to the United States, 10 millions, and 2,500,000 miles: and the total of the whole world is, of population, 435,800,000, and of territory, 9,687,000 square miles; so that the United States have the largest *home* territory of all the nations except Russia. China is not included in this, because it contains many parts barbarous and helpless. Britain possesses 150 millions of subjects in her Colonial Empire, and covers a dominion equal to nearly *one-fifth* of the whole surface of the globe, but her main strength must always depend upon the resources, intelligence, spirit and character of her native population in the British Isles.

PARLIAMENTARY HISTORY.

Chap. I. *Cash Payments—Bank Restriction—Bribery—Windsor Establishment—Abuse of Charity—Repeal of the Usury Law—The Plague—Trial by Battle Bill—East India Affairs—Prostitutes.*

HOUSE OF COMMONS.

Fd. 2.—Mr. S. Wortley presented a petition from certain bankers and manufacturers, praying the renewal of the Bank Restriction Bill.

Mr. Canning presented a similar petition from the merchants and bankers of Liverpool. There was one signature to this petition, which he wished to allude to, from its peculiarity: "Jas. Cropper willing that payments in specie may be postponed ; but not agreeing in the necessity that they should ever be resumed."

Mr. Tierney was happy to see that there was at least one individual who was not ashamed of openly declaring his opinion. This was the most honest signature he had ever seen to any petition. He only wished other gentlemen were candid enough to follow his example.

Mr. Tierney then rose to make his promi-

sed motion on this subject, and concluded a long and eloquent speech by moving, That a Committee be appointed to inquire into the effects produced on the exchanges with foreign countries, and the state of the circulating medium, by the Restriction on Cash Payments ; and to report whether any and what reasons exist, for continuing it beyond the period now fixed by law for its termination.

The Chancellor of the Exchequer said, he had been charged with a want of system in the financial arrangements which he had felt it is his duty to recommend to Parliament. Of the justice of this imputation the House might readily judge. He would challenge the R. Hon. Gent to mention any period equal in duration to that which had passed since the conclusion of the war, when so much was done either for diminishing taxation, or redeeming the public debt. Within three years £50,000,000. of taxes had been remitted—an amount certainly greater than he thought expedient. He had not approved of the repeal of every tax which had been withdrawn, but it could not be denied that a great and substantial relief had been rendered to the country. He would endeavour to explain the course of the proceeding which had been adopted, and what was in contemplation to propose. Undoubtedly, on the first day of the Session, his own impression was that it would be most expedient to continue the restriction for a short time without any inquiry. Since this opinion was formed, a communication was made to him and Lord Liverpool from the Directors, announcing that they had come to a resolution, that inquiry was preferable to an extension of the restriction for so short a period as had been proposed. Under these circumstances, but without abandoning the hope that cash payments might be resumed in 1820, he had judged it right to concur with the wishes of the Bank. The inquiry he should propose was at once more extensive, and the object of it more definitely explained, than that of the Rt. Hon. Gent. but as it was connected with an investigation of the affairs and property of the Bank, it was both just and necessary that the Committee entrusted with it should be *secret.* The Rt. Hon. Gent. concluded, by reading the motion, which he proposed as an amendment to the original one. The amendment was, that all the words after "appointed" be omitted, and that the following be substituted: "to consider the present state of the Bank, with reference to the expediency of the resumption of cash payments at the period fixed by law, and into such other matters as are connected with it."

Mr. F. Lewis could not doubt that the House entertained a common feeling with himself on the statement which had come from the Rt. Hon. Gent. (the Chancellor of the Exchequer). It appeared, after all that had passed, and all that had been heard on the subject, that the Bank was not prepared to resume cash payments.

Lord Castlereagh and Mr. Canning supported the amendment, and contended that a *secret committee*, chosen by *ballot*, was the fairest way of coming at the sense of the House.

Mr. Alderman Heygate and Mr. Bernall motion.

Mr. Tierney shortly replied to the arguments urged against his motion. After which, the House divided on the original spoke in favour of the original motion.

Ayes....................166
Noes....................277 ——
Majority for Ministers	109

The amendment was then carried, without a division. Some discussion took place after strangers were withdrawn, and we understand it was decided, that the committee was to be secret, and be formed by ballot.—Adjourned.

Feb. 4.—Sir R. Wilson presented a petition from a Mr. Brady, stating the following case of breach of privilege. The Hon. W W. Quin was *Custos Rotulorum* of the County of Limerick, and in virtue of that situation he had the gift of the office of Clerk of the Peace; an office of great importance, as the person who held it was charged with the register of freeholders. This office had been held for eleven years by T. W. Brady, the petitioner. Some time after Mr. Quin's appointment, he wished to give the clerkship to R. Smith, and offered to give Mr. Brady an allowance of £200 a-year, on condition that at every future election he should vote for Mr. Quin. The condition on which Mr. Smith was to be appointed to the office was, that he should give Mr. Quin his own vote, and the votes of 100 of his tenants. A paper to this effect was drawn up by Mr. Gould, a respectable barrister and King's Counsel, and signed by Mr. Quin; but both Mr. Brady and Mr. Smith rejected it with indignation. The circumstance then becoming public, Mr. Quin offered to sign a paper, giving Mr. Brady the salary without any condition annexed to it. But the petitioner thought he should abandon his duty, and be guilty of a high crime, if he did not represent so flagrant a case to the Hon. House. Sir R. Wilson added, that he was instructed to state, the petitioner was ready to prove at the bar of the House all the allegations contained in the petition. He hoped the House would not think that he had trespassed unnecessarily on their attention. A motion was then put and carried, that Mr. W. W. Quin be ordered to attend in his place on Thursday next.

On the motion of Mr. M. A. Taylor, an Address was voted to the Prince Regent, praying that he would adopt such measures as would give the four Northern Counties the benefit of an Assize twice a year.

Lord Castlereagh brought down a message from the Prince Regent, which the Speaker read to the following effect:

"G. P. R.—His Royal Highness the Prince Regent, acting for and on behalf of his Majesty, is graciously pleased to announce to your Honourable House, that the £58.000 appropriated to the maintenance of the Establishment and to the support of the honour and dignity of the Crown, having, by the lamented demise of the Queen, become applicable to the general services of the Civil list, the Prince Regent places this sum at the disposal of Parliament; at the same time he submits to the consideration of the House of Commons, the claims of several persons, which he leaves to the justice and liberality of Parliament; these claims are founded on the services of persons who were connected with her Majesty's department; and the House will not fail to grant them such allowances as are usual on occasions of similar affliction."

Lord Castlereagh prefaced his motion for a Committee to enquire into the state of the Windsor Establishment, by saying that there was now an annual sum of £158,000 at the disposal of the House, and it was the intention of the Ministers to propose, that the future establishment of the King should amount to only £50,000 per annum; and that £25,000 more be applied to pension off the old servants which were to be dismissed. Thus a saving would accrue to the nation of upwards of £80,000 per annum.

Mr. Tierney said, in the present burthened state of the country not one shilling should be voted unnecessarily. He thought, before the House agreed to allow an establishment of £50,000, some explanation *how* the money was to be expended should be given. For his part he could not conceive how it was to be expended. Fifty thousand pounds for the establishment at Windsor, for the support of his Majesty in his present unhappy state! His majesty, it was too well known, was incapable even of ordinary enjoyments. He could not, if he were rightly informed, speak or be spoken to; and his regimen was so very plain, that the tenth of £50,000, would be much more than sufficient to supply it, with all the necessary forms of attendance. But he had no objection to the committee; he was thankful for it; but it was not to the economical dispositions of Ministers he owed those thanks.

The Committee was then appointed.

Feb. 5.—Mr. Robert Ward presented a petition from several journeymen papermakers, complaining that they had been thrown out of employment in consequence of the general adoption of machinery in the manufacture of paper. The petitioners alleged, that the paper manufactured by machinery was of an inferior quality, and they prayed, therefore, that an act might be passed, ordering, that in all paper of this description it might be stated in the water-mark, that it was manufactured by machinery —Ordered to be laid on the table.

Mr. Byng presented a petition, signed by a number of respectable inhabitants of St. Paul's Shadwell, complaining of the exorbitant price and inadequate supply of water; and praying for leave to bring in a bill for the establishment of a new water-work company.—Ordered to be laid on the table.

Mr. Peter Moore presented a petition, praying for leave to bring in a bill for lighting the streets of Westminster with gas.—Ordered to be laid on the table.

Mr Brougham said, he held in his hand a petition from the minister, elders and inhabitants, of the parish of Moffat, in Scotland. It might be proper for him to state, before entering into the subject of the petition, that the minister and elders composed the session, or vestry of the parish, and were vested with an ecclesiastical authority The inhabitants who had signed this petition, about 300 in number, had taken the precaution of adding the age of each person over against the signature. The statement contained in the petition was to the following purport :—In 1369 the Reverend Mr. Johnson settled among them, and bequeathed £1,000. to Lord Johnson in trust, to be laid out in the purchase of land. The rents and profits of this land were to be laid out in building and supporting a school It was directed, first, that a yearly salary of £25. or £26. was to be paid to a schoolmaster: secondly, that £10. a year should be paid to the usher of the school; and thirdly, that from £7. to £8. a year should be paid to a writing master, it was a grammar-school; a sum was also provided for building a school-house. There was every reason to believe that these sums were at first laid out in terms of the devise. The house had been built, and the salary had been paid to the master regularly. At present however, instead of paying the second salary to an usher as directed in the devise, it was paid to the master; and the third salary directed to be paid to a writing master, was never paid at all. The overplus of the rents and profits had been directed to be paid into the hands of the kirk session for behoof of the poor of the parish; (the school, indeed, had been intended solely for the poor;) but no part of this estate had ever been so paid, nor was there any account how the surplus had been disposed of. The Rev. Mr. Johnson had devised another sum of £1000. to be laid out in a similar manner, for the support of eight poor scholars at the University of Edinburgh; but the scholars to whom these bursaries had been given for some time past, had been elected on a very different principle from that which was laid down in the devise. These were the subjects of complaint which the petitioners submitted to the House.

The petition was ordered to lie on the table.

Mr Madocks moved the second reading of the Welch Game Preservation Bill, and stated, that the present bill was merely for enabling proprietors of lands in Wales to appoint gamekeepers to preserve their game. Whatever lands they might possess at present, they could appoint no gamekeepers, unless they had manors.

The bill was read a second time, and ordered to be committed on Monday.

HOUSE OF LORDS.

Feb. 8.—Lord Kenyon presented a petition from certain cotton manufacturers, praying for a bill to limit the hours of labour in children.

The Bishop of Chester presented a similar petition from 5,226 persons at Bolton-le-Moor.

The Earl of Lauderdale opposed these petitions, and begged the subject might be deferred till there was a fuller House. It was therefore agreed to be postponed to the 22d Inst.

Feb. 10.—Lord Kenyon presented a petition from certain inhabitants of the city of Westminster, praying that the Insolvent Debtors' Acts may not be renewed, without some provisions for the better security of creditors.

The Earl of Liverpool laid on the table the papers relative to the war in India, referred to in the speech of the Commissioners at the opening of the Session. His Lordship next laid on the table papers relative to the negociations on the Slave trade; when

The Marquis of Lansdown enquired whether the Treaties concluded in 1817, between this country and Spain and Portugal, had been carried into complete effect; or, in particular, whether that part of the Treaty which related to the appointing of a mixed commission, and the sending it out, had been complied with. This measure was to have been carried into effect within a limited time from the exchange of the ratifications, he believed six or seven months, and that time was now expired.

The Earl of Liverpool said, that the commission was appointed; that on the part of Spain and Portugal it was arranged, but that the Commissioners on the part of this country were not yet sent out.

The Marquis of Lansdown next rose to move for an Address for correspondence between the Governor-General of India and Governor Raffles, on the subject of the island of Banca; instructions transmitted respecting the cession of that island; reports of Colonel Gillespie, Major Macpherson, &c.—Ordered.

The Malt and Sugar Duties Bill was brought from the Commons by Mr. Brogden, and read a first time.

HOUSE OF COMMONS.

Feb. 10.—Mr. Sergeant Onslow moved for leave to bring in a bill for the repeal of the laws which regulate or restrain the interest of money. He was happy to find his views supported by those persons who were most conversant with the subject, not only in England and in Europe, but in America. Usury was now applied only to what was paid for money above the legal rate of interest; but formerly the term was applied to all interest.—Early in our history, 10 per cent. was allowed to be taken; but in the reign of Edward IV. prejudices against usury became very violent, and this toleration was repealed. The consequence was, that money which might have been borrowed at 10 per cent. could not be obtained for less than 14. In Queen Elizabeth's reign, the 10 per cent. was again allowed, but with a declaration that to take any interest was a sin and detestable. Subsequent statutes afterwards regulated the subject, till at length the Act of Queen Anne reduced interest to 5 per cent. But through all those statutes the same sentiments prevailed, regarding interest as an evil that was only to be tolerated. This subject had lately been referred to a select committee, who had reported the result of their investigation. In times of distress the usury laws had been most grievously felt; mercantile interests had been much injured by them. One of the consequences of the usury laws was, that annuities were often had recourse to as loans. Another very injurious consequence was, that lands had suffered by disadvantageous sales, because no money could be borrowed at the market price.

Mr. Hume seconded the motion.

Leave was given to bring in the bill. It was immediately brought in, read a first time, and ordered to be read a second time on Monday, and to be printed.

On the motion of Mr Lushington, the bill for issuing 20 millions in Exchequer bills, for the year 1819, was read a first time.

Feb. 11—Sir J. Jackson moved for the appointment of a select committee to consider the validity of the doctrine that the plague is contagious.

Mr. W. Wynne considered committees of the House was not qualified to examine a question of medical science.

Mr. Robinson said, the motion was proper, since the question was materially connected with the Quarantine Laws, which were both severe and expensive in their operation, and which were entirely founded on the ancient belief that the plague was contagious. Many facts and discoveries had lately tended to cast doubts on the validity of that doctrine; and though the College of Physicians (to whom the matter had been submitted by Government) had declared in favour of the original and established opinion, he thought there were sufficient grounds

to enter into an investigation so important to the whole of mankind.

The motion was then agreed to, and the committee appointed.

Mr. Bennett obtained leave to bring in a bill to abolish the system of climbing boys.

Feb. 12.—The Attorney-General moved the second reading of the Trial by Battle Abolition Bill.

Mr. Denman said, he had but one objection to make to the Bill; he understood that it was intended to operate on all cases now pending; he submitted that it would be proper that the words "now pending" should be omitted; not that he considered it would be material in the present case, but if it were permitted now, it might be adverted to as a precedent on future occasions.

The Attorney-General explained. The bill was then read a second time, and ordered to a committee to report thereon on Monday next.

Mr. Canning laid upon the table a considerable volume of papers relating to the war in India; upon which

Sir R. Wilson moved, that there be laid before the House copies of all reports or other documents received by Ministers from the Marquis of Hastings, or Lieut.-Gent. Hislop, relative to the execution of the Killidar taken at the fort of Kilmare.—Ordered.

On the motion of Lord Morpeth, an account was ordered of the amount of the territorial debts of the East India Company at their several presidencies, according to the latest advices.

The Sheriffs of London presented a petition from the Lord Mayor and Common Council of London, on the subject of the female prostitutes in that City, and on the difficulty of putting down the many houses where they were harboured.

Mr Alderman Wood observed, that, as the subject was one of great importance to the health and morals of the rising generation, he hoped the law-officers of the crown would take it up, and put an end to an evil arising out of the confinement of those depraved females with paupers and others who had been guilty of no offences.

POLITICAL PERISCOPE.

Panorama Office, February 26, 1819.

It has been observed of History, that it delights in wars, revolutions, and disasters of mankind; but times of peace and prosperity it neglects: they do not afford matter for interesting particulars, or for well-rounded periods; they neither elevate the style, nor encourage speculation on causes or consequences; neither do they lead to philosophical reflections and profound disquisitions.

Placid history is very dull reading; and though it may now and then be diversified by a tempest or an inundation, yet the gliding by of day after day without difference, puts to silence exclamation and interjection; and almost deprives speech of one of its parts, and declension of one of its cases.

If history be thus deprived by a state of tranquillity, to what straits must be reduced the composer of a PERISCOPE, who, month after month, looking all around him, sees nothing to animate his pen; nothing striking, as the term is usually understood; nothing to rouse his spleen, his anger, his energy; but all is smooth, sedate, and silent.

Ah, we remember the time when every evening, the board met strong; when seven, at least, seated in due dignity, enquired anxiously of each other " *What news?*" when three messengers scouted from newspaper office to newspaper office, and after waiting two or three hours at each, returned with half a sheet of stamped paper, *printed on one side only,* and that so unintelligibly, as not seldom to defy the best reader's best spectacles.

Then was the table spread around with maps and memoirs of every description; from the twenty sheet Colossus of Germany to that less presuming delineation, which saved the British minister's life, by marking a road though which Mr. Drake escaped, while detachments of French chasseurs waited to intercept him, on all the roads marked in every map, save and except this single one.

Then to work went compasses and calculations;—" they were left by the latest accounts, at —— : " by this time they are arrived at —— and, possibly, even at ——." So much for Saxony and Germany; but, then, the Peninsula :—" here you see the road laid down by the French themselves, which a courier can pass in so many hours, all marked on it : His grace was left by the last dispatches, just here :—by this time ne is —— : but, how long has the vessel been on her passage?"

What a contrast is time present! We are reduced to home news ; and that neither very abundant, nor very dextrously made up : scarcely any thing more interesting than the elopement of the tall giantess shewn at the last fair with the little hunchback who discharged the official duty of Beef-eater, and invited company to lift themselves up—as he did,—to look the lady in the face, with the same degree of elevation as they inspected the cock on the church steeple.

Alas! Othello's occupation's gone!

and pastoral poetry may now take place of " the spirit-stirring drum, th'ear-piercing fife, and all the pomp and circumstance of glorious war." Well! we are friends of Peace; Peace, too, has her charms; and even as PERISCOPISTS, we hail, we admire, we adore the goddess.

Peace is the time when the interior condition of a country may be most accurately ascertained; when the correcting hand may be most efficaciously applied to those evils which *will* afflict the best constituted states. To describe a state as perfect, may be well enough in popular speech; but there the judicious must stop; and that which is deemed perfect to-day, will be found more or less out of order to-morrow.

Our readers will readily suppose that we heartily coincide with every endeavour to amend the enactments of our Criminal Code. There cannot be two opinions on the subject; but there may be more than two, on the best manner of accomplishing the purpose. Nor should it be forgot, that laws made to meet ordinary cases by punishment, are not adequate to the punishment of atrocious cases. The reader has often met with instances of crimes called *petty,* the commission of which, under certain circumstances, implied a hardened state of mind in the transgressor, to which a lenient visitation bore no proportionate retribution.

Inasmuch, then, as cases differ in their guilt, and crimes in their enormity, but the law cannot be so varied, when once enacted, as to meet an infinite variety of cases of the same description, we have to choose whether the law shall assign the severest penalty to the crime, generally,—leaving the chief magistrate of the realm to moderate its rigour, according to the minor demerits of a delinquent; or whether the law shall assign the slightest penalty, leaving another power to proportion the heavier suffering to atrocious offenders. To the latter proposition we give our decided negative : No judge, by our consent, shall augment the legal punishment; nor shall we commit that ungrateful task to the crown.

The crown is the fountain of mercy : so let the crown continue; but, to render the crown the source of increased severity, suits neither our feelings of British liberty, nor our sentiments on the respect due to the hereditary representative of the nation.

To make, or to amend laws when made, is not quite so easy a thing as some would fain persuade themselves and others. A striking instance of this is the system of the Poor-laws; all cry out against them ; the ignorant wonder they are not regulated—modified—repealed : the most sagacious most plainly see the difficulty; and they fear lest, while correcting one evil, they should encourage many. And always in free constitutions, should the danger of establishing improper precedents be ever present to the mind's eye of the legislator : for, as these are open to every man alike, there is no possibility of foreseeing in what manner they may be applied in time to come.

We may not, perhaps, disapprove entirely of certain proposals made at the present moment;—but we may be allowed to submit, that in our judgment the precedent would be dangerous: it would not terminate where even those who now support such proposals would desire.

There are not a few, who see no difficulty whatever in commanding the Bank to return to cash payments; but the well-informed know, that the mere agitation of the question, by inducing the Bank to exercise its prudence, has rendered money so scarce, that for a while the possessors of it could make after the rate of ten, or twelve, *per cent. per annum* : and some go so far as to say, that four or five *per cent*. additional was offered under the term *bonus*, or some other equally expressive, for a short time.

Suppose, for a moment, that the same prudence, pushed to excess, should induce the Bank to contract its issues from thirty millions to twenty; can the reader possibly estimate the difficulties under which this sudden failure of support would involve the whole mercantile world? Could their ships be sent to sea? Certainly not. What then must become of the sailors, the shipwrights, and the thousand other trades connected with ships? And if the ships did not go abroad, the manufactures they ought to carry out must needs stay at home; so the merchant would counter-order the manufacturer, and the manufacturer would counter-order his working hands:—of the consequences none can be ignorant.

That would be an extreme case; and the reader will discern in our letter from Petersburgh, a ray of more pleasing anticipation on the subject of bullion. That country has obtained silver enough to answer its purpose; it is now imported at a loss: of course the tide will turn, and silver will abide where it suffers no loss.

The same may be said of gold: to where it yields the greatest profit, thither it will flow; and those who observed that the Bank paid, on the last dividends, *guineas*, not *sovereigns*, for such smaller sums as are now paid in cash,—had an opportunity of discerning the power of calculation in reference to the relative value of the two species of coin.—But, where had these guineas been hoarded since their mintage? This subject would require a volume; but we cannot, at present, allow it more room. Though Britain be our dearest interests, yet we must dedicate a few lines to foreign affairs.

Since our last, which reported the death of the elder Queen of Spain, her husband, King Charles IV. has likewise deceased. He survived his queen only about a fortnight. We understand that he died at Naples, January 20, in the 71st year of his age.*

---

* CHARLES IV. was born at Naples, November 11, 1748. He was son of Charles II and of Maria Amelia of Saxony. He became Prince of Asturias in 1759, when his father succeeded to the throne of Spain, on the death his (the father's) brother, Ferdinand VI. He married at the age of 17, September 4, 17 Maria Louisa of Parma, whose sway over never ceased during their long union. He cended the throne December 14, 1788, reigned till March 19, 1808, the day of his abdication in favour of his son; an abdica which had nothing in it of a voluntary cha ter. When the melancholy journey to Bay took place, King Ferdinand withdrew his cl to the throne, which Charles IV. constrain superior force, surrendered immediately in hands of Buonaparte. It was, therefore, M 19, 1808, that terminated the reign of Ch IV. He had, during six years, a pensio 2,000,000 francs; but it was not regularly He resided a short time at Fontaineblean at Compeigne; he then established himself the Queen and the Prince of the Peace, at seilles; whence he went to Rome, in 1 After the fall of Buonaparte, Charles IV. solemnly renounced his Crown, in a treaty cluded with his son, the present King of who settled on him a pension of 3,000,000 f and agreed to pay his debts. At the bre out of the French Revolution, this mo made the most strenuous efforts to save t of his ally and relative, Louis XVI. He ed his ambassador to deliver a letter to th tional Convention, appealing to their mer was presented to that assembly on the e previous to the immolation of Louis; bu refused to open it, dreading that its c might inspire humanity in the less violent of some among them. When he receiv unhappy news of the King's death, Char clared war against the French Republi which, however, he was forced to make glorious peace; and afterwards to unite h with France against England. This cost mense losses, of which the battle of Traf one instance: nor could he maintain his intercourse with his colonies: the consequ of which are notorious.

SPAIN is certainly at this moment an interesting object to Political Speculators. We have too often alluded to her undeniable embarrassments, to add more than a mere recollection of them here.

FRANCE has, probably, reached that state at which she may continue stationary for some time. Her new ministry seem to go on smoothly enough, at least for the present.

We hear little from the interior of the Continent: the season is, no doubt, one cause; another is the little that transpires worthy notice.

Report had lately killed the Pope, the King of Sweden, and some other Monarchs: but we believe that they still continue to be inhabitants of this terrestrial globe.

The Grand Seignior, at Constantinople, lately indulged himself with the spectacle of putting to death the Chief of the Wahabees, and his principal adherents. The scene took place in his own palace; where also, were displayed at the same time, *a pleasing exhibition!*—a thousand heads, the spoils of victory. If we recollect rightly, Vitellius was the Roman Emperor who insisted that a dead enemy never had an offensive smell: if the Sultan of the Ottomans is of the same opinion, no doubt he had wherewithal to rejoice his olfactory nerves *con amore*.

From India we learn, that the chief instigator of the rebellion in Ceylon, with his Prime Minister, is taken by our troops; and consequently, that revolt, it may be hoped, is terminating.

There are various estimates of the ravages committed at Calcutta and its neighbourhood, by the *Cholera Morbus;* but none which supposes them to be less than 200,000 inhabitants.

We are anxious to hear from China; but have nothing fresh to report.

The Government of the United States of America has laid before Congress the papers necessary to elucidate the conduct of General Jackson, at and near Pensacola. Congress has appointed committees to report; and the General's rashness and violence have been decidedly condemned. The military execution of two British subjects, Arbuthnot and Ambrister, has been justly denounced as *murder;* and, as we hoped, the Government itself is discharged from all participation in the foul deed.

Here we close: Time will certainly compose a continuation, to which we shall have the honour to call the attention of our readers.

Commercial Chronicle.

Extracts from Commercial Letters, received from various parts of Europe.

MALTA.
New Regulations relative to Commerce.

THE Import Duty will hereafter be *one per cent, ad valorem: excepting,* on the commodities named in the new Tariff. Note, this Tariff comprises chiefly, such articles, as not being of general commerce, their value cannot be readily ascertained; also

COFFEE and SUGAR of Foreign growth; the former of which will pay 3 scudis per cantar, the latter 1¼ scudis per cantar, unless coming from Great Britain, or from the East or West Indies, in British bottoms. British Plantation Rum will hereafter pay on import 5 scudis per puncheon, but the Import Excise is now abolished.

The Export Duty heretofore levied is now abolished *in toto:* and vessels will no longer be required to deliver manifests outwards.

Merchant vessels are permitted to put into the quarantine port, and to remain there 48 hours, without being subject to any charge, save one *tari* per ton, for anchorage dues.

Malta, Jan. 16, 1819.

'There is none but Sicilian oil in the place, which is greedily taken at 17½ to 17½ per *cafiso*, equal to £76 16s. per ton on board. From the Ionian islands our advices anticipate a very bare crop, in Corfu. Refined Sugar is in much request. The market is very bare of Coffee: and the value of good ordinary is about 170s. per cwt. Black Pepper is in demand at 9d.'

St. Petersburg, Jan. 3-15, 1819.

'For some weeks past there has scarcely been any enquiry for Goods. Bad weather, bad roads, and high rate of carriage of goods into the interior, have checked purchases. The weather continues still in the same mild state, without frost; and *no snow on the ground*: and until it changes, there is little probability of much demand arising for any of the large stocks of Imports which are in the market, unsold. Indeed the state of our Import trade cannot be worse than it is; there is no demand for any article although there is an abundant supply. The only change we expect in our Tariff this year is, that the Silver Ruble will be reduced to 3¼ Paper Rubles, or perhaps to 3,70 copeeks.—The Loan has closed with somewhat more than 65 millions of Rubles (Bank-notes) subscribed; the import of silver will of course cease; as on late importations there has been considerable loss; and for silver now delivered in, government will only give notes due next November. Exchange 11¾d.

STATE OF TRADE.
Lloyd's Coffee-House, February.

The politics of the day have undoubtedly, at this moment, a considerable influence on the commercial world. It is the object of some politicians to depress the Bank, by way of punishment for the accommodation the Bank has afforded to ministers: it must be granted also, that the Bank has acquired great wealth within the last years, and when was wealth acquired without exciting a grudge? Be that as it may, the motion in parliament for enquiry into the affairs of the Bank has been met by the Directors with a readiness of communication that confirms the general confidence. None ever doubted whether all were fair and solvent; but to meet the possibility of doubt, the Bank readily submits to examination, and cross-examination; there is another possibility also which the Bank has the prudence to foresee and to meet, that of being ordered to resume cash payments.

With this in contemplation, the Bank is certainly narrowing its issues; they have been as high as thirty-two millions; they have been gradually diminished to below twenty-eight millions; it is probable they are, at this moment, lower; and report states the sum of twenty-five millions as a mark at which they are likely to stand for some time—the inference is obvious. In the first place, the smaller the amount of Bank notes in circulation may be, the less danger, certainly, exists of the possibility of a run on the treasury; in the second place, the inducement for dealers in bullion, &c. to import gold, or to keep at home gold imported, or to bring to sale gold in their possession, increases with the decrease of Bank-notes, for these dealers must pay their debts with something: with Bank-notes, if they be cheapest, but, if not with Bank-notes, then with coin; for gold in its raw state, as gold dust or as ingots, pays nobody, but when coined, it passes through the Bank, as the regular channel into public circulation. During this struggle of the Bank to obtain gold, and to provide against the worst, the discounts *done* by the Bank are extremely select, which is saying, in other words, what in common speech is more bluntly expressed "they *do* nothing:" the best paper of the best houses has recently been looked rather shy at; this obliges the merchants to sell, and those who are able to lay-down *the ready,* have very considerable opportunities of doing business to advantage at this moment; this obliges also those who had placed their cash in the funds or who had ventured on speculations in that lottery, to sell, at whatever rate; and hence, there being more sellers than buyers, and more urgent sellers than buyers, the Stocks have declined, and a progress marks their declination. nor must we here lose sight of the effects attributed to the great loans negociated by Foreign governments, trying losses have attended them to a considerable extent; add to these circumstances, the winding-up of the English loan, of which the last instalment was paid yesterday, the Bank having declined to hold it any longer; all these causes, operating together, have tried the strength of many purses. As usual, some of the strong have proved weak, while some of the weak have proved themselves strong.

The learned even derive satisfaction from the actual state of things; the English loan *is* paid; and therefore will no longer burthen the market; the Foreign loans are getting into more regular channels, and therefore will press more lightly: the examination of the Bank affairs will soon be over, and therefore the usual accommodations may be expected, though, in our opinion, cautiously. The merchants are looking forwards to the Spring trade, and symptoms already appear of those preparations, which a few weeks more will undoubtedly realize. It may be added that those houses which have been shaken, being now marked, those which have stood will be thought more respectable: in fact, we have reason to infer, that a pretty strict investigation of the accounts of every house connected with the Great House has taken place, and this under circumstances somewhat presaging further failures.

We now proceed, according to our custom, to specify some of the leading articles of mercantile dealings.

Standard Silver is marked at 5s. 7d. per oz. Gold is not marked.

It admits of no doubt, whether the price at which an article is raised and brought to market is a necessary price: and yet it may happen, from extraordinary pressure of a moment, that a price, less than that necessary price should be accepted.

COTTON has lately been sold at very reducedprices A sale is announced at the India-House, and what is somewhat remarkable, two other public sales are marked for the same day ; we presume that speculation will not fail of shewing itself on these occasions : the article is safe; and though the demand be languid, at this moment, it certainly will find its level in a reasonable time ; the finer kinds keep up their price. A considerable supply has lately arrived from the East Indies direct, by the private trade. *A propos* of the East Indies, we have seen letters from thence, which state, that the supply of European goods brought by the private trade chiefly, had been so great, that many sorts were disposed of at an absolute loss (reckoning invoice cost, and freight) of 50 per cent.—that others were selling at 30 *per cent.* loss—and the sales were pressed on those terms ; others in other proportions : a few articles, as Wines and other comforts for the table, with certain articles of dress, chintzes of pleasing patterns and other *personalities* yielded a profit, sometimes as high as 10 *per cent.* Our readers will infer, that unless the return cargo fetches a good price inEurope, the adventurers will have small occasion of triumph. Whether the spirit of rivalship connected with this trade has as yet reached its *acme* is more than we can pretend to give a determinate opinion on.

The buyers of Sugars are rather on the look-out to see what favourable business they may hit on, than actually forward to purchase ; this preserves an appearance of a hopeful market, but, at present, only the finer sorts are thought worthy of much notice ; the low browns and inferior are pressed forward by the holders, which is evidence sufficient that the number of sellers exceeds that of buyers. The deliveries from the Warehouses continue to be considerable, and by far the greater proportion is destined to home consumption.

The Refined market feels exceedingly the necessity of sale, in order to meet coming acceptances ; goods are offered at a very low rate for prompt payment, but this is supposed to be the only cause of the depression felt on the market: whence we infer, that as soon as that is removed the article will rise ; indeed, the expectation of this is general, and those who can lay down the purchase money need be at no loss for as many transfers of goods as they please.

COFFEE has experienced but little spirit lately, and during the last few days those who could hold have continued to hold

back forwhat they hope may prove better days while those who could not hold offered their commodity on very moderate terms: indeed these were so low that there were not wanting a few to embrace them, but unless the temptation was continued in its full force, consent was withheld ; in short, the whole has been heavy, and heavy it continues.

It deserves remark, that much the same is the state of things on the continent; the market is dull, consequently, there is no disposition to take advantage of the shade that overcasts the London Market; the continental holders, however, will not listen to abatement of prices, but keep up their spirits ; and this countenances the persuasion that the affair is only temporary ; whether they may feel the same pressure from the same cause as ourselves or whether the season may be the leading cause, may admit of much to be said on both sides.

The import of foreign Corn has been so abundant, that the ports are now shut against Foreign Wheat; but they continue open to other descriptions of grain, as yet : from British America Grain of all kinds is admissible.

Rice has lately found a favourable acceptance; the sale at the India House, last week, consisted of 6,000 bags; and not only was the whole cleared off, but the prices were higher than had been anticipated.

Silk appears to be a rising article ; and it is thought that the East India production will increase in value : There is a sale now depending, in which this opinion will be put to the test.

Indigo, as a material for dyeing, maintains its price : perhaps, we ought rather to state it as being on the advance, because the supply is not so much as expectation relied on.

BANKRUPTCIES SUPERSEDED, Jan. 30.

N. Walker, Dover, Brewer

J. Taylor, Whittington, Lancashire, cotton dealer

BANKRUPTS.

Allum R. Chatham, builder. *Sol.* James, Earl street, Blackfriars.

Barker J. Stratford, Essex, common brewer, *Sol* Smith, Finsbury square

Baylis D. Stroud, Gloucestershire, clothier. *Sol.* Young, New Corn Exchange, Mark lane

Bradley J. St. John's, Worcestershire, coal master. *Sol.* Bigg, Southampton buildings, Chancery lane

Burgis J. Southampton street, Covent garden, ornamental paper manufacturer. *Sol.* Castle, Cursitor street.

Cooper T. Kennett wharf, Upper Thames street, merchant. *Sol.* Crossley, Great James street, Bedford row

Fervall J. Birmingham, printer. *Sols* Swain and Co. Frederick's place, Old Jewry

Gleeson J. Cock hill, Ratcliff, potatoe merchant. *Sol.* Smith, Barnard's Inn

Greenslade R. Plymouth, builder. *Sol.* Drake and Co. Chancery lane

Henn I. Birmingham, screw maker. *Sols.* Hicks & Braikenridge, Bartlett's buildings

Hudson M. and G. Liverpool, slopsellers. *Sols.* Adlington and Gregory, Bedford Row

Jay J. Old Jewry, wine merchant. *Sols.* Taylor and Co. New Basinghall street

Jones J. Liverpool, merchant. *Sols.* Dacey and John, Palsgrave place, Temple bar

Lloyd T. and J. Winter, Blue Ball yard, St. James's street, wine merchant. *Sols.* Dennetts and Co. King's Arms yard, Coleman street

Macleod T. H. Pinner's hall, Winchester street, wine merchant. *Sol.* Hore, jun. Hatton garden

Perkins C. Perkins rents, Peter street, victualler, *Sol.* Jones, New Inn, Strand

Phillips R. Exeter, chymist. *Sol.* Bruton, Broad street

Price D. Watford, Hertfordshire, linen draper. *Sols.* Davies and Son, Lothbury

Reddall W. and T. Liverpool, and J. Reddall and R. Rainy, New York, America, merchants. *Sols.* Adlington and Gregory, Bedford row

Reddall T. Liverpool, merchant. *Sols.* Adlington and Gregory, Bedford row

Thompson E. Globe stairs, Rotherhithe, ship builder. *Sol.* Swain & Co. Frederick's place, Old Jewry

Wadley J. Coventry street, Haymarket, cheesemonger. *Sol.* Popkin, Dean street, Soho

Walker R. Newcastle upon Tyne, grocer. *Sols.* Atkinson and Wildes, Chancery lane

Wardale G. and F. Allhallows Wharf, Upper Thames street, oil crushers. *Sols.* Alliston and Hundleby, Freeman's court, Cornhill

White W. Chalford, Gloucestershire, linen draper. *Sol.* Chilton, Chancery lane

BANKRUPTS, Feb. 2.

Foulerton J. Upper Bedford place, Bloomsbury square, merchant. *Sols.* Knight and Freeman, Basinghall street

Gilchrist G. and J. M Liverpool, merchants. *Sols.* Blackstock & Bunce, King's Bench Walk, Temple

Hattersley M. Bilton with Harrowgate, Yorkshire, hotel keeper. *Sols.* Alexander and Holme, New inn

Hornby J Liverpool, merchant, *Sols.* Adlington and Gregory, Bedford row

Morgan J. M., G. M., and R. Morgan, Belle Sauvage yard, Ludgate hill, wholesale stationers. *Sols.* J. and A. Smith, Dorset street, Salisbury square

Mottram C. Pinners hall, Winchester-street, merchant. *Sols.* Stratton and Allport, Shoreditch

Pickman J. Deptford, malster. *Sols.* Parnther and Turner, London street, Fenchurch-street

Thompson T. Hambleton, Lancashire, tanner. *Sol.* Norris, John-street, Bedford-row

Towsey J. jun. and S. Lloyd, Blanford Forum, Dorsetshire, dealers. *Sols.* Wilson and Chisholme, Lincolns inn-fields

Towsey J. jun. Blanford-Forum, Dorsetshire, stonemason. *Sol.* Dean, Guildford street.

Wilbeam J. H. Dock-head, Surrey, distiller. *Sols.* Martin & Son, Vintners hall, Upper Thames street.

BANKRUPTCIES SUPERSEDED, Feb. 6.

B. Sargeant, Kingston-upon-Thames, carpenter

J. Twyford, Portswood-within-Brianington, Cheshire, cotton spinner

W. Chamberlayne, Leicester, hosier

S. Bryce, Liverpool, baker

BANKRUPTS.

Blyth R. Kingston-upon-Hull, corn merchant. *Sol.* Ellis, Chancery lane

Campbell P. Marylebone street, Golden square, wine merchant. *Sol.* Newcomb, Vine street, Piccadilly

Caumont P. Old Broad street, merchant. *Sols.* Blunt and Bowman, Broad street buildings

Healey R. Lower place, Rochdale, Lancashire, woollen manufacturer. *Sol.* Chippindale, Crane court, Fleet street

Jackson C. Upper Thames street, sugar factor. *Sols.* Smith and Henderson, Lemen street, Goodman's fields

Levy L. Great Prescot street, merchant, *Sol.* Lewis, Crutched friars

Lloyd T. Tibberton, Herefordshire, farmer. *Sol.* Pewtriss, Gray's inn

Marchant M. Poplar, cow-keeper. *Sol.* Howell, Symond's inn

Morgan W. and Matthews W. Newport, Monmouthshire, common brewers. *Sol.* Platt, New Boswell court, Lincoln's inn

Powell G. Little Trinity lane, Queenhithe, baker. *Sol.* Holmes, Great James street, Bedford row

Rothwell J. Mort-field, Halliwell, Lancashire, whitster. *Sol.* Meddowcroft, Gray's inn

Sayer E. Bath, tailor. *Sols.* Adlington and Gregory, Bedford row

Smyth E. St. Martin's court, St. Martin's lane, shoemaker. *Sols.* Mayhew and Co. Chancery lane

Whates R. Wapping street, anchorsmith. *Sol.* Orme, Stepney Church-yard

Wilks R. Chancery lane, printer. *Sol.* Arundle, Chancery lane

BANKRUPTS, Feb. 9.

Bacon R. jun. Barkway, Hertfordshire, miller. *Sol.* Gray, Tyson place, Kingsland road

Brown W. St. John street, cheesemonger. *Sols.* Dacie and John, Palsgrave place, Temple bar

Burn W. Exeter, draper. *Sol.* Brutton, Broad street, London

Burroughs, Great Hermitage street, Middlesex, spirit merchant. *Sol.* Pearson, St. Helen's place, Bishopsgate street.

Cullimore T. Wickwar, Gloucestershire, maltster. *Sol.* King, Sergeant's inn

Lewis W. Beak street, Golden square, woollen draper. *Sols.* Davies and Son, Lothbury

Lloyd W. Shrewsbury, tailor. *Sol.* Griffiths, Southampton buildings, Chancery lane

Longden J. Peak-forest, Derbyshire, meal and flour seller. *Sols.* Lowes and Cowburn, Temple

Mather J. Manchester, builder. *Sol.* Adlington and Gregory, Bedford row.

Matthews E. College hill, merchant. *Sols.* Dawes and Chatfield, Angel court, Throgmorton street

Medlam J. Huddersfield, Yorkshire, grocer. *Sols.* Fisher and Sudlow, Holborn.

Nayler M. and G. Darlington, Durham, leather dressers. *Sol.* Dixon, Gray's inn square

Oliver J. and Ingraham N. J. jun. Pinner's Hall, Broad street, merchants. *Sol.* Cranch, Union court, Broad street

Potts R. Holborn hill, haberdasher. *Sol.* Hodgson, Dyer's court, Aldermanbury

Robertson E. Manchester, cotton spinner. *Sol.* Ellis, Chancery lane

Stansfield J. Ardwick, Lancashire, merchant. *Sol.* Wiglesworth and Crosley, Gray's Inn

Taylor R. Witney, Oxfordshire, mealman. *Sol.* Gregory, WaxChandlers' hall, Maiden lane.

Wilkinson H. Liverpool, merchant, and F. J. Humble, Wavertree, Liverpool, master mariner. *Sols.* Taylor and Roscoe, King's Bench walk, Temple

BANKRUPTCIES SUPERSEDED, Feb. 13.

W. Peet, Basinghall street, merchant

BANKRUPTS.

Atkinson J. W. Mitcham, Surry, farmer. *Sol.* Nettleford, Norfolk street, Strand

Cawood D. Newton, Yorkshire, merchant. *Sol.* Foljambe, Wakefield

Crosse A. Ellesmere, Shropshire, grocer. *Sols.* Rosser and Co. Bartlett's buildings, Holborn.

Gale J. Paternoster row, wholesale stationer. *Sol.* Hurst, Milk street

Hopper C. Little Trinity lane, lace dealer. *Sol.* Unmey, Clement's inn

Martin W. Leadenhall market, cheesemonger. *Sol.* Russell, Lant street, Southwark

Penny G. and R. Thompson, Commercial Sale rooms, Mincing lane, brokers. *Sols.* Knight and Freeman, Basinghall street

Pitcher J. Upper Thames street, carpenter. *Sols.* Godmond and Black, Earl street, Blackfriars

Raffield J. Edward street, Cavendish square, dealer. *Sols* Draper and Bird, Exchange buildings, Royal Exchange

Randall J. Pancras street, Tottenham-court road, auctioneer. *Sol.* Collingridge, Secondaries office, Coleman street

Reed T. and J. Middlesma, Newcastle-upon-Tyne, merchants. *Sols.* Knight and Freeman, Basinghall street

Starbuck R. Milton, Kent, boot and shoe maker. *Sol.* Ledgwich, College hill

Twicker C. jun. Stoke newington, merchant. *Sol.* Maugham, Great St. Helen's

Upton G. Queen street, oil and colour merchant. *Sols.* Lee and Townshend, Three Crown square, Southwark

Watkinson W. Strand, boot and shoe maker. *Sol.* Jones, New inn

Wilkinson H. Liverpool, merchant. *Sols.* Taylor and Roscoe, King's Bench walk, Temple

BANKRUPTCIES SUPERSEDED. Feb. 16.

J. Job, Ivy lane, Newgate street, merchant

R. James, Bristol, cabinet maker

BANKRUPTS.

Cobbett W. jun. Kingsland road, common brewer. *Sols.* Lamb and Hawke, Prince's street, Bank

Dodsworth W. York, ship carpenter. *Sol.* Smith, Pump court, Middle Temple

Fish T. Bridport, victualler. *Sol.* Allen, Clifford's inn

Fricker C. jun. Stoke newington, merchant. *Sol.* Maugham, Great St. Helens

Highfield G. B. and C. Liverpool, merchants. *Sols* Blackstock and Bunce, King's bench walk, Temple

Johnson J. Lucas street, Commercial road, merchant. *Sol.* Willey, Welclose square

Lomas J. White Horse Inn, Fetter lane, tavern keeper. *Sols.* Mayhew and Co. Chancery lane

O'Hara M. Watford, Hertfordshire, innkeeper. *Sol.* Williams, Blackman street

Woods W. Haughton street, Clare market, coal merchant. *Sols.* Thomas and Kaye, Barnard's inn

Wright F. Budge row, merchant. *Sol.* Stratton and Allport, Shoreditch

PRICES CURRENT, *Feb. 20, 1819.*

	£ s. d.	£ s. d
American pot-ash, per cwt	0 0	to 2 0
Ditto pearl	2 11	0 0
Barilla	1 12	0 0
Brandy, Cogniac, bond. gal.	0 5	0 3
Camphire, refined....lb.	0 4 1	0
Ditto unrefined..cwt.	10 10	13 0
Cochineal, fine black, lb.	1 7	1 7 6
Ditto, East India	0 5	0 6 0
Coffee, fine bond....cwt.	7 2	7 8 0
Ditto ordinary	5 17 9	6 1 0
Cotton Wool, Surinam, lb.	0 1 7	0 1 8
Ditto Jamaica..	0 1 2	0 1 6
Ditto Smyrna ..	0 1 0	0 1 ½
Ditto East-India	0 0 8	5 1 1
Currants, Zant....cwt.	5 0 0	5 1 0
Elephants' Teeth 31	0 0	34 0
———Scrivelloes 20	0 0	28 0 0
Flax, Riga........ton 85	0 0	0 0 0
Ditto Petersburgh .. 68	0 0	0 0 0
Galls, Turkey....cwt..	9 0 0	9 1 0
Geneva, Holl. bond. gal.	0 3 0	0 9
Ditto, English........9	6 6	0 0
Gum Arabic, Turkey, cwt.	9 10 0	12 0
Hemp, Riga ...... ton 46	0 0	47 0
Ditto Petersburgh 41 10	0 0	42 0 0
Indigo Caraccas .. lb.	0 10 0	0 1 6
Ditto East India	0 7 8	0 3
Iron British bars .. ton.	13 0 0	14 0
Ditto to Swedish C.O.N.D. 21	0 0	22 0
Ditto Swed. 2nd sort 16	0 0	17 4
Lead in pigs...... fod	0 0 0	27 0 0
Ditto red...... ton	0 0 0	27 0 0
Ditto white......ton	0 0 0	40 0
Logwood......... ton 8	10 0	9 0 0
Madder, Dutch crop, cwt.	5 15 0	7 10 0
Mahogany.........ft.	0 1 6	0
Oil, Lucca..24 gal. jar	17 0 0	19 0
Ditto Florence, ½ chest	2 10 0	3 0
Ditto whale.........32	0 0	0 0
Ditto spermaceti..ton 85	0 0	0 0
Pitch, Stockholm .. cwt.	0 11 0	0 2 0
Raisins, bloom .... cwt.	0 0 0	4 10 0
Rice, Carolina bond....	2 5 0	0 0 0
Rum, Jamaica bond gal.	0 3 5	0 3 7
Ditto Leeward Island..0	3 1	0 3 3
Saltpetre, East India, cwt.	1 15 6	1 18 0
Silk, thrown, Italian, lb.	2 19 0	3 10 0
Silk,....raw,..Ditto...	1 16 0	2 8 0
Tallow, Russia, white ..	0 0 0	3 9 0
Ditto——, yellow..	3 8 0	0 0 0
Tar, Stockholm....bar.	1 0 0	1 2 0
Tin in blocks......cwt.	4 12 6	0 0 0
Tobacco, Maryland, lb.	0 0 11	0 1 4
Ditto Virginia	0 0	0 0 10
Wax, Guinea.....cwt.	9 0 0	9 10 0
Whale-fins (Greenl) ton 100	0 0	0 0 0

Wine:

		£ s. d.
Red Port, bond pipe .. 39		0 0
Ditto Lisbon 38		0 0
Ditto Madeira 60		0 0
Ditto Mountain 28		0 0
D.tto Cape........... 20		0 0
Ditto Sherry ..... butt 30	0 0 55	0 0
Ditto Claret .,........25	0 0 88	0 0

Fire-Office Shares, &c. Feb. 21.

Canals.

	£. s.	£. s.
Chesterfield ....Div. 5l..... 102	— —	— —
Coventry .... (Div. 44l.) .. 1000	— —	— —
Croydon 5 10	— —	— —
Crinan 2 12	— —	— —
Ellesmere and Chester (D.2l.) 68	— —	— —
Grand Junction ...(Div. 6l.).. 256	— —	— —
Grand Surry 55	— —	— —
Ditto (optional) Loan Div. 5l. 95 10	— —	— —
Huddersfield 13	— —	— —
Kennett and Avon 23 12	6 —	
Leeds and Liverpool (Div 10l.) 340	— —	— —
Lancaster......Div. 1l. 27	— —	— —
Oxford Div.31l. 630	— —	— —
Peakforest 63	— —	61 —
Stratford & Avon.......... 10	— —	— —
Thames and Medway 30	— —	— —

Docks.

Commercial .... Div. 3l. 10s. 63	— —	— —
East India........Div. 7l.... 183	— —	— —
London ....Div. 3l..... 81	— —	— —
West India ....Div 10l..... 187	— —	— —

Insurance Companies.

Albion...... 500sh..£50 pd. 45	— —	— —
County .... — —	— —	
Eagle.........50 5pd....... 2 10	— —	— —
Globe.........Div. 6l. 126	— —	— —
Hope.........50 5pd 4 4	— —	— —
Imperial 500 50pd. 92	— —	— —
London Fire 27	— —	— —
London Ship 21 5	— —	— —
Royal Exchange..Div. 10 .. 259	— —	— —
Rock....50..2pd......... 4 4	— —	— —
Union Fire Life..100l. 20 pd. 33	— —	— —

Water Works.

Grand Junction,...........44	— —	— —
London Bridge....Div. 3l. 10s.52 10	60 —	
Manchester and Salford 38	— —	— —
Portsmouth and Farlington 50l. 10 10	— —	— —
Ditto (New) 50l...Div. 6.....38	— —	6 2
South London;.............. 19	— —	— —
West Middlesex..100.........44	— —	— —

Bridges.

Southwark 58 10	— —	— —
Waterloo 10	— —	— —
Ditto Old Annuities 60 all pd ..36 10	— —	— —
Ditto New do 40 all pd. 25	— —	— —
Vauxhall Bonds, 97 pd.......96	— —	— —

Literary Institutions.

London, 75gs...............44	— —	— —
Russel, 25gs...............13	— —	— —
Surry, 30gs................10	— —	— —

Mines.

British Copper Comp. 100 sh...— —	— —	— —
Beeralstone Lead and Silver...,14 15	— —	— —
Butspill ......10 pd........	— —	— —
Great Hewas......15 pd......19	— —	— —

Roads.

Highgate Archway........... 4	— —	— —

Miscellaneous.

Auction Mart 21	— —	— —
Five per cent. City Bonds.....	— —	— —
Chelsea 10 sh. Div. Div. 12 .. —	— —	— —
Lon. Commer. sale Room 100p 34	— —	— —
Lon. Flour Comp. 14 pd...... 1 19	1 5	
East London..100l. sh ,p.....	— —	— —
Gas Light and Coke Company 75	— —	— —

	8 o'clock Morning	Noon	10 o'clock Night	Height of Barom. Inches.	Dryness by Leslie's Barom.	
Jan. 21	37	44	37	29,45	15	Fair
22	37	49	40	,36	15	Cloudy
23	38	53	44	,62	21	Fair
24	45	47	42	,47	19	Cloudy
25	42	47	40	,15	0	Rain
26	40	48	42	,42	17	Fair
27	42	49	46	,42	16	Foggy
28	42	54	39	,32	32	Fair
29	37	47	38	,42	24	Fair
30	44	44	40	,27	0	Rain
31	40	44	38	,40	12	Cloudy
Feb. 1	28	42	37	,52	14	Fair
2	29	37	28	,55	0	Snow
3	26	40	38	,54	12	Cloudy
4	37	45	42	,60	21	Cloudy
5	40	47	40	,56	0	Rain
6	44	50	45	,48	16	Fair
7	42	48	37	,38	23	Stormy
8	37	47	40	,83	22	Cloudy
9	45	50	50	,80	0	Rain
10	47	49	46	,89	29	Fair
11	46	52	47	,92	25	Fair
12	47	47	39	,56	0	Rain
13	45	46	38	,70	22	Showry
14	34	42	35	30,00	27	Fair
15	35	45	45	29,92	24	Fair
16	45	46	48	,49	0	Rain
17	50	54	50	,48	27	Fair
18	46	49	48ʰ	,49	26	Fair
19	50	53	40	,26	29	Fair
20	36	47	45	,70	27	Fair

London Premiums of Insurance.

Aberdeen, Dundee, Perth, &c. 15s. 9d. to 20s
Africa, 2gs.
Amelia Island, 0gs. to 0gs.
American States, 35gs. to 40gs.
Belfast, Cork, Dublin, 20s. to 25s.
Brazils, 2gs.
Hamburgh, &c. 20gs. to 25gs.
Cadiz, Lisbon, Oporto, 30s.
Canada 2gs. to 2½gs.
Cape of Good Hope, 2gs. to 2½gs.
Constantinople, Smyrna, &c. 2gs. to 50s.
East-India (Co. ships) 3gs.
———— out and home, 6gs.
France, 15s. 9d. to 20s.
Gibraltar, 25 to 30s.
Gottenburgh, 2½gs. to 2gs.
Greenland, out and home, 3gs. to 3½gs.
Holland 15s. 9d. to 20s.
Honduras, &c. 2gs.
Jamaica, 35s. to 40s.
Leeward Islands, 25s. to 30s.
Madeira, 20s. to 30s.
Malta, Italian States, &c. 35s. to 40s.
Malaga, 30s.
Newfoundland, 30s. to 35s.
Portsmouth, Falmouth, Plymouth, 15d. to 20s.
River Plate, 2gs.
Southern Fishery, out and home, 10gs.
Stockholm, Petersburgh, Riga, &c. 2gs.

LONDON MARKETS.

PRICE OF BREAD.

The Peck Loaf to weigh 17lb. 6oz. 4s. 0d
The Half ditto   ditto   8   11 2   0
The Quar. ditto   ditto   4   5 1   0
The half ditto   ditto   2   2¾ 0   6

POTATOES.

Kidney...... 8 0 0 | Ox Nobles .. 7 0 0
Champions .. 7 0 0 | Apple 7 0 0
ONIONS, per Bushel, 2s 0d to 3s 6d

MEAT.

Smithfield, per stone of 8lb. to sink the Offal

1819.	Beef s. d.	mut. s. d.	veal. s. d.	pork s. d.	lams s. d.
Feb. 27 ..	5 8	6 6	7 0	6 8	0 0
..	6 4	6 4	7 6	6 6	0 0
..	5 8	6 6	7 6	6 8	0 0
..	5 8	6 4	7 0	6 8	0 0

SUGAR.

Lumps ordinary or large 32 to 40 lbs... 101
Fine or Canary, 24 to 30 lbs. 120
Loaves, fine...................... 120
Powder, ordinary, 9 to 11lbs.......... 106

COTTON TWIST.

Feb. 19.   Mule 1st quality, No. 40 3s. 2d
————————————No. 120 7s. 9d
————2d quality, No. 40 2s. 9d
Discount—15 a 22½ per cent.

COALS, delivered at 13s. per chald. advance.

	Sunderland.		Newcastle.	
Jan. 27. ...	30s 0d to 41 0		31s 0d to 42 6	
Feb. 5. ..	33s 0	41 3	31s 0d	43 0
12. ..	42s 3	0 0	32s 0d	44 0
19. ..	30s 6	0 0	32s 0d	43 6

LEATHER.

Butts, 50 to 56lb. 24 | Calf Skins 30 to
Dressing Hides .. 21 | 45lb. per doz. 42
Crop hides for cut. 21 | Ditto 50 to 70.. —
Flat Ordinary .. 16 | Seals, Large.... 100
SOAP; yellow, 88s.; mottled 100s.; curd 000s.
CANDLES; per doz. 13s. 0d. ; moulds 14s. 6d.

Course of Exchange.

Bilboa	38½	Palermo, per oz 123d.	
Amsterdam, C.F.	11-7	Leghorn	51¼
Ditto at sight	11-4	Genoa	47¼
Rotterdam	11-8	Venice,	24-80
Hamb. us. 2¼	34	Naples	42½
Altona us. 2¼	34.1	Lisbon	58
Paris, 3d. d.	23-85	Oporto	65
Ditto, 2 us.	24-15	Rio Janeiro	64
Madrid	39-34	Dublin	10¼
Cadiz	40	Cork	10¼
Agio Bank of Holland, 2 per cent.			

HAY and STRAW.—AT SMITHFIELD.

	Hay. £. s. d.	Straw. £. s. d.	Clover. £. s. d.
Feb. 6 ..	7 7 0	2 16 0	9 0 0
13 ..	7 0 0	2 0 0	9 0 0
20 ..	7 0 0	3 0 0	9 0 0
27 ..	7 7 0	3 0 0	9 0 0

fear lest, while correcting one evil, they should encourage many. And always in free constitutions, should the danger of establishing improper precedents be ever present to the mind's eye of the legislator : for, as these are open to every man alike, there is no possibility of foreseeing in what manner they may be applied in time to come.

We may not, perhaps, disapprove entirely of certain proposals made at the present moment;—but we may be allowed to submit, that in our judgment the precedent would be dangerous: it would not terminate where even those who now support such proposals would desire.

There are not a few, who see no difficulty whatever in commanding the Bank to return to cash payments; but the well-informed know, that the mere agitation of the question, by inducing the Bank to exercise its prudence, has rendered money so scarce, that for a while the possessors of it could make after the rate of ten, or twelve, *per cent. per annum* : and some go so far as to say, that four or five *per cent.* additional was offered under the term *bonus*, or some other equally expressive, for a short time.

Suppose, for a moment, that the same prudence, pushed to excess, should induce the Bank to contract its issues from thirty millions to twenty; can the reader possibly estimate the difficulties under which this sudden failure of support would involve the whole mercantile world? Could their ships be sent to sea? Certainly not. What then must become of the sailors, the shipwrights, and the thousand other trades connected with ships? And if the ships did not go abroad, the manufactures they ought to carry out must needs stay at home; so the merchant would counter-order the manufacturer, and the manufacturer would counter-order his working hands:—of the consequences none can be ignorant.

That would be an extreme case ; and the reader will discern in our letter from Petersburgh, a ray of more pleasing anticipation on the subject of bullion. That country has obtained silver enough to answer its purpose; it is now imported at a loss: of course the tide will turn, and silver will abide where it suffers no loss.

The same may be said of gold : to where it yields the greatest profit, thither it will flow ; and those who observed that the Bank paid, on the last dividends, *guineas*, not *sovereigns*, for such smaller sums as are now paid in cash,—had an opportunity of discerning the power of calculation in reference to the relative value of the two species of coin.—But, where had these

guineas been hoarded since their mintage ? This subject would require a volume ; but we cannot, at present, allow it more room. Though Britain be our dearest interests, yet we must dedicate a few lines to foreign affairs.

Since our last, which reported the death of the elder Queen of Spain, her husband, King Charles IV. has likewise deceased. He survived his queen only about a fortnight. We understand that he died at Naples, January 20, in the 71st year of his age.*

---

* CHARLES IV. was born at Naples, November 11, 1748. He was son of Charles III. and of Maria Amelia of Saxony. He became Prince of Asturias in 1759, when his father succeeded to the throne of Spain, on the death of his (the father's) brother, Ferdinand VI. He married at the age of 17, September 4, 1765, Maria Louisa of Parma, whose sway over him never ceased during their long union. He ascended the throne December 14, 1788, and reigned till March 19, 1808, the day of his first abdication in favour of his son; an abdication which had nothing in it of a voluntary character. When the melancholy journey to Bayonne took place, King Ferdinand withdrew his claims to the throne, which Charles IV. constrained by superior force, surrendered immediately into the hands of Buonaparte. It was, therefore, March 19, 1808, that terminated the reign of Charles IV. He had, during six years, a pension of 2,000,000 francs ; but it was not regularly paid. He resided a short time at Fontainebleau and at Compeigne ; he then established himself with the Queen and the Prince of the Peace, at Marseilles ; whence he went to Rome, in 1811. After the fall of Buonaparte, Charles IV. again solemnly renounced his Crown, in a treaty concluded with his son, the present King of Spain, who settled on him a pension of 3,000,000 francs, and agreed to pay his debts. At the breaking out of the French Revolution, this monarch made the most strenuous efforts to save the life of his ally and relative, Louis XVI. He charged his ambassador to deliver a letter to the National Convention, appealing to their mercy ; it was presented to that assembly on the evening previous to the immolation of Louis ; but they refused to open it, dreading that its contents might inspire humanity in the less violent minds of some among them. When he received the unhappy news of the King's death, Charles declared war against the French Republic, with which, however, he was forced to make an inglorious peace ; and afterwards to unite his arm with France against England. This cost him immense losses, of which the battle of Trafalgar is one instance: nor could he maintain his usual intercourse with his colonies : the consequences of which are notorious.

SPAIN is certainly at this moment an interesting object to Political Speculators. We have too often alluded to her undeniable embarrassments, to add more than a mere recollection of them here.

FRANCE has, probably, reached that state at which she may continue stationary for some time. Her new ministry seem to go on smoothly enough, at least for the present.

We hear little from the interior of the Continent: the season is, no doubt, one cause; another is the little that transpires worthy notice.

Report had lately killed the Pope, the King of Sweden, and some other Monarchs: but we believe that they still continue to be inhabitants of this terrestrial globe.

The Grand Seignior, at Constantinople, lately indulged himself with the spectacle of putting to death the Chief of the Wahabees, and his principal adherents. The scene took place in his own palace; where also, were displayed at the same time, *a pleasing exhibition!*—a thousand heads, the spoils of victory. If we recollect rightly, Vitellius was the Roman Emperor who insisted that a dead enemy never had an offensive smell: if the Sultan of the Ottomans is of the same opinion, no doubt he had wherewithal to rejoice his olfactory nerves *con amore.*

From India we learn, that the chief instigator of the rebellion in Ceylon, with his Prime Minister, is taken by our troops; and consequently, that revolt, it may be hoped, is terminating.

There are various estimates of the ravages committed at Calcutta and its neighbourhood, by the *Cholera Morbus;* but none which supposes them to be less than 200,000 inhabitants.

We are anxious to hear from China; but have nothing fresh to report.

The Government of the United States of America has laid before Congress the papers necessary to elucidate the conduct of General Jackson, at and near Pensacola. Congress has appointed committees to report; and the General's rashness and violence have been decidedly condemned. The military execution of two British subjects, Arbuthnot and Ambrister, has been justly denounced as *murder;* and, as we hoped, the Government itself is discharged from all participation in the foul deed.

Here we close: Time will certainly compose a continuation, to which we shall have the honour to call the attention of our readers.

Commercial Chronicle.

Extracts from Commercial Letters, received from various parts of Europe.

MALTA.
New Regulations relative to Commerce.

THE Import Duty will hereafter be *one per cent, ad valorem: excepting,* on the commodities named in the new Tariff. Note, this Tariff comprises chiefly, such articles, as not being of general commerce, their value cannot be readily ascertained; also

COFFEE and SUGAR of Foreign growth; the former of which will pay 3 scudis per cantar, the latter 1¼ scudis per cantar, unless coming from Great Britain, or from the East or West Indies, in British bottoms. British Plantation Rum will hereafter pay on import 5 scudis per puncheon, but the Import Excise is now abolished.

The Export Duty heretofore levied is now abolished *in toto:* and vessels will no longer be required to deliver manifests outwards.

Merchant vessels are permitted to put into the quarantine port, and to remain there 48 hours, without being subject to any charge, save one *tari* per ton, for anchorage dues.
                              Malta, Jan. 16, 1819.

'There is none but Sicilian oil in the place, which is greedily taken at 17¼ to 17¼ per *oafiro,* equal to £76 16s. per ton on board. From the Ionian islands our advices anticipate a very bare crop, in Corfu. Refined Sugar is in much request. The market is very bare of Coffee: and the value of good ordinary is about 170s. per cwt. Black Pepper is in demand at 9d.'

          St. Petersburg, Jan. 3-15, 1819.

'For some weeks past there has scarcely been any enquiry for Goods. Bad weather, bad roads, and high rate of carriage of goods into the interior, have checked purchases. The weather continues still in the same mild state, without frost; and *no snow on the ground:* and until it changes, there is little probability of much demand arising for any of the large stocks of Imports which are in the market, unsold. Indeed the state of our Import trade cannot be worse than it is; there is no demand for any article although there is an abundant supply. The only change we expect in our Tariff this year is, that the Silver Ruble will be reduced to 3¼ Paper Rubles, or perhaps to 3,70 copeeks.—The Loan has closed with somewhat more than 63 mil-

M

lions of Rubles (Bank-notes) subscribed; the import of silver will of course cease; as on late importations there has been considerable loss; and for silver now delivered in, government will only give notes due next November. Exchange 11½d.

STATE OF TRADE.

Lloyd's Coffee-House, February.

THE politics of the day have undoubtedly, at this moment, a considerable influence on the commercial world. It is the object of some politicians to depress the Bank, by way of punishment for the accommodation the Bank has afforded to ministers: it must be granted also, that the Bank has acquired great wealth within the last years, and when was wealth acquired without exciting a grudge? Be that as it may, the motion in parliament for enquiry into the affairs of the Bank has been met by the Directors with a readiness of communication that confirms the general confidence. None ever doubted whether all were fair and solvent; but to meet the possibility of doubt, the Bank readily submits to examination, and cross-examination; there is another possibility also which the Bank has the prudence to foresee and to meet, that of being ordered to resume cash payments.

With this in contemplation, the Bank is certainly narrowing its issues; they have been as high as thirty-two millions; they have been gradually diminished to below twenty-eight millions; it is probable they are, at this moment, lower; and report states the sum of twenty-five millions as a mark at which they are likely to stand for some time—the inference is obvious. In the first place, the smaller the amount of Bank notes in circulation may be, the less danger, certainly, exists of the possibility of a run on the treasury; in the second place, the inducement for dealers in bullion, &c. to import gold, or to keep at home gold imported, or to bring to sale gold in their possession, increases with the decrease of Bank-notes, for these dealers must pay their debts with something: with Bank-notes, if they be cheapest, but, if not with Bank-notes, then with coin; for gold in its raw state, as gold dust or as ingots, pays nobody, but when coined, it passes through the Bank, as the regular channel into public circulation. During this struggle of the Bank to obtain gold, and to provide against the worst, the discounts *done* by the Bank are extremely select, which is, saying, in other words, what in common

speech is more bluntly expressed "they *do* nothing:" the best paper of the best houses has recently been looked rather shy at; this obliges the merchants to sell, and those who are able to lay down *the ready,* have very considerable opportunities of doing business to advantage at this moment; this obliges also those who had placed their cash in the funds or who had ventured on speculations in that lottery, to sell, at whatever rate; and hence, there being more sellers than buyers, and more urgent sellers than buyers, the Stocks have declined, and a progress marks their declination. nor must we here lose sight of the effects attributed to the great loans negociated by Foreign governments, trying losses have attended them to a considerable extent; add to these circumstances, the winding-up of the English loan, of which the last instalment was paid yesterday, the Bank having declined to hold it any longer; all these causes, operating together, have tried the strength of many purses. As usual, some of the strong have proved weak, while some of the weak have proved themselves strong.

The learned even derive satisfaction from the actual state of things; the English loan *is* paid; and therefore will no longer burthen the market; the Foreign loans are getting into more regular channels, and therefore will press more lightly: the examination of the Bank affairs will soon be over, and therefore the usual accommodations may be expected, though, in our opinion, cautiously. The merchants are looking forwards to the Spring trade, and symptoms already appear of those preparations, which a few weeks more will undoubtedly realize. It may be added that those houses which have been shaken, being now marked, those which have stood will be thought more respectable: in fact, we have reason to infer, that a pretty strict investigation of the accounts of every house connected with the Great House has taken place, and this under circumstances somewhat presaging further failures.

We now proceed, according to our custom, to specify some of the leading articles of mercantile dealings.

Standard SILVER is marked at 5s. 7d. per oz. GOLD is not marked.

It admits of no doubt, whether the price at which an article is raised and brought to market is a necessary price: and yet it may happen, from extraordinary pressure of a moment, that a price, less than that necessary price should be accepted.

Cotton has lately been sold at very reduced prices A sale is announced at the India-House, and what is somewhat remarkable, two other public sales are marked for the same day ; we presume that speculation will not fail of shewing itself on these occasions : the article is safe; and though the demand be languid, at this moment, it certainly will find its level in a reasonable time ; the finer kinds keep up their price. A considerable supply has lately arrived from the East Indies direct, by the private trade. *A propos* of the East Indies, we have seen letters from thence, which state, that the supply of European goods brought by the private trade chiefly, had been so great, that many sorts were disposed of at an absolute loss (reckoning invoice cost, and freight) of 50 per cent.—that others were selling at 30 *per cent.* loss—and the sales were pressed on those terms ; others in other proportions : a few articles, as Wines and other comforts for the table, with certain articles of dress, chintzes of pleasing patterns and other *personalities* yielded a profit, sometimes as high as 10 *per cent.* Our readers will infer, that unless the return cargo fetches a good price in Europe, the adventurers will have small occasion of triumph. Whether the spirit of rivalship connected with this trade has as yet reached its *acme* is more than we can pretend to give a determinate opinion on.

The buyers of Sugars are rather on the look-out to see what favourable business they may hit on, than actually forward to purchase ; this preserves an appearance of a hopeful market, but, at present, only the finer sorts are thought worthy of much notice ; the low browns and inferior are pressed forward by the holders, which is evidence sufficient that the number of sellers exceeds that of buyers. The deliveries from the Warehouses continue to be considerable, and by far the greater proportion is destined to home consumption.

The Refined market feels exceedingly the necessity of sale, in order to meet coming acceptances ; goods are offered at a very low rate for prompt payment, but this is supposed to be the only cause of the depression felt on the market: whence we infer, that as soon as that is removed the article will rise ; indeed, the expectation of this is general, and those who can lay down the purchase money need be at no loss for as many transfers of goods as they please.

Coffee has experienced but little spirit lately, and during the last few days those who could hold have continued to hold back for what they hope may prove better days while those who could not hold offered their commodity on very moderate terms: indeed these were so low that there were not wanting a few to embrace them, but unless the temptation was continued in its full force, consent was withheld ; in short, the whole has been heavy, and heavy it continues.

It deserves remark, that much the same is the state of things on the continent ; the market is dull, consequently, there is no disposition to take advantage of the shade that overcasts the London Market ; the continental holders, however, will not listen to abatement of prices, but keep up their spirits ; and this countenances the persuasion that the affair is only temporary ; whether they may feel the same pressure from the same cause as ourselves or whether the season may be the leading cause, may admit of much to be said on both sides.

The import of foreign Corn has been so abundant, that the ports are now shut against Foreign Wheat ; but they continue open to other descriptions of grain, as yet : from British America Grain of all kinds is admissible.

Rice has lately found a favourable acceptance ; the sale at the India House, last week, consisted of 6,000 bags; and not only was the whole cleared off, but the prices were higher than had been anticipated.

Silk appears to be a rising article ; and it is thought that the East India production will increase in value : There is a sale now depending, in which this opinion will be put to the test.

Indigo, as a material for dyeing, maintains its price : perhaps, we ought rather to state it as being on the advance, because the supply is not so much as expectation relied on.

Bankrupts in the order of their dates; with their Attornies.

BANKRUPTS, Jan. 26.

(Continued from p. 74.)

Aubert N. B. Lloyd's coffee-house, insurance broker. *Sols.* Reardon and Davis, Corbet court
Salter C. Jun. Portsea, baker. *Sols.* Sweet and Co. Basinghall street
Taylor W. Jun. Liverpool, merchant. *Sols.* Hurd and Co. King's bench walks, Temple

PRICES CURRENT, *Feb. 20, 1819.*

	£. s. d.	£. s. d
American pot-ash, per cwt	0 0 0	to 2 7 0
Ditto pearl	2 11 0	0 0 0
Barilla	1 12 0	0 0 0
Brandy, Cogniac, bond. gal.	0 5 6	0 6 3
Camphire, refined....lb.	0 4 10	0 5 0
Ditto unrefined··cwt.	10 10 0	13 0 0
Cochineal, fine black, lb.	1 7 0	1 9 6
Ditto, East India	0 5 0	0 6 0
Coffee, fine bond....cwt.	7 2	7 8 0
Ditto ordinary	5 17 0	6 1 0
Cotton Wool, Surinam, lb.	0 1 7	0 1 8
Ditto Jamaica..	0 1 2	0 1 6
Ditto Smyrna ..	0 1 0	0 1 ½
Ditto East-India	0 0 8	5 1 1
Currants, Zant....cwt..	5 0 0	5 10 0
Elephants' Teeth	31 0 0	34 0 0
——— Scrivelloes	20 0 0	28 0 0
Flax, Riga........ ton	85 0 0	0 0 0
Ditto Petersburgh ..	68 0 0	0 0 0
Galls, Turkey....cwt··	9 0 0	9 10 0
Geneva, Holl. bond. gal.	0 3 0	0 3 9
Ditto, English	9 6 6	0 0 0
Gum Arabic, Turkey, cwt.	9 10 0	12 0 0
Hemp, Riga ...... ton	46 0 0	47 0 0
Ditto Petersburgh	41 10 0	42 0 0
Indigo Caraccas .. lb.	0 10 0	0 10 6
Ditto East India	0 7 8	0 9 3
Iron British bars ·· ton.	13 0 0	14 0 0
Ditto Swedish C.C.N.D.	21 0 0	22 0 0
Ditto Swed· 2nd sort	16 0 0	17 0 4
Lead in pigs...... fod	0 0 0	27 0 0
Ditto red····· ton	0 0 0	27 0 0
Ditto white......ton	0 0 0	40 0 0
Logwood········ ton	8 10 0	9 0 0
Madder, Dutch crop, cwt.	5 15 0	7 10 0
Mahogany..........ft.	0 1 6	0 2 0
Oil, Lucca··24 gal. jar	17 0 0	19 0 0
Ditto Florence, ½ chest	2 10 0	3 2 0
Ditto whale..........32	0 0	0 0 0
Ditto spermaceti··ton	55 0 0	0 0 0
Pitch, Stockholm ·· cwt.	0 11 0	0 0 0
Raisins, bloom .... cwt.	0 0 0	4 15 0
Rice, Carolina bond····	2 5 0	0 0 0
Rum, Jamaica bond gal.	0 3 5	0 3 7
Ditto Leeward Island··0	3 1	0 3 5
Saltpetre, East India, cwt.	1 15 6	1 18 0
Silk, thrown, Italian, lb.	2 19 0	3 10 0
Silk,···raw,.. · Ditto···	1 16 0	2 8 0
Tallow, Russia, white ..	0 0 0	3 9 0
Ditto——— yellow··	3 8 0	0 0 0
Tar, Stockholm····bar.	1 0 0	1 2 0
Tin in blocks......cwt.	4 12 6	0 0 0
Tobacco, Maryland, lb.	0 0 11	0 1 4
Ditto Virginia	0 0 0	0 0 10
Wax, Guinea·····cwt.	9 0 0	9 10 0
Whale-fins (Green) ton	100 0 0	0 0 0

Wine:

Red Port, bond pipe ··	30 0 0	55 0 0
Ditto Lisbon ·········	38 0 0	44 0 0
Ditto Madeira········	60 0 0	70 0 0
Ditto Mountain········	28 0 0	33 0 0
Ditto Cape.··········	20 0 0	30 0 0
Ditto Sherry ······butt	30 0 0	65 0 0
Ditto Claret ··········	25 0 0	65 0 0

Fire-Office Shares, &c. Feb. 21.

Canals.	£. s.	£. s.
Chesterfield ....Div. 5l.....	102 —	— —
Coventry .... (Div. 44l.) ..	1000 —	— —
Croydon..................	5 10	— —
Crinan....................	2 12	— —
Ellesmere and Chester (D.21.)	68 —	— —
Grand Junction ...(Div. 61.)..	256 —	— —
Grand Surry	· 55 —	— —
Ditto (optional) Loan Div. 5l.	95 10	— —
Huddersfield	13 —	— —
Kennett and Avon	23 12	6 —
Leeds and Liverpool (Div 10l.)	340 —	— —
Lancaster......Div. 1l.....	27 —	— —
Oxford ......Div.31l.	630 —	— —
Peakforest	63 —	61 —
Stratford & Avon...........	10 —	— —
Thames and Medway	30 —	— ·
Docks.		
Commercial ....Div. 3l. 10s.	63 —	— —
East India........Div. 7l...	183 —	— —
London ....Div. 3l....	81 —	— —
West India ....Div 10l.....	187 —	— —
Insurance Companies.		
Albion...... 500sh..£50 pd.	45 —	— —
County	—	
Eagle········50 5pd.	2 10	— —
Globe........Div. 6l.	126 —	— —
Hope········50 5pd	4 4	— —
Imperial ····500 50pd.	92 —	— —
London Fire ··············	27 —	— —
London Ship ··············	21 5	— —
Royal Exchange··Div. 10 .·	259 —	— —
Rock······50..2pd·······	4 4	— —
Union Fire Life··100l. 20 pd.	33 —	— —
Water Works.		
Grand Junction............44	—	— —
London Bridge......Div. 3l. 10s.	52 10	60 —
Manchester and Salford 38	—	— —
Portsmouth and Farlington 50l.	10 10	— —
Ditto (New) 50l.··Div. 6····	33 —	6 2
South London.............	19 —	— —
West Middlesex··100········	44 —	— —
Bridges.		
Southwark ··················58	10	— —
Waterloo..................10	—	— —
Ditto Old Annuities 60 all pd··35	10	— —
Ditto New do 40 sh. all pd. ··.25	—	— —
Vauxhall Bonds, 97 pd.......	96 —	— —
Literary Institutions.		
London, 75gs.................44	—	— —
Russel, 25gs.................13	—	— —
Surry, 30gs. 10	—	— —
Mines.		
British Copper Comp. 100 sh.··	——	— —
Beeralvstone Lead and Silver..,.14	15	— —
Butspill .....10 pd............—	—	— —
Great Hewas.......15 pd.......10	—	— —
Roads.		
Highgate Archway·············	4 —	— —
Miscellaneous.		
Auction Mart................21	—	— —
Five per cent. City Bonds.....	— —	— —
Chelsea 10 sh. Div. Div. 13 ··	——	— —
Lon. Commer. sale Room 100p 34—	—	— —
Lon. Flour Comp. 14 pd.......	1 19	1 5
East London··100l. sh .,.....	——	— —
Gas Light and Coke Company 75	—	— ·

	8 o'clock Morning	Noon.	11 o'clock Night.	Height of Barom. Inches	Dryness by Leslie's Barom.	
Jan. 21	37	44	37	29,45	15	Fair
22	37	49	40	,36	15	Cloudy
23	38	53	44	,62	21	Fair
24	45	47	42	,47	19	Cloudy
25	42	47	40	,15	0	Rain
26	40	48	42	,42	17	Fair
27	42	49	46	,42	16	Foggy
28	42	54	39	,32	32	Fair
29	37	47	38	,42	24	Fair
30	44	44	40	,27	0	Rain
31	40	44	38	,40	12	Cloudy
Feb. 1	28	42	37	,52	14	Fair
2	29	37	28	,55	0	Snow
3	26	40	38	,54	12	Cloudy
4	37	45	42	,60	21	Cloudy
5	40	47	40	,56	0	Rain
6	44	50	45	,48	16	Fair
7	42	48	37	,38	33	Stormy
8	37	47	40	,83	22	Cloudy
9	45	50	50	,80	0	Rain
10	47	49	46	,89	29	Fair
11	46	52	47	,92	25	Fair
12	47	47	39	,56	0	Rain
13	45	46	38	,70	22	Showry
14	34	42	35	30,00	27	Fair
15	45	45	45	29,92	24	Fair
16	45	46	48	,49	0	Rain
17	50	54	50	,48	27	Fair
18	46	49	48ʰ	,49	26	Fair
19	50	53	40	,26	29	Fair
20	36	47	45	,70	27	Fair

London Premiums of Insurance.

Aberdeen, Dundee, Perth, &c. 15s. 9d. to 20s
Africa, 2gs.
Amelia Island, 0gs. to 0gs.
American States, 35gs. to 40gs.
Belfast, Cork, Dublin, 20s. to 25s.
Brazils, 2gs.
Hamburgh, &c. 20gs. to 25gs.
Cadiz, Lisbon, Oporto, 30s.
Canada 2gs. to 2½gs.
Cape of Good Hope, 2gs. to 2½gs.
Constantinople, Smyrna, &c. 2gs. to 50s.
East-India (Co. ships) 3gs.
———— out and home, 6gs.
France, 15s. 9d. to 20s.
Gibraltar, 25 to 30s.
Gottenburgh, 2⅛gs. to 2gs.
Greenland, out and home, 3gs. to 3½gs.
Holland 15s. 9d. to 20s.
Honduras, &c. 2gs.
Jamaica, 35s. to 40s.
Leeward Islands, 25s. to 30s.
Madeira, 20s. to 30s.
Malta, Italian States, &c. 35s. to 40s.
Malaga, 30s.
Newfoundland, 30s. to 35s.
Portsmouth, Falmouth, Plymouth, 15d. to 20s.
River Plate, 2gs.
Southern Fishery, out and home, 10gs.
Stockholm, Petersburgh, Riga, &c. 2gs.

PRICE OF BREAD.

The Peck Loaf to weigh 17lb. 6oz. 4s. 0d
The Half ditto ditto 8 11 ......2 0
The Quar. ditto ditto 4 5 ......1 0
The half ditto ditto 2 2¾ 0 6

POTATOES.

Kidney...... 8 0 0 | Ox Nobles .. 7 0 0
Champions .. 7 0 0 | Apple 7 0 0
ONIONS, per Bushel, 2s 0d to 3s 6d

MEAT.

Smithfield, per stone of 8b. to sink the Offal

1819.	Beef		mut.		veal.		pork		lams	
	s.	d.	s.	d.	s.	d.	s.	d.	s.	d.
Feb. 27 ..	5	8	6	6	7	0	6	8	0	0
..	6	4	6	4	7	6	6	6	0	0
..	5	8	6	6	7	6	6	8	0	0
..	5	8	6	4	7	0	6	8	0	0

SUGAR.

Lumps ordinary or large 32 to 40 lbs... 101
Fine or Canary, 24 to 30 lbs. 120
Loaves, fine...................... 120
Powder, ordinary, 9 to 11lbs.......... 106

COTTON TWIST.

Feb. 19. Mule 1st quality, No. 40 3s. 2d
———————————No. 120 7s. 9d
————2d quality, No. 40 3s. 9d
Discount—15 a 22½ per cent.

COALS, *delivered at 13s. per chald. advance.*

	Sunderland.			Newcastle.	
Jan. 27. ..	30s	0d to 41	0	31s 0d to 42	6
Feb. 5. ..	33s	6	41 3	31s 0d	48 0
12. ..	42s	3	0 0	32s 0d	44 0
19. ..	30s	6	0 0	32s 0d	43 6

LEATHER.

Butts, 50 to 56lb. 24 | Calf Skins 30 to
Dressing Hides .. 21 | 45lb. per doz. 42
Crop hides for cut. 22 | Ditto 50 to 70.. —
Flat Ordinary .. 16 | Seals, Large.... 100

SOAP; yellow, 88s.; mottled 100s.; curd 000s.
CANDLES; per doz. 13s. 0d. ; moulds 14s. 6d.

Course of Exchange.

Bilboa	38½	Palermo, per oz 123d.	
Amsterdam, C.F.	11-7	Leghorn	51¼
Ditto at sight	11-4	Genoa	47¼
Rotterdam	11-8	Venice,	24-80
Hamb. us. 2½	34	Naples	42½
Altona us. 2½	34-1	Lisbon	58
Paris, 3d.d.	23-85	Oporto	65
Ditto, 2 us.	24-15	Rio Janeiro	64
Madrid	39-34	Dublin	10¼
Cadiz	40	Cork	10¼

Agio Bank of Holland, 2 per cent.

HAY and STRAW.—AT SMITHFIELD.

	Hay.			Straw.			Clover.		
	£.	s.	d.	£.	s.	d.	£.	s.	d.
Feb. 6 ..	7	7	0	2	16	0	9	0	0
13 ..	7	0	0	3	0	0	9	0	0
20 ..	7	0	0	3	0	0	9	0	0
27 ..	7	7	0	3	0	0	9	0	0

Price of STOCKS, from 22d January, to 20th February, 1819.

1819. Jan.	Bank Stock.	3p. Cent. Reduced.	3 p. Cent Consols.	4p. Cent Consols.	Navy 5 p. Cent.	Irish 5 p. Cent.	Long Annuities.	Imperial 3 p. Cent.	Ditto Annuities.	India Stock.	India Bonds.	South Sea Stock.	Excheq. Bills.	Consols for Acc.
22	—	76¾ 9½	78¾	97¾	107½	—	20 7-16	—	—	—	88	—	20p	79⅛
23	270½	79¼	79 8⅞	98⅛	107¾	—	20 9-16	—	—	—	89	—	20p	79⅛
25	—	79⅛	78⅞	98¼	108⅛	—	20 9-16	—	—	—		—	20p	79⅛
26	272½	79⅛	78⅞	98⅛	107⅞	—	20 9-16	77½	—	—	88	—	20p	79⅛
27	272½	79⅛	78¾	98⅛	107⅞	—	20⅛	—	—	232¼	87	—	19p	79⅛
28	272½	79⅛ 8⅞	78¾	97½	107⅞	—	20⅛	—	—	—	86	86½	19p	79
29	—	79 8¾	78⅞	97½	107½	—	20⅛	77½	—	232½	84	—	15p	79
30	Mar	tyrdom of	of Cha	arles	the	First			—					
Feb.														
1	272½	78⅞	78½ 8	97⅞	107½	—	20⅛	77½	—	233½	81	—	13p	78¾
2	Puri	fication	of the	Virg	in M	ary.			—	—		—		
3	271½	78⅝	78¼ 7½	97⅛	106⅜	—	20 7-16	—	—	233½	82	—	17p	78⅛
4	—	77¾ 7½	77½ 7	96½	106¼	—	20 7-16	—	—	—	79	—	12p	78⅛
5	269	77⅝	77¼	95⅝	105⅝	—	20 5-16	75⅝	—	—	78	—	15p	77½
6	—	77⅝	76⅞ 7½	95¾	105¾	—	20⅝	—	—	—	78	—	16p	77⅝
8	—	77½	76⅞ 7	95¾	105¾	—	20⅝	—	—	—	79	—	18p	77½
9	269½	77½	77 6½	95¾	105¾	—	20 3-16	—	—	—	79	—	15p	77¼
10	—	78½ 6½	76½ 6	95½	105½	—	20 3-16	—	—	—	78	—	15p	77
11	269	76¼ 7½	76½	95¾	105¾	—	20 3-16	—	—	228	78	—	17p	76⅞
1[illegible]	—	77⅛	77⅛	96	106⅛	—	20½	75⅝	—	229	77	—	17p	76⅞
1	—	77⅝ 7	76⅞	95⅞	106⅜	—	20 3-16	—	—	—		—	18p	76⅞
13	—	77 6½	76⅞	95⅞	106⅜	—	20¼	—	—	—	71	—	18p	76⅞
15	268	76⅞ 7½	76⅞	95⅞	106⅞	—	20¼	—	—	229	70	—	18p	76⅞
16	269	77⅛	77 6¾	96½	107	—	20¼	—	—	—	74	—	18p	77⅛
17	—	77⅛	76⅞	96⅛	106⅞	—	20 5-16	75½	—	229½	63	—	18p	76⅞
18	268½	77⅞	77⅛ 6⅞	96⅛	107⅛	—	20 3-16	—	—	—	67	—	17d	77⅜
29	—	77⅞	76⅞	96	106⅞	—	20 5-16	—	—	229		—	18p	76⅞
6														

IRISH FUNDS.

Jan.	Irish Bank Stock.	Government Debenture 3½ per ct.	Government Stock, 3½ per ct.	Government Debenture 4 per ct.	Government Stock, 5 per ct.	Treasury Bills.	Grand Canal Stock.	Grand Canal Loan, 4 per ct.	Grand Canal Loan, 6 per ct.	City Dublin Bonds.	Royal Canal Loan 6per cent.	Omnium.
23	251	90⅝	83¼	—	108⅛	—	—	—	80	—	—	—
25	251	90¼	88¾	—	108⅛	—	—	—	—	—	—	
26	—	91¼	89¼	—	108⅜	—	—	—	—	—	—	
27	—	97½	89¼		108⅜			—	—	—	—	
30	—	91	88½	—	107⅛	—	—	52¾	—	—	—	
F. 1	—	91½	88½	—	107⅞	—	—	—	—	—	—	

Prices of the FRENCH FUNDS From Jan 20, to Feb. 18.

1819	5 per Cent. consols		Bank Actions.	
Jan.	fr.	c.	fr.	c.
19	67	90	1496	—
25	68	75	1422	50
30	69	85	1497	50
Feb.				
1	70	30	1500	—
6	70	85	1548	75
8	70	40	1525	—
13	69	70	1525	—
16	73		1525	—
18	69	80	1525	—

AMERICAN FUNDS.

	IN LONDON. Jan. 26.	Feb. 2. 9.	19.	AT NEW YORK. Jan. 3.	13.	20.
7 per Cent.	—	—	—	105	105	105
Bank Shares	24	24	23	108	112	93
Louisiana	—	—	—	par	par	par
Old 6 per Cent.	—	—	—	par	par	par
New 6 per Cent.	100	101	101	101	101	101

By J. M. Richardson, 23, Cornhill.

THE

LITERARY PANORAMA,

AND

National Register:

For APRIL, 1819.

NATIONAL AND PARLIAMENTARY NOTICES,

(British and Foreign,)

PROSPECTIVE AND RETROSPECTIVE.

CLIMBING BOYS.

REPORT

From the

BOARD OF WORKS

And

ARCHITECTS,

On the Use of

CLIMBING BOYS.

[*Ordered by the House of Commons to be printed, February* 1, 1819.]

The duties of Humanity are always interesting to the benevolent mind. When they can be perfectly discharged, nothing is more satisfactory; and even, when from adverse circumstances, they can be but imperfectly discharged, the very attempt has its pleasure, though the disappointment may be painful. The advantages of society are too numerous and too striking to need illustration here, but they are not obtained without accompanying disadvantages. The various ranks of life, which ever were, and ever must be, a natural consequence of society, imply, that while some are above the level of the generality, others will be beneath it: while some are exalted, others will be really and sometimes notoriously and conspicuously depress-

ed below that medium state, at which, perhaps, the *maximum* of the comfort of human life is most generally found. Great cities are, universally, instances of this diversity of station; they comprize the extremes of character and occupation. From this the metropolis of the British Empire is not exempt. While it gives employment to industry in a thousand forms, found no where else, and furnishes means of livelihood to thousands of individuals in ways peculiarly their own, and unknown to the public at large, it draws into its vortex characters of every description; and assigns them to labours which have no place in less populous towns; and to which, indeed, few, if any of the cities on the continent can furnish the parallel. Among these, some are engaged in by men, in the fulness of years and strength; use renders them—dangerous and even distressing as they appear to the considerate,—use renders them more than tolerable to those who follow them; these are not so eminently objects of pity, as youths and boys whose hard lot it is to follow businesses which combine with general hardships, many inevitably their own. These have no choice; they have no control over themselves; they are not their own property; and therefore on these the eye of compas

N

sion rests, with the closest attachment, with the most assiduous. and enforced observation.

The attention of the public to the condition of the climbing boys, by whom our chimneys are swept, was strongly excited by the benevolent Jonas Hanway, many years ago. The facts he then adduced, made a strong impression on the considerate; but the evil has increased with the increase of the metropolis, to an incalculable extent, since his days.· However, the subject was not lost sight of; and from time to time, the condition of these climbing boys has been pressed on the notice of the community. For this express purpose a society was formed about ten or twelve years ago; to which a reference may be seen in our sixth volume, O. S. p. 283: where the reader will find sentiments not foreign from those now submitted; together with the resolutions of the Master Chimney Sweepers at Sheffield, a town in which abundance of coal is consumed. They deserve general circulation. The society's proceedings came before us again, in our seventh volume, p. 1315.

At length, the matter obtained the interference of Government, and the exertion of legislative authority. Statutes were passed, ameliorating the condition of the boys, increasing the responsibility of the masters, bringing them forward to public view, and binding them to certain rules for their own government, and that of the striplings confided to their care. These enactments manifest the intentions of the legislature; and though they may be sometimes evaded, yet, on the whole they have proved beneficial.

But, the source of the evil still remained; and the object at present pursued is, the entire dispensing with this class of labourers It is beside our purpose to enquire particularly, whence comes the supply of these unfortunate children? in general they are orphans, cast on a friendless world; and of whom it may with too much truth be said,·

" The world is not their friend ; nor the world's law."

In a highly civilized state of society, society is the parent of him who has no parent; and the law, acting by the magistrate, is the guardian of him who has no natural guardian. Nevertheless, among the evils attendant on great cities, this is one, that the law and the magistrate cannot penetrate into all those obscure and intricate recesses of privacy and misery which abound. The duty is painful; the office is disgusting; it is equally thankless; and seldom is it permanently successful. If for the moment some apparent good is produced, a change of inmates, a new generation succeeds, and the evil resumes its course with aggravated vehemence. This, we say, is a grievance common to great cities: but, the particular evil now under consideration, is more prevalent in the British Metropolis, than in any other; and more than it was in former ages. This is owing to the immense consumption of pit-coal;—to the vast manufactories carried on in this seat of commerce; and to the extremely inconvenient constructions demanded by the necessary care to avoid encroachments on private property.

The smoke of pit-coal is more binding, more consolidating, than that of wood, or that of turf, or of peat, or of any other kind of fuel. When wood was the usual fuel in London, the chimneys were built large and open. They were easily swept, as they admitted a man and a ladder, inside of them: and this operation was necessary, (and of course was performed,) only at considerable intervals of time. As coal took the place of wood, chimneys were narrowed, and contracted. Neither were the constructions of those few manufactories which anciently existed around London, so· intricate as at present. Public prejudice was then against the use of coal; and though it *was* used, certainly, yet the opposition it had to overcome was considerable.

A writer in Queen Elizabeth's time, complaining of novelties, observes, that " our forefathers had no chimneys. There was in each dwelling-house only a place for the fire, and the smoke went out through a hole in the roof;—but, now, says he, there is scarcely a gentleman's house in England, that has not at least one fire burning in it." If we recollect rightly, the famous stone kitchen of the Abbot of Glastonbury, though intended to supply a prodigious consumption of victuals, has no chimney in it. What was called a rere-doss was then common; and up, and around this conductor the smoke rolled in huge volumes. There is extant in the records of one of Queen Elizabeth's Parliaments, a motion made by a member, reciting, " that many dyers, brewers, smiths, and other artificers of London, had of late taken to the use of pit-coal for their fires, instead of wood, which filled the air with noxious vapours and smoke, very prejudicial to the health, particularly of persons coming out of the country; and therefore moved that a law might pass to prohibit the use of such fuel (at least during the session of Parliament) by these artificers." It certainly was not a member for Newcastle that made this motion; but whatever he was, it may justly be asked, what would the worthy legislator say, could he behold the present state of the smoke of the beclouded metropolis, London, and its environs.

What would he say, could he behold the great numbers of steam-engines at work,—those notorious consumers of coal! What, to the immense breweries for exportation, the glass-houses, the soap-boilers, the tile-kilns, the waterworks, and lastly, the more modern gas-works, which with millions of chimneys from private houses, obscure the face of day, and hide the sun from the city more than the cloudiness of its natural climate. But, all these are instances of intricacy: our chimneys in private houses are not only narrower than they were, but they are also, higher than formerly. The continual consumption of coal requires frequent repetition of the act of cleaning the chimneys. The labour to clean

them is greater; and the necessity of providing against the danger of fire, is more urgent. There were no Insurance Companies in Queen Elizabeth's time; but now, those institutions have their rules; and the public find their interest in complying with them. The legislature has interfered, and the law must be obeyed. In short, since the time of Charles II. since the fire of London, and since the publication of Evelyn's book " *Fumifugium ;*" the purport of which was to prove coal-smoke harmless, the city is become quite another town from what it was; and with the change of manners, the city and the citizens, the houses and their inhabitants, have changed their character.

That chimneys have not been so constructed as to dispense with the use of climbing boys, is perfectly clear; that they cannot be so constructed, it is too much to say; but, that of the plans hitherto proposed for the purpose none has succeeded, is well known. Yet, this is the first requisite towards diminishing the number, and ultimately suppressing these instruments in the business. It is but justice to our Architects, to say, that they have long contemplated this purpose; more than forty years ago, Mr. Clavering, in his " Essay on the construction and Building of Chimneys," expressed himself to this effect,—" I must anticipate an objection that may be made, to the difficulty of sweeping the circular funnels, as it may be urged, that, by their roundness and smoothness, the boys can have no hold, and will not be able to get up them. I allow that they will not be so easily swept in this manner as a square funnel: and I sincerely wish, for the honour of this nation, that the sweeping of chimneys by boys was abolished. It is shocking to humanity, and disgraceful to a free and civilized nation, to doom poor destitute orphans to that slavish and cruel employment. Infants who have unhappily lost their parents, or who are unnaturally deserted by them, become the children of the public; and it is a savage abuse of trust, to drive them up these loathsome funnels, as soon as they acquire the use of their tender legs."

" The method I would recommend for sweeping circular funnels, is, to have a strong round brush, made full to the size of the funnel, and about two feet in length, with a staple at each end, for cords to be fastened to; if this is drawn up and down the chimney by a man at the top, and another below, the chimney will be swept clean in the most perfect manner, as it is practised in several parts of the north of England, where I have been; and, as I am informed, also, in Scotland and Ireland. A loose bunch of furze will clean a square funnel equally well."

" The ready way to perform this operation is to drop the lower end of the cord down the chimney, to the man below, with a piece of lead, or a stone fastened to it, and the brush to be put in at the top; and so pulling up and down by degrees all the way, which will perfectly clean the chimney."

Certainly, we have seen chimneys swept by similar means, often, in the country; but, in town there are hundreds of stacks of chimneys which rise very high above the roof, and afford no firm footing for a ladder;—these cannot be swept in this manner. They would be dangerous to the operators, dangerous to the inhabitants of the house, dangerous to passengers in the streets; and being attended with so many inconveniences, they would be seldom swept, and therefore their danger by the hazard of taking fire, would be incalculably augmented.

We must be cautious, that while our humanity exerts itself in favour of certain objects, it does not expose a greater number of objects of another description to augmented evils. We must be cautious also, that we do not introduce evils, intolerable in their nature, and never to be removed, in exchange for those, which, however vexatious, it may be hoped are not insuperable. We do acknowledge, and we sympathize with, those which attend the climbing boys;—such as, their perpetual filth, the cancer peculiar to the business, well known among the faculty; and above all the consideration, that after they are grown to years of maturity, the boys no longer are useful as climbers, and the business in which they have spent their days will not afford them an honest livelihood. On the other hand, we must take special care to place no impediments in the way against the necessary precautions to be taken as preventions of that most dreadful calamity, fire. A calamity not injurious to property, only, to an indefinite extent, but also to lives. A calamity of that insidious kind, that long lurks undiscovered and unsuspected; and when it once begins its ravages, extends undistinguishing ruin all around.

Our readers will observe, that since the days of Mr. Clavering, very little accession of skill has been obtained, on the subject. The ideas suggested by the professors to whose Reports the present thoughts are introductory, differ little from what that artist published. And indeed, this is a subject on which little assistance can be elicited from the usual course of studies pursued by Architects. The ancients have left us nothing worth notice: Vitruvius is no better than a blank: there are, certainly, chimney-sweepers at Vienna, at Paris (where they are inscribed on the back *ramoneur public*) but, in those cities wood is the chief fuel; in Amsterdam the chief fuel is peat; so that the devices of their inhabitants, or artists, or police, are by no means applicable to the state and condition of the city of London. In Germany and further north, stoves are in universal use; and stoves are cleaned by taking down the pipes which accompany them; but, a visible fire is proverbially an Englishman's companion; and the mere appearance of some kinds of stoves is an absolute negative to their adoption.

The subject appears to divide itself into two distinct considerations: humanity towards the poor little sweeps! a helpless, and much to be pitied race; and such a construction of chimneys, generally enforced, as shall supersede the labourers, who now, unhappily, are condemned to clean them. It might not be amiss, if some of our philosophical lecturers would turn their attention to the subject of chimneys : few things in domestic life are of greater importance ; —so far as the prevention of their smoking, or a cure for that nuisance, is in question, they are philosophical instruments : their proportions, their situations, and their other qualities, are worthy of every investigation.

And here, we might refer with advantage, to those contrivances for the consumption of smoke, which would remove great part of the evils complained of,—the nuisance to the neighbourhood, and the use of the climbing boys. Perhaps, if Parliament during the last few years, had made a rule of inserting in every act for incorporating certain companies, a proviso that they should consume their own smoke, the practice by this time would have become familiar. And though we cannot expect to see that practice carried universally into our domestic economy, yet, the hint once legalized there is no saying how far the ingenuity of our mechanics might have applied it. At any rate, those insufferably offensive nuisances which are but too visible, at certain times of the day, to a spectator who stands a few minutes on Blackfriars bridge would have been abated ; and the atmosphere of the metropolis would have been relieved from those volcanic eruptions which now terrify the valetudinarian, and choak up the lungs of infancy, and heedlessness.

The Reports presented as ordered, are so clear that nothing need be said by us in illustration. The proportion of chimneys swept by the machines now in use, will be noticed by the reader. The time consumed in the operation, with the number of persons employed about it, and the expences incurred, with a comparison of the same when climbing boys were employed, are not given.

We speak rather feelingly on these particulars, because, it seems, that of the attempts to sweep the PANORAMIC chimneys by machines, some did the business so imperfectly, that they may be said to have failed : others succeeded better ; but not completely :

and a climbing boy was necessary after all. Some were two hours in accomplishing nothing ; where less than one hour used to be time sufficient. But, there can be no question on the future improvements which these instruments will receive, under the fostering protection of the public. We wish they may ; and we shall heartily rejoice in the fact. We advise the friends to the cause to persevere ; it is the cause of humanity ; but, let them look well around them ; and carefully guard against that mistaken humanity, which while it attempts to correct one evil, gives occasion to the introduction of many.

Shall we be pardoned for repeating a story told by the facetious Dr. Moore, on this subject ?—A projector who thought that all was made for man, and therefore man had a right to direct the services of all at his pleasure, proposed that instead of the ball and rope let down from the top of the chimney, a goose, as being rather a heavy bird, should be substituted, and being as might be supposed, somewhat reluctant to entering a house by the opening at the chimney top, no doubt, she would ply her wings with great energy ; and effectually sweep the chimney in her descent. A lady who heard the proposal, pitied the poor bird *so cruelly* employed ! O, madam, said the author of the scheme, if you think it cruel on the poor goose, we will set her aside,— a COUPLE of ducks will do."

REPORT
OF THE SURVEYOR GENERAL
OF THE
BOARD OF WORKS,

Of the Experiments made for the Purpose of ascertaining the Practicability of superseding the Necessity of employing

CLIMBING BOYS

In the Sweeping Chimnies, by Means of the Employment of Machinery, made to the *House of Commons*, Feb. 1, 1819.

Office of Works, 15 *Jan.* 1819.

Sir,

I HAVE the honor to acknowledge the receipt of your letter, dated the 14th of March last, directing me, by command of Lord Sidmouth, " to ascertain by experiment, how far it is safe and practicable to supersede the practice of climbing boys in sweeping chimnies, by the use of machinery;" and I beg leave to acquaint you, for his Lordship's information, that upon the receipt of your letter, I proceeded, with as little delay as possible, to secure, by every means in my power, a fair and impartial trial of all the different machines that had been collected, for the purpose of sweeping chimnies without the aid of climbing boys.

From the many difficulties I had to encounter at the commencement of this undertaking, I found it necessary, in order to secure a faithful execution of the commands I had received, to appoint Mr. Davis, an active and intelligent clerk in this office, to superintend personally the progress of each separate experiment, and to give such directions and assistance, in the use of the different machines, as circumstances and situation might require.

It will not, I conceive, be necessary for me to enter into a detailed statement of all the numerous trials made by Mr. Davis, to sweep chimnies without the aid of climbing boys; and I shall therefore only submit, for his Lordship's information, the following list of experiments, where machinery has succeeded in effectually cleaning such chimnies, as presented particular difficulties in sweeping, from the size, situations, and peculiar construction of the flues.

	Swept by the Machine.	Swept by the Ball and Brush.	Total.
At Kensington Palace...	5	2	7
—the Queen's Palace ...	43	34	77
—Windsor Castle	20	—	20
—the Royal Mint	5	5	10
—the Speaker's house...	4	—	4
—Mr. Huskisson's house	13	4	17
—Mr. Nash's house ...	1	2	3
—Lord Liverpool's	9	2	11
	100	49	149

This statement contains, I believe, with some few exceptions, specimens, of nearly every difficult description of chimney that can be met with in the generality of either old or newly-constructed buildings, and will afford, in my humble opinion, sufficient evidence, that even at present by far the greater proportion of the chimnies throughout the country, can be effectually swept by machinery without the aid of climbing boys. There were, however, many chimnies that, from their very confined and horizontal construction, Mr. Davis could not succeed in sweeping, either with a machine or with the ball and brush; but this difficulty he thinks might be overcome by inserting iron registers or doors in some convenient part of such flues, where machinery might be used with ease; and if these registers are properly constructed and fixed, without either danger or inconvenience. The best constructed registers for this purpose that I have seen were exhibited here by Mr. Thomas White, of Air-street, Piccadilly, and by Mr. William Fetham, of Ludgate-hill. And the danger to which climbing boys are so constantly exposed when employed in sweeping narrow and intricate flues, would, in my opinion, in a great measure be obviated, were such iron registers or doors directed to be made at proper and convenient distances in every flue of this construction. The machinery that principally succeeded in the above experiments, was the invention of Mr. Smart, and has proved far superior in utility to any that have been submitted for trial upon the present occasion. This machine is simple in its construction, easily worked, can be repaired, when out of order, with little trouble or expense, and may be carried by a single person from place to place without any difficulty. During the progress of these experiments, I have had every possible assistance and advice, that the abilities and experience of Mr. Browne, the Assistant Surveyor General, and of Messrs. Nash, Soane, and Smirke, the architects attached to this department, could afford me upon this very interesting subject; and from the information I have obtained from these gentlemen, as well as from the observations I have been enabled to make in attending to several of the trials made with the different machines, I beg leave to offer it to his Lordship, as my most decided opinion, that the total abolition of climbing boys in the sweeping of chimnies, 'is at present impracticable, and could not be attempted without incurring much risk of danger to the general safety of the metropolis.

I shall beg leave to annex, for Lord Sidmouth's further information, copies of three letters, which I have received from the attached architects, upon the subject of superseding the use of climbing boys in sweeping chimnies: together with a copy of Mr. Davis's report to me, upon the several experiments he has made, to promote this very desirable object.

And have the honor to be,

Sir,

Your most obedient servant,

B. C. STEPHENSON.

———

Dover-street, December 31*st,* 1819.
SIR,

Having attended to several experiments made to sweep chimnies of intricate construction by machines, without the use of climbing boys, I am of opinion, that though it will be difficult, and perhaps impossible to construct a single machine which will clean every chimney, yet, by the use of various machines, almost any chimney may be swept clean; and that experience would, in a short time, render the operation quite easy: but I do not think the use of climbing boys can be wholly dispensed with, the pargetting or plastering of flues will require repairing; new buildings will require the mortar and knobs of bricks which stick to the plastering cleared away, which I think cannot be done by any other means than boys. I beg also to observe, that till the use of machinery shall by experience be made easy, and the adopting of the most efficacious form of the different machines shall be

ascertained, much damage will be done to the plastering or pargetting of the flues, which will require climbing boys to repair. I should advise also, that a clause be inserted in the Building Act, that all chimney funnels hereafter to be built, or old chimnies when taken down and rebuilt, should have the flues made circular in form; there would be then little difficulty in cleaning them with any machine; and if tubes, like chimney pots, were worked upon the walls as funnels for the smoke, they would be a great security against fire, having few joints and no plastering to require repair.

I have the honor to be,

Sir,

Your obedient servant.

(Signed)   JOHN NASH.

The Surveyor General
of the Office of Works.

———

Lincoln's Inn Fields, Jan. 4, 1819.
MY DEAR SIR,

In reply to your letter respecting climbing boys, I beg leave to state, that as far as my experience goes, a very large portion of the chimnies now constructed may be cleaned with machines; but that it will not be possible to do away entirely the service of climbing boys.

I am, dear Sir,

Your very obedient and faithful servant,

(Signed)   JOHN SOANE.
B. C. Stephenson, Esq.
    &c. &c. &c.

———

Albany, November 17, 1818.
SIR,

In compliance with your desire, that I should report to you my opinion upon the question of how far it is practicable to supersede the practice of climbing boys, in sweeping chimnies by the use of machinery, I beg leave to say, that I am not able to give an opinion founded on much personal observation on the subject; but the result of the very particular enquiries, and of the numerous experiments which you have caused to be made, prove, that machines, upon the principle of Smart's, may be employed with success in all common cases; but that the ball and brush let down from the upper part of the chimney-flue is the only process which has answered in every instance.

I have, however, learnt, from intelligent workmen in Scotland, where it has been long employed, that much injury is often occasioned by this operation at the turning of the flues, especially where they are separated only by a thin wall; and I do not think it would be practicable, by any regulation, to provide for the construction of chimney-flues in such a way as to obviate this important objection.

I am therefore, led to believe, that, although the use of machines may be very generally adopted, there is none hitherto invented which is so far free from objection in all cases, as to render it possible wholly to dispense with the use of climbing boys.

I have the honor to be,

Sir,

Your obedient and faithful servant,

(Signed) · ROBERT SMIRKE.

Lieut. Col. Stephenson.

———

Office of Works, Jan. 11, 1819.

SIR,

In obedience to the instructions, at various times received from you, on the subject of superseding climbing boys by the use of machines, I hereby enclose the results of the experiments made in consequence, with some observations and suggestions naturally presenting themselves in the detail.

It appears, that the whole of the flues at present in use, may be comprised in four classes; the first and most numerous are those which are carried up in

a perpendicular stack, the only bend in these flues being just sufficient to clear the opening of the flue above. The second, far less numerous, are those in which the fire-place is in a wall not continued higher than the next floor, and turning off with one bend (making two angles in the elevation) to a partition wall, in which the shaft is continued to the top. The third, still less numerous, are those in which the shaft is at some distance from the fire-place, having at least one angle on the plan, and which of necessity forms two bends in the elevation. The fourth class, which forms a very small proportion of the total number already constructed, are those having more than one angle on the plan, and being, for a part of the length, entirely horizontal.

For the first class, the machines already in use are quite efficient; they are also competent to sweep part of the second class; for the remainder of the second class, the ball and brush is perfectly efficient, unless any error in the construction has given the only bend in them a dip the contrary way. In the third class, where the ascent is at all preserved, the ball and brush still acts effectually; as it will also do in the fourth class, where there are no parts entirely level. The remainder of the fourth class comprehends those flues, which have several bends, and are frequently horizontal; and in these cases it is alike necessary to let in registers or doors, whether they are swept by boys or machines, there being no other security for the safety of the boys than this measure; which, when done, actually presents the means of of sweeping by a common machine.

As far as my experience has led me, I consider the proportions of the different classes nearly as under; out of 1,000 flues, 910 of the first class, 50 of the second, 30 of the third, and 10 of the fourth.

For the first and second classes, the machinery has been proved, at Kensington Palace, the Queen's Palace, the Mint, the Speaker's House, Lord

Liverpool's, Mr. Huskisson's, Mr. Nash's, and at the Office of Works; but a case has occured at the Queen's Palace, where a flue of the second class could not be swept by the ball and brush, and upon examining the external part of the chimney, by going between the timbers of the cieling and lead flat above, that part of the flue was out of a level, the end nearest the shaft being lower than that next the fire-place.

I have not seen a machine that will sweep many flues of the third and fourth classes; but have succeeded with the ball and brush at the several palaces and places above enumerated; and in the last week a chimney was swept at the Tower with the ball and brush in half an hour, which a boy was five hours sweeping a short time since, and in which, I am informed, a boy was once confined twenty-eight hours.

The necessity of putting doors in the remainder of those classes, has been proved at the Speaker's house, where, 'for want of them, they are obliged to cut tiles or take down part of the stone-work every time the servants hall chimney is swept by a boy; as well as at Somerset Place, where they have put doors in consequence of accidents occurring. Much has been stated by the parties interested, about the injury done to the pargetting by the use of the machinery and the ball and brush; but so far as the closest observation has enabled me to form an opinion, this is entirely without foundation; for in the use of the common machine less compression is required than is exerted by the boys to sustain their own weight; and with the ball and brush, unless there is a level, and the ball is wantonly thrown down instead of being lowered carefully, there can be no injury done. In the course of my own experience, I have never met with an instance of the necessity of employing a climbing boy to repair the pargetting of a chimney; and with respect to the coring of new chimnies, it requires only a determination on the part of the bricklayers to avoid the necessity of it.

It will appear, that the result of my experiments is, that all the really-difficult flues to clean are met with in large mansions or public offices, and that the middling and lower classes of houses are entirely free from them. The doors introduced in the flues can certainly be constructed to answer, by their locality, all the purposes of convenience, safety, and cleanliness.

The machines I have seen used are Messrs. Smart's, Bean's, Mumford's, Skinner's, Lee's and the Bath's; and these are nearly the same in principle and effect.

Smart's being most used in London, possesses from that circumstance, advantages the others have not; practice being required to give further confidence to the men employed.

The ball for conducting the brush is susceptible of improvement, inasmuch as making it lighter and larger, is found to increase its utility.

The machine from Scotland is not yet ascertained to possess more advantages than the others; but that being different in principle, it may be found capable of improvement.

I have the honor to be,'

Sir,

Your most obedient humble servant,

(Signed)   GEO. DAVIS.

B. C. Stephenson, Esq.
Surveyor General, &c.

━━━━━━━━━━━━━━━━━━

Travels in various Countries of Europe, Asia, and Africa. By Edward Daniel Clarke, L. L. D. Part III. Scandi_ naria, Section the first. 4to. with numerous plates, 4to. £4 14s. 6d. large paper, £8 8s. Cadell and Davies, London, 1819.

After a long silence, this learned and enterprizing traveller, with whose previous volumes our readers are well acquainted,* once more appears

* See LIT. PAN. O. S. Vol. ix. 842. xii. 958. xiii. *passim.* Vol. i. N. S. 53. 239, 500.

before the public, with a further portion of his researches. The same acute spirit of inquiry, which characterizes his former volumes, will be found in almost every page of the present; and though it does not treat of places and people interesting from the classical recollections they excite, yet it is in no respect deficient in that interest, which the faithful delineation of human life and manners, in regions comparatively unknown, never fails to excite.

Quitting England by way of Yarmouth, Dr. C. proceeded first to the celebrated island of Heligoland, of which we have some curious historical particulars. Thence he proceeded to Altona and Hamburgh, of which we have a pleasing description. Of the extensive commerce carried on at the latter place, some idea may be formed from the counting houses of the merchants, whose establishments have more the appearance of a national bank than that of the private counter of an individual. The worst part of Hamburgh is stated to consist in its narrow streets and their wretched pavement, which nuisance however is but little regarded, the use of carriages being almost universal. The houses are characterized by remarkable cleanliness, compared with which the houses of our metropolis (at least those of inferior tradesmen) would cut but a poor figure, notwithstanding our boasted cleanliness.

Dr. Clarke has communicated one article of information, which will not be lost upon those travelling epicures, who wander about the continent to gratify their palates. The luxuries of eating and drinking are no where more studiously cultivated, nor is there any place in Europe where larger sums of money are lavished to maintain them. At the same time, however, dinners are stated to be provided in the taverns, much neater and better than in those of London, and at one tenth of the price.

The manner in which provision is made for the poor, reflects the highest honour upon the people and the government. The poor are supported by vo-luntary contributions, and by taxes on public amusements. These contributions are deposited in the town hall, in five chests, respectively inscribed with the names of the five parishes of Hamburgh. Concerning the government of Hamburgh, which has often been vaunted as the most perfect example in the world of what a good government should be, Dr. Clarke obtained the following authentic particulars.

"Although considered as being *aristocratic*, it consists of three estates, controlling each other, and which may be compared to our King, Lords, and Commons. These three Estates are as follow :

"1st. *The Senate*, consisting of three estates within itself: the *first* of which is formed by four *burgomasters*, who are the principal magistrates of this city : the *second*, by four *syndics*, who have the administration of all foreign affairs; and the *third*, by twenty-four senators. Every assembly, whether of the three estates, or of the subdivisions of the first estate, has the power of electing its own members; that is, in case of the death of either of the burgomasters or syndics, the survivors elect another member.

"2nd. *The Antients*, or *Ober Alten,*—an assembly formed by the *Elders* of each parish : four of whom are chosen out of every parish. All laws proposed by the senate, must be approved by this assembly. In Hamburgh there are five parishes.

"3rd. *The Burghers* or *Citizens* of Hamburgh—answering to our freemen in borough towns. They never assemble but on great occasions; such as, the introduction of a new law, or the imposition of a new tax. Upon these emergencies, one hundred Burghers are elected, out of their whole body, by the Burghers themselves. Every Lutheran citizen also, who is a householder, and of course a Burgher, is amenable to the city taxes, and has a right to vote.

"In these three Estates is vested the whole legislative power of *Hamburgh :* but they have no power, either severally or collectively, to vote away a single *mark* of the public money: this can only be effected by an appeal from the Government to the Chamber of Finance. It is a very difficult thing, therefore, either to introduce a new law, or to levy a new tax; because the *Elders*, who have great influence, do not easily admit the propriety of making any alteration in customs which have been long established; and no appeal can be made to the *Burghers*, unless the *Senate* and *Elders* be of one mind."

The moral state of Hamburgh at this time (the spring of 1799) was highly creditable to the character of the inhabitants. The police, indeed, Dr. Clarke informs us, was " so well regulated, that an instance of murder had not occurred within the memory of many persons living*; and robberies had rarely happened. The firemen, who patrole the streets, have a custom, which exists also in *Constantinople*, of striking their long staves against the pavement. The watchmen always spring their rattle before they call the hour†.

From Hamburgh, our traveller proceeded through the duchy of Sleswick to Copenhagen, the metropolis of Denmark, with the description of which we need not detain our readers, and thence to Gothenburg, an important sea port belonging to Sweden, containing a population of about 15,000 souls, most of whom are entirely engaged in the com-

merce or very flourishing herring fishery of this city. From Gothenburgh, his route lay through Trolhaetta, and several intermediate towns to Stockholm, the capital of Sweden. Of the canal of Trolhaetta, the design of which is to effect a navigation between the Baltic and the Kattegat, we have an interesting account, for which we must refer our readers to Dr. Clarke's volume. Of the liberality of the Swedes to strangers, he experienced and has gratefully recorded many pleasing instances.

The architecture of Stockholm, though imposing to the eye, is little more than lath and plaster, " mere wood and mortar tricked out to look like corinthian pillars and stone walls." He visited the arsenal and senate house, which we shall not stop to describe, and has collected some particulars relative to the assassination of Gustavus III. by Count Ankarstrom, which cannot fail to interest our readers.

" To extenuate the enormity of this deed, and to keep as much as possible from view the real authors of the conspiracy, of which, the actual assassin, *Ankarstrom*, was but a mere instrument, the character of their victim has been blackened, and is still laden with all sorts of obloquy. Yet impartial men in *Sweden*, who, belonging to *no party*, may be considered as lookers-on, will not fail to discern in the " signs of the times" the developement of a drama which commenced only with the death of *Gustavus.*"

"It is said in *Sweden*, that the King, well knew to whom he was indebted for the blow inflicted by the hand of *Ankarstrom*. And if the opinion which the *Swedes*, notwithstanding their natural reserve, maintain before foreigners upon this subject be founded in fact, some future *Shakspeare* may find, in the mysterious circumstances connected with the death of *Gustavus*, a plot not unlike that of the Tragedy of *Hamlet;* for which we have been already indebted to the annals and characteristic manners of *Northern* nations. Yet to such a pitch have party feelings attained, with regard to this transaction, that the "memory of *Ankarstrom*" is sometimes given as a *toast*, even in *Stock-*

---

* " There is one remarkable exception to this. A woman of *Hamburgh*, about thirty years since, murdered her husband: and having packed up his body in several parcels, she hired a waggon to convey her, with the parcels and other luggage, to *Lubeck*. Near *Lauenburg*, she contrived, without being perceived by the driver, to push the parcels from the waggon, so that they fell into a very deep sand pit, on the road side. These were soon afterwards found, and led to her apprehension and execution; as contrary winds prevented her departure by any vessel from *Lubeck*.

"An execution of a thief took place in *Hamburgh*, in 1798-9, after he had been imprisoned *seven* years; and this was considered a very awful occurrence. But during the Revolution, and the troubles of *Hamburgh*, crimes became much more common."

† " Persons are stationed, all the night, in the windows of the several towers, to give notice in case of fire: and they blow a single note on the trumpet every quarter of an hour, to signify that *all is well*, and to denote their vigilance. In case of fire, the inhabitants put lights in their windows, as at *Copenhagen* and other Northern cities."

holm, and hailed with enthusiasm.* In the character of *Ankarstrom*, and in his conduct after condemnation, we may discern something of the hero: but how remote from every thing heroic was the act and the manner of the assassination of *Gustavus*, in whose death patriotism had not the smallest share. Private pique, party interest, and the most selfish views of ambition, all conspired together, and usurped the place of virtue. If the real history of the conspiracy should ever transpire, it will be manifest how low the assassin ranked among the members of a *party*, which extended, from the King's own relations, through all the ranks of society. Had it not been for this, *Gustavus* would have lived; and the mournful family of the misguided *Ankarstrom* might still have possessed their friend and parent. As a husband and a father, the latter was without reproach; and it may be imagined what was the anguish of his wife and children, when he was taken from them to answer for such a crime.* Among the various writers who have attempted to explain the motives for his conduct in this infamous murder, (at one time attributed to the influence of the *Parisian Jacobins*, and at another to the sect of *Illumines*,) there have not been wanted some who have ascribed it altogether to the King's own relations; and the belief that it might have been prevented by one of them, the most interested in the consequences of his death, is very general in *Sweden*†. This is not a question for our decision; neither shall we meddle with it, further, than to make known the opinions which prevail concerning it in the country where this event happenned. It is very certain, that

after *Gustavus* was no more, little desire was manifested, either to avenge his death, or to do justice to his memory. Of all the persons known to have been concerned as accomplices, *Ankarstrom* alone was put to death. Within four months after the affair happened, the *Opera House*, in which the King had been assassinated, was again opened; the *Court* appeared there with its usual splendour; and the very boards which had been stained by his blood, vibrated to the feet of the dancers. We made some inquiry of persons who had been eye-witnesses of all that passed upon the occasion, as to the behaviour of the King, when he found that the wound he had received was mortal. It had been said, that, upon receiving this intelligence, he was overpowered by his feelings, and gave way to his tears; but every thing we heard served to convince us of his great magnanimity. In the midst of his bitter agonies, he prayed that the lives of his assassins might be spared; and, in more tranquil moments, earnestly occupied himself in measures for the immediate benefit and for the future welfare of his country. In viewing the character of *Gustavus the Third*, his passion for the Arts, and his polished manners, we behold a Prince whose qualifications were more suited for the old Court of *Versailles* than for the throne of *Sweden*. The iron sceptre of the *Goths*, which his great ancestor, *Gustavus Vasa*, swayed in such a manner as to render *Sweden* formidable to surrounding nations, became, under the influence of his clemency, more impotent than a reed; and, consequently, there grew up beneath it all manner of civil dissentions and domestic conspiracies. Yet, amidst his defects and his vices, industriously exaggerated as they have been by his enemies, a certain elevation of soul was always conspicuous. The enterprising spirit with

---

* After we left the *Arsenal*, viewing a collection of pictures containing portraits of all the great men of *Sweden*, one of us said jocularly to a *Swede* who happened to be present,—"They are all here, as large as life! but where is the portrait of *Ankarstrom?*" To which he replied, with evident warmth of manner, "*Ankarstrom's* portrait is a *cabinet* picture; we keep it locked up *in our hearts!*"

* He was taken from his own bed, where he was found tranquilly reclined by the side of his wife:—"L'on trouva chez lui, paisiblement couché auprès de sa femme, qui paraissait n'avoir rien su de cet horrible projet." *Hist. de l'Assass. de Gustave III. p. 87, Paris, 1797.*

† "Cette opinion est si générale en *Suède* et chez tous les peuples du *Nord*, qu'un étranger de grande considération, à qui l'on montrait un tableau de la battaille de *Swenck-sund*, où le Duc le *Sudermanie* est représenté très-ressemblant et avec l'air de gaîté qu'un général éprouve à la vue d'une prochaine victoire, s'écria avec un sourire amer et sardonique: 'Ah! Dieu, comme le prince est frappant de vérité! on dirait qu'il vient d'apprendre l'assassinat de son frere." *Ibid. p. 129, Note.*

which he ascended the throne, lives recorded in history; nor has it been denied, that by those who make the great body of the people in *Sweden*, he was beloved while he lived, and regretted when he died."

The manner in which Ankarstrom was put to death is thus related.

"He was exposed upon a scaffold raised for the purpose, in front of the *Senate House*, upon the left of the pedestrian statue of *Gustavus Vasa*, and at the end of a street which here terminates in the square. The throng of spectators was immense. Several detachments of cavalry, with drawn sabres, preceded the cart in which *Ankarstrom*, surrounded by executioners, was conveyed from his prison. The streets were lined with infantry. After being publickly flogged, he was chained to a post, and left exposed, for several hours, to the view of all the people. Over his head were fastened, in a conspicuous manner, the *dagger* and the *two pistols* with which he went to the masquerade: and above all, appeared this inscription, in the *Swedish* language: "*Assassin of the King*." Several portraits of him have been sold: (that which has been engraved by Dr. C. is remarkable for the likeness it exhibits of the man; and it shows at the same time, the manner in which he was exposed, during three successive days, to the people.) He was five feet two inches high: his hair was black, short, and frizzled; his nose aquiline; and he had a firm and lofty expression of countenance; regarding the vast throng of spectators with an unmoved appearance of calmness and indifference. Being thus exposed for three days; upon the fourth day his right hand was struck off; after which he was beheaded, and his body separated into four quarters, which were exposed upon four wheels, in different quarters of the city. Five weeks after his execution, the remains of his carcase were visited by persons of distinction belonging to his party, and even by elegant women, as precious relics; and verses attached to those wheels were frequently observed, commending the action for which he suffered."

In his journey from Stockholm, through Sweden, to the confines of Lapland, our author traversed a fine country, which he has described with minute-

ness. The character of the Swedes, especially of those who dwell north of the 59th parallel of longitude, is pourtrayed in the most amiable point of view; a strong sense of religion pervades them, and every where he was received with kindness and hospitality. Upsal, celebrated for its university, and for the eminent naturalists to which it has given birth, Gefle, Sundswall, Umea, and Pitea, towns of considerable traffic, are all respectively described, with the intermediate country.

We extract part of his account of Upsal, which contains some particulars not noticed by preceding travellers.

"The antient name of this place was not that which it now bears. It was originally called *Arosia*, or *Oestra Aros*, to distinguish it from *Westeras*, or *Western Arosia*. In all the older chronicles and descriptions of *Sweden*, it appears under its original name; but when the Episcopal seat was removed from *Old Upsal*, the name was changed, and the *Eastern Arosia* became *New Upsal*. The antient history of *Upsal* has exercised the erudition of the most learned writers *Sweden* ever possessed. The best work upon the subject is that of *John Scheffer*: the most erudite observations are those of *Olaus Radbeck*: they are contained in his *Atlantica*; a work more frequently extolled than read; full of amazing learning, vainly employed to sustain the most vague and fanciful theories; and doomed to sleep under the same shelf with the equally ponderous volumes of *Athanasius Kircher*. A greater misapplication of time than would be necessary for the entire perusal of such a work, can only be that which would be required to write it; more useful information being contained in two little volumes of the *Delicia Suecia*, than in the whole of the *Atlantica*. According to *Rudbeck*, the etymology of the word Sal implied the *House, Portico*, or *Court of the Gods*; and Upsal, or *Upsaal*, signified *an open Court* of the same nature: but the city stood upon a river called *Sala*; and the more probable opinion is, that this very antient metropolis thence derived its appellation. Old *Upsal* was, however, the place renowned for the worship of the primeval idols of *Sweden*, and for the inauguration and residence of her earliest kings. In its neighbourhood, there are still shewn the remains of the Morasteen, *a circular range of stones*, where the ceremony of their election to the throne was solemnized, and where the date of it was recorded. This curious monument exists in the plain of *Mora*, about seven *English* miles from *Upsal*. The place was visited by *Mr. Coxe;* and more recently by the authors of the *Journal de Deux Fran.;ais*. There is a long account of the *Morasteen* in the *Upsalia Antiqua* of *Scheffer;* who has learnedly and accurately collected every information respecting the very antient custom to which its history relates. Such circular ranges of stones may be observed all over *Europe*. In *England*, it is usual to consider them as *Druidical ;* but the custom observed at the *Morasteen*, as it continued to a very late period, sufficiently explains their meaning and use. There is a relic of this kind at the *Altyn Obo*, near the side of the antient *Panticapæum*, upon the *Cimmerian Bosphorus*; where, perhaps, the *Bosporian* kings, or their predecessors of a more antient dynasty, were of old elected. The form observed in arranging the stones is nearly the same everywhere; a circular range, with one stone, larger than the rest, in the middle: and this, according to the description which *Olaus Magnus* has given of it, was found to be the case in the *Morasteen :* it consisted, says he, of " one large round stone, surrounded by about twelve others of smaller size, with wedge-shaped stones, raised a little from the earth." When *Olaus Magnus* saw the *Morasteen*, it still preserved its pristine appearance. In *Scheffer's* time, it had undergone considerable alteration. *Mr. Coxe* says, that he found ten stones yet remaining. The authors of the *Journal de Deux Francois* saw several, upon which the antient inscriptions were barely visible. They were then ranged around the inside of a chamber, only twelve feet square, within a small building upon the left-hand side of the road leading to *Stockholm*. Upon the *central stone*, the person to be elected king was placed, in the presence of an immense multitude; and, according to *Messenius*, it had been ordained by one of the *Swedish* kings, co-eval with our Saviour's birth, that the *election* of every

sovereign should, as usual, take place at *Morasteen*, but the ceremony of *inauguration* at *Upsal*, in a *temple* "shining within and without with gold," which he had there constructed for all *Sweden*. He was no less a personage than the renowned Frey, who was honoured as a divinity after his death; and whose name, according to *Pufendorff*, rather than that of the Goddess *Frea*, or *Friga*, being imposed upon one of the days of the week, appropriated for his worship, is still preserved in our word *Friday*. This is a point which may be settled by others: but we shall not quit the subject of the *Morasteen*, without noticing, that, in the *central stone* of such monuments, we may perhaps discern the origin of the Grecian (βῆμα) *Bēma*, or *stone tribunal*, and of the " set thrones of judgment," mentioned in Scriptures, (Psal. cxxii. 5.) and elsewhere, as the places on which kings and judges were elevated; for these were always of *stone*."

Numerous are the cataracts which agreeably surprise the traveller in Sweden and Norway; and the remarkable situation of the sawing mills by these different cataracts are among the most extraordinary sights he meets with. Dr. Clarke thus describes a sawing-mill, which he saw at the cataracts of the Dal, a few miles distant from Upsal.

" The mill here was as rude and picturesque an object as it is possible to imagine. It was built with the unplaned trunks of large fir-trees, as if brought down and heaped together by the force of the river. The saws are fixed in sets parallel to each other; the spaces between them, in each set, being adapted to the intended thickness for the planks. A whole tree is thus divided in planks, by a simultaneous operation, in the same time a single plank would be cut by one of the saws. We found that ten planks, each ten feet in length, were sawed in five minutes; one set of the saws working through two feet of the timber in a single minute. A ladder, sloping from the mill into the midst of the Cataract, rested there upon a rock; which enabled us to take a station in the midst of the roaring waters. On all sides of the Cataract, close to its fall, and high above it, and far below it, and in the midst of the turbulent flood, tall pines waved their shadowy branches, wet with the rising dews. Some of these trees were actually thriving upon naked rocks, from which the dashing foam of torrent was spreading in white sheets of spray. Another feature in this singular scenery was presented by artificial piers, projecting from the sides of the river, and constructed as snares for salmon; nets being attached to the piers. Among the living objects, were some of the children of the inhabitants, with their naked legs and red night-caps, perched upon the different crags over the Cataract, and calmly angling, with the utmost indifference either to the terror or the grandeur of the spectacle to which they were opposed. The bridge below the Cataract, although built entirely of timber, seemed strong, and well contrived to sustain the concussion to which it was liable. Its piers were defended by a series of treble wedges, such as we had never seen before. Many of our stone bridges in *England* have been carried away in situations where the pressure of the water has never equalled that which is here experienced, and where a similar mode of resistance might probably have saved them."

The structure in question, (of which Dr. C. has given a pleasing engraving,) is stated to be formed by the juxta-position of the trunks of trees, sloping towards the torrent, so as to meet it in this manner; one of these treble wedges being opposed in front of every pier. The upper tier of this projecting wedge, being hollow, is filled with large stones.

In his progress, our author had an opportunity of observing several Swedish forges at work: the excellence of the Swedish iron, he informs us, is in no respect owing to any improvement in the process of forging the metal; for in the simple machinery necessary for this purpose, the Swedes are rather behind than before other nations. It is the quality of the ore which gives such a decided superiority to their bar iron. This ore is a pure *protoxide*, so nearly in the *metallic* state, as to be highly magnetic, with polarity. It sometimes contains from 80 to 90 per cent. of metal: and as it requires very little manipulation to render it malleable, so it is much fitter for the purpose to which it is applied, than for casting, which would require an ore of less purity. Of Gefle, a flourishing port on the Gulph of Bothnia, we have the following description.

" It makes a considerable figure as it is approached : it lies in the midst of pasture-land, in a plain thickly planted with fir-trees, with which the town appears to be surrounded. Its church is a handsome building; and, like all the ecclesiastical structures in the *north* of *Sweden*, surprises the traveller by its grandeur. These edifices are all built by the peasants; among whom a great degree of emulation has been politically excited; the inhabitants of the different parishes endeavouring to outvie their neighbours in the stateliness, size, and beauty of their churches. *Gefle* is the principal town of *Gestricia*, and one of the best bordering on the *Gulph of Bothnia*, next to *Stockholm*. It contains ten thousand inhabitants, and is lighted with glass lanterns affixed to the houses. Vessels of four hundred tons burden are built here, and many large ships lie close to its quay. Those, however, of very considerable burden are obliged to be lightened in a bay about half a league from the river's mouth. This river, bearing the same name, runs through the town, which lies at a small distance from the sea. *Gefle* employs from sixty to seventy vessels in foreign commerce, besides a number of coasters. Its exports are, *bar-iron, timber, deal-planks, nails, tar, pitch,* and *potash :* its imports, *corn, hemp, flax,* and *salt.* One of the merchants, a *Mr. Hennis,* from whom we experienced very polite attention, had fifteen ships trading to different parts of the world. *Mr. Hennis* was engaged in a manufactory for refining *sugar ;* an article that bore, at this time, an enormous price in *Sweden ;* nearly all of it coming from *England.* Indeed, it was considered so rare, that we afterwards found we could not make a more acceptable present to the mistress of a family, than a lump of loaf-sugar. This manufactory had already proved very profitable to its owner, and the undertaking promised to enrich him. He had in his stable a young bear, which he was engaged in fattening for his table; and spoke of *bear's-flesh* as a great luxury. There was nothing, he said, of which the animal was so fond, as *molasses:* we saw him dip some brown paper in *molasses*, which the bear took between his fore paws, sitting upright, and licking off the treacle with his tongue, so delicately, that he eat the whole of it without tearing the paper. Our inn here much belied its external appearance, which was very cleanly : we found the inside infested with vermin. We had been told that the largest bugs in the world would attack us in *Lapland:* but it would be difficult to match those which were prodigal of their appearance in *Gefle.* The condition of an inn, probably frequented, too, by persons of all countries trading to this part of *Sweden*, ought to be no criterion of the state of the other houses in this town ; and to judge of them from their outward appearance, every one of them may be considered as a pattern of neatness. The *Town-hall* is large, and a very comely modern edifice. It was built by *Gustavus the Third*, who held his Parliament here, when *Ankarström* first tried to assassinate him ; but as the King kept himself at that time private, and surrounded by his guards, the design was frustrated. The streets are straight, and in good order. An officer of the Customs here examines the luggage of a traveller upon his arrival. Persons so employed, have great temptations to knavery, and they generally betray it; but in other countries they wait until money is offered, before they compromise their duty for a bribe. In *Sweden*, upon a promise of not performing it, they make a demand upon your purse ; being, however, easily satisfied, and quite contented to leave your baggage untouched, if you give them a few pence. We bought a fine live salmon, weighing twelve pounds, upon the banks of the *Gefle*, at the rate of two-pence the pound. After taking a walk by the side of the river, we returned to our inn; and although past ten o'clock, there was no appearance of night. We sat, at this hour, in a room with a single window, writing with as much light as if it had been noon; and *Mr.*

Hennis assured us, that a little to the *north* of *Tornea*, if we travelled expeditiously, we should yet find the sun above the horizon at midnight. The latitude of of *Gefle* is 60°. 42'. Few of the usual red-looking timber huts, or log-houses, were to be seen here : the dwellings were principally of a white colour : and the windows look green, as is commonly the case in *Sweden :* not owing to paint, but to the colour of the *Swedish* glass, which is of an inferior quality. Viewed from the streets, however, this green glazing has not an unpleasing appearance. The women seemed to have more beauty than commonly characterizes the *Swedish* females; who prone to industry, and a rigid economy, by severe labour, and a spare diet, consisting for the most part of bad food, become often deprived of charms they would otherwise possess; being what would be styled in *England*, hard-featured."

On leaving Gefle our author determined to travel through the night, as there was no danger of passing any object without seeing it; the *night-light* and the *day-light* being at that time nearly equal, and darkness having altogether fled for the present even in the gloom of the thickest forests, from *sun-set* till *sun-rise*, Dr. C. could read the notes of the common post book, printed in a very small type and in the Swedish language, without any light from the moon, which had then ended her last quarter.

In the forests, through which the Doctor and his companions travelled, he says " we saw *Ants' Nests* of such prodigious size, that we could hardly credit, either the accounts given of them by the inhabitants, or the evidence of our senses. They consisted of cones, formed by heaping together the small leaves and fibres of the pines, to the height of four or five feet. In examining the materials used by the ants in building such astonishing monuments of their industry and perseverance, we found branches which it would seem impossible for these insects to raise. Compared with the labours here manifested, what are all the works of man! The *Pyramids of Egypt*, exciting such amazement, that ignorant people have ascribed them to a race superior to the human, are by no means, when comparatively viewed, equally wonderful. Let the utmost accumulation of human strength, directed by the best intelligence, and called into action by the most powerful excitement, be so exerted as to produce even mightier monuments than any which the Antients have left, they would still be outvied by the cones which these little insects have built, as a nidus for their eggs and their offspring."

As it is impossible to give our readers an idea of Dr. Clarke's route, unless we could at the same time present them with the elegant maps which are interspersed through his volume, we shall close our account of his travels for the present, with the following interesting account of Böle, a small town in the north of Sweden, situated at no great distance from the Gulph of Bothnia.

" Here the houses are no longer painted red, as is common almost all over *Sweden* towards the *South*. They are literally *log-houses;* consisting of the mere timber laid together nearly as it has been felled; being roughly hewn with an axe, the only tool used in building, and without a nail in any part of them. Every man is his own carpenter and builder; working without saw, plane, chissel, nails, or hammer. Many new houses had been constructed here: we saw one which was building. The trunks of trees are piled longitudinally, and fitted at the corners by a sort of dove-tail work. All these buildings, viewed from a little distance, resemble piles of timber heaped for exportation. Every man's premises constitute, of themselves, a little village, surrounding a square court, the entrance to which is by a gateway. The owner has a separate house for every thing belonging to him; with such facility and speed are these houses built. Moss alone is used in caulking the interstices between the trunks of trees, where they do not fit close, to keep out the wind and winter frost. As a covering for the roof, they lay on, first, the bark of birchtrees, pressed down by poles placed transversely, and kept in their places by large

stones laid upon them. We saw some of the houses in *Upland* so laden with masses of stone, that the inhabitants seemed liable to dangerous accidents, if any of them should happen to fall, or if the roof were to yield to so much pressure, when it becomes old and rotten. Constructed in this manner, each farmer has a house for his hay, another for his corn, a third for his pigs, a fourth for his poultry, a fifth for his goats, a sixth for his sheep, a seventh for his cows, an eighth for his horses, and so for the rest of his stock. We saw no dwellings for poor persons: the peasants appeared to be all farmers, or to be members of some one family holding land in cultivation. Every dwelling has, by the side of it, a lofty ensign of the climate, in a high conspicuous rack for drying the unripened corn. These machines make a great figure all over the country, as they are close to every house; and sometimes there are two or three, or four of them to one dwelling, which are seen at a distance, and announce to the traveller the proportion of arable land in the occupation of the landholder whose dwelling he approaches. In this part of *Sweden*, bread is baked only twice the whole year; but in many other parts of the country only once; when a sufficient quantity for twelve months' consumption is prepared in the form of biscuits, which are spitted upon rods, and thus placed beneath the roof of every house; the biscuits being ranged in rows over the heads of the inhabitants, who, as they sit at their meals, take them down as they are wanted. This kind of bread is made, for the most part, of *rye* flour, seasoned with *aniseed:* it has an acid flavour, and to us was always unpleasant. It is generally eaten by the natives, either in milk, or with large lumps of butter. We had an *English* servant, who finding that the bread became worse and worse the farther we pursued our journey towards the *North*, was always longing for the very biscuit he had refused to eat in the province he left last; and ended with exclaiming, " It is a pity that all who grumble at their hard fare in *Old England*, were not sent abroad, to learn what it was to be well off at home." At *Böle*, we saw an infant swaddled quite after the manner used in

O

Lapland: it was lying upon the ground, packed up in a bag made of goats' skin; the hair being on the inside, and nothing but the head of the child visible. This part of the country is infested with *wolves,* which prove troublesome during the winter: but there are no *bears.*"

[*To be continued.*]

Narrative of a Residence in Algiers, By Signor Pananti, with Notes and Illustrations, by Edward Blaquiere, Esq. R. N. 4to. £2 2s. Colburn, London, 1818.

[Concluded from page 206.]

In our last number we left Signor Pananti, in the great *Bagno* for Christian slaves, of which he has drawn a most affecting picture. Painful as his own feelings must have been, his fortitude does not appear to have forsaken him till the next morning, when before sunrise the miserable slaves were summoned to work, and a Black Aga proceeded to rivet on the left ancles of the new victims an iron ring, the usual badge of perpetual servitude. At this dreadful investiture, though it was by particular favour permitted him to perform it with his own hands, he exclaims, in the strong and eloquent language of genuine passion, neither to be mistaken or counterfeited, "a cold sweat covered my forehead: my heart panted with anguish, my eyes no longer saw the surrounding objects; I attempted to speak, but could not articulate."

But while our author was looking forward only to a cruel bondage, a happy redemption was preparing for him: and through the benevolent and zealous exertions of Mr. Mc Donnel, the British consul, a second examination of Signor Pananti's case was instituted contrary to all known precedent. This most interesting crisis is described by him in the following very interesting and animated manner.

"The number of victims captured during the last cruise of the barbarians, amounted to two hundred. Being ordered, as soon as the fatal fetters were affixed, to proceed to the scene of our labours, a mournful silence marked our progress, which was attended by guards both in front and rear, armed with whips, frequently repeating, '*A trabajo cornuto; caro d'infidel a trabajo;*'—'To work! dog of a Christian, to work!' Thus escorted, we arrived at the public ovens, where two rusks of black bread were thrown to each of us, as if to mere dogs. I observed, that the old captives, who had arrived on the ground before our party, greedily snatched them up, and soon dispatched both with a frightful avidity. Arrived at the Great Hall of the Marine, we found seated there, in all the pride of tyrannic power, the various members of the executive government, including the Agas of Militia, the Grand Admiral, First Rais of the Squadron, the Cadi, Mufti, Ulemas, and Judges according to the Koran. We were then ranged along in regular succession, selected, numbered, and looked at with particular attention. With our eyes fixed on the assembly, and beating hearts, a profound silence reigned through the hall, when it was broken by the Minister of Marine, first secretary of state, calling out my name; I was then ordered to advance. On obeying, various interrogatories were put to me, relative to my occupation in England and other relations with that country. Having answered them in the best way I could, the minister pronounced the talismanic words, '*Ti star franco!*' 'You are free.' We are told that the most agreeable tones heard by human ears are those of well-earned praise, or of affection expressed by a beloved object. No! the sweetest voice which can possibly vibrate through the heart of a man, is that which restores the slave to liberty! To form an adequate idea of what I felt on this unforeseen and happy change of circumstances it will be necessary for the reader to conceive a victim with the bandage on his eyes, and fatal axe uplifted, whose ears are suddenly greeted with accents of grace and mercy!

"A case like mine was absolutely *unique* in the annals of Algiers; there being no example of a slave's liberation so immediately after his captivity, without ransom: the decrees of the barbarians being those of inexorable fatality. A soldier was ordered to knock off my irons: this done, he, in his turn, desired me to go and thank the minister; who, on my addressing him, shook me by the hand, adding many expressions of civility, and finally, ordering the dragoman to conduct me to the house of his Britannic Majesty's Consul. The first impulse of joy had fairly inundated my heart; when once more at liberty, I could move my limbs with some facility. But the next thought was for my unhappy companions, who, on the strength of my liberation, were induced to flatter themselves with the fond hope of being treated in a like manner. Next to my own safety, nothing on earth, could at that awful moment, have afforded me such heartfelt satisfaction. Departing slowly with my new guide, I stopped repeatedly, and looked back with wistful eyes, vainly anticipating the pleasure of seeing them follow; but the order was already given to conduct them all to labour; their respective occupations were even pointed out. I saw them hanging down their heads, with eyes suffused in tears; they advanced a few steps towards me, pressed my hand, sobbed adieu! and disappeared.

"Arrived at the British consulate, the dragoman left me; soon after which, my generous friend, the Chevalier Rossi, appeared; when, as it will be readily conceived, our meeting was a most agreeable surprise to both parties. In a short time we were joined by the Consul, whose countenance beamed all that serenity which arises from the performance of a good action; proving an old adage, that virtue is the best promoter of the circulating fluid, and consequent tranquility of mind. The name of this worthy minister, and the highly important services which he rendered me, will be eternally cherished in my heart. To the recollection of this great act of beneficence, will be united those of benevolence and kindness, which form the characteristic of true gentility, considerably enhancing all its favours. It is impossible for me sufficiently to applaud the eminent qualities of Mr. M'Donnel—courteous in his address and manners, with an elevated turn of thought and noble sentiments, uniting to the gentlest demeanour the dignified pride and decision of character which belongs alone to merit; to exquisite sensibility, a mind full of acumen to regulate its movements, and employ it for the most useful purposes; to

extensive knowledge, great application; to generous inclination, courage and activity;—in fine Mr. M'Donnel is one of those men who do honour to humanity."

Signor Pananti has drawn a very affecting picture of the wretched state of suffering to which all christians are exposed, who have the misfortune to fall into the hands of these African Barbarians. Were it not that the Knights of St. John had so completely lost the spirit of their chivalrous institute, and sunk into a degenerate effeminacy, which justly caused their fall, we could regret the dispension of that order as a loss to Europe. No one, we think, can peruse the following heart rending detail, without wishing that all the civilized powers of Europe may speedily form a crusade, and annihilate the power of the Barbary Pirates.

"Those who have never been at Algiers, nor witnessed the fate to which Christians falling into the hands of the Barbarians, are condemned, cannot form any idea of that the greatest calamity which fortune has in store for humanity; or into what an abyss of sorrow and wretchedness their fellow-creatures, thus situated, have been plunged. Even I, who saw and proved it, to a certain degree, in my own person, am at a loss for language equal to a description of what Christians feel and suffer, when precipitated into this dreadful situation.

"No sooner is any one declared a slave, than he is instantly stripped of his clothes and covered with a species of sack-cloth; he is also generally left without shoes or stockings, and often obliged to work bareheaded in the scorching rays of an African sun. Many suffer their beards to grow as a sign of mourning and desolation; while their general state of filth is not to be conceived. Some of these wretched beings are destined to make ropes and sails for the squadron, constantly superintended by keepers, who carry whips, and frequently extort money, from their victims, as the price of somewhat less rigour in the execution of their duty; others belong to the Dey's household, and many are employed by the rich Moors, who may have bought them at market, in the lowest drudgery of domestic employment. Some, like the beasts of burthen, are employed in carrying stones and wood for any public buildings that may be going on: these are usually in chains, and justly considered as the worst among their oppressed brethren. What a perpetuity of terrors, series of anguish, and monotonous days, must not theirs be!—without a bed to lie on, raiment to cover them, or food to support nature! Two black cakes, thrown down as if intended for dogs, is their principal daily sustenance; and, had it not been for the charity of a rich Moor, who left a legacy for that purpose, Friday, the only day they are exempt from work, would have seen them without any allowance whatever. Shut up at night in the prison, like so many malefactors, they are obliged to sleep in the open corridor, exposed to all the inclemency of the seasons: awoke at daylight, they are sent to work with the most abusive threats, and thus employed, become shortly exhausted under the weight and severity of their keepers' whips.

"Those destined to sink wells and clear sewers, are for whole weeks obliged to be up to their middle in water, respiring mephitic atmosphere; others, employed in quarries, are threatened with constant destruction, which often comes to their relief. Some, attached to the harness, in which beasts of the field are also yoked, are obliged to draw nearly all the load, and never fail to receive more blows than their more favoured companions, the ass or mule. Some are crushed under the falling of buildings; while others perish in the pits, into which they are sent to be got rid of. It is usual for one or two hundred slaves to drop off in the year for want of food, medical attendance, and other necessaries: and woe to those who remain, if they attempt to heave a sigh or complain in the hearing of their inexorable masters. The slightest offence or indiscretion, is punished with two hundred blows on the soles of the feet, or over the back; and resistance to this shocking treatment is often punished with death.

"When, in marching, a poor slave is exhausted by sickness or fatigue, and the cruelty of his usage, he is inhumanly abandoned on the high-road, to be insulted by the natives, or trod under foot by the passengers. They frequently return from the mountains with the blood trickling

from their limbs, which are, together with their whole body, covered with scars and and bruises. One evening, towards dark, I was called to by a hoarse voice; on drawing near, I beheld an unhappy being stretched on the ground, foaming at the mouth, and with the blood bursting from his nose and eyes. I had scarcely stopped, struck with horror and apprehension, when, in a faint voice, the word 'Christian! Christian!' was repeated; 'for Heaven's sake, have pity on my sufferings, and terminate an existence which I can no longer support!' 'Who are you?' was my reply. 'I am a slave,' said the poor creature, 'and we are badly treated!' An Oldak of the Militia, who was passing this way, overtook me hereabouts, and exclaiming in an angry tone, 'Dog of a Christian, how dare you stop the road when one of the faithful passes?' gave me a blow and a kick, which threw me down a height of several feet, and has left me in this condition."

To the above, we could add many other very curious and interesting details, but that we have scarcely space left for more than a very brief and hasty enumeration of the farther contents of the volume. The author being, by his release, in a situation to explore the greater part of the city of Algiers, and to make several excursions into the surrounding country, has availed himself of it, to procure for the public a great many very valuable and interesting particulars respecting the natural productions, government, and commerce, of the Regency; its revenue, population, and laws; interspersed with several lively and characteristic anecdotes, illustrative of the manners, and customs of the people; and concluded by a masterly disquisition on the propriety of expelling the pirate hordes from their fastnesses, and of colonizing Northern Africa from Europe. These we can now only recommend to the attention of our readers, with an unfeigned assurance that a very agreeable entertainment, and much information of a novel and highly important character, awaits them in the perusal of this part of Mr. Pananti's performance.

Mr. Blaquiere has executed his undertaking as editor and translator in a manner highly creditable to himself; and, in an appendix, has given an interesting memoir on the state of the Island of Sicily. Altogether, this is a very interesting work, and we doubt not will have,—what it amply deserves,—an extensive circulation.

An Inquiry, whether Crime and Misery are produced or prevented by our present System of Prison Discipline. By Thomas Fowell Buxton, Esq. M. P. 8vo. 5s. 12mo. 2s. 6d. Arch, London, 1818.

Notes on a Visit made to some of the Prisons in Scotland and the North of England,with some general Observations on Prison Discipline. By Joseph John Gurney, 12mo. 3s. 6d. London, 1819.

[Concluded from page 232 of this Volume]

In our last number, we presented to our readers some affecting statements relative to various prisons in England and Scotland. It were no difficult task, to select many others equally distressing; but, we shall spare our readers the pain of perusing such details; and shall now proceed to invite their attention to Mr. Bevan's observations on prison discipline.

On a general retrospect of the prisons, which our author visited and examined, it is impossible not to perceive that they have a tendency rather to increase than to diminish, rather to produce than to remove, misery and crime. Some of the prisons, described by him, for instance, Durham Old Jail and House of Correction, and the Jails at Haddington, Aberdeen, Glasgow and Carlisle,—are scarcely exceeded by any thing that is bad in the worst specimens noticed by Mr. Buxton. Others, again,—as the Bridewell at Aberdeen and the House of Correction at Preston,—approach in some respects to his standard of excellence; though they are not without

defects, which have hitherto prevented them from becoming, to the full extent, schools of reform. A third description of prisons, such as those at Wakefield, York, Edinburgh, Lancaster, Liverpool, and Manchester, presents to us a medium picture of good and bad qualities;—the proportion of what is good, varying of course in the different jails, and the whole leaving an impression not altogether of the most pleasing kind.

We pass Mr. Bevan's observations on the deplorable state of the Scottish prisons, and on the treatment of debtors and lunatics, under the existing law of Scotland, in order to call the attention of our readers to his remarks on the general subject, prison discipline, which for the most part have an equal reference to the prisons in that country and in England. These remarks are classed under the several heads of food, clothing, firing, sleeping, irons; cleanliness, inspection, superintendance, classification, instruction and employment. These topics are discussed with the same perspicuity and benevolence, which are visible in every page of Mr. Bevan's work. We shall select a few of his remarks on the *food, irons, classification, instruction and employment.*

I. *Food.*—" Insufficiency of food is an evil, which ought to be avoided in every prison. We are not justified in aggravating imprisonment, by sufferings to which the law gives no countenance; we are not justified in making inroads on the health of our prisoners: we are not justified in detaining them from their common means of livelihood, except we give them that which is necessary and sufficient for the due support of life. On the other hand, unnecessary indulgence either in the quantity or quality of food is very undesireable, and much opposed to a judicious system of prison discipline.

" The former of these evils is the frequent, and the latter the occasional consequence of a very prevalent practice— *that of allowing to the prisoners a daily sum of money for the purchase of victuals, instead of a certain portion of food.* The prisoners at Carlisle have no fixed quantity of bread; they have threepence-halfpenny per day. When bread is cheap; this sum will scarcely procure them a sufficient quantity; but when it is dear, they must experience something nearly approximated to starvation. The allowance of Doncaster jail is eightpence per day. This sum procures too little bread in times of scarcity, and too much in times of plenty. The rule ought to be, that the allowance of food be a fixed allowance, not depending on the price of provisions; and that in all cases it be sufficient, and *and not more than sufficient*, to maintain the prisoners in good health.

" It often happens, that criminals are supplied by their friends out of prison with articles of provision beyond the jail allowance. Were the rule which I have now recommended, generally adopted, it would become a question worthy of much consideration, whether this practice, especially in the case of tried prisoners, ought any longer to be permitted."

II. *Irons.*—" There is much more cruelty than justice in loading our prisoners with chains. The practice is cruel, because fetters not only prevent the wearer from standing or walking with ease, but very frequently produce excoriation. When prisoners are fastened to the iron bar as at Haddington, or to the bedstead as at Forfar, or to the wall of their cells as at Berwick, or to a ring in the floor as at Newcastle, the suffering produced by chaining becomes extremely aggravated.

" It ought also to be observed, that fetters have a strong tendency to create in the mind of criminals that feeling of their own degradation, which seldom fails to counteract the efforts made for their improvement.

" The injustice of the practice is very evident from this consideration;—that if the prisoner be untried, we have no right to subject him to any inconvenience beyond bare imprisonment; and if he be tried, chaining, according to the laws of this kingdom, seldom, if ever forms a part of his sentence.

" In many of the prisons which we visited, chains, except in cases of emergency, are entirely disused. In others, the insecurity of the yards or cells, is

pleaded as an excuse for them; but we observed, that in most of these cases, very simple alterations in the buildings would render them wholly unnecessary. One thing at least is certain, that a far better method than chaining for the prevention of escapes from prison, may be found in kind superintendence and constant employment."

III. *Classification.*—" It is a great evil when prisoners without employment are confined in very large companies. Riot, clamour, and all the tumult of ungoverned passions will be the almost inevitable conquence. This we saw exemplified in a deplorable manner at Wakefield, where, at the time of our visit to the house of correction, seventy turbulent felons were passing their lawless evening in a single apartment. This evil is however greatly increased, when the criminals, who, are thus herded together, are of totally different descriptions; when, for example, as at Perth, some petty offender against the revenue laws is obliged to live for many weeks together in the company of an atrocious murderer. The descent is so easy from petty offences to flagrant abuses, from lighter to deeper criminality, from the smaller to greater measures of sin, that the unvarying effect of such associations is an alarming increase of depravity. Of the dreadful augmentation which has taken place within the last twelve years in the number of crimes committed in Great Britain and Ireland, this above all others is an evidently prolific source.

" The young offender against the laws his country, whose conscience is yet alive, whose heart is not yet steeled against the impressions of religion, nor blinded to the awful consequences of sin, becomes, through his association with veterans in crime, lost to every good in himself, and terrible, in a tenfold degree, to society at large. He is no longer the trembling, solitary perpetrator of some secret misdemeanor, but a nucleus of crime, the centre of a spreading sore in the community, to which he belongs.

" This great evil loudly demands the care and interference of all, who have the power to prevent it; and certainly, it may be prevented by careful classification in in our prisons, connected with constant employment.

" With respect to the former object, a right classification of prisoners, in the variety of cases which will occur, depends so much on discernment and wise discretion on the part of jailors and visiting magistrates, that I should hesitate before I would propose very precise and definite rules. There are however certain broad lines of distinction which ought never to be sacrificed or forgotten. Female must be separated from male prisoners; debtors from criminals; the tried from the untried; adult from juvenile offenders. It is unquestionably necessary also, that those who have committed only misdemeanors, should in general be kept apart from felons. This however is a provision, which, under judicious care, will admit, in particular cases, of a little variation. It sometimes happens, that prisoners committed for a misdemeanor are notorious and desperate offenders, and much more fit to associate with the worst of felons, than with those of their own class. Amongst the felons, on the other hand, may occasionally be found individuals, young in crime and of a hopeful character. Such persons ought to be removed from the society of desperate villains, and kept in company with that class of criminals, which may be deemed less corrupted.

" There is one regulation connected with the subject of classification, which has hitherto been very rarely adopted, but which is undoubtedly of peculiar importance in promoting the great ends of prison discipline; namely, that female prisoners, where circumstances allow it, should be confined entirely apart from the men, in prisons appropriated to their own sex. In large cities, where female as well as male criminals are numerous, this regulation would be attended with signal advantages. When men and women are imprisoned within one inclosure, however carefully they may be separated, some correspondence will generally take place between them, and this correspondence will probably be productive of much evil to both parties. An instance has lately fallen under my notice, in a prison, in which debtors and criminals, men and women, are separately confined, of an acquaintance formed between a male criminal and a female debtor, which terminated, after they quitted the prison, in completing the moral ruin both of one and the other.

" The jailor at Wakefield informed us, that since his female prisoners had been confined in a house altogether distinct from the men's prison, both parties had become much more manageable than they were before that change took place.

" The Committee appointed by the last House of Commons, to inquire into the state of prisons in the metropolis, strongly recommended, in the Report which they submitted to the House, that a separate prison for females should be instituted in London. That this measure should be adopted, is greatly to be desired, not only on account of the metropolis itself, but as it may afford a beneficial example to other populous places. When our female criminals are superintended by officers of their own sex, and confined in separate prisons, they will soon be brought into a condition of much greater order than is the case with them at present; and the plans, which may be formed to promote their reformation, will be materially facilitated.

IV. *Instruction.*—" Some of the prisons described in the preceding part of this work,—for instance. the Bridewells at Glasgow and Edinburgh, are regularly attended by a school-master. This arrangement affords to the ignorant of the various ages, an opportunity of acquiring that scriptural knowledge, which may often be the means of turning them from darkness to light, and producing a real amelioration of character. In the great majority of these prisons, however, there is no provision of the kind; the weekly return of prayers and a sermon, is too often the only means of instruction afforded; and in many cases, even this is withheld. Thus, the ignorant inmates of our prisons are left to perish in their ignorance;—not a hand is held out to save them.

" In the course of our journey, we had occasion to remark that a considerable proportion of the criminals committed to our jails are able to read. I calculate, that in England, at least one-third of such persons have received some education, and nearly two-thirds none at all: in Scotland the proportion of criminals who can read is considerably greater. It must be acknowledged, therefore, that teaching to read is no certain antidote against the commission of crime. If connected, as it always ought to be, with instruction in the holy Scriptures, it is indeed a powerful means of good; but the heart of man is declared to be " deceitful above all things;" it is exposed on every side to temptation; and its depravity is not to be changed into purity, by any merely human contrivances. No wonder, therefore, that some amongst the many, who have been taught to read the Scriptures, but whose minds have not been actually brought under the influence of religious principle, are numbered with the perpetrators of crime; and as education becomes more universal, it must be expected that the *proportionate* number of our literate criminals will increase. It were, however, much to be lamented, did these considerations discourage us from promoting, by every method in our power, the religious instruction of the ignorant, whether they be bond or free. Such instruction may not always succeed in accomplishing its object; but no one can deny its having a *tendency* to encourage good, and to discourage evil. It is the most effectual instrument, which Providence has placed within our reach, for softening and improving the human mind, and preparing it for the work of the Divine Spirit; for eradicating from it the principles of falsehood, cruelty, and injustice, and implanting in it those of honesty, sobriety, and charity. If we make use of this instrument in a right disposition, we have reason to believe, that the blessing of the Almighty will rest upon our efforts; and although, through the influence of counteracting causes, those efforts may sometimes be foiled, yet we may well be encouraged by the conspicuous and important fact, that we find amongst the ignorant, not only the most numerous, but by far the most hardened and atrocious criminals.

" It is true, that effects, which arise out of many causes, are too often attributed to a single cause; but the comparative circumstances of England, Ireland and Scotland supply us with a convincing proof, that moral and religious education is one great source of virtue, one principal means, by which crime is prevented.

" The comparison evinces, that as education is increased, crime is diminished. In England, there is a medium quantity both of education and of crime; in Ireland there is less education and more crime; in Scotland, less crime and more education. It is calculated that in Scotland, crimes are ten times less numerous, in proportion to the population, than in Ireland. At Glasgow, where crime appears to abound more than in any other part of the former country, there is a large population of uneducated Irish.

" There are, therefore, the strongest and most obvious reasons, why the instruction of ignorant criminals should always form a part of the management, to which they are subject in prison. That which has so strong a tendency to prevent the commission of crime, may sometimes be no less effectual in restoring to the habits of virtue, those, by whom crime has already been committed.

V. *Employment.*—" The bias of all men to evil, is so powerful, that *if there be nothing to check and counteract its influence*, it will soon obtain the mastery over them. On these premises, for the truth of which I may appeal to universal experience, is founded the well known maxim, that " idleness is the mother of vice." A total absence of employment affords to the heart not under the guidance of good principles, an unlimited opportunity of pernicious thought and feeling; and we learn from the highest authority, " that out of the heart proceed evil thoughts, murders, adulteries, thefts, false witness, blasphemies."

" If these positions be true of mankind in general, they may be applied with increased force and precision, to that description of men and women, which we are accustomed to find in our prisons; persons already habituated to vice, and prone, beyond others, to entertain every evil imagination.

" On the other hand, we are in possession of scarcely any means of preventing the inroads of evil into the human mind, more powerful, or more sure, than constant, regular, and harmless occupation. Nor can there be any class of persons, for whom such occupation is more advantageous or more necessary than criminals in prison; for it may not only prevent the mischief of the present moment, but counteract the habits of idleness, to which they have formerly been accustomed; and it may also fix in them those contrary habits of industry and virtue, which will probably, in after life, prevent the repetition of their crimes. It ought also to be observed, that a great proportion of these persons have been destitute, before their imprisonment, of every honest means of livelihood. What then can be more desirable, than that they should acquire, during their confinement, a knowledge of some handicraft, which may procure for them, on their discharge, a reputable and inoffensive maintenance? Such a system will be productive of the most material benefits both to the criminal and to his country. The criminal will learn to live respectably, and will be enabled to live comfortably:—his country will, in the best possible manner, be delivered from those outrages, which disturb the peace and endanger the safety of society.

" There is another advantage arising from the employment of prisoners, which though not of equal moment, is by no means inconsiderable: this is *the saving of expense.* Although the prisoners in the Jail at Lancaster, and the House of Correction at Preston, are allowed for their own use a certain proportion of their earnings, it appears that at Lancaster, the public saves 900*l.* per annum, and at Preston, half the expences of the establishment, by means of those earnings. *As for the extensive and populous Bridewell at Glasgow, it now costs the public only one hundred pounds a year.*

" Thus morals, order and economy are alike subserved by the system of employing the inmates of our prisons."

We have quoted so largely from Mr. Bevan's instructive pages, that we have not room to give even the slightest sketch of his further observations on the employment of prisoners, and on *Visiting Committees.* The benefit of the latter, in Newgate, is too well known through the medium of the public journals, which have noticed the benevolent efforts of Mrs. Fry and her associates. The whole of his remarks on Visiting Committees deserve the most serious and attentive consideration of the affluent and humane who reside in the vicinity of large towns where there are prisons. On the whole, he concludes, (and we cordially accede to his conclusion),

" It may be confidently expected, that a system so fraught with advantages, and so clearly tending to the diminution of crime, and the peace of society, will gradually become prevalent among us; a system of order, employment, classification, and instruction, *protected* by the judicious superintendence of benevolent and unpaid visitors. It were greatly to be lamented, should indolence on the one hand, or prejudice on the other, prevent the progress of so beneficial and so interesting a work. If the visiting committees, which this chapter is intended to recommend, be formed under the immediate notice of the magistrates, which must of course be the case; and if their proceedings be conducted with prudence and perseverance, the feelings of distrust and jealousy, if any such be entertained, will soon make way for decided approbation and liberal support. All classes of Society may surely be expected to unite, in promoting an object, in which they are all alike most deeply interested.

" The great question is, Where are the labourers?

" Surely they may be found amongst benevolent and practical Christians of both sexes in every part of the kingdom. To them the appeal is made. If they feel it to be their duty to make the efforts which are here recommended;—if they know it to be a duty (as indeed they must) perfectly consistent with the will of Him, who came " to seek and to save that which was lost," they will be animated by that *spirit* which will enable them to cope with difficulties, and they will depend upon that *blessing,* before which all difficulties will subside.

" It must be repeated, that there is indeed much evil and much affliction in the world, which loudly demand the kind attentions and sedulous exertions of all, who wish well to their fellow creatures.

" Our Divine Master has declared to us a sufficient motive to all such efforts. " I was an hungered, and ye gave me meat ; I was thirty, and ye gave me drink ; I was a stranger, and ye took me in ; naked, and ye clothed me ; I was sick, and ye visited me ; I was in prison, and ye came unto me. *Verily, I say unto you, inasmuch as ye have done it unto one of the least of these my brethren, ye have done it unto Me.*"

In the confidence that his appeal to the Christian feeling, and principle will not be in vain, Mr. B. concludes his volume by suggesting the following resolutions as proper to be adopted on the formation of an association to visit any prison.

" 1. Permission having been obtained from the magistrates, it is agreed, that an Association be now formed for the purpose of visiting the prisoners in the jail of ———.

" 2. That the Association consist of two committees ; one of the ladies to visit the female prisoners ; and another of gentlemen, to visit the male prisoners.

" 3. That the two committees consist of the following persons.

" 4. That both classes of prisoners be visited daily ; and that the members of the committees visit in rotation and two together.

" 5. That the attention of the visitors be directed principally, to the making of suitable arrangement for the instruction of the ignorant and the employment of the idle.

" 6. That a time be set apart every morning for the reading of the Holy Scriptures with the several companies of prisoners.

" 7. That the most orderly of the prisoners be appointed to act as monitors— that regulations be made by the visitors to prevent all swearing and gaming in the prison—and that no effort be spared to promote, amongst the inmates, the habits of quietness, regularity, and submission.

".8. That the committees endeavour to exercise a kind care over those persons, who are discharged from the jail, and to assist in procuring, for such of them as appear deserving, some respectable means of maintaining themselves and their families.

" 9. That a fund be now raised to defray the expences, which will be incurred by this Association.

" 10. That the two committees submit a quarterly Report of their proceedings to the magistrates who superintend the jail.

With these resolutions we terminate our abstract of Mr. Bevan's truly christian and benevolent work ; which we are sure we need not recommend to the consideration of every humane and reflecting mind. The subject speaks for itself, and if our observations and extracts shall in any degree contribute to promote its circulation, it will be to us a source of the most pleasing recollection.

ΓΡΑΜΜΑΤΙΚΩΝ, &c. i. e. *A Course of Belles Lettres*, by Constantine Oikonomos, Professor of Philology, &c. vol. 1, 8vo. Vienna, 1817.

We have, on various occasions, called the attention of our readers to the growing spirit of inquiry, and progress of sound learning, among the modern Greeks. Few, very few, of the productions of their learned men have found their way to this country ; and we gladly avail ourselves of the assistance of a foreign pen, to present to the readers of this journal a short analysis of the work of M. Oikonomos, who justly holds a distinguished rank among the learned men that do honour to modern Greece. In 1813, this gentleman published (in Greek) an excellent treatise on Rhetoric. He has for several years past been a successful professor of Greek and Latin literature, and has formed a great number of excellent pupils. He is further said to be the *first* preacher in the churches at Smyrna, where he has acquired great celebrity by his resistless eloquence, which attracts to his sermons not only the Greek inhabitants of that opulent city, but also many of the Consuls and other Europeans of rank who are resident there.

Among this learned ecclesiastic's admirers, the present Archbishop of Smyrna, M. Anthimos, is particularly distinguished. This respectable prelate is a native of the island of Naxos, and the zealous friend of letters.

Lastly, M. Oikonomos, without having even quitted Greece, is profoundly skilled in general literature, and in the Latin, Italian, French, and German languages. The present patriarch of Constantinople has offered him one of the first professorships in the great Greek College established in that city; but he has hitherto refused to abandon the country of Homer, where gratitude and friendship have fixed him.

Such is the author of the course of Belles Lettres, now introduced to our readers, and of which, only one volume has yet appeared*. It is divided into two books, the first of which comprises twelve chapters (besides a brief introduction,) treating on the following subjects.

1. Definition and division of the fine arts;

2. Difference between the fine arts in general, and the fine and useful arts;

3. Of genius:—in the fine arts, that faculty imitates nature;

4. Nature defined;

5. Of enthusiasm, or that disposition with which genius imitates nature;

6. Of taste in general;

7. On the pleasures of taste, and on the sublime in general.

8. On the sublime in style;

9. Of the beautiful, in general;

10. Of the beautiful in style;

11. Of taste in the fine arts;

12. Taste has an influence on the manners of society, and on that account ought to be cultivated with especial care and attention.

The second book is appropriated to the art of poetry, which part of his sub-ject is discussed by this author in a strict method.

After a general introduction concerning the origin and nature of poetry, and its different species, M. Oikonomos speaks of the epopœa and of lyric poetry; he then gives a singularly just and luminous view of the principles and rules of the dramatic art; and passes in review bucolic poetry, the apologue, didactic, and satirical poetry, poetical epistles, and the epigram.

Such is a brief outline of the first volume of this interesting work, of which we regret that we cannot present to our readers a more minute analysis. The author has drawn largely from a great number of excellent writers, both antient and modern,—as Aristotle, Longinus, Dionysius of Halicarnassus, Quintilian, Rollin, Batteux, La Harpe, Dr. Blair, and especially from those who have adopted the critical system of the preceptor of Alexander. Every page of this valuable work displays the extensive and solid learning as well as the enlightened and exact taste of M. Oikonomos; who has appositely cited a great number of fine passages from the antient classic authors, and has also made frequent and impartial mention of the most celebrated English, French, Italian, German, Spanish and Portuguese writers.

In the publication of this work, M. Oikonomos has rendered a most important service to the Greek youth, who may be desirous of studying the beauties of the literature of their ancestors, and of transfusing them into their native mother tongue.

M. Oikonomos has dedicated his work to M. Alexander Mauros, of Paros, one of the richest merchants in Greece, and also one of its principal benefactors, who has made the greatest exertions to extricate that unfortunate country from ignorance and debasement.

The dedication is composed in a style, which, though it will perhaps appear somewhat novel to our English readers, is equally worthy of its learned author, and of the patriot to whom it is addressed.

---

*The other volumes, we understand, are in the press

"I do not honour you," says the author, on account of your wealth; I I do not admire you, for the friendship of the great; I do not congratulate you on account of your external qualities. The true merit of man consists in the practice of virtue; and it is virtue alone that intitles anyone to be honoured, congratulated, and admired: without it, however great a person may appear, he is essentially destitute of true greatness.

"Your singular virtue, most noble Alexander, gives you a claim to universal esteem. You are magnanimous, generous, and beneficent. You honour the Muses; you love your nation. The wise depositary of the gifts of Plutus, you make them subservient to raise up our unfortunate Greece; you are the support of our schools. At your expence it is that several young Greeks are studying the sciences in Europe. It is you, especially, who are endeavouring to augment the number of learned men, and to diffuse knowledge, in Greece. That country is grateful for the benefits you have conferred upon her. All Greeks bless your name, together with those of the Maruzzi, the Karaioanni, the brothers Zosimas; the Raplani, and all the immortal benefactors of Greece. But, so long as Smyrna shall exist, her college will more particularly acknowledge your munificence, &c. &c.

The preceding passages, (which are literally translated) are in no respect exaggerated, though they are dictated by profound sentiments of gratitude. In fact M. Mauros has, at his own expence, not only founded a free public school in his own native country, for the instruction of youth; but he has also made considerable donations to several colleges in Greece, and likewise supports a considerable number of professors and students.

Most of the Greek merchants, particularly those of Odessa, also contribute, according to their respective abilities, to raise prostrate Greece, and to revive in the Greek youth a taste for liberal studies, and a love of literature, the sciences and arts.

To the dedication succeeds a preliminary discourse which is addressed to the Greek nation. After offering some general considerations on the importance of classical literature and on the manner of studying it, the author particularly exhorts young men to apply themselves to the study of eloquence.

"By this," says he, "it is, that an orator conducts his fellow citizens into the paths of reason; makes them feel in a more lively manner the dignity of man; combats ignorance and error, which are the mortal enemies of the happiness of nations, and introduces into his country the knowledge of the arts and sciences."

M. Oikonomos proceeds to exhort his young countrymen to honour the true benefactors of their country, and those who sacrifice their life to the public good. He proposes, as models for their example, the learned patriarch of Constantinople, the Archbishop Ignatius, several prelates of the Greek church, who are eminently distinguished for their enlightened patriotism, and many noblemen and merchants, who are zealous promoters of instruction. He pays a just tribute of respect to Messieurs Theocletos and Kokkinaki, the editors of the "Literary Mercury," and also to Dr. Alexandrides the editor of the "Commercial Telegraph," and the "Literary Telegraph." These three journals, which are in the Modern Greek language, are printed at Vienna.

Equal commendations are bestowed upon M. Athanasius, the professor of Modern Greek at the Imperial Academy in the same city, who towards the close of the last year, published a prospectus of another Greek journal, to be intitled *Calliope*.

M. Oikonomos counsels his young countrymen to pay particular attention to the art of writing, and concludes his preliminary discourse with the following affecting address to them:—

"O ye, who love beauty,—young men of unfortunate Greece! listen to the last words of your friend—your country expects from you, works more perfect than mine—yes, my feeble labours will easily give place to yours.— I shall one day see my hoary hairs surrounded by a company of laborious pupils and more able professors. Then, with a trembling voice, and a soul intoxicated with joy, I shall sing with enthusiasm that beautiful song of the Muses and the Graces :

Every thing that is beautiful, is lovely, &c.

The History of the City of Dublin, from the earliest accounts to the present time, &c. &c. By Messrs. Warburton, Walsh, and Whitelaw, 4to. 2 vols. 5*l.* 5*s.* large paper 8*l.* 8*s.* Cadell and Davies, London, 1818.

[Continued from page 61.]

The pressure of other matter has caused us necessarily to suspend our report of this very interesting work; and we now gladly invite our readers attention to the second volume, which contains a rich fund of information to the philanthropist. A very considerable portion of it is occupied by details of the various religious and charitable institutions, the institution and support of which reflect such distinguished honour on the inhabitants of Dublin. The whole of these we have not room to specify; but we cannot pass in silence the numerous schools for instructing the children of the poor of every denomination.

From a Synoptical Table of the education of the *lower classes* in Dublin for the year 1816, it appears there are

	Children.
29 Protestant Schools, in which are educated - - - - -	3194
32 Catholic Ditto - - - - - - - - - - - -	5095
12 Schools of Dissenters - - - - - - - - - - -	906
12 Mixed Schools, for educating Children of *all* denominations	4402
85	13,597

The total expense of these various Schools is stated to amount 57,700*l,* Much as has been done in the city of Dublin in the way of education, it appears that *two* children out of *three* are still uneducated. The details of many of these schools are exceedingly interesting. We shall extract one or two for the gratification of our readers.

The income of the Dublin Free Schools in the year 1812 was 1155*l.* 14*s.* 9½*d* ; and the expenditure, 972*l.* 0*s.* 1½*d.*

"*Dublin Free School.*—The first Sunday-school established in this city, and in Ireland, was opened in 1786, by the Rev. Richard Powell, rector of Dundrum, in the parish of St. Katherine's, of which he was at that time Curate. The female children assembled in the parochial school-house, which the governors lent for that purpose ; and the boys were accommodated by the Earl of Meath, an anxious friend to the institution, with the use of the Court-house of the Liberties of Thomas Court and Donore. From 300 to 500 children of all denominations generally attended, and exclusive of the usual course of reading, writing, and arithmetic, the sacred scriptures were admitted and read, but without any selection, explanation, or comment whatever. In consequence of the gratuitous assistance of many respectable persons who were friendly to the infant institution, the expences were so moderate, that the collection made at an annual charity sermon preached in the Church of St. Catherine's, was sufficient to answer every demand. The accommodation, however, being not only indifferent, but insufficient for the continually increasing members in that poor but populous part of the city, an idea was conceived of erecting a school for the purpose, on a large scale, and with every necessary convenience. Among the promoters of the Institution, the Friends, or as they are usually denominated the Quakers, who in the parish of St. Catherine's are numerous, took an anxious and decided part, and in consequence, in a great measure, of the active and unremitting exertions of Mr. Ephraim Bewley, one of their body, so many respectable and opulent citizens were induced to contribute liberally, that in a short time a sum was subscribed nearly sufficient to defray the expence of the intended edifice, when the work was commenced, and in 1798 finished, with a rapidity that evinces the energy of that respectable body, and with a substantial plainness and neatness that does equal credit to their taste and good sense.

" This seminary, open to the children of all denominations of Christians, and therefore called the Dublin Free School-house, is situated in School-street, in the parish of St. Catherine: it is of a rectangular form, 156 feet by 37, of brick, and three stories high ; of these the basement story consists principally of stores rented by merchants in the vicinity, and on the two upper floors are the school-rooms, four in number, viz. two for males, and two females ; each 56 feet by 33, spacious, lofty, and well ventilated. The male and female schools have entrances perfectly distinct ; and are separated from each other by a spacious Committee-room, and an apartment appropriated to the superintendant, who by an ingenious contrivance of the architect, is enabled by a small change in his position, to command an uninterrupted view of the four schools, though on different floors.* While he sits, the entire of the male and female schools on the first floor are open to his inspection, as are those on the second floor when he stands: thus a constant sense of his superintending eye, contributes greatly to preserve order and silence ; while his communication with his assistants is correct, and unembarassed by the necessity of moving from one school to another to give his directions.

" From the commencement of this Institution in January, 1786, it was open for the admission of children on Sundays only until March, 1811, when the governors, anxious to extend its benefits to the utmost, opened it as a daily school also. Attendance from nine in the morning till one in the afternoon, and from three to six in the afternoon.

" This school has been for many years conducted on a plan which does not involve in its management any of those doctrines in which the different sects of Christians disagree ; and Mr. Joseph

* This plan is deemed so efficient for the purposes of superintendance, that it is adopted in some extensive manufactories in the Liberties.

Lancaster's system, admitting of the same latitude, has been latterly introduced, and we think judiciously : such a system, indeed, seems to be best adapted to the peculiar circumstances of the poor, in a district where Roman Catholics are to all other sects conjunctively as 9 to 1 ; and it has been attended with success. A sufficient knowledge in reading, writing and arithmetic, is rapidly, and at a very moderate expense, communicated to the objects of its care, and with it what is perhaps still more valuable, habits of order, cleanliness, and decency, to which we may add, of industry also among the females, in whose schools a mistress of superior qualifications superintends the working department : the remuneration here held out to the girls has been attended with very beneficial effects; they receive the entire of their earnings in clothes made in the schools ; their improvement in this branch, to which they dedicate two days in the week, is considerable, and has eventually produced a considerable increase of attendance.

" Since the commencement of the Weekly School up to the year 1814, 24,361 have been taught, and there are now on the books 578. Since the commencement of the Daily School, 8089 have been received, and there are no less than 796 in daily attendance. The proficiency and regularity of this mass of children are really surprising ; they are taken from the poorest classes of society, and pass from the licentious and irregular habits of the streets in the morning, and again return to them in the evening ; yet they suddenly conform, and implicitly submit to the discipline of one another, without apparent coercion or corporal punishment while they are in school, and the whole machinery moves with the utmost regularity under one superintendant.

" *Sunday and Daily School, North-Strand.*—In the same year and on the same principles as the preceding, was opened at the other extremity of the city, the Sunday School on the North-Strand, for the reception and instruction of the poor children of the parishes of St. Mary's, St. Thomas's, and afterwards of St. George's. It consists of a neat building, not so extensive or so arranged as the former, but having the advantage of a chapel, in which divine service is performed every Sunday to a numerous congregation, whose weekly contributions materially assist the establishment. The Governors finding, on inquiry, that the

children were for the most part unemployed during the week days, in a short
time opened it for the reception of day
scholars also. On this was engrafted a
School for Female Industry, which has
been very prosperous. Some of the regulations of these schools are peculiar,
and seem very well adapted to the circumstances of them *

"In consequence of their being strictly
enforced, this Institution, which is held
together by no fund but the annual voluntary contributions of individuals, has
continued to flourish for twenty-nine
years. During that period 7000 boys
and girls have been admitted, and there
are now 340 in attendance, being an
equal number of each sex ; of whom
one hundred of the most deserving are
annually clothed. The annual expence
amounts to £450. which is defrayed by
subscriptions, a charity sermon, and by
the profits of the children's work.

"*School for Young Sweeps.*—Among the
many projects which the exuberant charity of the metropolis has indulged in,
this school is the most fanciful. There
is certainly no class of the community
which has so much and so deservedly
excited public commisseration as that of
young sweeps, and we think the existence of such a trade is a reproach to
the police of any state where it is permitted ; but we think the only effectual
remedy would be to remove the cause.
The dismal effects can be but feebly
remedied, and the condition of a young
sweep is but little improved, because he

* As they are open to all religious persuasions, one of the masters is a Catholic,
who instructs his persuasion in their own
catechism, and conducts them every Sunday
to chapel. To induce an early attendance,
bread was distributed to those who came
soonest ; and after some time clothing, as a
reward ; to prevent the child from with-
drawing from the school when this was obtained, a note for the amount was passed by
the parent, on which he was liable to be sued.
Woolen cloaks are lent out to the most deserving girls during the winter months, which
are returned in spring ; those who keep
them best, receive a premium : one set of
cloaks has in this way served for five winters.
Advancement in education is considered not
a task but a reward ; and industry is made
preparatory to learning. No girl is allowed
to write till she has made a shirt. The superintendance of the schools naturally
devolves on the Chaplain, who does not
receive his salary unless he attends four
days in the week, to be certified by his signature in the visitors' book.

knows how to read and write. The incident which called the public attention to
this object, and gave rise to the establishment of this school, was as follows. A
master-sweep had been tried and convicted of cruelty to his apprentice. He
was sentenced to be publicly whipped ;
and the general indignation was strongly
excited by the circumstances which appeared in evidence. It was proved that
the child had been blistered with lashes
and burned with coals ; and when the
sores festered, to add to the poignancy
of fresh burnings, he was dipped in cold
water, and lashed and burned alternately.
He was brought into court, wrapped in
a blanket, covered with ointment, and
shortly after the trial died, it is said, of a
general mortification.

"At the next yearly meeting of the
Sunday School Society, this event excited much sympathy, and produced a
determination to relieve this most forlorn
and degraded class of society. In 1816
a society was founded, in which the lord
mayor, who was also member for the
city, took a leading part. At their first
meeting various enormities were reported
from the best evidence. Several instances
of murder, the constant practice of employing them to rob or steal by night ;
procuring young females, and using
them as boys : in effect, such a system of
cruelty, indecency, and moral depravity
was displayed, as degraded the present
state of these wretched children far
below the level of humanity, and precluded all hope, by rendering them
utterly unfit for any future state of society. To apply some remedy to these
melancholy evils, it was resolved, in the
first instance, to ascertain those master-
sweeps who retain children without
indentures, in order that steps might be
immediately taken to put such children
under the protection of the law. It was
next considered, that, as they cannot
pursue their trade, even if it was desirable, beyond a certain time of life,
when they attain too large a stature, and
as few can become masters, the great
majority, at an adult age, must be thrown
upon society, without knowledge, principle, or employment. To counteract
the present influence, and to qualify
them for something better hereafter, a
school was established to instruct them
in reading, writing, and arithmetic. The
trustee of Kellet's bequest readily
granted the large rooms of that school
for the purpose. Here they assemble
every Sunday ; a breakfast is provided
by the subscribers ; and they are sup-

plied with shirts, cloaks, caps, and shoes; premiums of soap, combs, and money are given to excite a sense of decency and a feeling of cleanliness, and on one day of the week, at least, these forlorn outcasts are admitted to the rights and raised to the level of humanity. About forty attend every Sunday, and some of them evince a great desire to learn.*

By far the greater number of schools and other charities, in Dublin, is supported by charity sermons,—a mode of collecting money for public objects, which, from the extent to which it is carried, the interest it excites, and the universality of the practice, is a distinguishing feature of the metropolis of Ireland. We have heard much, very much, of the liberality of the inhabitants of Dublin, and the account which the historians of that city have given of their charity sermons, more than confirms the statements which had previously reached us. From a comparison of the books of the several charities, for the collections of the year 1815, the historians inform us that no less

---

* One child had learned to read from the labels on the doors of the houses where he waited to be admitted, and another who was not able to walk, from an accident, was carried to school at his own request, on the back of his companion. We are concerned, however, to state, that the charity is for the present suspended by the interference of their own clergy of the Roman Catholic persuasion, who suspect an intention of proselyting the children. Now, besides the usual precaution of using the Bible and other books of instruction without note or commentary, care is taken here, that no Protestant visitor shall even hold the book out of which the child is instructed, lest he might be suspected of supplying an oral commentary to a book that had none, and instil any doctrine inimical to the Roman Catholic Church. None but monitors of their own persuasion teach them, or hold the book while they learn. We respect that care which the pastor of every persuasion ought to pay to the flock he is appointed to watch over, and if there was reason to fear that any system of proselytism was concealed under the garb of charity, we should applaud the precautionary jealously which defeated it even in the case of a degraded sweep; but it is not so; and we trust these forlorn outcasts will not be deprived of the new born sensations of comfort, cleanliness, and wholesome food, by an unfounded suspicion.

sum than 13,517*l.* 4*s.* 1*d.* was obtained in consequence of charity sermons at the various churches and chapels (Protestant and Roman Catholic) of that city. Having no poor rates to pay, the inhabitants of Dublin consider themselves exempt from a burthen which presses heavily upon their neighbours ; and therefore voluntarily impose upon themselves an annual contribution greater than any compulsory tax. Respecting the manner in which charity sermons are conducted in Dublin, we have the following interesting particulars.

"Every charity has its stated time of the year for an appeal to the public, and so anxious are the governors to prevent the interference of any other, that it is no unusual circumstance to see it advertised for several months before. As the selection of a preacher is of considerable consequence, the earliest application is made to one of those who are most popular, and his assistance very early secured, and notified accordingly As the day approaches, the whole parish is in commotion. Bills are posted, advertisements put forth, and letters every where circulated. Deputations of the parishioners set out in coaches to wait on the lord lieutenant, lord mayor, and other public or opulent characters to request their attendance. Ladies, the most remarkable for their rank and beauty, are appointed collectors. Every body takes an interest in the charity, as if it was a personal concern, and every means are taken to insure its success. It is sometimes usual even to close the churches in the vicinity, that the congregation may be compelled to that in which the sermon is preached. On the important day, if the preacher or the charity be at all popular, the church is generally crowded. It is held disreputable for any parishioners or other person connected with the charity, to absent themselves, and the additional congregation of strangers causes an overflow. Instances have frequently occured where a guard of soldiers has been obliged to keep order among the crowd who were kept out, and certain stewards with white wands to mark their authority, to regulate the tumultary congregation that had got in. Under such circumstances it is much to be regretted that scenes of irregularity, little according with the solemnity of the place, have sometimes occured, and the whole of the service which preceded the sermon been entirely unattended to. But when the preacher ascends the pulpit, the scene suddenly changes; the wave of the multitude subsides, and every auditor is fixed in wrapt attention. After the sermon, the ladies attended by white rods, proceed from pew to pew with a silver plate. The collection of each pew is poured into a bason held by her attendant, and the plate is presented empty to the next, that every one's donation may be conspicuous. Thus every engine is moved to increase the collection; and the charity of the congregation is so far from being the simple dictate of religion, that it is a mixed emotion, in which eloquence, pity, beauty and vanity have a considerable share.

" Among the many incidents which have occurred to mark the deep interest which the people of the metropolis take in charity sermons, we shall mention one which, though sufficiently known, is too remarkable to be omitted. On the 30th of March, 1794, a sermon was announced for the Female Orphan House to be preached by the Rev. Dean Kirwan, in St. Peter's Church. The popularity both of the preacher and the institution was great, and the church was crowded with even a more than usual concourse : when the preacher entered the pulpit a profound silence prevailed ; every one listened anxiously to catch those sounds which never failed to make upon them the deepest impression ; but they heard nothing : a sudden illness had seized the preacher, who was in a very feeble state of health, and he could do now no more than lay his hand upon his breast, and pointing with the other to his little flock, silently recommended them to the mercy of the congregation. The appeal was irresistible; and the mute eloquence of the preacher on this interesting occasion produced even more than his most laboured and powerful oratory. A sum exceeding 1000*l.* was in a few minutes collected in the church. It was on this occasion, we believe, that a watch was found on the plate ; the case was clasped on a bit of paper on which was a pencil-mark for 10*l.*, and the owner redeemed it next day, alledging that the sum he brought with him, and intended for the charity, he deemed insufficient for such an appeal. These are characteristic traits of the Irish disposition. A silent gesture produced more from a disappointed assembly, than they were

prepared to give to the most powerful appeal of reason and religion."

An account of this eminent preacher is given in a note, which we are tempted to extract, as it contains several circumstances, which are not known to the generality of the English readers.

" This extraordinary man was born in Galway, in 1754. He went at the age of seventeen to the Danish Island of St. Croix, in the West Indies, where he remained for six years. On his return he studied at St. Omer's, took orders, and became Roman Catholic chaplain to the Neapolitan Embassador, in 1778. After two years solemn deliberation, he conformed to the established church in 1787, and preached for the first time in St. Peter's Church in June in that year. Here immense crowds thronged to hear him, and on the following year the governors of the parochial schools came to a resolution, " that from the effects which the sermons of the Rev. W. B. Kirwan had from the pulpit, his officiating in the metropolis ought to be considered a peculiar national advantage, and that vestries should be called to consider the most effectual method of securing to the city an instrument under Providence of such public benefit." He was now presented to the prebend of Howth, and the parish of St. Nicholas without, and in 1800 to the deanery of Killala by Lord Cornwallis. Every testimony that could mark the admiration of the public was conferred upon him. Besides the immense contributions which his sermons called forth, his portraits were painted and engraved ; he was presented with addresses, pieces of plate, and the freedom of corporations; and in 1792, a man whose energetic oratory was congenial to his own, introduced him to the notice of the Irish parliament in these words. " This man preferred our country, and our religion, and brought to both genius superior to what he found in either. He called forth the latent virtues of the human heart, and taught men to discover a mine of charity in themselves, of which the owners were unconscious. He came to interrupt the repose of the pulpit, and shakes one world with the thunder of another. But in feeding the lamp of charity, he exhausted the lamp of life." The violence of his efforts had brought on a spitting of blood, and he fell a victim to his exertions, on the 7th of October, 1805. His funeral was attended by a long train of charity

P

children from the different schools in Dublin, which his eloquence had so eminently contributed to support and extend.'

"Kirwan was the founder of a new school of pulpit oratory in Dublin. His sermons were the result of much labour and attention. He committed them to memory with the most exact precision, but he delivered them in a manner so apparently unpremeditated that they had the effect of natural and unstudied elocution. On one occasion, some interruption to the service happened in a crowded church; when he returned home he composed a discourse on the propriety of behaviour in the house of God, which he determined should be his subject when next called on to preach. Supposing, however, that it would have more effect if it seemed unpremeditated, and to arise from some immediate cause, he gave out a different text, and commenced on another topic: what he had calculated on took place: the disturbance again occurred. He broke off the discourse he had begun, and abruptly thundered a reproof from the pulpit, the more solemn and impressive as it seemed sudden and unpremeditated. We had heard this mentioned as a proof that all his sermons were extemporaneous; but his great mind was above disguise, and he candidly communicated to us the real circumstance. His action has been taxed with extravagance; he literally " came to disturb the repose of the pulpit;" it was his custom to remove his cushion, that the sound elicited from the boards by his hands and feet might add to the effect of his empassioned delivery; strange as this was, the occasions were so appropriate, and accompanied by such energy of thought and potency of language, that the whole seemed perfectly natural and congruous. He had many personal deficiencies,—a weak voice, an oblique eye, and an unprepossessing countenance; but they were never noticed in the pulpit: the profound attention of his hearers remedied the one, and the ardent feelings of his mind, irradiated the other. His style of eloquence died with him. He had many imitators, but genius was wanting to sanction their attempts. They were principally distinguished by an extravagance of action, which is now happily banished from our pulpit, till some other Kirwan arise to give it currency. He has been succeeded by many charity sermon preachers, of another school, whose high attainments and ad-

mirable compositions adorn and promote the sacred cause in which they are exerted,—but " the mine of charity" is not wrought as it was wont to be. The voice " that shook one world with the thunders of the others" is heard no more; he that uttered it has been removed to that other world, and the mantle of Elijah has fallen upon no successor."

[*To be concluded in our next Number.*]

The Conversion of the World: or the Claims of Six Hundred Millions of Heathen, and the Ability and Duty of the Churches respecting them. By the Rev. Gordon Hall and Samuel Newell, American Missionaries at Bombay. Andover (N. A.) printed: London, reprinted, 12mo, 1s. 6d. Simpkin and Marshall, 1819.

As the season of the year is rapidly approaching, when the various benevolent Institutions, for diffusing religious knowledge among distant and Heathen Nations, will hold their respective Anniversary Meetings, we think it but an act of justice, at this time, to recommend to the notice of our readers the present eloquent and well written tract. Though primarily designed for and addressed to, the various churches, or denominations of christians, in the United States of America, the arguments which it contains are equally applicable to all countries, and to every society that is employed in the progation of christianity. The London Editor has, therefore, rendered an acceptable service to the British Public, in submitting this tract to their consideration; and he has confirmed and illustrated the observations of the original authors, by adding several useful notes. The following are the propositions discussed:

1. That it is the duty of christians to send forth the preachers of the gospel, in such numbers as to furnish the means of instruction and salvation to the whole world:

2. That the churches are able to furnish the requisite number of Mis-

sionaries for evangelizing the whole world :

3. That there are the most encouraging and important openings for the propagation of christianity in the various parts of the world : and

4. That although in this undertaking there are many difficulties to admonish, there are none to discourage, those who either promote it, or are employed in it.

Lest any of our readers should suppose that the authors of this publication are *enthusiasts* in the cause in which they have embarked, it may be proper to add, that, though they write with earnestness and fervour, yet their arguments are founded on undisputable facts, and are expressed with much energy and strength of language.

Practical Sermons on Various Subjects, chiefly designed to illustrate and enforce the principles of Christian Responsibility, 8vo. 7s. Cadell and Davies, London, 1819.

These Anonymous Discourses are stated to have been hastily and occasionally written in the intervals of more active occupation, and are published in aid of the declining funds of a very extensive and useful charitable Institution in Ireland. They do not, however, exhibit many marks of haste or defective composition : the subjects they embrace are seasonable at all times, but are especially so in the present age of religious profession. They are strictly practical, and though addressed to members of the Established Church of the United Kingdom, may be read with advantage by Christians of every denomination. Whoever the author is, we think he cannot be long concealed; and, from the intrinsic value of his discourses, we trust that their sale will essentially aid the interests of the Institution for whose benefit they are published. As this volume has been honoured with the approbation of the eminently learned divine, the Dean of Cork, (Dr. Magee), any recommendation of ours can add but little weight to his sanction. We cannot, however,

dismiss this handsomely printed volume, without stating that it forms an important, as well as useful accession, to our present stores of domestic divinity.

Speech of Lieutenant General William Thornton, in the House of Commons, on Thursday, the 7th of May, 1818, on his motion to repeal the declarations, against the belief of transubstantiation, and asserting the Worship of the Church of Rome to be Idolatrous. With authorities and illustrations, deduction and conclusion, royal 8vo. Longman and Co. London, 1818.

As the House of Commons decided against General Thornton's motion, it is not necessary that we should analize the various arguments and proofs, contained in his elaborate speech. It is written with great calmness, and exhibits much patient research : and, since the Roman Catholic question is about to be submitted once more to the consideration of the legislature,—while we feel assured that the enlightened characters, who compose the national senate, will not decide either hastily or inconsiderately, we think it but an act of justice to the author, to recommend his publication to the attentive perusal of all, who are interested in that momentous question.

A Summary Method of Teaching Children to Read, upon the principle originally discovered by the Sieur Berthaud, with an entirely new arrangement, calculated to adapt it to to the English Language. The whole illustrated by nine copperplates. By Mrs. Williams. The second edition, carefully revised and very materially improved, 12mo. 4s. 6d. half-bound. London, Printed for the Author, and sold by Longman and Co., 1818.

When the first edition of this truly useful and handsomely printed little work was announced, knowing by experience that there was no royal way to learning, we could not help suspecting that more was promised than either was or could be performed. A careful examination, however, of the present greatly improved edition, enables us to state, that it is admirably calculated to soften the difficulty of teaching, as well as of acquiring a knowledge of the *powers* and *sounds* of the different letters of our language. As the system of M. Berthaud, of which Mrs. W's works is an improvement, was honoured with the approbation of Madame de Genlis, her recommendation will doubtless have its weight with sensible and reflecting teachers.

Little Lessons for Little Folks; containing, 1. The Little Chimney Sweepers; 2. The Mistake; 3. The Widow and her only Son; 4. Ask and Learn; 5. Village Annals, or, Truth and Falsehood. By Mary Belson, 24mo. W. Darton, London, 1819.

We have been much interested in perusing these ' Little Tales ;' amusement and instruction are combined in them, in a very pleasing manner.

Food for the Young, adapted to the Mental Capacities of Children of Tender Years. By a Mother. 24mo. 2s. W. Darton, London, 1818.

Several striking incidents in the journies of eminent travellers are narrated in this handsomely printed little book, interspersed with instructive remarks and conversations, which appear to be excellently adapted to the capacities of infant minds.

Literary Register.

Authors, Editors, and Publishers, are particularly requested to forward to the Literary Panorama Office, post paid, on, or before the 19th day of each month, the titles, prices, and other particulars of works in hand or published, for this department of the Work.

· · · · · · · · · · · · · · · ·

BOOKS ANNOUNCED FOR PUBLICATION.

ANTIQUITIES AND THE FINE ARTS.

Mr. Britton's third Number of " *Chronological and Historical Illustrations of the Antient Architecture of Great Britain;*" containing eight engravings: also the fourth No. of " *The History and Antiquities of York Cathedral.*" The sixth No. to finish this Cathedral, is announced for the 1st of June.

The Victories of the Duke of Wellington, illustrated by a series of engravings from drawings, by Richard Westall, R. A.: the outlines engraved by Charles Heath, and colored in imitation of the original drawings, will appear this month in quarto.

The Englefield Vases; the first part of this work containing six plates engraved by H. Moses from the Vases in the possession of Sir H. Englefield, Brt. is just ready for publication.

The print of the Battle of Waterloo, by Burnet, from the capital Painting of Atkinson and Devis, will be ready for Delivery on the 1st of June, 1819.

Mr. J. S. Cotman, of Yarmouth, has in great forwardness, in folio, a Series of finished Etchings, with Descriptions, of the ecclesiastical and castellated Antiquities of Normandy, from drawings made by himself.

Shortly will be published, the fourth and final part ; being Nos. 10, 11 and 12, of the Architectural Perspective Views of every London Parish Church, being an elucidation of the Ecclesiastical Architecture of the Metropolis. The drawings are chiefly by Coney, whose merit as an Architectural draftsman, are well known.

BIOGRAPHY.

The Life of the late Right Hon. John Philpot Curran, Master of the Rolls in

Ireland. By his son, William Henry Curran, Esq. Barrister at Law, in 2 vols. 8vo. with a portrait.

Lord John Russell will soon publish, in a quarto volume, the Life of William, Lord Russell; with some account of the times in which he lived.

John Adamson, Esq. is preparing for publication, Memoirs of the Life and Writings of Luis de Camoens, in 2 vols. 8vo. illustrated with 9 engravings.

MEDICINE.

Mr. J. G. Mansford is printing, in an 8vo. volume, Researches into the Nature and Causes of Epilepsy, as connected with the physiology of animal life and muscular motion.

In the Press, and speedily will be published, in 8vo. illustrated with 5 plates, an Enquiry, illustrating the Nature of Tuberculated Accretions of Serous Membranes; and the Origin of Tubercles and Tumours in different Textures of the Body. By John Baron, M. D. Physician to the General Infirmary at Gloucester.

MISCELLANIES.

Mr. Burke, author of Amusements in Retirement, is printing in 4 octavo volumes, Meditations and Reflections on the Beauties, Harmonies, and Sublimities of Nature.

Mr. T. S. Peckston has in the press, a Practical Treaties on Gas Light, illustrated by plates; including an historical sketch of the rise and progress of the science.

A new edition of Mortimer's Commercial Dictionary is in the press, with revisions and corrections to the present time.

A Collection of Dr. Zouch's Works, with a Memoir by the Rev. Francis Wrangham, in 2 octavo volumes, will soon appear.

PHILOLOGY.

Mr. Thos. Yeates is printing a Syriac and English Grammar, designed for the use of British students; originally composed at the request and under the inspection of the late Rev. Dr. Buchanan.

POETRY.

The Iron Mask, a Poem; ascribed to the pen of J. D. Humphreys, Esq. great

grandson of the late Dr. Doddridge, and author of the Recluse of the Pyrenees; will be published in May.

THEOLOGY.

Sermons preached in St. John's Chapel, Edinburgh. By Daniel Sandford, D. D. one of the Bishops of the Scotch Episcopal Church, and formerly Student of Christ Church, Oxford, 8vo.

The Rev. William Pulling has in the press, a volume of Sermons, with appropriate Prayers, translated from the Danish of Dr. N. E. Balle, Regius Professor of Divinity at Copenhagen.

Mr. Joseph Ward is printing in a duodecimo volume, an Epitome of Scripture History, or a brief Narrative of the principal Facts and Events recorded in the Old Testament.

The Rev. Edmund Butcher, of Sidmouth, has in the press, a Third Volume of Sermons for the Use of Families.

In the press, and shortly will be published;—Remarks on the Foreknowledge of God; suggested by passages in Dr. Adam Clarke's Commentary on the New Testament. By Gill Timms.

TOPOGRAPHY.

In April will be published, the History of Ancient Wiltshire: Northern District. By Sir Richard Colt Hoare, Bart. F. R. S. and F. A. S.

A Geographical and Statistical Description of Scotland. By James Playfair, D.D. F. R. S. and F. A. S. E. Principal of the United College of St. Andrew, and Historiographer to his Royal Highness the Prince Regent, 2 vols. 8vo.

Collections for a topographical, historical, and descriptive Account of Boston and the Hundred of Skirbeck, Lincolnshire, by Mr. Pishey Thompson, will appear in the ensuing summer.

VOYAGES AND TRAVELS.

A Journey in Carniola and Italy, in the Years 1817, 1818. By W. A. Cadell, Esq. F. R. S. L. and E. 8vo., with engravings.

An Account of the Arctic Regions: including the Natural History of Spitzbergen, and the adjacent Islands ; the Polar Ice; and the Greenland-Seas ; with a History and Description of the Northern Whale Fishery ; illustrated by many Anecdotes of the Dangers of that Occupation. Chiefly derived from Researches made during seventeen Voyages to the Polar Seas. By William Scoresby, Jun. Member of the Wernerian Society. In 2 vols. 8vo. with numerous engravings.

Capt. Moritz de Kotzebue will soon publish, in 8vo. a Journey to Persia in the Suite of the Imperial Russian Embassy, in the year 1817.

Mr. Dodwell's long promised travels will certainly appear in May, accompanied with the first portion of his views in Greece.

Sir W. Gell's Itinerary of Greece, is also nearly completed.

. . . .

BOOKS PUBLISHED.

AGRICULTURE AND HORTICULTURE.

A Survey of the Agriculture of the Eastern and Western Flanders ; made under the authority of the Farming Society of Ireland. By the Rev. Thomas Radcliffe. With a map and numerous Plates of Implements, Buildings, &c. 8vo. 10s. 6d.

Facts and Observations relative to Canada. Proving that the British Colonies possess superior Advantages to Emigrants, compared with the United States of America. By Charles Frederick Grece, Member of the Montreal and Quebec Agricultural Societies, 8vo. 5s.

An Appendix to the Synopsis Plantarum Succulentarum cum Descriptionibus, Synonimis, &c. Auctore A. H. Haworth, F. L. S. 8vo. 5s.

FINE ARTS.

The Adventures of Hunch-Back, and the Stories connected with it (from the Arabian Nights Entertainments) with Seventeen illustrative Prints, engraved by William Daniell, from pictures painted by Robert Smirke, R. A. Imperial 4to. 6l. 6s.

BIOGRAPHY.

Biographia Hibernica, being the first volume of a Biographical Dictionary of the Worthies, from the earliest periods to the present times, edited by Richard Ryan, and embellished with a fine portrait of the late John Philpot Curran, 8vo. price 15s.

Memoirs of the Rev. Henry Martin, B. D. late Fellow of St. John's College, Cambridge, and Chaplain to the Hon. East India Company ; extracted from his private Journals, written at Cambridge, on his Voyage to India, in Bengal, and in Persia, in 8vo. 12s. boards.

EDUCATION.

French Pronunciation Exemplified ; and all the most elegant Figures of the French Language collected and explained, both in English and French. By E. Ch. Max. de Bellecour, 12mo. 5s.

A Sketch of Modern History from the Destruction of the Western Empire, A.D. 476, to the close of the Year 1818, together with a concise View of the Rise and Progress of the Arts and Sciences, and of Civilization in Europe; with a compendious Table of Chronology from the Creation of the World to the present Time. By A. Picquot, 12mo. 6s.

Conversations on General History, exhibiting a Progressive View of the State of Mankind, from the earliest ages of which we have any authentic Records to the beginning of the Year 1819. For the Use of Schools and Private Instruction. By Alexander Jamieson, 12mo. 6s.

Scenes in Asia for little Tarry-at-Home Travellers, by the Rev. L Taylor, illustrated by 84 engravings. Price 4s. plain, or 6s. coloured.

Scenes in Europe for little Tarry-at-Home Travellers, by the same Writer, illustrated by 84 engravings. Price 4s. plain, or 6s. coloured.

A Short Description of Sixty-four Birds, Beasts, Insects, and Fishes, such as generally excite the Curiosity of Young Persons, with a Copper-plate to each. Price 3s. plain, or 4s. coloured.

HISTORY.

Memorials; or the Considerable Things that fell out within this Island of Great Britain from 1638 to 1684. By the Rev. Robert Law. Edited from the MSS. by Charles Kirkpatrick Sharpe, Esq. 4to, 1l. 16s.

The History of France, Civil and Military, Ecclesiastical, Literary, Commercial, &c. &c. Continuing the History from the earliest Accounts to the Death of Henry III. A. D. 1589. By the Rev. Alexander Ranken, D. D. vols. 4, 5, 6, 8vo. 1l. 4s.

LAW.

Reports of Cases tried in the Jury Court, from the Institution of the Court, in 1815, to the Sittings at Edinburgh ending in March, 1818. By Joseph Murray, Esq. Advocate, 8vo. 15s.

The Penal Code of France, translated into English; with a Preliminary Dissertation and Notes, 8vo. 5s.

MECHANICS.

A Treatise on Spinning Machinery; illustrated by Plans of different Machines made use of in that Art, from the Spindle and Distaff of the Ancients to the Machines which have been invented or improved by the Moderns. With some preliminary Observations, tending to shew that the Art of Spinning, Weaving, and Sewing, were invented by the Ingenuity of Females. And a Postscript, including an interesting Account of the Mode of Spinning Yarn in Ireland. By Andrew Gray, Author of the Ploughwright's Assistant, and Experienced Millwright, 8vo. 10s. 6d.

MEDICINE, ANATOMY, AND SURGERY.

Practical Observations on the Treatment, Pathology, and Prevention of Typhous Fever. By Edward Percival, M. B. M. R. I. A. 8vo. 7s.

A Series of Engravings, representing the Bones of the Human Skeleton, with the Skeletons of some of the Lower Animals. By Edward Mitchell. Part I. imperial 4to. 1l. 1s.; royal 4to. 16s.

Observations on the Nature and Treatment of the Epidemic Fever, at present prevailing in the Metropolis, as well as in most Parts of the United Kingdom. To which are added, Remarks on some of the opinions of Dr. Bateman, in his late Treatise on this Subject. By Henry Clutterbuck, M. D. 8vo.

Essays on the Morbid Anatomy of the Human eye. By James Wardrop, F.R.S.E. Illustrated by coloured engravings, vol. 2, royal 8vo. 1l, 5s.

A Memoir on the Formation and Connexions of the Crural Arch, and other Parts concerned in Femoral and Inguinal Hernia. By Robert Liston, Fellow of the Royal College of Surgeons of London and Edinburgh, with 3 plates, 4to. 7s.

MISCELLANEOUS.

The Œdipus Romanus; or, an Attempt to prove from the principles of Reasoning adopted by the Rt. Hon. Sir William Drummond, in his " Œdipus Judaicus," that the Twelve Cæsars are the Twelve Signs of the Zodiac. Addressed to the higher and Literary Classes of Society. By the Rev. George Townsend, A. M. of Trinity College Cambridge, 8vo. 7s. 6d.

Observations on Penal Jurisprudence, and the Reformation of Criminals. With an Appendix; containing the latest Reports of the State Prisons of Philadelphia, New York, and Massachusetts; and other Documents. By William Roscoe, Esq. 8vo. 9s.

Facts and Observations toward forming a New Theory of the Earth. By William Knight, L. L. D. Belfast, 8vo. 9s.

Treasures of Thought, from de Stael Holstein: to which are prefixed, Cursory Remarks upon her Writings, and a Monody on her death. By the Author of Affection's Gift, &c. 18mo. 5s.

The Supplement to the Encyclopædia Britannica. Edited by Macvey Napier, Esq. F. R. S. L. and E. Vol. 3, part 2, 4to. 1*l.* 5*s.*

Kalila and Dimna; or, the Fables of Bidpai. Translated from the Arabic. By the Rev. Wyndham Knatchbull, A. M. 8vo. 14*s.*

NOVELS.

A Month at Stevens's. By a late resident, in 3 vols. 12mo. 1*l.* 1*s.*

The Priory of Birkenhead, a Tale of the Fourteenth Century. By Thomas Whitby, 12mo.

Oakwood Hall; a Novel. Including a Description of the Lakes of Cumberland and Westmorland, and a Part of South Wales. By Catherine Hutton, in 3 vols. 12mo. 16*s.* 6*d.*

A Traveller's Tale of the Last Century. By Miss E. I. Spence, in 3 vols. 12mo. 16*s.* 6*d.*

POETRY.

Emily, and other Poems. By Thomas Brown, M. D. Professor of Moral Philosophy in the University of Edinburgh, foolscap 8vo. 7*s,* boards.

The Autumnal Excursion; or, Sketches in Tiviotdale. With other Poems. By Thomas Pringle, foolscap 8vo. 6*s.*

Tom Crib's Memorial to Congress. With a Preface, Notes, and Appendix. By one of the Fancy. In foolscap, 8vo. 5*s.* 6*d.*

THEOLOGY.

Practical Sermons on Various Subjects, chiefly designed to illustrate and enforce the Principle of Christian Responsibility, 8vo. 7*s.*

An Analysis of the Fifth Book of Hooker's Ecclesiastical Polity; being a particular Defence of the Church of England. By the Rev. B. Kennicott, A. B. 8vo. 5*s.*

Sermons Preached in the Tron Church, Glasgow. By Thomas Chalmers, D. D. 8vo. 12*s.*

Familiar Dissertations on Theological and Moral Subjects. By the Rev. William Barrow, L. L. D. and F. R. S. 8vo. 10*s.* 6*d.*

Dr. Mant's Edition of the Book of Common Prayer, with Notes, Explanatory, Practical, and Historical, in one Quarto volume. Part I. price 4*s.* on medium paper, and 8*s.* on royal.

VOYAGES AND TRAVELS.

Travels through Denmark, Sweden, Lapland, Finland, Norway, and Russia, with a Description of the City of St. Petersburg, during the Tyranny of Emperor Paul. By E. D. Clarke, LL. D. Being the First Section of the Third and last Part of the Authors Travels in Europe, Asia, and Africa. With numerous engravings of Views, Maps, &c. Vol. 5, 4to. 4*l.* 14*s.* 6*d.* and a few copies on large paper, 8*l.* 8*s.*

A Tour through Sicily, in the year 1815. By George Russell, of his Majesty's Office of Works, illustrated by a Map and 18 interesting Plans and Views, 8vo. 1*l.* 1*s.*

The personal Narrative of M. de Humbolt's Travels to the Equinoctial Regions of the New Continent; during the Years 1799-1804. Translated by Ellen Maria Williams, under the immediate Inspection of the Author, vol. 4, 8vo. 18*s.*

A Statistical, Political, and Historical Account of the United States of America, from the Period of the first Colonization to the present Day, on a new Plan. By D. B. Warden, late Consul for the United States at Paris. With a new Map of the United States, and a Plan of the City of Washington, 3 vols. 8vo. 2*l.* 2*s.*

Foreign Literary Gazette.

America: United States.

Printing Press first established.

An article in our journal lately printed at the introduction of the press into South America, within these few years: it may not be amiss to notice that some time ago was published at Worcester, in the United States, a History of Printing in America, with biographical memoirs of the Printers, and description of the news-papers, &c. by Isaiah Thomas, 2 vols. 8vo., nearly 1000 pages. This work informs us, that the first printing press established in America, was by the Spaniards, at Mexico, about the year 1604: the first established in the United States, was at Cambridge in 1639. Without such authority it would hardly have been thought that the Spaniards might claim the precedency on this subject.

Denmark.

Paper, superior to common.

The haberdasher Ehrenhold, at Copenhagen, has discovered a method of making paper from the *Alga Marina;* which is reported to be superior in whiteness and strength to any paper prepared from linen rags.

The art of making paper from the *Alga Marina* is not a new invention; but, it is possible that in the improved state of Manufactures, and especially of Chemistry, a considerable improvement may be made on processes before imagined. There are several other plants, also, at present of no use from which very good paper might be made: but, we know not at what comparative expense.

Copenhagen: Botanic Garden.

Notwithstanding the disadvantages attending a northern climate, it is affirmed, that the Botanic Garden at Copenhagen, under the able direction of Professor Hornemann (who since 1801 fills the post of Principal) is nothing inferior to the establishments of the same kind which are at Goettingen, Vienna, Padua, Pavia, Turin, or Genoa: it even surpasses them in some things. It is particularly rich in Alpine plants, in plants from Norway, and Greenland. The herbal in the library of this garden was collected by the celebrated botanist Wall, predecessor of M. Hornemann; and is, beyond question, one of the most complete in Europe; it comprises more than 20,000 species, with their appellations and distinctions.

France.

The French critics, who of late, have been found somewhat hard to please, by the industrious class of labourers, called Novel-writers, have at length agreed to commend a certain "*Fanny Sandford,*" written by M. de Charlotte Kaufmann. The scene is laid in Great Britain, and *they say,* that the characters are well selected, and well preserved. They say too, that the progress of the action is natural, the interest is progressive; and the *dénouement,* is effected by those masterly touches of the pencil which strengthen the tone and vigour of the principal personages. The fair writer has intermingled a portion of criticism on the manners and customs of our countrymen; for which reason, principally, we have distinguished the work. We are afraid that the rule for wagering and betting, among us, affords but too much opportunity of severity to a foreigner, and too much scope to observers of human nature; such as writers of novels should be.

Notice on the diseases that might be expected among Cattle, from the heat and dryness of the last Summer: with methods of prevention and cure. By M. Heurtel. d'Aurbodal, Vetinerary Surgeon, Commissary for superintending the diseases of Animals, in the department of the *Pas de Calais.*

The Author of this Pamphlet was solicited by the Prefect of the Department, as directed by the Minister of the Interior, to give his opinion on a subject of unquestionable importance, and at once interesting to property and to humanity. We presume, that his labours cannot be made too public. This notice may afford valuable hints to other countries; and our own island is not so unlike the Department of the *Pas de Calais,* but what much useful and well adapted information might be

Q.

obtained from this contribution to the general stock of knowledge, by this intelligent writer.

GERMANY.
University Suppressed.

The University of Munster, in Westphalia, was suppressed by the Prussian Government, in July 1818. It was latterly attended by nearly three hundred Students. The salaries are continued to the Professors, till new nominations are made. The funds of the University amounted to 50,000 rix-dollars: these will be allotted to establishments for public instruction. The seminary for young persons training up for the church, the Gymnasium for education, and the school for instruction in Surgery, will be continued.

GREECE.
National Schools recommended.

M. Cleobulos, of Philippopoli, not long ago, published a letter in modern Greek, in which he describes to a friend, in a very clear and precise manner, the mechanism of the system of mutual instruction, (Bell and Lancaster's System.) He compares this method of instruction with that formerly practised; and shews how greatly the new mode excels the other, in point of economy, in point of progress made by the scholars, and further, in point of moral effects among the youth. M. Cleobulos, in consequence, desires his countrymen to adopt the new method: he concludes his letter by announcing a work on the subject; to which his compatriots look forward with great expectation.

National Schools patronized.

M. Rosetto Rosnovano, a young Nobleman of Moldavia, who not long ago travelled into England, taking France in his way, in order to inspect the various establishments for public education, and for beneficence, generally, and who has distinguished himself by his zeal and his intelligence in behalf of general instruction, has invited M. Cleobulos to Moldavia, to settle near him, for the purpose of establishing schools of mutual instruction in the Greek language. The invitation has been accepted; and M. Cleobulos is preparing to go into Moldavia, and to devote his talents to the undertaking.

HAITI.

Who would have thought some years ago, that we should have to register a Court Calendar from a Negro Empire in St. Domingo? Yet so it is: and it is not the least wonderful event of our times. We have now, therefore, to give a place to the *Almanach de la Republique d' Haiti*, for the year 1818. This *Almanach*, as the publisher thinks proper to term it, comprises the act of independence of the black nation, the correspondence between the Commissioners of France and the President of the Republic; the laws enacted by the Legislative Body, the revised Constitution of the State. Included are the names of the representatives of the various communes, who are in number thirty; those of the Senators, in number fifteen; and those of the ministers and functionaries of the State: to these are added, a view of the forces of this republic by sea and by land; with notice of two printing offices; one that of F. D. Chanlatte, the Author, or compiler of the volume, at Port-au-Prince; the other that of A. Laudun, at Aux Cayes.

Another work we cannot but notice; and it brings us acquainted with another printer at the Cape, P. Roux, to whom the world is obliged for an authentic copy of the *Code Henry*, or collection and digest of the laws established in the Black Sovereignty. It comprises the Civil Law, in 326 pages; the Commercial Law, in 47 pages; the Laws on Civil proceedings in 110 pages; the Criminal Laws, those for correction of offenders by the Police, in 75 pages; the Laws concerning Agriculture, in 32 pages; the Military Law, in 27 pages. The whole of these laws, formed into system, have been combined into one body, by an Edict of February, 20. 1812.

Constitution of the Republic of Haiti instituted December 27, 1806, and revised June 2, 1816, comprising 245 Articles; pp. 49.

It is impossible to avoid hinting, in consequence of these articles, at the advantages of an enlightened age: here are works produced by a negro population, a negro representation, a negro legislation, a negro Emperor, that would strike former ages with wonder. What would Justinian and

Ulpian have said, had they been told, that at some future time the negroes, whom they never thought of, but as slaves, should form a well-regulated and established Empire?—should compose a Code of Laws that should put to the blush their *Corpus Jus*—and *Corpus Juris*—and *Corpus Jurisprudentiæ*, by which the whole world was to be governed? Yet, this we behold: performed without any vast effort; and making no impression on the wondering powers of observers.

The principle of repetition and imitation accounts for all: the *Code Napoléon* preceded the *Code Henry*. The laws of Europe had their effect on the laws of the West Indies: the general diffusion of light, in the present day, illuminated by reflection the recesses of St. Domingo; the experience of the Old World, contributed instruction to the New World, and the orders, the ranks, the distribution of powers, the establishment of public officers, of public force, &c. &c. are the work of the Negroes of Africa, taught and trained, and arranged and influenced by the studies, the arguments, and the principles of Europeans.

ITALY.

Roman Jurisprudence: Fragments.

The Count of Bevilacqua, at Verona, has published a notice of the fragments of Roman Jurisprudence, discovered among the M. S. S. of the Library of the Chapter of Verona. These M. S. S. were thought to be lost, by Mabillon and Montfaucon, in the seventeenth century; but, since that time Maffei and the Canon Carinelli published a Catalogue of them. A part of these was carried into France in 1797; but restored in 1814.

We should not be surprized if the spoliations committed by the French, with the returns of the stolen goods, should give occasion to the publication of several catalogues of a like nature. It is not enough that the learned should know where certain documents and authorities once were: they desire information, also, where they now are; and where they may now be inspected.

Boccario, work of, reprinted.

The *Theseid* of Boccacio has lately been published at Milan, after a complete and correct manuscript. There existed before this only three editions; which were not only very rare, but very incomplete. The Editor is Sig. Giovanni Silvestri.

Adriatic Surveyed.

The Survey of the Adriatic Sea begun by Austrian and Neopolitan Officers, is continued with all possible perseverance. It is understood, that an English Officer, well experienced in Nautical Surveys, has a vessel under his command for the same purpose. We are certainly interested in this undertaking by our possession of Corfou.

PRUSSIA.

Animal Magnetism.

We have repeatedly reminded our readers that the practice of Animal Magnetism is still followed on the Continent; and that it is even studied as a science: the class of Physical Sciences of the Academy of Berlin, has proposed, by order of the Prussian Government, a prize of three hundred ducats, for the best Explication of the phenomena of Animal Magnetism, and of the experiments made down to the latest period, divesting them of the marvellous, which has hitherto been mingled with them. This is placing the subject, where it ought to be, in the hands of the intelligent; and as the Government has interfered in it, it may be hoped that considerable light may be obtained, and both opinion and practice be regulated by the sentiments of the judicious.

RUSSIA.

General state of Instruction.

It may be remarked of Russia, that the sciences, civil and military, are advancing with rapidity, and are giving a direction to the spirit of the nation, which at the same time, they contribute to develope, under the orders of the present Minister for public instruction. Nothing can be a more ready or more effectual means of promoting the civilization of the inferior classes of a people, than public schools, where instruction is communicated *gratis*. Within a few years more than two thousand such schools have been founded; several of which are conducted by young Russians, who had been sent into England, to acquire the methods of Bell and Lancaster. The generosity of the Emperor and the Empress mother towards these establishments is almost boundless; nor do they overlook any others having the same tendency. Their example is followed by many rich individuals. Count Shuwalow has endowed a Gymnasium, with a fund of 150,000 rubles. The counsellor of the mines, Demidow, has presented 100,000 rubles to the University of Moscow; and an equal sum to the two preparatory schools of Kiow and Tobolsk. To the preparatory school of Jaroslaw, with the Gymnasium, he has allotted another sum of the same amount, with considerable landed property. Count Schermetjew has given two millions and a half of rubles to found a hospital; besides a handsome present to the University of Moscow. The Great Chancellor Romanzow, has established on his estates, a great number of Lancastrian Schools: four churches for four different confessions of faith, are constructing at the same time, by his orders; and he also pays the expences of a voyage round the World, now in progress.

The Bible Societies, springing up in Russia, the Missionaries sent into various parts of that great Empire, receive not only protection, but, in various instances, considerable sums of money, as well from the Imperial family, as from individuals of exalted station. Even the Princes and the Chaus in the environs of Caucasus, of Georgia, and Mingrelia, contribute to the promotion of these objects: in which they are combined with the chiefs of the tribes which people Tartary and Siberia; nor must .we overlook the readiness of some among the Jews of these countries. At Irkutz, in Siberia, there are, as our readers know, schools for various purposes; as for Education, for teaching the Japanese language, —and for teaching navigation: there is also a library; which is, unquestionably, an institution, of which not many towns in Asia can boast.

Many of the tribes, especially the Tungooses and the Burates, some individuals of which have had opportunities of witnessing the astonishing effects of civilization, send their sons to these schools with great readiness. Most of the teachers have received their instructions at Irkutz.

Our pages witness a great number of similar facts; either old institutions invigo-rated, or new establishments patronized: or else, Collections added to those of public bodies; or assistance bestowed in various forms. It is not to be presumed, that every instance of generosity, reaches us in a shape of which we can avail ourselves; but, this is certain, speaking generally, that many tribes reputed still barbarous, no longer ago than the beginning of this century, now make rapid strides towards civilization; and that many circumstances concur, in a manner extremely favourable, to promote the object.

We lately hinted at the literary Institutions of the city of Odessa; we ought to distinguish the emulation that actuates the Greeks settled in this country, who retain a zealous regard to the interests of their original country. They have established by subscription among themselves, a school for the education of youth, that already enjoys a great reputation. They have appointed to it eight professors, at the head of whom are Messrs. Genadios and Macris, distinguished scholars. Besides the annual subscriptions of the Greeks to this school, there are four Insurance establishments, which are conducted by Greek merchants, who allot a certain portion of their annual profits to this object: the first allots as much as *thirty* per Cent. the second allots *twenty* per Cent. the third allots *seven* per Cent. and the fourth allots *five* per Cent.

These Institutions contributed to the school in the course of 1817, the sum of 53,892 rubles (say £10,000.) Several Merchants have contributed large sums for the purpose of establishing a Printing Office on a large scale, which may also essentially assist in propagating knowledge among the Greeks; they have in contemplation the establishment of a Hospital, to receive patients without distinction of country or creed.

The taste for theatrical entertainments, formerly so prevalent among the Greeks, is not wholly lost among their descendants: the Greeks of Odessa have represented the *Philoctetes* of Sophocles, translated into modern Greek, by M. Piccolo: who also has triumphed amid the applauses and the tears of his auditory, bestowed on his *Death of Demosthenes.* A ballet was given, founded on the modern incident of the *Souliots at Janina*, whither they were carried by the famous Ali Pacha, who had vanquished them by treachery.

Moscow: University.

That there is such a thing as reviving like a Phenix from the ashes of a former state, is strongly instanced in the present condition of the University of Moscow: concerning which, report affirms that the courses of public instruction have been, almost all, resumed with additional spirit and vigour. The destruction of this city by conflagration, had suspended these advantages: they are now favoured with additional patronage. The stipends of the Professors have been increased; the sphere of instruction has been enlarged; and the various branches have been better arranged. The students during 1817 might average two hundred. The Gymnasium annexed to the University, has also been restored to activity, and has equally been improved by additional studies, and a greater number of Professors.

SWITZERLAND.
Opposition to the Jesuits.

Lately has appeared at Paris, Opinions pronounced in the Great Council of Friburgh, January 16, 1817, and September 15, 1818, on the question of admitting the Jesuits; by M. Pierre de Landerset. Published by the friends of the Speaker: prefixed is a letter to M. le Comte Lanjuinais, Peer of France. This is an argumentative opposition to the admission of the newly revived Society of Jesus. The troubles to which the proposal for admitting these associates into Switzerland, gave occasion, are well known. The Jesuits prevailed, notwithstanding the temper, the courage, and the talent of this worthy magistrate. They have made various attempts to insinuate themselves in other countries; and they will succeed by fraud if not by force. Our opinion on the consequences, is well known.

TURKEY.

It is not often that we can treat our readers with literary intelligence from the banks of the Bosphorus: but the present article shews that even the Turkish press can produce works of consequence. The title is (in Turkish) *El Okeanus al-hassit*

fi terd schumetil-hamus al-mupit, &c. The Universal Ocean, or the ocean that includes every thing. Three large volumes in folio; printed at Scutan, near Constantinople, in 1817. Price at Constantinople 175 piasters.

The *Kamus* is the most complete Vocabulary of the Arabic language, that exists. The original Arabic occupied the presses at Calcutta, while this translation of it into the Turkish language was proceeding at Constantinople, under the direction of the learned *Abul-Kemel-Es-Seid-Ahmed-Assassin*, the same who translated and published at Constantinople in 1802 the *Burham Kalii*, or Persian Vocabulary.

The first volume comprises pages 943; the second 939; the third 973, of close printing, without any whites. The first was completed at the press in 1815, the second in 1816, the third in the Month of Moharren, in the year of the Hegira (or flight of Mahomet from Mecca) 1233. Answering to the Christian A. D. 1817. A very short time, certainly, in which to execute so great a work; and much to the credit of the presses at Scutari.

Che Gatherer.
No. XXVII.

"I am but a gatherer, and dealer in other men's stuff."

The Midnight Sun.

At Enontekis in Lapland, during the space of three weeks in every year, the minister informed Dr. Clarke, that he is able to light his pipe at midnight with a common burning glass; and, when clouds do not intervene, he may continue this practice for a longer time: but the atmosphere becomes clouded as the season advances. From the church, near his house, it is visible above the horizon at midnight, during seven weeks in each year; but the pleasure of this long day is dearly purchased by an almost uninterrupted night for the rest of the year; a continual winter in which it is difficult to dispense with the use of candles, during the space of three hours in each day.

Lapland Sermons.

The church was crowded, and even the gallery full: many of the wild nomade Laplanders being present in their strange dresses. The sermon was an extemporaneous harangue, but delivered in a tone so elevated, that the worthy pastor seemed to labour as if he would burst a blood-vessel. He continued exerting his lungs in this manner for one hour and twenty minutes, as if his audience had been stationed at the top of a distant mountain. Afterwards, he was so hoarse, he could hardly articulate another syllable. One would have thought it impossible to doze during a discourse that made our ears ring; yet some of the Lapps were fast asleep; and would have *snored*, but that a sexton, habited like themselves, walked about with a long and stout pole, with which he continued to strike the floor; and if this did not rouse them, he drove it forcibly against their ribs, or suffered it to fall with all its weight upon their sculls. (Clarke's Travels, Sect. III. Part I. p. 393.)

Charles I. and Lord Falkland.

One of the Lansdowne MSS. now deposited in the British Museum records the following singular affair respecting the unfortunate Charles I., and the accomplished Lord Falkland, who was slain in a skirmish in which he unnecessarily engaged, the day before the first battle of Newberry:—About this time there befel the King an accident, which, though a trifle in itself, and that no weight is to be laid upon any thing in nature; yet since the best authors, both ancient and modern, have not thought it below the majesty of history to mention the like, it may be the more excusable to take notice of. The King being at Oxford during the Civil Wars, went one day to see the public Library, where he was shewn, among other books, a Virgil, nobly printed and exquisitely bound. The Lord Falkland, to divert the King, would have his Majesty make a trial of his fortune by the *Sortes Virgilianæ,* which every body knows was an usual kind of augury some ages past. Whereupon the King opened the book; the period which happened to come

up was that part of Dido's imprecation to-Æneas, which Mr. Dryden translates thus ;—

Yet let a race untam'd, and haughty foes,
His peaceful eutrance with dire arms oppose;
Oppress'd with numbers in th' unequal field,
His men discouraged and himself expell'd,
Let him for succour sue from place to place,
Torn from his subjects, and his sons embrace,
First let him see his friends in battle slain,
And their untimely fate lament in vain ;
And when at length the cruel war shall cease,
On hard conditious may he buy his peace. ⎫
Nor let him then enjoy supreme command, ⎬
But fall untimely by some hostile hand, ⎭
And lie unburied on the barren sand.
                          Æneid, B. iv. l. 88.

It is said, King Charles seemed concerned at this accident, and that Lord Falkland observing it, would likewise try his own fortune in the same manner, hoping he might fall upon some passage that could have no relation to his case, and thereby divert the King's thoughts from any impression the other might have upon him. But the place that Falkland stumbled upon, was yet more suited to his destiny than the other had been to the King's; being the following expressions of *Evander* upon the untimely death of his son *Pallas,* as they are translated by the same hand :—

O Pallas ! thou hast fail'd thy plighted word
To fight with caution, not to tempt the sword:
I warned thee, but in vain; for well I knew
What perils youthful ardour would pursue,
That boiling blood would carry thee too far!
Young as thou wert in dangers—raw in war
O curst essay in arms,—disastrous doom,—
Prelude of bloody fields and fights to come.
                          Ibid. B. xi. l. 230.

Literary Abstraction.

Budæus one of the most learned men of the sixteenth century was engaged in deep study in his library, when his servant came running to him in a great fright, to tell him the house was on fire. " Go," said he, with perfect calmness, and hardly raising his eyes from his book, " and inform your mistress; 'tis her concern, you know I never interfere in domestic matters."

Americans and Frenchmen.

Dr. Franklin, while American Ambassador at Paris, undertook to refute a prevalent theory of American inferiority of talent from their size. He invited six of his own countrymen and six Frenchmen to dinner. As was expected, the Frenchmen, who were all profound philosophers, began to inquire into the causes of the declension of nature, vegetable, animal, and moral, in America. One said, the reason why man in particular became feeble in body and mind, was owing to the climate being too hot; another insisted that it arose from the climate being too cold; a third assigned, as the efficient cause, the too great quantity of rain; a fourth attributed the deficiency to too much drought; while the two last demonstrated that both man and beast were dwarfed in America, from a want of food in the country. Each Gallic disputant maintained his own side of the question with characteristic volubility for a length of time; when at last they all referred to Franklin for a philosophical solution of the cause, why all American creatures are so inferior to Europeans in size and strength? The Doctor very gravely desired his six countrymen to stand up, side by side; which they did, and exhibited a goodly spectacle; for they were all stout, well-proportioned, tall, handsome men: the half dozen Frenchmen were then requested to stand up, side by side; they did so, and presented a ludicrous contrast to the degenerate Americans: for they were all little, lank, yellow, shrivelled personages. They peeped up at their opposite neighbours, and were silent, though not satisfied. So says Mr. Bristed, but we must own that the prevalent form and tint of the Americans do not appear to us to be entitled to all the terms of admiration which he bestows on them. The American word *lengthy* describes the former, and the English term *sallow* the latter. Cobbet says, that a fresh-coloured cheek is a sure sign in America of an Englishman newly imported.

Loose Thoughts.

Mrs. Macaulay having published, what she called loose thoughts, Mr. Garrick was asked if he did not think it a strange title for a lady to choose? "By no means," replied he, "the sooner a woman gets rid of such thoughts the better."

Maundy Thursday.

On this day, a singular religious ceremony is celebrated by the Court at Vienna, which is thus related by Dr. Bright, in his travels. It is known in German Catholic countries by the name of the *Fusswaschung*, or the "washing of the feet." The large saloon, in which public court entertainments are given, was fitted up for the purpose; elevated benches and galleries were constructed round the room for the reception of the court and strangers; and in the area, upon two platforms, tables were spread, at one of which sat 12 men, and at the other 12 women. They had been selected from the oldest and most deserving paupers, and were suitably clothed in black, with handkerchiefs and square collars of white muslin, and girdles round their waists.

The emperor and empress with the archdukes and archduchesses, Leopoldine and Clementine, and their suites, having all previously attended mass in the Royal Chapel, entered and approached the table to the sound of solemn music. The Hungarian Guard followed in their most splendid uniform, with their leopard-skin jackets falling from their shoulders, and bearing trays of different meats, which the emperor, empress, archdukes and attendants, placed on the table, in three successive courses, before the poor men and women, who tasted a little, drank each a glass of wine, and answered a few questions put to them by their sovereigns. The tables were then removed, and the empress and her daughters, the archduchesses, dressed in black, with pages bearing their trains, approached. Silver bowls were placed beneath the bare feet of the aged women. The grand chamberlain, in a humble posture, poured water upon the feet of each in succession, from a golden urn, and the empress wiped them with a fine napkin she held in her hand. The emperor performed the same ceremony on the feet of the men, and the rite concluded amidst the sounds of sacred music.

Steam Baths.

There is not a village, nor indeed a dwelling in Lapland without a steam-bath; in which the inhabitants of both sexes assemble together in a state of perfect nudity, for the purpose of bathing, at least once every week; and oftener, if any illness occur among them. These steam-baths are all alike: they consist of a small hut, containing a furnace for heating stones rèd hot, upon which boiling water is thrown; and a kind of shelf, with a ladder conducting to it, upon which the bathers extend themselves in a degree of temperature, such as the natives of southern countries could not endure for an instant: here they have their bodies rubbed with birch boughs dipped in hot water; an office which is always performed by the females of each family, and generally by the younger females. It is to these baths, and to the natural cleanliness and temperate habits of the people, that the uninterrupted health they enjoy, may be ascribed.

School Squabbles.

At a public institution there was a matron named Bell, and another, whose severity and general manners obtained her among the Directors of the Charity the appellation of the Dragon. One day a violent squabble was heard in the room adjoining to that in which the Directors were assembled, and one of them was induced to put his head out to see what was the cause of the uproar. He did so, and instantly returned to his seat. " What was all that noise about, Sir, did you enquire?" " There may be a little more yet," replied Mr. S. " but you must not be alarmed, 'tis only *Bel and Dragon!*"

Vanity Reproved.

After one of Dr. Johnson's publications, James Boswell his Biographer, on the first of the ensuing month, repaired, according to custom to the lodgings of his idol, with the several magazines of the day, in order to read the strictures which were given on his performance. After perusing two or three criticisms, which were not of the most civil kind, the petulence of the Doctor got the better of his good sense, and he exclaimed peevishly, " Enough, enough, sir, now you have taken infinite pains to bring an account of what is thought of me individually; give me leave to ask what you imagine the world says of you and me conjointly," " Upon my

word, Doctor, I cannot pretend to say," answered Jemmy, " Why then I'll tell you," continued the Doctor, " They say that I am a mad dog, sir, and that you are the tin cannister tied to my tail." *(Davis's Olio.)*

HINTS, PLANS, and PROCEEDINGS
OF
Benevolence.

————————*Homo sum:*
Humanum nihil a me alienum puto.

CINGALESE PRIESTS.

Some interesting particulars of two Budhist Priests have lately been published by *Dr. Adam Clarke*, in a letter to the Committee of the *Wesleyan Foreign Missions.* They came from Ceylon, with Sir Alexr. Johnson, bringing with them only their sacerdotal robes, their books, and seven rupees (about 14s. english): the expence of their board and clothing is to be paid from the Missionary fund; but Dr. Clarke has undertaken to educate them, gratuitously. When they have acquired a sufficient knowledge of the principles of the Christian religion, they are to be sent back to Ceylon, to disseminate the gospel among their heathen brethren. The following are extracts from Dr. Clarke's letter.

The two Cingalese Priests *Munhi Rat Hana* and *Dherma Rama*, are cousins german; the first 27, the latter 25 years of age. They are meek, gentle, and submissive; very diligent in their studies, and have an insatiable thirst for knowledge, and particularly *religious knowledge.* They continue to improve in their writing, and will soon write a very elegant hand; their profiting in this is surprising, as they had never done any thing in this way before; their own writing gave them no advantage here, as that is a mere species of engraving with a steel point on the talipot leaf, which is the substance used instead of paper. They improve also both in reading and speaking English. Nothing but a thorough course of theological and philosophical

English reading, can ultimately conquer and remove all the false notions and deep-rooted prejudices relative to God and nature, found in that Priesthood. I say deep-rooted, because with false theology and philosophy they have had their minds imbued from their earliest infancy. Munhi Rat Hanna and Dherma Rama entered the temple when they were about five years of age, and before they could arrive at their high order in the Priesthood were obliged to learn several languages, not only the Cingalese in its purity, but also the Pali, Patois-Portuguese, Tamul, and Sanscrit; and to commit to memory *many thousands* of *Sloeas*, or verses, containing their Theology, Physic, Metaphysics, Traditions, History, Mantrass or Incantations, and their most curiously involved doctrine of the Metempsychosis, or Transmigration of Souls. From these they have derived all their principles of morality, theology, medicine, philosophy, and political economy. Till now they have had no opportunity of knowing better; these false principles had undisturbed empire in their minds. In a word, all their thoughts, ideas, and moral feelings were cast in this mould. They now see they were wrong in *many* things, and strongly suspect they were wrong in *all*. They wish for instruction; they devour it with the keenest appetite, and long, ardently long, to have their minds stored with nothing but what is *true* and *useful*. Against Christianity, they have not, as far as I am able to judge, one remaining prejudice; but they find it difficult to perceive the suitableness of many things, while they admit of their general truth. In a word, they want to perceive and comprehend the reasons of those things; and they have not, as yet, English sufficient to understand those arguments which I know would at once set their minds at rest on such points.

These men cannot be treated as *common heathens:* they are both *philosophers*, men of profound erudition in their way; with as far as I can judge, a powerful commanding eloquence. They are deeply read in the most speculative, most refined and purest ethics of the Brahman and Budhoo systems. In these respects, their acquirements are immense. I have myself read the *Oupnek'hat*, and some other works of this kind, and well knowing the subtle

and specious reasons which both these systems can bring forth in behalf of their ethics and philosophy, I do not a little wonder at the subjection of these men's minds to the general truth of the gospel.

They are both pretty nearly masters of the Cingalese Catechism; I mean Mr. T. Wood's Catechism, which has been translated into Cingalese, and to no part of this do I find them making any serious objection: indeed I have made it a maxim in their education, that "Christianity is indubitably true, comes immediately from God, and cannot be successfully controverted." This assumption I found it absolutely necessary to adopt from the beginning: on this I founded another, not less necessary to my difficult work, viz. that "all other systems of religion are false or forged; and on them no man can rely, but at the utter risk of his salvation." I told them, however, that I was at any time willing to enter into the *proofs* and *demonstrations* of these points, as soon as they were capable of comprehending the argument. Thus I became necessarily pledged to prove much, and satisfy many a scruple: but in this I found no other difficulty than their imperfect knowledge of English to comprehend the requisite argumentation. They never carp or cavil, nor start a difficulty that is not *serious* and *conscientious*. They pray often, and are very devout in prayer: and I am sure they have now, no object of adoration in heaven or earth but the true God; and his favour they seek through the only Mediator. Here, much is gained. The Budhoo system has, properly speaking, no *prayer:* because in fact it has no *God*. The decent regulation of the life, and the subjugation of the passions by a strong ascetic discipline, is their law of righteousness: and the sum of their religion. Under this kind of discipline these men were brought up from their infancy; and have, I believe, never been guilty of any acts of immorality. In consequence of this, I cannot expect them to mourn on account of sins which they have never committed. Swearing, lying, drunkenness, theft, uncleanness, &c. they have in the utmost abhorrence. They have the highest opinion of our *Decalogue*, and make it most conscientiously their rule of conduct.

Of the sincerity and purity of these men's motives, I have the most satisfactory evidence: they have sacrificed much in order to come and seek the Christian's God in a Christian land. They have lost, for ever lost, their temple and its revenues; and that high honour and reverence which they had, as high-priests, and highly learned among the highest orders, among their countrymen: and although they doubtless have suffered many buffettings on this account, yet there is not the most distant wish remaining to trace back their steps.

Dherma Rama is a young man of very high integrity, of an ardent and strong mind, wishing to sift every thing to the bottom; and never to take a *stand* any where till he is fully satisfied the ground will bear him. What he gets he keeps.

Munhi Ret'hana has a fine mind; is truly spiritual, meek, and affectionate: seeks God, I believe with his whole heart; and enjoys many consolations from his Spirit. All that are acquainted with them, esteem Dherma, and love Munhi.

They lately saw, for the first times in their lives, what they had often heard of, but could hardly credit; *water in a solid form.* I wrapped them well up, and took them out to the pond, about sixty or seventy yards from the house, that they might see this (to them) strange phenomenon. It had frozen keenly in the night; and they were struck with astonishment, to see that the water had become *solid,* and to see my nephew skaiting upon it. They said, "it will be of no use to tell this either to the Cingalese or Candians, for they can never believe it." They seem to view this as a farther evidence of the being of a God. My large copper sun dial was covered over with hoar frost, that had shot into crystallizations, representing the most beautiful foliage. At this they were beyond measure astonished; and after admiring it for some time, Dherma Rama took out his pencil, and with the blunt end, wrote on the icy incrustation, the following words (in Cingalese): *These leaves have been made by the Supreme God.*

Before I conclude, I will mention another circumstance relative to our Priests, which though apparently simple in itself, has led to some important results. It is well known that in the Budhoo and indeed Brahminical system of philosophy, the earth is considered to be a *vastly extended plain,* ever at rest, and immoveable: founded on an equal extent of *water,* and these upon *air,* which is itself either infinite, or founded on nothing! over this prejudice, which has more serious consequences than can well be imagined, our poor priests could neither *leap* nor *climb.* A simple circumstance the other day, has quite dissolved the fabric, and nearly annihilated this Cingalese world. While delivering a lecture on *Magnetism* to some young friends, and describing the nature, properties, and action of the magnetic fluid, and illustrating the doctrines laid down by experiments, the priests were greatly delighted: a new world seemed literally to be opened to their view. They understand some little of our doctrine of *gravitation,* by which we endeavour to explain so many *phenomena.* The flying of the steel filings to the magnet, and their adhering in an erect posture, surprised and confounded them. The course of the magnetic fluid, together with the *attractive* and *repulsive* influence of the poles of the same magnet, did not less surprise them; but when I set the *spinner* in very quick motion, and presented it to the end of a magnetized steel bar, by which it was instantly attracted, because suspended, and turned round its own axis with great velocity; they were fixed with wonder. To see such a substance revolving with such velocity, literally *unsupported,* and *hanging upon nothing,* Dherma Rama exclaimed, "I now believe what I never could before or comprehend: I see, I see that the earth is round; that it continues to turn round, and that it stands upon nothing!" I had at that time said nothing on the subject but his good sense, from the principles before him, led him to form the analogy, and make the deduction. This was to them both, another proof of the being and government of an all-wise and all-powerful God.

ANIMAL MAGNETISM.

The following communications to the "Archives of Animal Magnetism" a journal published in Germany, will shew to our readers, to what length, the Theorists of that country are capable of extending their reveries.

A woman was dying of a consumption, and the necessary manipulation for magnetising her was undertaken by her husband; but, after a trial of 24 days, no good effects resulted from it, in the way of expediting the cure, or arresting the disorder. Several strange phenomena, however, occurred during the experiment, in which the husband was equally concerned as the patient. The first effects of the *Medicine*, if it can be so called, was to render the woman more cheerful; but she soon became more fretful and peevish than before, and her husband, from being anxious, that she should recover, became suddenly the reverse, and confessed to the doctor, that he had lost the lively desire he had felt for her recovery, before he began to magnetise her. In short a *mutual dislike* was produced between man and wife, and the husband was ordered to give up the manipulation. About a week afterwards, the death of the patient was looked for every moment; but, at this time, Dr. Nasse observed a most singular tenaciousness of life, for the poor woman appeared *as if she could not die*. At one time pale, and almost breathless, she revived at another, opened her eyes, looked up, breathed strongly, seemed more lively and animated, and again sunk. These singular alternations were discovered, to depend upon the entrance and departure of her husband; and so clearly were they connected, that he insisted upon again renewing the magnetical operations. But the doctor, for what reason does not appear, would not permit this; but ordered the husband, the next time he left the chamber, to remain long enough away, as to allow his wife to terminate her sufferings by dying in peace!

OLD MAN OF THE MOUNTAIN.

Of this Assassin Chief, so well known in the history of the Crusades, some curious particulars are given in Marco Polo's Travels, which we shall quote, for the entertainment of our readers, from Mr. Marsden's recent translation of this very interesting, and, in many respects, authentic narrative.

He was named Alo-eddin, and his religion was that of Mahomet. In a beautiful valley, inclosed between two lofty mountains, he had formed a luxurious garden, stored with every delicious fruit and every fragrant shrub that could be procured. Palaces of various sizes and forms were erected in different parts of the grounds, ornamented with works in gold, with paintings, and with furniture of rich silks. By means of small conduits contrived in these buildings, streams of wine, milk, honey, and some of pure water were seen to flow in every direction. The inhabitants of these places were elegant and beautiful damsels, accomplished in the arts of singing, playing upon all sorts of musical instruments, dancing, and especially those of dalliance and amorous allurement. Clothed in rich dresses they were seen continually sporting and amusing themselves in the garden and pavilions; their female guardians being confined within doors, and never suffered to appear. The object which the chief had in view in forming "a garden of this fascinating kind, was this:" that Mahomet having promised to those who should obey his will the enjoyments of paradise, where every species of sensual gratification should be found, in the society of beautiful nymphs, he was desirous of its being understood by his followers, that he was also a prophet and the compeer of Mahomet, and had the power of admitting to paradise such as he should choose or favour. That none without his licence might find their way into this delicious valley, he caused a strong and inexpugrable castle to be erected at the opening of it; through which the entry was 'by a' secret passage. At his court, likewise, this chief entertained a number of youths, from the age of twelve to twenty years, selected from the inhabitants of the surrounding mountains, who shewed a disposition for martial exercises, and appeared to possess the quality of daring courage. To them he was in the daily practice of discoursing on the subject of the paradise announced by the prophet, and of his own power of granting admission; and at certain times he caused draughts of a soporific nature to be administered to ten or a dozen of the youths; and when half dead with sleep, he had them conveyed to the several apartments of the palaces in the garden. Upon awakening from this state of lethargy, their senses were struck with all the delightful objects that have been described, and each perceived himself surrounded by lovely damsels, singing, playing, and attracting his regards by the most fascinating caresses; serving him also with delicate viands and exquisite wines; until intoxicated with excess of enjoyment, amidst actual rivulets of milk and wine, he believed himself assuredly in paradise, and felt an unwillingness to relinquish its delights. When four or five days had thus been passed, they were thrown once more into a state of somnolency, and carried out of the garden. Upon their being introduced to his presence, and questioned by him as to where they had been;, their answer was, "in paradise, through the favour of your highness:" and then before the whole court, who listened to them with eager curiosity and astonishment, they gave a circumstantial account of the scenes to which they had been witnesses. The chief thereupon addressing them, said: "we have the assurances of our Prophet that he who defends his lord shall inherit paradise, and if you shew yourselves devoted to the obedience of my orders, that happy lot awaits you." Animated to enthusiasm by words of this nature, all deemed themselves happy to receive the commands of their master, and were forward to die in his service.

Poetry.

LINES,

Written on seeing a Model in the possession of J. Britton, Esq. from the Monumental

Bust of Shakspeare,

IN STRATFORD CHURCH.

By H. Neele.

HIS was the master spirit;—at his spells
The heart gave up its secrets: like the mount
Of Horeb, smitten by the Prophet's rod;
Its hidden springs gushed forth. Time, that
    grey rock
On whose bleak sides the fame of meaner bards
Is dashed to ruin, was the pedestal
On which his Genius rose; and, rooted there,
Stands like a mighty statue reared so high
Above the clouds, and changes of the world,
That Heaven's unshorn and unimpeded beams
Have round its awful brows a glory shed

Immortal as their own. Like those fair birds
Of glittering plumage whose heaven-pointing
    pinions
Beam light on that dim world they leave be-
    hind,
And while they spurn, adorn it (*); so
His "dainty spirit," while it soared above
This dull, gross compound, scattered as it flew
Treasures of light and loveliness.

   . . . . And these
Were "gentle SHAKSPEARE's" features; this
    the eye
Whence Earth's least earthly mind looked
    out, and flashed
Amazement on the nations; this the brow
Where lofty thought majestically brooded,
Seated as on a throne; and these the lips
That warbled music stolen from heaven's
    own choir
When Seraph-harps rang sweetest. But I
    tempt
A theme too high, and mount like Icarus,
On wings that melt before the blaze they
    worship.
Alas! my hand is weak, my lyre is wild!
Else should the eye, whose wondering gaze is
    fixed
Upon this *breathing bust*, awaken strains
Lofty as those the glance of Phœbus struck
From Memnon's ruined statue: the rapt soul
Should breathe in numbers, and in dulcet notes
"Discourse most eloquent music"

THE ROSE.

[*From Metastasio*]

O lovely rose, whose dewy leaflets blowing,
    Are tended by the genial breath of morn,
And o'er whose breast, the early breezes borne,
Have left in crimson hue thy garments glowing.

The same kind hand that watches now thy
    growing,
    Shall lead thee soon a purer scene t' adorn,
    Where freed for ever from the galling thorn,
Thou'lt bloom—alone thy fairer features showing.

* In some parts of America, it is said, there are birds which, when on the wing, and at night, emit so surprising a brightness, that it is no mean substitute for the light of day. Among the whimsical speculations of Fontenelle, is one, that in the Planet Mars, the want of a Moon may be compensated by a multiplicity of these luminous aeronauts.

Secure in loveliness that never dies——
  Nor snow, nor hail, nor warring winds are there,
Nor changing seasons, nor inclement skies ;
  But blooming safe beneath a kinder care,
Thou shalt in calm serenity arise,
  For ever fragrant, and for ever fair.

EPITAPH ON AN INFANT.

Innocens et perbeatus
  More florum decidi ;
Nil, Viator, fle sepultum
  Flente sum beatior.

Translated.

While innocent and therefore blest
Like dying flowers I sank to rest ;
Then weep not, for in peace I sleep
And happier am than you that weep !

                  T. G.

SATIRES IN INDIA.

(Concluded from p. 273.)

VIRGINIA sees a spark in ev'ry swain,
Sighs oft for Marriage, and may sigh in vain ;
The hated name of *Miss*—would still remove,
And throws dear looks in languishment of love !
And yet when first the damsel's charms appear'd,
To what a height her Marriage-views were rear'd,
'Twas then, indeed—' the wonder of her life,
' How paltry Subalterns could keep a wife !
' It seem'd quite strange, that foolish girls could bend
' Their thoughts so vilely low,—and condescend
' To marry, where perhaps a *Palankeen*,
' Or *Buggy* at the best, might chance be seen.
These thoughts of Grandeur lasted for a year :
No suitor came—no husband would appear.
And now alas ! when year on year creeps by,
And still VIRGINIA breathes th' unechoed sigh,
Fain would the Fair her former views forget,
And condescend to—*catch at a Cadet* !

PRECEDENCE is SUPERBA's dear delight,
Her busy thought by day—her dream by night ;
But see Superba plung'd in saddest tears !
Is fair Superba ill ?—nay cease your fears ;
The Lady only weeps, and sobs to see,
HONORIA married to a rich C. B. ;
And,—death to think !—dire incident of woe !
' *That thing* Honoria ! takes precedence now !'

SENESSA—still as blooming damsel gay,
Intent to catch each Fashion of the day,

Has scarce a thought, beyond some newer dress,
Or varied robe her dear lov'd form to bless :
How happy fly her busy morning-hours,
At *Smith's*—*Balmanno's*—*William's* fairy bowers,
Each Europe-letter that arrives, displays
Some novel Fashion's pattern, and its praise :
No matter then—the season, be it hot,
The mode, unsuiting to our sultry spot,
Still in that dress, she decks her fainting frame !
French hats and *Brussels* now her fancy claim.

And now young Beauty's style attracts her care ;
Its sylphid dress, that floats upon the air ;
Its arms of snowy white, to view display'd,
Its shape in *Houris'* loveliness betray'd ;
SENESSA sees—and thinks her form might prove,
Alike the semblance of aerial love !
She gives to view her long and shrivell'd arms,
Her straiten'd robe each gazer's eye alarms ;
And when thus disen'd forth, to woo the sight,
What is Senessa then ? a worse than fright !

OLIVIA is so delicate, her sigh
Betrays the helplessness of infancy ;
So lifeless, and alas ! her nerves so weak,
She scarcely can respire ! to hear her speak,
You'd think it is the whisper of some breeze
Wooing the trembling foliage of the trees ;
The punkah is too much,—then heat o'erpowers.
' Oh vile vile hookah ! pest of social hours !'
How languishing she looks : can such a form
Withstand the least rough shock of earthly
    storm ?
And yet Olivia hath a babe each year,—
Each day, unseen—a bottle of *strong beer* !

METISSA too is mild ; 'mid circling friends,
The softest languor ev'ry look attends ;
No angry glance e'er glistens from her eye ;
No inward passions can her words imply.
One fatal day, she dream'd no step was near,
No guest at hand, to lend a list'ning ear.
Ah me ! she gave a loose to angry tongue
A wild alarum in her chamber rung !
Her *Ayah* she chided, scolded, beat, abused,
And frantic ire her *angel-face* suffused.
Good heav'ns !—what language ! if Metissa
    guess'd
One half the meaning, her abuse express'd
She'd never dare an Eastern term again ;
But shrink in shame, and consciousness of pain !

LAURA is lovely, as the breathing morn,
While yet the sun's young tints the East adorn.
Image of sweetest delicacy's flower,
At ev'ry period—save the Tiffin-hour ;

And why not then?—nay prythee, cease to ask
For how unpleasing is the poet's task,
To paint, at such an hour, a pouting lip,
Where late the fancy seem'd but Love to sip,
Now, all besmear'd with Curry—hideous fright!
We turn disgusted from th' unseemly sight.

Where is the eye, so blind to ev'ry charm,
That hath not gaz'd on ARAMANTHA'S arm?
Who hath not said?—'May such an arm as this
'Wreathe round my form, in some lone hour of
    bliss!'
—And yet that charm can lose its power to please,
Its fairness vanish,—and its beauty cease,
When, half dismay'd, within her grasp, we see
The Hookah's monstrous snake held fearlessly.
That Type of eastern Luxury's excess,—
Emblem of aught, but female Loveliness.

When proud CECILIA condescends to play,
What seraph sounds allure the soul away:
How sweet, to catch the magic of her song,
While o'er her seat, the breathless listners throng!
But then alas! how sad to view the maid,
In all the consciousness of *Pride* arrayed
Which, 'mid its affectation, seems to say,
' Thus for applause, my sanction'd due, I play.'
Unwise CECILIA learn the better part—
To please the Ear, and yet secure the Heart.
Would you for ever charm the fleeting hour,
Prove but the wish to please, nor boast the
    power.]

Ah me!—if women knew their faultless worth;
When modest grace can draw each beauty forth;
When unaffected softness seems to bless,
And brightens still the charm of loveliness:
When Pride repels not, and no lure betrays;
But unreserve to all its ease conveys!
Silenc'd were then the Satirist's complaint;
Fled were the faults, that social pleasure taint.
The heartless Poet,—deaf to Beauty's sigh,
Durst not to Woman Character deny;
And Bards, too full of heart in ev'ry theme,
In ev'ry Fair would realise their dream!

National Register:

FOREIGN.
AMERICA: BRITISH.
Colony on a Spartan Plan.

The following curious notice is extracted from a Quebec paper.

Interesting to Thousands!—Colony of
Brotherly Union.

It is in agitation to found a Colony upon the ancient Spartan plan, sanctioned by Apostolical usage, of living in common, and enjoying a community of goods. In this establishment, as each will labour for all, and all for each, personal property will be unknown—and all lust of private gain, engendered by an imperfect organization of Society, will be sacrificed at the shrine of public felicity.

To carry this project into execution, a fertile tract of land, consisting of some thousands of acres, is on the point of being purchased and surveyed.

Husbandmen and artisans of every sort are invited to this Colonization. We tender the right hand of fellowship, to the honest and industrious of every description of people, whatever be their religious or political faith.

Want of funds will not furnish a reason for excluding any Colonist; and, on the other hand, it will be a fundamental law of this establishment, that whatever property may be, by adventurers, put into the common stock, will be considered as a loan, and refunded to them or their assignees on demand.

The Colony will be situated within the bounds of Lower Canada, and under the protection and controul of His Majesty's Government.

All persons who are willing to embark in this enterprise, are requested to address themselves to the Subscribers personally or by letter. They will specify their country, age, profession, number of children (if married) property, &c.

No letter will be received but from Principals, nor unless *post paid.*—Every letter to bear on its superscription the words, ' Colony of Brotherly Union.'

As soon as a sufficient number of applicants shall have enrolled their names, notice will be given by public advertisement to convene and digest a code of laws and regulations for the establishment.
    S. CLEVELAND BLYTH.

St. Constant, Lower Canada,
    Dec. 3. 1818.

The several Gentlemen who conduct the Public Papers printed in these Provinces, and the neighbouring States of America, are respectfully requested to give the above one insertion *pro bono publico.*

AMERICA: UNITED STATES.
Welsh Indians.

Mr. Owen Williams, a Welshman, residing near Baltimore, in the United

States, has lately given the following account of some Welsh Settlers in America, in a letter to the Editor of the New Times.

Sir—I am not a little surprised at the historical uncertainty expressed concerning the locality of a Welsh Settlement in North America.

The people in question are as well known to the inhabitants of the Western Continent, as the Welsh people are to the European world. During a residence of forty years in different parts of the United States, I have had dealings with some hundreds of them; and, in the year 1817, visited their settlements on the Madwga, or, as vulgarly called, the Paduca River, with one of the natives, a brave and intelligent man of the name of Austin Nerthog. These Indians, composed of two tribes, the Bridonee and the Madogee Indians, have their settlements on two promontories, called Kernan in latitude about 40 degrees north, and about 80 degrees longitude west. They are generally a tall and powerful people, of fair complexion, and of amiable manners; they have the use of letters, and are in possession of numerous manuscripts respecting their ancestors of this island, whom they call Brydon.

The language they speak is Welsh, much purer than that of the principality of Wales, as it is free from anglicisms: their religion is Christianity, deeply blended with Druidism: and their almost unvaried amusement consist of music and versification.

On my first acquaintance with these friendly people, which was above 30 years ago, I could hardly believe the individuals I conversed with. on account of these settlers having taken up a position so distant from the coast; to this they gave me the following answer, and which turns out to be the fact, that they first settled on the eastern coast at Llechein, now Lexington, and at other stations, and afterwards retired to their present settlements when the country became disturbed by a succession of invaders from the old world.

I trust, Sir, you will excuse the shortness and imperfection of this letter, as I am a plain man of business, and rather hurried, having to sail for America tomorrow. I must beg leave to add, that should any of my fellow-countrymen be inclined to visit the Welsh settlers at Kernan, it will give me great pleasure to assist them with every minute direction, if they will give a call on your obliged Servant as undersigned.

Fur merchant (a Native of Cardiganshire, S. Wales.) Fell's-point, near Baltimore, United States.

London, Feb. 21, 1819.

AUSTRIA.

Works of Art not to be Exported.

The exportation of paintings, statues, antiques, collections of coins and prints, rare manuscripts, first editions, and in general all articles of literature or the arts, which tend to the ornaments of a state, is prohibited throughout the whole Austrian empire, upon pain of confiscation, or a fine of double the value, with the exception of the works of the living artists.

Seduction.—Justice.

At a time when the question runs high whether or not our penal laws ought to be enforced to their utmost severity, we cannot refrain from giving the following anecdote of the Emperor of Austria, as contained in a recent letter from Vienna:—Some days before the Emperor's departure for Italy, he had an opportunity of displaying his love of justice, and full determination that the laws shall have their free course in all circumstances, and whatever may be the rank of the individual incurring their severity. A great Lord, enamoured of a young person. daughter of a respectable family, though of ordinary rank, seduced her, under a written promise of marriage, which he had no intention of fulfilling. The unfortunate girl lost her reason, and the father applying to her infamous seducer for the means of maintaining her while in that situation, was repulsed with contempt. He then carried his supplications to the foot of the throne, and the Monarch calling the degenerate nobleman before him, ordered him to take his choice of going to prison, and being punished with the utmost rigour of the law, or of settling an annuity on his unhappy victim. the principal of which to consist of 50,000 florins. The next day the annuity was granted.

FRANCE.

Paris.—New Prison.

The French Minister of justice proposes to build a new prison, exclusively for the reception of persons, charged with offences against the State. It is thought unbecoming that they should be degraded by confinement in the same place with common offenders.

Colony in Senegal

France is engaged in establishing a colony in Senegal, for the cultivation of cotton, indigo, coffee, and sugar. Great hopes are entertained of the quantity of colonial produce to be derived from it.

Arts and Manufactures.

By the royal audience of the 13th of February, on this subject, it is directed as follows :—

Article 1. There shall be a public exhibition of the products of the French industry, at periods to be determined by the King, and at intervals not exceeding four years.

The first exhibition shall take place in 1819, and the second in 1821.

2. The exhibition of 1819 shall take place on the 25th of August and following days, in the Halls and Galleries of the Palace of the Louvre.

3. All the manufacturers and artisans established in France, who wish to contribute to this exhibition, are required to send in their names to the Secretariat-general of the Prefectures, and their respective departments, at the period stated by the Minister, Secretary of State for the Interior.

4 Each Prefect shall appoint a jury, consisting of five members, to decide on the admission or rejection of the articles presented to them.

5. A central jury, consisting of fifteen members, shall be appointed by the Minister, Secretary of State for the Interior, to judge the products of industry. This jury shall point out the manufactures who may deserve either prizes on honourable notice.

6. The prizes are to consist of gold. silver, or bronze medals, according to the degrees of merit.

7. A specimen of each of the products mentioned by the juries, must be deposited at the Conservatory of Arts and Manufactures, with a particular inscription, indicating the name of the manufacturer or artisan by whom it has been sent.

INDIES : EAST.

Females Raffled for.

The following infamous advertisement appeared in Grunway's Daily Advertiser, printed in Calcutta, on the 6th Sept. 1818 :— " Be it known, that six fair and pretty young ladies, with two sweet and engaging children, lately imported from Europe, having the roses of health blooming on their cheeks, and joy sparkling in their eyes, possessing amiable tempers, and highly accomplished, whom the most indifferent cannot behold without expressions of rapture, are to be raffled for next door to the British Gal

lery. Scheme, twelve tickets, at twelve rupees each. The highest of three throws, doubtless, takes the most fascinating, &c."

ITALY.

Pompeu.—Discoveries.

The workmen employed in making researches among the ruins of this celebrated city, have lately discovered a bronze vase encrusted with silver, the size and form of which place it in the first rank of all the articles of this description which form so so interesting a part of the Bourbon Museum ; and also a bronze statue of Apollo, of admirable workmanship, which is indisputably the finest in the gallery. It would be impossible to describe the beauty of the form and the life of this figure, which is of the size of nature, and represents the god sacrificing with his avenging arrow the family of Niobe.

National Register:

BRITISH.

THE KING.

WINDSOR CASTLE, MARCH 6, 1819.

His Majesty has been generally cheerful throughout the last Month, but without any abatement of his disorder. His Majesty's bodily health continues good.

British Army.

An official return of the strength of the British army on the 25th of January, 1819, laid before the House of Commons, states the general total at 109,810 non-commissioned officers and privates, and 5,852 officers ; of which amount there are serving in Great Britain 15,248, exclusive of 5,516 Foot Guards ; Ireland 18,923 ; East Indies 18,281 ; troop-horses 11,276.

Navy Estimates.

These amount to 2,148,526l. 12s. 7d. Estimates have also been printed of the charge that may be necessary for the building and repairing of ships of war and other works, together with the sums that will be wanted for the Transport service, and by the Victualling Board, for the cost of provisions for the use of the army on board transports, and in garrisons abroad:

For the total charge for the ships is ···················· £1,145,430
For the improvements in the yards··· ················· 486,198
For army provisions ······ 419,319
For the Transport department ···················· 284,321

2,335,268

To which add the Navy Estimates ········· ······ 2,335,268

Total········ £4,483,724

Of the sum destined for the navy, the estimate of the half-pay, superannuations and pensions, &c. amounts to no less than 1,125,692*l.* 18*s.* 9*d.* The civil superannuations and pensions amount to 100,694*l.* 6*s.* 4*d.*

Gold Coin issued from the Mint.

The aggregate amount of gold coin issued from the Mint, in the course of the year 1818, was, in sovereigns, 2,347,230*l.* 7*s.* 6*d.* In half sovereigns, 515,143*l.* 2*s.* 6*d.* Amount of silver coin issued from the Mint in ditto, total aggregate, 576,189*l.*

Game Laws.

By a Return, made to Parliament, of the number of persons in custody, in England and Wales, for offences against the Game Laws, it appears that on the 26th of January last, in 75 prisons there were then in custody for such offences 522; of whom 99 had been committed under the Act 27 Geo III. Cap. 90: of the latter number the sentence of transportation for 7 years was passed upon 9: of imprisonment for 2 years upon 20; for 18 months, on 6; for 1 year, on 22; for 6 months, on 12; for 3 months, 5; for 2 months, 2: and there remain for trial, 23.

Prisoners sent to the Hulks, in 1818.

On the 1st of January, 1818, there were 2132 on board all the ships; since which period there have been received 3044; 2187 have been transported; 434 discharged by pardon or otherwise; five escaped; 57 have died; and 2493 remained in the hulks on the 1st of January instant." These statements are borne out by the reports of the Chaplains. The Report states, that the expense of the hulk establishment, from the 1st of July, 1818, to the 1st of January, 1819, including the fitting out of the Batavia as an hospital ship, was 38,471*l.* and the total amount of the earnings of the five ships for the same period was 19,690*l.*

British Herring Fishery.

The Report of the Commissioners for the Herring Fishery, of their proceedings for the year ending 5th of April, 1818, has been printed by order of the House of Commons. It concludes with stating, " the Commissioners think it is apparent that the character of the British Fishery is rising both at home and abroad; for while the quantity of herrings cured gutted is annually increasing, the quantity cured ungutted is every year diminishing, and that the demand has kept pace with the quantity they gut. They have also to mention, that while the exportation to the Continent of Europe has nearly-equalled that of the preceding year, and the exportation to Ireland and the West Indies has increased, a new market has opened in the West Indies, to which different shipments of herrings have been made both from Greenock and London; from the former with great success, but the result of the latter is not yet known, and they trust that India will soon become a permanent and valuable market for the consumption of British herrings."

Wheat, Beans, &c. Imported.

The quantity of wheat imported from foreign countries into Ireland, in the year ending the 5th of January, 1818, was 17,887 barrels; ditto, in the year ending the 5th of January, 1819, 14,647½ barrels. Of barley, in the former period, 120 barrels, ditto, in the latter, 1098 barrels. Of oats, in the former period, 8808 barrels; ditto, in the latter period, 952 barrels. Of beans, in the former period, 20 barrels; ditto, in the latter, 2½. Of flour, in the former period, 11,552 cwt.; ditto, in the latter, 1057 cwt.

The Rev. Samuel Lee.

It is with much pleasure we record the promotion of this learned man to the Arabic Professorship of Cambridge. Some account of him will be found in our last volume, page 1513.

At a congregation held on the 10th of March last, the Rev. Samuel Lee, of Queen's college, was admitted Master of Arts *by royal mandate,* and was afterwards elected Professor of Arabic, on the resignation of the Rev. John Palmer, B.D. of St. John's College.

Flying Hobby-Horses.

A substitute for walking has been already seen in this country. It has, however, been entirely surpassed by an Italian, who has made a sort of Pegasus

R

of the hobby horse, if we may believe the foreign papers, one of which says:— "A Mr. Brianza, at Milan, has invented a new travelling machine, which is said to be far superior to that of Baron Drais, and with which the traveller may go backwards or forwards. In the front of this vehicle, the Milan papers say, there is a winged horse, by the wings of which the carriage is put in motion."—The road from Ipswich to Whitton (says the Bury Paper) is travelled every evening by several pedestrian hobby-horses ; and no less than six are seen at a time, and the distance, which is three miles, is performed in 15 minutes. A Military Gentleman has made a bet to go to London by the side of the coach.—The crowded state of the metropolis does not admit of this novel exercise, and it has been put down by the Magistrates of Police, but it contributes to the amusement of the passengers in the streets, in the shape of caricatures in the print-shops.

Patent Safe-Coach.

Mr. H. Matthews, of Gretton-place, Bethnal-green, has invented a stage coach upon a new principle, which owes its origin to the numerous accidents that so much afflict the public, and is eminently calculated to allay future apprehensions. Its structure is light and elegant, and dissimilar to the usual forms, as it admits *neither passengers nor parcels on the roof :* the seats are about 6 feet 6 inches from the ground, and the luggage is under lock, secured from loss, and impervious to wet, placed at about 3 feet 6 inches, (instead of 8 feet 9 inches,) thus lowering the centre of gravity between 2 and 3 feet. It is impossible for it to lose its balance, being broader than the common coach, and allows more room for passengers. The wheels (nearly the size of the mails) are fastened on with a lock and key, putting to rest all apprehension of their " flying off." To prevent uncomfortable intermixture of different classes of persons, now prevalent on the outside of stage coaches, the front seats are devoted to those who choose to pay a halfpenny per mile more. The inside passengers, only four, sit as in arm chairs, without incommoding each other; and better views of the country are obtained than from a post-chaise, it being higher, and with more windows.

Roman Coins Found.

Last summer, as some workmen were employed at Vaynol, near Bangor, in removing some rubbish contiguous to a lime kiln, they discovered a large collection of Roman silver medals, and a pair of small antique brazen spurs, about two feet below the surface, by the side of a round grit stone. They are in a high state of preservation, and appear to have formed part of a collection, as they are of various dates. The ancient name of this part of the parish as appears from an old extant book of the See of Bangor, of the date of 1286, was Varchwel, a name which seems to desinate its proximity to a military station, and it is not improbable but that Vaynol was formerly a Roman villa, situated as it is, near the Roman Trajectus over the Menai. The number found was 73 ; and the historical period which they serve to illustrate, embraces an interval of 22 years, reckoning from the commencement of the reign of Vespasian to the death of Commodus. Of these there are 9 of the emperor Vespasian, 6 of Titus Vespasian, 3 of Domitan, one of which records the celebration of the *Ludi Seculares,* A. D. 84,) 3 of Nerva, 16 of Trajan, 10 of Hadrian, 1 of the Empress Sabina, his wife, 8 of Antoninus Pius, 7 of the Empress Faustina, 6 of M Aurelius Antonius, 1 of Commodus, and 3 which cannot be ascertained. The poor workman, who first made the discovery, was liberally rewarded for his honesty in communicating the same to the proprietor, T. A. Smith, Esq. in whose possession this classic treasure remains.

Curious Saxon Coin.

In the operation of digging for coal in the North Bastion of the fort at Ayr, constructed in 1654-5, by Cromwell, was found lately a gold coin, of nearly the size of half-a-crown, in good preservation, with the exception of being a little corroded on the edge, so as to render it very difficult to decipher the inscription round it. On the obverse is the figure of an angel, armed with a spear, the point of which is thrust into the mouth of a dragon, the other end being ornamented with the figure of a cross, the inscription, RICARD. DEI. GRA. REX. ANGL. & FRANC. On the reverse is the figure of a ship on the sea, having in the centre of it a shield with the arms of France and England quartered. From this shield is elevated a cross, the letter R on one side, and a rose on the other; the legend PER CRUCE. TUA. SALVA NOS. XPC. (or XPE. instead of XPC.) REDEMP. which may, perhaps, be read thus : *Per crucem tuam salve Nos Christe Redemptor.* The legend on both sides is in the Saxon character.

PARLIAMENTARY HISTORY

CHAP. II. *Windsor Establishment—Prisons—Children in Cotton Factories.*—

HOUSE OF COMMONS.

Feb. 22.—The house resolved itself into a Committee to consider the report of the Committee on the Windsor establishment.

Lord Castlereagh began by observing, that instead of moving to bring in a bill to alter the several acts on the subject, he thought that by moving a certain number of resolutions, the Committee would have the whole more clearly and fully in their view. He was then to move the following distinct resolutions. 1st, That for the Windsor establishment generally, instead of £100,000., £50,000. be appropriated. 2d. That annuities be given to the servants of her late Majesty to the amount recommended by the Committee. 3d. That £10,000. be given to the Duke of York, as to her late Majesty, for the expences attending the care of his Majesty's person. The 4th resolution was, in effect, that the £10,000. was not payable out of the privy purse. His Lordship then went into an exposition of each resolution, and concluded with stating that he had a communication to make from H. R. H. the Duke of York. Nothing could hurt his Royal Highness's feelings so much as to have his name connected with a money-vote in that house. Nothing but a sense of public duty could induce him to endure the painful feelings which arose from the donation of money to any of the Royal Family. But he was authorized by the Royal Duke to state, that nothing could induce him to accept what he considered the sacred private property of his Majesty.

Mr. Tierney expressed himself satisfied on the first and second resolutions, but as to the rest he thought the communication from the noble Lord at the end of his speech, was very ill advised. Mr. T. then went into a legal view as to the question, whether the King's privy purse was to be considered as private property, and contended, from a review both of the existing laws and various authorities which he cited, that it ought not to be so considered. He concluded, therefore, with moving, as

an amendment of the original resolution, that there should be added, "that the surplus out of the funds arising to his Majesty from the Duchy of Lancaster, and the £60,000 which was allowed for the privy purse, after the payment of the physicians and other incidental expences, be applied to the payment of the £10,000 to be given to his Royal Highness the Duke of York as the *custos* of his Majesty's person."

Mr. Tierney's view of the subject was supported by Mr. Banks, Mr. Protheroe, Mr. T. Wilson, Ald. Waithman, and Mr. Scarlett. Lord Castlereagh's opinion of the private property and unalienable nature of the privy purse, was defended by the Attorney and Solicitor General, Mr. Peel, Mr. Huskisson, and several other gentlemen; and the Solicitor General in particular stated, that if the House should agree to the amendment of the hon. gent. they would virtually appeal all the existing laws upon the subject. At length the question being put on the original motion of Lord Castlereagh, the House divided.

Ayes 281—Noes 186—Majority 93.

HOUSE OF LORDS.

Feb. 25.—Lord Sidmouth rose to call the attention of the House to the papers on the subject of Prisons, which, by command of his Royal Highness the Prince Regent, he had laid upon the table. Every pains had been taken to produce accuracy, and from the examination he had given them, he did not think there was any material deficiency; if there was, he should be happy to have it rectified without delay; about five-sixths of the returns had been received; and he was happy to say, that there had been a diminution of crimes during the last year, particularly in Middlesex. Some had conceived the state of the prisons as the chief cause of the increase of crime, but had they been unexceptionable, the pressure of the times must have occasioned an increase of crime. The state of the criminal law, as it respected punishments, would also demand their Lordship's attention. By some that law was held out as a sanguinary code: others had conceived that lenity in enforcing it was a great cause of the evil under which the country laboured. As to the supposition that the execution of the laws had become more sanguinary, it was completely contradicted by the returns on the table. It appeared, from the returns for the county of Middlesex and London, which commenced in the year 1749, down to the year 1805, that the annual average number of capital convictions was 62, and of executions 52. From the latter period to the present time, the average of convictions was 107, and of executions only 19. This statement certainly did not exhibit any thing like a sanguinary character in the execution of the laws. It might indeed be a question, whether in some instances they had not been administered with too much leniency. On this part of the question he could not help observing, that one means of remedying the evil of the increase of crimes, would be to take care that the punishments short of death were strictly enforced. He was sorry to say, that in consequence of unavoidable circumstances, the punishment of transportation had lost many of its salutary terrors. The number of persons liable to transportation had so greatly increased within the last seven years, that when they arrived at the place of their destination, it was difficult to find the means of classifying or properly disposing of them. In the hulks, however, a classification had taken place, religious instruction was administered, and constant and regular labour performed. A regulation had also within these three years been adopted, which had proved of the greatest advantage, with reference to the behaviour of the convicts. It had been thought proper to discharge those who behaved in an exemplary manner, upon certificates to that effect. The instances were few in which the persons so recommended were not pardoned; and he was happy to say, that the instances were also few in which the persons who had experienced that favour were found to return to their former situation. His Lordship concluded by moving the appointment of a Select Committee, to consider the papers laid upon the table, relative to the state of the prisons and of crimes, and to report thereon.

The Marquis of Lansdown was happy to hear the statements of the noble Lord, and that the enquiry came to them recommended by so high authority.

The question being put, was agreed to; after which the Committee was appointed,

and ordered to meet on Saturday next. Among the members are—the Lord Chancellor, the Lord President, the Marquis of Lansdown, the Earls of Carnarvon, Liverpool, Mulgrave, and Fitzwilliam, Lords Holland, Grenville, Beauchamp, Sidmouth, Auckland, Kenyon, the Bp. of Chester, &c.

On the motion of Lord Kenyon, the petitions from Bolton-le-moor, Stockport, Bolington, Holywell, and other places, praying for Parliamentary interference to regulate the hours of labour for children and persons employed in cotton factories, were read and entered as read. Some of the petitioners prayed that the regulations of Sir R. Peel's bill might be adopted.

Lord Kenyon said,—In rising to-night to propose the appointment of the Committee, which on a former occasion he had postponed, from a consideration of the thinness of the House, he was glad to see a greater number of noble Lords present than had on that occasion attended. The question now to be considered was one of the greatest importance. No less than 50,000 individuals were interested in its decision in Manchester and its neighbourhood. One-third of these persons were below 16 years of age, and consequently were unable to do any thing for their own protection. The noble Lord said he had made enquiries, since this subject was last before the House, into the improvements which were then said to be taking place without legislative interference. It had then been stated, that the master-spinners were willing to diminish the hours of labour of their own accord. This he had found was not correct generally. Some had indeed reduced the hours of labour at Stockport; but others not concurring, the former had been obliged to see their object defeated. At Bolton the hours had been shortened, but in Lancashire not a fourth of the factories had made any change, more than three-fourths of them working the children 14 hours and a-half a-day. With respect to the heat to which these children were exposed, the House would judge of the injury which it must occasion to their health, when he told them, on the report of a Magistrate who had particularly examined the factories, that it usually ran between 76 and 80 degrees of Fahrenheit, and sometimes amounted to 85. There were only two factories that were exceptions to this, that of Mr. Hollesworth, a member of the other house, and that of Macdonnel and Kennel. It would be for noble Lords to consider whether such a state of things did not call for enquiry and regulation. The noble Lord moved, therefore, that a Committee be appointed to enquire into the state and condition of children employed in the cotton manufactories, and to report thereon.

The Lord Chancellor thought that a general law ought to be passed for the regulation of all kinds of manufactories where children are employed.—After some conversation between the Bishop of Chester, Earl Grosvenor, Earl Liverpool, the Earl of Lauderdale, and Lord Holland, the original motion, which after the amendment was negatived (19 to 8) was carried without a division.

HOUSE OF COMMONS.

Feb. 25.—Lord Castlereagh moved that the report of the Committee on the Windsor establishment be brought up.

The report was brought up by Mr. Brogden, and read:

The first resolution, allowing £50,000. for the establishment, and the second, allowing £18,245. for annuities to her late Majesty's servants, were severally put, and carried. The third resolution, granting £10,000. to his Royal Highness the Duke of York, as *custos*, having been put,

Mr. Curwen said, he had hoped that on this point they would have received a disclaimer from his Royal Highness. Such a measure, he was convinced, would have given universal satisfaction. Whether the message which had been delivered from the Royal Duke, on this subject, had been intended to influence the house, he would not say, but he regretted that his Royal Highness should find it more difficult to take a sum from the privy purse, than from the pockets of the people at large. The discussion of this subject was extremely painful; but when it was forced on them, every other feeling must give place to the conviction that they had a sacred duty to perform to their country. When he saw that his Royal Highness received £4,000. a-year as Commander-in-chief, and that the whole emoluments of that

office could not be less than £10,000. a year; that he had from that house a grant of £20,000. a-year as Duke of York, and that he had various other emoluments to a great amount, he could not estimate his yearly income at less than £60,000. When he saw this, he thought the country, even if there were expences attending the office of *custos*, had a right to expect some little sacrifice on the part of his Royal Highness. But what were these expenses, about which so much had been said? He could see no expenses necessarily, but that of posting twice a-week to Windsor; and supposing that to amount to £500. or even to £1,000. a-year, which he conceived to be the utmost to which it could amount, what sacrifice was that, out of so ample an income?

Mr. F. Robinson justified the grant on the ground of its being accompanied with official duties, which duties his Royal Highness was now performing even before he knew the issue of their debate.

Mr. Williams proposed to reduce the sum to £5,000. per annum; but Lord Carhampton hoped his Royal Highness would copy the noble example of the Duke of Richelieu, and refuse it altogether.

The original motion was supported by Messrs. Peel, Martin, (of Galway) Cooper, J. Gordon, Freemantle, and Canning, the latter of whom pathetically alluded to the present condition of his Majesty, as deaf and blind in addition to other infirmities—"a ruin it was true, but a venerable ruin. His infirmities were any thing but an argument against his rights. He had been 'scathed by heaven's lightning,' but the blow which blasted had likewise consecrated him."

On the other hand, the grant was strenuously opposed by Messrs. Denham, Bernall, Long Wellesley, W. Wynn, Tierney, Scarlett, Brougham and other members.—On a division, the numbers were—

For the original resolution . . . 247
Against it 137
                                 ———
                 Majority 110

March 1.—Lord Castlereagh in rising, to call the attention of the house to the state of Prisons, observed that he should endeavour as shortly as possible to open to them the nature and object of his motion. The house would see that it would not be confined to the state of gaols alone; but that it was the intention of his Majesty's Ministers to take as large a view as possible of the other subject; that his motion would lead to the same satisfactory conclusion which others were anxious to arrive at.

The view his Lordship took of the subject was at all events more comprehensive, and it was impossible to look at the present state of the gaols without going at large into the general question. It would be first important to consider, whether it was or was not possible to repress and diminish crime. The question of crimes and punishments was unavoidably involved. No investigation of the kind could be instituted without examining the propriety of diminishing the more sanguinary laws, the necessity of some change in the system of the hulks, the advantages of penitentiaries, the plan of transportation, and the course of management in prisons; all these branches must be included, and not to enter upon them would be prematurely to pronounce a general sentence of degradation on the laws of the country: people out of doors would hastily conclude, that the whole system was unnecessarily harsh, and a false expectation would be raised of impracticable lenity. The Committee his Lordship should propose would in the first instance only consist of 21 members, but the number might be increased so as to facilitate dispatch in every possible way. What he was most anxious about was, that a broad and comprehensive report should be drawn up, upon which the house could act with propriety and safety. His Lordship admitted, that it appeared by the returns, that within the last 3 or 4 years, crime had increased to an alarming extent, almost in the proportion of two to one; and comparing the commitments of the last year with those ten years ago, in some classes of crime they were in the ratio of nearly three to one.. Such a view was in some respects appalling; at all events it would be most alarming and discouraging, if it could not be partially accounted for by various circumstances, which led to the conclusion, that the augmentation was attributable to temporary causes. In the first

place, the house could not fail to recollect that within the last 10 or 20 years, the whole system of the country had undergone a great alteration; the country, as it were, had swelled to an enormous size; the large towns had been increased beyond calculation. The manufacturing districts were more populous, and the inhabitants, being thrown together in stagnant masses, were of course liable to corruption. Yet, looking at the long catalogue of crime upon the table, it was evident that about half the total number of offenders were found in 5 out of 52 counties—Lancashire, Middlesex, Surrey, Warwickshire, and Yorkshire; and it was to be accounted for on a comparison of the rapid growth of the manufactures in comparison with the agriculture of the country.—The principal increase was within the last four years, and in that period also, the population had been augmented, not merely by natural causes, but an adventitious amount had been thrown back upon it from the army and navy; the soldiers, including militia, and sailors discharged and cast upon the face of the country, could not be stated at less than from 3 to 400,000, and this was an addition of so much to the mass of criminality and vice connected with temporary causes. It was not merely that these men were thrown out of occupations which were not manual, but that they were compelled to seek a livelihood in future, either by industry, to which they were not perhaps disposed, or by other means to which their habits might invite them. This had produced an additional pressure, which was not diminished by the low rate of wages and the resort to crime might, in some instances, be compelled by a sort of shame at receiving parish relief. It was, however, to be hoped, that the lapse of time of itself would operate a remedy, and contribute to the restoration of a more wholesome state to the great body of society. In the first place, it gave his Lordship sincere pleasure to observe, that there was in the country no increased principle of moral depravity; thus, although offences against property had multiplied extensively, offences against human nature, if he might so say, those of a blacker dye, had not augmented. Comparing them with former times, and making due allowance for differences in the amount of population, and for the nature and number of the difficulties to be encountered, it would appear that offences of a higher kind of enormity were even less numerous than they had been : for instance, the number of convictions in cases of murder had been fewer last year than perhaps at any former period of our history; in killing and maiming there had been no increase; the same of bigamy and manslaughter; rapes had not been more numerous last year than in the years preceding ; and the number of assaults, with a criminal intent, were still fewer. Unnatural offences and attempts had not been more frequent; so that those crimes that peculiarly marked moral depravity, had not only not experienced a proportionate increase, but, on the whole, were actually less than at former periods. The great mass of the growth of crime had been connected with the laws relating to property; forgeries, frauds, highway robberies, burglaries, and larcenies, had all augmented, and had given an undue character to the whole: the largest augmentation had been found in forgeries; but there was reason to hope that a remedy had been discovered, and would speedily be applied. With respect to the amount of convictions for forgery, it was observable, that though more had been found guilty in the few last than in preceding years, yet the returns proved that the executions within the last 8 or 10 years had been fewer than in the 8 or 10 years anterior. He would state one fact, which went to prove, that the growth of crimes was owing to temporary causes, viz. that there was no increase of *female* criminals: what increase there was had been confined to that sex, from a portion of whom it was rather to be expected, on the cessation of a long war, and the return to the arts of peace. The punishment of death certainly had increased in frequency in these kingdoms. At the close of the year 1805, the number of capital convictions was 350, and at the termination of last year 1,250. But this enormous increase was not without a drawback; for, referring to the commencement of the periods to which he had alluded, it appeared, that in one fifth of the capital cases, the law had been suffered to take its course; but in 1817, such had been the practice, with one case only in eleven, and in 1818,

one only in twelve. The merciful administration of the laws at present, very much retrenched the number of capital punishments. The number of persons executed last year, in Great Britain, was 97; and this number had not varied materially during fourteen years; and at that distance of time the number of executions in London and Middlesex alone, exceeded that of the whole country besides.—Now in order to meet and to remedy these evils, his Lordship remarked, the Committee must put their shoulders to the wheel, and deduce the origin and trace the progress of those evils, and devise a remedy. They must also consider how a secondary punishment may be found which shall at the same time be consistent with the morality and improvement of those who are in prison. He was sure the house would go along with him in observing with what mercy the laws had been administered during the present administration. That mercy had much weakened the impression of that salutary dread and terror which were intended by the laws to operate upon offenders. It was for the house to consider whether this had not become more a colonial question than one of crimes and punishments. It was an important consideration for that house, whether the colony he meant should be released from the burden of supporting those convicts, in whom transportation from their native country had failed to effect any moral improvement. The notion of going to Botany Bay, so far from impressing criminals with terror, had so completely different an effect, that many persons received that sentence rather as an indulgence than a punishment.

The Noble Lord concluded a most eloquent and elaborate speech with moving that "a Committee be appointed to enquire into the state of gaols and other places of confinement; and to inquire also into the best means to be taken for their improvement, and the prevention of crime."

Sir Js. Mackintosh rose, not to reply to the able speech of the Noble Lord, nor to anticipate inquiry; but gave notice that to-morrow (Tuesday) he should move for a select Committee, "to consider the operation and nature of the criminal laws relative to the capital punishment of felony."

Mr. Lawson thought the subjects of enquiry could not be separated. With respect to Botany Bay, he had reason to believe it had been in contemplation to settle a new colony, on a plan somewhat different, and that a survey had been ordered for that purpose.

Mr. C. W. Wynn chiefly objected to the vast extent of inquiry which his Lordship had marked out.

Ald. Wood thought it would take 6 or 7 years to go through the enquiry, and wished the evidence taken before former Committees might be laid before the present. As to the army and navy, 60 or 70 persons had applied together for passes home, but not one in 100 had been chargeable with crime.

Mr. F. Buxton expressed his satisfaction with the candid speech of the Noble Lord, who misunderstood him in supposing that the *exclusive* cause of crime was to be found in the state of penal laws and of the prisons; but certainly it was 'most unfortunate that prisons should be schools for crime, which he knew to be the fact.

The question was then put and carried. The following are the leading names on the Committee.

Lord Castlereagh, Sir J. Macintosh, Mr. Canning, Mr. Brougham, Mr. V. Fitzgerald, Mr. Bennet, Mr. S. Worthey, Mr. F. Buxton, Lord Clive, Mr. Holford, and Mr. Wilberforce.

On the motion of Mr. Bennet, the following orders were made : that five members do constitute a quorum : that the Reports of the Prison and Police Committees be referred to it; and that the Committee should have power to move from place to place, and to report their observations from time to time.

POLITICAL PERISCOPE.

Panorama Office, March 29, 1819.

There is nothing more amusing in the whole science of Politics, than to contemplate the change of opinion on the cant sayings, and the watchwords, of parties formed in a state. At a certain moment, while they are, as it were, fresh from the mint, the coinage of imagination, they are important ; and either wonderfully soothing and cheering, or inexpressibly defamatory, and even terrific. Even the slightest articles are at some times of moment ; and the most innocent notes of music, or the arrangement of them into a tune, become causes of heavy offence, not to say of criminal punishment. We were led into this train

of thought, by the circumstance of a Savoyard girl playing under our window, the other evening, on her hurdy-gurdy, a variety of old jacobin tunes, and among them, the famous air of " Charley over the water." And yet, how numerous soever were her auditors, not one among them, except a conclave of Panoramists, discovered the disloyalty, and *rebellion !* couched in the air she played. The era is gone by ; the generation to which the distinction applied, no longer exists ; and Time has imposed a silence equally expressive and instructive. Who now distinguishes, as once they were distinguished, the famous appellations of *Whig* and *Tory?* The families which formerly refused each other's alliance, have subsequently been so happily intermingled, that it would be difficult to determine whether *Whig* blood, or *Tory* blood, predominates in this or in that ; and as to pure descent, not blended with its opposite, there is scarcely any such thing known, to our acutest genealogists. All that modern ingenuity ventures to impute to such or such a character, whether peer or commoner, is, that he is an *in*, or an *out* ; a ministerial man, or an oppositionist. There is, moreover, a liberality, or at least, a latitude, allowed to opinion, even in these terms, for the public know well, that on certain questions, the opinion of the cabinet is divided ; and on certain others, the oppositionists never fail to supply a number of speakers on the ministerial side of the debate, and a number of votes, when the argument comes to a decision :—and the same *vice versa.*

It was a violent stretch of the royal prerogative, when, more than a century ago, no less than Twelve British peers were created in one day, in order to form a majority on a bill of some importance to the then minister ; but, who now gives himself the trouble to enquire, whether Lord A. or Lord B. is the representative of one of those twelve peers. His counsel, if he be a man of sense, is equally deferred to ; and his vote is counted, without reluctance, and without observation.

A much more violent stretch of royal prerogative has, since our last, been resorted to, in France ; no less than Sixty Peers having been added to the upper house, in one mass, by the king ; and among them not a few, whose names might have been thought of little recommendation to a legitimate monarch, recently settled on his throne. The step is singularly bold ; and either extremely judicious, or extremely otherwise. It appears to have been dictated by necessity; but the necessity itself is a legitimate occasion of regret. The monarch either felt, or feared, that he was reduced to the condition of a puppet, in the habiliments of royalty, and, therefore, he exerted that power most vigorously, if not furiously, with which the constitution had entrusted him, for self-preservation.

The crisis was brought on by a determinate opposition in the Chamber of Peers to the measures of government, and this extended to circumstances the most trivial, or the most wise. It decisively marks the displeasure of the king with those who think of violating the charter; and his resolution to abide by that instrument in his administration. It has had no other consequence, and pro will have none, except that of being followed by additional creations; and of forming a precedent, which nothing but an extreme case should originate, or should repeat.

The Finances of France have lately been the subject of an official report; the minister stated the sum required for the service of the year at 889,210,000 *francs* (about £37,500,000.) which he thought the existing taxes would supply; these he estimated at

	francs
The Land Tax	363,000,000
Stamps, &c.	181,000,000
Customs	13,000,000
Indirect Contributions	174,834,000
Post Office	22,460,000
Lottery	12,500,000
Rentes, in the Treasury, applicable	5,180,000
Salt Duty	5,389,000
Savings on Pensions and Salaries	11,900,000

The expences of collecting the duties on Stamps and Registry, amount to 17,000,000 *fr.* and the interest on the National Debt amounts to 232,000,000 *francs.*

The reader will observe the striking difference between the produce of some of these taxes and that of their representatives in Britain. The Customs are little above half a million sterling; the British Customs are twenty times as much: in revenge our Land Tax was never taken at two millions sterling; the French is fifteen times as much. Indeed the French minister confesses, that this tax bears heavily on some depart-

ments; and he hopes to regulate it, in part, after the present year: it must be acknowledged, that nothing can more strongly require it. The Salt Duty, which formerly was one of the most oppressive duties in France, or, perhaps, in the world, now produces a trifle more than £200,000. whereas salt in Britain figures for nearly a million and a half.

Nobody doubts whether the Salt Duties in Britain be not enormous: they amount, in fact, to *thirty-five times the value of the original article.* Either, then, the original article is unreasonably cheap; or these accumulations of duties render it unreasonably dear. To this consideration must be added, the excessive rigour of the excise laws on this article, as the administration of them, on some others, which deter prudent people from following occupations, which render them liable to ruinous vexations, from unintentional causes. Under the old *régime*, the imposition, the collection, and the arbitrary punishments, where the salt duties were in question, were still worse in France.

Reports of attempted vexations of the Protestants in France, have been again in circulation; we hope they have greatly exceeded the truth; but, on the whole, it seems to be evident, that the improvident vehemence of French feelings is not sufficiently controuled by cool deliberation, and self-restraint. Nothing could be a greater gratification to democratic levellers, than to witness the exuberance of what professes to be loyalty, direct its powers to the production of scenes, which have branded the name of France and Frenchmen, with all the ignominy and horror attached to the appellation of jacobin:—however, as yet, the king rules by the charter.

Spain is making the most powerful efforts her means afford, to equip a force that may operate effectually against her revolted colonies; she is hiring and buying ships from every where. Had this effort been made three or four years ago, we should have augured more favorably of its consequences; at present they are more than formerly precarious. There is, however, one thing against the colonists, which was not before; for the news is but recently arrived, that Spain has ceded the Floridas to the United States. The treaty is now laid before the Congress.

It is affirmed, that for this cession America pays *Five Millions of dollars* to Spain, or rather, to herself:—for it is said, that this sum is mostly to be paid among American citizens who have sustained losses by Spanish depredations. The pretence can deceive no one, in the least conversant with political negotiations; and a few weeks will shew, whether the bargain is not considered by the Americans themselves, as so much hush-money—which the censorious will call a bribe—to induce the American government to discountenance, and to forbear, all assistance to the insurgents in Spanish America.

After what has passed in the legislative body, in North America, we can believe any thing of the American government. Hitherto we have been cautious; because we considered that government as disapproving the acts of its agent, a military commander, taking on himself to *murder!* under colour of justice, not of law—for law he had none—two British subjects; who were not within his jurisdiction, and were not amenable to his authority. The committee to which the conduct of General Jackson, in the cases of Arbuthnot and Ambrister had been referred, condemned the general, in unequivocal terms: the Congress has refused to acquiesce in this condemnation, by a considerable majority.

And thus we have, from the American authorities themselves, a clear cause for describing the legislators of that country as void of every feeling of humanity, of equity, of rectitude, and of sound policy, too. For this decision now remains as a foul stain on the American character: it speaks volumes in condemnation of all Yankee pretences to justice and good faith, to honour and honesty, to mercy and liberality. It is the dictate of cowardice, sanctioned by the folly of intemperate ambition. It will have consequences; for, there are not wanting liberal spirits, and better-informed minds, among the American population, who will not cease to remonstrate against this violation of all order, decency, law, and justice. Their voice will be heard; and with these will be united a party, who, foreseeing the worst, will vent their apprehensions in Scripture language,— "Come out of her my people; that ye be not partakers of her plagues." The least effect this perversion of national character ought to have on our countrymen is, a resolution to avoid a country so debased, so degraded, in the eyes of justice and reason.

Again we return to that country, which, with all its imperfections, and they are many, is the object of our veneration and choice. We have little new to report since our last. A new parliament always brings to light some foul offence against the constitution. The people themselves are to blame: the want of integrity among individuals, is a leading cause of all public sufferings. National virtue, like national wealth, is the result of the virtue of individuals, combined into one aggregate.

Those who affect to see more deeply than others into political manœuvres, insist, that the allowance of £10,000. per Ann. to an illustrious personage, as *custos* of the sovereign, is a swindling transaction; for, say they, any other son would ———. But, it should be remembered, that the *custos* of his majesty's person, is *appointed* by the nation; is, in fact, the nation's deputy, to do that which the nation cannot do, in person. It is not as a son, but as a public person, as a person amenable to his constituents, the nation, for his conduct, as *their* agent, *their* representative, that the D. of Y. is *appointed.* It is, therefore, more analogous to the spirit of the constitution, that he should receive a stipend from the nation. While the nation gives, and the *custos* receives, the principle of responsibility is acknowledged. It is not the custody of a private individual that is in question, the laws in being are sufficient for that; but here is a new office created by a new law, and demanding new provisions; otherwise the nation might lose all interest in its sovereign.

We have hinted at the various petitions addressed to the legislature, desiring revision of various branches of the law; they are all of great importance. Our well-being depends on them, or their connections. Before long, much of the business in parliament will be so far advanced, as to allow of conjecture as to the form it may assume; at present, extensive observations would be premature.

The general state of Europe is tranquillity. We see little to disturb the peace. Long may it so continue. May commerce flourish; as every state is doing its utmost to accomplish; and may knowledge overspread the face of the world, introductory to the light of truth, as the dawn of Aurora gradually brightens into the full effulgence of the sovereign day.

Commercial Chronicle.

Extracts from Commercial Letters, received from various parts.

AMERICA.

Charleston, January 29, 1819.

" Upland Cotton which last month declined to 24 a 25 cents, advanced again, contrary to general opinion, and notwithstanding the scarcity of money, to 26 a 27 cents, and is now at 25 a 26 for first quality. Sea Island 50 a 53: demand slack. Rice 5¼ to 5⅞. Dollars per 100lb. Business in general in a very languid state."

BELGIUM.

Antwerp. March 9, 1819.

" Yesterday 1600 Bags fine Brazil Coffee were sold, at 14¼: except this parcel very trifling sales have taken place. Sugar is still on the decline. Cotton unsaleable at 14¼ to 15 for Bengal. Georgia 33 a 35. Pepper unsaleable. Discount 6 per cent. per annum.

RUSSIA.

St. Petersburgh, Feb. 11-23, 1819.

" Business very dull; the business at the Rostof Fair has been very inconsiderable. Sugar has declined, Common Crushed at 29; on long credit. English Double Loaves of good quality have been sold at 42. Tallow is looking down, Yellow Candle has been sold at 162. Clean Hemp can be bought on contract at 84: money. Exchange 11¼ a 11¾⅞. Silver money 3,71.

Riga, Feb. 11-23, 1819.

" The quantities of all descriptions of Grain actually contracted for, fall very short of those bargained for the same time last year: prices have not however given way so much as might have been expected. Flax is the only article for which there is any demand at the present moment.

STATE OF TRADE.

Lloyd's Coffee-House, March 20, 1819.

We should be very glad, undoubtedly, to remove every trace of that gloom, which our last Report was but too well adapted to produce in the mind of the reader; but, as yet, we must not indulge ourselves in that pleasure. We then hinted at expected disasters in the mercantile world; and events have corresponded to the hint, with a painful accuracy.

Symptoms too decisive to be mistaken, are described by the discerning, which indicate the continuance of commercial uncertainties. Not a few of the most considerable houses have been *talked of:* which is seldom without some cause, though not always with sufficient cause for what the too easily persuaded take on themselves to anticipate. There is something unspeakably cruel in propagating, and especially, in magnifying unfounded suspicions: those who can delight in it, have paid but little attention to the delicacy of Mercantile credit ; or, at least, have but little combined the feelings of humanity with their knowledge of the world.

It is nevertheless, true, that some of those houses at which rumour pointed, have come forward boldly, on late occasions; have discounted their own paper, and reduced their out-standing acceptances to a mere nothing;—Some also have paid their share of the loan without hesitation, or in advance: what more could they do ? That this was a pleasant operation, none can suppose; but, when character is in question, nothing is felt as an obstacle. We should be glad, were we able to say,— this example has been generally-universally followed: but it would be inconsistent with our better knowledge.

Many, if not most, of these monthly Reports, have stated the price of Exchequer Bills at a considerable *premium;* the present is under the necessity of announcing that description of public security at a *discount* It is true, the present bills are those at *two-pence* per day for the hundred pounds; whereas, those formerly alluded to, were either *three-pence* per day, or at least *two-pence halfpenny.* Yet, as these *two-penny* bills have been at a premium, their decline to a discount, is a strong indication of a pressure for money, somewhere.

Exchequer bills were a very convenient vehicle for obtaining *some* profit on any quantity of cash which a merchant might have in his hands, at the time. They afforded but a very moderate interest; but then, they were always accounted cash; they were convertible into cash, at an hour's notice; and they rested on the national credit as their basis. They were dealt in by all bankers; buying or selling, according to circumstances, and to the amount of cash in their strong chests.

The demand for them has decreased; either merchants or bankers, or both, have employment for their spare money in another way; and therefore, this way, is for the moment, declined. The same cause affects the prices of the Funds, generally: and though they have stood steadily, for some days past, yet we doubt whether any considerable, or rapid, rise, is speedily to be expected. It will be recollected, that they have not offered legal interest for money invested in them, for a long time past.

Bullion is rising in price: New Doubloons are, at present, 4l. 2s. per oz. and standard silver is 5s. 6d. per oz. This is not favourable to the interest of trade and commerce; the Bank, however, may observe, with some degree of satisfaction, that it is not the consequence of any enlarged emission of notes. We have not yet seen the intended new form of bank notes, which is to prevent forgery; report, however, continues to maintain its hope—perhaps we should rather say—its expectation.

The *Tea* Sale at the India-House has gone off with passable briskness, but on the whole 3d. or 4d. per lb. cheaper. The lower sorts have principally felt the decline; and the quantity of Congou being very considerable, while the demand for it has decreased, the reduction has greatly fallen on this sort of Tea.

We shall take this opportunity of registering the prices charged by the wholesale dealers to the trade.

Bohea 4s. 8d. to 4s. 10d.
Good ditto Congou Kind Leaf, 5s.
Common Congous, 5s. 7d. to 5s. 8d.
*Good Originals, 5s. 10d. to 6s.
Very good, 6s. 4d. to 6s. 8d.
*Fine Blackish Leaf, 6s. 9d. to 6s. 11d.
Fine Strong ditto, 7s. to 7s. 2d.
Souchong 7s. 4d. to 7s. 9d.
Good ditto, 8s. to 8s. 6d. Fine 9s.
Superfine, 9s. 6d. best 10s.
Good Caper 7s. 6d. to 8s.—Fine 8s. 6d.
Pekoe 9s. 6d. to 9s. 9d. Fine 10s.–Best 11s.
Good Common Twankay, 5s. 10d.
Ordinary lower.
*Fine ditto, 6s. to 6s. 2d.
Fine Brightish Leaf, do. 6s. 6d. to 6s. 10d.
*Hyson Kind, 8s. to. 8s. 6d.
Hyson, 9s. to 9s. 6d. Good do. 10s.
*Fine ditto, 10s. 3d. to 10s. 6d.
Superfine do. 11s. Best, 12s. 6d.
Gunpowder, 13s. to 13s. 6d.
Good ditto, 14s. Best 16s.
*Good West India Coffee, 2s. 6d.
Ordinary lower.
Fine ditto, 2s. 8d. to 2s. 10d.
Bourbon ditto, 3s. to 3s. 3d.
Good Turkey ditto, 3s. 3d. to 3s. 6d.
Best Ditto, 4s.
Sir Hans Sloane's Chocolate, 6s.
Churchman's Patent Ditto, 6s.
Best Plain ditto, 5s. to 5s. 6d.

Sugar has been rather flat within this little while; it seems, however, by the steadiness of the holders to expect an improvement in briskness; if not also in price. A few of the speculators who had stood their chance for a better market, have found themselves under the necessity of accepting a price, a shade under the currency of the day; and possibly, this may have some further slight consequences; though not, if our conjecture be correct, on the more competent houses. If a brisk demand should come, the rise of price will fully keep pace with it, and will be considerable.

The refiners have greatly diminished their stocks; not a few have even wrought themselves out of work; yet they do not immediately replace the goods they have sold. But, as their situation is known, it is known also, that they find no profit in standing still; and of this the market will not fail to retain a clear and infallible recollection. The grocers have been purchasing for the home trade, somewhat freely, though not in great quantities; their demands have chiefly had regard to the better qualities. In Foreign Sugars there is little doing.

The holders of *Coffee* have produced a sort of suspension in the market, by not bringing forward their goods for sale. There has scarcely been a public sale for these three weeks past; except of such articles as were somewhat damaged. The enquiry for private sale has been rather more free, in consequence; but, we believe, that no variation of prices have been effected. There certainly are buyers; but the prices at which they buy, being limited, they will only close a bargain where they perceive a shade of difference in their favour.

The demand for *Cotton* has lately depended pretty much on exportation; this has been lively and extensive. The home trade has been stocked sufficiently for some time. Very little, therefore, has been delivered from the warehouses, for home consumption; but the bulk has been chiefly in bond. We believe, that the Liverpool market is much in the same state; and considerable arrivals being looked for, the prices have rather given way. It is expected, that, when these vessels reach their port, the depression will be still greater; and it must be provided against.

The abundant supply brought by the private trade from India, has proved prejudicial to some of the speculators; and the newspapers have taken care to inform the public, that an express is gone over land to India, to countermand orders for shipping the article to England. This publicity has more than one object in view. We formerly suggested our expectation that India would prove a formidable rival to America in respect to cotton: we presume that the suggestion will be justified by events at no great distance.

We are sorry to learn that some branches of this trade have reason to fear a defi-ciency of employ for their working hands. If we are not misinformed, application has been made to government for assistance; and government replied, by enquiring whether the factories had not over-peopled the trade? Now, reason says, that for proprietors of works to take unlimited numbers of hands into employ, beyond a probable demand for their labour, is not a simple misfortune, for which the principals concerned have any just grounds to expect support from the public purse. If the men are too many, let them take service in other branches.

There is something, also, to be considered, whenever what is involved in Fashion comes under our contemplation. Fashions *will* change; but, to call on government to support those who suffer by the change, is to find plenty of work for the ruling powers. Extreme cases, only, can justify such interference; ordinary events—and what events are more ordinary than change of Fashion?—must find resources in their own vicinity.

The Cotton Trade is not the only to which the foregoing hints apply. We fear that the Silk Trade has little superior caution to boast of. Italian Silks are fallen in price 1s. to 2s. per lb. They have been indeed very high; but, at this time of the year the demand *should not slacken*, and the price *should not fall*. We shall be glad to find our apprehensions groundless.

Tobacco looks forward to an expected contract from the French government; and those dealers who are likely to be interested in that contract, have lately shewn somewhat of alertness to secure such parcels as have afforded beneficial terms. If they can purchase now to advantage, they answer more than one purpose; as they relieve the market, and will have occasion for a smaller quantity, when the moment arrives that they must buy, because they must deliver. Foreign orders in Town, are very limited as to the prices commissioned.

Hemp has found a rising market for some time past; principally owing to a limited stock on hand: of course, the holders not only expect the full price, but look for something additional. The supply will not arrive instantly; and, therefore, the prospect is, that those who want the article, must comply with the terms proposed.

FLAX continues steady; at prices little varied.

RUM, BRANDY, and HOLLANDS.—There has been little business done by private contract lately; the quantity of Rum wanted by the Navy Board (100,000 gallons) was contracted for yesterday, at a fraction under 3s. per gallon; the following are some of the prices at public sale.

12 to 16	. .	3s. 3d.	a 3s. 4d.
18 " 20	. .	3s. 5d.	a 3s. 6d.
25 " 30	. .	3s. 8d.	a 3s. 11d.

The market prices were previously nearly nominal: the depression may be stated 2d. to 3d. per gallon in low Rums, and 4d. to 6d. on the finer qualities.

Brandy has some enquirers; but, is on the whole, little varied.

GENEVA rather looking downward than upward.

There is some speculation in RICE, when it can be taken at a low rate: this chiefly refers to East India Rice, of which considerable parcels have lately changed hands. In Carolina Rice, nothing doing.

The Market is heavy for SPICES.

AVERAGE PRICES OF CORN FOR ENGLAND AND WALES.

Wheat, 79s. 4d.	Rye, 55s. 5d.
Barley, 59s. 7d.	Oats, 33s. 3d.
Beans, 65s. 5d.	Peas, 67s. 9d.

COUNTY OF ESSEX.

Agricultural Report, March 26, 1819.

The Wheat Plants still continue very luxuriant, and extraordinary as it may appear, it is a real fact, that a Wheat Ear has already this spring been taken from a field within a mile of the writer of this report. The latter planted Beans and Peas have been put into the ground in excellent order. Many pieces of stubble and fallowed Oats are already either drilled or sown, when the former wrought extremely well for the seed. Some of our lands intended for spring corn, must, for the want of frost this season, work tough, and the Barley sowing must be postponed for the present on the cold soils, but on the tender lands no impediment has occurred. Rye grass and Tares are getting forward, which is fortunate, as the Turnips are nearly done. The stock yards and barns are almost cleared of all kinds of grain.

Bankrupts in the order of their dates; with their Attornies.

BANKRUPTCY SUPERSEDED. *March* 2.

Trustam, J. King street, Goswell street, carpenter.

BANKRUPTS.

Beer, W. Plymouth dock, ironmonger. *Sols.* Darke and Co. Prince's street, Bedford row.

Bell, C. F. Castle court, Bethnal green, victualler. *Sol.* Parnell, Church street, Spitalfields.

Crickett, D. Hougham, Kent, timber merchant. *Sol.* Stocker, New Boswell court, Lincoln's inn.

Dobie, A. Liverpool, master mariner. *Sol.* Rowlinson, Liverpool.

Dyson, B. Doncaster, corn dealer. *Sol.* Lever, Holborn court, Gray's inn.

Kent, A. Deptford, baker. *Sol.* Williams, Curzitor street, Chancery lane.

Miall, M. Portsea, merchant. *Sols.* Alexander and Holme, New inn.

Pinkerton, T. Birchin lane, merchant. *Sols.* Rogers and Son, Manchester Buildings, Westminster.

Vigers, W. R. Austin friars, merchant. *Sols.* Knight and Freeman, Basinghall street.

Westwood, C. Bristol, merchant. *Sol.* King, Sergeant's inn.

BANKRUPTS, *Feb.* 23.

Boniface, C. jun. Chichester, mealman. *Sol.* Hume, Holborn court, Gray's inn.

Cushon, T. Minories, hat manufacturer. *Sol.* Mangham, Great St Helens.

Cox J. and J. Morgan, Gutter lane, glovers. *Sol.* Oldham, Earl street, Blackfriars.

French, W. Heaton-Norris, Lancashire, cotton manufacturer. *Sols.* Lowe & Bower, Southampton buildings, Chancery lane.

Greathead T. and W. Othwaite, Lamb street. *Sol.* Thompson and Oram, Leman street, Goodman's fields.

Gregson, W. Kingston upon Hull, merchant. *Sol.* Ellis, Chancery lane.

Harris G. and J. Edmonds, Birmingham, japanners. *Sols.* Alexander and Holme, New Inn.

Hope, T. Blakeley, Lancashire, bleacher. *Sols.* Hurd, Johnson and Chester, Temple.

Mitchell, T. Cowick, Yorkshire, linen draper. *Sol.* Egerton, Gray's Inn square.

Parker, J. Totton, Herts, dealer, money-scrivener. *Sols.* Young and Hughes, St. Mildred's court, Poultry.

Peake, S. jun. and J. Rothwell, Halliwell, Lancashire, calico printers. *Sol.* Meddowcroft, Gray's inn.

Powell, P. Knightsbridge, broker. *Sol.* Pember, Charlotte street, Blackfriars rd.

Shotter, F. Steyning, Sussex, auctioneer. *Sol.* Palmer and France, Bedford row.

Smith, T. R. Oxford, linen draper. *Sol.* Steel, Bucklersbury.

Street, J. F. Budge row, Stationer. *Sols.* Street and Wolfe, Philpot lane.

BANKRUPTS, *Feb* 20

Bourne, E. Austin friars, merchant. *Sols.* Kearsey and Spurr, Bishopsgate street, within.

Broady, W. Bromsgrove, Worcestershire, mercer. *Sols.* Fladgate and Neeld, Essex street, Strand.

Clarke, J. Stagbatch, Herefordshire, [far-mer. *Sol.* Jenkins, New Inn.

Cooper, E. Blandford forum, Dorsetshire, linen draper. *Sol.* Dean, Guildford street.

Dineley, J. Peopleton, Worcestershire, coal merchant. *Sol.* Beck, Devonshire street, Queen square.

Dunderdale, W. T. Manchester, merchant. *Sol.* Hurd, Temple.

Fox R. W. and W. P. Smith, Plymouth, merchants. *Sols.* Austice and Wright, Inner Temple.

Garner, W.Poulton-cum-Seacome,Cheshire, dealer in coals. *Sols.* Lowes and Cowburn, Temple.

Green, J. Maddox street, Hanover square, coach maker. *Sol.* Reynolds, Hertford street, Fitzroy square.

Hardman, J. Manchester, warehouseman. *Sol.* Kay, Manchester.

Jones, W. Shoreditch, earthenware and chinaman. *Sol.* Sutcliffe, Earl street, Blackfriars.

Kent, J. Stowmarket, Suffolk, beer brewer. *Sol.* Chilton, Chancery lane.

Neate W. Sweeting's alley, Cornhill, silver-smith. *Sols.* Rowland and Young, Lincoln's inn fields.

Peers J. Liverpool, merchant. *Sols.* Avison and Wheeler, Castle street, Holborn.

Phillips G. E. Plymouth, sadler. *Sols.* Anstice and Wright Inner Temple.

Prest W. and J. Woolner, Lawrence Pountney lane, corn factors. *Sols.* Druce and Son, Billiter square.

Revett, J. jun. Tolleshunt-Darcy, Essex, butcher. *Sols.* Milne and Parry, Temple.

Woodhouse J. and M. Mincing lane, West-India brokers. *Sol.* Weston, Fenchurch street.

BANKRUPTS, *Feb.* 27.

Adams S. and J. J. Wattleworth, Walsall, Staffordshire, factors. *Sols.* Price and Co. Old square, Lincoln's inn.

Bailey C. R. H. Swallowfield; Wiltshire, dealer. *Sols.* Fisher & Sudlow, Holborn.

Barfoot J. Arundel street,Strand, stationer. *Sols.* Paterson & Peile, Old Broad street.

Bass, J. Woodford, victualler. *Sol.* Hebler, Walbrook.

Bates J. Stockport, dealer. *Sol.* Meddowcroft, Gray's inn.

Churcher J. Bristol, hair preparer. *Sol.* King, Sergeant's inn, Fleet street.

Cousins J. Charlton street, Somer's town, cheesemonger. *Sol.* Rose, East street, Red Lion square.

Fareclough R. Farington, Lancashire, tanner. *Sol.* Blakelock, Sergeant's inn.

Gray G. Hammersmith, carpenter. *Sol.* Popkin, Dean street, Soho.

Hall R. S. Bank buildings, merchant. *Sols.* Blunt and Bowman, Broad street buildings.

Hatton J. Warrington, Lancashire, butcher. *Sol.* Hurd, King's Bench walk, Temple.

Heaford T. Stepney, dealer. *Sol.* Bousfield, Bouverie street, Fleet street.

Horner J. W. and J. Brockbottom, Lancashire, linen manufacturers. *Sol.* Blakelock, Sergeant's inn.

Kidd J. Castle Coomb, Wiltshire, butcher. *Sol.* Dax, Doughty street.

Leigh S. Strand, bookseller. *Sols.* Langham and Sons, Bartlett's buildings.

Loft G. Woodbridge, Suffolk, corn and coal merchant. *Sol.* Hine, Essex court, Temple

Maidstone, M. J. dealers. *Sol.* Norton, Commercial Chambers, Minories.

Paul J. Circus, Minories, merchant. *Sol.* Sweet, Basinghall street.

Sayer W. Bristol, corn factor. *Sols.* Clarke and Co. Chancery lane.

Stanley B. Woolwich, corn dealer. *Sol.* Chinn, Charles street, City road.

Stewart R. Liverpool, master mariner. *Sols.* Hurd and Co. King's Bench walk, Inner Temple.

Thick J. Islington, broker. *Sol.* Beckett, Noble street.

Woods E. R. Kelvedon, Essex, shopkeeper. *Sol.* Lewis, Clement's inn.

Worley J. Liverpool, wine and porter merchant. *Sol.* Leigh and Houseman, New Bridge street.

BANKRUPTCY SUPERSEDED, *March* 6.

Sansum S. Nailsworth, Gloucestershire, clothier.

BANKRUPTS.

Blake J. Parson's Green, Fulham, brewer. *Sol.* Buckle, Size lane.

Campbell D. B. Harper and A. Baillie, Old Jewry, merchants. *Sols.* Kaye and Co. New Bank buildings.

Carlisle, W. and T. Hodgson, Bolton-le-Moors, Lancashire, dealers in cotton yarn. *Sols.* Milne and Parry, Temple.

Chant J. Walsall, Staffordshire, flour seller. *Sols.* Avison and Wheeler, Castle street, Holborn.

Cheppett E. Walcot, Somersetshire, cabinet maker. *Sol.* Williams, Red Lion square.

Cole R. Friday street, haberdasher. *Sol.* Steel, Bucklersbury.

Cross J. H. Bristol, corn factors. *Sol.* Edmunds, Lincolns inn.

Harvey W. jun. Clifton, Gloucestershire, Boarding house keeper. *Sols.* Adlington and Gregory, Bedford row.

Hendry M. Kingston-upon-Hull, merchant. *Sols.* Rosser and Co. Bartlett's Buildings.

Herbert T. Checquer yard, Dowgate hill, cotton merchant. *Sol.* Lewis, Crutchedfriars.

Knowles J. Stroud, Gloucestershire, innholder. *Sol.* Nix, Cook's court, Lincoln's Inn.

Leslie A. Size lane, Bucklersbury, provision Merchant. *Sols.* Gregson and Fonmereau, Angel court, Throgmorton street.

Norris H. Bolton-le-Moors, Lancashire, confectioner. *Sol.* Ellis, Chancery lane.

Pigot W. Ratcliff-highway, grocer. *Sol.* Heard, Hooper's square, Leman street, Goodman's fields.

Starkey W. Bethnal-green-road, bricklayer. *Sols.* May and Co. Bethnal-green-road.

Steine J. Butcher row, East Smithfield, rectifier. *Sols.* Lane and Bennett, Lawrence Pountney hill.

Taylor T. Leadenhall street, master mariner. *Sols.* Taylor and Reeves, Great James st. Bedford square.

White J. and W. French, Devonshire street, Kennington, dyers. *Sol.* Younger, Wellclose square.

BANKRUPTS, *March* 9.

Bamforth J. jun. Warn-upon-Dearne, Yorkshire, butcher. *Sols.* Alexander and Holme, New inn.

Fourdrinier J. and C. J. Rickmansworth, paper makers. *Sol.* Richardson, Clement's lane, Lombard street.

Heath R. Cheltenham, carrier. *Sol.* Bridger, Angel court, Throgmorton street.

Jammieson J. Globe street, Wapping, master mariner. *Sol.* Hatchison, Crown court, Threadneedle street.

Mercer J. Heath street, Commercial road, mariner. *Sol.* Charsley, Mark lane.

Power T. F. London street, merchant. *Sol.* Osbaldeston, London street.

Stephens J. Dublin, merchant. *Sols.* Adlington and Gregory, Bedford row.

Tuckett J. and E. H. Bristol, grocers. *Sol.* Thomson, Field court, Gray's inn.

BANKRUPTCY SUPERSEDED, *March* 12.

Barfoot J. Arundel street, Strand, fancy and ornamental stationer.

BANKRUPTS.

Barfoot J. Arundel street, Strand, fancy and ornamental stationer. *Sols.* Paterson and Peile, Old Broad street.

Booth J. Gloucester, china and earthenware-man. *Sol.* Walston, Hatton garden.

Burton W. Cornhill, auctioneer. *Sols.* Collins and Waller, Spital square.

Cameron J. Manchester, merchant. *Sol.* Makinson, Middle Temple.

Cottam G. Manchester, plasterer. *Sols.* Adlington and Gregory, Bedford row.

Evans W. S. Chapel street, Lamb's Conduit street, bricklayer. *Sol.* Blakelock, Serjeant's inn, Fleet street.

Grime J. Bolton, Lancashire, upholsterer. *Sols.* Appleby and Sergeant, Gray's Inn square.

Guy T. Liverpool, broker. *Sol.* Norris, John street, Bedford row.

Hayhurst W. Rimington, Yorkshire, cotton manufacturer. *Sol.* Hurd & Co. Temple.

Howe J. Finsbury place, livery stable keeper. *Sols.* Longdill and Butterfield, Gray's Inn square.

Lamb, J. R. Pilkington, Lancashire, calico printer. *Sol.* Hay, Essex street, Manchester.

Lawes T. Amesbury, Wiltshire, corn dealer. *Sol.* Sandys and Co. Crane court, Fleet street.

Masters J. Dartford, grocer. *Sols.* Pownall and Fairthorpe, Copthall court.

Morton J. Ainsworth, Lancashire, cotton manufacturer. *Sols.* Adlington and Gregory, Bedford row.

Mycock H. Manchester, provision dealer. *Sols.* Appleby and Sergeant, Gray's inn square.

Nelson T. and E. Smith, Bolton, Lancashire, bed quilt manufacturers. *Sol.* Meddowcroft, Gray's inn.

Price T. Liverpool, baker. *Sols.* Adlington and Gregory, Bedford row.

White S. Turnham green, victualler. *Sol.* Henson, Bouverie street, Fleet street.

Trahair T. Newlyn West, Cornwall, baker. *Sol.* Rivington, Fenchurch street.

BANKRUPTCY SUPERSEDED, *March* 16.

Gunn J. Eton, Buckinghamshire, coach maker.

BANKRUPTS.

Burraston W. Worcester, hop merchant. *Sols.* Cardale and Young, Holborn court, Gray's inn.

Chaster G. Gomersal; J. Chaster, Knottingley; and T. Chaster, Dewsbury, Yorkshire, corn dealers. *Sol.* Evans, Hatton Garden.

Cocksedge T. A. Woolpit, Suffolk, merchant. *Sol.* Toms, Copthall court, Throgmorton street.

Cook W. P. Plymouth, merchant. *Sols.* Allaston and Hundleby, Freeman's court, Cornhill.

Fenner B. Fenchurch street Chambers, flour factor, *Sols.* Parnther and Turner, London street, Fenchurch street.

Houghton J. E. Fetter lane, builder. *Sol.* Deykes, Thavies inn.

Jones, G. E. Bedford, bookseller. *Sols.* Swain and Co. Frederick's place, Old Jewry.

Lea W. Birmingham, victualler. *Sols.* Long and Austen, Holborn court, Gray's inn.

Newton H. Marshall street, St. George's in the fields, tailor. *Sol.* Goodall, Southampton buildings, Chancery lane.

Whitmarsh H. H. Wingham, Kent, malster. *Sol.* Star, Canterbury.

Williamson T. Leigh, Lancashire, provision dealer. *Sol.* Shaw, Ely place, Holborn.

BANKRUPTS, MARCH 20.

Barter R. and H. Bishop's Waltham, grocers, *Sols.* Amory and Coles, Lothbury

Bennett J. A. Tabberer, and C. Scudamore Manchester, woollen cord manufacturers. *Sols.* Adlington & Gregory, Bedford row

Brodie H. Liverpool, linen draper. *Sol.* Hurd, King's Bench walk, Inner Temple

Burchall R. Ashton, Lancashire, dealer. *Sol.* Makinson, Middle Temple

Ellis R. Dean Street, Southwark, provision broker. *Sol.* Richardson, Clements Inn

Emanuel A. Plymouth Dock, navy agent. *Sol.* Walker, New Inn

Fenner R. Paternoster row, bookseller. *Sol.* Sweet, Basinghall street

Fisher G. Liverpool, merchant. *Sols.* Clarke and Co. Chancery lane.

Garland J. Austin friars, merchant. *Sols.* Bourdillon and Hewett, Bread street, Cheapside

Hollman J. Mile end road, brewer. *Sol.* Thomas, Fen court, Fenchurch street

Murray J. Bishopsgate street, cordwainer. *Sol.* Redit, King's road, Bedford row

Needes J. Brick lane, Spital-fields, coal merchant. *Sol.* Lang, Fenchurch street

Pearse W. Oat lane, Blackwell-hall-factor. *Sol.* Stevens, Sion-College-gardens

Pell J. C. Harding and W. Willock, Fazeley, Staffordshire, cotton spinners. *Sol.* Eastham, Lawrence lane, Cheapside

Ratcliffe T. J. J. and R. Manchester, calico printers. *Sol.* Kay, Manchester street

Sykes, J. jun. J. Sykes and W. Redfearn, Almondbury, Yorkshire, fancy manufacturers. *Sol.* Battye, Chancery-lane

Watson H. Stepney green, merchant. *Sol.* Wright, Fenchurch street

Williams D. Bath, saddler. *Sols.* Dax, Son and Co. Doughty street

Wright W. Kirkdale, Lancashire, victualler. *Sols.* Dacie and John, Palsgrave place, Temple bar

BANKRUPTS, MARCH 23.

Brumwell R. Newcastle-upon-Tyne, hatter, *Sol.* Brooksbank, Grays-inn-square.

Fleming T. Limehouse, sugar-refiner, *Sols.* Paterson and Peill, Old Broad-street.

Groning R. Broad-street-buildings, merchant, *Sols.* Blunt and Bowman, Broad-street-buildings.

Haward J. Liverpool, flour-dealer, *Sol.* Smith, Holborn-court, Gray's-inn.

Hunt I, Cheltenham, brandy-merchant, *Sol.* Bridger, Angel-court, Throgmorton-street.

Parkinson T. sen. T. Parkinson, jun. and I. Lilley, Sculcoates, Yorkshire, raff-merchants, *Sol.* Rosser, Bartletts-buildings

Moule H. Bath, baker, *Sols.* Adlington and Gregory, Bedford-row

Rugg J. Bristol, victualler, *Sol.* Edmonds, Exchequer-office of Pleas, Lincoln's-inn.

Stanley, R. Horridge-end, Derbyshire, flour-dealer, *Sols.* Wills & Co. Warnford-court.

Tatum W. and E. Palmer, Fish-street-hill, paper-stainers, *Sol.* Hodson, Old-jury

Wood S. Bolton, Lancashire, baker, *Sol.* Meddowcroft, Gray's-inn.

S

PRICES CURRENT, *March* 20, 1819.

	£.	s.	d.	£.	s.	d.
American pot-ash, per cwt	0	0	0 to 2	7	0	
Ditto pearl	2	15	0	2	16	0
Barilla	1	12	0	0	0	0
Brandy, Cogniac, bond. gal.	0	5	6	0	6	3
Camphire, refined....lb.	0	4	10	0	5	0
Ditto unrefined··cwt.	10	10	0	13	0	0
Cochineal, fine black, lb.	1	7	0	1	9	6
Ditto, East India	0	5	6	0	6	0
Coffee, fine bond....cwt.	6	0	0	6	10	0
Ditto ordinary	5	17	0	6	1	0
Cotton Wool, Surinam,lb.	0	1	5	0	1	7
Ditto Jamaica	0	1	2	0	1	6
Ditto Smyrna	0	0	11	0	1	1
Ditto East-India	0	0	6	0	0	9½
Currants, Zant....cwt.	5	0	0	5	10	0
Elephants' Teeth	32	0	0	36	0	0
——— Scrivelloes	21	0	0	30	0	0
Flax, Riga........ton	83	0	0	0	0	0
Ditto Petersburgh	64	0	0	0	0	0
Galla, Turkey.... cwt··	9	0	0	9	10	0
Geneva, Holl. bond. gal.	0	3	0	0	3	8
Ditto, English	9	6	6	0	0	0
Gum Arabic, Turkey, cwt.	9	10	0	12	0	0
Hemp, Riga ...... ton	46	0	0	50	0	0
Ditto Petersburgh	45	0	0	46	0	0
Indigo Caraccas .. lb.	0	10	0	0	10	6
Ditto East India	0	7	8	0	9	3
Iron Briish bars ·· ton.	13	0	0	14	0	0
Ditto Swedish C.C.N.D.	21	10	0	22	0	0
Ditto Swed· 2nd sort	16	0	0	17	0	4
Lead in pigs....... fod	0	0	0	26	0	0
Ditto red······ ton	0	0	0	27	0	0
Ditto white......ton	0	0	0	40	0	0
Logwood·········· ton	8	10	0	9	0	0
Madder, Dutch crop, cwt.	6	0	0	6	5	0
Mahogany..........ft.	0	1	6	0	2	0
Oil, Lucca··24 gal. jar	17	0	0	19	0	0
Ditto Florence, ½ chest	2	10	0	0	0	0
Ditto whale	36	0	0	37	0	0
Ditto spermaceti··ton	85	0	0	0	0	0
Pitch, Stockholm ·· cwt.	0	11	0	0	0	0
Raisins, bloom .... cwt.	4	2	0	4	10	0
Rice, Carolina bond····	2	5	0	0	0	0
Rum, Jamaica bond gal.	0	0	0	0	0	0
Ditto Leeward Island··0	0	0	0	0	0	0
Saltpetre, East Iudia, cwt.	1	15	6	1	17	0
Silk, thrown, Italian, lb.	2	19	0	3	8	0
Silk, ···raw,... ·Ditto··	1	16	0	2	4	0
Tallow, Russia, white ..	0	0	0	2	16	0
Ditto———, yellow··	3	8	0	0	0.	0
Tar, Stockholm....bar.	1	0	0	1	1	0
Tin in blocks........cwt.	4	12	6	0	0	0
Tobacco, Maryland, lb.	0	0	11	0	1	6
Ditto Virginia ······	0	0	0	0	0	10½
Wax, Guinea······cwt.	9	0	0	9	10	0
Whale-fins (Greenl) ton	80	0	0	85	0	0
Wine :						
Red Port, boud pipe ··	39	0	0	55	0	0
Ditto Lisbon	38	0	0	44	0	0
Ditto Madeira	60	0	0	70	0	0
Ditto Mountain	28	0	0	33	0	0
Ditto Cape	20	0	0	30	0	0
Ditto Sherry ······butt	30	0	0	65	0	0
Ditto Claret ·····..····	25	0	0	65	0	0

Fire-Office Shares, &c. *March* 20.

	£.	s.	£.	s.
Canals.				
Chesterfield ....Div. 5l.....	102	—	—	—
Coventry .... (Div. 44l.) ..	1050	—	—	—
Croydon	4	—	—	—
Crinan	2	2	—	—
Ellesmere and Chester (D.2l.)	68	—	—	—
Grand Junction ...(Div. 9l.)..	257	—	—	—
Grand Surry	55	—	—	—
Ditto (optional) Loan Div. 5l.	94	—	—	—
Huddersfield	13	—	—	—
Kennett and Avon (Div.17l.6s.)	22	—	—	—
Lancaster	28	—	—	—
Leeds and Liverpool (Div 10l.)	340	—	—	—
Oxford ....Div.31l.	630	—	—	—
Peakforest	60	—	—	—
Stratford & Avon	23	—	—	—
Thames and Medway	26	10	—	—
Regents	45	—	39	—
Docks.				
Commercial......Div. 3l. ...	52	—	—	—
East India ....Div. 10l.	185	—	—	—
London ...... Div. 3l.....	78½	—	—	—
West India ....Div.10l....	180	—	—	—
Insurance Companies.				
Albion ....Div. £5...	45	—	—	—
Atlas ·········---·Div. 6l.···	4	10	—	—
Birmingham Fire	400	—	—	—
Eagle ···················	2	10	—	—
Hope ···················	4	4	—	—
Imperial, ···················	89	—	—	—
London Ship ··············	21	—	—	—
Provident···············	13	—	—	—
Royal Exchange··Div. 10 ..	250	—	—	—
Sun Life	22	10	—	—
Union Fire Life ··Div. 6l....	33	—	—	—
Water Works.				
Grand Junction	41	—	39	—
London Bridge....Div. 2l. 10s.	58	—	—	—
Manchester and Salford	38	—	—	—
Portsmouth and Farlington....	9	—	—	—
South London	19	—	—	—
West Middlesex··100········	42	—	—	—
York Buildings········..···	20	7	6	—
Bridges.				
Southwark	58	10	—	—
Waterloo	10	—	—	—
Ditto Old Annuities Div. 8l.···	34	—	—	—
Ditto New do Div. 7l.	25	—	—	—
Vauxhall Bonds, 96 95	30	28	—	—
Literary Institutions.				
London, 75gs.	44	—	—	—
Russel, 25gs.	12	12	—	—
Surry, 30gs. ················	10	—	—	—
Mines.				
Beeralstone Lead and Silver....	12	10	—	—
Great Hewas......15 pd.....	17	—	—	—
British Copper Comp. 2l. 10s..	50	—	—	—
Cliff down	5	10	—	—
Wheal Goodluck ....1pr.··	—	—	—	—
Albion Copp. Mine	10	—	—	—
Roads.				
Dover Street	20	10	—	—
Highgate Archway	4	—	—	—
Miscellaneous.				
Auction Mart	21	—	—	—
Lon. Commer. Sale Rom.......	24	—	—	—
Golden Lane Brewery..50l. sh.	13	—	—	—

METEOROLOGICAL TABLE.

	8 o'clock Morning	Noon	11 o'clock Night	Height of Barom. Inches	Dryness, by Leslie Barve.	
Feb. 21	47	47	42	28,99	0	Stormy
22	39	46	40	29,80	20	Showry
23	40	40	34	,30	0	Rain
24	32	41	28	,36	17	Cloudy
25	31	41	35	,65	10	Fair
26	30	40	36	,45	12	Cloudy
27	37	47	41	,30	24	Fair
28	40	41	37	,25	10	Cloudy
Mar. 1	35	40	40	,20	0	Rain
2	42	44	40	,36	0	Rain
3	40	40	40	,55	22	Cloudy
4	37	45	42	,82	25	Fair
5	42	46	40	,95	10	Showry
6	44	48	40	,85	27	Fair
7	41	46	40	30,00	25	Cloudy
8	40	46	40	,01	30	Fair
9	42	47	40	,02	29	Fair
10	40	47	40	,01	21	Cloudy
11	41	48	46	,04	28	Cloudy
12	46	50	40	,10	29	Cloudy
13	44	47	42	,23	27	Cloudy
14	42	49	39	,24	29	Cloudy
15	37	55	40	,09	35	Fair
16	46	56	50	29,94	30	Fair
17	44	47	40	30,12	31	Cloudy
18	37	52	40	,09	30	Fair
19	47	51	44	29,52	47	Showry
20	44	54	39	,62	26	Showry

London Premiums of Insurance.

Aberdeen, Dundee, Perth, &c. 15s. 9d. to 20s.
Africa, 2gs.
American States, 30s. to 35s.
Belfast, Cork, Dublin, 20s.
Brazils, 30s. to 35s.
Hamburgh, &c. 15s. to 20s.
Cadiz, Lisbon, Oporto, 20s.
Canada 2gs. to 2½gs.
Cape of Good Hope, 2gs.
Constantinople, Smyrna, &c. 35s. to 40s.
East-India (Co. ships) 3gs.
——— out and home, 6gs.
France, 10s. 6d. to 15s. 9d.
Gibraltar, 20 to 25s.
Gottenburg, 1½gs. to 2gs.
Greenland, out and home, 3gs. to 3½gs.
Holland 12s. 6d. to 15s. 9d.
Honduras, &c. 2gs.
Jamaica, 35s.
Leeward Islands, 25s. to 30s.
Madeira, 20s.
Malta, Italian States, &c. 35s. to 40s.
Malaga, 25s. to 30s.
Newfoundland, 30s. to 35s.
Portsmouth, Falmouth, Plymouth, 15s. 9d.
River Plate, 2gs.
Southern Fishery, out and home, 10gs.
Stockholm, Petersburgh, Riga, &c. 20s.

LONDON MARKETS.

PRICE OF BREAD.

The Peck Loaf to weigh 17lb. 6oz.	..... 4s. 0d
The Half ditto	ditto 8 11	 2	0
The Quar. ditto	ditto 4 5	 1	0
The half ditto	ditto 2 2¾	 0	6

POTATOES.

Kidney...... 8 0 0 | Ox Nobles .. 7 0 0
Champions .. 7 0 0 | Apple 7 0 0
ONIONS, per Bushel, 2s 0d to 3s 6d

MEAT.

Smithfield, per stone of 8b. to sink the Offa

1819.	Beef s. d.	mut. s. d.	veal. s. d.	pork s. d.	lamb s. d.
Feb. 27 ..	5 8	6 6	7 0	6 8	0 0
..	6 4	6 4	7 6	6 6	0 0
..	5 6	6 6	7 6	6 8	0 0
..	5 8	6 4	7 0	6 8	0 0

SUGAR.

Lumps ordinary or large 32 to 40 lbs...	100
Fine or Canary, 24 to 30 lbs.	120
Loaves, fine.........................	126
Powder, ordinary, 9 to 11lbs..........	101

COTTON TWIST.

Feb. 19. Mule 1st quality, No. 40 2s. 10d
————No. 120 7s. 0d
————2d quality, No. 40 2s. 7d
Discount—25 a 30 per cent.

COALS, delivered at 13s. per chald. advance.

	Sunderland.	Newcastle.
Feb. 26. ..	32s 3d to 41 6	32s 6d to 44 0
Mar. 6. ..	34s 3 42 3	31s 6d 43 0
14. ..	37s 6 42 9	31s 0d 42 3
20. ..	31s 6 42 0	31s 6d 42 6

LEATHER.

Butts, 50 to 56lb. 24	Calf Skins 30 to
Dressing Hides .. 18	45lb. per doz. 36
Crop hides for cut. 19	Ditto 50 to 70.. —
Flat Ordinary .. 16	Seals, Large.... 100

SOAP; yellow, 90s.; mottled 102s.; curd 106s.
CANDLES; per doz. 13s. 0d. ; moulds 14s. 6d.

Course of Exchange.

Bilboa	38	Palermo, per oz 123d.
Amsterdam,	11.7	Leghorn	51¼
Ditto at sigh	11·4	Genoa	47¼
Rotterdam	11·9	Venice,	24·80
Hamb. us. 2½	34 4	Naples	41¼
Altona us.	34·5	Lisbon	57½
Paris, 3d. d.	23·85	Oporto	58½
Ditto, 2 us.	24.10	Rio Janeiro	61
Madrid	39·½	Dublin	12
Cadiz	39·½	Cork	12

Agio Bank of Holland, 2 per cent.

HAY and STRAW.—AT SMITHFIELD.

	Hay. £. s. d.	Straw. £. s. d.	Clover. £. s. d.
Feb. 6 ..	7 7 0	2 16 0	0 0 0
13..	7 0 0	2 0 0	9 0 0
20..	7 0 0	3 0 0	9 0 0
27..	7 7 0	3 0 0	9 0 0

Price of STOCKS, from 22d February, to 20th March, 1819.

1819.	Bank Stock.	3p. Cent. Reduced.	3 p. Cent Consols.	4 p. Cent. Consols.	Navy 5 p. Cent.	Irish 5 p. Cent.	Long Annuities.	Imperial 3 p. Cent.	Ditto Annuities.	India Stock.	India Bonds.	South Sea Stock.	Excheq. Bills.	Cons. for Acc.
Feb.														
22	269	77⅞ 7	76⅝ ⅝	96	106½	—	20 3-8	—	—	—	67	—	10p	76⅜
23	267½	77 6¼	76½ 5⅞	95¼	106	—	20 3-8	—	—	—	68	—	13p	76¼
24	—	75⅝ 6¼	74⅞ 5⅜	95¼	105¾	—	20 1-8	—	—	—	66	—	11	75¼
25	266	76½ 5⅝	75⅝ 4⅞	95⅝	105⅞	—	20 1-8	—	—	—	66	—	10	76⅛
26	266	75⅞ 4⅞	75¼ 4¼	95¼	105⅞	—	19 9-6	74⅛	—	228	58	—	9	76
27	—	74⅞ 3⅜	74⅝ 2¼	92⅞	104⅛	—	20⅛	—	—	—	30	81½	4d	74⅛
Mar.														
1	—	73⅞ ⅛	73¼ 2¼	92⅝	104⅛	—	19 9-6	—	—	—	30	—	4d	74⅛
2	262	73⅛ 4¼	72⅞ 3¼	92⅝	104	—	19 3-4	—	—	221	20	—	7d	74¼
3	—	73⅝ 4⅝	73⅞ 4⅜	93⅝	104⅜	—	Shut	—	—	222	30	—	7d	74¼
4	—	74⅝ 64⅝	74⅜ 3⅜	93⅝	104⅝	—	—	—	—	222	40	—	3d	74⅝
5	Shut	74¾ ¼	74⅛ 3⅛	94⅛	107⅞	—	—	73⅛	—	—	40	81⅝	2d	74⅜
6	—	75⅜	74⅜ ⅜	94	105	—	—	—	—	—	34	—	1d	74⅜
8	—	Shut	74⅛ ⅛	Shut	105½	—	—	—	—	—	34	—	1d	74⅜
9	—	Shut	74⅛ ⅛	Shut	105⅛	—	—	—	—	—	34	—	2d	74⅜
10	—	Shut	73⅞ 4⅛	Shut	105⅝	—	—	—	—	—	34	—	2d	75
11	—	75⅜	74⅛ ⅛	Shut	105⅝	—	—	—	—	—	35	—	1d	74⅞
12	—	—	74⅛ ⅝	74½	105¼	—	—	73⅜	—	—	36	—	2d	74⅞
13	—	—	75⅛ ⅛	—	105⅛	—	—	—	—	—	37	—	2d	74⅞
15	—	—	74⅜ ⅜	—	105⅜	—	—	—	—	—	39	—	2d	74⅞
16	—	—	74⅜ ¼	—	105¼	—	—	—	—	—	40	—	1d	74⅞
17	—	—	74⅛ ⅛	94½	104⅞	—	—	73⅝	—	—	40	—	2d	74⅞
18	—	—	74⅛	—	104⅝	—	—	—	—	—	38	—	1d	74⅝
19	—	75⅛	74⅛ ⅛	—	104	—	—	73¼	—	—	37	—	par	74⅜
20	—	—	73⅞ ⅝	—	105	—	—	—	—	—	36	—	2d	74⅞

IRISH FUNDS.

Feb.	Irish Bank Stock.	Government Debenture 3½ per ct.	Government Stock, 3½ per ct.	Government Debenture 4 per ct.	Government Stock, 5 per ct.	Treasury Bills.	Grand Canal Stock.	Grand Canal Loan, 4 per ct.	Grand Canal Loan, 6 per ct.	City Dublin Bonds.	Royal Canal Loan 6per cent.	Omnium.
27	253	90⅝	88⅞	—	107⅛	—	—	—	—	—	—	
M 4	249	90⅛	—	—	106⅝	—	21½	—	81½	—	—	
5	—	91⅛	—	—	106⅞	—	—	—	—	—	—	
8	—	97⅞	89¼	—	107⅛	—	—	—	—	—	—	
13	251	91	89¾	—	107	—	—	—	—	—	—	
18	—	91½	89	—	107½	—	—	—	81¾	—	—	

AMERICAN FUNDS.

	IN LONDON Mar. 5.	Mar. 9. 12.	16.	AT NEW YORK. Feb. 19.	4.	12.
7 per Cent.	—	—	—	105	105	105
Bank Shares	21 7 6	21 7 6	21 7 6	98	98	93
Louisiana	—	—	—	par	par	par
Old 6 per Cent.	—	—	—	par	par	par
New 6 per Cent.	101	101	101	101	101	101
3 per Cent.		63	63	66	66	66

Prices of the

FRENCH FUNDS

From Feb. 22, to Mar. 22.

1819	5 per Cent. consols fr.	c.	Bank Actions. fr.	c.
Feb. 22	69		1500	—
27	67		1490	—
Mar. 3	68	50	1487	50
6	66	55	1487	50
9	65	20	1490	—
13	66	35	1500	—
16	66	75	1500	—
20	66	45	1492	50

By J. M. Richardson, 23, Cornhill.

THE

LITERARY PANORAMA,

AND

National Register:

For *MAY*, 1819.

NATIONAL AND PARLIAMENTARY NOTICES,

(British and Foreign,)

PROSPECTIVE AND RETROSPECTIVE.

CATHOLICS IN FOREIGN STATES.

REPORT

From the

SELECT COMMITTEE

On the Regulation of

ROMAN CATHOLIC SUBJECTS

IN FOREIGN STATES.

[*Ordered by the House of Commons to be Printed, 25th of June, 1816.*]

It may be very true that the intercourse of man with his Maker, should be perfectly free, and is an affair wholly between the individual, and the Supreme, to whom it is addressed: against this, as an Abstract Proposition, we would be the last to utter a single sentence. But, if we trace the course of History, we shall find, that Legislators and Statesmen, have ever esteemed it a part of their office to superintend, or at least, to watch very carefully, the Public exercise of Religious rites, and the Public avowal of Religious principles. And this solicitude has equally influenced Governments under the form of Theocracy, in which the Divinity was understood to be the Ruler, the Presiding Power, the *dernier resort*, in civil affairs, as well as in sacred; and those of the most savage

tribes, in which recourse was had to incantation and fantasies, varied by a thousand modes, in order to ascertain the will of the Deity, and to derive advantage from a foreknowledge of events which the sagacity of the human mind anticipated, as very probable, and therefore predicted as absolutely certain. All history bears evidence to this; from the inspirations by the nymph Egeria vouchsafed to the Roman Numa, and the miracle of the Sacred Shields, to the more refined establishments of the immortal city, and the numerous Colleges of Priests, endowed and patronized by the Senate of Rome, in later ages; and by the Emperors, when the Senate was all but annihilated. The sway of the Sovereign became, at length, combined with the influence of the Sacerdotal Dignity; and the Emperor united in his person the Tribunitial power, derived from the people, together with the authority of the *Pontifex Maximus*, derived from the ancient religion, patronized through succeeding ages by the State.

Nor was this combination unknown to the Jewish establishment, though originally founded on very different principles. The Maccabees were at once priests and princes; and if the Herods did not assume the priesthood, yet they placed and displaced the High

Priests, in a manner, at their pleasure. Even the Sacred vestments were withheld from the custody of those who were to wear them on the solemn feasts; and the restoration of these to their proper guardians, was celebrated as a favour obtained from the alien, the stranger Governors of the once independent and still haughty Hebrew nation.

While things were thus circumstanced, a new Religion sprang up in Judea, which was destined to cause an entire revolution in the public mind. Simple at first, and professing to be in nothing allied to worldly honours and grandeur, it gradually made its way in opposition to whatever the establishments of the world could present as most formidable. The Jewish authorities persecuted it: the Heathen, who, at first regarded it with indifference, as merely an extravagant branch from the despicable stem of Jewish superstition, contemned it in its early stages; but afterwards, grieving at the inroads it made on their long consecrated observances, they employed whatever diabolical fury could invent, in the shape of tortures and sufferings, to repel it. Their efforts were vain; and the population of the known world became acquainted, in a greater, or a less degree, with the Religion of Christ; and more or less it was professed in every part. At length, it triumphed. The Jews, who resisted it were destroyed, and the sacred structure in which they trusted, was demolished; the Gentiles were out-numbered, if not converted: the temples were forsaken; the victims were not presented; and the dignity once attributed to the worshippers of Jupiter Capitolinus, and the Fortune of the Cesars, was transferred to the descendants of those who formerly met early in the morning to perform their rites, if possible without observation, and without disturbance.

The era of prosperity, presented an era of difficulties: for, the civil government was placed in circumstances absolutely new; or if not absolutely new with respect toi tself, yet absolutely unprecedented with respect to Christianity. Constantine professed himself a Christian: Constantine interfered in Christian affairs: he advised Christian bishops; he also commanded Christian bishops; he took cognizance of Christian complaints, brought before him; and he appointed his civil officers judges in cases of Ecclesiastical delinquency. Constantine professed himself a Christian: but he was not yet baptized. He even presided, as Emperor, in the famous Council of Nice, (A. D. 325,) while yet of no higher rank in the church, than a humble Catechumen. What authority, what precedents, had Constantine for this interference? Was it merely an assumption of power as Emperor? Or, since we read of no protest against it, or of any complaint vented on the occasion, was it the obvious duty of the assembled council to submit to their Sovereign, and was it agreeable to what the Bishops knew had already occurred?

To ascertain this we must carry our researches somewhat higher: and we hint at this the more willingly, because Mr. Brown, in his " Historical Enquiry into the Ecclesiastical Jurisdiction of the Crown,"[*] has merely touched, and that very obscurely, on the antient State of Christianity in Britain; and has begun his authorities with the more obvious, and better known instance of Constantine.

Britain was the first country in which Christianity was established:——but, when we say " established," we do not mean to affirm that it was universally received. Undoubtedly, there was a considerable mass of the population (probably the majority) that long adhered to their former profession; and we well know that the Druids, the Bards, and the Ovates, for ages continued to possess a preponderance in the hearts, if not in the judgments of thousands, and tens of thousands of their countrymen: in fact, the influence of their maxims is not extinct among us, at this day.

We had occasion, some years ago,[*] to submit an Historical Sketch of the original Introduction of Christianity into Britain, by means of the captive Britons, carried with Caractacus to Rome. We even suggested the possibility, that the LIN-*us* of the Apostle Paul is the *Cy-*LIN-*us* of the British Triads; we might have gone further, and, with little risk of error, might have added, that this LIN-*us*, the first Bishop of Rome, was a Briton: for, if our conjecture do not fail us, there were *two* first Bishops of Rome; one attached to the Christian converts from the Jewish nation; the other attached to the associated converts from among the Gentiles. And this clears up the confusion found among the ancients, in respect to the first bishop of the Imperial city. Irenæus, Eusebius, Jerom, and the ancient Catalogues of the Popes place LIN-*us*, after Peter,—then Anacletus, and then Clement: while Optatus, Rufinus, Augustine, and other Latin Writers, place Clement immediately after Linus, and Anacletus after Clement. The Apostolic Constitutions say, that Linus was appointed by St. Paul, and Clement by St. Peter: so that our notion of *two* first Bishops, is not wholly without authority: for, that work, though not Apostolic, is certainly ancient; and the writer *should not* be deceived in what regards the see of Rome. Epiphanius conjectures, that Clement declined Episcopal office, during the life of Linus; who was bishop from A. D. 65 to A D. 77, twelve years.

If Linus was a Briton,—if he was of the royal family of Britain,—if Bran, his grandfather, was the first, who with Aristobulus, the disciple of St. Paul, brought Christianity into Britain, there can be no occasion of wonder, that a frequent intercourse was maintained between Britain and Rome; and when we read, that several of the British Princes, after the invasion of the island by Julius Cæsar, and especially after the expedition of Claudius, were educated at Rome, (either in whole, or in part,) the difficulties which some have found in the *familiarity* between the countries entirely disappear. For instance, Coel, the son of Meurig, received his education in Rome, and had " been familiarized to the Roman customs and manners," say the British writers. This agrees with what Tacitus relates of the policy of Agricola; and was indeed, one of the principal advantages derived from sending chiefs, or the sons of chiefs, as hostages, to the seat of Empire. Coel was succeeded by his son Lles (or *Lucius*,) whose disposition resembled that of his father. He continued in amity with the Roman Government; he even paid his stipulated tribute, although, say the British Histories, he was sufficiently powerful to have withheld it. To this King the *introduction* of Christianity has been attributed; that is wrong; but had the *settlement* of Christianity been attributed to him, it would have been right. Nor is there any thing very marvellous in the story (reported by Nennius,) of his sending to Rome,— where it will be remembered, his father was educated,—for Christian teachers; either in addition to those of his own people, or desiring to compare their accounts of Ecclesiastical matters, before he determined on a definitive arrangement in behalf of Christianity.

Be that as it might: there is nothing unnatural, in his maintaining relations with a see which had been superintended by one of his ancestors, in Apostolic times, (about 50 or 60 years before,) and, if he further *designed* to replace the Druidical priesthood by Christian instructors, generally, and if he really did *begin* to assign Druidical lands, or temples to the support of Christian worship, and the Christian interest, as such, where is the cause of astonishment? He might *begin*,—he might partially execute,—that which he did not live to accomplish; and after ages would, and very probably did, without reserve, attribute to him, that which he intended, that which he sanctioned in the first instance, by his authority, and possibly, exerted his influence to render permanent, and to increase, as well

---

[*] See LIT. PAN. O. S. vol. II. p. 837. Comp. N. S. Vol. VIII. p. 1056-57.

after his death, as during his life. He died at Gloucester, A. D. 136. He was King of the Silures, and great grandson of Caractacus. The *conversion* of Lucius by divines sent from Rome, is a monkish imposition, or rather misapplication of an historical fact;—but truth may be the basis of the tale, though the additions be mere perversions, whether intentional, or from ignorance.

The power of Lucius, in all probability, did not extend beyond the country of the Silures, over which he was King; yet his example could not remain unknown, or unnoticed, or without its influence, among his cdntemporaries and his successors.   It is true, that he has been called " *Sovereign of all Britain ;*" and the title might continue in the family of Caractacus, and therefore might belong to him; but, it would be very difficult to prove that he enjoyed the power of sovereignty ; the utmost we can fairly allow him, is deference, or influence.

Christianity, however, continued to spread in Britain, under and after his fostering care, and from the number of churches destroyed in the Dioclesian persecution, it must have prevailed. And now we come to the time of Constantius and his son Constantine. The universal tradition of the Britons, with the unvarying assertions of the British Historians, is, that Constantine married Helen, surnamed *the Prosperous*, a British lady, daughter of Coel Coedhebawg, Earl of Gloucester: that he lived, and died, at York, where Constantine was born.

We are not ignorant, that this has been disputed. We cannot investigate it here ; but, even without this fact, the remark is obvious, that Constantine had not only beheld the interference of heathen Emperors, as head of the State, in behalf of the heathen rites and religious establishments ; but, he had also contemplated in Britain, at least one example of a Christian Prince, interfering as head of his country, in behalf of Christian rites and establishments. Now Lucius had so interfered,

not only without blame, but with much and general praise. The Clergy whom he patronized, could not immediately forget him ; and the regulations he promulgated, apparently, continued to be conformed to, long after his decease. Of this, Constantine could not be ignorant ; whence we infer, that Britain furnished the first instance of protection afforded by the State to the Church ; as it furnished the first instance of a Royal family, converted to the Christian faith.

We do not forget the story of Abgarus, King of Edessa; but, it forms but a feeble rival to this descent of religious profession in the Royal family of Britain, and this royal provision for the perpetuity of the Christian faith. Undoubtedly, protection by the King implied submission by the Christian ministers, whom he protected; for, to suppose that he introduced, or admitted, or that they so much as thought of assuming an independent power, is to suppose what could not possibly exist at the time.

We are greatly mistaken if the power of the King of the Silures extended to the introduction of an independant priesthood: the British Constitution then abhorred, as the British Constitution now abhors, such an *imperium in imperio*. The nation then met by its representatives; and since these representatives, or, at least, very many of them were Druids, or Druidically inclined, the power of the King was necessarily limited ; and his designs would have been counteracted, had they been so grossly unconstitutional. It should be remembered, also, that, as a tributary King, the Romans had paramount authority in his dominions ; and the Roman authority was sufficiently opposed to Christianity, at this period, and long after. These considerations are independent of the question whether *Diocesan* Bishops were known at this time ; and whether the instructors sent from Rome to Lucius, would, or could, assume the character of Diocesan Bishops.

It is not, indeed, beyond question, whether, in the comparatively much later age of Constantine, 'all the Bishops at Nice, who obeyed his summons, were Diocesans. But, it is certain, that in a previous assembly held at Arles, in France, by the Emperor's order, the British Church was represented by three British Bishops, a Presbyter, and a Deacon.[*] And the consent of our Ecclesiastical Historians, is pretty general in the probability that Britain had Bishops in the Council at Nice.

Great indeed, was the difference between the importance attached or attachable to the actions of Lucius and of Constantine; the first was Sovereign of a part only of an island at the extremity of the Roman Empire, and was himself an acknowledged tributary to the Roman Power; the other was head of the most extensive dominions, as well in the east, as in the west, and his dictates would reach throughout many provinces, and even many nations. Constantine had summoned Bishops from all parts; and the whole assembly, met by his orders, exceeded the number of two thousand persons. The Emperor did not pretend to assume authority in matters of faith; but, he maintained his claim to oversee the external affairs of the church, and to preserve the public peace; then in no small danger, from the controversies and contentions of Churchmen.

The removal of the seat of Empire to Constantinople, left Rome, the Imperial city, very much to itself; and succeeding events diminished the power of the successors of Constantine so greatly, that the bishop of Rome, as a public person, could hardly avoid exercising, mediately, or immediately, an increasing portion of that authority which was necessary for governing the city and its vicinity, and which pro-

perly belonged to the Sovereign. Rome also, was 'the seat of learning, the centre of learning to all the provinces of the Empire which had become familiar with the latin tongue; and these being harassed and disturbed by invaders, and becoming almost wholly military, the ecclesiastical power of the Roman Pontiffs gradually assumed the supremacy, not only over Italy, but over all professing the name of Christ; and at length boldly claimed as its right, derived from the Prince of the Apostles, that paramount authority which the Princes of the Earth had suffered to glide away from their grasp.

To this, subjugation however, the Greek emperors were less reduced than Sovereigns in the west of Europe: and the successors of Constantine, though many of them were feeble minded, yet preserved a dignity independent of the Popes, to whom they acknowledged no canonical obedience; and on whom they occasionally conferred not submission, but protection.

The representative of these successors in the Eastern Empire, is now the Emperor of Austria, who, being ci-devant, the Emperor of Germany, was acknowledged chief among Christian Potentates, and in his titles, at least, preserved a shadow of the dignity of the Holy Roman Empire. It is, therefore, not merely a fair question—but it is an important question to ask,—What is the nature, and the state of that authority and influence, which this representative of Constantine allows to the Roman Pontiff, in his dominions?

And this question is now of peculiar importance;—the Catholics of our country are urging claims, which have been repeatedly canvassed, which may again be canvassed, but which must not be admitted without great deliberation. They are taking advantage of a new Parliament, to try once more their strength in the Legislative Assemblies. They demand privileges which are not to be measured by those which their Church enjoys in any other nation, whether that nation be Catholic or Protestant. This proposition is of a nature to be established by evidence;

---

[*] The Bishops which signed are the following:
EBORIUS Episcopus, de civitate Eboracensi Provincia Britannia.
RESTITUTUS Episcopus, de Civitate Londinensi, provincia supra scripta.
ADELFIUS Episcopus, de civitate Colonia Londinensium.
EXINDE Sacerdos Presbyter.
ARMENIUS Diaconus.

and this evidence has been provided for us by the authority of Government, and the industry and influence of its agents in foreign countries.

The Report before us, has been characterized by Representatives of Catholic Powers, as the severest blow ever struck at the Catholic interest in Britain. It is an official account of the sentiments of their Sovereigns, *as Sovereigns*, as heads of great political bodies; and it manifests such a jealousy of the presumptions and pretensions of the Court of Rome, as becomes truly exemplary, and never to be lost sight of. Nor is this jealousy less than general, all over Europe: the documents are furnished from the Public authorities of Austria and Germany, of Italy, of France, of Spain and Portugal, of Switzerland, of Prussia, of Denmark, of Sweden, of Russia; in short, of all Christendom. It comprises the opinions of the most learned Jurisconsults, and Historians; documents issued on particular occasions, as well as standing orders, and unyielding principles. Were it only as containing particulars of the State of the Catholic Religion in the countries referred to, it well deserves to be of the acquaintance of our readers; but, as affording an object of comparison with the demands of the dissatisfied among our own Catholics, its importance is greatly enhanced.

This document will furnish materials for three papers. The subject naturally divides itself into a consideration of the conduct of powers Catholic, and powers Protestant: which should be followed by an application of their principles of policy to ourselves; or, at least, a comparison of their maxims and regulations with our own. The contracted limits of our pages warn us against further enlargement at present; and however reluctant, we must close. The Public will accept an apology for the slight view which it is in our power to communicate, of a document containing five hundred and forty-four folio pages, with a supplement of fifty pages, mostly on a small type. We have often experienced the indulgence we now solicit; and on that indulgence we must again depend.

. . . .

REPORT

From the

SELECT COMMITTEE,

To whom the Official Papers relating to Regulation of the

ROMAN CATHOLICS,

In the Several States of Europe, &c. have been referred, &c.

[The following is part of the Report by the Committee, in reference to the election or appointment of Bishops, in the dominions of the Emperor of Austria.]

"The *Austrian* bishops are nominated or appointed by the Emperor, which appointment is in lieu of the election, or postulation of the chapters of their respective cathedrals, and has the same effect; the Papal confirmation being afterwards obtained through the Austrian minister at Rome. To this mode of election the archbishop of *Olmutz* forms the sole exception; the right of chusing him vesting entirely in the chapter of his see.

"As king of *Hungary*, the Emperor has the sole right of appointing not only the archbishops and bishops, both of the *Latin* and *Greek* churches, but also *titular* bishops and prelates for those chapters and monasteries in the *Turkish* dominions, which once formed a part of that kingdom.

"In *Hungary*, all bishops appointed by the sovereign, immediately perform every part of their functions which relate to jurisdiction, before they have been confirmed by the Pope. . . . .

"It is positively enjoined by the *Austrian* law, that, at the consecration of a bishop, the episcopal oath shall neither be given, nor taken, in any other than its original and proper sense, of a mere canonical obedience to the Pope, in nowise infringing upon the rights of the Emperor, or on the duties, as subjects, to which the bishops are sworn by the particular oath of allegiance and fidelity to their sovereign, which they are obliged to take after their nomination, and previous to their taking the pontifical oath. . . . .

" All papal reservations have been done away with, both in *Austria* and in *Hungary;* by the laws of which latter .State it is provided, that " no one shall attempt to procure to himself the presentation or collation to any ecclesiastical benefice from any other than the king, or those who have the right of patronage." The Austrian bishops are bound to make the provincial government acquainted with the name, country, place of education, progress, morals, &c. of every candidate for orders; exhibiting due testimonials, and the requisite title, previous to his ordination." . . . .

" The PLACITUM REGIUM, as admitted in *Austria,* is, " the right of requiring that all ecclesiastical statutes and ordinances be submitted to the state before their publication, and of prohibiting their promulgation whenever they are found to relate to objects not essential to the legitimate ends of the church, or obnoxious to the interest of the state. And this right extends not merely to rescripts or regulations of discipline, but to those also which are dogmatical; as something might be added to them in the mode of their publication or penal sanction, which is not a point of doctrine."

In execution of this power it is provided by the Austrian laws, " That all Papal rescripts, as well originals, as authenticated copies, are to be laid before the provincial government, and afterwards transmitted to the supreme tribunal, along with the opinion of the attorney-general, and of the provincial government. That this is to be observed not only with regard to newly emitted bulls, briefs, or other regulations of the Pope, but also with regard to Papal rescripts of former times, at whatever period they may have been issued, so that whoever desires to make use of them is bound to obtain the imperial *placet*." . . . . Also,

That " no person is allowed to apply for an indult from the Pope for the celebration of any new festival, or for any new act of devotion, without permission from the Emperor."

. That " kinsmen, relations in prohibited degrees, are forbidden to apply to the Ecclesiastical court for any dispensation, without having previously obtained the consent of the sovereign for that purpose.':

That, " if (in such cases) the bishop thinks the Papal dispensation necessary, especial leave to apply for it at *Rome* is to be obtained from the sovereign; which leave is generally granted, on condition that the said dispensation is to be had *gratis*." . . . .

That " Exemptions from episcopal jurisdiction, are of no avail when they are in contradiction to the general laws of the country, or when it cannot be shewn that they have been confirmed by an imperial *placet*, which is absolutely required for the execution of any Papal ordinance, though of ever so long standing." . . .

That " though bishops may visit slight offences of the clergy, which incur no civil punishment, with some temporal chastisement of a gentle nature, such as a moderate confinement and fasting, yet it is only in consequence of their having a licence to do so from the Emperor." . .

Advices of a subsequent date appear to have been received from authentic sources, intimating that the *Austrian* government persists in the resolution of " not permitting the publication of any Papal rescripts or pastorals from any foreign bishop, without the application of the *Regium Placitum;* and that the edict, on this head, has been renewed; as the Congregation *della Riforma* was desirous to revive certain *ultramontane* claims."

[The following Extracts are from the Evidence annexed. Robert Gordon, Esq. his Majesty's Minister at Vienna, writes to Sir John Cox Hippisley,

" The kingdom in the north of Italy, which had been annexed to the Emperor's dominion, is speedily to be brought under the same administration of ecclesiastical law; and the Pope's authority has already been rejected in the late changes which have been made touching these matters, in the Milanese.

" The present Emperor follows literally the spirit which Joseph II. displayed in securing his government from Papal influence, and he lately was on the point of promulgating an edict to forbid the establishment of Jesuits throughout his dominions, but has been withheld by a wish not to offend the Court of Rome, when his object might be otherwise attained. He is contented therefore to remain silent, as long as none offer to settle themselves in his country, and is resolved to refuse permission to each individual who may hereafter express such a wish."

[It is impossible not to coincide with this wise determination of the Emperor of Austria.

Among other documents annexed, are copious extracts from a very learned and laborious work, entitled "*Enchiridion Juris Ecclesiastici Austriaci:*" A Manual, or Text Book, of the Ecclesiastical Law of Austria," originally published in German, and afterwards translated into Latin, by George Rechberger, Doctor in Law, Chancellor of the Bishopric of Lintz, 1809. Of this treatise we can offer here, only a specimen.]

Rights falsely ascribed to the Church— direct or indirect power in Temporals.

"There have been some who have ascribed to the Pope, as king of all kings, a direct power over all temporal concerns. An opinion so highly injurious to the civil power has been solidly refuted by Bellarmine. But, by a singular inconsistency, he himself substituted another power of the church over temporal concerns, which he calls an indirect one; and in Catholic kingdoms, where church and state constitute, as he says, a single christian commonwealth, he attributes that power to the Pope, as head of the church. This power, he asserts, refers to all civil concerns which have any relation to the spiritual object of the church, and must be measured accordingly. It is in consequence of this power, he adds, that the Pope may depose sovereigns, who, by any heresy, or other ecclesiastical crime, obstruct the salvation of souls, and that he may absolve their subjects from their

allegiance. But both these opinions are most plainly contrary to the true principles of the nature and limits of both powers; to the express words of holy writ; to the doctrine of the fathers; and to the example of the ancient church[*]."

[What our Countrymen may think of this doctrine, it is not difficult to divine: especially, as we find that the right of levying tolls and taxes is by other casuists held to be null and void, till it has received the acquiescence and sanction of his Holiness at Rome. The attention of the Austrian Government extends to inferior Ecclesiastics also.].

Election of Prelates (not being Bishops) in Austria.

The mode of proceeding in the elections of prelates had been settled in Austria by an agreement between the Emperor Rodolph II. and Urban bishop of Passau, of November 6th, 1592; but is now newly regulated by a particular Imperial Statute of September 10th, 1805.[†] Whenever a prelature becomes vacant, commissaries are deputed by the provincial government to the college where the vacancy has taken place, to make an inventory of the effects of the deceased, which commissaries, in order to assert its jurisdiction, affix the seal of the civil government of the province in a convenient place, and appoint a provisional administrator of the estate. The bishop likewise appoints an administrator in spirituals, and generally entrusts this office to the dean, or to the prior of the monastery. The chapter then sends their petition to the court, for permission to proceed to the election of another pre-

---

* This subject is copiously discussed by *Bossuet*, in his Defence of the Declaration of the French Clergy, lib. i. sect. 2. *Dupin* de Antiq. Eccl. Discipl. Diss. vii. Anonym. de Potest. Eccl. et Tempor. propos. 1. Natal. Alexand. Diss. 2, in Hist. Eccl. Sect 11 & 12.

* The same regulations are to be observed at the election of Abbesses, and other superiors in female convents, when their office is for life. June 23d, 1806. (For the kingdom of Gallicia.)

late. As soon as the consent of the court is obtained, the imperial commissaries and the bishop jointly fix the day for the election, against which both the imperial and episcopal deputies repair to the chapter where the vacancy has occurred. The commissaries of the bishop direct the election itself in the way prescribed by the canons ; they communicate the name of the elected candidate to the commissaries of the Emperor, and if there be no objection started on their part, they publish the name of the elected prelate in their presence, and on the person elected consenting to accept the office, they confirm him in the name of the bishop, and proceed to his installation in spirituals, after he has pronounced his profession of faith, and taken the usual oath of canonical obedience ; and when this is done, the imperial deputies add the installation in temporals. The provincial government makes its report of the whole business of the election to the court for the Emperor's approbation. As for the particular observances in every such election they are accurately stated in the aforesaid statute.

The Effects of Nomination.

"The effects of nomination are, 1st, That nomination previous to its admission by the Pope, only gives a *right* TO *the thing*, so that a nominee, possessed of the required qualifications, may not be rejected by the Pope; the nominor may however, without infringing any right of the person first named, present a more deserving object. 2d, Nomination admitted by the superior, holds in the room of confirmation or institution, and gives a *right* IN *the thing*, and thus ratifies the spiritual marriage, and gives the power of administration.

On the Denial of Christian Burial.

" As the being forbid entering any church, and being deprived of christian burial, is a kind of ecclesiastical censure, it certainly cannot take place without a previous cognizance of the cause, followed by a judicial sentence, and attended with the consent of the Sovereign. Public officers, who were formerly obliged to bring testimonies to their superiors of having confessed at Easter, are exempt from this law, in consequence of the abuses to which it gave rise. April 21st, 1788.

The Analysis of Human Nature; or, an investigation of the means to improve the Condition of the Poor ; and to promote the happiness of mankind in general; comprising, also, the progress and present state of political, moral, and religious society. By S. Phelps, author of a "Treatise on the importance of extending the British Fisheries."† 8vo. 2 vls. £1 1s. Simpkin & Marshall, London, 1818.

It has been the distinguished honour of Great Britain, to have given birth to the ablest writers on political economy. Much as has been accomplished towards elucidating and simplifying that important branch of Science, by the works of Adam Smith, Steuart, Messrs. Ricardo, Malthus, and others, they have not so entirely exhausted the subject, as to afford no farther topics for subsequent writers. The author of the work now under consideration has discussed a great variety of important matters ; and has brought to the task a spirit of practical benevolence that pervades every page of his volume, together with a research both deep and successful, and an acquaintance with the state of every country which can afford any elucidation of the various points he has treated of—such as we do not often witness in treatises on political science.

The volumes before us contain (as their title implies) a series of disquisitions embracing almost every branch of political economy ; in which the ameliorating of the condition of our own poor justly holds a most prominent place. After some general remarks on the state of the poor and of the industrious classes, as well as of society in general, and the various opinions which have been offered with regard to the relief of the poor, Mr. Phelps devotes a considerable portion of his first volume to an examination of the principle of population,—the ratio of the increase of population compared with that of food, —and the effects of population in savage

† For an analysis of this valuable work, see pp. 189—200, of the present volume.

and in civilized life. The celebrated principle of Mr. Malthus,—that "the human race have a tendency to increase faster than food can be provided for them,"—is here controverted, we. will not say with complete success, but certainly with no small degree of ability. As our opinions on most of these important topics have already been given in different volumes of the Literary Panorama, we shall not enter into any comments or details on this part of our author's work, but shall select a few passages, which we think will impart both instruction and gratification to our readers.

Mr. Phelps's argument against Mr. Malthus's theory of '*moral restraint*' is, briefly, that it is at variance with the apparent plan of the Supreme Being.

"An increase of population, as I believe, is an increase of wealth and happiness, to an industrious and civilized nation, under good government; and although it may produce more, "animal wants," as it is termed, yet, at the same time, it provides more means to supply them; for there was never yet a country without subsistence for its inhabitants, when there were sufficient hands able and willing to work, and allowed to labour.

"Those philosophers who state the contrary, (and they are not many,) appear not to have considered, that when man was created, a reasoning faculty was given him, with hands to work, as well as an organ of individuality, and powers of the mind, to direct his operations; but not so with the brute, that can neither sow nor increase the harvest, nor extend the supply which nature has provided for his subsistence, without the aid of man.

"The earth will always supply the wants of its inhabitants, if cultivated with energy and distributed with prudence and justice; but if the field be kept from the labourer, and tyranny obstructs the hand of industry, our animal wants may then exceed the supply of nature, and man may be destitute of subsistence, by being deprived of the efforts of his labour.

"He who has a belief in a Supreme Being, must also have a confidence in his divine and infinite wisdom, and feel conscious that nothing was ever made by him in vain;—that there never was, nor ever will be, that being created, for which no provision is made for its support:—that it is the fault of man, opposing the will of God, when examples are found to the contrary."

"The question then comes to this, Is there more wealth, more means of subsistence, less poverty, and more happiness, in proportion, in a thinly populated country, than where there is a numerous population? Those who pretend that there is, should show where it exists. And is not the supply of subsistence, as well as every thing else, according to the demand and means of purchase, or the effort used in procuring it? For, who will cultivate the earth beyond the extent of his own wants, if he cannot dispose of the surplus produce of his labour? And to what a state would the agriculture of this country be reduced, if the population were reduced to half its present number? Would not the cultivation of the lands be improved, if the population were increased; and would there not then be sufficient food, if no corn were allowed to be imported? And would there not be a greater demand for labour?

"If it could be proved of any country, that it could not supply food, by the utmost efforts of industry, for its inhabitants, why then it might be affirmed, that in such a country there is an excess of population, and some check to population, or emigration, must certainly be necessary; and some people, perhaps, may insist that such is the present state of Great Britain, but which appears by no means to be the case. There is certainly a vast number of people out of employ, but there is also no proper encouragement given to find them employment; and there is a great deal of misery which few people endeavour in the proper way to relieve. Some will say, that there are not the means;—but the causes of this will be discussed hereafter.

"It has been asserted, as already stated, "that all the good and well-situated lands of this country, being already appropriated and occupied, capital and subsistence can no longer be kept up to the population." It may be allowed, that all the good and well-situated lands are occupied; but it cannot be said, that even these are all appropriated to yield food for man. A great part may be said to be applied to not only the comforts, but to the luxuries and extravagancies of life. It requires as much food to support a horse, or at least as much land to produce it, as would subsist a large family, or even several families, if it were cultivated to the utmost extent, and made to yield the most productive food for man. But, independently of all this, there are more lands uncultivated in the United Kingdom, than would subsist double the number of its present inhabitants, if properly laboured and cultivated; and this assertion must not be put down by the popular cry, that they are not worth cultivating, or that it would require more expence and more labour than they are worth. This is the very thing we want. Land and labour will be always better than spontaneous productions, which create idleness.

"The reason why there is not more land cultivated in this country is, that either there are not sufficient hands to do it, at the price they would be paid, or that there is not sufficient capital employed in that branch of industry. As this is a commercial and manufacturing country, the industry and capital of the country are most directed to those objects, by which more profit on capital and labour can be obtained than in agriculture.

"There is no want of food when there is money to pay for it. The supply of food, like other things, is always according to the demand; and nothing but money, or the means of barter, is ever known to be deficient; but if corn could not be imported, all hands would then soon turn to agriculture, and it would be soon found that there would be no occasion for importations of corn, or want of subsistence for the population.

"Did any one ever know, where there was a decrease of population, that there was a greater plenty of riches, food, or comfort? Look into history, and behold to what state even empires may be reduced, when their population is decreased. Was Greece more happy when the population of her states decreased? And did not Roman greatness decline with the decrease of her population? Has there been

greater plenty in Egypt since her towns and people have been destroyed, and the whole country has exhibited a picture of deserted villages.

"Rome was destroyed by importing corn from her provinces and subject countries, by turning all the lands of Italy into pasture, and thus taking all the people from the pursuits of agriculture, and giving them the habits of idleness. The Romans could get corn without labour, and therefore they had no inclination to work; but when corn was not to be obtained by these means, the people retorted upon their government, that had ruined them by such indulgencies. When the royal Cincinnatus worked in the field, Rome was happy. Look at the mighty Syracuse, where luxury and wealth had once no bounds; when her population decreased, her former festive boards could scarcely supply the wants of a pauper.

"Even in the frigid zone, and under the rigour of an arctic climate, there are proofs that a populous community is best for human happiness and comfort. When the shores of Iceland, for instance, were covered by a numerous and independent people, as they once were, they could then supply their own wants, without the help of other nations; but since the hand of tyranny and oppression has reduced their numbers, they are often exposed to the misery of want and famine.

"It does not require the aid of metaphysical knowledge, or of very profound philosophy, to show what will be sufficient to supply the wants of nature, or of an extensive population. Industry, favoured by freedom, justice, and wise regulations, will do the whole. But if we must come to geometrical and arithmetical calculations, and admit that two and two make four, and four and four make eight, and eight and eight make sixteen, which is stated to be the ratio of the increase of population; we must also admit that four pair of hands will supply food for at least eight persons; and that the more hands there are to work, the greater will be the plenty and ease for the population; and the more hands there will be to spare for cultivating and adorning the neglected part of the country, and for adding to the comforts and luxuries of life.

" But they say that population increases by geometrical rule, and subsistence does not; that there is a limit to the latter, and not to the former. How do they know this? Who can prove that there is no limit to the number of the human species? The quantity of land, which we know of, cannot certainly, according to our present knowledge and understanding, be made to yield more than a certain quantity of food; but this is no proof that it may not yield more by further intelligence. We can produce more from the earth than untutored savages; and future ages may make discoveries, and produce what is unknown to us. Sir Walter Raleigh added to our means of subsistence by the introduction of potatoes, and greater discoveries may yet be made than this, should there be occasion for them. But if the earth will supply enough subsistence for its inhabitants, enough must be sufficient, and it is all that is required; and, it may be repeated, that no proof has ever yet been given to the contrary of the earth being capable of yielding sufficient subsistence for its inhabitants, and probably never will, where there is a proper reward and encouragement for labour.

" A Mr. Higinbottom, professor of music, at Overbury, in Yorkshire, lately died. He was father, grandfather, and great grandfather to 305 children. He was followed to his tomb by nine of his own children, whose united ages amounted to 533 years, and 59 grand children, and numerous other relatives.—Were all men to produce a progeny like this, if it continued without variation, and it increased by geometrical ratio, population would certainly soon press against the means of subsistence; but perhaps, in the course of the same space of time, in which this progeny has been raised, the family of the Higinbottoms may be entirely extinct. "*Sic transit gloria mundi.*"

In the chapter "on the effect of population in savage life compared with that of civilization," we have the following interesting passage.

" But there is also, unfortunately, to be found, much savage barbarity in countries where food is plenty, and where the means of producing it are known, but where the people are either too idle, or their government too despotic and unjust, to protect individual property, or suffer labour and industry to be exercised with security, or the labourer to live by his exertions. This is the most barbarous and savage state of society.

" Trace the line where Eden once stood; the fertile banks of Pison, Gihon, Hiddekel, and Euphrates, and say what tribes of savages can exceed the barbarity of the people in these fallen countries? This race of Cain sell their own children from their mother's arms, rather than labour for their support, or teach them how to labour for themselves. This is bad enough, but something worse is still behind. Civilized nations, who are continually complaining of population pressing against the means of subsistence, have been purchasing these slaves to do the work which they were too idle to perform themselves. One should suppose by the rule laid down of the increase of population, that in those countries where such numbers were exported and destroyed, population must thus have been reduced to a very low ebb indeed; and that, now, since the practice is checked, it must become very numerous. But this does not appear to be the case. Also those countries, where such multitudes of human beings were imported, ought by this rule to have been overpeopled, for they have never been in want of subsistence; they have never been badly fed, nor is the climate injurious to their constitutions. Every thing was done to preserve their lives, because they cost the purchaser dear, and yet the population has always been declining, and only to be kept up by fresh importations, at an immense expence. This shows that so inhuman and unnatural a traffic could not succeed; and that it must always have defeated its own purposes. Neither has the population of Africa been lessened or benefited by this traffic, nor have the civilized countries, whose views were to increase the labourerers of their lands, obtained their end.

" It may be said that they found it cheaper to purchase, than to breed these labourers; but this does not appear to have been the motive, or consideration, which encouraged this trade. Every encouragement has always been given to the increase of these people; for one slave, born on an estate, was considered worth many purchased; but they could not make them breed, so as to keep up the population to the demand for labour. The inhuman traffic could not prosper; but it will now most likely be seen, that the population of these countries will increase, and flourish; and a proof of it is given in St. Domingo. The population of the African countries will most likely decline, instead of increase, as there will be no demand for this produce of human traffic; but whether the purchasers or venders of this abominable merchandize were most to blame, or which were the greatest savages, is difficult to determine."

Since, in the opinion of Mr. Phelps, population in this country does not press upon the means of subsistence, the causes of the poverty and distress which partially exist, naturally present themselves to investigation. These he has examined at considerable length, and has traced them, with much ability, to the inadequate remuneration of labour, arising in part from the abuse of the poor laws (especially the existing workhouse system) and in part from the great importation of foreign corn. This subject is discussed with so much fairness, that we shall extract the passage for the gratification of our readers.

"Daniel de Foe, Sir F. M. Eden, and others, have been quoted to prove the inefficacy of establishing workhouses for the poor; but this has been taken in too general a sense, for many proofs may be given to show, that where they have been properly managed, they have lessened the poor rates more than one half in a short space of time. Workhouses, or houses of industry, are however only fit receptacles for those who have no home or employment out of them; for every poor person can be best and most advantageously assisted and supported in his own cottage, if proper means be taken; but if they have no habitation, and must pay as much for a wretched and miserable lodging as would half support a family, which is the case in great towns, what else is to be done with them? The life which poor people lead, in poor houses, is in general miserable in the extreme. They all know this, and most of them will endeavour to keep out of such places if they can; but in cases of real and temporary distress, the poor of a country must be in a most deplorable state, without such receptacles and establishments; but which, no doubt, should be under better management and regulations than they are at present.

"The object of workhouses should only be to give temporary relief and employment to those who cannot find it elsewhere, but it should never be made permanent, or continue longer than is absolutely necessary, and only until other employment can be found, which should be the solicitous care of the governors and managers of such places to endeavour to procure. In such a way, these receptacles would be of great good, and if the name of any thing but charity were attached to them, they would be still more useful. It would give a character to people above the degradation of parochial relief, which the poor should always be taught and encouraged to avoid and abhor. The individual as well as public good, which this would produce, would soon render itself visible. People would only apply for work at these places, when they could not procure employment by other means, and when they did apply, no disgrace or shame would be attached to such application, as it would be a proof of their industrious inclination, and give that security and recommendation of character which are not always to be obtained by the ordinary means of enquiry.

"The comforts of the labouring poor must necessarily depend on the funds destined for the maintenance of labour*. This is indisputable, but it will not always be in proportion to their increase. Funds are always drawn to the most profitable objects, and as agriculture is not always the most profitable, though the safest and best pursuit in the end, it is oftentimes neglected. It is the erroneous principle of great gain and immediate profit, that is the great check to agriculture, and the facilities which are given to the importation of corn are also hurtful to agricultural industry. Speculators keep up the price of corn, in order to keep it above the importation rate, and however fallacious reports may be, of monopolies in other things, it

*Essay on Population, vol. ii. p. 190.

certainly exists by collusion in this article, and no doubt in many others, and those who ought to have the profit, are excluded from it, otherwise the mischief would not be so great. The great capitalists take the whole, and swallow up the fruit of rightful justice and wearied industry, which is an evil difficult to be remedied.

"The condition of the labouring classes cannot certainly be very essentially improved, while their habits remain the same as at present, farther than by giving them a greater command over the means of subsistence; but this is of less value to them than permanent employment, and a permanent change in their habits. It may be difficult to fix the price of labour, because this will always depend upon the demand; but, when it is reduced below the standard at which poor people can properly subsist, it then becomes unjust, and the evil must fall upon society some way or other. It is then the duty of society to step forward, and endeavour to increase the demand for labour, which will always soon bring it to its fair and just recompense.

"It has been said that manufacturers, by inspiring a taste for comforts, tend to promote a favourable change in the habits of a people, and this way counterbalance all their disadvantages. The labouring classes of society, in nations merely agricultural, are generally on the whole poorer than in manufacturing nations, though less subject to those occasional variations which, among manufacturers, often produce the most severe distress. The reason of this is, that agricultural labour is the worst paid, and manufacturing labour either over or under paid, according to the demand, and the manufacturing people, owing to bad habits, are inclined to live according to their best means, and never provide for the worst; and these are the people whose habits are with the greatest difficulty to be amended; but it can be done, as has been proved by Mr. Owen, and if all people were to follow his example, in this respect, in every line of life, we should not long have to complain of an excess of population, or of the poverty and distress of the country; and when saving banks are properly established, among all classes of people, it will remedy this evil; for, when once people begin to save, they will be no longer dissolute and improvident.

"It has been laid down by Aristotle, Dr. Smith, and others, that land and labour constitute the wealth of nations. This is true, but labour constitutes the greatest part; for, without labour, land would yield little to the wealth, power, or comforts of a state, or people. This we may see clearly evinced in Spain, Russia, America, and other extensive territories. No more land will be cultivated than there are people to consume its produce, unless it can be exported, and it is not very wise in any country to import corn, when the lands of the country would produce sufficient for the subsistence of its inhabitants, and when, at the same time, there is not sufficient demand for their labour. But if, at the same time, it be a manufacturing and commercial country that imports corn, and there be sufficient employment for the people, and demand for the manufactures of the country, corn may be taken in exchange for such merchandize, and not injure society or the industry of the country; but if money is to be paid for the corn imported, and there is not sufficient employment for the population of the country, it is then an evident disadvantage which no object of commerce can ever compensate, or any thing but immediate necessity justify.

"It is more convenient to import corn than cattle, or any animal food, on account of the difficulty of transport of the latter; but it is of more advantage to the labour and industry of a country to import cattle, or any animal food, or produce, than corn, excepting fish, which is a source of industry, as well as supply of subsistence, not properly considered, or encouraged, in this country. There are different descriptions of labouring classes of people, in this and every country. The policy of nations, however, is generally to support and encourage one staple article, or some particular branch of industry or another, but never the whole together. Sometimes it is the fashion, in this country, to think of nothing but agriculture, and it becomes so much the mania, that every one turns his thoughts to it. Then something or other checks this rage; and instead of making it a moderate and steady pursuit, people desert it, to lead a more idle life, or turn to some more favourite amusement. Thus the agricultural poor are neglected. and must be supported by their parishes, unless they can find some other employment. Wearied out with the bad support they get, and the low price of their labour, the agricultural poor fly to towns and manufactories for employment, and if they are disappointed there, their misery is complete. They then turn out ill, and vice and crime are the corresponding consequences. The policy of the Chinese ought to teach us better wisdom. With them the most revered pursuit is agriculture; which certainly should rank first, as the general and most useful occupation of men; but every branch of industry should be supported, for a people to be happy.

"The price of corn depends upon the supply of the markets, or upon the plenty or scarcity which is brought to market, and not upon the quantity that there may be in the country, and whether plenty is produced by growing more corn in the country, or by importations from abroad, the effect in price will be the same; but there will be a material difference as to the agricultural interest and industry of the country; for that money which is sent abroad to purchase corn, will, by growing more corn in the country, be employed in useful industry, and productive labour at home. Nothing can countenance the importation of corn, but where there are not hands to raise it, or lands to produce it, in sufficient quantity for the population; which has never yet been known in any country. It was this bad policy which destroyed the Roman empire, and has been the ruin of Spain and other countries, and has also been one of the greatest injuries to this country; for although it may be said to make a barter or exchange for manufactured goods or other articles, yet it never comes in return of payment for such goods. For the importers of corn are seldom exporters of woollens or cotton goods, and never, perhaps, make their payments this way; nor do the people in foreign countries take our woollens or cottons, merely because we take their corn. They take those articles only because they have a necessity, or occasion for them, therefore it is a feeble policy to admit the importation of corn but when there is an

absolute necessity for it, and it cannot be produced at home. When we have, or could have, enough of our own, why should we purchase it of others? As every nation looks to its own interest and benefit, and should to the industry and happiness of its own people, this is a subject of the highest importance to the welfare, happiness, and improvement of this country. Do what we will, we cannot bring the price of provisions in this country to a level with that of other countries, whilst we have an enormous debt and taxes, without injuring the agricultural and landed interests of the country, by importations of corn, and thus lessening the demand, as well as lowering the price of agricultural labour. How are proprietors of lands or farmers to pay poor rates, taxes, tithes, and labour, and a dear price for all other articles, if they cannot sell their corn at a fair price? And if they cannot profit by it, they cannot be expected to grow corn, nor will they employ labourers, or till the land, as they otherwise would do. Thus society in general suffers for it. Better to pay a reasonable price for corn, than suffer the industry of the country to be checked, or the demand for the labour to be lessened. Give us employment, say the labouring people, and we do not regard the price of corn. But without employment it is little advantage to them that corn should be cheap; for they cannot purchase it at any price without employment, and must either starve or live upon charity, if they are deprived of the means to purchase it.

"The argument made use of in favour of the importation of corn is, that the poor people would have a greater plenty, and those not interested in agriculture would thereby be greatly benefited; but no more corn will ever be imported than will find a market, nor will more be raised than is consumed; but there will always be enough, and sufficient raised within the country, by provident care and judicious encouragement; therefore it amounts to the same thing whether corn is imported or not, in regard to supply, price, or quantity. When things are excessively dear, there is always less consumption and more economy, and when they are excessively cheap, there is more waste, and, in a short time, less supply; because neither corn, nor any other article, will be raised, or produced, longer than it will yield the grower or procurer its cost, with some profit."

We have not time to analyse our author's facts and arguments concerning the value of labour, and on money compared with the value of labour, but we cannot pass in silence his observations on the origin of crime and on juvenile delinquency.

In the valuable evidence communicated to the House of Commons, sometime since, by Mr. Poynder (who from his official situation had ample and peculiar opportunities of making observations) that gentleman ascribed the origin of crime in most cases to the habit of drinking spirituous liquors. Mr. Phelps, while he gives full weight to the statements of Mr. P., observes that there are other causes besides drinking spirituous liquors, which lead to crime: for instance, idleness, bad example, extravagance, evil communications, poverty, distress of mind, as well as corrupt nature, unreformed, or a want of proper education, morality and religion. At the same time there is no doubt but that strong liquors have great influence, not only in stimulating to action, but also in aggravating the circumstances attending the commission of crime. In this part of his work, Mr. Phelps has incidentally communicated some valuable information relative to the manufacture of porter, at the same time that he vindicates the brewers from the attacks lately made upon them.

" Formerly beer used to be kept to a proper age, and porter was then considered as a wholesome and nutritious beverage. Porter was probably made, originally, from very high dried malt; but it is said, that its peculiar flavour cannot be imparted by malt and hops alone. As long ago as in the reign of Queen Anne, brewers were not to mix sugar, honey, Guinea pepper, essentia bina, coculus indicus, or any other unwholesome ingredient in beer, under a certain penalty; from which we may infer, that such was the practice of some brewers, even at that time; and writers, who profess to discuss the secrets

of the trade, mention most of these, and some other articles, as essentially necessary. The essentia bina is sugar boiled down to a dark colour and empyreumatic flavour; and, when mixed and fermented with the beer, can certainly have nothing in its quality which may be deemed pernicious, if it contained nothing worse. Broom tops, wormwood, and other bitter plants were formerly used, before hops were introduced into this country, but are now prohibited to be used in beer made for sale. There is no reason to suppose that these ingredients could do any harm, and might be useful; but now we know not what is the mixture or ingredients put into beer, under the term of finings; but this we know, that beer is sent out in a state which must be very prejudicial to the health of every one who drinks it. Formerly it was kept to be one or two years old, until the vinous fermentation was completed by slow degrees. Now it is sent out, sometimes at the end of a fortnight, and is a mixture of new and old sour beer, the fermentation being incomplete in the one, and forced a second time in the other. In this state, people drink it whilst it is in a second fermentation, or commencing the process of the acetous fermentation, and overcharged with carbonic acid. Nothing can be more hurtful to the health and constitution; and what is worse than all, if a little proper finings be thrown into it, let it appear ever so clear, a sediment will be deposited, which will be disgusting to look at, and much worse to taste. The business of brewing being now a perfect monopoly, in a few hands, the brewers purchase almost all the public houses that are licensed, and therefore the publicans are obliged to sell whatever kind of beer the brewers chuse to send them. All they aim at is, to contrive to make it a little palatable, and to create thirst more than quench it. It has the effect which Mr. Poynder describes, of making persons heavy, stupid, and senseless; and, on account of this quality, people drink it, to sodden and compose, or stupify, their senses, and drown their cares, without considering the quality of the pernicious drugs they have been swallowing.

"Beer appears to have been of ancient use, and was generally considered to be peculiar to northern nations; but Mr. Park found that the art of making malt, and brewing from it very good beer, was known among the negroes in the interior parts of Africa. There appears however a very unjust, as well as just, attack upon the brewers at present; and as beer, properly made, would be an essential article of comfort and support to the poor, it behoves every person to give whatever information he may possess upon the subject. When people see something wrong, and are unacquainted with the cause or reason why, they are apt to form conjectures without foundation or real existence, and such seems to be the attack upon the brewers, though not without reason, in some respects. The present system, or practice, of brewing and preparing beer for sale, is certainly wrong, and injurious to the public. I would not wish to be understood to arrogate to myself any superior knowledge in this respect; but, as it so much affects the comforts of the poor, I should conceive it unpardonable to conceal what I know upon the subject; and having made the art of fermentation my study for more than twenty years, in making wines abroad, and on beer and wines at home, I may probably be able to give some information that may be useful. · By former accounts, and by what may have been confirmed by observation, within the time of remembrance, beer was formerly kept to a proper age before it was offered for sale, and the vinous fermentation was suffered to proceed, by slow degrees, as in making wine; now it is sent out at the end of a fortnight, if necessary, mixed with stale sour beer, and perhaps with various drugs in the finings.

"Mr. Beaumont states, "that beer was formerly drawn off entire into butts, and kept twelve or eighteen months in a store cellar, before it was delivered for use. It is still called "*entire*," but the great brewers now draw their beer off into immense vats, into which they also empty sour beer, which is frequently bought of small beer brewers. An imitation of the age of eighteen months is thus produced in one day. But this mixing is apt to produce the acetous fermentation : to neutralize the acidity, alkali is added. The liquor, thus formed has none of the heartening and strengthening qualities of old beer. Labouring men, who drink beer, not for amusement, as their superiors

do, but to bear up, under their great toil, are miserably deceived by these saline mixtures. Such beer rather weakens than strengthens. Where men already labour under disease, their complaint will be aggravated, not healed, by such drink. This," he says, "is the most general adulteration of modern beer; but the report of the seizing officers, and the excise returns mention, that drugs of a very nauseous, and some of a very pernicious, quality are still vended by persons, as a trade, and bought by the lesser brewers and the publicans. Mr. Beaumont concludes that beer, as it regards labouring men, or those who have tender bowels, is the most pernicious liquor, perhaps, that can be drank."

"With respect to mixing new and old sour beer together, it is undoubtedly an art, or trick, practised in all the breweries, and is a very pernicious one. The acid beer both forces and stops the regular vinous fermentation of the new beer, before the spirit or strength is properly developed, and gives it only a fictitious appearance of age and strength. This is the process of making sparkling Champagne; but the generous wines, or good beer, have a different process. The vinous fermentation goes on by slow degrees, and the great art is to prevent the commencement of the acetous fermentation, which is best done by frequent racking from the dregs or sediment.

"It has been observed, that alkalies are used to neutralize the acid in the mixed beer, which most likely is true, and perhaps caustic alkali is used, which, if in excess, is very hurtful; but the mild alkalies, in small quantities, would be far from being a pernicious saline mixture, as it has been called; it would from a diuretic salt, or acetit of soda, or potash, which is by no means injurious, and therefore would be less corrosive and hurtful to the stomach than sour beer. There are certainly many drugs in some beer which may be named, but they do not appear to be hurtful.

"All fermented liquors naturally contain an alkali, and it is this which forms the tartar deposited from wine, which, being entirely deprived of it, becomes weak, vapid, and sour. Alkali has the property of throwing down all earthly and foul matter, in beer or wine. If a small quantity of carbonat of soda be dissolved in some warm beer, and thrown into a decanter full of the clearest and finest porter from the public houses, or at least such as I have tried, and the mixture be shaken, an immense deposit will soon fall down, nauseous and disgusting in appearance, taste, and smell; but, afterwards, if the clear part be taken off and bottled, it will become delicious beer, and, if well made in the first instance, will keep for any number of years.

" It would have the same effect if brewers were to use a small quantity of the carbonat of soda with their finings, dissolved in warm beer; for warm beer, wine, vinegar, water, or any other liquid, will keep a cask of that liquid from decomposition, and purify and ameliorate it in a shorter space of time than by any other method. Wine, beer, and all fermented liquors, are best mellowed and purified in large vats; and if the brewers were to treat their beer in this way, and keep it in vats from six to nine months, racking it from dregs at least three times, the public would be supplied with a very different quality of beer, and the brewers would also be benefited in the end. An addition of old wine mellows new wine amazingly, and the same with beer; but a mixture of sour beer is a practice that should not be suffered; it should go to the vinegar makers. The method here recommended may require greater capital or stock in beer, but the brewers would be more honestly and justly paid by these means, than by the large capital which they now employ in purchasing public houses; for he would best succeed who made the best beer, and kept it to the proper age, with the best management.

The essay on police, poverty, imposition, casual and indiscriminate charity, and prostitution, contains many interesting facts, and much information that cannot but excite painful sensations in the mind of the reader. Mr. Phelps concludes his first volume with some important observations on the influence of the female character upon society, from which we are tempted to extract the following impressive passages.

" It is in the power of women to form, or reform, the characters of men. As most men may be led away by their allurements, so the most vicious would yield to their persevering kindness and virtuous entreaties. The education and conduct of females are, therefore, of as much or more consequence than those of males, though not so regularly attended to. A virtuous woman is the greatest blessing to, and most valuable part of, the

human species; but women are not treated as their merit deserves and their value requires. With them the power lays to civilize or to corrupt mankind; to make them good, or to incline them to be vicious. Every care then should be taken, by all good governments, to protect the female character, to support virtuous endeavours, and to check the inroads to licentiousness.

"A virtuous woman is a treasure to her husband, and cannot be too much prized; but how can women be expected to be virtuous, unless their husbands show them the example, or at least do not counteract it? When the dignity of their character is injured or degraded, it is but too natural that they should retaliate, and make reprisals in their turn. None should enter the marriage state, who are not determined to obey its laws. The crime of inconstancy is fully as bad in the man as in the woman, because the woman is the weaker vessel; and, therefore, the husband ought not to oppose, by a contrary example, what he is so eminently desirous of preserving in his wife. Inconstancy is certainly more fatal on the female side than in that of men, but this is no excess. Men may be said to be open to more temptations, and are led away by intoxication and other incitements, but superior men are not to be corrupted by such means. It must, however, be allowed, that inconstancy in men may not do as much visible injury as that of women; but the immorality, operating in different and various ways, may produce as much vice and mischief. The most horrible and fatal consequence of female inconstancy and depravity is, that it exposes the woman to other infamy, which must be supported by falsehood and deceit, by fostering children upon the wrong father, and so infamy seems capable of being compared with this; and how a woman can endure to see a husband she has injured, caressing a child which she knows is not his own, seems past comprehension: the blush of conscience, one should suppose, would some time or other discover the guilt, which the most abandoned mind could not always conceal. It is however often said to occur; but let us hope, that the belief is more frequent than the real occurrence. Happy is the married pair, who have full confidence in the virtue and honour of each other.

" It is certainly known, by experience, that the accretion of some of the worst evils originates from an illicit intercourse with bad women; and yet this source of evil, if not encouraged, is evidently tolerated by the policy of most countries, to prevent, as is said, greater evils. This is a sort of doctrine, however, that cannot be supported, or be substantiated, by either any direct or imaginary reason or proof; for what is the evil to which prostitution will not lead? The abandonment of virtue, as the term implies, stamps on the forehead of the fallen victim "*the abandoned character*" which is seldom to be erased. When the path of virtue is departed from, the way opens to a field of vice, to which there is no limit. The wretched fugitive, driven by maddening frenzy or by wild despair, haunted by frightful thought, impelled by goading necessity, urged by brooding melancholy, cloyed, or corrupted, by insatiate guilt, stops at no step to temperate its thirst, or dissipate its care. While the rising dawn of virtue carols in the morn with new delight, the trumpeter of guilt ushers in light accompanied by all the attributes and fiends of black despair, ready for any evil. The wandering fancy, thus from virtue fled, stops at no bounds; the mind is formed for any work, and those that stop half way in sin are not arrested by any principle of virtuous thought, but by that of fear, or not being urged on by further necessity; for, if necessity impelled them, they would run the whole chain of human evil. This is evidently evinced by the growing magnitude of vice and prostitution. There is a chasm to be filled up, which virtue leaves, and this the distempered brain knows not how to fill. The fever lurking fiends torture the cankered heart with knawing anguish; and, if they have their hold, Virtue then takes her flight from the tainted spot, never to return. No calm temper rests there. Pining restleness either fans the flame, by new and foul desires, or animates its gloom by conscious terror. The heated mind finds no relief. Conscience heightens the maddening thought, the ill-fated wanderer rushes on to desperate deeds, sinks in the abyss of ruthless sin, or, fainting in the toil of endless gloom and cheerless hope, yields to despair a wretched life.

"If human nature is ever to be improved, or society ever to be made better, it must be by the encouragement of virtue, particularly in the female sex; and this is not to be done by abandoning them to guilt or despair, or by screening or countenancing those who are their seducers. The most abandoned prostitutes continue in the practice, generally speaking, only because they have no protection or alternative. Money is their sole object, necessity their incentive; for the most depraved have no pleasure in that course of life, than which nothing can be more deplorable. Can the miseries they experience proceed from inclination, or be the objects of their desire? Can the police, or the government of a country, then be good, or the people of such country be truly humane, who can see thousands of these wretched beings suffering under all the extremities of guilt and misery, and view them with regardless attention and indifference? There is an honest and bounteous principle and nobleness in the possessors of true virtue, that would wish to see it manifested and conspicuous in all others, as well as in themselves; and those who owe little to virtue who have never had the trial or occasion to resist temptation.

"There is scarcely an instance of a prostitute, either in high or low life, emanating from a well-regulated and virtuous family. If some exceptions are to be found, they proceed from the want of early care and proper education, or from the arts of seduction and bad example in others, in the first instance. It is quite time that governments and human wisdom should not look upon these wretched beings as necessary evils. Society can never be bettered by such principles. This is the root of all evil, and the way to stop its growth can only be by the better care and instruction of the rising generation, to bend the plant to its right direction, and to nourish and protect it in its progress; for if virtue can ever be established, as the only good and means by which human nature can be supported, or mankind can prosper, the odium of vice will then not only become disgusting, but be incapable of existence. This seems to be the true principle by which society can be benefited and improved.

"The evils of life seem to proceed as much from error and necessity, or the want of support in virtuous actions, as from ignorance or want of good principle. The best *police*, therefore, that can be established in any country, is to promote virtuous actions; for the punishment of the guilty can afford little encouragement to be penitent; relieve by its terrors the sufferings of distress, or conduct the untutored mind to purity of action. While the calls of nature and necessity are allured by the glowing temptations of profligate or vicious prosperity, and the sober suits of modesty and virtue are left unheeded and neglected, the police, or policy of a nation, which admits of such principles, must have more the show of terror than of justice. The mode to better the condition of mankind, and to benefit society, is not by the punishment of crime, but by such public and private institutions as best tend to fix the early and true principles and support of moral happiness and conscious virtue.

(To be continued.)

The Reports on the Present State of the United Provinces of South America; drawn up by Messrs. Rodney and Graham, Commissioners sent to Buenos Ayres by the Government of North America, and laid before the Congress of the United States ; with their accompanying documents ; occasional notes by the Editor ; and an introductory discourse, intended to present, with the reports and documents, a view of the present State of the Country, and of the progress of the Independents. With a map. 8vo. 9s. 6d. Baldwin, Cradock and Joy, London, 1819.

There is no country, which at present is more deserving the attention of Britons, than the provinces on the Rio de la Plata. They contain an immense extent of fertile soil, blessed with a salubrious climate, and fitted for the growth of every species of produce. Under a liberal government, they must soon teem with inhabitants and wealth : the progressive increase of their raw commodities will create a demand for manufactures to supply the consumption of a rapidly increasing population. To England therefore they open the prospect of a constantly increasing market for the sale of her goods. Without looking forward into the future, our present commerce with those provinces is considerable : and as it is of no small importance that we should be well acquainted with a region, with which we already have so great a commercial intercourse, the present publication is well calculated to diffuse correct notions relative to the situation

and resources of the provinces on the Rio de la Plata. It consists, first, of an introductory discourse, containing many appropriate observations on the character of the revolution in those provinces, the mode in which it will probably terminate, the policy to be pursued by England, and the system on which it is likely that the United States will act. These remarks are followed by the reports of Messrs. Rodney and Graham : as we have already given the latter entire, * and as Mr. G's. observations are confirmed in all substantial points by the elaborate memoir of Mr. Rodney, we shall only call the attention of our readers to Mr. R's. observations on the state of religion, and the administration of the different branches of municipal law, and education, in the provinces just mentioned.

" On the subject of religion, especially, the change in the public mind has been very great. The Catholic faith is established as that of the state, but there are many advocates, both in conversation and in writing, of universal toleration. Some members of congress are said to be strongly in favour of it; but the ignorant and superstitious part of the people, together with the regular clergy, would not be satisfied with such a measure—while the liberality prevailing among the better informed classes is such as to secure a virtual toleration for the present. Besides, from the circumstance of there being no sects in the country, such a provision may wait the progress of liberality in public opinion. In fact, the human mind has been set free on all matters of a general abstract nature, although the liberty of the press is circumscribed in some degree with respect to strictures on public measures and men, and the established religion ; but there is neither inquisition nor previous licence. They acknowledge the Pope as a spiritual head merely, and do not think him entitled to any authority to interfere with their temporal concerns. His Bull in favour of the King of Spain against the colonies, which may be almost regarded as an excommunication, produced little or no sensation.

" The number of monks and nuns was very great in Buenos Ayres, when compared with other portions of the Spanish dominions. They have diminished since

---

* See pp. 1. –18 of the present volume.

the revolution. There was at one time a positive law passed, forbidding any one to become a monk or a nun; but they were obliged to repeal it, and it was afterwards passed with some modifications. The restrictions substituted, aided by public opinion, have nearly produced the desired effect. Few of the youth of the country apply themselves to the study of theology, since other occupations, much more tempting to their ambition, have been opened to their choice. Formerly the priesthood was the chief aim of young men of the best families, who were desirous of distinction; as, in fact, it constituted almost the only profession to which those who had received a liberal education could devote themselves; which will readily account for the circumstance of so many of the secular clergy directing their attention at present, almost exclusively to politics. The regular clergy, who are not permitted by the nature of their profession, to take part in the business of the world, or to hold secular offices, are many of them Europeans; but those of them who are natives, take the same lively interest in passing events, with the other classes of the community.

"They have gone cautiously to work in reforms in the different branches of their municipal laws, and the administration of them. The number of offices has been considerably diminished, and responsibility rendered more direct and severe. The judiciary system has undergone many improvements, and nearly all the leading features of the law, which did not harmonize with the principles of free government, have been expunged, though some of the former evils still remain. The barbarous impositions on the aborigines have been abolished—the odious alcavala, and other obnoxious taxes, modified, so as to be no longer vexatious—slavery, and the slave trade, forbidden in future—and all titles of nobility prohibited, under the pain of loss of citizenship.—The law of primogeniture is also expunged from their system. In the provisional statute, as has already been stated, nearly all the principles of free representative government are recognized, accompanied, it is true, with certain drawbacks, for which they plead the necessity of the times, but which they profess their intention to do away, on the final settlement of the government—a consummation anxiously desired by all classes of inhabitants. The example of France has warned them not to attempt too much at first; they have followed the plan of the United States in

the introduction of gradual reforms, instead of resorting to violent and sudden innovations and revolutions.

"Next to the establishment of their independence by arms, the education of their youth appears to be the subject of the most anxious interest. They complain that every possible impediment was thrown in the way of education previous to the revolution; that, so far from fostering public institutions for this purpose, several schools were actually prohibited in the capital, and the young men were not without restraint permitted to go abroad for their education. There was a college at Cordova, at which those destined for the bar, or the priesthood, completed their studies, upon the ancient monkish principles. Another, called San Carlos (now the Union of the South), had been opened at Buenos Ayres, but was afterwards converted into barracks for soldiers. It is an immense building, more extensive, perhaps, than any which has been dedicated to learning in this country; and it has lately been fitted up at a very great expence. The school was to have opened in May or June last, on a more modern and liberal plan of discipline and instruction. The library of the state is kept in an adjoining building; it occupies a suite of six rooms, and contains nearly 20,000 volumes, the greater part rare and valuable. It is formed out of the library of the Jesuits, the books collected in the different monasteries, donations from individuals, and an annual appropriation by the government, and contains works on all subjects and in all the languages of the polished nations of Europe. A very valuable addition has been lately made of several thousand volumes, brought to Buenos Ayres by M. Bonpland, the companion of the celebrated Humboldt.

"Besides the university of Cordova, at which there are about 150 students, there are public schools in all the principal towns, supported by their respective corporations. In Buenos Ayres, besides an academy in which are taught the higher branches, and the college before mentioned, there are eight public schools, for whose support the corporation contributes about seven thousand dollars annually; and, according to the returns of last year, the number of scholars amounted to 864. There are five other schools exclusively for the benefit of the poor, and under the charge of the different monasteries. These are supplied with books and stationary at the public expense. There are also parish schools in the country, for the support of which a portion of the tithes has been lately set apart. It is rare to meet with a boy ten or twelve years of age, in the city of Buenos Ayres, who cannot read and write. Besides the scholars thus instructed, many have private tutors. In addition to all this, I must not omit to mention the military academies supported by government at Buenos Ayres and Tucuman, at which there are [is] a considerable number of cadets.

"There are no prohibited books of any kind; all are permitted to circulate freely, or to be openly sold in the book stores; among them is the New Testament in Spanish. This alone is a prodigious step towards the emancipation of their minds from prejudices. There are several bookstores, whose profits have rapidly increased, a proof that the number of readers has augmented in the same proportion. There had been a large importation of English books, a language becoming daily more familiar them. Eight years ago, the mechanic art of printing was scarcely known in Buenos Ayres; at present there are three printing offices, one of them very extensive, containing four presses. The price of printing is, notwithstanding, at least three times higher than in the United States; but, as there is no trade or intercourse with Spain, all school books used in the country, some of them original, are published at Buenos Ayres; the business is, therefore, profitable and rapidly extending. There are many political essays, which, instead of being inserted in the newspapers, are published in loose sheets; there are also original pamphlets, as well as republications of foreign works.

"There are three weekly journals or newspapers published in the city, which have an extensive circulation through the United Provinces. They all advocate the principles of liberty and republican forms of government, as none other would suit the public taste. The year before last, it is true, one of the papers ventured to advocate the restoration of the Incas to Peru, with a limited monarchy, but it was badly received. No proposition for the restoration of hereditary power of any kind, as far as I could learn, will be seriously listened to for a moment by the people. Even the ordinary language has changed. They speak of "the state," "the people," "the public," "country," and use other terms, as in the United States, implying the interest that each man takes in what appertains to the community.

The reports of Messrs. Rodney and Graham are followed by a copious appendix, the contents of which we have not room to enumerate: they consist chiefly of State Papers and other documents, which were communicated, with noble frankness, to the North American Commissioners, by the Secretary of State of the Buenos Ayres Government. The provisional regulations, to be observed until the adoption of a Constitution, will be read with particular attention: but the most interesting articles in the present dearth of authentic information relative to the Provinces on the Rio de la Plata, is an Historical Sketch of the revolution there, from the 25th of May, 1810, until the opening of the National Congress on the 25th of March, 1816, by Dr. Gregorio Funes, and continued by him at Mr. Rodney's request, so as to bring the sketch down to the battle of Maipo. To this historical fragment we attach much value: it has every appearance of being written with impartiality, and is the more important as the historian is himself an eye-witness of, and deeply interested in, the events which he has recorded. As the battle of Maipo has in all probability, contributed to secure the independence of Chili, we shall subjoin Dr. Funes' account of that sanguinary conflict and of the circumstances by which it was preceded.

"While San Martin and O'Higgins were endeavouring to reduce the last strong hold of the Spaniards in Chili, the fortress of Talcaguana, the Viceroy of Lima, with all possible despatch, threw fifteen hundred men into that place, which in point of strength may be compared to Gibraltar. The army of Chili, under the command of San Martin, was increased to nearly double its number by the new levies among the Chilians; but time was requisite to train and discipline them. O'Higgins took possession of the town of Conception, of which Talcaguana is the sea-port. Here, a great part of the summer was passed away in skirmishes, in which the enemy were generally worsted. San Martin was, however, occupied in designs of greater magnitude; he was unremittingly engaged in preparing to strike the same blow in Peru which had so successfully paralysed the power of Spain in Chili. The want of transports was the principal cause of delay, as a march through the desert of Atacama would be impracticable. The Viceroy dreading the enterprise of San Martin, and knowing the materials by which he was himself surrounded, conceived it most prudent to risk the fate of Peru in Chili. Accordingly after an effort, which in the present fallen state of the Spanish power might be considered great, he collected about five thousand men, which were hastily embarked for Talgacuana under Osorio, leaving Peru entirely defenceless. Osorio had scarcely reached that place, when he commenced preparations for proceeding directly to the capital of Chili: he calculated with confidence on the superiority of his troops over those whom experience had not yet taught him to respect; he also flattered himself with being able to overtake the army of O'Higgins, before it could form a junction with San Martin. Osorio, taking with him nearly all the garrison of Talcaguana, together with two thousand of the natives of Chili, marched rapidly through the province of Conception with an army of nearly eight thousand men. Before he passed the Maule, the patriot army had already formed a junction, and consisted of an equal number of regulars, besides considerable bodies of the militia of the country. In a few days it was completely organized and consolidated; but so large a body of men, when collected, soon began to experience considerable wants. The capital of Chili confidently trusted to the abilities and valour of San Martin, while the circumstance of the wants of his army, when made known to them, afforded an opportunity of displaying a magnanimity which we have unjustly supposed to have been buried beneath the ruins of Greece and Rome. San Martin announced that his army was ready to take the field against the enemies of the country, and that all were willing to sacrifice their lives in its defence, but that it was in want of bread and other supplies. The effect which this intimation produced in the noble-minded people of Chili, is best displayed in the reply which they made through the different officers of the municipality and corporations.

"Your Excellency," said they, "has just informed us that our brethren in the field of battle are in hourly expectation of being called upon to shed their blood and sacrifice their lives for our preservation. Your Excellency recalls to our recollec-

tion the sad image of Chili, laid waste for two years and a half, with an atrocity truly Spanish; whilst our children, our fathers, and our wives, who (terrified at the chains and gibbets preparing for them by the monsters that have reached the plains of Talca) turn their tearful eyes towards the brave that, on the banks of Tangeuca, have sworn to perish sooner than behold their desolation. But your Excellency, at the same time, intimates to us that these brave men are in want of bread and other supplies, in order to support with vigour the arms destined to exterminate our enemy, and that the public fund having been exhausted, there scarcely remained a sufficiency for the hospital, where the wounds received for our defence are to be healed. And what does your Excellency expect will be the reply of the Chilians to a representation so mournful and affecting? That all our fortunes, without reserve, belong to *our country*. That from this moment we request your Excellency will be pleased to accept the spontaneous offer of whatever silver we have in our possession, together with the vow which we make before our country and the universe, that so long as the war shall last, and the wants of Chili may require it, there shall not be seen a single article of plate in our houses.

"The people of Chili are unwilling that the silver of the churches should be touched, until that which belongs to individuals shall be entirely exhausted, we shall then humbly say before the Supreme Being, *To preserve the precious gifts of life and liberty, which thou hast bestowed upon us, we present ourselves naked, to implore thy protection, while we endeavour to support thy ordinances with the aid of those things which we had set apart to adorn thy worship; our vows and ardent adoration shall henceforth be the most pure and becoming homage we can offer Thee.*

"In the mean while, will your Excellency be pleased to accept the offer on the part of the secular and regular clergy, of whatever articles of plate belong to them in particular, and which do not appertain to the ceremonies of religion, and whatever belongs to the magistrates and corporate bodies, which we offer in our name and in the name of the people of Santiago.

"Your Excellency will therefore be pleased to accept these offerings, and to inform our brethren that they may rely on the utmost exertions of our gratitude."

"This unexpected but sublime display of gratitude was replied to by the Director in a suitable manner: accepting their offer, he declared himself unable to find expressions sufficiently strong to do justice to the magnanimity of their conduct; but for the purpose of commemorating so glorious an action, he ordered the following inscriptions to be engraven on the two columns which adorn the eastern and western entrances of the city:

" *On the 5th of March*, 1818, *the people of Santiago voluntarily stripped themselves of all their plate and utensils of silver, protesting that they would acquire no others until their country shall be out of danger.*

"*Nations of the universe! Strangers who enter Chili, say whether such a people deserve to be slaves.*"

"The patriot army lost no time after its junction, in marching to meet the enemy. The army of Osorio had already passed Talca; it was not long before a continual skirmishing took place between the invaders and the patriots. These were kept up for several days, until the 19th, when an affair of some importance took place between the advanced corps under O'Higgins, and a part of the Spanish army, in which the latter was compelled to fall back with considerable loss, being pursued into the very streets of Talca. The whole Spanish force had been compelled to fall back upon its steps. Osorio now discovered that his contempt of San Martin's army had led him into error; it was so much superior to his, particularly in cavalry, that the chances of success would be decidedly against him; knowing that in all probability San Martin would attack him the next morning with his whole force, and that if defeated, with a large river and numerous bodies of Militia in his rear, retreat would be no longer possible. In this critical situation, by the advance of General Ordones, he determined to select two thousand of his best troops, and try the fortune of a night attack, which, if successful, would enable him to retire without fear of pursuit. The principal part of the army had in the evening halted within a short distance of Talca: the remainder of the infantry having arrived, and the ground being reconnoitred, orders were given about nine o'clock, for each division to occupy the position assigned to it. The right wing had already been posted, and the left was also in motion, when the enemy rushed upon them in the most furious and unexpected manner; the baggage and artillery were first thrown into confusion, which was soon communicated to the troops on

their march; these, after a short resistance, broke and dispersed in every direction, in spite of the exertions of their leaders. The Director of Chili, who commanded in person, was severely wounded in the arm, in his efforts to rally them. The right, however, under the immediate command of that excellent officer, Colonel Las Heras, retired in good order, and together with some other bodiés, collected by the exertions of San Martin and his officers, continued the contest for some time, but were compelled at last to give way. The next morning presented a spectacle truly melancholy: an army, of which the day before our country might justly have been proud, the best appointed that had ever taken the field on the side of independence in South America, stripped of its artillery and baggage, and more than one half dispersed, and this without having been beaten.

" San Martin conducted the fragments of his army to the narrow pass of Angulemu, which lies on the route to Santiago, and which the enemy could not avoid without making a very considerable circuit. Here he remained in the most painful situation, deprived of his baggage, and his men in want of every thing. In the mean time the stragglers, dispersed through the valleys of Chili, spread the most disheartening accounts among the inhabitants, and so complete was supposed to have been the defeat of San Martin, that the partizans of Spain, wherever any of them happened to be, could scarcely refrain from openly declaring themselves. San Martin with the Director, whose presence was required in the capital, made it a hasty visit for the purpose of inspiring confidence in the people, and of procuring the means of recompensing his army. He now judged it most prudent to fall back upon the capital, where his army could be recruited with greater celerity, and intending in case of defeat to retire into the city, which the Director was actively engaged in placing in a state of defence. The army, under the creative hand of San Martin, with a celerity almost incredible, in the course of a few days, and after a march of eighty leagues, once more presented a formidable front on the plains of *Maipo*. The most animated proclamations were circulated through the country by him and the Director; hope was seen to revive, and the patriot army was animated by a desperation gathered even from its late disgrace.

The news of this lamentable occurrence, arriving at the same time with that of the misfortunes of the eastern shore, cast a gloomy shade over Buenos Ayres. The most melancholy anticipations filled the breast of every American, while the Spaniards among us discovered their joy, on some occasions, with very little discretion. Our apprehensions induced us to believe that the affairs of Chili were still worse than the government had been willing to communicate: the very importance of the contest in that country was enough to produce doubts in the minds of the most sanguine. Osorio finding the success of his attack to have so far exceeded his expectations, determined to follow up his blows, but having himself experienced a considerable loss, he was somewhat retarded in setting off; his march was notwithstanding rapid, having approached the Maipo in twelve days after the dispersion of the patriot army. On the 3d and 4th of April there were frequent skirmishes, and early in the morning of the fifth the two armies came in sight of each other; the body of the Spanish forces having crossed the Maipo. The whole morning was passed in manœuvring; each chief in vain endeavoured to gain some advantage over his opponent. San Martin rode incessantly along his lines, addressing each individual corps, and infusing into them his own feelings, while the patriotic songs and marches resounded through the army Seeing, at last, that there was no probability of his being attacked that day by the Spaniards, and finding his men roused to the highest pitch of enthusiasm, he gave orders to advance. With the exception of a small height, which the enemy had occupied with some pieces of artillery, the ground was nearly level and well adapted to military manœuvres. The infantry was placed under the command of General Balcarce, Colonel Las Heras on the right wing, and Colonel Alvarado on the left; the artillery and cavalry posted on each wing, and a strong reserve in the rear under Colonel Quintana. In this order the army moved towards the enemy, who opened a dreadful fire from his infantry, and from several pieces of artillery posted on the small elevation before mentioned, but without arresting its progress; a body of the enemy's cavalry charged at the same time, but were driven back by that of the patriots who pursued them even under their guns. The action now became general and bloody; our line, at last, appeared to vacillate, but at this moment the reserve being ordered up,

the whole returned to the charge, and with an irresistible impetus carried every thing before them. The resistence of the enemy was, however, so obstinate, that they had to be literally pushed from the ground with the bayonet. The regiment of Burgos, composed of the best troops of Spain and twelve hundred strong, was not broken until after repeated charges, which San Martin is said to have led in person. The remnant of the enemy's force then threw themselves into some narrow lanes, made by walls, and under their shelter commenced the contest anew, but were at length entirely overcome. This action lasted from noon until six o'clock in the evening, and was contested on either side with a courage and firmness worthy of the great prize which was at stake; not merely the independence of Chili, but perhaps of South America. The history of wars furnishes us with few instances of a victory more complete; the whole Spanish army was annihilated; artillery, military chest, every thing belonging to it fell into the hands of San Martin. Its chief alone fled with some horsemen, when he saw that the day was lost. Ordonez, the second in command, 198 officers, 3,000 rank and file, surrendered their arms; and 2,000 of their dead covered the field of battle. The loss of the country did not exceed 1,000 in killed and wounded. The capital, from its extreme depression, was now elevated to the highest pitch of joy. The streets, before silent and fearful, were suddenly filled by the inhabitants, like the blood, which, after some moments of deep suspense and anxious fear, rushes again from the heart to the extremities of the body. The scene which ensued can only be conceived by those who have witnessed the sublime effusions of popular feeling, when each thinks his own happiness, that of his posterity, his friends, and his country, are entirely involved. There was a general and almost universal exclamation, " At last we are independent !" while San Martin was hailed as the genius of the revolution."

The public, in general, and the mercantile interest in paaticular, are much indebted to the editor for the publication of the present volume. It contains a large mass of authentic and important, as well as interesting information; and the editor's preliminary remarks are well adapted to diffuse correct notions relative to the real situation of the provinces on the Rio de la Plata.

The History of the City of Dublin,
from the earliest accounts to the
present time, &c. &c. By Messrs.
Warburton, Walsh, and Whitelaw,
4to. 2 vols. 5*l.* 5*s.* large paper 8*l.* 8*s.*
Cadell and Davies, London, 1818.

[Concluded from page 392.]

The account of the various charitable institutions presented to our readers
in our last number, and which do honour to the inhabitants of Dublin, is
followed by a sketch of the Literary
Societies, and public Libraries, that
adorn the capital of the sister island.
These are six in number, viz.

1. *The Royal Irish Academy.*—This
society had existed, for many years
under the name of the *Historico
Physical Society* ; and, having increased in number and respect-
ability, it was deemed necessary to
give it a corporate form, in order to
ensure its future permanence, and
character. Accordingly, in the commencement of the year 1786, it was
incorporated by an Act of Parliament
of Ireland, under the name of the
Royal Irish Academy for the study of
Polite Literature, Science, and Antiquities. At present

" It consists of a patron, who is the
King, a visitor, who is the chief governor
of Ireland ; a president and vice-presi-
dents, a treasurer, two secretaries, and a
council of twenty-one, which is sub-
divided into three committees, of science,
polite literature, and antiquities. The
committee of science meets on the
first Monday of every month—of polite
literature on the second—of antiquities
on the third— and the Academy at large
on the fourth, at eight o'clock in the
evening. All members are invited to
attend and assist at the meeting of the
committees. The Academy-house is
situated on the west side of Grafton-
street, nearly opposite the provost's
house. It is a large edifice not distinguished by any architectural ornaments
but furnished with a library and suitable
apartments. That in which the Academy meet is a spacious room, ornamented with striking portraits of Lord Char-
lemont and Mr. Kirwan. To stimulate
exertion by the incentive of reward and

reputation, the society occasionally propose prizes for the best compositions on
given subjects, and periodically publish
their Transactions, in which the most
approved essays in the different departments of literature are laid before the
public. In this way twelve quarto
volumes have appeared, in which
are to be found many curious and
valuable papers on subjects very interesting to the country, the greater part
of which would never have existed, or
enriched the literature of Ireland, if not
called forth by the incentives, and preserved in the Transactions of this society.
The mode of admission is by ballot, and
the terms five guineas entrance, and two
guineas per annum ; there are at present
180 members. The rent and taxes of the
house, amounting to 166*l.* were defrayed
by an annual grant from government.
The present grant from parliament is 300*l.*
besides 400*l.* for the perfect repair of the
house."

2. The *Kirwanian Society* was
founded in 1812, and assumed for its
appropriate appellation, the name of
the great Irish Chemist, Richard Kirwan. Its members are about forty in
number, and their attention to the cultivation and advancement of Chemistry,
Mineralogy, and other branches of
Natural History, as well as to keeping
alive a spirit of philosophy in Ireland.
Although this society is but in its
infancy, it is silently proceeding in
its march. Already has it acquired a
philosophical apparatus, and has commenced the formation of a valuable
library. Several ingenious essays have
been read at its meetings; and from
the zeal and activity of its members we
are authorized to expect, in due time,
many valuable contributions to chemical and mineralogical science.

3. The *Gaelic or Hiberno-Celtic Society* was established by a few patriotic individuals, for the express purpose of promoting the study of the
native irish language. The account of
this society is drawn up in a singularly
interesting manner, for which our
readers will consult the work now
under consideration.

4. *The Library of Trinity College,*
the use of which is confined to graduates, was founded by the donation

of the patriotic english soldiers in the year 1603; who, having defeated the spaniards at the battle of Kinsale, were determined to commemorate their victory by some permanent monument; and collected among themselves the sum of 1800*l.*, to purchase books for a public library in the then infant establishment of Trinity College Dublin. The disposal of the money was confided to the illustrious Archbishop Usher, who proceeded to London, and made the necessary purchases. From this commencement the library has gradually increased by various donations, so that it now forms a very noble collection of books.

" The first donation to the library was Usher's own collection, consisting originally of 10,000 vols. After his death, Cardinal Mazarine, and the King of Denmark, wished to purchase it, but Cromwell would not suffer it to be brought out of the kingdom. The soldiers at that time in Ireland wishing to emulate those of Elizabeth, purchased it in the same manner; but Cromwell again interfered, and would not suffer them to present it to the college. It was therefore deposited in the Castle, whence many valuable books and MSS were stolen. At length, on the Restoration, it was given to the college, but not before the collection was reduced, both in the number and value of its books. It is said to have been given ex dono Car. II. though he had no other merit in the donation than complying with the original intentions of the purchasers.

The following presents the state of the library, as to the number of books and manuscripts, and by whom they were presented.

MSS. ROOM.

Usher A. Biblia Sacra, partes Bibliorum Commentarii.
    B. Breviaria, Missalia, Ecclesiæ Romanæ Rituales, Patres sancti et scriptores orientales.
    C. P. Sancti.—Scriptores Systematici, Scholastici, Polemici.
    D. Catalogi, Philosophi, Medici, Historici.
    E. Genealogiæ, et Historiæ Hiberniæ Ecclesiasticæ et Civilis.
Stearne F. Codices ejusdem argumenti, et Theologi.

G. Historici et Theologi cum MSS. quæ præcipue tractant de rebus forensibus.

The MSS are preserved in a room at the east end of the library, whence they are not permitted to be taken. The room is never to be opened, nor the MSS to be inspected, unless in the presence of the librarian. These precautions are required by the statutes, as well with a view to their preservation, as to render them as authentic documents as possible. They are all in good preservation.

Number of printed Books.

Usher's	6,401
Hallison's	4,109
Gilbert's	12,749
Other books	309
	23,568

Other side, not including Smith's	11,850
Smith's	629
	12,479

Total	36,047

Of Manuscripts.

Usher's	693
Stearne's	135
Stearne's and Alexander's	77
Others	102
	1,007

Printed books and prints	104
Total	1.111

The above account was taken in the year 1787; since that time great additions have been made to the library, particularly the collection of M. Fagel, pensionary of Holland, amounting to upwards of 20,000 volumes; it cost 8,000*l.* granted by the trustees of Erasmus Smith. When the French invaded Holland, in 1794, the collection was removed to England, where it was purchased by the College, with the above grant. This library is included in the bookseller's act, and receives a copy of every new publication. The total number is now supposed to amount to near 100,000 vols.

We will only add to this account that among the Biblical MSS. are the celebrated Codex Montfortianus and a Codex Rescriptus, containing a very antient and valuable fragment of St. Matthew's Gospel, of which a correct and elegant fac-simile was a few years ago published by the Rev. Dr. Barrett.

5. *Marsh's Library* was founded in 1707, by Narcissus Marsh, then Archbishop of Dublin. The books, which compose this collection, originally formed the library of the celebrated Bishop Stillingfleet, and was purchased by Marsh for this purpose.

The books are arranged in two long galleries, which meet each other at a right angle; in the first are the books of Stillingfleet. The second gallery contains the donations of others; at the angle is the reading room, in which the librarian sits, and commands a view of the whole library. Originally all gentlemen and graduates had free access, but some abuses occasioned more limited restrictions.* None can be now admitted but such as can produce a well attested certificate, and no book can be removed from its place unless in the presence of the librarian. Extraordinary precautions were also taken to preserve the books. Each was fastened by a chain, terminated by a ring, which ran upon a wooden rod. This rod was close and parallel to the shelf to which the book belonged, and the chain was sufficiently long to suffer the book to rest upon any part of the reading desk below. The chains have been removed, but the rods yet remain to indicate the structure of this precautionary contrivance. The library is open every day, except Sundays and holidays, from 11 till 3; and notwithstanding these apparent precautions and restrictions, few persons will find any

difficulty in obtaining free access to it.* It is governed by trustees appointed by act of parliament, who make annual visitations; yet the public derive but little benefit from it. The books are extremely old, and on such subjects as but little interest the general reader, and the sum of 10l. a year, allowed to purchase new ones, is altogether inadequate for any such purpose. To this may be added, the remote situation, so distant from the general haunt, and so uninviting, deters many from attempting to avail themselves of it. In effect, the solitary individual now and then found in it, is a melancholy proof of its inutility, though it appears to have been, fifty years ago, in high estimation.

6. *The Dublin Library Society* was founded by a few public spirited individuals in the year 1791. As it is managed on the same liberal plan as the Westminster Library and similar establishments in London, we need not detain our readers by detailing the manner in which it is conducted. The same remark will apply to the Dublin Institution, founded in 1811, and containing a public library, together with arrangements for Lectures, &c. like the Royal, London, and Surry Institutions.

The length, to which this article has already unavoidably extended, prevents us from giving any account of the "Dublin Society," and the "Farming

---

* The cause of these restrictions is thus stated in an inscription near the entrance, dated October, 1750. "A considerable number of books having been, from time to time, stolen from the library, by persons under the denomination of Gentlemen, claiming a privilege to read in it, according to the statutes, To guard against the thefts of such *infamous villains*, in future, no person will be admitted unless he produce a well attested certificate to the librarian, of his being a scholar and a gentleman. An honest porter is appointed to watch and search every person leaving the library." This practice, however, is not continued.

* In the reign of Anne, an act passed for regulating this library. It enacts, among other provisions, that it be vested in trustees, with the primate and archbishop of Dublin, the chancellor and chief judges, the deans of Trinity and St. Patrick's, the provost and their successors, for ever. The property to be unalienable, free from taxes and incumbrances, unless particularly changed in future acts. The librarian to be appointed by the archbishop, to be a priest and A. M. Books hereafter to be given, if duplicates, may be changed or sold, and others bought. Librarian to keep the building in repair, or be suspended, and his income applied by the archbishop. Governors to visit second Thursday in October, yearly. 6 An. cap 9, sect. 2. 3 5. &c. The sum of 250l. per annum is allowed to the librarian, out of which he keeps the building in repair. The number of books amount to about 25,000 vols. Among them are some valuable works on oriental literature, with a large proportion of polemic divinity. The Bampton Lectures are among the few recent purchases.

Society," to whose noble and patriotic labours Ireland is most deeply indebted.

Of the various manufactures, which have been carried on in Dublin, at different times, that of Linen alone is carried on to any extent. The commerce, corporation, and the different courts of law, both civil and ecclesiastical, are described at considerable length ; together with the numerous new buildings which of late years have been erected in the city and its environs. The biographical accounts of artists and literary men, natives of Dublin, though concise and interesting, present many names which are an ornament to literature. A copious appendix consisting chiefly of tables and other statistical information, terminates these handsomely printed volumes, which are illustrated with numerous elegant maps, plans, and views.

Parliamentary Letters, and other Poems. By Q. in the Corner, 8vo. 4s. 6d. Baldwin, Cradock and Joy, London, 1818.

This little volume contains much pleasing Satire, and several Minor Poems, that are both elegant and useful. The " Parliamentary Letters,' are supposed to be written by an Electioneering Candidate, to his friend in London, soliciting advice of the latter (which is consequently given) in what manner he is to act, in conducting his election, and also how he should demean himself, when he should have obtained a seat in Parliament. We shall select one or two passages from the replies of the adviser, which will give our readers a favourable idea of the spirit and manner that characterize these epistles.

It now shall be my aim to represent
The most prevaling pleas of discontent ;
To store your mind with murmurs, and to teach
How much those murmurs ornament a speech :
In war you should exclaim, " 'Twere better far
" To live all slaves, than bear the ills of war ;
" Taxes and burdens of all kinds increase ;
" On any terms 'twere better to have peace."
Condemn the gift of pensions, and applause,
For loss of limbs, in so absurd a cause ;
Declare defeat is certain ;—or pretend
Defeat would be an eligible end ;
Let laurels flourish round a foreign brow,
We demand peace,—obtain'd—no matter how.

It also is your duty to bestow,
In artful language, praises on our foe ;
He fights our country ; but a liberal mind
Discovers countrymen in all mankind ;
Should England fall, and bear another name,
—England or France ;—to us t'were all the same.

If war, and its anticipated ill,
Bring peace and glory, you may murmur still ;
If public men give dinners,—take offence
At your low means, and their magnificence ;
Forget the services they did the state,
And grumble at their services of plate :
In all rejoicings, search out a pretence
For blaming fetes, and folly, and expense ;
Look coldly on, and show that you despise
Such childish sport, such vulgar prejudice.

I know, dear Ben, it is your cruel fate
To be by birth descended from the great ;
But 'tis your interest *to feel,—or feign,*
For birth an insurmountable disdain ;
Despise all honorary claims, and sport
With ribbons, titles, stars of every sort ;
With great humility your rank disclaim,
And view your noble pedigree with shame ;
Your ancestors were British Peers ; what then?
We need no more *Right Honourable men* ;
And whilst you shade the honours they have won,
Be famed as their *dishonourable son.*

Go tell the mob—(but hold I'm not discreet,
Mob is a slavish word, grown obsolete :)
Go tell the multitude, you offer cures
For all their griefs,-and that those griefs are yours.
And if they boast no grievances, point out
Some new distress they *ought* to grieve about :
Use high-flown words and beautiful bombast ;
Say ills disgrace times present and past ;
Proclaim to all, your projects are pursued
For patriotic ends and public good ;
Let every sentence harrow up the soul,
With Want, Oppression, Famine and Controul ;
Let tales of woe unmerited be heard,
And rank rebellion lurk in every word ;
Talk loud and long, and only just withdraw
In time to shun the vigilance of law ;
And in each prudent pause it will appear
That more is Understood than meets the ear :
Spare none in place,—or, if one man is spared,
Show you would talk high treason,—*if you dared.*

Lead those you seem to serve : the multitude
Are led with ease to evil or to good ;
Whate'er may be their present idol's aim,
Worthy or worthless, theirs will be the same :
And those who, with enthusiastic zeal,
Now talk of loyalty they seem to feel ;
To-morrow, led astray, with hearts as warm,
Will pelt nobility, and cry reform.
Let their worst passions labour for your use,
For all their errors find some fit excuse,
And whilst they serve your purpose and maintain
The daring schemes of your seditious brain ;
Whilst by their crimes you boldly hope to rise
To that high state you outwardly despise ;
Whilst they believe you seek *their* good alone
—More worldly wise, you struggle for *your own.*

These are my counsels : now, my friend, go forth,
And let my pupil's actions prove their worth ;
Let your consistency be firm and strong ;
Oppose all measures, *whether right or wrong* :
Say ministers, and all who aid them too,
Have nothing but emolument in view ;
Would vote for Beelzebub,—be bought or sold ;
Would rather steal " *than eat their mutton cold.*"

If you should doubt my judgment, look around—
Some perfect specimens may soon be found,
Who act as you must do, and boldly storm
About their injuries, and seek reform ;
Who speak of liberty, and prove that each
At least possesses liberty of speech.

. . . .

You ask if, after all the ills you find
In *place-receivers,* you could change your mind :
Yes,—if a tempting offer should appear,
Some thousand comfortable pounds a year,—
You may accept them all, nor fear disgrace,
Your former scruples would be *out of place* ;
Say learned men have kindly set you right :
You see the matter in its proper light ;
Nor can the change be called a dereliction,
It only proves you're *open to conviction.*

Let not expensive dinners give you pain—
This is a tax which greatness must sustain ;
Your voters have no interested views,
But turtle feasts 'twere madness to refuse ;
And their huge appetites a proof will give
In this they need no representative.
Besides, when mortal men on business meet,
Without a dinner all seems incomplete :
At JUSTICE MEETINGS, where grave sages sit
Arranging roads or rates, as they think fit ;
At PARISH MEETINGS, where in long debate
Churchwardens frown in enviable state ;
At CORPORATION MEETINGS, where 'tis just
Paving and lighting should be well discuss'd ;
At QUARTER DAY, when lawyers are intent
Collecting in due form a client's rent ;—
In fact, whate'er is done by saint or sinner,
Nothing will prosper if there's not a dinner.

Your aunt is worthy of her nephew ; now
'Tis time to decorate the female brow
With lasting laurels ; and your aunt shall claim
The glory of establishing their fame.
Oh ! let her hasten to secluded shades,
And found a college for scholastic maids ;]
Let caps and gowns their lovely persons grace ;
Not fashion's dress, but suited to the place ;
Their volubility of tongue and pen
Will far exceed the oldest, ablest men ;
She most will charm who most intently tries
To take degrees, or struggle for a prize ;
And we shall boast, midst those who 'aid our cause,
Spinsters of Arts, and *doctresses of laws.*

Avoid all those who party views reject,
Who always vote as conscience may direct ;
But worship those who, kings and realms to shake,
Boldly oppose, for opposition's sake ;
And, to obtain the sanction of the throng,
Vociferate " whatever is,—is wrong."

When all your plans have prosper'd and you find
Your potent spells regenerate mankind ;
When your reforming influence imparts
Foreign propensities to British hearts ;
When opposition to your voice is sin,
When all your foes are *out,* and you are *in* ;
When you possess importance, pension, place,
Your ministers---all ministers of grace ;
When your decree is law ;—-you may engage
The age to come will be a golden age.

From the Minor Poems, which are partly Sentimental and partly Sportive, we extract the following verses

TO A LADY,

From whom the Author had received a Purse of three colours.

———

THREE days you laboured to unite
Three colours, beautiful and bright :
Three times you raised my hopes, and said
---For me the *triple* web was made ;
Three times it seem'd before you gave it,
'Twas *three* to one I ne'er should have it ;
Three doubts, *three* fears, were quickly past ;
Thrice welcome came the purse at last.

Three thanks I give ; which can't reveal
One *third of* what I ought to feel ;
Yet wanting some more strong device,
In *three* short words " I thank you" *thrice.*
I own I'm at (in lines like these)
Sixes and *sevens, more than threes* ;
And *you* may think their folly such,
Three of them would be *three* too much ;
Yet credit this, my joy shall be
To drink your health in---*three times three.*

We are greatly deceived if this little volume does not become a favourite with the public : its sentiments are correct, and its versification is for the most part both easy and pleasing.

═══════════════════════════════════

A Brief Treatise on Prisons, intended for the Use of Sheriffs, Magistrates, Grand Jurors, and other Persons interested in the Management and Construction of Prisons, illustrated with an enlarged design of the New Goal about to built at Dover. By Richard Elsam, Architect, 4to. 6s. J. Taylor, 1819.

At a time like the present, when, notwithstanding the law displays its terrors in every Court of Justice, and religion publishes its prohibitions in every place of worship, crimes of all sorts appear to increase, we hail with gratitude as a benefactor to his country, any individual, however humble his efforts may be, who endeavours to stem the torrent of vice, by suggesting measures which have a tendency to the suppression of those enormities which spring from the depravity of human nature ; but when men of the profession of the author lend their as- sistance to the work of human refor- mation, we have double occasion to rejoice, because the goodness of their intentions is seconded by the power which they derive from their intelligence, and talent to carry those intentions into effect.

This valuable little work, on the management and construction of our prisons, is addressed to the two Houses of Parliament; and we sincerely hope that it will meet with the attention which it deserves. By all, it will be found interesting and instructive; and more especially by those, for whose use it is in particular designed. Without a due construction of prisons, it is impossible that they can be properly managed : and without a proper management, the advantages of the most judicious construction must be lost. This the author has explicitly pointed out; and he has further shewn what are the proper remedies for the evils, which he exposes and deplores.

Commentaries on the Laws of England, principally in the Order, and comprising the whole Substance of the Commentaries of Sir William Blackstone, 8vo. £1. 1s.   J. Butterworth and Son, London, 1819.

Upwards of fifty years have elapsed, since Blackstone published his justly admired Commentaries on the Laws of England : and though successive editors of them, since the learned judge's decease, have pointed out the various alterations which have been made in the Statute law, yet, a work was wanting, which should exhibit a comprehensive and luminous summary of the laws of England, as they actually exist. This has been accomplished in the publication now before us, which, while it assumes Blackstone's work as its basis, has reduced his materials to a better form ; has corrected their errors ; supplied their defects ; and retrenched their superfluities. At the same time, the editor, (whom we understand to be an eminent civilian) has not only given to them additional clearness and precision in point of language and arrangement, but has also ingrafted, as far as was practicable, the most important

modern *Statutes and Decisions ;* and has further substituted much new and appropriate matter, in lieu of that which the lapse of half a century has rendered obsolete.   In many instances where the editor differed in opinion from the commentator on points of law, particularly in the fourth book which treats on Public Wrongs, he has inserted new matter, grounded on the best legal authorities : so that, though Blackstone has been adopted whenever it was practicable, nearly one half of this large volume has been recompiled. The following synopsis of its contents will exhibit the arrangement adopted by the editor.

INTRODUCTION.

Sect.
1. On the Study of the Law.
2. Of the Nature of Laws in general.
3. Of the Laws of England.
4. Of the countries subject to the Laws of England

BOOK I.

Of the Rights of Persons.

Chap.
1. Of the absolute Rights of Individuals.
2. Of the Parliament.
3. Of the King and His Title.
4. Of the King's Royal Family.
5. Of the Councils belonging to the King.
6. Of the King's Duties.
7. Of the King's Prerogative.
8. Of the King's Prerogative.
9. Of Subordinate Magistrates.
10. Of the People, whether Aliens, Denizens, or Natives.
11. Of the Clergy.
12. Of the Civil State.
13. Of the Military and Maritime States.
14. Of Masters and Servants.
15. Of Husbands and Wives.
16. Of Parent and Child.
17. Of Guardian and Ward.
18. Of Corporations.

BOOK II.

Of the Rights of Things.

Chap.
1. Of Property in general.
2. Of Real Property; and first, Corporal Heriditaments.
3. Of Corporal Heriditaments.
4. Of the Feudal System.
5. Of the ancient English Tenures.
6. Of the modern English Tenures.
7. Of Freehold Estates and Inheritance.
8. Of Freeholds not of Inheritance.
9. Of Estates less than Freeholds.
10. Of Estates upon Condition.

Such are the plan and contents of this valuable compilation; which contains an accurate and compendious view of the constitution and legal polity of England; that will be found useful not only to the legal student, but also to every one who is desirous of acquiring a general acquaintance with with these important topics.

Observations on the Automaton Chess Player, now exhibited in London. By an Oxford Graduate, 8vo. 1s. Hatchard, London, 1819.

The Automaton Chess Player, now exhibiting at Spring Gardens, has withstood the first players in Europe, and

excited universal astonishment. Although every part of the interior mechanism is exhibited to public scrutiny,
no one has yet succeeded in discovering the principle of its action. The
Automaton plays with any of the company inclined to oppose it; and such is
its experience on the board, that the
Knight may be set at pleasure on any
of the sixty-four squares, and the Automaton will move it successively to
every square of the board, without
touching the same square twice.

The design of this well timed pamphlet is, to give some idea of the construction of this most ingenious piece
of mechanism; the history of it is thus
related.

"The celebrated piece of mechanism,
called the Automaton Chess Player, was
the invention of Wolffgang de Kempelen,
a Hungarian gentlemen, Aulic Counsellor
to the Royal Chamber of the domains of
the Emperor in Hungary. His genius for
mechanics appeared in early life; and
when matured by study and experimental
observation, to which the leisure that his
employment afforded him was chiefly
devoted, displayed itself in various inventions and improvements of great public
utility.

"Being at Vienna, in the year 1769, upon
business of office, he was invited, by order
of the Empress Maria Theresa, to be present at certain experiments of magnetism,
which were to be exhibited before herself
and the Imperial court, by a Frenchman,
of the name of Pelletier. During the exhibition, M. de Kempelen, who was honoured with the familiar conversation of
the Empress, dropped a hint that he
thought himself competent to construct a
piece of mechanism, which should produce
effects far more surprising and unaccount-
able than those which she then witnessed.
The curiosity of the Empress being strongly raised, she expressed a lively desire to
see his idea carried into execution, and
drew from him a promise that he would
gratify her wishes without delay. M. de
Kempelen kept his word; and within the
space of six months completed his Automaton Chess Player.

"At Vienna, where it was first produced,
it excited the highest astonishment and
admiration of the Empress and her court,
and of many illustrious and scientific persons, who examined its extraordinary
powers. The report of them quickly
spread; and the newspapers of the time
speak of them in unmeasured terms of approbation. The inventor, however, with
that indifference to popular favour which
characterizes true genius, not only declined
making a public exhibition of his Automaton, and refused considerable pecuniary
offers from persons desirous of purchasing
it; but in his ardour for prosecuting some
new mechanical pursuit, actually laid it
aside, and even proceeded in part to take
it to pieces.

"In this disordered state it remained
during many years, when, on the occasion
of a visit made by the Grand Duke Paul,
of Russia, with his consort, to the court of
Vienna, the Emperor Joseph II. recollecting the invention of M. de Kempelen, signified a wish that he should exhibit it for
the gratification of these august persoa-
ages. In the course of five weeks, the
numerous repairs which it required, were
completed by the indefatigable genius of
its inventor; and on being produced before
the Imperial visitors, it excited no less astonishment and admiration than at its first
appearance. Upon this occasion, M. de
Kempelen was urged and prevailed upon
to satisfy general curiosity by exhibiting it
publicly in Germany and in other countries. Accordingly, the Emperor having
granted him permission to absent himself
from the duties of his employment during
two years, he travelled with his Automaton, into various parts of Germany and to
Paris; and in the year 1785, he visited
England. At his death, which took place
about the year 1803, the Automaton came
into possession of his son, who sold it to
the present exhibiter, a man, apparently
of great ability in the science of mechanics,
and inferior only to M. de Kempelen himself."

This pleasing little tract will form an
useful companion or manual to those,
who go to see the performances of this
wonderful piece of mechanism; and to
their attentive perusal we cordially recommend it.

X

Illustrations of Affection; with other
Poems. By G. H. Toulmin, 8vo. 6s.
Longman and Co. London, 1819.

The influence of affection, domestic and
national, is illustrated in this volume by
numerous pleasing pictures, which are delineated, for the most part in easy verse.
We select the following sketch of the
invasion of Switzerland by the French
republicans, not as being the best specimen in the book, but rather because
it is one that may be more easily detached, and also contains an accurate
imitation of the celebrated Swiss Song,
the *Rantz des Vaches.*

Where craggy frontlets, cloud-capt, pierce the
 sky,
Mountains stupendous, snow-crown'd tow'ring
 high;
From cavern sluices, rushing down amain,
Impetuous torrents hurry to the plain—
Form the long lake, irriguous on proceed,
Then gently flowing lave the verdant mead.
Land of the brave! where valor's dauntless eye,
Peers above storms thy spirit—Liberty!
Helvetia! freedom's slime, thy archives wall,
Acts of bold emprise, and *Affection* tell!

When *Jura's* rocks, responsive to the sound,
Echo'd the war-cry to the vales around;
Sublime on hills, in scatter'd masses driv'n,
The bale-fire smoke incessant rose to heav'n—
Then like the *avalanche,* destructive, wide,
The cavern rocks and heights a host supplied
To crush proud usurpation, and to free—
Their native land from *Gallic* perfidy.
Maidens and children—matrons! all appear'd,
Where Liberty her standard boldly rear'd;
No craven fears subdued, supreme imprest,
The patriot virtues dwelt in every breast;
Affection ardent—love of country reign'd,
Nerv'd the weak arm, the timid heart sustain'd.
—Her garments deftly on, for speed array'd,
The youthful virgin gave the timely aid;
Her lover wounded, prov'd *Affection,* truth,
Reviv'd by tepid draught the fainting youth;
Kneeling, supported, check'd life's ebbing tide,
And while she aided, by the death-shot died!
E'en children shar'd the perils of the fray,
The bloody honours of the glorious day;
Amid the ranks, by mothers, sisters sent,
With viands tott'ring, cheerful, fearless went;
And ere return'd, stroll'd heedless where around
The cannon's bullet struck the battle ground;
When spent its force, the heavy trophy seiz'd,
And carried to the hamlet, breathless, pleas'd.
Conspicuous o'er the scene with gestures proud,
Matrons on hills beheld the fighting crowd—
Wav'd to and fro their kercheifs in the air,
As fortune favor'd, breath'd the fervid pray'r—
With animating cries, and clam'rous joy,
Husbands and sons, excited to destroy;
But when retir'd the foe, *Helvetia* free,
Low murmur'd sighs, and tears of ecstacy,
In woman, plaintive, eloquent, exprest,
Affection still, was inmate of the breast!

Land of the giant mountain, lowly glen,
Terrific storm, and nurse of armed men;
The mind on eagle pinions soars to trace
From thy bleak summits, amplitude of space;
Delighted roves thy verdant rocks among,
By freedom sacred, and the classic song;
In *Uri* views the lengthen'd, shadowy vale,
And lists to hear the legendary tale.
Still does the peasant shew with patriot joy,
Where stood the father and the gallant boy,
When power vindictive, stern, the parent led,
To shoot the apple on his darling's head;
With triumph speaks the dextrous archer's aim,
How true to strike the whizzing arrow came,
Affection's triumph, when the father found.
Escap'd from death—the child was free from
 wound!
The tyrant's wrath—when fallen on the green,
Of *William Tell,* another shaft was seen!
The tumult-shouts of approbation wide,
When said 'twas meant to pierce his (*Gresler's*)
 side—   }
Freedom! thy triumph when the tyrant died!

Dear are his legends, various—strange,
O'er years remote and glory's act they range;
Pictur'd by rocks familiar to his sight,
In youth and manhood seen with fond delight.
On the bold ledge sublime, where scarce the eye
Can trace the site, as pendant in the sky—
Dear is his simple, lowly cabin—there,
Vig'rous by toil, he breathes the mountain air;
Remote from noise, except when thunders loud
Percussive roll—and flames the battle cloud;
Sublime he sees the vivid, glancing ray,
Around—beneath—the arrowy light'nings play;
Dear is his native land! *Affection* true—
Clime, distance, absence, never can subdue;
In other lands he wakes the sylvan strains,
And thus in simple melody complains :—

THE SWISS SONG, RANTZ DES VACHES,
    IMITATED.

O! when shall I see, now distant from me,
  The sweet blooming bow'rs
  Of infancy's hours;
The scenes of my youth—*Affection* and truth;
  Our snow-piled mountains,
  The crystalline fountains,
Our valleys of freedom, the pride of the earth!;
O! when shall I be, Helvetia, with thee,
The clime of my sires! the land of my birth!

Dear objects of love, wherever I rove,
  My father, my mother—
  My sister, my brother—
And her lov'd so well, the young Isabelle!
  Memory's fond treasures,
  Of infantile pleasures
In valleys of freedom, the pride of the earth!
O! when shall I be, Helvetia, with thee,
The clime of my sires! the land of my birth!

The historical allusions, in the poem,
are illustrated by notes, which contain
many pleasing anecdotes, particularly
of the force of affection in the softer
sex.

The minor poems are on various subjects, and possess considerable merit.

Exchiridion Romæ: or Manual of Detached Remarks on the Buildings, Pictures, Statutes, Inscriptions, &c. of Ancient and Modern Rome. By S. Weston, F. R. S. S. A. foolscap, 8vo. 5s. 6d.   Baldwin and Co., London, 1819.

An elegant, useful, and instructive manual, for those who design to visit the antient capital of the world, as well as for those, whose travels must be limited to the fire-side.

The Alchemist.   By the Author of the "Metamorphoses," &c. 18mo. 2s, 6d. W. Darton, London, 1818.

The triumph of truth and falsehood, and of sincerity over duplicity, are pleasingly illustrated in this well-written tale, which furnishes many examples of conduct, in scenes that are likely to occur in private life; at the same time it inculcates the necessity of economy and the payment of just debts, in opposition to that profusion and extravagance, which appears to be the leading characteristic of the present age.

Emigration; a Poem, in Imitation of the Third Satire of Juvenal, 8vo. 1s. 6d.   Hone, London, 1819.

He must be a bold adventurer in the regions of poesy, who shall attempt an imitation of Juvenal's third Satire, after Dr. Johnson's admirable poem, intitled "London." From the pictures of the miseries attendant on improvident emigration which recent travellers in America have presented to the public, we confess, that we do prefer our country with all its real and *imaginary* evils, to any other in the world. We do not suppose that this anonymous author will gain many converts to his sentiments, or induce many *reflecting* persons to quit the comforts of Old England, for the precarious and *uncomfortable* life of a backwood's-man in North America. His poem is evi-

dently the production of a superior mind; and though we cannot but disapprove of its subject, justice requires us to add, that *even after Johnson*, it is both an animated and able imitation of Juvenal,

Thoughts on the Funding and Paper System, and especially the Bank Restriction, and resumption of Cash Payments, as connected with the national distresses; with Remarks on the Observations of Mr. Preston, and Sir John Sinclair. Addressed to the Landed Interest. By N. J. Dennison, Esq. 8vo. 3s. 6d. Hone, London, 1819.

A dispassionate and well-written tract, which will doubtless be read with interest, whenever the question relative to the Bank Restriction shall again be agitated.

An Analysis of the Fifth Book of Hooker's Ecclesiastical Polity, being a particular defence of the Church of England. By the Rev. B. Kennicott, A. B. 8vo. 5s.   Rivington, London, 1819.

This analysis or abridgment appears to be faithfully executed, and will doubtless prove useful to candidates for the Clerical Office, for whose use it is immediately designed. It may also be read with advantage, by those who are desirous of seeing the arguments, which may be urged in behalf of the established church, briefly and perspicuously stated.

Elements of Medical Logic, illustrated by Practical Proofs and Examples; including a Statement of the evidence respecting the contagious nature of the Yellow Fever. By Sir Gilbert Blane, Bart. 8vo. Underwood, London, 1819.

Medicine being an art beset with every species of fallacy, it is of the utmost importance that those who engage in it, should be aware of this; and that they should so discipline their minds, by a knowledge of the laws of evidence and the rules of investigation, as not to fall into either of the extremes of scepticism or credulity, to both of which the human mind, in different circumstances, is so prone. Dr. Blane has therefore conferred no small benefit on the medical profession, by expanding with perspicuity and accuracy, the physiology, pathology, and therapeutics of the medical mind;—in other words, in what medical truth consists, what are the difficulties that have obstructed its progress, and by what means they may be obviated. To medical men, whose opinions are so often required by coroners' inquests, this volume will be found an invaluable manual.

Literary Register.

Authors, Editors, and Publishers, are particularly requested to forward to the Literary Panorama Office, post paid, on, or before the 19th day of each month, the titles, prices, and other particulars of works in hand or published for this department of the Work.

BOOKS ANNOUNCED FOR PUBLICATION.

ARTS, FINE.

The History and Antiquities of Westminster Abbey, Part VII. by E. W. Brayley, is now ready for publication; together with Thirty Views in Islington and Pentonville, from drawings by Mr. Pugin, with historical and descriptive sketches by the same author.

BIBLIOGRAPHY.

Early in May, will be published, by Richard Baynes, a Catalogue of Old and New Books. Part I. containing a large collection of Theology and Sermons, including the valuable library of a minister deceased, amongst which are many of a rare occurrence, with a collection of original MSS. Sermons.

BIOGRAPHY.

The Life of Andrew Melville: containing Illustrations of the Ecclesiastical and Literary History of Scotland, during the latter part of the sixteenth and beginning of the seventeenth century. With an Appendix, consisting of Original Papers. By Thomas M'Crie, D.D. Minister of the Gospel, Edinburgh, and Author of the Life of Knox. 2 vols. 8vo.

The Life of Sir Thomas Bernard, Bart. By the Rev. James Baker, his Nephew and Executor, with a portrait, 8vo.

The Life of the Rt. Hon. R. B. Sheridan, from a variety of interesting Documents, and original Communications. By Thomas Moore, Esq. Author of Lalla Rookh, 4to.

EDUCATION.

Conversations on Geology, in a duodecimo volume, will soon appear.

HISTORY.

The Court of England, in 1626. Being a Translation of Marshal Bassompiere's Account of his Embassy to London, with Notes and Commentaries, 8vo.

Miss Lucy Aikin has nearly ready, in an octavo volume, Memoirs of the Court of King James the First.

A Narrative of the Sufferings and Fate of the Expedition to the Rivers Orinoco and Apure, in South America; which sailed from England in November 1817, and joined the patriotic Forces of Venezuela and Caracas. By G. Hippisley, Esq. late Colonel of the first Venezuelan Hussars, in the Service of the Republic, and Colonel Commandant of the British Brigade in South America, with portraits and a map, 8vo.

MINERALOGY.

Mr. Wm. Phillips has in the press, a new and greatly improved edition of his Elementary Introduction to Mineralogy, in a small octavo volume.

MISCELLANIES.

Mr. J. F. L. Williams will soon publish, in two octavo volumes, illustrated by engravings, an Historical Account of Inventions and Discoveries in those Arts and Sciences that are of utility or ornament to man.

On the 1st of June will be published, handsomely printed in 8vo. with engravings, price 7s 6d. sewed, Number 1, of The Edinburgh Philosophical Journal, exhibiting a View of the Progress of Discovery in Natural Philosophy, Chemistry, Natural History, Practical Mechanics, Geography, Statistics, and the fine and useful Arts.—To be continued Quarterly.

The Court and Parliament of Beasts; translated from the Animali Parlanti of Giambattista Casti. By Stewart Rose, foolscap, 8vo.

Letters of the Rt. Hon. J. Philpot Curran. to H. Weston, esq. written on his first coming to London, in 1773, are in the press.

A Collection of Letters, relative to public events in the latter half of the 17th century, from the originals in the archives of the Rawdon family in Ireland, with an introduction and notes, is printing.

Mr. J. Goodwin, Veterinary Surgeon to the Prince Regent, will soon publish, an Account of the various Modes of Shoeing Horses employed by different nations, in octavo, with plates.

Dr. Busby is engaged on a General History of Music, from the earliest times to the present, with the lives of eminent composers; intended to form two octavo volumes.

NOVELS.

Emmeline; an unfinished Tale, with some other Pieces. By the late Mrs Brunton, Author of Self-control, and Discipline. To which is prefixed, a Memoir of her Life, including some Extracts from her Correspondence, post 8vo.

Anastasius, or Memoirs of a Greek. Written by himself, in 3 vols crown 8vo.

PHILOLOGY.

A Copious Greek Grammar. By Augustus Matthiæ, Doctor in Philosophy, Director of the Gymnasium, and Librarian of the Ducal Library at Altenburg: Honorary Member of the Academy of Sciences at Erfurt, of the Latin Society at Jena, and of the Society of Sciences and Arts at Mentz. Translated into English from the German, by the late Rev. E. V. Blomfield, M.A. Fellow of Emanuel College, Cambridge. The Work is printing at the Cambridge University Press, and will form 2 volumes in 8vo.

POETRY.

Tales of the Hall. By George Crabbe LL. B. 8vo.

Scenes from History; the Abencerrages or Civil Wars of Grenada; the Widow of Crescentius, &c. in Verse. By the Author of Modern Greece, &c, &c. foolscap 8vo.

E. D. Baynes, esq. translator of Ovid's Epistles, has in the press, Pastorals, Ruggiero, and other Poems.

THEOLOGY.

The Rev. Edward Cooper has another volume of Practical Sermons in the press; containing with the four already published, a course of Family Sunday Reading for two years.

Speedily will be published Thoughts on Baptism, as an Ordinance of Proselytism; including observations on the Controversy respecting Terms of Communion.

A new edition, corrected and enlarged, of Dr. Gray's Connexion between the Sacred and Heathen Writers, is in the press.

TOPOGRAPHY.

Mr. Geo. Weir is preparing for the press, Historical and Descriptive Sketches of Horncastle, and several neighbouring parishes, in Lincolnshire, with engravings.

On the Topography and Antiquities of Athens. By Lieut. Col. W. M. Leake, with plates, 8vo.

VOYAGES AND TRAVELS.

First Impressions; in a Tour upon the Continent, in the Summer of 1818, through Parts of France, Italy, Switzerland, the Borders of Germany, and a Part of French Flanders. By Marianne Baillie, 8vo.

Sketches Descriptive of Italy, in 1816 and 1817. With a Brief Account of Travels in various Parts of France and Switzerland, in the same Years. In 3 vols. foolscap, 8vo.

Journey over Land from the Head Quarters of the Marquess of Hastings in India, through Egypt, to England, in the Years 1817-18; with an Account of the Occurrences of the late War, and of the Character and Customs of the Pindarries. To which are added, a Description of the Sculptured Mountains of Ellora, and of the recent Interesting Discoveries within the Tombs of the Pyramids of Egypt. By Lieut-Col. Fitz-Clarence, with maps, plans, and views, 4to.

Journal of an Expedition over Part of the (hitherto) Terra Incognita of Australasia, performed by Command of the British Government of the Territory of New South Wales, in the Year 1817. By John Oxley, esq. Surveyor General of the Territory, and Lieutenant of the Royal Navy. With an entirely new map, and other plates, 4to.

A Memoir and Notice of a Chart of Madagascar, in the Archipelago, or Islands northeast of that Island; drawn up according to the latest Observations, under the Auspices and Government of his Excellency Robert Townshend Farquhar, Governor, Commander in Chief, Captain-General of the Isle of France, &c. &c. By Lislett Geoffroy. With the Chart, executed by Arrowsmith, 4to.

Travels in Nubia and in the Interior of North Eastern Africa. Performed in the Months of February and March, 1813. By J. L. Burckhardt. To which are prefixed, a Life of the Author, and a portrait. Published by the African Association, 4to.

. . . .

BOOKS PUBLISHED.

FINE ARTS.

Senefelder's Lithography, a Complete History of Lithography, from its Origin down to the present Time, by the Inventor, Alois Senefelder: containing clear and explicit Instructions in all its Branches: accompanied by Fourteen illustrative Specimens of this Art, 4to. 1l. 6s.

Picturesque Views of the celebrated Antiquities of Pola. By Thomas Allason, Architect. Engraved by W. B. Cooke, George Cooke, Henry Moses, and Cosmo Armstrong, royal folio, 3l. 10s.

Hakewill's Views in Italy, illustrative of Addison, Eustace, Forsyth, &c. The Fifth Number, 12s. 6d.

The Antiquities of Sicily, consisting of the most interesting Views, Plans, &c. with Descriptions; etched by Pinelli of Rome, from Drawings by John Goldicutt, Architect, Member of the Academy of St. Luke, at Rome, part I. 1l. 5s.

BIOGRAPHY.

The History of Seyd Said, Sultan of Muscat: With an Account of the Countries and People of the Shores of the Persian Gulf, particularly of the Wahabees. By Shaik Mansur, a Native of Rome, who, after having practised as a Physician in many Parts of the East, became Commander of the Forces of the Sultan of Muscat, against the Geovasseom and Wahabee Pirates. With a plan of Muscat, royal 8vo. 12s.

The Third and Last Volume of Memoirs of John, Duke of Marlborough; with his Original Correspondence, collected from the Family Records at Blenheim, and other authentic Sources. By William, Coxe, M. A. F. R. S. F. S. A. With portraits, maps, and plans, vol. 3, 4to. 3l. 3s.

CHEMISTRY.

A Manual of Chemistry; containing the principal Facts of the Science, arranged in the Order in which they are discussed and illustrated in the Lectures at the Royal Institution. With a Prefatory History of the Science. By T. W. Brande, Secretary to the Royal Society, and Professor of Chemistry in the Royal Institution. With upwards of 100 woodcuts, plates, &c. in 8vo.

COMMERCE.

To be completed in Six Monthly Parts, forming one large volume, 8vo., a General Commercial Dictionary, comprehending Manufactures, Trade, Navigation, and Agriculture, as connected with Commerce; with Abstracts of the Laws relating to the Regulation and Protection of Trade and Merchandise. By Thomas Mortimer, esq. A New Edition carefully revised throughout, with considerable Additions and Improvements, part I. 8vo. 6s.

CRITICISM.

Lectures on the English Comic Writers, delivered at the Surrey Institution. By William Hazlitt, 8vo. 10s. 6d.

DRAMA.

Hamlet and As You Like It. A Specimen of a New Edition of Shakspeare, royal 8vo. 15s.

EDUCATION.

Exercises for Greek Verse: consisting of extremely literal Translations, from the Anthologia, Apollonius Rhodius, Theocritus, the Fragments of the Comic Poets, Aristophanes, and Euripides; with short Notes. By the Rev. Edmund Squire, M. A. Master of Felsted School, post 8vo. 7s.

Introductory Latin Exercises to those of Clarke, Ellis, and Turner; designed for the younger Classes of Learners. By Nathaniel Howard, 12mo. 2s. 6d.

A Grammar of Logic and Intellectual Philosophy, on Didactic Principles, for the Use of Schools and Private Students. By Alexander Jamieson, 12mo. 6s.

The Young Logician's Companion; comprising Questions and Exercises on the above Grammar, 12mo. 1s. 6d.

GEOLOGY.

A Refutation of Prominent Errors in the Wernerian System of Geology. By Joseph Sutcliffe, A. M. 8vo. 1s. 6d.

HISTORY.

The Annual Register, for the Year 1808; being the Eighth of the New Series, 8vo. 1l.

A History of England, from the First Invasion by the Romans, to the Accession of Henry VIII. By the Rev. John Lingard, Author of the Antiquities of the Anglo-Saxon Church, in three large volumes, 4to. 5l. 5s.

Aspin's Universal History, part XIII. 4to. 4s.

LAW.

A Systematical Arrangement of Lord Coke's First Institute of the Laws of England, on the Plan of Sir Matthew Hale's Analysis, with the Annotations of Mr. Hargrave, Lord Chief Justice Hale, and Lord Chancellor Nottingham ; and a New Series of Notes and References, to the present Time ; including Tables of Parallel Reference, Analytical Tables of Contents, and a copious Digested Index. By J. H. Thomas, esq. 3 vols. royal 8vo. 4l. 4s.

MEDICINE, ANATOMY AND SURGERY.

The Hunterian Oration for the Year 1819, delivered before the Royal College of Surgeons in London. By John Abernethy, F. R. S. Surgeon to St. Bartholomew and Christ's Hospitals, 8vo. 2s. 6d.

Synopsis Zoo-Nosologiæ ; or, Conspicuous View of Medical Science, exhibited in Tables and Aphorisms on Anatomy, Physiology, Nosology, and Therapeutics, in Four Parts; with an entirely New Classical Nomenclature. By Thomas Parkinson, M. D. 12mo. 5s. 6d.

MISCELLANIES.

Essays, Biographical, Literary, Moral, and Critical. By the Rev. John Evans, 12mo. 5s. 6d.

A Twelve Months Visit to Newgate, 12mo.

NOVELS.

Old Tapestry. A Tale of Real Life, in 2 vols. 12mo. 12s.

Zeal and Experience : a Tale, in 2 vols. 12mo. 10s. 6d.

The Esquimaux; or Fidelity, a Tale. By Emily Clark, in 3 vols. 12mo. 16s. 6d.

Redmond the Rebel; or They Meet at Waterloo, in 3 vols. 12mo. 16s. 6d. bds.

POETRY.

Lines written at Ampthill Park, 4to. 5s. 6d.

The Poetical Remains of the late Dr. John Leyden, with Memoirs of his Life. By the Rev. James Morton, 8vo. 12s.

Peter Bell: a Tale in Verse. By William Wordsworth, esq. 8vo.

POLITICS AND POLITICAL ECONOMY.

A Second Letter to the Rt. Hon. Robert Peel, M. P. for the University of Oxford, on the Causes of the Increase of Pauperism, and the Poor Laws. By one of his Constituents, 8vo. 3s. 6d.

A Letter to the Hon. Thomas Brand, M. P. for the County of Hertford, on the Practicability and Propriety of a Resumption of Specie Payments. By Erick Bollman, M. D. 8vo. 3s. 6d.

The Speech of the Rt. Hon. George Canning, President of the Board of Control, &c. &c. in the House of Commons on Thursday March 4, 1819, in proposing Votes of Thanks to the Marquis of Hastings and the British Army in India, 8vo. 1s. 6d.

THEOLOGY.

Lyra Davidis; or, a New Translation and Exposition of the Psalms: grounded on the Principles adopted in the posthumous Work of the late Bishop Horsley ; viz. that these Sacred Oracles have for the most Part an immediate Reference to Christ, and to the Events of his first and second Advent. By the Rev. John Fry, B.A. 8vo. 18s.

Scripture Compared with Itself, in Proof of the Catholic Doctrine of the Holy Trinity; and (by necessary Induction and Consequence) of the Personality and Divinity of the Holy Ghost; and of the Divinity of our blessed Saviour, equal to the Father in the Unity of the Godhead. In a Letter to a Friend. By John Vaillant, esq. M. A. Late of Christ Church, Oxon. Barrister at Law. 8vo. 2s. 6d.

A Supplement to the Ninth Portion of the Warburtonian Lectures: containing Answers to certain Objections, edited in the " British Critic," in Relation to that Work; and serving to introduce a considerable Body of additional Evidence, adapted to illustrate and corroborate, still further, the particular Points objected to by the Critic. By Philip Allwood, B. D. Fellow of Mag. Coll. Cambridge, 8vo. 7s.

Vital Christianity, exemplified in a Series of Letters, addressed to Young Persons. By J. C. Seymour, esq. 8vo.

An Important Case Argued, in Three Dialogues, between Dr. Opium, Gallio, and Discipulus, 12mo.

The Revival of Popery; its Intolerant Character; its Political Tendency; its Encroaching Demands and Unceasing Usurpations, described in a Series of Letters to William Wilberforce, Esq. M. P. By William Blair, esq. A. M. 8vo. 7s. 6d.

TOPOGRAPHY.

A General History of the County of York. By Thomas Dunham Whitaker, LL. D. F. S. A. Vicar of Whalley, and Rector of Heysham, in Lancashire. Part I. 4to. 2l. 2s. large paper, 4l. 4s.

VOYAGES AND TRAVELS.

A Voyage of Discovery, made under the Orders of the Admiralty, in his Majesty's Ships Isabella and Alexander, for the purpose of exploring Baffin's Bay, and of inquiring into the probability of a North-west Passage. By Captain John Ross, K. S. R. N. Commander of the Expedition. With thirty-two coloured plates, maps, &c. in 4to. 3l. 15s. 6d.

A Narrative of the Expedition to Algiers, in the Year 1816, under the command of the Rt. Hon. Viscount Exmouth. By Mr. A. Salame, a Native of Alexandria in Egypt, Interpreter in his Britannic Majesty's Service for the Oriental Languages, who accompanied his Lordship for the Subsequent Negotiations with the Dey. Published by Permission. With plates, 8vo. 15s.

The Reports of the Present State of the United Provinces of South America; drawn up by Messrs. Rodney and Graham, Commissioners sent to Buenos Ayres by the Government of North America, and laid before the Congress of the United States; with their accompanying Documents; occasional Notes by the Editor, and an Introductory Discourse, intended to present, with the Reports and Documents, a View of the Present State of the Country, and of the Progress of the Independents, with a map of South America, 8vo. 9s. 6d. boards.

A Journey from Moscow to Constantinople. With a continuation of the Route to Jerusalem, the Dead Sea, Petra, Damascus, Balbec, Palmyra, &c. in the Years 1817, 1818. By William Macmichael, M. D. F. R. S. one of Dr. Radcliffe's Travelling Fellows, from the University of Oxford. With six plates, 4to. 1l. 11s. 6d.

Account of the Mission from Cape Coast Castle to the Kingdom of Ashantee; with a Statistical Account of that Kingdom, and Geographical Notes of other Parts of the Interior of Africa. By Thomas Edward Bowdich, Conductor and Chief of the Embassy. With sixteen coloured plates, maps, wood-cuts, &c. in 4to. 3l. 3s.

A Voyage up the Persian Gulph, and a Journey over land from India to England, in 1817; containing an Account of Arabia Felix, Arabia, Deserta, Persia, Mesopotamia, the Garden of Eden, Babylon, Bagdad, Koordistan, Armenia, Asia Minor, &c. &c. By Lieutenant William Heude, of the Madras Military Establishment. Illustrated by plates, 4to. 1l. 5s.

foreign Literary Gazette.

BELGIUM.

Schools of Instruction.

The council of Regency of the city of Antwerp, has opened a Subscription, headed by all its Members, for the purpose of establishing a School of mutual Instruction for five hundred Scholars.

The municipal council of the town of Bruges has also opened a Subscription list, the proceeds of which will be employed in establishing a School for the Poor; in which the new method of teaching will be employed.

New Journal.

Belgium will also derive further advantages in favour of Literature, from the publication of a *Bulletin* of information, Literary and Scientific, which will appear monthly.

FRANCE.

Numbers and Characters of the Journals: with incidental Remarks.

It may be possible in France, but it would be impossible in England, to compose such a work as *Notices Historical and Bibliographical of all the Journals and Periodical Works published* in 1818. The names of contributors to most works of reputation among ourselves, are concealed with some care; and we have known writers disbanded from a corps, because their names were becoming too public. Whether this be right or wrong, we do not say; but, it is well known, that a Review in which each writer was expected to avow his article (under the late Mr. Cumberland) advanced to a very few numbers, before it closed. It is not so in France; there the public is as well informed on the subject, as here our Stamp-Office is, by means of the Securities given for all Newspapers. One consequence is, that the adverse opinions occasionally given respecting works, lead to squabbles and recriminations, to the great amusement of the Public; but, little to the advantage of the Belles Lettres, generally speaking.

Be that as it may, the Author of this work announces that it comprises a Notice

of all the Journals, Works, or Collections, that have been published periodically,—that have been born,—that have lived, or have died, during the course of the year. I have given under each of them bibliographical details, and sometimes anecdotes: I have named their Editors; in short, I have denoted with precision the *tone of colour* of each journal, its leading opinions, and the party division to which it belongs.

The author divides his subject into twelve sections: 1. Daily Journals, of which he reckons *eight*. 2. Political and Literary Journals, not published daily, *four*. 3. Journals and Collections purely literary, *nineteen*. 4. Journals and Collections either wholly religious, or chiefly so, *seven*. The author includes in this division, a work called *Hermes* or *Masonic Archives*; which seems somewhat strange; but his apology is, that he could not find where else to put it. 5. Journals or collections which combine politics, literature, and the arts, of these *sixty-two*. 6. Journals devoted to the Sciences, Philosophy, Natural History, Mathematics, &c. *sixteen*. 7. Journals of Medicine and the Medical Sciences, *fourteen*. 8. Journals principally legal, Maritime, Commercial, and Military, *seventeen*. 9. Journals made up of Advertisements, Play-bills, and other notices, (for Paris only,) *eight*. 10. Journals in foreign, or in the dead languages, *five*: that is to say, *one* in the Portuguese, *three* in the English, and *one* in Latin. 11. Journals refering to Music, *four*. 12. Country Journals; these are calculated at more than a hundred. In Britain they are nearer to three hundred. The whole of the Journals published in Paris, amounts annually to *one hundred and fifty.*

This pamphlet is well adapted to meet the natural curiosity of the French people; it swarms with proper names, and should it be fortunately preserved, may convey to posterity, numbers which otherwise would never have been known. It will also interest the bibliographers, who will find in it curious and useful details. It is acknowledged, that many men who have risen to eminence in the republic of letters, have begun their labours in periodical journals: it must also, be confessed, that many men of no ordinary talents, do at

Y

this time, contribute to the information and amusement of the public, in periodical journals; and that journals have no small influence on the public mind, and feeling, since they are read by thousands, who read nothing else. Our pages, also, announce the institution of new journals, in almost every part of the world, and seldom a month passes, in which two or three are not reported. On the whole, therefore, the effect of this description of literature cannot but be exceedingly great: it has taken fast hold of the public mind, and will, no doubt, retain a decided and operative influence. That this should always be correct, were too much to expect; but, that it is beneficial on the whole, we presume does not admit of doubt.

Were it possible that similar means of information had descended to us from the ages of antiquity, with what delight should we peruse the *pros* and *cons* of those times. We now scarcely know what confidence to put in any historian of the few which have come down to us; and, at least, we desire to ascertain his party, before we trust him. More than that, we endeavour by comparing several historians to discover the bias of each; and the differences we endeavour to adjust by some balance, either real or imaginary. In short, though Napoleon disclosed his dread of the truth, when he ordered castrated editions of the principal ancient writers to be printed, and adopted *in usum Scholarum,—in gratiam juventutis,* yet his plea that they were vitiated by party spirit, was but too well-founded in the infirmities of Human Nature. Had periodical journals existed, one would have corrected another; and where the whole were under a censure so strict as that established by the ex-Emperor, those foreign countries which were in opposition to his tyranny, would not have failed to preserve a very different version of all important events and documents, whether proclamations, addresses, mystifications, or bulletins.

GERMANY.

Universities Patronized.

We know not well what to make of the present organization, or disorganization of the University of Germany. If reports may be credited, the character and conduct of the Students in several of them is extremely unfavourable, and even atrocious. We allude to the late fightings in some: and to the murder of M. Kotzebue; said to have been planned in another. It is understood that the Prussian Government has found itself under the necessity of closing and remodeling some, (see our last Number,) and of keeping a strict watch over others.

Elsewhere, the disposition of Government to favour literature has been productive of considerable advantages to similar institutions.

The three Universities of Wurtzburgh, Erlangen, and Landshut, have lately been much patronized by the Bavarian Government. The first has received a new organization: the number of its Professors is augmented; and its Library has received considerable accessions of literary treasures. The University of Altdorf, which was suppressed in 1809, has been combined with that of Erlangen; the library of which, has received by this union, an addition of 40,000 volumes. The Government has also made a present to this University of the residence formerly occupied by the Dowager Margravine Caroline of Brandenburgh, at Bayreuth. The garden of this residence is to be converted into a Botanic Garden, and the buildings which surround it will be employed in those clinical operations which are at once benevolence to the poor, and Schools of instruction to the Student. Several highly estimable men of learning and of skill have been called from different foreign countries to fill the vacant chairs in the University of Erlangen. As to that of Landshut, the funds of its income have been equally augmented, and the prosperity of this University increases in a rapid progress; as also does that of the others.

Perhaps our readers are hardly aware of the importance attached to the selection of Professors in the Universities of Germany; but, the fact is, that when opportunities offers by means of vacancies in the chairs, it is the interest of Government to obtain the most celebrated and most popular Professors to fill them. Hence, sometimes, arises a competition of no small interest, for the acquisition of a distinguished man of letters: for it is well understood, that not only will such a one be followed by Students, and the University where he presides will be thronged, but the effects of his reputation and skill may become permanent; and their benefits may be experienced in succeeding generations; to the great advantage of the State, as well as of the University.

Greek Learning: New Editions.

The great Dictionary, German and Greek of the learned Hellenist, Schneider, in two volumes quarto, has lately been reprinted at Leipsick, at the very moderate price of 25s. to Subscribers, and 40s. to non-Subscribers. This work is spoken of as the most complete of its kind; and this edition as being carefully revised.

New Journal Announced.

At Weimar a new journal is announced, under the title of *Vorvaerts* (Forward). It will include as well Politics, as general Science.

GREECE.

Munificence in favour of Science.

M. Koumas, Director of the New Greek College at Smyrna, is arrived at Vienna, for the purpose of causing several works to be printed. He has already published the first two volumes of his *Course of Philosophy*, composed in Modern Greek; to which is prefixed a letter to M. F. Mauros, containing salutary advice to his Compatriots, and exposing the fallacies of those friends to Despotism, who oppose the propagation of knowledge and learning. The same author has translated into Modern Greek, and published them for the benefit of his countrymen, *Schell's Elementary Chronology*, translated from the French; and *Tenneman's Abridged History of Philosophy*, translated from the German. These are dedicated to M. Nicolaides, a Greek Merchant, settled at Odessa, who has paid the expences of publishing these works for the advantage of the rising generation. More than three hundred copies of them have been given by order of M. Nicolaides, to young Students, who have distinguished themselves, by their promptitude in learning, and by their good conduct and fair character.

HOLLAND:

Foreign Colonies.

Lately has been published at Amsterdam, by Major General J. Van den Bosch, a General View of the Dutch Establishments in Asia, America, and Africa, considered with respect to the Kingdom of the Netherlands, and also Philosophically, &c. The subject is certainly interesting, and susceptible of much elucidation if it be correctly treated, and free from that selfish bias which too often renders the speculations of European writers little better than useless.

INDIES: EAST.

The following Works have been published from the Calcutta Press, during the course of one year; 1817-18. The exertions made, and making, to provide for the good government and well being of the natives, cannot be too highly appreciated; and in this view every work is important, whether it be in its nature preparatory only, or adapted to the purposes of the finished student, and official character.

An Elementary Analysis of the Laws and Regulations, enacted by the Governor in Council, at Fort William, in Bengal, for the Civil Government of the British Territories under that Presidency. Vol. III. By John Herbert Harrington; President of the Council of the College of Fort William, and late Professor, under that institution, of the Laws and Regulations.

The History of Timour, in the original Arabic, written by Ahmud Bin Moohummud of Damascus in Syria, generally known by the name of Ibno Arab Shah. Collated with four Manuscript Copies of the work, and corrected for the Press, by Shykh Ahmud-oobno Moohummud il Ansareyool Yumeenee Yuosh Shirwanee, a native of Arabia, now employed in the Arabic Department of the College of Fort William, Calcutta; Printed at the Press of the Editor, 1818.

" The present edition was undertaken at the recommendation of Dr. Lumsden, the Persian and Arabic Professor, who found the errors in the editions of Golius and Manger, so very numerous and perplexing, that it was only by means of conjectural emendations in every page, that he was able to peruse the work. These errors will be found corrected in the present edition, which has been carefully collated with four valuable Manuscripts, and the Editor anxious, to render the work as extensively useful as possible, has inserted the vowel 'points throughout.' *Extract from the Preface of Captain Lockett.*

Hatim Ta,ee, a romance in the Persian language: Revised and corrected under the superintendence of James Atkinson, Esq. and published, with the approbation of the College Council, for the use of the Junior Students in the College of Fort William, Calcutta, 1818

" The illustrious personage, whose marvellous adventurers are recorded in the following Romance, was equally celebrated among mankind for his wisdom, his valour, and his liberality. The surname of Ta,ee, which he bore, was common to his ˙tribe. He flourished before the birth of Moohummud, and his sepulchre may still be seen at a village, called *Aooaredh.* in *Arabia.*

" The examples of the liberality of Hatim are almost universally known. The most famous of them is that which relates to an Ambassador of the Greek Emperor, who was sent express to demand, on the part of his master, the most valuable horse in the possession of Hatim. The noble-minded Arab, before he was acquainted with the object of the mission, and owing to the hardship of the times, having nothing in his house which might enable him to give a suitable entertainment to his guest, ordered his finest horse to be killed for that purpose! This circumstance is recorded by D'Herbelot as an example of the highest generosity. The wonderful feats described in the present volume, are intended to illustrate the same disposition.

" In selecting these wild and fabulous tales for publication, the object was to supply the Junior Students in the College of Fort William, with a Class Book at once easy, correct, and amusing. The work has no˙ pretensions to elegance of style ; it is, however, highly popular among the Natives, and it appears to be well calculated for the purpose of familiarizing the beginner with the idiom and

structure of ˙the Persian language, and preparing him for the study of more difficult compositions."—*Preface.*

The Kuzeedu of Ibno Zohyr, in the original Arabic, with a commentary by Shykh Ahmud, the learned Editor of the Kamoos, Timour, and other works. This Poem is one of the most celebrated in the Arabic language and indispensibly requires to be accompanied by a commentary, without which it cannot be read by a foreigner, and scarcely perhaps by very many of the Arabs.

The Annals of the College of Fort William, containing the following heads:

1st. The Marquis of Wellesley's Minute in Council, establishing the College.

2d. Report of a Committee, (consisting of Messrs. Barlow, Harington, Kirkpatrick, Edmonstone, and Blaquiere), appointed in July, 1800, to ascertain the progress made in the Hindoostance and Persian languages, by the Junior Civil Servants, who were directed in February, 1799, to attend Mr. Gilchrist, for instruction in those languages.

3d. An account of all the Public Disputations that have been held from the commencement of the Institution to the present time, together with the Discourses of the Visitors delivered each year.

4th. The Statutes of the College now in force.

5th. A general list of all works patronized, or encouraged by the College, or alluded to in the speeches of the Visitors, classed and arranged under their respective languages, intended to show at once what has been accomplished under the auspices of the Institution.

6th. A list of the names and designations of the present College Council, the Officers, Professors and Examiners, who have at any time been employed since the first institution of the College.

7th. An alphabetical list of the Students, Civil and Military, shewing the date of their admission, the period of leaving College, the rank held by them in the scale in general proficiency of their year, and lastly in what page or pages of the book their names are mentioned.

By Thomas Roebuck, Captain in the Madras Native Infantry, Examiner in the

College of Fort William, and late Assistant Secretary to the Council of the College of Fort William.

Boorhani Qatiu, a Dictionary of the Persian language, explained in Persian; Alphabetically arranged according to the system of European Lexicons: comprising the whole of the Words, Phrases and Metaphors, in the Furhungi Juhangeeree, the Mujmuool Foors of Soorooree, the Soormu,e Sooluemanee, and the Suhah ool Udwiyu, together with many Words and Terms, from the Puhluvee, Duree, Zhund o Pazhund, Greek, Syriac, Arabic, Turkish, and other languages; with a short Grammar prefixed, by Moohummud Hoosuen Ibni Khuluf Oot-'Tubreezee, poetically styled Boorhan : To which is added, an Appendix; consisting of the Moofhuqat of the Boorhani Qatiu; the Khatimu or Appendix to the Furhungi Jehangeeree, together with a collection of Words, Phrases, Metaphors, and Proper Names, extracted from the Buhari Ujum, and various other authorities. The whole arranged, collated with 13 Copies of the Work, carefully corrected, revised, and the Text occasionally illustrated with Persian Notes. By Thomas Roebuck, Captain in the Madras Native Infantry; Examiner in the Bruj Bhasha, Persian and Arabic Languages; Acting Assisting Hindoostanee Professor in the College of Fort William, and Member of the Asiatic Society. With the assistance of ten learned Natives.

ITALY.

The Tiber to be Explored.

We learn from Rome that expectation is alert respecting the success of the undertaking to explore the bed of the Tiber, in search of Antiquities ; and at the same time to deepen and cleanse that river. The Subscription for this purpose is patronized by several persons of rank ; and the operations are expected to begin on the first of June, under the direction of Sig. Naro.

Agriculture Patronized.

Four Schools of Practical Agriculture have lately been established in the Neapolitan province of Moliso; the country of the ancient Samnites.

PRUSSIA.

Noble Present : Botany.

The Herbal of the celebrated Botanist, Wildenow, has lately been purchased by the King, who has presented it to the University of Berlin.

RUSSIA.

New School in Georgia.

The chief of Georgia inaugurated on the 15th of November last, a School which the Russian General Yermolow, had caused to be built at Teflis; for the education of the children of the superior classes in that province.

SPAIN.

Schools of Instruction, Patronized.

The System of mutual Instruction, known among us, as that of Bell and Lancaster, has lately been translated into Spanish, and published at Madrid. King Ferdinand has accepted the dedication of this work; and has taken the publication under his protection. We may, therefore, hope that he will also take the Schools founded on it, under his protection also; the result of which cannot but be of essential, in fact, of vital benefit to Spain.

SWEDEN.

Ancient Hieroglyphics, on Rocks.

Hitherto we have looked for Hieroglyphics in Egypt only; but a learned man of the University of Lund, M. Brunins, has discovered a considerable number of inscriptions cut in rocks : of these he has published a *Programma,* which induces the learned to hope for the speedy appearance of a more detailed work on the subject. According to the best estimate that can now be formed of them, they are Hieroglyphics of very remote antiquity.

If the reader should recollect what has been said on the written rocks of North America, in the State of Massachusetts, if we rightly recollect, this article will appear to combine an interest, not obvious at first sight. As those inscriptions are on rocks exposed to the action of water, it has been doubted whether they were the works of people of remote antiquity, or cracks and crevices produced by the abrasion of the stream, &c, during a lapse of ages. If any similarity should be found between the characters of these in Sweden and those in America, the subject may receive elucidation. That it was customary to inscribe important memorials on rocks, intended to inform distant posterity, appears from the allusion of the Patriarch Job, who speaks of it as a customary thing,—and, no doubt, very ancient, even in his day.

The Gatherer.

No. XXVIII.

" I am but a gatherer, and dealer in other mens' stuff."

A Froggish Concert.

To a person coming at once from England, says a recent traveller (Dr. Clarke), the appearance is new and strange; but that which offered the greatest novelty to our party, was the loud and incessant chorus of myriads of frogs, the whole way from Lubeck to Eutin. To call it croaking, would be to convey a very erroneous idea of it, because it is really harmonious; and we gave to these reptiles the name of *Holstein Nightingales.* Those who have not heard it, would hardly believe it possible for any number of frogs to produce such a powerful and predominating clamour. The effect of it, however, is certainly not unpleasing; especially, after sun-set, when all the rest of animated nature is silent, and seems to be at rest. The noise of any one of them, singly, as we sometimes heard it near the road, was, as usual, disagreeable, and might be compared to the loudest quacking of a duck; but when, as it generally happened, tens of thousands, nay millions, sang together, it was a choral vibration, varied only by cadences of sound, something like those produced upon musical glasses; and it accorded with the uniformity which twilight cast over the woods and waters.

Chesterfield and Lamb.

The late residence of the Duke of York, in Piccadilly, now the Albany, was originally built by Mr. Lamb, the grandfather of the present Member for Westminster. When it was first completed, Mr. Lamb remarked to the witty Earl of Chesterfield,

that he did not know how to distinguish it properly as the family town residence, because it would appear rather awkward to call it *Lamb House.* " The difficulty, my dear Sir," replied the Peer, " is easily removed, by calling it *House Lamb!*"

Origin of Ranks.

Alexander Barclay, a priest of Devonshire, who died at a great age in 1532, wrote the much quoted but indifferent *Ship of Fools,* but is more memorable for having been the earliest writer of Eclogues in our language. His description of rural life presents a miserable picture of the peasantry of that age. The speakers in one of his Eclogues (says Mr. Campbell, in his " *Specimens of British Poets,*" lie littered among straw, for want of a fire to keep themselves warm; and one of them expresses a wish that the milk for dinner may be curdled, to save them the consumption of bread. In one of his moral apologues, Adam, he tells us in verse, was one day abroad at his work——Eve was at the door of the house, with her children playing about her; some of them, while she was " kembing," says the poet, prefixing another particle, not of the most delicate kind, to describe the usefulness of the comb. Her Maker having deigned to pay her a visit, she was ashamed to be found with so many ill-dressed children about her, and hastened to stow a number of them out of sight; some of them she concealed under hay and straw, others she put up the chimney; and one or two into a " tub of draff." Having produced, however, the best-looking and the best-dressed of them, she was delighted to hear their Divine Visitor bless them, and destine some of them to be Kings and Emperors, some Dukes and Barons, and others Sheriffs, Mayors, and Aldermen. Unwilling that any of her family should forfeit blessings while they were going, she immediately drew out the remainder from their concealment; but when they came forth, they were so covered with dust and cobwebs, and had so many bits of chaff and straw sticking to their hair, that, instead of receiving benedictions of promotion, they were doomed to vocations of toil and poverty suitable to their dirty appearance. Such is Mr. Barclay's account of the origin of different ranks in society; from which it appears, that we poor fellows who are born to labour in this world, inherit the destiny from our earliest progenitors being, perhaps, stuck, into the " draff tub !"

Anecdote of Foote.

This facetious actor, while passing down St. James's Street, was suddenly accosted by a person whom he had seen before, and who begged to ask his advice under very peculiar circumstances. " What is the matter, my dear fellow ?" said Foote. " Why," said the other, " I have just been thrown out of that window," pointing to a window in an upper story of a house, still devoted to pursuits similar to those followed on that day. " In the name of fortune," cried Foote, " what could have led to this ?" " Oh," said the other, " I was playing at cards, and being accused of cheating, without any further hesitation I was seized by the neck, and chucked into the street. I shall certainly go to a lawyer and bring an action— wouldn't you advise me to do so ?" " No," says Foote, " I would not indeed advise you to do any such foolish thing." " What then ?" said the other. " Why," concluded Foote, " nothing can be more foolish than to go to lawyers upon such occasions, for they generally get all the money, and their clients all the disgrace : but if you will take my advice in future, when you are disposed to play in the same way, take care that you keep on the ground floor, and then if you should be thrown out of the window, your fall will not be so great."

Horse Advertised.

A parish clerk in a chapel-of-ease, at Meltham, in Yorkshire, being ordered to advertise a horse, thus described it : " Stolen, or otherwise conveyed from Hallam, near Bedlam, a horse 15 hands high, *four* white feet and *a black one.* God save the King with a pack-saddle on his back !"

Shut the Door !

Among the peculiarities of the late Dr. Burney, were two of a very innocent kind ; the first was, the possession of the best wine, of the best vintage ; the next, a dread of a fresh current of air. Shut the door ! was the first salutation uttered by him, to any one who entered his apartment, and but few of his associates ever neglect-

ed this rule. This custom, it seems, did not abandon him even on the most critical and trying occasions ; for it is said, that having been robbed while returning home one evening in his own carriage, along the Greenwich-road, by a couple of footpads, who were more eager in obtaining his money than contributing to his accommodation, he called them back in a peremptory tone, and while they were wondering at what he wanted with them, he exclaimed in his usual manner, and with his own peculiar emphasis, " Shut the door !" A voice accustomed to command produced the desired effect, and he was instantly obeyed.

A Lapland Interior.

We now advanced, says Dr. Clarke, and threw open the door of the tent : it was full of inmates, about seven persons in all, two men and two women, besides children. We presented them with two offerings most likely to ensure a welcome ; namely, brandy and tobacco ; the women swallowing the former, as greedily as the men, who, as it is well known, will almost part with life itself for the gratification of dram-drinking. We now seated ourselves with them in their tent. They had dark hair and tawny skins, but there was no appearance of filthiness. Their shirts were made of leather ; their scull-caps either of woollen cloth, or of black plush ; their shoes seldom worn in summer, were of the same nature as the labkas of the Russians, made of matted birch-bark. The outer garments of men and women resemble a Capuchin's cowl, fastened round the waist with a sash. This outer covering is only worn when they are abroad ; and then they carry provisions in the large pouch which the bosom affords : this is moreover their summer dress. After we had sat for some time, a girl came in, who had been tending the rein-deer ; her father being on the outside, in close conversation with our Pipping, our Lapland interpreter. We had previously given to this man the remainder of our brandy, about a pint, thinking he would husband it with great care ; and we had seen him place it behind him, upon his bed, near the skirting of the tent. As soon as the girl entered, we called to the Pipping, desiring him to prevail on the father to allow his daughter a taste of the brandy, as she had lost her share by being absent. The old man made no answer; but upon our repeating the request, he slily crept round the out-side of the tent, until he came to the spot where the brandy was; when thrusting his arm silently beneath the skirting, he drew it out, and swallowed the whole contents of the bottle at a draught. We now offered to buy some rein-deer cheese, which is white, and not unlike the Cottenham cheese, made near Cambridge: he said he would supply us with any quantity for brandy, but refused money. Another Lapp brought us some of the cheese as a present, hoping to get a dram; but our stock of spirituous liquor was already consumed. The brandy seemed, moreover, to have effect; for the chief looking very wise, began to sing. We begged for a Lapland song, and it was granted. With both his fists clenched, and thrusting his face close to that of Mr. Pipping, as if threatening to bite him, he uttered a most fearful yell: it was the usual howl of the Laplanders, consisting of five or six words repeated over and over, which when translated, occur in this order:

Let us drive the Wolves!
Let us drive the Wolves!
See they run :
The Wolves run!

The boy also, our guide, sang the same ditty. During their singing they strained their lungs so as to cause a kind of spasmodic convulsion of the chest, which produced a noise like the braying of an ass. In all this noise there was not a single note that could be called musical; and it is very remarkable, that the Laplanders have not the smallest notion of music. (*Travels in Sweden, Lapland, &c.*)

Seeming to Dine.

A Prince who was much celebrated at the Court of Bonaparte, one day ordered a table sufficient to contain 60 covers. The tradesman having brought it, his Highness directed that it should be placed in the dining-hall, in order that he might see whether it was large enough. The Prince laid it was too small for 60 persons to sit down to it conveniently. The tradesman was of a different opinion. After a long discussion, he resolved to put the question to the proof. He sent one of his valets to the masons who were then employed at

some building in the Place de Carousel, with an order that sixty of them should immediately come to him. The workmen were at first surprised at this sudden invitation, and thought that his Highness wanted to have some work executed in a great hurry.—They washed their hands and faces, put on their coats, and repaired to the Prince. They were introduced into the dining-hall. The Prince had sixty plates put on the table, and as many chairs placed round it. He ordered them to sit down; their astonishment was redoubled, but they obeyed. The greater part of them supposed that Monseigneur had received good news from the armies, and that he was about to drink to the health of the warriors, and they were in the best disposition to officiate on the occasion, when the Prince ordered them to perform the following manœuvres:— " Raise your elbows—appear as if you were drinking—seem as if you were cutting something on your plates—stretch out the right arm." After the sixty workmen made every movement in imitation of persons at an entertainment, his Highness being satisfied that the table could contain sixty guests, sent these people back to their work, undertaking to indemnify them for the time they had lost.

Increase of Attornies.

In the Rolls of Parliament, A. D. 1445, is a petition from the Commons of two counties in England, stating that the number of *attornies* had lately increased from *six* or *eight* to *twenty-four*, whereby the peace of these counties had been greatly interrupted by suits. The commons therefore petition, that it may be ordained that there shall be no more than *six* common attornies for Norfolk, the same number for Suffolk, and *two* for the city of Norwich. Any other person acting as an attorney to forfeit *twenty shillings*.

<hr>

HINTS, PLANS, and PROCEEDINGS

OF

Benevolence.

————————*Homo sum :
Humanum nihil a me alienum puto.*

NATIVE EDUCATION IN INDIA.

It is only of late, that experience has produced a general conviction of the great importance of schools in our Indian possessions ; and, the rapidity with which education is advancing in this immense empire offers the most complete proof of the practicability of the system pursued and affords the most encouraging. prospects of the moral and religious improvement of the rising generation in this remote, but highly interesting quarter of the world. We have often alluded to this subject in our former numbers, and at p. 260 of the present volume, will be found a notice of the " Bombay Native Schools," and a p. 262 some particulars of very useful institutions, the " Calcutta School Book Society."

It is now our pleasing task to record, that the education of the hundred millions of people in India under the influence of England, begins to fix the attention and to receive the support, not only of Societies, but of all classes of persons : the British Governments, and some of the native authorities, the Governor General, the Bishop of Calcutta, Chaplains, Missionaries, Military Officers, European Ladies and Gentlemen, resident in India, and even the rich natives themselves, all unite to promote the education of children. Already. from thirty to forty thousand native children, are receiving those blessings of education, which are to redeem them from the idolatry of their forefathers, and to render them useful members of society. And this number is continually and rapidly increasing. Can superabundant wealth be better employed than in fostering and promoting this great and good work.

The necessity of education is affectingly demonstrated to every intelligent observer, by the Serampore Missionaries, in the following excellent observations, taken from their " Hints."

Not only are the people, in general, destitute of every just idea of God ; but they can scarcely be said to be fully impressed with the importance of a single principle of morality. They have no just idea of the objects of nature so constantly before them—of the sun, moon, and stars —of the clouds, the winds, the rains— of the earth, on which they dwell—of the groves, the trees, and plants, which surround them—of the domestic animals, which they nourish ; nor, in a word, of the flowing stream, the buzzing insect, or of the plant which creeps over their lowly shed. To them the sun retires behind a mountain ; the rain from heaven is given by a god whom they are in the

habit of despising and vilifying ; the rainbow is the bow of Rama ; the river is a deity ; the birds, the beasts, and even the reptiles around them, are animated by the souls of their deceased relatives. Falsehood and uncleanness are nothing ; perjury a trifle ; and a failure in fidelity and probity, often a subject of praise : while ablution in the water of a river is deemed a due atonement for almost every breach of morality.

The wretched Schools which they have in their towns and villages are so few, that, on the average, scarcely one man in a hundred will be found who can read a common Letter. Printed books they have none, unless a copy of some book of the Scriptures should have found its way among them : and, as to manuscripts, they have scarcely one in prose ; but, if they possessed a multitude, their ignorance of their own language would render the perusal of an inaccurate and ill-written manuscript too formidable a task to be often attempted. Thus, with a regular, and copious language of their own, nearly all who are ignorant of Sanscrit (which is not understood by one in ten thousand throughout India) are in a state of ignorance not greatly exceeded by that of those savage hordes which have no written language ; while numerous causes combine to sink them far below most savage nations, in vice and and immorality.

Add to this, that their knowledge of Arithmetic is scarcely less wretched. What avails their possessing Treatises in Sanscrit, both on Arithmetic and Geometry ? From these the common people derive about as much advantage as though they were written in Chinese. Hence, though some of them, through long habit, are expert in calculation, (as is the case with many in England unacquainted with a single rule of Arithmetic,) at School they learn even the four fundamental rules in so wretched a manner, that an English Boy of eight years old would, in a few minutes, resolve a question in multiplication or division, the solving of which would cost them an expence of time scarcely to be credited.

The complete absence of all just ideas is the chief cause of that degradation of public morals so evident in this country. The doctrine of the Metempsychosis, carried to the extent to which it is in India, while it seems to exalt man to the state of a God, by terming him an identical part of the Deity, in reality sinks his ideas of the Deity to the level of every thing immoral and degrading; while men's maintaining that God does every thing within them, takes away all reverence for Him. and sets them free from every tie of moral obligation. The idea of the soul's passing from body to body, strips death of every thing awful, and humanity of every thing tender; and, instead of elevating the minds of Hindoos above terrene objects, renders them insensible to the finest feelings of human nity, and causes them to set scarcely any value on human life, even though it be the life of those who gave them existence. Thus those two grand principles, piety and humanity, which are the foundation of all virtue, both public and private, and which enter into the essence of religion, are almost extinguished in the mind of a Hindoo, by the natural operation of the system which he holds: and when to this we add that disregard of justice and all good faith, and that proneness to knavery, falsehood, and deceit, which instantly follow the absence of piety, justice, and humanity, we have before us all the great features of depravity visible in their general character.

The School Book Society, to which we have before alluded seeks to improve the natives in a knowledge of their own language, by the distribution of suitable tables and elementary works, which possess every advantage in point of legibility and appearance. On this subject the Baptist Missionaries have suggested some very important points; and they have, in a great measure accomplished, what they suggested Some of these very sensible observations we shall subjoin, as they cannot be too widely circulated. If generally acted upon, they could not fail of producing the happiest results.

Their *System of Arithmetic* should be improved; and they should be made acquainted with the simplest and easiest method of solving those practical questions which are now so abstruse to them. This would be useful beyond merely enabling them to manage an account: the precision of thought and the habit of reasoning, which a thorough acquaintance with the fundamental principles of numbers tends to produce, are not useless, in strengthening the mind, and in fitting it for further advances in knowledge.

To this might be added a concise but perspicuous *Account of the Solar System;* preceded by so much of the laws of motion, and of attraction and gravity, as might be necessary to render the Solar System plain and intelligible.

This abstract of the Solar System might be followed by a compendious *View of Geography.* In this part it would be proper to describe Europe particularly. because of its importance in the present state of the world; and Britain might be allowed to occupy that pre-eminence among the nations which God has given her.

To these might be added a number of popular truths and facts relative to *Natural Philosophy.* In the present improved state of knowledge, a thousand things have been ascertained, relative to light, heat, air, water, meteorology, mineralogy, chemistry, and natural history, of which the Ancients had but a partial knowledge, and of which the Natives of the East have as yet scarcely the faintest idea. A knowledge of these facts would rectify and enlarge their ideas of various objects of nature around them; and might inflame a few minds, of a superior order, with an unquenchable desire to know why these things are so; and thus urge them to those studies, which, in Europe, have led to the discovery of these important facts.

To this view of the Solar System of the Earth, and of the various Objects which it contains, might, with advantage be added such a *Compendium of History and Chronology,* as should bring them acquainted with the state of the world in past ages, and with the principal events which have occurred since the Creation. It should commence with the Creation; and describe the primitive state of man, the entrance of evil, the corruption of the antediluvian age, the Flood, and the peopling of the earth anew from one family. The compiler should avail himself of all the light thrown on this subject by modern research and investigation: he should particularly notice the nations of the East; incorporating, in their proper place, the best accounts of both India and China. He should go on to state the call of Abraham; the giving of the Decalogue; the gradual revelation of the Scriptures; the settlement of Greece, and its mythology; the Trojan War; the Four great Monarchies; the Advent of the Saviour of Men; the persecution of the Christian Church; the rise of Mahomedanism; the origin of the Papacy; the invention of printing, of gunpowder, and of the mariner's compass; the Reformation; the discovery of the passage to India by sea; and the various discoveries of modern science: Such a synopsis of History and Chronology would exceedingly enlarge their ideas relative to the state of the world ; certainly not to the disadvantage of Britain, which God has so exalted as to render her almost the arbitress of nations.

Lastly. it would be highly proper to impart to them just ideas of themselves, relative both to body and mind, and to a future state of existence, by what may be termed a *Compendium of Ethics and Morality.*

Although this Compendium of Ethics is mentioned last. it is not necessary that the communication of ideas so important in their nature, should be deferred till all the rest be acquired : it might be better to intersperse them among those already mentioned, that they might take deep root in the mind.

If we would therefore wish to improve the public morals of our Indian Fellow-Subjects, this must be attempted by the introduction of a remedy suited to the nature of the disease ; by imparting to them that knowledge relative to themselves, to their responsibility for their actions, their state both here and hereafter, and the grand principles of piety, justice, and humanity, which may leaven their minds from the earliest youth.

Should any one say, " Effect this by at once introducing the Holy Scriptures into these Schools ;" the measure is not so much objected to on account of any danger attending it, as from its not appearing to be the most efficient method which can be adopted. That the Scriptures contain every degree of information relative to the nature of man, his relation to God, and a future state, no one can deny But is it to be expected, that an Indian Youth, totally unacquainted with the nature of the book, and the reading of whose parents and contemporaries has never been equal to a twentieth part of its contents, should be able, under the direction of a Heathen Teacher, to select precisely those truths which would meet the deficiency of his own ideas? It seems necessary, that those important facts, relative to the nature of man, a future state, our responsibility to God, &c. with which we in Europe are familiarized from our earliest infancy, should be laid down in a way no less clear and definite than those which relate to the solar system, natural philosophy, geography, and history. The Compendium containing these ideas might be drawn up in the words of Scripture, or otherwise ; the

plainest and easiest language being adopted, and that of Scripture preferred when peculiarly suited, as in the case of a multitude of instances, to express the idea to a child.

We have not space to dilate further on this very interesting branch of the " Hints of Benevolence ;" but must refer our readers for a mass of curious information on this subject, to the " Missionary Register," for March, 1819, in which will be found among a variety of other matter, a Survey of the meritorious labours of the Christian Knowledge Society, the Danish Mission, the Church Missionary Society, the Baptist Mission, the London Missionary Society, the American Board of Missions, the Wesleyan Missions, the Hindoo College at Calcutta, and the Calcutta School Book Society.

INTERESTING INTELLIGENCE FROM THE BRITISH SETTLEMENTS IN INDIA.

CALCUTTA.

ASIATIC SOCIETY.

The following description of the localities, where the river Ganges rises to day, will be read with great interest, not as a geographical document only, but as connected with the religion and tribes of the Hindoos. Our readers know, that the Ganges is a sacred stream ; that it is understood to issue from the foot of a Goddess ; that the Gods are supposed to rejoice at its appearance ; and that many places of worship, temples, &c. stand, or did stand, in the vicinity. The reference made by Capt. Hodgson's guide, of the icicles, to the pair of Manades, shews the lively imagination of the people, as well as the prevalence and strong hold obtained by superstition ;—by that superstition of which Capt. Hodgson was now at the spring and source.

On Monday Evening, August 10, a Meeting of the Asiatic Society was held at Chouringhee, the Most Noble the

Marquis of Hastings, President, in the chair.

On this occasion the journal of a survey to the heads of the rivers Ganges and Jumna, by Captain Hodgson, 10th Regiment of Native Infantry, was presented by the President. Captain Webb's survey in 1808, having extended from the Doon Valley to Cajane, near Reital, Captain Hodgson commences his scientific and interesting labours from the latter place, which by a series of observations he found to be in latitude. 30° 48′ 28″ N. The village of Reital, consists of about 35 houses, which are built of wood, and are two, or three stories high. He left Reital, on the 21st of May, 1817. On the 31st he descended to the bed of the river, and saw the Ganges issue from under a very low arch at the foot of the grand snow bed. The river was bounded to the right and left by high rocks and snow, but in the front, over the debouche, the mass of snow was perfectly perpendicular, and from the bed of the stream to the summit, the thickness was estimated at little less then 300 feet of solid frozen snow; probably the accumulation of ages, as it was in layers of several feet thick, each seemingly the remains of a fall of a separate year. From the brow of this curious wall of snow, and immediately above the outlet of the stream, large and hoary icicles depended. The Gangoutri Brahmin who accompanied Captain Hodgson, and who was an illiterate mountaineer, observed that he thought these icicles must be Mahadeo's hair, from whence, as he understood, it is written in the Shaster; the Ganges flows. Captain Hodgson thinks that the appellation of Cow's mouth is aptly given to this extraordinary debouche. The height of the arch of snow is only sufficient to let the stream flow under it. Blocks of snow were falling on all sides, and there was little time to do more than to measure the size of the stream; the mean breadth was 27 feet, the greatest depth about 18 inches, and the shallowest part 9 or 10 inches. Captain Hodgson believes this to be the *first appearance in day light* of the celebrated Ganges! Zealous in the prosecution of his inquiries, he attempted to proceed forwards, but was obliged to return, having frequently sunk in the snow, one

time up to his neck, and there being evident marks of hollows beneath.

The height of the halting place near which the Ganges issues from under the great snow bed, is calculated to be 12914 feet above the sea, and the height of a peak of the Himalaya, called St. George, by Captain Hodgson, is estimated to be 22,240 feet above the surface of the sea.

Captain Hodgson in his account of the course of the river Jumna, observes, that at Jumnoutri, the snow which covers and conceals the stream, is about 60 yards wide, and is bounded to the right and left by mural precipices of granite, it is 40½ feet thick, and has fallen from the precipices above. He was able to measure the thickness of the bed of snow over the stream, very exactly, by means of a plumb line, let down through one of the holes in it, which are caused by the steam of a great number of boiling springs at the border of the Jumna. The thickness was 40 feet 5¼ inches. The head of the Jumna is on the south west side of the grand Himalaya ridge; differing from the Ganges, inasmuch as that river has the upper part of its course within the Himalaya, flowing from the south of east to the north of west, and it is only from Sookie, where it pierces through the Himalaya, that it assumes a course of about south 20 west. The mean latitude of the hot springs of Jummoutri appears to be 30° 58′. Captain Hodgson made this observation April 21, 1817.

HEIGHTS OF THE HIMALAYA MOUNTAINS; AND OF PERPETUAL SNOW.

Capt. Webb some time ago transmitted to Mr. Colebrooke his observations on the Himalaya Mountains; from which that gentleman, as well as Capt. W. calculated their heights. He observes in a subsequent letter, that these heights were obtained *Barometrically* as well as *Geometrically;* and, that the agreement between these two modes of measuring, was very satisfactory. On the whole Capt. W. infers, after making all proper allowances for refractions, bearings, or other supposeable causes of error.

1st. That 11,000 feet is an elevation, beyond that at which perpetual snow rests on the sides of the Himalaya.

2d. That a "good grassy plain" at the foot of the Neetee Pass, may be estimated at 6000 feet, and the summit of the pass itself, at 9500 feet.

Captain Webb compares these speculations with a Test, not inferior to the Meteorogical Phenomena; viz. Barometrical Observation.

Barometrical height of places in the Bhoteea Purguna of Jawahir, as computed from observations made in June 1817.

	Feet.
Reelakot Village, above Calcutta	10653
Murtolee	11327
Mapau	1108?
Panchoo	11284
Milum	11405
Ditto Temple	11681
Birjoo Village	11314
Boorphoo	10836

Between the Village Milum, and the Temple, are extensive fields of a kind of Barley, (Oo'a) and Buckwheat.—He procured some plants of Spikenard, (Jatamansi) from at least 1500 feet above Milum Temple.

The road from Milum to Tartary leads along the banks of a rapid mountain stream (and is consequently a continued ascent), four days journey for laden sheep and goats, and crossing the Snowy Chain on the fifth march. This road opens in July, at which time the Bhoteeas find pasture for their sheep and goats, (though no fuel) even at the fourth halting ground—which allowing only 500 feet of ascent for each, will carry the limit of vegetation to 13500 feet.

On the 21st of June, 1817, Captain Webb's camp was 11630 feet above Calcutta, on a clear spot surrounded by a rich forest of Oak, Pine, and Rhododendra.—The surface covered with rank vegetation as high as the knee—and very extensive strawberry beds in full flower. Currant bushes remarkably numerous in blossom.—Soil a fat black mould.

On the 22nd of June, at 1 P. M. he reached the summit of Pil-goenta Churhaee, 12642 feet above Calcutta.

The thick dense mist prevented his distinguishing distant objects—there was not the smallest patch of snow near him—and the surface, a fat black mould, from beneath which, at this altitude, the rock frequently peeps forth, and is here covered with Strawberry plants! (not yet in flower.) Dandelion, Butter-cups, and a multitude of small flowers.—The shoulder of the hill on the left, rose 400 or 450 feet above him, without a vesture of snow, enamelled with flowers to the very top, and shutting out from view the still higher parts of the ridge.—On the right the hill declines to a forest of Birch, Alpine, Rhododendron and Raga Pine about 500 feet, or less below. The hollows and dips of the hill, (much lower than the summit), where the drifting snow had accumulated in unusual quantities during the winter, still remained half filled, but with a mean temperature of 50°, their contents would of course quickly dissolve.

The Goatherds who were with Captain Webb, gave assurances that in July and August their flocks would be led to pasture on this ridge, (which continued to ascend to the eastward), as far above Pilgoenta Ghat, as that Ghat was higher than his camp on the 21st instant, (or 1000 feet,) which again brought the limit of vegetation to nearly the same elevation as before inferred.

But of this fact Captain Webb meant to require occular demonstration.

By comparing these altitudes with those obtained by M. Walhenberg, [Comp LIT. PAN. O. S. vol. 10. p. 1016.] Very instructive results may be obtained. The line of perpetual snow in the Alps and Switzerland is 7,000 or 8,000 feet; in the Pyrenees 8,100 feet; in Lapland it begins at 4,00 feet above the level of the sea.

SCULPTURE FROM PERSEPOLIS.

A letter from Lieutenant Taylor, was read, presenting in the name of Captain Bruce, a specimen of the Sculpture of Persepolis, taken from the principal staircase of the Palace, the sides of which are ornamented with figures in various costumes, each apparently bringing some gift to the monarch of the age, in which the structure was raised. The air of the whole series of ornaments on the staircase, and generally throughout these memorable ruins, are said to bear a resemblance to the ceremonies practised even at this day before the King of Persia on the anniversary of the *Nowroz*, at the vernal equinox, when individuals bearing gifts from the Vice-roys of the different provinces of the Empire are displayed, in an extended and successive line, in the presence of the monarch and his courtiers.

HOSPITAL FOR LEPERS.

A Hospital for the reception of Lepers has lately been projected; and we are glad to learn, that it is likely to meet with very considerable support from the liberality of the public. The number of wretched creatures labouring under leprosy, in and about Calcutta, calls for a measure of this kind, as the nature of the disorder precludes them from receiving benefit from any of the charitable institutions already established.

MADRAS.

LITERARY SOCIETY.

On Tuesday Sept. 8th, the Members of the Literary Society held their first evening Meeting at their Rooms, on the Mount Road, the Honorable Sir John Newbolt, President, in the Chair.

The President having congratulated the Members of the Society on the success which had attended their first endeavours to collect a library, the liberal donations to which, might be observed, he regarded as evincing a confidence in the public mind, with regard to the ultimate success of the Institution; proceeded to deliver to the Meeting an interesting Address, in the course of which he took a rapid and masterly sketch of the manner in which oaths are administered in different Countries, particularly in India.—The President, remarked, that the subject had been suggested by his professional pursuits, and he concluded with expressing a hope that his observations might prepare the way for further research into a matter not only very curious in itself, but of vital importance to the interests of public justice.

The President also repeated to the Meeting, as connected with the subject of his discourse, a paper which had been drawn up in the English Language; by Mohummud Teepoo, the Mohummudan Interpreter of the Supreme Court, on the opinions entertained respecting oaths by the best Commentators on the Mohammudan law. The paper was read to the Meeting, and, both in the order of its arrangement, and in the style of the composition, it reflected great credit on the talents of the writer.

A paper was read to the Meeting, by Sir George Cooper, containing some highly curious and interesting observations on the articles of Indian merchandize enumerated in a rescript in Justinian's Digest of the Roman law.

The Acting Secretary presented to the meeting, on the part of Mr. B. Babington, a paper communicated by a Gentleman who has lately visited Palestine, containing an elegant and striking description of the ruins of Jaresh, a city of the ancient Decapolis, [said to be Pella Edit.]

A letter was read from Mr. Heath, at Salem, forwarding a valuable donation of books: and the Acting Secretary acquainted the Meeting that several Gentlemen had lately contributed very largely to the Library of the Society.

His Excellency Sir Thomas Hislop; J. M'Kerrell, W. M'Taggart and C. M. Whish, Esquires; were elected Members of the Institution, and it was resolved that Sir Thomas Hislop should be requested to accept the situation of a Vice-President of the Society.

CHILDREN KIDNAPPED FOR BASE PURPOSES.

The following paragraph will not surprize those of our readers who recollect certain others which have appeared in our pages: The issuing of four writs in one day, with the acknowledged frequency of the crime throughout India, speaks sufficiently plainly the degraded state of morals and moral feeling, among a people of which some writers, not sufficiently acquainted with them, have spoken too highly.

The fourth and last Law Term for the present year,—the Advocate General moved for a Writ of Habeas Corpus, directed to Shah Begum, to bring up the body of a child, which had been stolen from its Mother, and had been seen in the house of this person.—The Learned Advocate in moving for this Writ, observed that he understood it to be a very prevalent and common practice at this place, and indeed, generally over India, for persons to kidnap young children of the poorer class of inhabitants, and sell them to the higher orders to be brought up as slaves and prostitutes. The motion was granted, and three other Writs of a similar nature, issued were at the same time.

BOTANICAL ACQUISITION,
FROM NEW SOUTH WALES.

The Ship Lady Castlereagh, Captain G. Weltden, from Hobarts Town, the 26th of June, and Sydney the 1st of July, has arrived with a detachment of His Majesty's 46th Regiment.

Captain Weltden has brought out a very fine collection of plants from New South Wales, for the Queen of England; and one for the emperor of Austria.—They are in beautiful preservation, and are taken care of by one of the Kew gardeners, sent out for that purpose.

BOMBAY.
SICKNESS COUNTERACTED.

We have been cautious in communicating the most extensive intelligence that had reached us, respecting the ravages of the *Cholera Morbus* ; but, we have the greatest pleasure in repeating the following paragraph, from the Bombay Courier of August 8, 1818.

We are happy to be able to state, that all the accounts from the Deccan received during the last week, relative to the Cholera Morbus, concur in the statement, that the practice adopted has been most successful in preventing the fatal effects of this dreadful malady. In cases wherein the application for relief was made in time, not more than one in a hundred had died; but the disease had been generally fatal wherever any considerable delay had occurred in administering the medicines.

Where the disease attacked Europeans, copious bleeding has been adopted, and an early use of the hot bath had been found most beneficial in abating the violence of the spasms; which in some instances attacked the patients with such intensity, that it was necessary for the medical assistants to hold them down.

The disease is generally considered by the profession to be disappearing : in Poona, there have been only a very few cases, and it was supposed that in these instances the patients had arrived in that city with the seeds of the disease about them. We trust the very heavy rains we have had during the last week, will relieve us from all anxiety of a visitation of this fearful epidemie.

EXCESSIVE RAINS.
Bombay, Sept. 5, 1818.

The fall of rain here during the last month has not been excessive. The rains however, at Tinnah and on the continent in our immediate neighbourhood, have been very heavy; particularly on the 19th ult., when the rivers of Panwell and Apta overflowed their banks and did considerable mischief. We are sorry to learn, that, at Panwell, fifteen persons were drowned, and fifty houses destroyed. At Apta one hundred and fifty houses were swept away by the flood, several others were considerably damaged, and many gardens destroyed. We are happy to add, that, by the exertions of the Collector's people, no lives were lost at the latter place.

We are also informed that the rains throughout Guzerat have proved unusually heavy.

CEYLON.
SLAVES EMANCIPATED.

His Excellency the Governor has given Deeds of Emancipation to all the Slaves employed in the Leper and Pettah Hospitals, under the Superintendant of the Poor Funds. This measure is to be considered as indicating his Excellency's determination to promote the general abolition of that odious degradation of our

Fellow creatures, since in regard to the Slaves just now emancipated, they were Slaves only in name, for by his Excellency's particular directions they received the same wages as free Servants.

Poetry.

ODE TO ENTERPRIZE,

By Dr. E. D. Clarke,

Author of Travels in Sweden, Lapland, &c.

I.

On lofty mountains roaming,
  O'er bleak perennial snow,
Where cataracts are foaming,
  And raging north winds blow ;
Where hungry wolves are prowling,
  And famish'd eagles cry ;
Where the tempests loud are howling,
  And lowering vapours fly.

II.

Then at the peep of morning,
  Bedeck'd with dewy tears,
Wild weeds her brows adorning,
  Lo! ENTERPRIZE appears :
While keen-eyed *Expectation*
  Still points to objects new ;
See panting *Emulation*
  Her fleeting steps pursue !

III.

List, List, Celestial Virgin !
  And oh! the vow record !
From groveling cares emerging,
  I pledge this solemn word :—
By deserts, fields, or fountains,
  While health, while life remains,
O'er LAPLAND's icy mountains,
  O'er Afric's burning plains ;

IV.

Or, midst the darksome wonders
  Which Earth's vast caves conceal,
Where subterranean thunders
  The miner's path reveal ;
Where, bright in matchless lustre,
  The lithal flowers* unfold,
And, midst the beauteous clustre
  Beams efflorescent gold ;

* Chrystals, the blossoms of the mineral world ; disclosing the nature and properties of stones, as those of vegetables are made known by their flowers.

V.

In every varied station,
  Whate'er my fate may be,
My hope, my exultation
  Is still to follow thee !—
When age, with sickness blended,
  Shall check the gay career ;
And death, though long suspended,
  Begins to hover near.

VI.

Then oft in visions fleeting,
  May thy fair form be nigh,
And still thy votary greeting,
  Receive his parting sigh ;
And tell a joyful story,
  Of some new world to come,
Where kindred souls, in glory,
  May call the wanderer home !

EPIGRAM.

I scarce can blame thee, foolish Fly,
Vent'ring too near Elmira's eye,
For, giddy Fly, thou still delightest
To wanton where the beams are brightest,
And many a gaudy insect round
Doth court the death that thou hast found.

AN OLD ENGLISH COTTAGE,

[By Mr J. Smith.]

Sprinkled all o'er Augusta's smoky vale,
  Fringing her roads full rightly as I guess,
Beflower'd around, and white from head to tail,
  Upright and prim as beau in summer dress,
Are scores of *things* where citizens inhale
  Their country breathings, nick-named " cottages:"
Away! I hate them—'tis no treat to me
To see such apings of humility.

I like the pretty little homely thatch
  Where lives a poor man—no, not very poor—
But such a man I mean as well can catch
  From oven-mouth 'bout once a week or more,
Of wholesome wheaten bread, a goodly batch
  To feed his children with—suppose there's four—
Suppose there's six—ne'er mind—God bless him
  with 'em ;
Provided he sufficient hath to give them.

Where all the live-long day right merrily
  The simple housewife plies her daily care ;
Because, while her good man's a-field you see,
  'Tis right the woman has her proper share :

1 love to see her busy as a bee
 With things that *are not*, well as things *that are*;
Lo! while she sings and spins, the bubbling pot
Proclaims for supper there's something hot.

I like it standing where it full can catch
 The healthful breeze that blows some common
  o'er,
Where, from its half clos'd little wicket hatch,
 We view a wide expanse of hill and moor;
A slip of leather to upraise the latch,
 A bunch of woodbines drooping o'er the door.
Hark! two or three pigs are squeaking in the sty;
Look! two or three shirts are hanging up to dry.

And oh! the pipe—brown jug—and summer seat
 Close by the garden-gate, where shadowing
  come,
Brim-full of tuneful birds and zephyrs sweet,
 Thick boughs that boast the apple and the plum.
I love to see the windows clean and neat,
 Half smother'd o'er with spice geranium—
I do not mind a broken pane or two,
Providing there's no petticoat thrust thro.'

A well-hedged garden—nicely planted out
 With herbs of all sorts, and flowers not a few,
In comely order spread, or bunch'd about—
 Here the sweet pea, and there the bitter rue;
And on the larger beds the emerald sprout
 Of winter greens that cup the silver dew,
The bright red carrot, onion sweet and dry,
Potatoe, turnip hard, and crinkled brocoli.

And oh! to see the chicks all budge to school!
 What if they pout? pish! nothing is the matter
It shews th' unbending wife is skill'd to rule
 As well in decent learning, as the platter;
To see the ducks come " gabbling o'er the pool,
 To claim their crumbs—O! 'tis a goodly
  clatter;
Nay more, for, seeing that, one's thoughts do
 go forth,.
That they have useful hens, and eggs, and so
 forth.

———

TO THE SUN.

Hail, genial Orb! whose rays prolific spread
O'er the wide bosom of creative earth;
Whose fervid influence gilds the mountain head,
And swarms the seeds of Nature into birth.
To thee the Persian offers up his vow,
Efficient means which make his bosom glow,
Whose pow'r expands his leaves and fills his
 boughs,
And makes the blossoms of his orchard grow.

Brighten'd by thee, his long espaliers shoot,
His Melons swell beneath thy vertic ray,
His Vineyard spread, and prodigal of fruit,
Oppose their blushes to the rip'ning day,
Happy to trace of Heav'n th' unerring laws,
Confess th' effect, and glorify the cause.

———

LINES BY MISS RADCLIFFE.

Oh! say, canst thou so soon forget
 Our early pledged affection,
While yet in happier hours we met?
 Hail! guiltless retrospection!

Canst thou forget *thine own* request,
 In accents mildly breathing,
Ere yet we heard the stern behest
 Which fate was wildly wreathing?

Canst thou forget that wizard dream,
 Which presaged much to-morrow?
Oh! cherish'd, lov'd, distracted theme
 The gall of future sorrow!

Canst thou forget that vivid gleam
 Our wayward path that lighted?
But oh! the crash—delusive beam
 Our every hope was blighted.

The vow thine anguish wrung from me
 On record stands in Heaven;
In lone devotion still to thee
 The pledge of faith is given.

═══════════════════════

GERMAN UNIVERSITIES

THESE, it will be seen, instead of being the peaceful abode of that science and literature which prepare youth for the great duties of life, are little better than hot-beds of lawless principle and conduct; the ignorance of the nurslings of faction which they contain is as gross as their morals. The melancholy termination of the life of Kotzebue, offers but too convincing a proof of these observations, and gives a peculiar interest to the following narrative, which we extract from a very excellent and amusing book of Travels, entitled "An Autumn near the Rhine."

Nothing can be imagined more striking than the contrast between an English and

Z

a German University. In the former, the Gothic buildings, the magnificient colleges, the noble libraries, the chapels, the retired walks, the scholastic grace of the costume, are all so many interesting indications of the antiquity, the munificence, and the dignity of the institution. The University of Heidelberg is one of the most distinguished in Germany—but the constitution of a German University has necessarily no monument of architecture, no appendage of dignity, scarcely any decent building connected with it. The *Universitat Gebaude*, or public building, containing the library and the lecture-rooms of the Professors, barely comes under this last description. An Englishman might pass the town a dozen times without remarking any traces of its institutions, unless he happened to encounter a string of swaggering mustachioed youths, their hair flowing on their shoulders, without cravats, with pipes in their mouths, parading the streets with a rude impudence. These are the students, who resemble each other in all the Universities, in main points, both of costume and character. It is hardly necessary to say this is not an academical costume. A German student would disdain, as a pert young gentleman of this number told me, to wear a dress not of his own free choice; and his choice, under the influence of a luminous patriotism, takes the direction of reviving the *alt Deutsche kleidung*, or the old costume of the worthy Germans three centuries ago. ‘ *They* were sturdy patriots and right good Germans, and stuck up for our liberties against the Emperor Charles and the Princes. *We* want some of this spirit in our days— therefore we will begin by copying them in their dress, and thus we shall introduce it.' This is the reasoning of the independent philosophers from fourteen to five and twenty, who attend lectures, if they please, when they please, and on what they please, in the Professors' rooms, at the Universities.

The Universities are, with slight variations, constructed upon the same plan. They are not, as in England, composed of Colleges, where the students are obliged to reside, forming large households under the controul of a Head; and submitting to wholesome regulations, both as to conduct and study. A German University

is little more than a place where there is a good library, and a collection of Professors, who read lectures to those who choose to attend them. They afford bare opportunities for study—with few facilities, no compulsion, no discipline, no subordination. The Professor reads his lecture, the student pays him for it. If he attends it, which he does or not as he likes, he walks off at the conclusion as independant of the Professor as a man of his drawing-master, at the end of the hour's lesson. There are, besides, private tutors who can be engaged for assistance, at leisure hours.

At Heidelberg, the University is divided into four faculties, divinity, jurisprudence, medicine, and philosophy. Each department has several Professors; and a Pro-Rector, chosen annually among them, is the actual head of the University. The Grand Duke of Baden, in whose territory Heidelberg is comprised, is the nominal head under the title of Rector. There are a smaller and greater Senate chosen from the Professors, the former of which meets every fourteen days for transacting the business of the University—and four *Ephori*, who are said to superintend the industry and morals of the students, to correspond with their parents, &c. But these last have an office of little efficacy. Their admonition is without authority ; for, short of the power of the police in criminal offences, the students are subject to no power whatever of punishment or controul. They can, consequently, neglect all study, and push their excesses to the verge of a breach of the law in defiance of Rector, Ephori, and Professors. Offences which overstep this bound are liable to punishment by the University police; for the University is not subject to the ordinary police of the country—a University *Amtmann* (bailiff) and beadles, supplying the place to the University of the ordinary provincial bailiff and *gens d'arme*. The consequence is, the broken windows, riots, and disturbances, with which the students annoy the citizens, are visited very lightly by the University Magistrates, who often observe them with a secret satisfaction as symptoms of a spirit of independence, which they hope may be one day turned to better purposes. With such license, it is not to be wondered that the students find the authorities of the law nearly as much employment as our students give to the gentler advice and correction of the Hea ls of Houses, Proctors, &c. In some Universities the students are almost as much the terror and nuisance of the nighbourhood, as the worthy associates of Robin Hood or Rob Roy, were to the inhabitants of the scenes of their exploits. In an inn where I slept at Manheim, it was discovered, one morning, that one of these young gentlemen had decamped by his bed-room window, taking with him the sheets of his bed. At Heidelberg, where there are many of noble and respectable families, they are rather better behaved than usual; and a lady of the town, told me she found them 'tolerably quiet, considering.'

The students live in lodgings, at the houses of the shopkeepers in the town; a system which, if their superiors possessed controul over their conduct, would almost entirely fraustrate it. They dine at the tables d'*Hôte* of the inns, to which they are good customers. I dined with an acquaintance of their number, at a table filled with them. Their manners were, in general, as coarse and as 'rude as their appearance; they had all the air of low mechanics, or persons much less civilized. Some of them were young nobles—others had the ribbons of orders in their button-holes; and they often wear the cockade of their country in their caps or hats, which is sometimes the symbol of a provincial patriotism, much of akin to the national one indicated by their clothes. Since the flame of national feeling has been kindled by late events, the distinctions of country are, however, *professedly* abandoned. The separate associations of the students from different states are done away; and they now loudly assert that they form but one body of *Germans*. But it is easier to assume the title than to suppress national prejudices, or neutralize distinctions of character. The light subtle Prussian is little formed to harmonize with the fat phlegmatic Bavarian or Austrian; and if the students of different states mix in amusements pretty indiscriminately, a quarrel (an event of the commonest occurrence) draws out their provincial prepossessions, and ranges the parties accordingly.

The number of students at Heidelberg,

for the last spring *semestre*, or course of lectures, was above 400 — Goettingen sometimes musters 1200. The Professors at Heidelberg are now in high repute; and on their attraction depends the fulness of the University. When a favourite Professor departs, sometimes nearly half a University follow him. The students generally enter very young—many at sixteen or seventeen; for as every young man, intended for the civil service of any prince, must spend two years, by way of qualification, at a University, the object of parents is to qualify them for office as early as possible. Raw children from the Gymnasium are, consequently, sent to the University, rather to get over these two years than for the purpose of study. Finding themselves here, all at once, their own masters, and exposed to every temptation, they naturally follow the stream, assuming the vices and caricaturing the consequence of full-grown men. The necessary two years are often spent in drinking, gaming, rioting, and insulting others, more from the intoxication of liberty, than from vicious inclination. The pride of premature manhood makes them jealous of their little dignities, and ape the punctilios of false honour. Perpetual duels are the consequence, which have all the ill effect of brutalizing the feelings, without the questionable advantage of exercising courage; for their execution is, in general, ludicrously devoid of danger.

The breasts and faces of the doughty combatants are cased in pasteboard, in the security of which panoply, they chivalrously engage with small rapiers till incensed honour is satisfied, sometimes by the first sprinkling of blood; at others by nothing less than a wound of a certain length and depth, to be ascertained by measurement of the seconds. New comers are beset, on their matriculation, with incitements to quarrel, till they put their valour beyond dispute, in one of these combats. Sometimes bodies of disputants (often of different countries) settle their differences by a combat *en masse*. These fights generally terminate in slight wounds; but more fatal consequences are by no means unfrequent. In spite, however, of constant disturbances, and now and then a death occasioned by them, they are still freely permitted, like all other excesses, from the fear of checking the exuberant fervour of youth.

All titles and distinctions of rank are dropped among the students for the common appellation of *Bursch* (Fellow); and when, on giving some particulars of our universities to a student, I mentioned the distinction of costume, &c. given to noblemen, this spark of liberty exclaimed—' that would not be suffered among us—we are all equal—we have no distinctions.' I could not help smiling, when I reflected that, after his two years swing of lawlessness and equality, this young man was destined for a pastor's cure or some petty office under a despotic government, where he would find himself pinned down in the third rate circles, and encompassed by the barriers of rank on all sides.

No place can be more delightfully situated as a retreat of study and science than Heidelberg, enclosed as it is between picturesque ranges of mountains; the majestic and placid Neckar in the valley; the castle ruins on the declivities above the town, which are covered with the luxuriant hanging gardens of the castle, whose terraces, thickets and umbrageous walks, afford solemn and silent retreats for study, and prospects over the Rhine and the Neckar valley of the most ravishing and varied beauty. The castle is an immense mass of rambling ruins, of architecture of different centuries and descriptions, whose mouldering remains rear their ragged masses with a most striking effect, overhanging the Neckar, and embosomed in the wild shrubberies and woods 'which cover the slope of the mountain. The town is old, dark, and irregular, and presents few traces of the consequence it enjoyed till the early part of the last century as the residence of the splendid court of the Electors Palatine.

National Register:

FOREIGN.

AMERICA : BRITISH.
Productions of Canada.

Mr. Grece, in his publication on Canada, where he has long farmed extensively, strongly recommends that country to English emigrants, in preference to most parts of the United States of America. The land in Canada, when well managed, is very productive; and the chance of securing, besides a good living, ultimate independence to the farmer, certain. The spring and summer months being very warm, not unhealthfully sultry, the rapid advance of vegetation is almost incredible to those who have not actually witnessed it. Wheat has sometimes been sown as late as May 11th, and harvested in the August following, the produce weighing upwards of 63lbs. per bushel. Lime stone is abundant, and various other manures easy to be obtained. Cherries, chesnuts, walnuts, hickory, hazel, and filbert nuts, being natural to the soil, grow wild; as also grapes, gooseberries, strawberries, raspberries, blue berries, cranberries, and black currants. All the superior European fruits flourish there, and orcharding is most successful. The following returns of the various crops are given by Mr. Grece, as from the ordinary farming of the country, which is capable of great improvement:—Drop of wheat, from 25 to 30 bushels per acre ; buck wheat, 15 to 20; rye, 15 to 25; barley, 15 to 30; oats, 32 to 40; Indian corn, 30 to 50: horse beans, 25 to 35; potatoes, 250 to 500 bushels per acre ; carrots and parsnips, from 700 to 900; turnips, from 300 to 700 bushels ; cabbages, from 18 to 25 tons; hay, from one and a half to two and a half tons. Game in immense quantity and variety, and no game laws.

AMERICA: UNITED STATES.
Influence of Bible Societies.

The Fifth Report of the Virginia Bible Society has an eloquent passage on this subject:—The four quarters of the world witness the liberality and zeal of Christians employing their united efforts in promoting the highest interest of their fellow creatures. And it is a scene of moral grandeur, which none can contemplate without feelings of rapture and exultation. On glancing over the history of mankind, and especially surveying the events of the last twenty-five years, in which the highest energies of the human mind and the utmost force of man's physical power has been employed in the work of destruction, it is delightful to turn and behold so many institutions springing up in all parts of the world, which, by the unity of their design, the benevolence of their purpose, and the salutary tendency of all their means and results, are calculated to excite common feelings in all who bear the Christian name, to soften and subdue the malignant passions of the heart, and to bestow the blessings of civilization and a pure religion on all who dwell on earth.

The Bible Society enables Christians of every different form of worship to unite in promoting true religion. It is but one *Institution* in Europe, Asia, Africa, and America. It is the same in Britain and Russia, in Bengal and the United States of America. Surely we may well rejoice, when we see an Association breathing the spirit of Heaven itself, stretching its arms over seas and continents, holding in its embrace the most distant nations, and infusing into them its own charities. The time is not distant, when the blessed effects of this book shall be felt from the Atlantic to the Pacific Ocean; when the lessons it gives shall be learned, the hopes which it inspires be enjoyed, the consolations which it affords be received, by free men, spread through our vast regions, and making the western wildernesses vocal with the praises of Him 'who was, and is, and is to come,' the only true God, our Saviour."

Important to Emigrants.

We learn that the "British Emigrant Society" have purchased a large body of land, in Susquehannah County, of Dr. R. H. Rose; and are taking measures to settle it with farmers from England. Susquehannah will become one of the most populous and wealthy counties in the state. The gentlemen who have purchased, had previously visited Illinois, and preferred, I think wisely, the hills; vales, and living streams, of Pennsylvania, to the sickly prariries and stagnant waters of the west. The Englishmen who remove to Susquehannah may still eat their roast beef, and retain the native rose upon their checks ; but for an English lady who cares the least of her beauty, or that of her daughters, it would be madness to bury herself in the pestilent prairies of Illinois. Breathing the miasmata of the prairies, and drinking their stagnant waters, would quickly blast the finest bloom in Christendom. We hope to see the settlements increasing in the counties all along the northern line of the state ; not from motives of personal interest (as is impertinently insinuated in the *Wash-*

ington City Gazette), but because we know the country to be healthy, the waters sweet, and the lands fine ; because we wish to see Pennsylvania increase the number of her free, prosperous, and happy people ; and because, if we could check the torrent of unreflecting emigrants, who, attracted by the specious but deceptive tales of speculators, are precipitating themselves upon the fever-prairies of the west, and induce them to settle where reason so cordially invites by the fairest promises of health and prosperity, we are sure that we should render them a service, and be entitled to their blessing.—*American Paper*.

FRANCE.

Amelioration of Prisons.

The *Moniteur* also contains a royal ordinance, approving the institution of a " Royal Society for the amelioration of prisons." This ordinance consists of 23 articles, regulating the manner in which the said Society shall carry into effect, throughout the whole kingdom, the purposes for which it has been specially created. The King declares himself the Protector, and authorizes the Duke d' Angouleme to become the President of the Society. The statutes and regulations of the Society, as well as the list of the founders, are ordered to be submitted to the royal approbation.

The funds and revenues arising from the contributions of the said Society shall he exclusively dedicated to the amelioation of prisons.

A general council of 24 members, chosen by the Minister of the Interior, and submitted to the approbation of his Majesty, from among the members of the Society, is to take upon itself the executive labours of the institution. This council is already elected, and their names published. They are the Dukes de la Rochefoucault, d' Albufera, and Broglie, M M. le Baron Benj. Delessert, le Marquis de Marbois, Marq. d'Aligre, Marq. de Catelon, Vicomte Montmorency, Count Chaptal, Baron Pasquier, Counts Daru, Mollien, de Saint-Aulaire, and Bigot de Priameneu, M. Roy, Baron Delaitre, Abbe Desjardins, M. Guizot, A. de la Borde, M. Cottu, and M. Pariset. The members of this council are to be renewed by thirds every five years.

The 6th article thus describes its functions :—" They are to communicate to the Minister of the Interior their sentiments upon every part of the administration and internal management of the prisons of the kingdom, and especially in what relates to classifying the prisoners according to their age, their sex, and the nature of their crimes; the various kinds of labour proper to be adopted in prisons; the distribution of the profits of that labour; the internal discipline of the prisons; the health, safety, religious instruction, and moral reformation of the prisoners, together with their food and clothing; lastly, the enlargement, general construction, and alterations which may appear necessary or useful in the buildings themselves.

"The 8th article states, that in addition to these functions the Council shall be required to examine and state the actual condition of all the prisons of the kingdom, and to suggest to the Minister of the Interior the means of applying successively to the different prisons the general principles of which it shall have recognized the convenience and utility.

The remaining articles contain a series of farther regulations for furthering the great object of the Institution.

Roman Medals.

On the 1st of March, some Monks, of one of the Convents at Namur, working in a piece of ground belonging to the Convent, found, about a foot under ground, a vessel of baked earth, which contained about 2000 Roman medals or coins. Most of them are of bronze, and some of silver. Among these medals, which have not yet been well examined, there are some of Gallienus, of Gordian, Claudius, &c. They are in the possession of the Directors of the Convent, to whom the Monks delivered them. The vessel is broken into a multitude of small pieces. The place where they were found is about a quarter of a league from Namur. It is a small hillock above the calcareous rocks which border the left banks of the Meuse, directly above the hermitage of Saint Hubert, which is marked upon Ferrari's map.

Indies: West.

Marriage of Slaves Established.

It had been long a prevailing notion, that slaves were incapable of contracting marriage, and more especially without the consent of their owners. Marriage has, therefore, but seldom been encouraged; and polygamy, with all its baneful consequences on morals, domestic comfort, and the relations of life, prevailed throughout the whole of the West India Islands. A clergyman in Nevis, conceiving slaves competent to marry, ventured to publish the banns of matrimony between two, in the parish church. The marriage was interdicted by the authorities of the island, and the clergyman appealed to the Bishop of London. His Majesty's Ministers being consulted, the opinion of the law officers of the crown was taken, who stated, "That the ecclesiastical law had always held that slaves were competent to marry without any reference to the authority of their masters."

Otaheite.

Present State.

The following is, we believe, the latest intelligence from these islands:—A vessel named the Macquarrie left Otaheite on the 24th of April, 1817, with a portion of her cargo, consisting of fifty or sixty tons of pork, excellently cured. In order to complete a full cargo of this, she had visited Morea (Eimeo,) one of the Society Islands, where the Missionaries have lately dwelt, but had opened no trade with the natives. From thence she went to Huaheine, and thence to Ulitea, where she procured a further supply of the same article of provisions. She afterwards touched at Bolabola, where she received the principal part of her cargo, and after visiting Mobidde, returned again to Eimeo, and at length completed it, after about ten months, as she left Otaheite in April, 1817, and did not finally quit Eimeo until February, 1818. The difficulty of procuring a cargo was extremely great, owing to various causes, one of which was, that the women are now allowed to eat pork as well as the men, which formerly was not the case, and the consumption is consequently increased, or perhaps doubled. The war that has almost desolated the main island of Taheite (Otaheite,) in the next place produced a universal lassitude with respect to a property that was always open to spoliation and destruction, and of course but little stock was bred; whilst the general state of poverty that prevailed, scarcely left the means of supporting themselves. Their war was conducted perfectly upon a marauding system—burning and pillaging, but with the loss of a very few lives. An army of 300 was considered a numerous force; and although they had a number of muskets, and know tolerably well how to use them, yet they do but little execution with them, and if two or three fall, the main body immediately give way, and fly in all directions. They have a great quantity of poultry, such as cocks and hens, a few Muscovy ducks, and a number of goats. The Missionaries have a few head of horned cattle, and a few sheep; but hogs and the bread fruit constitute the chief dependence of the islands. The banana seems to have been indigenous to the islands; the sweet tropical potatoe, the pumpkin, and melon, are cultivated with success; and Captain Campbell has, we understand, during his late excursion, sown among the islands of the loquet, the peach, the celery, and other garden seeds. Cotton is of spontaneous growth among most, or all of the islands, and its quality very various. The country, which is beautiful in itself, has derived luxuriance from its intercourse with the British nation; the aborigines, who, but a few years, or indeed but a few months since, were idolaters, are now said to be converted to Christianity; their idolatry is past; their wars are at an end; and under the guidance of their missionary friends and brethren, they promise to become a good and happy people. The inhabitants of Bolabola made Captain Campbell a present of their Deity, which consisted of a log of wood from five to six feet long, and two or three inches thick, with a number of faces carved upon it. They parted with it as a proof of their reformation, and a token of contempt towards their former prejudices. Pomarec has not been re-invested with absolute power; the Chiefs are still afraid that he might abuse it; but he is so much the convert to Christian principles, that the fear is supposed to be ungrounded. He resides on a small spot a few hundred yards distant from Taheite; and seems in the enjoyment of perfect content of mind, distributing books to all his countrymen that apply for them, and indiscriminately bestowing his favours upon those who had been enemies, as well as upon his approved friends. In fact, so wonderful has been

the change wrought upon the minds of the people, according to these accounts, that the happiest result may be anticipated from it.

RUSSIA.
Reduction of Duties.

The following is an extract of a letter from the Agent of the Russian Company in London, by which it will be seen that the important reduction of 10 per cent. on all goods imported and exported from Russia has taken place. It will also be observed, that rum is allowed entry on the same terms as other spirits:

PETERSBURGH, Feb. 23.——An Ukase has been issued, directing, that in the levying of duties in the different Custom-houses, for the year 1819, the silver roubles shall be taken at three roubles and 60 copiques Bank notes, which make a reduction of 10 per cent. on the duties of all imports and exports, excepting on those that pay *ad valorem*. Some persons having claimed the right to pay duties on goods imported last year, and still in the Custom-house, at the new rate of three roubles and 60 copiques, it has been decided that the old duty shall be charged on all goods which shall have been received at any Custom-house previously to the receipt of the present order.

I have further to announce, that the order from the department of Foreign Commerce to the Petersburgh Custom-house, dated 8th February, has been made public, authorizing the importation of rum at the same duty as is levied on brandy and arrack, viz. 10 roubles per anker (silver); and I hope to be enabled to send a copy and translation of the Ukase by an early conveyance.

In the mean time it is necessary to understand, that the duty on all spirits is levied according to their strength; that the lowest duty is 10 roubles per anker, and if below, and not above what is here denominated 10 degrees.

If above 10, and not above 15 degrees, is considered pure spirit, and pays 20 silver roubles per anker.

Military Cordon.

The Russian Government, imitating that of Austria, is, it is said, about to establish a permanent military cordon on the frontier towards Turkey, and the places occupied by this line of posts are to be exempted from the jurisdiction of the respective provincial Governments.

SPAIN.

Schools encouraged.

The Madrid Gazette states, that Ferdinand VII. has been paying the best homage that can be paid to the memory of his Queen, by visiting one of the institutions of which she was a munificent patroness, for the education of children of both sexes, and in which 170 girls and 200 boys are instructed in all branches of useful education, and in the principles of moral and religious control.   The King, after a long and minute inspection, took his leave, first making a handsome contribution, and promising, with much emotion, in the name of God and his Queen, to be a constant protector to the establishment.

National Register:

BRITISH.

THE KING.

WINDSOR CASTLE, APRIL 3, 1819.

His Majesty continues to enjoy a good state of bodily health, and has been tranquil and cheerful through the last month ; but his Majesty's disorder remains undiminished.

The Revenue.

Produce of the Revenue, exclusive of property, or unappropriated War Duties, in the April quarters of the year :

1817.	1818.	1819.
9,510,211*l*.	10,249,207*l*.	10,481,916*l*.

In the War Duties continued, there is, under the head of Excise, an increase in this quarter, beyond the corresponding quarter last year, viz. 897,203*l*. to 936,494*l*.

The amount of the Irish Revenue for the quarter is not yet known.   The year's Revenue presents an increase of above 1,800,000*l*. beyond that of the preceding year.

Total Revenue for the year ending the 5th of April, 1818, 47,271,631*l*.

Total Revenue for the year ending the 5th of April, 1819, 49,056,563*l*.

Net produce of the Revenue of Great Britain in the years ending 5th of April, 1818, and 5th April, 1819, together with an income and charge of the Consolidated Fund.

The total consolidated fund for the year, viz. 5th of April, is, 42,235,726*l*.

In the Customs for the quarter there is an increase of 115,686*l*.—in the Excise an increase of 226,073*l*.—in the Post-office an increase of 19,000*l*.—in the Stamps, Assessed Taxes, and Land Taxes, a decrease of 130,000*l*. which deducted from the increase,·leaves an increase in the quarter of 232,709*l*.

The charge on the consolidated fund for ·the corresponding quarter last year, was 8,827,741*l*.   The charge on the present quarter is increased to 9,770,000*l*. leaving a deficiency of 148,300*l*.

An account of the total, real or declared value of the produce and Manufactures of the United Kingdom, exported from Great Britain during each of the three years, ending the 5th Jan. 1819:—

1817.	1818.	1819.
42,955,256*l*.	43,626,253*l*.	48,903,760*l*.

Total and official value of Foreign and Commercial Merchandise exported from Great Britain to all parts of the world:—

1817.	1818.	·1819.
14,545,964*l*.	11,534,616*l*.	12,287,274*l*.

An account of the total value of all articles imported into Great Britain during each of the three years ending the 5th Jan, 1819, as calculated at the official rates of valuation:—

Foreign and colonial merchandise.

1817.	1818.	1819.
26,406,634*l*.	29,962,913*l*.	35,880,983*l*.

Produce of Ireland and the Isle of Man.

1817.	1818.	·
3,698,931*l*.	4,002,318*l*.	4,276,651*l*.

Total value of imports.

1817.	1818.	1819.
20,105,565*l*.	33,965,231*l*.	40,157,634*l*.

State of Crimes, 1805-1818,

An official return, printed by order of the House of Commons, presents in one view an accurate representation of the state of crimes made capital by the law in the several years from the year 1805 to the year 1818, inclusive.   From this it appears that the total number of persons convicted were as follows:

	Convicted.	Executed.
For Burglary	1874	199
Larceny (value 40s.)	1119	17
Forgery	501	207
Horse-stealing	852	35
House-breaking . . .	761	17
Murder	229	202
Highway robbery .	848	118
Sheep-stealing . . .	896	43
Other capital offences	1350	197
	8430	1035

Expense of Convicts.

Annual expence of the transportation of convicts to New South Wales and its dependencies, and of the establishments there:—

1816	£216,291	8	7¼
1817	232,585	9	6¼
1818	178,939	19	4¼

Cattle consumed in London.

The consumption of sheep and lambs in London, in 12 mnoths, has been lately estimated at the number of 1,062,700; the number of horned cattle slaughtered, at 164,000; and of horse-hides produced at Leadenhall-market, 12,000

Potass from Potatoe Tops.

Lord Cloncurry, in order to promote the manufacture of potass from potatoe tops, has offered a premium of 50l. for a quantity not less than 1000lbs. sold in a merchantable state in Dublin; being little less, it is proved, than 40s. per acre for what has hitherto been altogether useless.

Cure for Superstition.

Miners are known to be a superstitious race. Their superstition, however, is sometimes made a pretext for idleness. There is a recipe for curing this species of the disorder. In some extensive mines in Wales the men frequently saw the Devil, and when once he had been seen, the men would work no more that day. The evil became serious, for *Old Belzebub* repeated his visits so often, as if he had a design to injure the proprietor. That gentleman at last called his men together, and told them that the Devil never appeared to anybody who had not *deserved* to be so terrified, and that as he was de-

termined to keep no rogues about him, he was resolved to discharge the first man that saw the Devil again. The remedy was as efficient as if he had turned a stream of holy-water into the mines.

Virginia Nightingales.

In the course of the last month, a person walking in the fields near Colwick, Nottingham, last week, made a curious discovery of four birds lying together, and with every appearance of having been dead a considerable time. Their beautiful red plumage and uncommon appearance denoted that they were not natives of this Island, and on taking them home, they proved to be Virginia nightingales. They have been stuffed, and have been inspected by several naturalists.

Recent Legal Decisions.

Foreign Property.—In an important case that occured lately, the Vice-Chancellor laid a it down that foreign monarch, government or corporation, has no political or independent character here, but in the courts of law are the same as private individuals, and can sue and be sued as such. The property of a foreign monarch, government, or corporation, stands likewise in the same relation. The only privileged characters in England are the ambassador, envoy, and suite. But should any person in the suite engage in business, it causes a forfeiture of the diplomatic privilege. Such is the law of the land. A consul general is no privileged character, and much less, deputy, agents, &c.

Machinery.—It has been held that where certain parts of a machine has been put up by the tenant during his term, and were capable of being removed without either injuring the other parts of the machine or the building, and had been usually valued between the outgoing and incoming tenants, that they were the goods and chattels of the out-going tenant, for which he might main trover.

Coroner.—A Coroner, under 25 Geo. c. 29, s. 1. is not entitled to any compensation for the miles travelled by him in returning to his usual place of abode from taking an inquisition.

Conspiracy.—An indictment charged that defendants conspired, by divers false pretensions and subtle means and devices, to obtain from A. divers large sums of money, and to cheat and defraud him thereof : held that the gist of the offence being the conspiracy, it was quite sufficient only to state that fact and its object, and not necessary to set out the specific pretences.

Parish Officers.—The statute 51 Geo. III. c. 80. extends to parishes where there are three officers only, one of whom acts as churchwarden as well as overseer ; and therefore an indenture in such a case, signed by two parish officers, one of whom acted in double capacity, has been held to be valid.

Sheriff.—The Sheriff has no right to claim extra expenses, to which he may have been put, in summoning jurors residing at a distance from each other, for it is part of his general duty as sheriff to summon the jury.

PARLIAMENTARY HISTORY

CHAP. III. *Thanks to Marquis Hastings— Penal Code—Regulations of Mad- Houses—Bank Balances—Husbandry Horses Bill.*

HOUSE OF LORDS.

THANKS TO MARQUIS HASTINGS.

March 2.—The Earl of Liverpool rose pursuant to notice, to move the thanks of the House to the Marquis of Hastings, and the officers and troops under his command in India. His Lordship stated, that the military measures of that country originated in self-defence, and the predatory excursions of the Pindarees to the amount of 30,000, had been borne with as long, or longer perhaps than could be justified, considering the mischiefs they spread around them: and it was not till they had invaded the Presidency of Madras, and began to lay waste the country, that our army had commenced hostilities against them; but when commenced, the army acted with such distinguished bravery and effect, as soon to decide the contest, and restore tranquility to the country.

The Marquis of Lansdown was happy to agree to the motion, except so far as referred to the execution of the Killedar of Talnier, after he had surrendered, which he considered as contrary to justice, and the principles of war among civilized

nations. He wished therefore to make this exception.

Lord Holland perfectly agreed with the Marquis of Lansdown, and the first resolution of thanks to the Marquis of Hastings past unanimously; but on the vote of thanks to Sir T. Hislop who executed the Killedar, the Earl of Liverpool suggested, that Government themselves were not satisfied, and had sent out for farther information.

The Duke of Wellington spoke in the highest terms of the whole conduct of the Marquis of Hastings, and the military bravery of Sir T. Hislop. After some conversation, the Marquis of Lansdown qualified his amendment, and the vote was past unanimously, saving an opinion of the particular fact referred to, the consideration of which was deferred till farther information be received.

HOUSE OF COMMONS.

PENAL CODE.

March 2.—Sir J. Mackintosh brought forward his motion for the appointment of a committee to inquire into, and investigate, such parts of the Penal Code as relate to capital punishments. The noble lord (Castlereagh) agreed in the necessity of enquiry, and for a committee: they only differed as to the mode; he contended for a more extended mode of enquiry than the noble lord did: and here he would guard himself by saying, he had no intention to propose a new code; such a proposition would be wild and visionary. He did not propose to do away the punishment of death, which he considered as necessary for self-preservation against incorrigible offenders. He had no intention to abridge judicial discretion, which he considered as wise; neither had he any intention to limit the exercise of the royal prerogative of mercy, but to restore that power most fully to the crown. His object was to bring the practice and the letter of the law to agree, and to do away uncertainty; to set criminal law and virtuous feeling in unison, which at present were at variance; and wherever such was the case, ill must follow. These were the objects he hoped to gain by the appointment of his committee. Now with respect to what he should recommend to the consideration of the committee, he should propose that murder, stabbing, arson, piracy, and all offences striking at human life, should be left out of the question; but he would ask whether any man alive would say that cutting a hop bine or an ornamental tree in a gentleman's grounds, should be punished with death; whether going to masquerade with the face blacked, or destroying the head of a fish-pond, should be adjudged by our criminal code offences for which death should be inflicted. With respect to the effect which the mitigation of capital punishment had on offenders, he was of opinion it only made the punishment of transportation light, when they reflected on having escaped that of death, to which by law they were liable. The effect of heavy penalties had deterred many from prosecution, as well as of those likely to become witnesses. But the knowledge of this had a very opposite effect on the minds of the criminals at the time of committing offences. Last session, an honorable gentleman (Mr. J. Smith) said, that the bankers were deterred from prosecuting for forgery on account of the punishment of death. The same was the case in the secretion of property by bankrupts. The severity of our revenue laws also tended to prove what Lord Bacon had said long ago, that severity of penalty would always deter from inflicting punishment. He was not against the punishment of death; but that guardian of men's lives and properties was daily impaired by its being denounced from the judgment seat, without its possibly being put in execution. The honorable member concluded by moving for a select committee to enquire into the criminal law, as far as it regards capital punishments.

Lord Castlereagh applauded the very temperate and candid manner in which the honorable and learned gentleman had handled this subject. He flattered himself that their opinions were not very different, although he was afraid the impression would go abroad, that the honorable and learned gentleman considered our laws in a sanguinary light, as far as the administration of them was concerned. But he was happy to find that the honorable gentleman did not intend to propose any new criminal code, nor to take away from the Executive Government the great right of pardoning offences. He was of opinion, however, that the course proposed was not likely to lead to any practical result. He again contended, that it was impossible for any committee to enquire into two subjects at once. Let the enquiry be carried forward with as little delay as possible; but let it go on before one committee, and not be divided into parts. For these reasons he felt it his duty to move the previous question on the motion of the honorable and learned gentleman.

Mr. Buxton thought it impossible that the committee appointed could enquire into the state of all the prisons, the whole police, the hulks, transportation, and a new colony of the Antipodes, if they were to enquire into the state of the new criminal law. The want of religious instruction was the great cause of the increase of crime. He hoped the House would agree to send the enquiry into the criminal code to a distinct committee, as he was of opinion that our criminal laws did greatly tend to increase of crime. He said, that from Parliamentary documents, it could be seen that it was ten to one that an offender was not taken, fifty to one that he was not prosecuted, a hundred to one that he was not convicted, and more than a thousand to one that he was not executed. The effects of executions were next to nothing; and any one might satisfy himself that from the conduct and conversation of those present at such terrible exhibitions; and the prisoners themselves always said, after an execution, " Well, we can't pity him, he is now in Heaven," thus shewing that no effect was produced on them. He appealed to the petitions of those very men who were the greatest losers by depredations, who were the loudest in claiming a revision of our penal laws. Something must be done, and ought to be submitted to a separate committee.

Mr. Wilmot spoke for the motion of the honorable and learned gentleman; but he wished his committee should be delayed until the noble lord's committee had made its report, because the question of secondary punishment would bear strongly on the determination of this question.

Mr. Wilberforce was impatient that the laws of our country should possess the respect of, as well as authority over, our countrymen. The honorable member was of opinion, the system of solitary confinement would prove most advantageous and efficacious, since it would afford to an offender time for reflection and amendment, and would probably restore him to society a better man. This had been the opinion of Mr. Bentham and of Mr. Basil Montague, to whom the public were greatly obliged. It had also, he believed, been the opinion of both Mr. Pitt and Lord Melville—men . well qualified to judge on this subject. After it had undergone the consideration of such men as these, surely no one could justly accuse the House of taking up the question rashly, and without consideration. He could not conclude without strongly recommending an enquiry into the state of the settlement of New South Wales, as the state of Botany Bay would have a great effect on the manners and morality of all the surrounding country.

Mr. Canning was ready to allow that the law, as it at present stood, was such as ought not to continue. It was, as it were, a nuisance which should immediately be abated. In the statement of his learned and honorable friend, he had understood him to go almost the length of saying, the punishment of death should only be retained in the case of murder. He feared all hopes of effecting this would prove visionary. Would to God they were not—would to God such a system could possibly be adopted; but that, he was persuaded, could not be done without introducing other punishments so severe and disgusting, that, in this country, they would be worse and more revolting to the feelings than death itself. On the whole view of the subject, he thought the House ought to have its substitutes ready before they talked of repeal, and not put it in the power of any miserable malefactor to say, "What! execute me under laws upon which you yourselves have pronounced the sentence of condemnation?" The right honorable gentleman concluded by repeating his opinion, that the plan recommended by his noble friend would be far more efficacious than that suggested by his hon. and learned friend.

The Attorney-General defended the present system.

Sir J. Mackintosh briefly replied, and proceeded to read the names of the members whom, should he succeed in his motion, he proposed to nominate for his committee:—Mr. Bathurst, the Attorney and Solicitor-Generals, Mr. Alderman Wood, Lord Althorp, Dr. Phillimore, Mr. Wynn, Mr. Courtney, Mr. Macdonald, Mr. Scarlett, Mr. Abercrombie, Mr. Finlay, Mr. Lyttleton, Mr. Bennett, Mr. Wilberforce, Mr. Brougham, Lord Nugent, Mr. Vernon, Mr. Buxton, and Mr. Howorth.

The House then divided, when the numbers were—For the original motion, 149; against it, 128; majority, 19.—Adjourned.

REGULATION OF MADHOUSES.

March 10.—Mr. C. W. Wynn, in submitting his motion for leave to bring in a bill upon this subject, observed, some years had now elapsed since an enquiry into the subject had developed such scenes of gross abuse as had seldom fallen within the knowledge of the legislature; but it could scarcely be imagined, that after such abuses had come to light, and two reports had been published upon them, that they had not been followed up by measures calculated to afford a remedy. They had repeatedly passed measures for the purpose of applying the remedy, but those measures had been lost in the House of Lords. The honorable gentleman then moved for leave to bring in a bill to repeal the Acts of the 14th and 55th of his present Majesty, and for making such other alterations as might be necessary for the better regulation of madhouses. The question was put and carried.

BANK BALANCES.

Mr. Grenfell, in the absence of the Chancellor of the Exchequer, asked the honorable gentleman (Mr. Lushington) opposite, when it was intended to introduce the measure of the Bank Balances and Exchequer Bills' deposits. He would appeal to the House, whether the conclusion which might have been fairly drawn from what the right honorable gentleman had said on the 2d of February, and on last Friday, was not that 6,000,000l. would be available to the public services in the way he had then described? But instead of 6,000,000l. being applicable to the services of the public, in the way stated, the House would find, that the public would not have the benefit of half that sum.

Mr. Lushington had no hesitation in saying, his right honorable friend (the Chancellor of the Exchequer) had declared, that the 6,000,000l. would be applicable to the service of the public, and that the result would prove the correctness of his calculation.

Mr. Tierney remarked, that his right honorable friend (Mr. Grenfell) had said no more than what the House would find would turn out to be the fact; that after all the boasting about the 6,000,000l, there would not be a sum of more than 3,000,000l. or from that to 4,000,000l. so applicable.

Mr. Lushington brought in a bill to render the growing produce of the Consolidated Fund available to the public service. He thought it necessary, in introducing this bill, to guard against misconception with regard to it, by stating, that its object was to render a sum of 6,000,000l. available to the public service, 3,200,000l. or 3,300,000l. of which were to be applied to the discharge of arrears, and 2,700,000l. in part payment of a sum of 3,000,000l. due to the Bank. The bill was then read a first time.

HUSBANDRY HORSES BILL.

March 12.—On the motion of Mr. Lushington, the House resolved itself into a committee upon this bill.

Mr. Stuart Wortley had a clause to propose at another period of this bill, to which he was happy to understand there would be no objection; it was to except from the operation of the tax brood mares. These had hitherto been taxed, when he conceived they ought to have been considered like other stock; for it was well known that in many parts of the country, particularly in the county where he resided, (Yorkshire,) there were several persons who kept mares for no other purpose but breeding. He thought that that ought to be encouraged, and that the tax upon them ought to be removed.

Several clauses were then brought up, and agreed to.

After a few observations from Mr. Wynn, which were not audible in the gallery,

Mr. Stuart Wortley said, (in allusion to what had fallen from Mr. Wynn,) that nothing could be, more ridiculous than the whole system of the assessed taxes, from the manner in which surcharges were at present made. He hoped that his Majesty's Ministers would take this matter into their consideration, so as that these taxes might be compounded for by a certain sum.

Mr. Lushington said, he had no doubt his right honorable friend (the Chancellor of the Exchequer) would pay attention to what the honorable gentleman had suggested.

The bill then passed through the committee, and the report was received, and ordered to be taken into further consideration.

POLITICAL PERISCOPE.

Panorama Office, April 27, 1819.

THE Science of Politics is one of those in which men become wiser and wiser every day, and yet this wisdom does not attain perfection; nor is it productive of unmingled felicity to the present, or to any generation. On the contrary, there is a strong disposition in the human mind to look back, and to estimate former times as more felicitous than the present.

On what does this disposition depend? Is it because present troubles are felt, not so those of our forefathers? But, why then do we not feel present enjoyments? and why place them on our estimate of things below that degree on which we place enjoyments long departed?

Some have supposed, that this disposition is, if not peculiar to our countrymen, yet felt by them with greater force than by any other people. And attempts have been made to account for it, by considering it as one of the attendants on public liberty; as part of the spirit of a free people; and among those indulgences which apertain to John Bull and his children, as well by privilege as by habit.

But, in truth, our countrymen are not so different from the rest of mankind as this theory supposes. Other people also look back to past times with regrets founded on comparison. So long ago as the days of Solomon, that wise monarch observed it, and observed it with censure. Perhaps he had even felt the force of this disposition; and be cautious against indulging it, those who might peruse his aphorisms with intention to profit by them.

It is, however, somewhat disheartening to statesmen to labour without receiving that reward which is always included in praise; or, in other words, being thought criminal in all they do; or, in other words again, being held responsible for the success of every measure; and for the consequences of their proposals, notwithstanding those innumerable accidents to which all mortal undertakings are liable.

Perhaps the true solution of this enquiry may depend on the difference between the talent required to look forward, with accuracy, and that which is required to look backward. To contemplate past events, exacts no preter-natural powers; to anticipate what is about to happen, is a gift bestowed on few. Every writer may become a historian; while to Tiresias, the blind! alone is entrusted the faculty of foresight.

The present partakes of apprehension: a sense of possible change, if the present be prosperous, intermingles itself with that prosperity; and if the present be adverse, a fear of the continuance of that adversity, contributes to render its sufferings more acute. Such is the nature of the human mind: such is the constitution of the thinking part of our nature; and, as our countrymen are eminently a thinking people, such is the character of their political argumentations and feelings.

It were the easiest thing in the world to prophecy pleasing events; but, the course of terrestrial affairs warrants no such unmingled predictions. Pure evil is seldom the lot of any time. Neither is pure good. A mixture of good and evil, of necessities and supplies; of difficulties, and of powers to solve those difficulties; of improvements in some points, and of deteriorations in others, characterizes the conditions of private life; and characterizes too, the labours and the feelings of political duty.

While affairs are, as it were *in equilibrio*, we deem it most adviseable to hope the best. We trust, that the important examinations and consultations now in progress, will issue in much good to the community; and days to come will feel the benefit of measures taken to obviate the heavier impediments to national happiness, which are too conspicuous at this time to need enumeration.

To the present Parliament, and the present Session of Parliament, are looking—all who wish well to the Interests of Religion, as connected with the Rights of Conscience, and the Prosperity of the State, for both these are involved in the Catholic Claims:—all who consider the character of the country as combined with the present state of our currency, and the security of our paper credit, these await the measures to be taken by the Bank;—all who feel—and who does not feel the burden of the Poor rates, with the melancholy proportion of persons receiving assistance, to that of persons compelled to afford assistance.

Now all these interests are surrounded with difficulties; not one of them presents the prospect or the possibility of *plain sailing*.

The Public voice, so far as we can collect it, is clear for the admission of Catholics to the full exercise of their Religion; but, for withholding from them Political power. There are not wanting those who think that, as Britain has prospered under Protestant ascendancy, so under Catholic re-action, should that take place, Britain will sink into utter insignificance, and non-importance.

Others add particulars of National Dissentions, and their consequences, at which we shudder to think. We *will* not foresee them; and we trust, no occasion will arise by which the possibility of their existence may be realized.

Not less difficulty attends the return to a metallic currency. It is said, that the Report of the Special Committee on the Bank Affairs, has been attended with much trouble. Some go so far as to say, it has been agreed on, as to its purport, and again set aside;—the knowing ones affect to whisper—more than once. Here we are silent: we see, and we acknowledge the difficulties of giving advice, to be acted on, in the case.

Nor can any plan be proposed to meet the exigencies of the rates for supporting the Poor, that will give universal satisfaction, that suits one place injures another. It is the natural consequence of that multiplicity of interests, which England now embraces. A determinate time of resilence is a good criterion of proper applicants: yet labour seems also to form a just consideration :—those who have spent their strength in a parish should naturally look to that parish for reciprocal advantage, when required by circumstances.

There are certain minor matters also in progress for the *benefit* of the nation. Those may differ from this statement who find themselves *minus* a few thousands—(we shall be understood in the .city)—but they have only their own ambitious or avaritious schemes to blame.

We confess ourselves to be shocked at the ferocity that has shewn itself lately, in the commission of crime: it has disgraced our country: it now disgraces other countries, in fact, Europe at large.

We *do* think that there is *some* truth in reports of most malignant attempts against sovereigns and rulers. Murder has lately been too familiar in the world. If it has been cherished among the better instructed classes of society, it is a bad sign —in short, the worst of signs. Among banditti it were in its place perhaps ; not so in civilized life.

We hear of little that is interesting from foreign parts, as to public matters. But, we are sorry to hear it from a foreign part of an accession to our Royal Family, in that of the Duke of Cambridge (the Duke of Clarence has not had equal good fortune) and other pregnancies are reported. The Duchess of Kent is arrived in England in a hopeful way—all in good time. We know that some politicians affect to tremble for France. Others see every thing most gloomy on the side of Spain. Germany embarasses some; and Italy perhaps others.

We ourselves strongly sympathize with the Pope in all his mortifications; and if the Grand Seignior did but know how many sleepless nights our anxiety for his *waning* crescent costs us!—But, commend us especially to the head of the " Celestial Empire," of the blue sky that environs the whole earth: his realm has lately been afflicted with a drought, and he has besought his gods in vain. · An individual has presented to him a paper of advice, recommending him to break in pieces his whole set of gods, as a proper punishment for their pertinacious obduracy. He has sent the individual into banishment; and

to say truth, not' without cause: gods are not to be treated so harshly. We appeal to the Tribunal of Ceremonies, whether the ancient laws of the Chinese empire did not prescribe, in the first place, A " humble Petition and Remonstrance," next " a Chiding," drawn up by the Chief Bonzee of the Royal Temple; but read and repeated by the Emperor, in person : then, indeed, followed, according to the custom of the country, a good hearty flogging, *bien appliquée*; which even might have brought hearts of stone to their sense of feeling:—but as to dashing a whole set of gods to pieces at once—the mere idea overcomes us—*usque ad animi deliquium* —we can no more.

Commercial Chronicle.

Extracts from Commercial Letters received from various parts.

ITALY.
Palermo, March 22d, 1819.

" All the crops promise well; wheat might be shipped at 36s. on the coast, and at Girgenti 40s. but if no foreign demand takes place, expect a decline."

Malta, March 18th, 1819.

" Coffee is moving to 140 a 145 Scudi per cantar; Pepper .rather dull, but no quantity on hand ; Grain is looking up a little. There is an absolute want of Oil for the consumption of the place—the present scarcity arises from a short crop in Barbary and the Greek Islands, and the prohibition of the export in Sicily."

AMERICA.
Charleston, March 2d, 1819.

" A little advance has taken place in Upland Cotton, several prime parcels having been sold at 26 cents; Sea Island 50 a 60 ; Rice 4¼ to 5 dollars, but dull; Specie 3 per cent. premium. The exports last month were 14000 bales Upland Cotton, 19000 bales Sea Island, 9,800 tierces Rice; the stock of low Cotton however, accumulates; the whole quantity of Upland Cotton exported from Charleston since the 1st of October is above, 40,000 bales."

RUSSIA.

St. Petersburg, March 11-23d, 1819

" The demand for imports is very trifling, and chiefly confined to the consumption of the place; the carriage duty being double the usual rate is one cause; coffee continues steady. Exchange 11¼d. Silver Rubles 3,71. 6 per cent. Stock 90 per cent.

STATE OF TRADE.

Lloyd's Coffee House, April 20, 1819.

To a stranger the sight of so many busy faces as the various departments of the business transacted in these rooms present is not merely interesting by its novelty, but also on that connection which it maintains with all the world. No wind can blow that does not affect some individual in this assembly; no letter can arrive from a foreign part that does not concern some one whose name is annexed to an adventure that has been guaranteed here.

The practice of insurance is not a mode of business derived from the ancients; but, whether from Venice, or from Genoa, in their most flourishing times, neither of those cities could shew any thing to be compared with the scene before us. Perhaps Amsterdam was once the nearest approach to it; but Amsterdam never had, certainly has not now, the facilities for business, the readiness, the dispatch, and the command of capital, which enable Lloyd's to stand foremost of all similar institutions. Many also are the shrewd guesses, and the peculiar pieces of intelligence, which here find circulation; and usually they are founded on good information, if not on absolute knowledge.

Cross but a street, and you enter on a new scene, of as equal bustle, and greater noise, at the Stock Exchange. Not every report *formerly* circulated there, could be depended on as authentic; nor was every appearance, whether of forwardness, or of reluctance, worthy of confidence. What vast sums are daily in motion in both these places! And these again lead us to the Bank; where prodigious amounts pass and repass, every hour, every moment, by means of a few strokes of the pen. Such is commerce! and such especially is credit! the value of a nation rests on the word, or on the signature of a British merchant, or of an official Director.

But the motions of the Bank are contemplated at this moment with peculiar anxiety. When the Bank suspended payments in gold, the stroke was sudden; it was suspected by very few, and expected by fewer still: but the resumption of cash payments is a subject of conversation among all parties; and all parties reason on it as best suits themselves. The expectation is very general, that cash payments *will* be resumed; but, the previous steps and the determinate method are not agreed on. We have very good reason to think that some time ago the Bank was well prepared to meet the exigency: but prudence forbids those who know from speaking.

It is certain, that under the system lately pursued of paying the amount of smaller sums in cash, the constant drain prevented that accumulation which a bold stroke demands. For, supposing that the Bank should determine on issuing the sum of ten millions in specie, on a certain day, after a momentary surprize the public would on many, if not on most, occasions, have recourse to Bank paper. All the larger payments would be made in Bank notes. No man would carry a thousand guineas about him, nor even a hundred, when a single note would effectually represent that sum, and would be equally acceptable to a *payee.*

It is more a Political question than a Commercial one, what would be the consequence of a vast influx of gold on the public? Would it affect property? Would it affect credit, national, personal? Would it remain in the country, or would it find its way to foreign countries? Beyond all doubt, while gold was in circulation there was a constant emission of it to foreign parts: but what did foreign parts give for it? Certain of their commodities And it returned again to Britain, on the same principle: for, what did Britain give for it? Certain of our national commodities.

There would, undoubtedly, be somewhat of a *push* at first; but, after that quantity of foreign commodities which speculation might assign to British consumption was received; what should induce the sending abroad of much additional gold? Could foreigners deprive us of it, by sending hither goods which found no buyers? And would not foreign parts also remit gold to their country? for surely they would not suspend their habits of purchasing British goods, because it might suit their convenience to pay for them with British specie.

That the governments of nations, to answer certain political purposes, might find it to their interest to give, on special occasions, a much greater quantity of national industry for gold, than they would deem either prudent or just, at. all times, is likely enough; but, when the emergency is over, the action will cease. France is said to have coined five millions of louis d'or from British gold: how did France acquire it? Did not other countries contribute a share? or, is the trade in gold wholly in the hands of Britain? We believe, that the principal supply of Europe passes through British hands: this cannot but be profitable in one respect; perhaps in more than one.

Be that as it may, the Parliament, on the recommendation of the *Secret Committee*, to whom the enquiry has been referred, has passed an act by which the emission of gold from the Bank is wholly stopped; and only very small sums in silver, merely change under twenty shillings, are allowed to be paid. As the Committee's Report is not before the public, this act has been passed in confidence: it has as yet had little other consequence, than creating a general hope and expectation of something efficient at no distant day.

The Funds, which are affected by a something or a nothing, have certainly felt the effects of the various conjectures on the subject: they. have declined, and there are those parties interested in their decline, who take care to add the certainty—Aye, the absolute certainty—of a heavy loan. Why so? because they themselves are at the moment out of stock; and they hope to buy cheaper—cheaper' and then they will rise again, to be sure they will.

It is not entirely to what we have hinted at, that the present indifferent state of the Commercial markets is to be attri-

buted. We have not concealed from ourselves, or from our readers, the dangers inseparable from *our* speculation. These have fallen with insupportable weight on two eminent Cotton Houses, one at London, the other at Manchester: the consequence is a kind of blank disposition, the effect, no doubt, of prudence, throughout the market. This is no more than natural: in the first place, the usual purchases of these houses are now suspended; and their absence is felt: and secondly, since they are injured, by having overbought themselves, others cannot but take warning.

We have, therefore, to report the demand for *Cotton*, slack at this moment; although it was brisk not many days ago. The exporters took off freely; and . the speculators were not idle: so that, between both the holders were encouraged to ask a higher price; and much business was done at a farthing per lb. additional. It is probable, that the sympathy will be only temporary; and that the usual commissions will revive, will reanimate the market, in a reasonable time.

Coffee has been, as it were, locked up from public sale, for, at least, two months past; and private contract has taken no more than was immediately wanted. At length, a sale or two has been submitted, and the opinion seems to have been well founded, that the demand was languid, and the general prices giving way. Much, however, must always be referred to the quality of the article; what is inferior, or what is any way damaged, must expect to meet a dull sale and low prices. The finer qualities, being somewhat rare, and certainly not seen every day at market, obtained fair prices, and rather higher than lower. The market generally must be stated depressed.

The holders of *Sugar* are desirous to sell; consequently, they find themselves under the necessity of giving a turn in favour of the buyer. Even the best qualities have experienced this necessity; especially where any suspicion was afloat, that the holder *must* sell. The public sales have felt the same effect of indifference in the buyer, and though sales have been made, yet they exhibited little vigour, and no urgency. The same remark affected the refined market: the buyers are cautious, while the refiners do their utmost to attract notice, and to do business.

The *Provision* trade is not brisk, except for parcels of prime Beef, which is scarce. Prime Pork is also scarce; but not equally in demand. The prices of Butter are nearly nominal; but are, it is understood, reduced, and perhaps are likely to continue, &c.

Corn fluctuates, but on the whole it is lower, and does not appear to rise, notwithstanding the supply of prime English grain is not abundant; and that of Wheat may be stated as rather scarce. The imports have been extensive; prime Barleys have fetched good prices. Oats lower. Much enquiry after Beans—Egyptian Beans — and considerable anticipations contracted for, said to be at an advance; supposed of two shillings.

Rice of a good quality is in request: the best Carolina meets purchasers without difficulty. It does not appear that East India Rice is equally sought after: it is more abundant, and less in favour.

Spices are heavy and declining: Company's Black Pepper has been sold at 7d. Pimento 8d. to 8½d.

Indigo is at present nominal; waiting the event of a considerable sale at the India House.

Spirits in general are reported heavy; the current price can be with difficulty obtained; and some indulgence must be shewn to the buyer, by way of inducement.

The lengthening, or rather lengthened, days, have reduced the demand for *Tallow*, to a mere trifle: this is no more than is usual at this season of the year. *Hemp* and *Flax* have few buyers; and consequently few sellers. Real purchases are reported to be rare.

Tobacco rather hangs on hand: a sale has been attempted; but the prices obtained for such lots as were sold, which was but a small proportion, were not very tempting to additional adventurers by means of the hammer.

Bullion is marked at the following prices:—

Foreign Gold, in bars	-	-	£4 2 0
New Dollars -	- - -	-	0 5 5
Silver, in bars standard	-		0 5 6

Average prices of Corn for England and Wales.

Wheat	76s. 6d.		Barley	54s. 10d
Rye	53s. 9d.		Beans	59s. 10d
Oats	32s. 2d.		Pease	62s. 4d.

HAMBURGH.

April 2d, 1819.

Coffee.—Prices have declined considerably during the last month, owing to the unfavourable accounts from London, and the large parcels pressed upon the market.

Cochineal.—Prices maintain themselves pretty well, our stocks being small, but there is very little demand; the black generally sells more readily than the other descriptions.

Cotton.—The fall in the London Market has produced a bad effect on our prices. The low prices of Bengals have, however, induced some speculators to come forward, and Cottons that had only fetched 13¾ gt. got up to 14. We received the other day 400 Bales Boweds from Charleston, the greater part of which was immediately sold at 26 to 27 gt.

Indigo.—Scarcely any thing doing in Bengal Indigos. Prices have, however, experienced but a very trifling depression, and we are of opinion that they will soon get up again: Spanish Indigos are, on the contrary, very much pressed upon the market, and would not find buyers at our quotations.

Rice.—New Carolina of which about 1800 Casks are already arrived, is held at 30m. but only a trifling quantity has been sold, and that at 29m. Old is offered at 23 to 26m. There is a great deal of Italian and Brazil Rice in the market; the former is worth 17 to 18 m. and the latter 19 to 21 m. East India Rice could be bought at 12 to 16 m.

Sugar.—Prices of this article have again declined, and low as they are at present, we think it likely they will still decline.

Our stocks are very large: this week we have had an arrival of 6 Cargoes from Bahia and Rio de Janeiro.

Tobacco.—Kentucky Tobacco is lower, and a good quality may be obtained at 5¼ m. Maryland is scarce, and well supported. Some large purchases have been made in Porto Rico, and prices have advanced about ½ gt.

Tea.—The ordinary qualities have declined considerably.

TRIESTE.

March 8th, 1819.

THE demand for Sugars continues languid, and the extensive quantities on hand discourage the purchasers. The prices for Refined Goods are entirely nominal; those for crushed Lumps have declined of late, and some sales of inferior quality were made at 33f to 34f; small parcels of 5 to 10 Hhds. sold at 35f to 37f. In raw Sugars, very little is doing, and white Pernambuccos are offered at 32¼ to 33f.

Coffee is looking down, and the unfavourable accounts of the London and Hambro' markets had the effect of depreciating the prices with us; good ordinary St. Domingo is offering at 70f to 71f, ordinary at 68f to 69f, but few purchasers are coming forward.

Our Cotton Market is exceedingly dull, and a further decline in the price has taken place. Bengals are offered at 40f to 42f, without finding purchasers.

The demand for Twist continues languid, and no sales to any extent have been made for some time past.

COUNTY OF ESSEX.

Agricultural Report, March 26, 1819.

The sowing of Spring Corn may be said to be completed, except in a few instances, where the Turnips are not cut off, and all in a desirable and husbandlike manner; fallowed Oats in places have experienced an inconvenience from the insect. The Barleys have escaped at present, and must be considered fuller plants than the former. The Peasare flourishing and strong, but Beans do not appear so healthy, as might be expected. The sup-

ply of Spring Seed must be early, and with some the horses are already pastured for a few hours in the day.

Bankrupts in the order of their dates; with their Attorneys.

BANKRUPTCY SUPERSEDED, *March* 27.

R. Starbuck. Milton-next-Gravesend, boot and shoe maker

BANKRUPTS.

Baker S. Brighton, linen draper. *Sols.* Lamberts and Co. Gray's Inn.

Barnett A. Berners street, glass dealer. *Sol.* Cappage, Old Broad street

Barton W. St. Saviour's Church yard, Southwark, upholsterer. *Sols.* Rogers and Son, Manchester buildings, Westminster.

Booth J. Chapel-en-le-Frith, Derbyshire, common brewer. *Sols.* Milne and Parry, Temple

Brooke N. Duke street, Lincoln's Inn fields, shoe manufacturer. *Sols.* Amory and Coles, Lothbury

Buckland T. Langley, Buckinghamshire, brick maker. *Sol.* Berkeley, Lincoln's Inn

Burmester J. W. and C. L. Vidal, New London street, merchants. *Sols.* Barrows and Vincent, Basinghall street

Bush, Wick and Abson, Gloucestershire, dealer. *Sol.* King, Sergeant's Inn, Fleet street

Canstat N. Upper East Smithfield, chymist. *Sol.* Isaacs, Bury street, St. Mary Axe

Chamberlain W. Bristol, corn factor. *Sol.* King, Sergeant's Inn, Fleet street

Dalgairns P. and E. Winslow, St. Mary-at-Hill, ship and insurance brokers. *Sols.* Clarke & Faulkner, Sadler's Hall, Cheapside

Dampier E. Primrose street, Bishopsgate without, seed crusher. *Sols.* Druce and Son, Billiter square

Dickinson W. Scalby, Yorkshire, coal merchant. *Sols.* Fisher and Sudlow, Holborn

Dunnage H. Colchester, miller. *Sol.* Williams Cursitor street, Chancery lane

Goddard M. Stannylands, Cheshire, farmer. *Sols.* Rosser and Co. Bartlett's buildings

Harman T. C. Wisbeach, linen draper. *Sols.* Sweet and Co. Basinghall street

Hellicar T. and J. Bristol, merchants. *Sols.* Lambert and Co. Gray's Inn

Hornshaw T. Halifax, grocer. *Sol.* Battye, Chancery lane

Johnson J. Sheffield, draper. *Sol.* Duncan, Holborn court, Gray's Inn

Macdonald R. Frant, Sussex, shopkeeper. *Sols.* Rowland and Young, Lincoln's Inn fields

Miller R. Old Fish street, bookseller. *Sols.* Lane and Bennett, Lawrence Pountney hill

Mountjoy R. Hanwell Nursery, Ealing, seedsman. *Sol.* Rooke and Co. Armourers' hall, Coleman street

Sibley J. Abchurch lane, drysalter. *Sol.* Birkett, Cloak lane

Stalker D. and A. D. Welch, Leadenhall st. slopsellers. *Sols.* Kearsey and Spurr, Bishopsgate street, within

Tatum W. and E. Palmer, Fish street hill, paper stainers. *Sol.* Hodgson, Old Jewry

Thistlewood G. Muscovy court, Tower hill, flour factor. *Sol.* Druce and Son, Billiter square

Turner W. London road, stationer. *Sols.* Jones and Roche, Charles street, Covent Garden

Webb, A. Hammersmith, coach proprietor. *Sol.* Goram, Orchard street, Portman sq.

Whatton J. Liverpool, cattle dealer. *Sols.* Dacie and John, Palsgrave place, Temple bar

Whitebrook J. Chester, shoe maker. *Sols.* Drew and Sons, Bermondsey street

BANKRUPTS, *March* 30.

Anderson H·W· Cushion court, Broad street, merchant· *Sols.* Willis and Co. Warnford court, Throgmorton street

Barnes J. Portsea, builder. *Sols.* Alexander and Holme, New Inn

Bigg J. and C. Hatfield, Hertfordshire, common brewers, *Sols.* Nicholson and Platt, Hertford

Cotterill E. M. & C. G. Vine street, Liquorpond street, bacon merchants. *Sols.* Nind and Co. Throgmorton street

Gaunt J. and T. Armley, Yorkshire, woollen manufacturers. *Sol.* Few and Co. Henrietta street, Covent garden

Harding S. T., C. Oakes, and T. Willington, Tamworth, bankers. *Sols.* Hicks and Braikenridge, Bartlett's buildings, Holborn

Moore T. B. Denmark court, Strand, paper stainer. *Sols.* Alexander and Holme, New Inn

Pearson J. Portsmouth, mercer

Pegrom M. and J. Artillery street, dealers, *Sol.* Walker, Lincoln's Inn fields.

Relph W. Lewknor, Oxfordshire, farmer. *Sols.* Rose and Slater, Gray's Inn.

Simpson F. Huddersfield, woolstapler. *Sol.* Beckett, Noble street, Foster lane.

Stubbs, W. Leek, Staffordshire, innholder. *Sols.* Long and Austen, Holborn court, Gray's Inn

BANKRUPTCIES SUPERSEDED, *April* 3.

J. Revett, jun. Tolleshunt Darcy, Essex, butcher

H. Brodie, Liverpool, linen draper

BANKRUPTS.

Buchanan D. S. M. Smith, and F. Ashley, Liverpool, merchants. *Sol.* Adlington and Gregory, Bedford row

Dixon J. Ivybridge, Devonshire, merchant. *Sols.* Darke and Co. Princes street, Bedford row

Fisher W. Union place, Lambeth, master mariner. *Sol.* Hayward, Took's court Cursitor street

Gilpin W. Villiers street, Strand, army clothier. *Sol.* Teasdale, Merchant Tailors' hall, Threadneedle street

Gompertz A. Lombard street, merchant. *Sol.* Elliot, Fenchurch street

Hancock W. Bury St. Edmunds, Suffolk, cabinet maker. *Sols.* Amory and Coles, Lothbury

Isaac J. Fareham, Southampton, leather seller. *Sols.* Dyne and Son, Lincoln's Inn fields

Lewis W. and J. A. Henderson, Little Tower street, wine merchants. *Sols.* Kearsey and Spurr, Bishopsgate, within

Nayler B. Sykehouse, Yorkshire, tanner. *Sol.* King, Castle street, Holborn

Owen J. & H. D. Great St. Helen's, Bishopsgate street, merchants. *Sol.* Crosley, Great James street, Bedford row

Pickbourn J. North street, City road, drug grinder. *Sol.* Hutchinson, Crown court, Threadneedle street

Somers W. Newcastle-upon-Tyne, flour dealer. *Sols.* Bell and Brodrick, Bow Church yard

Wathen C. Salter's Hall court, merchant. *Sol.* Clarke, Little St. Thomas Apostle

BANKRUPTS, *April* 6.

Carr C. Bridge st. Westminster, jeweller. *Sol.* Upsdell, Fenchurch street

Clancy W. Cornhill, provision merchant. *Sol.* Crosley, Great James street, Bedford row

Gallimore W. Norbury, Derbyshire, tanner. *Sol.* Barbor, Fetter lane

Hawkins S. Milton, Southampton, dealer. *Sol.* Langton, Hare court, Temple

Jones R. Cheapside, woollen draper. *Sol.* Farren, Threadneedle street

Panton S. Milton-next-Sittingbourne, Kent, miller, *Sols.* Brace and Mosins, Essex court, Temple

Pearse J. Plymouth dock, sadler. *Sols.* Anstice and Wright, Inner Temple

Saxby J. R. Hawkhurst, Kent, hop merchant. *Sols.* Gregson and Fonnereau, Angel court, Throgmorton street

Smith B. Birmingham, steel toy maker. *Sols.* Clarke and Co. Chancery lane

Swainston J. Kendal, Westmorland, morocco leather manufacturer. *Sols.* Hurd and Johnson, Inner Temple

Thornley S. Levenshulme, Lancashire, and J. Beckton, Manchester, manufacturers. *Sol.* Ellis, Chancery lane

Travers J. Lambeth, coal merchant. *Sols.* Brace and Selby, Surrey street, Strand.

Wainewright W. Liverpool, merchant, *Sol.* Ellis, Chancery lane

Wroath D. Truro, Cornwall, smith. *Sols.* Price and Co. Lincoln's Inn

BANKRUPTS, *April* 10.

Bartlett J. Frome Selwood, Somersetshire, clothier. *Sol.* Edmunds, Exchequer office of Pleas, Lincoln's Inn

Bensly C. Stroud, Gloucestershire, mercer. *Sol.* Price, Exchequer office, Lincoln's Inn

Bentley S. Horton, Yorkshire, worsted manufacturer. *Sol.* Nettlefold, Norfolk st. Strand

Buckley H. Junction, Yorkshire, inn keeper. *Sols.* Milne and Parry, Temple

Cooper J. Scholes, Yorkshire, slate merchant. *Sol.* Brigg, Southampton Buildings, Chancery lane

Cruse T. Chatham, brewer. *Sol.* James, Bucklersbury

Davies G. Tenby, Pembrokeshire, merchant. *Sols.* Alexander and Holme, New Inn

Gowland M. J. Whitby, Yorkshire, porter merchant. *Sol.* Edmunds, Exchequer Office, Lincoln's Inn

Griffiths M. J. and R. Bristol, masons. *Sol.* Edmunds, Exchequer Office of Pleas, Lincoln's Inn

Howard R. jun. Woolwich, brewer, *Sols.* Wiltshire and Co. Winchester House, Old Broad street

Hurrell S. Minories, corn dealer. *Sols.* Clutton and Carter, High street, Southwark

Jackson M. Bolton, Lancashire, cotton manufacturer. *Sol.* Meddowcroft, Gray's Inn square

Kilby J. York, common brewer. *Sol.* Eyre, Gray's Inn square

Peake S. Pendleton, Lancashire, wine merchant. *Sol.* Meddowcroft, Gray's Inn sq.

Watt J. J. Ratcliffe highway, surgeon. *Sols.* Eicke and Evans, Aldermanbury

Wood E. Bolton, Lancashire, brazier. *Sol.* Meddowcroft, Gray's Inn.

BANKRUPTS, *April* 13.

Abram R. Liverpool, merchant. *Sol.* Chester, Staple Inn

Cope R. Worcester, victualler. *Sols.* Price and Co. Lincoln's Inn

Dolphin E. Cheadle, Staffordshire, plumber and glazier. *Sol.* Barbor, Fetter lane,

Fletcher R. B. Blackburn, Lancashire, manufacturer. *Sols.* Bonnell and Dixon, St. Swithin's lane

Glover E. and E. Warrington, Lancashire, brewers. *Sol.* Chester, Staple Inn

Gunton J. St. James's street, Westminster, picture dealer. *Sol.* Turner, Percy street, Rathbone place

Jones C. E. Kentish town, tanner. *Sol.* Carter, Lord Mayor's Court office, Royal Exchange

Pearson J. Leicester, commission agent. *Sol.* Beverley, Garden court, Temple

Pritchard J. Bristol, grocer. *Sols.* Poole and Greenfield, Gray's Inn square

Young P. and R. Anderson, Wapping, sail makers. *Sols.* Blunt and Bowman, Broad street buildings

BANKRUPTS, *April* 17.

Aslat A. White Lion, Lambeth, victualler. *Sol.* Popkin, Dean street, Soho

Brammer C. Woodhouse, Yorkshire, mans mercer. *Sol.* Battye, Chancery lane

Burcher T. Mitchel-Dean, Gloucestershire, timber dealer. *Sol.* King, Sergeant's Inn, Fleet street.

Collinson, E. Crooked lane, oil merchant. *Sols.* Allitson and Hundleby, Freeman's court, Cornhill

Douthit S. Liverpool, merchant. *Sols.* Blackstock & Bunce, King's Bench walk, Temple

Elmer G. Mistley, Essex, merchant. *Sol.* Cocker, Nassau street, Soho

Forbes A. B. Bristol, draper. *Sols.* Price and Co. Lincoln's Inn Old Buildings

Heal W. Bradford, Wiltshire, inn keeper. *Sols.* Dax and Co. Doughty street

Hoyland J. Knottingley, Yorkshire, grocer. *Sol.* Blakelock, Sergeant's Inn, Fleet st.

Hull C. Moneyers street, Hoxton New town, riband manufacturer. *Sols.* Knight and Freeman, Basinghall street

Martin J. St. Philip and Jacob, Gloucestershire, druggist. *Sol.* Poole and Greenfield, Gray's Inn square

Milnes R. Mirfield, Yorkshire, coal merchant. *Sol.* Lake, Dowgate hill

Perkins J. B. Carpenter's hall, London wall, ironmonger. *Sols.* Clark and Co. Chancery lane

Rothwell J. Arnold, Nottinghamshire, hosier. *Sol.* Sykes New Inn.

BANKRUPTCY SUPERSEDED, *April* 20.

B. Smith, steel toy maker

BANKRUPTS.

Bentley S. Horton, Yorkshire, worsted manufacturer. *Sol.* Nettlefold, Norfolk st. Strand

Booth T. Newark-upon-Trent, and A. Booth, Nottingham, tallow chandlers. *Sol.* Knowles, New Inn

Campbell J. White Lion court, Cornhill, merchant. *Sol.* Rivington, Fenchurch street buildings

Dixon J. Wellington, Shropshire, mercer. *Sols.* Baxter and Bowker, Gray's Inn pl.

Farmer W. Walsall, Staffordshire, inn holder. *Sols.* Turner and Holmes, Bloomsbury square

Fletcher B. Burnley, Lancashire, plumber. *Sols.* Stocker and Co. New Boswell court

French J. jun. Bristol, clothier.

Jarman W. jun. Knightsbridge, paper hanger. *Sol.* Hudson, Winkworth place, City road

Messent P. Quaker street, Spitalfields, silk weaver. *Sol.* James, Bucklersbury

Samuels E. I. Great Prescot street, Goodman's fields, lapidary. *Sol.* Isaacs, Mansell street, Goodman's fields

Slade J. Frome Selwood, Somersetshire, clothier. *Sol.* Williams Red Lion square

Turner W. Llangollen, Denbighshire, and A. Comber, Manchester, cotton spinners. *Sol.* Ellis, Chancery Lane

Whitton J. Kingston-upon-Hull, merchant. *Sol.* Rosser and Co. Bartlett's buildings, Holborn

Wood T. Nottingham, grocer. *Sols.* Hurd and Johnson, Temple.

sun becomes a powerful cause of blindness.

There remains, however, one point to be cleared up : for, as the Pope interposes his judgment on the *permissibility* of books, who can tell how closely that judgment may affect ourselves ? For aught we know the PANORAMA itself may figure on the list of prohibited books, either now or hereafter ;— and then—what will become of all our hopes of being made SAINTS ? Or, if we should be happy enough to arrive within ken of St. Peter, at heaven's gate, and he should incline to turn the key in our favour—which, by the bye, is rather doubtful, all things considered—just as we are crossing the threshold, perhaps, up comes a decision from the Censors of the Vatican, and the whole corps is remanded to a place too dreadful to think of!!!

" In the bull of 1515 Pope Leo X. not only renewed the attempt of Alexander VI. against the civil government, but even joined to the sword of the church, or excommunication, the temporal penalties of confiscation, fines, and suspensions (from office). He suddenly introduced a new public law, which laid the foundation for the usurpations that followed soon after, and opened the door to the censure of books, the court of Rome presently beginning to meddle with the examination of works which had nothing dogmatic in them, and to inflict punishments foreign to the power of the church.

" The bull of 1520, and that *In Cœna Domini* of Adrian and Clement, caused disturbances of another kind ; for as they prohibited all heretical books in general, without mentioning the names of their authors, under the penalty of excommunication, it was necessary not only to know the books with regard to their doctrine, but also that every one should be a judge of that doctrine ; and as this private judgment never could be uniform, the confusion may be easily imagined which resulted from such general and indefinite prohibitions.

" These spiritual and political disturbances called forth efficacious means to guard against them ; and as the temporal power was really sacrificed in the aforementioned bulls, it was the first that thought of the wholesome and happy regulation of the *Indices Expurgatorii* (lists of those books which the Popes think fit to prohibit) which has since been adopted by the church.

The regulation of the *Index* insured the temporal power against the infection of its subjects by satyrical, seditious and heretical writings, at the same time preventing the ill understood policy of the court of Rome, from forbidding along with those books the reading of those authors who supported the rights of the states, and settled the just limits of the priesthood.

We hinted at some of the prohibitions contained in the last edition of the *Index*, in vol. viii. p. 1667, N. S. and we hinted at the reasons, too, of such prohibitions ; valid, they certainly are, in all points, as any Jesuit could prove, with the greatest ease ;—were they not all employed on matters more analogous to the spirit of their Order, of which the present Report contains evidence, in a memorandum by Lord William Bentick, dated so long ago as January 1813. To what extent conversions have since been effected,—who can tell ?

" With respect to *young English or Irishmen who have come to Sicily to obtain holy orders*, it appears that *since the restoration of the Jesuits in Sicily, about six or seven years, these restless and active brethren, have procured in all nineteen eleves from the British islands ; of these, five have returned in holy orders, two died in Palermo, and nine are now here.*

" The objects which the Jesuits may have had in view, in thus extending their search for pupils, are of course as various, as are the branches of their wily policy ; but as it has been boasted, that *one of them who has returned* (and who by the way was accounted half mad when here, and may therefore be a good fanatic) *has laboured successfully in the work of conversion, one may be permitted to conclude, that hopeless as such a pursuit must be, it has not been entirely left out of their speculations.*"

	8 o'clock Morning	Noon.	11 o'clock Night.	Height of Barom. inches	Dryness by Leslie's Barom.
Feb. 21	40	47	40	29,87	41 Fair
22	40	49	40	,85	40 Fair
23	41	50	42	,78	22 Cloudy
24	47	56	46	,73	36 Fair
25	46	52	40	,70	30 Showry
26	41	53	45	,70	39 Fair
27	47	54	46	,96	26 Showry
28	47	54	45	,88	10 Sm. Rain
Mar. 29	49	56	47	,77	27 Showry
30	47	59	49	30,06	30 Xhowry
31	51	58	50	,20	31 Cloudy
1	50	62	52	,24	46 Fair
2	52	65	54	,25	62 Fair
3	53	66	47	,07	63 Fair
4	47	56	49	,22	41 Fair
5	47	56	48	,14	45 Fair
6	44	50	49	29,81	47 Fair
7	49	62	51	,78	40 Fair
8	52	53	47	30,00	0 Rain
9	47	53	42	,10	32 Fair
10	43	62	47	29,84	40 Fair
11	52	58	44	,43	38 Fair
12	46	47	46	,36	0 Rain
13	52	52	44	,37	25 Rain
14	49	57	47	,54	51 Fair
15	51	59	51	,49	39 Fair
16	52	57	49	,27	41 Windy
17	50	55	46	,50	45 Stormy
18	49	55	44	,77	38 Stormy
19	46	55	50	,74	30 Showry
20	54	59	55	,70	27 Sm. Rain

London Premiums of Insurance.

Aberdeen, Dundee, Perth, &c. 10s. 6d to 13s. 9d.
Africa, 2gs.
American States; 30s. to 35s.
Belfast, Cork, Dublin, 15s 9d. to 20s.
Brazils, 30s. to 35s.
Hamburgh, &c. 12s. 6d. to 15s.
Cadiz, Lisbon, Oporto, 20s.
Canada 2gs. to 2½gs.
Cape of Good Hope, 2gs.
Constantinople, Smyrna, &c. 35s. to 40s.
East-India (Co. ships) 3gs.
——— out and home, 6gs.
France, 10s. 6d. to 15s. 9d.
Gibraltar, 20s. to 25s.
Gottenburgh, 15s. 9d. to 20s.
Greenland, out and home, 3gs. to 3⅓gs.
Holland 10s. 6d. to 12s. 6d.
Honduras, &c. 2gs.
Jamaica, 35s.
Leeward Islands, 25s. to 30s.
Madeira, 20s.
Malta, Italian States, &c. 30s. to 35s.
Malaga, 25s. to 30s.
Newfoundland, 30s. to 35s.
Portsmouth, Falmouth, Plymouth, 10s.6d.15s.9d.
River Plate, 2gs
Southern Fishery, out and home, 10gs.
Stockholm, Petersburgh, Riga, 15s. 9d. to 20s.

PRICE OF BREAD.

The Peck Loaf to weigh 17lb. 6oz.		4s.	0d
The Half ditto ditto 8 11		2	0
The Quar. ditto ditto 4 5		1	0
The half ditto ditto 2 2¾		0	6

POTATOES.

Kidney	8 0 0	Ox Nobles	7 0 0
Champions	7 0 0	Apple	7 0 0

ONIONS, per Bushel, 2s 6d to 3s 6d

MEAT.

Smithfield, per stone of 8b. to sink the Offa

	Beef	mut.	veal.	pork	lamb
1819.	s. d.	s. d.	s. d.	s. d.	s. d.
Mar. 27	5 8	6 6	7 0	6 8	0 0
	6 4	6 4	7 6	6 6	0 0
	6 0	6 8	7 6	8 0	0 0
	5 8	6 4	7 0	6 8	0 0

SUGAR.

Lumps ordinary or large 32 to 40 lbs...	100
Fine or Canary, 24 to 30 lbs.	118
Loaves, fine.........................	118
Powder, ordinary, 9 to 11lbs..........	104

COTTON TWIST.

Feb. 19. Mule 1st quality, No. 40	0s. 0d
———————————No. 120	0s. 0d
———— 2d quality, No. 40	0s. 0d
Discount—0 a 0 per cent.	

COALS, delivered at 13s. per chald. advance.

	Sunderland.		Newcastle.	
Mar. 27.	31s 6d to 42 0	31s 6d to 42 6		
April. 6.	33s 6	41 6	31s 0d	41 6
12.	34s 0	41 6	32s 6d	41 6
19.	31s 0	41 0	32s 6d	40 6

LEATHER.

Butts, 50 to 56lb.	24	Calf Skins 30 to	
Dressing Hides	18	45lb. per doz.	3d
Crop hides for cut.	20	Ditto 50 to 70..	—
Flat Ordinary	16	Seals, Large,...	100

SOAP; yellow, 90s.; mottled 102s.; curd 106s.
CANDLES; per doz. 13s. 0d.; moulds 14s. 6d.

Course of Exchange.

Bilboa	38	Palermo, per oz	153d.
Amsterdam,	11-6	Leghorn	51½
Ditto at sigh	11-3	Genoa	47½
Rotterdam	11-7	Venice,	25
Hamb. us. 2½	34 0	Naples	41¾
Altona us.	34-1	Lisbon	57
Paris, 3d. d.	23-80	Oporto	57
Ditto, 2 us.	24-10	Rio Janeiro.	60½
Madrid	38-½	Dublin	14
Cadiz	39-	Cork	14

Agio Bank of Holland, 2 per cent.

HAY and STRAW.—AT SMITHFIELD.

	Hay.	Straw.	Clover.
	£. s. d.	£. s. d.	£. s. d.
Mar. 6	6 15 0	2 16 0	8 0 0
13	6 15 0	3 0 0	8 0 0
20	7 0 0	3 0 0	8 0 0
27	7 7 0	3 0 0	8 0 0

Price of STOCKS, from 22d March, to 20th April, 1819.

1819. Mar.	Bank Stock.	3 p. Cent. Reduced.	3 p. Cent. Consols.	4 p. Cent. Consols.	Navy 5 p. Cent.	Irish 5 p. Cent.	Long Annuities.	Imperial 3 p. Cent.	Ditto Annuities.	India Stock.	India Bonds.	South Sea Stock.	Excheq. Bills.	Consols for Acc.
22	Shut	75½ ⅝	74½ ⅝	95	104⅝	—	Shut	—	—	—	35	—	1d	75
23	—	—	74½	Shut	104⅝	—	—	—	—	—	27	—	5d	74⅞
24	—	—	74⅝	—	104⅝	—	—	—	—	—	27	—	3d	75
25	—	75⅞	75 74⅞	—	104⅞	—	—	—	—	—	—	—	4d	75
26	—	—	74⅞	—	105	—	—	73⅞	—	—	24	—	4d	75
27	—	75⅛	74⅞	—	105	—	19 15-16	—	—	—	24	—	3d	75
29	—	75⅛	74⅞	—	104⅞	—	19 15-16	—	—	—	22	—	5d	74⅞
30	—	—	74⅞	—	105	—	Shut	—	—	—	20	—	5d	74⅞
31	—	—	74⅞	—	105	—	—	73⅞	—	—	20	82⅝	3d	75
Apr.														
1	—	75⅝	74⅞	—	105⅛	—	—	—	—	—	30	—	pa	75⅛
2	—	—	74⅞	—	105⅛	—	—	74	—	—	37	—	1p	75
3	—	—	74⅞	—	105⅛	—	—	—	—	—	40	—	3p	75⅛
5	—	—	75¼	—	105¾	—	—	—	—	—	40	—	3p	75¼
6	254	74⅛ 3¾	75 4½	93	105⅝	—	19 3-16	73⅞	—	—	39	—	3p	75⅛
7	254	73⅝	74⅞ ⅜	92⅞	105¾	—	19 3-8	—	—	—	38	—	4p	74¾
8	254	74 3¾	74⅞	92⅞	105¾	—	19 7-16	—	—	—	39	—	2p	74⅞
9	Good Friday													
10	253	73¾ ⅝	74½ ¼	92⅛	101⅞	—	19 3-8	—	—	—	40	—	2p	74½
12	Easter Mond													
13	—	73¼ 3	74 3⅝	—	105⅛	—	19 3-8	—	—	—	41	—	1p	74⅛
14	253½	73 2¾	73⅞	92	105⅝	—	19 1-4	—	—	—	40	—	1p	73⅞
15	253½	73⅛ 2⅝	74 3¼	91⅛	105¼	—	19 1-16	71½	—	221	39	—	1p	74⅛
16	252	72⅛ 1⅞	73¼ 2½	91⅛	105⅛	—	19 1-16	71¼	—	—	39	—	4d	73¼
17	252	72⅛ 1⅞	73 2⅞	90⅞	105⅛	—	19	72	—	221	38	—	5p	73⅛
19	—	72⅛ 2	73 2⅝	90⅞	105	—	19	72⅜	—	—	36	—	3p	73
20	252	72⅛ 1⅝	72⅞ ½	90⅞	105	—	19	—	—	220½	38	—	4p	73

IRISH FUNDS.

Apr.	Irish Bank Stock.	Government Debenture 3½ per ct.	Government Stock, 3½ per ct.	Government Debenture 4 per ct.	Government Stock, 5 per ct.	Treasury Bills.	Grand Canal Stock.	Grand Canal Loan, 4 per ct.	Grand Canal Loan, 6 per ct.	City Dublin Bonds.	Royal Canal Loan 6 per cent.	Omnium.
1	249½	88¾	86⅝	—	—	—	—	—	—	—	—	—
3	249½	89¼	86⅝	—	107½	—	—	—	—	—	81⅝	
8	250½	90	87⅝	—	—	—	—	—	—	—	81⅞	
9	250½	90	87⅝	—	—	—	—	—	—	—	81⅛	
12	250½	89	86⅞	—	107½	—	—	—	—	—	—	
13	—	88½	86½	—	107⅛	—	79¼	—	—	—	—	

Prices of the FRENCH FUNDS From Mar. 22, to Apr. 22.

1819	5 per Cent. consols fr.	c.	Bank Actions fr.	c.
Mar. 20	66	45	1492	50
22	66	55	1500	—
27	65	50	1525	—
29	65	40	1515	—
Apr 3	66	95	1537	50
6	67	10	1530	—
10	67	50	1540	—
12	67	45	1540	—
17	66	95	1532	50

AMERICAN FUNDS.

	IN LONDON. Apr. 8.	13.	16.	AT NEW YORK. Feb. 1.	2	Mar. 9.
7 per Cent.	—	—	—	105	106	—
Bank Shares	24	—	—	98	112½	—
Louisiana	—	—	—	par	par	—
Old 6 per Cent.	—	—	—	par	par	—
New 6 per Cent.	99	99	99	101	102½	—
3 per Cent.		62½	62½	66	65	

By J. M. Richardson, 23, Cornhill.

THE
LITERARY PANORAMA,
AND
National Register:
For *JUNE*, 1819.

NATIONAL AND PARLIAMENTARY NOTICES,

(British and Foreign,)

PROSPECTIVE AND RETROSPECTIVE.

CATHOLICS IN FOREIGN STATES.

REPORT

From the

SELECT COMMITTEE

On the Regulation of

ROMAN CATHOLIC SUBJECTS

IN FOREIGN STATES.

[*Ordered by the House of Commons to be Printed, 25th of June,* 1816.]

[Continued from page 493.]

THE Sovereigns of independent kingdoms not seldom act on principles diametrically opposite, in the conduct of their public affairs: taught by experience to know that what suits the system of Policy in one place, or under certain circumstances, is absolutely contrary to the interests of both prince and people, elsewhere. When, therefore, we find a general inclination among princes to pursue the same line of conduct, to preserve the same systematic precautions on any given subject, and to admit or refuse their consent to certain things, on the same general principles—when they all plead the same rights, and all assign the same reasons in support of those rights, we may be sure that the causes of this uniformity are cogent, important, and unyielding.

If there be any thing to which this constant view of the proper course of policy to be pursued, may be appropriated, rather than to another, it is to that line of conduct, which the Potentates of Christendom have followed in respect to the influence, the exertions, and the assumptions of the Papacy. That the Bishop of Rome, under the influence of the circumstances by which he was surrounded, at the time, should become not only the ecclesiastical, but also the civil governor of the Roman city, and the Roman territory, is not wonderful; and may be easily accounted for, by natural causes: While Rome was the seat of empire, the *Pontifex Maximus* was controuled, and more or less corrected, by the Imperial presence; nor was the influence of the Bishop of Rome less controuled by the political power of the state. When that was removed, and when Christianity became triumphant, the Bishop of that city gradually assumed the ascendancy, and ultimately, the supremacy. He demanded submission from the Clergy of the East, as well as from the Clergy of the West, and the Patriarchs of the primitive Churches of Jerusalem, and of Antioch, with that of the now Imperial city, Constantinople, were required to yield obedience to the see of Rome. This was too much for human nature to endure. Those sees maintained their precedence; and the Bishop of Rome became schismatic to all who spoke the Grecian, or the Eastern languages. Where the Latin language had obtained more extensive influence, and was intermingled among the native dialects of the people, the Pope, affecting to be the head of the Latin Church, possessed himself of much of the admiration and veneration of the public. But, it was not till after his artifices had established the profession of celibacy by the Catholic Clergy, that his power was effectually formed into absolute tyranny; nor had it surmounted all opposition, and firmly rivetted its chains on the people, till the institution of the Order of the Jesuits. That Order, now justly held in horror by most, and beheld with jealousy by all, for a while supported the most preposterous propositions and pretences of the Holy See. At last, the conduct of its body, with the misconduct of various of its members, became so intolerable, as well to the public at large, as to Sovereigns and Statesmen, that the world saw with joy the suppression of the Order, and obtained a glimpse of long looked for freedom from Romish artifice.

That Order has been revived by the present Pope: the consequence will be, that all the pretences, the prevarications, the subtleties, and the hypocrisies of that Order will revive with it. Evidently, the jealousies, the precautions, of Sovereigns must revive to meet it. What they did to counteract its machinations before, they must again do, to counteract its machinations at present. It is, therefore, a part of political and practical wisdom to enquire what maxims were formerly adopted, and to what degree they were acted on, by the Rulers of various Countries, who professed their adherence to the See of Rome. We have partly attended to this in a former paper; and have partly considered what were the rights of Sovereignty insisted on, and acted on, by the Emperor of Austria; because, he being head of the Germanic

body, and the leading prince among those who interest themselves in the concerns of the See, one of its principal supporters, and one by his situation, most closely connected with the Papacy, no imputation of unfriendliness could possibly attach to him. If then, we found HIM insisting on the right of nominating Ecclesiastical Superiors, of various grades, and of controuling Ecclesiastical Institutions, if HE held Popish authority, at a certain distance, and as it were, in jeopardy, he has prepared us for a proper contemplation of the conduct of other powers respecting the same authority.

To what straits, and even humiliations, a government may be exposed, by the intrigues of the Papacy, might be exemplified in the necessity which several governments have found themselves under, to forbid the entrance of Papal Bulls into their dominions. Our own history affords instances of this: for the public records of England contain a diploma granted by King Richard II. to one Valeton, to search all vessels, in order to find out those who imported Bulls, and other writings of the Pope; and in the reign of Edward III. all the ports were watched by order of the King, to intercept Papal Bulls. The Kings of Spain, too, have been obliged to issue orders commanding that on whoever, coming into the kingdom, a certain expected Bull was found, the crime should be expiated by the gallows, *instanter:* even though the King's own sister should assume the protection of the culprit. But, the most complete history given in these papers, of such an incident, is one that took place in the Venetian States: the document is equally curious and instructive.

" The republic of Venice had at that time another war to support, which was more vigorously carried on, namely, the war which the Pope made against that republic by means of the thunders of the church. On the 24th of May, on the festival of Whitsuntide, Sixtus IV. had published against Venice a bull, by which he ordered all the monks to leave that excommunicated city within three days. The Council of Ten were informed of it. They caused all who came from Rome to be watched, in order to seize this bull in their hands. They rendered the rectors of parishes responsible for all bills or papers that might be found posted up at the doors of their respective churches ; and *they ordered the Patriarch and all the Venetian clergy to transmit, unopened, to the Inquisitors of the state, any Bull that might be addressed to them by the Holy See. These commands were strictly obeyed,* The excommunication, still sealed up, was delivered to the Council of Ten by the Patriarch, without any Venetian whatever knowing of the circumstance.[*] This council ordered all the cardinals and prelates who were vassals of the state, to meet at Venice on the 15th of July, under the penalty of having the revenues of their benefices seized in case of non-compliance, and there to hold a provincial council. At the same time *an appeal* was lodged with Hieronymus Lando, the titular patriarch of Constantinople, *to a future council, from the sentence of excommunication. The Patriarch in consequence of this appeal suspended the interdict, and sent a summons to the Pope himself to appear before the future Council.* Some resolute men posted this summons up, on the bridge of St. Angelo, and *against the doors of the Vatican,* and of the Rotonda, This boldness however caused the death of the watchmen, whom the Pope caused to be hung for not having prevented the posting up of the summons[†]. All the Venetian priests who were at Rome were recalled under the penalty of being deprived of their benefices, and *the Pope opposed to this summons* an edict, by virtue of which the prelates and priests who should attempt to leave Rome might be sold as slaves[‡].

Now, we suppose that our readers will agree with us in feeling the extreme impropriety of such indignities offered to Princes : — indignities, for which the authority supposed to be granted to the Pope in spirituals, offers not the shadow of an excuse. It may be said, perhaps, that the temper of republican Governors, (for Venice was then a Republic) is unfavourable to the *just* interests of the Papacy : or, that,

on great and remarkable occasions the interference of the Pope is desirable, not to say necessary. The following history shews that the slightest incident may occasion broils and misunderstandings, and squabbles with the Holy See.—What would the members of our popular clubs, whether *Pittite,* or *Foxite,* feel, under the terror of apprehension that a commemoration dinner, with a few glasses of wine, enjoyed for the good of their Country and Constitution, should call forth the thunders of the Vatican ?

" It had always been customary to allow all sorts of popular diversions and dancing at the festival of the church of *Udlingenschwil,* in the canton of Lucerne, by the express permission of the supreme magistrate. The rector, *Christian Leonce Ander Matt,* a native of Zug, a man of an inconsiderate officious zeal, forbade this dancing in the year 1726, under the penalty of spiritual pains. The magistrate, in order to have his authority respected, sent the public crier about to promulgate anew his permission to dance, as being a temporal concern, of the cognizance of the civil authorities. The dance took place without any violation of decorum. On the following Sunday the rector preached a fulminating sermon against the dancers, of whose names he had procured a list : and after having *twice* read the gospel of the ten leprous men, he compared the dancers with these, and he bade them, in the words of the gospel to go show themselves unto the priests, to confess their sins somewhere else, and to bring him a written certificate of their confessors that they had so confessed. Other imprudent expressions having escaped him in the pulpit, the rector was summoned before the great council. The nuncio of the Pope (*Dominicho Passionei*) took a lively interest in the affair, and excited both the Pope and the bishop of Constance to proclaim the summoning of the rector as a profanation of the rights of the church. The bishop ordered the rector not to appear before the civil court, and the fear of ecclesiastical censures having caused him to comply with this injunction, he was condemned to leave for ever the canton and territory of Lucerne within four and twenty hours. The inhabitants of *Udlingenschwil* were ordered to proceed to the election of a new rector ; whereupon the bishop insisted upon *Ander Matt* being

---

re-established in his rectory, and his offence being judged before the consistory ; and he refused the admission of the elected rector. The nuncio of the Pope likewise quitted Lucerne early on a Sunday without taking leave, and retired to *Altorf*, in the canton of *Uri**. He published a violent account of this pretended violation of the rights of the church ; which induced the council of one hundred at Lucerne to complain to the Pope of the indiscreet departure of the nuncio, of his improper interference in the business of the rector of *Udlingenschwil,* and of his distorted representation of the whole affair. They begged his Holiness would not sacrifice them to the ill-will of those who wished to ground their own elevation on their ruin; that the dance, which had caused such scandal, was a mere temporal concern, which from time immemorial had always been allowed, or prohibited by the civil magistrate; that the conduct of the rector in this respect was a sedition against the constituted authorities of the country; that the summoning of a clergyman was an emanation of the rights of sovereignty, and the banishment of the guilty priest connected with those rights.

"The bishop of *Constance* remonstrated to the senate of Lucerne, that the exemption from the civil jurisdiction was not a personal concern, but the property of the clergy in general; that the jurisdiction of the bishops had been instituted by Christ, sanctioned by the apostles, practised by the fathers, and confirmed by the emperors. The senate answered, that the exemption from civil jurisdiction which had been granted to the clergy by the benevolence of emperors and kings, and which the senate acknowledged, never could be stretched to the ruin of the civil power ; that the object of this immunity was to enable clergymen more calmly to attend to their vocation as pastors and teachers, and to lead a pious life, and not to serve as a cover for malice, sedition, and revengeful animosity ; that the refractory conduct of the rector, and the interference of the nuncio and of the bishop, has no good end in view. The whole of the Helvetic confederacy having offered their mediation, the senate of Lucerne inquired, whether they were ignorant of the antiquity of the right of the cantons to judge their clergy?

And when the bishop pretended in a farther remonstrance, that the supreme magistrate had no authority to judge the clergy ; that clergymen, from the instant they took orders, ceased to be natural subjects, and were free from all slavery ; the senate replied, that the supreme authority had been wantonly insulted by the banished priest, and that such an insult could be punished by none but the supreme magistrate.

" When the court of Rome, the bishop of *Constance,* and the nuncio, made further attempts to induce the senate to submit to their views, the senators of Lucerne took a solemn oath to preserve the rights of the state, and not to be deterred by any menaces, papal excommunications, or other means : And in order to act still more in unison, they assembled all the citizens of the city of Lucerne, acquainted them with every step they had taken in the affair, and informed them of the opposition of the court of Rome, and its menaces. Animated with an ardent zeal for the preservation of the rights inherited from their forefathers, the citizens thanked the senators for the ardour with which they had defended those privileges, begged that they would continue zealous in maintaining them, and promised to assist them with their blood and treasure in case of need."

This contention ended by a compromise : the banished priest continued in banishment ; and the priest chosen to succeed him gave place to another successor. — But, the Swiss were not always so condescending,

" During the great quarrel between the emperor and the Pope, in the Year 1247, Zurich, Uri, Schwitz, and Underwalden continued faithful to the emperor (whose subjects they were,) in spite of the excommunication of the Pope. The refractory priests who refused to officiate, were expelled from Zurich, and their property confiscated ; and when the Pope afterwards permitted those priests to return to the town and officiate, they were not admitted. Zurich prefered to be eighteen years without any divine service, rather than to submit to any infraction of their civil rights."

" Eighteen years without divine service !" And this, because the Pope assumed a power of which he ought not, as a Christian bishop, to be so much as suspected—a power to judge *in temporals.* Nor was this assump-

---

* Pasquin at Rome exhibited on this occasion this witticism:
Lux olim Lucerna fuit, lux Uria nunc est.

tion confined by the Pope to the comparatively minor states which compose the Helvetic confederacy. A polite note of his Holiness to the King of France, shews explicitly enough how far the Pope could extend his *civil* interference: while the no less complimentary answer of his Majesty the King of France, exhibits his courtly manners to great advantage:

"Boniface, bishop, servant of the servants of God, to Philip, king of France, fear God, &c. We wish you to know that you are subordinate to us both in spiritual and temporal concerns.———

Econtra.

"Philip, by the grace of God king of France, to Boniface, acting as Pope, little or no greeting. Your superlative foolishness is hereby informed, that in temporal concerns we are not subordinate to any one."———

After this specimen of singular *politesse*, the reader will be little surprised to learn that Papal Bulls were treated with but moderate respect in France; and, indeed, elsewhere. It is scarcely possible that he should not have heard of the famous Bull *In Cœna Domini*, and of the contentions to which it gave rise. They were not confined to one country. They extended, more or less over Europe. In some places the Bull was received in parts; in others it was rejected in the whole. Such were the scandals occasioned by a mandate which continues to form part of the Roman ritual; and of which the following is a brief history.

"Pope Pius IV. lived but a short time after the conclusion of the Council of Trent, dying on the 9th December 1565. On the 7th of January 1566, Cardinal Michele Ghisilieri, surnamed Alessandrino, because in 1504, he was born in the village of Bosco near Alessandriaĵ.

was elected in his place. He was a monk of the order of St. Dominick; and, by the good offices of Cardinal Caraffa, was made commissary of the Inquisition, and because he exercised that office with great severity and boldness, when Caraffa came to be Pope, in 1517, he made him a cardinal. Ghisilieri being raised to the Papacy, took the name of Pius V. and having imbibed the maxims of Paul IV. he was a terrible enemy to the sectarians; and in the beginning of his Pontificate, he caused Giulio Zoanneto, and Pietro Cornesecco to be burnt, only because it had been discovered that they kept a correspondence with the sectarians in Germany, and in Italy with Vittoria Colonna and Giulia Gonzaga, who were suspected of heresy. The most learned Aonio Paleario had the same unhappy fate, who, when he heard his sentence, said, *Inquisitionem esse sicam districtam in literatos*. Pius had conceived too high an opinion of the papal dignity, and, on the contrary, too low of the imperial; and, like Paul IV. he was persuaded, that he could exert the authority of the Holy See over princes, more than was consistent with spiritual power. He looked upon himself to be superior to them in every thing, and made it a matter of conscience to keep up that authority; therefore whatever he did was out of pure zeal for religion and discipline: so that by this severity of manners, and his having furnished such great sums for carrying on the war against the Turks, he acquired the reputation of sanctity, and in our time we have seen him canonized by Pope Clement XI.

"In the beginning of the second year of his Pontificate he issued out that so famous and remarkable bull, *In Cœna Domini*, which every year on Holy Thursday is published in Rome; whence that day takes its name. He published it in the year 1567. The following year he published another, wherein he added many things, and made it much more terrible.† He commanded that all the christian world should obey it, without any other publication but that made in Rome; that every year on Holy Thursday it should be read from the pulpit in all parishes to the people; that copies of it should be affixed on the doors of all churches and confessionaries; and that it should be the rule of discipline and

---

* The Pope writes: "Bonifacius, episcopus, servus servorum Dei Philippo Francorum Regi Deum time, &c. Scire te volumus quod *in spiritualibus et temporalibus nobis subes.*"
† To which the king answers: "Philippus Dei gratia Francorum Rex Bonifacio se gerenti pro summo Pontifice salutem modicam seu nullam. Sciat tua maxima fatuitas *in temporalibus nos alicui non subesse*"
‡ Thun. lib. 39. Hist.

* Idem, loc. cit.
† We find both these Bulls in tom. 4. of Chioccarello's MS. Giurisd.

conscience, not only to the bishops, but to the penitentiaries and confessors. It contains many articles; for that which is handed about, and is seen upon the confessionaries, is curtailed and very much abridged.

"This bull, besides an infinite number of extravagancies, intirely overthrows the power of princes, deprives them of the sovereignty of their dominions, and subjects their government to the censure and correction of Rome. Besides those from the 19th article to the 29th, we read in *Toledo's Summa de instruct. sacerdotum* eighteen articles, all tending to that end.

"In the 19th article, all favourers of heretics are excommunicated, thereby putting it in the Pope's power to excommunicate christian princes, who, either for the defence of their dominions, or other reasons of state, should make leagues with heretics and infidels; giving the people to understand, that the prince that does so, has not a sound faith, and may be dethroned, as Henry III. of France, a catholic prince, was served, only because he took the people of Geneva under his protection, which gave the Jesuits a handle to teach, that the people might rebel against him.[*]

"In the 20th article, all those are excommunicated who appeal from the decrees, sentences, and other orders of the Pope to a general Council. All universities, colleges, and chapters that hold or teach that the Pope is subject to a general Council, are excommunicated and interdicted; so that, not only all the articles established in this bull, but all the constitutions, decrees and sentences of the court of Rome, are to be obeyed and received under pain of excommunication and interdiction.

In the 21st article, all princes are excommunicated, who in their dominions lay on new tolls, taxes and customs, or augment the old, excepting in cases where they are allowed by law, or by special licence obtained from the apostolic see.

In 1582, in the government of the Duke D'Ossuna, the pernicious effects of this doctrine too manifestly appeared; for it having been resolved by all the *Seggi* of the city of Naples, excepting those of Capuana and Popolo, to lay a new duty of a ducat upon each hogshead of wine that should be drank, the people in a tumultuous manner declared that they would not pay it, in which they

were encouraged by many spiritual fathers, who openly declared, all those that had had a hand in laying on that duty, were guilty of a mortal sin; and among the rest, there was a Spanish capuchin, named Fra' Lupo, who, with great fervency, declaiming in all the corners of the city, and preaching and protesting to all, that the judgments of God would light upon them if that duty should be paid; the viceroy was forced to turn him immediately out of the city. But notwithstanding, the people could never be brought to consent to it, and the duty was laid aside; and the year following all means possible were used, in order to dispose them to give a new donative of 1,200,000 ducats:[*] Whence proceeded that pernicious doctrine of the casuists, with which they direct the consciences of men, and insinuate to them from their confessionaries, that it is lawful for the people to cheat the custom-house of the duties, because they are imposed without the papal license.

"In 1568 the city of Naples, in order to prevent the raising the price of bread higher than it is at present, having fallen upon an expedient to give the corn to the bakers at a lower price than it cost the city, in consideration of which the bakers were to pay a carlino[†] for each bushel they should bake, whereby the city would have gained more than 60,000 ducats yearly; and a proclamation having been issued for the payment of the said carlino per bushel, 108,000 ducats had been offered for two years, and some resolved to offer 120,000, which would have made up the city's loss in the price of corn: and a day being appointed for entering into a contract with whoever should offer most, the *Seggio* of Nido retracted on account of the bull *In Cœna Domini,* whereby all those are excommunicated who impose taxes or customs in their dominions, saying, that they were likewise liable to the excommunications contained in the same bull; and those who were about to enter into the said contract were also under the same apprehension, although the churches, clergy, and ecclesiastical persons were exempted from this tax.

Now, if the question were not on so momentous a concern as Religion, we

---

* Richer. Apolog. Jo. Garsen, pag. 194.

* Tom Costo, por. 3. del Compendio al Collen. lib. 3.

† About Sixpence.

doubt not but what there are many among us who would like well enough to appeal to his Holiness against new taxes; who would delight to see the Chancellor of the Exchequer *pitted* against Pope Pius; or the Lords of the Treasury against the Treasurers of the Church. Would the Pope, indeed, furnish *the necessary*, and relieve us fom forty or fifty millions of unfunded debt, though it might terrify " the Jews" of the Stock Exchange, we should feel ourselves much obliged to him; and as it passes for a maxim, never to be questioned among the true Sons of the Church, that " the Church's Treasury is always full," the only difficulty would be to persuade the Bank Directors to discount bills drawn on *that* Treasury; which, notwithstanding their habits of meditating much more on their interest here, than on their interests hereafter, they might possibly be induced to do, by a kind epistle *sub plumbo*, with the seal of the Fisherman's ring, and the Apostolic Benediction annexed, in the first place;—or, in case of contumacy, a hearty sentence of anathema, and excommunication; with curses in abundance, and a glowing ————ation at the close.

Such a document, most certainly, we should advise might be " *preserved:*" and for the proper explanation of this term, we beg leave to refer to a very laudable custom in Spain, where Bulls that are " suspected of being suspicious" are most reverendly attended by the proper officers, and with triple congees equally profound and expressive, are carefully deposited in a chest with three keys, among the *arcana imperii*. Such an instance we have in this Report, on occasion of a Bull sent from the Pope, confirming the nomination of a Bishop, in which the misjudging eyes of Spanish jealousy saw, or fancied they saw, a something, or several somethings, altogether foreign to the subject, and incompatible with the welfare of the State.; for the Bishop was enjoined to do————but, what signifies what the Bishop was enjoined to do? when the King's Advocate, who

judges, *ex officio*, on such affairs, perversely reported, and petitioned, that,

" The rescript received from Rome, of his Holiness Pius VII. confirming the election made by his majesty, of the reverend father in God D. Isidoro de Celis, (heretofore a regular priest of the order instituted for the comfort of the dying,) to the bishopric of Segovia,—he says the Bull sent to his majesty, enjoined him to recognise the new bishop, should be kept in the royal archives, for the security and preservation of the royal prerogative; for as to the persons newly elected to bishops sees, they need not any such bull to authorize them to take possession.

" The bull of Vasallos, directed to those of the bishoprick of Segovia, is likewise to be *preserved* [*retener*;] to which effect the king's advocate interposes a corresponding supplication for his Holiness, for many obvious reasons; since neither the provincial council in former times, when the metropolitan used to confirm the canonical elections of bishops; nor the Holy See, after the reservations, ought to interfere in these temporal lordships emanating from the crown.

" So that a note should be inserted in this bull, stating, that it ought to be kept [*preserved—retenida*,] *in order that it may not in any way, or at any period of time be used;* and instead of it should there at any time be vassals in the bishopric of Segovia, the royal cedula investing him with the temporal lordships of this see will be sent to the new prelate.

That the King's advocate was mistaken in what he saw, or fancied he saw, or that he saw double on this occasion, or that he was troubled with visions of ghosts and hobgoblins, is beyond all doubt: for, that the Pope should insert into a bull of confirmation, any thing not relevant to the subject, or that he should covertly, introduce principles, or expressions, in such Bulls, which he would not dare to introduce openly, or, with any view to turn them to his advantage afterwards, is a suspicion not to be endured. And in fact, such suspicion could only arise in minds hardened by too frequent, and too elaborate contemplation of Papal Bulls; as too long a contemplation of the sun becomes a powerful cause of blindness.

There remains, however, one point to be cleared up : for, as the Pope interposes his judgment on the *permissibility* of books, who can tell how closely that judgment may affect ourselves ? For aught we know the PANORAMA itself may figure on the list of prohibited books, either now or hereafter ;— and then—what will become of all our hopes of being made SAINTS ? Or, if we should be happy enough to arrive within ken of St. Peter, at heaven's gate, and he should incline to turn the key in our favour—which, by the bye, is rather doubtful, all things considered—just as we are crossing the threshhold, perhaps, up comes a decision from the Censors of the Vatican, and the whole corps is remanded to a place too dreadful to think of!!!

" In the bull of 1515 Pope Leo X. not only renewed the attempt of Alexander VI. against the civil government, but even joined to the sword of the church, or excommunication, the temporal penalties of confiscation, fines, and suspensions (from office). He suddenly introduced a new public law, which laid the foundation for the usurpations that followed soon after, and opened the door to the censure of books, the court of Rome presently beginning to meddle with the examination of works which had nothing dogmatic in them, and to inflict punishments foreign to the power of the church.

" The bull of 1520, and that *In Cœna Domini* of Adrian and Clement, caused disturbances of another kind ; for as they prohibited all heretical books in general, without mentioning the names of their authors, under the penalty of excommunication, it was necessary not only to know the books with regard to their doctrine, but also that every one should be a judge of that doctrine ; and as this private judgment never could be uniform, the confusion may be easily imagined which resulted from such general and indefinite prohibitions.

" These spiritual and political disturbances called forth efficacious means to guard against them ; and as the temporal power was really sacrificed in the aforementioned bulls, it was the first that thought of the wholesome and happy regulation of the *Indices Expurgatorii* (lists of those books which the Popes think fit to prohibit) which has since been adopted by the church.

The regulation of the *Index* insured the temporal power against the infection of its subjects by satyrical, seditious and heretical writings, at the same time preventing the ill understood policy of the court of Rome, from forbidding along with those books the reading of those authors who supported the rights of the states, and settled the just limits of the priesthood.

We hinted at some of the prohibitions contained in the last edition of the *Index*, in vol. viii. p. 1667, N. S. and we hinted at the reasons, too, of such prohibitions ; valid, they certainly are, in all points, as any Jesuit could prove, with the greatest ease ;—were they not all employed on matters more analogous to the spirit of their Order, of which the present Report contains evidence, in a memorandum by Lord William Bentick, dated so long ago as January 1813. To what extent conversions have since been effected,—who can tell ?

" With respect to *young English or Irishmen who have come to Sicily to obtain holy orders*, it appears that *since the restoration of the Jesuits in Sicily, about six or seven years, these restless and active brethren, have procured in all nineteen eleves from the British islands ; of these, five have returned in holy orders, two died in Palermo, and nine are now here.*

" The objects which the Jesuits may have had in view, in thus extending their search for pupils, are of course as various, as are the branches of their wily policy ; but as it has been boasted, that *one of them who has returned* (and who by the way was accounted half mad when here, and may therefore be a good fanatic) *has laboured successfully in the work of conversion, one may be permitted to conclude, that hopeless as such a pursuit must be, it has not been entirely left out of their speculations.*"

The Dessert, a Poem; to which is added the Tea, with notes and engravings. By the author of "the Banquet,"* 8vo. 5s. 6d. Baldwin, Cradock, and Joy, and T. Hookham, Jun. 1819.

The man of genius, it has been said, *takes* his place in society, it is not *given* him. He may conceal his name, his rank, his station; his talents are not so easily hid. Various are the surmises started respecting the author of the " Banquet:" although we hail the appearance of a new production from the pen of this agreeable unknown, we confess it does not better enable us to pierce the veil of mystery under which he continues to shroud himself.

The Banquet has been attributed to various writers; but whether, as we have heard it asserted, it is the composition of a well-known favorite of the public, or whether the work of a rising candidate for Fame, we confess our ignorance and our inability to attribute it with any degree of probability to any modern poet of our acquaintance. By this avowal we mean no disparagement to the Banquet, nor do we insinuate a comparison injurious to the merits of contemporary poems: we allude only to a feature, a character of originality, a vivacity of manner, a vein of *learned pleasantry*, if we may so call it, which distinguishes the style of this author's poetry, and stamps it with a character of genius peculiarly his own. The easy and playful freedom however which he is wont to assume, is apt now and then to degenerate into a curelessness of manner, of which we would warn him to beware. Led away by an exuberance of fancy, he seems sometimes almost to soar above both his subject and his readers; on the whole it is easy to perceive he is a bard indulging himself in intercourse with the muses, less for the entertainment of the public than for his own gratification. Those indeed, who roam unrestrained, and unchecked, thro' the haunts of Parnassus, are some-

times led to forget how closely they are watched by the argus eyes of unsparing criticism, ready to detect the slightest trespass on a domain which would be too alluring " had she not marked it for her own," had she not vowed vengeance on the head of the intruder who dares to disregard the severity of her penal code.

We do not however, feel ourselves authorized to pronounce any such denunciation in the present instance; on the contrary, we would invite our poet by a little attention to the hints we have thrown out, to pursue the path he is so successfully treading, and in which we feel little hesitation in predicting to him the success due to his talents.

We are supported in our opinion by that of the Northern Bard,. whose unqualified approbation, as may be gathered from the dedication to him of the present work, has not been withheld from the merits of the Banquet.

In this second display of his poetic powers, the author affords his readers little less entertainment than on a former occasion; the Banquet would not have been complete without a Dessert: " I have therefore," says the lively writer, " thought it incumbent upon me to endeavour to supply the former deficiency, and to spread the board again before my indulgent reader with such delicacies as still remained in the already exhausted stores of a sterile imagination."

The imagination of no man ever less merited the accusation of *sterility*: It is rather of the opposite quality, we have to complain, yet we may still admit there is less of whim and humour in this work than in the preceding; the Dessert is more chastely elegant—the craving appetite has been satisfied, and the elegant superfluities of refined luxury replace the more substantial profusions with which the table was lately covered.

Although we feel strongly inclined to quote a few extracts from such parts as have appeared to us to boast superior claims to notice, we feel some hesi-

---

* See an analysis of this poem, page 211 to 216 of the present volume.

tation in deranging the regularity and delicate freshness of this well-ordered Dessert; we fear to rob the peaches of their bloom, or the wines of their flavor, lest by culling from the one, or dipping into the others, we should deprive our readers of the relish they ought to bring to the repast.

As the appetite, however, is likely to be excited rather than palled by a view of the ornamental apparatus of the feast, we will indulge in a short quotation where the brilliancy of the service of glass is described in peculiarly happy colours.

How smooth the surface, luminous the mass !
What scintillating streams of light illume,
And with their vivid pencils tint the room !
Some to the ceiling mount and mock the eye,
With fancied rainbows in a mimic sky ;
Low on the floor, some disregarded fall,
Some paint the pictures on the storied wall.
The modest violet with a tend'rer hue,
Retires behind bold indigo and blue,
Blended with these the gaudy yellow seen,
Delights the view with eye-reviving green.
The glaring orange with its tawny glow
And limitary red, complete the bow.
What art to fashion thus the brittle block
To graceful forms, from the mis-shapen rock !
The convex cover, the tureen concave,
And vase serener than the chrystal wave.
The omphaloptic stud,—cerulean cup
Where Jove from Ganymede might nectar sup.
Diaphanous decanter, bowl enchas'd,
With imitative stars and crescents grac'd ;
By cunning finger, wheel, and lathe, and sand,
Endow'd with full prismatic powers they stand.
Tho' lavish hand of opulence and power,
Shou'd shed of gems the inestimable shower,
In vain wou'd their contrasted lustre vie,
With rays of this coruscant galaxy.

Previous to this dazzling display, something of a *sweeter* nature is offered in so luxurious a detail of elaborate confectionary, corrected nevertheless, here and there with such occasional mixture of satirical acerbity, as to prevent the luscious treat from cloying on the palate.

See sugar there that with the rainbow vies,
To grottos sink, to spiry temples rise :
Secure in crystallis'd Palazzo's stow'd,
Slim biscuit figures make their sweet abode ;
In fresh-baked bricks, St. James's turrets lower,
And in thick battlements of ice, the tower :
On Gallic toys the English eye regales,
The Louvre, Bagatelle, Madrid, Versailles.
The Loves and Graces, and their Paphian queen
Shower *comfits* down, in hail of red and green.
From secret lurking place the urchins strike,
And bid you covet *what* and *whom* they like.
Warm with fresh fire tho' torrified and hard,
Amours of Sappho, Werter, Abelard ;
Of Ovid, of Propertius, and Tibullus,
Candied and clarifi'd the sweet Catullus ;

Group'd with Lestrygones the Laocoon,
Phyllis, her almond-tree and Demophoon,
A coal-brown Proserpine and black Corœin,
Hoary with frost young Cycnus and Adonis ;
Here Asia's florid birds, her ape and monkey,.
And there Silenus on unsaddled donkey :
Astride Bucephalus, young Ammon enters
With sirens, elephants and hippocentaars :
Elizabeth, Rousseau, the Swiss Lavater, .
L' Heros de Quatre-Bras, and Henri quatre.
Objects like these, astonishing as rare
Shall edify your noble guests, and fair.

Be cautious how with ardour indiscreet
You overturn these trophies of the great :
At least allow some qualified existence
To what of hundreds makes the frail subsistence
Destructive heroes who with fire and sword,
So many thousands when alive *devour'd*,
When dead, *as meet*, shall furnish on this plan
Support for nobleman and artisan.
These too must fall, in dust again must lie,
What monument of art can Time's sharp tooth
	defy !

A fitter regimen for your's prescribe ;
More tempting presents your attention bribe.
Lo ! nodding branches bend with auburn fruit,
That grow all seasons, and all fancies suit :
The citron's smooth, the pine's hirsuter coat,
The cherry paste, the strawberry compote :
Pellucid plum and apricot opaque,
The Norfolk biffin and the Savoy cake,
And mass wherein the blushing damsons freeze
Their mellow pulp to well-dissembled cheese :
Amber ginseng, and purified cringoes,
Regalias, and imperials and meringue's.—

Nor genius curb, till charms to charms unite,
Fruits tempt the tongue, and flowers the eye
	invite ;
The dish by ruddy-cheek'd Pomona crown'd,
Let Flora deck with lily-fingers round.
Your centre rise pyramidal and bold,
Where mimic gems may rival real gold.
The loving myrtle and fraternal vine,
With leaves alternate broad and slender twine ;
As if some brawny youth with manly grasp
His slim-arm'd sister round the waist should
	clasp.—
The humble hare's-foot may run round the plinth,
Hounds-tongue, hawk's-beard, hearts-ease or
	hyacinth.
The pallid jasmine to contrast the rose,
To shame the lily, the carnation blows :
Here wan from arctic snows Linnæa sink,
Camellia's there, Japan's fair blossoms shrink ;
Whilst from the Icelandic-moss, congealing bed !
The bright Reaumuria lifts her tropic head.
Relish, admire, bewilder'd connoisseurs,
All these are yours—all these are comfitures !
Go on and cultivate the sweet parterre,
Who but would think the Hesperides were there :
Our herbal such, can any mortal miss
To imbibe a taste for botany like this ?
Sweetest of studies, oh ! delicious hour,
How greedily our *lesson* we *devour !*

We come now to a part interesting to most of our readers ;—there is something in the name of " Tea" congenial to the feelings of the English ; and the word " tea-table" never fails to conjure up so many images of home born comforts and delights, that it is sure to create a pleasing association of ideas to our minds. How often when basking in the sun-shine of more favored skies, and feasting on the luxuries of foreign climates, has the British traveller sighed at the recollection of his long lost but never to be forgotten tea-table at home! frequently as this domestic scene has furnished a topic of interest, our bard has found the secret of setting it in an entirely new light. After the superb scenery with which our eyes and senses have been regaled, we here find an agreeable repose; the wholesome influence of our favourite beverage is offered to allay the fumes of more costly liquors, and we yield to the invitation, when

" The mantling cup bewitching beauty fills,
The flavorous drop Affection's hand instills."

Here it is indeed that the British fair shines forth in all her charms. However fashionably dissipated at other times, she here assumes, or at least appears for a season to assume, the domestic character, that ever fascinating garb of innocence and virtue! The winning yet nameless grace with which an Englishwoman presides at her tea-table can never be equalled by the foreign fair, however practised in the arts of pleasing. The author has felt this, and the delicate compliment he here takes the opportunity of paying to his beauteous countrywomen while it must effectually recommend him to their favor, shall for the present close what we have to say on a subject which has perhaps already led us farther than we intended.

Come, sprightly daughters of this favor'd Isle,
With these enchanting streams the eve beguile ;
Let amber currents glitter as they flow,
And tawny tides refreshing odours blow.
Tho' brilliantly they shine and warm and pure,
More clear your eyes can sparkle and allure ;
Those vapours fragrant as the wave is bright,
Yet sweeter breathe your accents, and invite.
With marge emboss'd the babbling fountain stands,
And golden vases court your silver hands :
The glittering cover lift, and lo, beneath,
Sweet as your breath, and snowy as your teeth,
The elastic forceps draws the crust refin'd,
To enrich the honey on your lip design'd.—
Vain boast !—the essence of the Ortygian hive,
Distils no drop that with that balm shall strive.

Such the sweet dish, the liquor, and the hand,
What cynic—nay, what stoic could withstand ?

How shall the bard, whose thirst Apollo arms,
Resist this sorcery of confederate charms ?
What nerves can brave the batteries of those eyes
When hidden trains of gunpowder surprise ?

These flints refin'd with fiercer fire within,
Now boast, like you, their alabaster skin ;
No wonder, in these calices, the work
Of Hebe's hand that Cupid likes to lurk ;
And when your fingers launch the unerring dart,
It strikes the tongue and quivers in the heart.
The mantling cup, bewitching beauty fills ;
The flavorous drop, Affection's hand instils ;
And from the top as cordial balm we skim,
Arch Smiles and Graces hover round the brim.—
Ah ! who would wish his senses to regain
Who from such philters life and love can drain ? ;

The notes, though they do not present so great a variety of classical elucidation as the Banquet, (the subjects of these poems indeed does not admit of them,) are nevertheless both ingenious and pleasing, and combine both amusement and information. We select one, in which the author has given nearly all that is known with correctness relative to the tea-plant.

Kempfer's designation of Tea is, Thea frutex, folio cerasi, flore rosæ sylvestris fructu unicocco, bicocco et ut plurimum tricocco.——Leaf like the cherry, flower like the dog-rose ;

The Chinese call it Theh, the Japonese tshanok, the Russians tchai.

The plant is evergreen, but not odoriferous ; the outer bark is offensive, the leaves astringent and bitter, and when taken fresh from the tree, have a convulsive effect on the nerves. The best Tea in Japan is grown at Udsi near Mesco. Udse tschai—tacke jsacke tschai.—Imperial tea —a purveyor from the Court attends to the growth, management, and transportation of this precious article,—sees that the rows in which it is planted are regularly swept twice a day, that the gatherers are fed upon no offensive food that might contaminate their breath, that they perform regular ablutions in hot and cold baths, and above all, that their hands are covered with the finest kid gloves before they break the leaves, which they select one by one from the first buds in spring. This Tea is curled on irons, not like our curling irons, but large plates on which the leaves are rolled by the hand, they are then pounded and drank in hot water. Tea loses so much by the voyage, that the above writer says, he could never get any fit to drink out of Japan.

The Emperor of China is no less choice in his Tea than his neighbour.

Linnæus reckons two species of Tea. Thunbergh only one with two varieties, class polyandria, order monogynia.

The Tea plant flourishes in Tonquin, Japan, and the north and south of China, but like the ware which contains it, that which is manufactured at Nankin is the best.

At three years old the leaves are fit to gather, the stem has then attained the height of about six feet, and is cut down.

The bohea or black is rather more dressed and washed and curled than the green, which gives the further more colour and less flavour, and renders it less deleterious as well as less palatable: of the latter there are three sorts, viz. imperial, hyson, and singol: of the former five; souchong, cambo, congo, pekoe, and common bohea.

The Chinese make their tea with boiling water, but dilute it afterwards with cold, and take it without any adventitious admixture whatever.

Giavanni Botero is the first European who speaks of this plant; his work was published in 1590. He does not however mention the word Tea, and only describes the use made of it in China. Tea was first brought to Europe by the Dutch in 1610, to England by Lord Arlingtou in 1666, a year in which the metropolis suffered from three fatal scourges, fire, pestilence, and *poison.* The effects of the two former are almost forgot, those of the latter seem more lasting. Green Tea was first used in 1715, when it was as high as 60s. a pound.

If Tea resembles the rose, coffee is still more like the jasmine.

The word Coffee, which with little variation obtains in the European languages, seems derived from the Turkish cahoube.

Whether the adoption of this vegetable to domestic use is owing to the piety of a chief of Arabian dervises or monks, or of muftis who wished to extend his prayers beyond the bounds of ordinary devotion, is not ascertained, but we are told its powers were first discovered by the effect it had on goats which had eaten of it, and were kept capering all night.

The best Coffee grows to three times the height of Tea, stems erect, bark brown, leaves oblong, oval flowers in axillary clusters, pure white, fragrant, transient; the fruit like a cherry but growing in bunches. It may be raised from seeds but they must be sown as soon as ripe. It is supposed to excite a cheerfulness which lasts many hours, and which is not succeeded by langour or debility, to diffuse over the whole frame a glow of health, and a sense of ease and well being, which are extremely delightful; existence is felt to be a positive enjoyment, and the mental powers are rendered uncommonly active and acute.

It will be thought unfortunate, perhaps, that the writer of this note did not take a larger dose before he began. *Pour égayer la matiere,* and to prove its enlivening powers therefore I shall subjoin the anecdote of a Mr. Leauté, Docteur en Medicine de la Faculté de Paris.

He was called in one day to attend a person who appeared to be in a very dangerous condition. The patient had applied to a notorious quack for the cure of an obstinate cough, with which he had been long incommoded. The mountebank prescribed his remedy, and a most *efficacious cure* it proved, for it not only stopped the cough and expectoration, but all other secretions also. Phlebotomy was resorted to, veins were opened in the legs and arms, but without effect. The circulation had been completely arrested; the lymphatics clogged, and the blood seemed to be set and coagulated. But our skilful Esculapius was not to be thus baffled; he administered six large consecutive dishes of the strongest coffee, unadulterated with sugar or cream, and in less than one hour by its powerful operation the blood flowed freely from the aper-

tures, and the sufferer was immediately restored to health, and spirits. What became of the cough is not mentioned.

Letters from the North of Italy, addressed to Henry Hallam, Esq. By William Stewart Rose, Esq. 8vo. 2 vols. 18s. Murray, London, 1819.

Mr. Rose is advantageously known to the public as a poet, of no contemptible rank; and though we cannot but regret that his pages are frequently disfigured by flippant remarks, conveyed in a flippant style, yet we are in justice bound to state that he has presented the public with much curious and valuable information relative to Italy, and Italian Literature, that would otherwise have remained in obscurity.

Our travellers object was, to make trial of the celebrated baths of Abano, in the vicinity of Padua, for a paralytic affection, which had deprived him of the use of one side: and he proceeded from Paris by the *Voiturier,* which he recommends, upon the whole, as being the best mode of travelling across the Simplon into Italy. In describing his journey over that stupendous mountain, he takes occasion to introduce some pleasing anecdotes relative to the benevolent Monks of St. Bernard and their celebrated dogs. For these we shall gladly make room.

" You will hear with pleasure, that the race of these useful beasts (I mean the dogs) is not, as I understood in England, extinguished; there existing a fine race of puppies, who, literally speaking, promise to tread in the steps of their progenitors.

" The merits of these, though in themselves sufficiently great, have, however, been much exaggerated. They neither carry provisions to the strayed, nor go, unaccompanied, in search of those buried in snow. But they are endowed, as it should appear, with a very extraordinary instinct, which enables them to distinguish the solid path, though covered with snow, where the deviation of a step might plunge their followers into an abyss. They are, therefore, to be considered as the guides of the mountain, and it was in the discharge of this duty that the most experienced of the tribe found their grave. A courier, who was passing the St. Bernard, stopped at the convent for shelter, and after a short stay, insisted on proceeding. As the weather was dangerous, the good monks all but knelt to him, to divert him from his purpose: but he was an old stager and was obstinate. They, therefore, did all they could for his protection, and furnished him with three men and three dogs for guides, these three dogs being the only ones fit for service, the rest of the family consisting of two bitches who gave suck. The party had not proceeded far, when they were overwhelmed by an *avalanche*, and to complete the catastrophe, the courier's brother and brother-in-law, who had come out to meet and assist him, were buried in another, on the opposite side of the mountain.

" To return to the dogs.—Though they do not proceed alone to disinter the buried, they do indeed, by scratching, indicate where they are to be found; but most dogs, and particularly our sheep dogs, will do the like to carcasses of any animal, covered by the snow.

" The utility of the convent of St. Bernard, in the situation in which it is placed, is so obvious, that whilst Bonaparte smoked out all the drones of the plains, he left several mountain-convents, and by endowing this with an additional estate in Lombardy, most considerably increased its revenues. In this he did well; for independently of the general hospitality which is exercised by the monks, the ordinary expences of the establishment must be enormous in a place which is inaccessible by carriages, and where a pound of wood literally bears the same price as a pound of bread. A very different system has been followed by the successors of Buonaparte.

" A magnificent building which he had begun, a sort of caravansera, on the top of the *Simplon*, has been left half finished, but things are infinitely worse on *Mount Cenis*. Buonaparte had there, as well as here, constructed several houses, termed *refuges*, at different distances, for the shelter of passengers in dangerous months, and endowed them with slight privileges, such as that of selling wine and provisions, duty free.—It was amongst the early acts

of the King of Sardinia to abrogate these, and the *refuges* of *Mount Cenis* are lost to the traveller.

" To return to the monks of St. Bernard.—Of the mode in which they spend their revenues, as well as of the manner in which they fulfil the objects of their institution, the anecdote which follows may serve as a specimen. An enterprizing English party, consisting of men and women, took shelter in the convent during a fall of snow. The monks fed them and their horses as long as they could, giving up their bread to the beasts, when they had no more crude grain to bestow on them. The guests had then, therefore, no choice but to decamp. But how to get the horses over the snow, which was yet too soft to support them? The ingenuity and activity of the monks found an expedient. They turned out with their servants, and placing blankets before the animals, which were carried forwards and extended afresh, as soon as passed over, conducted men, women, and beasts in safety over the mountain."

Mr. Rose, having now entered Italy, was hastening by the direct route to the place of his destination; but, on stopping to bait at a certain town, a few stages beyond Aronna, he was turned back from the Austrian states in consequence of some informality in his passport, and was obliged to make a retrogade movement. He therefore pursued his journey over the Bocchetta, to Genoa. The following description of the effect which the Coup d'oeil of that magnificent city produced on his mind, is, perhaps, one of the best passages in his Letters.

" Genoa," he says, " is most impressive in its general exterior. The figure which it forms, approaches nearly to that of a crescent. It is backed, as I have before observed, by a mountain, which is fringed here and there with low oak-wood and olives, and it looks down upon a beautiful bay."

" Imagine, then, to yourself, a city, with something of a theatric form, at the base of a mountain, the sloping sides of which are gay with suburban palaces, and gardens full of colonnades of trellis work, covered with the red oleander now in one blaze of bloom; add an atmosphere and a sun, precisely such as you see represented in the vivid paintings of the Venetian school, and you have such as I saw it in the month of August."

After staying a few days in this interesting spot, Mr. Rose proceeded, by Stradella, Tortona, Cremona, Mantua, Verona, and Padua, to Abano: and as his account of the mud baths is both curious and new, we shall select it for the gratification of our readers.

" The muds," he informs us, are taken out of the hot basons in which they are found, " and applied, either generally, or partially, as the case of the patient may demand. These are thrown by, after having been used, and, at the conclusion of the season, returned to the hot fountains, where they are left till the ensuing spring, that they may impregnate themselves anew with the mineral virtues which these are supposed to contain. The most obvious of these, to an ignorant man, are salt and sulphur. The muds are, on being taken out, intensely hot, and must be kneaded and stirred some time before they can be borne. When applied, an operation which very much resembles the taking a stucco cast, they retain their heat without much sensible diminution for three-quarters of an hour, having the effect of a slight *rubefacient* on the affected part, and producing a profuse perspiration from the whole body: a disposition which continues more particularly in the part to which they have been applied, when unchecked by cold. Hence heat is considered as so essentially seconding their operations, that this watering-place, or rather mudding-place, is usually nearly deserted by the end of August; though there are some who continue to wallow on through the whole of September.

" The baths, though sometimes considered as a remedy in themselves, are most generally held to be mere auxiliaries to the muds, and usually but serve as a prologue and interlude to the dirty performance which forms the subject of the preceding paragraph, they being supposed to open the pores and dispose the skin to greater susceptibility."

These powerful applications, it appears, are sometimes successful, but Abano has no other recommendation; the air is damp and heavy, and the absence of all usual means of diversion renders it the dullest of all dull places. Our invalid, however, endeavours to pass away the time by making several excursions into the surrounding country; but in these, though it would not be entirely without its reward, we cannot afford space to accompany him: for the same reason we must also pass by his elaborate dissertation on the Malaria, its causes, treatment, and effects; together with the very affecting and apparently faithful picture which he has drawn of the extreme misery of the lower orders in Italy; both of which he dates from Abano. His next remove is to Vicenza, and from the observations he makes there, and in the neighbourhood, on the variety of character in the Italian provinces, on Palladian architecture, on the Improvisatori, &c. we could easily select some very amusing notices, did we not conceive that our readers would rather thank us for the novel and very curious account with which he presents his correspondent, in his last communication from the town above mentioned, of the inhabitants of the Sette Communi, or seven commons, a part of the Vicentine territory. Of this singular race, of whom we believe very little was previously known in this country, we learn from Mr. Rose's very interesting detail, that " they occupy a district containing about eighty-six square Italian miles.

" This area is almost entirely mountainous, and the spot where stands the capital, Asiago, is eight hundred toises above the level of the sea. The whole space, which, in addition to the seven burghs, contains twenty-four villages, is bounded by rivers, alps, and hills. Its most precise limits are the Brenta, to the east, and the Astico to the west; which rivers were called by the Romans, the greater and lesser Medoacus,

" Terrarum septem tractus jacet inter utrumque Medoacum : hic major dicitur, ille minor."

To the north, it has for boundary the Tyrolian Alps, looking towards Valsugna, and to the south, the hills of the line of Morastica as far as Cantrano. These are volcanic, but the tract of the Seven Communes is, itself, calcareous. The population of this, previous to the last dreadful year of pestilence and famine, consisted of thirty thousand souls, but is now diminished to twenty-five thousand.

" The moral character of this people, who till lately enjoyed a comparatively free government, is, like that of most freemen, and more especially of free mountaineers, simple, frank, and good. For the rest, their customs savour of a race long insulated from their neighbours.

" Some of these (but such are principally confined to the less civilized villages) remind one of some of the Celtic usages. Thus they *wake* their dead the night before interment, performing certain games about the bier. If a traveller dies by the way, they plant a cross upon the spot, and all who pass by cast a stone upon his cairn. Some go on certain seasons in the year to the high places and woods, where it is supposed they worshipped their divinities; but the origin of the custom is forgot amongst themselves, they alledging no better reason for the practice than that their fathers did so before them. If a man dies by violence, instead of clothing him, as the dead are usually clothed, they lay him out, with a hat upon his head, and shoes upon his feet, seeking to give him the appearance of a way-faring man ; perhaps as symbolizing one surprised in the great journey of life. If a woman dies in child-birth, they lay her out, set off with all her bridal ornaments. Such are some of the most remarkable of their customs and observances.

" This people, in the simplicity of their modes of life, are sufficient to themselves, cultivating all the productions of agriculture, except the vine, which their mountains are too cold to produce, and manufacturing all necessary articles ; in some of which they drive an export trade to Venice and the circumjacent cities. But the general mode of life is pastoral and migratory. When their mountains are covered with snow, (as they have now been some time,) they descend, in search of warmth and herbage, to the plains, and you may see their beasts feeding on the ramparts of Padua, and the masters hutted under the walls. The same way may be observed of them in all the odd corners and suburbs of Vicenza, and various other low-land towns.

" There is something very remarkable in the physiognomy of this people, who bear about them evident marks of Teutonic origin. This is a wide word ; and, there are those who trace them up to a more certain stem, and will have them to be the remains of the wreck of the Cimbri, defeated by Marius and Catullus. This opinion derives some countenance from Strabo, who, in his fifth book, amongst some other races, whom he plants in this tract of country, specifies the " *Simbri, è quibus nomini Romano hostes extiterunt alique*." But it is always 'to be remembered that he speaks of different nations occupying the country I am describing, and of the scattered Simbri, or Cimbri, as only one amongst several. But, if the region was occupied at first, as it should appear, by various tribes, these mongrel mountaineers mixed their blood, in after times, with several other swarms, issuing out of what has been called the great northern hive. Ancient historians have recorded many such local irruptions, and above all, that in the time of Theodoric ; who assigned to a quantity of northern men, habitations and lands amongst these mountains.

" Instead therefore of considering these people as legitimate sons of the Cimbri, it is surely more consonant to all the evidence of history, to say that the flux and reflux of Teutonic invaders at different periods, deposited this back-water of barbarians; who have no better title to the denomination they have assumed, than the inhabitants of Kent and Sussex have to a Belgic, or those of Suffolk to a Danish origin.

" It should seem, that the fidelity with which they served the lords, to whom they became subject, had won from these petty tyrants many privileges at an early period of modern Italian story, and there exist authentic monuments of those accorded them by the Viscontis and Scaligers. They did not experience less indulgence from the Venetian republic on falling under her dominion ; for, though they were subjected as to many points, to the provincial government of the circle in which they lay, they in many other respects legislated for themselves, and may be said to have had a parliament of their own, whose place of sittings is still to be seen in the town of Asiago. It will, however be scarcely necessary to add, that the Sette Communi lost their privileges on being subjected to the yoke of Austria. They are now entirely subjected to the provincial government of Vicènza."

[*To be continued.*]

Travels in Canada and the United States, in 1816 and 1817. By Lieut. Francis Hall, 14th Light Dragoons, H. P. 8vo. 14s. with a map. Longman and Co. London, 1818.

Mr. Hall is a lively and pleasing writer, whose remarks sometimes degenerate into flippancy, but who has collected a rich harvest of curious and amusing anecdote, as well as of interesting information, relative to the countries he has described. And he has taken notice of many particulars, which preceding travellers in the United States have either passed in silence, or had not similar opportunities of ascertaining.

Our author quitted England on the 20th of January, 1816, and arrived at New York, early in March, whence he proceeded through Albany to Canada. As this part of his route is well known to most readers, we shall not detain them by extracting any of his descriptions of New York and other places that are familiar to them, but shall confine our selections to such circumstances as are not generally known. The following is part of his character of the Americans, which is by no means over-charged.

" One table for meals is stage-coach fare even in England: one bed-room, containing a dozen beds, may be tolerated in a country new to the luxuries of travelling; but the spirit of sociality is a little excessive, when, as I have been told, it enjoins the traveller to halve his bed with whoever arrives too late to procure one for himself. I had often occasion to observe, the Americans have no idea of a private chit-chat betwixt two persons. I several times fancied myself engaged tête-à-tête, when on raising my eyes, I have found a little circle formed round us, fully prepared with reply, rejoinder, or observation, as opportunity might occur: let me, however, add without any intention of rudeness: Impertinence I never met with, though they have sometimes rather a startling plainness in their manner of conveying their sentiments. On our arrival at Poughkeepsie, a plain man stepped from the crowd round the inn-door, and addressing himself to the gentleman I was accompanying, (who had been appointed to the administration of Lower Canada,) wished him joy of his arrival, congratulated him on the peace between the two nations, and concluded by hoping he would not follow the examples of his predecessor; a kind of schooling, to which I believe their own rulers are no strangers. In fact, the art of government, that tremendous state engine, is no mystery here; both men and measures are canvassed with equal freedom; and setting aside the bias of party feeling, with a degree of good sense and information, most probably unique in the mass of any nation on earth. The late war was spoken of with equal detestation by all parties; and so far did they seem from assuming any credit for engaging in it, that each party most studiously shifted the odium to the other. I could perceive none of that rancour against the English which some Englishmen seem anxious to discover.* Individually I met with all civility from all parties; I observed, indeed, among some of the shop-keepers of New York, an indifference towards their customers, more resembling the listlessness of the Portuguese, than the polite alacrity of a London tradesman; but I have no reason to think we came in for a greater share of it from being Englishmen: the want of competition produces the same effect, both on the tradesman and inn-keeper, to whom it gives an air of independence, very commonly attributed to much profounder causes.

* It is a curious circumstance that, while we accuse them of favouring the French, French writers invariably attack them for their rooted, and, as they deem it, blind partiality to the English. Vide Volney, Beaujour, &c.

The inn-keepers of America, are, in most villages, what we vulgarly call, "topping men," field officers of militia, with good farms attached to their taverns, so that they are apt to think, what, perhaps in a newly settled country, is not very wide of the truth, that travellers rather receive, than confer a favour by being accommodated at their houses. They always give us plentiful fare, particularly at breakfast, where veal-cutlets, sweetmeats, cheese, eggs, and ham, were most liberally set before us. Dinner is little more than a repetition of breakfast, with spirits instead of coffee. I never heard wine called for; the common drink is a small cyder; rum, whiskey, and brandy, are placed on the table, and the use of them left to the discretion of the company, who seem rarely to abuse the privilege. Tea is a meal of the same solid construction with breakfast, answering also for supper. The daughters of the host officiate at tea and breakfast, and generally wait at dinner. Their behaviour is reserved in the extreme, but it enables them to serve as domestics, without losing their rank of equality with those on whom they attend. To judge from the books I frequently found lying about, they are well-educated; the landlord of an inn at Waterford was very particular in inquiring of a gentleman who was with me, for the most accomplished schoolmistress of New York, with whom to place his daughter; the same man, after shrewdly commenting on the conduct of some of the first political characters of the country, summed up his eulogium on his favourite, by saying, " I make no objection to his lying and intrigues, for all politicians will do the same." I cannot pretend to say how far this is practically true in America, but I have reason to think the sentiment at least too general. The spirit of speculation, in all professions of life, seems to go far towards weakening the finer feelings of political honour and integrity. The indolent habits of the Spaniard are thought to be favourable to the fidelity and honour observable in all his transactions; the commercial activity of the Chinese degenerates into knavish trickery. It is for the Americans to consider, to which extreme they are verging, and to remember above all, that the vital spirit of repub-

licanism is virtue—but this is going deeper than I have any pretension to do at present; I have seen but a little portion of the mere surface.

" An English traveller is frequently surprised to find the highest magistrates and officers of the nation travelling by the same conveyances, sitting down at the same table, and joining in conversation with the meanest of the people; borrowing from his own prejudices of rank, he is apt to fancy all the great world amusing themselves in masquerade. I entered, casually, in conversation, on board the steam boat, with a man whose appearance seemed to denote something betwixt the shop-keeper and farmer, though his conversation marked him superior to both. He was the high sheriff of a county. I remember, among other observations, his remarks on the unhappy condition of the greater part of emigrants into America, particularly the poorer Irish, who are induced by flattering representations to strain every effort to procure a passage to New York, or some sea-port town, where they are left in total ignorance, both of the country most fit to settle in, and of the means of getting to it, until their little stock is either wasted by delay, or plundered by sharpers, and themselves reduced to beggary, or the lowest drudgery of society.* It is very rare to find a native American begging, or indeed to find any condition resembling beggary throughout the States, except in the sea-port towns, in which these naked wanderers are collected."

Mr. Hall's account of Canada is dispatched in little more than one hundred pages. He has briefly described the prominent features of the country through which he passed, and has given, upon the whole, a pleasing view of that province and its inhabitants.

The following character of the French Canadians, we think, will be read with interest.

" After quitting the neighbourhood of Montreal, we see little of the French Canadian; he is succeeded by settlers of a

---

* I have heard Americans complain, that almost all their crimes and misdemeanors are committed by persons of this description.

character very different; and with whom he is generally placed in humiliating contrast. He gains little by travellers; few enter his cottage, or inquisitively scan the character of an ignorant and superstitious race, who aspire to little more than to walk in the steps of their priests, and forefathers. Certainly if intellectual power be the sole measure of human merit, their's lies in little compass.—Ignorant they unquestionably are, though I doubt whether they have a right to such extreme. pre-eminence in this respect, as Englishmen are usually liberal enough to assign them: Schools are common through the Province, and the number of colleges seems proportioned to the population: the gentry and tradesmen appear not much inferior in information, to the country gentlemen and tradesmen of wiser nations; and if the share of the peasant's intellect exceeds not much that of the ox he drives, he may claim fellowship in this respect, with the peasant of almost every country on the globe, except the United States. He is certainly superstitious, that is, he believes all his priest tells him— no great peculiarity. Let not, however, those qualities be overlooked, which give a grace to his poverty, sweeten the cup of his privations, and almost convert his ignorance into bliss.——Essentially a Frenchman, he is gay, courteous and contented: If the rigors of a Canadian climate have somewhat chilled the overflowing vivacity derived from his parent stock, he has still a sufficient portion of good spirits, and loquacity, to make his rulers, and neighbours seem cold and silent: To strangers and travellers, he is invariably civil, seeming to value their good-work beyond their money: He is reckoned parsimonious, because all his gains arise from his savings: He is satisfied with the humblest fare, and his utmost debauch never exceeds a "coup" of rum, and pipe of tobacco, taken with a dish of gossip, the only luxury in which he can be accounted extravagant. The influence of the priests is probably injurious, as it affects mental improvement, beneficial with respect to morals. Religion, or rather superstition, and morality, are so blended in the mind of the Canadian, that were the former shaken, considerable time must elapse before any basis could be raised on which to

found the latter. At present, great crimes are almost unknown, and petty offences are rare; I have indeed heard the lower classes accused of a propensity to pilfer, but I am inclined to think, few instances of this kind occur, except from the pressure of extreme want. The late war, by calling out a considerable proportion of the population to serve in the militia, has produced an evident change in the manners of the young men: I always found two invariable symptoms of a man's having *served;* a little more intelligence, and a great deal more knavery. But if the war did not mend their morals, it certainly raised their character: They exhibited a high degree of courage in the field, and an affectionate zeal towards their governor, whom they believed their friend: a striking instance of this occurred early in the war. While Sir George Prevost was at Montreal, a body of several hundred peasants, from the remotest settlements of the province, came to wait on him; each man was armed with whatever weapon he could procure on the spur of the occasion, and all were clothed and provisioned for immediate service: An old man, who had been a soldier in the revolutionary war, was at their head, who thus addressed Sir George: "My general, we heard you were in difficulty, and have marched to your assistance; I have served myself, and though an old man, do not think I am quite incapable of duty."—Sir George, strongly affected with this instance of attachment, accepted their services, and they acted as a separate body during the whole of the campaign.

"The Canadians bear a considerable antipathy to the Americans, whom they denominate, "*Sacres Bastonnais.*"* I believe it to arise principally from religious prejudices; in proof of which, there is a striking anecdote related in the life of Franklin, who made an attempt to bring them over to the revolutionary cause. At this day, even the better informed among them are fully persuaded that the American government is constantly plotting their ruin, and the destruction of the mighty city of Quebec. I was witness to a curious exemplification of this feeling: A young Canadian, by no means illiterate,

---

* Bostonese. Inhabitants of Boston.

informed me one morning, with a very grave face, that a tremendous plot had been discovered—to destroy the whole city by blowing up the powder magazine; that a train had been found ready laid, and no doubt existed of an American's being at the end of it. I took the trouble to trace the source of this report, and found it to originate in an order to mend a broken door belonging to the magazine. A fire never happens in the town, (and they happen very often,) but the " *Bastonnais*" are the incendiaries.——Petty quarrels betwixt the natives and the Vermontese keep this feeling alive; and the English may well say of it, in the words of Sir Lucius O'Trigger, " 'Tis a pretty quarrel as it is, and explanation would spoil it." "

Re-entering the United States, Mr. Hall proceeded in a southerly direction through the western country of New York, by the Niagara Frontier to Philadelphia. The present state of the celebrated falls of Niagara is pleasingly described : and the general appearance of the country is represented as flourishing. The following account of the Mohawks, who are considered as the head of the six confederated tribes of Indians of the Grand River, communicates some particulars which we do not remember to have seen elsewhere.

" They (the Mohawks) were strongly attached to the British interest, and first followed Sir William Johnson into Canada, under their chieftain, " the Monster Brandt." The Monster had, however, some good qualities. He accustomed his people to the arts of civilized life, and made farmers of them. He built a church, and translated one of the Gospels into the Mohawk language; for, like Clovis, and many of the early Anglo-Saxon and Danish Christians, he contrived to unite much religious zeal with the practices of natural ferocity. His grave is to be seen under the walls of his church. I have mentioned one of his sons : he has also a daughter living, who would not disgrace the circles of European fashion : her face, and person are fine and graceful : she speaks English, not only correctly, but elegantly ; and has, both in her speech and manners, a softness approaching to Oriental langour : she re-

tains so much of her own dress as to identify her with her people, over whom she affects no superiority, but seems pleased to preserve all the ties, and duties of relationship. She held the infant of one of her relations to the font, on the Sunday of my visit to the church. The usual church, and baptismal service was performed by a Dr. Aaron, an Indian, and an assistant priest ; the congregation consisted of sixty or seventy persons, male and female : many of the young men were dressed in the English fashion, but several of the old warriors came with their blankets, folded over them, like the drapery of a statue; and in this dress, with a step and mien of quiet energy, more forcibly reminded me of the ancient Romans than some other inhabitants of this continent, who have laid claim to the resemblance. Some of them wore large silver crosses, medals, and other trinkets, on their backs and breasts; and a few had bandeaus, ornamented with feathers. Dr. Aaron, a grey-headed Mohawk, had touched his cheeks and forehead with a few spots of vermillion, in honour of Sunday : he wore a surplice, and preached at considerable length; but his delivery was unimpassioned and monotonous in the extreme. Indian eloquence decays with the peculiar state of society to which it owed its energy.

" The Mohawk village stands on a little plain, looking down upon the Grand river; upon the alluvion of which the inhabitants raise their crops, chiefly of Indian corn. Their houses are built of logs, rudely put together, and exhibiting externally a great appearance of neglect, and want of comfort. Some few are in a better condition : the house belonging to Brandt's family resembles that of a petty English farmer ; Dr. Aaron's was neat and clean. The Doctor, who had been regularly ordained, and spoke very good English, told me the village had been injured much by the war, which had put a stop to its improvements, and dispersed the inhabitants over the country. This is probable enough : the Indians advance towards civilized life with a forced motion, and revert to habits of warfare, and wandering, with a natural rebound. The Cayugas seem to have made less progress than the Mohawks, towards domestic accommodation: the fire is still in the middle of their dwellings: the earth, or a block of wood, suffices for chair, and table; and planks, arranged round the walls, like cabin births, form their beds. They seemed very cheerful, though with little reason; for their crop of Indian corn, which they were now drying and husking, had been spoiled by premature frost, and in common with all the other Indians of the settlement, their only resource against starvation, was the British Commissariat. They confine themselves to the cultivation of Indian corn, because it requires little labour, and of that sort which may be performed by women; the consequence is, that a single frosty night strikes them with famine, or at least throws them for support upon the magazine at Kingston. The evil and remedy proceed from the same source: an habitual dependance on our bounty destroys, by rendering needless, all exertion towards self-support. But from the system of Indian tutelage results the necessity of guardianship, that is, of the Indian department, through which some thousands of the public money are annually filtered: plentiful harvests on the Grand River would destroy golden crops of place and patronage.

" I had little opportunity of observing their manners and character. It may be conjectured that European intercourse is fast obliterating the characteristic features of their former social system. Their increased knowledge of our arts, and enjoyments, has been probably followed by a proportionate increase of wants, and desires, and these, by the usual accession of their concomitant passions. It is likely they are less brave, less temperate, less sagacious, and less ardent in their social affections, than their woodland ancestors; but also less cruel and revengeful, more selfish, and more religious. In the vicinity of their settlements they have the character of being inoffensive neighbours, and of living peaceably among themselves, except when under the occasional influence of intoxication. Their manners seemed to me remarkable for nothing so much as for that quiet self-possession, which constitutes the reverse of vulgarity. Their women, before strangers, are extremely timid: most of those who lived

at any distance from the church, came mounted, with their husbands walking by their sides; a symptom, perhaps, that the sex is rising among them into an European equality of rights, and enjoyments.

" The whole of the settlements are reckoned to furnish about five hundred warriors, to our Government. These, if not the best, are certainly the dearest of our allies: beside the support of themselves and their families during the war, several thousands are expended annually in cloathing, and nick-nacks, under the name of presents. Every accidental loss, from failure of crops, or other disasters, they are in the habit of expecting should be made good by the liberality of their " Great Father," whose means and generosity they are well disposed to consider as unbounded; an idea which his agents are little careful to repress. During the late war they behaved with the cautious courage of German auxiliaries, evidently considering it their first interest to spare themselves, their second, to serve their father; a mode of conduct which was nearly resented by the more enterprising warriors, of the West, who had taken up the hatchet from a strong feeling of necessity, and hatred to the encroachments of the Americans. Among these, the most distinguished was Tecumseh, a Shawnee chieftain, whose courage and commanding talents recommended him, early in the war, not only to the notice, but to the personal esteem, and admiration of Sir Isaac Brocke.* Tecumseh perceived the necessity of a general Indian confederacy, as the only permanent barrier to the dominion of the States. What he had the genius to conceive, he had the talents to execute: eloquence, and address, courage, penetration, and what in an Indian is more remarkable than these, undeviating temperance. Under better auspices, this Amphictyonic league might have been

---

* The General, one day, presented him with the sash he had worn on his own person. Tecumseh received it with great emotion, and begged the General to consider, that if he refrained from wearing it himself, it was from an anxiety to prevent the jealousy, which such an honour conferred on a young chieftain, might excite, among the older Indian captains; but that he would send it to his family, to be preserved as an eternal memorial of his father's friendship.

effected; but after the death of his friend and patron, he found no kindred spirit with whom to act; but stung with grief and indignation, after upbraiding, in the bitterest sarcasms*, the retreat of our forces, he engaged an American detachment of mounted riflemen, near the Moravian village, and having rushed forward, singly, to encounter their commanding officer, whom he mistook for General Harrison, he fell by a pistol ball. The exultations of the Americans on his death, afford unerring, because unintended evidence of the dread his talents had inspired."†

The present state of Philadelphia is discussed in four sections, which treat on its architecture, fine arts, society, goal and penal code. At Washington, which may be considered as the capital of the American Union, our traveller made some stay, and attended some of the deliberations of the congress.

" Strangers who intend staying some days in a town, usually take lodgings at a boarding-house, in preference to a tavern: in this way, they obtain the best society the place affords; for there are always gentlemen, and frequently ladies, either visitors or temporary residents, who live in this manner to avoid the trouble of house-keeping. At Washington, during the sittings of Congress, the boarding-houses are divided into messes, according to the political principles of the inmates, nor is a stranger admitted without some introduction, and the consent of the whole company. I chanced to join a democratic

mess, and name a few of its members with gratitude, for the pleasure their society gave me :—Commodore Decatur and his lady, the Abbé de Correa, the great botanist and plenipotentiary of Portugal, the Secretary of the Navy, the Secretary of the Navy Board, known as the author of a humorous publication, entitled " John Bull and Brother Jonathan," with eight or ten members of Congress, principally from the Western states, which are generally considered as most decidedly hostile to England, but whom I did not on this account find less good-humoured and courteous. It is from thus living in daily intercourse with the leading characters of the country, that one is enabled,to judge with some degree of certainty of the practices of its government; for to know the paper theory is nothing, unless it be compared with the instruments employed to carry it into effect. A political constitution may be nothing but a cabalistic form, to extract money and power from the people ; but then the jugglers must be in the dark, and " no admittance behind the curtain." This way of living affords too the best insight into the best part of society ; for if in a free-nation the depositiaries of the public confidence be ignorant, or vulgar, it is a very fruitless search to look for the opposite qualities in those they represent; whereas if these be well informed in mind and manners, it proves at the least an inclination towards knowledge and refinement, in the general mass of citizens, by whom they are selected. My own experience obliges me to a favorable verdict in this particular. I found the little circle into which I had happily fallen, full of good sense and good humour, and never quitted it without feeling myself a gainer on the score, either of useful information or social enjoyment.

" The President, or rather his lady holds a drawing-room weekly, during the sitting of Congress. He takes by the hand those who are presented to him; shaking hands being discovered in America to be more rational and manly than kissing them. For the rest, it is much as such things are every where, chatting, and tea, compliments and ices, a little music, (some scandal, I suppose, among the ladies,) and to bed. Nothing in these assemblies more attracted my notice, than

---

* " I compare," said he, speaking of the author of this retreat, " our father to a fat white dog, who in the season of prosperity carries his tail erect on his back, but drops it betwixt his legs, and flies at the approach of danger." On another occasion, when by way of pacifying his remonstrances with a metaphor, in the Indian manner, our commander professed his readiness to lay his bones by his side, " Tell the dog," said the angry warrior, " he has too much regard for his carcass, to lay his bones any where."

† The officer who shot him was a Colonel Johnson, who had been himself severely wounded the moment before. Tecumseh bore a personal enmity to General Harrison, to whom he attributed the slaughter of his family; and vowed that when they met, one of them should be left on the field.

the extraordinary stature of most of the western members; the room seemed filled with giants, among whom, moderately sized men crept like pigmies. I know not well, to what the difference may be attributed, but the surprising growth of the inhabitants of the western states is matter of astonishment to those of the Eastern, and of the coast line generally. This phenomenon, which is certainly a considerable stumbling-block to the Abbé Raynal's theory, may probably be resolved into the operation of three positive causes, and one negative, namely, plentiful, but simple food, a healthy climate, constant exercise in the open air, and the absence of mental irritation. In a more advanced stage of society, luxurious and sedentary habits produce in the rich that enfeeblement of vitality, which scanty food, and laborious and unwholesome occupations bring upon the poor. The only persons to be compared with these Goliahs of the West, were six Indian chiefs from Georgia, Chactaws or Chickasaws, who having come to Washington on public business, were presented at Mrs. Maddison's drawing-room. They had a still greater appearance of muscular power than the Americans; and while looking on them, I comprehended the prowess of those ancient knights, whose single might held an army in check, " and made all Troy retire."

" The sittings of Congress are held in a temporary building, during the repair of the Capitol : I attended them frequently, and was fortunate enough to be present at one interesting debate on a change in the mode of Presidential elections : most of the principal speakers took a part in it: Messrs. Gaston, Calhoun and Western in support of it; Randolph and Grosvenor against it. The merits of the question were not immediately to be comprehended by a stranger, but their style of speaking was, in the highest degree, correct and logical, particularly that of Mr. Western of New Hampshire, whose argumentative acuteness extorted a compliment from Mr. Randolph himself, " albeit unused to the complimenting mood." Mr. Grosvenor, both in action and language, might be considered a finished orator, as far as our present notions of practical oratory existed. Mr. Randolph, whose political

talents, or rather political success, is said to be marred by an eccentric turn of thought, which chimes in with no party, seems rather a brilliant than a convincing speaker; his elocution is distinct and clear to shrillness, his command of language and illustration seems unlimited; but he gave me the idea of a man dealing huge blows against a shadow, and wasting his dexterity in splitting hairs: his political sentiments are singular: he considers the government of the United States as an elective monarchy; " Torture the constitution as you 'will," said he, in the course of the debate, " the President will elect his successor, and that will be his son whenever he has one old enough to succeed him." No expressions are used, either of approbation or the contrary; whatever may be the opinion of the House, the most perfect attention may be given to each member ; nor, however long he may speak, is he ever interrupted by those indications of impatience so common in our House of Commons. This may reasonably be accounted for by supposing, that their average speeches are, in themselves better ; or more agreeably, by conjecturing that the American idea of excellence is put at a lower standard than our own. Both the talents, however, and behaviour of the members, seem worthy of the government, and of what America is, and may be. Their forms of business and debate nearly resemble those of our parliament; always excepting wigs and gowns, a piece of grave absurdity well omitted : for 'tis surely an odd conceit, to fancy the dignity of the first officers of States attached to, or supported by, large conglomerations of artificial hair."

A considerable part of Mr. Hall's volume is appropriated to the State of Virginia. At Monticello, he met with a hospitable reception from Mr. Jefferson the late President of the United States.

" I found Mr. Jefferson tall in person, but stooping and lean with old age, thus exhibiting that fortunate mode of bodily decay, which strips the frame of its most cumbersome parts, leaving it still strength of muscle and activity of limb. His deportment was exactly such as the Marquis de Chastellux describes it, above thirty years ago ; " At first serious, nay even cold," but in a very short time relaxing into a most agreeable amenity; with an unabated flow of conversation on the most interesting topics, discussed in the most gentlemanly, and philosophical manner. I walked with him round his grounds, to visit his pet trees, and improvements of various kinds: during the walk, he pointed out to my observation a conical mountain, rising singly at the edge of the southern horizon of the landscape: its distance he said, was forty miles, and its dimensions those of the greater Egyptian pyramid; so that it accurately represents the appearance of the pyramid at the same distance; there is a small cleft visible on its summit, through which, the true meridian of Monticello exactly passes: its most singular property, however, is, that on different occasions it looms or alters its appearance, becoming sometimes cylindrical, sometimes square, and sometimes assuming the form of an inverted cone. Mr. Jefferson had not been able to connect this phenomenon with any particular season, or state of the atmosphere, except, that it most commonly concurred in the forenoon. He observed, that it was not only wholly unaccounted for by the laws of vision, but that it had not as yet engaged the attention of philosophers, so far as to acquire a name; that of looming, being in fact, a term applied by sailors, to appearances of a similar kind at sea. The blue Mountains are also observed to loom, though not in so remarkable a degree.*

"It must be interesting to recall and preserve the political sentiments of a man who has held so distinguished a station in public life as Mr. Jefferson. He seemed to consider much of the freedom and happiness of America, to arise from local circumstances. "Our population, he observed, "has an elasticity, by which it would fly off from oppressive taxation." He instanced the beneficial effects of a free government in the case of New Orleans, where many proprietors who were in a state of indigence under the dominion of Spain, have risen to a sudden wealth, solely by the rise in the value of land, which followed a change of government.

* Vide for a more detailed account of this phenomenon in Notes on Virginia, p. 122.

Their ingenuity in mechanical inventions, agricultural improvements, and that mass of general information to be found among Americans of all ranks and conditions, he ascribed to that ease of circumstances, which affords them leisure to cultivate their minds, after the cultivation of their lands was completed.—In fact, I have frequently been surprised to find mathematical and other useful works in houses which seemed to have little pretention to the luxury of learning. Another cause, Mr. Jefferson observed, might be discovered in the many court and county meetings, which brought men frequently together on public business, and thus gave them habits both of thinking and expressing their thoughts on subjects, which in other countries are confined to the consideration of the privileged few. Mr. Jefferson has not the reputation of being very friendly to England: we should, however, be aware, that a partiality in this respect, is not absolutely the duty of an American citizen; neither is it to be expected that the policy of our government should be regarded in foreign countries, with the same complacency with which it is looked upon by ourselves : but whatever may be his sentiments in this respect, politeness naturally repressed any offensive expression of them : he talked of our affairs with candour, and apparent good-will, though leaning, perhaps, to the gloomier side of the picture. He did not perceive by what means we could be extricated from our present financial embarrassments, without some kind of revolution in our government: on my replying, that our habits were remarkably steady, and that great sacrifices would be made to prevent a violent catastrophe, he acceded to the observation, but demanded, if those who made the sacrifices, would not require some political reformation in return. His repugnance was strongly marked to the despotic principles of Bonaparte, and seemed to consider France under Louis XVI. as scarcely capable of a republican form of government; but added, that the present generation of Frenchmen had grown up with sounder notions, which would probably lead to their emancipation."

Of the Virginian character, generally, Mr. Hall's impressions are not favourable.

" They seem, especially the plantation-bred Virginians, to have more pretension than good sense: the ,insubordination, in which they glory, both to parental and scholastic authority, produces, as might be expected, a petulance of manner and frothiness of intellect, very unlike what we may imagine of the old Romans, to whom, in their modesty, the Virginians affect to compare themselves.—Having given four Presidents to the United States, they are fain to suppose they have obtained a monopoly of genius, as well as of power, and hold in true regal disdain the honest simplicity of their Yankey brethren. These observations do not, however, apply to the inhabitants of the Upper Country, who seem to be generally a race of plain and industrious farmers, with both the sound sense, and unaffected manner, peculiar to this class of people throughout the Union.

" As the Virginians feel destined to govern, and as persuasion is a necessary instrument for this purpose, eloquence is their favourite study; but one of their countrymen is best able to describe their efforts and success:— ' The people of this State insist upon it, that they have the patent right for making speeches. Eloquence, indeed, (of some sort or other) is almost the only road to fame and influence in the State. Every youth, of course, who has been led to believe that he has any talents at all, immediately turns his whole attention to the science of spouting. The consequence is, that the land is literally over-run with orators of all sorts and sizes, almost as numerous and noisy as the frogs in the plague of Egypt.—In the first place, we have the political spouters, who are found in every hole and corner of the favoured land; but particularly in the court-yard and tavern. The tavern, especially, seems to be a very favourite haunt of these young orators; whether it is that the long porch invites them by certain classical associations, from its resemblance to the schools of some among the ancient rhetoricians; or, rather, as others suppose, that the bar-room contains some secret stimulants of eloquence, more sovereign than all the precepts of Quintilian. It is, indeed, very amusing to hear one of these talking Jacks (as you may call them), when it has been properly screwed up, seated by the fire, and unwinding itself in long discourses upon liberty, the rights of man, the freedom of the seas, general suffrage, or something of that sort. Its whole conversation is one incessant harangue. Indeed, to speak strictly, it never converses at all; but declaims upon you without any reasonable allowance for the delicacy of your ears. And yet, really when it cocks its feet up against the mantle-piece, its favourite oratical attitude, and lets out, as they call it, you can form no idea how eloquent it is.— Next in order to these comes the ' Fourth of July Orators,' or they would doubtless prefer to be styled, the Qrators of the Human Race.' These men who set up once a-year (generally in very hot weather) to proclaim their independence with a loud voice, and abuse the British *en amore.* In fact, they sometimes carry their malice so far, as to vent their spite upon the very language they speak in, its unoffending parts of speech, and innocent rules of syntax, only because they are English, I presume. Nothing seems to be requisite for the perfection of these things, but a plenty of hard names, abuse against tyranny and oppression, a panegyric upon liberty, and five or six apostrophes to the dead heroes of the revolution; the whole accompanied with an entire new set of mouths and faces made on purpose for the occasion. Add to this, the words selected for this service must all be as long as possible, *sesquipedalia verba:* or tri-syllables at least; and none under that size should be received, any more than a man under six feet could have been admitted into the King of Prussia's tall regiment. I can only say of them, as poor *Desdemona* said of the mad speeches of her jealous husband,

" I understand a fury in the words ;
" But not the words ——"

' But besides these engaging speakers, we have still another class of orators, called Slang-whangers, who are also sometimes known by the name of Stump-orators, from their generally choosing to deliver their harangues from the stump of a tree, or a horse-block, or some other appropriate place of this sort. For you must know, these are the men who undertake to regulate elections, and to change the votes in the court-yard, before the opening of the poll. I have observed they are all passionately fond of the word Republican; which seems to comprise all the excellence of oratory in itself, and is generally looked upon as a very good substitute for both reason and common sense.' "

[*To be concluded in our next.*]

Tom Crib's Memorial to Congress; with a preface, notes and appendix: By one of the Fancy, 8vo. 5s. 6d. Longman and Co. London, 1819.

Though not announced in the title, it is impossible not to ascribe this jeu d'esprit to the facetious author of the "Twopenny Post Bag," and the "Letters from the Fudge Family,"—Mr. Thomas Moore. Having established his claim to rank with our most valued poets, he now chooses "*desipere in loco;* and having, with a master's hand patronized the dazzling splendours of the gorgeous palaces of the East, he has now described with equal force the *flashy* brilliancy of his newly-adopted haunt, the Finish. Sated with sweets, and tired of roaming over

"The delightful province of the Sun,"

and inhaling the breathing odours of Paradise, the poet, having " on this fair mountain leave to feed," descends, and,

"Lighted earthward by a glance That just then broke from Morning's eyes,"

is content to "batten on the moor" of coarse vulgarity, and inhale the whiffs of stale debauch which overpower the perfumes of the flowers of Covent-Garden. Often has Mr. Moore recorded his bitter displeasure against the illustrious head of our Government, and his principal advisers; but being, it appears, apprehensive that something offensive had been left unsaid which, in the new character of " One of the Fancy," he might utter with effect—and perhaps from an anxiety to shew that he can appear in the character of Thersites to as much advantage as in that of Anacreon—he has presented us with Tom Crib's Memorial to the Congress of Europe. We do not discover

any advantage which the author has gained by the assumption of this character, unless indeed it can be called one, that his attacks upon the royal object of his hatred, being directed chiefly against the size of his person, might be thought to be in very bad taste by the class of society to which Mr. Moore belongs, whereas they lose none of their force from such considerations when they come ostensibly from one of the St. Giles's fraternity. As a *jeu d'esprit*, however, the Memorial is spirited and entertaining; displaying much wit, which comes naturally from the author, and much learning, which for the sake of a few puns, one or two of which are very good, is forced somewhat awkwardly into the service, and is indeed the

" Rich armour worn in heat of day."

We here by no means intend to allude to the author's more rare proficiency in the Cant and Flash languages, which is most appropriately displayed, and will render the work highly valuable to the lexicographers of future ages.

The objects of the satire are chiefly persons for whom we, in common with the greater part of the nation, entertain unfeigned respect; they are wise and good men, but we do not object to a joke at their expense, notwithstanding. "Because they are virtuous shall there be no more cakes and ale?"

Besides the 'memorial,' from which we shall not make any extracts, there is an appendix containing sundry 'fancy' pieces, executed in the same style and spirit. One of these is a translation, from the fifth Book of the Æneid, of Virgil's description of the boxing, *alias* 'milling match' between Dares and Entellus: as our readers may like to see how the Roman bard appears, clothed in the ' fancy lay,' we shall select this part of Mr. Moore's volume for their perusal.

WITH *daddles* (1) high uprais'd, and *nob* held back,
In awful prescience of th' impending *thwack*, [1]·
Both *Kiddies* (2) stood—and with prelusive *spar*,
And light manœuvring, kindled up the war!

---

(1) Hands.
(2) Fellows, usually young fellows.

The One, in bloom of youth—a *light-weight*
  blade——
The Other, vast, gigantic, as if made,
Express, by Nature for the *hammering* trade ;
But aged, (3) slow, with stiff limbs, tottering
  much,
And lungs, that lack'd the *bellows-mender's* touch.

Yet, sprightly *to the Scratch* both *Buffers* came,
While *ribbers* rung from each resounding frame,
And divers *digs*, and many a ponderous *pelt*,
Were on their broad *bread-baskets* heard and felt.
With roving aim, but aim that rarely miss'd,
Round *lugs* and *ogles* (4) flew the frequent fist;
While showers of *facers* told so deadly well,
That the crush'd jaw-bones crackled as they fell!
But firmly stood ENTELLUS—and still bright,
Though bent by age, with all THE FANCY'S light,
Stopp'd with a skill, and *rallied* with a fire
Th' Immortal FANCY could alone inspire !
While DARES, *shifting* round, with looks of
  thought,
An opening to the *Cove's* huge carcase sought,
(Like General PRESTON, in that awful hour,
When on *one* leg he hopp'd to—take the Tower!
And here, and there, explor'd with active *fin*(5)
And skilful *feint*, some guardless pass to win,
And prove a *boring* guest when once *let in*.

And now ENTELLUS, with an eye that plann'd
Punishing deeds, high rais'd his heavy hand ;
But, ere the *sledge* came down, young DARES
  spied
Its shadow o'er his brow, and slipp'd aside—
So nimbly slipp'd, that the vain *nobber* pass'd
Through empty air ; and He, so high, so vast,
Who dealt the stroke, came thundering to the
  ground !—
Not B—CK—GH—M, himself, with bulkier
  sound,(6)
Uprooted from the field of Whiggish glories,
Fell *souse*, of late, among the astonish'd Tories !(7)
Instant the *Ring* was broke, and shouts and
  yells
From Trojan *Flashmen* and Sicilian *Swells*
Fill'd the wide heav'n—while touch'd with grief
  to see
His *pal*, (8) well-known through many a *lark*
  and *spree*, (9)
Thus *rumly floor'd*, the kind ACESTES ran,
And pitying rais'd from earth the *game* old man.
Uncow'd, undamag'd, to the *sport* he came,
His limbs all muscle, and his soul all flame.
The memory of his *milling* glories past,
The shame, that aught but death should see him
  grass'd,

All fir'd the veteran's *pluck*—with fury flash'd
Full on his light-limb *customer* he rush'd,
And *hammering* right and left, with ponderous
  swing, (10)
Ruffian'd the reeling youngster round the *Ring*—

Nor rest, nor pause, nor breathing-time was
  given,
But, rapid as the rattling hail from heav'n
Beats on the house-top, showers of RANDAL's
  shot (11)
Around the Trojan's *lugs* flew, peppering hot !
'Till now ÆNEAS, fill'd with anxious dread,
Rush'd in between them,' and, with words well-
  bred,
Preserv'd alike the peace and DARES' head,
Both which the veteran much inclin'd to *break*—
Then kindly thus the *punish'd* youth bespake :
" Poor *Johnny Raw* ! what madness could impel
" So *rum a Flat* to face so *prime a Swell* ?

" See'st thou not, boy, THE FANCY, heavenly
  Maid,
" Herself descends to this great *Hammerer's* aid,
" And, singling *him* from all her *flash* adorers,
" Shines in his *hits*, and thunders in his *floorers* !
" Then, yield thee, youth,—nor such a *mummy* be,
" To think mere man can *mill* a Deity !"
Thus spoke the Chief—and now, the *scrimmage*
  o'er,
His faithful *pals* the *done-up* DARES bore
Back to his home, with tottering *gams*, sunk
  heart,
And *mugs* and *noddle pink'd* in every part, (12)

While from his *gob* the guggling *claret* gush'd,
And lots of *grinders*, from their sockets crush'd,
Forth with the crimson tide in rattling frag-
  ments rush'd !

Κεσκιον ἡ κεφαλη σευ, Απολλοφανης, γεγενηται,
  Η των εντιλισεων βιβλαριον τα κατω.
Ολαις μυριμιαις τρυπημαῖα λοξα και ορθα,
  Γραμμαῖα των λυρικων Λυδια και Φρυγια.

(3) Macrobius, in his explanation of the various properties of the number Seven, says, that the fifth Hebdomas of man's life (the age of 35) is the completion of his strength ; that therefore, pugilists, if not successful, usually give over their profession at that time.

(4) Ears and eyes.

(5) Arm.

(6) As the uprooted trunk in the original is said to be " cava," the epithet here ought, perhaps, to be " *hollower* sound."

(7) I trust my conversion of the Erymanthian pine into his L——ds——p will be thought happy and ingenious. It was suggested, indeed, by the recollection that Erymanthus was also famous for another sort of natural production, very common in society at all periods, and which no one but Hercules ever seems to have known how to manage. Though even *he* is described by Valerius Flaccus as—" Erymanthei *sudantem pondere monstri*."

(8) Friend.   (9) Party of pleasure and frolic.

(10) This phrase is but too applicable to the *round hitting* of the ancients, who, it appears by the engravings in Mercurialis de Art. Gymnast. knew as little of our *straight forward* mode as the uninitiated Irish of the present day. I have, by the by, discovered some errors in Mercurialis, as well as in two other modern authors upon Pugilism (viz. Petrus Faber in his Agonisticon, and that indefatigable classic antiquary, M. Burette, in his " Memoire pour servir a l'Histoire du Pugilat des Anciens") which I shall have the pleasure of pointing out in my forthcoming " Parallel."

(11) A favourite blow of *the Nonpareil's*, so called.

(12) There are two or three Epigrams in the Greek Anthology, ridiculing the state of mutilation and disfigurement to which the pugilists were reduced by their combats. The following four lines are from an Epigram by Lucilius, Lib. 2.

Literally, as follows : " Thy head, O Apollophanes, is perforated like a sieve, or like the leaves of an old worm-eaten book ; and the numerous scars, both straight and cross-ways, which have been left upon thy pate by the cestus, very much resemble the score of a Lydian or Phrygian piece of music." Periphrastically, thus :

Your noddle, dear Jack, full of holes like a sieve,
Is so figur'd, and dotted, and scratch'd I declare,
By your *customers'* fists, one would almost believe
They had *punch'd* a whole verse of " The Wood-
  pecker" there !

It ought to be mentioned, that the word " *punching*" is used both in boxing and music-engraving.

The Analysis of Human Nature; or, an investigation of the means to improve the Condition of the Poor; and to promote the happiness of mankind in general; comprising, also, the progress and present state of political, moral, and religious society. By S. Phelps, author of a " Treatise on the importance of extending the British Fisheries." 8vo. 2 vols. £1 1s. Simpkin & Marshall, London, 1818.

[Concluded from p. 515.]

The education of Children is an object of the highest importance. The welfare of families, the preservation of States, and the happiness of Society, depend wholly upon the nature and principles of the education of youth. This momentous topic is treated at very considerable length by Mr. Phelps, who has brought to the discussion the same spirit of practical research and benevolent feeling, which characterize the first volume of his work. We select the following remarks on the system of tuition, which at present most generally prevails.

" Education, either among the poor or higher classes, does not consist in, or simply imply, reading, writing, or a knowledge of the arts and sciences; it implies a great deal more, and what is more to the purpose: it implies the fitting of youth, so as to conduct themselves in the world with honour and advantage, both to themselves and to others, and according to the rank which they may hold in society. The system of education now established in this country is excellent, so far as it regards the teaching of reading, writing, and accounts; but, perhaps, a great deal more might be done with respect to morality and religion, and in preparing youth according to the rank and situation in which they may be placed in public or private life.

"Youth, who have nothing to depend upon for their support but their labour, industry, and good conduct, should be instructed in the best way by which they can perfect those views. Reading, writing, and arithmetic must now be necessary and useful to the lowest ranks of people; and a youth who has a natural genius for more learning, will generally afterwards, with these advantages, acquire it of his own accord. But no youth will acquire the habits of life fitted for his station, unless he be taught them; and this necessary part of his education is more difficult to be taught him than reading, writing, and arithmetic. The morals and manners of youth are, therefore, a more necessary and more valuable part of their education than either Greek or Latin.; but, if a boy learn his book, little notice is in general taken of the remainder part of his tuition.

"The world cannot now be kept in ignorance; but youth will bend, either the right way or the wrong, according to the inclination that may be given them. The best lessons for youth are, to prepare their minds for the vicissitudes of life, and to show them the effects of good and evil conduct, in whatever situation and sphere they may happen to be placed. It is this study which seems to contribute most to the happiness of mankind, although it is that which appears to be the most neglected in the modern system of education.

"Nothing is more dangerous than to educate the youth of wealthy parents, and such as have great expectations, with those of humbler pretensions and prospects in life, unless both are educated under the same principles and discipline, and with perfect equality. But even then, the rich would naturally give notions to the poorer youth, which they ought not to possess; and the youth in humble life might narrow or lower the degree of character which ought to be supported in the rich, by confining and straitening the liberal notions which they ought to hold in estimation as the best recommendations of their elevated situation. But, notwithstanding, if both were educated in a strict line of rectitude, and taught that society requires of every man his services, according to his means, these lessons would do good to both, by approximating the two characters, which are generally separated by false notions of distinction. The rich youth would thereby be taught that, if his companion should prove a better man than himself, he will be the most valued in society; and the poor youth would be taught that his deficiency in wealth may be made up to him, by emulation in his character.

"In human life there is certainly no struggle so hard as that of a man, without capital and connexions, contending against those who have both; but perseverance and prudence will often obtain what the want of them cannot even preserve, and thus the fluctuations which are seen in the affairs of men. A proper rule for conduct in life is, therefore, the best instruction that can be given to youth; and, although not the only essential, it is probably the most material part of education. Habits of prudence and industry are the best lessons to be given to those who must support themselves by their labour; and they are even necessary for those who may support themselves without them.

"The teaching of youth how to get their bread with honesty and industry, and how to conduct and comport themselves through the various trials and privations of life, are the most essential parts of the education of the lower orders of people. This is what is termed, by writers on political economy, "turning the physical powers of men to the best advantage;" and which applies to both sexes. The accumulation of wealth has been considered, by political economists, to depend nearly as much on female effort and prudence as those of men; for, although they have not so much to do with income, they have, in most cases, the greatest control over expenditure. Prudence and economy are therefore necessary lessons to be taught to both sexes, and to every rank and class of society.

"It has been said, that the practice in this country is, to make education expensive, but not to make it complete. Few people learn what they ought to learn, and most people learn what they ought never to know. Modern education is also said to elevate the minds of people above their situations; and that it only teaches them to hope for things which, probably, they can never obtain. And it may be well, if it can be so said and be confirmed, without the hazard of a discovery to the contrary, that modern education tends

more to debase than to elevate the human mind.

"The intention of correct education is, to refine, to improve, and to exalt the human character; but if the coarser and sterner principles of human nature should be thought preferable to those of civilization, and if ignorance should prove to be more conducive to human happiness than sublime intelligence, cultivated intellect, and the attainment of knowledge, there is certainly no better way of making people happy than by the neglect of education. But if man is to be made better, or to be considered as possessing more exalted powers than the brute, and if the mind is to be esteemed of more value than the body, it is correct education alone that can develop human excellence.

"It is however true, that a man of brutal manners will always be a brute, whatever may be his wisdom or understanding; but this only shows that one part of his education has been neglected; and even such a character is not so contemptible as an empty coxcomb, who appears certainly to savour most of the modern principle of education. If men, through habit or fashion, will condescend to assimilate themselves to the brute creation, the bear is certainly not the most amiable animal to imitate; but it is still more ridiculous to be bowing into a room with all the grimace of a monkey, and to be chattering with the loquacity and ignorance of an ape. True education, however, will show itself in a different way, by displaying the powers and dignity of the human mind; by exalting the man, rather than by suffering him to descend to the character of a brute."

The power and tendency of good or bad education cannot prove themselves more than in religion and politics. Mr. Phelps, after treating on this topic at some length, applies it especially to the little republic of Geneva. He remarks that

"At a time when the Bible and Missionary Societies are extending their influence in all parts of the world, and by their exertions communicating the knowledge of the Gospel to heathen and savage tribes, it is surprising to observe the great departure from the doctrines of Christianity which prevails in what is termed civilised nations, and particularly in the church of Geneva; a church so interesting to every Protestant, as having been the cradle of the reformation. The reports lately given of the departure from the true faith, in the church of Geneva, do not appear to be derived from uncertain documents, or from the religious opinions of individual members of its body, but from recent public acts of the company of its pastors.

"1st. The ancient catechism of Geneva taught expressly the doctrine of the *divinity* of Jesus Christ. This catechism was withdrawn from that church some years ago, and its place has been recently supplied by another catechism, which maintains a guarded silence with respect to the divinity of Christ.

"2nd. In 1805, the company of pastors introduced into the churches of Geneva a new version of the Bible, in the publication of which they not only omitted the confession of faith of the reformed churches of France and Geneva, which had been prefixed to all their former Bibles, but they also made many very important alterations in the translation itself, particularly in parts relating to the divinity of Christ, to original sin, and to the personality and offices of the Holy Ghost. This version is still used in their churches.

"3rd. These acts were followed by another of a still less equivocal character, by which the pastors of Geneva endeavoured, as far as they were able, utterly to exclude from their churches the peculiar doctrines of Christianity. By a rule of their company, passed by them so recently as May 3, 1817, all candidates for holy orders are required solemnly to promise that they will abstain from preaching in the churches of the canton of Geneva on the following subjects:

"1st. On the manner in which the divine nature is united in the person of JESUS CHRIST.

"2nd. On original sin.

"3rd. On the manner in which *grace* operates, or on efficacious grace.

"4th. On predestination.

"This rule has been twice acted upon; a candidate has been refused ordination, and a minister has been prohibited from preach-

ing, for objecting to subscribe to it. These acts, however, although authorised by a great majority of *pastors*, leave no room for the exercise of that charity "which thinketh no evil," nor of that liberty of conscience which repels hypocrisy; but they render it too evident, that the present church of Geneva is essentially departed from the orthodox doctrines of its predecessors.

"It should be remembered that Geneva is a university, to which youth, from different parts of Europe, and particularly from the reformed church of France, are sent to be instructed in theology; and that the professors are chiefly, if not exclusively, chosen from the company of the pastors. Of this company, consisting of twenty-five persons, not more than five hold the orthodox faith. The remainder unite in opposing it. The consequence of this state of the church of Geneva, on the minds of the students, may be easily conceived. By far, the greater number of them have imbibed the doctrines of their instructors, and by whose means the infection will, most probably, be carried into other churches and countries, and the evil be extensively diffused.

"Hac fonte derivata clades
"In patriam populumque fluxit?" !

"Such is the force of education and example, to which the mind bends and yields, giving the broad ear to extraneous novelty, and closing its organ against the sounds of established truth. But this is neither orthodox, nor liberty of conscience, which knows no evil, nor the voice of nature; for "nature," as Aristotle observed, "works not after the niggardly fashion of Delphic cutlers, who can shape the same knife for various and often dissimilar purposes."

The chapters on government, the administration of government, and on Finance, are replete with information. From the latter we extract the following account of the rise, progress, and present state of the National Debt.

"According to the history of the public debt and revenue of this kingdom, from the time we had first recourse to the ruinous expedient of perpetual funding, the reduction of the public debt, in time of peace, has never borne any proportion to its accumulation in time of war. It was by the war, which began in 1668, and was concluded by the treaty of Ryswick, in 1697, that the foundation of the present enormous debt of Great Britain was first laid. On the 31st December, 1697, the public debts of Great Britain, funded and unfunded, amounted to £21,515,740. A great part of those debts had been contracted upon short anticipations of the public revenue, and some part upon annuities for lives; so that before the 31st of December, 1701, or less than four years, those had been partly paid off, and partly reverted to the public the sum of £5,121,041; a greater reduction of the public debt than has ever been produced since that period, in so short a space of time. The remaining debt, therefore, amounted to only £16,394,701.

"In the war which began in 1702, and which was concluded by the treaty of Utrecht, the public debts were still more accumulated. On the 31st of December, 1714, they amounted to £53,681,076. The subscription into the South Sea fund, of the short and long annuities, increased the amount of the public debt, so that, on the 31st of December 1722, it amounted to 55,282,978l. The reduction of the debt began in 1723, and went on so slowly, that on the 31st of December, 1739, during seventeen years of profound peace, the whole sum paid off was no more than 8,328,354l. The capital of the public debt then remaining amounted to 46,954,623l.

"The Spanish war, which began in 1739, and the French war which soon followed, occasioned a further increase of the debt, which on the 21st of December, 1748, after the war had been concluded by the treaty of Aix-la-Chapelle, amounted to 78,293,313l. The most profound peace of seventeen years had, therefore, only reduced the national debt 8,328,354; a war of less than nine years increased it 31,338,689. During the administration of Mr. Pelham, the interest of the public debt was reduced, or at least measures were taken for reducing it, from *four* to *three* per cent; the sinking fund was increased, and some part of the public debt was paid off.

"In 1755, before the breaking out of the war, the funded debt of Great Britain amounted to 72,289,673l. On the 5th of January, 1763, at the conclusion of the peace, the funded debt amounted to 122,603,336l. The unfunded debt was also stated at 13,927,589l.; but the expence occasioned by the war did not end with its conclusion by peace, so that, though on the 5th of January, 1764, the funded debt was increased, partly by a new loan, and partly by funding a part of the unfunded debt, to 129,586,789l. there still remained, according to the well-informed author of the Considerations on the Trade and Finances of Great Britain, an unfunded debt which was brought to account in that and the following year, of 9,975,017l. In 1764, therefore the public debt of Great Britain, funded and unfunded together, amounted, according to that author, to 139,516,807l. The annuities for lives too, which had been granted as premiums to the subscribers to the new loans in 1757, estimated at fourteen years purchase, were valued at 472,500l.; and the annuities, for long terms of years, granted as premiums likewise in 1761 and 1762, estimated at twenty-seven and a half years purchase, were valued at 6,826,875l. Thus, during a peace of about seven years continuance, the prudent administration of Mr. Pelham was not able to pay off an old debt of six millions; during a war of nearly the same period of time, a new debt, of more than seventy-five millions, was contracted.

"On the 5th of January, 1775, the funded debt of Great Britain amounted to 124,996,086l.; the unfunded debt, exclusive of a large civil list debt, amounted to 4,150.236l. making together 129,146322l. According to this account, the whole debt paid off, during eleven years of profound peace, amounted only to 10,415,474l.; and even this small reduction of debt was not all made from the savings out of the ordinary revenue of the state; several extraneous sums, altogether independent of that ordinary revenue, contributed towards it. Among these were, an additional shilling in the pound, land tax, for three years; two millions received from the East India Company, as indemnification for their territorial acquisitions; and, one hundred and ten thousand pounds, received from the Bank, for the renewal of their charter.* To these may be added, several other sums which, as they arose out of the war, should be deducted from the expence of it, namely, 690,449*l.*, the produce of French prizes; 670,000, composition for French prisoners; and, 95,500*l.* produced from the sale of *ceded islands ;* making together, a total 1,455,949*l.* This sum, with other savings and means, of the same kind, amounted to more than five millions; so that the whole debt paid off during eleven years of peace, out of the savings of the ordinary revenue of the state, did not amount, upon an average, to more than half a million a year. The sinking fund, however, was considerably augmented during that peace, by the debt which was paid off, by the reduction of the redeemable four per cents to three per cents, and by the annuities which had fallen in; and it was supposed, at that time, that, if peace had continued, a million annually might have been spared out of it, in discharge of the debt.

"Then came on the American war, and at this time it was declared and generally believed, that the country could not support itself for seven years. However, it did support itself, and added to the public debt more than one hundred millions; so that, during a peace of eleven years, little more than ten millions of debt was paid off; during a war of seven years, an additional debt of more than one hundred millions was contracted. At the commencement of the American war, it was stated by one author, that it would be altogether chimerical to expect that the public debt should ever be completely discharged, by any savings which were likely to be made from the ordinary revenue of that time ; and it appears that he was right, for there have been no proofs shown to the contrary ; and it would have required a hundred years of profound peace to have accomplished it ; instead of which, seven years from that period, involved

---

* The Bank proprietors then paid one hundred and ten thousand pounds for a renewal of their charter, and now receive three millions a year for doing the public business ; therefore, it was money well spent by them.

the country in an additional debt, which would have required another hundred years to discharge it by the same means.

"Another author, at that time, represented the public funds of the different indebted nations of Europe, particularly those of England, as the accumulation of a great capital, superadded to the other capital of the country, by means of which its trade was extended, its manufactures multiplied, and its lands cultivated and improved, much beyond what they could have been by means of that other capital only. This author is not named, but he was highly condemned, at that time, for the opinion he had delivered upon the subject. However, time has shown, that he also was perfectly right ; for as our necessities have increased, so have our means. Who could have believed, except this unknown author, in the year 1775, when the country was considered to be undone, that the government of the country could increase the public debt six hundred millions more than it was at that time ; that they could have the credit to borrow such a sum, or that the people could have the means or possibility of furnishing it ? The proof is, that the industry of the country must have rapidly increased the capital of the country, during the war, otherwise this immense sum could not have been raised.

"What would the desponding writers of 1775 now say of paying off the public debt ? If some writers are correct and can prove, as they assert, that the public debt promotes industry, it would, perhaps, be best never to pay it off ; which agrees with the sentiments of most of the stockholders, and people of this country who feel the advantages of possessing stock and paying no taxes ; but those who do not like taxes, and yet are obliged to pay them, are, most likely, of a different opinion. Most people like stock, and few like taxes ; it is therefore, no wonder that most people, who have the means, vest their property in the former, which seems the only way to avoid the latter ; but there seems to be something wrong in this system, which does not bear equally on all classes of people. It is a kind of political bribe against the industry of the country ; or saying, in other words, if you will lend government your money, you shall not be taxed; but if you lend it to other people, you must expect to pay taxes."

In the chapter on Colonization and Commerce, Mr. Phelps strenuously advocates freedom of trade, and urges the equity of the colonies contributing to the general support of the Empire.

"It is not natural that eighteen millions of people, composing the population of the United Kingdom, should bear the whole burden of taxes and expences, and leave above fifty millions of British subjects free, without contributing any part towards the support of the empire, at least if they have an equal participation of benefits. Every colony, or settlement, necessarily contributes, more or less, to increase the expence of the general government; and if it do not contribute its share towards defraying this expence, an unequal burden must fall upon the other part of the empire. It is, in fact, comparatively, but a small part of the community, and those least able to bear it, that endure the burdens of the whole British empire. If despotic governments have a sovereignty over the whole property of the people, they can only contribute according to their means; what they do not save the government cannot get. A free people called, should not be taxed upon a worse principle than this; but they certainly are in general, for whatever may be their privations, they must pay taxes.

"Colonies can be of no benefit, unless they contribute to the revenue, commerce, and industry of the parent state; but which they would always do, under proper regulations. Perhaps it might have been as well for this country, if it had never possessed any colonies, without better regulations. The American colonies, or the Americans, involved England in full forty millions of debt to protect them, and full one hundred millions, afterwards, in trying to keep them in subjection. We are now more valuable to each other, as friends, than we were as relations. If colonies cannot, or will not, contribute to the expences of the state that protects them, they had better be left to themselves. But necessity has no law: we have now an immense empire, an immense debt, and an immense load of taxation, with an immense population; and it is not feeble means, or feeble efforts, that can support or relieve the one or the other.

"All colonies should naturally contribute to the general support of the empire; but they should have equal benefits and privileges, and become a united people. They should have their representatives in the senate, so as to have a general interest in the state; their rights should be every way equal, without distinction. Their industry, commerce, and property, should be encouraged and protected by the same laws, and they should all be equally concerned and benefited by the general welfare of the empire. Prosperity would grow up with such a system. A unity of interests would be formed, which no circumstances could divide. The surplus population of one part of the great empire would remove to the other, as circumstances or occasions may invite them; their mutual wants would be supplied, and thus a natural intercourse would be kept up, for the general benefit of all.

The two last chapters treat on the perceptions of sense, on the moral and social nature of man, on the powers of the human mind and intellect, the perfectibility of man, and the confirmation of a future state. We confess that we did not expect to find these topics in a work, expressly devoted to political economy; they are, however, treated with ability, though rather desultorily. We noticed several passages, which we could wish to have selected; but we have already extracted so largely, in the present as well as in the preceding number of our journal, that we have not room for any additional observations. Our object has rather been to invite attention to Mr. Phelps's very valuable work. More practical wisdom and less fanciful theory we have not often seen in any of the modern treatises on political economy.

Lectures on the Principal Evidences, and the several dispensations of Revealed Religion; familiarly addressed to young persons, with select references to the most valuable Treatises on each subject. By W. Roby, 8vo. 8s. fine paper, 10s. Longman, and Co. London, 1819.

A benevolent and active concern for the rising generation, forms one distinguishing feature of the present times. The lowest classes have now the opportunity of receiving gratuitous instruction, sufficient to qualify them for the successful cultivation of their intellectual powers. An increasing disposition to read is the natural result; and this circumstance dictates the vast importance of furnishing youth with suitable books;—books that may inform their judgments, and captivate their minds, without depraving their hearts. Numerous publications, admirably adapted to these purposes, have of late years issued from the press: and Mr. Roby has added another to the number, which is well fitted to guard the minds of those, who, advancing to maturity, are ready to enter on the business of life, against the insidious arts of infidelity.

These Lectures were originally delivered from the pulpit, as weekly discourses. They are divided into four parts, embracing the evidences and dispensations of Revealed Religion in all their branches. Novelty of argument is not to be expected on a subject which has so often been discussed. The evidences adduced are treated in a clear, perspicuous, and attractive manner. Many pleasing anecdotes are incidentally introduced, illustrative of the author's arguments; and the value of his work is considerably enhanced by the insertion of judicious references to the most valuable treatises on each subject, for the information of those who may have the opportunity or the desire of prosecuting further inquiries. We should regard this work as a valuable accession to British Literature at any time; but it is peculiarly seasonable at the present crisis, when principles subversive of social order and religion are circulated through the medi-

um of the press in the cheapest forms, and with the utmost assiduity.

The blessedness of those who die in the Lord.—A Sermon, delivered April 5th, 1818, at Ebenezer Chapel, Bristol, on the occasion of the death of Mr. James Bundy. By Thomas Wood. 8vo. 2s. Bristol, Printed: Longman and Co. London.

A Biographical Sketch of the Life and Character of the late Mr. James Bundy, whose active benevolence and Ministerial Fidelity, procured to him a large share of public confidence and much personal esteem. By Thomas Wood, 8vo. 2s. Bristol, printed: Longman and Co. London.

Funeral Orations were pronounced over the illustrious dead, among the Greeks and Romans: a similar practice has been adopted by Christians, and continues to this day. When confined to persons, whose lives have been distinguished for their benevolence, their piety, or other eminent virtues, we conceive this practice to be both useful and beneficial. The discourse under consideration is well adapted to display the happiness attending a life of true piety. The individual, who gave occasion to it, and of whom we have an interesting memoir, appears to have been a person of rare disinterestedness and uncommon benevolence. Rising from humble poverty, to affluent circumstances, he employed himself in various ways, in doing good; of which we have numerous pleasing instances. One of these we transcribe, as it suggests to those who have the means, a simple and efficacious mode of assisting the industrious poor.

"On Saturday evenings he regularly visited the market,—not as an idle observer, but to do good to the poor. If he beheld a poor person at a butcher's stall, inquiring the price of a piece of meat and then turning away for want of more money, he would call him back, 'saying what can you afford to give?' on being told how much, he would produce the additional sum, and purchase it for the poor man. He would then go in pursuit of other persons of the same description and assist them in like manner. Thus he spent the Saturday evenings, relieving promiscuously the wants of the poor, who, in return for his humanity and benevolence, offered up prayers and poured blessings upon him. After he had gone round distributing his bounty, he would then purchase pieces of meat for his own poor, or those indigent families whom he visited at their own houses. When he had finished this work of charity and labour of love, he would return home with a glad heart, and recount the blessings he enjoyed above others."

Christian Missions, an enlightened Species of Charity; or, a Vindication of the Policy and Expediency as well as Benevolence of the Royal Letter, authorising Subscriptions throughout the Kingdom in aid of the venerable Society for propagating the Gospel. Respectfully addressed to the Members of the Society, and to the Reverend the Clergy, who are about to plead its cause. By the Rev. S. C. Wilks, A. M. 8vo. 2s. 6d. Rivingtons, London, 1819.

Mr. Wilks is already advantageously known to many of our readers as the Author of two volumes of valuable "Christian Essays."* In the present well written tract he has successfully and ably vindicated the enlightened policy of Christian Missions. He observes with great truth that

" There was a time when to be liberal in alms-giving was considered as almost all that was necessary to constitute true charity. This period is gone by: the enlarged deductions of modern science, and the necessity of husbanding the resources of charity, with a view to the best application of them, have tended to bring to light the injurious effects of many schemes,

---

* See an account of this Work in the Literary Panorama, Vol. VII. N. S. p. 596.

which were, doubtless, originally planned with a truly benevolent intention; so that there is danger lest, in the eagerness of discovery and reform, we revert to the opposite extreme, and learn to consider the efforts of Christian charity as of little or no importance, or even as positively injurious to the great family of mankind.

" It is true, perhaps, that never was the virtue of charity more extensive, or more popular, than at the present moment; yet it cannot but be evident, that, in the attempt to reduce what is naturally little more than an unguided impulse of the mind to a regular and enlightened system, there is danger of confining this Christian virtue in undue trammels, and of narrowing too much the sphere of its exertions. Warped either by incorrect ideas of political economy, or by false deductions from true premises, there are not wanting persons who decry almost every species of charity; who tell us, plainly, that the various plans pursued for the amelioration of the human race are useless, or even mischievous; that the world will ever remain what it has ever been; that the same, or nearly the same, measure of vice and want, of irreligion and misery, will always exist; that the efforts of charity only remove the burden from one to another; and that, in short, true wisdom dictates that we should leave the world where we found it, under the guidance of laws over which we can exercise no effectual controul.

" There are few persons, much acquainted with the present state of society, who have not occasionally to encounter arguments of this description; and that not only from men who are glad to exhibit their science as a cloak for their want of charity, but even from others, whose indifference to the necessities of their fellow-creatures is not the *cause* but the *effect* of their misapplied speculations;—men who *would* perhaps have been charitable, had they not taken up an unfounded opinion that charity is useless. Persons of these and similar descriptions naturally keep aloof from the various excellent institutions, which reflect so much honour upon this age and nation. Nor is this all: the patrons and friends of such institutions are viewed by them as persons whose affections are more expanded than their understandings, and who, in pursuing a local or partial object, are not aware of its general bearing upon the state of society, and of its ultimate effects upon the human race."

From the consideration of these circumstances, our author is led to define in what truly enlightened christian charity does consist, viz. that it springs from right motives, and consequently blesses the giver—that it also benefits the receiver,—and that it is not calculated to injure others. This definition is illustrated in various points of view, with much force and clearness of argument; and the author then proceeds to shew that the objects proposed by the various religious institutions, which do honour to British liberality and benevolence, fairly come under that definition.

The application of these arguments and considerations is then made to the cause of missions generally, and particularly to that Society, for whose benefit the royal letter (alluded to in the title page*) has been obtained. The Course of Doctrine, which a Christian Missionary ought to inculcate, is next stated, with considerable eloquence and with fervent but rational piety. We have dwelt the longer on this pamphlet on account of its immediate interest, and also because of the claims which the Society, advocated by it, has upon the liberality of every one who is desirous of promoting the temporal and eternal happiness of his fellow mortals.

Letters from a Father to his Son, in an Office under Government, including Letters on Religious Sentiment and Belief. By the Rev. H. G. White, A. M. foolscap 8vo. 6s. 6d. Asperne, London, 1819.

The object which the eloquent Author of this impressive and well written volume had in view, in composing it, was the desire of promoting the welfare of a son, whom he was anxious to guard from the snares and temptations to which inexperienced youth are exposed on their entrance into public life, where the evil influence of bad example is too frequently found to bear down the resolves of virtuous intention, and to

* See this Letter and a brief notice of this Society, in p. 714.

surprise the best constituted mind into a surrender of its purest convictions of duty to certain habits of associated life, which, however tolerated by custom, are too apt to weaken the first principles of prudence, and to betray ingenuous youth into incautious compliance.

With this motive most of the letters, now under consideration, were written and inserted in a respectable contemporary journal,* where we read them as they successively appeared, with much pleasure; and that pleasure has not been diminished on the re-perusal of them. The five last of the collection, are now added, for the first time, "from a consciousness" (says the author) "that all moral precept, as enforcing our obligations towards Society and ourselves, must be deprived of its most important support, if not blended with a religious sense of the relation in which we stand towards God."

Although this volume is chiefly designed for young men in public offices, it contains much important precept that is of *general application*. Every page breathes the solicitude of a father, anxious to promote the welfare of his son; and this circumstance imparts a tone of affectionate earnestness that cannot fail to make a deep impression on the minds of well disposed youth. We have not often met with so much practical wisdom, clothed in so pleasing a form; and we dismiss this handsomely printed volume, with our cordial recommendation of it as a valuable manual for young persons, who are just entering into public life.

Edward and George; or Lessons from real life, for Children of early years. 18mo. 2s. Darton and Co. London, 1818.

The Promised Visit: including an account of the various methods of manufacturing Paper in different countries. To which are annexed fifty questions, with a view to impress the subject on the youthful mind. By the Author of the "Dew Drop." 18mo. 1s. 6d. Darton and Co. London, 1818.

Winter Scenes, to amuse and instruct the Rising Generation. By M. H. 18mo. 1s. 6d. Darton and Co. London, 1818.

These are very interesting and well written books; and are excellently adapted to convey instruction and amusement in the most pleasing form. They are each ornamented with an appropriate engraving, and will form an acceptable present to young persons.

Literary Register.

Authors, Editors, and Publishers, are particularly requested to forward to the Literary Panorama Office, post paid, on, or before the 19th day of each month, the titles, prices, and other particulars of works in hand or published for this department of the Work.

. . . .

BOOKS ANNOUNCED FOR PUBLICATION.

ARTS, FINE.

Thirty Views in Islington and Pentonville, from original drawings by Mr. Augustus Pugin, with concise descriptions of each subject, by E. W. Brayley; 4to.

BIBLIOGRAPHY.

The Rev. T. F. Dibdin is preparing a Bibliographical, Antiquarian, and Picturesque Tour in Normandy, France, and Germany, in three volumes, to arrange with his Decameron.

BIOGRAPHY.

Mr. Oliver Cromwell, a descendant of the family, will soon publish, Memoirs of the Protector, Oliver Cromwell, and of his sons Richard and Henry, with some original letters and other family papers.

In the Press, and speedily will be published, Memoirs of John Tobin, Author of "The Honey-moon," &c. &c. With two unpublished Plays and other Selections from his MSS. By Miss Benger, Author of Memoirs of Mrs. Elizabeth Hamilton, &c.

In the press, and will be published in a few weeks, in 1 vol 8vo. with a Portrait, An Account of the Life of James Crichton of Cluny, commonly called the admirable Crichton; with Notes, and an Appendix of Original Papers. By Patrick Frazer Tytler, F. R. S. E.

The Rev. J. Evans, of Islington, has on the eve of publication, his Memoirs of the Rev. William Richards, L.L.D. with some Account of Roger Williams, founder of Rhode Island, and first assertor of complete Religious Liberty in the United States of America. The work is inscribed to the Marquis of Lansdown.

CHEMISTRY.

Dr. Harrington, Author of Fire and Planetary Life, from which all the new and improved Nautical Tables have been taken, has in the press, and will publish shortly, An extension of his Important Theory and System of Chemistry, elucidating all the phenomena, without one single anomaly.

HISTORY.

Annals of Scotland, from the Accession of Malcolm III, in the year 1057, to the Accession of the House of Stewart, in the year 1371. To which are added, Tracts relative to the History and Antiquities of Scotland. By Sir David Dalrymple, Bart. of Hailes, 3rd edition, in 3 vols. 8vo.

MEDICINE.

Dr. Bateman will soon publish, Reports on the Weather and Diseases of London, from 1804 to 1816, comprising practical remarks on their causes and treatment.

Mr. W. A. Pearkes is printing, Popular Observations on the Diseases incident to Literary and Sedentary Persons, with hints for their prevention and cure.

Dr. F. Swediaur is printing, a Treatise on the Symptoms, Effects, and Nature of the Treatment of Syphilitic Disorders.

Preparing for publication, An Essay on the Diagnosis, Morbid Anatomy, and Treatment of the Diseases of Children; by Marshall Hall, M. D. F. R. S. E. &c.

MISCELLANIES.

In the press and speedily will be published, a new edition, corrected throughout, of Grey's Memoria Technica, to which is added, Dr. Lowe's Table of Mnemonics, in 1 vol. 12mo.

A new edition of Debrett's Baronetage of England, corrected and continued to the present Time.

New Italian Journal.—L'Ape Atalians a Londra. Giornale per le colte persone de la Gran Brettagna e d'Italia, in 8vo.

Literary Register. [710

A Number will appear regularly on the 15th and 30th of each Month. The Price to Subscribers for Three Months will be 2s. each Number, to Non-subscribers 3s. Numbers 1. and II. have already appeared.

In a few days will be published in 2 vols, foolscap 8vo. Hints on the Sources of Happiness, addressed to her Children by a Mother, Author of " Always Happy," &c.

John Gamble, Esq. Author of Irish Sketches, &c. &c. will shortly publish, Views of Society and Manners in the North of Ireland, in a Series of Letters written in the year 1818.

Mr. Partington of the London Institution is preparing materials for a History of that Establishment, with plates, &c. to which will be prefixed a Biographical Memoir of the late Professor Porson, with Anecdotes, Jeux d'esprit, &c. to be entitled Parsoniana.

Shortly will be published, in demy 12mo. The Wandering Jew, being an authentic account of the manners and customs of the most distinguished nations, interspersed with anecdotes of celebrated men at different periods since the last destruction of the Temple of Jerusalem, in a narrative supposed to have been written by that mysterious character.

NATURAL HISTORY.

The eleventh volume of Dr. Shaw's Zoology will appear in a few days.

Dr. W. E. Leach has nearly ready for publication, a Synopsis of the British Molluscæ, being an Introduction to the method of arranging the shells of Great Britain according to the structure of the animals, with descriptions, and illustrative engravings.

NATURAL PHILOSOPHY.

The Author of Conversations on Chemistry, &c. has a new work at press, entitled, Conversations on Natural Philosophy, in which the Elements of that Science are familiarly explained and adapted to the comprehension of Young Pupils, illustrated with plates, by Larry.

NAVIGATION.

A new edition of Mr. Darcy Lever's Young Sea Officer's Sheet Anchor, or a Guide to Practical Seamanship, in 1 vol. 4to. with considerable improvements, will appear in a short time.

NOVELS.

A Third Series of Tales of my Landlord. Collected and arranged by Jedediah Cleishbotham, Schoolmaster and Parish-clerk of Gandercleugh. Con-

taining the Bride of Lammermuir, and a Legend of the Wars of Montrose. In 4 vols. 12mo. To be published in the first week of June.

A Romance on the subject of Robin Hood is preparing for publication.

POETRY.

A Translation of Paradise Lost into Welsh, in the same metre as the original, by W. Owen Pughe, will be published in the course of the ensuing month. The unparalleled copiousness of the antient British Language, has enabled the translator not only to keep verbally to the meaning of the author, but generally to preserve even his varied pauses and other ornaments, and at the same time to avoid all literal elisions.

Mr. John Lawson, author of the Maniac, has in the press, Orient Harping, a desultory poem, in a foolscap 8vo. volume.

Shortly will be published, in 1 vol. 8vo. The Lay of Agincourt, and other Poems.

The Vestriad or the Opera, a mock epick poem, in five cantos, with Notes and engravings, by the Author of the Banquet, the Dessert, &c. &c.

Poems founded on the Events of the War in the Peninsula, written during its progress and after its conclusion, by the wife of an officer, who served in its campaigns, will soon appear, in an 8vo. volume.

A new edition of Ossian's Poems is preparing for publication, with notes, critical, historical, and explanatory, by Mr. Wm. Beauford.

Mr. Bird is preparing for the press, a second edition of his poem, the Vale of Slaughden.

Mrs. Kentish, Resident at St. Salvadore, in Brazil, has in the press, through the medium of her friend, K. Pringle, esq. of Liverpool, a collection of about 120 Poems, which will be compressed into a small handsome 8vo volume.

Mr. W. S. Rose is preparing a translation of the Orlando Furioso of Ariosto, with a life and notes.

The Author of " Night," a descriptive poem, will soon publish, Tales of Night, in rhyme, comprising Bothwell, Second Nuptials, the Exile, and the Devil on Shealfden Pike.

POLITICAL ECONOMY.

John Clay has in the press, a Free Trade Essential to the Welfare of Great Britain, or, An Inquiry into the Cause of the present distressed State of the Country, and the consequent Increase of Pauperism, Misery, and Crime. To which are added some observations on Two Letters to the Rt. Hon. Robert Peel, M. P. by one of his Constituents. The first on the pernicious effects of a valuable standard of value. The second on the Causes of the increase of Pauperism, &c. &c.

THEOLOGY.

The Rev. Christopher Benson has in the press, an Inquiry into the True Time of the Birth, Baptism, and Crucifixion of Jesus Christ.

A new version of some of the Epistles of St. Paul and of the Epistle of St. James, is about to be submitted to the Public in a cheap and unostentatious form. The translator has had Campbell in view as to the arrangement and manner of the work, and much care and pains have been bestowed to exhibit the sense of the Apostles, faithfully, clearly, and according to the present idiom of our language.

Sermons. By the Rev. C. R. Maturin, Curate of St. Peter's Dublin, in 8vo.

The Rev. Harvey Marriott has in the press, Homilies for the Young, in two duodecimo volumes.

TOPOGRAPHY.

A Description of the Western Islands of Scotland, including the Isle of Man: comprising an Account of their Geological Structure; with Remarks on their Agriculture, Economy, Scenery and Antiquities. By J. Macculloch, M. D. F. L. S. In 2 vols. 8vo. with a Volume of illustrative engravings in Quarto.

A History of the Castle, Priory, and Church of Kenilworth, is printing in a 4to. volume, illustrated by engravings.

VOYAGES AND TRAVELS.

Mr. Playfair is printing in two 8vo. volumes, France, as it is,—not Lady Morgan's France.

Mr. Robert Walpole has in the press, Travels in various Countries in the East; being a continuation of his Memoirs on European and Asiatic Turkey.

. . . .

BOOKS PUBLISHED.

ARTS, FINE.

Number V. of Volume III. (being the concluding Number) of Claude's Liber Veritatis; containing Twenty-two Prints after the original Drawings of Claude le Lorrain, in the Collection of his Grace

the Duke of Devonshire, executed by Richard Earlom, in the Manner and Taste of the Drawings. Proof impressions 2l. 12s. 6d., Prints 1l. 11s. 6d.

The Seventh Number of Mr. J. P. Neale's Illustrated History of Westminster Abbey, is just published.

BIOGRAPHY.

The Life of the late Rt. Hon. John Philpot Curran, Master of the Rolls in Ireland. By his Son, William Henry Curran, Esq. Barrister at Law. With a Portrait and Fac-similies, in 2 vols. 8vo. 1l. 4s. boards.

BOTANY.

Fuci; or Coloured Figures and Descriptions, in Latin and English, of the Plants referred by Botanists to the Genus Fucus. By Dawson Turner, Esq. F R.S. F. L. S. &c. &c. The 48th and last Number, 4to. 7s. 6d.

EDUCATION.

Hints for the Improvement of Early Education and Nursery Discipline, 12mo. 3s. 6d.

Introductory Greek Exercises, to those of Neilson, Dunbar, and others; arranged under Models, to assist the Learner. By Nathaniel Howard, 12mo. 5s. 6d.

The National Spelling-Book; or Sure Guide to English Spelling and Pronunciation, compiled from the Dictionaries of Walker, Sheridan, and Jones; the Syllables divided agreeably to their approved Methods, and arranged on such a Plan as cannot fail to familiarise the Art of Spelling and Pronunciation, remove the difficulties, and facilate general improvement in the English Law. By B. Tabart. Printed on a large and clear type, 1s. 6d. bound.

HISTORY.

The Fifth Edition, with a Continuation to the present time, of The History, Civil and Commercial, of the British West Indies. By Bryan Edwards, Esq. F. R. S. S. A. In 5 vols. 8vo. with a 4to. vol. of plates, 3l. 15s.

Proceedings in Parga, and the Ionian Islands; with a Series of Correspondence and other justificatory Documents. By Lieut. Colonel de Bossett. With a Map, 8vo. 7s

HORTICULTURE.

Memoirs of the Caledonian Horticultural Society, with numerous plates, 2 vols. 8vo. 1l. 5s.

LAW.

A Practical Treatise on the Criminal Law, adapted to the Use of the Profession, Magistrates, and Private Gentlemen. By Joseph Chitty, Esq. of the Inner Temple, Barrister at Law, 4 vols. royal 8vo. 5*l*. 5*s*.

The Trial of Augustus Bogle French, John French Burke, and Matthew Welch, for a Conspiracy; in the Court of King's Bench, before Lord Chief Justice Abbott and a Special Jury, on Wednesday the 9th of December, 1818.—To which are added the further Proceedings on the 27th of January, and 1st and 3rd of February, 1819, and the Sentence. Taken in Shorthand by Wm. Brodie Gurney, Esq. Shorthand Writer to both Houses of Parliament, 8vo. 5*s*.

The Attorney's Clerks' Assistant; containing Plain and Easy Directions for Levying Fines, and Suffering Recoveries, arranged under an entirely new system, in the immediate order in which they are proceeded with throughout the several stages, 8vo. 3*s*.

MANUFACTURES.

The Theory and Practice of Bleaching, with Oxymuriatic Acid; as now practised by some of the most eminent Bleachers, Paper-makers, &c. &c. in which an attempt is made to explain the Nature of that Process, shewing its immediate Connexion with the old Practice of Exposure upon the Grass and to point out the Cause and Failure of it. Also, an Analysis of the several Methods, now in use for the Bleaching of Woollen Cloths and Silks. By a Chemist, 8vo. 3*s*.

MEDICINE.

An Inquiry, illustrating the Nature of Tuberculated Accretions of Serous Membranes; and the Origin of Tubercles and Tumours in different Textures of the Body. By John Baron, M.D. Physician to the General Infirmary at Gloucester. Illustrated by five plates, 8vo. 14*s*.

MINERALOGY AND GEOLOGY.

Familiar Lessons on Mineralogy and Geology; explaining the easiest Methods of discriminating Minerals, and the Earthy Substances, commonly called Rocks, which compose the Primitive, Secondary, Flœtz or Flat, and Alluvial Formations: to which is added, a Description of the Lapidaries, Apparatus, &c. By J. Mawe. With engravings, and a coloured plate, 12mo. 5*s*.

MISCELLANIES.

The Encyclopædia Edinensis; or, Dictionary of Arts and Sciences, and Miscellaneous Literature. To be completed in Six Volumes 4to. and illustrated by 180 plates. By James Millar, M.D. vol. 3, part I, price 8*s*.

A Letter respectfully addressed to his Royal Highness the Prince Regent, on Occasion of the Death of her late lamented Majesty. By Lysias. Price 1*s*. 6*d*.

A Treatise on the Kaleidoscope; containing an Account of the Principles and Construction of the Instrument, and of its Application in various Forms to the useful Arts. By David Brewster, LL D, F R. S. 12mo. with Seven Plates, 6*s*. boards.

Useful Knowledge; or, a Familiar Account of the various Productions of Nature, Mineral, Vegetable, and Animal, which are chiefly employed for the Use of Man. Illustrated by numerous Figures, and intended as a Work both of Instruction and Reference. By the Rev. William Bingley, A. M. The Second Edition, with considerable Alterations and Additions, and with a new set of 16 plates, in 3 vols. 12mo. 1*l*. 1*s*.

The Journal of a Soldier of the 71st or Glasgow Regiment, Highland and Light Infantry, from 1806 to 1815. 12mo. 5*s*.

NOVELS.

The Aubid, an Eastern Tale, by James Atkinson. Esq. 8vo. 3*s*. sewed.

The Black Robber, a Romance. By Edward Ball. In 8 vols. 12mo. 16*s*. 0*d*. boards.

The Sisters of St. Gothard, a Tale. By Elizabeth Cullen Brown. In 2 vols. 12mo. 10*s*. 6*d*. boards.

Gogmagog-Hall, or the Philosophical Lord and Governess, a Satirical Novel, by the Author of Prodigious! or Childe Paddie in London, 3 vols. 1*l*. 1*s*.

POETRY.

The Commemoration of Handel, (Second Edition) and other Poems: to, which is added a Prospectus of a Translation of Virgil, partly original, and partly altered from Dryden and Pitt, with Specimens. By John Ring, 8vo. 0*s*.

Greenland and other Poems. By James Montgomery, 8vo. 10*s*. 6*d*.

The Triumphs of Religion; a Sacred Poem. In Four Parts. By Miss Cope, Author of the Suicide, a Poem. The Second Edition, considerably enlarged, price 7*s*.

Peter Bell, a Tale in Verse. By William Wordsworth, Esq. 8vo. 5*s*. 6*d*.

POLITICAL ECONOMY.

Letters of Daniel Hardcastle to the Editor of the Times Journal, on the Subject of the Bank Restriction, the Regulations of the Mint, &c. with Notes and Additions by Richard Page, 8vo. 6s.

The Oppressed Labourers; the Means for their Relief, as well as the Reduction of their Number, and of the Poor Rates, presented to Public Notice Dedicated, in the First Instance, to the Agricultural Societies of Great Britain, 8vo. 1s. 6d.

Observations on the Poor Laws; their Policy vindicated against the Aspersions cast upon them by numerous Authors; the State of England compared with that of Ireland, Scotland, and France; &c. &c. By James Macphail, 8vo. 2s.

A Remonstrance, addressed to the Author of Two Letters to the Rt. Hon. Robert Peel, on the Effects of a Variable Standard of Value, and on the Condition of the Poor. By an English Gentlemen, 8vo. 2s 6d.

THEOLOGY.

An Historical and Critical Inquiry into the Interpretation of the Hebrew Scriptures, with Remarks on Mr. Bellamy's new Translation. By John William Whittaker, M. A. Fellow of St. John's College, Cambridge, 8vo. 9s.

Christian Missions, an Enlightened Species of Charity; or, a Vindication of the Policy and Expediency as well as Benevolence of the Royal Letter, authorising Subscriptions throughout the Kingdom, in aid of the venerable Society for propagating the Gospel. Respectfully addressed to the Members of the Society, and to the reverend the Clergy who are about to plead its Cause. By the Rev. S. C. Wilks, A. M. Author of Christian Essays, and of the St. David's Prize Essay for 1811, on the Clerical Character, &c. 8vo. 2s. 6d.

Elementary Discourses; or, Sermons addressed to Children. By John Burder, M. A. 12mo. 4s.

The Protestant's Catechism on the Origin of Popery, and on the Grounds of the Roman Catholic Claims. By the Bishop of St David's. The Second Edition, 1s.

Sermons preached in St. John's Chapel, Edinburgh, by Daniel Sandford, D. D. One of the Bishops of the Scottish Episcopal Church, and formerly Student of Christ Church, Oxford, 8vo. 12s.

Thoughts on Baptism, as an ordinance of Proselytism; including Observations on the controversy respecting term of Communion, 8vo. 4s.

Scripture Costume, exhibited in a Series of engravings, representing the principal Personages mentioned in the Sacred Writings, drawn under the superintendance of Benjamin West, Esq. President of the Royal Academy, by R. Satchwell: with Biographical Sketches, and Historical Remarks on the Manners and Customs of the Eastern Nations, elephant 4to. 5l. 5s.

Just published, Remarks on the Foreknowledge of God; suggested by passages in Dr. Adam Clarke's Commentary on the New Testament, by Gill Timms, 8vo. 2s. 6d.

TOPOGRAPHY.

A Geographical and Statistical Description of Scotland. By James Playfair, D D. F. R S. and F. A S. E. Principal of the United College of St. Andrews, and Historiographer to his Royal Highness the Prince Regent, in 2 vols. 8vo. with an elegant and accurate Sheet Map of Scotland, 1l. 4s. boards.

A Statistical, Historical, and Political Description of the Colony of New South Wales, and its dependent Settlements on Van Dieman's Land: with a particular Enumeration of the Advantages which these Colonies offer for Emigration, and their Superiority in many respects over those possessed by the United States of America. By W. C. Wentworth, Esq. a Native of the Colony, 8vo. 5s.

VOYAGES AND TRAVELS.

An Account of the Kingdom of Nepal, and of the Territories annexed to this Dominion by the House of Gorkha. By Francis Hamilton (formerly Buchanan) M. D F. R. S. L. E. and Fellow of the Societies of Antiquaries, and of the Linnean and Asiatic Societies, 4to. with engravings, 2l. 2s. boards.

A Classical Tour through Italy and Sicily, tending to illustrate some Districts which have not been described by Mr. Eustace in his Classical Tour. By Sir Richard Colt Hoare, Bart. Second Edition. in 2 vols. 8vo. 1l. 4s.

Foreign Literary Gazette.

AMERICA: UNITED STATES.

New Institution: Medical.

At New Orleans there seems to be a disposition to emulate the studies of Europe. We, some years ago, gave notice of an Institution for Religious purposes, for circulating the Bible among the neighbouring population. Another Society has more recently been formed, for the purpose of promoting Medical Science. Several Physicians and Surgeons, chiefly French, and educated at the Schools of Paris, Montpellier, and Strasburgh, who have settled at New Orleans, have lately established in that city a Medical Society. This Institution, though yet in its infancy, is constantly consulted by the neighbouring authorities, and obtains a place in the confidence of the public, which no doubt will be justified and confirmed by the talents of the professors associated.

This Society has lately published two pamphlets: one of which is entitled, Sketch of the proceedings of the Medical Society of New Orleans, from August 1817 to January 1818. The second is a Report made to the Medical Society of New Orleans concerning the Yellow Fever that reigned in that city in the manner of an epidemic, during the Summer of 1817. Both these pamphlets are dated April 1818.

This Society, embodied by an act of the legislature, February 16, 1816, has lately sent over several diplomas of corresponding members, to eminent medical practitioners in Europe, especially to those of the faculty in France.

Literary Institution: Historical.

Historical Society of New York.—(January 8, 1819.) This is an Institution, that, perhaps ought to have been formed long ago, and while there was a possibility of recovering and preserving some of the traditions received from the early settlers, and possibly from the original inhabitants. The object of this Society is to cultivate the Natural History, the Ecclesiastical History, and the Civil History of America in general: but especially of the City and Province of New York. It has already formed a library consisting of works analogous to the purpose of its formation, consisting of ten or twelve thousand volumes; also, a cabinet of the most valuable, or most rare productions of the American continent: and thirdly, a collection of portraits of such persons, whether natives or foreigners, as have distinguished themselves by services done to America, or by writings in which they have treated on subjects relating to transatlantic interests. In the sitting of December 7, 1818, Mr. Verplank read a discourse, which the Society ordered to be printed, and it has appeared under the title of an Anniversary Discourse delivered before the New York Historical Society, by Julian C. Verplank, Esq 8vo. New York, 1818.

AUSTRIA.

Animal Magnetism forbid.

Our pages have repeatedly noticed the attention paid by the Governments on the Continent to the progress and practice of Animal Magnetism. We learn from German publications, that in the month of November last, all the Physicians not matriculated at the University of Vienna, were called together, in order to be officially informed of a Resolution taken by the Supreme Powers, by which the practice of Animal Magnetism is generally prohibited throughout the Dominions of the Emperor of Austria. Several of the Doctors of Vienna, who are known to be empirical practitioners of this art, have been publicly censured, and threatened with an entire suspension of their functions, in case of their continuing to have recourse to the operations of Magnetism. Directions to the same effect have been given to all the Governors of Provinces, as well as to all houses and hospitals established for the recovery of health, in the Austrian Monarchy.

Gas Lights.

The attempts made to light the streets, &c. of Vienna, by means of hydrogen gas, have afforded the most satisfactory results.

Mosaic safely arrived.

The famous Mosaic of which we have repeatedly spoken, has arrived safely at Vienna. It is a copy of the famous Last Supper by Leonardo da Vinci, executed by Professor Raffaelli of Milan, who is also arrived at Vienna. The dimensions of it are 28 feet by 18, which is the size of the original. The Professor has a double merit in this work: that of having applied with the most exemplary and admirable patience and address, an Art which hitherto has been confined to small compositions, and also, that of having preserved, to a comparative immortality, a work so valuable, that has long been on the point of perishing from mere old age.

While we are applauding a performance so considerable as this triumph of the art of painting in Mosaic, may justly be deemed, we ought not to lose sight of that noble specimen of the art of Engraving by which its principal beauties have lately been circulated throughout the world. It is true, Volpato's print has not the colours of the original; but, in every thing else it presents with great accuracy the conceptions of the original author.

BELGIUM.

Royal Historiographer : History.

M. Stuart, preacher at Amsterdam, and Historiographer of the Kingdom of the Netherlands, has been commanded by the Government to compose Annals of the Kingdom, in the Dutch language. He has already published a Roman history, and a history of the French Revolution; both of them large works.

DENMARK.

University of Copenhagen.

Our Library has lately received a present of Books, Chinese, Hindoo, and Arabic, &c. printed at Calcutta : To which is added a copy of all the translations of Scripture, which have been made at Calcutta. We owe these valuable acquisitions to the attention of M. Wallich, a learned Dane, now Director of the Botanic Garden at Calcutta. He has added, from his own Library, sixty five works, mostly of price, and rare in Europe. The Directors of this Library have charged M. Wallich to make their acknowledgements to the government of Calcutta, and to the Missionaries there ; and in return have sent to the English College at Fort William an assortment of works on the ancient literature of the North of Europe.

Sepulchre of Christ, opinion on.

Bishop Munter, one of the most learned men of Denmark, has lately addressed a letter to M. Gregoire, formerly Bishop of Blois, in which, among other things, he notices the conjecture of Dr. E. D. Clarke, respecting the tomb of Jesus Christ. He says "a learned Englishman, Mr. Clarke, who has visited Palestine, believes that he has found near Jerusalem a tomb which might be that of our Lord. I rather think he is mistaken in his hypothesis; for, the tomb of J. C. was cer-

tainly cut in the rock in the ??????? of Gihon, near the road lead??? ?? ????, and not in the mountain of S??. There are in certain adjacent place? ??? Jewish tombs with the inscripti?? ? "the Holy Sion," which is very gener?. Mr. Clarke insists that Golgotha was ????? ground, but, it is much more pr???e, that it was the place of public exec??? as almost all interpreters have expla?? it. As our readers know, this opinion ?? been supported in the Panorama, and ?? are happy to find our sentiments co?? firmed by those of a man so convers?? with scripture subjects, as Bishop Mun?er.

Ancient Version of Scripture, reco??

The Bishop informs his correspond??? that when he was at Wurtzburg he found in a MS. of the description call? *Palimpsestes,* the original writing of w??? was almost, but not entirely effaced many fragments of a version of the Scri? tures prior to that of Jerom, common?? called the *Old Italic.* Dr. Feder ha? copied almost all the passages that cou?? be decyphered, chiefly portions of the prophets Jeremiah, Ezekiel and Daniel. He is too far advanced in years to fini?? this undertaking, which demands goo? eyes. But, so much as he has been abl? to read is not uninteresting, because ? fills up several *lacunæ* in Sabatier's edition; and proves at the same time how just?? Augustine and Jerom had estimated thes? versions ; for these fragments differ great?? ly from such corresponding parts as are found in Sabatier. They are not of the *old Italic ;* for the *perspicuitas* sentenc??, which characterized that version is want? ing. I rather suppose them to be of *African* origin. Dr. F. having allowed me to use his labours, I have copied them. and am preparing them for publicatio?. —There is, in the library of the Seraglio, at Constantinople, an Arabic translation of the *Politeia* of Aristotle : this I learn from the *Allgemeine literatur zeitung* of Leip? sic. It is very important for the servic? it may do to Ancient History.

FRANCE.

Statement of the Works published in Franc? during the course of the Year 1818.

FIRST CLASS.

PHYSICAL & MATHEMATICAL SCIENCES.

Physics	6
Chemistry	24
Mineralogy	3
Botany	14
Zoology	7

We have inserted the foregoing tables not only as records of the labours of literature in France, and as shewing, in some degree, the direction of the public mind, but, also, as examples of a convenient and systematic arrangement of materials for literary history. The various branches of literature are now so numerous, and the difficulty of attending to them all is so considerable, that an orderly scheme directing to the proper situation of any particular subject, is a convenience by no means despicable. Whether a similar scheme exhibiting at one view the literary performances of our own country, and in like manner, of other countries, were not desirable, is a consideration to be taken, at present, *ad referendum.*

Two Professorships, one for the Mantchou, the other for the Sanskrit, have been added to the College of France, by Louis XVIII.

Two new professorships have been established in the Royal Academy of Arts: one for History and Antiquity, intended chiefly for the branches of Painting and Sculpture; the other for Historical Art, adapted to the study of Architecture.

Public Libraries, history of.

Researches concerning public Libraries, antient and modern, to the foundation of the Mazarin Library, and on the causes which have contributed to the increase of the number of books. By M. Petit-Radel. This subject is important in the history of General Literature: it includes the consequences of the invention of Printing; and contrasts with the difficulty of forming collections of books while they were only to be obtained in MSS.

It is well known that the origin of printing dates from about the time of the taking of Constantinople, in 1453. M. Petit-Radel pays particular attention to the very early and rapid circulation of the Classics, both Greek and Latin. He also enumerates as far as possible the MSS. of Classic Authors still extant in Italy and in France. He traces the first appearance of these works, in print; with their effect in forming various collections, for the use of Students. Nevertheless, Public Libraries, as such, were first founded in the seventeenth century: as the Bodleian Library, at Oxford; the Ambrosian Library at Milan; the Angelical Library, at Rome; and the Mazarine Library, at Paris, founded in 1648. The Author traces the History of this foundation, from its own Archives. Since the Revolution this library has received augmentations to the amount of 50,000 volumes.

Antiquities found : Dry Summer.

Among other consequences of the dryness of the last Summer, the extraordinary lowness of water in the river Rhone, laid dry much of the marshy lands near that river, wherein was formerly found the beautiful statue known by the name of the Venus of Arles. The inhabitants recollecting their former good fortune, have taken advantage of circumstances to direct their researches and diggings in the same spot; and they have met with success. Among other things obtained, is a Vase, three feet high, of elegant form and workmanship; also, fragments of Architecture, lamps, cinerary and lachrymatory urns, coins, a medal of Constantine, &c.

Theatrical Novelties ; various.

At Paris were presented during the course of 1818 one hundred and thirty four new pieces, on the various Theatres of that city. The Opera, or as it is more loyally styled, the Royal Academy of Music, gave two Operas and three Ballets, —the Theatre Francois gave seven new Comedies; Feydeau gave eleven Comic Operas; Favart gave twenty-two Comedies; the Vaudeville gave twenty two Comedies, historical facts, vaudevilles, anecdotes, episodes, reviews, &c.; the Variétés gave twenty pieces of divers characters : the Theatre of Porte St. Martin gave thirteen Melodramas, Comedies or Vaudevilles; the Gaieté fourteen ; the Ambigu ten; the Olympic Circus, although shut during a great part of the year, gave five new pantomimes.

Of these hundred and thirty-four novelties, not so many as fifteen have held possession of the Theatre; and not so many as five have merit sufficient to justify their reception as stock pieces.

Experimental Farm : resolved on.

The Royal Society of Agriculture of the department of the Higher Garonne, persuaded that the best theories ought not to be generally received, until after they have been subjected to the test of positive experiment, has undertaken to establish a farm for the purpose of making such experiments in Agriculture as to the majority of the body may appear to be useful.

GERMANY.

At Breslau has been published, by J. G. Busching, Researches on the life of the Germans in the middle ages; including their Arts, and the extent of their knowledge, with lithographic prints; the first volume.

New Religious Journal.

The Bible Society at Strasburgh has charged M. C. G. Krafft with the Editorship of a journal in the German language, in which accounts will be given of the dissemination of the Holy Scriptures, and of the general state of Christianity among all nations.

New Publication.

At Leipsick has lately commenced publication *a General Repertory of the most recent Literary works of Germany*, including also foreign countries. It is formed by the contributions of several men of letters; and gives a rapid view of the principal contents of the most valuable productions in most branches of literature.

GREECE.

Architect : Studies of.

Letters from Corfou dated in January last, inform us that, M. Gerasimos Pizzamanos, a native of Cephalonia, and formerly pupil of M. Percier of the French Institution, and of the French Academy at Rome, has returned from traversing various districts of Greece and Asia Minor, where he has visited numerous monuments of Antiquity. He is now at Corfou, with his port-folio filled with a great number of beautiful drawings. The Government confided to him the undertaking of furnishing plans for the palace of the Grand Master of the new Order of St. Michael and St. George; and his designs having been adopted, he has also been employed to make drawings for a new Grand College, and for other public establishments; in which, no doubt, he will display additional proofs of his natural talent, cultivated and improved by extensive study and much reflection ; and we may again see the Fine Arts of Greece revive, and perhaps establish themselves, in their native soil.

ITALY.

The Emperor of Austria has given directions for the Establishment at Milan, of a professorship of Chemistry applicable to the Fine Arts.

At Naples the art of. *Lithography* has obtained patronage; and presses are established for the practice of it; from which valuable results are expected.

RUSSIA.

Manufactures : liberty of following.

It is, probably, known to our readers, that not every individual of the community in Russia was allowed to engage in such manufactures and arts as his inclination might lead him to : that was a privilege attached to the nobility, and to men of business, who were members of the first and the second body of Artisans. The Emperor Alexander has removed this obstacle to the free exercise of genius, by an Imperial Ukase, dated December 28, 1818. O. S. by which the peasantry of the Empire are allowed to establish manufactories and warehouses at their own pleasure. This cannot but prove an additional stimulus to industry.

This order contains five articles, the first of which exempts peasants who establish works, during the first four years of the existence of such works, from all imposts to which peasants engaged in commerce are subjected by the laws of February 11, and December 19, 1812.

New Institution : Mineralogical.

The extensive Empire of Russia contains, beyond all question, Minerals of various, and of the most valuable kinds, concealed in different parts of its soil. To discover them is difficult ; to work them profitably is still more difficult. The Emperor has, however, endeavoured to meet this difficulty by extending his patronage to a Society instituted for the purpose of exploring the Mineral riches of Russia. This Society is yet young : it celebrated January 7, the second anniversary of its foundation, with much solemnity. It has been observed, that among its members may be found the knowledge of all languages. This particular cannot but prove of essential use to a country the districts of which are so unlike each other ; and where the indications of peculiar productions will naturally be expressed by very unlike denominations and terms ; and where, also, the peasantry in the neighbourhood, and others equally ignorant, are likely to be the persons from whom the first intelligence of the contents of the soil around them, may be obtained. The language of science, though now general throughout the world, is not sufficient for the discoveries wished for in localities so barbarous, and so difficult of access.

SWEDEN.

New Publications.

M. Liljegren has lately published at Stockholm, the first volume of *Scandinavian Fables*, with historical notes : including the fable of Gange-Rolf. The volume is ornamented with several plates.

Dr. Djuberg, has published at Stockholm, a *Geographical Dictionary of Scan-*

dinavia, by Scandinavia intending the now United Kingdom of Sweden and Norway.

Cataract, extensive.

The mines of Sweden have long been known as the great source of wealth to that country ; and with design to promote them more effectually, Commissaries have been sent into Lapland in order to institute mineralogical researches. A late Report of these Commissaries takes particular notice of a cataract in the Lulen, which may well pass for the largest in Europe. It is nearly a quarter of a league in breadth. The neighbouring inhabitants call it *Neomcleaiskae ;* the hare's leap.

DISCOVERIES OF ANTIQUITIES IN EGYPT.

An occasional visit to the British Museum has reminded us that we have not yet noticed, in a regular manner, the labours performed under British patronage, with their results, in that scene of wonders the land of Egypt. The Egyptian Room in our National Repository has received an interesting addition in a colossal bust, very improperly, and indeed, unhappily, called a " young Memnon." Whatever it really was, it is a wonderful instance of art and labour. It demonstrates the truth of travellers' accounts concerning other colossal figures, since the whole statue could not be less than sixty or seventy feet high. The features are placid and even prepossessing,—always considering the effect of the distance at which it was intended to be seen. They are wrought with great perseverance, and are well finished. A colour is added to stain the lips, &c. The top of the mitre is broken off ; also parts below the shoulders, which were blasted by the French with gunpowder, to diminish the weight ; yet the French left it where they found it. It may weigh about twelve tons : and was moved by M. Belzoni by mere strength of human arms, combined in numbers, with indefatigable perseverance, a distance of two miles, to the Nile. Those who are acquainted with the Djerms of that river, will wonder by what means it was got on board, and brought off.

The following article describing other exploits of this singular discoverer, is partly copied from a contemporary journal, and partly enlarged from a foreign communication. The whole contains unusual interest.

From Thebes M. Belzoni proceeded to Nubia, to examine the great Temple of Ybsambul [Ibsambul, Ebsambul, or Absimbul], which lies buried more than twice its height in the sands near the second cataract. On this occasion, however, he was unable to effect any thing, and therefore returned to Thebes, where he employed himself in new researches at the temple of Karnack. Here, several feet under ground, he found surrounded by a wall a range of sphynxes, about forty in number, with heads of lions on busts of women, of black granite, and for the greater part beautifully executed. Mrs. Belzoni succeeded in digging up at the same place a white marble statue of Jupiter Ammon holding a ram's head on his knees. And on his second journey to Thebes in 1817, M. Belzoni discovered a colossal head of Orus, of fine granite, larger than the Memnon, measuring ten feet from the neck to the top of the mitre with which it is crowned, exquisitely finished and in fine preservation. He carried with him to Cairo one of the arms belonging to this statue. As he succeeded so well in removing the Memnon, may we not hope that he will be encouraged also to attempt the removal of this head, and that we may ere long see it placed beside its colossal brother in the British Museum?

After this, M. Belzoni proceeded again to Nubia, and, in spite of many hindrances and much inhospitality which he experienced, succeeded in opening the celebrated temple of Ybsambul, which no European had ever before entered. In this temple (the largest and most wonderful excavation in Egypt, or in Nubia) he found fourteen chambers and a great hall, and in the latter, standing, eight colossal figures, each thirty feet high. The walls and pilasters are covered with hieroglyphics beautifully cut, and groups of large figures in fine preservation. At the end of the sanctuary he found four sitting figures about twelve feet high, cut out of the natural rock and well preserved. Belzoni's labour may be

conceived, when we state that on commencing his operations the bed of loose sand which he had to clear away was upwards of fifty feet deep. He carried hence two lions with the heads of vultures, and a small statue of Jupiter Ammon. From the superior style of sculpture found in this temple to any thing yet met with in Egypt, Mr. Salt infers that the arts descended hither from Ethiopia.

M. Belzoni, by a kind of tact which seems to be peculiarly his own, discovered, on his return to Thebes, six tombs in the valley of Biban El Moluck, the Tombs [or rather Gates] of the Kings, (in a part of the mountains where ordinary observers would hardly have sought for such excavations,) all in a perfect state, not having been viewed by previous intruders, and giving a wonderful display of Egyptian magnificence and posthumous splendour. From the front entrance to the innermost chamber in one of them, the length of passage, cut through the solid rock, is 309 feet: the chambers, which are numerous, cut in a pure white rock, are covered with paintings *al fresco*, well executed, and with hieroglyphics quite perfect, and the colours as fresh as if newly laid on. In one of these chambers he found an exquisitely beautiful sarcophagus of alabaster, nine feet five inches long, three feet nine inches wide, and two feet one inch high, covered within and without with hieroglyphics in intaglio, sounding like a bell, and as transparent as glass—supposed by M. Belzoni to have been a depository of the remains of Apis. In the innermost room he found the carcase of a bull embalmed with asphaltum, which seems to give some confirmation to his idea. We are happy to learn that this matchless production is now on its way to England, to be placed by the side of the sarcophagus supposed to have contained the remains of Alexander. Mr. Salt, assisted by Mr. Beechey (son of the well-known artist of the same name), has, with much labour and care, copied several of the paintings within this tomb, which will by and by be given to the public. These paintings are quite fresh and perfect. The colours employed are "vermillion, ochres, and indigo;" and yet they are not gaudy, owing to the judicious balance of colours and the artful management of the blacks.

It is quite obvious [says Mr. Salt,] that they worked on a regular system, which had for its basis, as Mr. West would say, the colours of the rainbow; as there is not an ornament throughout their dresses where the red, yellow and blue are not alternately mingled, which produces a harmony, that in some of the designs is really delicious.

It is a curious fact, that in one of the Theban tombs two statues of wood, a little larger than life, were found as perfect as if newly carved, excepting the sockets of the eyes, which had been of metal, probably copper.

We have to mention another successful labour of M. Belzoni, perhaps the most singular, because, to all appearance, absolutely hopeless and unpromising—the opening of the second pyramid of Ghiza, known by the name of Cephrenes. According to Herodotus, (whose information has generally been found correct,) this pyramid was constructed without any internal chambers. M. Belzoni, however, believed the fact might be otherwise; and having reasons of his own for commencing his operations at a certain point, he began his labours, with so much foresight as actually to dig directly down upon a forced entrance. But even after this success, none but a Belzoni would have had the perseverance to pursue the labour required to perfect the discovery. It was by attending to the same kind of indications which had led him so successfully to explore the six tombs of the kings in Thebes, that he was induced to commence his operations on the north side. He set out from Cairo on the 6th of February, 1818, pretending (as he did not wish to be interrupted by visitors) that he was going to a neighbouring village. He then repaired to the Kaia Bey, and gained permission; the Bey having first satisfied himself that there was no tilled ground within a considerable distance of Ghiza. On the 10th of February he began with six labourers in a vertical section, at right angles to the north side of the base, cutting through a mass of stones and cement which had fallen from the upper part of the pyramid, now so completely agglutinated together as to spoil the mattocks, &c. employed in the operation. He persevered in making an opening fifteen feet wide, working downwards, and uncovering the face of the pyramid. During the first week there was but little prospect of meeting with any thing interesting; but on the 17th one of the Arabs employed called out with great vociferation that he had found the entrance. He had in fact come upon a hole into which he could thrust his arm and a djerid six feet long. Before night they ascertained that an aperture was there about three feet square, which had been closed irregularly with a hewn stone: this being removed, they reached a larger opening, filled with rubbish and sand. M. Belzoni was now satisfied that this was not the real but a forced passage. Next day they had penetrated fifteen feet, where stones and sand began to fall from above: this was removed; but still they continued to fall in large quantities, when after some more days labour he discovered an upper forced entrance, communicating with the outside from above. Having cleared this, he found another opening running inward, which proved on further search to be a continuation of the lower horizontal forced passage, nearly all choked up with rubbish: this being removed, he discovered about half way from the outside a descending forced passage which terminated at the distance of forty feet. He now continued to work in the horizontal passage, in hope that it might lead to the centre, but it terminated at the depth of ninety feet; and he found it prudent not to force it further, as the stones were very loose over head, and one actually fell, and nearly killed one of the people. He therefore now began clearing away the aggregated stones and lime to the eastward of the forced entrance; but by this time his retreat had been discovered, and he found himself much interrupted by visitors.

On the 28th of February he discovered at the surface of the pyramid a block of granite having the same direction as that of the passage of the first pyramid, or that of Cheops; and he now hoped that he was not far from the true entrance. Next day he removed some large blocks, and on the 2d of March he entered the true passage, an opening four feet high and three feet and a half wide, formed by four blocks of granite, and continued descending at an angle of about 26° to the length of

104 feet five inches, lined all the length with granite. From this passage he had to remove the stones with which it was filled; and at its bottom was a door or portcullis of granite (fitted into a niche, also made of granite) supported at the height of eight inches by small stones placed under it. Two days were occupied in raising it high enough to admit of entrance. This door is one foot three inches thick, and with the granite niche occupies seven feet of the passage, where the granite work ends, and a passage, twenty-two feet seven inches leading towards the centre commences; at the end of which is a perpendicular descent of fifteen feet. On the left is a small forced passage cut in the rock, and above on the right a forced passage running upward and turning to the north thirty feet, just over the portcullis. At the bottom of the perpendicular, after removing some rubbish, he found the entrance of another passage which inclined northward. But quitting this for the present, he followed his prime passage, which took a horizontal direction, and at the end of it, 158 feet eight inches from the above-mentioned perpendicular, he entered a chamber forty-six feet three inches long, sixteen feet three inches wide, and twenty-three feet six inches in height, for the greater part cut out of the rock; and in the middle of this room he found a sarcophagus of granite, eight feet long, three feet six inches wide, and two feet three inches deep inside, surrounded by large blocks of granite, as if to prevent its being removed. The lid had been opened, and he found in the interior a few bones which he supposed to be human: but some of them having been since brought to England by Capt. Fitzclarence, who was afterwards in this pyramid, and one of them (a thigh bone) having on examination by Sir Everard Home been found to have belonged to a cow, we may doubt whether any of them ever belonged to a human subject. The size indeed of the coffin seems better fitted for the reception of a cow than of a man.

On the west wall of this chamber is an Arabic inscription, testifying that this pyramid was opened by the Masters Mahomet El Aghar and Othman, and inspected in the presence of the Sultan Ali Mahomet the 1st, Ugloch (a Tartaric title, as Uleg Bey, &c.); and on other parts of the walls inscriptions, supposed by M. Belzoni to be in Coptic.

He now returned to the descending passage at the bottom of the above-mentioned perpendicular. Its angle is about 26°: at the end of forty-eight feet and a half it becomes horizontal, still going north fifty-five feet, in the middle of which horizontal part there is a recess to the east, eleven feet deep, and a passage to the west, twenty feet, which descends into a chamber, thirty-two feet long, nine feet nine inches wide, and eight and a half high. In this room were only a few small square blocks of stone, and on the walls some unknown inscriptions. He now returned to the horizontal part; and advanced north, ascending at an angle of 60°; and in this, at a short distance from the horizontal part, he met with another niche, which had been formerly furnished with a granite door, the fragments of which were still there: at forty-seven feet and a half from this niche, the passage was filled with large stones to close the entrance, which issues out precisely at the base of the pyramid. All the works below the base are cut in the rock, as well as part of the passages and chambers.

By clearing away the earth eastward of the pyramid, he opened the foundation and part of the walls of an extensive temple, which stood before it at the distance of forty feet; and laid bare a pavement composed of fine blocks of calcareous stone, some of them beautifully cut and in fine preservation. This platform probably goes round the whole pyramid. The stones composing the foundation of the temple are very large—one which he measured was 21 feet long, 10 high, and 8 in breadth: (weight 120 tons.)

———

M. Belzoni, to whom the world is indebted for so many discoveries, is a native of the Papal States. About nine years ago he was in Edinburgh, where he exhibited feats of strength, and experiments in hydraulics, musical glasses and phantasmagoria, which he afterwards repeated in Ireland and the Isle of Man, whence he proceeded to Lisbon, where he was engaged by the manager of the theatre of San Carlos, to appear in Valentine and

Orson, and afterwards in the sacred drama of Sampson. For such characters he was admirably adapted, being in his 25th year, six feet seven inches high, remarkably strong, and having an animated prepossessing countenance. He afterwards performed before the Court at Madrid, whence he proceeded to Malta, where he was persuaded by the agent of the Pasha of Egypt to visit Cairo. Here he built a machine worked on the principle of the walking-crane, to irrigate the gardens of the Pasha by raising water from the Nile. Three Arabs with M. Belzoni's servant (an Irish lad whom he had taken with him from Edinburgh) were put in to walk the wheel; but on the second or third turn the Arabs being either frightened or giddy jumped out, and the Irishman had his thigh broken; which put an end to this undertaking. On this failure happening, and while meditating on trying his fortune in search of antiquities in Upper Egypt, Mr. Salt arrived in Cairo; and on the representation of Sheik Ibrahim, who had witnessed his extraordinary powers, conceived him to be a most promising person to bring the head of the young Memnon to Alexandria. They came to terms; and how well he succeeded in this first work has been proved by the head being now in the Museum.

As an instance of the confidence which his determined perseverance inspires in others, we need only mention, that in his second journey to Nubia Mr. Beechy accompanied him. Having engaged a party of natives, he set about uncovering the temple where two colossal statues showed their heads above the sand. They worked tardily for a few days and then ceased, alleging that the feast of Rhamadan had commenced; nor could any argument persuade them to resume their labour. In this emergency, Belzoni, Beechey and the Irishman set to work themselves; but they soon found that by order of the Aga they could not, for money or by entreaties, procure a supply of provisions. The object was to compel them to return the following season to spend more money. Having, however, in their boat, a bag of millet, the party pursued their labour, living on this fare and the Nile water; and after twenty-one days severe labour, effected their object, in uncovering and gaining access to the interior of the temple.

We consider Mr. Salt, who has been indefatigable in his own researches, and unsparing in encouraging those of others, as most fortunate in having secured the assistance of so able an explorer as M. Belzoni. By their exertions, and those of M. Caviglia, the British Museum is likely soon to become the richest depository in the world, of Egyptian antiquities. Mr. Salt has possessed himself of many gems in this line. Among others he has got down to Cairo the famous stone discovered by the French, with eight sculptured figures; another beautiful head of granite, as perfect, and with a finer polish than that named the young Memnon, not quite so large, but perfect; a sitting figure, exquisitely wrought, and as large as life; several statues of basalt; thirty rolls of papyrus, and an immense number of smaller articles.

. . . .

In the mean while the French have also continued and invigorated their researches in Egypt: of the success of one of their countrymen, M. Caillaud, they have communicated several reports. That young *Savans* is lately arrived at Marseilles, after having spent nearly four years in Egypt, traversing it in various directions: his excursions have included also parts of Nubia, the Deserts on the east of the Nile, towards the Red Sea; and on the west, the great Oasis, &c. From Syenna to the great Cataract of the Nile, he visited various temples built in the Egyptian style: of which several are partly hollowed out of the natural rocks and hills.

In the great Oasis, the temples he has inspected appeared to him to be, some of Egyptian, and others of Grecian construction: in the latter he observed several vaults, or arcades well executed, whereas the arch does not occur in works truly Egyptian. His attention was also fixed by antique tombs, distinguished by their extent and elevation; nor less by the interesting ruins of a Roman fortification. He has collected a variety of Greek inscriptions, some of which are of great interest.

M. Calliaud is the gentleman who has had the good fortune to discover an antient city seven or eight leagues distant from the Red Sea; and about thirty or forty south of Cosseir. It is hereabouts, that D'Anville places the Emerald Mines known to the Ancients; and this traveller found in the vicinity numerous traces of extensive mining operations. He descended into one of these mines, a hundred fathoms deep, that communicated with galleries still deeper; the researches he made led him to the discovery of emeralds in no small quantities still lying in their native beds; and induced the Pacha of Egypt to order further labours and works to be carried on, when the discovery was authenticated and confirmed to him.

The antient city already mentioned is not far from this mine; the Ababdes call it *Schette;* and it is distinguished by having preserved many private houses; while most antient cities which have been discovered, present only public edifices, as temples, palaces, and other constructions of magnitude. Various inscriptions, placed in and about the temples of this city, leave no doubt of its having been founded by the Ptolemys; and one of these temples, it appears, was erected in honour of Berenice. The architecture is Greek; but intermingled with Egyptian ornaments.

From this city to the Nile lies a valley, in which is an Egyptian temple, and fortified works, marking it as a station for Caravans, in the time of the Ptolemys; and possibly, in the more antient times of the Pharaohs: on several rocks along the road are inscriptions in hieroglyphics: the valley terminates at the Nile, in the vicinity of the ruins of Elethyia.

M. Caillaud has also traced, not far from the Emerald Mines, a portion of the celebrated route from Coptos to Berenice, which is mentioned by Pliny: he particularly distinguished two stations, supposed to be those of *Hydreum Jovis,* and *Aristornis,* which were the fifth and the sixth. The course of the passage through these leads towards Coptos; and the Ababdes affirm that four other stations of a similar description, are found in the way from these to Coptos. This road leaves the emerald mines twelve or fifteen leagues to the east; and M. Caillaud has no doubt but what in following it to the south east (which we are sorry this gentleman himself did not accomplish) it would lead to the ruins of Berenice.

It is most probable, that this traveller's narrative will be published; when we may be able to lay before our readers, a more satisfactory account of his remarks.

In the mean while, it may not be amiss to observe, that by means of the persevering exertions made and making, we shall ultimately become acquainted pretty fully, with a Country, that a few years ago was known only to the literati, to those who could afford to purchase the expensive works of Pococke, Norden, &c. and to those whose early recollections led them to the connections of the histories of Joseph, of Moses, and of the Israelites, with the river Nile, and the land of Goshen.—The arts and the antiquities of Egypt, will soon become as familiar to us, as those of Italy and Greece.

STEAM VESSELS FOR CONVEYING FISH.

The following appears to us to be such a proper application of the power of machinery to a desirable purpose, that we think it our duty to promote the intention by publishing it. The supplies furnished by the bounties of the Ocean are inexhaustible; and should be directed to furnish the tables of the poor with plenty, at a cheap rate, as well as to furnish those of the rich with delicacies, the prime of the season.

The application of the power of the steam-engine to navigation is now proposed to be extended to the important object of furnishing the metropolis with a regular and constant supply of fresh fish at a cheap price. The variable manner in which the London market is supplied with this valuable article of food—its scarcity at one time, its over-abundance at another, and its dearness at all times—have long been matters of public complaint; and are undoubtedly more the result of those detentions to which the fishing packets are necessarily exposed from their dependence on the winds and tides, than of any combination or artifice (as is vulgarly supposed) among the dealers in the article. A fishing company has accordingly been formed, for the conveyance of fish from the coasts to the metropolis, whose vessels are to be strongly built, sea-worthy, and fast-sailing sloops, with the additional power of proceeding at option by sails or steam separately or united. They are to be fitted up with wells and suitable valves, so that the fish will be brought to Billingsgate alive in pure sea water, at all seasons of the year, and London thus enjoy a luxury to which it has been hitherto a stranger. The construction of the vessels and engines has been intrusted to Mr. George Dodd, author of a work on Steam-Packets and Steam-Engines.

Cħe Gatħerer.

No. XXIX.

" I am but a gatherer, and dealer in other men's stuff."

Anecdote of Dr. Wolcott.

This gentleman, better known by the name of Peter Pindar, was always a welcome guest at the house of a very worthy family some years since, resident in—— Place; but being in the habit of keeping late hours, he sometimes disconcerted them by his unseasonably protracted sittings: and having one evening replied to a friendly remonstrance on the subject, " I will *if I live* go at eleven in future," he was jocosely answered by the young lady who superintended the economy of the house, that she should certainly send him off *dead or alive* if he attempted to transgress again. Next day the young ladies received from him the following lines, which, from their playful humour, and the allusion to his foible, are highly characteristic of the facetious bard :—

Tell me, sweet girls of——Place,
   If at the Opera, or the Play,
You mean this night to add a grace,
   And steal a heart or two away ?
If not, I sip my tea with you at seven,
   Dead or alive I'll leave you at eleven !

About this time a little compact was entered into, by which a servant of the house was each night to bring the Doctor's hat and cane into the parlour on the clock's striking eleven, as a signal for his departure. But the Doctor, as is well known, was remarkable for his convivial powers, particularly for his humorous stories; and it happening not many evenings after, that the clock struck the hour in the middle of one of his best; the servant's usual summons was omitted—which the Doctor no sooner observed than he exultingly declared the treaty broken, and himself absolved from the engagement, and he followed up his declaration by nearly sitting out the night.

Japanese Prayers.

On their high roads, every mountain, every hill, every cliff, is consecrated to some divinity ; at all these places, therefore, travellers have to repeat prayers, and frequently several times over. But, as the fulfilment of this duty would detain pious travellers too long on the road, the Japanese have invented the following means to prevent this inconvenience. Upon these spots, consecrated to divinities, they set up posts, in case there are none already there, to mark the distances. In these posts a long vertical cut is made, about an arsheen and a half, above the ground ; on which a flat round iron plate turns like a sheave in a block. Upon this plate the prayer is engraved, which is dedicated to the divinity of the place ; to turn it round, is equivalent to repeating the prayer, and the prayer is supposed to be repeated as many times as it turns round. In this manner the traveller is able, without stopping, and merely by turning the plate with his fingers, to send up even more prayers to the divinity than he is obliged to do.

Discovery of Galvanism.

This extraordinary agent, from its effects on animals, was originally called *animal electricity*. It received its name from Professor Galvani, of Bologna, to whom we are indebted for this discovery, in which, however, as in many others, accident had no small share. His wife, who was in a declining state of health, was using a soup made of frogs as a restorative. Some of the animals, being skinned for the purpose, were lying on a table in the laboratory, when one of his assistants chanced to touch with a scalpel the crural nerve of a frog that lay near the conductor; upon which the muscles of the limb were strongly convulsed. This effect was noticed by the lady, a woman of superior understanding and science, and communicated to her husband on his return home. He repeated the experiment, which he varied in every possible way, first with artificial and then with the atmospherical electricity. In the course of his experiments with the latter, he suspended some frogs by metallic hooks from iron palisades, and observed that the muscles were frequently and involuntarily contracted, when no electricity appeared in the atmosphere. Having duly considered the phenomenon, he found that it had no connexion with the changes in the state of the electricity in the atmosphere; but might be produced at pleasure, by applying two pieces of metal to different parts of the animal and bringing them into contact. This effect may be increased by arming the nerve with a metallic coating, by which means a larger portion of the nerve is brought into contact with the metal. Zinc and copper, and zinc and gold, operate much more powerfully than other metals, though any of them produce the effect. Galvani also ascertained that a combination of two metals acts with greater force than a simple metal. From all his experiments, which commenced in 1791, the Italian philosopher concluded, that the phenomena of galvanism were owing to electricity generated in the animal organs, and that metals served only as conductors to it. This theory, however, subsequent investigation has proved to be erroneous.

Spoiling a Boy.

A Fantee boy having fractured his leg, and his dissolution appearing inevitable, the parents, in great distress, applied to the surgeon of an English outfort, who amputated the limb, and after much wearying attendance, to the surprise of every one, restored the boy to health. The family then brought him into the fort, and laying him down in the hall, addressed the surgeon (who was in charge of the fort) thus: " As Master cut off poor boy's leg, and so spoil poor boy for work, we come to ask Master how much he think to give poor boy to keep him."

Clerical Wit.

The facetious Watty Morrison, as he was commonly called, was intreating the commanding officer of a regiment at Fort George to pardon a poor fellow sent to the halberds. The officer granted his petition, on condition that Mr. Morrison should accord with the first favour he asked. The favour was to perform the ceremony of

baptism for a young puppy. A merry party of gentlemen were invited to the christening. Mr. Morrison desired Major —— to hold up the dog. " As I am Minister of the Kirk of Scotland," said Mr. Morrison, " I must proceed accordingly." Major——said he asked no more. "Well, then, Major, I begin with the usual question: *you acknowledge yourself the father* of this puppy ?" The Major understood the joke, and threw away the animal. Thus Mr. Morrison turned the laugh against the ensnarer, who intended to deride a sacred ordinance.

Lapland Calendar.

January.—The most intense cold took place between the 3rd. and the 7th. The greatest depth of Snow, 1½ of a Swedish ell.

February.—Snow falling, with violent wind, from the 9th to the 13th.

March.—Extreme cold from the 8th to the 13th.

April.—The first rook seen on the 15th. Several rooks made their appearance on the 23rd. The ways become passable; wild geese begin to appear.

May.—The partridge (Charadrius apricarius Linn.) and the Motacilla œnanthe Linn. appeared on the 5th. The season for travelling in sledges ended on the 8th. The rivulets began to flow on the 9th. First rain appeared on the 11th; and at the same time the Lumme (Colymbus Lumme) made its appearance. The ice began to break up on the 14th. Swallows appeared on the 15th. The ice disappeared on the 17th. The spring floods in the rivers then at their height. Upon the 18th sowing began: the plains beginning to look green. The last snow fell on the 19th. Upon the 23rd planted potatoes. Cuckoo heard on the 25th; and perch began to spawn. Birch-leaves began to appear on the 27th, and the plains to exhibit an uniform green colour. The last spring frost happened on the night of the 30th.

June.—The earth white with snow on the 4th. Pasturage commenced in the forests on the 7th. Snow and heavy hail on the 13th. The first summer heat on the 15th. First thunder on the 18th: at this time sowed the kitchen garden. Meaquitos in vast numbers on the 22nd. Inundations from the highest mountains on the 26th, at this time the leaves of my potatoe-plants perished with cold.

July.—First ear of barley on the 26th. Haymaking began on the 30th. The first star visible on the 31st, denoting the re-approach of night.

August.—First frosty night towards the 17th. Harvest began on the 20th. Birch leaves begin to turn yellow on the 23rd.

September.—Hard frost towards the 6th. Swallows disappear on the 11th. Ground frozen, and ice upon the banks, on the 12th. First snow fell on the 21st, and remained upon the mountains. Cattle housed on the 24th. Lakes frozen on the 26th.

October.—Leaves of birch and osier not altogether fallen on the 3rd. Lakes frozen on the 5th; the river, on the 6th. Upon the 9th not a rook to be seen. The earth again bare on the 22nd; and the ice not firm on the 26th. Durable frost and snow on the 27th.

November.—Upon the 19th, travelling in sledges commenced.

December.—The greatest degree of cold from the 16th to the 22nd inclusive. The depth of the snow now equalled 1 Swedish ell, and 18 inches. (See Dr. Clarke's Travels.)

The Conscientious Courier.

By a singular regulation, the government couriers in Austria are ordered, when they are charged with dispatches sealed with only one seal, to go at a walking pace, if with two seals, to trot, and if with three to gallop. A courier, bearing a dispatch with three seals, passing lately through a garrison town, was requested by the Commandant to take a dispatch to the Governor of the next town, to which he willingly agreed; but perceiving, when he received it, that it had but one seal, he refused to take charge of it, saying, "that the regulations ordered him to walk his horse, with such a dispatch; and as he had another, with which he was ordered to gallop, he could not possibly take them both!"

Medicine for Conquerors.

Buonaparte said one day to the physician, Desgenettes, "Medicine is an art of assas-

sins," 'And what does your Majesty think that of conquerors is,' was the reply, which for a moment confused even the Corsican.

Hanging a Man.

In the Corsican war, the inhabitants of the Island took a French officer-prisoner, and were going to hang him: but the latter addressed them. "You probably imagine that by hanging me you will cause the King my master much sorrow. With respect to myself, I am prepared for every thing; but so much I must say, that the King of France will not trouble himself in the least on my account, and that he will not even know that you have hanged me." 'Nay, if this be the case,' replied the Corsicans, 'we will not hang you!'

Midsummer Custom.

The custom observed in most Catholic countries, of making bonfires on the eve of St. John, the Baptist, is still preserved in Ireland, though somewhat on the decline. An addition to it prevails here, however, never, we believe, seen abroad, that the children and cattle are made to pass through the fire; grown people will also not unfrequently do it voluntarily; it is considered a certain preservative against disease or accident. When the fire is dying away, the old women assemble round, and each takes away a burning stick to carry home with her, which is to bring a blessing on the house, and is carefully preserved till the next year. It is reckoned very dangerous to be exposed to the air after sunset on this day, for the *evil-ones* are about, and are then endowed with particular power to harm any body. At all times it is thought hazardous to be near a wood at night, but the risk is never so great as on St. John's eve! See Plumtree's Residence in Ireland, and Time's Telescope for 1814, p. 142, for 1817, p. 164, and for 1818, p. 139.

Imperial Breakfast.

On setting out for his campaign in 1806, Bonaparte happened to breakfast at the Postmaster's House at Claye. There they had made the most splendid preparations for his reception, and perhaps the whole history of that little commune does not furnish another instance of so princely a repast. Not far from thence lived the old Duke of P——, shut up in an ancient *chateau,* by a series of restrictions which his family had caused formerly to be imposed upon him, and debarred by a little imbecility from the different kinds of emancipation which the Revolution had given to the whole world. The old man, grown silly and almost paralysed, conceived great joy at being permitted, under these circumstances, to approach the personage whose journal was the daily source of his pleasure, and who came not to make war upon paralytics. Having provided himself with a small sack of Moka coffee and an harangue, which had, on a former day, been manufactured by the clearest head of his village, he set out for Claye, and placed himself in his elbow chair, in the passage which led to the Postmaster's house. Bonaparte, smarting under a long fast, was hastening to his breakfast, and was but little disposed to pay much attention to the Duke of P——, who astounded him alike with the variety of his compliments and the length of them. Through form sake, however, he took from him his discourse, and precipitated himself into the breakfast-room, leaving the old man astonished at such a reception, which he had calculated upon would be much more warm. On his return after breakfast, through the same passage, he was again accosted by the old applicant, who with a voice rendered doubly comical by his stammering, cried out, " If you are not disposed to receive my compliments, at least, be good enough to tell me how you liked my cof—cof—cof—cof—." 'Ere he had time to organize the perfection of the sound, Bonaparte, who knew nothing of his coffee, was thrown off his centre, and with his suite, indulged in a burst of merriment at the old gentleman's expence, which was, however, very conducive to digestion.

HINTS, PLANS, and PROCEEDINGS
OF
Benevolence.

———————Homo sum:
Humanum nihil a me alienum puto.

SOCIETY FOR PROPAGATING THE GOSPEL IN FOREIGN PARTS.
King's Letter.

The Members of the Church have now an excellent opportunity afforded to them for displaying their zeal in promoting the attempts to diffuse the light of the gospel throughout the British Dominions of Asia, by the grant of the following "King's Letter" which has already been forwarded to the greater part of the different Dioceses.

It is now forty years, since a similar application was made ; at which time, (the year 1779) we are informed, that this pious and charitable Society would have been completely stopped, had it not resorted to such a mode of exciting public attention.

In the year 1778 the Society were obliged to sell £1600 reduced Bank Annuities, and also to borrow £1000 at £5 per cent to answer their current expenses; large advances of money having been made for the relief of the persecuted and exiled American Clergy. We are sure that the present appeal to the generosity of an enlightened public will not be made in vain; and we trust that the Members of the Church will, by their timely assistance, afford the Society the means not only of making some great and decided effort, but that the Society's Annual Contributions will gradually increase, and thus widely extend the sphere of its usefulness.

In the Name and on the behalf of his Majesty.

GEORGE, P. R.

MOST Revererend Father in God, our right trusty and right entirely beloved councillor, we greet you well: whereas the Incorporated Society for the propagation of the Gospel in Foreign parts have, by their petition, humbly represented unto us, that King William the Third, of glorious memory, was graciously pleased to erect the said corporation by letters patent, bearing date the 16th day of June, 1701, for the receiving, managing, and disposing of the charity of such of his loving subjects as should be induced to contribute towards the maintenance of an orthodox clergy, and the making such other prevision as might be necessary for the propagation of the gospel in foreign parts :

That the very great expences necessarily attending that good work having frequently much exceeded the income of the Society, they have been obliged, at several times, to make humble applications to our royal predecessors :—to her Majesty Queen Anne, in the years 1711 and 1714—to his Majesty King George the First, in the year 1718—in 1741 and 1751 to his Majesty King George the Second, our royal grandfather—and to ourselves in the year 1779, for permission to make public collections of charity; which applications were most graciously received, and permissions granted for the purposes aforesaid, by which means the Society was enabled to carry on the good designs for which they were incorporated.

That during the period of forty years which have elapsed since their last application, the funds of the Society have been faithfully expended in promoting the erection of Churches and Schools—in dispersing bibles and prayer books, with other books of devotion—in supporting and maintaining within our provinces in North America and elsewhere, a constant succession of Missionaries, Catechists, and Schoolmasters, by whose means the comfort and benefit of pastoral care and instruction, of public prayer, and preaching of God's word, and the due administration of the holy sacraments, have been secured to many of our subjects in those parts, and many thousands of Indians and Negroes have been instructed and baptized in the true faith of Christ :

That, induced by a variety of favourable circumstances, the Society are desirous of extending the range of their labours, and of using their utmost endeavours to diffuse the light of the gospel, and permanently to establish the christian faith in such parts of the Continent and Islands of Asia as are under our protection and authority; but that, owing to the state of their funds, which are altogether unequal to the expences of such an undertaking, they are unable, without further assistance from our good subjects, to proceed in the execution of their designs : the Society, therefore, confiding in our great zeal for our holy religion, and our known affection to all our subjects, most humbly pray, that we would be most graciously pleased to grant them our royal letters, directed to the Lords Archbishops of our Kingdom, for a general collection of charity within their several provinces, for the good uses of the Society for the propagation of the gospel in foreign parts : we, taking the same into our royal consideration, and being always ready to give the best encouragement and countenance to undertakings which tend so much to the promoting true piety and our holy religion, are graciously pleased to condescend to their request; and do hereby direct you, that these our letters be communicated to the several Suffragan Bishops within your province, expressly requiring them to take care that publication be made hereof on such Sundays and in such places within their respective Dioceses, as the said Bishops shall appoint ; and that upon this occasion, the Ministers in each Parish do effectually excite their parishioners to a liberal contribution, whose benevolence towards carrying on the said charitable work shall be collected in the Church immediately after divine service, and in the course of the week following, at the dwellings of the several inhabitants, by the Churchwardens and Overseers of the Poor, assisted, as far as may be, by the Minister and such other respectable Inhabitants as may be prevailed upon to attend for that purpose ; and the Ministers of the several parishes are to cause the sums so collected to be paid immediately to the Treasurer or Treasurers for the time being of the said Society, to be accounted for by him or them to the Society, and applied to the carrying on and promoting the above-mentioned good designs ; and so we bid you very heartily farewell.

Given at our Court, at Carlton House, the 10th day of February, 1819, in the Fifty-ninth year of our reign.

By the command of His Royal Highness The Prince Regent, in the name and on the behalf of His Majesty.

SIDMOUTH.

ARCHBISHOP of CANTERBURY.
For a Collection for the Society for propagating the Gospel in Foreign Parts.

STATE OF INSTRUCTION IN RUSSIA.

Nothing can be a more ready, or more effectual means of promoting the civilization of the inferior classes of a people, than public schools, where instruction is communicated *gratis.* Within a few years, more than 2000 such schools have been founded ; several of which are conducted by young Russians, who have been sent into England, to acquire the methods of Bell and Lancaster. The generosity of the Emperor and the Empress mother towards these establishments is almost boundless ; nor do they overlook any others having the same tendency. Their example is followed by many rich individuals. Count Sherwalow has endowed a Gymnasium, with a fund of 150,000 roubles. The counsellor of the mines, Demidow, has presented 100,000 roubles to the university at Moscow; and an equal sum to the two preparatory schools of Tiow and Tobolsk. To the preparatory school of Jaroslaw, with the Gymnasium, he has allotted another sum of the same amount, with considerable landed property. Count Schermetjew has given 2,500,000 roubles to found a hospital, besides a handsome present to the University at Moscow. The great Chancellor Romanzow, has established on his estates, a great number of Lancastrian Schools, four Churches for four different confessions of faith are constructing at the same time, by his orders; and he also pays the expences of a voyage round the world, now in progress. *(Philanthropic Gazette.)*

SCHOOLS IN GREECE.

M. Cleobulos, of Philippopoli, not long ago, published a letter in modern Greek, in which he describes to a friend, in a very clear and precise manner, the mechanism of the system of mutual instruction, (Bell and Lancaster's system.) He compares this method of instruction to that formerly practised, and shews how greatly the new mode excels the other, in point of economy, in point of progress made by the scholars, and further, in point of moral effects upon the youth.

M. Rosetto Rosnovano, a young nobleman of Moldavia, who not long ago, travelled into England, taking France in his way, in order to inspect the various establishments for public education, and for beneficence, generally, and who has distinguished himself by his zeal and his intelligence in behalf of general instruction, has invited M Cleobulos to Moldavia, to settle near him, for the purpose of establishing schools of mutual instruction in the Greek language. The invitation has been accepted.

IMPRISONMENT FOR SMALL DEBTS.

The Society for relief of persons imprisoned for small debts, at their annual general Court on the 7th Instant, reported that the number of debtors released, and discharged by them from 62 prisons, during the past year was 1138, who had 883 wives and 2187 children; the average expence of whose liberation cost only £2. 17s. 2¼d. each.

At this meeting 68 prisoners were relieved for the sum of £228. 9s. 7d. Of 92 cases, 23 were rejected, and 6 deferred.

Provisional Committee for Encouragement of Industry and Reduction of Poor's Rates.

The Committee desires to be assisted by the reflecting and patriotic of the commercial, manufacturing, and mechanical portion of the community, in the devising and eliciting such modes of employment for the unoccupied as will not interfere with existing occupations.

2. For the further prevention or diminution of Poors'-rates, the furnishing occupation for all capable of work.

3. The best means of equalising as much as is practicable the existing inequality of wages in manufacturing districts.

The Committee is also desirous to obtain from their countrymen generally, judicious opinions as to the means of preventing the unhappy consequences and heavy expenses attendant on removals of parochial poor.

B. WILLS, Secretary.

King's Head, Poultry.

INTERESTING INTELLIGENCE FROM THE BRITISH SETTLEMENTS IN INDIA.

CALCUTTA.

SCHOOLS ESTABLISHED.

The Rev. Dr. Middleton, Bishop of Calcutta, is now zealously endeavouring, and with good prospect of success, to spread the knowledge and practice of Christianity in the East Indies. Among other good works, he is now establishing schools, in his widely-extended jurisdiction, for the moral and intellectual improvement of the native population; and the inhabitants have generally manifested a disposition to avail themselves of these means of instructing their children. This is a most important fact; and both religion and humanity may rejoice at the results likely to flow from an education founded on Christian principles. The native powers are also well disposed towards this head of our Indian Church; and some of them have given him assurances of protection to the Missionaries he may send into their dominions. Such, indeed, is the good opinion entertained at home of his zeal, tempered as it is with sound judgment and discretion, that no ordinary degree of alacrity is shewing itself in assisting him in these undertakings.

. . . .

NEW SOUTH WALES.

COMMERCE.

Advices from Sydney are received to the 25th September. The Isabella, Gloria, and Maria, convict ships, had arrived safe, with their crews and convicts in the best condition. The regulation by Government, restraining the commanders of such vessels from taking out investments of goods, as formerly, appears to have been quite unexpected at Sidney; and it was generally supposed a material rise would take place in all articles exported from this country.

The following report of the state of the Colony was brought by the David Shaw, which arrived lately from Port Jackson direct, entirely freighted, by the principal house in the Settlement, with a valuable cargo of oil, fur, seal-skins, and wool, produce of the territory, and its adjacent shores.

PRODUCE—POPULATION.

The autumnal rains of March and April have this season caused only a partial overflow of the South Creek. The price paid to Government for the supply of their stores with fine fresh meat was 6d. per lb.; and 10d. per bushel for wheat;—a fine milch cow could be purchased for 10l.

The annual muster, concluded at the date of 1817, gave the following results:—

Total number of souls in
New South Wales 17,165
   Van Dieman's Land . . .   3,214

Population of the territory . 20,379

There were 14,500 acres of wheat in cultivation in New South Wales; 1250 acres of potatoes, barley and oats; and 11,700 acres of maize. The following

are the quantities of stock exclusively in New South Wales, viz.

Horses 2,850
Horned Cattle 38,650
Sheep 66,700
Pigs 11,400

Of the above 20,379 souls there were 4,000 male convicts; 2,340 women prisoners, and 850 of their children; and upwards of 4,000 men and about 500 women having been forwarded thither, from this country and Ireland, since June of the last year. Thus, including the settlers who have since gone out, the entire population of the territory may now be estimated at 25,000 souls. In 1812, the total number of inhabitants were only 12,471, by which it will appear they have been doubled in six years!

MISSIONARIES.

By the last advices received from Otaheite the island was in tranquillity. The Missionaries, says a Sydney Gazette, were in the full enjoyment of their health, and every wished-for success is attending their labours, all the islanders being converted to Christianity! Speaking again of these islands, another Gazette says. A great majority of the natives can read, and delight in perusing the various tracts printed for them in their own dialect: furnished by nature with subsistence from the most trifling labour, they bestow much of their time in reading, and even in writing, corresponding with each other on the leaf of the plantain and the banana. There are very few families without one or more readers.

The Church Missionary Society have also, through the personal indefatigable exertions of the Rev. Mr. Marsden, formed an establishment on the north island of New Zealand; and it is an interesting proof of the reciprocal services commencing between ourselves and the fine race of men inhabiting the above islands, that an advertisement of the departures in the Sydney Gazette, of March 9, specifies the names of twelve New Zealanders and six Otaheitans, who compose part of the crews of two colonial brigs, then on the eve of sailing for the coast fisheries. (*Philanthropic Gazette.*)

CHINA.

NEW VICEROY.

From China, we learn, the Viceroy has been recalled by the Emperor of China and sent to a distant part of the Empire for the alledged purpose of quelling by his wisdom and activity a rebellion which is said to be raging with great fury at the extremity of the kingdom. The removal, however, is attributed with greater appearance of truth and probability, to the immense wealth amassed by the Viceroy at Canton, which is supposed to have excited the avarice and rapacity of the Ministers about the Court. This new Viceroy arrived at Canton in January last, and is reported to be of a more mild and accommodating disposition than his predecessor. It will probably however be soon found that he differs little from others of his Countrymen in power.

POLICE AND CRIMINAL LAWS.

From the Pekin Gazette, August 9, 1817,

Chow, the Yu-she (or Censor) of Honan, kneels, to report, with profound respect, in the hearing of his Majesty, the following circumstances, and to pray for his sacred instructions.

The clear and explicit statement of punishments is a means of instruction to the people ; the infliction of punishments is a case of unwilling necessity. For all courts there are fixed regulations to rule their conduct by, when cases do occur that require punishments to be inflicted in questioning. Magistrates are not, by law, permitted to exercise cruelties at their own discretion.

But of late, district Magistrates, actuated by a desire to be rewarded for their activity, have felt an ardent enthusiasm to inflict torture. And though it has been repeatedly prohibited by Imperial edicts, which they profess openly to conform to, yet they really and secretly violate them.

Whenever they apprehend persons of suspicious appearances, or those charged with great crimes, such as murder or robbery, the Magistrates begin by endeavouring to seduce the prisoners to confess, and by forcing them to do so. On every occasion they torture by pulling, or twisting round the ears (the torturer having previously rendered his fingers rough by a powder) and cause them to kneel a long while upon chains. They next employ what they call the

Beauty's Bar,* the Parrot's Beam,† the refining furnace‡, and other implements expressed by other terms which they make use of. If these do not force confession, they double the cruelties exercised, till the criminal dies, (faints) and is restored to life again, several times in a day. The prisoner unable to sustain these cruelties, is compelled to write down or sign a confession (of what he is falsely charged with) and the case any how is made out, placed on record, and with a degree of self-glorying is reported to your Majesty.. The Imperial will is obtained, requiring the person to be delivered over to the Board of Punishments, for further trial.

After repeated examinations, and undergoing various tortures, the charges brought against many persons are seen to be entirely unfounded.

As for example, in the case of the now degraded Taeu-tae, who tried Lew-te-woo ; and of the Che-chow, who tried Pih-keu-king. These Mandarins inflicted the most cruel tortures, in a hundred different forms, and forced a confession. Lew-te-woo, from being a strong robust man, just survived ; life was all that was spared. The other, being a weak man, lost his life, he died as soon as he had reached the Board at Peking. The snow-white innocence of these two men was afterwards demonstrated by the Board of Punishments.

The cruelties exercised by the local Magistrates examining by torture, throughout every district of Chih-le, cannot be described ; and the various police runners, seeing the anxiety of their superiors to obtain notice and promotion, begin to lay plans to enrich themselves. In criminal cases, as murder and robbery, in debts and affrays, they endeavour to involve those who appear to have the slightest connexion. The wind being raised, they blow the spark into a flame, and seize a great many people, that they may obtain bribes from those people, in order to purchase their liberation. Those who have nothing to pay are unjustly confined, or sometimes tortured, before

---

* A torture said to be invented by a Judge's wife ; and hence the name. The breast, small of the back, and legs bent up, are fastened to three cross bars, which causes the person to kneel in great pain.

† The prisoner is raised from the ground by strings round the fingers and thumbs, and suspended from a supple transverse beam.

‡ Fire is applied to the body.

being carried to a Magistrate. In some instances, after-undergoing repeated examinations in the presence of the Magistrate, they are committed to the custody of people attached to the Court, where they are fettered in various ways, so that it is impossible to move a single inch : and without paying a large bribe they cannot obtain bail. Their oppressions are daily accumulated to such a degree and for so long a time, that at last death is the consequence.

The death warrants to be signed by his Majesty, at the autumnal execution, amount this year to 935 In this number is included the lowest class of capital crimes. The share which Canton had in these this year is 133 ; but to the whole number executed in Canton during the year, the word *thousands*, it is said, must be applied : some say 3000. If the truth be equal to 1000, it is a shockingly awful number of human beings for one province to sacrifice to the laws, in the space of one year. I omit the word justice, for human laws and justice are not always the same. What is the reason why so many fall victims to the sword of the law ? Is it wholly the fault of the people ? or does a share rest with the ruling part of the community ?— (*Indo-Chinese Gleaner.*)

REBELLIOUS ASSOCIATIONS.

Pekin, Oct. 7, 1817.—One of the Imperial kindred is charged with being connected with a Society, whose nature and object are said to be rebellious.

Associations of a secret nature (for the government disallows of any,—the association of five persons is illegal) seem to increase in China. Their names are very various. The one referred to above is called " The great ascending Society ;" others are (2.) " The Society of glory and splendour," (3) " The Union of the three great powers, viz. Heaven, Earth, and Man." Other names are quaint and ludicrous, such as (4.) " The white jackets," (5.) " The red beards," (6.) " The short swords," and so on. The (7.) " white water-lily" is of long standing. The third one prevails much in Canton, and the new Viceroy, Yuen Tajin, has commenced with great severity against them. Between 2 and 3000 have, it is said, been recently apprehended. At the rite of initiation into this Society, which is performed by night, they make a paper effigy of the reigning Emperor, and require the noviciate to cut it in pieces.

The Foo-yuen, (or Vice Governor of the province of Fob-keen,) has been dismissed ; but no farther inquiry into his conduct is to take place. When he received this communication, he wrote to his Majesty, that he was going immediately to Pekin, " To put his head in the mire by the side of the road as his Majesty passed by, to render thanks for his divine goodness." However, his Majesty has commanded, " the Governors of the intervening provinces to take no notice of him, and has forbidden him to proceed on his intended pilgrimage. " Go home," says the Emperor.

The death of the acting Viceroy's wife, is to day thus announced on a slip of red paper, issued with the daily paper.

The lady of his Excellency the Foo-yuen has gone to ramble amongst the immortal. In consequence of his Excellency's son not being at Canton, (to attend to the reception of his friends, who come to sacrifice and pour out libations to the departed,) it is determined on the 16th, 17th, and 18th days of the moon, to perform the rites of sacrifice, and to chant prayers, at the hill of the goddess Kwan-yin, situated on the north side of the city of Canton.

PERSECUTION OF CHRISTIANS.

A Tartar Public Secretary and his coachman have been apprehended and delivered over to the Board of Punishments, on the charge of being Christians. The Secretary acknowledged that his grandfather became a Christian, but that when, in the tenth year of the present reign (1806), the profession of that religion was disallowed, he had recanted.

That this statement is unreal, is argued from his not calling for Pagan priests during his mother's illness, nor performing certain ceremonies after her death ; as also from his not offering incense at the gates of his house to the presiding spirit. The prosecution is conducted by some of the first people at Court, in consequence of the statements of an informer. Fifteen persons are implicated most of them hold offices in the government.

RELIGIOUS MEETINGS PROHIBITED.

It has been stated to the Emperor, that in Keangnan, there is a temple on the hill, called Maou-shan, to which thousands of men and women resort twice a year, in spring and in autumn, to burn incense, and give thanks to the gods. Similar meetings occur also in Keang-se, Yan-hwuy, and Che-keang. His Majesty prohibits all such proceedings, and disallows people going beyond their own district for religious purposes, because all such meetings occasion a waste of time and money, are injurious to morals, and afford pretexts for illegal associations. Those who shall form societies, and collect money, are ordered to be taken up and punished.

Poetry.

A FRAGMENT,
WRITTEN IN 1815.

OH! yield me heav'n, some soft persuasive strain,
Some mighty opiate for the torn heart's pain,
Which, like Nepenthe in the goblet thrown,
May soothe the soul, and all its tumults drown.
And be it, dear one! to thy ******* given,
To wean thee now from Earth, and guide to heav'n;
To bid thee smile, amidst this world's wide strife,
And live, expectant of another life.

Ah gentle ****, what a state is ours!
The thorns how sharp, how fleeting all the flow'rs!
Our woes how true, how little worth our gain!
Factitious joys!—Mere intervals from pain!
Tell me, my ****, in this mortal sphere,
What *is* there worthy of a hope or fear?
By *others* ills, too soon *our* fate we know—
Poor trembling Pilgrims, in a world of woe!
Slaves in the same dull round of misery,
We breathe, we toil, we hope, despair—and die!

Thou dotard man! half animated clod!
Prone on delusion, thoughtless of thy God!
Why toil'st thou thus? what anxious to procure?
What gift is certain, or what blessing pure?
For health and strength, as heaven's first boon,
      we crave:
This day brings vigour—and the next a grave!
Is 't *Beauty?* least secure of human joys!
Disease first mars it—then old age destroys,
Honour what art thou? mere delusive thing!
Bought from a mob, or borrowed from a king!
In semblance great, while slander skulks unknown;
Blows but one blast—and all the phantom's gone?
Of *Wit* who boast ye? Earthly minions, say!
That frothy venom of a thing of Clay!,

By nature planted in the breast of youth, :
A guard to reason, and a guide to truth :
But see it soon, perverted from its end,
Bid some betray their God, and some their friend.

Oh! filthy world! Oh! chaos of all ill!
Replete with crimes, and reproducing still!
Turn thee my **** from this fearful sight,
This cave enveloped in eternal Night ;
See! Faith waits smiling for the just and good,
To lave their spirits in th' eternal flood ;
The safe sure road of endless bliss to show,
And smooth their passage from this world of woe.

Oh mighty mystery! least understood!
What is the Essence of that Sovereign good,
Which lasts eternal in unknown excess,
And free's our nature from its Bitterness!
Oh say! what Faculty to man is given
To taste the joys, prepared for him in Heav'n,
What guardian sprites the shriven soul await,
To fit it, trembling, for its new found state?
Doubtless we leave below all mortal sense,
And glow unveil'd in Angel Excellence.
What Eye could bear the presence of its God?
What Ear, the anthems of the blest abode?
No! every sense expires in one great sense,—
One mighty power of lasting excellence.

Oh **** best and dearest, kindly given!
Thou choice, and only gift of pitying heav'n!
Leave we the world, its sorrows and its crimes,
Glide we, unnoticed, thro' these troublous times,
Proving that state, which none but fond Hearts
      know
Denied the Joys of Heav'n, yet free from Earthly woe ;
Content the lot of lowly ones to prove,
Our Hope,—*Hereafter* ; and our treasure—*Love*,
Oh grant us, Fate! some home, some humble spot,
Within all peace, and all without forgot!
This our Petition, and our only Pray'r,
Apart from all, our Hermitage to share:
There may we wait, with humble hope the hour
Of Virtue's triumphs o'er the Dæmon's pow'r ;
And, stealing softly from this world of pain,
One pillow serve us, and one grave contain.

AN OCCASIONAL EPILOGUE.

Before the fatal knot is fairly tied,
Before I change the Widow for the Bride—
Once more at this tribunal I appear,
Nor doubt your favour to a Volunteer.

' Such am I now,—though not by martial laws
' I volunteer it: in the Drama's cause
' Enroll'd, in a new corps I range my suit,
' Nor doubt your kindness to a fresh Recruit.
' But fresh recruits are apt to feel dismay'd
' Upon their first appearance on parade,
' And so did I—but soon you calm'd my mind—
' I ever found you liberal, ever kind
' Ye Critics General of this dread review,
' My doubts and fears arise alone from you ;
' Suspend awhile your judgment and your rod,
' And do not vote me of the *awkward squad.*
' Say, is the day my own ? how goes my cause?—
' You need not speak — I'll judge by your
      applause.'

Ladies—I one proposal fain would make,
And trust you'll ear it for your country's sake :
While glory animates each manly nerve,
Should British women from the contest swerve?
No!—we'll form a female *Army of Reserve,*
And class them thus : Old Maids are *pioneers,*
Widows *sharp-shooters—* Wives are *fusileers ;*
Maids are *battalion—*that's—all under twenty,
And as for *light troops—*we have those in plenty;
Vixens the trumpet blow, Scolds beat the drum—
When thus prepared what enemy dare come?
Now, Brother Soldiers—dare I, Sisters, join?
If you this night together would combine
' To save poor me from anxious hope and fear,
' And send out Mercy as a Volunteer—
' To whose white banner should the Critics flock,
' My faltering spirits might sustain the shock :
' Give to my efforts, then, this glorious sanction—
' Your smiles, your plaudits, and your appro-
      bation.' "

WOMAN.

Yes, sweet are woman's tears,
When feeling bids them flow ;
When anxious hopes and fears
In woman's bosom glow.

Let man proclaim his power,
His giant strength display ;
'Tis woman rules the hour
Of anguish and dismay.

She bids each sorrow cease,
When keenest woe assails ;
She softly whispers peace
When man's assistance fails.

Then rosy chaplets bind
Round woman's brow alone ;
The world may prove unkind,
If woman's smile we own.

SONG.

[From Carolan ; a Tale.]

Within this breast a sorrow dwells,
  Which happy lovers never know ;
Within this breast a transport swells
  Of joy, attended still by woe !

Within this breast still lives a maid
  Whom hope to my fond arms had given,
And long my love and joy's delay'd
  For her—a favourite of Heaven !

Within this breast lives many a pain
  Of disappointed love and joy :
Within this breast lives hope---ah, vain !---
  Whom wild despair does still annoy.

Within this breast springs many a sigh,
  Urg'd by Affections tenderest glow,
And love's and pity's sympathy---
  Ah, oft the source of grating woe.

Within this breast how oft have sprung
  The tenderest raptures love could seal ;
How often has this breast been wrung
  By woes---which none but lovers feel.

Within this breast, while reason beams
  Upon the active senses clear,
Her lovely form shall live in dreams
  Of hop'd-for joy,---to me yet dear. '

FINE ARTS.

THE BRITISH GALLERY.

The Italian, the Flemish, the French
and the Spanish Schools, are all fully represented in this parliament of genius—
all ages, and the perfections of almost
every great master, have their specimens
here. It contains 156 pictures of every
description, and of the foremost class in
each. The liberality of the Prince Regent
has contributed some of the finest Gaspar
Poussins in existence, besides productions
of Titian, Claude, Rubens, Vandyke, Par-
megiano, del Sarto, Tintoretto, Holbein,
and the splendid Cartoon of The Sacri-

fice. He has also sent some fine Cuyps, Rembrandts, Potters, &c. &c.; the Duke of Wellington some excellent Flemish drolls, and masterpieces of Snyders, together with two examples of Platza, a painter unknown to us. The Earl of Carlisle is the donor of many interesting pictures; the Earl of Darnley of some grand Salvators; the Marquis of Bute of an incomparable Hobbima, &c.; the Right Hon. Charles Long of Teniers' Misers, &c.; Viscount Ranelagh a delicious Cuyp.

OIL AND WATER COLOURS.

The fifteenth exhibition at Spring-gardens displays much talent in both the branches of the art to which the exhibition is devoted. Among them are some fine landscapes by Stark, Miss H. Gouldsmith, Prout, Deane, Linnell, T. Fielding, Varley, C. Fielding, Robson, &c. The miniatures are numerous, and many of them well executed. Among the water-colour pictures in the historical style is 'Falstaff acting the King, from the first part of Henry IV.', by Richter; which, both in conception and execution, possesses very considerable merit.

ROYAL ACADEMY.

We have not room for more than an enumeration of the most striking pictures, in this annual exhibition of the talent of British Artists. 38. Portrait of Chantrey, by Raeburn; 48. Theatrical Portraits, by G. Clint; 86. View of Rotterdam, by Calcott; 104. Entrance of the Meuse, a masterly sky, by Turner; 143. Lending a Bite, a humorous little thing, by Mulready; 153. The Penny Wedding, one of Wilkie's best painted and most characteristic compositions; 157. The Stolen Kiss, from Guarini, Pastor Fido, West; 163. Portraits of three Messrs. Lyell, a charming picture, Phillips; 164-5-6. An Interior and Designs for Boccace, exquisitely done, by Stothard; 169. Venus Anadyomene, a beautiful piece, by Howard; 175. Morning Fishermen, one of Collin's most perfect landscapes; 206. Richmond Hill, an uncommon and splendid work, by Turner; 212. Highland Chief, by Raeburn; 232. Captain Manby, in a fine broad style, J. P. Davis; 269. The Post Office,

E. V. Rippingille; 309. Jacob's Dream, by W. Allston, equal to the foremost productions of the season; 310. Aladdin, richly coloured, by Stewardson; 341. Sir Roger de Coverly, a very clever thing, by C. R. Leslit; 404. A Lady in a Raben's manner, R. R. Reinagle; 453. Calandrino, a droll story from the Decameron, H. P. Briggs; 461 and 469. Landscapes by Samuel and Hoffland; 603. Village Feast, W. Kidd; 640. A Wood-Cutter and his Daughter, Drummond; 676. In miniature, Sir Gregor Mac Gregor and other large portraits, by Steele; and several brilliant and sweet productions, by A. Robinson, Chalen, W. H. Watts, Newton, &c. Enamels by Bone in his best manner, and a large and fine copy by Muss, &c.:—In Sculpture, 1179. A Peasant Girl, by Westmacott; 1181. Statue of Dr. Anderson for Madras, Chantrey, and some fine busts, &c.

ON THE ARABIC LANGUAGE,

As now spoken in Europe, in Asia, and in Africa.

To the Editor of the Literary Panorama.

SIR,

In this enlightened age, when our intercourse is increasing with nations remote from our own, and possessing different religions, languages, laws and customs;—when the Ambassadors of the Mahommedan potentates of Europe, Asia and Africa, are resident in our metropolis; all understanding the *Arabic Language*:—when, with a knowledge of this language, a person may travel and hold colloquial intercourse with the inhabitants of Turkey, with the greatest part of Asia, and with Africa;—and lastly, when we consider the valuable and immense stores of Arabian Literature, of the best periods which still remain unexplored;—is it not remarkable, that in this powerful and opulent country, there should not be found, with all our boasted learning and eagerness of research, as many as three or four Englishmen capable of writing and conversing intelligibly in that beautiful and and useful language. The extent of this disgraceful ignorance would be scarcely credible, were there not proofs beyond doubt that our principal seats of learning are as deficient in this knowledge as scholars in general are, and that letters or public documents written in that language have been, in vain, sent to them for translation. See the P. S. to my letter. What I have long considered as chiefly tending to diminish the desire of acquiring this language, is an opinion dogmatically asserted, and diligently propagated, that the Arabic of the East and West, are so different from each other as almost to form distinct languages; and to be unintelligible to the inhabitants of either of those regions respectively. *Having always doubted the truth of the assertion, I have endeavoured from time to time during the last ten years, to ascertain whether the Arabic spoken in Asia be the same as that spoken in Africa*, (westward to the shores of the Atlantic ocean,) but without success and even without the smallest satisfactory elucidation, until the arrival in London last winter of the most *Reverend Doctor Giarve, Archbishop of Jerusalem ;* and this gentleman has given such incontestible proofs of his proficiency in the Arabic Language, that his opinion on this important point, cannot but be decisive; accordingly on presenting to the Reverend Doctor some letters from the Emperor of Marocco to me, desiring, that he would oblige me with his opinion, whether the Arabic in those letters was the same with that spoken in Syria; he replied in the following perspicuous manner, which I think decides the question.—" *I can assure you that the language and the idiom of the Arabic in these letters from the Emperor of Marocco to you, is precisely the same with that which is spoken in the East.*"

It is, therefore, now ascertained that the Arabic language spoken in the kingdom of Tafililt, of Fas, of Marocco, and in Suse or South of Barbary, is precisely the same language with that which is now spoken in Syria, and Palestine in Asia;—countries nearly 3000 miles distant from each other. And, from information since obtained, there appears to be no doubt that the Arabic Language spoken by the Arabs in Arabia, by the Moors and Arabs in India and Madagascar, and by the Moorish nations on the African shores of

the Mediterranean, are one and the same language with that spoken in Marocco; subject only to certain provincial peculiarities, which by no means form impediments to the general understanding of the language; not so much indeed as the provincial peculiarities of one country of England differ from another.

Unwilling to trespass further on the time of your readers, I shall in a future letter notice the considerable misconstructions and errors into which the ignorance of this language has !led European travellers in Africa; of which I shall state some examples that have occured in a recent publication respecting that country.

I am, &c.

JAMES JACKSON.

Circus, Minories,
13th *May,* 1819.

P. S. There is a letter from the reigning Emperor of Marocco (Mully Soliman ben Mohammed) to our revered Sovereign in the Western Arabic (See Appendix to *Jackson's Account of Marocco, &c.* p. 320) which was sent to the University for translation, and after remaining there as Dr. Buffé informed me, about two months, was returned without a translation. It was then sent to the Post-office for the same purpose, but with similar ill success: Dr. Buffé who had been the bearer of it (from the Emperor) to the Secretary of State, then called on me, and requested a translation which I declined giving, unless I should be requested so to do by the Secretary of State.—This letter contained friendly overtures, and afforded a most favourable opportunity to open an advantageous negociation with Marocco, and a mutual exchange of good offices; but from ignorance of the language the opportunity was lost . The late Mr. Spencer Perceval having expressed to my Lord Redesdale, or to Mr. Mitford, late of the Audit-office, the regret he felt at not being able to procure a translation, my friend Mr. Mitford, mentioned my name to his relation as a person competent to translate. Accordingly I received a letter from Mr. Perceval, requesting a translation into English which I delivered to that gentleman a few days afterwards, but the original Arabic letter of which I made a translation did not reach me till several months after it had been received by the minister! In the mean time the Emperor made repeated enquiries of the *Bashaw of El Garb*, of the *Governor of Tangier*, and of the *British Consul*, for a reply to this letter, when his Imperial Majesty was actually informed by some of the Members of the *Divan*, that the King of England had no power; but that the power was vested in the hands of the Ministers of the Crown; whereupon the Emperor determined never to write again to a Christian King in the Arabic Language, and with regard to Great Britain, I believe he has faithfully ever since kept his word! Some time before this letter was written, I being then in Marocco, the Emperor's Minister asked if the Emperor his master were to write an Arabic letter to *Sultan George, Sultan El Ingleez* (these were his expressions) whether they were capable of translating it into English; as the Emperor did not wish the contents to be known to his Bashaw at Tangier, nor to the British Consul, as it would necessarily be, if written in English; I replied that there were learned men at the Universities capable of translating every learned language in the known world; and, accordingly, the letter above alluded to, was written in Arabic and addressed to his Majesty. An additional proof of the desire which the Emperor *then had* to conceal its contents, was, that it was written in *his own hand-writing;* which I am competent to declare, having letters from him in my possession,—and being acquainted with the Emperor's hand-writing and style.

FORGED NOTES.

The Society of Arts having opened a Committee for the purpose of ascertaining whether there exist any means, within the compass of the fine or mechanical arts, not of totally preventing the forgery of Bank notes (for that is obviously impossible), but of increasing the difficulty of imitation, and thus of checking the prevalence of the crime, plans from various quarters were sent in, and infor-

mation of no trifling value was obtained by oral testimony, both from the Members of the Society and from strangers. The report of this Committee has lately been published; and after remarking on the facility afforded by the present Bank of England notes to forgery, they enter into various plans for rendering it more difficult: the most important part of their observations is the following:

From the testimony of professional artists, it appears extremely difficult to produce the effect of type-printing by common engraving. If, therefore, it be granted that a note composed of type can only adequately be imitated by type, the present forgers must either associate typemakers in their schemes, or learn an entirely new art. The smallest kind of type, called Diamond, is so difficult of execution, and so little in demand, that (as appears from the testimony of Mr. Caslon) there are not more than four or five persons in England who can cut the punches for it. By fixing upon an unusual form for the type, in which, for example, the letters shall lean the contrary way to Italic type, and making it penal to execute any such, except for the Bank of England, a great difficulty in the first instance will be opposed to the forger. It does not appear that the most expert artist can execute more than two punches in a day. Now it would be easy to combine 1,200 or 1,500 different letters or characters, and forms of letters and characters, in one note, and to repeat each letter and character several times. It would therefore be necessary that the forger should either be himself a first rate artist, or secure the co-operation of such; and that he should employ from two to three years in furnishing himself with materials. That he then should acquire the art of the letter founder, or expose himself to the additional risk of a second associate in his fraud, in order to obtain from the punches a font of types. But security in a high degree against forgery, is not the only advantage attending the use of typography; for if with this latter the process of stereotyping be combined, we obtain absolute identity through an infinite number of impressions, without any necessity of renewing the original punches, combined with all the difference in rapidity of production between letter-press and copper-plate printing. It appears, therefore, as the result of this investigation, that there are at least three or four practical methods of constructing Bank-notes, each of which will, in a greater or less degree, prevent the successful competition of the forger—namely, the highest perfection of design and engraving, executed on steel—the adoption of figured borders, like the American notes—the union of variety, evenness, and mathematical accuracy, in engine engraving—and the perfection of type combined with stereotype. But the employment of any one of the three first of these modes is not in the least incompatible with the combination of any other or of all the three; and this combination is in fact contemplated by the authors of all those communications that have been approved by the Society. In the same manner analogous combinations of wood engraving, and works of art cut in the same manner, or struck on metal, are capable of being united with printing-type. Thus means appear to be accessible to the Bank of England of rendering the forgery of their notes in a high degree more difficult than at present. The problem estimated by the Society to the investigation of this Committee appears to be resolved; and although it is not in the nature of things that a person who cannot read should be protected from imposition by the most clumsy forgery, yet to all others the security thus offered appears to be so nearly complete as to invite a fair trial of its practicability.

National Register:

FOREIGN.

AMERICA: UNITED STATES.

Extent of Territory.

From Mellish's map referred to in the late negociations with Spain, it appears that the whole territory of the United States, extending from the Atlantic to the Pacific Ocean, is about equal to 2,256,955 square miles: of which that part lying east of the Mississippi, and including the Floridas, is equal to 942,130 square miles.

If the whole domain were as populous as Connecticut at the last census (1810,) it would contain a population of 135,417,300 persons.

Great Experiment.

A new steam vessel, called the Savannah Packet, of 300 tons burden, has been built at New York, for the express purpose of conveying passengers across the Atlantic. She is come to Liverpool direct. A trial had been made with her from New York to Savannah; she went to Staten harbour and back in one hour and fifty minutes. She is calculated to bear 20 inches of steam, and will pass any steam-boat in the American rivers. Her cabin is furnished in a most elegant style; there are 32 state-rooms; the cabins are on an entire new principle, those for the ladies being entirely distinct from the gentlemen. She is commanded by a Captain Rogers, one of the first engineers in the United States. She sailed from Savannah, on the 30th of April, for Liverpool.

FRANCE.

Prizes offered.

The Society for the encouragement of National Industry in France, have offered the following prizes:—Improved manufacture of sewing needles, 3000 francs—dressing of flax and hemp without soaking, 1500—new method of silvering the back of mirrors, 2,400—dying wool scarlet by madder, without cochineal, for artificial diamonds and precious stones, 1200 francs—preservation of alimentary substances, according to M. Appert's process, 2000 francs—best mode of salting provisions, 2000 francs—construction of a country windmill, 4000 francs—for planting the northern pine, 1000 francs—for planting the Scotch pine, 1000 francs—These have been offered before, and are not yet merited.

The following are other prizes:—For the completion and performance of the *miria*, (a machine for raising water,) 1000 francs—for the construction of new water-wheel, 3000 francs—a mill for cleaning Indian corn, 600 francs—for the establishment of wells for obtaining water by filtration, two prizes, 1800, and 3000 francs—preparation for materials adapted to the arts of engraving, 1500 francs—

a substance that may be cast in a mould like plaister of Paris, and of great durability, 2000 francs—manufacture of Russia leather, two prizes, 1500 and 3000 francs—to the maker of the hydraulic press that shall have been substituted for the common presses of oil and wine, 2000 francs.

Eulogium of Mr. Bowditch.

At the late Annual Public Meeting of the four Academies of the Institute at Paris, Mr. Walckenaer, a distinguished member delivered the most flattering eulogium on Mr. Bowditch, the conductor of the British Mission to Ashantee, in a geographical memoir about to be published.

Cheats in all Trades.

The Gazette de France says, some owners of large depots of wine, in a village which we will not name, have adopted a most adroit scheme for obtaining advantageous sales. They get wine shoots brought from the Northern departments, that have been nipped by the frost, and then industriously spread the news that the vintage has been destroyed. On this the merchants flock to their cellars, and purchase eagerly at high prices; but the fact is, that the vines have not suffered, and every thing promises one of the finest years that France has even seen.

Abundant Crops.

We hear from Marseilles, under date of the 1st of May, that the corn, the vines, and fruit trees all over Province, promise an abundant produce. The abundant rains which fell in April, and the general weather which followed, have filled with joy the hearts of the husbandmen and proprietors.

INDIES: WEST.

State of Hayti.

From a recent work by M. de Lacroix, we learn that Agriculture has not yet reached the degree of perfection it had attained in 1789, but it is making rapid advancement towards complete regeneration. The revenues of this Colony exceed one hundred millions. The annual resources of the two governments amount to forty-eight millions, and their expenditure to eighteen. The armies of the two chiefs of St. Domingo amount to 48,000 men. One third of this force is kept constantly under arms; and in case of attack, it

could be quadrupled. The population of Hayti is calculated at 500,000 souls, 480,000 of whom are blacks or creoles. In 1789, the population amounted to upwards of 600,000, including 40,000 whites and 40,000 creoles. Of the former but few now remain, and the latter do not exceed 25,000. The morals of the people are improving, and public instruction is protected and encouraged.

National Register:

BRITISH.

THE KING.

WINDSOR CASTLE, MAY 1, 1819.

" His Majesty's bodily health continues to be good, and he is generally in cheerful spirits; but his Majesty's disorder is undiminished."

Presents brought by the Persian Ambassador.

A Gold Enamelled Looking Glass, opening with a Portrait of his Persian Majesty; the object of which was to exhibit, at one view, the portraits of two Sovereigns; the one in painting, the other by reflection; and around which were poetical allusions.

A Gold Enamelled Box.

A magnificent costly Sword, celebrated in Persia for the exquisite temper of its blade; the sheath ornamented with emeralds, rubies, and diamonds.

Carpets of Cashmere Shawl, composed of four distinct pieces; the principal Carpet is in length 17 Persian yards, breadth 9 yards. They were manufactured for the King of the Afghans, who sent them as a present to the Shah, and who, without hesitation, sent them, as the greatest rarity he possessed, to the Prince Regent. In Persia they are inestimable, such a specimen of manufacture being there hitherto unknown.

Two carpets of Herat.

A large Painting of his Persian Majesty.

Ten magnificent Cashmere Shawls, of various sizes and denominations.

The Arabian horses brought by his Excellency to England as a present to the Prince Regent, were drawn up in the Court.

Important Documents.

An Appendix to the Bank Report of the House of Commons, contains various important documents relative to the commercial and monied operations of the United Kingdom. The following results are extracted from some of them:—

The total amount of Bank-
notes in circulation on the
20th ult. was   -   -1.27,456,900
Which was an increase since
the 6th of the same month, of   3,047,130
On Feb. 11, 1819, the 1l.
and 2l. notes in circulation
amounted together to the
sum of   -   -   7,445,102
It is calculated that of these the 2l. notes do not bear a greater numerical proportion to the ones than 1 to 7 or 8.

Between the 29th of Feb. 1816, and the 31st of Aug. 1818, nearly five millions of foreign property appear to have been drawn out of our funds:—
At the former of these periods
the whole sum was   -   1.17,334,458
At the latter   .   -   12,486,913

Difference - 1.4,847,545
Added to which is the difference of terminable Annuities, viz.—
At the former period   -.   1. 6,363
At the latter   -   5,791

Difference -   1. 572
The Importations of Grain
into England appear to have
amounted in value in 1818,
to the enormous sum of   1. 13,271,629
Whilst those of 1815 were
only   -   -   2,192,685

Difference - 1. 11,078,944

Sinking Fund.

An important return has just been made to the House of Commons on the subject of the National Debt. It is, we believe, one of the papers moved for by Mr. P. Grenfell, for the purpose of ascertaining how far the public would be gainers, were the Commissioners for the reduction of the National debt, instead of laying out their funds in buying up the already existing debt of the country, to employ it (as by act of Parliament they are authorised) in contracting for the whole or part of any new Loan that may

be wanted for the public service. The year which has been selected for data on this point, is that ending the 15th of June, 1816. The amount of the Sinking Fund for that year was in money 13,407,298 l. 2s. 4d. and there was raised by Loan for the service of the same year the sum of 36,000,000l. Now it appears that these 13 millions and odds, having been laid out in the purchase of old 3 per Cents. the capital stock acquired, or, in other words, redeemed, was only 22,532,505 l. 3s. 9d; whereas, had the Commissioners paid the money into the Exchequer in exchange for such portion of the new Loan of 36,000,000l. as would have been deliverable to them at the rate and on the terms upon which that loan was contracted for, and raised, the capital stock which they would have acquired, in the Three and Four per Cents. would have amounted to 24,569,428 l. 10s. 7d. The nett loss, therefore, which this country suffered by the mode in which the Fund was appropriated, was no less than 2,156,928 l. 6s. 10d.

Beautiful Sculpture.

The Albion, 74, lately arrived at Portsmouth, has brought to England a group, by Canova, in Parian Marble, of the three Graces, (natural size) of Hebe, Bacchantes, Nymphs, and of the Muses, taken from the most celebrated antique models, and executed under the eye of Canova, in white marble, which are intended to be placed in an elegant Temple of the Muses, recently erected in Woburn-park, the seat of his Grace the Duke of Bedford. Some of these figures cost his Grace 3,000 l. each. The cases containing them were not suffered to be opened at the Customhouse, from the danger there would be of breaking them; but the duty will be paid when fixed on their pedestals. There has also been landed from this ship, a magnificent collection of medals and coins, for the British Museum; and a curious and elegant collection of weights and measures, for Lord Castlereagh, by which, we understand, his Lordship hopes to illustrate a plan which he has had some time in progress, to equalize the weights and measures among all civilized nations. Various packages of alabaster figures, vases, antiques, models, and groups, for numerous of the nobility, manufactured at the po-

tories, and artists, have also been landed, with several casts from antique basso relievos, &c.

Students at Cambridge.

It appears by the University Calendar for the present year, that the total number of members of this university, whose names are on the boards, is 3698, being 250 more than the preceding year, and an increase of 1576 since 1804, when the number was 2122.—In order to admit more members of the university at St. Mary's church, the pulpit has been removed, and is placed nearer the organ; alterations have also been made in some of the college chapels for the accommodation of a greater number of students.—*Cambridge Chronicle.*

Velocipede improved.

The velocipedes have something so ridiculous in their appearance, as well as difficult in their management, that the modest and the idle will be equally deterred from the use of them; but there is so much ingenuity in the principle of their construction, that one would lament to see them wholly abandoned. We learn that a vehicle has been constructed which has more of the ingenuity and usefulness, without any of the disadvantages of this mechanical invention. It is calculated to accommodate three persons: the front compartment is constructed in the same manner as the common velocipede; the centre consists of a convenient seat, fitted up like the seat of a gig; and the third portion is behind the centre, in the shape of a dicky. It is worked by the person in front, and the one behind, the person in the middle sitting perfectly easy. The man in front has work of the same kind to do as the rider of the common velocipede; the one behind sits in the dicky, with his foot supported by a foot-board, and the exertion he has to make is to turn with each hand the wheels beside him: for this purpose a handle is fixed to the axis of each wheel, and which is turned round in the same manner as a common hand-mill. The machine combines ingenuity with use, and must produce admiration. It is particularly available in private roads, and gentlemen's parks. It was exhibited last week to the Duke and Duchess of Kent, who both expressed the highest satisfaction at so ingenious a contrivance.

A *velocipede*, on a new construction, is said to be building by an artist at Hereford. It is to have beams or bodies on springs, and four wheels, which will insure its safety. It is to quarter on the roads like other carriages, and, with four impellers, it is supposed that it will proceed with astonishing rapidity; but its peculiar recommendation is to be, the conveyance of two ladies and two impellers, at the rate of six miles the hour.

Bridge over the Menai.

The third Report of the Select Committee on the road from London to Holyhead has been printed: The Committee adopt, and strongly recommend, Mr. Telford's plan of an hanging iron bridge across the Menai Strait. Each of the two principal piers will be 60 by 40½ feet at high water mark, having a foundation of rock. Upon the summit of each of these will be erected a pyramid of cast metal, for the purpose of raising the cables from which the bridge is to be suspended. The bridge, which is to hang between these two points, will be 522 feet long, and 30 feet wide. The entire length of the bridge will be 560 feet. The expence is estimated at 70,000l.

Curious Calculation.

It is calculated that the national debt, in 1l. Bank of England notes, taken at the round sum of 800,000,000l. and at the rate of 512 to the pound, will be found to amount to the enormous weight of 618 tons, 2 qrs. and 9 lbs.; which, allowing 2 cwt. 2 qrs. to each man, would require upwards of 5,500 able-bodied porters to carry it away—or more than 200 waggons, with four horses.

Subterraneous Garden.

A curious account of a subterraneous garden, formed at the bottom of the Percy Main Pit, Newcastle, by the furnace-keeper, was communicated at the last quarterly meeting of the Caledonian Horticultural Society. The plants are formed in the bottom of the mine, by the light and radient heat of an open stove, constantly maintained for the sake of ventilation. The same letter communicated an account of an extensive natural hot-bed, near Dudley, Staffordshire, which is heated by means of the slow combustion of coal at some depth below the surface. From this natural hot-bed a gardener raises annually crops of different kinds of culinary vegetables, which are earlier by some weeks than those in the surrounding gardens.

Soap Caution.

The Public have long been imposed upon, by the article of soap being manufactured of inferior materials, to cover the deception of being sold upon cheap terms; but the following simple experiment will detect the imposition, and prove that genuine soap, from its superior quality and strength in washing, is the cheapest.

Experiment.—Take half an ounce of soap, cut it small, and melt it in half a pint of boiling soft water; put it in a pail, and, with a flat piece of wood, gently stir up the liquor to raise a lather, then add half pint measures of boiling water, and keep stirring each quantity as it is added, until the mixture ceases to raise a strong frothy lather. Be particular in setting down the number of half pints of water used, before the froth begins to disappear, for then the soap has taken as much water as its strength will bear; and by thus comparing soaps of different manufacturers, that which will take the greatest quantity of water is the most genuine.

To try the Quality of Soap.—Take two ounces of any soap, cut it small, and put it into a pint basou; fill it full of boiling water, and stir it till the soap is dissolved; then cover it up, and set it a little distance from the fire for 12 hours; then take it away, and let it cool and settle; turn it out on a plate, and all the impurities of the soap will be found at the bottom : good soap should have no sediment.

PARLIAMENTARY HISTORY.

CHAPTER IV.

Criminal Laws in India—Marriage Act—Catholic Petitions—Salt Duties—Royal Household Bill — Game Laws — Civil Contingencies' Deficiency.

HOUSE OF COMMONS.

CRIMINAL LAWS IN INDIA.

March 16. — Mr. Hume in rising to move certain papers relative to India, stated, that the object was of vast importance as relating to the judicial system, under which 70 or 80 millions of souls were placed—mere justice was sold at a high price to the natives, from the tedious and expensive manner in which all their law proceedings were conducted. The consequence was an enormous encrease of crime, insomuch that the depravity of the inhabitants of Bengal was beyond all bounds. He concluded with moving for reports of the criminal proceedings in the several presidencies, from 1810 to the present time.

Mr. Canning, on account of the immense volume of papers called for, recommended the confining them to those on the hon. member's list numbered 1, 4, 6, and 10; which would be more than could be brought under review in the present session.

Lord Morpeth supported the motion, and remarked, that our best security for India, was in the equity of our proceedings, and the protection afforded the inhabitants.

Sir W. Burroughs thought much allowance must be made for the difficulty of administering equal and impartial justice, to so great a number of people divided into so many religious sects—Hindoos, Mahometans, Chinese, Arabs, and Christians.

Mr. Hume in reply, adverted to the miserable state of the police in India, which was founded on the system of espionage, every office having its regular set of spies and informers, and at so great an expence were the laws administered, as to amount to one eleventh of the whole revenue of India. The several papers named by Mr. Canning were ordered, and he also offered all the farther private information in his power.

MARRIAGE ACT.

March 17.—Dr. Phillimore, in pursuance of notice, rose to ask for leave to bring in a bill to amend the 26th Geo. III. commonly called the Marriage Act. He observed, that as he had introduced the measure last year with the full approbation of the House, it would be unnecessary for him to do more than state the outline of it. It related to the marriages of infants—1. by license: 2, by bans. The House was aware that, by the existing law, the marriage of a minor by license without consent, was at all times absolutely void, even after the lapse of many years: the Court had no discretion, and most distressing cases sometimes occurred, where the parties even sought to avail themselves of their own perjury, to free themselves from the connection they had formed. The remedy for this was extremely simple : it was to limit the period for the avoidance of the marriage by parents or guardians, to the minority of the party, and where the party himself sought relief, to one year after the celebration of the marriage; after this time had elapsed, it ought not to be disturbed. With respect to the marriage of infants by bans, it was generally considered that that formality was a proclamation; but in so large a city as London, it was impossible that it could be effectual, where bans might be put up in a distant and obscure situation. The hon. member meant, that an actual residence of one fortnight should be necessary in the parish where the bans were published. Leave was then given.

HOUSE OF LORDS.
CATHOLIC PETITIONS.

March 17.—The Marquis Downshire presented three petitions in favour of the Catholics. The first of these petitions, (said the noble marquis) was from the Protestant inhabitants of Dublin, praying for the removal of those disabilities which still disqualified their Catholic Brethren by interdicting their constitutional claims. Another petition to the same effect had also been consigned to his custody from the Protestant Freemen of Dublin, worthy of that spirit of intelligent toleration which was fast obliterating the prejudices of less liberal eras. The first of these petitions was not only numerously signed, but it was signed by men of consideration and property, and was, he conceived, well deserving of their lordships' attention. The third petition was from the Protestant Dissenters of Belfast. His lordship spoke in high terms of the loyal conduct of the Catholics during the last 27 years, and of their tolerant spirit, and hoped they would be granted the required relief.—The petitions were read, and ordered to lie on the table.

ROYAL HOUSEHOLD BILL.

March 19.—On the Speaker's putting the question that the amendments to this bill be read a second time,

Lord Folkestone objected to the clause by which the sum of 10,000*l.* was to be allowed to the Duke of York, on account of his having the care of his majesty's person. He thought this sum was much larger than the expenses to be incurred rendered necessary. He therefore moved that the clause should be expunged.

The motion was supported by Mr. Lyttelton and Mr. Protheroe, who said, he had always felt great respect for the personal character of the Duke of York; but he had felt, as he had before expressed, that in a discussion of this kind the influence of his name and family had not been used with the utmost delicacy; it was a

fair inference that ministers had impressed the mind of his Royal Highness with sentiments not congenial to it. He regretted that so painful a subject had been brought under discussion, and was convinced that it would have done much greater honour to ministers, if they had come down to the House with a statement, that under existing circumstances his Royal Highness, however just his claim, could not think of adding a new weight to the burdens of the people.

On a division there appeared, for the amendment of Lord Folkestone, 97; against it, 156; majority, 59. The bill was then ordered to be read a third time on Monday next.

GAME LAWS.

On Mr. Brand's moving the second reading of the bill for the amendment of the game laws, Sir John Shelley rose to oppose it, and moved that it be read this day six months; which, being put and negatived, a warm conversation arose upon the principle of the bill, in which Mr Wilberforce, the Hon. Mr. R. Clive, Mr. L. Wellesley, Mr. Coke, Mr. Bankes, Col. Wood, and Mr. Frankland Lewis, bore a distinguished part, the former observing, that "as the present game laws now stood, all the purchasers of game were the absolute encouragers of vice! Mr. Brand defended the principle of his bill, which he said was founded upon the resolution of a former Parliament, that "game belonged to the owner of the soil;" and his object was gained, if the moral feeling of the House were awakened to the system of game laws, which was opposed by the concurrent interests of the lower orders. On a division of the House, there appeared a majority of 27 for the second reading.

CIVIL CONTINGENCIES DEFICIENCY.

On the Chancellor of the Exchequer moving that the report of the Committee of Supply on the Civil Contingencies Deficiency be taken into further consideration,

The Hon C. Hutchinson said, that the expenses which the House were now called upon to sanction, were the most unnecessary and extravagant that had ever been presented to parliament. But the item to which he objected most was, the sum of 22,610*l.* 15*s.* 1*d.* for snuff-boxes, to make as presents to foreign ministers; and so far, he had been informed, was this absurd practice carried, that the coachman appointed to drive an Imperial Grand Duke, lately on a visit to this country, had been presented with one. He concluded by moving a resolution, that the sum of 22,610*l.* 15*s.* 1*d.* for presents to foreign ministers, was extravagant and ought not to be again incurred.

The Speaker suggested, that as the resolution now before the House was that the sum of 97,154*l.* 8*s.* 9¼*d.* be granted to his Majesty to make good the deficiency in the grant of parliament for the civil service of 1818, the course of proceeding would be to read that resolution a second time, for the purpose of moving an amendment upon it. The form of the amendment would then be a resolution to deduct the 22,510*l.* 15*s.* 1*d.* which was the amount of the vote objected to, from the larger sum of 97,154*l* the whole grant proposed.

Mr. Hutchinson said, that as the charge had been already incurred, he did not propose to disallow it, or to deduct it from the resolution now before the House; but he proposed his resolution for the purpose of expressing the disapprobation entertained against this part of the expenditure.

The Speaker again suggested, that if this was the object of the hon. gent. he could accomplish it best by proposing a separate resolution, after the question before the House was disposed of. This would be more conformable to the usual practice, than moving it in the shape of an amendment. This course was adopted, and the resolution, that the House agree in the opinion of its committee, that 79,154*l* 8*s.* 9¼*d* be granted to his Majesty for making good the deficiencies in the civil service of 1818, was put from the chair.

Lord Castlereagh denied that there had been any waste of the public money, and contended that there was no impropriety in giving presents to the ministers of foreign courts; such a practice was authorized by custom, and was pursued by all nations, except the United States. To speak of himself, he (Lord Castlereagh) could say, that out of 22 presents given to the agents of this country, during the last two years, only five had come to him. The situation of diplomatists was not very enviable or gainful, and therefore ought not to be curtailed of any of its advantages. He knew few instances of their making themselves rich—they were not paid so well, considering the expenses to which they were exposed, as other public servants. He would not, therefore, consent to withdraw this advantage without replacing it by another, and he could think of no other more appropriate or economical. Some of them, he was aware, disposed of these presents for immediate profit; but the greatest part of the gentlemen who were honoured with them, preserved

them as memorials of the transactions in which they had been engaged. " If I might speak of myself as an instance (said the noble lord) I would say that I have kept all the memorials of this kind I have received, in the shape in which they were given; and shall transmit them to my family as property which they will prize higher than any thing else I can leave them."

The original resolution was then put, and agreed to, Mr. C. Hutchinson said, his object would at present be answered by having his resolution on the journals. It would go against the precedent being established. He gave credit to the noble viscount for what he had heard, and had no intention of imputing any thing personally to him, and to the practice which had prevailed.

Sir F. Burdett moved, that the report of the Trial by Battle Abolition bill should be re-committed, in order to afford him an opportunity of moving certa'n amendments, by which the right of the subject might be preserved, in cases of appeal for murder, against the privilege of the crown to grant pardons in such cases: his motion being supported by only three, was consequently lost, and the report of the bill was received.

SALT DUTIES.

March 18.—Mr. Calcraft brought the subject of the salt duties before the House. He admitted that the state of the country would not admit of the repeal of a tax that brought in a million and a half yearly to the revenue; but he contented himself with moving for an account of all the salt delivered duty free in England for the last year, and the purposes to which it had been applied. A short discussion took place, during which Mr. Curwen stated, that since the last year there had been an increase of salt applied to agricultural purposes, which had been found to answer in the most satisfactory manner. The motion was agreed to.

Sir. M. W. Ridley brought forward his proposition for an address to the Prince Regent, praying his Royal Highness to make a reduction in the number of junior Lords of the Admiralty. The hon. bart. in a temperate speech, argued that the reduction now proposed by him of the junior lords to four, might well be adopted; since, during the war, whilst our naval force was constantly from 120,000 to 120,000 men, and the number of ships in commission was 1,000, six junior lords had been found sufficient to perform all the duties of the department: surely now, when our naval force amounts to but 137 vessels of different descriptions, and the vote of seamen was confined to 20,000, four junior lords might suffice to perform all the ardous business of the office. The motion was supported by Sir I. Coffin, Mr. Calcraft, and others. Ministers, however, preserved a determined silence, and Sir C. Cockburn was the only speaker in opposition to the motion. On a division, the motion was lost by a majority of 84, the numbers being for the motion, 164; against it 145.

POLITICAL PERISCOPE.
Panorama Office, May 27, 1819.

To suppose that Nations should be exempt from vicissitudes similar to those which befall individuals, in a world proverbially uncertain, were to manifest a pitiable ignorance of the real state of things. The seasons range alternately over the globe; and the vegetable beauties which the present month displays to the delighted eye, are not destined to that perpetuity which a mere gazer on them might wish for his continued gratification. The severities of winter are over; but, they will return; and the heats of summer, with the droughts of autumn, will assume their proper place, and influence. Human life, also, varies; sometimes it demands the utmost exertion of fortitude; while at other times, real prosperity and still more flattering appearances justify enjoyment, though they cannot warrant reliance. Why then, should not nations experience similar variations? Why should not their fortitude be tried, on some occasions, as well as their gratitude on others? Why should not their internal strength be put to the test, as well as their external prowess?

The circumstances of the British nation, at this moment, demand the union of fortitude of mind with gratitude of spirit. Whoever would form a just estimate of them, must not lend his ear without reserve to the representations of party men; nor confide implicitly on the rumours and reports, and conjectures and inferences, which are circulated as unquestionable, by speculative politicians of warm heads and cold hearts; who, generally speaking, are always the most forward to impose their opinion. It is no more than natural, that the momentous discussions now pending in the National council, should occupy all minds, and divide the sentiments of the public. It is

not every man's lot to obtain that information, without which nothing deserving the name of a judgment can be formed. It is not in every man's power to reason rightly on correct information, when he has obtained it; nor to sift the real facts which justify his confidence, from the superficial assumptions, which, at least are problematical, and may, or may not, be realized. There is much truth on both sides; but the medium is the most secure. It is necessary that these opposing truths be allowed to qualify each other; to correct each other, as to quality or quantity, or both; as to degree, or to application; as to influence or to urgency; as to their present action, or as to their expected consequences.

We have repeatedly submitted our opinion, that the questions before the Parliament are of vital importance to the nation. What can be more important, than that which has assumed the name of Catholic Emancipation? A question, on which, as it is well known, the most profound Statesmen differ, and agree to differ. What can be more important than the condition of the Poor at this moment, and the correction, or renovation, or invigoration of that system of laws, by which they are to be governed? On this, too, the most competent persons, the best qualified by theoretical reasoning, or by practical administration, differ, and differ essentially. To treat the poor with contumacy, were to violate the first principles of humanity, together with the positive injunctions of religion. To lead them to depend on fallacies, or what common prudence pronounces uncertainties, and what can be only temporary, and what must fail them, eventually, is to augment their sufferings beyond what God and Nature intended; and to aggravate, beyond bearing, at some future day, what should now be met with wisdom and vigour, with candour, but also with decision.

While are writing, it should seem that the rich are in a state of greater agitation than the poor; in a state of greater uncertainty; and many more are the aching heads and hearts of those who ride in their coaches, at the date of this paper, than of those who look on them, as they are driven along the road, and who wonder at the caprice of Fortune, in bestowing such superabundance on some, and withholding the necessary from others.

To our readers these events can occasion no surprise: we had warned them of the approaching struggle between the financial department of the state, and the description of men known as principals on the money market. The public funds have felt the effects of this contest; and have rapidly declined, in a proportion so considerable, that those who are the most deeply interested in them cannot but be much mortified. To them, it is no child's play; to them the consequences may be more than serious, they may be destructive; and the man who rose up rich, but a few days ago, may find himself in the Gazette a few days hence. From this anxiety the poor are free; they have their troubles; but they are not so sudden; and habit has prepared them to meet such troubles by prudence, and to counteract them by industry.

We remember to have bought Stock at *ninety six*, and to have sold out that same stock at *forty seven!* Can we, then, but sympathize with those who are now under the necessity of complying with the the state of Stock Market; and are selling at *sixty six* or *sixty seven*, what they bought at ten or twelve per cent. higher?

Since our last, the Committee on the Affairs of the Bank have made their Report; and they have also sketched out a plan by which that Institution may, or rather *must*, return to the long wished for resumption of payments in cash. As the law stands, no payment *in Silver* can be made beyond *forty shillings;* so that all Bank Notes of higher value must be paid in *Gold.* The consequence will be, possibly, a small loss to the Bank, on one part; and possibly, a small loss to the Public on the other part. But, after the whole is over— we leave it on record, as our opinion—the judicious will look back, not without surprize, on the present difficulties felt or feared, and will wonder at what there was so terrific in *that*, which they will find accomplished by a moderate exertion of sagacity, spirit, and firmness.

The plan proposes, that since the Bank cannot pay in *coined gold*, at the mint price, it shall be allowed to pay in *uncoined gold*, at a price to be fixed, above the mint price. The present price of gold is *four pounds* and *six-pence* per ounce. The plan allows the Bank, after a certain period, to pay ingots of gold stamped (not

coined) at four pounds *one shilling* per ounce. If the price of gold should fall to four pounds,[*] it is evident, that nobody will apply to the Bank, and pay the additional *shilling*: the Bank may keep their gold; should the price of gold rise to *one shilling* and *six-pence* above the four pounds, the Bank will lose the difference. And this difference will be calculated on such a quantity as the Bank bought at a certain price, and such a quantity as it delivers at a stipulated rate; which, supposing its whole issues were demanded—a most incredible supposition!—would make not *three* per cent. loss on the whole: but, much more probably, the loss on the whole would not exceed *one* per cent. if so much. And this is the terrific object, the Medusa's head, that has turned certain persons into stone! What proportion would such a loss of *one* per cent. bear to the profits realized by the Bank, within a few years last past? It will be observed, that this plan is no novelty: it is acted on by the Bank of Hamburgh.

The Committee propose, that not later than the 1st. of Feb. 1820, the Bank shall begin to pay their notes in portions of not less than the value of 60 ounces of gold, in bars assayed and stamped, at the rate of 4*l.* 1*s.* the ounce: that the next payment, which is to take place before the 1st. of October, 1820, shall be in bars similarly assayed and stamped, at the rate of 3*l.* 19*s.* 6*d.* and the third after the 1st. of May, 1851, in bars, at the Mint price, of 3*l.* 17*s.* 10½*d.* the ounce. After these preliminary steps, the Committee have a confidence, that at the end of two, or at the most three years, cash payments may safely be resumed. In this part of the Report, the Committee recommend the repeal of all penal laws relative to melting and exporting the coin. After solemn debates bills are brought into Parliament to this effect.

The prospect is, that the competition in matters of Finance, which now exists among the Governments of Europe, will close, with this plan; and gold, with other commodities will find, and keep, a level. It is impossible, however, on this subject, to avoid remarking the uncertainty of supplies of this metal from the mines of Spanish America; we doubt much, whether the proportion of produce be not fixed by nature, which is paramount to all law, in

[*] It is since fallen to 80.

such a manner that gold may be scarce, while silver is abundant.

So far as the state of our Commerce may be accepted as a branch of politics, our readers will perceive, from our "State of Trade, that things are rather flat, in the Mercantile world; the fact is, that Speculation has exhausted its means: we need say no more. It will be admitted, too, that in some places, the industrious are suffering; but, on the cause of this, opinions differ; they differ, also, on the point, whether such sufferings be general.

It is no more than natural, to compare the Financial State of Foreign Countries with our own: from the French Report on the Public Finances, we learn, that the annual expenditure of France, including interest and payment of the public debt, and the regular charges of existing establishments of the public service, amounted, for the last year, to 878,109,575 francs, or £36,587,898; and that the Budget for the current year is estimated at 889,210,000 francs, or £37,050,416. —Under the necessity of providing for such a heavy expenditure, notwithstanding the famous ruin spread by the *Assignats*, and National Bankruptcy, we do not think France will be forward to disturb the peace of Europe. It is understood, that French Commerce improves; but, it appears that great complaints are made of want of employ for the workmen in certain manufactures. Is it not somewhat remarkable, that this complaint should be general?—that every where part of a population, supposed to be superfluous, should be quitting the land of its nativity, being unable to obtain adequate support?

The same Report may serve for more countries in Europe. Where the inhabitants live on the land, and depend on Agriculture, they complain of the low market price, at which they must sell their produce: where manufactures employ the population, they complain of rivals, and their underselling. The cause is, the dependence, now inevitable, of one country on another, for supplies. It is one consequence of Commerce.

It is very likely that our readers should have paid somewhat more attention than they otherwise might, to the rumours of *Discussions* between Russia and Sweden, from the recollection of hints formerly thrown out, and not obscurely repeated

in the PANORAMA; that there was in Sweden a strong feeling in favour of the son of Gustavus, we know, from the authority of Gustavus himself; and from other incidents. That the young prince has acquiesced in his father's abdication *for the family*, is not true. That Charles John has behaved well on the throne, we have no inclination to doubt. Nevertheless, the time may come when the song once sung in England, of "the King shall enjoy his own again," may be translated into Swedish, and become popular. It would be the strangest thing in the world—no, it would *not* be the strangest thing in the world—if Russia and America, though apparently at the greatest possible distance from each other, should be found guilty of approximation, and eventually squabble. The Russians have ships out, surveying the western coast of America, and intent on enlarging their settlements on that coast: the Americans are sending out a vessel, well manned and armed, to see what the Russians are about; (for such is its real destination, though thinly veiled under other pretences) being intent on suffering no settlements but their own. This looks like nothing *now*: Time may tell another tale.

It is certain the American Government is fostering schemes of ambition: the evils suffered by Europe from the tyranny of Colossal power, have not proved a warning to America: future generations will lament this failing.

South America continues to be a scene of bloodshed; it is astonishing, considering the little real assistance obtained from the Mother Country, by what means the Royalists still hold out; if the victories claimed over them, were so decisive as some affect to believe. On the other hand the Patriots said to be slain, have lived to become again the assistants.

On surveying the general state of the World, there is one gratification—and it is a great one—that, whatever be the political state of things, superficially seen, there is a power gradually making its way, that is destined to produce conspicuous effects: we mean, the power of KNOWLEDGE. Where is the spot on the face of the earth, to which this power has not penetrated? Where is the clime so cold, the people so barbarous, the island so remote, that has not been visited by this power? or, that has not the prospect of being visited by this power, now become its neighbour? KNOWLEDGE is the basis of strength, whether moral or political. It is so much to the honour of our native country, that this power has been fostered by her, at home, and has been sent by her abroad, that we shall close this paper with the gratifying reflection. To what extent it may prove a blessing to mankind, none can say; but, no small portion of mankind, when acknowledging whence they received it, will unanimously, cheerfully, and decidedly, ascribe it to BRITAIN.

. . . .

The Royal Family has an accession, by means of a daughter born to the Duke of Kent.

Commercial Chronicle.

Extracts from Commercial Letters, received from various parts.

AMERICA.

Charleston, April 13th, 1819.

" Rice of fair middling quality may be bought at 3¼d. dollars; and good merchantable Upland Cottons, a 16 a 17 cents.

Exports from Charleston, from 1st October, 1818, to 1st April, 1819.

Bales of Cotton.	Uplands.	Sea Islands
To Liverpool . . .	31000	3400
London . . .	1200	
Greenock . . .	8600	1300
France	10000	450
Coastwise . .	5000	
Other places .	800	250
	56000	5400

Rice.	Tierces.
To Liverpool	2072
London	2437
Other parts of Gr. Britain	2330
France	1696
Antwerp	1505
Hamburg	2470
North of Europe	607
Cowes, and a Market . .	4007
Coastwise	7137
West Indies	10477
	34738

ITALY.

Naples. April 27th, 1819.

" Oil is in calm; but it is said the crop will be rather short from the want of rain, which having now come on, will very much benefit the crops of Corn."

Palermo, April 17th, 1819·

" Rain has fallen plentifully in the Provinces; and we hope it will ensure that favorable result to the Corn harvest which present appearances lead to expect."

INDIA·

Calcutta, October 15th, 1818

" Our accounts from the interior, state the crop of Cotton to be the most luxuriant ever known. If we couple this information with a most extended cultivation, and a present stock of last year's growth, of more than 100,000 Bales, we cannot be wrong in putting down for a certainty, that a great reduction in price will take place when the new crop comes down, in February; so great, we anticipate, as probably to exclude the competition of any other country in the European market.

" It is now certain that the present crop of Indigo will not exceed 65,000 Maunds, and holders are firm in their demands of 20 per cent. advance on the prices of last season.

" The trade in Piece Goods is gradually declining, as European Manufactures of like description are found to be cheaper, of better quality, and of equal durability: *they are making their way rapidly in the provinces of this populous Country.*"

The Americans always looked on the opening of the trade to India as a measure particularly destructive to their commerce, and they now find it almost impossible to compete with us, in consequence of the low rate of freight, and the duties imposed on their India ships. It is expected in America, that the staple articles of this country will hold their prices, or even rise; in this opinion they are confirmed, by finding that advanced price on those commodities exists, not only in London, where it commenced, and where it was attributed to the mercantile speculations of a number of individuals, who had no other way of employing their capital, but that the rise had been found to obtain in a proportionate ratio throughout the continent of Europe. The effect has been immediate on the American markets. The old stock of cotton is entirely sold off; and it is expected that the new crop (the bulk of which will be brought into market in December,) will sell at the opening of the market, at 30 cents. (16d.) per lb. which is 4 cents. more than it did last year. This of course will shew much in favor of the cotton shippers of this country, as, although, the mercantile people of Great Britain are aware, that 50,000 bales more are expected from the American crop of 1817, than that of 1816; the holders of cotton in Liverpool, we are informed, are firm in their belief, that it will maintain its present advanced price, or, perhaps, even rise. We may expect a very great rise on cotton in the India market, as no less than 40 American vessels are gone, or going round the Cape chiefly for that article, besides the ships which have gone for pepper and coffee, which will probably not get full cargoes, and will be obliged to fill up with cotton. Enough of ships, is stated, have gone to Java from America alone, to carry away the whole spice crop; and they will rather give 12 Dollars a pecul, that return without a cargo. Good Indigo sent from this country has done well in the United States, though a large quantity of inferior quality had been sent from South America; but that commands no sale, as long as there is good in the market

Salt-petre is cheaper in America than in England. The Americans have sent a larger quantity of specie, than usual, to China, to be invested chiefly in silks, as, from the bad crops and increased consumption, that article has nearly doubled its price in France and Italy.

The amount of woolens is imported from England into the United States is said to be £3,500,000.

STATE OF TRADE.

Lloyd's Coffee House, May 20, 1819.

Perhaps we cannot better open the present paper than by a letter which we copy from a Bengal paper, wherein the spirit of speculation, with the fallacies adopted in the arguments of speculators, are strongly evident.

Now, true it is, that the Americans expected to find in the Cotton furnished by India, a rival of the most formidable kind; but, true it is not, that the price of Cotton would keep up, and perhaps, " even rise." On the contrary, as our readers know, our Reports for some months past have stated a dull sale, and abated prices. With

these the reader will please to connect the intelligence of our abundant crop, as stated in our letter from Calcutta.

The demand for Cotton has been so disproportionate to the import, that the sale price has hardly paid the expences on the article, to say nothing of its first cost; and we have been assured, from very respectable quarters, that assortments of Cotton are making up in Britain—*for China!*—The most distant of Countries, surely, and the very last to which it might have been predicted that Britain should send Cotton. Such is Commerce! East-India Cotton, after being sent across the globe, westward, is again sent across the globe eastward; and to a country itself producing cotton in abundance!

We have, however, to report a rise in this article, from its lately depressed state; which if it does not altogether place it where it was, and where the Importers would wish it, yet relieves, in some measure, the anxieties of the market. The fact is, that in this Commercial Country, there are usually men of a speculative turn who take off a considerable portion of any commodity, when the price at which it can be obtained offers the prospect of an adequate advantage on a future day. Speculators of this description, have been somewhat forward within these few days; and together with a somewhat enlivened demand for exportation, have given a favourable turn to the market.

It is understood, that the business done has been even extensive; and the prices have risen about a halfpenny per lb.; which on the quantity sold justifies consideration, and affords hopeful presages. Of some kinds the market was absolutely cleared; and more Pernambucos would have found purchasers, could they have been delivered. How long this favourable state of this article—favourable at least, by comparison with what it was—may continue, none can tell; but we learn that the Liverpool market has experienced a corresponding rise; and we may now hope, that what we hinted in our last, at the subsidence of the sympathy with the misfortunes of certain eminent dealers, will be realized, without that long delay which some ventured to anticipate.

The Bengal letter was right in its statement respecting the dearth of Silk, in Euraps; but, the writer could not foresee the uncommon dryness of the last summer; and all who know any thing of the nature of the silk worm, know, that humidity in any form, is even fatal to it, while a dry atmosphere, is friendly. A dry atmosphere also contributes to bring to perfection the food furnished by the Mulberry tree, and thus it is in more senses than one favourable to the production of Silk. Accordingly, this commodity, which had been very high, has resumed a rate not extremely different from its former currency.

The Bengal letter alludes to the value of Indigo in the United States; but, that also is much changed; and India must look for its principal market in Europe; which quarter of the globe will long continue to be the seat of talent, taste, and fashion. At present, the demand for Indigo is not very brisk, though it is not absolutely without motion. There have been small profits realized on purchases made at the last sale at the India House; but, generally speaking, the better profits are yet to come. India, alone, has the power of supplying all the world with this article; and there can be no doubt of its continued endeavours to improve the quality of the production, to the utmost.

East India Drugs generally have experienced but a moderate sale lately; and have varied very much, according to their quality and condition. There have been enquiries after East India Rice; but, the offers made were not equal to the expectation of the holders. At a late Public Sale the whole quantity of Java Rice (ordinary) to the amount of nearly 6,000 bags, was withdrawn, finding no purchasers. The nominal prices were from 10s. 6d. to 11s. 6d.

A parcel of Italian Rice was offered for; but, we believe, was not sold: fine Carolina realized 29s. in bond.

Coffee has again made its appearance in Public Sales; but, either the holders expect it to fetch too high a price, or the buyers expect to obtain it at a price too low; for they seldom agree, of late, sufficiently to do business together. Making all allowances for the irregularity of purchasers, and the differences of opinion and judgment between one dealer and another, we may report the average of the market as having experienced a further decline.

In short, though some parcels, perhaps capriciously, or favoured by Fortune, or coming from favourite names, have supported the highest terms, yet on the whole the market is sufficiently depressed to deter most holders from trying the effects of sales. It is thought probable, that the demand will continue limited for some time; in consideration partly, of the supply for home consumption having been answered; while that for exportation is not at present lively.

New Sugars have partially made their appearance at Market. The quality of those as yet shewn is not remarkably excellent; nevertheless, they have had the effect of somewhat damping enquiries, as those who incline to purchase wait till they obtain further intelligence. However that may be, these Sugars have been offered at moderate rates; and even have sold heavily at a reduction of 1s. to 2s. from what had been the currency. Foreign Sugars especially, have felt this; for, to say truth, there is little, or nothing doing in them. At a recent Public Sale, the offers were not within several shillings of the prices at which the Sugars were withdrawn; and after about half the quantity announced had been submitted to the company, without meeting with purchasers, the whole was withdrawn, to stand another chance, under better auspices.

The low prices at which Sugars may be obtained are, certainly, favourable to the Refiners, to whom the dealers now look for customers. But, at this moment there does not seem to be much disposition to enter with any spirit into the market. There are, indeed, those smaller orders in progress which the home trade of the country always commands; but, extensive commissions, or speculations on a commanding scale, are suspended. Good Sugars, are, however, comparatively scarce; probably, from being in hands able to hold them, who look forward with anticipations of a favourable nature; such at least, is our suspicion of the cause. The effect is the same: good Sugars rate high, in comparison with those of inferior qualities.

The demand for Rum is, at this moment, trivial; and Brandy may be purchased lower; but there seems to be no great alacrity in catching at the terms on which it is offered. Geneva is heavy.

Tobacco has lately furnished a supply for exportation; and therefore is now in but little request. Indeed, it must be re-collected of every commodity, that after a considerable delivery, there must ensue a pause, till fresh orders arrive from some other quarter, and are in a course of execution. This, sometimes, influences a Report drawn up at a certain period; and casts a dulness over it, which a few days may dissipate.

With these reflections our article must close. It would be perfectly easy to speculate on probabilities, and to anticipate what may happen; but, to give such anticipations as truths, and to desire the dependence of our readers upon them, would be delusive; and might be dangerous. The utmost we can do,—the utmost that any ought to do, is, to catch the rumours of those opinions which occasionally issue from merchants and dealers of the best information; and, correcting the opinion of one by that of another, or combining the whole, to exhibit a general view of the state of things, as they appear at the time. Any day may make essential alterations in the markets, as in the weather; but, this forms no impeachment of the correctness of the register, or of the accuracy of the weather glass.

The prices of Silver are marked at Standard Silver in bars . . . £0 5 5
New Dollars 0 5 3¼

The price of Gold is not marked; and probably, must wait the event of the operations of the Bank, before it be definitively settled.

Average Prices for Corn in England and Wales.

Wheat	73s.	5d.	Oats	29s.	11d.
Rye	47s.	11d	Beans	54s.	7d.
Barley	46s.	8d.	Peas	52s.	11d.

COUNTY OF ESSEX.

Agricultural Report, May 24, 1819.

In such a Season as this, it must be considered not at all requisite to enumerate every particular grain now growing, as every species of field produce is in extreme forwardness, and to all present appearance, the result must be, a heavy harvest, at least a great quantity of Straw. In some parts of this County, the Hay harvest is already began, which also is in great abundance. The Tare crop also is in favour

of the farmer, and should the weather prove fine, much of this sort will be made into stover, as a substitute for the loss of Clover.

Bankrupts in the order of their dates; with their Attornies.

BANKRUPTCY SUPERSEDED, *April* 24.
W. Watkinson, Strand, boot and shoemaker

BANKRUPTS.

Atherton J. Warrington, Lancashire, cabinet maker. *Sols.* Mason and Hoasman, New Bridge street

Bradshaw J. Carlisle street, Soho, tailor. *Sols.* Lowe and Bower, Southampton buildings, Chancery lane

Cooke W. Birmingham, merchant. *Sols.* Long and Austen, Holborn court, Gray's inn

Ellerby T. Poole, Dorsetshire, linen draper. *Sols.* Sweet and Co. Basinghall street

Folder J. Savage gardens, Tower hill, merchant. *Sol.* Wilde, College hill

Harris H. Bradford, Wiltshire, baker. *Sols.* King and Lukin, Gray's Inn square

Harris R. Wood street, Spitalfields, stationer. *Sol.* Isaacs, Bury street, St. Mary axe

Holbrook G. Fleet market, poulterer. *Sol.* Kiss, Cliorffd's Inn

Hunter J. and J. Orr, Barge yard, Bucklersbury, merchants. *Sol.* Barton, Bow church yard

Jordan R. and J. Smith, Stratford, Essex, and I. Litchfield, Leadenhall street, coach proprietors. *Sol.* Wilkinson, Cornhill

Laing C. Garford street Limehouse hole, ship-chandler. *Sols.* Dennett and Co. King's Arms yard, Coleman street

Lloyd J. Carnarvon, Shopkeeper. *Sols.* Adlington and Gregory, Bedford row

Moon J. Acres barn, Lancashire, cotton merchant. *Sols.* Milne and Parry, Temple

Nightingale J. and T. Byrne, George street, Portman square, tailors. *Sols.* Fielder & Bartley, Duke street, Grosvenor square

Palmer J. Wellingborough, Northamptonshire, wine merchant. *Sols.* Forster and Warner, Lime street, Fenchurch street

Penfold J. Watling street, warehouseman. *Sol.* Birkett, Cloak lane

Radford E. Strand, tailor. *Sol.* Lewis Clement's Inn

Robinson T. and T. H. and R. Hancock, Manchester, cotton merchants. *Sol.* Ellis, Chancery lane

Self R. H. Whitecross street, grocer. *Sol.* Willett, Tokenhouse yard, Lothbury

Taylor T. Bristol, tobacconist. *Sols.* Lambert and Co. Gray's Inn

Turk T. Rose street, Newgate market, butcher. *Sol.* Lewis, Clement's Inn

Watt J. Preston, manufacturer. *Sol.* Ellis, Chancery lane

BANKRUPTCIES SUPERSEDED, *April* 27.
J. Mott, Hadleigh, Suffolk, miller
J. Simpson and T. Fleming, Mark lane, merchants

BANKRUPTS.

Ackland T. sen. Greenwich, butcher. *Sol.* Suter, Greenwich

Daniell H. Warren street, Fitzroy square, coach maker. *Sol.* Abraham, Great Marlborough street

Deakin T. and T. Dyer, Birmingham, dealers. *Sols.* Clarke and Co. Chancery lane

Dunderdale H. and W. T. London, merchants. *Sols.* Hurd and Johnson, King's Bench walk, Temple

Edwards W. Manchester, manufacturer. *Sols.* Adlington and Gregory, Bedford row

Gray J. Drury lane, commission agent. *Sol.* Willett, Tokenhouse yard, Lothbury

Hepke T. and H. O. V. Post, St. Mary hill, merchants. *Sols.* Smith and Rickards, Basinghall street

Holroyde J. Halifax, Yorkshire, factor. *Sols.* Bennell and Dixon, St. Swithin's lane

Lavell J. Lower row, Lambeth, grocer. *Sol.* Wright, Fenchurch Street

Levet W. Shadwell, grocer. *Sols.* Amory and Coles, Lothbury

Lough R. Upper Ground street, Blackfriars road, brass founder. *Sols.* Bleasdale and Co. Hatton court, Threadneedle street

Marks J. Bath place. New road, chinaman. *Sol.* Lewis, Clement's Inn

Messiter R. Bristol, cloth and wool dealer. *Sol.* Edmunds, Symond's Inn, Chancery lane

Morton R. M. Shepton Mallet, grocer. *Sols* King and Lukin, Gray's Inn square

Parker W. Bridgewater, malster. *Sols* Alexander and Holme, New inn

Peers R. Warrington, Lancashire, grocer. *Sols.* Mason and Housman, New Bridge street

Pierce R. Exeter, stonemason. *Sols.* Darke and Co. Princes street, Bedford row

Richardson S. Nicholas lane Lombard street, merchant. *Sol.* Smith, Bedford row

Smith T. York, butter factor. *Sol.* Eyre, Gray's Inn square

Thomson S. Redcross street, Cripplegate, calenderer. *Sols.* Palmer and France, Bedford row

Tupman J. Great Russell street. Bloomsbury, watchmaker. *Sols.* Jones and Bland, Great Marylebone street

Wharton W. and I. Leominster, common carriers. *Sol.* Becke, Devonshire street, Queen square

Williams E. Birmingham, victualler. *Sol.* Edmunds, Exchequer office, Lincoln's inn

Wilson T. John street, Clerkenwell, carpenter. *Sol.* Jones, Brunswick square

BANKRUPTCIES SUPERSEDED, *May* 1.

W. Dixon, jun. Liverpool, wine merchant

T. Fleming, Limehouse, Middlesex, sugar refiner

BANKRUPTS.

Ainsworth J. Bolholt, Lancashire, whitster. *Sols.* Adlington & Gregory, Bedford row

Bates J. Leyburn, Kent, miller. *Sols.* Brace and Selby, Surry street, Strand

Bound R. Sopley, Southampton, miller. *Sols.* Bremridge and Barnes, Dyer's buildings, Holborn

Chapman J. Margate, baker. *Sols.* Bell & Brodrick, Bow Church yard

Davis D. New Bond Street, jeweller. *Sols.* Mayhew and Co. Chancery lane

Dyer W. sen. Aldersgate street, goldsmith. *Sol.* Upsdell, Church passage, Fenchurch street

Earl T. Kingston-upon-Thames, cord dealer. *Sols.* Clare and Dickinson, Pancras lane, Bucklersbury

Fisher T. Liverpool, master mariner. *Sols.* Dacie and John, Palsgrave place, Temple bar

Gorton J. H. and J. and W. Roberts, Tottington, Lancashire, cotton spinners. *Sols.* Clark and Co. Chancery lane

Hodgson R. Fleet street, oilman. *Sol.* Guy, Howard street, Strand

Hunter J. Barge yard, Bucklersbury, merchant. *Sol.* Barton, Bow Church yard

Illingworth J. Leeds, woollen cloth manufacturer. *Sol.* Wilson, Greville street, Hatton garden

Jones S. O. Princes street, Lambeth, potter. *Sols.* Evitt and Rixon, Haydon square, Minories

Kitchingman J. Cateaton street, merchant. *Sol.* Gylby, Berners street, Oxford street

Lawrence R. Minety, Wiltshire, grocer. , *Sols.* Blake and Son, Cook's court, Carey street

Meaden W. Bath, coachmaker. *Sols.* Bennell and Dixon, St. Swithin's lane

Orr J. Barge yard, Bucklersbury, merchant. *Sol.* Barton, Bow Church yard

Parsons A. Montagu Mews South, Montagu square, horse dealer. *Sols.* Fielder and Bartley, Duke street, Grosvenor square

Puxley J. Aldermanbury, carpenter. *Sol.* Gray, Tyson place, Kingsland road

Ramsay J. North Shields, ship owner. *Sols.* Mitchell and Francis, Sun court, Cornhill

Rees W. Margham, Glamorganshire, grocer. *Sol.* Price, New square, Lincoln's Inn

Ridley R. Basing lane, carpenter. *Sol.* Hudson, Winckworth place, City road

Rossiter E. Warminster, Wiltshire, clothier. *Sol.* Edmunds, Symond's Inn

Statham P. and J. Ardwick, Lancashire, dyers. *Sol.* Ellis, Chancery lane

Steemson T. Kingston-upon-Hull, ship-builder. *Sol.* Rosser, Bartlett's buildings

Tuson J. Cannon Street road, St. George's in the East, builder. *Sol.* Lewis, Crutched friars

Williams W. G. Throgmorton street, auctioneer. *Sols.* Alliston and Hundleby, Freeman's court, Cornhill

Wood R. Hart street Bloomsbury square, paper hanger. *Sol.* Hudson, Winckworth place, City road

Yandall E. Kingsland, coach proprietor. *Sol.* Gray, Tyson place, Kingsland road

BANKRUPTCY SUPERSEDED, *May* 4.

T. A. Cocksedge Woolpit, Suffolk, merchant

BANKRUPTS.

Blackburn W. and P. C. S. Rousseau, City road, Finsbury square, corn dealers. *Sols.* Smith and Son, Dorset street, Salisbury square

Bourne S. Leck, Staffordshire, ironmonger. Sols. Long and Austen, Gray's inn

Brooke G. Leckwood, Yorkshire, woollen manufacturer. Sol. Battye, Chancery lane

Cooper G. Walton-upon-Thames, brewer. Sols. Rogers and Son, Manchester buildings, Westminster

Dixon W. jun. Liverpool, wine merchant. Sols. Lowe and Bower, Southampton buildings, Chancery lane

Ewbank J. Little Bush lane, Cannon street, bottle merchant. Sol. Harrison, Bucklersbury

Fox R. jun. Norwich, silk mercer. Sols. Taylor and Roscoe, King's Bench walk, Temple

Goode T. Leominster, Herefordshire, draper. Sol. Pearson, Pump court, Temple.

Grimsby J. B. Kingston-upon-Hull, haberdasher. Sol Rosser, Bartlett's buildings

Hahn S. Bishopsgate street, tavern keeper. Sols. Alliston and Hundleby, Freeman's court, Cornhill

Hall W. Highgate, victualler. Sol. Howell, Symond's Inn

Henderson J. and J. Morley, Ludgate hill, linendrapers. Sol. Hartley, New Bridge street

Jepson W. and C. Wignall, Liverpool, turpentine distillers. Sols. Adlington and Gregory, Bedford row

Lindsey W. J. W. and A. Hewer, Bath, silk mercers. Sol. Hodgson, Old Jewry.

Mallinson D. and T. Septon, Yorkshire, clothiers. Sol. Jacomb and Bentley, Basinghall street

Manning W. Bristol, dealer. Sol. King, Sergeant's Inn, Fleet street

Pyer G. Newport, Monmouthshire, shopkeeper. Sols. Poole and Greenfield, Gray's Inn square

Slingsby J. Manchester, calico printer. Sol. Kay, Manchester

Warne W. Great Queen street, Lincoln's Inn fields, boot maker. Sol. Jones, New Inn

Watts W. P. Gosport, victualler. Sol. Flashman, Ely place, Holborn

Wild R. Craven street, Strand, tailor. Sol. Pasmore, Warnford court, Throgmorton street

Wilson E. Newcastle-upon-Tyne, merchant. Sols. Atkinson and Wildes, Chancery lane

Wotherspoon M. Liverpool, merchant. Sols. Lowe and Bower, Southampton buildings, Chancery lane

Wyatt T. St. John street, Smithfield, stage coach master. Sol. Williams, Blackman-st.

BANKRUPTCY SUPERSEDED, May 8.

J. Bennet, A. Tabberer, and C. Scudamore, Manchester, woollen cord manufacturers

BANKRUPTS.

Appleyard J. Kingston-upon-Hull, bricklayer. Sol. Hicks, Gray's Inn square.

Ball J. Poole, shoemaker. Sols. Alexander and Helme, New inn

Basham C. Norwich, coachmaker. Sols. Tilbury and Langdale, Falcon street, Falcon square

Beckett J. and J. Roberts, Silver street, Wood street, City, Blackwell hall factors. Sol. Butler, Cornhill

Bevis T. Oxford street, coachmaker. Sol. Carlon, High street, Marylebone

Blachford R. Little Tower hill, stationer. Sol. G. Abbott, Mark lane

Firth M. Cooper bridge, Yorkshire, lime burner. Sol. Battye, Chancery lane

Foot B. Half-moon Tavern, Gracechurch street, victualler. Sol. Reardon and Davis, Corbett court, Gracechurch street

Gottreux J. Mincing lane, broker. Sols. Blunt & Bowman, Broad-street Buildings

Jackson R. W. Melksham, Wiltshire, grocer. Sol. Hannan, Covent garden

Lansdedell J. Northampton square, victualler. Sols. Robinson and Hine, Charterhouse square

Langston R. sen. Manchester, cotton merchant. Sol. Ellis, Chancery lane

Levar J. Ashby-de-la-Zouch, Leicestershire, draper. Sols. Long & Austen, Gray's inn

Lowe G. Manchester, merchant. Sols. Willis and Co. Warnford court

Lowe G. and R. Cohen, Manchester, fustian manufacturers. Sols. Hurd and Johnson, King's Bench walks

Martin M. D. Burlington arcade, Piccadilly, jeweller. Sols. Cardale and Young, Holborn court, Gray's Inn

Rhoades T. jun. Queen street, Hoxton, glass mounter. Sols. Bennett, Tokenhouse yard

Shepherd M. Fareham, Hampshire. Sols. Alexander and Helme, New Inn

Prattimos W. and A. L. Bewdley, grocers. Sols. Benbow and Alban, Lincoln's inn

Smith E. Tothil street, dealer. Sols. Alexander and Helme, New Inn

Smith W. Newcastle-upon-Tyne, grocer. Sols. Amory and Coles, Lothbury

Thompson J. Joiner street, Southwark, victualler. Sol. Pratt, Harper street, Kent road

Vander Kieft A. W. Narrow wall, Lambeth, oil merchant. Sols. Boardillion & Hewitt, Bread street, Cheapside

Walker B. West Smithfield, tailor. Sol. Carpenter, Church passage, Old Jewry

Watt J. Preston, linen draper. Sol. Ellis, Chancery lane

BANKRUPTCY SUPERSEDED, May 11.

J. O. Parr, Liverpool, Merchant

BANKRUPTS.

Austin J. Aldersgate street, corn dealer. Sol. Barber, Chancery lane

Ball T. Keyford, Somersetshire, woolstapler. Sols. Bridges and Quilter, Red Lion sq.

Barlow J. Bolton-le-Moors, Lancashire, druggist. Sols. Adlington and Gregory, Bedford row

Bromley J. jun. Stafford, shoe manufacturer. Sols. Price and Co. Lincoln's Inn

Doraing D. Worsley, Lancashire, inn keeper. Sols. Adlington and Gregory, Bedford row

Elliott W. jun. Tunbridge wells, cheesemonger. Sol. Osbaldeston, London street, Fenchurch street

Flaction F. Berwick street, Sòho, jeweller.
Sols. Mayhew and Co. Chancery lane

Goode J. Liverpool, merchant. *Sols.* Avison
and Wheeler, Castle street, Holborn

Golding J. Colchester, tanner. *Sol.* Nelson,
Barnard's Inn, Holborn

Highton J. & J. Brewer, Broadway, Blackfriars, warehousemen. *Sols.* Swain and
Co. Frederick's place, Old Jewry

Holder F. Whyle, Herefordshire, auctioneer.
Sol. Hach, Furnival's Inn court, Holborn

Norris T. White Hart yard, Drury lane,
victualler

Read J. and J. Hellyer, St. Mary hill, Eastcheap, merchants. *Sols.* Montrion and
Luccock, King's Arms yard, Coleman st.

Wood B. Narborough, Leicestershire, hosier. *Sol.* Taylor, John street, Bedford
row

BANKRUPTS, May 15.

Abrahams L. and A. Camomile street, oil
merchants. *Sol.* Lewis, Crutched friars

Birt W. Bristol, broker. *Sols.* Poole and
Greenfield, Grays Inn square

Blake T. Cowes, Isle of Wight, brewer.
Sol. Bogue, Clement's Inn

Drown R. and G. H. Harris, Botolph lane,
wholesale ironmongers. *Sol.* Oakley and
Birch, Martin's lane, Cannon street

Cohen G. A. St. Swithin's lane, merchant.
Sols. Bennell and Dixon, St. Swithin's lane

Dawson G. and Longden W. Silver street,
colour manufacturers. *Sol.* Fisher, Staple Inn

George W. otherwise Hunt, Frome, Selwood, Somersetshire, clothier. *Sol.* Williams, Red Lion square

George S. and R. Webb, Bristol, sugar refiners. *Sols.* Clarke and Co. Chancery lane

Halmshaw J. and J. Swallow, Heckmond-
wike. Yorkshire, carpet manufacturers.
Sol. Evans, Hatton garden

Hartley C. Whitehaven, joiner and cabinet
maker. *Sols.* Lowden and Helder, Clement's Inn

Hornby G. Liverpool, brewer. *Sols.* Blackstock and Bunce, Temple

Kain R. Curtain Road, Shoreditch, and
Cath W. H. New Union street, Little
Moorfields, merchants. *Sols.* Stratton
and Allport, Shoreditch

Moss B. Chamber street, Goodman's fields,
watch maker. *Sols.* Mayhew and Co.
Chancery lane

Mountague D. West street, West Smithfield,
soap manufacturer. *Sols.* Alliston and
Hundleby, Freeman's court, Cornhill

Peeke T. Great Coggershall, Essex, corn
factor. *Sol.* Clarke, Little St. Thomas
Apostle

Richardson T. King street, Spitalfields,
silk weaver. *Sols.* Few and Co. Henrietta
street, Covent garden

Scudamore C. Manchester, woollen cord
manufacturer. *Sols.* Adlington and Gregory, Bedford row

Shoobridge C. Kensington, draper. *Sol.*
Wilde, College hill

Sowden R. Canterbury, linen draper. *Sols.*
Walker and Rankin, Old Jewry

Smithson R. Whalley, Lancashire, butter
factor. *Sol.* Makinson, Temple

Swanzy J. Austin friars, merchant. *Sols.*
Dennetts and Co. King's Arms yard,
Coleman street

Taylor T. Guildford, liquor merchant. *Sol.*
Child, Upper Thames street

Williams P. G. Princes street, Marylebone,
painter. *Sol.* Righey, Golden square

Yates G. Tottenham Court road, plumber,
Sol. Turner, Percy street, Bedford square

BANKRUPTCY SUPERSEDED, May 18.

R. B. Fletcher, Blackburn, Lancashire, manufacturer

BANKRUPTS, May 18.

Beardsworth J. and Bealey J. Blackburn,
Lancashire, cotton manufacturers. *Sols.*
Milne and Parry, Temple

Clunie R. A. Berwick-upon-Tweed, corn
merchant. *Sols.* Swain and Co. Frederick's
place, Old Jewry

Cox J. St. John street, linen draper. *Sol.*
Dobson, Jun. Chancery lane

Cummings J. Osborn street, Whitechapel,
brewer. *Sol.* Argill, Whitechapel road

Dickinson J. Manchester dealer. *Sols.* Hurd
and Johnson, Temple

Duffil J. Bromsgrove, Worcestershire, grocer. *Sols.* Fladgate and Neeld, Essex st.

Evans S. Bristol, victualler. *Sols.* Poole
and Greenfield, Grays Inn square

Goldney T. Chippenham, Wiltshire, clothier.
Sols. Few & Co. Henrietta street, Covent
garden

Hirst A. Beverley, Yorkshire, worsted manufacturer. *Sols.* Lamberts & Co. Gray's
Inn square

Langton R. London, merchant. *Sol.* Chester, Staple Inn

Lee W. Bolton, Yorkshire, cloth manufacturer. *Sol.* Battye, Chancery lane

Lewis J. Mincing lane, merchant. *Sols.*
Noy and Hardstone, Mincing lane

Midgley R. Harden, Yorkshire, worsted
manufacturer. *Sols.* Few and Co. Henrietta street, Covent garden

Mumford E. Liverpool, silversmith. *Sols.*
Dacie and John, Palagrave place, Temple
bar

Oughton J. Deretend Mills, Aston, Warwickshire. *Sol.* Hall, Great James street,
Bedford row

Powell, J. and E. Holborn hill, oilmen.
Sol. Mott, Essex street

Richards J. E. C. and J. Martin's lane, cannon street, merchants. *Sol.* Wright, Fenchurch street

Swanzy, Austin Friars, merchant. *Sols.*
Austin and Co. King's Arm's yard, Coleman street

Titterson C. W. and J. Foster lane, button
sellers. *Sol.* Jones, New Inn

Williams G. Brighthelmstone, carpenter.
Sols. Palmer and France, Bedford row

Zimmer J. Welbeck st. Cavendish square,
merchant. *Sols.* Oakley and Birch, Martin's lane, Cannon street

PRICES CURRENT, *March* 20, 1819.

	£. s. d.	£. s. d.
American pot-ash, per cwt	0 0 0	to 3 4 0
Ditto pearl	2 15 0	2 16 0
Barilla	1 10 0	0 0 0
Brandy, Cogniac.bond.gal.	0 5 6	0 0 0
Camphire, refined....lb.	0 4 10	0 5 0
Ditto unrefined--cwt.	10 10 0	12 0 0
Cochineal, fine black, lb.	1 10 0	1 12 0
Ditto, East India	0 5 6	0 6 0
Coffee, fine bond....cwt.	5 0 0	5 3 0
Ditto ordinary	4 10 0	4 12 0
Cotton Wool, Surinam,lb.	0 1 3	0 1 5
Ditto Jamaica..	0 0 0	0 0 0
Ditto Smyrna ..	0 0 11	0 1 0
Ditto East-India	0 0 6	0 0 8½
Currants, Zant....cwt..	5 0 0	5 10 0
Elephants' Teeth	32 0 0	37 0 0
——— Scrivelloes	21 0 0	30 0 0
Flax, Riga........ton	80 0 0	0 0 0
Ditto Petersburgh ..	58 0 0	0 0 0
Galls, Turkey.... cwt··	9 0 0	9 10 0
Geneva, Holl. bond. gal.	0 3 0	0 3 3
Ditto, English	0 14 6	0 15 6
Gum Arabic, Turkey, cwt.	9 10 0	12 0 0
Hemp, Riga ...... ton	46 0 0	48 0 0
Ditto Petersburgh	45 0 0	46 0 0
Indigo Caraccas .. lb.	0 9 6	0 10 0
Ditto East India	0 8 9	0 9 1
Iron British bars·· ton.	13 0 0	14 0 0
Ditto Swedish c.c N.D.	21 10 0	22 0 0
Ditto Swed· 2nd sort	16 0 0	17 0 4
Lead in pigs...... fod	0 0 0	23 10 0
Ditto red····· ton	0 0 0	27 0 0
Ditto white......ton	0 0 0	40 0 0
Logwood·········· ton	8 10 0	9 0 0
Madder, Dutch crop, cwt.	6 0 0	7 0 0
Mahogany..........ft.	0 1 6	0 2 0
Oil, Lucca··24 gal. jar	17 0 0	19 0 0
Ditto Florence,½ chest	2 10 0	0 0 0
Ditto whale·····	33 0 0	0 0 0
Ditto spermaceti··ton	96 0 0	100 0 0
Pitch, Stockholm ·· cwt.	0 11 0	0 0 0
Raisins, bloom .... cwt.	3 15 0	4 0 0
Rice, Carolina bond····	2 5 0	2 10 0
Rum, Jamaica bond gal.	0 3 3	0 3 4
Ditto Leeward Island··0	2 9	0 2 11
Saltpetre, East India, cwt.	1 13 6	1 17 0
Silk, thrown, Italian, lb.	2 17 0	3 0 0
Silk,···raw,.. Ditto··	1 14 0	2 0 0
Tallow, Russia, white ..	0 0 0	2 19 0
Ditto———, yellow··	3 8 0	0 0 0
Tar, Stockholm....bar.	1 0 0	1 1 0
Tin in blocks......cwt.	0 0 0	4 15 0
Tobacco, Maryland, lb.	0 0 11	0 1 6
Ditto Virginia ······	0 0 7	0 010½
Wax, Guinea·····cwt.	9 0 0	12 0 0
Whale-fins (Greenl) ton	80 0 0	100 0 0
Wine:		
Red Port, bond pipe ··	39 0 0	55 0 0
Ditto Lisbon ··········	38 0 0	44 0 0
Ditto Madeira ·········	60 0 0	70 0 0
Ditto Mountain·········	28 0 0	33 0 0
Ditto Cape.........·..	18 0 0	26 0 0
Ditto Sherry ······butt	30 0 0	65 0 0
Ditto Claret ···········25	0 0	65 0 0

Fire-Office Shares, &c. March 20.

	£. s.	£. s.
Canals.		
Coventry .... (Div. 44l.) ..	1080 —	— —
Croydon	4 —	— —
Crinan	2 12	— —
Ellesmere and Chester(D.21.)	62 —	— —
Grand Junction ...(Div. 91.)..	252 10	— —
Grand Surry	55 —	— —
Ditto (optional) Loan Div. 5l.	94 —	— —
Huddersfield	13 —	— —
Kennett and Avon(Div.17l.6s.)	22 —	— —
Lancaster...............	26 —	— —
Leeds and Liverpool (Div 10l.)	345 —	— —
Oxford ......Div.31l.	630 —	— —
Peakforest	60 —	— —
Regents.................	45 —	— —
Stratford & Avon..........	23 —	— —
Thames and Medway	26 10	— —
Trent & Mersey..Div. 70l..	1600 —	— —
Docks.		
Commercial......Div. 3l. ..	55 —	— —
East India ....Div. 10l.	185 —	— —
London .... Div. 3l.....	77 10	— —
West India ....Div 10l.....	185 —	— —
Insurance Companies.		
Albion ....Div.£5.···	45 —	— —
Atlas ··········Div. 6l.····	4 12 6	—
Birmingham Fire ··········	400 —	— —
Eagle ················	2 10	— —
Hope ················	4 2	— —
Imperial ················	88 —	— —
London Ship ············	21 —	— —
Provident................	13 —	— —
Royal Exchange··Div. 10 ..	250 —	— —
Sun Life..................	22 10	— —
Union Fire Life ··········	33 —	— —
Water Works.		
Grand Junction..............	43 —	— —
London Bridge....Div. 21. 10s	58 —	— —
Manchester and Salford	38 —	— —
Portsmouth and Farlington....	9 —	— —
South London ··········	20 —	— —
West Middlesex ···········	41 10	— —
York Buildings.............··	24 —	— —
Bridges.		
Southwark ··················	57 —	— —
Waterloo...................	10 —	— —
Ditto Old Annuities Div. 6l.··	34 —	— —
Ditto New do Div. 7l.	25 —	— —
Vauxhall (Bonds, 95)	28 —	— —
Literary Institutions.		
London, 75gs.··············	44 —	— —
Russel, 25gs. ··············	13 —	— —
Surry, 30gs. ··············	10 10	— —
Mines.		
Beeralstone Lead and Silver....11	—	— —
Great Hewas......15 pd.....	23 —	— —
British Copper Comp. 2l. 10s...50	—	— —
Cliff down ....···	5 —	— —
Wheal Goodluck ....1 pr.··	20 —	— —
Albion Copp. Mine	10 —	— —
Roads.		
Dover Street	20 10	— —
Highgate Archway············	5 —	— —
Miscellaneous.		
Auction Mart.................	21 —	— —
Golden Lane Brewery..801. sh.	13 —	— —
Ditto 50l. Share ············	8 —	— —

	8 o'clock Morning	Noon	11 o'clock Night	Height of Barom. Inches.	Dryness by Leslie's Barom.	
April. 21	54	58	44	29,72	30	Cloudy
22	46	51	45	,00	18	Sm.Rain
23	46	51	44	,77	16	Sm.Rain
24	51	48	44	,67	0	Rain
25	46	46	42	,80	10	Cloudy
26	46	51	41	30,16	33	Fair
27	45	50	40	,21	40	Fair
28	46	55	46	,23	51	Fair
May. 29	48	55	44	,05	52	Fair
30	47	60	45	29,93	63	Fair
1	51	62	50	,89	61	Fair
2	55	67	55	,76	84	Fair
3	62	69	56	66	82	Fair
4	56	64	55	,59	56	Showry
5	55	66	56	,70	76	Fair
6	58	68	51	30,05	84	Fair
7	55	64	55	,13	69	Fair
8	59	72	56	,10	74	Fair
9	60	74	55	,17	88	Fair
10	57	68	54	,24	60	Fair
11	56	61	58	,21	56	Rain
12	60	67	55	,10	66	Rain
13	56	66	54	,10	65	Fair
14	56	64	50	,17	64	Fair
15	55	61	50	,12	60	Fair
16	50	66	55	,12	64	Fair
17	58	69	56	29,95	76	Fair
18	60	69	57	,99	79	Fair
19	57	62	56	,64	0	Rain
20	56	60	55	,67	0	Rain

London Premiums of Insurance.

Aberdeen, Dundee, Perth, &c. 10s. 6d to 15s. 9d.
Africa, 2gs.
American States, 25s. to 30s.
Belfast, Cork, Dublin, 12s. 8d to 16s 9d.
Brazils, 30s. to 35s.
Hamburgh, &c. 10s 6d to 12s. 6d.
Cadiz, Lisbon, Oporto, 15s. 9d. to 20s.
Canada 2gs.
Cape of Good Hope, 2gs.
Contantinople, Smyrna, &c. 35s.
East-India (Co. ships) 3gs.
——— out and home, 6gs.
France, 10s. 6d. to 15s. 9d.
Gibraltar, 20s.
Guttenburgh, 12s. 6d. to 15s. 9d.
Greenland, out and home, 3gs. to 3½gs.
Holland 7s. 6d. to 12s. 6d.
Honduras, &c. 2gs.
Jamaica, 30s.
Leeward Islands, 25s.
Madeira, 15s. 9d. to 20s.
Malta, Italian States, &c. 30s.
Malaga, 25s.
Newfoundland, 30s.
Portsmouth, Falmouth, Plymouth, 10s. 6d.
River Plate, 2gs
Southern Fishery, out and home, 10gs.
Stockholm, Petersburgh, Riga, 15s. 9d.

PRICE OF BREAD.

The Peck Loaf to weigh 17lb. 6oz. 3s. 6d
The Half ditto ditto 8 11 ......1 10
The Quar. ditto ditto 4 5 ......0 11
The half ditto ditto 2 2¾ 0 5½

POTATOES.

| Kidney...... 8 0 0 | Ox Nobles .. 7 0 0 |
| Champions .. 7 0 0 | Apple ...... 7 0 0 |

ONIONS, per Bushel, 2s 0d to 3s 6d

MEAT.

Smithfield, per stone of 8lb. to sink the Offal

1819.	Beef s. d.	mut. s. d.	veal s. d.	pork s. d.	lamb s. d.
April 27 ..	5 8	6 0	7 0	6 8	0 0
May. 3 ..	6 4	6 4	7 6	6 0	0 0
10 ..	5 6	6 6	7 6	6 8	0 0
17 ..	5 8	6 0	7 0	6 8	6 8

SUGAR.

Lumps ordinary or large 32 to 40 lbs... 95
Fine or Canary, 24 to 30 lbs. 115
Loaves, fine........................... 115
Powder, ordinary, 9 to 11lbs.......... 100

COTTON TWIST.

Feb. 19. Mule 1st quality, No. 40 0s. 0d
——————No. 120 0s. 0d
——————2d quality, No. 40 0s. 0d
Discount—0 a 0 per cent.

COALS, delivered at 13s. per chald. advance.

	Sunderland.			Newcastle.	
April. 26. ..	31s 0d to 40 0			32s 6d to 40 0	
May. 4. ..	42s 9	0 0		43s 0d	0 0
11. ..	39s 0	41 3		51s 0d	41 9
18. ..	32s 6	40 0		30s 0d	41 0

LEATHER.

Butts, 50 to 56lb. 24	Calf Skins 30 to
Dressing Hides .. 18	45lb. per doz. 38
Crop hides for cut. 20	Ditto 50 to 70.. —
Flat Ordinary .. 16	Seals, Large..... 100

SOAP; yellow, 90s.; mottled 102s.; curd 108s.
CANDLES; per doz. 13s. 0d. ; moulds 14s. 6d

Course of Exchange.

Bilboa	37½	Palermo, per oz	123d.
Amsterdam,	11-9	Legborn	51
Ditto at sight	11-6	Genoa	47
Rotterdam 2-us.	11-10	Venice,	25
Hamb. us. 2½	34 8	Naples	41
Altona us.	34-9	Lisbon	56
Paris, 3d. d.	24.30	Oporto	57
Ditto, 2 us.	24.60	Rio Janeiro	60½
Madrid	38	Dublin	12½
Cadiz	38-½	Cork	12½

Agio Bank of Holland, 2 per cent.

HAY and STRAW.—AT SMITHFIELD.

	Hay. £. s. d.	Straw. £. s. d.	Clover. £. s. d
Mar. 6 ..	6 15 0	2 16 0	8 0
13 ..	6 15 0	3 0 0	8 0 0
20..	7 0 0	3 0 0	8 0 0
27..	7 7 0	3 0 0	8 0 0

Price of STOCKS, from 21st April, to 20th May, 1819.

1819.	Bank Stock.	3 p. Cent. Reduced	3 p. Cent. Consols.	4 p. Cent. Consols.	Navy 5 p. Cent.	Irish 5 p. Cent	Long Annuities.	Imperial 3 p. Cent.	Ditto Annuities.	India Stock.	India Bonds.	South Sea Stock.	Excheq. Bills.	Consols for Acc.
Apr.														
21	—	75¾	72⅔ 1¾	99	104⅓	—	18 7 8	—	—	—	37	—	5p	72¼
22	252	70⅞ 1½	72 1⅝	89⅞	104⅛	—	18 3 4	—	—	—	35	—	6	72⅛
23	251½	71⅛	71⅞ 2⅛	90	104⅛	—	18 3-4	—	—	—	35	—	4	72⅜
24	—	71⅛	72¼	90⅛	104⅝	—	18 13 16	—	—	—	31	80½	5	72⅜
26	—	71⅛	72⅛	90⅛	105	—	18 13-16	—	—	220	30	—	4	72⅜
27	252	72⅛ 1½	73 1⅞	91⅛	105⅛	—	19	—	—	—	29	—	10	71
2	252	71	71⅞ 2⅛	90⅛	104⅞	—	18 7-8	—	—	220	27	—	10	72⅛
29	251½	71⅛	72⅜ 2	90⅞	105⅛	—	18 13-16	—	—	—	28	—	9	72⅜
30	251½	71⅝	72⅛ 2	90⅞	105¼	—	18 13-16	—	—	—	28	—	10	72⅛
May														
1	—	71¾	72¼ 2	90½	105	—	—	—	—	—	—	—	10	72⅜
3	251	71¾	72¼ 2	90⅛	105	—	18 13-16	—	—	—	29	79½	9	72⅛
4	251½	71⅛	72⅛ 2	90⅛	105	—	18 13-16	—	—	219	30	—	11	72⅛
5	—	71⅛	72 ⅛	90⅛	105	—	18 13-16	—	—	218½	28	—	11	72⅜
6	—	71⅞	72⅝	90¼	105½	—	18 3-4	—	—	219½	29	79½	10	72⅜
7	250½	71⅛ 70⅞	72 1⅞	90	105⅛	—	18 11-16	69⅞	—	—	29	—	9	72⅛
8	250	71	71⅞ 2	90	104⅞	—	18 3 4	—	—	—	28	—	8	72
10	250	71⅝	72⅛ 1⅞	90	104⅞	—	18 3-4	—	—	—	28	—	8	72⅛
1	249	71⅝	72⅛ 1¼	90⅛	105	—	18 3-4	—	—	—	25	—	5	72⅛
12	239	71 70¾	71⅞	89⅞	104⅞	—	18 11-16	—	—	—	27	—	8	71⅞
13	240	70¾ 71	71⅝	89⅞	104⅞	—	18 5-8	—	—	218	27	—	9	71⅞
14	237	71⅛ 70⅞	71⅞	89⅞	104⅞	—	18 5-8	—	—	218	29	—	10	71⅞
15	237½	71¼ 71	72 1⅞	89⅞	105	—	18 5-8	—	—	217½	29	—	11	72
17	Princess of Wales born													
18	238½	71 70⅞	71⅞ ⅛	89⅛	105	—	18 9-16	—	—	218	30	—	9	71⅞
19	—	70⅞ 71	71⅛	89⅛	105	—	18 5-8	—	—	—	31	—	8	71⅞
20	238½	70 ⅞	71⅞	—	105	--	—	—	—	—	30	—	7	71⅞

IRISH FUNDS.

	Irish Bank Stock.	Government Debenture 3½ per ct.	Government Stock, 3½ per ct.	Government Debenture 4 per ct.	Government Stock. 5 per ct.	Treasury Bills.	Grand Canal Stock.	Grand Canal Loan, 4 per ct.	Grand Canal Loan, 6 per ct.	City Dublin Bonds.	Royal Canal Loan 6 per cent.	Omnium.
Apr. 30		88½	85⅛	—	107⅓	—	—	—	78	—	—	
M. 3	219	87⅞	85	—	107⅓	—	—	—	78	—	—	
6	217	90	84⅓	—	107⅓	—	—	—	77	—	—	
10	—	90	84⅞	—	107⅞	—	—	—	—	—	—	
14	—	89	84	—	—	—	—	—	77	—	—	
18	—	85½	83½	—	107	—	—	—	—	—	—	

Prices of the FRENCH FUNDS From Apr. 19, to May 18.

1819	5 per Cent. consols fr.	c.	Bank Actions fr.	c.
Apr 19	66	65	1533	50
24	66	80	1510	—
27	66	95	1500	—
May 1	66	85	1512	50
8	66	25	1500	—
10	67	25	1508	75
15	66	70	1512	50
18	67		1540	—

AMERICAN FUNDS.

	IN LONDON. May 11.	14.	21.	AT NEW YORK. Mar. 13.	Apr 9.	24
7 per Cent............	—	—	—	106	106	106
Bank Shares	—	24l. 10s.	24l. 10s.	114	105	102
Louisiana	—	—	—	par	par	par
Old 6 per Cent.	—	—	—	par	par	par
New 6 per Cent.......	par	par	102½	101	101	101
3 per Cent............	—	—	—	66	66	63

By J. M. Richardson, 23, Cornhill.

THE

LITERARY PANORAMA,

AND

National Register:

For *JULY*, 1819.

NATIONAL AND PARLIAMENTARY NOTICES,

(British and Foreign,)

PROSPECTIVE AND RETROSPECTIVE.

CATHOLICS IN FOREIGN STATES.

REPORT

From the

SELECT COMMITTEE

On the Regulation of

ROMAN CATHOLIC SUBJECTS

IN FOREIGN STATES.

[*Ordered by the House of Commons to be Printed, 25th of June, 1816.*]

[Concluded from page 652.]

IF the Policy of Catholic Sovereigns respecting the wily pretences and presumptions of the head of the Catholic (Latin) Church, has been uniformly vigilant and even jealous, if they have been constantly on the watch to discover, and on the alert to counteract, Papal sophistry and devices, there can be no wonder that Protestant Princes should conduct themselves towards his Holiness with a reserve, and suspicion, systematic, to say the least, and occasionally even severe. The power assumed by the successor of St. Peter to dethrone kings, at his pleasure, the language held by mortal man, "by ME Kings reign, and Princes decree justice," was too arrogant to be borne; and the dictates of self-preservation,—the first law of nature, the indispensable condition of existence,—justified

that fearful scrutiny into all Papal proceedings, which less presumptuous, and less insidious conduct, might have rendered unnecessary.

Protestants have departed from the Doctrines and dogmata of Popery in various degrees. Some have thought that the further they receded from whatever was *Papistical*, the nearer they approached to the truth of Christianity; while others supposed, that in dismissing the *corruptions* of the Romish system and practice, they carried their principles of Reformation as far as policy permitted, or as duty required. For, it must be recollected, that although the balance of opinion did, on the whole, preponderate in favour of Protestantism, yet it was not then—nor is it now—without a strong and weighty counterbalance, in various connexions, and among many people. The freedom of thought and of enquiry that has subsequently been established by the propagation of Protestant principles, the stronger light in which certain things have been since viewed, the increasing convictions, and the continued experience of later days, are advantages in our favour, which, by the very nature of events and circumstances, could not be enjoyed by those eminent men by whom the Reformation was principally promoted.

The liberality of the present day is not
the work of Popery; there is no principle admitted, or acknowledged, by
the Holy See, that might lead to real
liberty of spirit, or might relieve the
understanding from the galling shackles
of superstition, or priestly imposition.
It is confessed, with as much pleasure
as the fact will justify, that Popery
itself has derived some benefit from the
re-action of the Reformation in sundry
of its parts ; the reflection of light has
somewhat diminished its darkness;
but, its ruling principles, its conducting
maxims, its pretensions, its insinuations,
its over-bearing assumptions, continue
unchanged.   They were originally advantages taken of ignorance, to render
that ignorance subservient to Ecclesiastical Dominion ; they continue the
same.   Can it be the duty of States,
and Statesmen to forego all the blessings attendant on knowledge, to return
to blindness, after having enjoyed various degrees of light, after having felt
the importance, as well as discerned
the advantages of national information,
and open inquiry ? If this be abhorrent,
not endurable, not even admissible in
imagination,—it is no more than natural to enquire, by what means shall these
advantages be secured to those Governments which have obtained them ? how
shall they be perpetuated ? how shall
they be most effectually and vigorously
improved ?

Amidst the abundance of British
liberty, the well understood privileges
of our own land of freedom, opinions
will differ, they cannot but differ, more
or less, on every subject.   It is part of
our national constitution ; and by habit
is become, as it were, part of our personal constitution.   But, on the subject
of Religion, opinion usually acquires a
firmness, and is held with a determination, seldom shaken by opposition; in
such cases the judgment of a referee is
eminently advantageous.   Somewhat
in this light we view the question,—
" How do other Protestant Powers
conduct themselves towards Catholics? There is Prussia, there is Denmark, there is Sweden, there are Protestant Cantons among the Swiss—on what

principles is their policy founded ? and
what is their practice? The enquiry is
instructive ; and the instruction will not
be lost on the thinking part of the public.   Neither will it be lost on the Catholics themselves : for, no reason has
yet been assigned by them, why members of their body in Britain should be
placed on a rank more elevated than
that of their brethren abroad ; why they
should here enjoy privileges which there
are denied them ; and why they should
claim under our mixed Government and
limited Monarchy, stations of authority
and influence which the wisdom of
other Sovereigns refuses them.   The
appeal is made to Foreign States.   It
is not influenced by the party spirit of
our own population; by the force of
prejudice, arising from circumstances
peculiar to Britain;—it is made to the
Policy of the European World, at
large.

If we direct our attention to Prussia,
we find that Government availing itself
of the services of all its subjects, without exception ; for such was the intention of the sagacious and *military* Fre-
deric :—but, then, it prohibits all intercourse between its subjects and the
Court of Rome, except through the
channel of the Prussian Government ;
it prohibits even communications on
matters purely spiritual.   This Government maintains an Agent at Rome;
but, forbids a nuncio of the Pope from
appearing in Prussia.   Nay, so far does
the State exert its power, that

" The minister of state at the head
of the home department manages
the affairs which concern the catholic
churches. He appoints the clergymen to
the vacant churches. No bull of the
Pope, or any other publication whatever,
can be admitted without having been previously submitted to the examination and
approbation of the minister of the home
department, who makes in such bulls or
writings, any alteration which he thinks
comformable to the general principles of
the king's government.

" All catholics are admitted to fill scientific situations.

" The Government is authorised to see
that the Revenues of the Church are properly laid out !"

Besides this, it has taken effectual measures to regulate the Monastic Orders, those indefatigable and sworn supporters of the Papacy.

" All the convents in the Prussian dominions, such as they existed in 1810 were suppressed in that year, and the State took possession of their property. At present there exist no convents in this kingdom, except some very few, and very small endowed, in its Polish territory: no persons will be allowed to take the vows in them in future; and they will be incorporated into each other by degrees, as their present members are reduced in number, until they finally expire. The *Grey Sisters*, the *Compassionate Brethren*, and the *Ursulines*, are maintained; and a small portion of the revenues of the suppressed convents have been assigned to them. The two former of these orders devote themselves to the service of the hospitals; and the latter is solely occupied in education.

" The members of these orders cannot, at once, bind themselves by religious vows for life. They may, at the age of twenty, take vows for three years; when that time is expired, they may renew them for the like period; at the end of that second period, they may repeat them for a third of equal length: and when this is completed, they are then at liberty to bind themselves by such vows for life.

" No insinuation or request has been addressed to this Government, for the revival of the order of the Jesuits, and probably, from the certainty, that it would on no account be listened to."

By these regulations, a considerable security is given to parents for the continuance of their children with them, in the state of their family. They cannot *easily* be deluded into conventual seclusion; a delusion that is by no means uncommon in Catholic countries. The State has also interfered in other domestic connexions :

" Catholic priests are bound to communicate the dispensations in cases of marriage, received from their spiritual superiors, to the civil magistrate of the province to which they belong; and if they do not choose to perform the marriage ceremony in a case allowed by the laws of the country, but for which they have not obtained a dispensation from their superiors, they must submit to the marriage not being performed by another clergyman."

" In mixed marriages, the baptism of the male children is to be performed by the clergyman of the father's religious profession : that of the female by the clergyman of the mother's side."

These are important considerations; and they are considerations which greatly involve the welfare, the peace, and even the existence of families, and of the state itself, also; but they have not been duly canvassed and estimated among us, as parts of the present question.

In Denmark the prohibition of Roman Catholics, of Priests and Jesuits, was extremely strict :

" According to a fundamental law, his majesty king Christian the Vth, commanded that the Evangelical Lutheran religion, should be solely permitted in the state of Denmark. And he further ordained, that no Roman catholic, or any other from the established religion *deviating confessors,* must be tolerated in this country, and that no monks, jesuits, and the like papistical persons (who at that time in particular were suspected of endeavouring to subvert the inhabitants of the country from the established religion) must, at the forfeit of their lives come into his majesty's land and dominions, and that those who knowingly housed or afforded them place to exercise their Roman catholic rites, were to be punished like those that house and harbour outlaws.

" Foreign ministers who resided here, and were acknowledged as such at his majesty's court, and confessed a foreign religion, were allowed free exercise of religion in their houses, for them and their attendants, however, with this proviso, that no sermon must be preached but in their own language, and that their priests must not preach, distribute the sacrament, or undertake any other office belonging to their religion, to other persons than to the foreign ministers and their attendants, though other persons who wish to partake in divine service were of the same confession.

"The great services which the chevalier Hugues de Terlon, ambassador of France, rendered to Christian the Fifth, determined his majesty, by a letter patent, dated September 26th, 1761, to grant him permission to build a residence, with a church or chapel, in the town of Copenhagen, in which he as well as his successors were to have permission to exercise the Roman catholic worship, and also to add a cemetery. But on the other side the ambassador engaged by bond *(lettres reversales)* that this permission should not be abused by making any processions or any exterior ceremonies used by the Romish church; and that he would take care that all catholics who came there were firmly attached to the king of Denmark; and if at any time this should give umbrage, that he should not have recourse to the protection of the king of France, or of any other prince, inasmuch as this favour had been accorded without their intercession, and that it depended solely on the king of Denmark to give such orders as he should judge necessary for his services. The ambassador was at liberty to have four chaplains, either secular or regular; and every catholic inhabitant of Copenhagen had right to attend mass at the French chapel, to receive the sacrament, and to be married by the French clergyman, but on the condition that every such marriage should immediately be declared to the magistrate of the town.

"At Copenhagen. A chapel (free from taxes) has been granted to the catholics by a convention with the empress queen Maria Theresa, who in return gave the Danes permission to have a Lutheran chapel at Vienna. This chapel is at present served by two catholic priests, under the protection of the Austrian minister. The service is in the German language. The French catholic chapel, under the protection of the French minister, does not exist any longer.

"At *Frederica*. As every christian obtains by the privilege granted this town, the 11th March 1682, art. 1st. the free exercise of his religion, the catholics availed themselves of it. They built a church, which was served by two Jesuits as long as that order existed; but as they accompanied the exercise of their religion with public ceremonies, they were expressly forbidden to do so, by the edict of the 17th June, 1707. As the Jesuits made some converts, whom they afterwards sent out of the country in 1745, a fine was imposed on them of 1,000 crowns, if they did not bring them back; and they were at the same time informed, that if they made any such attempt in future, the liberty of worship would be taken from them.

"The free exercise of their religion was granted by an ordinance of the 17th Nov. 1786, art. 1st, to all Christians who were inclined to establish themselves at *Reikerig* in *Iceland*, though theirs should be different from the established religion. The catholics are therefore at liberty to exercise their religion there, but, up to the present time, they have not availed themselves of it.

"The free exercise of their religion is also granted to the catholic inhabitants of the Danish isles of *St. Croix, St. Thomas*, and *St. John*, in the *West Indies*, by an edict dated the 20th Sept. 1754, with the right of building as many churches as they please, and to name as many priests and ecclesiastics as they judge necessary (with an exception against Jesuits, who may not go there).

"No catholic proprietor of negroes is at liberty to prevent them from frequenting the protestant churches, or the community of Moravians, unless they are baptised in the catholic religion.

"The catholics have had a church at Tranquebar, on the coast of Coromandel, since the the 16th century, and another at Poreirie, a great village in the territory of that town. Catholic missionaries have endeavoured to spread their doctrine amongst the Indians, but they have been surpassed in zeal by the protestant missionaries, brought up at the famous paedagogium of Halle, in Germany.

"At *Altona*, the catholics obtained from Frederick III. on the 16th May 1658, the free exercise of their religion, with the exception of grand ceremonies and processions; they obtained at the same time permission to build a church, which in 1768, was declared free from taxes; and also of having a burying ground. On the 17th Dec. 1736, the right was given them of sending for their priests and ecclesiastics from any place they chose, and no impediment was to be thrown in the way of their correspondence with, or obedience to, their provincials and superiors. And lastly, they obtained, on the 28th March 1757, the permission, in case a catholic should marry a protestant, that the nuptial ceremony may be performed by a catholic priest, provided the parties are agreed, otherwise it is forbidden."

A considerable degree of mutual accommodation is practised in the Kingdom of Hanover: there the Lutheran persuasion is established; nevertheless, the Catholic is not overlooked: one instance of their *mutuality* is sufficiently singular.

• " In the parish of Goldenstedt, in the county of Diepholz, where Lutheran and Catholic inhabitants are mixed, they celebrate their public worship on the Sunday morning in the same church and at the same time, but in the afternoon and on week days, the catholics worship alone. At the commencement of the service, Catholics and Lutherans, who are seated promiscuously, are besprinkled by the catholic priest with holy water, and during mass the protestant clerk sings with the congregation Lutheran hymns, which must cease, when the host is lifted up, and when the mass is ended; then the Catholics sing, and afterwards again the Lutherans; and thus they take their turns several times during the service. The catholic priest sometimes in one part of the parish performs the marriage ceremony and baptism, for protestants.

" Both persuasions have the same burial ground, and at all burials the Roman catholic priest and the Protestant clerk attend, and the former offers the prayers. All fees, except those for burials, are paid by the Lutheran inhabitants to the clergymen of the adjoining protestant parishes. The building of the church, though belonging to both parties, is kept in repair by the catholics only; the protestants contribute to the repairs of the steeple. The revenues attached to the church are administered by each party separately, the poor fund only is common to both. The catholic priest stands (or stood formerly) under the bishop of Munster, the protestant clerk under the jurisdiction of the Elector of Hanover.

" The catholic priest is prohibited from baptizing a child, unless the father be a catholic, or a legal marriage compact has fixed the mode of education of the children ; he may not marry, unless the male at least be a catholic, and the female have agreed to enter the catholic church; all natural children must be educated as Lutherans.

" Catholic priests enjoy the same exemption from taxes as the protestant clergy. The fees must be paid to the protestant clergy, who must certify the payment of them, before the catholic priest has a right to perform any of the acts for which they are paid."

There is, certainly, something extremely pleasing in the benevolence of parties toward each other, though differing in opinion on certain subjects : the alternate use of a place for public worship, mutual assistance when required, community in charitable institutions, and equal distribution to the poor, these are laudable : but, whether our countrymen, especially certain jealous sects among us, would *quite* approve of an indiscriminate sprinkling with Holy Water, at the commencement of Divine Service, we must be allowed to think, very questionable. Yet even in Hanover the Catholics are not fully equalized with their Lutheran brethren. In case of desiring a dispensation for marriage, they are not permitted to apply to the Pope, or to a Catholic Archbishop; but to the Lutheran Consistory, at Hanover. Catholic children may be sent to Protestant schools ; but not Protestant children to Catholic schools.

It is well known, that the Cantons of Switzerland, are divided into Protestant and Catholic, and some are mixed : of course, various degrees of toleration, or equalization, are established among them. Lucerne may be looked on as the model of those where the Catholic Religion is dominant; Berne is the leading Protestant canton ; and Argau maintains universal equality and toleration.

"The liberties enjoyed by the Catholic States of Switzerland are principally founded on established usages and ancient precedents, a confirmation of which was wrung from the impotence or gained from the good-will of the Court of Rome, by the exertions of the people during the course of ages. To these liberties it appears that the Swiss are still resolved strictly to adhere; a proof of which was lately strikingly manifested in the conduct of Lucern towards the Holy See, in the affair of the abbot of St. Gall, that Government having on that occasion evinced the most determined opposition to the encroachment attempted by the Pope on the rights of the secular power.

"The principal kindred points of conduct amongst all the confederate cantons, are :—

1. "The exercise of a strict superintendence and controul over all religious establishments, by the supreme secular power.

2. "The right of examining into the mode of acquiring and disposing of all ecclesiastical and monastic property.

3. "Liability of all such property to all burdens imposed by the State on secular possessions.

4. "Subjection of all bulls, pastoral letters, &c. to the *Placet* or *Exequatur* of Government, prior to their publication.

"The extreme jealousy and watchfulness hitherto constantly felt and exercised by the Government of this country, in all matters where the spiritual and temporal power were brought into a state of collision with each other, and where the former may have endeavoured to extend its authority at the expence of the latter, have been the means of preserving this free and happy country from innumerable evils and embarrassments which have fallen on others where that vigilance was wanting. It is to be hoped that neither threat nor intrigue will ever induce them to alter their conduct."

It may not be amiss here to notice the protection afforded to the Catholic Clergy, by the Protestant Canton at Berne.

"The same oath of allegiance is administered indifferently to Protestants and Catholics.

"The Government allows 72,000 French francs per annum, from the public treasury, for the maintenance of the Catholic clergy in the districts belonging to the ancient see of Bâle, recently annexed to the canton of Bern.

"The curés are divided into three classes, according to their extent and population. To the first class is attached an annual stipend of 1,200 Fr. fr.;—to the second 1,000—and to the third 800. According to this proportion of re-partition amongst 69 curés, an annual sum of 63,400 Fr. is employed.

"Besides the foregoing salaries the rectors of Porentru, St. Ursanne, Seignelegier, Delémont, Courendelin and Lauffon, enjoy a high pay *(haute paye)* of 500 Fr. fr.: each under the denomination of cantonal rectors.

"Those ecclesiastics, who, being incapacitated by age or infirmities, from discharging the duties of their office themselves, are obliged to find a curate, receive an indemnity of 500 Fr. fr. per annum.

Those rectors, who serve a second church, from want of a pastor to it, are entitled to half the pay of that cure; the other half, added to the remaining balance of the 72,000 francs, goes to form a fund of reserve for pensioning those ecclesiastics, who, from age or infirmity, are rendered incapable of serving any longer.

"Besides these pecuniary advantages, each commune is bound to furnish its respective rector with a house and small garden, the keep of a cow, and sufficient fire-wood for domestic purpose."

The reader will easily draw the proper inferences from these documents. In no Catholic Dominion, in no Protestant Dominion, are Papal injunctions or decrees, or Bulls, or Pastoral Letters, admitted without strict and official revision : In some places they are not admitted in any shape, so great is the jealousy of the Government: And if any information on Ecclesiastical matters, refering to the Catholics, be necessary to such places, it is given in the form of anonymous articles, in the Newspapers,—" We hear from such a place, that his Holiness has ordered, that ——." In no well governed State are the Monastic Orders allowed to escape regulation and inspection: they are controuled in all: they are annihilated in many. The prohibitions of the Order of the Jesuits are most strict; and are founded generally, on the misconduct of its members. There is no difficulty in directing these principles with others, inseparably connected, to the regulation of Catholics among ourselves. When that body of our fellow subjects is prepared to submit the election of their bishops to the opinion of the British Government, when they can bring themselves to obtain favours from Rome, through the medium of the British Government, when their Monastic Institutions shall be regulated by the Government, and when they shall consider themselves more as good subjects, and less as good Catholics, then will the difficulties of which they now complain, give way; and they may congratulate themselves on the certainty, the proximity of Catholic Emancipation. In the mean while, they may learn from these documents, that ALL Protestant States think SOME restrictions necessary over their Catholic population—AND SO MUST BRITAIN THINK FOR HERSELF.

Calmet's Dictionary of the Holy Bible, with the Fragments, containing Illustrations of Scripture Incidents and Expressions, selected from the most authentic Histories, Travellers, &c. containing many Occurrences and Observations, extremely interesting and highly entertaining: with Plates of Views, Maps, Plans, Dresses, &c. 4to. Parts I. to VIII. price 6s. each. The Fourth Edition. Taylor, 1819.

When a work has reached a fourth edition, it is clear that the public must have acknowledged its merit, and have pronounced on its character; so that criticism can have little more to do than to notice the attention paid to the execution of the copy sent for inspection. Every Biblical Student is well acquainted with the name and authority of the

uncommonly laborious CALMET; and we need not occupy our pages with repeating what has been said a hundred times over, that his Dictionary of the Bible stands foremost among works of a like nature, and that it well deserves a place on the shelves of every library. The general reader will find occasion to consult it from time to time, and even frequently, for his personal satifaction; while the enquiring mind, and especially the mind intent on accurately understanding Holy Writ, with its connections, and evidences, will not fail to derive much gratification, as well as advantage from a familiar acquaintance with it, and a prompt consultation of its articles.

By comparing the present edition with those which have preceded it, we find that a great number of new articles are inserted in the Dictionary: and by attending to the brackets, which distinguish the additions made by the present Editor, from the original text, we perceive that the whole has been revised with great diligence, and many corrections, or completions are adopted, which, though frequently consisting of a few lines, or even of a single line, add much to the importance of the work, and form a considerable accession on the whole. Some of them, indeed, are longer than the original article; but, more commonly they supply information obtained from works published in later times.

It appears to us, that the Geographical articles are the most improved; and the histories of several of the principal places are succinctly brought down to their modern state. The original appellations of many towns, &c. are with great labour, deduced from more probable causes and roots, than formerly; and the explanations transmitted by Jerom, but not obtained by him from the purest sources, are with evident reason, relinquished, for others derived from the nature of the country, from local situation, from ancient occurrences, idol temples, &c. &c. by which they assist in elucidating the history of past ages, as well as the Geography of particular cities and districts.

The Natural History should have been more correctly, and more frequently referred to the Linnæan system, than it yet appears to be; but, perhaps, the Editor felt the difficulty of identifying the subjects of Holy Writ, in this department of Science: or, he may yet accomplish it, in some succeeding part of his undertaking. It must at the same time be confessed, that the Disciples of Linnæus, themselves, have not always agreed on this matter; and that errors, if admitted into a work of such authority as Calmet, would have very injurious and lasting consequences. Nevertheless, we must be allowed to remind the Editor of the importance that attaches to this branch of the Dictionary; and of the *duty* that devolves on him, in consequence.

The History of Persons seems to have undergone but little variation; and to say truth, little could have been added, without prolonging the articles beyond reason or utility. The same may be said of that vast mass of information which the learned author had collected, on the rites, ceremonies and manners of the Jews, and Orientals; their principles and prejudices, civil and religious, &c. &c.

A considerable portion of these Parts is composed of articles originally published under the humble title of *Fragments*; and this title they still retain. We have heard them spoken of with great applause; and from the specimens before us, we incline to think that they well merit the encomium. They comprize miscellaneous illustrations, always ingenious, and often new, of scripture incidents, without order or connexion, generally. They are for the most part short, or concise; but some of them approach toward the nature of Dissertations. An infinity of remarks, and illustrations of passages, which are not to be found in the Dictionary, are introduced in these detached essays; which form articles, not less entertaining than instructive.

On the whole, we do not scruple to pronounce this edition, likely to become the standard of this valuable work. We understand that the American press has reprinted the former editions, *verbatim;* and has copied the Plates, without addition; also, that other repetitions were in contemplation. It was, therefore, high time that the London press should maintain, or resume, its superiority; and the Editor proposes to enrich the Plates given with this copy, with corrections, additions, and perhaps, novelty. Our recommendation can add little to the popularity of this Encyclopædia of Biblical Knowledge; but, we cannot conclude our report without wishing success to this edition, and to the worthy Editor health and ability to continue and conclude his laborious and anxious undertaking.

The New Testament, in Hebrew; by the London Society for promoting Christianity among the Jews. 8vo.

To enable the Jewish people to peruse the records of the great Christian Teacher, in a language familiar to them, has been the wish of many learned men. It was attempted by Hutter, who published the New Testament in twelve languages, and among them Syriac and Hebrew (1600; reprinted in 1603.) Dr. Robertson, at Edinburgh, also reprinted this version, not very many years ago, with sundry corrections, which were not always improvements. This was repeated by Dr. Caddick, whose labours were contented with *verbatim* fidelity. The Society has aimed at something higher; and the language of their version is more biblical than that of former versions. It has, however, felt the disadvantage of being composed amidst the diversities of Christian Sects; for instance, the term *Baptist* and *baptism* were at first expressed by the regular *Hebrew* words of the like signification; but subsequently they have been exchanged for the *Greek*, which is more Christian, certainly, but not more Judaic. Perhaps, scrutinizing critics may also find certain, almost inevitable inaccuracies among the points; but, these are trifling blemishes in a work that deserves much commendation for general accuracy to of execution, and the greatest benevolence of intention.

Facts and Observations respecting Canada, and the United States of America; affording a comparative view of the inducements to emigration presented in those Countries. To which is added an appendix of Practical Instructions to Emigrant Settlers in the British Colonies. By Charles F. Grece, Member of the Montreal and Quebec Agricultural Societies, &c. 8vo. 7s. Harding, London, 1819.

The present rage for emigration to North America has been the means of eliciting much valuable information relative to that Country, which we have seized the earliest opportunities of laying before our readers ; but it has also produced much merely literary speculation, numerous ridiculous blunders, and not a few wilful misrepresentations. The facts and observations, communicated to the public by Mr. Grece, are drawn from the most authentic sources, and result from the best possible data, —viz. his own personal knowledge acquired by sixteen years residence in Canada, and the most unequivocal information of those who have resided in, or visited those parts of the transatlantic Continent, which he had not been able personally to inspect.

The experience thus obtained by our Author, has enabled him to present a correct and circumstantial view of the various agricultural productions of the Canadas, which is highly interesting to all who have it in contemplation to emigrate to America. The great influx, indeed, of *Native Americans* into these countries for many years past, may be considered a strong proof, in addition to the other circumstances brought forward in Mr. Grece's work, of the great advantages which these colonies possess over their own country for settlers. The population in the townships of Lower Canada, he informs us, is composed of two thirds Americans : and he states that they are the best people to employ in the woods,

being well acquainted with the clearing of new land, and also able to make the necessary utensils and implements required in a new settlement. The inference, very naturally deduced by our author, is, that if the Americans find it advantageous to settle in the Canadas, Englishmen must have a greater interest in emigrating thither, as they fall into Society with laws and habits similar to their own.

After exposing the misrepresentations contained in one of Mr. Birkbeck's publications, Mr. Grece proceeds to give a view of the favourable Climate of the Canadas, and to detail the present state of these fertile provinces, as compared with that of the United States; and the comparison is in every respect favourable to our colonies. We shall select a few particulars for the gratification of our readers.

1. *Price and quality of Land.*

" The quantity of land in Canada, yet in a state of forest, is capable of containing and supporting some millions of souls. Its quality is equal, if not superior, to any in the eastern States, and its price far below that of the western territory.

" Some lands are held by a tenure similar to our English copyholds; but a great part is freehold. Copyhold farms are subject to an annual rent of $1\frac{1}{4}$ bushel of wheat, for every 100 acres, besides four shillings and two pence in money. On the alienation of lands, 8 *per cent.* is paid by the buyer to the lord of the manor. The tenants are compelled to go to the lord's mill to grind the grain for their own consumption, paying a toll of 1-14th of the grain so ground.

" The Roman Catholics continue to pay tythes to their own clergy : this amounts, however, but to 1-26th, and that of grain and pulse *only*, every other production being entirely free from tythe : neither are there any assessed or land taxes exacted from the farmers of the Lower Province.

" The freehold land is held by the same tenure as in England.

" Farms of 100 acres, with a small loghouse, and a barn, thirty acres of the land being previously prepared for cultivation, may be bought for from £150 to £200. In the townships, which are very extensive, and in many parts not more than fifty or eighty miles from the city of Montreal, the great emporium of the Canadas, farms may be bought on the above terms.

" Land in a state of nature may be bought for from ten shillings, to two pounds per acre, at a credit of from five to ten years, paying 6 *per cent.* interest to the owner. This land, to be cleared, and made fit for sowing, will cost about three or four pounds per acre more, in the Lower Province; in the Upper Province, about six pounds per acre: labour not being so plentiful there."

2. *Expences of Cultivation.*

" The usual price of labour on farms, is from one shilling and eight pence, to two shillings and six pence per day, with board : if without board, four shillings and two pence. An annual farming servant, besides board and lodging, has from £15 to £24 wages *per annum ;* and a woman servant of all work, from £6 to £12 *per annum.*" ·

Mr. Grece has given a detail of one year's expence of cultivating a farm of 100 arpents, equal to about 80 English acres, in the vicinity of Montreal, for which we must refer our readers to his volume, as well as for the particulars relative to the rotation of crops and the proper seasons for putting them into the ground, and their subsequent culture.

3. *Prices of provision at Montreal and Quebec.*—These are nearly alike.

" Beef is from 4d. to 6d. per lb. Mutton, 6d. to 7½d. Veal 5s. to 12s. per quarter; pork, 6d. per lb. turkeys, 5s. each ; geese, do. ducks, 2s. 6d. fowls, from 10d. to 1s. 3d. eggs, from 8d. to 1s. 6d. per dozen. Fresh and salt fish are to be had at a proportionate rate. Butter, from 1s. to 1s. 8d. per lb. cheese, from 5d. to 10d. per lb. potatoes from 1s. to 1s. 8d. per bushel; wheat, from 5s. to 7s. 6d. per bushel; barley, from 2s. 6d. to 4s. 2d. rye, from 4s. to 5s. buck wheat, from 3s. to 4s. 2d. Indian corn, from 4s. to 5s. oats, from 1s. 8d. to 2s. 6d. horse beans, from 5s. to 10s. pease, from 3s. 4d. to 5s. French beans, from 8s. to 12s. per bushel ;

hay, 3s. 6d. per hundred pounds weight. The price of horses is from £15 to £25 ; a yoke of oxen, from 15 to £25 ; cows, from 5 to £10 each. These prices are Halifax currency, being 18s. sterling per £."

" The usual retail prices, (Halifax currency), of grocery and liquors, in Canada, are as follows :—Tea from 4s. to 5s. 6d. per lb. coffee 1s. 3d. loaf-sugar 1s. West India sugar from 7d. to 9d. maple sugar, produced in the country, from 4½d. to 6d. per lb. Rum 4s. 6d. per gallon, Hollands gin from 7s. to 8s. brandy from 10s. to 13s. wine the same. Madeira, 16s. per gallon, Teneriffe, from 6s. to 9s. Spanish from 4s. to 5s. 6d. Vinegar 5s. per gallon, and porter 1s. 8d.

" Salt is sold in Canada at from 2s. 3d. to 2s. 6d. per bushel, tobacco and snuff from 1s. to 1s. 3d. per lb. candles 1s. soap 8d. or 9d. but these two last articles are made in most of the families."

The Commerce of the Canadians and their facilities for exports are very considerable, and superior to those offered in the American Union. Mr. Grece has communicated much valuable information to persons of every class, who designing to emigrate to the Canadas, whose comforts will be essentially promoted by attending to his suggestions. His contrast between the dangers, difficulties, and inconveniences, attendant on settling in the American Union, and the facilities and comforts to be found in the Canadas, deserves to be read by them with the deepest attention.

To the lovers of field sports it will certainly be no mean recommendation, that, in the Canadas, they *are free to all,* while the friendly aid rendered by the native Canadians, as well by the American settlers, essentially contribute to smooth the difficulties necessarily incident to emigration.

A copious appendix is subjoined, containing various details relative to the husbandry of Canada, which will afford considerable interest to those whose views are directed to a settlement in that Country.

From the preceding analysis of this work, our readers may easily collect our opinion of its value. It is a cheap and unassuming volume, and in a small compass presents a mass of authentic and valuable information respecting a part of the British Empire, the advantages of which are comparatively unknown to a great majority of Englishmen.

The Delphin Classics, with the Variorum Notes. (Intitled the Regent's Edition.) Nos. 1, 2, 3, 4, 8vo. £1. 1s. each, large paper, £2. 2s.

It is with singular pleasure that we enter on this article, for it is, what rarely falls to our lot in our critical department, with unmixed feelings of approbation. That a work of such magnitude should have been projected in our country, at a time too when all other countries in Europe were " so shaken" and " so wan with care," breathless and powerless as it were from their long struggles in the grasp of war, must be a subject of laudable pride to every Englishman; that it should have been encouraged by a list of subscribers, numerous beyond all precedent, to a work of its nature and extent, affords occasion for additional exultation,— an exultation in which both public and private gratification may be indulged; for, at the same time that we must rejoice at such an indisputable proof of the wealth and munificence of our nation, we may be allowed to be glad also that the effects of it will reward the spirited exertions of the Editor, who in this, as in all his other undertakings of an expressly classic nature, has acquitted himself of his duty with a liberality and care, which at once prove his attachment to the cause of literature, and his scrupulous adherence to the performance of every thing for which he had pledged himself.

A complete, and at the same time uniform Edition of the *Latin Classics* has been for many years a desideratum in literature, not only in this country, but on the continent also. The *Delphin* Edition, originally compiled, from

the most learned authorities, for the use of the Dauphin of France, has long been esteemed the best that was ever published ; and an undeniable proof of its being so, is the eagerness with which imperfect sets of it are bought up, for perfect ones can no longer be procured. This Edition is however so far from being perfect, that the tables of errata would form a volume in themselves—the works of Claudian alone having five closely printed pages at the end of it, dedicated solely to the purpose of correcting the errors of the press.

The great improvements in the typographical art which have been made within the last century, and the variety of information on subjects of classical learning which has accrued to us within the same period of time, as well from the researches of antiquaries and travellers, as from the labours of scholars, among whom those of our own country claim honourable place, who have been contented to display the treasures of their own minds only in elucidating the productions of the minds of others, authorized us to expect that this new and corrected Edition of the Delphin and Variorum Classics, would, both in a mechanical and literary point of view be a lasting monument to the honor of the State of Letters in England in the beginning of the nineteenth century. We are happy to say that our expectations have been in all respects amply fulfilled in the parts of the work already laid before the public. The excellence of the paper, and the beauty of the type, particularly as seen in the magnificence of the large paper copies, will recommend it immediately to such *epicures* in books as must have their eye as much delighted as their understanding, whilst to the scholar it will be more strongly recommended by the correctness of the text, and the judicious arrangement of the notes, the ordo, and various readings from the original Delphin Edition, which are placed under it; whilst at the end of each author we are presented with the notes relative to his performances, from the best Variorum Edition, with the addition of *Literaria Notitia*, relative to himself from the Bipont Editions, thus truly concentrating as was promised to us, in one mass, the excellencies of the *Delphin*, the *Variorum* and the *Bipont* Editions.

Under all these advantages we cannot but look on this work as one calculated to reflect the highest credit on its projector and supporters, both in our own country and in the eyes of our continental neighbours; who have hitherto seemed to think the ground of Classical Literature their own unalienable possession. The fact is, that the very perfection to which the typographic art has attained within the last few years, has been perhaps purchased at the price of inquiry to the cause in whose service its greatest attractions ought to be employed.—Considered too much as a mechanical art, it has been confined too exclusively to the hands of mere mechanics, and the mention of a printer, instead of conveying such ideas of learning and liberality as are still inseparably connected with the names of Aldus, Stephens, Plantin, Bowyer, &c. &c. forms no other association in the minds of modern readers, than that of types, ink, and hot-pressed paper, and all the other material of the employment. We would however, willy hope to reckon an increased attachment to the different departments of classical learning, which we have regretted to see, has of late years been treated in our own country with a degree of indifference almost amounting to apathy, or else with still more disgusting and reprehensible ridicule. To inquire into the causes of this defection from works, which by their merit have been handed down to us with reverence from the earliest ages of civilization, would open too wide a field of discussion—whether it be owing to the prevalence of an ill-founded austerity of feeling, such as in the age of Oliver Cromwell caused it to be reckoned among the crimes of Charles Ist. that he made the works of Shakspeare the companion of his solitary hours, or whether it be from that excess of self-conceit in the school of modern poetry that

it wishes to disclaim the idea of borrowing figures or allusions from any that have preceded it, and which certainly succeeds so far as to produce many of a nature that never yet had models and never will have imitators,— we cannot now stop to enquire; but we trust the transient chill which a mistaken zeal, or an over-weening vanity has been able to spread over the fairest flowers of antiquity, will be rapidly dispersed by a more general cultivation of taste and learning. Every new form, under which the works that have made our greatest poets, historians, and orators, are presented to the public, is a new service to it; and never yet have they been laid before it in a form combining at once such elegance and such comprehensiveness as in Mr. Valpy's Edition of the *Delphic Classics*, which we think must be regarded, in every family in which it may find a place, (and that is in almost every family of rank and attainments in the kingdom) as a valuable addition to its library, and a never failing source of reference and mental gratification.

A Tour Through Sicily, in the year 1815. By George Russell, of His Majesty's Office of Works. Illustrated by a Map and Eighteen Plates. 8vo. £1. 1s. Sherwood and Co. London, 1819.

This is an elegant and interesting publication. The Author, (in common with many other Englishmen,) having been driven from Rome by the approach of the French army in 1815, proceeded in company with some intelligent German gentlemen, to embark for the Island of Sicily. We shall not detain our readers with any observations on the voyage, or the general account of that island, which occurs in the earlier part of the volume, but shall introduce them to the City of Palermo, of which we have a pleasing description. Among the various objects of attraction which this place contains, Mr. Russell failed not to visit the celebrated repository of the dead, in the Capuchin Convent, situated in its environs. In this cemetery,

"The fathers and brothers of the order, after their decease, are placed in rows, perfectly upright, their backs being supported against dwarf walls, erected for that purpose. They are habited in the same same sort of dress they had been accustomed to wear during their natural life, and bear a ticket on their breast, which denotes the time of their decease, and likewise their age.

"In this *cimiterio* we beheld, horribly exemplified by the varied appearances of more than five hundred human bodies, the grim tyrant death in all his different stages of decay, from the most perfect human, although cold and lifeless form, to, literally speaking, the mere skeleton. After the skeletons fall to pieces, the bones are carefully collected and symmetrically arranged against the walls, and the teeth are set in a species of mosaic work, and form the front of the altar.

"While contemplating this region of the dead, and expressing our surprise at the sight of so many human beings who once lived and moved, our *cicerone* placed his finger under the chin of one whose face we were then earnestly viewing, and raised the body from the ground, as though it had been of paper; so light had this withered emblem of mortality become."

Literature and Science are described as being at a low ebb; foreigners, however, and especially the English, are received with hospitality and attention. But the inhabitants, being under the domination of the Popish Clergy, are exceedingly superstitious. The tutelary idol of Palermo is one Saint Rosalia, whose grotto our author visited. Her festival is celebrated with the utmost pomp and most extravagant rejoicings: though Mr. Russel had not an opportunity of witnessing its celebration, he has given us a lively description of it, derived from authentic sources, which we think will gratify our readers.

"The voluptuous and perhaps monotonous life of the inhabitants of *Palermo* is interrupted by the annual *fête* of *Santa Rosalia*, certainly the most brilliant and enthusiastic display of devotion which exists at the present day in *Europe*. But as we frequently find at the opera, that the splendour exhibited in the ballets and *fêtes* often obscures the general interest of the spectacle, so in these rejoicings, we equally lose sight of *Santa Rosalia*, if, at the end of the fifth day, after a most tumultuous procession, we did not behold the shrine of this holy saint.

"The car upon which this shrine is borne is decorated, or rather overloaded with ornaments of every species; it is drawn by forty mules, and filled by a considerable number of musicians. This enormous machine, certainly the richest and most magnificent ever put in motion, commences its march on the first day, without the shrine, from the *Marina*, and tremblingly traverses the *Cassaro* from the *Porta felice* to the royal palace, situated at the other extremity of this street. A grand display of fire-works here takes place, and the amusement of the day terminate by the *Cassaro* being splendidly illuminated.

"This street, decorated alternately with porticos and fountains along its whole length, which is upwards of a mile, upon a plan rather concave, presents, on this occasion, a *coup-d'œil* of the most pleasing nature.

"The people quietly promenade the *Cassaro* until midnight, when they retire, and the coaches of the nobility arrive and take possession. The gravity of the *Sicilians* is conspicuous during the celebration of this festival: they partake of all its gaieties and pleasures without manifesting the slightest external symptoms of delight; and the various ceremonies pass off with a perfect regularity which never requires the interference of the police, although upwards of one hundred thousand persons are assembled together on the occasion.

"The principal amusements of the second day consist in their races: youths about twelve years of age ride the horses without saddle or bridle, and it is astonishing to see with what address they keep their seats. The horses are assembled and arranged behind a cord, where there is considerable difficulty to retain them: the animals being full of ardour, and, as it were, conscious they are going to contend for the prize, seem to strive to prevent each other from getting the foremost.

, " Upon one of the senators, who is stationed in a species of booth, sounding a bell, the little jockeys instantly mount, and sit well advanced towards the shoulders, with their head almost reclining upon the neck of the horse. At the second sound the cord falls; the horses then set off, and by the discharge of a cannon, the people are informed that they are on the way; the crowd immediately opens, and leaves a free passage for them to pass. Another senator, who is stationed at the extremity of the course, adjudges the prize, after which, the little jockey who has been successful is carried in triumph, decorated with a golden eagle suspended around his neck, amid the acclamations of the assembled people.

" The horses are generally the property of rich individuals, and are trained and fed the whole year for this express purpose. The races occupy part of three days; the first is between country horses, the second between mares, and the third, which is by far the most rapid, between *Barbary* coursers.

" The amusements of the second day are completed by the car returning from the royal palace to the *Marina*, stopping almost every ten places in order that the numerous spectators may enjoy the music: the car, as well as the *Cassaro*, are again most splendidly illuminated.

" The third day commences with another race, and the car also repeats its journey from the *Marina* to the palace. In the evening there is a grand display of fire-works upon the *Marina*; and the buildings contiguous to the port, as well as the *Cassaro*, are again illuminated in such a superb manner, that, viewed from the bay, it fills the imagination with the idea of an enchanted city.

" The diversion of the fourth day again commences with the course. Without comparing these races with those which take place in *England*, yet, from their rapidity, they are in no respect less interesting: the horses generally run the whole length of the *Cassaro*, which is upwards of a mile, in less than a minute and a half.

" The evening of this day is particularly distinguished by a spectacle altogether new, and of which it is impossible to form an idea without having witnessed it. This superb spectacle is the illumination of the cathedral, which is executed in a manner truly enchanting. The interior of this vast edifice is so decorated, that the most pleasing effects are produced by merely introducing such trifles as fringes, garlands of various coloured papers, silver tissue, little pieces of glass, and many other articles of even less value: the whole is, however, so well arranged, and the church is lighted with so much taste, that, upon entering, it presents to the imagination the idea of being within the precincts of a fairy palace.

" The fifth and last day is celebrated by a long and continued procession, which commences shortly after the setting of the sun, and continues till one hour after midnight. It is upon this occasion that all the taste of the inhabitants of *Palermo*, for religious spectacles, is fully developed. Every confraternity or religious order bears in this procession a portrait or image as large as life of its particular saint. The charge of arranging the different toilettes is wholly left to the nuns, who never fail, in dressing *Judith* or the *Holy Virgin*, to pay great attention *à la dernière mode*, or, in other words, to the last fashion imported from *Paris*.

" These representations of the different saints, enlivened by artificial rays, and ornamented with all sorts of garlands, are carried on a frame constructed of timber, which is borne on the shoulders of thirty or forty men, who consider they are achieving their own eternal salvation by carrying their particular saint faster than those behind, and thus gaining time to make counter-marches and evolutions: at last *Santa Rosalia*, in her triumphal car, solemnly traverses the *Cassaro*. ,The presence of their protectress considerably increases the universal joy of the people: as the holy saint approaches, every knee bends in pious adoration; and thus terminates this most splendid *fête* of *Santa Rosalia.*"

The present state of Segeste, and of Selinus, certainly one of the most splendid and magnificent cities ever founded by the Greeks, and also of Girgenti, the antient Agrigentum, is described at considerable length; but we have not room for any passages from this part of the volume, and selection would impair the interest which the lover of classical literature and antiquities would take in the perusal of them.

Having heard much, during his residence at Girgenti, respecting the singular kind of volcano, on the summit of Mount Macaluba, situated about six miles thence in the interior of the country, our Author and his companions accordingly visited this phenomenon; and, as it has not been noticed by any preceding English travellers, we shall extract his description of it.

" This volcano of air, if we may so express ourselves, whose effects resemble those which have fire as their principal agent, has its moments of calmness as well as those of great fermentation and labour; it produces, too, like other volcanos, earthquakes, subterraneous thunder, and violent eruptions; which last have, at times, thrown the matter so emitted more than one hundred feet above the summit of the craters.

" The base of *Macaluba* is nearly circular, and its height is about two hundred and fifty feet, taken from a valley which surrounds it: this valley is, however, considerably elevated above the level of the sea. Its summit is about half a mile in circumference, and terminated by a plain presenting rather a convex surface; it is besides extremely steril. On this summit are a considerable number of little conic heights, the largest of which may be about nine feet in diameter; and on the highest part of these cones, which are in general under five feet, are craters, whose depth we were unable to ascertain, being unprovided with a plumb-line, or any other contrivance by which such a purpose could be effected. The soil appeared externally to be composed of clay, rather dry and cracked, and the hollow sepulchral noise, caused by the action of walking, excited our most serious attention, and reminded us that in all probability we were then over an immense gulf of liquid mud, separated only by a thin covering of clay.

The interiors of the craters is moist, and out of which there constantly issues a species of brown diluted clay, which, after reaching the height of the lips or highest part, forms into little demi-globules; a few

moments after this formation has taken place, these globules break, and the confined air which they retained dispels itself; the diluted clay then runs down the flanks of these heights, and extends itself more or less on every side. Upon introducing a pole about twelve feet long into several of the craters, we found it produced a kind of noise not unlike that of distant thunder: we observed upwards of one hundred and fifty of these craters in full action, besides many which had ceased to throw up the argillaceous matter, and our *cicerone* informed us that their number were continually varying, some, as he said, " dying away, and others as constantly breaking forth."

" It is generally believed, that in all volcanic eruptions fire acts as the principal agent: in this of *Macaluba*, however, the result is very different; for after minute examination, not only on the summit, but round the sides and base, we could perceive no trace of any such element having been concerned either in the formation or working of this surprising production of nature: neither could we discover the least particle of any matter that had undergone the action of fire. We next immersed our thermometer in several of the craters, naturally expecting to find the temperature much higher than in the open air; but here also we found ourselves greatly deceived, the reverse being the result of the experiment. The thermometer so immersed, about nine o'clock in morning, stood at 64° according to *Fahrenheit ;* but on being exposed to the atmosphere, it immediately rose to 72°: after this experiment, we no longer sought the igneous element."

Of Castro Giovanni, which stands on the site of the once celebrated Enna, we have a classical and antiquarian description, as also of the Lake of Proserpine, and of the singularly romantic valley of Ipsica; places, which have been wholly unnoticed by those accurate travellers, Brydone and Swinburn. The antient and modern state of Syracuse, of Catania, of Taormina (the antient Taurominium) and of Messina, together with the Cyclopian and Æolian or Lipari Islands, are respectively described at considerable length, and illustrated with numerous beautiful views. Of Mount Etna, which our author was prevented from ascending by ill health, he has given an interesting and scientific account from his fellow travellers; but want of room compels us to omit several highly interesting passages, which we could wish to have extracted for the gratification of our readers.

The work is handsomely printed, and the maps and plates which accompany it, contribute not more to illustrate than adorn it. Mr. Russell's Tour fills up an important chasm in classical topography, and justly claims a place in every well selected library.

Travels in Canada and the United States, in 1816 and 1817. By Lieut. Francis Hall, 14th Light Dragoons, H. P. 8vo. 14s. with a map. Longman and Co. London, 1818.

[Concluded from page 685.]

Our last number terminated with this intelligent traveller's portraiture of the general character and habits of the inhabitants of the State of Virginia. It now remains that we notice his accurate and interesting account of Slavery, as it at present exists in the United States. Degraded, as we have reason to fear the condition of the Negroes is, in many of the West Indian Islands, their situation in Virginia is wretched in the extreme. The view which Mr. Hall has given of the *Code Noir* of that State, is deplorable indeed: And as information concerning the actual condition of Slaves in the American Union is little attainable by a cursory traveller, we shall select a few passages on this subject.

" The law by which slaves and free-men of colour are governed in the Carolinas (and I believe the same, or a similar code prevails in all the Slave States) is a Provincial Act past in 1740, and made perpetual in 1783. It commences by a heart chilling enunciation;

' Whereas in His Majesty's Plantations, &c. Slavery has been allowed, be it enacted, 'That all negroes, mulattoes, &c. who are, or shall hereafter be, in this province, and all their issue and offspring, born, and to be born, shall be, and are hereby declared to be, and remain for ever hereafter absolute Slaves.' A clause follows from which the most iniquitous oppressions are at this day deduced; ' It shall always be presumed that every negro is a slave unless the contrary can be made appear."

" The 9th clause gives two justices of the peace, and three, of five freeholders, the power of trying slaves for capital offences, and of carrying their sentence into effect; that is of inflicting such manner of death ' as they shall judge will be most effectual to deter others from offending in like manner.'

" The 13th clause admits the evidence of all free negroes, and of any slave, against a slave ' without oath.'

" Clause 14th. ' And whereas slaves may be harboured, &c. by free negroes, and such free negroes may escape punishment for want of sufficient and legal evidence against them, be it enacted, That the evidence of any free Indian negro, &c. or slave, without oath, shall in like manner be allowed and admitted against such free negroes, &c.'

" The 34th clause prohibits any master from suffering a slave to traffic on his own account, thus cutting off the most unobjectionable mode by which the slave of a benevolent master might ascend, through an equality of condition, to an equality of rights with the white man.

" The 37th clause presents an exquisite specimen of that legislative cant and cruelty with which the governments of all nations, from time to time, edify their country and mankind; ' And whereas cruelty is not only highly unbecoming those who profess themselves Christians, but is odious in the eyes of all men who have any sense of virtue and humanity, therefore to restrain and prevent barbarity from being exercised towards slaves, be it enacted, That any person wilfully murdering a slave shall forfeit 700l. currency, (i. e. 100l. sterling:) and if any person shall on a sudden heat and passion, or by undue correction, kill his own slave, or slave of another person, he shall forfeit 350l. currency, (i. e. 50l. sterling.)"

The 38th, 39th and 40th clauses breathe a similar spirit, and the 45th inflicts a penalty of 100*l*. currency for teaching a slave to write.

"Such," observes this enlightened traveller, "is the code by which Christians govern Christians; nor is it, in any point a dead letter. The fears of the proprietors are tremblingly alive, and racked with the dread of an insurrection, in which they must expect the measure they have meted. A military police is constantly kept up in Charleston, and every man of colour, whether slave or free, found in the streets after dark, without a pass, is taken up, and punished. In fact, the condition of the free man of colour is scarcely preferable to that of a slave: subjected to the same mode of trial, exposed to the same jealous surveillance, carefully excluded from all the rights and privileges of citizenship, and surrounded by every kind of snares, both legal and illegal, his freedom seems but a mockery superadded to oppression. The statute declares that every man of colour shall be presumed a slave: every newspaper is a commentary on the injustice and barbarity of this enactment; every day men of colour are advertised as taken up on a suspicion of being slaves: they are committed to jail, and if no owner appears, are sold to pay expences."

But the direct operation of this sanguinary law is not all the freeman of colour has to dread. The humane exertions of some gentlemen at the Charleston bar have lately detected a singular system for kid-napping *free* negroes, and selling them as slaves into Kentucky, or any state at a distance from their connections. The agents, were a justice of the peace, a constable, and a slave dealer.

"The process was as simple as unblushing villainy could devise. A victim having been selected, one of the firm applied to the justice upon a sham charge of assault, or similar offence, for a writ, which was immediately issued and served by the constable, and the negro conveyed to prison. Here, without friends or money, he is to await his trial for some unknown crime, charged against him by some unknown accuser: no wonder if in this desolate condition his spirits sink, and his fears

anticipate the worst: the constable now appears, exaggerates the dangers of his situation; explains how small is his chance of being liberated, even if innocent, by reason of the amount of the jail fees and other legal expences; but he knows a worthy man who is interested in his behalf, and will do what is necessary to procure him his freedom, upon no harder condition than an engagement to serve him for a certain number of years. It may be supposed, the negro is persuaded; 'influenced perhaps, (as the counsel for the defendants observed, on the trial,) by the charms of a country life." The worthy slave dealer now appears on the stage. The indenture of bondage is ratified in presence of the worthy magistrate and constable, who share the price of blood, and the victim is hurried on ship-board to be seen no more.

"This traffic had been long carried on, when humanity discovered and exposed it in a court of justice; but since, by the present law, there is no such offence as man-stealing, it could be punished as false imprisonment only. Should not however the shame of discovery produce a stronger impression on the parties engaged in this iniquitous traffic, than can be expected from their depraved habits, it is more than probable, it will be continued to be carried on with keener, and perhaps more atrocious dexterity than before."

It is not to be supposed that much attention is paid to the comforts of the Slave population of the Southern States. Mr. Hall, in treating of this subject, professes to confine himself to "matters of public notoriety," that admit of no dispute; and therefore afford true bases, on which to discuss the question of their physical enjoyments. Their huts are miserable in the last degree, built of logs or unsquared trunks of pine trees, so carelessly put together, that, as our author travelled by night, the fire light shone through every part of them, as through wire lanterns. To augment their daily toil (and it is no light addition) they are obliged to cut and fetch wood, and have their nights' rest perpetually broken by the obligation of keeping up their fires. The furniture of these huts is composed of a few goods and wooden utensils : as for bedding,—the Negroes are supposed to require none, and their clothing is almost invariably ragged and miserable in the extreme. Their food consists of rice and Indian meal, with a little dried fish; and is, in fact, " the result of a calculation of the cheapest nutriment, on which human life can be supported."

" I have heard, indeed," continues this intelligent traveller, " of the many luxuries the negro might enjoy were he not too indolent; of the poultry and vegetables he might raise round his hut ; but his unconquerable idleness masters all other feelings. ¡ I have seldom heard an argument against the negroes that was not double-edged. If they are, indeed, so indolent by nature that even a regard for their own comforts proves insufficient to rouse them to exertion, with what colour can it be asserted that they feel it no misfortune to be compelled to daily labour for another? Is the sound of the whip so very exhilarating that it dispels at once indolence and suffering? But I admit the fact of their indolence. The human mind fits itself to its situation, and to the demands which are put upon its energies. Cut off hope for the future, and freedom for the present, superadd a due pressure of bodily suffering, and personal degradation, and you have a slave, who, of whatever zone, nation, or complexion, will be, what the poor African is, torpid, debased, and lowered beneath the standard of humanity.

" To enquire if, so circumstanced, he is happy, would be a question highly ridiculous, except that the affirmative is not only gravely maintained, but constitutes an essential moral prop of the whole slave system. Neither they who affirm, nor they who deny, pretend to any talisman by which the feelings of the heart may set in open day ; but if general reasoning be resorted to, since pain and pleasure are found to be the necessary result of the operation of certain accidents on the human constitution, the aggregate of our sensations (that is, our happiness or misery) must be allowed to depend on the number and combination of these accidents. ' If you prick us, do we not bleed? If you tickle us, do we not laugh? If you poison us, do we not die?'

" Should there be any unknown principle in the negro's constitution, which enables him to convert natural effects into their contraries, and so despise contingencies, whether of good or evil, he may pride himself on having over-past the glory both of saints and stoics; but the fact would no more justify his oppression, than did the stubborn endurance of Epictetus, the barbarity of his master, who broke his leg. It would be too much first to inflict a cruelty, and then to take, credit for the patience with which it is supported; but the fact itself is, in this case, more than doubtful. That to a certain point the feelings of the slave grow callous under bondage, may be conceded: this is the mercy of Nature : but that they are wholly extinguished, by suffering, is contradicted by facts of too palpable evidence ; one of which is, that it is no uncommon thing for negroes to commit suicide. This I heard from a gentleman of Charleston; and I have since met with the still more unexceptionable testimony of a friend to the Slave Trade.

" Dr. Williamson, in his ' Medical and Miscellaneous Observations, relative to the West India Islands,' observes, ' Negroes anticipate that they will, upon death removing them from that country, be restored to their native land, and enjoy their friends' society in a future state. The ill-disposed to their masters, will sometimes be guilty of suicide; or by a resolute determination resort to dirt-eating; and thence produce disease, and at length death.' i. 93. This is the kind of man who, should he ever hear of the death of Cato, would call it the result of ' an indisposition towards his master, Cæsar.'

" I remember to have once heard a person assert, from his own experience, that a cargo of Africans expressed great pleasure on finding themselves made slaves, on their arrival in America. A further explanation, however, removed the seeming improbability of this anecdote. They imagined they had been purchased for the purpose of being eaten, and therefore rejoiced in their ignorance, when they discovered they were only to be held in bondage."

The force of this reasoning it is impossible to resist. It may be evaded by sophistry, opposed by selfishness, or questioned by prejudice or ignorance: but its truth and justice will be self-evident to the mind of every candid and intelligent observer.

Of the oppression, tyranny and injustice exercised towards the wretched victims of transatlantic cruelty, we have a striking instance in the following narrative of the trial and execution of a Negro, which took place during Mr. Hall's stay at Charleston, in South Carolina.

"A man died on board a merchant ship, apparently in consequence of poison mixed with the dinner served up to the ship's company. The cabin-boy and cook were suspected, because they were, from their occupations, the only persons on board who did not partake of the mess, the effects of which began to appear as soon as it was tasted. As the offence was committed on the high seas, the cook, though a negro, became entitled to the benefit of a jury, and with the cabin-boy, was put on his trial. The boy, a fine looking lad, and wholly unabashed by his situation, was readily acquitted. The negro's turn was next. He was a man of low stature, ill-shapen, and with a countenance singularly disgusting. The proofs against him were, first, that he was cook; so who else could have poisoned the mess? It was indeed overlooked, that two of the crew had absconded since the ship came into port. Secondly, he had been heard to utter expressions of ill-humour before he went on board: that part of the evidence was indeed supprest, which went to explain these expressions. The real proof however was written in his skin, and in the uncouth lines of his countenance. He was found guilty.

Mr. Crafts junior, a gentleman of the Charleston bar, who, from motives of humanity, had undertaken his defence, did not think a man ought to die for his colour, albeit it was the custom of the country; and moved in consequence for a new trial, on the ground of partial and insufficient evidence; but the judge, who had urged his condemnation with a vindictive earnestness, intrenched himself in forms, and found the law gave him no power in favour of mercy. He then forwarded a representation of the case to the President, through one of the senators of the State; but the senator ridiculed the idea of interesting himself for the life of a negro, who was therefore left to his cell and the hangman. In this situation he did not however forsake himself; and it was now, when prejudice and persecution had spent their last arrow on him, that he seemed to put out his proper nature, to vindicate not only his innocence, but the moral equality of his race, and those mental energies which the white man's pride would deny to the shape of his head and the woolliness of his hair. Maintaining the most undeviating tranquillity, he conversed with ease and cheerfulness, whenever his benevolent counsel, who continued his kind attentions to the last, visited his cell. I was present on one of these occasions, and observed his tone and manner, neither sullen nor desperate, but quiet and resigned, suggesting whatever occurred to him on the circumstances of his own case, with as much calmness as if he had been uninterested in the event; yet as if he deemed it a duty to omit none of the means placed within his reach for vindicating his innocence. He had constantly attended the exhortations of a Methodist preacher.*, who for conscience-sake, visited 'those who were in prison;' and having thus strengthened his spirit with religion, on the morning of his execution, breakfasted as usual, heartily; but before he was led out, he requested permission to address a few words of advice to the companions of his captivity. 'I have observed much in them, he added, which requires to be amended, and the advice of a man in my situation may be respected.' A circle was accordingly formed in his cell, in the midst of which he seated himself, and addressed them at some length, with a sober and collected earnestness of manner, on the profligacy which he had noted in their behaviour, while they had been fellow-prisoners; recommending to them the rules of conduct prescribed by that religion, in which he now found his support and consolation.

---

* The church builders in Charleston are too happy in a monopoly of salvation to afford a salaried clergyman to the jail, and the salaried clergyman of the city cannot afford to contaminate their piety, by entering, unpaid, the abode of crime and misfortune.

" Certainly, if we regard the quality and condition of the actors only, there is an infinite distance betwixt this scene and the parting of Socrates with his disciples; should we however put away from our thoughts, such differences as are merely accidental, and seize that point of coincidence which is most interesting and important; namely, the triumph of mental energy over the most clinging weaknesses of our nature; the negro will not appear wholly unworthy of a comparison with the sage of Athens. The latter occupied an exalted station in the public eye; though persecuted even unto death and ignominy, by a band of triumphant despots, he was surrounded in his last moments by his faithful friends and disciples, to whose talents and affection he might safely trust the vindication of his fame, and the unsullied whiteness of his memory: he knew that his hour of glory must'come, and that it would not pass away. The negro had none of these aids; he was a man friendless and despised; the sympathies of society were locked up against him; he was to atone for an odious crime, by an ignominious death; the consciousness of his innocence was confined to his own bosom, there probably to sleep for ever: to the rest of mankind he was a wretched criminal; an object perhaps of contempt and devastation, even to the guilty companions of his prison house; he had no philosophy with which to reason down those natural misgivings, which may be supposed to precede the violent dissolution of life and body: he could make no appeal to posterity to reverse an unjust judgment.—To have borne all this patiently, would have been much: he bore it heroically.

" Having ended his discourse, he was conducted to the scaffold, where having calmly surveyed the crowds collected to witness his fate, he requested leave to address them. Having obtained permission, he stept firmly to the edge of the scaffold, and having commanded silence by his gestures, ' you are come,' said he, ' to be spectators of my sufferings; you are mistaken, there is not a person in this crowd but suffers more than I do. I am cheerful and contented, for I am innocent." He then observed, that he forgave all those who had taken any part in his condemna-tion, and believed that they had acted conscientiously from the evidence before them; and disclaimed all idea of imputing guilt to any one. He then turned to his counsel, who with feelings which honoured humanity, had attended him to the scaffold; to ' you, Sir,' said he, ' I am indeed most grateful, had you been my son, you could not have acted by me more kindly;' and observing his tears, he continued; ' this, Sir, distresses me beyond any thing I have felt yet. I entreat you will feel no distress on my account, I am happy;' then praying Heaven to reward his benevolence, he took leave of him, and signified his readiness to die; but requested he might be excused from having his eyes and hands bandaged; wishing, with an excusable pride, to give this final proof of his unshaken firmness: he however, submitted on this point, to the representations of the sheriff, and died without the quivering of a muscle.

" The spectators, who had been drawn together, partly by idle curiosity, and partly by a detestation of his supposed crime, retired with tears for his fate, and execrations on his murderers."

We will not weaken the effect, which the preceding narrative must awaken in the minds of our readers, by any comments we might offer. We have already extracted so largely from this interesting volume, that we have not room to notice his truly excellent observation on the American character and government, which are treated at considerable length and with much ability. We cannot however withhold from our readers his reflections on the pernicious effects of Slavery on the character of the inhabitants of the Southern States.

" Land cultivated by slaves requires a considerable capital, and will therefore be divided among a small number of proprietors. Experience too, shews that the quantity of labour performed by slaves, is much below that of an equal number of free cultivators; the number of persons deriving support from the soil, will consequently be less: but the loss is not in quantity only, the quality is proportionably deteriorated. He who commands the sweat of others, will be *little* inclined to toil himself* ; the inclination will diminish with the necessity. The fact is so consonant with the remark, that in the Southern states, the fisheries, and all branches of active exertion, fall into the hands of the New Englanders : so much so, that the city of Charleston is supplied with fish by smacks from Marble-head and Boston. Climate might be supposed to have a partial influence in producing this effect, were not such individuals as are compelled by the nature of their occupations to rely much on their own efforts, found no ways inferior in attainments and application to the same description of persons in the more temperate portions of the Union. Nay, have not almost all the sultriest regions of the globe been alternately the seats of sloth and enterprise?

"The same distribution of property which renders labour unnecessary to its proprietor, is no less fatal to its mental improvement. Experience informs us, that means and leisure are less powerful excitements to study than the spur of necessity, and hope of profit Information will be first sought, that it may be useful, it will afterwards be pursued for the pleasure of the acquisition only. The planter has therefore been ever reckoned among the least enlightened members of society ; but says a proverb, those whom the devil finds idle, he sets about his own work. Dissipation must be always the resource of the unoccupied, and ill-instructed

"If the political effects of slavery are pernicious to the citizen, its moral effects are still more fatal to the man. 'There must doubtless,' (says Mr. Jefferson,)' be an unhappy influence on the manners of the people, produced by the existence of slavery among us. The whole commerce between master and slave, is a perpetual exercise of the most boisterous passions; the most unremiting despotism on the one part, and degrading submissions on the other. Our children see this, and learn to imitate it, for man is an imitative animal. The parent storms, the child looks on, catches the lineaments of wrath, puts on the same airs in the circle of smaller slaves, gives loose to the worst of passions, and thus nursed, educated, and daily exercised in tyranny, cannot but be stamped by it with odious

peculiarities. The man must be a prodigy who can retain his morals and manners undepraved by such circumstances." Notes p. 241.

"We know the time of prodigies is past, and that natural effects will follow their causes. The manners of the lower classes in the Southern states are brutal and depraved*. Those of the upper, corrupted by power, are frequently arrogant and assuming : unused to restraint or contradiction of any kind, they are necessarily quarrelsome ; and in their quarrels, the native ferocity of their hearts break out. Duelling is not only in general vogue and fashion, but is practised with circumstances of peculiar vindictiveness. It is usual when two persons have agreed to fight, for each to go out regularly and practise at a mark, in the presence of their friends, during the interval which precedes their meeting; one of the parties therefore commonly fall."

We cannot close our account of this work, without tendering our thanks to Mr. Hall for the amusement and instruction which his volume contains. It contains the most copious view of the legal and actual condition of the Slave, as it exists in the United States, that is any where extant: and breathes throughout a liberal spirit of inquiry as well as of just sentiment that does equal honour to his head and his heart.

Travels in various Countries of Europe, Asia, and Africa. By Edward Daniel Clarke, L. L. D. Part III. Scandinavia, Section the first, 4to. £4 14s. 6d. large paper, £8 8s. Cadell and Davies, London, 1819.

[Concluded from p. 359.]

We left our entertaining and intelligent traveller on the confines of Lapland. His journey through that com-

---

* "Of the proprietors of slaves, a very small portion indeed, are ever seen to labour." *Jefferson's Notes,* p. 241.

* The stage drivers, for instance, are more inhuman, and much inferior in decency of behaviour to the negroes, who are sometimes employed in the same capacity; so that it seems not improbable that the effects of slavery, upon the lower orders at least, are more debasing to the governing class, than to the governed.

paratively unknown country is equal in point of interest to any of his former volumes. We have not room to notice all the singular and striking particulars, which occur in this part of his volume: we shall therefore, select a few of the more remarkable for the gratification of our readers.

The Laplanders or *Laps*, as they are always called by the Swedes, enjoy many peculiar privileges, and may be considered almost as in a state of freedom. They are not compelled to provide quarters for soldiers marching: they pay little or no tax; and live and act according to the usages of their forefathers. In the judgment of Dr. Clarke, they constitute, the only remaining branch of the antient inhabitants of Finland, and perhaps of Sweden: and the absolute certainty of their Asiatic origin is conspicuous in all that belong to their persons, in their complexion, pliant postures, diminutive stature, air, and manner. The names, which they bestow upon their rivers and lakes (Swedish antiquaries assert) are found upon the borders of Persia; and they pretend that, of the ten tribes of Israel led captive into Assyria, a portion migrated to the North, where they bestowed their own appellations upon the mountains, lakes, and rivers. They even add, that the Lapland language approaches near enough to the Hebrew, for the two people to understand each other's speech: but the truth of this must be left entirely to future investigation.

As Dr. Clarke travelled when the sun shone most intensely in the Arctic regions, he experienced all the inconveniences of a tropical climate from Mosquitoes: but on this subject we shall let our author speak for himself.

" The boats, used to conduct travellers up the *Lapland* rivers, may be considered as under a similar regulation to that of the *post-horses;* relays being appointed at certain stations. They are worked entirely with poles, after the manner which we call *punting.* When the boatmen, who had with such excessive labour conveyed us from *Ofver Tornea,* reached the

end of their station at *Jouxnge,* the people were all absent, and there was no one to go with us any farther: hearing which, the same men cheerfully volunteered their further services; and offered to proceed another station, as far as *Soasaten,* if we would give them each two glasses of brandy, to which we gladly assented. It was now seven o'clock, but the sun still shone in his might, high above the horizon. On the opposite shore, women were calling their cattle from the forest, by blowing the *lures;* a long line of white cows appeared moving through the trees, answering to every call of the *lure,* and, by their lowing, seeming to imitate the sound of the distant summons. There is a forge for making *bar-iron,* at *Soasaten;* large masses of the semi-fused ore being beat out into bars. The ore is brought to them from a place about twelve *Swedish* miles up the river. We visited this forge. A single hammer only was employed: figures like what one imagines of the *Cyclops,* of gigantic stature and fierce aspect, with sinewy arms and bare bodies, were engaged in supplying the anvil with the tough and almost liquid ore from the furnace. The Director invited us to his house; and conducted us into a neat apartment, the walls of which were covered with hangings of gilt leather. This room, like every other place, was filled with *mosquitos;* but owing to some cause we could not explain, no person here was bitten by them; which enabled us all to enjoy a little refreshing rest. It is evident that blood cannot be the natural food of these insects; because they are often found most abundant in situations where there is hardly a trace of animal existence: and in some experiments which we made, by allowing them to take their fill of what they seek with such avidity, we found that it cost them their lives. If they be watched after they have imbibed a sufficient quantity of blood, they fly with difficulty, endeavouring to escape, and become afterwards dull and benumbed, until they turn upon their backs and die. Yet, in their thirst for blood, they will penetrate between the hairs of a dog's back, or those of a cow, and fix themselves in such number as to form a living mantle upon the animal's skin. So powerful is the little flexible *proboscis* with which they make their punctures, that it will penetrate very thick leather; the gloves upon our hands not being a sufficient protection from their attacks. Finding that all the covering we could use was of no avail, and that the incessant torment inflicted by these insects became intolerable, we were almost tempted to follow the advice of the natives, and to cover our faces, necks, hands, and arms, with a mixture of *cream* and *tar;* a practice adopted by the celebrated *Ledyard,* when he visited this country, and whose example we were ultimately constrained to imitate. However revolting this may appear to persons who judge of a *mosquito scourge* by the gnats and summer-flies of *England,* (1) it is a penance that all will gladly undergo who visit *Lapland* during this season of the year; especially as the stranger has always the precedence at a *mosquito* court; the natives being neglected and deserted by them, that they may cover the new-comer with their swarms. The method by which an apartment is cleared of them in *Lapland* is, in itself, scarcely more tolerable than their presence: for this purpose, every person is made to lie down upon the floor, with his face to the earth; then dried birch-boughs being kindled, the whole room is kept full of a dense smoke, until the *mosquitos* have escaped; when every aperture being closed, the inmates may remain, if they can exist in such an atmosphere; being, as it were, hermetically sealed in a deal box, and almost in a state of suffocation: but if, during this time, the door, or window, should be opened for an instant, a cloud of noisy *mosquitos* rush in, and fall by thousands upon their prey. A sturdy *English* groom, who attended us as servant, was driven to such desperation by them, that being at last compelled, not only to make his appearance beneath a veil, but with his skin tarred, and festering wounds upon his hands and legs, he was with difficulty

restrained from throwing himself into the river. We cannot wonder, therefore, that the poor *Esquimaux* Indians of *North America,* who are nearly allied to the *Laplanders,* (2) should consider these insects as personifications of the *evil* principle, and always speak of them as the winged ministers of hell; being ignorant that they rank among the bountiful gifts of Heaven, and are, in fact, one of those wise provisions of Nature which have been admirably calculated for the wants of the countries where they are found. *Linnæus,* to whose discerning eye this truth was first disclosed, terms them, in his expressive language " *Lapponum calamitas felicissima;* " since the legions of *larvæ,* which fill the lakes of *Lapland,* form a delicious and tempting repast to innumerable multitudes of aquatic birds; and thereby providentially contribute to the support of the very nations which they so strangely infest."

At Pello, where our author dined, he saw the winter sledges, lying in readiness for the Tornea trade.

"These sledges are all drawn by reindeer; but so tractable is this animal, that a single person in the foremost sledge guides fifteen following at the same time. With these sledges were also the sort of skates used very generally throughout *Lapland* and *Finmark,* which are called *skider.* The *skiders* are made of wood: those which we measured here were seven feet and a half in length, and four inches broad. It is said, that, using these *skiders* they will overtake *bears,* and even *wolves,* in full flight."

The Laplanders have no idea whatever of music; neither have they any national dance. Their tents, with the exception of their form which is conical, scarcely differ from those of our English gypsies. In the centre is the fire place, over which two chains, fastened to two transverse bars of wood, serve to suspend their kettles.

"These *nomade Laplanders* devour more animal food than those who dwell in settled habitations, and cultivate the soil:

---

(1) Dr. *Shaw* believed that the *Mosquito* of *Lapland* only differs from the common *Gnat,* in deriving additional vigour from a warmer and moister atmosphere. This may, perhaps, be true; or they may be *varieties* of the same *species* of *Culex;* but we have adhered to the distinction of names now generally adopted, in calling the former *Mosquito.* The smaller species, called *Midge,* or *Culex pulicaris,* sometimes causes, by its bite, more swelling and inflammation, even in *England,* than any insect of this *genus.*

(2) According to the account given by the *Moravian* Missionaries, a *Laplander* may be employed as an interpreter with the *Esquimaux.*

with them, also, the means of subsistence are always abundant; but they are a pigmy swarthy race, of stunted growth and most diminutive stature, and by no means to be compared in strength or size with those of their countrymen who work harder and fare worse. When they lie down to sleep, they contract their limbs together, and huddle round their hearth, covered by a rug; each individual hardly occupying more space than a dog. We had been for some time in this little tent, when, observing something move among the rein-deer skins upon which we sate, we discovered a woman sleeping close to us, of whose presence we were before ignorant: yet the diameter of this conical tent, at its base, did not measure more than six feet; and its whole circumference, of course, did not exceed eighteen feet, which is the usual size of the Lapland *tugurium*, both in summer and winter; although in winter they be better fenced against the inclemency of the climate. Over our heads were suspended a number of pots and wooden bowls. To form the entrance of one of those tents, a part of the hanging (about eighteen inches wide at the bottom, terminating upwards in a point) is made to turn back, as upon hinges. (3) Such are the dwellings of those among the *Laplanders* who are called wealthy, and who sometimes possess very considerable property. In addition to the hundreds of *rein-deer* by which they are attended, and to whose preservation their lives are devoted, they have sometimes rich hoards of silver-plate, which they buy of the merchants: but fond as they are of this distinction, their plate is always buried; and the secret of its deposit is known only to the *Patriarch* or *chief* of every family. When he dies, the members of his family are often unable to discover where he has concealed it. Silver-plate, when offered to them for sale, must be in a polished state, or they will not buy it: for such is their ignorance, that when the metal, by being kept buried, becomes tarnished, they conceive that its value is impaired; and bring it to the merchants (who derive great benefit from this traffic) to be exchanged for other silver, which being repolished, they believe to be new. A person, therefore, who should only instruct a *Laplander* in the art of scouring silver-plate, if he taught him nothing else, would be entitled to his gratitude, and save for his family an annual expenditure equivalent to many head of *rein-deer*.

" From the tent we went to visit the *dairy*, one of the most curious sights belonging to the establishment. It consisted of nothing more than a shelf or platform raised between two trees, supported by their stems and overshadowed by their branches, neatly set out with curds and cheese as white as the milk from which they had been recently made. They were placed either in wooden frames or on splinters of wood, or in nets hanging from a pole placed longitudinally over the platform. About fifty yards from the tent were the *rein-deer*, in their inclosures, running about, and apparently tame: when we entered the inclosure, they came and stood by us. The males were separated from the females. These inclosures consisted of the trunks of fir-trees, laid horizontally one upon another, without being stripped of their branches. In the centre of each inclosure there was a fire burning, to keep the flies and musquitos from the cattle. When we first entered, our little dog put about fifty of the rein-deer to flight: they scampered off into the forest, and as quickly returned; which enabled us to judge of the astonishing speed with which they travel, exceeding that of any animal we had ever seen: they darted between the trees like arrows, and over deep bogs with such velocity as not to sink through the yielding surface. The boy, who had conducted us, vaulted upon the back of one of them, having a rein-deer skin for his saddle, and two sieves by way of stirrups. When it is necessary to catch any of these animals it is done by merely throwing a cord over their horns. Some of the females were milked; and the women presented us with the milk, warm: it was thick, and sweet as cream; we thought we had never tasted any thing more delicious: but it is rather difficult of digestion, and apt to cause the head-ache in persons unaccustomed to it, unless it be mixed with water. At this time the rein-deer were all casting their hair, which

---

(3) This description of a *Lapland Tent* agrees, in all its parts, with a *North-American Wigwam*.

made their skins look as if they were mangy. Their horns, covered with soft hair, seem to yield to the touch, and par- take of all the warmth of the animal's body : this soft cuticle was now falling off in ribbands, which hung loose about their ears, leaving the horny part red and sore in several places."

At Enontekis, a town situated in 68¼ degrees of North latitude, at the source of the river Muonio, Dr. Clàrke was hospitably received by Mr. Grape the minister, to whom he had letters of in- troduction, and whom he found to be a man of learning and general knowledge. By this gentleman he was directed to ob- jects most worthy of notice, and received from him much curious statistical infor- mation relative to this part of Lapland, as well as the character, manners and pursuits of the *Lapps*.

"The soil every where in the neigh- bourhood, and throughout the parish of *Enontekis*, is unfavourable to agriculture. It consists of *sand* and *clay*, but chiefly of *sand*. Nevertheless, the pastures around the church and buildings belonging to the village appeared rich, and were covered with good crops of hay. Mr. *Grape*, how- ever, was of opinion that ages might elapse before the natives will be induced to pay any adequate attention to the cul- tivation of the earth. The principal ob- stacle arises from the *fisheries* upon the *Norwegian* coasts; a great part of the youth, at the age of fifteen or sixteen, emigrating to those shores, where the means of subsistence are abundant, and easily obtained : and the rest adopting the nomade state of the *Laplanders*, and living after their manner. A little *barley* is almost the only species of grain sown: they have not even attempted to sow *rye*, which is so commonly in use in *Sweden;* and *wheat* is altogether unknown. The sowing season commonly begins in *May;* and the harvest is got in, at the latest, before the end of *August;* but sometimes the growth is so rapid, that it takes place much earlier. The grain is harrowed into the ground by means of a wooden rake, or at best with an iron hoe, and the crop reaped with a sickle. Sometimes the whole of the grain used for seed is lost, and the crop never ripens: in middling

crops, the amount does not exceed the *triple* or *quadruple* of the seed sown; and in the best harvest, the average may be reckoned at about a *sextuple :* but such seasons are very rare. Hence it must be evident, that the food of the natives does not consist in *bread*: indeed, the only *bread* known among them is often nothing more than the bark of trees. The inha- bitants are divided into what are called *Colonists*, or *Peasants*, and *Laplanders*. The former are *Fins ;* and the *Finnish* language is universally spoken, although the *Lapland* tongue is every where under- stood : but in the whole parish of *Enon- tekis* there were only two women who understood *Swedish*. The *Log-houses* are small and low, affording different dwelling- places for winter and summer. The winter habitation is called *Pöerte :* it con- tains a large stone oven, without flue or chimney, the smoke being dispersed throughout the room ; there being no aperture for its escape, except through a small hole in the roof, or through the door- way. In summer, they inhabit a house with windows; and these frequently have chimneys. Almost all the *Colonists* have a chamber set' apart for the reception of strangers. Instead of candles, they make use of splinters of deal, about four feet in length; and these are called *Pærtor*. The principal means of subsistence among the *Colonists* are, fish, and the produce of the forests. The *fishing*-season commences when the ice is melted, about the middle of *June*. Then they quit their dwellings, and do not return before the end of *July*. During this time they are seen, upon the banks of the rivers and lakes, hard at work with their nets. A single net will sometimes enable its owner to procure from 350 lbs. to 400 lbs. weight of *Salmon- trout*, called *Lavaret*, and from eight to twelve barrels of a species of fish called *Saback*, or lesser *Lavaret ;* but the greater part of those employed in *fishing* do not take above half this quantity. There are generally three men to each net. In this manner *Pike* are, also caught. Dried *Lavaret* is used as a substitute for bread. Towards the end of the *fishing*-season begins the work of *salting* the fish. Very little *salt* is used, to the end a slight degree of putrefaction may take place ; when an acid being thereby generated, the fish becomes, in their opinion, more nourishing, and has a better flavour. That portion which they do not keep for home consumption is sold to the *Lapps*, or it is carried to *Kangis* fair, where they exchange it for *grain*; a measure of *fish* for an equal measure of *grain*. After harvest, the *fishing* employment is renewed, nets being chiefly used; but even by angling a good fisherman will, in the course of the year, catch half a barrel of fish; and in this way, *salmon* are sometimes taken. But the fishing for salmon after the *tenth* of *September* is prohibited; for which a curious reason is assigned, that " the *salmon*, now become poor, may return back to the sea, and conduct a fresh supply of fish up the rivers in the ensuing year." In winter, *fishing* is carried on beneath the ice of certain lakes.

" The produce of the *forests* consists in the capture of *wild rein-deer*, which is the most profitable. An adroit hunter will, in some years, take not less than ten or twelve of these animals. They are caught in spring and in autumn. In spring, when the yielding surface of the snow gives way to the feet of the *rein-deer*, the hunter pursues them in *skiders*, killing them either with his dart or with a gun. After the festival of the *Virgin Mary*, this chace is prohibited; because the *rein-deer* are then lean, and their hides are of no value. In autumn, they are commonly caught by the feet, with snares; or they are shot. Traps and snares are also laid for *foxes*, *hares*, *white-partridges*, and *water-fowl*.

" The manufactures of a people in such an incipient state of society are, of course, little worth notice; yet a very considerable quantity of *glue* is made both among the *Colonists* and the *Laplanders*. This is obtained from *rein-deer's* horns, boiled down to a jelly during two days and a half, and afterwards dried in the shade. From three and a half to four portions of the *horns* yield one of *glue*. A little *tar* is also made, merely sufficient for their own consumption; the scanty and dwindled growth of the forests in this *latitude* not being adequate to the production of any greater quantity. Another produce of the forests is the food they afford for the cattle. It was mentioned to us as a remarkable circumstance, that as much provender is required for the *sheep* as for the *cows*. The number of *cows* in each colony, of course, varies, from five to ten, and even to twenty. Of *sheep* there may be found as many as fifty. For the maintenance of their cattle, hay and dried

boughs are used; and above all, the *Lichen rangiferinus*, or white *rein-deer* moss, without which, however excellent the *hay* be, the *cows* do not yield either so much milk, or of such good quality. During the nights of *summer*, the cattle are penned in folds, called *Tarrha*; in which fires are kindled, to keep off the mosquitos, by means of smoke. From the beginning of *June* until the middle of *September*, they are allowed, during the day-time, to roam the forests for food. Each *colony* has its own troop, also, of *rein-deer*, from ten to thirty, fifty, and even an hundred. The whole of this statement applies only to that portion of the inhabitants who are called *Colonists*: of the *Laplanders*, properly so called, we shall speak more fully in the sequel. By a *colonial* establishment is meant nothing more than a farm, supporting sometimes a single family: in other instances, two or three. The *Colonists* are either *Finlanders*, or bankrupt nomade *Lapps* who have been ruined by the loss of their *rein-deer*; but whoever is disposed to settle in *Lapland*, has only to chuse his situation, provided it be six miles distant from the nearest village. The moment he has built his hut, all the land, including the produce of all the lakes, rivers, forests, &c. for six miles round, becomes his own, by right of possession. The *Colonists* pay an annual tribute of twenty-nine rix-dollars to the crown: the *Laplanders* pay only twenty-seven. The first tax was fixed in 1747; the last, in 1694, to be collected by an equal levy among the tributaries, without augmentation or diminution, whether their number be increased or diminished. The administration of the territorial justice, the gathering of the tribute, and the annual fair, commence in the middle of *February*. The two first are completed in three or four days; but the fair lasts ten days. This fair is made by the *Tornea* merchants, who come hither to sell flour, salt, tobacco, coarse and fine cloth, hides, hemp, cordage, silver drinking-vessels and spoons, guns, caldrons, axes, &c. The *Colonists* traffic with them by exchanging the skins of rein-deer, foxes, hares, squirrels, ermines, &c.; also dried *pike* and *salmon-trout*, and a little *butter*, which the *Tornea* merchants carry afterwards to *Norway*. The distance to *Tornea* from *Enontekis* Church is 287 British miles by land, and 296 by water; the journey being performed at this season of the year, in sledges, drawn by *rein-deer*. The commodities brought for sale by the *Laplanders* to the fair at *Enontekis* consist of rein-deer and sheep skins, and rein-deer flesh; *pelisses*, called *Lapmudes*;

boots, shoes, gloves; various articles of furriery, such as the skins of white and red foxes, gluttons, martens, sables, otters, and beavers; they bring, also, cod and stock fish, fresh and frozen, or dried, which they have caught themselves, or bought in *Norway.*

"The number of inhabitants, at present, in the whole parish of *Enontekis,* amounts to 870 persons; of which number 434 are males, and 436 females; that is to say, 268 *Colonists,* and 602 tributary *Laplanders.* In this list are included 175 married couple, six widowers, nineteen widows, 170 unmarried persons under the age of fifteen years, and 325 children. The number of births annually may be averaged at thirty; and of deaths from ten to fifteen and twenty. In 1758, the number of deaths amounted to forty-five; but this is recollected in the country as a very remarkable circumstance. A single person, at the time of our visit, had attained the age of eighty years, which is also uncommon. The most common diseases are, pleurisy, fever, pectoral disorders, and opthalmia. In the whole parish of *Enontekis* there were, however, but three blind persons, and one of this number became so in consequence of the small-pox. Hardly one in ten among the *Laplanders* have ever had this disease: when once infected with it, they generally die, owing to want of proper treatment Their domestic medicines are few and simple; and it is remarkable that the *Laplanders* are, in this respect, more skilful than the *Colonists;* industriously seeking for such things as experience has taught them to make use of in disorders to which they are liable, both external and internal. *Camphor, castor oil, asafœtida* and *turpentine* dissolved in *brandy,* are considered as the best remedies in all internal complaints; and for disorders of the head, or in cases of pleurisy, they have recourse to cupping; or they suck the part affected so as to draw blood. Bleeding is very generally practised; and, for this purpose, it is usual to open a vein in one of the feet, rather than in any other part of the body. The climate, although extremely frigid, is not unwholesome. The coldest summer ever remembered was that of 1790, when not a sheaf of barley, or of any kind of grain, was harvested; even in the *August* of that year the snow remained unmelted, and in the same month fresh snow began to fall. The annual depth of the snow varies from three to four feet *English.* According to an average, founded upon eight years' observation, either rain or snow falls every three or four days throughout the year.

The winds, especially in *autumn,* are very impetuous: among these, the *north-west* is the prevailing, and the most violent. Whirlwinds have been sometimes experienced, but they are rare: for the last twelve years there had not been a single hurricane. The appearance exhibited by the *Aurora Borealis* is beyond description magnificent; it serves to illuminate their dark skies in the long nights of winter: but, what is most remarkable, it is distinctly stated, by Mr. *Grape,* that this phænomenon is not confined to the *northern* parts of the hemisphere, but that its appearance to the *south* of the *Zenith* is no uncommon occurrence. The *latitude* of *Enontekis,* accurately estimated at the point where the church stands, is 68°. 30'. 30": its *longitude,* 39°. 55'.

The remainder of this volume comprises a most amusing account of the manners and habits of the Laplanders, and of the Author's Tour in Norway. The description of Trönyem, the capital of the latter country, (which is miscalled Drontheim in every map and book of travels that is extant except the work now under consideration) is particularly interesting. This portion of Dr. Clarke's Travels closes, like the preceding volumes, with various useful tables: it is printed, and the illustrative engravings are executed, in the same style of beauty and correctness, that characterize the volumes already before the public; to which it is in no respect inferior, in point of the information it communicates,

---

The History and Antiquities of the See and Cathedral Church of Winchester; illustrated with a series of engravings of views, elevations, plans and details of the Architecture of the Edifice, &c. By John Britton, F. S. A. with 30 engravings, 4to. £3 3s.

Mr. Britton is so well known as a distinguished Antiquary and illustrator, and his works have been so often before us, and deservedly commended, that we need do little more on this occasion, than announce the continuation of his diligence and care. This volume forms one of his series of illustrations of English Cathedrals; and is worthy of taking its place among its fellows. It consists, as usual, of descriptions of the Edifice and its parts, of memoirs of eminent prelates and persons, who have adorned the See, with other Antiquarian and Ecclesiastical documents.

But, this volume is distinguished by a preliminary view of the introduction of Christianity into Britain, in which the writer differs much from that which we have thought it our duty to take. Mr. B, in our opinion, finds difficulties where there are none. He acknowledges that " the first conversion of the Britons to Christianity, is involved in the greatest obscurity;" yet he expects if St. Paul, or his agents, introduced the Gospel, direct testimony of that fact. It may be observed, in answer, that with the exception of the Countries mentioned in the Memoirs of the Apostles collected by St. Luke, we scarcely know to whom to attribute the first conversion of any country; nor the time when: that the agreement of the Greek writers with the ancient British Triads, and of these Triads with the whole current of Roman history for the time, are evidences superior to suspicion, if not to scruple, and mutually support each other : that the " evidence of Pliny, as to the fact of the Druidical superstitions of Britain being extremely prevalent, even so late as fifty years after the death of Claudius," is not conclusive ; for nobody supposes that Christianity, though introduced, or even supported by royal patronage, was general, or was established, in the modern sense of a national establishment.

The distinction is equally obvious and necessary: the Gospel was advantageously introduced; in process of time, it acquired many converts, and at length became the prevailing religion of the country. But, this was slow, gradual, and subject to incidental interruptions, as in all other countries. We must not be misunderstood, as if we inclined to support the fables of the Monkish Historians : nor shall we warrant that the foundation of Winchester Cathedral was laid by King Lucius, A. D. 169. It is possible enough, that he might establish a chapel in his palace; but the notion of a Cathedral, except

as to what afterwards became its site, is absurd. This answers Mr. B's objection as to the absence of a recorded succession of bishops : there might be, and probably there was, a succession of instructors, whose names are lost to history ; and we pass without reply " the total silence of the Roman historians, as to any Christian hierarchy being established in this island, during the first three centuries of the Roman dominion here."

In the seventh century the ecclesiastical history of Winchester becomes clearer; and the foundation of a new church was certainly laid before A. D. 643. in which year King Kinegils was buried within its pale. Alfred was crowned King in Winchester Cathedral, A. D. 872 ; and ancient writers report that he preferred the very herdsman who had concealed him at Athelney, " he having obtained some competency in learning," to the bishoprick of Winchester, A. D. 879. The last bishop, prior to the Norman invasion, was Stigand, who had the boldness to head the men of Kent, when they demanded from the Norman William a full confirmation of their ancient liberties. This was treason enough in the eye of the Conqueror; and was punished accordingly. It is probable, however, that this Bishop was supported in his opinion, if not in his action, by the Saxon clergy, generally ; whence arose the necessity and policy of new laws and new manners ; by which Winchester was affected, in common with other religious establishments.

' " In the Councils held at Winchester in 1070, 1071, and 1076, the clergy, with Lanfranc at their head, formed a series of Canons, or laws, levelled at the Saxons, and framed to justify and protect themselves. Among the alterations now effected, was the new modelling of the laws, language, and customs of the kingdom. Every thing was to be Norman, and even the English or Saxon language was to be abolished : Winchester was the residence of the Court, and we may safely infer, was fully occupied by the officers, priests, and followers of the king. A new royal castle was commenced here: the curfew, or eight o'clock bell, was first rung at

Winton, to warn all persons to retire to bed, or to extinguish fire at that hour: and a command is said to have been issued hence to depopulate the entire tract or district which now forms the New-Forest: that inquisitorial edict of ascertaining and registering the whole landed property of the realm in the '*Domesday Book,*' or '*Roll of Winchester,*' was issued from this City, A. D. 1083, and here that important record was kept: but another more material event, as relating to our present subject, and the stability of the See, was the commencement of a large and magnificent Cathedral, by the Norman bishop, in 1079. The old historians clearly intimate, that he began the church from its foundation, and raised it at his own expence, although the same writers admit, that the former edifice, by Ethelwold, had not been erected more than a century. Some of these also relate that the bishop employed a little finesse at the very beginning of his work, but which, according to Dr Milner, "proved the greatness of the undertaking, and generosity of the Conqueror." The prelate, wanting timber for his new fabric, solicited some from the monarch, who granted him as much from his wood of Hanepinges, or Hampege, near Winchester, *as he could cut down and carry away in three days.* Taking advantage of this unqualifying grant, he employed all the men, horses, carts, &c. he could obtain, and levelled and carried away the whole of the said wood, or "forest," within the prescribed time. This act, Dr. Milner says, so prodigiously incensed the monarch, that he refused to see the bishop; but the latter, in disguise, contrived to obtain an interview, and explained that he had not exceeded the monarch's prescribed time of three days, &c. when the king mildly remarked, '*Most assuredly, Walkelyn, I was too liberal in my grant, and you too exacting in the use made of it.*' It appears that this event occurred in the last year of the Conqueror's life; and it is said that the bishop continued the building for seven years after that event, when, 1093, the Church and conventual offices were so near completion, that "almost all the bishops and abbots of England assembled in this city to honour the solemn dedication of them, which took place July 15, being the festival of St. Swithun, the patron saint of the place."

The present church was built by Walkelyn, say the historians, *from the foundation;* but there is some difficulty in determining what they intended by the term; it is possible, that in some places he might really lay a new foundation, while in others he built only from the level of the ground. A very intelligent letter from Mr. Garbett, the gentleman appointed to superintend the repairs of the church, attempts to assign to each succeeding Bishop his portion of the construction; but not always to the conviction of Mr. B.

The exterior of Winchester Cathedral presents few beauties, or attractive features.

"The Interior, however, will amply compensate for any defects or deficiencies of the outside. This presents several architectural and sculptural excellencies: this displays a variety of truly interesting and important subjects, for professional and critical examination. Whilst the fine and sublime architecture of Wykeham, in the Nave and ailes, produces the most impressive effect, and claims general admiration; the substantial, plain, and large works of Walkelyn, in the tower and transepts, are imposing and simply grand. In the north Transept, lately cleaned and restored, we see the effect and character of this style, in nearly its pristine state. Every member is in unison with the rest: each is large, bold, and unadorned. The bases, capitals, clustered columns, or piers, and the single shafts, are devoid of all ornament, and appear to be entirely designed for their proper places and necessary uses. The arches, likewise plain, are composed of squared stones, and formed wholly for strength and utility, without any pretension to beauty. On the contrary, in the carving of the Stalls, and the wood-work of the Lady Chapel and Langton's Chapel, we see a redundancy of ornament prevail. The designers seem to have wantoned in a licentiousness of fancy, and thought they could not surcharge their works with too much variety, or introduce an excess of decoration. Still these parts of the edifice afford us much delight, even from this very caprice. The eye wanders from one form and object to another, in search of novelty, and the mind is kept in constant and pleasing exertion by analyzing and appropriating the whole. The elaborate and sumptuous ALTAR-SCREEN is full of architectural members, and is certainly very beautiful. It is covered with niches, canopies, buttresses, pinnacles, crockets, pediments, &c. and when in its original colour and condition, with statues and costly ornaments, must have been surprisingly splendid. The monumental *Chantries* for Fox, Beaufort, Waynflete, Wykeham, and Edington, have all their peculiar beauties, and each presents a specific style in design and detail: that of Edington has, perhaps, the least interest as a whole; but its statue is the most elegant of any in the Church. Wykeham's altar-tomb, and some of its interior parts, are fine specimens of the age; Fox's chantry is a superb example of monumental architecture; gorgeous in its design, and exquisite in execution. Those for Beaufort and Waynflete seem placed in opposition to each other, like rival beauties, to court admiration: each consists of a pyramidical series of canopies, crocketed pinnacles, niches, tracery, buttress piers, &c. raised on, and supported by, open arches, piers, and panelled screens. Each also occupies a corresponding arch, and each is formed to enshrine and surmount the altar tombs and statues of the deceased prelates. It may be confidently asserted, that the combined group of chantries, screens, and clustered columns, in this part of Winchester Church, is not equalled by any spot in England, or in Europe. Every remove of the spectator, as he wanders round this part of the building, presents these objects differently grouped, differently combined, and with varied effects of light and shade. With such a splendid feast before him, it is not to be wondered if the architectural enthusiast, indulges himself to excess, and almost satiates his senses.

Among the most remarkable and laboured of these ornaments the Screen for the High Altar must, undoubtedly, be placed.

"With its original altar, and Catholic embellishments, this screen must have been magnificently rich and splendid. Its furniture, &c. are thus described by Dr. Milner, from an inventory printed in the Monasticon, from the report of the commissioners in the time of Henry the Eighth; the nether part, or antependium of the high altar, consisted of plated gold, garnished with precious stones. Upon it

stood the tabernacle and steps, of embroidered work, ornamented with pearls, as also six silver candlesticks, gilt, intermixed with reliquaries, wrought in gold and jewels. Behind these was a table of small images, standing in their respective niches, made of silver, adorned with gold and precious stones. Still higher was seen a large crucifix with its attendant images, viz. those of the Blessed Virgin and St. John, composed of the purest gold, garnished with jewels, the gift of Bishop Henry de Blois, King Stephen's brother. Over this appears to have been suspended from the exquisite stone canopy, the crown of King Canute, which he placed there, in homage to the Lord of the Universe, after his famous scene of his commanding the sea to retire from his feet, which took place at Southampton.

Such were the accompaniments of the Royal Crown of Canute, rather than of the Christian place of worship. But, while we pity the mistaken zeal which assigned ornaments so gorgeous, and so unmeaning, to ecclesiastical structures, we must not condemn without discrimination: the zeal might be honest though mistaken. Mr. B. well observes, that,

"To appreciate the character of Wykeham, we must divest ourselves of many notions (prejudices indeed they may justly be termed) resulting from the state of things in our days, compared with that exhibited in England four centuries ago. Many acts and measures then considered to be beneficial, judicious, and meritorious, may now be regarded in a very different light. Of the value of the religious, scientific, and eleemosinary institutions of former times, we cannot properly form an adequate estimate: we may, therefore, imagine that much of Wykeham's munificence might perhaps have been better employed. It must not, however, be forgotten, that monastic institutions (besides contributing their proportion to the exigencies of the state) supported the whole body of the poor; exercising hospitality to all, furnishing schools for the gratuitous education of youth, and hospitals for the reception of the sick and infirm. To the industry of the monks, prior to the discovery of printing, we are indebted for multiplied copies of the scriptures, and of the ancient classic and ecclesiastic writings; and also for the histories and records of past times in general. It has been unfortunate for Wykeham that he was, more on account of his place and influence than from his personal character, peculiarly obnoxious to a person so powerful as John of Gaunt; but Edward held him in singular favour; for, as Godwin observes, in the greatness of his authority the king found two notable commodities, one, that without his care all things were ordered so well as by a wise and trusty servant they might; the other, that if any thing fell out amiss, wheresoever the fault were, he had opportunity to cast all the blame upon the Bishop of Winchester.

"His will, made fifteen months before his death, extends to all orders and degrees of men, and answers every demand of piety, gratitude, affection, and charity, Dying in September, 1404, he was interred in the chantry he had erected in this Cathedral."

From this specimen, our readers will perceive the liberal sentiments of the author; which he further manifests in a willingness to relieve the memory of Cardinal Beaufort from the imputation of his death-bed despair; so powerfully illustrated by Shakespeare. Mr. B. observes that the features of his effigy are *placid:* the bard, nevertheless, is supported by the Chronicles.

We could with great pleasure prolong our extracts; but prudence forbids. It is sufficient praise to rank this publication among the others for which the British public, and especially the lovers of our National Antiquities, are obliged to the author.

The History and Antiquities of the Abbey Church of St. Peter, Westminster. By J. P. Neale, Parts III to VI. 4to. each Part 16s.

This work, at its first appearance,* was reported by us with approbation; and we are happy to find, from Mr. Neale's advertisement annexed to the subsequent Parts, that it has met with "general approval," and "almost unprecedented support;" derived in part from "names the most distinguished for rank and talent in this country."

This is evidence sufficient that the public has confirmed the opinion we expressed, and we have little more to do on this occasion, than to congratulate Mr. N. on the conclusion of the first volume; and to wait for the termination of the whole, in a second volume.

As is well known, the main interest of such works depends on the plates, and graphic illustrations, which we cannot transcribe, or analyze; however desirous we may be to do them justice. We must, therefore, content ourselves with describing them as meritorious, well conducted, and honourable to the state of the arts among us.

The history of the Deans includes many illustrious scholars and churchmen; and from the natural connexion of the Abbey with the Court, much of the dangerous influence of the latter on the dignitaries of the former, is presented to the reader. We must, nevertheless, make allowances for the reluctance of the narrator to detract from the character of men so eminent by station as the Deans of Westminster. This appears principally in modern times. Atterbury is mildly dealt with, at the expence of the Prime Minister Walpole; but Walpole certainly knew more of Atterbury's proceedings than he thought proper to proclaim to the world; and we learn from Dr. King's Anecdotes* that plots and *intentions* by the partizans of the exiled family were incessant. To any politician, this is saying enough in justification of Walpole's partial concealment. On the merits of later Deans, the learning of Dr. Pearce, the zeal and talents of Dr. Horsley, the classic attainments, and elaborate researches of Dr. Vincent, we could enlarge with pleasure. To the latter, must be ascribed the honour of first earnestly recommending the restoration of Henry VIIths Chapel, which is now carrying on under the direction of a Committee appointed by the House of Commons.

We certainly consider Westminster Abbey as a national structure, and wish it to be always kept in a state of repair and of cleanliness, creditable in the eyes of foreigners, as well as of natives. There is a solemnity connected with the building, with the consideration of the illustrious dead whose monuments surround its walls, and speak powerfully to every principle of mind, with the public services there performed, and with the national engagements there contracted, which cannot but strongly affect all who wish well to their King and Country, to the British Constitution, and to the interests of the British Empire, at large. It well deserves commemoration.

Peak Scenery, or Excursions in Derbyshire: made chiefly for the purpose of Picturesque Observations, &c. By E. Rhodes, royal 4to. part I. price £1 14s. For the Author, 1818.

It is true, that there are scenes so impressive in their nature, or their constituent parts, that the eye and the heart, however uninformed, cannot but feel and acknowledge their beauty or their sublimity. But it is also true, that not only such scenes when beheld by the eye of taste properly instructed, are *enjoyed* with a more copious delight, but that objects little, if at all, exalted above the ordinary, communicate to such powers, sensations, and pleasures, of which only such powers are susceptible. The extent of a prospect is obvious to all: the beauty of a prospect, with the causes, or the operating principles, of that beauty, is restricted to few. Hence the difference of judgment between artists and casual spectators; and hence the aptitude of artists to find beauties in uncouth forms, ruins, sheds, rough coated animals, stumps of trees, &c. which to other beholders are rude, perhaps offensive.

Almost every county in England has its peculiar features, and consequently its beauties; but among the most striking, by the effects to which they afford scenery and *play*, are such as abound in rocks, mountains, dales and impetuous streams. These are works of Nature; and Nature seems, occasionally, to take a pride in shewing them under the most striking effects, merely because they are her work.

Derbyshire has much of this character: it comprises ridges of mountains, from which the view is most extensive, and which in return become objects of great interest, whether forming the more proximate back ground, or varying the lines of the remote horizon. Our author did well to wander in Derbyshire, for the purpose of picturesque observation: and in company with such a friend and such an artist as Mr. Chantrey, he could not fail of intermingling improvement with pleasure. That all the subjects introduced are grand or striking, cannot be affirmed; that the taste and skill of the designer has imparted to them an interest, need not be denied; and to say truth, the sight of them induces us to substitute the painter for the poet,

> who gives to airy nothings
> A local habitation and a name.

Mr. Rhodes has shewn himself highly sensible to the different styles of beauty in Nature; and, strange as some may think it, he finds beauties too where Nature never placed them. If any suspect that the pencil of the designer suggested some of these to him, *as beauties,* perhaps they will not greatly err. But, we shall suffer him to speak for himself.

"It may here be observed that picturesque beauty is not necessarily confined to any peculiar species of landscape: it belongs not exclusively either to a flat or a hilly country. The happy intervention of light and shadow may atone for the absence of variety of form; and impart this delightful quality to scenes and objects apparently at variance with those acknowledged principles on which it is understood to depend: hence it may be found, not only amongst the dales of Derbyshire, but in the level counties of Leicester and Lincoln, where the sight, uninterrupted by hills, freely expatiates over an extensive range of well cultivated country. It is refreshing to the spirits, and gratifying to the eye, to wander over ground like this, where no objects intervene to disturb that calm sublimity of feeling, produced by contemplating an expanse of prospect, terminating only with the limited powers of human vision; and where one prevailing tone of colour, broad and bold in the foreground, harmoniously unites an infinity of detail, that gradually softens into the blue mists of distance, and imperceptibly melts into the horizon."

As a contrast, and a contrast sufficiently strong, we add our author's opinion on some of the objects in Middleton Dale.

" The romantic pictures of this dale are often essentially improved by the fires of the lime-kilns, with which it abounds; the volumes of smoke sometimes throw an obscurity over the objects in Middleton Dale, which increases their effect, and occasionally imparts a sublimity to the scene: sometimes they roll darkly beyond the broadly-illuminated surface of the boldest projections; sometimes the turretted summits only of the rocks are seen gleaming with light, while all below is involved in the indistinct and shadowy medium that floats at their base.

It is the imagination that imparts these " essential improvements :" that clouds and mists, especially in motion, may augment the grandeur of a scene, must be allowed; but the smoke or the reek of a lime kiln, is ill calculated for that purpose. It adds, no otherwise, than as it takes off that absolute stillness, that lifelessness, which is inseparable from bare rocks and naked projections.

We give Mr. Rhodes credit for considerable powers of description : he looks forward in his rambles, with the anticipations of a traveller; he looks backward with the eye of an artist, he takes occasion to connect histories of persons and places, not without discrimination, though we think some of them might have been spared. The character of Miss Seward imparts an interest to Eyam, the place of her residence; the character of Mr. Mompesson, with the history of the plague, imported into the village from London, though already

well known, bears repetition: and we cannot suppress our anger at the insensibility of the later generations of rustics, who have allowed themselves to violate those honourable memorials of Human Nature, the grave stones, and trees, which formerly marked the places where fortitude, charity, and piety had taken up their "dread repose."

We find a pleasure in repeating that to Mr. Howard is owing the recovery and preservation of the cross in Eyam church-yard : that great philanthropist, though intent on superior things, yet felt that such " unregarded reliques," though " overgrown with docks and thistles," were not beneath his notice. It was wise in the parishioners of Eyam to take his hint, and obey his wishes.

We desire now to direct the attention of our readers to the operation of natural causes; and first to the effects of the famous Earthquake of Lisbon, as felt in the mines of Derbyshire.

" About eleven o'clock in the forenoon of the first of November, 1755, as Francis Mason sat in a small room at the distance of from forty to fifty yards from the mouth of one of the engine shafts, he felt the shock of an earthquake, which raised him up in his chair, and shook some pieces of lime and plaster from the sides and roof of his little hovel. In a field about three hundred yards from the mine he afterwards observed a chasm or cleft in the earth, which he supposed was made at the same time : its direction was parallel to the vein of ore which the miners were then pursuing, and its continuation from one extremity to the other was nearly one hundred and fifty yards. Two miners who were employed in the drifts about sixty fathoms deep when the earthquake took place, were so terrified at the shock that they dared not attempt to climb the shaft, which they dreaded might run in upon them and entomb them alive. They felt themselves surrounded with danger, and as they were conversing with each other on the means of safety and looking for a place of refuge they were alarmed by a second shock much more violent than the one preceding. They now ran precipitately to the interior of the mine: it was an instinctive movement that no way bettered their condition ; it only changed the spot of earth where they had previously stood ; but their danger and their fears were still the same. Another shock ensued, which after an awful and almost breathless interval of four or five minutes was succeeded by a fourth and afterwards by a fifth. Every repercussion was followed by a loud rumbling noise, which continued for about a minute; then, gradually decreasing in force, like the thunder retiring into distance, it subsided into an appalling stillness more full of terror than the sounds which had passed away, leaving the mind unoccupied by other impressions, to contemplate the mysterious nature of its danger. The whole space of time included between the first and the last shock, was nearly twenty minutes. When the men had recovered a little from their trepidation, they began to examine the passages, and to endeavour to extricate themselves from their confinement. As they passed along the drifts they observed that pieces of minerals were scattered along the floor, which had been shaken from the sides and the roof, but all the shafts remained entire and uninjured.

We recommend a comparison of this dangerous situation of miners below ground, with that of a ship's company out at sea, as given in our third volume, O. S. p. 730. Such are the effects of Earthquakes; and such the distances to which their tremendous vibrations are active. Various opinions have been held on the causes of these phenomena: a phenomenon not less perplexing, and equally to both Vulcanist and Neptunist, was formerly, and possibly, may be still found in the mines of Derbyshire. Whether any thing similar occurs in the lower strata of the globe, may afford matter for reflection: at a greater depth its powers would acquire augmented force.

" Haycliff mine, now no longer worked, was once the grand depository of that extraordinary phenomenon in the mineral world, provincially called, Slikensides. The external appearance of this curious species of Galena is well known wherever mineralogy has been studied. At the present time good specimens of it are extremely

rare, and can only be met with in cabinets which have been long established. In those mines where it has most prevailed it exhibits but little variety, either in form or character. An upright pillar of limestone rock, intermixed with calcareous spar, contains this exploding ore: the surface is thinly coated over with lead, which resembles a covering of plumbago, and it is extremely smooth, bright and even. These rocky pillars have their polished faces opposed to each other, sometimes they nearly touch, sometimes they are farther apart, the intervening space being filled up with smaller portions and fragments of spar and particles of lead ore, which is every where intersected with narrow veins of a whitish colour, and a powdery consistency, that run in oblique directions amongst the mass.

" The effects of this extraordinary mineral are not less singular than terrific. A blow with a hammer, a stroke or a scratch with a miner's peck, are sufficient to rend those rocks asunder with which it is united or embodied. The stroke is immediately succeeded by a crackling noise, which is sometimes accompanied with a sound not unlike the mingled hum of a swarm of bees: shortly afterwards, an explosion follows so loud and appalling that even the miners, though a hardy race of men and little accustomed to fear, turn pale and tremble at the shock. This dangerous combination of matter must consequently be approached with caution. To avoid the use of the common implements of mining, a small hole is carefully bored, into which a little gunpowder is put and exploded with a match, which gives the workmen time to withdraw to a place of safety, there to wait the result of their operations. Sometimes not less than five or six successive explosions ensue at intervals of from two to ten or fifteen, minutes, and occasionally they are so sublimely awful that the earth has been violently shaken to the surface by the concussion, even when the discharge has taken place at the depth of more than one hundred fathoms.

" When the Haycliff mine was open, a person of the name of Higginbottom, who was unused to the working of Slickensides and not much apprehensive of danger, was repeatedly cautioned not to use his pick in the getting of the ore. Unfortunately for himself he paid little attention to the admonitions of his fellow-miners. He struck the fatal stroke, that by an apparently electrical communication set the whole mass instantaneously in motion, shook the surrounding earth to its foundation, and with a noise as tremendous as thunder, scattered the rocky fragments in every direction, through the whole vacuity of Haycliff mine. Thick boards of ash, at the distance of twenty or thirty paces, were perforated by pieces of rock six inches diameter. The poor miner was dreadfully cut and lacerated, yet he escaped with life."

The work is elegantly printed ; and the whole is a pretty specimen of modern taste.

The Vestriad, a Poem, in Five Cantos. By Hans Busk, esq. author of the Banquet, Dessert, &c. With Notes, and Plates, 8vo. 12s. London, Colburn.

Among the airy tribes, that, borne on dusky pinions, come with such winged speed at this season of the year, to hover round our heads, court our admiration, and stun our ears with such a variety of *discordant* melodies, and which then for the most part again recede into that obscurity whence they emerged, it is not an easy nor is it a very grateful task, to endeavour to distinguish the full clear and sweet, and affecting note that charms the ear and reaches to the heart—and this is the more difficult, since, in the ardour of their flight, the generality of these Songsters aim at making a striking, rather than a lasting impression, and at reaching a lofty rather than a permanent position.

They weave the dazzling splendour of their plumage before our eyes, in all the intricate mazes that a sickly fancy can suggest, or which a perpetual agitation can produce, and rely on the perplexity of the combinations, like the chance turn of the kaleidoscope, to ex-

hibit appearances that shall have the semblance of novelty, and acquire the praise of excellence.—For ever soaring to an unattained and unattainable height, they exhaust that strength that would have supported them in the elevation, for which nature designed them, and they sink below mediocrity, into contempt.

They spur their Pegasus to such a height,
They leave the astonished reader out of sight ;
Then quicker than they rose, enfeebled fall ;
On their five nerveless feet—too lame—to crawl.

That these observations will apply to a great proportion of modern poets, (some of whom are basking in the sunshine of ephemeral reputation) many of our readers (we think) will be readily disposed to admit. But to particularize would be as unnecessary as it would be invidious.

Nothing can be to us more discouraging, more tiresome and disgusting, and nothing can more effectually prevent

The spirit of a wandering wit,
That dangerous point with daring hand to hit ;
By all attempted, but attained by few,
The grand, sublime, the natural, and true !

than those petty artificers by which vanity is archly laying snares for admiration, and of which pride generally becomes the first victim—than those eternal struggles to produce the wits—astonishing and rare—that restless search for some tall bombastic metaphor—those laborious throes of genius which distort the features of composition, frighten discretion from her seat, and which, as they excite the most painful anxiety while they last, generally terminate in abortive disappointment and futile inanity.

We may well say—*nil intentatum nostri liquere poetæ :* but every body may not be disposed to add,

Nec minimum, meruere decus,—
Vestigia Græca * * * * ausi deserere.

It is not therefore without considerable satisfaction, and a mixture of some exultation, that we announce a production in the present time, which is so little open, as the one before us, to these objections and animadversions. Of the former works of this author we have had occasion to speak favourably,* and we are happy to see, that the hints, we took the liberty of throwing out, do not require to be repeated. We are fully persuaded that every man of taste will hail with us a work of which the arrangement is so classical, the versification so harmonious, and the style so captivating :—where, notwithstanding the exuberance of witty allusions——humorous combinations and imagery—the judgment of the Poet goes hand in hand with the good sense of the reader; and where we are not called upon at every turn, as is the fashion of the moment, to mount the clumsy *velocipede* of a puerile imagination to perform that excursion which the play of ordinary faculties, and the spring of moderate exertion can accomplish with far greater grace, dexterity, and ease.

We cannot better exemplify our feelings in the subject, than by applying to himself the compliment he has paid to the judicious and successful attempts of one of his heroes.

Where measured increments of rapid force,
Raise and support and regulate his course.
His passive feet, his judgment seems to tether ;
Not launch at once into the skies together ;
Affect the limits of a humble sphere,
And check the circuit of their safe career.
* * * * * * * * * *
But slow, subsaltive graze the level floor,
And promise little to perform the more.
                                    Canto V.

That the subject is well calculated to become the vehicle of elegant satire, the poet has ingeniously and ably illustrated in a copious and well-written preface, full of that epigrammatic force and animation which so eminently distinguish his compositions whether in verse or prose.

This preliminary discourse which we think is not likely to suffer the fate the author, (with a moderation real or affected) apprehends ; of being " read last or not at all," concludes with an epigram of which the elegant modern latinity speaks it from the pen of an ancient born after his time, and we have no

* See p. 211—216, and 653—660 of the present volume.

doubt the reader, in favor of the modesty, will adopt the mutuality, of the wish it contains.

The plot of this entertaining Poem is extremely simple, but on that account, surely not the less admirable, and as laying its foundation in the revolution which has taken place, in manners and taste, commemorates the age in which it has been composed. – In the Arts, the Sciences, and Belles Lettres, the precision, formality and rigid subjection to rule and discipline of the *old modern* school, has given way to a freer, more dégagé, and more energetic style, partly acquired from a cultivation of the antique, and (analogous and consequent to that) partly from a study of nature, which has led to a relish only for what is really beautiful, excellent, and true. This reformation as far as dancing is concerned, somewhat farther seems to constitute the ground-work of his performance.

The name of Vestris appears to have been taken as more familiar than any other of his tribe, to distinguish the hero of the old school, that of Duport, whose excellence has lately been so highly appreciated in this country, to denote the progress of the new school.— A slip which the former is supposed to have made during a trial of skill in a ballet expressly constructed for the occasion, developes at once the object and catastrophe of the piece.

The machinery, by which this easy story is supported and conducted to a happy termination for the theme, though not for the principal character, is also free from intricacy and embarrassment.

To give consequence to the Hero, he is introduced as invested with the character of the *operatic* Jupiter, enjoying the Apotheosis which Paris has unthinkingly bestowed, and giving laws to fashion and taste throughout Europe.

Terpsichore alarmed for the true interests of her art, raises up a rival to this despot of the dance, and sends the phantom of her Protégé to disturb the Hero's slumbers. In the character of Telemachus he seeks for advice and consolation from his mistress Encharissa; but, not finding the relief he expects, resolves on a trip to England.

Terpsichore "pursues with mortal hate, the immortal man," and descends to the bottom of the sea in search of Neptune; whom she inspires with a love for the art, and persuades him to swim a fluent minuet with her; and taking advantage of his admiration of a submarine ballet, raises such a storm as she imagines must overwhelm the packet—Venus interposes, and sends her sons to smite the monsters of the deep, who " who in more gentle vortices embrace," and a calm ensues. The Hero lands at Dover, is conducted to London, introduced to the Queen,—in a conversation with whom the Poet takes the opportunity, after the manner of the Second Book of the Æneid and of the Henriade, of relating what could not so well have been introduced into the body of the work. In the mean time France becomes impatient for the return of Vestris, who after having recruited his purse, his confidence, and his hopes, again crosses the channel, determined to meet his antagonist and his fate.

" Prepared to fall, or vanquish all his foes."

To his infinite mortification he finds himself betrayed by his mistress, outshone by his rival, and deserted by his admirers.

In consequence of this, he summons a council, which is most humorously described, and in which a plan is proposed to circumvent and destroy his enemy.

By the advice of his protectress however he first takes

—The road from day-light and from Paris,
To Pluto's gloomy realm, direct that carries:
For every Hero, while he's yet alive,
Is doomed to take this memorable drive.
Herein, who break the law of their creation,
Renounce all prospect of deification.

He then solicits the aid of the infernal spirits—and receives their assurances of assistance and co-operation in the meditated stratagem.

" Vestris approaching, sends them in his name;
' What, the great Vestris !' all at once exclaim.

Aw'd by the mighty sound the reverent troop,
Low to the ground, in solemn homage stoop:
Then thus accost him :—' God of Dancers, why
Leav'st thou the zenith of thy wholesome sky
To plumb the caverns of this black abyss,
The grave of light, antipodal of bliss?
Say wouldst thou ought of these thy lowly friends?
Say can their wrath anticipate their ends?
Thy flaming ministers shall fly to arms,
And fill the Opera-house with vain alarms.
Is it some Nymph rebellious to thy reign,
Alike who causes and who mocks thy pain;
Or Beauty treacherous to her maiden vow,
Thou fain wouldst punish, and thou know'st not
  how?
Wouldst thou consign her to our claws impure,
To *kill* the fair delinquent or to *cure* ?
Shall we with cords her winged feet detain,
Print on her ivory skin a bloody stain,
Her roving eye-balls from their sockets tear,
Or apparitions raise to fix them there?
Shall we on mattresses expressly laid,
From Leucas' rock precipitate the maid?
' Or shall we'—' Hold,' the visitor replies;
It is not here, my friends, the grievance lies—
There is no Nymph rebellious to my reign,
Alike who causes and who mocks my pain;
Nor barbarous maid, and faithless to her vow,
I fain would punish, tho' I know not how:
Nor were there, would I to your claws consign;
In such a cause your aid I should decline.
The sex I honour to my latest breath,
Nor punish their delinquency with death.
Ah! would for *Love* or *Money* here I came.'"

He then returns from Elysium to Paris, which ends the fourth Canto.

The fifth opens with night; scene the Opera,—Zephyr prepares to carry off Psyche.—The demons spring their mine.—Terpsichore interposes.

Lo! with a super-human bound he springs.
Clears the wide gap and claps his smoking
  wings.
Zephyr his flight and equipoise maintains,'
Nor stops, nor starts, nor murmurs, nor com-
  plains;
Transcendent towering with unruffled mien,
He circumvolitates the prostrate scene.
Thus, near fall'n battlements of antique towers,
The quivering lapwing chides the evening hours;
Measures the ruined pile in airy rings,
And sweeps the time-worn fragments with his
  wings.

The Hero enraged at this disappointment resolves to rely on himself alone, and sends

A formal challenge in laconic prose.
In sable edgings mourns the snowy page;
The flaming wax a type of burning rage:
The sugared syllables well varnished flicker;
The words drop vinegar and gall the thicker.
Each letter bears the character of woe;
And mutes funereal form a solemn row.
The combatants prepare their arms and feet,
Enliven'd Paris hails the expected treat.

The description of the crowd within and without; of the new Ballet, of the Contest for the Armour of Achilles, in which the new Ajax and Ulysses display all their skill and intrepidity, bring on the Denouement before pointed out, and some appropriate similes, reflections, and few episodical lines finish the canto and the poem; which, to use the author's expression concerning Acis and Galatea, is a scene of fascination and splendour throughout: nor are we aware that the language contains any thing in this class of composition that can be compared with, much less that surpasses it, in beauty and force, expression and finishing.

After saying so much, it will be unnecessary to make any long extracts of what appear to us the most brilliant passages in this engaging work, and we shall content ourselves with mentioning that the parts we should have selected, if our limits had permitted, would have been from the Invocation—the Russian Embassy—the description of the Phantom—the Portrait of Eucharissa—her Interview—Neptune's floating Palace and Attendants—Origin and Progress of Dancing—Character of the French—of whom the Author in a former work has aptly said

What nation ever cut, that History quotes,
So many capers, and so many throats!

The opening of the Third Canto—The Night and Silence—The Boudoir Scene—Personification of that Law—Ballet—Affiche—Press at the Opera Door—the Buckler of Achilles—Hecatompadon, &c. &c.—all of which are admirably delineated.

We do not however, intend to affirm that it is a faultless production: neither do we mean to say that we consider it subject to the same severe rules of criticism as works of a graver character

Versibus exponi tragicis, res comica non vult.

One rule has been observed—which is in our opinion a great recommendation, tho' the contrary is too often the modern practice.

Parcere personis—dicere de vitiis.

Where, on the whole, there are so many prominent and shining parts, whatever may be done by envy or detraction, it can never be the province or

wish of just criticism, to collect a few scattered imperfections or blemishes into the focus of observation, for the sake of obscuring the lustre of a work, which is calculated to live in the admiration of every reader of taste and discernment, and which with all its playfulness of manner and vivacity of intelligence, developes a force of pleasing and instructive satire, and bears a stamp of thought and moral reflection, which we are the more delighted, as we are the more surprised to find it in a poem of this description, and which we often look for in vain, in books of a more serious class, with pretensions of the highest cast. To elucidate this, we shall devote the space left us for quotation to the episode of the Sibyl in the fourth canto, which carries its own eulogium and that of the work along with it.

Long had he stood to view their execution;
To quit the scene still wanting resolution;
But lifting up his eyes, surpris'd he sees
A slipshod Sibyl stretch'd beneath the trees.
Cold was her aspect, not more cold the stone,
On which she rested, meagre and alone:
A scanty cloak of tawdry red and blue,
Half shew'd her limbs, and half concealed from view.
A nose prolong'd beyond the usual size,
And pointed chin inverted to the skies,
Proclaim'd a head, if not by nature wrong'd,
To this extenuated shade belong'd.
Her hair dishevell'd o'er her shoulders hung,
A chequer'd kerchief on her neck was flung:
A tinsel flounce, unript by thorns and time,
Tarnish'd the robe it garnish'd in its prime;
Two tatter'd mitts, that never were a pair,
Display'd two wither'd hands that once were fair;
One leathern slipper, and one shoe of jane,
Crippled her feet, unequal to sustain;
A silken ridicule fell down her side,
Store of her wealth, and remnant of her pride.
Unable to the stars to lift her head,
Yet, in their science most profoundly read:
Pleas'd her borometries and signs foretell
Fortunes to those—who seldom pay her well:
Luxurious fare her promises dispense,
She practises herself strict abstinence:
Vast palaces she gives, and best of roses;
On straw herself abstemiously reposes:
To every passenger his wish bestows,
Her portion want, and wakefulness and woes;
From all her fifty-two depicted leaves,
Not one good omen for herself retires,
Whilst in their black and scarlet lines she reads,
How every mortal but herself succeeds.

Shock'd at the sordid sight, his courage sinks;
Three paces back reluctantly she shrinks;
Heroes retreat,—three paces and no more.
We call them cowards if they go to four.
His wonted fortitude again returns;
To dip into futurity he burns.

'What tho' no Trojan would her tales believe!
The Muse Terpsichore my vein inspires;
She gave these rags and these prophetic fires:

She can at will impoverish or enrich,
And made me actress ere I was a—witch.
A dancer, I too figur'd on the boards;
I know what this bewitching art affords:
The sweet seductions of the stage have felt,
Could storm with fury, or with pity melt.
Like yours, my joyous morn unclouded rose,
Like mine, your evening ray in mist must close.
Sad, sad conformities our lots combine,
And fate assimilates your end to mine.
One thing there lacks to make your likeness true,
She yet has made—no conjuror of you.
Like you, I danc'd as soon as I was born;
Like you, in raptures past my rosy morn;
Blithe as the lark I floated in the sky,
Warbled as well, and soar'd almost as high:
Where Pleasure led, for ever on the wing,
By Princes ogled in the dazzling ring;
Flatter'd at feasts, and follow'd up and down,
The stage's Phœnix, minion of the town.
This leg which feebly props its tottering load,
Once the firm axis of my figure glow'd;
The incessant whirl upon the pointed toe,
Oft the turned ankle, calf or knee would show,
While the hemm'd skirts centrifugally through
Concentric orbits, glitter'd as they flew;
Or wand'ring spirally with bullion'd rim,
In clinging drapery clasp'd the swelling limb.
These eyes in sunken sockets that expire,
Could once the frigid breast of age inspire,
The heart with transport warm, or bid it languish
With fell despair, with jealousy or anguish.
These lips, round which these sightless wrinkles curl,
Once vied with rubies, and were set with pearl:
And when the neighbouring dimples deign'd to smile,
Would the mild hearts of Emperors beguile.
This bosom, tann'd by many a scorching sun,
In snowy lustre was surpassed by none;
The soft contour would roving eyes ensnare;
The little Loves and Sports would nestle there.
In my stunn'd ears perpetual plaudits rang;
Fond suitors sigh'd, and amorous poets sang:
The one would live for ever in my arms,
And one insur'd me everlasting charms:
With hands unsparing shower'd their venal praise;
With myrtle crown'd my brow, their own with bays;
Extoll'd my sweet perfections to the skies,
And gave me Dian's lip and Hebé's eyes.
The intoxicating fumes o'erpower'd the brain;
I danc'd, I reel'd, I waltz'd and reel'd again.
My thousand charms were echo'd in their rhymes
To the same tune, an hundred thousand times.
Smitten with their productions, as with me,
They promis'd both an immortality.—
Their vows they broke, the verses, torn, forgot,
Each line I twisted to a papillote.
Fool that I was to heed their fickle breath,
Or care for what an idle poet saith!
Too soon, were my confiding hopes betray'd;
Too soon, my blushing cheeks began to fade:
Phœbus with spots and freckles marr'd my face,
In spite of all his versifying race.
My faithless lovers fled, and with the rest,
The Loves themselves forsook their downy nest:
They fled, alas! regardless of their duty,
When, midst the bevy rose a brilliant beauty,
Whose brighter light these eyes could ill endure,
Tho' to my sight not like a Cynosure;
But judging them by astronomic rule,
Resembling more the baneful Canicule.
Tho' from the horizon scarce emerg'd to day,
Her blaze of charms eclips'd my parting ray:

My setting orb, now gods and mortals shun,
And haste to kneel before her rising sun.
My cause abandon'd and my strength decay'd,
My fortunes and my steps moved retrograde:
Object of private scorn and public scoff,
All my celestial beauty soon fell off;
In these deep furrows can be trac'd no line
Of those attractions peerless and divine;
No golden offerings at my shrine were paid;
No bulse of diamonds at my feet was laid:
My youthful follies had consum'd my wealth,
Impair'd my vigour, and destroy'd my health: }
The thousands lavish'd to indulge my taste,
Were idly scatter'd in pernicious waste:
Years of disgrace had fixed a mortal stain,
But years of labour, nothing left but pain:
Of all my boasted charms the shameless price
Was earned in terror, and was spent on vice:
The day's receipts scarce lasted till the morrow,
And nought remain'd for sickness, age, nor sorrow:
The Queen of Paphos, fallen from her clouds,
Saw no assembled monarchs press in crowds,
No Mars, nor son of Mars before her kneels:
Alas! her very shoes are out at heels!
The dotard's last fond stipend is cashier'd;
Flora flew off, and Hebe disappear'd.
On my last legs, and shuffling in my gait,
For eleemosynary sous I wait,
Which kindred spirits may perchance supply,
That mete the scanty dole of Charity.
Pity my lot, and hence that wisdom learn,
Which I from infamy and misery earn;
My threat despis'd,—most clearly I foresee
A heavier fate impending over thee."

　　The spectre spoke, and vanish'd from his sight,
As some tall shadow flits before the sight,
When, 'thwart the moon-beam, misty clouds obtrusive,
Sicken the eye, and mock with ray illusive.

The Notes contain some very necessary and pleasant elucidations and illustrations of the subject; but, whether founded on acute observation, or extensive reading, they are always enlivened with a sprightly pleasantry which is natural and peculiar. On running them over we find the charm which sound learning, divested of pedantry, ever inspires; and we acknowledge at the end, that we have been instructed and beneficially employed, tho' we only thought of being agreeably entertained.

Of these notes we had marked various passages for selection, but are compelled to omit them for want of room. If flowing verse, happy invention, ingenious satire, and the rare but felicitous union of fancy with classical literature,—give any claim to popularity, we think this beautifully printed poem must command—as it most justly deserves—an ample share of public favour.

Rational Reform on Constitutional Principles: addressed to the good sense of the English Nation. By George Carr, Esq. Barrister at Law. 8vo. Baldwin, Cradock, and Joy, London, 1818.

After the failure of so many plans of reform, practical only in increasing the corruption which they profess to diminish, by giving undue colours to the exercise of authority; it is impossible not to receive the political suggestions of any subsequent writer, without a considerable degree of suspicion. We have, however, been agreeably undeceived in examining the reasonings and statements of Mr. Carr. The subjects he has discussed, are, the Legitimacy of Government,—the Borough System,—the Unity of the executive power,—National Charters, Constitutional Rights,—Responsibility of Ministers,—Taxation and Legislation.—These topics are treated with calmness and with candour: the results of his speculations, indeed, will not be relished by the furious sticklers for Revolution. He has fairly reprehended abuses that *do* exist; but he has also shewn that the political changes, which are absolutely necessary, are really few in number, and may be accomplished without much difficulty. The work evinces sound constitutional knowledge, which is conveyed in perspicuous language, and contains many important facts, that are alike interesting to the lawyer and the politician.

The Doctrine and Practice of Attachment in the Mayor's Court, London: with various corrections and additions, particularly of two chapters, respecting the method of authenticating powers of Attorney, and other documents, under the Mayoralty Seal, and of removing plaints in replevin by certiorari. Second Edition. By Henry Ashley, Gent. of the Lord Mayor's Court Office, Royal Exchange, London. 8vo. 7s. 6d. Maxwell, London, 1819.

This volume presents much information on a topic, which (we have reason to be-lieve) is comparatively but little known. The process of Attachment is, perhaps, the cheapest, as well as the most prompt and efficacious remedy for the recovery of debts, that is encouraged by the laws of England. An attachment for £20,000 as well as for £20, may be made in ten minutes, at the trifling expence of £1 14s. Within the space of five days, and for less than £4, judgment may be obtained, and the amount of the creditor's demand be paid over to him. It is not confined solely to the Citizens of London, but it may be adopted in many cases by others; and it is a branch of the law, that ought to be well understood by all who are engaged in commercial pursuits, especially the inhabitants of this great metropolis. The treatise before us is extremely easy and familiar; and in this second edition, the editor has made many valuable alterations and improvements.

A new Theoretical and Practical Grammar of the French Tongue; with numerous instructive Exercises. By C. Gros, 12mo. 5s. bound. G. & B. Whittaker, London, 1819.

The elements of every branch of knowledge should be delivered with the greatest care and circumspection, as being the foundation on which the whole superstructure is erected. Nor can these elements be properly explained but by those, who are well acquainted with the science: for, in order to know the best method of laying down those elements, we ought to have a previous knowledge of their use and application.

The Grammar now before us is an improvement upon that of the late Abbé Leirzac, one of the most accomplished critics in the French language, of whom France could boast. It appears to have been executed by a gentleman, who has thoroughly studied the structure and genius of that language; and who is both able and willing to communicate the result of his researches to the public. This work is clear and comprehensive in its arrangement; the examples are judiciously selected, and, we think that they are well calculated to remove the difficulties which attend the study of the French tongue. It is therefore with pleasure, that we recommend the present grammar to those, who are desirous of becoming proficients in that universal language.

Select Sermons, with appropriate Prayers; translated from the original Danish of Dr. Nicolay Edinger Balle, Court Chaplain and Regius Professor of Divinity at Copenhagen. By the Rev. W. Pulling, M. A. F. L. S. 8vo. 10s. Ogle & Co. London, 1819.

The discourses of Professor Balle have long enjoyed very high and deserved popularity in Denmark ; and, in our judgment, Mr. Pulling has conferred no small favour on the English language by translating them into it. They treat on the most important doctrines of the Christian Faith, and are expressed with a considerable degree of energy, simplicity, and earnestness. It may be proper to add that the doctrinal sentiments are those of the Lutheran Church, which, in all material points, harmonize with the views entertained by the majority of professing Christians in this Country. We regard these Sermons of the Danish Divine, as a valuable accession to the ample stores of practical discourses, with which our language so happily abounds.

The Youth's Spelling Pronouncing and Explanatory Theological Dictionary of the New Testament; in which all the words of the four leading parts of speech are arranged under their respective heads, with the pronunciation annexed, and the explanation given in as simple, clear, and concise a manner, as possible. To which is added an Essay, by way of introduction, on the several parts of speech, and also a correct alphabetical index, 12mo. 7s. fine paper, 9s. Booth, London, 1819.

A judicious compilation, well calculated to assist those who are engaged in the

gratuitous instruction of youth in Sunday Schools, as well as those individuals, who are engaged in the several national, parochial, and other Schools, where the children are taught to read the Scriptures only, but particularly the New Testament.

A Treatise on Midwifery; developing New Principles, which tend materially to lessen the sufferings of the Patient, and shorten the duration of labour. By John Power, Accoucheur, &c. Member of the Royal Medical Society, of Edinburgh, 8vo. Underwoods, London, 1819.

We have examined this work with the deepest attention and interest, from the encouraging prospect, held out in the title page, of lessening materially the sufferings of the patient during parturition ; a desideratum, which every person of benevolent feelings must anxiously wish to see established. The Doctrinal part is not better written than in many obstetrical treatises that are extant: and we think that it might have been curtailed without disadvantage. The method recommended by the author in the twenty fourth and twenty fifth pages of his work, by which the fair patient may be spared an inconvenient and unpleasant examination, may (if Mr. P's statements may be depended on) be useful in certain cases. It has also the merit both of ingenuity and of novelty, though we cannot help entertaining some apprehension that it is not so certain as he professes to believe.

Mr. Power has given a kind of Nosological view of the varieties of the parturient state, which evinces considerable reading and precision : and then proceeds to exhibit his mode of lessening the sufferings of the patient. The principal Novelty of the work is the introduction of friction with the addition of internal remedies as a powerful means of mitigating the pains incident to parturition. The author supports the treatment he recommends with much ingenuity : time only can determine whether it will be found as efficacious, generally, as he seems to expect.

2 S

Practical Illustrations of the Progress of Medical Improvement, for the last thirty years; or Histories of Cases of Acute Diseases, as Fevers, Dysentery, Hepatitis, and Plague, treated according to the principles of the doctrine of Excitation, by himself and other practitioners, chiefly in the East and West Indies, in the Levant, and at Sea. By Charles Maclean, M. D. Lecturer on the Diseases of Hot Climates to the Hon. East India Company, 8vo. 7s. Black, Kingsbury & Co. London, 1818.

Though we cannot accede to ALL this author's theoretical notions, *we may* confidently announce this work as a valuable contribution to medical literature; which cannot fail to be highly useful to students, and to professional men who are actively engaged in practice in hot climates.

A Year and a Day, a Novel, in two volumes. By Madame Panache, 12mo. 2 vols. 12s. Baldwin, Cradock, and Joy, London, 1818.

A lively delineation of the *tracasseries* of fashionable life. It affords a striking exemplification of the misery that inevitably attends a course of dissipation. The language is greatly superior to that in which Novels are commonly written; and the interest of the tale is sustained to the very last.

Letters on History, addressed to a Beloved God-child, in two parts. By the author of 'Affection's Gift.' Part I sacred, 12mo. 5s. Colchester; Swinborne and Walker: Baldwin & Co. London, 1819.

It reflects no small honour on the instructors of the present age, that most of the works, which are avowedly written for the rising generation, are of a class,—not only superior in point of composition to those of the last and preceding centuries; but are also calculated to impart more correct

information as well as sound principle to the young reader. We consider the present handsomely executed volume, as a pleasing and valuable addition to the juvenile library. It treats on the importance of religious principle, on the authenticity of the gospels, &c. and on the Prophecies;—and presents a concise but well written sketch of Sacred History from the earliest period to the close of the Apostolic Age. Brief notices of the contents of the several Books of the Old and New Testaments are also interspersed, together with a short account of the Music of the Hebrews. Although the author makes no pretensions to novelty of argument, she has the rare merit of compressing much important information into a small compass; and has introduced a variety of appropriate as well as natural and impressive remarks. In short, we know not a more acceptable present that can be made to young persons, especially females, who are about to enter into the world, where they are exposed to a variety of temptations, and particularly to the insinuation of opinions unfavourable to the interests of Religion and Virtue.

Literary Register.

BOOKS ANNOUNCED FOR PUBLICATION.

BIOGRAPHY.

The Life of the Right Rev. Thos. Wilson, D. D. Bishop of Sodor and Man. By the Rev. Hugh Stowell, 8vo.

EDUCATION.

The School of Improvement; two Juvenile Dramas, 18mo. with plates.

The Accidents of Youth, consisting of short stories calculated to improve the Moral Conduct of Children, and to warn them of the many dangers to which they are exposed, illustrated by engravings, 18mo.

HISTORY.

To be published in a few days, in royal 8vo. The Historiæ Brittorum, commonly attributed to Nennius, from a Manuscript lately discovered in the Library of the Vatican Palace at Rome, with an English Version, a Fac-simile of the Original, Notes, and Illustrations. By the Rev. William Gunn, B.D.

MEDICINE.

Dr. H. W. Carter is printing, an Account of some of the principal Hospitals in France,

Italy, Switzerland, and Netherlands; with remarks on the diseases of those countries.

Sir Wm. Adams has in the press, a Treatise on the Modes of restoring Vision by the Formation of an Artificial Pupil.

MISCELLANIES.

Hareach, the Wandering Jew, being an Authentic Account of the Manners and Customs of the most distinguished Nations, interspersed with anecdotes of Celebrated Men of Different Periods since the Destruction of the Temple of Jerusalem, &c. with maps and plates, 12mo.

The History of Gog and Magog, the Champions of London, containing an account of the origin of many things relative to the City, 18mo. with plates.

NOVELS.

Mrs. Taylor, of Ongar, has in the press, the Family Mansion, a tale.

New Tales of My Landlord, the Third Series, containing The Bride of Lammermoor, and A Legend of Montrose, in four volumes.

THEOLOGY.

The Rev. Dr. Nares will soon publish a volume of Sermons preached before the University of Oxford, on the Three Creeds, the Trinity, and the Divinity of Christ.

Dialogues, Letters, and Observations, illustrative of the purity and consistency of the Doctrines of the Established Church, will soon appear.

TOPOGRAPHY.

The Rev. John Hodgson, of Jarrow, has in the press, in six quarto volumes, a History of the County of Northumberland.

The Rev. Joseph Hunter has nearly ready, in a crown folio volume, the History and Topography of the Parish of Sheffield.

A Clergyman late of Oxford having made a Tour to Claremont, with part of his family, is preparing the same for the press with reflections suggested on the occasion, serving to illustrate the peculiar genius, character and pursuits of the late illustrious and lamented Princess Charlotte, designed for the improvement of the young.

VOYAGES AND TRAVELS.

Mr. Grieseke will soon publish, in German and English, an account of his eight years residence in Greenland, illustrated by charts and views.

John Crawford, esq. late British resident at the court of the sultan of Java, is preparing a History of the Indian Archipelago, with illustrative engravings.

Thomas Hodgkin, esq. has in the press, in two octavo volumes, Travels in the North of Germany, describing the present state of the country, particularly in the kingdom of Hanover.

. . . .

BOOKS PUBLISHED.

TRANSACTIONS OF SOCIETIES.

Transactions of the Royal Society of Edinburgh. Illustrated by engravings. Vol. 8, part 2, 4to. £1. 5s.

Transactions of the Royal Society of Dublin. Vol. 11, part I, 4to. 15s.

COMMERCE.

New Interest and Discount Tables. By Joseph King, foolscap folio, £1. 16s. half-bd.

DRAMA.

Tragic Dramas, chiefly intended for Representation in Private Families. To which, is added Aristodemus, a Tragedy from the Italian of Vincenzo Monti. By Francis Burney, 8vo. 9s. 6d.

EDUCATION.

The Child's Introduction to Thorough Bass, in Conversations of a Fortnight, between a Mother and her Daughter of Ten Years old, illustrated by Plates and Cuts of Music. In small 4to. 8s.

A Critical Examination of Cobbett's English Grammar, 1s. 6d.

The Young Christian Instructed, a reprint of Stebbin's Christian Instructed, or Catechism, with Notes from the Old Divines, revised by Mr. Wilkinson, of Christ Church, Oxford, 1s.

GEOLOGY.

A Critical Examination of the First Principles of Geology; in a Series of Essays. By G. B. Greenough, President of the Geological Society, F. R. S. F. L. S. 8vo, 9s.

HISTORY.

The Annual Register; or, a View of the History, Politics, and Literature of the Year Year 1818, 8vo. 16s.

Howell's State Trials, Vol. 26, royal 8vo. £1. 11s. 6d.

The Court of England in the Reign of Charles the First. Being a Translation of Marshal Bassompierre's Account of his Embassy to London, with Notes and Commentaries, 8vo. 9s. 6d.

Statistical Annals: embracing Views of the Population, Commerce, Navigation, Fisheries, Public Lands, Post-office establishment, Revenues, Mint, Military and Naval Establishments, Expenditures, Public Debt and Sinking Fund of the United States of America: founded on Official Documents, commencing on the 4th March, 1789, and ending on the 20th April, 1818. By Adam Seybert, M. D. A Member of the House of Representatives of the United States, from the State of Pennsylvania, &c. 4to. £3. 13s. 6d.

Proceedings in Parga and the Ionian Islands, with a Series of Correspondence and other Justificatory Documents. By Lieut. Colonel De Bosset, with a map, 8vo. 7s.

MISCELLANIES.

A Review of a Work entitled Remarks on Scepticism, by the Rev. Rennell, A. M. By D. Wylke Edwinsford, esq. of Caermarthenshire, 5s.

Memoirs of the Life of Miss Caroline Elizabeth Smelt, late of the City of Augusta, Georgia, in the 17th year of her age. By Moses Waddel, D. D.

NATURAL HISTORY.

The Entomologist's Useful Compendium; or, an Introduction to the Knowledge of British Insects. By George Samouelle, A. L. S. with 12 plates, £1. colored £1. 18s.

NOVELS.

The Authoress, a Tale. By the Author of Rachel. With a frontispiece 8vo. 5s.

No Fiction; a Narrative founded on Recent and Interesting Facts, 2 vols. 8vo.

PHILOLOGY.

The Greek is published of the Polyglott Grammar, in Ten Languages, by the Rev. F. Nolan, in which the genius of the principal Ancient and Modern Languages is explained upon an uniform plan, and by a new and simple principle of Analysis, applied to the improvements of the latest and most approved Grammarians: Four Grammars, the Greek (as above) and Latin of the Antient Part, the French and Italian of the Modern Part, are already published, and may be had separately. The Hebrew, Chaldee, and Syriac will appear next.

This work forms a Grammatical Apparatus to the Polyglott Bible and Common Prayer, publishing by Mr. Bagster.

POETRY.

The Waggoner, a Poem: to which are added, Sonnets by William Wordsworth, esq. 8vo. 4s. 6d.

Tales of the Hall. By the Rev. George Crabbe, LL. B. 2 vols. 8vo. £1. 4s.

Mazeppa; a Poem. By the Rt. Hon. Lord Byron, 8vo. 5s. 6d.

THEOLOGY.

Select Scriptural Proofs of the Trinity, arranged in Four Discourses: delivered in the Chapel of Trinity College, Dublin. to which are annexed, Notes and Illustrations. By the Very Rev. Richard Graves, D. D. M. R. I. A. Dean of Ardagh, &c. &c. 8vo. 7s.

The Baptists Self-convicted, by the Rev. William Anderson, of Dunstable, in his remarks on the Editor of Calmet's Dictionary of the Holy Bible. By the Editor of Calmet, 8vo. 2s.

TOPOGRAPHY, VOYAGES, AND TRAVELS.

A Topographical Dictionary of Scotland. By David Webster, 8vo. with map, 14s.

A Narrative of a Journey to Persia, in the Suite of the Imperial Russian Embassy, in the year 1817. By Moritz de Kotzebue, illustrated by plates, 8vo. 12s. boards.

A Memoir and Notice of a Chart of Madagascar, in the Archipelago, or Islands north-east of that Island. By Lislet Geoffroy. With a Chart, executed by Arrowsmith, 4to. 1s.

Foreign Literary Gazette.

AMERICA; UNITED STATES.

Statistics: Emigrants.

It appears from Statistical Tables collected at New York, that the number of white inhabitants has increased in the following ratio. In 1790, there were 27 blacks to 100 whites; in 1800, there were 20, and in 1810, there were 19 to the 100 whites. The number of emigrants in 1794 was estimated at 10,000; in 1817, at 22,240; of which 11,977 were from England or Ireland: 2,901 were from British Colonies: 4,169 were from Germany or Holland: 1,245 were from France: 58 were from Italy: 1,569 were from American Islands: and from divers other countries the number was 321.

AUSTRIA.

Military History.

The Archduke Charles has lately published at Vienna, *a History of the Campaign of 1799 in Germany and in Switzerland.* This work, says the illustrious author, in his preface, may be considered as a sequel to that which he published in 1813, under the title of *Principles of Strategia, illustrated by the Campaigns in Germany in 1796.* Marshall Jourdan (the opponent of the Archduke) has also published, by way of reply to the latter work, *a History of the Campaign of 1796.* And it may be hoped that a History of the Campaign of 1799, will also be published on the part of the French.

FRANCE.

School for Naturalists and Botanists.

The King has lately created, on the proposition of the Minister of the Interior, a School for Young Naturalists; it is attached to the *Jardin du Roi,* and directed by the professors of that establishment. The intention is, that after having received instruction sufficient, these students should visit different parts of the world, at the expense and for the advantage of the state.

The excursions they will undertake will be conformable to Itineraries traced by the Professors; avoiding countries already sufficiently known. All their researches will be directed to useful ends. This institution, which promises happy results, is a seed, in its nature abundantly prolific; but, which eventually may develope itself to the great profit of the philosophic world: and perhaps may prove the germ of an association of Naturalists, in more countries than one.

On the Re-establishment of the Jesuits in France, under the name of *Pères de la Foi* (Fathers of the Faith.)—*Considerations on the Jesuits,* by L. Magnier.

The legal re-establishment of the Jesuits in certain neighbouring nations, with their clandestine introduction into France, where they already direct several colleges, imparts a lively interest to works of which they are the subject, especially if written with wisdom and moderation. Following the example of the celebrated and unfortunate La Chalotais, of Servan, of Montclar, it is in its Constitutions that the Author studies the Society. M. Magnier presents but a small number of facts, but drawn from good authorities. He might have insisted on the truly Jesuitical tactics by which they have once more reared their head in France, under another name, and have assumed false colours: nothing wonderful in Jesuits; nothing commendable in honest men.

Universal Alphabet.

M. Volney, Peer of France, well known by former works, has lately published a volume on the application of the European Alphabet to the languages of Asia; he describes it as an elementary work useful to all travellers into the Oriental Continent. This writer had already published a tract entitled Simplification of Eastern Languages, or a new and easy method of learning the Arabic, the Persian, and the Turkish Languages, by means of the European characters. Paris, 1795.

By means of the Roman alphabet with certain additional signs, the author proposes to express all the Asiatic idioms, and thereby to facilitate our researches into the dialects, the History, the Sciences, the Arts and the immense literary treasures of Asia; at the same time, these acquisitions would support and enlarge the commercial connexions of Europe with the original country of the human race.

This work is dedicated to the Academy at Calcutta. The first part of it comprizes the definitions as well of the general system of sounds pronounced, as of the system of letters, or signs by which those sounds are expressed. In the second part the author considers all the vocal enunciations and tones used among Europeans. They amount to nineteen or twenty vowels, and thirty two consonants, almost the same as those of the richest languages of Asia; the Sanscrit particularly, according to several of its alphabets.

The twenty-five, or twenty-six letters of the Roman alphabet are not adequate to the notation of all the variations of voice. But this alphabet has the valuable advantage of offering the most simple forms, and of being employed throughout Europe, in America, and in all the European colonies of Asia. M. Volney proposes to render it universal, by obtaining from itself other simple signs, necessary to mark additional sounds.

In the third part of his work the author reduces his theory to practice, by applying it to the Arabic alphabet, which is one of the most complicated of the Asiatics, though not so vicious in its application as the thousand-hyphen'd Sanscrit. The same process applies to the Turkish, the Persian, the Syriac, the Hebrew, the Ethiopian, &c.; and even to Sanscrit and the Chinese.

The curious in Etymology will find in this work many new and learned applications of the powers of the letters: and we have somewhat enlarged on its nature, because it may prove extremely useful to the preparatory studies of our youth destined for Asia; not to notice the additional assistance it may afford to the practical conduct and advantage of gentlemen, whose situations oblige them to daily intercourse with Asiatics of various provinces, some of whose languages are acquired with difficulty, or but imperfectly, after much labour and time spent in studying them.

GERMANY.

Public Institutions: Universities.

We have lately reported unpleasant events, as originating in, or being connected with, the Universities of Germany; the reader, therefore, will be but little surprised to learn, that the number of students is considerably diminished. Formerly Gottingen reckoned more than a thousand students; now it has only 770; Halle has 500; Breslau has 366; Heidelberg has 363; Giessen has 241; Marburgh has 197; Kiel has 107; Rostock has 160; Greifswalde has 55; Landshut has 640; Tubingen has 698; Berlin has 942; Leipsick has 911; Jena has 634; Vienna has 957; and Prague has 880. The whole number is 8,421, in the sixteen principal Universities of Germany.

GREECE.

State of Literature

The progress of that civilization which is the constant attendant or consequence of letters, continues to be rapid. The number of schools of the second order, Gymnasia, augments daily. The principal establishments of the kind are at Smyrna, at Kydonios (a small town of eight or ten thousand inhabitants, opposite the island of Lesbos) and in the island of Chios. A young man a native of Kydonios, mentioned above, has staid long enough in the printing-office of M. Didot, at Paris, to perfect himself in the art of printing. Also, a daughter of the Professor of the Gymnasium in that town, named Erianthia, not more than eighteen years of age, has translated into modern Greek, Fenelon's work on the Education of Daughters.—The inhabitants of Chios have held meetings for the purpose of raising subscriptions in order to establish a Public Library.

HOLLAND.

Public Instruction: gratis.

We learn from the last annual Report of the Schools for giving gratuitous instruction at Amsterdam, that in the eleven Schools of this description, three thousand six hundred and fifty children received the rudiments of education, *gratis* : to which may be added, about eight hundred others who received instruction in the Evening Schools.

ITALY.

Typographic Art and Industry.

In the course of last year was published a complete collection of the typographic characters of the celebrated Bodoni, who died at Parma, in November 1813. This is the noblest monument that can be erected to so skilful an artist, as it shews the extent of his talent, and his taste. This collection stands alone, not only distinguished by the individual beauty of each letter, but also by the harmony that prevails throughout the characters, when arranged in a series. It includes two hundred and ninety one alphabets of Roman type; one hundred and two of Greek type; eight of Hebrew; three of Rabbinical characters; two of Chaldee; six of Syriac; two of Samaritan; two of Arabic; one Turkish · two Tartar; two Persian; one Ethiopian; two Coptic, with the great letters; two Armenian, with the great letters; two Etruscan; two Phenecian; one Punic; two Polo-nese; one Servian, with the great letters; one Gothic, from the text of Ulphilas; two of Thibet; one Brahminical; one Malabar; two German, with the great letters; and seventy one of Russian types; in all four hundred and thirteen alphabets, which Bodoni not only cast, but for which he also engraved the matrices. To these must be added, the great variety of ornaments, of Arabic cyphers, notes, &c., to enable us to conceive aright of the industry, the labour, and the skill by which a single man could bring to perfection such multifarious undertakings, The title of this collection of specimens is *Manuale Tipographico del cavaliere Giambatista Bodoni. Parma, press a la Vedova*, 2 vols. folio. To the first volume is prefixed a good likeness of Bodoni.

PRUSSIA.

New Canals Projected.

Very great preparations are made for the approaching execution of vast plans, already approved by the Government, intended to multiply the benefits of water communication, by means of the rivers formed by nature, and to perfect the navigation of the streams, to the utmost *capabilities* of the Prussian territories. The first president, M. de Winke is one of the most active promoters of this enterprize; and the labours necessary to effect it, will begin immediately, under the direction of Lieut. Col. the Chevalier Kremer. This officer who has great reputation in this branch, was formerly in the service of Norway; from which he has removed to that of Prussia. These undertakings, will of course, occupy a number of years.

RUSSIA.

Don Cossacks : Reading Society.

At Neutscherkesk, the chief town of the Don Cossacks, the Hetman, Andrew Denisow, has instituted a society for purposes of instruction. and amusement. The reading of journals and other periodical works, whether in foreign languages, or in the Russian, forms the principal object of the members of this society; who are principally officers and nobles. Adjoining the reading room are apartments for conversation, and for play.

The nature and advantages of such institutions are so well known among us, that nothing need be said on them; but the satisfaction at finding the means of improvement in literature and sociability established in a country so remote, does not allow us to pass over the fact in silence. ¦

SPAIN.

Interests of Spain and her Colonies.

At Paris has been published in one volume 8vo. An *Essay on the Commerce and Interests of Spain, and of her Colonies,* by F. A. de Christophoro d'Avalos. The Author was formerly in the Spanish Ministry; which, with the subject of his work, is recommendation sufficient of his performance. His observations are well founded on Spanish industry, with the causes of its decay; on the encouragement required by the Arts; on the Population, the Clergy, the Religious Orders, &c. The author considers impartially the advantages and disadvantages accruing to Spain, from the discovery of America, with the consequences dependent on the loss of America as a source of wealth. This essay affords means for estimating the present state of Literature in the country of Calderon, of Lopez, and of Cervantes, and glances at the reforms to be expected from the impulse of European civilisation, and the progress of knowledge; reforms absolutely necessary both to governors and governed.

SWEDEN.

New Public Literature.

Among the many improvements which have taken place under the administration of Charles John, the reigning Prince, must be distinguished a new Collection of Hymns, intended to take the place of those heretofore in use, which were introduced in 1695; also, a new Public version of the Bible:—the New Testament part of which is already completed; a New Code of Laws is also in great forwardness, some of its parts being finished; as is also, a Military Institution for the Regulation of the Army, chiefly as to its economy. The capital also expects to acquire additional facilities for public instruction of the superior kind, by an important establishment, under the name of a Gymnasium.

TURKEY.

Code of Laws: Moldavia.

Not long ago was published at Jassy, by order of the Prince Regent, Skarlatto Callimachi, a Code of Laws, extracted from the Basilicæ, and modified by the present usages of Moldavia. This Code is written in modern Greek, and also in Moldavian. It issued from the press founded by M. Eustathios, first Physician to the Prince, and supported by other enlightened individuals. The Prince has also assigned an annual rent, to the great College at Smyrna.

The Gatherer.

No. XXX.

"I am but a gatherer, and dealer in other men's stuff."

An Ashantee Dinner.

The King received us in the market-place, and enquiring anxiously if we had breakfasted, ordered refreshment. After some conversation we were conducted to a house prepared for our reception, where a relish was served (sufficient for an army) of soups, stews, plantains, yams, rice, &c. (all excellently cooked) wine, spirits, oranges, and every fruit. The messengers, soldiers, and servants, were distinctly provided for. Declining the offer of beds, we walked out in the town, and conversed and played drafts with the Moors, who were reclining under the trees; the King joined us with cheerful affability, and seemed to have forgotten his cares. About two o'clock dinner was announced. We had been taught to prepare for a surprise, but it was exceeded. We were conducted to the eastern side of the croom, to a door of green reeds, which excluded the crowd, and admitted us through a short avenue to the King's garden, an area equal to one of the large squares in London. The breezes were strong and constant. In the centre, four large umbrellas of new scarlet cloth were fixed, under which was the King's dining table (heightened for the occasion) and covered in the most imposing manner; his massy plate was well disposed, and silver forks, knives, and spoons (Colonel Torrane's) were plentifully laid. The large silver waiter supported a roasted pig in the centre; the other dishes on the table were roasted ducks, fowls, stews, pease-pudding, &c. &c. On the ground on one side of the table were various soups, and every sort of vegetable; and, elevated parallel with the other side, were oranges, pines, and other fruits; sugar-

The Gatherer.

candy ; Port and Madeira wine, spirits and Dutch cordials, with glasses. Before we sat down the King met us, and said, that as we had come out to see him, we must receive the following present from his hands, 2 oz. 4 ackies of gold, one sheep and one large hog to the officers, 10 ackies to the linguists, and five ackies to our servants.

We never saw a dinner more handsomely served, and never ate a better. On our expressing our relish, the King sent for his cooks, and gave them ten ackies. The King and a few of his captains sat at a distance, but he visited us constantly, and seemed quite proud of the scene ; he conversed freely, and expressed much satisfaction at our toasts. " The King of Ashantee, the King of England, the Governor, the King's Captains, a perpetual union (with a speech, which is the sine qua non) and the handsome women of England and Ashantee." After dinner, the King made many enquiries about England, and retired, as we did, that our servants might clear the table, which he insisted on. When he returned, some of the wine and Dutch cordials remaining, he gave them to our servants to take with them, and ordered the table-cloth to be thrown to them with all the napkins. A cold pig, cold fowls (with six that had not been dressed) were dispatched to Coomassie for our supper. We took leave about five o'clock, the King accompanying us to the end of the room, where he took our hands, and wished us good night. We reached the capital again at six, much gratified by our excursion and treatment. See *Bowdich's Mission*, and compare LIT. PAN. vol. vii. p. 492.

Sagacity of the Rein-Deer.

The only food of the rein-deer, during winter, consists of moss and snow: and the most surprising circumstance, in the history of this animal, is the instinct, or the extraordinary olfactory powers, whereby it is enabled to discover the former when buried beneath the latter. However deep the snow may be, if it cover the lichen rangiferinus, the animal is aware of its presence the moment he comes to the spot; and this kind of food is never so agreeable to him as when he digs for it himself. In his manner of doing this he

is remarkably adroit. Having first ascertained, by thrusting his muzzle into the snow, whether the moss be below or not, he begins making a hole with his fore feet, and continues working until at length he uncovers the lichen. No instance has ever occurred of a rein-deer making such a cavity without discovering the moss he seeks. In summer their food is of a different nature: they are then pastured upon green herbs, the leaves of trees, &c.

Tribute to Johnson.

The most triumphant record of the talents and character of Johnson, is to be found in Boswell's life of him. The man was superior to the author. When he threw aside his pen, which he regarded as an incumbrance, he became not only learned and thoughtful, but acute, witty, humorous, natural, honest, hearty, and determined. It is to be observed, that Johnson's colloquial style was as blunt, direct, and downright, as his style of studied compositions was involved and circuitous. His good deeds were as many as his good sayings. His domestic habits, his tenderness to servants, and readiness to oblige his friends; the quantity of strong tea that he drank to keep down sad thoughts; his many labours, reluctantly begun and irresolutely laid aside; his honest acknowledgement of his own, and indulgences to the weaknesses of others; all these, and innumerable others, endear him to the reader, and must be remembered to his lasting honour. (*Hazlitt.*)

Greenland—Population.

According to the accounts received by the Missionary College, at Copenhagen, the whole population of Greenland, as far as it is known, in the Seventeen Danish Colonies, on the West Coast, amounts to 5836 souls. The coasts alone are inhabited; the interior of the country being covered with eternal ice. The population has increased since 1789 by 714 souls. The number here given is according to the enumeration made in 1818.

Japanese Worship.

On entering their temples, they proceed to a basin, or small pond, filled with water, in order to wash before they offer up their services. Next to that is a coffer, where they may deposit alms. In front of the central building is the next spot, where they prostrate themselves before the majesty of the God. Here, in front, sit the priests, clad in rich habits. On the door of this central building hangs a gong, on which every worshipper strikes at his first arrival, to inform the God that he is come to worship him: after which, the votary looks through a window where hangs a mirror, as a symbol that as he sees his own countenance, so does the God see his heart and thoughts—and this seems to end the ceremony.

Absence of Mind.

The justly celebrated Lessing was frequently very absent. Having missed money at different times without being able to discover who took it, he determined to put the honesty of his servant to a trial, and left a handful on his table. " Of course you counted it ?" said one of his friends. ' Counted it ?' said Lessing, rather embarrassed, ' no; I forgot that.'

The following is a similar trait. In a public sale there was a book which Lessing was very desirous of possessing. He gave three of his friends, at different times, a commission to buy it any price. They accordingly bid against each other till they had got as far as 90 crowns; there having been no other bidder after ten crowns. Happily one of them thought it best to speak to the others, when it appeared that they all had been bidding for Lessing, whose forgetfulness in this instance cost him 80 crowns.

Lapland Character.

Every individual, who has visited Lapland, must have remarked one characteristic common to all the Lapps;. namely, their mild and pacific disposition. When inflamed by spirituous liquor, their intoxication betrays itself by acts of intemperance; but never by anger, malice or cruelty. It is manifested only in an elevation of spirits, amounting indeed to madness; in shouting, jumping, and laughing; in craving for drams with hysteric screams, until they fall senseless on the ground, in a total disregard of all that belongs to them, offering any thing they possess for brandy, in raging lust, and total violation of all decency in their conduct, suffering

at the same time kicks, cuffs, and blows, insult and provocations of any kind, without the smallest irascibility. When sober, they are as gentle as lambs; and the softness of their language, added to their effeminate tone of voice, remarkably corresponds with their placable disposition. *(Clarke's Travels.)*

Scruple of Conscience.

An old German Knight, in the first half of the 47th century, when enormous goblets were among the chief ornaments of the rooms and tables of the nobles, sat once at table next to his young wife in a numerous company, where the bottle went continually round, and a large goblet was to be emptied each time, on pain of being contemned as a false brother by the guests, who were used to be very strict in this point. The wife, who had received a more polished education, whispered to her husband, when it again came to his turn to empty an enormous glass, to pour the wine secretly under the table. " The others will see it," said he. His wife, therefore, just as he was raising the glass to his mouth, snuffed out the candle, and repeated her request. Instead of complying, he said, with a kind of solemnity, " God sees it," and emptied his goblet.

Act against Luxury.

There is an old act of Parliament, passed during the protectorate of Cromwell (1657), entitled, " An Act for punishing of such persons as live at high rates, and have no visible estate, profession, or calling, answerable thereunto." The preamble recites, that " whereas divers lewd and dissolute persons in this Commonweath, live at very high rates and great expenses, having no visible estate, &c. to maintain themselves in their licentious, loose, and ungodly practices, but make it their trade and livelihood to cheat, deboyst, cozen and deceive the young gentry and other good people of this Commonwealth, be it enacted," &c. The authority given to Magistrates under this act was curious. Every justice of the peace, mayor, or other head-officer, might issue his warrant to bring such person before him, and require bail for his appearance at the next General Sessions, and in default of such bail, send him to prison till it was provided.

They were then to be indicted at the said sessions, " for living at high rates and great expenses, having no visible estate, profession, or calling, answerable thereunto; and upon conviction they were to be sent to the House of Correction, and kept to hard labour for three months. Upon a second conviction for the same offence, they were to be committed as aforesaid, and detained till discharged by the justices in open sessions. If this law were now in force, how amazingly crowded would be our different Houses of Correction! and how would our taverns, our theatres, promenades, be thinned of sharpers, dandies and dandizets!—a motley group, who ape their betters' dress and manners, and "feed on air," or on the produce of their tortured wit.

Italian Lottery.

The Lottery in Italy, as in France, is determined by the coming up of certain numbers on the same ticket, which if they accord to the extent of 2, 3, or 4, with those the adventurer has previously chosen, the prize is less or more valuable. The choice of figures on which to play naturally enough gives rise to a variety of superstitions, and there are books published which shew the relation of every occurrence, whether in vision or in every-day-life, to numbers in the lottery. Thus, for example, I meet in my morning's walk a mangy dog, a man in a pea-green coat with a cocked hat, or a with a rouged face under a beaver one: I return home and consult my books, and find that the mangy dog is 12, the pea-green man 16, and the rouged face under a white hat 30. But I should have said that every odd circumstance whatever has a double signification. Thus if I dream that my dog bites me, I recur to my books for an explanation of what this is significative; and here I find, perhaps, that in my dog's biting me is prefigured an injury to be received from a friend, and that the same thing is connected, by some mysterious link, with No. 62. But as the magic volume cannot of course supply a provision for every possible case, I must, if abandoned by my spells, find a resource in the powers of my own ingenuity. Let us put a case: I see a human figure on one of the highest pinnacles of the Alps. I seek an explanation in my conjuring book in vain. How then am I to read the emblem? I see a man as high as human daring and address can carry him, what can this signify, but that I am to mount as high as is possible in the lottery scale? The case is clear, and I pay 90. [The highest No.] *Rose's North of Italy.*

HINTS, PLANS, and PROCEEDINGS
of
Benevolence.

——————*Homo sum :*
Humanum nihil a me alienum puto.

ENCOURAGEMENT OF INDUSTRY.

The Provisional Committee for Encouragement of Industry and Reduction of Poors Rates, has ascertained from a multitude of the most intelligent replies to its circulated Scheme of Inquiries, that an eminent mean of improving the condition of the Labouring Class, and diminishing Pauperism, would be to afford Labouring Poor small portions of land on easy terms. That this practice promotes industry—furnishes employment to the rising race—prevents a dependence on parish aid, having in some districts operated to the keeping down, in others almost to the utter extinction of Poors Rates—is most favorable to morality, and prevents lesser offences, tending to greater crimes.

It has, therefore, great satisfaction in addressing the public on the present occasion. The Act intituled, "An Act to amend the laws for the relief of the poor, pages 7 and 8, enacts as follows :—

"And whereas, by an Act passed in the 43rd year of the reign of Queen Elizabeth, the Churchwardens and Overseers of the poor are directed to set to work certain persons therein described: and whereas by the laws now in force sufficient powers are not given to the Churchwardens and Overseers, to enable them to keep such persons fully and constantly employed: be it further enacted, that it shall be lawful for the Churchwardens and Overseers of the poor of any parish, with the consent of the inhabitants thereof in vestry assembled, to take into their hands any land or ground which shall belong to such parish, or to the Churchwardens and Overseers of the poor of such parish, or to the poor thereof, or to purchase, or to hire and take on lease, for, and on account of the parish, any suitable portion or portions of land within or near to such parish, not exceeding twenty acres in the whole; and to employ and set to work in the cultivation of such land, on account of the parish, any such persons, as by law they are directed to set to work, and to pay to such. of the poor persons so employed as shall not be supported by the parish, reasonable wages for their work; and the poor persons so employed shall have such and the like remedies for the recovery of their wages, and shall be subject to such and the like punishment for misbehaviour in their employment, as other labourers in husbandry are by law entitled and subject to.

"Provided, and be it further enacted, that, for the promotion of industry amongst the poor, it shall be lawful for the Churchwardens and Overseers of the poor of any parish, with the consent of the inhabitants in vestry assembled, to let any portion and portions of such parish land as aforesaid, or of the land to be so purchased or taken on account of the parish, to any poor and industrious inhabitant of the parish, to be by him or her occupied and cultivated on his or her own account, and for his or her own benefit, at such reasonable rent, and for such term as shall by the Inhabitants in vestry be fixed and determined."

The Committee therefore hopes that parishes and parochial officers will proceed to the selection of suitable objects, and to the division, and distribution of the land, whereby, besides the labouring class, a great number of manufacturers will also be found to avail themselves. Wherever there may be found a surplusage of land, parish farming may successfully be resorted to, to furnish employment for the unoccupied. And it will be considered necessary to remark, that though in a very large proportion of instances the limited amount of land to be hired under this bill will be inadequate, yet it is not doubted that the advantages which will necessarily arise from the adoption of this grant, will

induce the legislature to remove every obstacle to a requisite supply.

It remains to invite all who have the means, to assist our poor with small portions of land, every rank partaking the benefit. Parish officers are invoked to do their utmost in behalf of the community: noblemen, magistrates, gentlemen, occupiers of land, will answer the call to an universal co-operation. On this grand principle of economy, demonstrative proof will be afforded that subjects of general utility occupy the public mind.

For the Committee,

BENJAMIN WILLS, Hon. Sec.
King's Head, Poultry, May 10, 1819.

BRITISH AND FOREIGN BIBLE SOCIETY.

The Report details the progress of the Bible Societies in the different countries on the Continent, and in the Indies, &c. and states that the number of Bibles issued at cost and reduced prices, from the 31st of March, 1818, to the same period in 1819, was 123,247 Bibles, and 136,784 Testaments, making in the whole 260,031 copies, being an increase beyond the issues of the preceding year, of 65,930 Bibles and Testaments; making, with those issued at the expence of the Society, from various presses upon the Continent, a total of more than Two Millions Three Hundred Thousand Bibles and Testaments.

The total net Receipts of last year were £94,306 17 10
Including Aux. Soc. £56,604 3 3
Do. Bibles, Test. &c. 27,499 2 10
Total net payments . . 92,237 1 4
Besides which the Society was under engagements to the amount of £70,000 more.

EDUCATION OF THE POOR.

The first Report of the Commissioners on the Education of the poor, has been printed. It consists of 261 folio pages, and includes 275 cases in London, Westminster, Southwark, Middlesex, Berkshire, Oxfordshire, Hertfordshire, Surrey, Sussex, and Kent. The cases, for the most part, from the extreme poverty of the foundations, are devoid of interest. It rarely happens that Schools which have considerable property are without special visitors, and it will be remembered, that all such, by a clause introduced in the House of Lords, were withdrawn from inquiry. The Commissioners, however, very properly decided, that the exemption did not extend to those instances, where the special visitors had themselves the administration of the funds. This decision brought the case of Tunbridge School under their review, which will be found the most important one in the Report. It seems the Skinners' Company are both the visitors of this School, and the trustees of its estates; that they have regularly made all the fixed payments under the donor's grants, with some small increase, but the whole surplus rent, amounting to several thousand pounds per annum, have been appropriated to the uses of the Company. The Commissioners state, that the right of the Company, in treating the surplus as their own, can only be solved by a judicial decision. Some documents are published, from which it appears, that they originally took the estates for the maintenance and benefit of the School, and if this is proved, the public will be indebted to this inquiry, for the creation of a new establishment, with advantages, in the School and at the Universities, equal, if not superior, to any that are to be found in the greatest foundations in the kingdom.

EDUCATION OF THE POOR IN IRELAND.

In their last report, the Committee announced the building of a school-house, in Kildare-street, in Dublin, and expressed a hope, that it would be ready at the commencement of the present year: this hope, they regret to say, has not been fully realized; but as the interior of the school-rooms is now nearly completed, they expect they will shortly be opened for the reception of 1000 children, 500 boys and 500 girls. This school which is to contain in each room 500 boys and 500 girls, independently of its affording instruction to so great a number of the poor of Dublin, will exhibit in its internal arrangement, a system capable of adaption to all schools, for the instruction of any number of pupils; and, being on so large a scale, will exhibit the system of instruction in its greatest perfection, at the same time answering all the Society's objects, so far as regards the training of masters; for which purpose, a school, constructed on an extended plan, is absolutely necessary.

BAPTIST IRISH SOCIETY.

The fourth Report of this Society mentions that the number of Schools (exclusive of Sunday Schools) was 65, containing about 3860 children. They have since increased to 75 Schools, some of which are supported at 8*l.* per ann. each to the Society, the resident gentry providing the other moiety of the expense. In some instances, where the Schools amount to upwards of 100 children, the masters receive 20*l.* per annum. There are at present in all the Schools upwards of 5000 children.

INTERESTING INTELLIGENCE FROM THE BRITISH SETTLEMENTS IN INDIA.

CALCUTTA.

Proposed cultivation of Saugor Island.

The following plan appears to us of so much importance that we have thought proper to lay it before our readers, at large.

Pursuant to a Notice given in the Public Papers, a meeting took place on the forenoon of Tuesday Sept. 15, at the Exchange Rooms, to consider of the best means of clearing the Island of Saugor, and to draw up an outline of the scheme for providing the funds, and fixing the terms on which this laudable undertaking was to be effected.

Charles Trowers, Esq. Collector of the 24 Pergunnahs, opened the meeting, by observing that although he had had no official communications with the Government on this subject, yet he was persuaded of their wishes and intentions to give every facility to the execution of any approved plan for the clearing and cultivating the Island of Saugor. The principal members of the mercantile community of Calcutta met this assurance by a correspondent readiness to promote so useful a work.

Dr. Dunlop, then read a paper setting forth the advantages which may be expected to ensue from this useful undertaking, both during its progress and after its completion, exclusive of the profits to be derived from the cultivation of the soil, and the benefits which invalids may hope to receive there, from the salubrity of the sea air, and accommodation for sea water baths, warm and cold; it is projected to establish a depôt for marine stores, a market for fresh provisions, to supply ships to the latest period of their departure, a post office, packet boats, telegraphs, &c.

A Map of the Island from the hand of an Engineer Officer of the Honorable Company's Service, drawn in 1811, was produced, and by this it appeared that the Island was about 20 miles in length, and 5 in general breadth, being broadest towards the southern, and narrowest towards the northern extremity. The shores are bordered with Jungle, but it is said, from the authority of persons who have traversed the Island in hunting parties, that the interior of the Island presents many spots covered with wild grass only, and that the traces of tanks, temples, habitations, and former cultivation are visible in many parts, all which would be favourable to the undertaking of clearing it. Small branches of the Hooghly River, both from Lacam's channel, and from near the New Anchorage, intersect the Island in various directions, and at the S. W. end is a spring of good fresh water, which is now enclosed in a tank and marked as a watering place for ships, in some of the latest charts. It is estimated that such parts of the Island as are thickly covered with jungle, would take six rupees per biggah to bring into a state fit for cultivation. If the whole surface of the Island was of this description the sum necessary to be raised for this purpose would not be less than from 12 to 15 lacs of rupees. But the great proportion of land in the interior which is covered with a grass Jungle only, and which the mere setting fire to would effectually clear, has induced a pretty general impression that from two to three lacs of rupees would be fully adequate to the purpose.

The sum at present fixed on to be raised by Subscription, has been therefore named at two lacs and a half—and this is divided into 250 shares of 1000 rupees each. The conditions proposed were that the Island should become the sole and exclusive property of the Sharers for a period of

thirty years from the 1st of January next, and all benefits arising from it within that period to be entirely their own, but that after that period an annual rent of 4 annas per biggah was to be paid by the holders of the land to Government.

A portion of the continent opposite to Mud Point, near the northern extremity of Saugor Island, and on the eastern side of the river, was some years since granted by the Government to private individuals, for a period of seven years free of rent, and after that period to pay at the rate of 7 annas per biggah. This has succeeded so well as to have continued in uninterrupted cultivation ever since, and may be taken therefore as a presumptive argument in favor of the same beneficial results arising from the clearing of Saugor.

Many of the wealthiest and most respectable natives of this city have testified their willingness to assist in the restoration of an Island venerated by them as a place of sanctity and former population. Before the meeting dispersed upwards of 70 shares were filled up. (Since 130.)

COMPARISON OF SHIPS;
India Built and Europe Built.

In comparing a Ship built at Bombay with those built at Calcutta, it must be premised that a Bombay built Ship of 25 years of age, is as good as a Calcutta built one of 15, depending not on the science or workmanship, but on the wood alone, this assertion cannot be doubted, when we can point out many Bombay and Surat built Ships, of 25, 30, 32, and 40 years standing, whilst there is scarcely a Bengal built Ship of 20 years now afloat.

This being admitted the

Bombay Ships stand as . . No.	1
Surat Ships when built by competent persons	2
Cochin Ships ditto ditto . . .	3
Damaun Ships ditto ditto . . .	4
Calcutta built	5
The H. C. 800 and 1200 Ton Ships	6
Eng. River built Ships 2 to 600 Tons	7
Ditto out ports 2 to 600 . . .	8
American Ships 2 to 500 . . .	9
Java built Ships	10
Chittagong	11
Pegu	12

The above statement, relates only to their relative durability, and when constructed by professional and scientific men. Ships whose planks are nailed or bolted, are no doubt safer than those whose planks are only secured with tree nails, this was verified in Bombay by Mr. Stalkart, in 1801, when a Ship of 400 Tons with tree nails, was built at Colabah, under his immediate inspection, but though the timber was as good as any that Bombay produced, and the utmost science was displayed in her construction, she never was a good Ship.

The Ships built at Calcutta, must from the circumstance of the wood being inferior, always fall behind, not only to Ships built at Bombay, but to those built at Surat, Cochin or Damaun, by professional men.

HOAX: DECEPTION GENERAL.

The whole native population of Calcutta, and many European ladies and gentlemen in their train, was induced to visit Wazeer Ally's tomb on Tuesday Oct. 26, by a report that it had been seen to shake. A guard of Europeans and Sepoys was on the spot, to prevent, we suppose, the confusion and mischief which this confluence of curious and credulous spirits might occasion. We state this of course, merely for distant readers, and as an additional instance of the superstitions of this country.

NEW ROUTE TO EUROPE.

A Gentleman is now in Calcutta, who is about to proceed to Petersburgh by a route, which we believe, no native of England or France has heretofore attempted; after entering Persia, instead of passing by the usual track, through Ghilan and Daghistan, to Astracan, it is his intention to proceed on the Eastern side of the Caspian, through the provinces of Korassan and Karasm, and the country of the Usbecks, Turcomans and Kirgees, round the northern shores of the Caspian, until he reaches the Wolga. It is desirable that there should be adventurous and enterprising spirits to visit countries, which have been unexplored by the scientific traveller; and we shall be happy to learn that this gentleman may find among the wild and predatory hordes he may visit, enough to compensate him for his exertions.

INTELLIGENCE FROM PERSIA.

Slave Trade Continued.

In Sept. 1818, a Ship and a large Bugulah were at Bushire, from Muscat, with no less than from 7 to 800 African slaves, males and females, for sale. These wretched victims were occasionally led about the streets in search of purchasers. Thus while we are urging all the powers of Europe to abandon the abominable traffic in slaves, little notice is taken of its being carried on to such an extent in the Persian Gulf. The Joassimees this year are said to have captured 40 sail of Boats from Zanzibar, whose cargoes were principally slaves, each boat at the lowest appears to have had from fifty, up to 2 or 300. The whole of these sufferers were distributed amongst the Pirate Chiefs, and will probably form part of the crews of the Piratical Boats.

Zanzibar is perhaps as fine an Island as in any part of the world, and a perfect garden, enjoying a most salubrious climate. The Cinnamon, Cloves, and Nutmegs, which have been carried there, thrive as well as in their native country,—indeed there are large Plantations of them now, a few boxes of Plants of Cinnamon and Cloves had just been received at Bushire, when our letters came away. The Island is subject to Muscat, and is the most valuable of, its dependencies. The slaves are principally brought from thence, and a few from the western shores of the Red Sea, Abyssinians, and Nubians.

MADRAS.

LITERARY SOCIETY.

At the last meeting of the Literary Society, three papers were presented from different members. The first is some account of Cutch, by Captain Macmurdo: little has hitherto been known respecting this district; and Captain Macmurdo's paper, at the same time that it fills up a blank in the geography of India, and connects the survey of Guzerat with the branches of the Indus, gives a very lively description of the peculiar manners and customs of the people, and adverts to some interesting points in the natural history of the country. Infanticide, we are sorry to say, prevails in Cutch, to a great extent, and the number of female children who are annually murdered from this abominable practice, Captain Macmurdo supposes cannot be less than one thousand; it is to be hoped, that the benevolent interference of the British government will be attended with the same success there, which has so happily crowned its efforts in Guzerat. Captain Macmurdo's paper is a valuable addition to our Indian knowledge, and we are particularly glad to observe in this paper, and in one lately presented by Captain Dangerfield, some attempts to illustrate the natural history ; a subject as yet but very little explored in this country.

The second paper contains some observations by Captain Vans Kennedy, on the history and failure of the scheme of a Universal Religion, attempted to be introduced by Acbar. The paper is written with great perspicuity, and affords some translations from native accounts, of the religious disputations held by Acbar's order, and in his presence, between the learned of the several sects.

The last paper is an account by Captain Elwood, of the caste of Niaheas, a singular race of people, who derive their origin from five brothers, who fled to the Concan, from the neighbourhood of Oudipoor.

CEYLON.

NATIONAL RELIC LOST AND RECOVERED.

The following account places a new particular of Ceylonese Superstition in a conspicuous point of view. We have inserted the reflections of the writer, without any variation of his language or sentiments. Those who have been in India can judge on their propriety.

The precious Relic on which the destinies of the Kandyan Monarchy are supposed to depend, was deposited by Lieut. Col. Kelly, on the 11th at the Temple of Nettawelle, on the road between the Ferry of Wattapologa and Kandy. A fortunate time is to be discovered for its removal, when it will be conveyed in a procession and restored to the Great Temple in Kandy.

There is something, it must be confessed, revolting to common sense, to see the boasted reason of man degraded into the folly of attaching immense consequence to a piece of worthless bone. It is still more disgusting to a sincere Christian to see the victims of an abject superstition bending in adoration before an imaginary Relic. But we must be careful not to suffer these natural feelings to hurry us into rash and precipitate measures. There is little hope of reclaiming a bigotted Heathen from those errors which he has been learning all his life, by thwarting his prejudices with sudden acts of compulsion. Such conduct would only rivet the chains of his superstition; it is not violently depriving him of his processions and his adorations and his offerings of flowers, that would dispose him to listen to the doctrines of a purer religion. His errors must be treated with gentleness and the means of removing them put within his own reach, for he will be disposed to use them as soon as he feels that they are not forced upon him, but he is fairly left to judge for himself.

The Kandians are a people that have had perhaps less intercourse with Europeans than almost any other nation of India, they ought therefore to be treated with peculiar discretion; and if they are convinced that their security is dependent upon their possession of a certain piece of bone, why should not that bone be restored to their Temple with ceremony and pomp?—It is to their future tranquility under the stable permanence of a British Government that we must look for their moral and religious improvement.

This high valued Relic appears by the deposition of one of the party to have been stolen from the Temple, several months ago, by two priests and three other persons; the informer has give a minute account of the manner in which the several caskets in which it was secured, were broke open, but there is nothing at all interesting in the detail.

It was recovered by Ensign Shoolbraid near Pubilia, in the same jungle where he took Madugalle; he was informed by the people, who so much assisted him, that a Buddhist Priest had been seen lurking about the forest: and he desired them to seize and bring the Priest before him.

This they soon performed, and with him they brought three other men looking like Coolies, who appeared to be carrying a great deal of baggage. Ensign Shoolbraid asked what the contents were of all their bundles, &c., he was answered, "the Priest's clothes," but that officer not accustomed to meet Buddhist Priests in the jungle, with such a wardrobe, had the bundles opened, and upon examination they were found to contain the Relic and all the Interior Caskets, richly ornamented with Jewels; the large outward case which is silver gilt, and of considerable size, had been of course left in the Temple to prevent any suspicion of the theft.

Ensign Shoolbraid went directly with his Priest and his prize, and delivered both up to Lieutenant Colonel Kelly, at Nalande.

PENANG.

LANGUAGES NUMEROUS.

The following is a list of no less than thirty-four distinct Languages of Europe, Asia and Africa, said to have been spoken at the same period (1808) in this small colony. The catalogue has been kindly furnished us by a friend, who, however, does not vouch for its accuracy—neither do we.

English, Erse, French, Italian, German, Spanish, Portuguese, Dutch, Danish, Swedish, Russian, Latin, Greek,—Arabic, Persian, Armenian, Malayan, Parsee, Hindoostanee, Bengallee, Chinese, Siamese, Achinese, Javanese, Bugguese, Cingalese, Chooliah, Burmah, Ratta, Talinga, Guzarat, Malabar,—Abyssinian, Caffrarian.

JAVA.

Extract from a letter dated Batavia,
8th September, 1818.

The Americans are pouring in here every day, and in consequence of the great demand for our produce, Coffee is now up to 19 a 20 Spanish dollars per pecul; Sugar 8½ to 9, and all other goods in proportion; there is but little Tin now here, and no Copper, the Japan ships not having yet returned. All other goods are dear in proportion, excepting Europe arti-

cles, which are both abundant and cheap. Bengal goods, are rather heavy just now, and find a sale but slowly. At a late Auction Sale, Gurrahs and the 3rd sorts were purchased at 40 dollars per corge. Opium is not much in request at Batavia, the farmers having already secured a considerable supply of both Bengal and Turkey Opium. At Samarang some good sales have been made as high as 1650 Dollars per chest.

Freights are not to be had either for Europe or elsewhere, and there is no appearance of their being bettered soon.

Alceste Reef.—The loss of His Majesty's ship Alceste, commanded by Captain Murray Maxwell, in her return from China, through the straits of Gaspar, having given alarm to navigators, as to the safety of the passage through the channel, we have great pleasure in laying before our readers, an original and authentic description of that reef, as ascertained from angles taken over the keel of the Alceste, which still marks the situation of the wreck.

The highest part of the West Island bore S. 22, 20′ W. distant four miles and eight-tenths. A remarkable White Rock forming the Northern end of the Middle Island, S. 18. 30′ E. distant one mile and three-tenths. The highest part of Middle Island, forming a peak, S. 2. 0′ E. The shoals off this part of Middle Island, consist of several narrow but long patches of coral, forming channels with from six to ten fathoms of water between them, but too intricate for shipping to navigate.

The Alceste's keel is lying about ten yards from that of the Portuguese ship Amelia, which was wrecked here in 1816. No other dangers exist on the outside of these wrecks, which are under the surface of the water, in two and three fathoms depth. The soundings coming from the Northward very gradually decrease to ten fathoms near the Reefs. With the pitch of the Reef bearing East, at the distance of two miles are twenty fathoms water.

One mile west of West Island are two patches of rocks, nearly even with the water's edge, lying on a bank, the general soundings are from six to ten fathoms.

Ross's Rock bears W. from the peak of Middle Island, distant four miles and half from West Island. Navigators, taking care to avoid the above-mentioned dangers, will find these Straits of Gaspar, preferable to those of Banca.

We are happy to add that a Survey of these Straits, as well as of Clement's straits, the shoals North of Gaspar Island, the Southern parts of the Straits of Banca, and the Dogger bank, had been made during the last season, and that it had been ascertained, that there was a good channel inside the bank which lies off Point Romania and the Water Islands. This channel is three or four miles in breadth, and will be of great advantage to ships leaving China in the N. E. monsoon, enabling them to get into the Straits of Sincapore with facility and safety in dirty weather.

CHINA.

Our last advices from this Empire mention nothing further of any interruptions of the Public Peace: but the following hint shews sufficiently the tenure of our trade with China.

The Hong Merchants, it is said, were about to impose an additional duty on cotton and other articles of trade imported by foreigners, in order to raise the sum of 300,000 tales, to be presented to the Emperor, but the supercargoes, it is added, had already remonstrated against this measure, and it was confidently hoped that their remonstrance would be attended to, and the proposed increase of duty not levied.

NEW SOUTH WALES.

POPISH VICAR APOSTOLIC EXPELLED.

A correspondent informs us that the Reverend Jeremiah O'Finn having arrived at New South Wales, with the commission of Vicar Apostolic, was ordered by Governor Macquarrie to leave the settlement immediately, and on his absconding to evade this order until reference should be made to Europe, he was detected, seized and sent under a guard of soldiers on board a ship which sailed for England the same day. We find that 500 free settled inhabitants of Sidney have addressed a remonstrance on the subject, to

the local Government on behalf of the Roman Catholics of the place. The question cannot of course be ultimately decided but by the Government at home, without whose special authority no agent of the Pope ought to have appeared in the colonial settlement in question. For, the right which the Irish Catholics have undoubtedly to demand from the legislative power of the United Kingdom the free exercise of their religion, does not constitute a right on the part of any foreign power, to interfere in these domestic differences, or to appoint agents unknown to, and unauthorised by, the supreme Government, at home.

NATURAL HISTORY: ANIMALS.

The Batavia has brought from New South Wales, a peculiar wild dog, with two rows of teeth.

Also an animal of the species Phoca, lately named Platipus, with a horny snout like the bill of a duck.

The former is alive, and not unlike one of the wild dogs of this part of the world. The Platipus, is in spirits, but not in very good preservation.

COIN RETAINED.

A mode of keeping the current coin in circulation has been practised with much success in New South Wales. The coin in circulation are chiefly Spanish dollars, and a piece of the size of a sixpence, is punched out of the middle of them, which is also put in circulation under the denomination of Dumps, and valued at 15d., the Dollar however loses nothing of its value, and is by this means, retained in circulation, as it is of more value in the Colony than elsewhere. The Chinese also disfigure and mutilate the Spanish dollars for the same reason :—their laws are very rigid against the exportation of even bullion, and it is only owing to the venality of the officers of the customs, that a single ounce gets out of the country.

MANILLA.

SCARCITY OF COIN: NEW DUTY.

From the very great scarcity of money, owing to the non-arrival of the usual ships from Acapulco, where it was conjectured they had been detained in consequence of information having been received of the

Insurgent Privateers infesting the Eastern Coasts of Luconia, a duty of thirteen per cent. was about to be levied on all monies exported from Manilla.

To those acquainted with the course of traffic between Manilla and the English Settlements, this tariff may appear of trivial moment, and not otherwise detrimental to the foreign trader, than our laws, which prohibit the exportation of British Coin from Great Britain. But when it is considered that Manilla is not only a country of consumption itself, but the intermediate Port between the South American Provinces, which are similarly circumstanced, and India; and that less than one part out of ten of the returns to this country is made in goods, and the rest in bullion, it will be apparent that this duty must, if continued, considerably affect the British merchant.

National Register:

FOREIGN.

America: United States.

National Mint.

From official documents, transmitted to Congress during the last session, it appears, that the total amount of gold, silver and copper coinage, at the Mint of the United States, from the date of its establishment up to the end of the year 1817, was 14,183,768 36-dollars; and that the amount of gold coins made during the year 1818, was 242,940 dollars; of silver, 1,070,427, 50 dollars; of copper, 52,320 dollars; making a total amount of 1,365,687,50; which, added to the aggregate of coinage in former years, makes up the amount coined up to the first day of the present year 15,549,456 dollars. It further appears, that the nett amount chargeable to the coinage of gold, silver, and copper, from the commencement of the Institution to December 31, 1818, including the costs of lots, buildings, and machinery," was 514,946 dollars.

Scientific Expedition.

A steam-boat is to be launched at Pittsburg, to be employed in an expedition to the Yellow Stone River, the object of which is to obtain a history of the inhabitants, soil, minerals, and curiosities. Major Long, of New Hampshire, topographical engineer; Mr. Graham, of Virginia; Mr. Wm. H. Swift, of Massachusets, from the Military Academy; Major Biddle, of the Artillery; Dr. Jessup, mineralogist; Dr. Say, botanist and geologist; Dr. Baldwin, zoologist and physician; Mr. Peale, of Philadelphia, landscape-painter and ornithologist; Mr. Seymour, ditto; and Major Fallow, of the Indian department, form the expedition. The boat is 75 feet long, 13 beam, draws 19 inches water, and is well armed: she carries on her flag a White Man and an Indian shaking hands, the calumet of peace, and the sword. Her machinery is fixed to avoid the snags and sawyers of the rivers The expedition departs with the best wishes of the friends of science.

The Floridas.

It is believed (for our knowledge of the Floridas is very defective) that few, if any of the navigable rivers take their rise in the United States; but the coast is indented with two spacious bays that will afford security for shipping; particularly the large and capacious bay of Hillsborough, which will admit any vessel over the bar, not drawing over twenty four feet water. The principal part of the soil in the peninsula abounds in pines, called the yellow pitch-pine tree, which is excellent timber for shipping: the peach and the mulberry orchards thrive in this soil remarkably well: it is likewise abundant in grass. In the vicinity of the soil so productive of the pine, there is to be found soil of another quality: it abounds in maple oak of seven different species, all of which grows in great abundance; walnuts, chesnuts, mulberry, and maple; it is likewise favourable to the cultivation of the indigo plant: figs and oranges are likewise found in this soil; but the latter fruit is not of the first quality. Nor are the savannahs of Florida destitute of interest, although in the wet seasons they are almost impassable, yet they are productive of grass of which cattle are extremely fond: in this soil dwarf oaks and junipers are numerous. The river swamps (by which we are not to understand marshes, but low grounds subject to inundation) abound in corn, rice, indigo, in great profusion;—of timber, the maple, hickory, oak of various kinds, birch, beech, willow, the sumac, the myrtle and the locust, thrive in these low grounds. There is another species of soil of a light and spongy texture, intermixed with vegetable fibre, which trembles to a considerable extent on the approach of man or beast, and in which the latter are sometimes swallowed up, and irrecoverably lost. Here is found very fine clay fit for manufacturing, bituminous earth coal, fossil, marl, iron, lead, chalk, chrystal, and white topaze. The Floridas abound in esculent plants; wheat, rye, barley, maize, buck-wheat, and rice, cotton, tobacco, peaches, pears, and apples; pitch, turpentine, hemp, all articles of naval stores abound in this country, and perhaps the finest ship timber in the world. The lakes, bays, and rivers, present excellent fisheries, in all which places several kinds of the most valuable fish are found in abundance —Such is an imperfect outline of the soil and natural productions of the Floridas.— *American Paper.*

GREENLAND.

Siliceous Wood.

A species of siliceous fossil wood was found by a serjeant of artillery, who accompanied Captain Sabine, near the top of a hill, in Hare Island, on the west coast of Greenland, in Lat. 70 deg. 26 min. It had been part of the trunk of a pine tree, about four inches in diameter. The hill is in the interior of the island, about four miles from the shore, and is considerably more than 900 feet above the level of the sea, being higher than an intermediate hill, the elevation of which was ascertained barometrically.

RUSSIA.

Volcanic Island.

A new Volcanic Island has been raised among the Aleutian Islands, not far from Unalaschka. This phenomenon appeared in the midst of a storm, attended with flames and smoke. After the sea was calmed, a boat was sent from Unalaschka, with twenty Russian hunters, who landed on this island, June 1st, 1814. They found it full of crevices and precipices. The surface was cooled to the depth of a few yards, but below that depth it was still hot. No water was found on any part of it. The vapours rising from it were not injurious, and the sea-lions had begun to take up their residence on it. Another visit was paid to it in 1815; its height was then diminished. It is about two miles in length; they have given it the name of Bogulslaw.

SAXONY.

Jews expelled.

Accounts from the frontiers of Saxony give the following particulars of the ex-

pulsion of the Jews from Meiningen:— From ancient times the town had the privilege that no Jew should reside there; latterly several Jews had established themselves there, without any opposition from the government. Some time since, circumstances being changed, the magistrates thought it advisable to enforce the old regulations, and all Jew beggars and petty dealers received orders to quit the town, which they did. Some rich Jewish families remained; and the magistrates were asked whether they should be further tolerated? The magistrates thought themselves not competent to decide this question, and called an assembly of the citizens. This assembly had scarcely heard what was the matter in debate, when some of them resolved to cut the knot at once, collected some empty waggons standing in the market, obliged the Jews still remaining to pack up their goods, and to put themselves with them in the vehicles, which stood ready to convey them over the frontiers. The immediate cause of the event is said to have been, that a Jew, contrary to the ancient custom, which did not permit persons of his nation to acquire real property, had purchased a house in the town of Meiningen, [and desired to have his name registered as the proprietor.

SPAIN.

Lancasterian Schools.

On the 30th of March last the King signed the order for establishing one school in each of the towns of the kingdom. The King has named a Director General of all the schools on the Lancasterian plan in Spain, and a Committee of 12 Grandees of Spain to protect the said schools: at present there are only 9 members—the Duke of Infantado, President for life; the Duke of Montemar, the Marquis of Cerralbo, Marquis of Santa Cruz, Duke of Villahermosa, Secretary; the Dukes of Medinauli, San Fernando, Counts Altamira and Santa Coloma. All the Schools in Spain are to be subordinate to the central school established in the capital. This central school is to be sustained by the Committee only (being an offer they made to the Government.) This school which will consist of 300 children, and has already 207, was opened the 4th of this month (May), in which many children entered without knowing their letters; has about 30 at present well established as apprentices. Government was astonished at the great rapidity with which the children learnt, and the great economy that was observed. The King has favoured the school twice with his presence; the last time his Majesty was accompanied by our late beloved Queen, and both times he was pleased to express his great satisfaction, and determination to protect the plan. His brother, the infant Don Carlos, has also honoured the school with a visit. The Duke of Frias, who is at present in Paris, has given gratis his ball-room, in which the central school is now established, and his Grace is to be one of the members of the Committee.

National Register:

BRITISH.

Population of London.

It appears from official documents that London within the walls contained, in 1701, 139,300 inhabitants; in 1750, 57000; in 1801, 78,000; and in 1811, only 57,700 —It also appears, that in 1813, London within the walls contained 97 parishes, having 67 churches, and a population of only 55,484 persons; while Westminster and its liberties, Southwark, and 12 out-parishes of the metropolis, contain 27 parishes, 27 churches, and a population of 686,655 persons!

Waterloo Prize Money.

Commander-in-Chief 60,000*l.*; General Officer 1,250*l.*; Field Officer 420*l*; Captain 90*l.*; Subaltern 33*l.*; Serjeant 19*l.*; Rank and File 2*l.* 10*s.* The Duke of Wellington's share is equal to 50 General Officers, 143 Field Officers, 666 Captains, 2,158 Serjeants, 24,000 Rank and File.

Steam Vessels.

The scheme to propel the vessel constructed according to Lord Cochrane's directions, by the application of steam to machinery operating under water, has, it is understood, totally failed. An experiment was last week made to compress the water by means of air-tunnels fixed in the paddle-cases, but it was without effect. This is the second failure in the attempt to work machinery under water; and a considerable sum of money, besides a year, have been expended.

Iron Boat.

There is now building at Glasgow, on a plan of Mr. Creighton's, a vessel of malleable iron, intended as a passage-boat for the Great Canal Company. This boat though composed of iron, will be, it is computed, from four to five tons lighter than the same dimensions in wood, as well as much superior in strength.

Linen from Nettles.

Some experiments on the preparation of linen and thread from the floss of nettles, have been made lately in Ireland. The thread in colour, strength, and fineness, is equal, if not superior, to that obtained from flax, and the linen has the appearance of common grey linen.

Maple Sugar.

Some years ago experiments were made in France for extracting sugar from the Maple tree; but the object was subsequently neglected, and even abandoned. M. Bodard has, however, recently received from Bohemia some important information on the subject. An incision was made in a maple tree, from which a quantity of syrup issued. This syrup afterwards produced sugar, which, it is said, rivals that of the beet-root or the cane.

The Box-tree a Poison.

It is not perhaps generally known, that the box-tree is a strong poison. The box borders of several beds in a garden at Wittering Lodge, near Lincoln, were lately thrown upon some manure in which nine strong pigs were rooting, four of whom died from eating the noxious leaves, notwithstanding castor oil and other antidotes were administered.

Polar Expedition.

In one of the ships belonging to the Hudson's bay Company, which recently left the river for their settlements, Lieutenant Franklyn, late Commander of the Trent, in the expedition to reach the North Pole, has taken his passage for the purpose of exploring that part of America to the northward of Hudson's bay. The route this officer is to take will be nearly the same as that pursued by Mr. Hearne, in 1770, who stated that he reached the sea at the entrance of Copper Mine river. Lieutenant Franklyn will be accompanied by about five Europeans, one of whom is a surgeon; and on their arrival at the Copper Mine river are to pursue such further course as may appear proper.

During the voyage of discovery last year to Baffin's bay, a bottle was thrown into the sea from the Alexander, Lieutenant Parry, on the 24th May, when that ship was off Cape Farewell. It contained the latitude and longitude the ship was then in. About three months since the bottle was found on the island of Bartragh in Killala·bay, and an account of it forwarded to the Admiralty. It is supposed it must have floated at about the rate of eight miles per day across the Atlantic.

The celebrated Maltebrun has just published some interesting remarks on the undiscovered parts of the world. Speaking of the voyage to the South Pole, he considers the project useless, but advises the attempt to be made in sledges and ice boats. The floating masses of ice encountered by Cook and others, from 50 to 70 deg. and which were supposed to form part of a moving enclosure, behind which lay an open sea, and perhaps a chain of island to the south points of the known lands, and to have been carried towards the low latitudes by the current said to run constantly from the Poles to the Equator, he imagines to have been detached parts of an immense continent of ice, carried by a finely temporary polar current towards the tropic. Following up the supposition of this continent, he says, " the peninsulas and promontories of such a continent would naturally fall into the sea after a succession of warm seasons, and cause this phenomenon."

Churches in Scotland.

A Committee of the General Assembly of the Church of Scotland, has represented that in that country there are 47 parishes in need of churches or chapels; and 88 other parishes but ill provided with religious instruction. It appears also that within the last 7 years, many parishes have added a sixth or more to the number of their inhabitants.

Enormous Pudding.

Lately at Paignton Fair, near Torbay, a plum-pudding, of an extraordinary size, was prepared and placed on a car, fancifully decked with ribbands, laurel, &c. and drawn through the town by eight oxen; it was then cut up, and distributed among the populace, conformably to an ancient custom, neglected many years, but thus pleasantly revived. An immense concourse from the neighbouring parishes assembled to witness the ceremony, and enjoy the amusements of the fair. The ingredients which composed this massy pudding were 400lb. of flour, 170lb. of beef suet, 140lb. of raisins, and 20 doz. of eggs: it had been kept constantly boiling in a brewer's furnace, from Saturday morning until Tuesday morning; tin pipes were passed through it to convey the heat, so that the middle and every part should be thoroughly dressed.

Adulteration of Flour.

Among the means of adulterating flour, great use has lately been made of bones, the price of which has accordingly advanced within these few years from ten-pence a bushel to eighteen-pence, to the first purchasers. The collecting of bones is in fact pursued as a regular trade in the Metropolis. The admixture of fine pulverised clay in the prime necessary of life, is a practice unfortunately not unknown in many parts of the kingdom.

The presence of any foreign substances in flour and bread may, however, be detected by common and ordinary processes within the reach of every person. Pure and unadulterated flour may be known by any of these methods:—

1st. Seize a handful briskly, and squeeze it half a minute; it preserves the form of the cavity of the hand in one piece, although it may be rudely placed on the table. Not so that which contains foreign substances, it breaks in pieces more or less; that mixed with whiting being the most adhesive, but still dividing and falling down in a little time. Flour mixed with ground stones, bones, or plaster of Paris, loses its form at once, and the more bran there may be in it, the sooner it will be flat on the board.

2nd. Having dipped the fore-finger and thumb partially in sweet-oil, take up a small quantity of flour; if it be pure, you may freely rub the fingers together for any length of time; it will not become sticky, and the substance will turn nearly black; but if whiting be mixed with the flour, a few times rubbing turns it into putty, and its colour is thereby very little changed.

3rd. Drop the juice of a lemon, or good vinegar, upon flour; if the flour be pure, it remains at rest; if adulterated, an immediate commotion takes place. This is the readiest method for detecting the presence of stone-dust and plaster of Paris.

Lastly, genuine flour will longer keep the impression even of the grains of the skin, than that which is adulterated, the latter very soon throwing up the fine marks. Let a person of a moist skin rub flour briskly between the palms of both hands; if there be whiting among it, he will find resistance; but with pure flour none.

Bone Manure.

A Stamford paper, referring to the arrival of several vessels at Grimsby from the Continent with bones, observes, that the eagerness of English agriculturists to obtain this manure, and the cupidity of foreigners in supplying it, is such as to induce the latter actually to rob the sepulchres of their forefathers. Bones of all descriptions are imported; but what confirms the above observation is, that pieces of half-decayed coffin tire are found amongst them; and those skilled in anatomy have no hesitation in pronouncing many of the bones to have belonged to human subjects. Our brave countrymen who fell at Waterloo, and were there consigned in undistinguished thousands to huge graves, there is no doubt (from the nature of the traffic which is carried on) have, after laying down their lives in defence of the liberties of their country, had their ashes used for enriching the soil.

Growth of Larch.

The following communication has lately been addressed to the Board of Agriculture, on the properties of the Larch:—
Ten years ago the Duke of Athol transmitted to the Commissioners of Naval Revision some observations on the Larch. The larch was introduced into Scotland, in the year 1738, by a Highland gentleman, Mr. Menzies, who brought a few small plants from London, some of which were standing in the year 1807; and the largest then measured thirteen feet in circumference. His Grace has been in the constant habit, for more than 30 years, of using larch of various ages for different purposes, and he positively affirms, that the thinning of his plantations employed for pailing, rails, and hurdles, " are more durable than oak copse wood of 24 years' growth." He builds all his ferry-boats and fishing-vessels of larch; and after a lapse of years, they have proved sound, when the ribs, which were made of oak, have become decayed. In mill-axes, also, larch has been substituted for oak, with the best effect, and in cutting up cogs which had been repaired with it 20 years before, they were discovered to be as sound and as fresh as at first. The value of larch is not to be estimated merely by its intrinsic qualities, but also by its aptitude

to soil and situations where few other trees can live. On the very summit of the lower range of the Grampian Hills, from 1000 to 1200 feet above the level of the sea, on a barren soil, composed of mountain schist, slate and iron stone, and where even the Scotch fir cannot rear its head, the larch grows luxuriantly; " and in considerable tracts," says the Duke, " where fragments of shivered rocks are strewed so thick that vegetation scarcely meets the eye, the larch puts out as strong and vigorous shoots as are to be found in the vallies below, and in the most sheltered situations." The larch is an Alpine tree, and it will not thrive in wet situations, but its comparative value is exceedingly greater than the Scotch fir, where it finds a congenial soil. The Duke sold a larch that was fifty years old for 12 guineas, while a fir of the same age, and in the same situation, was not worth more than 15s. In addition to the valuable properties of this tree, some experiments have been made to prove that the bark of the larch may be used for tanning, with as much advantage as that of the oak itself.

Important to Farmers.

By the Act 59 Geo. III. cap. 13, the the reduced rates of duties on husbandry horses are continued for two years longer: and such horses may be used in the following manner, without subjecting them to the *guinea duty* as heretofore, viz. they may be lent or let for purposes of agriculture—for the making or repairing of roads —for drawing coal, wood, peat, or turf, for fuel in private houses, but not for sale, Butchers may use a *second* riding horse, in their trade for *one guinea.* Ponies for riding or drawing carriages, *not exceeding* 13 *hands high*, to pay only two guineas whatever number may be kept; which will be a great accommodation to persons with families; for, suppose a person to keep one hore chargeable at 2l. 17s. 6d he can for the use of his family keep a pony for 2l. 2s. making together 4l. 19s. 6d. instead of 9l. 9s. as heretofore. Mares solely kept for breeding are wholly exempt. Bailiff's horses to pay only 2l. 10s. each. Tenants coming into the occupation of their farms at or after Midsummer, who never used their horses before that time, may appeal and be discharged for the moiety of the duties on such horses.

PARLIAMENTARY HISTORY.

CHAPTER V.

Water Companies—Copyright Act—Poor Laws—Misapplication of Poor Rates—Friendly Societies—Bankrupt Laws—Poor of Ireland.

HOUSE OF COMMONS.

WATER COMPANIES.

March 2.—Mr. M. A. Taylor brought up the report of the Committee which had been appointed to inquire into the truth of certain allegations contained in a petition from the Parish of Mary-le-bone, against the water companies of the metropolis. The hon. gent. complained of the inconvenience arising from the present system of having the metropolis carved into three divisions; one of which was to be served by the New River Company, another by the Grand Junction Company, and a third by the West Middlesex Company. They each raised their rates at pleasure, and if any person refused to pay their price, immediately left him without water.—The report was laid on the table.

Mr. Taylor thought, that as the water companies had contrived to avoid all former statutes, one ought to be made to compel them to supply water on reasonable terms. He would willingly join any gentleman in framing an act of that description. He hoped that he should have the support of the ministry on this occasion, as he had when he introduced the metropolis paving bill. If it had not been for the kindness of the Speaker and the support of Government, it would have cost him in fees to the house, and other expenses, between 4,000*l.* and 5,000*l.*

COPYRIGHT ACT.

Mr. Lambton begged to state the substance of a petition that had been intrusted to him by the booksellers and publishers of London and Westminster, praying for a repeal of the Copyright Act. It was enough to mention the names of Messrs. Longman and Co., Rivington, Murray, and Mawman, to secure it attention; in short, it had been signed by all the respectable booksellers of the metropolis. It appeared, between the years 1814 and 1818, the house of Longman and Co, had lost, by the operation of the Copyright Act, no less than 1,885*l.*, while Mr. Murray had lost in the same period, 1,275*l.* It was stated that the delivery of 11 copies of only 5 works, including Dugdale's Monasticon, and the History of St. Paul's would occasion a loss of 2,198*l.* and 11 copies of Dodwell's Scenes, at the trade price, would be worth 275*l.* Under these circumstances, the prayer was the repeal of the act.

The petition was brought up, laid upon the table, and ordered to be printed.

PENITENTIARY.

In a Committee of Supply, among other sums, 60,000*l.* were moved for towards finishing the Penitentiary at Millbank, and 21,000*l.* for the expences of the expences of the establishment, both which were carried, after some conversations between Mr. Long, Ald. Wood, and other members. Also 50,000*l.* for completing the Caledonian Canal, between Inverness and Fort William.

TRIAL BY BATTLE.

The Attorney-General's bill for abolishing trial by battle, was read a third time and passed. Sir R. Wilson and Ald. Wood opposed the suppression of the right of appeal, but were not supported.

POOR LAWS.

March 25.—Mr. S. Bourne, in introducing his bill to regulate the settlement of the poor, observed, that it might be necessary to render the subject perfectly intelligible, that he should treat it somewhat historically: the first statute establishing a compulsory assessment for the poor, was the 14th Elizabeth, and it was further regulated by the 43d Elizabeth, and the law remained unaltered until the 13th and 14th Car. II. which was in truth the foundation of the superstructure which had spread so wide, and excited so much dissatisfaction. It was required, among other things, by this last statute, that before settlement could be gained by a pauper, by a residence of 40 days, he must give notice in the church of his coming to reside. This enactment imposed heavy fetters on the free circulation of labour, and by an act of William III. certificates from parish officers were substituted. As these certificates were granted, or refused, merely at the option of the overseers, the evil was only partially removed; and down to a very late date, and through what were called the best times, it had continued in the power of the parish officers to remove any labourer or family, without cause assigned, from one end of the kingdom to the other. This immense power was, [however, partly restrained by Mr. Rose's bill for the encouragement of friendly societies, in 1793, and further limited by Mr. East's act of 1795, which, although making a most important change, and doing more for the benefit of the lower classes than had been accomplished since the Revolution, had passed *sub silentio*, without any expression of national gratitude. Notwithstanding the great reduction in the wages of the poor within the last few years had had the effect of reducing things to nearly the same condition as before 1795 ; and the intricacies in which settlements were involved were all restored. The evils attending the present system were threefold: 1. The enormous expences incurred by parishes, in prosecuting or defending appeals, and in removing paupers; 2. The injustice under which parishes laboured, to which old paupers were sent back, after they had spent their youth and strength elsewhere; 3. The hardship upon the paupers, who, having resided many years and formed connexions at a distance, were sent home to their parishes, and separated from all their friends and consolations, to die in a remote poorhouse. This last was by far the greatest evil. What he proposed was, that as settlement was now gained by residence combined with other circumstances, in future it should be acquired by residence only, and the difficulty was to fix what period of residence should confer a settlement. In the bill he should introduce, he should propose that three years' residence in a parish should gain a settlement to a pauper. A separation of an aged pauper from his friends and neighbours would then be avoided; provided within a certain period he went before a magistrate, and made oath to his residence. In case of dispute, he proposed that an appeal should lie, not to the quarter sessions, but to two magistrates, by which much expen-

sive litigation would be spared. Another point to be settled should be, what period of absence should defeat the settlement : he should suggest that the blank should be filled up with 90 days. This question, however, might be more precisely settled in the Committee. This was the general outline of the measure which he had to submit. He should now therefore conclude by moving for leave to bring in a bill to regulate the settlement of the poor.

Mr. Atkyns · Wright feared that the principle of allowing parties to gain a settlement for themselves by residence, would be attended with many mischievous consequences.

Mr. Curwen declared, that the general outline of the measure corresponded with his own ideas of what might be beneficially done upon this branch of the subject. To him it appeared equally cruel and unjust to refuse a settlement to those whom long service or residence in a particular place had inspired with a desire of obtaining it. If the bill which had already passed the House, should become a law, he did not see how they could withhold their sanction from the present. The bill would likewise tend greatly, in his opinion, to diminish litigation.

Mr. Western was decidedly in favour of the principle of the bill, its object being, as he understood, to facilitate to the labourer, the means of carrying his industry to the most advantageous market, and to prevent his being torn from the place where he found it his interest or his happiness to reside. So far the measure had his approbation—it would render the inquiry before a magistrate simple and easy of determination, and must necessarily put an end to a great deal of the existing system of litigation. At the same time he was not prepared to say, that it would not open other sources of litigation, and give rise to fresh difficulties in practice. He knew no satisfactory reason why the poor should not be permitted, without the forfeiture of any legal benefit, to repair from one place to another, according to the demand for their labour. Leave was given to bring in the bill.

MISAPPLICATION OF POOR-RATES.

Mr. S. Bourne then rose to move for leave to introduce another measure directed also to the amendment of the Poor laws. This bill had been under the consideration of the last Parliament, but there had not been sufficient time for correcting and modifying its objectionable clauses. This he hoped would be now found to have been done, and that it was not ill calculated to produce its end, which was to prevent a very considerable misapplication of the poor's-rates. The House must be well aware that one of the greatest evils arising out of the present system, was the payment of the wages of labour out of those rates. A man with, perhaps, a family of six children, represented to the parish officers that he was not able to maintain more than two. By the acts of Elizabeth and of George I. there was a case in which the children above the number of two, ought to be set to work in the parish workhouse; but under all the circumstances, it was not surprising that this practice should not be resorted to: the bill was intended to provide for placing these children to work and sustaining them, instead of giving to their parents a relief which was often squandered and not applied to the benefit of the children. This conduct of parents was not, indeed, of new occurrence; it had been remarked in the reign of William III. by Mr. Locke, who had recommended the regulation adopted in the present measure. The experiment had been made in some parishes, and the applications for relief had become less numerous. One advantage would certainly be gained in the due application of the funds, and a third and more material one would be realized in those parishes where charitable institutions existed, by placing the children in schools where industry might be combined with education. He thought it must be an overstrained humanity which would urge that there was any thing harsh in separating the children from parents who could not feed, and much less educate them. It must be recollected that persons in a higher sphere of life, place their offspring at some distance from their home, for the purpose of instruction, and not unfrequently send them out of the realm. The bill would also provide, that no relief should for the future be given to any able bodied labourer in employment—a provision, which, he hoped, would point out the necessity of granting him more adequate wages.

Mr. Mansfield said, he should certainly feel it his duty to object to the latter provision of the bill. He had been that day

attending a Committee, before whom a case was proved, of a great number of labourers, the best of whom by working 15 or 16 hours a day could not earn above 7s. a week.

An hon. Member, whose name we could not learn, made a few observations, which were distinctly audible in the gallery.

Mr. Ricardo thought, that the two great evils for which it was desirable to provide a remedy, were, the tendency towards a redundant population, and the inadequacy of the wages to the support of the labouring classes: and he apprehended that the evils now proposed would not afford any security against the continuance of these evils.

After a few observations from Mr. J. Maxwell, leave was granted to bring in the bill.

FRIENDLY SOCIETIES.

Mr. T. Courtenay rose to move, pursuant to the notice which he had given on a former evening, for leave to bring in a bill for the further encouragement and protection of Friendly Societies. He thought there was no necessity for shewing that the existing regulations respecting these societies were very defective. Of late years it had been said by high authority, that to encourage poor people to lay by their earnings under an ensurance of this nature, was a bad thing ; and that those whose property was very small should not enter into a mutual guarantee. He thought the reverse; and if he might be allowed, he would illustrate his opinion by what was familiar to him professionally. He who had great property, and only a small portion of it embarked in an enterprise, did not ensure ; but he who had his all embarked, however small it might be, would be unwise if he did not ensure it. He wished the house to understand, that all he contended for was, to allow those who chose to secure their earnings in this manner, as others did in saving banks. It was a great satisfaction for him to know, that he who was entitled to the greatest praise from his country for his exertions in the establishment of savings banks, and who had published a book on the subject, had declared his opinion of the total incompetency of savings banks alone ; but had proposed to him, before the Committee on the poor-laws', that they should be united to friendly societies. He alluded to Mr. Duncan, who might indeed be called the father of savings banks. It was objected by some, that the meetings of these societies in public-houses induced them to spend a great deal of money. If the accounts were to be examined by the quarter-sessions, it would be easy to prevent this; but for his part, he was not for depriving them of those convivial meetings, which were thought necessary to every charitable institution.

Leave was granted to bring in a bill.

Mr. T. Courtney also obtained leave to bring in a bill for the establishment of parochial benefit societies.

BANKRUPT LAWS.

April 2.—Mr. J. Smith, in moving the second reading of the Bankrupt Laws' Amendment Bill, stated, that his first great object would be to take such a proper care of the bankrupts' property, as to ensure the creditors, as well as the bankrupt himself, against that loss which they now so frequently sustained from the manner of proving debts. A great object would also be, to do away the facility with which fraudulent bankrupts could at present obtain their certificates; to alter the law which inflicted the punishment of death in many instances of fraud under these acts, and to ensure an adequate allowance to the bankrupt himself on the dividend. The want of such regulations had been complained of in several petitions, and was proved before the Committee in 1817. The Committee then proceeded to examine several respectable merchants and traders of the metropolis, and also solicitors, a great part of whose business was connected with bankrupt commissions; and from all they received the concurring opinions, that the present state of the bankrupt laws was wholly inefficient to their object. In the next year the Committee had the testimony of some of the most experienced of the Commissioners, Mr Montague, Mr. Cullen, and some others, who all agreed that the laws were insufficient. Mr. Smith then proceeded to offer remarks upon several points in detail. The first was to define accurately who were and who were not subject to the laws of bankruptcy, from which he would exempt those whose subsistence depended chiefly on mental and manual labour, as artists, artizans, attornies, &c. and others, whose dealings did not usually require credit by means of bills of exchange, &c. In the next place Mr. Smith would make stoppage of payment for seven days (except in cases of sudden illness) or absence from business without providing for such payment, omitting to put in bail, or remaining 14 days in prison, acts of bankruptcy. He wished to guard against conspiracies among the friends or creditors of the bankrupt, and to protect assignees against them. He proposed to strengthen the powers of Commissioners, to enforce order in the meetings, and to allow them to strike out any debt, even after proving, that appeared to them unjust. He proposed also to assist the assignees by appointing an agent (as in Scotland) to make up and examine the bankrupt's books, called debts, &c. The capital punishment affixed to concealment, he would repeal, as by its severity it often deterred creditors from prosecuting. He would farther empower Commissioners to look into the bankrupt's affairs previous to failure, and punish gross extravagance by withholding his certificate.

Mr. Smith wished farther to guard against the too common practice of perjury in hiring persons to prove fictitious debts, who afterwards signed the certificate as *bona fide* creditors. On the other hand he would grant to all bankrupts an allowance, in proportion to their dividend, and a farther allowance for their trouble in assisting to collect debts, so as to make it every bankrupt's interest to be honest. He wished to protect, not only Commissioners but Messengers in the performance of their respective duties; but he gave up the idea of allowing to the Commissioners any fixed salaries, as he found it generally disapproved.

Mr. Abercromby, Sir J. Newport, and Mr. Ald. Waithman said a few words in support of the general principle, and the great zeal and diligence of the hon. mover in preparing it. The bill was then read a second time and referred to a Committee of the House.

POOR OF IRELAND.

April 6.—Sir J. Newport proposed the revival of a Committee, to enquire into the state of disease, and of the Poor in Ireland. The ravages of disease had for the 2 or 3 last years been quite unprecedented in Ireland. During the last 12 months 3500 individuals had been admitted into the hospital of the place which he himself represented; and in the hospitals of Dublin, Cork, and Waterford there had been no less than 43,000 patients during the last 15 months. The resources to which their late Committee had applied for relief, had produced great benefit ; and he therefore hoped that the House would resort to it again, engrafting upon it such improvement as they think just and proper. One of the objects which he had in view was the proper application of labour to the cultivation of bogs and morasses, which were so common in the central parts of Ireland. It appeared from the report on this subject, that there were no less than 2,830,000 acres in this condition, of which 1,000,000 had been snrveyed, levelled, and reported by the Commissioners. If any act therefore could be proposed to enable individuals to reap advantage from this waste land, it would be a great point gained to the general prosperity of the country and its inhabitants. In certain districts, whose population amounted to 3,840,000 inhabitants, the number of persons engaged in agriculture was to that of the persons engaged in manufactures and handicraft trade, as 488,000 to 164,000. If, therefore, it can be shown that one million of acres can be brought into cultivation, a great relief would be given to the agricultural part of the population.

Mr. C. Grant, jun. seconded the motion as one of the utmost importance. He considered the ravages of fever as arising from their low diet, and want of fuel. They had however been greatly relieved by a grand impulse of general benevolence. The clergy of the established church had distinguished themselves by the most exemplary exertions, and the Catholic priesthood had not been found inferior to their Protestant brethren. One instance had fallen within the sphere of his own knowledge. A Catholic priest was called upon to visit a small cabin, in which six individuals were lying, all violently affected with the typhus fever The priest had no other means of receiving the dying man's communications, than by throwing himself on the wretched pallet upon which the sick man lay, and thus inhaling contagion from its source. The conduct of the medical profession was also beyond all praise : men of rising talent and celebrity had devoted themselves to an exclusive and gratuitous attention to the poor. Nor was this philanthropy and benevolence confined to them alone. A gentleman of the name of Mahony, at Cork, had watched nights and days by the bed-sides of the wretched sufferers, who were too poor to pay for nurses. Many landed proprietors had done the same, and had received a noble return in the gratitude of their tenantry. Those who had been absent from their

estates, had lost an opportunity which he hoped would not soon occur again under similar circumstances, of fixing themselves in the affections of their dependents ; and were as deserving of pity, for the love which they had lost, as resident proprietors were of envy for the gratitude which they had obtained.

After a few words of approbation from several other members, the motion was agreed to, and the Committee appointed.

BIOGRAPHICAL MEMOIRS OF EMINENT PERSONS DECEASED.

March 30. At the advanced age of 81, SIR WALTER FARQUHAR, Bart. Physician to his Royal Higness the Prince Regent, and for a long period distinguished by his consummate skill and ability in the medical practice. He was, if possible, still more distinguished for those domestic virtues which marked through a long life, in an eminent degree, his valuable character. As a son, he was a pattern of filial piety ; a most affectionate brother, an exemplary and tender husband, a father almost adored by his children, for his wisdom and goodness ; a warm and steady friend, scarce to be equalled, in his exertions of kindness, or to bring forward merit wherever he found it. He was the patron of the friendless ; and distress, even accompanied by error, was never disregarded by him. More free from frailty himself than most men, he was charitable and lenient in his judgment of others; and although always doing some good, declining the praise attached to it.

Feb. 4, 1819. At his house in Dean Street, Soho, in the 32d year of his age, Mr. GEORGE HENRY HARLOW, Portrait and Historical Painter. He had recently returned from Italy. He was in the bloom of life, and possessed a genius for the Art of Painting, which it is no extravagant panegyric to say, had few equals, and still fewer living superiors. During his whole life, it was Mr. Harlow's custom to sketch at the moment every thought that occurred to him, and seemed deserving of being so embodied. He thus accumulated port folios of treasures, the materials for almost every emergency. A practice of collecting and, as it were, realizing ideas in this way, cannot be too much recommended either to artists. or authors. His first Historical picture piece was Bolingbroke's entry into London, which was never exhibited. The first which was exhibited at the Royal Academy, (except the portrait of his mother, was the quarrel between Elizabeth and her favorite Essex, in which Majesty so far forgot itself as to strike a subject. We do not remember any other subject in the higher walks of art, between this, which was painted ten or twelve years ago, and the Hubert and Prince Arthur which was at the British Gallery about four years since.

The splendid picture of the Kemble family, in the characters of Katherine, King Henry, Wolsey, &c. was originally begun on a small scale, but the Artist became so enamoured of his theme as he proceeded, that he enlarged his plan, and produced the present admirable work, which he consigned to Mr. Welsh, the composer for 100 guineas. The last great work exhibited by Mr. Harlow, was Christ healing the woman who had an issue of blood. It possessed great merit, though not on the whole so fine as some of his former efforts. Mr. H. obtained a well earned and high reputation by his unrivalled portraits upon a small scale. Those of Mr. West and Mr. Northcote will be long remembered as chef-d'œuvres. His talents seem to be unbounded, and with the exception of landscape, we are not acquainted with any branch of the art in which he did not excel.

On the 22d of June, 1818, Mr. Harlow set out on a tour of improvement, to Italy; and re-landed at Dover the 13th of January 1819. This, but for its termination, was to him a fortunate and glorious journey. In Italy he made many friends, and received many honors from the various Academies. During this short interval of absence he made an entire copy of the Transfiguration, and executed a composition of fifteen figures of his own conception, which was at the request of the celebrated Canova publickly exhibited at his own house, and afterwards at the Academy of St. Luke's. Soon after Mr. Harlow's arrival in town he was seized with the malady commonly called the mumps. At first it did not threaten any consequence more serious than a few days confinement at home, but perhaps from an anxiety to get rid of so unpleasant an external appearance, at an important period for active exertion, the disease was checked and thrown inward. It speedily assumed a dangerous aspect, and at length ulcerated so as to preclude the possibility of administering nourishment of any kind, and even to prevent utterance.

* * * * * * * * * * *

March 3, 1819, at Manheim, in his 48th year, by the hand of the Assassin Sandt, the celebrated AUGUSTUS VON KOTZEBUE. He was born at Weimar, where his father was Secretary of Legation, in the service of the Duke, and where his mother still lives. He was remarkable when quite a child for his vivacity and sensibility, and was not yet six years of age when he made his first attempts at poetry. His love of the dramatic art was early excited by the then very good company of players at Weimar, in which were the families of Seiler, Brandes, Boeckh, and Eckhof. At this period Kotzebue attended the Gymnasium, where Musæus, afterwards his uncle, obtained great influence over him by his instructions and example. He was not quite sixteen years old when he went to the university at Jena, where his love for the drama found new encouragement in a private theatre. From attachment to his sister, who married in Duisburg, he went for a time to the university there; whence he returned, in 1779, to Jena, studied jurisprudence, without however ceasing to live for the theatre, and to compose various pieces. He soon after passed his examination, and became an Advocate. He now enjoyed the entire friendship of the worthy Musæus, and attempted, as he had already done, with Wieland, Goethe, Hermes, and Brandes, to imitate Musæus, an example of which is his "I, a History in Fragments." At Leipsig he printed a volume of Tales, and went thence in 1781 to St. Petersburgh, whither he was invited by Count Goerz, Prussian Ambassador at that court. He became secretary to the Governor-general Bawr; and the latter being charged with the direction of the German theatre, Kotzebue was again in his element. His first dramatic work, Demetrius Iwanowitsch, was performed with great applause in the German theatre at St. Petersburgh, in 1782. His "Sufferings of the Ortenberg family" (1785,) and "The collection of his smaller Essays" (1787,) first shewed in a brilliant manner his agreeable and diversified style; but it was especially his two plays, "Misanthropy and Repentance," and "The Indians in England," which gained the poet the highest reputation in all Germany. His ill health obliged him, in 1790, to make a journey to Pyrmont, where is ill-famed "Doctor Bahrdt with the Iron Forehead," which he published under the name of Knigge, lost him a great part of the esteem which the public had conceived for him. After the death of his wife he went to Paris, and then for a time to Mentz. He then obtained his discharge, and retired, in 1795, to the country, where he built the little country seat of Friedenthal, eight leagues from Narva, in Esthonia. The "Youngest Children of my Humour," and above twenty plays, belong to this period. He was then invited to Vienna, as poet to the Court theatre. Here he published a great part of his "New Plays," which fill above twenty volumes. As various unpleasant circumstances disgusted him with his place at Vienna, he requested his discharge, after an interval of two years, and obtained it, with an annual pension of 1000 florins. He now went to live again at Weimar, but resolved to return to Russia, where his sons were educated in the Academy of Cadets, at St. Petersburg. Baron von Krudener, the Russian Ambassador at Berlin, gave him the necessary passport; but he was arrested on the Russian frontiers (April 1800,) and, without knowing for what reason, sent to Siberia; a happy chance delivered him. A young Russian, of the name of Krasnopulski, had translated into the Russian language Kotzebue's little drama, "The Body Coachman of Peter the Third," which is an indirect eulogium of Paul I. The translation was shewn in MS. to the Emperor Paul, who was so delighted with the piece, that he immediately gave orders to fetch back the author from his banishment, and distinguished him on his return with peculiar favour. Among other things he made him a present of the fine domain of the crown, of Worrokull, in Livonia; gave him the direction of the German theatre, and the title of Auric Counsellor. M. von

Kotzebue has given a romantic account of his banishment, well known all over Europe under the title of "The most remarkable Year of my Life." After the death of Paul I. Kotzebue requested his discharge, and obtained it, with a higher title. He went to Weimar, where he lived a short time, and then to Jena. Various misunderstandings which he had with Goethe, vexed him so much, that he went in 1802 to Berlin, where he joined with Merkel to publish the Journal called Der Freymuthige. Kotzebue and Merkel wrote against Goethe and his adherents, Augustus, William Schlegel and Frederick Schlegel; and as M. Spazier, at that time editor of the "Journal for the Fashionable World," espoused the cause of the latter, there arose a very violent paper war. A more serious consequence of the misunderstandings between Kotzebue and Goethe was the removal of the Literary Journal of Jena to Halle, and the establishment of a new Literary Journal at Jena. In 1806 he went, for the purpose of writing the history of Prussia, to Konigsberg, where he was allowed to make use of the archives. His work on the history of Prussia, published at Riga, 1809, in four volumes, is certainly not an historical masterpiece, but deserves attention, particularly for the original documents printed in it. The year 1806, so unfortunate for the Prussian monarchy, obliged him to go to Russia, where he never ceased to combat the French and their Emperor with all the arms which a writer possessed of so much wit could command particularly in his journal "The Bee." The public in Germany were the more eager after his published works, as the French hardly permitted a free or bold expression to be uttered in Germany. As under these circumstances his political writings had excited a very high degree of attention, he appeared, on the great change in the political affairs of Europe in 1813, to be peculiarly qualified to maintain among the people their hatred of the French. Raised to the rank of Counsellor of State, he attended the Russian head-quarters, and published at Berlin a Journal, called "The Russian and German Journal for the People." In the year 1814, he went to Konigsberg as Russian Consul-General in the Prussian dominions, where, besides several political pamphlets, comedies and little dramas, he wrote a history of the German Empire, which is said to be very partial. In 1816 he was placed as Councellor of State in the Department of Foreign Affairs in St. Petersburg, and in 1817 received the commission to go to Germany, in order to send reports directly to the Emperor Alexander, on the State of Literature and Public Opinion in Germany. He settled, for this purpose, at Weimar, where he published at the same time a Literary Journal, in which he constituted himself judge of all writings in every branch of literature which he thought worthy of notice, and at the same time delivered his opinions on politics and on the spirit of the times in a manner which his opponents accuse of being in the extreme partial and illiberal. His Cossack-like tactics, say they, with which he made war on all liberal ideas, especially the wishes of the people for representative constitutions, freedom of the press, &c. in the name of sound reason, of which he fancied himself the representative, gained him great applause with a certain class of readers. But it drew upon him the indignation of no inconsiderable part of the nation, particularly the ardent minds of the German youth; and in this tendency of his latest literary labours, we must doubtless look for the chief cause of his violent and tragical death.

. . . .

April 25, 1819, at Paris, FRANCISCO MANUEL, the celebrated Portuguese Poet, at the age of 84. From his earliest youth he had successfully cultivated almost every branch of literature. Having profoundly studied the best Portuguese classical authors, his works were imbued with a portion of their beauties, and his literary productions helped to revive among his countrymen a taste for the noblest studies. His odes which are full of enthusiasm, are remarkable for bold traits and sublime flights of genius. In his translation of La Fontaine's Fables he overcame difficulties which were before thought insurmountable owing to his perfect knowledge of the French and Portuguese languages. Unfortunately, it is met with respect to talent only, that he may be compared to other celebrated poets; fame smiled more kindly on him than fortune. The Marquis de Marialva, the Portuguese ambassador to the French Court, whose kind patronage Manuel had long enjoyed, befriended him in his last illness, and afforded him all the assistance that might be expected from his benevolent disposition, and his love of literature and the fine arts.

. . . .

Jan. 13, 1819, at his house in Somer's Town, in his 81st year, Dr. JOHN WOLCOTT, well known to the literary world under the name of *Peter Pindar.* It is needless to expatiate on the character of his works as they are universally known. Nature has seldom afforded a more original genius, and his mind was stored with various knowledge. He was well acquainted with the Greek language, and was a sound scholar in Latin. He spoke French with facility, and had made considerable progress in Italian. He drew his imagery from Nature and Life, which he had observed with vigilance and accuracy. Perhaps hardly any Poet since Shakspeare has illustrated his works with more abundant allusions derived from the sources of Nature. He had seen much of the world in various parts, and excelled in the imitation as well as delineation of character. His satirical humour was exuberant; and in reference to our revered Sovereign, it is impossible to palliate, or rather, not strongly to reprobate, the freedom, to use the mildest word, which he took with the Royal Character; but such is the ignorance, malevolence, and bad taste of the world, that his works were more popular on that account than for the original humour, wit, tenderness, and often sublimity, by which they are characterized. He never attacked any person after he became acquainted with him. He retained his faculties to the last, and was able, till within a very few days of his death, to dictate verses from his bed, which were strongly marked by his former strength and humour.

He was a sound critic in poetry and painting; and his sketches of landscape evinced a degree of taste which, if poetry had not engrossed so much of his attention, might have rendered him no inferior artist.

LIST OF PATENTS.

Augustus Applegarth, of Nelson-square, Great Surrey-street, Surrey, Printer, for certain improvements in the art of casting stereotype or other plates for printing, and in the construction of plates for printing bank or bankers' notes, or other printed impressions, where difficulty of imitation is a desideratum, April 23, 1818.

Edward Lillie Bridgman, of Goswell-street-road, St. Luke's, Middlesex, Tallow-chandler; for certain improvements in making coffins, and in machines for conveying coffins for interment, and appendages to the same in the church and burial grounds, April 23, 1818.

George Tyer, of Homerton, Middlesex, Gentleman; for a chain-pump, May 2, 1818.

Joshua Rowe, of Torpoint, Cornwall, Merchant; for certain improvement or improvements, or process or processes applicable to the printing of cotton and other cloths, and to other purposes, May 4, 1818.

Sir Thomas Cochrane, Knight, commonly called Lord Cochrane; and Alexander Galloway, of Holborn, Middlesex, Engineer; for the working or making a manufacture, being a machine or machines for removing the inconvenience of smoke or gases generated in stoves, furnaces, or fire-places by the ignition or combustion of coals or other inflammable substances, and in certain cases for directing the heat, and applying such smoke or gases to various useful purposes, which will be of great public utility, May 4, 1818.

Thomas Jones, of Bradford-street, Birmingham, Warwickshire, Iron-founder, and Charles Plimley, of Birmingham, aforesaid, Refiner; for an improvement to blast engines and steam engines, May 7, 1818.

William Bush, the younger, of Bermondsey, Surrey, Engineer; for an improvement in the method of drying and preparing of malt, wheat and other grain, May 5, 1818.

Wolf Benjamin, of Plymouth-dock, Devonshire, Umbrella-manufacturer; for a composition varying in colour, with a peculiar method of applying, for the pur-

pose of rendering canvass, linen, and cloth durable, pliable, free from cracking, and water-proof; and also for preserving every kind and description of wood from wind or weather, whether applied to ships, houses, or manufactories, and for all purposes where paint, varnish, or tar are used for the purpose of preservation or beauty, and whether applied to cannon or or iron of every description, May 5, 1818.

Thomas Todd, of Swansea, Glamorganshire, Organ-Builder; for certain improvements in rolling of iron, and making wire, nails, brads, and screws, May 7, 1818.

William Church, of Turner-street, Commercial-road, Gentleman; for certain improvements in or upon the machinery for making nails and spikes of various forms and dimensions, and also wire and screws of iron, copper, brass, or any other suitable metal, May 7, 1818.

Henry Constantine Jennings, of Carburton-street, Fitzroy-square, St. Marylebone, Middlesex, Esq.; for an improvement in the mariner's compass, May 7, 1818.

Robert Eccles, of Edinburgh, Esquire; for certain improvements in the masts, sails, and rigging of ships or sailing vessels, May 9, 1818.

Thomas Brown Milnes, of Lenton, Nottinghamshire, Bleacher; for certain improvements on machinery for the finishing of Cotton, Angola, and lamb's-wool stockings, and other frame-work goods; also the application of known powers to the working of the said machinery, May 19, 1819.

Maurice St. Leger, of St. Giles's, Camberwell, Surrey, Gentleman; for an improved method of making lime, May 19, 1819.

Thomas Hills, of Bromley, Middlesex, Merchant, and Uriah Haddock, of the City-terrace, City-road, Middlesex, Chemist; for an improvement in the manufacture of sulphuric acid, May 19, 1819.

Thomas Motley, of the Strand, Middlesex, Patent Letter Manufacturer, one of the people called Quakers, for certain improvements on ladders, May 19, 1819.

John Dyson, of Watford, Hertfordshire; for certain apparatus for the culture and tillage of land, May 26, 1818.

profess to be most enamoured of the comforts and enjoyments of the " good old times."

The Agricultural interest, will, doubtless, think hardly, of the tax on Malt ; but then the Agricultural interest has obtained, what our pages witness it has been many years soliciting, a tax on Foreign Wool imported. If it were just in Lord Sheffield, and those who thought with him, to desire this tax, let them calculate whether the benefits they formerly professed to expect from it, do not preponderate against the probable consequences of the additional tax on malt.

To come to plain figures:—the Chancellor of the Exchequer finding the combination forming what is technically called " the Jew's list," becoming unmanageable, not to say, too formidable, has proposed to take half a loan of £24,000,000. for the services of the present year, from the Commissioners of the Sinking Fund ; thereby rendering the very extensive preparations of the Jews (who had reckoned on nearly double the amount) completely useless. They had reduced the price of stocks very low, in order to make the better bargain ; they had disposed of all their stocks, and refused to buy, insomuch that they borrowed one of another, to enable them to deliver stocks to which they were bound—but, in vain; the loan instead of being £36,000,000. is only £12,000,000. and thus the Jews are *Jew'd !!!*

Besides this, the Chancellor of the Exchequer, knowing that temporary expedients are not calculated for durability, has determined to adopt a more effective system of finance ; and having made free with the Sinking Fund, on one hand, he has determined to strengthen it on the other hand. The surplus of the Sinking Fund, under the management already hinted at, was about £2,000,000.; and the Minister proposed to raise it to *five millions,* annually, by laying on taxes to the amount of *three millions,* on the following articles :—

	£
Consolidation of Customs, including duty on Wool	500,000
Additional Duty on Malt	1,400,000
on British Spirits	500,000
on Tobacco	500,000
Additional on Coffee and Cocoa	130,000
on Tea	130,000
on Pepper	30,000
Total	3,190,000

Very little of this *ought* to be felt by the poor: nor will the prices of the articles rise so high, generally speaking, as they were during the war.

The internal regulation of the kingdom proceeds; *some* progress has been made in that difficult question, the Poor laws, by regulating the qualifications of settlement. The Catholic question is at rest, for the session; and, though decided by a very small majority in the Commons, yet was opposed by a very considerable one in the Lords. The Bank affairs have, also, met with their ultimate regulation.

The Government has determined to preserve, if possible—we doubt the possibility—a perfect neutrality between the contending Spanish provinces in South America and the Mother Country. We are by no means easy on this subject: we see no escape from arbitrary power, either on the right hand or on the left. We regret, exceedingly, the blood shed, and the cruelties committed, on both sides; and if there be any truth in the report that a descendant of Montezuma has made his appearance in the province of Mexico, it is by no means calculated to diminish our regret. The name will have great influence among the Indians,—hitherto disregarded by both the Royalists and the Insurgents,—although, in fact, the chief who assumes it, should have no nearer relation to Montezuma than Buonaparte had to Charlemagne.

The Negro Empire of Hayti will always furnish an example not to be lost on the transatlantic world; and America, (the United States) has had a proof of this, in a plan laid by the Negroes of Georgia to massacre their masters, and set up for themselves: in short, no reason can be alledged, if liberty be worth struggling for, why the Negroes, Slaves, of North America, or the Indians, long oppressed, in South America, should not struggle for liberty, as well as their masters who have European blood in their veins.

We told our countrymen, freely, that those who ventured to South America, must expect to meet, in the climate, an enemy that gives no quarter. We understand, that of eight hundred English troops which had arrived there, one in four had died almost immediately.

It is said, that beside the cession of Florida to America by Spain, Spain has offered to cede Cuba to Britain. The acquisition would certainly be favourable to our interests; but, it would have consequences, not distant from what we have been hinting at, supposing it to be true; for which we do not vouch.

Not only the negroes of St. Domingo, and Georgia, with the Indians of Mexico, have felt their spirit stirring, but, the Caffres and the Bushmen of South Africa have taken arms, and have made inroads on the settlements of the Europeans. They have considered all the cattle possessed by their neighbours as fraudulently obtained from their true and rightful owners—themselves—and have swept off the whole.

Scarcely are we suffered to breathe from the calamity of Pindaree warfare, when our attention is called to Caffre hostilities. It must be so, where a state has numerous colonies: perhaps, the issue may prove, that as the Cape formerly assisted India: so India may now assist the Cape. The consequences are not of difficult divination.

We shall not on this occasion do more than advert to the state of Europe generally. The King of France has lent himself to the recall of those marked characters whose temper and principles paid no respect to Royal blood: we wish him well; but we augur no good from this.

The King of Spain has been busying himself in prohibiting certain books from the perusal of his loyal subjects : bad books are bad things: few things are worse: yet, we are no friends to prohibitions, unless consequent on the verdict of a jury.

The King of Prussia has met with an accident that perhaps may disfigure his face for life: it happened while amusing himself at one of those (lately fashionable at Paris) *divertisemens,* called Russian mountains. Kings should be cautious as well in their sports and pastimes, as at their Council boards.

The Emperor of Austria has employed a few weeks of leisure in visiting his Italian dominions, also Rome, Naples, &c. If his Majesty has exerted the same spirit of observation as the Grand Dukes did in England, his subjects, as well as himself, will profit by his excursion.

The King of Saxony will probably give a Queen to Spain, in the person of a princess of his family.

The disputes between Sweden and Denmark on the subject of *meum* and *tuum,* it is understood, are compromised: Denmark does not get all she wished, but gets it sooner than she expected.

And now, having run over so great a portion of the globe, on what part of it shall we fix, as capable of affording a greater share of human good than a certain little island affords? placed geographically in the temperate zone, rarely visited with those pestilential distempers which at this moment are hurrying their thousands to the grave, in some places; yielding the necessaries of life in no niggardly portion, raised by arts and sciences to an enviable height in the scale of nations, fearing nothing from external foes, at peace with all parts of the globe, and in all parts of the globe respected as an ally, confided in as a merchant, or esteemed as a friend:—no: we shall not forsake Britain; British people may forsake themselves;—but, their *wisdom !!!* shall have no sanction or support from the LITERARY PANORAMA.

Commercial Chronicle.

STATE OF TRADE.

Lloyd's Coffee House, June 20, 1819.

The State of Trade has been considerably slack, for some time past, owing to a variety of causes. The most public cause was the unsettled state of affairs between the Bank and the Community at large. While those affairs were pending, and before they had assumed that shape on which opinion might be formed, and arguments might be founded, the mercantile world were in uncertainty as to what accommodation it might expect, and consequently, as to what accommodation it might afford. Every prudent person would rather keep within, than exceed what he considered his fair and honest power; and he found his security in his caution. It must be added, that not a few of the more adventurous speculators had paid the forfeit of their rashness, and these examples became warnings to others.

At present, the action of those causes has greatly abated. Confidence has never been shaken as to the solidity of the Bank; and now the accommodations granted by that establishment to Commercial men are fully equal to what they have lately been. The public, too, begins to see through the mists which imagination had magnified into thick clouds, and the mountains of difficulty are sunk to prominences, preparatory to their dwindling to mole-hills. The Bank is to have its choice, whether it will pay in *stamped* gold, or in *coined* gold; and we venture to foretell, that very few refiners at the mint will be employed in stamping, and very few porters at the Bullion Office in delivering, ingots of gold, of the magnitude of sixty ounces. The Bank will meet all demands upon it, with a good grace, and current money.

We cannot with equal assurance say the same on the second cause at which we have hinted;—the sufferings of speculators. The accounts of such dealers are not wound up in an instant: as they looked forward to profits, so their creditors must look forward to proceeds. We do not say that all concerns will eventually prove to be total loss; of which, nevertheless, we find ourselves bound to say, they are at the moment, entire suspension. We know several houses, which have recently completed their payments of twenty shillings in the pound; but, the interval of two or three years, or more, since they suspended payments, has been sufficiently, not to say fatally, distressing to tradesmen, and others, whose property was involved in the affairs of such houses.

The Chancellor of the Exchequer has favoured Commerce with a visitation in the shape of new Taxes. It so happens, that at this moment they will little affect the consumer. For instance, TEA is further taxed 4 per cent.: but, an article already taxed 96 per cent. will scarcely feel the addition. And moreover, the Tea Sale, now recently closed, at the India House, has on the whole, gone off lower than the previous average; so that prices will nearly, or altogether, preserve their former level. Much the same may be said on Coffee: the article had suffered a great reduction; and it will not be the effect of the duty, if it reaches its price of some time back. We are given to understand, also, that the price of Beer, is rather kept from falling, to the consumer, than really heightened by the new tax on Malt; so that this season it will not be felt: but what may result from fluctuating harvests, no man will venture to foretell.

We proceed now to notice a few of those more important commodities in which, usually, the greatest changes occur. We have already hinted at the lower prices of Teas, taken generally;—with these we ought to connect the diminished expenses of shipping, freight, &c. compared with what they were during the war. The article may afford equal profit, though sold at reduced prices.

SUGAR has taken a start: the demand has been, for some days, unusually brisk: nor is it yet fully satisfied. The holders expected, and obtained, higher prices; and the cautious were far from being forward to sell. The buyers have so long refrained, that they are now out of stock, and are known to be so. Good qualities —which are rather scarce—were all taken off at a considerable advance, as soon as exposed to sale.

The Refined Market was so inconsiderable in point of shew, and so unable to deliver immediately, that those who had somewhat of quantities, and were fortunate also, in qualities, did business to whatever extent they pleased. The advance on the whole may be stated at 3s. to 4s. per cwt. The home trade has taken off much: and, besides what orders for exportation have already been executed, it is known that there are others in town.

COFFEE has risen in a greater proportion than Sugar. What a few days ago was worth only 95s. or 96s. now fetches 108s. or 109s. The holders are even firm at higher prices; and the request is steady. It is however, to be observed, that caprice has some share in this state of things; and that some qualities have greatly the advantage of others, without any apparent cause, or real difference.

COTTON is beholden at present to export orders for the support of its prices: the sale for home consumption has been but moderate, and in fact, somewhat languid: but, considerable quantities have been transferred, in bond, for immediate shipping. The Manchester trade is dull: and is likely to feel the consequences of this dulness ; owing to circumstances which it might have been hoped would have ceased to operate ere now; but, which certain good natured souls take delight in perpetuating, and exciting from bad to worse. At Liverpool, therefore, Cottons have declined. The supply has not, very lately, been equal to what it was some time ago; and this, with the rumour of a short supply expected from India, will, most likely, produce an effect in favour of such holders as wait a reasonable time.

Government has advertised a Contract for 80,000 gallons of RUM; and suspicion whispers that the quantity taken may eventually prove more extensive. This has benefited the Leewards at market, in greater proportion than the Jamaicas; and somewhat of bustle and enquiry has taken place in consequence. This was increased by means of an expectation of a new import duty on Rum; but that, together with a talked-of additional duty on Sugar, has been suspended. It is, certainly, prudent to wait the effects of the duties fixed on, before others, if dispensable, are finally imposed. If the home manufacture under these additions suffer from the competition of imported goods, those imports must expect to undergo a countervailing charge, in some shape or other,—either by the Customs or by the Excise.

Brandy and Hollands continue much as before. Tobacco is looking forward to a movement; but, this is not so near as to raise the present price.

Hemp continues to give way; and may be stated lower, say 20s. to 40s. Tallow rather rising.

Britain has been called the country of supply; and it is certain that the quantity of manufactured goods she can deliver, is astonishing; but other countries are be-

coming every year more and more countries of supply, or else the imports into Britain could never have been furnished. The wonderful quantity of Cotton imported during last year, is a striking proof of this: say, approaching 700,000 bales: Ships are laden with Cotton to be returned to the East: we are even assured that ships are freighted with Spices to be returned to the East; but, we have not been able to trace the fact.

The quantity of Corn imported last year was about the value of *ten millions sterling*: the countries which have furnished this, are surely countries of supply. There is then, a strong disposition throughout the world to engage in Commerce, and to pay for foreign articles by the exchange of commodities raised at home. This, if we rightly conjecture, will increase. The competition in some things will become more and more animated, and whatever else it produces, probably the perfection of the manufacture will be one result. We have repeatedly inculcated this on the minds of our readers: we repeat it, as the dictate of a judgment founded on no slight grounds:—THE PERFECTION OF THE MANUFACTURE IS THE ONLY MEANS BY WHICH TO MAINTAIN OUR STANDING. As to any other events, which by possibility may rise above the horizon, those who witness them will, very probably, look back to this paper, and compare its date, with what they witness; they will prove, if we guess rightly, of no small importance to the nation, and to National Commerce.

COUNTY OF ESSEX.
Agricultural Report, 24th June, 1819.

Much labour has been bestowed in hoeing and weeding, yet the Fields will be foul at Harvest. The late fine rains have not lessened that inconvenience, yet have been of the greatest use to all Spring Corn. Our Barley and Oats were nearly at a stand, till the recent showers, which came just in time to help them, and many of the early sown Barleys are in the ear. The Wheat is very fine, but notwithstanding the sharp white frosts and cold winds, the lice are getting quite prevalent on the Pease, and should not some storms of lightning and thunder soon ensue, the Beans must likewise suffer. Tares are in abundance, throughout the County. Turnip sowing is generally commenced; the lands in excellent order for the Seed, and all the fallows are in a desirable and husband-like state. The appearance of the Hop bine is mostly promising. Wool is advancing in price.

PRICES CURRENT, *June* 20, 1819.

	£. s.	d.	£. s.	d.
American pot-ash, percwt	0 0	0 to	2 2	0
Ditto pearl	2 12	0	2 14	0
Barilla	1 10	0	0 0	0
Brandy, Cogniac, bond. gal.	0 5	6	0 0	0
Camphire, refined .... lb.	0 4	9	0 5	0
Ditto unrefined ·· cwt.	10 10	0	12 0	0
Cochineal, fine black, lb.	1 10	0	1 11	0
Ditto, East India	0 5	6	0 6	0
Coffee, fine bond cwt.	5 8	0	5 10	0
Ditto ordinary	4 18	0	5 0	0
Cotton Wool, Surinam, lb.	0 1	3	0 1	5
Ditto Jamaica..	0 0	0	0 0	0
Ditto Smyrna ..	0 0	11	0 1	0
Ditto East-India	0 0	6	0 0	8
Currants, Zant .... cwt..	5 0	0	5 10	0
Elephants' Teeth	32 0	0	37 0	0
———— Scrivelloes	21 0	0	30 0	0
Flax, Riga .... ton	75 0	0	0 0	0
Ditto Petersburgh ..	58 0	0	0 0	0
Galls, Turkey .... cwt··	9 0	0	9 10	0
Geneva, Holl. bond. gal.	0 3	0	0 0	0
Ditto, English	0 14	6	0 15	6
Gum Arabic, Turkey, cwt.	9 10	0	12 0	0
Hemp, Riga .... ton	46 0	0	47 0	0
Ditto Petersburgh	42 0	0	43 0	0
Indigo Caraccas .. lb.	0 9	6	0 10	0
Ditto East India	0 8	9	0 9	1
Iron British bars·· ton.	13 0	0	14 0	0
Ditto Swedish c.c.N.D.	21 10	0	22 0	0
Ditto Swed· 2nd sort	16 0	0	17 0	4
Lead in pigs ...... fod	0 0	0	25 10	0
Ditto red ······ ton	0 0	0	27 0	0
Ditto white ...... ton	0 0	0	40 0	0
Logwood ·········· ton	8 10	0	9 0	0
Madder, Dutch crop, cwt.	6 0	0	0 0	0
Mahogany .... ft.	0 1	6	0 2	0
Oil, Lucca·· 24 gal. jar	17 0	0	19 0	0
Ditto Florence, ½ chest	2 10	0	0 0	0
Ditto whale ··········	33 0	0	0 0	0
Ditto spermaceti·· ton	90 0	0	0 0	0
Pitch, Stockholm ·· cwt.	0 11	0	0 0	0
Raisins, bloom .... cwt.	3 15	0	4 0	0
Rice, Carolina bond ····	1 15	6	0 0	0
Rum, Jamaica bond gal	0 2	2	0 2	4
Ditto Leeward Island ··0	2	5	0 2	7
Saltpetre, East India, cwt.	1 13	6	1 17	0
Silk, thrown, Italian, lb.	2 17	0	3 0	0
Silk, ··· raw, ... Ditto··	1 14	0	2 0	0
Tallow, Russia, white ..·	0 0	0	2 19	0
Ditto——, yellow··	3 5	0	0 0	0
Tar, Stockholm .... bar.	1 0	0	1 1	0
Tin in blocks ...... cwt.	0 0	0	4 6	0
Tobacco, Maryland, lb.	0 0	11	0 1	6
Ditto Virginia ······	0 0	7	0 0	10½
Wax, Guinea ...... cwt.	9 0	0	12 0	0
Whale-fins (Greenl) ton	110 0	0	120 0	0
Wine :				
Red Port, bond pipe ··	39 0	0	55 0	0
Ditto Lisbon	38 0	0	44 0	0
Ditto Madeira ········	60 0	0	70 0	0
Ditto Mountain ········	28 0	0	33 0	0
Ditto Cape	18 0	0	26 0	0
Ditto Sherry ······ butt	30 0	0	65 0	0
Ditto Claret	25 0	0	65 0	0

Fire-Office Shares, &c. March 20.

Canals.

	£. s.	£. s.
Coventry .... (Div. 44l.) ..	1008 —	— —
Croydon	4 —	— —
Crinan	2 2	— —
Dudley ····(Div. 2l. 10s.) ·	59 —	— —
Ellesmere and Chester (D.2l.)	68 —	— —
Grand Junction ...(Div. 9l.)..	230 —	— —
Grand Surry	50 —	— —
Ditto (optional) Loan Div. 5l.	94 —	— —
Huddersfield	13 —	— —
Kennett and Avon (Div. 17l.6s.)	21 15	— —
Lancaster	27 5	— —
Leeds and Liverpool (Div 10l.)	345 —	340 —
Oxford ...... Div. 31l.	630 —	— —
Peakforest	60 —	— —
Regents.................	39 —	— —
Stratford & Avon	23 —	— —
Thames and Medway	27 —	— —
Trent & Mersey .. Div. 70l ..	1800 —	— —

Docks.

Commercial ...... Div. 3l. ..	55 —	— —
East India .... Div. 10l.	180 —	— —
East Country	20 —	— —
West India ...... Div. 10l.	182 —	— —

Insurance Companies.

Albion .... Div. £5.···	45 —	— —
Atlas .... Div. 6l.···	4 10	— —
Birmingham Fire	400 —	— —
Eagle ··················	2 12 6	— —
Hope ··················	4 —	— —
Imperial	88 —	— —
London Ship	21 —	— —
Provident ··············	13 —	— —
Royal Exchange·· Div. 10 ..	250 —	225 —
Sun Life	22 10	— —
Union Fire Life · ·· (Div. 6l.)	33 —	— —

Water Works.

Grand Junction	42 —	— —
London Bridge .... Div. 2l. 10s.	58 —	— —
Manchester and Salford	38 —	— —
Portsmouth and Farlington	9 —	— —
South London	20 —	— —
West Middlesex ··········	41 10	— —
York Buildings	24 —	— —

Bridges.

Southwark ··················	55 —	— —
Waterloo	7 —	— —
Ditto Old Annuities Div. 8l. ...	33 —	— —
Ditto New do Div. 7l.	23 —	— —
Vauxhall Bonds .... ·	93 —	— —

Literary Institutions.

London, 75gs.	45 —	— —
Russel, 25gs.	12 —	— —
Surry, 30gs.	10 —	— —

Mines.

Beeralstone Lead and Silver....	9 10	— —
Great Hewas ··········	16 17	— —
British Copper Comp. 2l. 10s...	50 —	— —
Cliff down	5 —	— —
Wheal Goodluck .... 1pr.··	20 —	— —

Roads.

Dover Street	20 10	— —

Miscellaneous.

Auction Mart	21 —	— —
London Corn Sale Rooms	18 —	— —
Golden Lane Brewery .. 80l. sh.	7¾ —	— —
Ditto 50l. Share	12 —	— —

METEOROLOGICAL TABLE.

		8 o'clock Morning	Noon.	11 o'clock Night.	Height of Barom. Inches.	Dryness by Leslie's Barom.	
May.	21	55	59	54	29,52	57	Stormy
	22	56	64	55	,80	47	Fair
	23	58	63	52	,97	50	Fair
	24	55	57	50	,98	0	Rain
	25	50	63	47	,94	39	Fair
	26	50	58	44	,97	36	Cloudy
	27	48	58	46	,87	36	Fair
	28	47	56	45	,95	60	Fair
	29	46	54	44	,99	63	Fair
	30	47	58	49	30,05	58	Fair
	31	49	59	54	,17	52	Cloudy
June.	1	56	62	56	,15	61	Showry
	2	57	68	57	10	66	Fair
	3	58	69	58	,02	60	Fair
	4	59	67	56	29,94	48	Sm. Rain
	5	60	69	56	30,14	66	Fair
	6	60	70	57	,10	68	Fair
	7	56	68	57	29,70	60	Fair
	8	59	69	57	,70	40	Fair
	9	60	69	57	,75	60	Fair
	10	58	66	55	,86	49	Showry
	11	56	68	50	30,05	42	Fair
	12	55	64	55	,08	40	Showry
	13	56	68	54	,04	58	Fair
	14	56	69	53	,02	50	Showry
	15	54	61	52	29,84	0	Rain
	16	54	57	51	30,04	47	Fair
	17	53	67	53	,15	46	Fair
	18	54	60	50	,08	0	Rain
	19	60	70	56	,22	48	Fair
	20	58	68	57	,28	63	Fair

London Premiums of Insurance.

Aberdeen, Dundee, Perth, &c. 10s. 6d to 15s. 9d.
Africa, 2*gs.*
American States, 25*s.* to 30*s.*
Belfast, Cork, Dublin, 12*s.* 8*d* to 15*s* 9*d.*
Brazils, 30*s.* to 35 *s.*
Hamburgh, &c. 10*s.* 6*d* to 12*s.* 6*d.*
Cadiz, Lisbon, Oporto, 15 *s.* 9*d.* to 20*s.*
Canada 2*gs.*
Cape of Good Hope, 2*gs.*
Contantinople, Smyrna, &c. 35*s.*
East-India (Co. ships) 3*gs.*
——— out and home, 6*gs.*
France, 10*s.* 6*d.* to 15*s.* 9*d.*
Gibraltar, 20*s.*
Gottenburgh, 12*s.* 6*d.* to 15*s.* 9*d.*
Greenland, out and home, 3*gs.* to 3½*gs.*
Holland 7*s.* 6*d.* to 12*s.* 6*d.*
Honduras, &c. 2*gs.*
Jamaica, 30*s.*
Leeward Islands, 25*s.*
Madeira, 15*s.* 9*d.* to 20*s.*
Malta, Italian States, &c. 30s.
Malaga, 25s.
Newfoundland, 30*s.*
Portsmouth, Falmouth, Plymouth, 10*s.* 6*d.*
River Plate, 2*gs*
Southern Fishery, out and home, 10*gs.*
Sockholm, Petersburgh, Riga, 15s. 9d.

LONDON MARKETS

PRICE OF BREAD.

The Peck Loaf to weigh 17lb. 6oz. 3s. 5d
The Half ditto ditto 8 11 ......1 8½
The Quar. ditto ditto 4 5 ......0 10¼
The half ditto ditto 2 2¾ 0 5⅛

POTATOES.

Kidney......	8 0 0	Ox Nobles ..	7 0 0
Champions ..	7 0 0	Apple	7 0 0

ONIONS, per Bushel, 2s 0d to 3s 6d

MEAT.

Smithfield, per stone of 8b. to sink the Offal

1819.	Beef s.	Beef d.	mut. s.	mut. d.	veal. s.	veal. d.	pork s.	pork d.	lams s.	lams d.
May. 27 ..	5	8	6	0	7	0	6	8	0	0
June 3 ..	6	4	6	4	7	6	6	6	0	0
10 ..	5	6	5	6	6	6	5	8	0	0
17 ..	5	4	5	4	6	4	5	4	6	8

SUGAR.

Lumps ordinary or large 32 to 40 lbs... 92
Fine or Canary, 24 to 30 lbs. ....
Loaves, fine..........................
Powder, ordinary, 9 to 11lbs.......... 98

COTTON TWIST.

June 19. Mule 1st quality, No. 40 0s. 0d
——————No. 120 0s. 0d
———2d quality, No. 40 0s. 0d
Discount—0 a 0 per cent.

COALS, *delivered at 13s. per chald. advance.*

	Sunderland.	Newcastle.
May 25. ..	33s 0d to 40 0	33s 6d to 41 0
June 2. ..	34s 0 41 0	33s 6d 40 9
8. ..	32s 3 40 9	31s 6d 40 9
16. ..	33s 0 39 9	33s 3d 39 9

LEATHER.

Butts, 50 to 56lb.	22	Calf Skins 30 to 45lb. per doz.	36
Dressing Hides ..	20	Ditto 50 to 70..	—
Crop hides for cut.	20	Seals, Large....	100
Flat Ordinary ..	16		

SOAP; yellow, 86s.; mottled 98s.; curd 102s.
CANDLES; per doz. 12s. 0d.; moulds 13s. 6d.

Course of Exchange.

Bilboa	36	Palermo, per oz	150d.
Amsterdam,	11-11	Leghorn	50¾
Ditto at sight	11-8	Genoa	46
Rotterdam 2-us.	11-12	Venice,	26
Hamb. us. 2½	35	Naples	40¾
Altona us.	35-1	Lisbon	54
Paris, 3d. d.	24-50	Oporto	55
Ditto, 2 us.	24-80	Rio Janeiro	
Madrid	37	Dublin	14½
Cadiz	37-½	Cork	14⅝

Agio Bank of Holland, 2 per cent.

HAY and STRAW.—AT SMITHFIELD.

	Hay. £.	s.	d.	Straw. £.	s.	d.	Clover. £.	s.	d.
May 27..	6	6	0	2	14	0	7	0	0
June 5..	6	6	0	2	14	0	7	0	0
12..	6	4	0	2	16	0	8	0	0
19..	6	0	0	2	16	0	8	0	0

Price of STOCKS, from 21st May, to 20th June, 1819.

1819.	Bank Stock.	3 p. Cent. Reduced.	3 p. Cent. Consols.	4 p. Cent. Consols.	Navy 5 p. Cent.	Irish 5 p. Cent.	Long Annuities.	Imperial 3 p. Cent.	Ditto Annuities.	India Stock.	India Bonds.	South Sea Stock.	Excheq. Bills.	Consols for Acc.
May														
21	237	70¾ 69¼	71⅛ 70½	78¾	104¼	—	18 7-16	68½	—	216	29	—	7p	71½
22	230	68½ 7¾	69⅞ 8½	76¼	104	—	17 3-4	66	—	211	16	—	4	69⅛
24	232	67 66¼	67⅞ 7⅛	75½	102¾	—	17 1-8	64½	—	207	20	—	8	68
25	214	66½ 5½	67⅛ 5⅛	74¼	101½	—	17	—	—	206	5	—	7	67½
26	217	64½ 6½	65 7½	74½	101	—	17 1-16	65	—	205	14	—	1	68
27	221	67½ 6½	68½ 67	75¼	102	—	17 5 16	64⅞	—	—	12	—	1	68½
28	221	66¾ ½	66¼ 7½	74¾	101¼	—	17 1-4	64⅝	—	211	9	—	1	67⅛
29	219½	65⅞	65⅛	73¾	100¾	—	—	—	—	211	9	—	1	66½
31	219	65⅝	66⅞	73¼	100¼	—	—	—	—	211	—	—	1	65⅞
June														
1	219	65½ 5	66⅝ 5⅝	73¼	100¼	—	—	63½	—	211	2	—	1	66⅝
2	218	65⅝ ½	65⅞ 6½	73¼	100¼	—	—	—	—	210	3	73½	1	66½
3	217	65⅞ ⅜	65⅞ 6¼	73¾	100½	—	17 1-4	—	—	210	4	—	4	66½
4	—	65⅝ 69	Shut	—	100¼	—	—	—	—	—	2	—	6	70½
5	230	69¼ 70⅝	—	78½	103⅝	—	18 5-8	—	—	—	1	—	7	71½
7	—	68½ ⅞	—	77	106	—	—	—	—	—	—	—	4	69¾
8	—	69⅛	—	78½	104⅝	—	18 9-16	66½	—	—	2	—	8	70⅜
9	226	70 8½	—	76¾	106½	—	18 5-16	—	—	—	2	—	5	71
10	221	67⅞	—	75⅝	106	—	17 7-8	—	—	—	2	—	4	69½
11	—	69½ 8½	—	77⅝	—	—	—	—	—	—	3	—	2	70½
12	220	67½ 8	—	76⅝	—	—	18 1-16	—	—	—	4	—	8	69½
14	—	68½ ½	—	76⅝	—	—	18 1-8	—	—	—	5	—	5	69½
15	220	68½ 7½	—	76½	—	—	18 1-16	66½	—	—	2	—	2	69½
16	218	67⅞	—	75⅞	104½		17 7-8	—			3			68¾
17	219½	68½ 8	—	76½	104⅝	—	17 15-16	66⅝	—	—	2	—	—	69
18	220	68⅝ ½	—	76⅝	—	—	18 1-16	—	—	—	2	—	—	69⅞
19	—	68⅝ ⅜	—	76⅝	—	—	18 1-16	—	—	—	1	—	—	69⅛

IRISH FUNDS.

	Irish Bank Stock.	Government Debenture 3½ per ct.	Government Stock, 3½ per ct.	Government Debenture 5 per ct.	Government Stock, 5 per ct.	Treasury Bills.	Grand Canal Stock.	Grand Canal Loan, 4 per ct.	Grand Canal Loan, 6 per ct.	City Dublin Bonds.	Royal Canal Loan 6 per cent.	Omnium.
M24	—	—	—	—	—	—	—	—	—	—	—	—
29	—	—	82	106½	—	—	—	76½	—	—	—	
Ju.3	—	79¾	—	103	107½	—	—	—	74	—	—	
7	228	—	79¾	105½	107½	—	—	—	75	—	—	
11	231	88½	86¾	108	107½	—	—	—	77	—	—	
14	236	86½	83½	107¾	107½	—	—	—	—	—	—	
16	—	—	82	106¾	106¾	—	—	—	—	—	—	

AMERICAN FUNDS.

	IN LONDON. June 11.	14.	21.	AT NEW YORK. Apr. 13.	May 9.	24
7 per Cent.	—		—	106	106	106
Bank Shares	24l. 10.	24l. 10s.	24l. 10s	102	102	102
Louisiana	—	—	—	par	par	par
Old 6 per Cent.	—	—	—	par	par	par
New 6 per Cent.	101	a	101	101	101	102
3 per Cent.	—	—	—	66	66	63

Prices of the
FRENCH FUNDS
From May 19, to June 18.

1819	5 per Cent. consols fr.	c.	Bank Actions fr.	c.
May.				
18	67	—	1510	—
22	67	—	1506	25
25	66	95	1505	—
29	66	85	1505	—
June				
1	66	85	1510	—
5	67	—	1505	—
12	68	20	1516	—
15	67	90	1510	—

By J. M. Richardson, 23, Cornhill.

NATIONAL REGISTER: FOREIGN.

CONTENTS.

CONTENTS.

INDEX.

Lightning Source UK Ltd.
Milton Keynes UK
UKHW02n0824190818
327370UK00002B/182/P